The Bahamas Cruising Guide

with the
Turks and Caicos Islands

Second Edition

A DOLPHIN–NOMAD BOOK

Mathew Wilson

INTERNATIONAL MARINE

Camden, Maine

International Marine/
Ragged Mountain Press

A Division of The McGraw·Hill Companies

The name International Marine and the International Marine logo are trademarks
of The McGraw-Hill Companies. Printed in the United States of America.

ISBN 0-07-135327-5
Library of Congress Cataloging-in-Publication data available.

Questions regarding the ordering of this book should be addressed to:
The McGraw-Hill Companies
Customer Service Department
PO Box 547, Blacklick, OH 43004
Retail customers: 1-800-262-4729 • Bookstores: 1-800-722-4726

Additional Content and Research
Port Information: Janet Wilson
Photographs including aerial photography (unless otherwise credited): Mathew Wilson

Book Design, Production, and Advertising
Chief Executive: Alexander Kahan; Editor: Susan Hale; Design: Molly Allen;
Cartography: Joe Faucher and Chris Adams; Electronic photo enhancement: David Morin;
Support: Hope Thompson, Rachel Benoit, and Lauri Berkenkamp.

Dolphin–Nomad Publications, PO Box 875, Norwich, Vermont 05055
Tel: 802-649-1995; fax: 802-649-2667

On the Cover
The colors of the Bahamas are evident in this photograph of Governor's Harbour, Eleuthera.

Publication history: Second Edition 1999

Imprint is last number shown: 9 8 7 6 5 4 3 2 1

Table of Contents

Table of Charts

Table of Yellow Pages

v

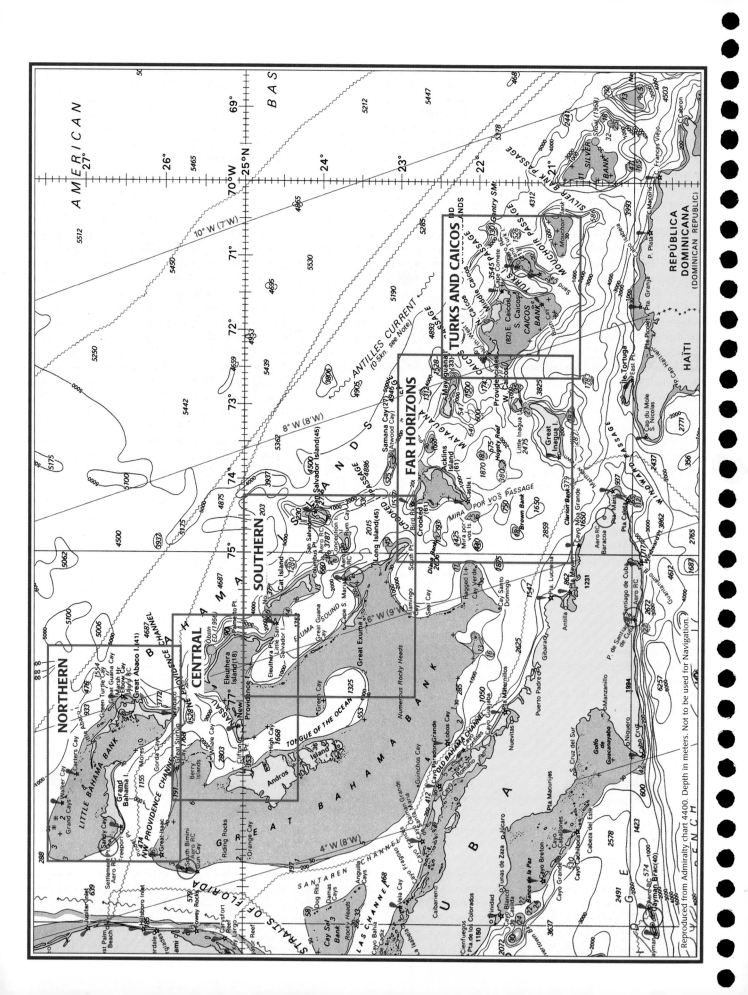

Reproduced from Admiralty chart 4400. Depth in meters. Not to be used for Navigation.

Preface

About This Guide

OUR aim has been to produce the one guide to the Bahamas and Turks and Caicos Islands that every captain and first mate will want to have on hand. Our purpose is to hold the hand of the first timer and refresh the memory of the veteran, and help you with your planning and your day-to-day cruising in the Bahamas and the Turks and Caicos, or your passage making through the area. As the **Contents** show, the first part is devoted to general information, the background you need to know. Then the main part of the book deals with the Bahamas in four convenient parts, and the Turks and Caicos Islands form a sixth part:

- **The Northern Cruising Grounds.** The Little Bahama Bank passages, the Abacos, and Grand Bahama.

- **The Central Cruising Grounds.** The Bimini Islands, the passages across the Great Bahama Bank, the Berry Islands, Nassau, Spanish Wells, Harbour Island, Eleuthera, and North Andros.

- **The Southern Cruising Grounds.** The passages across the Yellow Bank, the Exuma Cays and the Exuma Islands, the Out Islands north of the tropic of Cancer (23° 30' N), and Long Island.

- **Far Horizons.** The Bahamas south of the tropic of Cancer, the more remote areas likely to be of interest only to those on passage to and from the Caribbean, and to the seasoned and dedicated explorer. Essentially these are the islands that are on your path to or from the Turks and Caicos, and included with this we touch briefly on South Andros and the Jumentos Cays.

- **The Turks and Caicos Islands.** Providenciales, the Caicos Bank, Grand Turk Island, and the Turks Bank. This is a vital staging area, or potential refuge, if you are on passage to or from the Caribbean.

Areas hazardous to navigation that have never been regarded as cruising grounds are not covered other than in passing reference. Immediately following each section are **Yellow Pages** that cover the shoreside in capsule form, listing all the facilities you're likely to need from marinas, bars, and restaurants, to shoreside accommodations, just in case you have shore-based guests. We conclude each Yellow Page review with a list of **Things To Do In . . .**

Three sections of colored reference pages follow the main parts of the Guide.

- **The Blue Pages** concentrate on Navigation, Seamanship, and Preparation.

- **The Green Pages** deal with the Environment, Recreation, and allied subjects likely to be of General Interest to the cruising visitor.

- **The Buff Pages** provide an "across the board" reference section covering virtually all matters of concern to every captain flying a Bahamian or British courtesy flag, from Immigration and Customs, through medical facilities, to duty free shopping.

And finally the **Appendix** is a reference compendium in tabular form, with a Waypoint Catalog, Conversion Tables, and the like. At your fingertips if you want it.

With a target area spanning some 2,000 nautical miles, we've had to be selective and hold back from gunkholing up every creek. Although we reckon you could use this Guide as a single source, we've always believed in the safety of multiple references. Don't hold back from adding to your bookshelf. There are some fine special-to-area guides out there. Make use of them.

A book dates from the time it goes to print. Other than geography and history, sooner or later almost everything will change, but in successive editions we'll keep pace with those changes, and we'll not let this Guidebook become outdated. Enjoy your time in the Islands! We hope we'll meet you there sometime, somewhere along the line.

With our best wishes for fair winds and following seas,

Mathew Wilson

Janet Wilson

Acknowledgements

THIS Guide marks the achievement of targets we have long set. Revised, updated, and improved, our changes also reflect the comments, suggestions, and wishes of everyone we've met in the Bahamas and in the Turks and Caicos, and on shore in the United States, the United Kingdom, and elsewhere over the last two years. Our list of thanks covers only a fraction of this population, and is drawn primarily from our mailbox. We have enjoyed talking to you all, and hearing your views.

We thank Kelly Dobbs of the North Palm Beach Marina, Jack Holobinko of *Jac Flash*, Keith and Sally Huzyak of M/V *Besame*, then en route to the Dominican Republic, Clarence and Toni King, Don Langer of *Mare Cavaliero*, Gary Miller of *Dad Bear*, Ron Morrisseau of *Metaphor*, Bruce Nelson of Oceanus Sail & Drive, Bill O of *V Lucky Lady*, Doug Newbegin of *Wren of Aln*, Martin Pinkard of *Janeva*, Sten Tonnesson of Key Biscayne, Major General (R) Drake Wilson of *Boundless II*, and Frank Young of Coral Gables for their contributions. Joe Kirkby of *Moro* suggested that two Abaco anchorages generally regarded as safe for short-term use, Hole-in-the-Wall and immediately south of the Hawksbill Cays, are potentially dangerous and should not be contemplated. Both of these, like so many Bahamian anchorages, are fine in settled weather *in the right season*, but do not come anywhere close to offering any kind of refuge. On much the same subject Herbert Hucks of the *Old Bahama Bay Resort and Marina* reported that two yachts anchored off West End in early 1998 dragged their anchors and went on the rocks when the weather stepped up. The holding there is poor, thin sand over rock. This shallow bay has always been a bad risk as an anchorage. It's usable in the short term in settled weather, for two or three hours or so before setting off across the Gulf Stream to return to Florida, simply for pre-positioning if you plan to set sail at night and don't want to exit the marina in darkness. Don't use this bight as an anchorage.

Ivan Forster of *The Lady Hamilton*, a 41-foot Morgan classic, gave us the benefit of his pioneering marking of the Exuma Cays Normans Pond entry and exit routes. In Cat Island Tom Johnson of *Nipigon* helped us chart the Hawk's Nest entry, and explore the creek to advantage. In North Eleuthera we re-ran the Devil's Backbone Passage with Wilf and Sylvia Rudd in their 42-foot Nordic Tug *Moxie*, with Edsel Roberts at the helm. It was a convincing demonstration of the vital importance of local knowledge given in what most of us would consider No-Go conditions, an east–northeast wind gusting in the 20s, with 4-foot breaking seas and little or no color showing in the water.

Our thanks for help in the Turks and Caicos Islands go to many people. To Lindsey Musgrove and Valerie Jennings in Grand Turk, and Ralph Higgs in Providenciales, all members of the Tourist Board. To Tomlinson Skippings and Judith Garland for their valuable help in allowing us to use their maps and information on the National Parks. To Norman Watts, for his help with surveys of the North Creek entry channel in Grand Turk, and a special thank you to Brian Riggs, the Director of the Turks and Caicos Museum, who held out a guiding hand in Grand Turk Island.

In Providenciales, our principal mentors were Bengt Soderquist of Provident Ltd; Art Pickering, whose dive operation is based in Turtle Cove; and Bob Pratt of South Side Marina. Their immense local knowledge was invaluable.

We much appreciate the guest articles written for this edition by Tom McGrath, of Corning Community College, on Bahamian reefs, and Arne Molander of Montgomery Village, Maryland, with his Columbus landfall proposal. We thank the Bahamas Ministry of Tourism, the Bahamas Port Authority, the Bahamas Telecommunications Corporation, BASRA, Bluewater Books and Charts, Mobile Marine Radio, the Turks and Caicos Tourist Board, the United States Coast Guard (Camslant in Chesapeake), and Nick Wardle of Coral Harbour for their cooperation in our research for this Edition. Finally, in this long list, we thank the Salvador Dali Museum in St. Petersburg, Florida, for letting us use a reproduction of Salvador Dali's high-impact work, the *Discovery of America by Christopher Columbus* in our feature on **The Columbus Controversy**.

This new definitive edition of *The Bahamas Cruising Guide with the Turks and Caicos Islands* is the creation of a talented team. Molly Allen's attractive clear, clean, and balanced design, the cartographic skills of Joe Faucher, and Chris Adams's deceptively simple maps, together with Susan Hale's patient, incisive editing, have resulted in a book that eclipses its best-selling forerunner and is, by any standard, **A Millennium Edition.**

1999 Bahamas and Turks & Caicos Hurricane Report

GLOBALLY 1999 has been marked by an extraordinary number of natural disasters, severe storms, floods, and earthquakes, which have affected many parts of the world. The Bahamas has joined the list of disaster areas. This year two hurricanes, *Dennis* and *Floyd*, have tracked along the line of the Turks and Caicos Islands and the Bahamas. The first, *Dennis*, was relatively harmless. The second, the mid-September *Floyd*, ravaged the eastern and central Bahamas.

Hurricane *Floyd's* Track of Destruction

Entering the area of interest of this guide, Hurricane *Floyd* passed some 150 miles north of the Turks and Caicos, generating 50-mph winds and spawning a tornado in North Caicos, which destroyed six houses. Developing in strength *Floyd* continued to track to the northwest, carving a path that passed some 50 miles to the east of San Salvador, Cat Island, and Eleuthera. By September 14, the center of the hurricane was over Abaco. *Floyd* exited the Bahamas still heading on its northwesterly course to threaten the Carolinas and the East Coast of the United States.

In magnitude *Floyd* rated on a par with the 1992 Hurricane *Andrew*. It hardly mattered whether the eye of the storm passed over you, or passed offshore. *Floyd's* storm span covered 500–600 miles, its sustained wind speed hit 155 mph, and storm-strength winds extended out as far as 300 miles from the center. San Salvador, Cat Island, Eleuthera, Harbour Island, Spanish Wells, Great and Little Abaco Islands, and the Abaco Cays suffered widespread severe damage. Grand Bahama Island, the Berry Islands, Nassau and New Providence Island, North Andros, the Exuma Cays, Great Exuma Island, Rum Cay, and Long Island were also hit hard. At the time we write parts of Abaco, Eleuthera, Spanish Wells, Harbour Island, Cat Island, and San Salvador are still without power, water, sewage, and full telecommunications facilities. It is almost incredible that loss of human life in the Bahamas was minimal. Only one man died, through drowning, in Grand Bahama.

Recovery

A Bahamas Disaster Relief Fund was established. Power line teams from St. Vincent and the Grenadines, Barbados, St. Lucia, Antigua and Barbuda, Grenada, the Cayman Islands, and Anguilla set to work in the Bahamas. The Pan American Health Organization worked with Bahamian Government Health teams on disease prevention, and restoring water and sewage facilities. The US Coast Guard provided transportation and delivered water and other supplies, and the American Red Cross worked with the Bahamas Red Cross on hurricane relief. Within two weeks much of the Bahamas was back in business. Rebuilding is now going ahead, fueled by the waiving of import duties

on construction and allied materials. But it remains that *Floyd* was near-catastrophic in its impact.

The Impact on the Cruising Community

The easternmost islands are going to need at least six months to rebuild and recover. The scars of *Floyd*, like the marks of Hurricane *Andrew*, are going to be visible for a long time. Widespread loss of mature trees has already altered the profile of many places, and agriculture, particularly in Grand Bahama and Long Island, will take twelve months or more to get back on line, due to wind damage and salt saturation from storm surge.

On the marine side it will take a long time before we know the true extent of the changes that have come about. The most dramatic has been the severing of Elbow Cay close to the Abaco Inn. We can expect sand to have moved, although this occurs every season. This coming year it's likely we'll find the changes have been more dramatic. Many marinas have lost docks, and there has been severe damage to shoreside facilities. We give details later in this report, under the headings of each geographic cruising ground.

The Pace of Recovery

The pace of post-*Floyd* recovery is now dependent on adequate funding and the availability of construction equipment, building materials, and labor with the necessary skills. The geographic spread of the devastated area and transportation problems engendered by dealing with something like well over sixty hard-hit settlements and islands will inevitably be a critical factor. Our prediction is that by the end of January the more frequented cruising destinations closest to mainland help (the Abacos and Nassau) will be back in business. The cosmetic side will come later. Much the same will apply to the commercial infrastructure in each island. The Exumas will not be far behind. It will be a longer haul in Eleuthera, Cat Island, and San Salvador.

There is no reason why you should not plan to cruise in the Bahamas in the Millennium Year. There are cogent reasons why you should go there. Don't write them off as a cruising ground. Your greatest contribution to the recovery of these people and their islands is to go there, and accept shortfalls and limitations if some aspects are not as they were. Your presence alone is supportive. But try to do more than that. Take gifts for the children, dine ashore, hold back on self-sufficiency and buy some of the things you'll require in their stores, listen to their needs and think whether there is more that *you* could do to help them recover, later on, when your cruise ends . . .

We'll now turn to our detailed reports on the Bahamas post-*Floyd*. The main body of this Guide remains not just a record of what was, but also the target of what will be. We shall not draw the line and assume that permanent change has come about until at least one year has passed.

The Northern Cruising Grounds

The Mainland Abacos

Fox Town lost its Batelco tower, and over one hundred homes were destroyed in the Fox Town–Coopers Town area. Treasure Cay took a storm surge of 8 feet. Marsh Harbour was flooded, and suffered extensive waterfront damage. Little Harbour was reported as virtually destroyed with its dock and foundry gone, and Pete Johnson's house destroyed. Sandy Point was hard hit, and had no power, communications, or water, very little food, and was cut off entirely as the southern Abaco highway was blocked and washed out in part. Houses were destroyed along the length of Little Abaco and Great Abaco Island, and waterfront properties destroyed or severely damaged. Virtually all fishing boats were lost, miles of power lines were down with poles broken. Distribution systems were damaged, and Abaco lost its 3,000-acre citrus harvest.

Treasure Cay Marina is open, but is operating at reduced capacity at this time. In Marsh Harbour the Boat Harbour Marina, Conch Inn Marina, Marsh Harbour Marina, and the Triple J Marina are temporarily closed as we write this report. The Conch Inn Marina will reopen in late October, Marsh Harbour Marina in November, and Boat Harbour Marina in December. The Harbour View Marina has forty slips open, and all facilities available.

The Abaco Cays

Spanish Cay was reported as devastated. In Green Turtle Cay the wind was logged at 160 mph. Bluff House suffered severe damage, as did the Green Turtle Club, but both are forecasting that they will be back in business by November or December. Boats were sunk, docks were wrecked, and restaurant, bar, and other facilities damaged. Boats hauled for storage were blown off their blocks at the Abaco Shipyard on Black Sound. New Plymouth was flooded, and Mike's Bar was badly damaged. In Great Guana Cay the Guana Beach Resort burned down. Man-O-War Cay and Elbow Cay were hard hit. Hope Town came through well enough to send relief supplies to Sandy Point, but Elbow Cay was "washed over" and virtually cut in two just south of the Abaco Inn. The Sea Spray Marina was badly damaged. All the houses along the beach south of Hope Town were either taken by storm surge or wave action, or left hanging over the ocean. The famous Hope Town lighthouse remains intact.

Walkers Cay Marina has sixty-five slips open, and is in business. Spanish Cay is closed at this time. In Green Turtle Cay, the Green Turtle Club Marina is temporarily closed. We believe Bluff House Marina falls in the same category. We have no reports on the Black Sound marinas at this time, and we have no specific Man-O-War reports. In Hope Town the Lighthouse Marina is open and in service as normal. The Hope Town Harbour Lodge, the Club Soleil, Hope Town Hideaway Marina, the Abaco Inn, and Seaspray Re-

sort are all temporarily closed as we write. On Guana Cay the Guana Beach Resort is temporarily closed, but the Guana Seaside Village is aiming to re-open in December. We have no report on Orchid Bay.

Grand Bahama Island

Grand Bahama, which accounts for 50 percent of the Bahamas vegetable crop, will not recover its agricultural production for at least a year. In addition there was some loss of pine, hardwood, and other trees. Severe floods affected the north coast including the International Airport, which was under 6 feet of water at one time. Additionally, high winds damaged the terminal building. The eastern end of Grand Bahama suffered some damage, and West End had flooding but, as we hear at this time, no substantial damage. Freeport took storm surge measured at 15 feet. This said, recovery has been fast.

In Port Lucaya both the Port Lucaya Marina and the Lucayan Marina Village report that they are in service, undamaged, and operating as normal. Xanadu Marina reports that its fifty slips are available, and all its normal facilities are on offer. All support businesses in the Freeport–Lucaya area, stores, boat supply stores, and hospitals, are now operating normally. The airport has been re-opened, and tourist traffic has resumed.

The Central Cruising Grounds

The Bimini Islands

Minimal damage has been reported. Apparently *Floyd* struck at Tropical Storm strength. The Bimini Big Game Club and the Bimini Sands Marina report that they are fully operational. We have no other reports.

The Berry Islands

Floyd struck at full hurricane force. The Government Dock at Bullocks Harbour (Great Harbour Cay) was damaged. Roads were washed out, and there was major beach erosion. We have not heard from Great Harbour Cay Marina. In the southern Berrys, Chub Cay Marina reports that it is operational with all slips in service.

Nassau and New Providence Island

Winds logged at 120 mph, storm surge, and heavy rain in pre-dawn darkness took out sea walls, road, and structures along West Bay Street in the Sauders Beach–Brown's Point area, Rock Point south of Delaporte Point, and the Orange Hill area. Damage to buildings, although widespread, was not severe. A large number of mature trees were uprooted all over the island. Sandals, the Ocean Club, and the Sheraton Grand hotels all closed temporarily to make repairs. On the marine side some mailboats were beached, and many boats were damaged.

On the Nassau side of Nassau Harbour both Nassau Yacht Haven and the Nassau Harbour Club marinas are operational, and have all facilities in service. East Bay Marina suffered severe damage, which may take some months to make good. On Paradise Island the Atlantis Marina, Hurricane Hole, and the Paradise Island Harbour Club Marina are operational.

Spanish Wells, Harbour Island, and Eleuthera

Eleuthera shared with the Abacos the unenviable distinction of being the hardest-hit area in the Bahamas, with widespread damage to buildings and utilities. Power, water, sewage, and telecommunications services were totally disrupted. One report we have says that the Glass Window bridge is impassable, and once again North Eleuthera has been parted from the main island.

In Spanish Wells the most severe damage was on the marine side. Fishing vessels and other boats sank in the harbor or were beached by the hurricane, and the Spanish Wells fishing fleet has taken severe losses. In the first stages of the hurricane Spanish Wells reported gusts registering 185 knots and a 10–15-foot storm surge in the harbor. We believe that the Spanish Wells Yacht Haven is temporarily closed at this time.

In North Eleuthera both Upper and Lower Bogue, and The Current, all hard hit by Hurricane *Andrew* in 1992, were severely damaged once again, suffering both structural damage to public buildings and houses, as well as serious flooding, and lost power, telephone, and water. The Gene's Bay Dock (the ferry dock for Spanish Wells) was destroyed. All North Eleuthera farms have been severely damaged.

Harbour Island lost docks and road on the western side of the island, and serious erosion occurred on the eastern beaches. A large number of hotels, businesses, and houses suffered structural damage. Valentine's Marina suffered damage (as did the Resort) and is closed temporarily for repairs. The Harbour Island Club Marina is also temporarily closed. Both hope to be back in business by January 2000.

In Central and South Eleuthera the road in the James Cistern area was cut. Hatchet Bay lost houses. In Governor's Harbour Cupid's Cay was swept clean. Batelco, Barclays Bank, the clinic, and Customs were all hit, and other buildings and houses were damaged. Winds of 135 mph were registered. Palmetto Point lost roadway to washouts, and houses. In Tarpum Bay the Methodist Church, serving as a hurricane refuge, lost its roof and had to be abandoned. "Miraculously," (in the words of the Prime Minister, the Right Honorable Hubert Ingraham), "no one was injured." Rock Sound lost its airport terminal building, and suffered extensive damage to commercial buildings and houses, with flooding in low-lying areas. Cemeteries in Hatchet Bay, Tarpum Bay, Green Castle, and Wemyss Bight were devastated and graves exposed.

The Rainbow Inn is forecasting a November opening. The Club Med reckons it will be back in business in July 2000. These dates probably serve as a good indication of the timespan Eleuthera will require to recover from the effects of Hurricane *Floyd*.

Andros

North Andros suffered coastal damage as the result of high seas and storm surge, particularly between Mastic Point and Morgans Bluff. Roads inland were blocked by fallen trees and debris. A number of houses suffered roof damage from high winds. Morgans Bluff reported damage to its Regatta Village area, and to its water and sewage treatment plant. In Fresh Creek the Lighthouse Marina is open and normal service has resumed.

The Southern Cruising Grounds

The Exuma Cays

The Highborne Cay Batelco antennas were damaged. We have no other details of the Exuma Cays at this time, other than that Sampson Cay has some fourteen slips (out of twenty-five) operational. In Staniel Cay, the Staniel Cay Yacht Club is open and in business. The Happy People Marina is temporarily closed.

Great Exuma Island

The George Town Government Dock was seriously damaged, and storm surge undermined the causeway connecting Great Exuma Island to Barraterre. In George Town Exuma Docking Services report that they are fully operational. Exuma Dive Centre and and Minns Watersports are reported to be in business, as is the Club Peace and Plenty, which lost some of its dock.

Cat Island

Cat Island was hit very hard indeed. The eye of Hurricane *Floyd* passed right over Arthur's Town. All communication with Cat Island was lost for 24 hours. Damage to buildings and houses was widespread and severe, and 40 percent of the homes on the island were reckoned damaged at the first count. All low-lying parts of the island suffered flooding either from storm surge or rain, and the road between Tea Bay and Knowles was washed out. Water supplies were disrupted, as was power and telephone. In the eight miles between Tea Bay and Smith's Bay over forty poles carrying telephone and power lines were down. Similar extensive damage extended further along a ten-mile stretch from Bennett's Harbour to Orange Creek. Hawk's Nest is in operation and the eight slips in their marina are in service.

Long Island

Coastal flooding in all low-lying areas washed out roads and damaged property, particularly in Millerton, Deals, Simms, Salt Pond, and Deadman's Cay. The Government Docks at Glenton, Salt Pond, and Clarence Town were damaged. In the north both the Cape Santa Maria Resort and the Stella Maris Resort reported no structural damage, but the Cape Santa Maria Resort closed for two weeks to clear storm debris strewn over Calabash Bay beach. Stella Maris Marina reports having fifteen slips in service, and all facilities available to boaters. We have no report from Clarence Town.

In Long Island the worst long-term damage was to agriculture where all crops have suffered, particularly banana and citrus. Long Island is the main agricultural producer in the Bahamas, and wind damage coupled with salt water inundation indicate that Long Island's agriculture will not recover for at least a year.

San Salvador

The "Columbus Island" suffered severe damage. *Floyd* struck at night, power failed immediately, and all communications were cut. A mile and a half of the Long Bay coastal road south of Cockburn Town was washed out. Both the Club Med and the Riding Rock Resort were badly damaged, and were out of business. Buildings around the island suffered structural damage. The Riding Rock Inn Marina is temporarily closed.

Rum Cay

The Rum Cay Batelco tower was nearly lost. We have no further report from Rum Cay.

Far Horizons

Crooked Island

The Government Dock at Landrail Point was destroyed. Otherwise only minimal damage was reported. Pittstown Point Landings is, we believe, closed temporarily.

Long Cay, Acklins Island, Mayaguana, and Great Inagua all reported minimal damage.

The Turks and Caicos Islands

The Turks and Caicos were singularly fortunate. Hurricane *Dennis*, as a Tropical Storm, dumped 12 inches of rain on Grand Turk over one night, flooding several areas for two days, but there was no other damage. *Floyd*, as we said in our introduction, passed 150 miles north of Grand Turk Island generating 50-mph winds (the storm had yet to develop to its near-record full strength) and spawned a tornado in North Caicos that damaged some six houses. There is no more to report. Business in the Turks and Caicos, as we write this report, is as normal.

A Summing Up

THE North Atlantic–Caribbean hurricane season is reckoned to run from June 1 to November 30. Statistically August, September, and October are the worst months. Our publication date is set for December 1999. The lead time required to get a book on the bookshelves requires that we go to print in mid-October with, technically, six weeks of hurricane season still to run, so bear in mind the date at the end of this report. Be aware too that our report is bound to be incomplete, and may well be in-accurate. It was compiled when telephone links in the Bahamas were still severed, airfields and airstrips were out of service, and many of the hardest-hit areas were still virtually isolated.

Looking Ahead in a Positive Way

There is no hindrance to your mobility, your enjoyment of the rightly famed waters of these islands, and your exercise of the freedom of the seas, which is why we all go boating. What may change is your approach to your cruising. You must be aware of what to expect, and where you may find that full facilities have not yet been restored. Call to find out the state of your intended destinations. Now, after *Floyd*, it may make sense to book your slip or mooring well ahead, as dock space may be limited in the short term. A preliminary check on the Internet (www.Bahamas.com) can bring you up to date with marina facilities. Go to the *Destinations and Hotel Status Report*. You'll find a *Marina Status Report* there that may be helpful. Go to our web site (www.bahamasguide.com) to see whether we have updated information to give you.

Once again, we encourage you to cruise in the Bahamas in the coming year. Many of the places we know were hit by *Floyd* and suffered damage. But never underestimate the determination of a people to recover from natural disaster. By the start of Year 2000 most of the places we list as temporarily closed will be back in business. On our part we must just accept that some shoreside facilities may be compromised in the short term. It just requires planning further ahead, checking, being more prepared for it, and a degree of greater self-sufficiency coupled with a willingness to aid their recovery, whether that comes by spending money there, or helping in a more concrete way. One passing hurricane, since time began, has never taken away the sunlight, nor altered water colors and visibility, nor have high winds wiped the smile of welcome from the face of an Island Nation.

Don't hold back. The Bahamas and the Turks and Caicos are still there. Waiting for you! Enjoy your time in the Islands. We'll be there, and we'll see you there too, we hope.

info@bahamasguide.com

It will take us all months of voyaging in the islands before we know exactly what has changed in terms of appearance, size, shape, and depth. We will update and revise this Guide during the currency of each edition as we build up our information bank. Will you let us know what *you* discover as you cover the islands in your cruising? Use our web site and this Guide as your notice board to share what you've found, and we'll gratefully acknowledge your contribution on behalf of the Bahamas-bound cruising population.

Part I

Introduction

Stop Dreaming . . . Start Planning

The Lessons of 500 Years of Voyaging in Bahamian Waters

Ocean water, about 60 feet deep, west of Memory Rock.

Chapter 1
Stop Dreaming . . . Start Planning

NASA

Berry Islands. Photograph taken at an altitude of 234 nm, 25° 08' N 077° 09' W. Skylab, Mission 4.

What Are These Islands?

LOOK down from Space. Extending southeast from the east coast of Florida you'll see an ocean area of brilliant colors, turquoise seas, white sand, and specks of emerald, a scattering of islands and cays divided into contiguous groups by the dark sapphire blue tongues of deeper water. The larger islands stretch out for perhaps 100 miles in length but most of the cays are tiny, strung in chains like bracelets laid out under the spotlight of the sun.

Islands, Cays, and Keys

Let's get these Bahamian names right at the start. A *cay*, pronounced *key*, is a small, low-lying island, probably coral-fringed, mostly sand on a limestone-coral base. The word comes from the Spanish *cayo* (with the same meaning), which the early Spanish explorers took from Taino, language of the Arawaks, the indigenous island people whose extinc-

tion they brought about. It joins many other words, like barbecue (*barbacoa*), canoe (*canoa*), and hammock (*hammaca*) with the same origins. In the United States the word cay still survives today (misspelled) in the name Key West (*Cayo Oeste*, the westernmost cay).

As for an island, well, that's an island. Something bigger. You could say so big that if you're on one of the cays, it seems like a continental shore. Indeed Great Abaco Island, in the cays, is often referred to as "the mainland."

All around this magic area, save for one side, there is the deep water of the southwestern North Atlantic Ocean. It is some of the deepest ocean water in the hemisphere. On one side a narrow strait, the Florida Strait, separates the area from the east coast of Florida. Just 65 miles wide, the Florida Strait is far more than the continuance of the ocean around the islands: it's the mainstream course of one of the greatest maritime rivers in the world, the Gulf Stream. Immensely powerful, 45 miles wide here, the Gulf Stream flows north at 2.5 knots with the dynamic and thermal energy to create nightmarish seas from contrary north winds and, distantly, give the fortunate shores of its European landfalls exotic plants and mild winters, a climatic imitation of lands a thousand miles to their south.

A Cruising Ground?

If you draw lines around the Bahamas, you'll find that you've drawn a box that looks square on the map. Try it. Place your first line at 072° 30' W in the east, and the second at 079° 20' W in the west. In the north your line runs along 27° 25' N. In the south it's 20° 50' N.

Inside your box the islands run catty-corner, from the northwest to the southeast. If you try to count them you'll lose count around the 700 mark. If you try to work out the area contained within your square you'll settle for something like 90,000 square miles. Most of it is water. Perhaps it's simpler to say the islands are spread over something like 700 miles of ocean and circled with 900 square miles of coral reefs. And that ocean is deep. Within sight of land it is 10,000 feet deep, and the land by contrast is no more than 206 feet at its highest point.

But is it all ocean? No way. The Spanish called the area the *gran bahamar,* the "great shallow seas." There's nothing like it. It's a great tableland of limestone, coral, and sand, a raised reef-fringed platform on the edge of the Atlantic Ocean. Depths average 10–30 feet over much of the Bahamas but on all sides the ocean dropoffs plunge to depths your depth sounder will never register. The waters of the great shallow seas are something else, offering both clear sailing and a maze of reefs, coral heads, isolated rocks, and sandbores often too complex, and too subject to seasonal changes in the case of the sand, to be recorded accurately on a chart. The islands, as we've said, are low lying, and average no more than 100 feet in elevation. This can give you identification problems, although their vegetation makes them

Pigeon Cay, Abaco.

Where You Could Go

Where Everyone Goes
Marsh Harbour, Abaco
Hope Town, Abaco
Port Lucaya, Grand Bahama
Nassau, New Providence Island
George Town, Exuma

Where the Sailboats Get Together
Marsh Harbour, Abaco
Staniel Cay, Exumas
George Town, Exuma

Where the Cruise Ships Go
Gorda Cay (re-named Castaway Island), Abaco
Freeport/Lucaya, Grand Bahama
Nassau
Great Stirrup Cay, Berry Islands
Little Stirrup Cay, Berry Islands
Princess Cay (Bannerman Town), Eleuthera
West Bay (re-named Half Moon Bay), Little San Salvador

Where to be Street Wise
Nassau
Hatchet Bay, Eleuthera
George Town, Exuma

relatively easy to pick up.

In the Bahamas safe navigation depends vitally on the colors we saw from Space: the deep blues, the turquoise, the white, and the browns of reef and sea grass, and it also depends on the no-less-vital illumination of the sun. The Spanish, after losing seventeen treasure ships off the coast of Abaco in 1595, wisely avoided the sea they had named. It was no place for lumbering galleons, for them it was no place to be during the Northers of the winter months, and certain death if they were caught there by the hurricanes of the summer and early fall.

It's no bad thing to carry a sense of history as you cruise in Bahamian waters, but for us it's very different from the horror area dreaded by the Spanish. The Bahamas rates with the Virgin Islands, the Aegean, and Polynesia as one of the top boating destinations in the world. What more could you add to your wish list than 82°F water so crystal clear you can count the starfish on the bottom 30 feet below your keel, more places to explore than you can possibly visit, with conditions just demanding enough to hone and prove your nautical skills, be it in a sailboat or a power boat?

It's the stuff of holiday dreams: sun, white sand, and palms, with more stars in the soft black velvet of the night skies than you'll have ever seen. Something like 20,000 US boats cruise in the Bahamas each year. The figures tell the story of how it is now.

Where to Go?
A Cruising Ground Analysis

IT'S a truism to say that the geography of the Bahamas has a profound effect on the cruising grounds the Bahamas offers. Generally where you have strings of small islands (the Abacos, Berrys, Exumas) you have good cruising grounds with infinite possibilities, whatever the weather. You can find places to explore, anchorages to tuck yourself into, and landfalls where you can get around on foot, or explore further by dinghy.

The big islands (Grand Bahama, Nassau, Eleuthera) are very different. Generally you have straight runs of open coast, few (if any) hidey-holes to explore or to use for shelter in adverse weather, and too much territory (if you want to see the sights) to get around other than by taxi (at high cost) or by taking a rental car. Eleuthera is perhaps the archetypal example of the "big" island seen in cruising terms.

Long and thin as it is, Eleuthera presents two coasts, the east (Atlantic) coast and the west (Eleuthera Bight) coast. The Atlantic coast has no shelter, near continuous offshore reefs, and is not a cruising ground. The west coast has only three true, all-weather havens for the cruising boat, Hatchet Bay, Cape Eleuthera Marina, and Davis Harbour. In between there are places (Pelican Cay, Governor's Harbour, and Rock Sound) where you can find some kind of shelter, but overall you are fine traveling up and down the west coast of Eleuthera *if* the prevailing southeast winds are the weather of the day, and if this is so, you can safely anchor off most of the small villages; but in unsettled weather you have just those three options as your safety net.

Andros Island, the largest of the Bahamian islands (over 100 miles in length and 40 miles wide), favored with the third-largest barrier reef in the world, would appear at first sight to be the most promising cruising ground you could imagine, but it's just not so. Much of Andros is a wilderness of mahogany and pine forest, scrub, marsh, tidal inlets, and flats. The barrier reef really is a barrier, and navigation inside the reef is hazardous.

Crew changes and the location of the nearest airport may well be a governing factor, and this, coupled with time available, often sets your limits. The decision of where to point

The Tropic of Cancer

The line of latitude running along 23° 30' N that marks the limit of the sun's summer migration into the Northern Hemisphere (it's the tropic of Capricorn that sets the reverse limit in the south). Cross these lines and you're in the Tropics. In other words, coming from North America, you've got *south*. Real south. But more of this later under **The Far Horizons**.

What Are You Looking For?

Bimini

Closest to the USA
Abacos
Andros
Berry Islands
Bimini Islands
Grand Bahama

Best for Air Services to the USA
Abacos (essentially Marsh Harbour and Treasure Cay)
Bimini Islands (Bimini and Cat Cay)
Grand Bahama (Freeport)
Nassau (Paradise Island and Nassau International)
George Town
Providenciales, Turks and Caicos

Best for Many Islands and Short Cruise Legs
Abacos
Exumas

Atlantis Casino, Nassau
Janet Wilson

Best for High Life
Grand Bahama
Nassau

Best for Short Legs and Ports of Call
Abacos

Best for Pretty Towns and Settlements
Abacos
Eleuthera

Hope Town, Elbow Cay, Abaco

Best for Diving
Andros
Bimini Islands
Out Islands
Turks and Caicos

Best for Sports Fishing
Abacos
Andros
Bimini Islands
Eleuthera

Best for Exploring
Abacos
Exumas
Out Islands
Turks and Caicos

Bahamas Trophy
Ministry of Tourism

Best for Real Adventuring
Andros
Out Islands
Turks and Caicos

Best for Getting Away from Everyone Else
Andros
Berry Islands
Out Islands
Turks and Caicos

Palmetto Point, Eleuthera

your bow when you set off for the Bahamas is only yours to take. Your choice, as ever, must rest on what you want. Perhaps, if we give our assessment by categories, it may help your decision-making process.

What About the Time Factor?

Remember the meaning of time is entirely related to two factors, one under your control (at least in your initial choice of boat), and the other quite out of your control. The first is the passage speed and therefore the cruising range of your boat. The second is the weather. If you're unlucky, you might get holed up somewhere for eight days or so. It can happen. But let's assume that if time counts, you are not in a 30-knot express cruiser but a boat that will average somewhere between 5 and 8 knots on passage. Your time and space considerations (from the east coast of Florida) will come out to something like this:

One Week to 10 Days
Northern Abacos
Bimini Islands
Grand Bahama
Berry Islands

At Least Two Weeks
Abacos
Bimini Islands and the Berry Islands

Place Names

BAHAMIAN and Turks and Caicos names can be confusing on two counts. The first is repetition. One day we'll do a count and see how many Crab Cays, Sandy Cays, and Sandy Points and the like we can list. Some doubles can come up far too close to each other, such as the Crab Cay off the northeastern tip of Little Abaco Island and the Crab Cay just north of Green Turtle Cay, but mostly you can figure out which one to focus on.

The spelling of names is another minefield of confusion. Over the last three hundred and fifty years place names have been spelled one way, then another, then maybe even a third way. This knock-on effect still shows in our charts today. Is it Man of War or Man-O-War? Powel or Powell? Generally we have tried to use the "newspaper" spelling of place names as it is right now. So from time to time our text names and our chart names will be slightly different versions.

Finally, where variants in naming exist we try to give them. In the Turks and Caicos the pass we now call Sandbore Channel was once known as Caicos Creek. Big Sand Cay is often known as Sand Cay. And so it goes. Just hang in there with us.

One Month
Anywhere in the Northern or Central Cruising Grounds

Over a Month
You can reach the Far Horizons. But if the weather factor is not in your favor, you may find that just one month is not long enough.

Ocean Approaches

FOR the ocean voyager there are as many routes into the Bahamas as there are navigable passes through the fringing reefs and gaps between the islands. On the shorter approaches from the Florida coast your departure port and route is decided when you've chosen your destination cruising ground, and your entry port options follow from this.

If you're coming from the south after a longer bluewater passage you may wish to make your entry port a place where most conventional commercial facilities are available, rather than fastening on a relatively isolated Out Island settlement, but your options are always dictated by your eventual destination. Whatever you choose to do, it's sensible to keep your approach voyage into the Bahamas low stress.

- Don't arrive off your first landfall during the night. Use daylight to advantage.
- Keep the position of the sun in mind when you work out the time of your passing into shallow water. You want it behind you.
- Keep the navigation simple.

The routes we've chosen are the most common approaches. Those involving an initial Gulf Stream crossing will be covered in greater detail under **Crossing the Gulf Stream** on page 17.

From the West (Florida)

FOR THE ABACOS
Bound for the Abacos, the most popular approach is to head for West End in Grand Bahama, clear in there, and then enter the Little Bahama Bank the next day by way of Indian Cay Passage. This will take you to the Abacos by way of Mangrove and Great Sale Cays. As Indian Cay Passage carries no more than 5.5 feet at mean low water (MLW), if you have a deep keel you may have to discard this option and take the Memory Rock approach.

The way by Memory Rock is favored by those who wish to take their approach as a straight shot to the Abacos and clear in at their destination. You enter the Little Bahama Bank either just north or south of Memory Rock, and carry on to Great Sale Cay if you have to overnight on the way. Once you reach the Abacos, your entry ports could be

Walkers Cay, Green Turtle Cay, or Marsh Harbour.

A popular alternative to these two routes is to head for Lucaya in Grand Bahama and take the Grand Lucayan Waterway to gain access to the Little Bahama Bank at Dover Sound, to the south of Mangrove Cay. Be warned that there is a fixed bridge with only 27-foot clearance on the canal, and the Dover Sound Channel carries only 4 feet of water at MLW. If you can make use of this shortcut, however, the saving in time is appreciable.

FOR GRAND BAHAMA

If you're making for Port Lucaya, the only way to go is to take it as a direct run from your Florida departure port.

FOR NASSAU AND THE EXUMAS

If you're bound for the southern Berrys (Chub Cay), Nassau, the Exumas, or Eleuthera, the Bimini Islands are well placed to serve as your first staging point and entry port (your choices are either Alice Town on North Bimini, or Cat Cay). One way or another, your route will take you through Gun Cay Cut before you cross the Great Bahama Bank to the Northwest Channel Light. From there your route goes on to Chub Cay and, if you wish, straight on to Nassau.

Alternatively you could set your course to pass north of the Bimini Islands to Great Isaac Light, and make Nassau your entry port. You'll have deep water all the way, plenty of sea room, and no navigational problems. All you have to decide is whether you want to stop in the northern Berry Islands on the way, or take the Northwest Providence Channel down to Nassau.

Fort Lauderdale and Miami are the favored departure points for these routes.

The Gulf Stream Factor

Setting out for the Bahamas from Florida inevitably dictates a Gulf Stream crossing at the start of your voyage. For slower boats the further south (within reason!) you make your departure point the better. You'll want to gain the advantage of the push of the Stream. If you fight it, your crossing will become a tough crablike crawl across the Florida Strait.

From the South and the Southeast (the Caribbean and the Turks and Caicos)

Whatever your original start point, the Virgin Islands, Puerto Rico, or the Dominican Republic, the Turks and Caicos Islands lie squarely in your path to the Bahamas, and Providenciales makes an ideal stopping point if you want to break your journey. From then on the simplest and most straightforward plan is to select George Town on Great Exuma Island as your entry port. Your route will take you in deep water to the east of Acklins, Crooked, and Long Islands before you turn west toward George Town on your final leg.

There are two places of concern. The first is the passage between the Plana Cays and the northern end of Acklins Island. You have plenty of sea room there, but you must make sure that you are not being set closer to land than you'd wish. The second is to resist the temptation to round Cape Santa Maria on the northern tip of Long Island too closely. Stand well out before making your turn to the west. The Cape was previously supposed to mark the northern limit of the blind wanderings of Christopher Columbus immediately after his Bahamian landfall in October 1492. Now it is generally believed that he never got this far north, although he did reach Long Island. Had he continued northward, as he had been heading, he might well have discovered America. Instead he turned south, and found Cuba.

From the Southwest (Havana and the Gulf of Mexico)

Perhaps the southwestern approach is the easiest of them all. Just ride with the Gulf Stream as if you were a Spanish galleon and turn to the east when you reach the right latitude to make your chosen landfall.

Charts

A full list of charts covering both the Bahamas and the Turks and Caicos, including electronic charts, is given in **Appendix A**. These are obtainable from Bluewater Books and Charts in Fort Lauderdale (see their advertisement), BOAT/US, and West Marine, as well as marine stores specializing as suppliers of marine charts. Small marine stores often carry charts of their local areas.

Terrapin *making a Bahamian landfall.*

Seven Days Out of Marsh Harbour

A TASTE OF THE SOUTHERN ABACOS

A suggested itinerary for a week you'll never forget.

DAY 1   DAY'S RUN 10–15 NM
MARSH HARBOUR TO GREAT GUANA CAY

■ Anchor in Fowl Cay Land and Sea Park. Snorkel. Lunch.
■ Anchor off Guana Beach Resort. Overnight.

Day's Attractions

- Sufficient passage time to acclimatize new crew.
- Snorkeling in a marine park.
- Explore and overnight in Great Guana Cay.

Suggestions
- Swim off Seven Mile Beach.
- Have sunset drinks at Nippers Beach Bar.
- Dine under the palms at Guana Beach Resort.

DAY 2   DAY'S RUN 13–14 NM
GREAT GUANA CAY TO HOPE TOWN

■ Sail to and anchor in American Harbour, Man-O-War Cay (the southern harbour). Explore Man-O-War Cay.
■ Move on to Hope Town. Anchor off, or in the harbor (if there is space/mooring available). Overnight.

Day's Attractions
- Visit Man-O-War Cay.
- Get to know Hope Town. You'll fall in love with it!

Suggestions
- Lunch at the Man-O-War Pavilion.
- Visit the Sail Shop in Man-O-War Cay.
- Swim off the beach at the Hope Town Harbour Lodge and then enjoy their happy hour.
- Dine ashore.

DAY 3   DAY'S RUN 13–14 NM
HOPE TOWN TO LYNYARD CAY

■ Snorkel the Pelican Cays Land and Sea Park.
■ Anchor off South Lynyard Cay. Overnight.

Day's Attractions

- A reasonable distance to run with some interesting jinking around Tilloo Bank. You'll need your navigator at your side, and to give her a break you could stop at Tahiti Beach on the way.
- There's miles of beach off your anchorage.

Pelican Cays.

Suggestions
- Don't miss snorkeling in the Pelican Marine Park.
- Try the reef between Lynyard Cay and Goole Cay in the morning.

DAY 4   DAY'S RUN 1.5 NM
LYNYARD CAY TO LITTLE HARBOUR

■ Enter Little Harbour at Half Tide or with greater depth. Take up one of Pete's moorings.
■ Explore Little Harbour. Overnight.

Day's Attractions
- Little Harbour itself.

Suggestions
- See Pete's Gallery, the Lighthouse, and the Johnston Cave.
- Snorkel the Little Harbour Reef.
- Dinghy around the Bight of Old Robinson.
- Make sure at you're at Pete's Pub for sundowners.

Dinghies at Pete's Pub, Little Harbour.

DAY 5 — DAY'S RUN 19–20 NM

LITTLE HARBOUR TO CHEROKEE SOUND TO LITTLE HARBOUR

- ■ Day trip down to Cherokee Sound for a picnic and swimming.
- ■ Return to your Little Harbour mooring. Overnight.

Day's Attractions
- • An ocean sail.
- • A great picnic site.

Suggestions
- • Take the chance to explore Cherokee settlement in your dinghy.

Cherokee Sound.

DAY 6 — DAY'S RUN 14–15 NM

LITTLE HARBOUR TO HOPE TOWN

- ■ Take a new route to Hope Town. Overnight.

Day's Attractions
- • A good sail (there's a choice of two routes going north, the Abaco mainland side or the ocean side of the Sea of Abaco).

Suggestions
- • Visit the Hope Town lighthouse. Climb to the top.
- • Walk every street in Hope Town. Find your dream house.
- • Dine somewhere you didn't go last time.

For complete information about routes, anchorages, and shoreside facilities and attractions, see Chapters 5 and 6 (pages 59–62 and 75–88), and the accompanying Yellow Pages.

DAY 7 — DAY'S RUN 5–26 NM

HOPE TOWN TO MARSH HARBOUR

- ■ If time is available, a final sailing circuit: Hope Town–Bakers Bay on Great Guana Cay– Marsh Harbour.

Day's Attractions
- • A chance to stretch your wings in a final sail.

Suggestions
- • Take your last chance for snorkeling (in Fowl Cay Park?).
- • Swim with the dolphins in Bakers Bay.
- • Dine that night in Marsh Harbour.

A Hope Town gateway.

THE PLUSES IN OUR SEVEN-DAY MARSH HARBOUR PROGRAM

- • The itinerary is infinitely variable. Within limits, it can be taken in any order to suit mood and weather.

- • Distances are short to maximize time for other activities. Most days that amounts to two or three hours of boating, and the rest is relaxing, swimming, and play time. If you have young children, that's even more of a plus.

- • Some more extended passages are included to let the enthusiastic mariners test their skills and spread their wings.

- • No repeats (even with the Hope Town re-visit). There's enough in each stop to make you wish you'd had two or three weeks, not just one.

- • If bad weather breaks in, you have plenty of options. No problems there.

Man-O-War Cay.

Chapter 2
The Lessons of 500 Years of Voyaging in Bahamian Waters

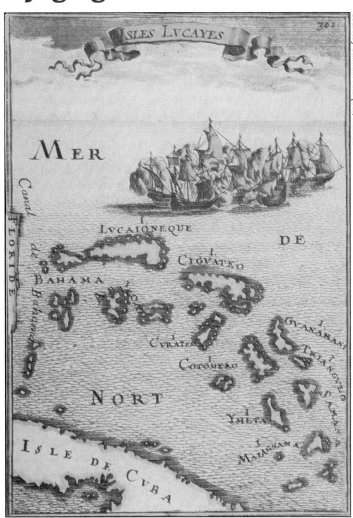

Courtesy Balmain Antiques, Nassau

Ocean Approaches. One of the first charts of the Bahamas, drawn by the French map maker Alain Manesson Mallet (1630–1706). The shape of Cuba had been fairly accurately established by the Spanish by 1650, but the Bahamas were still unexplored, uncharted, and a high-risk area.

Weather

AS we all know, high winds and high seas have an over-riding effect on what you can, or cannot, do in a boat. We cover **Climate**, that is prevailing meteorological conditions, which in the Bahamas falls into three zones, in our **Green Pages**. While of interest to the cruising visitor, climate is more likely to concern you if you're wintering or buying property in the Bahamas. Sources of daily **Weather Broadcasts** and weather information, which you will need, are listed in tabular form in **Appendix C**.

In any travel agency they'll tell you the Bahamian climate is near-perfect. In the winter (mid-December to mid-April) the temperature is between 70 and 80°F (21–26°C). In the summer (mid-April to well into the fall) the daytime temperature is between 80 and 90°F (26–32°C). A 10° difference. That's all. Humidity throughout the year runs 75–80 percent, but there's almost always a cooling breeeze. Even in summer, the heat and humidity rarely clamp down. Days and hours of sunshine per day are high throughout the year with the summer index winning over winter. As for rainfall, the summer brings squalls and thunderstorms that produce short bursts of torrential rain, but even in the gray weather produced by a Norther in winter, rainfall rarely lasts long.

What about hurricanes? The Bahamas, like the east coast of the USA and the islands of the Caribbean from Barbados northward, lie in the hurricane zone. June to November is the hurricane season, and August, September, and October are the high-risk months. Does this count the Bahamas out for summer cruising? The answer is no. You can expect maybe two bad storms a year, they'll tell you, but you'll get plenty of warning. This said, winter or summer, hurricane season or not, it makes sense to study Bahamian weather patterns before you set out.

The Bahamian Winter

The North American mainland is the primary driving force behind Bahamian winter weather. What happens in Canada and the continental US inevitably affects the Bahamas, sometimes a day or two later, sometimes almost at once. If an Alberta Clipper brings sub-zero temperatures right down across the Eastern States, you'll feel the cold as far south as George Town in the Exumas. If winter storms driving down from the northern quadrants blast Florida, the prevailing southeast Bahamian winds lose out and the North American "Norther" will take over, dominating what happens in the Abacos, Nassau, and as far south as the Out Islands. Sometimes the effects of a Norther will be felt as far south as Puerto Rico.

NORTHERS

This change to a winter weather pattern starts around mid-November. The wind cycle is largely predictable. In the Bahamas, as on the east coast of Florida, the wind first veers to the south and then to the southwest as a cold front starts driving down from the north. As the cold front comes closer the wind shifts to the northwest, then to the north, and then to the northeast. The strongest winds come just ahead of the cold front. During a Norther you can expect wild seas over the Gulf Stream and steep waves over the Banks. Wind strengths can reach Force 8 (34–40 knots), occasionally higher, and Force 6 (22–27 knots) is what you'll experience in the early period before the front arrives.

A Norther can last for days, or blow through within 24 hours. Sometimes a second Norther follows on the heels of the first so fast the wind shifts from northeast or east to northwest, and you get no break. Sometimes, just about when you think it's blown out, a Norther recharges itself and you get another two days.

As the Norther works itself out, the wind moves around to the east, and then stabilizes where it would like to be, in the southeast.

RAGES

You must also be aware that rough seas can build up within hours on the barrier reefs fringing the Atlantic Ocean, and normally navigable passages through the reefs become impassable. This is the deadly sea state the Bahamians call a "Rage." If there's any risk of Rage conditions you must take the threat seriously. It's always prudent to seek out local advice before setting out on a passage through the reefs at any time, winter or summer. Distant North Atlantic storms can create swells that will produce the same phenomenon. You

will not survive to relate the experience if you attempt to force your way through a reef passage in a Rage.

KEEPING AN EYE ON THE WINTER WEATHER

Northers are never surprises. Just pay attention to North American weather. Eastern US weather forecasts and Nassau Radio give you ample warning of what is going to happen. In the Bahamas you'll note that wind shift, see the dark clouds build up, and then you'll get the wind and the rain.

What this cycle dictates is that you take careful note of the weather pattern before you cross the Gulf Stream, and in the Bahamas you work out where you'll go for shelter in the event of a Norther before you move on another stage in your cruising itinerary. Depending on the wind state, a Norther does not necessarily keep you penned in a harbor or captive in your anchorage. Sailboats can take advantage of the wind direction, and power boats, given the right sea state, can go largely where they will.

The Northers can make the winter sound like a no-no season for cruising in the Bahamas, but it's just not true. Normal winter conditions are your 70–80°F temperatures, Force 3–4 (7–16 knot) southeast winds, sun every day, and occasional squalls to wash the salt off your decks (you'll appreciate that, for fresh water is expensive in the islands). The famous colors of the water are there, the water temperature is around 73–75°F, and winter water visibility is 60–100 feet on average.

Northers can break this pattern and give you days when you're holed up, waiting to move on; but when they come, the Northers often bring exceptional clarity of air, a light that gives the Bahamas the intensity of a color slide, and a chill in the night air that's sometimes welcome. If you get cabin fever waiting out your first, second, or third Norther, work your way south. The further south you go, the less you'll be troubled by the tail-ends of the storms that plague the commuters of the Mid-Atlantic States and the citrus growers of Florida in the winter months.

The Bahamian Summer

By May the Northers of winter will be history and the summer wind pattern settles to the influence of the southeast Trade Winds far to the south, giving wind from the southern quadrants for most of the time. The wind strength settles to average around 5–12 knots, enough to give you your sailing, and calms at night are more frequent than they are in the winter. Water temperatures rise in summer to around 85°F, and water visibility drops slightly to average 50–70 feet.

THUNDERSTORMS

Thunderstorms are a feature of the summer months. Anvil-headed cumulonimbus clouds build up over solar super-heated land and shallows, and you can expect everything that goes with a thunderstorm when they let loose, rain that seems as heavy as lead pellets, hail, lightning, thunder, and violent (60-knot) downdrafts. Microbursts with winds over 100 knots are not unknown but are mercifully rare events.

The towering summer anvil heads are one-off one-cloud dramas. Isolated thunderstorms are always obvious, one-hour affairs for the most part, and normally develop and hit their point of discharge in the late afternoon. Out in the ocean, on a bluewater passage, you can expect a thunderstorm to "go critical" during the night hours. If you're on passage stay well clear of a developing thunderstorm. Radar, if you have it, is a great bonus for thunderstorm avoidance. If you can determine which way a thunderstorm is moving (this is where radar really helps) try to pass it on the side away from the direction of its motion (ie, go where it has been, not where it is going). If you are at risk, take your canvas down and batten down.

There is a fairly reliable way to predict in the morning whether there will be scattered thunderstorms later in the day. About mid-morning, say ten o'clock, check the sky for small puffy white cumulus clouds. Around noon look again to see if the clouds have thinned out somewhat by appearing to stack themselves on top of each other so they look like tall lumpy cylinders. If they have, you may expect them to continue to scatter, but a few of them will grow into thunderstorms by late afternoon. As they develop, they will be visible for many miles, so observe their positions and direction of motion and be ready to take evasive action if necessary. Usually it is wiser to start your course deviation sooner rather than later, not only from a safety standpoint, but also to minimize the total distance to be sailed in the diversion.

LIGHTNING STRIKES

How likely is it that you might be struck by lightning? Statistics published by the Marine Insurance division of BOAT/US give these figures (the base being any given year):

Auxiliary Sail	0.6%	6 out of 1,000
Multi-hull Sail	0.5%	5 out of 1,000
Trawlers	0.3%	3 out of 1,000
Sail only	0.2%	2 out of 1,000
Cruisers	0.1%	1 out of 1,000
Runabouts	0.02%	2 out of 10,000

You always hope it will never happen to you. The chances are, statistically, that it never will. We've been hit once, in the Bahamas. We'd left our boat secured in the inner harbor of Sampson Cay for a week to fly back to the States. When we returned we found the induced surge of a near-miss lightning strike had taken out our electronics and "fried" our gel cell batteries. Just carry insurance, and have faith in those statistics.

Above, an approaching front, the clear sign of a marked imminent change. You are in for a complete reversal of the conditions you've been enjoying. Expect temperature change, an immediate increase in wind, the wind to veer, and low visibility. As the marked edge of the front passes through, the weather will settle into a new pattern (depending on whether it's a warm front or a cold front). If it's only a weak front, the disturbance in the more normal regular weather pattern may be brief, perhaps a matter of hours, or even less.

Below, the darkening weather of a rain squall. At best just rain, but never take it on trust. The front-like line of rain may carry high wind, sudden changes of wind direction, and gusts that are surprisingly strong. Be prepared to take it. Rain in sub-tropic and tropic waters is rarely just a gentle shower.

WATERSPOUTS

In the summer months you'll also see waterspouts that, although they may move erratically, can usually be avoided. Don't be tempted to sail through one. A waterspout is a marine tornado, short-lived normally, but still dangerous.

DON'T BE SURPRISED BY THE WEATHER

Bahamian weather never ceases to surprise. Yes, there are patterns to the winter months and patterns to the summer months, but we've crossed the Little Bahama Bank in early March in dead calm, literally counting starfish on the bottom as we passed. In late May, when the summer pattern should have been established, we've had 7 inches of rain in 24 hours at Man-O-War Cay together with 45-knot winds, and this "nasty" came as part of a three-day package of unrelenting gray skies, rainstorm after rainstorm, with winds flicking round the clock like a cow's tail in the black fly season.

Maybe we have changed the world's climate in the last century. But on the whole the Bahamas has a weather factor that still rates it as one of the best cruising areas you can find. Have faith. Bad weather never lasts forever, and the good days and the good weeks are magic.

Towering, turbulent clouds, a highly visible danger signal. Expect thunder and lightning, heavy rain, visibility of less than 300 feet, a marked drop in temperature, and wind that at worst could hit gusts of between 40 and 60 knots. It will not last, but unless you are in safe, deep water, well clear of land and reefs, it is a threat to be taken seriously. Take precautionary action early (anchor somewhere safe, batten down). Your warning is the clouds. The accompanying fall in barometric pressure usually comes as it hits.

Hurricane Season

The North Atlantic–Caribbean hurricane season runs June 1 to November 30. August, September, and October are the worst months. Seasonally, an average of ten depressions or tropical waves develop into tropical storms and reach "name" status. On average, eight of these will become severe storms and ultimately reach hurricane status.

No one would wish to risk being caught by a hurricane, but in many ways the hurricane months offer the best cruising in the Bahamas, and are not necessarily ruled out of your voyaging calendar as a high-risk period. Hurricane forecasting is accurate and will give you, from the first warnings of the development of a tropical wave, plenty of time to think ahead. When the warnings move up a notch into a tropical depression you should really focus on the weather and your planning moves into an active phase. It follows that to understand the dynamics of the hurricane development and learn the rules of hurricane avoidance, you must first be familiar with the language of the hurricane season.

TROPICAL WAVES

A tropical wave is a trough of low pressure. A wave shows itself with falling barometric pressure, overcast skies, and the arrival of a succession of mini-fronts, high wind, rain, and thunderstorms, with periods of relative calm and rain in between. A tropical wave is born in the Atlantic and its movement is always westward and northward. The trough can pass through quickly, or may linger, nearly stationery, for days. You could say that a wave is an embryonic hurricane. If the pressure dropped dramatically and the winds started to revolve around the center of low pressure, that's exactly what you would have.

The forecast of a wave may persuade you to sit out its passing in comfort rather than set out on your next passage, and it will interrupt your sunbathing. If you're at sea, a wave is no severe threat to your safety but it does bring with it all the characteristics of a succession of line squalls, which means reefing if you're under sail, closing hatches, and concern for the dinghy you may be towing.

TROPICAL DEPRESSIONS

A tropical depression is the next stage. It's the development of the wave into a system of clouds and thunderstorms with a definite circulation, always counterclockwise in the Northern Hemisphere. Top sustained winds are no more than Force 7 (28–33 knots) but gusts will be stronger.

TROPICAL STORMS

A tropical storm is the next step in the evolution of a hurricane. By now it's getting serious. At the outset sustained winds are up to Force 9 (41–47 knots), and gusts will be stronger. The counterclockwise rotation continues, and the storm will have a recognizable center. It's important to real-

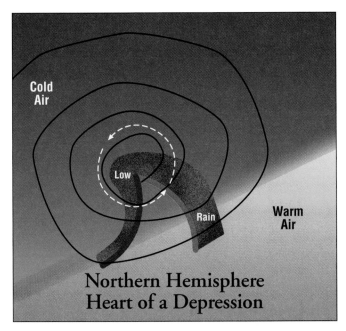

Northern Hemisphere Heart of a Depression

ize that the rotation of the storm is not simply circular but takes the form of a spiral, with the wind working inward toward the eye of the storm. This understanding plays a part in your storm evasion tactics if you're caught out at sea. A severe tropical storm moves into the Force 10 or Force 11 field with wind strength increasing to 63 knots.

The forward speed of a storm usually averages around 10 knots in its early days, and its course, which can be erratic, usually holds west and north. Warm water generally gives a tropical storm the energy burst it needs, and the Gulf Stream often becomes a hurricane interstate highway for this reason.

HURRICANES

When the sustained wind speed of a tropical storm exceeds 63 knots you are in the Force 12 bracket and you have a hurricane. From then on, although hurricanes are classed in order of magnitude as the wind speed goes up, from a cruiser's point of view it hardly matters. The highest recorded gusts have hit 175 knots, but the start point, 64-knot winds, is bad enough. The forward speed of a hurricane is likely to average 20–25 knots. A speed of 40 knots has been known. The message is that you cannot outrun a hurricane.

WIND SPEED AND WAVES

Wind and waves are the commonly understood lethal agents of a hurricane. What may not be known by many is that a doubling in wind speed results in four times the increase in wind pressure. Take a baseline of 0.1 pounds force per square foot for a 5 mph (4.3 knot) wind and, quite apart from wave action, the devastating force of a hurricane or major storm in terms of pure punch can be understood.

STORM SURGE

Above high winds and waves, hurricanes carry with them a third agent of destruction called storm surge. A dome of water up to 20 feet high is "vacuumed" skyward by the spiral rotation of the hurricane. This massive pile-up of water may have as much as a 100-mile diameter. When the hurricane hits land, particularly if this coincides with high tide, storm surge is often the principal cause of hurricane death and damage.

STORM WARNINGS

The hurricane warning system is simple, and always gives the area to which the forecast applies. You should start taking an active interest in weather forecasts when you hear that a Tropical Depression has developed, and from then on plot its progress until it is no longer a threat (we have a **Weather Plotting Chart** in **Appendix C** on pages 444–445). Long before you might find yourself listening to a Tropical Storm Watch (or even worse a Hurricane Watch) you should

				Hurricane Categorization
Category	Pressure	Wind Speed	Probable Surge	Conditions and Type of Damage
1	Above 980 mb (Above 28.94 in.)	64–83 knots (74–95 mph)	4–5 ft.	Visibility much reduced. Maneuvering under engines just possible. Open anchorages untenable. Danger of poorly secured boats torn loose in protected anchorages.
2	965–979 mb (28.50–28.91 in.)	84–96 knots (96–110 mph)	6–8 ft.	Visibility close to zero. Boats in protected anchorages at risk, particularly from boats torn loose. Severe damage to unprotected boats and boats poorly secured and prepared.
3	945–964 mb (27.91–28.47 in.)	97–113 knots (111–130 mph)	9–12 ft.	Deck fittings at risk and may tear loose, anchor links can fail, and unprotected lines will chafe through. Extensive severe damage.
4	920–944 mb (27.17–27.88 in.)	114–135 knots (131–155 mph)	13–18 ft.	Very severe damage and loss of life.
5	Below 920 mb (Below 27.17 in.)	Above 135 knots (Above155 mph)	Above 18 ft.	Catastrophic conditions with catastrophic damage.

have anticipated the weather, and be out of the danger area. The final countdown goes in stages:

Tropical Storm Watch	36 hrs
Tropical Storm Warning or Alert	24 hrs
Hurricane Watch	36 hours
Hurricane Warning or Alert	24 hrs

PLAYING IT SAFE IN THE HURRICANE SEASON

If you're cruising through the islands during the hurricane months, the rules you must follow are:

- Plot the location of every hurricane harbor or potential hurricane hole along your route.

- Set out with the extra ground tackle and extra dock lines on board to secure your boat against a severe storm, be it at anchor, in mangroves, or wherever.

- As we've said, listen to a reliable weather forecast service at least once every day. Remote as it may seem, you must know what's happening in the North Atlantic Ocean between 07° and 20° N, and in the southwest Caribbean Sea in much the same latitude.

SECURING YOUR BOAT

In securing your boat the guidelines are straightforward common sense.

- Mangroves are ideal. Canals are good. Any land-locked water is better than open water. Try to get away from other boats. Their lines may not hold.

- Secure your boat. Use every line you have and all your ground tackle. Allow for storm surge.

- Reduce windage. No canvas or curtains of any kind should be above deck.

A fishing vessel left high and dry by a hurricane.

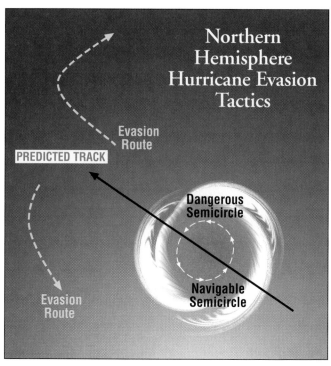

Northern Hemisphere Hurricane Evasion Tactics

- Batten down, and leave the boat. Find shelter ashore. Don't stay on your boat. Consider flying out of the Bahamas. Your life counts. The boat can take care of itself; and you have insurance, don't you?

IN THE WORST CASE

If you are caught at sea, your survival tactics are totally dependent on accurately plotting the position and course of the hurricane, and plotting radial distances from its center (the eye of the hurricane) to establish estimated danger zones:

Distance from the Eye	Wind Speed
150 miles	Force 8 (34–40 knots)
100 miles	Force 11 (56–63 knots)
75 miles	Force 12 (over 64 knots)

Every hurricane develops its own unique intensity and footprint. These figures are no more than a generalization, but indicative of the wind speed and sea state you can expect. It's also vital to know your position in relation to the eye and the predicted track of the hurricane so that you can decide which way to turn. The one vital question is this: Are you in the *dangerous* semicircle, or the *navigable* semicircle?

If you don't know where the center of the hurricane is and can't plot it, if the wind is veering, you're in the *dangerous* semicircle. If the wind seems steady, or starts to back, you're in the *navigable* semicircle.

THE DANGEROUS SEMICIRCLE

The most dangerous half of the storm is the *northern* semicircle, the part that lies to the north of the path of the hurricane. It's called the dangerous semicircle because if you're caught in this area, you're in the path of the hurricane and its spiral rotation will take you deeper into its center. Your only hope is to try to break away to north, and then get behind the worst of it.

Your immediate evasive action is to get away with all the speed you can make, keeping the wind 10–45° on your starboard bow, and keep altering to starboard to take you above and eastward away from the storm.

THE NAVIGABLE SEMICIRCLE

The southern semicircle is known as the *navigable* semicircle, simply because your chances are better there. The hurricane will be moving away from you rather than toward you, and the direction of the wind will blow you away from the storm.

Your immediate evasive action is to turn to bring the wind on your starboard quarter, make all possible speed, and keep turning to port to pass below and eastward away from the storm.

CLOSING THOUGHTS ON WEATHER

Hurricanes are the most destructive of weather hazards, but they happen relatively rarely, and are now predicted and tracked hour by hour. Today it's the missed forecast and the "harmless thundershower" and other oversights and miscalculations that cause most of the lost boats and lives. Alcohol and arrogance, sometimes in deadly combination, can act in concert with the weather leading to tragedy. Sitting out a thunderstorm in the lee of an island, or returning to port early because of freshening unfavorable winds may seem overly cautious. But you can still enjoy "being there," and you'll live to enjoy another day!

Crossing the Gulf Stream

FOR any vessel crossing to the Bahamas from the east coast of Florida, or returning to Florida, the Gulf Stream is the dominant navigational consideration. Don't imagine it as a current. It's a 45-mile-wide river, more powerful than you think. You can't see the wash of its speed as if you were standing on a river bank, but it's always there, flowing northward at an average speed of 2.5 knots, day and night, in every season. It's hard to believe at first that it even exists when you look east from a Florida beach, out over the ocean.

In winter you can sometimes mark the Gulf Stream by the steam rising from its warm waters, degrees warmer than the colder coastal water. In winter too, and whenever a Norther is blowing, the sea horizon is often jagged, sawtoothed. That's when there are "elephants" out there, giant square waves, high seas kicked up by the Stream's determination to win its way north against the wind, come what may.

In summer you can identify the Gulf Stream by a color change to an ultramarine deep blue in which sometimes, if the sun is right, you will see light dancing in its depths. You can guess you're in the Stream when you see corn blond patches of Sargasso weed drifting north. You know you're there when the water temperature clicks up something like 2° above the shoreside ocean temperature, and your GPS shows you moving 2 to 5 knots faster to the north than your knotmaster indicates. Fishermen, tuned to the rhythm of ocean life, can fix the boundaries of the Gulf Stream by the run of pelagic gamefish.

Planning to Cross the Stream

Crossing the Gulf Stream in any kind of craft can best be compared to the progress of an ant crossing an airport moving walkway. The ant might well have wanted to make a direct crossing but, during its transit, inevitably the ant will be taken past its target. For every hour you are in the influence of the Stream you will be carried about 2.5 nm to the north. Like it or not. Your first concern is to minimize the time you'll be in Gulf Stream water if you're crossing from a departure point more or less on an equal latitude to your destination. If you're coming up from the south, then it's different. You want to stay on that walkway for as long as possible, getting a free ride to help you north before you turn off.

NOAA weather broadcasts give daily information about the Stream, its width, speed, distance offshore at different points, and its temperature, but for navigation it's sensible to assume that the entire distance you have to run from departure point to a destination lying anywhere along the

Gulf Stream Crossing Principal Routes

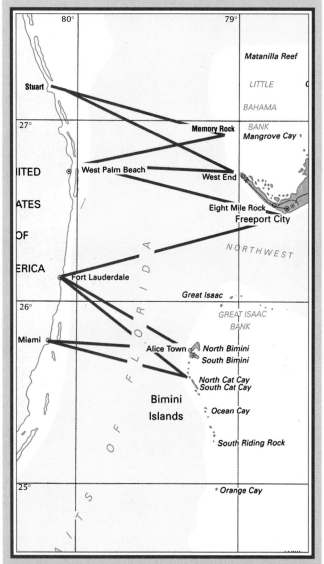

Route To/From		Headings	Distance
Florida	**Bahamas**		**NM**
Stuart	Memory Rock	100°/280° M	56
Stuart	West End	115°/295° M	66
Palm Beach	Memory Rock	079°/259° M	49
Palm Beach	West End	094°/274° M	53
Palm Beach	Freeport/Port Lucaya	105°/285° M	75
Fort Lauderdale	Freeport/Port Lucaya	070°/250° M	83
Fort Lauderdale	Bimini	119°/299° M	48
Fort Lauderdale	Gun Cay Cut	127°/307° M	52
Miami	Bimini	095°/275° M	42
Miami	Gun Cay Cut	106°/286° M	43

Distances exclude inshore close approaches at the start and end of a passage.

079° 15' W line of Longitude will be subject to that 2.5-knot north-flowing current. Listen to NOAA's Gulf Stream information. Plot the edge of the Stream on your chart, its width, its speed, and record the temperature. Note when you're in the Stream, and when you leave it. If nothing else it will add interest to your passage across the Florida Strait, and you'll add to your store of knowledge.

The Gulf Stream Crossing Routes

The need to minimize the time you spend in the Stream, unless you're prepared to accept a long haul, effectively means you should set out from Florida no further north than Stuart (the St. Lucie Inlet). To set a southern limit, for in theory there are no problems in riding the Gulf Stream all the way north from its start, let's say no further south than Angelfish Creek at the north end of Key Largo. In this start zone area the hazards of most of the Florida East Coast inlets, Jupiter, Boynton, Boca Raton, and Hillsboro, dictate that unless you have up-to-date local knowledge, the right kind of craft, and a favorable tide, sea state, and wind, your departure ports come down to six options, of which the best (rated for simplicity of navigation, and pre-departure backup facilities) are marked with an asterisk (*):

- **Stuart*** (St. Lucie Inlet)
- **The Port of Palm Beach*** (Lake Worth Inlet)
- **Fort Lauderdale*** (Port Everglades Entrance)
- **Miami*** (Miami Harbor Entrance)
- **Key Biscayne** (Key Biscayne Channel)
- **Key Largo** (Angelfish Creek)

In the Bahamas your landfalls and immediate ports of entry are:

- **West End, Grand Bahama** (for the Abacos).
- **Port Lucaya, Grand Bahama** (for Grand Bahama itself, the Abacos, and the Berry Islands).
- **Alice Town in North Bimini** (for the Biminis, the Berry Islands, Nassau, and beyond).
- **North Cat Cay** (for the Biminis, the Berry Islands, Nassau, and beyond).

You can elect to continue on across the Little Bahama Bank or the Great Bahama Bank without staging or even clearing in at these first landfalls, but when you cross the West End–Bimini line you have crossed the Gulf Stream.

These are the best routes to minimize disadvantageous time in the Gulf Stream. You can make your own variations and there's no reason why a boat shouldn't leave Miami destined for West End, but to set out from Stuart or Palm Beach bound for Gun Cay Cut wouldn't make sense, especially for a slow boat.

You can make your own way to the Bahamas outside the area covered by these routes, but it might not be wise unless you're prepared for a voyage of exploration. In particular, south of South Riding Rock and Castle Rock Light (20 nm south of North Cat Cay) you're on your own. There are no navigational aids, and the accuracy of the charts is suspect. If you're approaching the Bahamas from anywhere further afield than the east coast of Florida, the Gulf Stream is not your particular concern.

Weather

The Gulf Stream is a constant, reckonable force. The weather is not. Listen to the forecasts. Believe the bad ones. Don't trust the good ones! Go to the beach and look out over the ocean. What's it doing out there?

The most difficult and dangerous time for any vessel to cross the Gulf Stream is when the wind is from the north, and that includes the northeast and the northwest. Whether you are running a 180-foot motor yacht or an 18-foot sailboat doesn't matter—this is *definitely not* the time to cross. Remember that Gulf Stream flowing north at anything up to 5 knots. When the wind blows from the north it's like rubbing a cat the wrong way, all the fur kicks up and the result is the "elephants" we mentioned. High ugly waves as closely spaced as elephants in a circus parade. If it's like that, enjoy the chance to finish the job list you never completed. Take your crew to brunch, lunch, or dinner. See a movie. The Gulf Stream is *not* where you want to be.

Wait until the forecast is good and it *looks good*, too. Even then, be prepared to take unexpected weather. If it's uncertain, don't take a chance on the weather and try to grab what seems to be a window if you haven't got the speed to get there fast in safety. We all know the pressure of deadlines, you only have *x* days for your holiday, or you've got a flight to meet somewhere, but your safety comes first. The

Cherokee Sound. Approaching storm.

Florida Strait, because of the Gulf Stream, can become a very hazardous stretch of water if the weather turns against you. In the wrong weather it can be a killer.

Tactics

There are some three or four different ways of working out your crossing tactics to minimize the effect of the Gulf Stream or take advantage of it. For the first timer we give a work sheet in **Appendix A** on page 429 that shows one way you can go about this, which may be helpful.

LANDFALLS AND WARNINGS

To the north of West End, the tall casuarina trees of Sandy Cay (9 nm south of Memory Rock and 7 nm north of West End) are a useful marker. West End's water tower is prominent, and its 150-foot Batelco tower has red lights at the top and at its midpoint. There's a light on Indian Cay, immediately north of West End, but it's often hard to pick up. Freeport has approach buoys, as do the marinas between Freeport and Port Lucaya.

In the south, tiny uninhabited Great Issac Island has a reliable 23-nm-range light. Gun Cay has a lighthouse that works some of the time. But it remains that your arrival in Bahamian waters, unless you're taking the Northwest Providence Channel route on to Nassau, should be timed for daylight. It's better for you, for lights can fail or be obscured in rain, it's less stressful, and it's safer. More detailed navigational advice is given in the separate island group sections of this Guide.

RETURNING TO FLORIDA

Navigation on the return passage to Florida poses no landfall problems. You'll pick up the loom of the lights of the East Coast anything up to 50 nm out at night, and condominium and office tower blocks around 10 nm out, depending on your height above the water. You can't miss Florida. There's 360 miles of it right in front of you.

The Gulf Stream Rules

It remains to list the "rules" of making a successful Gulf Stream crossing:

- Never set out in adverse weather, or risk outrunning the onset of bad weather. Be especially wary of winds from the north. You want pussy cat conditions, not a wildcat!

- Always time your arrival in the Bahamas for daylight. Preferably between dawn and noon.

- Don't single-hand. *If* something happens to you, Murphy's Law will take over. Self-preservation is the name of the game, not macho image-making. The Florida Strait is no place to be when you're in real trouble.

- If you're crossing in a small boat, go in convoy with similar boats or with another boat whose cruising speed matches your *achievable* speed, which, depending on the sea state, may be very different from the speed you can achieve in calm water.

- If you're making the crossing for the first time, or you're anxious about it (you may have reservations about the competence of your crew if something happened to you), team up and make your passage in company with another of your kind. Then get together for a celebration meal after your safe arrival!

- Always have enough fuel (even on a sailboat) to motor the full distance against head seas and arrive with not less than 20 percent of your fuel remaining.

- Always have a working VHF radio with a backup (handheld?) VHF.

- Ideally have GPS as your navigation system, for Loran becomes progressively inaccurate in the Bahamas.

- Check that you have a working depth sounder, working lights, a flashlight, an air horn, charts, binoculars, distress flares and smoke, and a Type I lifejacket for every person on board.

- If you're on a sailboat or an open boat, have a safety harness or fitted tether for every person on board with a secure anchor point.

- If you can afford an EPIRB (Emergency Position-Indicating Radio Beacon), have one, preferably a 406 MHz EPIRB.

- Let a friend know when you are leaving. Call when you arrive. *If you don't call after your forecast arrival within a time equal to one third of your anticipated passage time, the friend should contact the Coast Guard.* Make sure your friend knows the make, length, color, and callsign of your boat, your route, your time of departure, and how many people you had on board. Even better, leave them your Float Plan (see the **Appendices** on page 428).

Navigation in the Islands

AS the captain of a Spanish galleon might have told you, in the Bahamas you need just about every aid to navigation you can get your hands on, as well as your own wits and skill. With the combination of bluewater ocean passages (however short) and coastal work in waters where reefs, rocks, and sandbanks are part of the tapestry of each leg you run, this is just about true.

The one navigational system we've never had to employ in the Bahamas is celestial, but we've carried a sextant for years and perhaps we should have kept in practice, just in case. Top of our list is the most basic requirement of all: charts, even though these may be dated. With the charts you'll want your parallel rules, dividers, pencils, and so on. There's nothing very extraordinary in this, and of course you'll need a pair of binoculars and a hand-bearing compass (as well as a fixed compass on the boat). If you have this much, and your skills in eyeball navigation (see the next section), you're pretty well set and could go anywhere. But we live in an age of electronics, and why not take advantage of it? Our preference is the most accurate navigation system yet devised, GPS, and electronic charting.

The Global Positioning System (GPS)

The Navstar/GPS system is a satellite-based US government radio navigation system designed to provide global all-weather 24-hour position data. While intended for use by navigators worldwide, the GPS system was and is under the control of the US Department of Defense.

Claiming that national security was at stake the Department of Defense superimposed a special mode known as Selective Availability (SA) on the satellite broadcast made available for civilian users (1575.42 MHz), which deliberately introduced timing errors to make the system less accurate than the broadcast available for the military. The Pentagon reserves the right to impose SA whenever they wish, and for safe navigation it must be taken that SA, which has been imposed almost continuously since 1991, is in force the whole time.

At first your natural reaction is to conclude that SA puts the civilian user at risk, and that its imposition is unjustifiable in the context of national security. These conclusions are probably true, but the improved accuracy of the military system would not necessarily give the civilian user the ability to

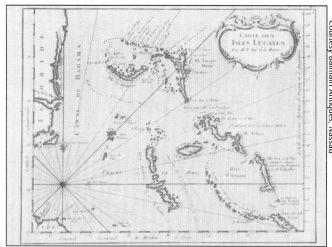

A chart of the Bahamas by Jacques Nicholas Bellin, 1751.

navigate by GPS alone through a narrow passage at night or with zero visibility. The reason is that most of the world's charts are based on hydrographic surveys carried out in the last century and the charts are only as accurate as the charting methods of the day could make them. As it stands now, President Clinton, convinced that SA should be deactivated, has ruled that a review of its justification should be held in 2000. If SA is continued past the year 2000, the case for its retention is to be re-examined annually for five years.

GPS without SA imposed will give position fixes accurate to +/- 15 meters (49.2 feet). With SA imposed you must reckon on accuracy of +/- 100 meters (328 feet) 95 percent of the time. In other words, you will know that you are within a football field's length of a known place on the surface of the world. Putting it in other words, GPS draws a circle with a radius of 328 feet around the position of your GPS antenna, and you are somewhere inside that circle. For the other 5 percent of the time you will be close but somewhere outside that circle.

The GPS positions we have plotted are circles with a radius comparable to a GPS position with SA imposed, but there is no guarantee that the center of our circles is an accurate fix. Our plotting, like yours, is subject to the limitations of SA and sometimes inaccurate charts, and all you will know is that we were somewhere near there, and that the position we have marked is the point at which we reckon conventional navigation must take over.

Differential GPS

The US Coast Guard, in the interest of safe coastal navigation, has introduced a supplemental radio broadcast system called Differential GPS, which removes the errors produced by SA and results, if you have a DGPS receiver, in a position accuracy between 5 and 8 meters (16–26 feet). In effect it is pinpoint accuracy. Before you come to rely absolutely on DGPS, you will want to be well aware that the DGPS beacons cover US coastal waters only. They do not, at this time, cover the Bahamas.

The introduction of DGPS does not itself solve the ongoing problem caused by inaccuracies in charts, and the wise navigator will realize that DGPS accuracy can take him or her closer to known dangers than it's prudent to venture.

GPS Datum

The GPS Datum used in this Guide is WGS84. This is compatible with the National Oceanic and Atmospheric Administration (NOAA) NAD83 Chart Datum.

Don't be surprised if your GPS and the chart you are using disagree on positioning, but remember the chart, in its depiction of coastline, offshore hazards, and depths will be good. Nonetheless, you are wise to take note of the dating and latest updating of the chart you're using, and look carefully for any warning notices about its accuracy.

The Ultimate Warnings

ALL charts, paper and electronic, are only as accurate as the survey on which they are based, and the extent of the updating that has taken place since that first survey. It's not unlikely, in areas unfrequented by commercial shipping and therefore lower on the priority list for chart updating, that GPS and chart fail to match. We've "been" on dry land chartwise more than once while still happy, and safely afloat, in navigable water. In all coastal and inshore navigation you must place primary reliance on your own eyes, your depth sounder, and your radar. And use that autopilot only when you're absolutely certain that your projected course lies in safe, deep, obstruction-free water.

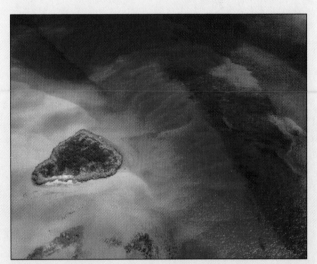

Eyeball navigation. The Wide Opening, northern Exuma Cays.

Remember too that the GPS isn't infallible. Not all GPS receivers will give the same figures for the same spot. Their accuracy depends on the number of satellites they can process, your field of view, the position of the satellites you've acquired at that time, and, we'd guess, the quality of the equipment you're using. Much of the time we run three different GPS receivers and none agree exactly. We may all have variations there.

At the end of the day it's Eyes, Eyes, Eyes, and Common Sense that count!

Finally, we must state that we take no responsibility for the accuracy of our waypoints, nor can we guarantee that a course line drawn between any two waypoints will give you safe, navigable, obstruction-free water. The ultimate responsibility for pilotage is yours.

Waypoints and Units of Measurement

GPS on its first introduction was programmed to work in the conventional navigation position fixing of degrees, minutes, and seconds. The wider use of GPS, particularly for land surveying, led to a change in which seconds were replaced by thousands to give pinpoint accuracy. Some marine GPS instruments have followed this trend, and most of these omit the third figure from the read-out to keep it simple (and display hundreds). This can lead to confusion if you're not certain what those two terminal figures represent. If the figures go above 59, it's the sure indication that you are working in hundreds.

We have no wish to appear reactionary or be fighting a rearguard action against progress, but we feel inclined to stay with seconds. We feel that 1 second, just over 100 feet, say two or three boat lengths for the majority of us out there on boats, is as accurate a measurement as you can reasonably work with and achieve at sea. Perhaps the more overriding reason is that a large number of charts still carry latitude and longitude measured in degrees, minutes, and seconds. If you make use of charts (which you should), it makes it easier to stay in the same system, otherwise you have to convert those thousands into seconds before you can start plotting.

Waypoints are given step by step throughout our text, and a full Waypoint Catalog is in **Appendix B**. So that you're able to work with no hindrance, whatever your units of GPS measurement, we list all our waypoints in both systems of measurement, and in our **Appendix,** under **Conversion Tables and Useful Measurements** on page 452 we provide you with a bridge between both systems. In truth we run both in tandem, and have no problems switching between them.

It remains that GPS is a superb system for passage making. It guarantees you the ability to make landfalls exactly where you want 100 percent of the time, and it will do this regardless of the weather and whether it is day or night. Thereafter you must rely on the old tried and trusted aids to navigation: your own eyes, your chart, sketch chart, or air photograph, the depth, your log, and your radar.

Traditional Navigation

Navigation Marks

The nature of their world dictated that the Bahamians, born and brought up within sight of the sea, nurtured on a diet of conch, lobster tails, and fish, and more often than not "bused" to school by boat, would become highly competent seamen. The establishment of navigation marks has never been a high priority in the Bahamas. They know their reefs, channels, and cuts from childhood and can read their waters as if the colors were a map spread before them.

In the last century navigation marks set up by their British overlords were regarded with suspicion and at times destroyed or deliberately misplaced, for the only source of income for many islanders came from wrecking and the profits of salvage. There are navigation marks in the islands today, but their maintenance is not always the highest priority. Regard them as a bonus. Treat them with caution.

It's essentially chart, compass, depth, and your eyesight that counts. Radar can help, particularly with landfall identification, but your own eyes are vital. In the Bahamas the best rule to follow is *if you can't see, don't move.* In other words, don't risk running inshore passages at night, or in bad weather, and particularly if all the Bahamian colors are lost and you can't read the water.

The Effects of Wind and Wave

Coral is so slow growing that a reef will hardly gain visible height in a thousand years, but sand and sandbars move with currents and swells, and are moved in storms. Just as the bars and shoals of the Florida East Coast inlets are never constant, so the underwater profile of much of the Bahamas is always changing.

Be aware that no chart can serve as more than a warning that shoal waters exist in a general area and can never show you the passes through the shoals in the year that you are cruising there. Be aware that severe storms, such as Hurricane *Andrew* in 1992 and Hurricane *Floyd* in 1999, can change the contours of the seabed, obliterate navigation marks, which may not be replaced for years, and uproot every tree, which will change the profile and appearance of an island. Elbow Cay in the Abacos was cut in two by Hurricane *Floyd*.

Batelco Towers

What you will find, more often than not, is that the essential similarity of the low-lying Bahamian cays and islands make identification difficult, and sometimes really confusing. There are few natural land features that are

Batelco towers, George Town, Great Exuma.

prominent enough to help you fix your position. Time and time again it's the man-made features that will count, the silos around Hatchet Bay in Eleuthera, and the new water tanks that have been built in places like Grand Cay and Spanish Wells. The greatest aid of them all are the radio towers erected by the Bahamas Telephone Corporation. These Batelco towers, faint against the sky at a distance, are the certain indicator of a settlement. Once you've picked up your Batelco tower, you've got it made. We list them in **Appendix B** on page 441.

Eyeball Navigation

Most of us have heard about eyeball navigation. It's the magic art of reading depth contours by color "the way you've got to do it while you're there, otherwise you'll be on the reefs." As a first timer it sounds like the kind of skill that can only be acquired after three seasons, or maybe after you've left at least three keels lying on Bahamian reefs. The reality is very different.

Eyeball navigation is no more than using your eyes to pick your way forward, rather than taking a course off the chart and panicking when your depth sounder shows 4 feet of water. It's the same way you'd chose a route up a mountainside on land. You use your eyes and common sense to bend your route to suit the land, to take the easiest course, the best path, rather than blundering uphill on a set of compass bearings.

Navigating the Bahamas is eyeball stuff. You know where you want to go. Just use your eyes, steer your course looking ahead so that you can see the Bahamian equivalent of trees and rocks way ahead, rather than just 2 feet ahead of your bow pulpit. There's no magic about it. You could say it comes naturally. It's not difficult. Why? For one all-important reason. The dangers are color-coded. All you have to know is the color code.

For eyeball navigation we're talking about six colors, blue, green, yellow, brown, black, and white, and some shades in between: turquoise and aquamarine. The last is the color that makes Bahamian waters seem like nowhere else on earth, a transparent green with a touch of blue in it that looks as if it's being floodlit from below. Estimating depth in ocean water with the clarity of a Florida spring seems impossible at first. Are you in 5 feet, or is that starfish 18 feet down? But you soon learn that color is the give-away.

Before you start, you need polarized sun glasses. This brings two advantages. The first is that you cut surface reflection and you can see into the water. The second is that the colors are enhanced. Only polarized lenses will do this for you. You could add a third advantage, but any good pair of sunglasses will give you this: sunglasses cut glare, and prevent you being temporarily blinded if you swing around into the sun, or, even worse, have to hold a course into the sun.

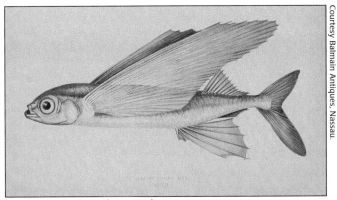

Antique print. A Flying Fish.

Sunlight

The position of the sun is the key to eyeball navigation. You need the sun to bring the colors of the water alive, and you need the sun as a searchlight working to your advantage rather than as a blinding light in front of you. The optimum is to have the sun fairly high in the sky and behind you. The worst situation is to find yourself making your way through unknown waters into a rising or a setting sun. Don't take it on, unless you're certain that the depth, all the way, is more than safe for your boat draft.

Overcast days and rain make eyeball navigation difficult. If you have a tricky passage immediately ahead and you're caught by a rain squall, hold off until you can read the water. Even on sunny days the shadows of moving clouds can suddenly confuse the underwater map you're reading. But if those dark patches are in motion, you know they're clouds. Again you may have to hold back until you can see what the cloud shadow has been concealing.

The Colors

Now let's turn to the main colors. Let's take the sequence color by color showing the variations as they come, as you'll find them after crossing the Gulf Stream. First, deep blue water. Classic bluewater. Deep blue is absolute safety. Safe deep ocean water. Light blue is the kind of depth, around 30 feet, you get at the edge of the Banks. You are safe, however surprised you may be to suddenly see everything on the bottom as clearly as if there were just 3 feet of water under your keel.

Green water is starting to become shallow, the color changing from dark to light as the depth decreases. Green is Banks water, going from 30 feet down to 15 or 12 feet. The paler the shade of green, the more shallow the water will be. Yellow, running into white, is shoal water. Reckon it to be 5 feet or less, and go slowly if you're running in deliberately to beach your boat. Otherwise avoid water that has taken on more yellow or white than green. Perhaps pale aquamarine could be a way to describe the warning color, the color

1. *Safe, deep ocean water (San Salvador).*

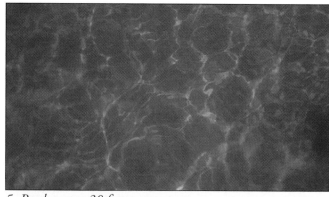

5. *Bank water, 30 feet or more.*

2. *Going from ocean to shore or bank (Semana Cay).*

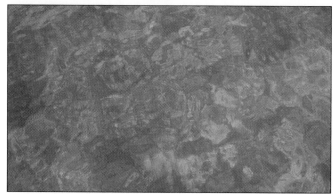

6. *Bank water, 12–15 feet.*

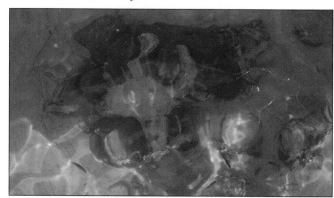

3. *Ocean shoaling to reef (Semana Cay).*

7. *A small coral head.*

4. *Broken coral, 9 feet.*

8. *Coral or limestone rock just under the surface.*

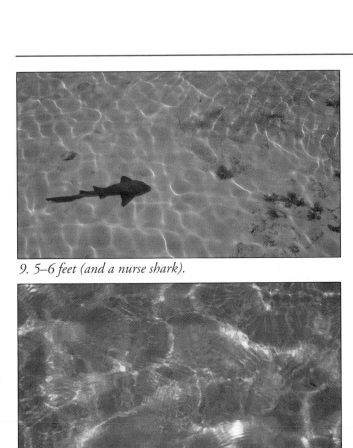

9. 5–6 feet (and a nurse shark).

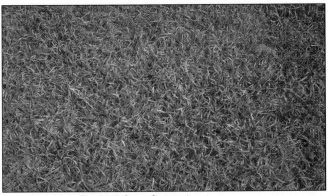

10. Warning color of reef or grass (most likely grass).

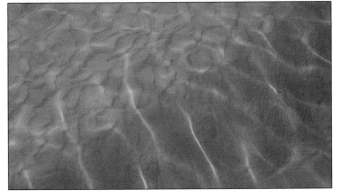

11. Grass (under 3–4 feet of water).

12. Upper left, 1–2 feet; lower right, 3–4 feet.

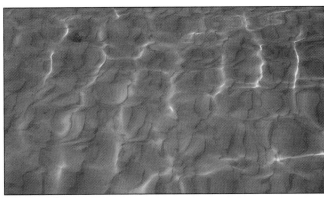

13. 3–4 feet.

14. 1 foot.

15. Sand exposed at low water.

16. The very edge of the beach.

that makes the prettiest photographs when it's set against a distant strip of darker blue deep water, or the sand and palms of a Bahamian beach.

Brown rings alarm bells. It could be grass, but it might well be a coral reef. Avoid it or slow down. Don't chance your luck. If it's grass, you'll learn that the edge of the brown is not as sharp as it will be if it's a coral reef. Grass, which shows dark on the bottom, can be your greatest confusion factor. Until you get used to it, and can second guess where grass should be, or could be, or will be, you can mistake grass for coral. The only way to learn is to get behind the wheel. Dark brown or black certainly rings an alarm bell. It's the color of a coral reef. Closer to the surface it will show sharp edges as you get nearer, but deeper features remain less distinct.

Dark bown or black is also the color of an isolated coral head. It's always a tough shot to guess whether it's two feet under the surface or ten feet down. It's best to reckon, unless you're in good deep water, that each coral head is a threat and avoid it. As you get closer to a coral head, if the surrounding bottom is grass, you may see a ring of sand around it where foraging fish have scoured the bottom.

Finally white comes in the alarm bell category. It's sand. Generally white will turn out to be a sand bore, but it can be a shelving beach. Sometimes in shoal water the aquamarine tint of the water makes it hard to see a sand bore that has built up close to the surface. If you're lucky a sand bore will show a dry white spine but, like an iceberg, there's more under water than you can see on top. Stay well clear. White may also signal a "fish mud," an area of sand stirred up by a school of fish rooting around. But don't guess that it's a fish mud because no sand bores are shown on your chart in that area. Go cautiously. Study our pages of water photographs. These give you an idea of the way it is.

Pulling the Navigation Package Together

Except for safe, deep-water passages, you don't sail at night in the Bahamas. You need your eyes, and you need your skill at reading the water. GPS is useful only for marking the waypoints along your deep-water passages. Once you get into shallow water, or near shallow water, forget GPS.

What can help you? Essentially two things. The first we've already mentioned. It's your sunglasses. Polarized lenses. The second is height above water. You don't have to have a tuna tower, but the higher you are above the water, the better you'll be able to see. An aft cockpit sailboat is not necessarily disadvantaged. A lookout on the bow can pilot you through the shallows. We've done this with a lookout seated on the spreaders. It worked well.

Follow the Mailboats

Our final advice is the old Bahamian advice: "Follow the mailboats." Not only take note of their routes, but also their departure times, normally when the sun is high in the sky. At least up to December 1998, this was our last word on navigating in the Bahamas. Why up to that date? That was when the mailboat *Lady Mathilda* ran aground on Hogsty Reef in the southern Bahamas.

The mailboat Eleuthera Express.

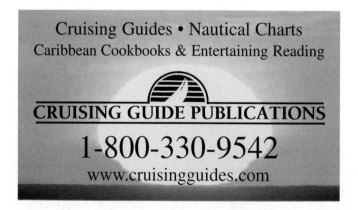

Part II

The Northern Cruising Grounds

The Little Bahama Bank

The Northern Abacos

The Central Abacos

The Southern Abacos

Grand Bahama Island

Bank water, about 30 feet deep, Little Bahama Bank.

Northern Cruising Grounds
Principal Routes

Map labels: Matanilla Shoal, Matanilla Reef, Walker's Cay, Grand Cay, LITTLE BAHAMA, Strangers Cay, Carters Cays, Lily Bank, Little Sale Cay, Moraine Cay, Fish Cays, BANK, Great Sale Cay, Memory Rock, Mangrove Cay, Pensacola Cays, Little Abaco, Fox Town, Cedar Harbour, Crab Cay, Powel Cay, Cooper's Town, Nun Jack Cay, Crab Cay, Sandy Cay, Cave Cay, Mangrove Cay, Basin Harbour Cay, Green Turtle Cay, New Plymouth, Whale Cay Channel, Wood Cay, Water Cay, Riding Point, Norman Castle, Great Guana Cay, Treasure Cay, Scotland Cay, Indian Cay, WEST END, Settlement Point, Lucaya Estates, High Rock, McLeans Town, Big Joe Downer Cay, Man of War Cay, Eight Mile Rock, Peterson Cay, GRAND BAHAMA, Sweeting's Cay, Woolen Dean Cay, HOPE TOWN, MARSH HARBOUR, Tilloo Cay, Pinders Point, FREEPORT, Snake Cay, Pelican Harbour, Pelican Cays L and Sea Park, The Marls, Linyard Cay, Little Harbour, Mastic Point, Hard Bargain, The Bight, Moore's Island, Cherokee Sound, N.W. Providence Channel, ABACO, Great Isaac, The Brothers, Gorda Cay, Crossing Rocks, Little Isaac, Great Isaac Bank, Middle & East Isaac, Sandy Point, Rocky Point, Hole in Wall, Great Stirrup Cay, Channel

ROUTE TO/FROM		HEADINGS	DISTANCE NM	PASSAGE
Stuart, Florida	Memory Rock	100°/280°M	56	Gulf Stream crossing
Stuart, Florida	West End	115°/295°M	66	Gulf Stream crossing
Palm Beach, Florida	Memory Rock	079°/259°M	49	Gulf Stream crossing
Palm Beach, Florida	West End	094°/274°M	53	Gulf Stream crossing
Palm Beach, Florida	Freeport/Port Lucaya	105°/285°M	75	Gulf Stream crossing
Fort Lauderdale	Freeport/Port Lucaya	070°/250°M	83	Gulf Stream crossing
Freeport/Port Lucaya	Mangrove Cay	see text	33	Lucayan Waterway
Freeport/Port Lucaya	Little Stirrup Cay (Berry Islands)	138°/318°M	55	NW Providence Channel
Memory Rock North	Walkers Cay	070°/250°M	41	Little Bahama Bank
Memory Rock South	Mangrove Cay	086°/266°M	28	Little Bahama Bank
Mangrove Cay	Great Sale Cay	086°/266°M	21	Little Bahama Bank
West End	Walkers Cay	see text	45	Little Bahama Bank
West End	Mangrove Cay	see text	28	Little Bahama Bank
Walkers Cay	Great Sale Cay	see text	20	Little Bahama Bank
Great Sale Cay	Crab Cay	see text	41	Little Bahama Bank
Crab Cay	Green Turtle Cay	see text	16	Sea of Abaco
Crab Cay	Treasure Cay	see text	30	Sea of Abaco
Treasure Cay	Marsh Harbour	see text	12	Sea of Abaco
Green Turtle Cay	Hope Town	see text	23	Sea of Abaco
Hope Town	Little Harbour	see text	15	Sea of Abaco
Little Harbour Bar	Hole-in-the-Wall	197°/017°M	33	Atlantic coastal
Little Harbour Bar	Great Stirrup Cay (Berry Islands)	see text	73	NE Providence Channel
Little Harbour Bar	Little Egg Island (Eleuthera)	176°/356°M	50	NE Providence Channel

Distances exclude inshore close approaches at the start and end of a passage. The notation "see text" indicates multi-leg passages that are fully covered in the text.

Chapter 3
The Little Bahama Bank

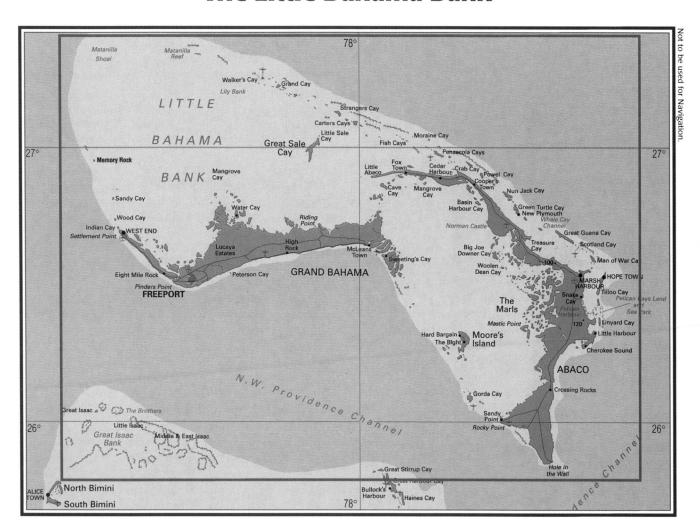

The Little Bahama Bank

THE Little Bahama Bank is the northernmost of the shallow seas that give the Bahamas its unique character. Measured from west to east along Latitude 27° N (just north of Memory Rock to the barrier reef east of the Abaco Cays) it's some 85 nm. Measured from north to south, dropping down the line of 078° 30' W (just west of Walkers Cay to the shoals off the north coast of Grand Bahama) it's about 35 nm. You can add in the Sea of Abaco, which runs between Great Abaco Island and the Abaco Cays. That's another 55 nm. The shallows between the east end of Grand Bahama and Little Abaco Island, the area lying south of Little Abaco Island and west of the Marls, is also a part of the Little Bahama Bank. This sector of the Bank, a mess of mud banks, sand ridges, and shoals, is no cruising ground.

Other than taking a circuitous ocean route, the only way to reach the Abacos is by crossing the Little Bahama Bank.

The Little Bahama Bank offers depths that average around 15 feet and, provided you keep to the proven routes, no particular navigation problems. Your primary concern is to be somewhere secure by last light. It's possible to transit the Little Bahama Bank at night, but the cays are low lying with outlying reefs and shoals, there are uncharted rocks and sandbars, the effects of tidal currents are guessable but not predictable, and there are few navigation lights. Unless you want to get in touch with your insurance agent early in your cruise, we'd give night passage making over the Banks a miss.

If you haven't the speed to cross the Bank and reach your destination in daylight, you must anchor out. But maybe not "out" in the middle of nowhere. The salvation of the Little Bahama Bank (if you can put it that way) is Great

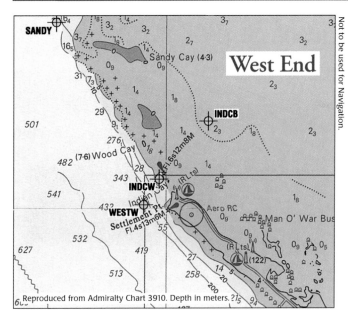

Reproduced from Admiralty Chart 3910. Depth in meters.

Not to be used for Navigation.

Sale Cay, an uninhabited island (at which it's lawful to anchor if you haven't cleared in), located at just about the midpoint of the Bank. So your decision making hinges, as ever, on your destination, your choice of entry port, your boat, and the weather. Whatever these parameters, the Little Bahama Bank offers a broad compass of options.

West End

West End is in Grand Bahama Island, and on the face of it, we should include it in that section. We don't. Why? Look at the chart. West End occupies a strategic position. You could say that it's the Bahamian gateway on the Florida-Abaco route. Sure there's an alternative, which is to go by way of one of the Freeport-Lucaya marinas in Grand Bahama and the Grand Lucayan Waterway, but this is not mainstream for most boaters. Not least anyone unable to accommodate a bridge clearance of 27 feet at high water. So if you look at the West End route, you have two simple choices: either to stage in West End before crossing the Little Bahama Bank, or to carry straight on across the Bank.

So let's call West End the Port of Entry to the Little Bahama Bank, and we'll cover it here. First measure your distances and look at your courses, and you'll realize that West End (if nothing else) could be a vital refuge. For the sailboat, it's just right. At the end of your Gulf Stream crossing endurance, and a shot in the arm before you set off across the Bank. Many power boaters take the same kind of reasoning. Despite its strategic geographic location and its entry port status, for a long time West End won little favor other than as a stop made out of necessity, for the only marine facility, the old Jack Tar marina, had fallen into a state of acute decline. Now all this has changed. West End has two marinas, both new, and one of them, the Old Bahama Bay, seems set to feature on our list of the best marinas in the Bahamas.

Approaches and Marinas

West End is an easy landfall. Its water tower (sited between the marina and the airfield) is prominent, and its radio mast also shows, perhaps more clearly at night with its red lights. To the north, Sandy Cay's tall casuarina trees will show up early on your horizon but don't be seduced by the landfall, for Sandy Cay lies 8 nm north of West End. It's a useful safety net, and we've been grateful for it more than once in bad weather. If you do miss your landfall off West End, remember that a reef line extends north from West End along the continuous western edge of the Little Bahama Bank. Abruptly that deep blue ocean color will change to green. Keep in the blue water. If you hit it right, our West End approach (WESTW) places you just off Settlement Point ready to turn in to Old Bahama Bay marina, or to carry on through Indian Cay Passage (INDCW), to the Little Bahama Bank.

The second West End marina, Harbour House Marina, is in West End settlement and can be reached only from the Bank. In either direction, whether you are inbound from the ocean or westbound across the Bank, your turn point for West End settlement comes up at a midpoint in Indian Cay Passage. See our entry on this marina.

Old Bahama Bay

In mid-July 1997 West End Resort took over the Jack Tar property, nailed up their sign as Old Bahama Bay, and started an ambitious total reconstruction. The original two channels leading into the commercial basin and the marina have been reduced to one channel, and the commercial basin, which many may remember, no longer exists as a separate entity. A new 130-slip marina, with entry port facilities, is in service. A restaurant will open next, together with a fifty-room cottage-type hotel. See our **Yellow Pages** for the fine details.

Alongside this the plans call for the sale of lots and the construction of private houses on the interior canal basins. To date a number of lots have been sold and house con-

ENTRY POINTS FROM FLORIDA		
Memory Rock North		
MEMRN	26° 59' 15"/250 N	079° 08' 00"/000 W
Memory Rock Light		
MEMRK	26° 57' 00"/000 N	079° 07' 00"/000 W
Memory Rock South		
MEMRS	26° 55' 00"/000 N	079° 07' 00"/000 W
Sandy Cay		
SANDY	26° 49' 30"/500 N	079° 05' 30"/500 W
West End		
WESTW	26° 42' 00"/000 N	079° 01' 00"/000 W
Indian Cay Passage West (Ocean side)		
INDCW	26° 43' 00"/000 N	079° 00' 26"/433 W

The final figures in each waypoint show seconds (00") and thousands (000) of a minute.

struction has started. In time we may see the reopening of the airport, possibly reduced to just one 6,000-foot runway, and the taking up of an option to develop the remaining 2,000 acres of Jack Tar land. In the meantime the superb mature trees and plantings laid down in the original development have been preserved. What has been achieved to date is looking good.

OLD BAHAMA BAY MARINA

The entrance to Old Bahama Bay Marina is straightforward. The entry channel is marked and is obvious. It's shoal close inshore, so don't hug the coast, and remember that a reef extends southward from Indian Cay. Stay in the blue and you'll be fine. On entry the fuel dock comes up to starboard just before you come into the main marina basin.

West End, Old Bahama Bay Resort, from the north.

THE HARBOUR HOTEL AND MARINA

Harbour Hotel and Marina		
HARBH	26° 41' 22"/366 N	078° 57' 58"/966 W

We give the GPS position of the marina not for navigation, but so that you can plot its position, for it's hard to pick out from far off. The Harbour Hotel Marina is a Texaco Starport development fronted on to the old West End Harbour House hotel, which has been extended not only by the marina but also has a new bar, restaurant, and showers. Depth inside the marina is good, 8.5 feet at MLW by our reckoning. A breakwater around the marina gives adequate protection from the north through to east and southeast much of the time, but would not serve in bad weather. It needs beefing up, and building higher. The work is planned. See our **Yellow Pages**.

The shoal areas off West End set absolute limits on your approach to West End settlement. If you've never been there before, choose high water, reasonably good visibility, and a day with no significant wave state. The approach route starts in the Indian Cay Passage. Your turn point is when Sandy Cay bears around 340–350°M, which is, if you're incoming from the ocean, about 0.6 mile after the second marker (INDC2). Coming from the Bank it's just after passing the second westbound marker (INDC3). On turning for West End take the Batelco tower as your heading, around 160–170°M, and keep Sandy Cay behind you all the way. Close in you'll pick up the Starport sign off your port bow, and you can turn for the marina. (The white church is your indicator if you can't pick out the sign. The marina lies to the left of the church). You should find 6 feet at MLW on this route, but there are some shallow patches. Say 4 feet at times. Read our section on the **Indian Cay Passage** before taking this approach (see page 33).

There is an alternative route. That is to hug the shoreline from the Old Bahama Bay entry channel, aiming to pass about 100 feet off the old dock on the Old Bahama Bay Bankside beach, and keep inshore all the way to West End settlement. You'll have 4–6 feet at MLW.

We reckon that Harbour Hotel Marina is fine for small power boats, particularly outboards, but the approaches are not attractive if you are plus of shoal draft, nor is the marina really suited to any craft over 30 feet LOA.

Clearing In—Your Options in the Abacos

If you have put in to West End, obviously you'll clear in there for it's an entry port and you get the formalities over and done with right at the start of your cruise. However, if you decide to bypass West End, not having cleared in doesn't prevent you from anchoring at uninhabited cays, such as Great Sale, or indeed anchoring off anywhere. Just keep that Q flag flying until you've cleared in.

Abaco Entry Ports

Not to be used for Navigation.

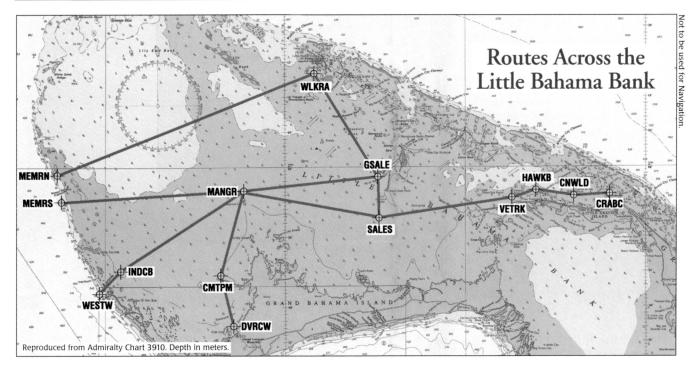

Reproduced from Admiralty Chart 3910. Depth in meters.

Routes Across the Little Bahama Bank

If you look at our route map, you can see you have a number of places where you can pass safely through the barrier reefs and shoals on to the Little Bahama Bank. Just one mile north of West End there's the Indian Cay Passage. Sandy Cay, 8 nm north of West End, is a second choice. The Memory Rock area, some 16 nm north of West End, offers routes both north and south of Memory Rock. On the Bank, Mangrove and Great Sale Cays are both waypoints and route intersections; and Great Sale Cay is a staging anchorage. But if you have the cruise speed and the endurance, you can make it across the Bank by any route without stopping.

Let's assume that you're incoming, bound for either Walkers Cay or Green Turtle Cay, the two main start points for cruising in the Abacos. The best direct route from Florida to Walkers Cay is by way of Memory Rock. Bound for Great Sale you can choose either West End or Memory

LITTLE BAHAMA BANK TRANSITS

Mangrove Cay			Sale Cay South		
MANGR	26° 57' 00"/000 N	078° 37' 00"/000 W	SALES	26° 52' 49"/828 N	078° 14' 30"/500 W
Cormorant Point Marker			Mid-Carters		
CMTPM	26° 44' 38"/631 N	078° 40' 49"/812 W	MCRTR	27° 03' 00"/000 N	078° 01' 00"/000 W
Dover Channel West			South Carters Cay		
DVRCW	26° 36' 48"/803 N	078° 38' 28"/462 W	SCRTR	27° 00' 00"/000 N	078° 01' 00"/000 W
Walkers Cay Approach			Fish Cays		
WLKRA	27° 12' 55"/913 N	078° 25' 27"/451 W	FISHC	27° 01' 19"/324 N	077° 49' 00"/000 W
Triangle Rocks			Veteran Rock		
TRIRK	27° 11' 00"/000 N	078° 25' 00"/000 W	VETRK	26° 55' 45"/750 N	077° 52' 16"/275 W
Sale Cay West			Hawksbill Cays		
SALEW	27° 04' 00"/000 N	078° 14' 30"/500 W	HAWKB	26° 56' 48"/805 N	077° 48' 30"/500 W
Sale Cay North			Center of the World Rock		
SALEN	27° 03' 22"/375 N	078° 11' 10"/167 W	CNWLD	26° 56' 05"/091 N	077° 41' 40"/671 W
Great Sale Cay			Crab Cay		
GSALE	26° 58' 45"/750 N	078° 14' 30"/500 W	CRABC	26° 56' 00"/000 N	077° 36' 00"/000 W
Great Sale Anchorage			Allans-Pensacola Cay		
GSANC	26° 59' 52"/867 N	078° 12' 54"/900 W	ALPEN	26° 59' 15"/250 N	077° 42' 15"/250 W

The final figures in each waypoint show seconds (00") and thousands (000) of a minute.

Rock. The approach routes on to the Bank decide that one for you. You have three options.

- **Indian Cay Passage**, just north of West End, carries 5.5 feet at Low Water. It's a marked channel, but its marks have disappeared in the past, and strong cross currents can take you aground if you allow yourself to get pushed out of the channel.

- **Sandy Cay** is the West End area alternative to Indian Cay Passage, some 8 nm north of West End. The best route we've found lies about 5 nm north of Sandy Cay. It carries 6 feet at Low Water and requires eyeball navigation. Taking this entrance on to the Bank will add about 10 nm to your run to Mangrove Cay. We see no advantage in going the Sandy Cay way, whatever your destination, but we include it simply because it's there.

- **Memory Rock**. If you require greater depth than that offered by the two passages we've mentioned, you must gain access to the Little Bahama Bank by way of the deeper passages north or south of Memory Rock where you should be able to find 6 feet or more without difficulty. Memory Rock, some 16 nm to the north, is remote from the track to or from West End, but it serves the routes between the Florida ports north of Palm Beach and the northern Abacos.

West End–Indian Cay Passage–Mangrove Cay–Great Sale Cay

INDIAN CAY PASSAGE

From West End after leaving the marina head for our Indian Cay Passage west waypoint (INDCW) on something like 033°M, keeping a quarter of a mile off Indian Cay and the reefs. After just about a mile you'll see Indian Cay Rock with its light. Indian Cay Passage opens up to the north of it. There's a piling standing in the channel with a board like an arrow pointing north (to tell you to pass north of that mark). If you're incoming from the ocean you can ignore West End and simply head for that INDCW waypoint.

We mark the pass opening into the channel with our Indian Cay pass (INDCP) waypoint, which is a quarter of a

INDIAN CAY PASSAGE

Indian Cay Passage West (Ocean side)		
INDCW	26° 43' 00"/000 N	079° 00' 26"/433 W
Indian Cay Passage Pass		
INDCP	26° 43' 10"/166 N	079° 00' 15"/250 W
Indian Cay Passage 2nd Mark		
INDC2	26° 43' 42"/698 N	078° 59' 46"/773 W
Indian Cay Passage 3rd Mark		
INDC3	26° 44' 45"/750 N	078° 59' 10"/166 W
Indian Cay Passage Barracuda Shoal		
INDCB	26° 45' 51"/847 N	078° 58' 00"/000 W

The final figures in each waypoint show seconds (00") and thousands (000) of a minute.

mile on 045°M from INDCW. The passage marker is the first of three similar pilings marking the south side of the channel. Leave it to starboard as you enter on to the Bank. At your entry point a reef (which is often hard to see) extends south from Wood Cay for well over 1 nm, so don't assume you have all the distance between that first piling and Wood Cay as your channel. As it is, the shallowest water in the area is around Wood Cay.

We've listed waypoints in our catalog but do NOT use them to negotiate Indian Cay Passage. The only way is to go visual. If you fool around trying to navigate by GPS you may well run aground. Keep close to the marks all the way, and it's better to steer by them, taking them one by one, rather than setting courses. The tidal flow runs across this channel. At mid-tide you'll probably find yourself being carried to the right or left, so navigate by keeping your eyes on the marker astern as well as the marker ahead. This last piece of advice is for real. You cannot hope to stay in a channel unless you check your direction both by the markers ahead of you and the markers astern.

You have three Indian Cay Passage channel markers, that first entry mark by Indian Cay Rock and then two

Transit Distances	
West End–Mangrove Cay–Great Sale Cay	49 nm
West End–Walkers Cay	45 nm
Memory Rock–Mangrove Cay–Great Sale Cay	49 nm
Memory Rock–Walkers Cay	41 nm
Great Sale Cay–Walkers Cay	20 nm
Great Sale Cay–Green Turtle Cay	57 nm

Indian Cay Pass, from the north.

Fish Muds

THE Little Bahama Bank has one natural phenomenon that can get you over-excited about sandbars and shoal water, and that's a Fish Mud. Hundreds of bonefish take it into their collective heads to go shoveling up the sand moving across the Bank in search of delicacies, and the end result is water the color of green tinged milk. From any distance off you could swear that it's a sandbar.

On our last updating trip in the area we were told that winter storms had brought sand between Mangrove Cay and our South Sale waypoint. We were heading over the reverse course that day, as it happened, and sure enough around 26° 54' 59"/988 N 78° 27' 02"/032 W the "sand" was there. We criss-crossed it and found plus or minus 13 feet of water all over. That's a Fish Mud. BUT if you don't know the area, just be wise. If you think it's sand, slow down. Inch up close to it. Check it out, and be safe.

more. All are left to starboard. Then one final marker comes up, which is on Barracuda Shoal. Keep this marker about 0.5 mile to port as you're making your way on to the Bank. If you're in doubt, steer 045°M from the third Indian Cay Passage mark for 1.5 nm and this will keep you in the channel and safely off that shoal. When you pass the Barracuda Shoal marker you can alter course for Mangrove Cay and use your GPS then. You'll have some 21.8 nm on 059°M to run to our Mangrove Cay (MANGR) waypoint.

West End–Sandy Cay–Mangrove Cay–Great Sale Cay

The Sandy Cay route on to the Little Bahama Bank is not marked. It carries about 5.5 feet at Low Water and you must rely on your skill in reading the water by its color, choosing your own route. Sandy Cay itself is a private island. Visitors, if you had thought of taking a break there, are not welcome.

Set out from West End as if you were going to take Indian Cay Passage and then run northwest to Sandy Cay in deep water. You have about 6 nm to go. Don't try to go south of Sandy Cay. There's only one break in the reef there and the area is very shoal. Go to the north and make your turn to the east about 1.5 nm to the north of Sandy Cay. Look at your chart to get an idea of what's ahead of you, and then go in slowly using your eyes. When you're safely past Sandy Cay and have a comfortable 12 feet of water under you, alter for Mangrove Cay or Walkers Cay.

Memory Rock

Memory Rock, 16 nm to the north of West End, is a plug of rock hardly big enough to support a shack, but there's a light on it. It's a stake light, not a lighthouse, and it may, or may not, work. There's a shipwreck on the reefs about two miles to the south of it, and another two wrecks about six miles to the north. None of these are visible. Within a hand span, sometimes two miles, sometimes less, the depth contours along the edge of the ocean-bank interface change from the deep, thousand-foot midnight blue of the Florida Strait to the pale green of six feet over the Little Bahama Bank.

What's the particular importance of Memory Rock? It just happens to be on one of the best routes from Florida north of Palm Beach, say Palm Beach, Jupiter, and Stuart, to Walkers Cay, Great Sale Cay, and the more distant Sea of Abaco. But it's not Memory Rock itself that's the magnet. It's the passes north or south of the Rock, where you can find good, deep water to take you safely on to the Bank, or out into the Gulf Stream.

That's Memory Rock. There's no one there. Not even a blade of grass. No facilities. Just a light that should be giving a single white flash every three seconds from dusk to dawn, but you should never see that. Why? You should do all your running in the Bahamas during daylight, and ideally, so that you can read the water, you should be passing

Memory Rock, from the east.

Memory Rock between 9 a.m. and 4 p.m. But, if you go there to fish, that could be different. Some do.

Memory Rock–Mangrove Cay–Great Sale Cay

The Memory Rock routes on and off the Bank, like the Sandy Cay route, have no marks and you're on your own, relying on your eyes. We favor going north of Memory Rock, but we've taken the southern route in a 49-foot boat with a 4-foot draft on a high tide. There are shoal areas lying 2.5 nm east of Memory Rock across both approaches, but the chart shows these and you should have no problems. Once you've passed the shoals you can alter for Mangrove Cay.

Memory Rock–Walkers Cay

Cross on to the Bank north of Memory Rock. Then head straight for our Walkers Cay approach waypoint (WLKRA) on a heading of 070°M, which you hold for 40.2 nm. From here you have about 1.5 nm to run on a heading of around 045°M to reach the start of the Walkers Cay entry channel. Go visual when you get to that last waypoint. Forget the GPS. See **The Approaches to Walkers Cay** under **Options After Great Sale Cay** on page 38 for details of the final approach to Walkers Cay.

Mangrove Cay

Mangrove Cay, which runs north-south just 20 nm east of West End, is low lying, uninhabited, and barely 0.75 nm in length. The cay has a marker stake just north of it (26° 55' 30"/500 N 78° 37' 22"/368 W). A shoal area extends south of the cay for slightly more than twice the length of the visible land. Mangrove Cay can provide a lee if you are caught out by weather, but other than this, Mangrove is no more than a transit waypoint between West

End or Memory Rock and Great Sale Cay, and on the route to or from the Grand Lucayan Waterway to its south.

MANGROVE CAY–GRAND LUCAYAN WATERWAY

From our Mangrove Cay waypoint (MANGR) head south on 195°M for 12.8 nm to Cormorant Point (CMTPM), where a lone piling gives you the reassurance that you're on a regular route, and not going on and on into a horizonless void.

The shallow bight you are crossing extends from West End to the Cormorant Point peninsula with Crishy Swash and Mangrove Cay to its immediate north. Closer in to Grand Bahama Island it's known as Dover Sound. The north-running hook of land, of which Cormorant Point is a western outlier, is the widest part of Grand Bahama. The shore is low-lying, broken up by swamp, mudflats, and small islands, and barely shows for much of the time. The entrance to the Grand Lucayan Waterway, masked by Crab Cay to the west and Sandy Cay to the east, is not evident until you are right there. The MLW depth over much of this area can be taken as 6 feet, but keep at least 3–4 nm offshore, for there is a definite shoal depth contour running parallel to the coast.

From Cormorant Point you continue on 171°M for 6.4 nm to the Lucayan Waterway–Dover Channel mark (DVRCM), which is another lone piling. From there you head 144°M for 1.8 nm to the posts marking the west entrance to the Dover Channel.

The half-mile-long Dover Channel runs close to west–east (290°–110°). It's marked by seven pairs of marker poles (number five, incoming from the west had lost its twin when we were there last), and the outer markers at each end have lights (red right returning from the west).

This channel is narrow and open to wind from the north.

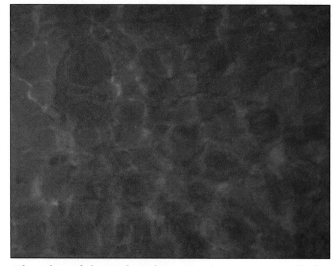

The colors of the Little Bahama Bank: ocean water, 60-foot depth, west of Memory Rock.

It's also shallow (as little as 6 feet at best and maybe 4 feet at worst). You can't hammer through it at speed to counter a side wind, for you may dig your stern in too deep and take the water you need right out of the channel. Go for the best compromise speed if you have a side wind, but keep moving. You'll notice there's a prominent sandy spoil ledge on the south side of the channel.

After the last pair of posts, incoming, turn to starboard by two concrete posts and you're in the Grand Lucayan Waterway. See **Grand Bahama Island, The Grand Lucayan Waterway** on page 112 for complete details.

GREAT SALE CAY

Great Sale Cay runs north–south for 7 nm (counting in its southern reef) and is barely a mile broad at its widest point.

Great Sale Cay anchorage, from the west.

A long tongue of reef and coral heads extending 2 nm south from the southern tip of Great Sale Cay is a definite hazard to navigation and is difficult to see until it's too late. Stay well clear. Great Sale Cay is low lying, covered in scrub, and is not particularly attractive, although it has a sand beach and the swimming in the anchorage is fine. The east side is low coral and the west is mangrove fringed. There are insects so sunset barbecues are not a good idea (we've tried). Great Sale Cay is uninhabited.

The anchorage, nearly a mile wide at its entrance, runs northward for nearly a mile. It carries 7–8 feet of water along its eastern side over sand and grass. The holding is adequate, but not good in some parts. You should dive to check your anchor. The anchorage shoals to the north and to the west, where you can find mostly grass and 4 feet of water. Great Sale anchorage, open to the south and west, is exposed to wind from every direction as the land is so low lying. It does offer protection from high seas from all directions other than the southwest quadrant, but in high winds you can expect to find yourself in quite a chop, and dragging anchors are not unknown. During the sailing season you may find yourself in company with fifteen or more yachts there, but we have, on occasion, found ourselves the sole occupants and then wondered what had happened in the world outside that we'd missed!

North of Great Sale Cay is Little Sale Cay, marked with a light, and Sale Cay Rocks, all of which are obvious.

Options After Great Sale Cay

After Great Sale Cay you're free to head in any direction. In this Guide we give advice on just two alternatives, Green Turtle Cay, and Walkers Cay, which are the most popular destinations as Abaco cruise start-points.

Great Sale Cay–Crab Cay–Green Turtle Cay

There are no problems on this route, which, of all the longer Abaco passages, remains one of our favorites. At the start run straight to our South Sale (SALES) waypoint on a heading of 180°M for 5.8 nm. Even if you can't see that reef extending south from Great Sale Cay, don't be tempted to cut corners and turn early for Veteran Rock (or the reverse if you are heading west). We have, and were scared stiff, and in those days we drew just 2 feet 6 inches fully laden.

Reproduced from Admiralty Chart 3910. Depth in meters.

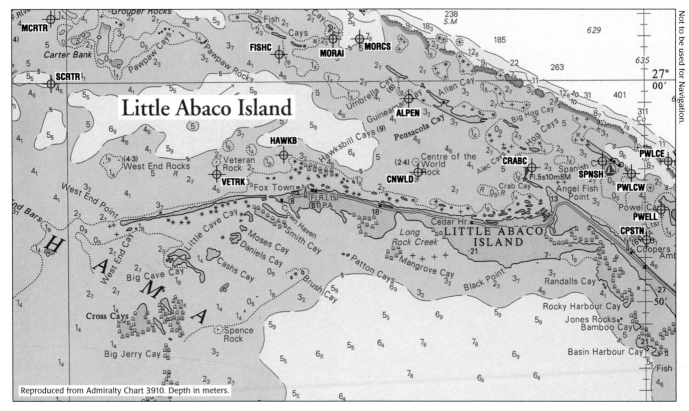

Reproduced from Admiralty Chart 3910. Depth in meters.

Thereafter it's all straightforward. After South Sale there's a 20-nm leg to Veteran Rock (VETRK) on 082°M. You may not see Veteran Rock. Don't edge toward it thinking you need it as a mark. It's awash at high tide. Stay well clear. It's 3.4 nm to Hawksbill (HAWKB) on 073°M. When you get to the Hawksbill Cays don't be tempted to run too close, for rocks and shoals lie to the north of them. The next leg, 6.1 nm on 097°M, to Center of the World Rock (CNWLD), which is highly visible as a great doughball of a rock in the middle of nowhere, should keep you clear of the outlying Hawksbill reefs. After Center of the World it's 5 nm on 091°M to reach our Crab Cay (CRABC) waypoint, passing north of Crab Cay with its marker.

At this point you've left the Little Bahama Bank, and you're in the Sea of Abaco. So that we complete the sequence of the run to Green Turtle Cay, we'll go on. At Crab Cay turn southeast for 6.11 nm on 119°M to place you off Coopers Town. Your course favors the west side of the Sea of Abaco because shoal areas lie between Spanish, Powell, Ambergris, and Nunjack Cays to the east. If you're visiting these cays you take an inshore route closer to the cays themselves (see **Chapter 5, The Central Abacos, Allans-Pensacola to Treasure Cay** on page 51). After Coopers Town change to 134°M for 8.6 nm to reach a position just over 2 nm northwest of Green Turtle Cay. That's it. Then close the distance to choose your landfall, White Sound, Black Sound, or the anchorage off New Plymouth. For greater detail see the Central Abacos chapter we quoted.

Great Sale Cay–Triangle Rocks–Walkers Cay

This is a straightforward passage. From our Great Sale waypoint it's 15.4 nm on 323°M to take you to our Triangle Rocks waypoint (TRIRK). Just watch that you are not set southwesterly on this leg, which would take you on to Triangle Rocks. At our Triangle waypoint alter to 348°M and hold it for just under 2 nm until you reach our Walkers Cay approach (WLKRA).

The colors of the Little Bahama Bank: bank water, 30-foot depth.

THE APPROACHES TO WALKERS CAY

One of the Walkers Cay landmarks is its radio tower. This tower is dwarfed by a much larger Batelco tower, almost a mini-Eiffel Tower, on Grand Cay to the south. Don't be fooled and take the Grand Cay Batelco tower as your heading. Remember Walkers Cay, with its cluster of rocks, is the "Land's End" in the chain of islands that open up in front of you. You should see the gleam of white hulls in the marina long before you notice the Walkers Cay radio tower. Our approach waypoint WLKRA places you 1.5 nm off the entrance to the entry channel. From this waypoint your heading will be about 045°M. Soon you'll pick the first of the stakes marking the marina entry channel. The stakes are not the grand approach path you might expect. There are only a handful of them, set far apart and single. If you're entering on a low tide, just go slowly and carefully. You gain deeper water after the last stake. For details on Walkers Cay see the next chapter, **The Northern Abacos, Walkers Cay to Allans-Pensacola Cay.**

The Waters of the Abacos

One explanation may help those new to the Bahamas, and to the Abacos. Properly speaking the Little Bahama Bank is the area of shallow seas that run to the north of Great Bahama Island and surround the Abacos. In practice we talk about the Bank as the area to the north of Grand Bahama and Little Abaco. The shallow seas between Great Abaco Island and the chain of Abaco Cays to the east is known as the Sea of Abaco, or sometimes as Abaco Sound. The Northern

Abacos, with no "mainland" to their west, front directly on the Little Bahama Bank.

Most of the passages we describe in the next chapter, **The Northern Abacos, Walkers Cay to Allans-Pensacola Cay** are in Little Bahama Bank waters. We deliberately avoided including these passages in this chapter as we wanted to focus on Little Bahama Bank transits.

In this Guide we now turn to the Abaco Cays and Great Abaco Island. Although the northernmost waters are still technically Little Bahama Bank, it makes the business of cruising more simple if the whole is regarded as one straight run down the line of the Abacos, from Walkers Cay all the way south to the southernmost point in the Sea of Abaco at Little Harbour.

Dolphins on the Little Bahama Bank.

YELLOW PAGES

This area received the full force of Hurricane *Floyd* in September 1999. Be aware that reconstruction and the restoration of normal services after a Category 4 Hurricane may take a considerable period of time to complete.

WEST END

MARINAS

OLD BAHAMA BAY
Tel: 242-346-6500 • Fax: 346-6546 • VHF 16

The strategic position of West End has always made it seem a reassuring and safe haven en route to the rest of the Bahamas after a turbulent Gulf Stream crossing, but it is rapidly becoming a destination in its own right as this new 200-slip full-service marina is completed. State-of-the-art docks with **Customs** and **Immigration** on site, a restaurant and bar, swimming pool, private airport, and small cottages will be ready during the millennium year. Gone is the old Jack Tar Marina, with its sadly decaying air of the last few years; here is a an exciting development for West End, with first-class facilities for boats and their owners and friends. Who knows, you may even be tempted to purchase one of the attractive new homes and stay forever?

Slips	75 at time of writing.
Max LOA	Up to 120 ft., up to 175 ft. when all docks completed.

MLW at Dock	8 ft.
Entry Channel	13-ft. depth, newly constructed.
Dockage	50¢ per foot during construction, monthly rates on request.
Power	100A, 50A, and 30A available.
Fuel	Diesel, gasoline, and oils at the fuel dock.
Propane	Available from *RF Grant Electronics* in West End.
Telephone	Payphone on the dock.
Cable TV	Hookup available
Customs and Immigration	At the *Customs House,* with the dockmaster's office.
Showers	Will be new showers and toilets.
Laundry	$1 in quarters for washer or dryer.
Restaurant	Overlooking the harbor, on the second floor of the *Customs House.*
Provisions	Limited groceries in West End settlement.
Ice	$3 per bag.
Pump out	Will be available.
Credit Cards	Visa, MasterCard, and Amex.

HARBOUR HOTEL AND MARINA
Tel: 242-346-6432/6433/6434 • VHF 16

This small marina in the settlement of West End fronts the original *Harbour Hotel,* now painted bright pink and slowly being refurbished. The restaurant, bar, laundry, and showers are all new. The marina is slightly protected from the northeast by a low sea wall, although it is still fairly exposed. Because of its shallow approaches, it is best suited to those with smaller fishing boats or center console boats, who enjoy coming across from Florida for a weekend to fish and stay at the hotel. There are plans to have a dive boat and dive shop, and for a marina shop to sell bait and tackle, with a few groceries.

Slips	14 boats up to 60 ft., 30 boats up to 30 ft.
MLW at Dock	8 ft., very shallow approach at low water.
Dockage	$20 per day up to 30 ft., 50¢ per foot per day over 30 ft.
Power	50A and 30A available; $10 per day.
Fuel	Diesel and gasoline; fuel dock open 7 am to 10 pm.
Water	$5 per day.
Telephone	Payphone on the dock.
Showers	Yes, very clean.
Laundry	Yes
Restaurant	*Harbour Hotel Restaurant,* open 7 am to 11 pm.
Swimming	Pool for hotel and marina guests.
Accommodations	*Harbour Hotel,* rooms from $60.
Dockmaster	Morton Wilchcombe
Manager	Godfrey Nairn

SERVICES & SHOPPING

Bakery
Seaside Bakery Tel: 346-6013 • VHF 16 "Seaside Bakery" or "Tony" Stella Hepburn bakes bread daily, as well as pies, banana bread, duff, peas 'n rice, and johnny cake. Her husband, Tony, who drives a taxi, will deliver to your boat if you call ahead.

Churches
St. Michael's Catholic Church   Sunday Mass
Church of God of Prophecy
St. Mary Magdalene Church

Abandoned boat and conch shell mound, West End settlement.

Clinic
Open 8 am to 5 pm, Monday to Friday; Dr. Fernandez close by.
Groceries
J & M Grocery   Tel: 346-6222   On the waterfront, with limited supplies.
Hardware
R F Grant Electronics   Tel: 346-6207   24-hour service; repairs, plumbing, and propane.
Liquors
Butler and Sands Liquor Store
T & J Liquor Store
Marine Supplies
Leo Moxey   VHF 16 "Calypso II"   Can help you fix an engine, and will answer distress calls.
Police
In the turquoise painted building next to *Batelco*.
Post Office
Open from 9 am to 5 pm, Monday to Friday.
Telephone
Outside the *Batelco* office, next to the radio mast.

RESTAURANTS

The Buccaneer's Club   Tel: 349-3794   Serves Swiss and Bahamian food, and offers free transportation.
Harbour Hotel Restaurant   Tel: 346-6432   Open daily for lunch at the bar and poolside, and dinner in their new dining room.
Harry's American Bar and Restaurant at Deadman's Reef
Tel: 349-2610   Open noon to 11 pm with a complimentary drink and free transportation.
Paradise Cove at Deadman's Reef   Tel: 349-2677   Serves hamburgers, hot dogs, and snacks, and offers a secluded beach, snorkel rental for $10, and beachfront accommodations.
The Star   Tel: 346-6207   Local flavor, a 1940s time capsule.
Yvonne's Cafe   Open all day, eat in or take out.

GETTING AROUND

Airport
The nearest operational airport is Freeport, a $50 taxi ride; the West End airport may be reopened to commercial traffic.
Taxi
Tony Hepburn   Tel: 346-6013 or VHF 16 "Tony" or "Seaside Bakery"

ACCOMMODATIONS

Harbour Hotel and Marina on the waterfront in West End
Tel: 242-346-6432   Twelve simple rooms from $60 per night.
Old Bahama Bay will have cottages close to the marina. Check with them for availability.

THINGS TO DO IN WEST END

- Take the dinghy across to Indian Cay and enjoy the little beach all to yourself.
- Go for a swim or dinner at Deadman's Reef, which will show you more of Grand Bahama Island.

- Dive the *Sugar Wreck*, in just 20 feet of water, or snorkel the offshore reef, just southwest of Old Bahama Bay.
- Dance the night away in the *Harbour Hotel* disco on Friday, Saturday, and Sunday nights.

Chapter 4
The Northern Abacos
Walkers Cay to Allans-Pensacola Cay

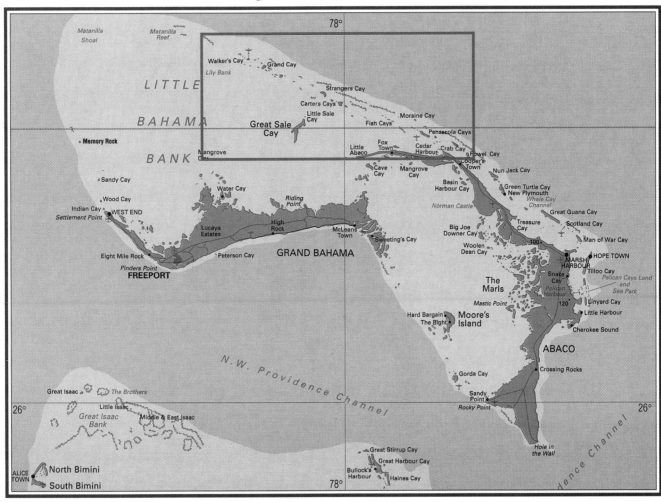

Ocean Passes

THERE are relatively few easily navigable ocean passes through the Abaco reefs out into the open Atlantic. We deal with these area by area, in each chapter, but see our warning on Rages on page 59. The passes in this northern section are primarily of use to the ocean-bound sports fisherman.

Walkers Cay Channel

WLKCN	27° 19' 05"/086 N	078° 29' 42"/699 W
WLKCS	27° 13' 48"/795 N	078° 29' 10"/175 W

The northernmost pass is the old Walkers Cay Channel between the Atlantic Ocean and the Little Bahama Bank. From Walkers Cay itself the "play safe" route would take you first running visual up the Walkers Cay approach

channel to our WLKRS waypoint, then on to our WLKRA approach waypoint (1.5 nm on around 227°M with an incoming course of 047°M). After that head for WLKCS. That's 3.4 nm on 285°M outgoing or 105°M incoming. Then after WLKCS you're in the ocean channel. WLKCN lies just over 5 nm off in blue water on a heading of 355°M outgoing (that's 175°M incoming).

Walkers–Gully Rocks–Seal Cay Channel

SELCN	27° 16' 14"/239 N	078° 21' 35"/582 W
GLRKS	27° 15' 18"/309 N	078° 23' 25"/423 W

The shortest route out to the ocean from Walkers Cay is to turn east, parallel Walkers Cay for a short distance, and then head out on 060°M (incoming 240°M) between Walkers Cay and the Gully Rocks. You have about 1.8 nm to run to reach deep blue water.

Seal Cay Channel

| SELCN | 27° 16' 14"/239 N | 078° 21' 35"/582 W |
| SELCS | 27° 15' 20"/341 N | 078° 21' 45"/758 W |

One of the three Walkers Cay ocean passes, the Seal Cay route involves turning east out of Walkers Cay, passing south of Gully Rocks and Tom Brown's Cay, and then swinging northward between Tom Brown's Cay and Seal Cay. At that point (SELCS) you have about 1 nm to run to SELCN on 010°M (incoming 190°M). Coming from Walkers Cay we see no particular advantage in this route.

Moraine Cay Channel

| MORCN | 27° 03' 53"/886 N | 077° 44' 49"/824 W |
| MORCS | 27° 02' 06"/109 N | 077° 44' 49"/824 W |

There's a good, clear and wide pass out into the ocean to the northeast of Moraine Cay. From our MORAI waypoint (which is not a mandatory waypoint on this pass course) head due east for about 1 nm to reach our MORCS waypoint. Then head out due north for just under two miles to clear the reef line. Incoming from MORCN you'll be coming in due south, and can either turn for Moraine Cay, or join the main Abaco Cays course line running northwest–southeast to the west of Allans-Pensacola.

Walkers Cay

If you're into sports fishing, Walkers Cay is the place to be. Along with Bimini, Treasure Cay, and Marsh Harbour, Walkers Cay rates as one of the world centers for the sport and everything there takes its pattern from the life style of the sports fishing fraternity. At tournament times it's jumping and wall-to-wall with boats, and if you're searching for peace and quiet, you're unlikely to stay long (that's if you can get dock space). Like West End and Bimini, Walkers Cay has a strategic location, which is worth factoring into your cruise planning. Many people, particularly those coming from the East Coast north of Stuart, reckon it's ideally sited as a Port of Entry, and alternatively, offers the best jumping-off point for them on returning home. It's a full-service marina, has good accommodations, and a good restaurant. See our **Yellow Pages**.

Approaches

One of the Walkers Cay landmarks is its radio tower. This tower is dwarfed by a much larger Batelco tower, almost a mini-Eiffel Tower, on Grand Cay to the south. Don't be fooled and take the Grand Cay Batelco tower as your heading. Remember Walkers Cay, with its cluster of rocks, is the "Land's End" in the chain of islands that open up in front

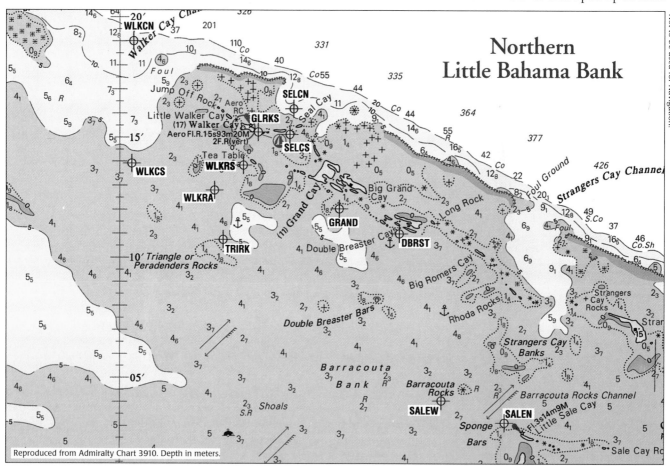

Reproduced from Admiralty Chart 3910. Depth in meters.

of you. You should see the gleam of white hulls in the marina long before you notice the Walkers Cay radio tower. Our approach waypoint WLKRA places you 1.5 nm off the entrance to the entry channel. From this waypoint your heading will be about 045°M. Soon you'll pick the first of the stakes marking the marina entry channel. The stakes are not the grand approach path you might expect. There are only a handful of them, set far apart and single. If you're entering on a low tide, just go slowly and carefully. You gain deeper water after the last stake.

Moving on from Walkers Cay

From Walkers Cay you're well poised to start a leisurely cruise southeastward, visiting each cay in turn. Your distances from potential anchorage to potential anchorage are short, your navigation is going to be a combination of eyeball and GPS (for you have to make some doglegs to avoid shoals and reefs), and you'll see little of civilization as we know it in the northern Abacos.

For your planning, first let's list the places where you can get fuel or provisions:

Walkers Cay	fuel and provisions (marina)
Fox Town	fuel (but depth at dock is less then 4 feet)
Spanish Cay	fuel and some provisions (marina)
Coopers Town	fuel and some provisions (open to weather)
Green Turtle Cay	fuel and provisions (well served with options)

Your primary concern should be the weather, for as it is over all the Bahamas, there are few anchorages that are good under all conditions. Against this, if the weather does start to change, the distances are so short you can run for a safer place within a few hours. There's no need to get paranoid about being caught out.

Walkers Cay to the Grand Cays— The High Water Short Cut

This is a simple, short run to be taken when the tide favors you. We reckon you have 6–8 feet at High Water. You don't have to take the marked channel out of Walkers Cay. On

NORTHERN ABACOS I

Walkers Cay Approach		
WLKRA	27° 12' 55"/913 N	078° 25' 27"/451 W
Walkers Cay		
WLKRS	27° 14' 00"/000 N	078° 24' 09"/148 W
Grand Cays		
GRAND	27° 12' 00"/000 N	078° 19' 30"/500 W
Grand Cays Anchorage		
GCANC	27° 13' 10"/166 N	078° 19' 18"/299 W
Double Breasted Cays		
DBRST	27° 11' 00"/000 N	078° 16' 30"/500 W

The final figures in each waypoint show seconds (00") and thousands (000) of a minute.

Walkers Cay, from the east.

leaving the marina turn southeast on an initial heading of around 130°M, aiming to leave Elephant Rock (lying just southwest of 27° 14' N 078° 22' W) on your starboard side.

Pass between Elephant Rock and Burying Piece Rock, which will be on your port side. You'll be running on a line offshore of Burying Piece Rock, aiming now to leave Sandy Cay (just southwest of 27° 13' N 078° 20' W) on your port side. Don't be tempted to pass between Sandy Cay and Little Grand Cay. Even at the high-water mark you may find only 4 feet there.

You'll see that just level with the north end of Sandy Cay there's an opening between Grand Cay and Little Grand Cay (the Batelco tower is there and a prominent blue water tank with a white top that looks like a silo). Ignore the opening. Continue your heading, watching for the rocks south of Sandy Cay, until you pass the 078° 19' W line. At that time you'll see two more openings lying between Little Grand Cay and Felix Cay. Don't take the first. Go for the second. You'll see that it has a marker on the starboard side, and there's a prominent white house on Big Grand Cay behind it. Richard Nixon used to stay there to unwind while he was President.

Walkers Cay to the Grand Cays—The Regular Route

Take the marked channel out of Walkers Cay and when you reach the Walkers Cay approach waypoint (WLKRA) set a course of 168°M for our Triangle Rocks waypoint. (TRIRK). You have 1.9 nm to run. From Triangle Rocks turn for Grand Cays on 078°M for 4.9 nm. When you reach the Grand Cays waypoint (GRAND) head for the center of Felix Cay, which lies in front of you, and take the second opening that will open up off your port bow. For the final stages of your approach, follow the guidelines we've given under the **High Water Short Cut** route, above.

The Grand Cays, from the north.

Grand Cays

THE GRAND CAY GROUP

The Grand Cay group consists of five main islands (Grand, Big Grand, Little Grand, Rat, and Felix Cays) with a settlement on Little Grand Cay marked with the prominent Batelco tower. About 200 people live there. The waters around the cays are shallow, a mix of bonefish flats, mangrove channels, and ocean beach. It's dinghy country, with good water colors, but the cays are not particularly beautiful and we've been plagued by flies there. Other than going to the Grand Cays out of curiosity, we feel there's little that you'll find rewarding, but Rosie's (see our **Yellow Pages**) cracked conch is reputed to be "the best ever."

THE GRAND CAY ANCHORAGE

Go slowly in to the Little Grand Cay anchorage, favoring the starboard side of the approach channel. Off the settlement you'll find 6–7 feet of water with patches of 8 feet over sand and grass. Don't be tempted to work your way further inshore without checking it out first in your dinghy. Your distance run from Walkers Cay to get to Grand Cay will be about 8 nm.

It's a good anchorage but open to wind and fetch from the northwest and southeast, and wind and current can chase you 360 degrees around. Make sure you have plenty of space to swing, and don't be surprised if you drag when the tide changes. Use two anchors if your primary doesn't reset all that well, or if you're not sure that it has set properly. Stay clear of the fairway in to the settlement (the deeper water on the starboard side as you enter), despite its attractive depths. The cowboys come home from Walkers Cay too fast to avoid you at night. Use your anchor light, **at or near**

deck level, so that it can be seen by someone in a small fast-running boat. (This advice holds, as a matter of sensible prudence, for the Bahamas at large, and our preferred anchor lighting is to use both a conventional masthead light and a light at deck level). An incidental note: we've never seen so many rays cruising around an anchorage.

Grand Cays to the Double Breasted Cays

Choose a time close to high water. On leaving the Grand Cays anchorage head back to that Grand Cays approach waypoint and then head 110°M for 2.8 nm to the anchorage area off the Double Breasted Cays (DBRST).

Double Breasted Cays

We have friends who have long said that Double Breasted is one of their favorite stops in all the Bahamas. If you want a place to go gunkholing in the time-honored fashion of the true cruising boat, beachcomb, swim, snorkel, fish a little, and be amazed at the colors and clarity of the water, we join them in placing Double Breasted high on our list.

THE DOUBLE BREASTED CAYS ANCHORAGES

We've been wary of working in too close to the Double Breasted Cays and prefer to anchor off, using our dinghy to explore. But if you want to anchor close in, feel your way. Stand off about 100 yards to the east of the reef (covered by 2 feet of water at MLW) leaving it on your port side. Once you're past the reef, take a northerly heading until you're 200 yards off the rocky islets ahead. That's your anchorage. Beware: there's a submerged rock at 27° 22' 39"/650 N 078° 16' 59"/983 W. Don't circle out too far finding your ideal spot. If you drop your hook there you'll have protection from the west through the north. The downside is that you're not protected from the prevailing winds, and it can be rolly. The holding is fair, gravelly sand with some grass and rock, and you don't want to get too close in to the land, for the water depth gets down to around 5 feet at MLW.

Double Breasted Cays, from the north.

INNER ANCHORAGES (WATER CAY AND THE POND)

Getting in and out of the Water Cay–Pond area is not difficult, but it's potentially hazardous. Once you're there, you'll be in a kind of private marine paradise. If you elect to work your way in, anchor off first, wait for the tide, and while you're waiting, check the route in your dinghy. Don't make your move until you've done this, and you've got good light so that you can get the eyeballing right.

From the rocky islets bear around to the west and follow the dark water (6–7 feet at MLW) all the way in. Pass midway between the first sandbar on your port side and the rocky islet to starboard. Then continue on to pass midway between Water Cay to port and another rocky islet to starboard. After Water Cay you'll come to a second sandbar on your port side. If you reckon you've had enough inshore work at this point, you can anchor either on the north side of Water Cay or the north side of this second sandbank in 6–6.5 feet of water.

If you want to get in to the pond, it becomes testing from this point on. Ahead of you to port you have the sandbar, and to starboard an opening in the line of rocky islands you've been passing. You want to round the sandbar turning to port, but must first pass a boat length away from the gap, squeezed between the opening itself and the sandbar. This gap carries a strong tidal flow. It's fine at slack water. At any other time you're either going to be sucked out to sea by an ebb tide, or pushed right on the sand by a flood tide. Hence the desirability of Slack Water. Once you've met this challenge, just make your way around Water Cay into the pond to the south of Water Cay. Set two anchors. The current runs fast through the whole Water Cay–Pond anchorage area.

BIG ROMERS CAY, RHODA ROCKS, STRANGERS CAY, AND JOE CAYS

Big Romers Cay, Rhoda Rocks, Strangers Cay, and Joe Cays form, by any standard, a difficult area of banks, shoals, rocks, and reefs. It could well be a gunkhole fanatic's idea of heaven, but for the cruising yachtsman it could be unrewarding, and possibly prematurely aging, to choose it as a playground.

After visiting Double Breasted, even if we're intent on cruising the Abaco chain cay by cay, we leave this stretch to the locals. Of course you can make your way around these cays and Rhoda Rocks if you set your mind to it, but we take a diversion and go on to Carters Cay by way of Little Sale Cay. The reverse applies running south to north.

Double Breasted Cays–Little Sale Cay–Carters Cay

From Double Breasted Cays head 148°M for our Little Sale Cay north waypoint (SALEN), which will take you on a run of 8.9 nm safely past Barracouta Rocks (on your starboard side) to a point northwest of Little Sale Cay. Then turn on to 092°M to run 9.0 nm to a point 1 nm due south of Carters Cay, which we've called Mid-Carters (MCRTR). From then

Cracking conch in Carters Cay.

on you go visual. Turn north. After 1 nm you're at our Carters Cay waypoint (CRTRS). Work your way in.

LITTLE SALE CAY

Little Sale Cay, together with Sale Cay Rocks, present a line of rock running east–west three quarters of a mile north of Great Sale Cay. You could say it's a barrier line spread out along Latitude 27° 02' N for just about 4 nm. Little Sale itself, standing rocky and sturdy with a light on its west headland is an unmistakable landmark. It's one of the best Little Bahama Bank waypoints, but don't forget those four miles of rocks and shoals extending eastward from it.

Carters Cay

If you like offbeat, forgotten places, Carters Cay hits the spot. Once a US missile-tracking station, Carters Cay has nothing in terms of civilization but its ruins. No one lives there, but Bahamian fishermen come to camp there, with generators to give them light and charcoal grills as their kitchens, using the abandoned barrack blocks and a set of shacks as their base. Over two or three days they'll fill their boats with lobster and conch for sale as far away as Freeport. They keep much to themselves, if you find them camped there, but will be happy to talk if you take the time to greet them.

Wander around Carters Cay. You may get the feeling that you've found the site of Dr. No's bid for World Domination in a James Bond movie. But above that, Carters has a magic that's captivating. It's partly its fantastic deep-water anchorage, partly the ease of access by dinghy to the ocean reefs on one side and the Banks rocks on the other, partly the colors of the water, partly the sense of peace and isolation. If this kind of thing appeals, go there.

THE CARTERS CAY ANCHORAGE

From our Carters waypoint feel your way in past the very obvious sandbars, leaving them to port. Head for the center

Carters Cays, from the east.

high tide as you can, and that goes for your departure too. Despite all our concern for depths, we've grounded at mid-tide, and the sandbanks and the shoal areas change. No air photograph, no chart, and no guide book can really help you. As ever in the Bahamas, you're on your own in many places. It's character building.

GROUPER ROCKS, PAWPAW CAYS, AND PAWPAW ROCKS

If you look at your chart, you'll see that to take a boat on any kind of direct track from Carters Cay to the Fish Cays and Moraine Cay could cut short your cruising time in the islands. The shallows of the Carter Cays Bank, with Grouper Rocks, the Paw Paw Cays, and Paw Paw Rocks, dictates that you must drop south from Carters Cay to gain deeper water before continuing on your travels. Of course you may play it as you wish, and there are ways around this area other than the routes we suggest, but rather like our avoidance of the Rhoda Rocks tangle, we leave this territory to the locals.

Moving on from Carters Cay you have two options. You can run south of the Carters Bank to the Fish Cays, and then head for Moraine Cay or Allans-Pensacola. Alternatively you can drop southeast to the Hawksbill Cays (and Fox Town), at which point you have three choices. One is to head for Moraine Cay. If this is your primary destination, you've gone out of your way. The second is go to Allans-Pensacola. Again you don't really need to visit Hawksbill on your way. The third is to make for Crab Cay and head south in the Sea of Abaco. It all hinges on what you fancy doing, and maybe on wind and weather too. We'll cover both options.

of Gully Cay, and then turn to port to head toward the mark on the little rock that will be on your bow. Keep about one–two boat lengths off Gully Cay. Then round the end of Gully Cay, not too close inshore, and anchor between Gully Cay and what is plainly the remains of some kind of military camp on Big Carters Cay. You'll have the luxury of 20 feet of water there. Don't go in too far to the east for it shoals. Don't opt for mid-channel, for the tide rips through it. You are safe where you are. Only a Norther will give you a rough time.

But if you do go there, time your arrival for as close to

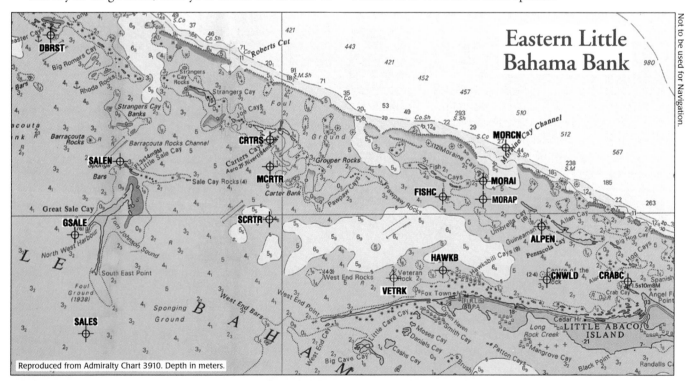

Reproduced from Admiralty Chart 3910. Depth in meters.

Carters Cay–Fish Cays–Moraine Cay

Drop due south from Carters Cay to our South Carters waypoint (SCRTR), passing through Mid-Carters on your way. That "all-Carters" leg amounts to 4 nm. At South Carters turn east onto 083°M for 10.7 nm, which will take you to a waypoint south of the Fish Cays (FISHC). Then you have 2.5 nm to run on 096°M, bringing you to our Moraine Cay approach waypoint (MORAP). Turn due north. Moraine Cay is on your bow, one mile off.

FISH CAYS

The Fish Cays are nothing to write home about. There are beaches on the ocean side, but otherwise they offer neither good anchorages, nor anything particularly exciting to explore.

Moraine Cay, from the northeast.

MORAINE CAY

Moraine Cay, privately owned but open to visitors, is a prime *must-see* day stop in this part of the Abacos. The beach on the west side, which you reach from your anchorage by dinghy, is postcard material. A sweep of good sand (despite a ledge of rock close inshore), and a 180-degree panorama that encompasses ocean reef, every color of Bahamian water, and a horizon that sometimes just merges limitless into the sky. Behind you there's nothing but one small island, white sand, and some palms. This place you would write home about.

APPROACH TO MORAINE CAY

Go in visual from our approach waypoint and anchor off the beach in about 8 feet of water. This anchorage is not an all-night stop unless you're certain of your weather, for it's exposed and would be no fun in winds from southeast through southwest. As for the north, protected though it may be, you wouldn't want to be there in a Norther.

Moraine Cay to Allans-Pensacola Cay

This is a straight run of 3.8 nm on a course of 117°M from Moraine Cay. Heading southeast, after passing Umbrella Cay to port, you'll see little Guineaman's Cay also to port, our waypoint set near the northern tip of Allans-Pensacola, and the anchorage will open up as you continue on. See our detail later in this chapter on **Allans-Pensacola Cay**. Heading northwest to Moraine Cay it's the reverse sequence.

Carters Cay to Hawksbill Cay

Drop south from Carters Cay to South Carters (SCRTR), passing through Mid-Carters. That "all-Carters" leg amounts to 4 nm. At South Carters turn southeast on 106°M for 11.5 nm for our Hawksbill Cay (HAWKB) waypoint.

THE HAWKSBILL CAYS

The Hawksbill Cays run west–east on a line just about 1 nm north of Fox Town, which is on Little Abaco Island. They act as a barrier to north winds if you are tucked up under their south side, and the anchorage just south of the westernmost beach on Hawksbill Cay can serve you well.

Our Hawksbill waypoint is safely off the west end of Hawksbill Cay. When you get there, swing westward in a lazy half-circle to pass well away from a rock with a marker on it, and come in to the anchorage on the 26° 56' N line to anchor under the westernmost end of Hawksbill Cay. You'll have around 8–9 feet of water, and relatively good holding. You are open to east and west, but if the wind stays below 15 knots you'll be okay.

NORTHERN ABACOS II		
Mid-Carters		
MCRTR	27° 03' 00"/000 N	078° 01' 00"/000 W
Carters Cay		
CRTRS	27° 04' 00"/000 N	078° 01' 00"/000 W
Carters Anchorage		
CTANC	27° 05' 03"/050 N	078° 00' 07"/116 W
South Carters Cay		
SCRTR	27° 00' 00"/000 N	078° 01' 00"/000 W
Fish Cays		
FISHC	27° 01' 19"/324 N	077° 49' 00"/000 W
Moraine Cay Approach		
MORAP	27° 01' 02"/043 N	077° 46' 07"/123 W
Moraine Cay		
MORAI	27° 02' 06"/108 N	077° 46' 07"/123 W
Hawksbill Cays		
HAWKB	26° 56' 48"/805 N	077° 48' 30"/500 W
Allans-Pensacola Cay		
ALPEN	26° 59' 15"/250 N	077° 42' 15"/250 W

The final figures in each waypoint show seconds (00") and thousands (000) of a minute.

Hawksbill Cays to Moraine Cay

If you went south to Hawksbill Cay from Carters and decide you want to see Moraine Cay, it's an easy run. A course of 027°M will take you 4.7 nm to our Moraine Cay approach waypoint. But be warned. Use this route at High Water. The final mile or so of this leg is shoal reducing to 4 feet at MLW.

FOX TOWN (LITTLE ABACO ISLAND)

Fox Town, which has fuel and provisions, is unlikely to feature on your list as a provisioning stop. For a start it carries barely 4 feet at the local docks, and the approach, through a chain of inshore islets and rocks that parallel the Little Abaco Island coast, will put you off. But of course you can dinghy in.

You'll find a smart little settlement, a state-of-the-art clinic, and two gas stations, one at each end of town (both ready to dispense marine fuel from their own docks). There's a mini-supermarket, one restaurant, and two unnamed bars. There's Batelco, a post office (open three days a week only), and a police station. See our **Yellow Pages**.

Hawksbill Cays to Allans-Pensacola or Crab Cay

Moving on from Hawksbill to either Allans-Pensacola Cay or Crab Cay into the Sea of Abaco are short, easy runs. Allans-Pensacola is 6 nm on 066°M. The route to Crab Cay is two legs, or we take it that way, simply because the Center of the World Rock lies roughly at the midpoint. It's obvious and we doubt that you're going to hit it, but a great lump of rock is the archetypal waypoint, so we make use of it. Hawksbill to Center of the World (CNWLD and safely south of it) is 6.1 nm on 097°M. Continuing on to Crab Cay (CRABC) is 5 nm on 091°M.

ALLANS-PENSACOLA CAY

Lying northwest–southeast across Latitude 26° 59' N, Allans-Pensacola is one of the Bahamian destinations where location wins. It's at the right spot on the chart, and sooner or later most people go there after crossing the Little Bahama Bank, or before setting out across it. At one time two separate cays, Allans Cay and Pensacola Cay were linked in a spur-of-the-moment marriage by a hurricane. The end result has provided an anchorage, which, as we've said, is ever popular.

The unified cay is some 3 nm long. Other than the ruins of yet another US missile-tracking station, there's nothing on the island. The beaches on the ocean side are good, and the cuts between Allans-Pensacola and little Guineaman's Cay, to its north, are one of our favorite areas for gunkholing.

THE ALLANS-PENSACOLA ANCHORAGE

The bay that forms the Allans-Pensacola anchorage, entered from the northwest, is nearly a mile in length. Only the first half of this is usable as an anchorage, for it shoals at the southeast end. Favor the inshore side to avoid Allans Cay

Rocks. You don't want to take your boat further south than the headland by Allans Cay Rocks, unless you have shoal draft. It's a good anchorage, protected from everything but the west and northwest to north, with around 6–8 feet of water and fairly good holding (but dive to check that anchor). It can be crowded in the cruising season.

In the south of Allans-Pensacola there's a narrow creek-like entrance to a rocky channel that leads in to a landlocked basin surrounded by mangroves. It appears to be an ideal hurricane hole, and you may well be able to creep into it on a high tide if you don't draw too much.

CENTER OF THE WORLD

In the **Little Bahama Bank** chapter we described Center of the World as "highly visible as a great doughball of a rock in the middle of nowhere." That's it.

Allans-Pensacola to Crab Cay

From Allans-Pensacola down to Crab Cay to gain access to the Sea of Abaco is a straightforward run to the southeast, 6.4 nm on 120°M.

CRAB CAY

Crab Cay, a thin northwest–southeast island at the northern tip of Great Abaco Island (the "mainland") marks your entry point into the Sea of Abaco. Barely a mile in length there's nothing there but a light on its northern tip, and your route lies just to the north of that light. South of Crab Cay the northern spur of Abaco is called Angel Fish Point. Don't try to cut between the two. There's a propeller-and-keel-shearing ledge of rock there, linking Angel Fish Point to Crab Cay. Seeking shelter, we've worked our way behind Crab Cay, but it's shallow. We wouldn't recommend it.

Allans-Pensacola anchorage, from the south.

YELLOW PAGES

This area received the full force of Hurricane *Floyd* in September 1999. Be aware that reconstruction and the restoration of normal services after a Category 4 Hurricane may take a considerable period of time to complete.

WALKERS CAY

Walkers Cay is the home of sports fishing! As the northern-most island in the Bahamas, with its good facilities and airport, it also offers a northern Port of Entry and jumping off place for the Abacos. All facilities are found in and around the marina and hotel complex. **Customs** and **Immigration** (353-1211) are at the airport and can be called from the marina on arrival. They are open from 9 am to 5 pm, or on request.

MARINA

WALKERS CAY HOTEL AND MARINA
Tel: 242-353-1252, 800-327-8150, or 954-359-1400
• Fax: 353-1339 • VHF 16 and 68

Slips	73
Max LOA	Over 100 ft.
MLW at Dock	5 ft.
Dockage	$1.35 per foot per day, including power.
Fuel	Diesel and gasoline.
Water	30¢ per gallon.
Telephone	Outside the liquor store.
Showers	Yes
Laundry	Yes, ask at the hotel.
Credit Cards	All cards accepted.

SHOPPING

Groceries
Sea Chest Grocery
Gift shops
Sea Below Dive and Gift Shop
Treasure Chest Gift Shop
Liquors
Walkers Spirit

RESTAURANTS & BARS

Conch Pearl Dining Room Open daily from 7:30 am for breakfast, and 7:30 pm for dinner.
Lobster Trap Restaurant & Lounge Open from 11 am to 3 pm for lunch in the winter season, and for dinner during the summer. Indoor or outdoor dining, and a lounge with pool table.
Marlin Bar Open from noon to closing.

GETTING AROUND

Airport
The airport has a 2,400-foot paved runway and sea plane ramp.
Chalk's International Seaplanes daily, except Tuesdays, from Fort Lauderdale. Charter flights from Marsh Harbour and Treasure Cay.

SPORTS

Charter Boats
Bonefishing: 18-foot Hewes Skiff, $305 per day; reef fishing: 23-foot Hoog, $300 per day, $200 for a half day; deep-sea fishing: 50-foot Hatteras, $700 per day, $400 for a half day.

Diving
Sea Below Dive Shop Tel: 352-1252 Two-tank dive $75, resort course $125, snorkelers $20; rental equipment available, with three dive boats and eleven full-time staff. Bonefishing, deep sea fishing, shark rodeos, secluded island picnics, tours of a tropical fish hatchery, and cookouts for dive groups.

Dive Sites
If sharks and barracudas hold a fascination for you, the dive sites around Walker's Cay are definitely in the five-star league. One of the most exciting dives is watching the Shark Rodeo at *Spiral Cavern* where literally dozens of sharks of different species come in to feed, or Shark Canyon with its sleeping sharks, while *Barracuda Alley* and the *Pirate's Cathedral* both attract large barracuda. You can take an hour-long Shark Awareness Class before your dive, which includes lessons in shark behavior and history.

Fishing
Offshore, reef, or bonefishing.

Shuffleboard

Swimming
Salt- and freshwater pools with Jacuzzi.

Tennis
Two all-weather tennis courts.

ACCOMMODATIONS

Walkers Cay Hotel Tel: 242-352-1252 62 rooms from $100 per night, suites and villas from $200, MAP $37.50 per person. Special package deals for small boaters, divers, and private pilots. Call 1-800-WALKERS.

THINGS TO DO IN WALKERS CAY
- Join in the action—charter a boat or find a friend with a sports fisher, and go deep sea fishing.
- Take your dinghy and spend a day gunkholing around Grand Cay.
- Go diving—there are some fantastic dive sites.

Walkers Cay.

GRAND CAY

When you have anchored off and come in with your dinghy to the pier in front of *Rosie's Place*, you will find a small settlement, with just about 200 inhabitants, many of whom work at Walkers Cay. Apart from *Rosie's Place*, there is little ashore to attract the cruising visitor, but the gunkholing and fishing around Grand Cay is great.

SERVICES & SHOPPING

Accommodations
Rosie's Place Island Bay Motel   Tel: 242-353-1200 •
VHF 68 "Love Train"

Beauty Parlor
Rachel's Hair and Nails

Church
Shilo Baptist

Clinic
Grand Cay Community Clinic   Open 9 am to 1 pm, Monday through Friday, closed Wednesdays and weekends.

Fuel
Diesel and gasoline.

Groceries
Father and Son Grocery and Drug Store   Open 7 am to 9 pm Monday to Saturday, to 7 pm on Sunday.
L & S Restaurant and Grocery   Open daily for fresh bread, cakes, and canned food. Let them know in advance if you want to eat there.
Rosie's Place and Grocery   A small selection of groceries.

Restaurant
Rosie's Place and Grocery   A bar, pool table, and television, but you must order meals ahead of time.

Telephones
Outside the clinic and outside *Rosie's Place.*

THINGS TO DO IN GRAND CAY

- Go bonefishing on the flats.
- Try Rosie's cracked conch.
- Count the sting rays and the starfish in the anchorage.

FOX TOWN

If you anchor off and take your dinghy in, friendly people and some surprising, almost Spanish-style villas welcome you to Fox Town. There is only 3 feet of water at low tide off the *Foxtown Shell* fuel dock, and 2.5 feet of water off the *Texaco Starport* at MLW, so call ahead for advice on how to get in to either fuel dock. They both monitor VHF 16, and will be happy to guide you in.

SERVICES & SHOPPING

Accommodations
Millie's Guest House   Tel: 242-365-2046   Next door to the *Valley Restaurant*, there are five rooms, including an efficiency apartment, all with air conditioning and private bathrooms, from $45 to $53 per night, depending on the number of beds in the room.

Sponges drying in the sun.

Barber Shop
Claudine Jackson   Tel: 365-2071   For men and women.

Churches
St. Chad's Anglican Church
Zion Baptist Church

Clinic
Tel: 365-2172   The smartest building in Fox Town, a short walk south of the fuel docks. Dr Biney visits from Coopers Town on Tuesdays. Nurse Romer is there full time.

Fuel
Foxtown Shell   Tel: 365-2046 • VHF 16   6.5 feet of water at high tide at the dock, and 3 feet at low water. Open daily from 7 am all day; open from 7 to 9 am and 2 to 6 pm on Sundays, with diesel and gasoline. Credit cards accepted with a surcharge. Groceries available next door, ice $5 and $2 per bag, *Valley Restaurant* at the dock, with a telephone.
Foxtown Starport   Tel: 365-2021 • VHF 16   8 feet of water at full high tide, 2.5 at low water. Open daily from 7 am to 7 pm, closed 10 am to 2 pm on Sundays, with diesel and gasoline. Ice $5 per bag, bottled water $2 per gallon. This fuel station is run by Daniel and Lilian Parker; Lilian reads the weather report in the mornings. Listen for her on VHF 16, switching to VHF 72, if you are in the area at around 7 or 8 am.

Groceries
M & M Grocery Store   Tel: 365-2046   Open at the *Fox Town Shell* fuel dock and filling station, from 7 am to 9 pm daily, and from 7 to 9 am on Sundays. Frozen meats, bread, water, sodas, shoes, saucepans, toys, and some fruit and vegetables.

Marine Repairs
Delgarna Parker or Rand Parker, Lilian Parker's sons, can help you with engine repairs. Call them on the *Starport* number, or on VHF 16.

Police
Next door to the post office.

Post Office
Open 9 am to 5 pm Monday, Tuesday, Thursday, and Friday.

Restaurant
Valley Restaurant at the *Foxtown Shell*   Tel: 365-2046   Open from 7 am to closing, serving Bahamian fish, chicken, pizza, and burgers, with cracked conch a specialty. This cool and clean, simple restaurant is owned and run by Judy Mae Russell and her sister Maria Edgecombe. There is a pool table and television, with a deck overlooking the water planned.

Telephones
At *Batelco* (Fax: 365-6290) and outside the *Valley Restaurant.*

Chapter 5
The Central Abacos
Allans-Pensacola Cay to Treasure Cay

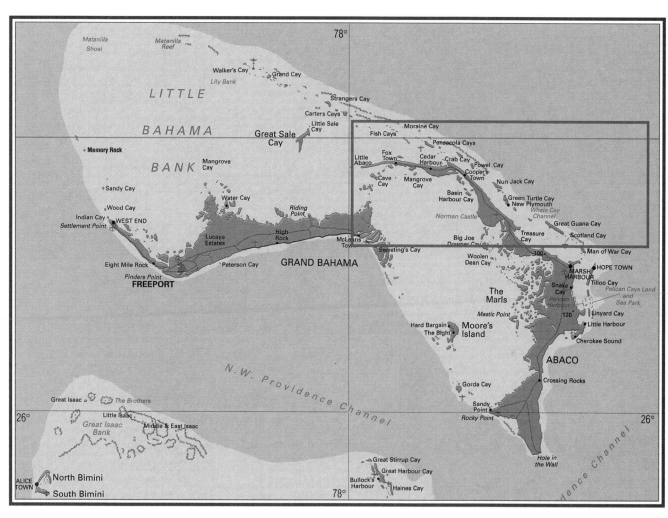

Ocean Passes

OF the three ocean passes in the central Abacos, the most well known is Whale Cay Passage. Shoal water between Whale Cay and mainland Great Abaco Island dictates that everyone continuing southward down the Sea of Abaco must make a necessary diversion at this point into the Atlantic before continuing on their way south.

Powell Cay Channel

| PWLCE | 26° 56' 22"/365 N | 077° 28' 42"/699 W |
| PWLCW | 26° 55' 53"/889 N | 077° 30' 45"/759 W |

There are, in truth, two passes through the reefs going north and south of Spanish Cay. We don't favor the northern one, which is tight and needs perfect conditions. We prefer the

pass between Spanish Cay and Powell Cay, known as the Powell Cay Channel. From Spanish Cay Marina head 115°M (NOT on autopilot!) to pass south of Goat Cay to our PWLCW waypoint. There's a shoal on your starboard side. Then swing on to 075°M, with just under 2 nm to run to clear the reefs. Incoming it's 255°M to clear the reefs, and then head for the marina, swinging around Goat Cay and avoiding that shoal to port, on something like 295°M.

Nunjack Channel

| NUNCN | 26° 52' 52"/864 N | 077° 23' 06"/096 W |
| NUNCS | 26° 50' 52"/877 N | 077° 24' 22"/376 W |

There's a good wide ocean pass to the north of Manjack Cay just south of the Ambergris Cays. You have 20 feet of depth there and something like a mile in passage width go-

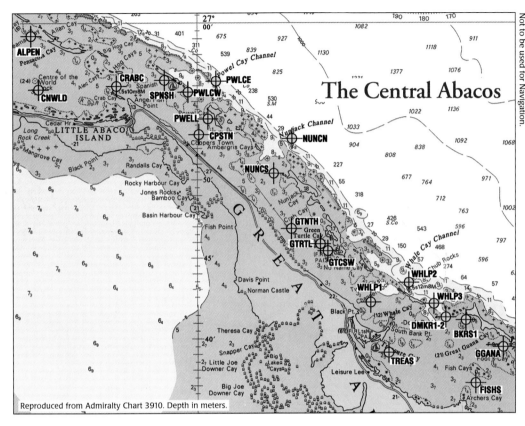

Reproduced from Admiralty Chart 3910. Depth in meters.

WESTERN CHANNEL WHALE CAY PASSAGE

The first two waypoints (WHLP1 and 2) will take you in or out through Whale Cay Pass if Green Turtle Cay or the northern part of the Sea of Abaco is where you are, or where you want to go. Your headings between these two points are 068°M outgoing and 248°M incoming, with 2.6 nm to run. At WHLP2 outgoing you must turn on to a heading of 345°M, and on an approximately reciprocal incoming course to pass safely northwest of the Chub Rocks, which are clearly visible. In the pass itself you have just 12 feet at MLW, which is sufficiently shoal to produce a wicked sea state if anything significant is happening out in the Atlantic. This apart, there are no problems.

ing through the reefs, but there is just one bad isolated rock south of Ambergris Cay. You'll see it. Head out on 030°M, and come in on 210°M, with about 2 nm to run.

Whale Cay Passage

Whale Cay Passage 1			
WHLP1	2 nm SW	26° 42' 30"/500 N	077° 17' 00"/000 W
Whale Cay Passage 2			
WHLP2	offshore N end	26° 43' 30"/500 N	077° 14' 15"/250 W
Whale Cay Passage 3			
WHLP3	offshore S end	26° 42' 30"/500 N	077° 12' 25"/417 W
Whale Cay Passage 4			
WHLP4	inshore S end	26° 42' 15"/250 N	077° 12' 10"/166 W
First Deep Channel Marker			
DMKR1		26° 42' 00"/000 N	077° 12' 00"/000 W
Second Pair of Markers			
DMKR2		26° 41' 52"/866 N	077° 11' 53"/883 W

Whale Cay Passage is probably the best-known ocean pass in the Abacos, simply because at this point the Sea of Abaco is effectively barred to transit by an area of shoals extending from Great Abaco Island across the Sound to Whale Cay. We cover this in detail under **The Treasure Cay Triangle, The Whale Cay Passage** on page 58. Here we treat Whale Cay Passage as two separate ocean passes, the Whale Cay Passage (or Western Channel) to the north, and the Loggerhead Pass (or Eastern Channel) to the south of Whale Cay.

significant is happening out in the Atlantic. This apart, there are no problems.

EASTERN CHANNEL (OR LOGGERHEAD PASS)

Four waypoints serve to take you in or out through the Loggerhead Channel (to the south of Whale Cay). If you use no more than the first waypoint (WHLP3), you are set up to choose your own line to pass the Loggerhead Bars on the northeastern side. However if the sea state is kicking up, you may well prefer to seek deeper water and pass to the south of the Loggerhead Bars. In this case the next three waypoints (WHLP4, DMKR1, and DMKR2) kick in. These, and our continuing Baker's Bay waypoints (see **The Whale Cay Passage** on page 59), mark your course if you're coming from or bound to Marsh Harbour, or the southern part of the Sea of Abaco. The Loggerhead Bar is the only problem area in this pass, simply because it is shallow and can produce uncomfortable seas even in moderate conditions. Chub Rocks, offshore to the northeast, are no direct threat, but you must still be aware of them, both outgoing and incoming.

Allans-Pensacola to Green Turtle Cay

Allans-Pensacola Cay is fully covered in the previous section of this Guide, **The Northern Abacos, Walkers Cay to Allans-Pensacola Cay** on page 48.

If you look at the chart, you'll note that a series of shal-

Flame trees in Spanish Cay.

low banks lie in the Sea of Abaco off the southwest tip of Spanish Cay, the Ambergris Cays, and the north end of Manjack Cay, all of which combine to dictate two primary options as you head south. The first is to stay on the western side of the Sea of Abaco, and run along the coast of Great Abaco Island. The second is to stay on the eastern side, paralleling the cays.

We covered the route from Crab Cay to Green Turtle Cay in our section titled **The Little Bahama Bank, Options After Great Sale Cay** on page 36, a route that takes you down the western side of the Sea of Abaco before you alter your heading for Green Turtle Cay. Putting it in US East Coast highway terms, you could call this Great Abaco–side route the I-95 of the Abacos. Its drawback is that it sweeps you right past the cays you may want to visit.

The alternative route, staying on the eastern side of the Sea of Abaco, could be called the A1A. It's the beach route. Slower, maybe. But you can stop everywhere. This sounds absolute, but it's not quite like that. Of course you can switch from one side to the other as you wish, but it's useful to look at it this way in passage-making terms. For ease of reference we'll repeat part of the western route. Initially both routes running south from Allans-Pensacola Cay are the same up to Angel Fish Point.

Allans-Pensacola Cay to Angel Fish Point
From Allans-Pensacola Cay a straight run of 6.4 nm on 126°M takes you to Crab Cay, and Angel Fish Point comes up almost immediately after that, just over a mile further on 125°M. This is your decision point. Head for Spanish Cay, or stay off the coast of Great Abaco Island?

THE HOG CAYS
The Hog Cays, which you pass on your way from Allans-Pensacola to Crab and Spanish Cays, are another ground for dinghy expeditions and picnics, but not an area where you are likely to want to anchor for any length of time. This said, Big Hog Cay has some tempting beaches. At this time a well-protected pond on the southernmost Hog Cay has a Department of Fisheries sign prohibiting entry.

Angel Fish Point to Green Turtle Cay (the I-95 Route)
From Angel Fish Point hold 125°M for 5.1 nm to Coopers Town. After Coopers Town change to 139°M for 8.6 nm to place you 3.5 nm northwest of Green Turtle Cay, and then close the distance, altering to around 125°M to place you ready to choose your landfall, either White Sound, Black Sound, or the anchorage off New Plymouth.

Great Abaco Island

COOPERS TOWN
If you're on the I-95 route through the Sea of Abaco, you'll have no problems stopping off at Coopers Town. Low lying though it is, as always its Batelco tower (200 feet here) is the giveaway. Simply slow down, make your way closer inshore, and anchor off. If you need fuel, then go in to the fuel dock there.

If you're on the A1A route, getting to Coopers Town from Spanish Cay requires a kind of dogleg because of the bank off the southwest tip of Spanish Cay. On leaving the

CENTRAL ABACOS I		
Crab Cay		
CRABC	26° 56' 00"/000 N	077° 36' 00"/000 W
Spanish Cay		
SPNSH	26° 56' 30"/500 N	077° 32' 15"/250 W
Powell Cay		
PWELL	26° 54' 19"/317 N	077° 29' 05"/083 W
Coopers Town		
CPSTN	26° 53' 00"/000 N	077° 30' 00"/000 W
Ambergris Cay Warning Stake		
AMSTK	26° 51' 35"/583 N	077° 25' 50"/833 W
Manjack-Crab Cay Anchorage		
MANCR	26° 49' 03"/050 N	077° 21' 47"/783 W
Green Turtle North		
GTNTH	26° 47' 00"/000 N	077° 23' 00"/000 W
Green Turtle Cay		
GTRTL	26° 46' 00"/000 N	077° 21' 00"/000 W
Green Turtle Cay Southwest		
GTCSW	26° 45' 30"/500 N	077° 20' 30"/500 W

The final figures in each waypoint show seconds (00") and thousands (000) of a minute.

Spanish Cay Marina, head about 219°M straight across toward the Great Abaco shoreline. You'll see a strip of sand beach, if you want to keep a landmark, slightly south of where your heading is taking you. You'll end up a comfortable distance offshore after running for 2.48 nm and your position then will be 26° 54' 43"/716 N 077° 32' 47"/783 W. Turn to run southeast parallel to the coast until you reach Coopers Town. The total distance is some 6 nm.

Coopers Town anchorage, if you can call it that (for there's no anchorage at all in the proper sense), is bad news when the wind is from the north, east, and southeast. Forget it then. It also shoals close to the shore (what coastal waters do not?) but you are really limited by this. If you doubt it, note the length of the Coopers Town docks.

There's a Shell dock in Coopers Town, but very little else that you're likely to require.

Angel Fish Point to Spanish Cay (the A1A Route)

From Angel Fish Point you have 2.6 nm to run on 073°M to reach Spanish Cay.

SPANISH CAY

The entry to the Spanish Cay Marina is marked by two pilings painted red (on your starboard side) and green (for your port side). We are not entirely certain what may greet you as you enter the marina. After a period of gradual deterioration, having hit a high standard in 1996–97, Spanish Cay fell apart at the seams, and changed hands in May 1999. The marina itself is large, and has good depth. The docks at the time we were there, literally on Day 1 of the new ownership, needed

work, as did virtually everything else we saw. This said, the original Spanish Cay was well run, had good shoreside facilities, showers, two bars and restaurants (one on the Sea of Abaco side and one on the Atlantic coast), good beaches, and an accommodating and friendly staff. We see no reason why this state should not be brought back, and we know that it's the intention of the new owner to make Spanish Cay second to none.

Spanish Cay, 3 miles in length, is the property of a development consortium and is in its fourth incarnation. The resort and marina, once known as The Club at Spanish Cay, and then as The Inn at Spanish Cay, may retain this name. In any event they will answer as Spanish Cay Marina on VHF 16. The complex as a whole boasts a 5,000-foot airstrip at the northwest end, and a club house, hotel-type rooms, the two restaurants we mentioned, and its sixty-five-slip marina at the southwest end. The island is divided into lots, some with houses built, most still for sale. The most outstanding feature of Spanish Cay is its plantings. It has benefitted from being in private hands and the island is a mini subtropical paradise of native and not-so-native trees, palms, and flowering shrubs.

Spanish Cay–Powell Cay–Ambergris Cays– Manjack Cay–Green Turtle Cay (the A1A Route)

To take AIA south, turn to port when you leave Spanish Cay Marina and run parallel to the breakwater. Keep going, eyeball it between the little island on the south tip of Spanish Cay and the bank that will be on your starboard side, and cross the first gap opening up to the ocean. Watch out for the rocks on the northwest tip of Powell Cay, ignore the little beach on the northwest, and your first option in potential anchorages comes up along the run of Powell Cay's sweep of beaches facing the Sea of Abaco. The distance from Spanish Cay Marina is roughly 4 nm, and if you want a rough position for reassurance, take 26° 54' 19"/316 N 077° 29' 05"/083 W or something like that. You'll find you have 6–8 feet of water.

You'll note that we are not giving courses or waypoints on this route. Navigation here must be done in the old way, using your eyes and common sense.

POWELL CAY

Powell Cay, about 1.5 nm in length, has fine beaches and unusually, its northern stretch of

Spanish Cay Marina, from the southeast.

Powell Cay Channel, from the south.

beach is divided by the first real elevation in land height that you'll have seen in the Abaco Cays, a seemingly great rock headland. Powell is uninhabited but far from unfrequented, for it's a popular stop with cruising visitors. It's also within easy reach of Coopers Town, just 2.5 nm away across the Sea of Abaco. If there are a number of boats anchored off Powell Cay, your congregation may well attract an opportunistic mobile snack bar from Coopers Town, which will set itself up near the pier.

To reinforce the popularity of Powell Cay with cruising visitors, the plus side is the good holding (penetrable sand and some grass), protection from the north through southeast, the Powell Cay beaches, and the snorkeling on the Atlantic-side reef. Cap this with the space of the Powell Cay anchorage ground, where it never feels crowded, and you have a winner. The shelling is reputed to be good on the southern beaches, but if you want to go down there, take your dinghy. A considerable area of shoal lies off the south end of Powell Cay, which extends to and includes Bonefish Cay. What's the downside? Wind from the west. Don't stay under those conditions (you won't want to, as soon as the wind shifts). Anything more? Yes. Anchor far enough offshore to escape the mosquitos.

Moving on from Powell Cay head southwest at the start to avoid the shoal area we've mentioned, and give yourself some offing from the two Ambergris cays, unless of course you want to anchor off and take your dinghy in to explore. From the south of Powell to the isolated rock 0.75 nm southeast of the southern tip of Ambergris Cay, the whole area is a mess of rock and reef. It's dinghy territory, not a playground for big boats.

BONEFISH CAY
Bonefish Cay has a crashed airplane to its southwest in some 5 feet of water, part of which just shows.

THE AMBERGRIS CAYS
When you reach Little Ambergris Cay you'll have run something like 8.6 nm from Spanish Cay. Both Ambergris cays have good beaches, but there are beaches just as good that offer a more user-friendly approach. As it is, Ambergris Cay is privately owned, so that counts it out. Watch out for the shoal area between the two cays, and look particularly for the shoal and rocks that run out for nearly half a mile southwest from the southern end of Ambergris Cay. There's a warning stake on one of the outermost rocks. Its position is approximately 26° 51' 35"/583 N 077° 25' 50"/833 W. After Ambergris you cross a 2 nm gap giving on to the ocean (of which the first half mile is unusable because of one outlying rock) before you reach Manjack Cay.

MANJACK CAY AND CRAB CAY
Manjack Cay has reasonable anchorages at its northern end, although there are shoal areas there. The best anchorage is in the bight formed by Manjack and Crab Cays where you'll fine good protection from the northeast through to the south and around 8 feet of water. Your position here will be around 26° 49' 03"/050 N 077° 21' 47"/783 W, and by then you'll have run some 14 or 15 nm southeast from Spanish Cay.

Green Turtle Cay
Green Turtle Cay runs for 3 nm from northwest to southeast, parallel to Great Abaco Island and 3 nm out in the Sea of Abaco. The Atlantic side of Green Turtle presents an almost straight, unindented coast to the ocean, fringed with reefs and coral heads. The Abaco side has two bays in the north, and those two deeply indented sounds, White Sound in the north and Black Sound in the south, which we've already mentioned. The southeast corner of the island has a fine shallow bay, Gillam Bay, perfect for beachcombing. New Plymouth, the main settlement, is on the southwest tip of the island.

For many of those who know it, Green Turtle Cay is rated the number-one destination if you want a laid-back, relaxed island with everything you dream about. A pretty little settlement town in New Plymouth, plenty of choice in restaurants and bars from the high priced to basic, two small resorts in Bluff House and the Green Turtle Club, apartments and houses to rent, great beaches, and the safest anchorages in the Abacos. All of this is packed into three miles. How has it kept its magic? Like many of the best places, you can only get there by boat. At risk of drawing the world into an island that has largely held its unique inheritance, character, and integrity intact, we must admit that Green Turtle Cay has always been one of our favorite destinations, and rather than be accused of escapism, we'll keep secret the length of time we've spent there in the last few years.

Approaches

Some 3 nm southeast of the Manjack–Crab Cay anchorage you'll find yourself positioned off the entrance to White Sound in Green Turtle Cay, with the entrance to Black Sound a tad further on and the anchorage off New Plymouth dead ahead on your bow. As you approach White Sound you'll notice the Bluff House Resort to port as you come from the north, and a dock for both fuel and where day trippers may secure. The main purpose of this dock was to accommodate the fuel tanker, and the Bluff House Marina, with what you might call its regular fuel dock (linked to the seaward one by pipeline), lies inside White Sound.

WHITE SOUND

There are no problems in entering White Sound. There's a marker at the entrance to the dredged channel leading into the Sound, and you'll have little problem recognizing the channel for it is well dredged, has a clean sand bottom, and is well marked. It offers 5 feet of water at MLW, is about a boat length in width (say around 30 feet), and leads you to the Green Turtle Club Marina, to starboard, or the Bluff House Marina, to port. Between the two docks there's an anchorage, with moorings also available. Don't be tempted to poke your way into the east extension of White Sound when you see it open up to starboard about halfway up the entrance channel, despite the mooring buoys you'll see there. Although there is perhaps 6 feet of water inside, the threshold carries barely 3 feet. More about this later.

BLACK SOUND

Entering Black Sound your initial landmark is a large, two-storied house on the higher ground immediately behind the Black Sound entry channel, which looks a little like a barrack block: squared off, plain, and unadorned. The entry channel is marked by a post to port, and a NO WAKE sign to starboard. This sign is the smaller of two signs that are to starboard. Between the NO WAKE sign and the Black Sound promontory there is another larger sign, which is on the reef. Yes, there is a reef that runs between that NO WAKE sign and the promontory, which is not obvious at high water. At low water it shows. Don't be fooled into thinking that the post is someone's mooring piling and the entry lies between the two signs. That would be a *big* mistake.

As a guide, if you can't see the reef to starboard as you enter Black Sound, you'll have some 5 feet in the channel. If you can see the reef, the channel depth will reduce to 3 feet at MLW.

There may or may not be a line of marker buoys to lead you in, but the deeper water is obvious. Take a gentle curving course to starboard and line up to pass up the center line of the Sound. Abaco Yacht Services are to port, and to starboard you have the Other Shore Club (with a fuel dock), and further on, the Black Sound Marina. There are some

White Sound, from the north.

Black Sound, from the southeast.

Black Sound entrance.

(or was at the time we write) of two Sea Tow craft whose mission, essentially, was to cover the northern Bahamas. See our **Yellow Pages.**

NEW PLYMOUTH SETTLEMENT CREEK

New Plymouth, as we've said, lies directly ahead and you can see where those who've anchored off have chosen to lie.

COMING FROM THE SOUTH OR GOING ON SOUTH

If you are approaching from the south, or heading that way for Whale Cay Passage, take note that there is a shoal area immediately south of the point on which New Plymouth sits. Stand out to get well clear of this.

New Plymouth, from the southwest, with Black Sound at the top of the photograph.

Anchorages and Marinas

Your choices of anchorages lie principally in the choice between the two Sounds and New Plymouth. White Sound has moorings and normally is fairly full. The buoys in the inner pond (some fifteen in total) were placed there by the Green Turtle Club. We have reservations about them, concerned as we are about the depth of water over that access sill and the nature of the mooring itself, a concrete block, which we do not believe would hold in bad weather. There are also moorings in Black Sound. See our **Yellow Pages** for contact details.

If you choose to anchor off New Plymouth there are no problems in settled weather from the east. You'll see the Settlement Creek entrance markers to the town dock area and you must stay clear of the approach channel to the New Plymouth waterfront and clear of the routes that the Bolo ferries, operating from New Plymouth, will take from the adjacent ferry dock on their runs to Black and White Sounds and their crossings to mainland Abaco. Anchoring off New Plymouth you're exposed to the north and the west. The Government Dock, used by commercial shipping, lies on the west side of New Plymouth, and you wouldn't want to anchor in this area. The flow of traffic would not be good for you, nor would your anchoring be good for the commercial carriers. And if the weather changes from the prevailing winds, you're exposed to the south, west, and north.

Going to New Plymouth by dinghy you use the town dock to the right (as you approach it) of the Bolo Ferry dock. There's a small shed on the dock (it's the Green Turtle Cay Fire Station), a Batelco telephone kiosk, a trash dumpster, and a "Welcome to New Plymouth" sign. To run in, use the Settlement Creek entrance markers, going in on the Bolo ferry route. Your dinghy dock is on the right side of the town dock, behind the T.

Your choices in marina rest on the broad option of the two Sounds. In White Sound it's the Green Turtle Club Marina, or the Bluff House Marina, in the process of considerable expansion as we write. Both are good and have everything you will want, but you are remote from New Plymouth by land. The water route there, by dinghy, is the best way to go. Black Sound has the Other Shore Club and the new Black Sound Marina. The Other Shore Club has fuel. Abaco Yacht Services are a repair and storage yard.

NO NAME CAY

No Name Cay, immediately southeast of Green Turtle Cay, is uninhabited, has a good offshore reef, but otherwise has nothing to offer. You might land on its beach out of curiosity during your Green Turtle gunkholing, for No Name is barely a stone's throw off Gillam Point. However, if you want to bring a deeper draft boat closer to No Name Cay, beware of the shoals extending southeast from Green Turtle Cay. There are also shoals running southwest from the southern tip of No Name Cay, and a further shoal area between these two areas.

The Treasure Cay Triangle

The Treasure Cay Triangle is the name we've given the area of the Sea of Abaco that has Treasure Cay as its apex and the full span of the Whale Cay Passage as its baseline. The heart of the triangle is the no-go part of the Sea of Abaco, the barrier of shallows around Treasure Cay Bank, the Sand Bank Cays, and Dont Rock, which makes a diversion out into the Atlantic around Whale Cay a necessary way to continue your cruise, both north and south, on your all-Abaco itinerary. This barrier across the Sea of Abaco between Treasure Cay and Whale Cay at once dictates your approach to routes to Treasure Cay,

Atlantic Beach, Green Turtle Cay.

as well as your route between Green Turtle Cay and Great Guana Cay and destinations further south.

We covered the Whale Cay Passage under **Ocean Passes** on page 52, for it is the principal central Abaco–Atlantic pass. It also doubles as a necessary part of the Sea of Abaco north–south route. If you are shoal draft, there are two alternatives. The first is to parallel the west coast of Whale Cay, where there is some 3 feet of water, maybe more, at MLW, staying just offshore and reading your way as you go. The other is to cross the main sandbar to the east of the Sand Bank Cays and Dont Rock, again feeling your way. This second route is a real *if*. There may be 2 feet there at MLW. It could be dry. The sand changes, each year. We've taken a cata-

maran sailboat across there, and came close to sitting on the sand for an hour or two. If you really want to check it out, why not take an inflatable first? It's easier to push.

If you do consider either of these two alternatives to Whale Cay Passage, they are not rough weather alternatives. You need good light and calm conditions to read your way, and any chop will not only make eyeballing it impossible, but could have you striking bottom in the troughs.

There is an inshore route to Treasure Cay from the north that takes you past the Sand Bank Cays and around Dont Rock. The temptation to go this way, rather than going around Whale Cay Passage is irresistible at first sight, particularly if Whale Cay Passage is impassable due to weather. Forget it. Yes, it can be done. We've done it. But it's shoal draft, even at high water. The sands continually move in this area, and there's no "safe" course. The probability of your grounding is so high we'd count it as a certainty. In short, if it's calm, it's a hazardous passage. If there's any kind of sea running, it's dangerous.

Whale Cay and the Whale Cay Passage

Whale Cay, 2 nm south of No Name Cay, is famous for its passage out into the ocean rather than the island itself. This uninhabited cay runs for 1.5 nm and occupies a strategic position in navigational terms, for it lies at the very point that the Sea of Abaco becomes too shallow, due to sandbanks, for most cruising boats to negotiate. As we've said, if you're heading for Hope Town or Marsh Harbour, the only route (albeit a fair-weather route) is to dogleg out into the Atlantic around Whale Cay and then continue your passage down the Sea of Abaco. Your brief excursion into the Atlantic will add another eight waypoints to your catalog and 5 nm or so to your distance run, all legs counted.

To the north the passage is wide enough to cause no anxiety, but there are rocks to be spotted and it's relatively shallow, some 12 feet deep. To the south the passage is shallow but has a deep entrance channel dredged for cruise ships in a failed venture to develop Baker's Bay at the northwest end of Great Guana Cay into a tropical island adventure stop.

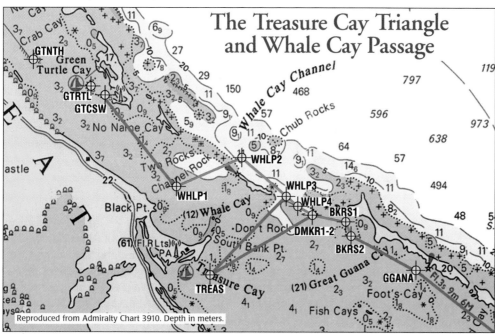

The Treasure Cay Triangle
and Whale Cay Passage

Not to be used for Navigation.

Reproduced from Admiralty Chart 3910. Depth in meters.

The Whale Cay Passage Step-by-Step

First of all, check the weather the day you intend to do the Whale Cay Passage. Call anyone in the area on Channel 16 and ask what Whale Cay conditions are like. If everything's OK, go for it. The first leg from Green Turtle down to Whale Cay, 4.69 nm on a heading of 144°M from just off Settlement Point, is easy. Just remember that there's a considerable area of shallow water to the south of Green Turtle Cay. Get some distance out before you turn south toward Whale Cay.

The Whale Cay Passage is a simple three-leg diversion around Whale Cay, followed by two further legs that take you up the disused cruise ship channel to Baker's Bay on the northwest tip of Great Guana Cay.

Whale Cay Passage 1

WHLP1	26° 42' 30"/500 N	077° 17' 00"/000 W

At WHLP1 turn on to 064°M to head out through Whale Cay Channel for 2.88 nm. To port are Two Rocks and Whale Cay Channel Rocks. To starboard you'll pass the north tip of Whale Cay. Ahead, as a marker, you'll see Chub Rocks.

Whale Cay Passage 2

WHLP2	26° 43' 30"/500 N	077° 14' 15"/250 W

At WHLP2 turn on to 127°M for 1.92 nm, running offshore and parallel to Whale Cay.

Whale Cay Passage 3

WHLP3	26° 42' 30"/500 N	077° 12' 25"/417 W

At WHLP3 turn inshore on 149°M for 0.06 nm until you reach the approach to Loggerhead Channel (the southern Whale Cay pass, named for the bars in that area).

Whale Cay Passage 4

WHLP4	26° 42' 15"/250 N	077° 12' 10"/166 W

At WHLP4 you're at the entrance to the dredged channel.

Deep Channel Markers

DMKR1	26° 42' 00"/000 N	077° 12' 00"/000 W
DMKR2	26° 41' 52"/866 N	077° 11' 53"/883 W

At this point you hardly need your GPS. Our two waypoints are simply for guidance. You can see the line of markers along the deep-water channel (don't get fooled by some markers that will be off to starboard), you can see the sand of Baker's Bay on your port bow and the main spoil island on your starboard bow.

Baker's Bay Waypoints

BKRS1	26° 41' 25"/417 N	077° 10' 15"/166 W
BKRS2	26° 41' 05"/085 N	077° 10' 05"/085 W

On a heading of 116°M you'll reach our first Baker's Bay

The greatest knock-on effect of the shallowness of the Whale Cay Passes is that in high seas, particularly Northeasters, and whenever distant Atlantic storms have generated heavy swells, the water piles up on the Whale Cay shoals producing dangerously rough conditions, known locally as a "Rage." These are powerful, turbulent, and lethal seas.

In unfavorable weather under *no* circumstances should you even *think* of poking your nose out to check what it might be like out there. If someone has a deadline, a flight to catch from Marsh Harbour or something like that, change it to Treasure Cay, or take the Bolo Ferry to Treasure Cay and a taxi on to Marsh Harbour. The reverse applies, of course, if you're the other side of Whale Cay heading north.

waypoint. The distance on this leg is 1.67 nm. Check your heading, but use the channel markers. Our two Baker's Bay waypoints serve to direct you between the Baker's Bay spoil banks, which will come up on your starboard side, and Baker's Bay to port. At the first waypoint turn on to 162°M and hold it for just 0.37 nm to reach the second waypoint. Here you're at the end of the deep-water channel with the mooring buoys intended for the cruise ships.

Great Guana Cay

You've made it to Great Guana Cay. Rather than go on at once there are three places where you might well wish to stop and beachcomb for a while, or maybe even anchor.

DAY ANCHORAGE OFF THE NORTHWEST BEACH

From the cruise ship channel just south of Gumelemi Cay pick a northerly course that will allow you to pass midway between Gumelemi Cay and West End Cay. You'll have a minimum of 8 feet MLW all the way. Once you pass about 200 yards off West End Cay, turn to starboard and parallel the beach. One-half mile up the beach you'll find a good anchorage in 12 feet over fine sand, just 200 feet off the beach. This day anchorage, best when the wind is southeast, is one of the loveliest beaches in the Bahamas.

BAKER'S BAY

Baker's Bay, on the southwest side of the north end of Great Guana Cay, is the site of the failed commercial development. Why not anchor there and enjoy the beach and the swimming? At last count four dolphins, two mothers and two calves, once part of the circus trained to entertain cruise ship passengers, are still in the area. The dolphin pens, where they were once held, remain. The best anchorage is the south-

Gumelemi Cay, from the south.

east corner of the bay in the lee of the point, where you'll have 6 feet or more. The holding is adequate, in sand and some grass. This is a much-favored stop for those who have completed the Whale Cay Passage heading south, and those who are waiting to pass through it on their way north.

THE SPOIL BANKS

The Spoil Banks are a popular stop, known for their shelling. If nothing else, it's an encouraging example of how nature, once given a free hand, can reclaim and make good the waste of mankind. The best anchorage is in the lee of the main spoil bank, 1 nm west of Baker's Bay. This is a fair-weather stop.

Baker's Bay to Great Guana Cay Settlement

The straight-line course to take you from Baker's Bay to the entrance to Great Guana Cay's settlement bay with its public dock and the Great Guana Beach Resort's dock is 122°M. The distance to run is just 3 nm. On your way you'll pass the Guana Seaside Village resort with its dock. Although no marina facilities are offered, nor moorings, you are welcome to stop there for a drink or a meal. You can pick up Guana Seaside Village by the Batelco-like mast standing higher up behind it, and by its long dock. Its approximate position, if you want to plot an inshore mark on your chart, is 26° 40' 40"/666 N 077° 08' 05"/ 085 W.

GREAT GUANA CAY

Great Guana Cay is higher than the average Abaco cay, a rolling island, 5.5 nm in length with a nearly continuous Atlantic beach. Great Guana's superb beaches, and its distinction of being the last of the large Abaco Cays to suffer development, made it one attractive destination. Over the

last two years, destiny has arrived. Nipper's Beach Bar has become one if the "in places," attracting the crowd from Marsh Harbour and Hope Town. The Abaco-side Guana Seaside Village is in business, and on the ocean side, the Dolphin Beach Resort is in full swing. The Orchid Bay Yacht Club development, with eight houses about to be built at the time we write, is hitting a high batting average. Despite all this, the small settlement remains small, and unspoiled. And there's still a lot of Great Guana Cay out there. As of now, Guana Harbour (the proper name for the settlement) remains largely untouched and the island population has still held at around the eighty mark.

Near the southeast of Great Guana Cay there's a private harbor that reportedly was carved out by a landowner hoping to sell waterfront lots with their own docks. As yet it's undeveloped. One captain who by invitation was allowed to ride out Hurricane Bertha there in 1996 said that it offered superb protection. Add it to your panic list of potential hurricane refuges.

Great Guana Cay Anchorages and Marinas

The best anchorage is just off the Great Guana Beach Resort in the bay behind Delia's Cay and the small point that shields the Great Guana settlement area and the docks from view as you come down from the north. On your approach look out for the submerged rock at 26° 40' 05"/083 N 077° 07' 20"/333 W, which is marked by a stake, but don't rely on the stake being there. Don't cut between the rock and Delia's Cay, for a submerged reef connects them. In the anchorage you'll find good holding in 8–10 feet of water. You're well protected from the east and southeast, although you may get some surge, but it would be untenable in a Norther. You can dinghy in from here to the Great Guana Beach Resort's dinghy dock.

A second potential anchorage may attract (and may even be in use by some boats) inside the settlement bay (optimistically called Guana Harbour), but the holding here is not good. In good weather, with nothing coming out of the Sea of Abaco from any direction, sheer weight on the bottom may keep you in place. But if the Delia's Cay anchorage is a No-Go, the bay certainly is out of the question, and your only options are to go for one of the two marinas, or move on.

GREAT GUANA BEACH RESORT MARINA

The Great Guana Beach Resort Marina, together with the public dock, are inside the bay to port as you enter, with the Guana Beach Resort dock coming up first. The basic facilities of this marina have been improved with the conversion of the single T to a fuel dock, but other than that, and shore power, there's little there, certainly no water, and no shoreside facilities. You can negotiate with the resort and gain the use of a room if you want a shower. The depth there, other than

CENTRAL ABACOS III		
Great Guana Cay		
GGANA	26° 39' 31"/519 N	077° 07' 22"/374 W
Treasure Cay Entrance		
TREAS	26° 39' 30"/500 N	077° 15' 45"/750W
Fish Cay South		
FISHS	26° 37' 14"/232 N	077° 09' 16"/270 W

The final figures in each waypoint show seconds (00") and thousands (000) of a minute.

at the inshore slips, will give you 6 feet at MLW. The downside is that in anything other than good weather the dock suffers from a total lack of shielding, other than from the north. We've had nights there when the effect of surge has made sleep impossible. This apart, if you're simply paying a day visit, and eat in their restaurant or on their patio, they'll ask you for a $10 deposit on securing, but will refund it as a credit against your restaurant bill. See our **Yellow Pages**.

We've always reckoned that the Guana Beach Resort has one of the best sites, both in location and with its existing palm grove planting, in the Bahamas. The pity is that so far it has failed to realize this potential.

ORCHID BAY MARINA

Immediately to starboard, protected by a half circlet of white stone breakwater, is the new (February 1999) Orchid Bay Yacht Club and Marina. Its entry is obvious, as is its Texaco fuel dock at the head of the first dock. The marina is the flag bearer of a far larger planned development, on a site extending from the Sea of Abaco to the ocean front, whose emphasis will be on low-density private housing. A significant parcel of central land has been set aside as a Nature Reserve. A restaurant and, later on, a small hotel are also in the cards.

The sizeable marina (sixty-four slips) has all the facilities you'd expect at the top end of the market, an approach of 9 feet at MLW, and depth in the slips gradually shoaling from that 9 feet down to 4.5 feet inshore at MLW. See our **Yellow Pages**.

Treasure Cay

Treasure Cay (the "sounds good" name came with tourist development) is not a cay at all, but very much a part of mainland Great Abaco Island. It's both a resort community, served by a local airport with Customs and Immigration, and a

full-service marina, primarily devoted to sports fishing.

From the North. The safest route from Green Turtle Cay or the north, although it seems a diversion, is to take Whale Cay Passage to our waypoint 4. From there head toward the Great Abaco shoreline on a course of 239°M, which will bring you to our Treasure Cay approach waypoint, just 1 nm southeast of the entrance to Treasure Cay Marina. This course takes you safely southeast of Dont Rock, which is easy to see, and northwest of a shallow bank that lies less than a mile southeast of Dont Rock. Your distance to run on this leg from the Whale Cay Passage waypoint is 4.18 nm. When you get close to the Treasure Cay entrance you'll see the Treasure Cay welcome sign.

From the South. Approaching Treasure Cay from the south, our Fish Cay waypoint is the focal point on all routes to Treasure Cay, unless you elect to go by way of Great Guana Cay and our Whale Passage waypoint. From our Fish Cay waypoint it's 7.48 nm on a heading of 298°M to our Treasure Cay approach waypoint. To get to the Fish Cay waypoint from Marsh Harbour it's 4.8 nm on a heading of 318°M. From North Point Set Rock it's 7.1 nm on 295°M, and from Man-O-War it's 5.4 nm on a heading of 283°M.

After the Treasure Cay welcome sign you'll pick up a series of white pilings marking a sandbar on your starboard side and another sandbar, which may or may not show, to port. Stay between the markers and you'll have 7 feet of water all the way into the marina. On your way in you'll pass the Treasure Cay fuel dock to port, which is separate from the marina.

Seven Mile Beach, Great Guana Cay.

Treasure Cay, from the northeast.

If you're into fishing, you'll certainly have Treasure Cay on your visit list but it's highly likely to feature there for other reasons, as well. It's a good place to change crew or pick up guests, for the airport is almost on your doorstep. Treasure Cay has a great beach (some say it's world class), and for beach lovers it's well worth a lazy morning or an afternoon in the sun. What else? We hope you never have to head for Treasure Cay purely for this last reason, but think seriously about going there if you're in the area and a severe storm is coming your way. We have friends who moored their 42-foot trawler to two Treasure Cay moorings when Hurricane *Bertha* roared up the Abacos in 1996. The moorings held and the boat came through it, undamaged, in over 60 knots of wind. The network of Treasure Cay canals are another "hurricane hole" option you might want to keep on your "What If?" panic list.

YELLOW PAGES

This area received the full force of Hurricane *Floyd* in September 1999. Be aware that reconstruction and the restoration of normal services after a Category 4 Hurricane may take a considerable period of time to complete.

SPANISH CAY

Spanish Cay is a privately owned island with all the makings of a tropical paradise. Under new ownership, the marina will once again provide cruising boats with an ideal setting in which to relax and enjoy the welcome and hospitality that is found here. All the facilities are centered around the marina and hotel complex. **Customs** and **Immigration** will be available to clear you in after September 1999.

MARINA

SPANISH CAY MARINA
Tel and Fax: 242-365-0083 • VHF 16

Slips	60
Max LOA	Over 100 ft.
MLW at Dock	8 ft.
Dockage	$1 per foot per day.
Power	$25 per day for 50A, $15 per day for 30A.
Fuel	Diesel and gasoline.
Water	25¢ per gallon.
Telephone	No public telephone.
Showers	Very clean, located by the restaurant.
Ice	Available from the marina store.
Swimming	New fresh-water pool under construction.
Marina Store	Open from 8 am to 6 pm.
Office	Open from 8 am to 6 pm.
Credit cards	Visa and MasterCard.

SERVICES

Airport
Only private or chartered aircraft use the 5,000-foot runway.
Accommodations
The Inn at Spanish Cay Tel: 242-365-0083, 954-779-3155, or 888-722-6474 A small luxury resort with villa suites and seven apartments.
Cart Rental
$10 per hour, $35 per day
Restaurant and Bar
The Point House Tel: 359-6622 • VHF 16 Overlooking the marina and the Sea of Abaco. Open for lunch and dinner in a tropical garden setting. Dinner reservations preferred.
The Wreckers Bar An imaginative building on stilts set out over the water on the ocean side of the island, currently being rebuilt for weekend functions. Serves light snacks and drinks.
Liquors
The Ship's Store Liquor, gifts, a few snacks, and some marine supplies.

SPORTS

Diving
There are reefs only half a mile from shore, as well as some exciting dives between Spanish Cay and Green Turtle Cay. Within reasonable distance, the wreck of the *San Jacinto* lies in about 40 feet of water, though badly broken up and covered in fire coral. This early American steamship sank in 1865 while on a blockade patrol. There are also caverns that play host to schools of fish and have some lovely swim-through caves, while *Meghan's Reef* has magnificent and unusual corals rising close to the surface.

Tennis
There are four tennis courts available.

THINGS TO DO IN SPANISH CAY

- Take a golf cart ride around the island and try to decide on which lot you would build your dream house.
- Count the number of different trees and shrubs that have been planted on the island. How many can you name?
- Swim off one of the five Spanish Cay beaches or walk part of the seven miles of glorious coastline.
- Enjoy a romantic dinner under the stars in the tropical garden overlooking the Sea of Abaco.

GREEN TURTLE CAY

One of the best-loved Abaco cays, and certainly a favorite cruising destination, Green Turtle remains a joy and a delight. The early settlement of New Plymouth has a timelessness and charm that has much to offer, with good restaurants, well-stocked stores and a thriving community of friendly people used to visiting boaters. Both White Sound and Black Sound provide sheltered moorings and marinas, while many boats of deeper draft prefer to anchor off New Plymouth. Good beaches, good friends, and a warm welcome complete the idyll. Green Turtle Cay is a Port of Entry for the Bahamas; the **Customs** and **Immigration** office (Tel: 365-4077) is on Parliament Street in New Plymouth. It is open weekdays 9 am to 5 pm, closed on weekends unless specially requested. To find it, tie up your dinghy at the town pier, and walk up the street past Laura's Kitchen and the Shell Hut to the Albert Lowe Museum, take a left and walk a few yards to the office, up the steps next to the post office.

MARINAS IN WHITE SOUND

GREEN TURTLE CLUB AND MARINA
Tel: 242-365-4271 • Fax: 365-4272 • VHF 16
This is a well-maintained marina, in a lovely, sheltered position at the head of White Sound, with all the facilities that the *Green Turtle Club* offers. With its own fishing tournaments, yacht club, and outstanding beaches within walking distance, it is one of the most attractive marinas in the Abaco Islands.

Slips	35
Max LOA	100 ft.
MLW at Dock	7 ft.; only 5 ft. in the channel at low water
Dockage	80¢ per ft. per day, $22 minimum charge; 70¢ per ft. per day monthly in advance.
Power	$18.50 per day for 50A, $12 per day for 30A.
Fuel	Diesel and gasoline; open from 8 am to 4:30 pm.
Water	30¢ per gallon.
Telephone	In the clubhouse, where there is a fax machine and copier for use during office hours, from 8 am to 4 pm.
TV Hookup	$5 per day, $25 deposit for the connector.
Showers	Complimentary to marina guests, $40 deposit for the key.

GREEN TURTLE CAY DIRECTORY

1. Green Turtle Club and Marina
2. Bluff House Club and Marina
3. Dolphin Marine
4. The Other Shore Club
5. Abaco Yacht Services
6. Black Sound Marina
7. Roberts Marine
8. Brendal's Dive Center
9. Bluff House fuel dock on Sea of Abaco
⛽ Fuel

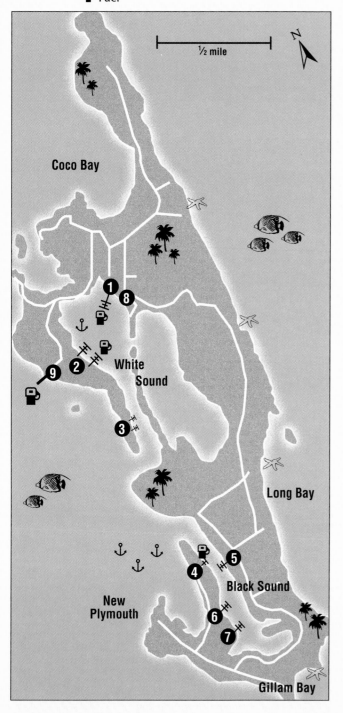

Laundry	Tokens at reception; $3.50 per machine.
Restaurants	On the *Green Turtle Club* terrace, and in their elegant dining room for dinner.
Provisions	Marina store open from 8 am to 5 pm daily, selling ice, beverages, snacks, and a few marine supplies.
Swimming	Freshwater pool, solar heated in winter
Mail	The Club will send and hold mail for you.
Gift Shop	There is a small boutique in the clubhouse.
Rentals	Bicycles, sailboats, and windsurfers.
Dive Shop	*Brendal's Dive Center* Tel: 365-4411 • VHF 16 Two dive boats, a sailboat, kayaks, windsurfers, and a glass-bottom boat. Scuba instruction from beginner courses to advanced open-water certification, underwater photography, night dives, CPR and first aid course; dive and snorkel equipment to rent; all-day trips with seafood beach picnics and rum punch. One-tank dive from $50, open water diver certification course $450.
Cart Rental	*D and P* have carts and scooters available.
Bicycles	From *Brendal's Dive Center.*
Accommodations	At the *Green Turtle Club*, rooms from $145 per night, villas from $260; MAP $36.
Credit Cards	Visa, MasterCard, Discover, and Amex accepted.

BLUFF HOUSE BEACH HOTEL AND MARINA
Tel: 242-365-4247 • Fax: 365-4248 • VHF 16 •
E-mail: BluffHouse@oii.net

At the time of writing, *Bluff House Marina* had not caught up with the hotel renovations. This is a very friendly, family-owned and run hotel, with secluded coves and beaches and a great restaurant. The new villas overlooking White Sound and the marina are very appealing, and the deck surrounding the dining room and entrance to the hotel is a great improvement, but the docks were feeling their age and needing attention. Dockmaster Michael Sawyer hoped that the dock reconstruction would start soon, so call ahead for an update. Their fuel docks on both White Sound and the Sea of Abaco are open from 7 am to 4 pm daily, and accept Visa, MasterCard, and American Express.

Slips	50, after rebuilding is complete.
Moorings	4 at $8 per night.
MLW at Dock	8 ft., but only 5 ft. in the approach channel into White Sound at low water.
Power	$20 per day for 50A and $10 per day for 30A.
Fuel	Fuel docks on White Sound and the Sea of Abaco, open daily from 7 am to 4 pm.
Water	20¢ per gallon.
Telephone	At the hotel.
Showers	There will be, plus a laundry.
Restaurants	At the time of writing, there is the main restaurant up in the hotel serving excellent dinners. Reservations, with choice of menu, are required by 5 pm. Lunch is served daily at the *Palms Beach Bar* where Kevin and the Gully Roosters play for the Thursday night barbecue.
Ice	$3 a bag.
Swimming	Pool at the hotel, and a beach below *Bluff House.*
Accommodations	*Bluff House Beach Hotel*, suites from $135, villas from $275 per night.
Credit Cards	Visa, MasterCard, and Amex accepted.

Bluff House and Green Turtle Club Marinas, White Sound, Green Turtle Cay.

MARINAS IN BLACK SOUND

THE OTHER SHORE CLUB
Tel: 242-365-4338/4226 • VHF 16
One of the friendliest small marinas in the Abacos, Alan and Trudy Andrews have been welcoming guests to *The Other Shore Club* for over 30 years. Now with the help of their daughter Babs, and son Cleeve, and dockmaster Kevin McIntosh of Gully Rooster fame, the welcome and charm continues. It is a pleasant walk through the garden around to New Plymouth.

Slips	15
Moorings	4 moorings, $7 per night.
Max LOA	50 ft., but 100 ft. alongside the fuel dock.
MLW at Dock	6 ft.; only 4.5 ft. in the channel at low water.
Dockage	50¢ per foot per day.
Power	$17 per day for 50A, $10 for 30A.
Fuel	Diesel and gasoline; fuel dock open from 7:30 am to 4 pm.
Water	Reverse osmosis water for 25¢ per gallon.
Telephone	By request, in the dockmaster's office.
Showers	$3 each
Ice	$3.50 a bag.
Accommodations	There is a house, cottage, and an apartment for rent at The *Other Shore Club*. Call Babs at 365-4226.
Credit Cards	Visa, MasterCard, and Amex accepted. Five percent discount for cash.
Dockmaster	Kevin McIntosh

BLACK SOUND MARINA
Tel: 242-365-4531 • VHF 16
This small, quiet marina is tucked away past *The Other Shore Club* on the west side of Black Sound. It is attractive with well-landscaped grounds, picnic tables, and barbecue grills for guests set out under the trees, only a few minutes walk into New Plymou*th*.

Slips	15
Max LOA	55 ft., with 65 ft. on the T-dock.
MLW at Dock	7 ft.; only 4.5 ft. in the channel at low water.
Dockage	70¢ per foot per day.
Power	$18 per day for 50A, $12 for 30A.
Water	25¢ per gallon.
Showers	$3; only one shower, but clean.

Laundry	$4 for the one washer or dryer.
Ice	$4 a bag.
Storage	Monthly rates available.
Credit Cards	Visa and MasterCard.
Dockmaster	Reggie Curry is at the office from 8 am daily, and on Sunday mornings from 9 am.

SERVICE MARINAS

DOLPHIN MARINE   White Sound
Tel: 242-365-4262 • VHF 16
Evinrude and Johnson sales, service, and parts, with factory-trained mechanics. Boston Whalers in stock. OMC and DONZI, and *Brownie's Third Lung* diving equipment.

GREEN TURTLE SHIPYARD at ABACO YACHT SERVICES
Black Sound
Tel: 242-365-4033 • Fax 365-4216 • VHF 16 • CB 11
• E-mail: ays@grouper.batelnet.bs
This is a full-service yard with good mechanics, a travel lift, forklift, and small-boat hoist, and long-term dry dockage while you are away from the Bahamas. But reserve space for dry storage ahead of time. Sea Hawk Islands 44 tin-based paint is available. Yamaha sales and repairs on site. They also have a token-operated laundromat, the only one on Green Turtle Cay, except for the *Green Turtle Club*, which is for marina guests only. The yard is open from 7:30 am to noon and 1 pm to 4:30 pm, Monday to Friday.

Dockage	55¢ per ft. per day without power, 65¢ per ft. per day with power.
Water	25¢ per gallon.
Showers	$3
Laundry	$4 tokens from the office for the washing machines, and $3.50 for the dryers.
Ice	$3 a bag.
Dry Storage	$4.25 per ft. per month.
Labor	From $25 per hour, painting $37 per hour, Yamaha mechanics $48 per hour.
50-ton Acme Travel Lift	Up to 30 ft. in length, $100. Prices increase according to boat length for haul and launch. Pressure cleaning starts at $65, and blocking at $55 for boats up to 30 ft.
Small Boat Hoist	From $46 to $60 depending on length, up to 25 ft.
Catamaran Haul and Storage	Up to 30 ft., $115.50. Prices increase according to boat length.
Catamaran Dry Storage	$6.50 per foot per month.
Accommodations	There is a house for rent.

ROBERTS MARINE   Black Sound
Tel: 242-365-4249 • VHF 16
Workshop with complete engine service, inboards and outboards, and a diesel mechanic on site. They have a few slips available for transient boats, and three moorings for $5 a night, or monthly. Boat sales and rentals, marine accessories, batteries and ice. Johnson dealer. Their store, *Roberts Hardware* (Tel: 365-4122 and VHF 16), in New Plymouth is well stocked with marine supplies, household goods, building supplies, and paints.

SEA TOW   Black Sound
Tel: 242-365-4649/4226/4338 or 362-1236 • VHF 16
Judson Thompson and Stafford Morrison can help you if you need towing anywhere. From Hole in the Wall to Green Turtle Cay, to Nassau and back to Florida if necessary. They have a tug, tow boat, and barge with pumps, and guarantee 24-hour service. They also offer yacht deliveries to the Caribbean and yacht management.

NEW PLYMOUTH

SERVICES

Bank
Barclays Bank Parliament Street   Tel: 365-4144
Open from 10 am to 1 pm on Tuesdays and Thursdays.

Churches
Methodist Church   Services at 11 am and 7 pm on Sundays.
Miracle of God Church   Sunday services at 11 am.
New Plymouth Gospel Chapel   Completed in 1995, winning top honors in the Institutional category from the Institute of Bahamian Architects. Services at 10 am and 8 pm on Sundays.
St. Peter's Anglican Church   Dates from 1786, and has Sunday services at 11 am and 8 pm.
Roman Catholic Mass at the *Green Turtle Club*, Thursdays at 11 am.

Clinic
Tel: 365-4028   The clinic is on the street running down opposite the *Sand Dollar Shop*. Nurse Barbara Reckley is on duty from 9 am to 3 pm, Monday to Friday. Dr Swan is there on Tuesdays and Thurdays.

Couriers
Fedex deliveries can be arranged via ferry from Marsh Harbour.

Dentist
Tel: 367-4070 or 365-4548   Call to make a Saturday appointment.

Doctor
Dr Robert Sonn at the *Sunlight Medical Center*   Tel: 365-4409 • Fax: 365-4455   In emergency call 340-7243, then give the operator beeper number 340-8083 with your name and telephone number and the nature of the emergency. Or you can call Dr Sonn's home at 365-5423.

E-mail
Sid's Grocery provides access to your E-mail for a $2 connection charge, and $1 per minute after that.

Hairdresser
Hubert's Cuts 'n' Curls   Parliament Street Tel: 365-4100

Museums
Albert Lowe Museum Tel: 365-1494   Open 9 am to 11:45 am and 1 pm to 4:30 pm, Monday through Saturday. Admission $3, with a gift shop and the Schooner Gallery in the cellar beneath this 200-year-old house. A must-visit.
New Plymouth Town Jail   Renovations are underway here, with new roof beams and new cell doors. There is even talk of a Junkanoo exhibit in one of the cells.

Police
Parliament Street

Post Office
Tel: 365-4242 Between customs and the library, which, at time of writing, is due to move into the restored cookhouse in the grounds of the administrator's office, on Parliament Street. Open from 9 am to 5 pm, Monday to Friday.

Rest Room
Next door to the library.

Telephones
There is a card phone on the public dock, and direct-dial phone outside the library, next to the post office on Parliament Street. There is also one outside the Batelco office at the top of the hill leading out of New Plymouth, and two more inside. The office is open from 9 am to 5 pm, Monday to Friday.

SHOPPING

Boutiques
Bluff House Boutique at *Bluff House Beach Hotel*.
Green Turtle Club Boutique, in the lobby of the Clubhouse.

Fresh Flowers
Creative Native   Tel: 365-4206 • Fax: 365-4372   Wonderful fresh flowers, sold by the bunch or as an arrangement, as well as silk flowers, hand-crafted Christmas decorations, unique gifts, and Abaco Ceramics.

Galleries
Alton Lowe Art Gallery Tel: 365-4624/4094   Alton Lowe's own paintings and carved Bahamian boat models by Ventrum Lowe, as well as sculptures and paintings by James Mastin, at the head of Black Sound. Call ahead for an appointment. They have their own dock, and a lovely garden that is also used in summer for theater performances.
Ocean Blue Gallery   Tel: 365-4234   Featuring many local and island artists, open within the Plymouth Rock Liquors and Cafe.

Gifts and Souvenirs
Sand Dollar Shop Parliament Street Tel: 365-4221   Original handcrafted jewelry, designed and manufactured by 9th-generation Abaco artists, as well as souvenirs, T-shirts, gifts, and sportswear.
Shell Hut On the street up from the public dock Tel: 365-4188   Offers a selection of T-shirts, souvenirs, post cards, and some clothing. Open from 9 am to 5 pm, Monday to Saturday.
Tropic Topics Variety Store   Straw work, T-shirts, souvenirs, and ice cream.
Vert's Model Ship Shoppe Next to Curry's Food Store, open when Vert is there.

Groceries
Curry's Food Store Tel: 365-4171   Open 8 am to noon, and 1 pm to 5:30 pm, Monday to Friday; to 8 pm on Saturdays. Also T-shirts, wonderful fresh bread, and custom wood carvings. They have their own dinghy dock.

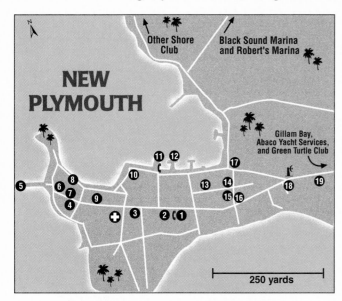

NEW PLYMOUTH DIRECTORY

1. Customs, Post Office, Telephone, and Library
2. Albert Lowe Museum
3. New Plymouth Inn
4. Roberts Hardware and Marine Store
5. Commercial Dock
6. Liquor Store
7. Barclays Bank
8. Anglican Church
9. Sid's Grocery and propane
10. Curry's Food Store
11. Public Dock and Telephone
12. Ferry Dock
13. B & M Seafood
14. Bert's Sea Garden
15. The Blue Bee Bar
16. Town Jail
17. The Wrecking Tree
18. Batelco
19. Rooster's Rest
✚ Clinic

The old jail, New Plymouth.

Lowe's Tel: 365-4243   Open 7:30 am to 6 pm, Monday to Friday, to 8 pm on Saturdays. Gifts as well as groceries.

Sid's Food Store Tel: 365-4055   Open 7 am to 5:30 pm, Monday through Friday; to 7:30 pm on Saturdays. Well stocked with everything including fresh fruit and vegetables, pharmacy, some hardware, greeting cards, and souvenirs. Propane refills may take a couple of days. Scott Lowe is very good to boaters, and now offers an E-mail service from the store, charging $2 for a connection, and $1 per minute after that.

Hardware

New Plymouth Hardware Tel: 365-4305 • Fax: 365-4372 • VHF 16   Open 7:30 am to 4:30 pm, Monday to Friday; 8 am to noon on Saturdays. Household goods and some marine hardware. No credit cards accepted. They will let you use their fax machine, and they also build docks.

Roberts Hardware & Marine Tel: 365-4122 • VHF 16   Hardware and building supplies, paints, charts, rope, ice, and fishing and diving supplies.

Liquors

Plymouth Rock Liquors Parliament Street Tel: 365-4234   Open 9 am to 6 pm, Monday to Thursday; to 9 pm on Fridays and Saturdays. They will deliver to the town dock. At lunch they serve sandwiches and light meals. The *Ocean Blue Gallery*, featuring many local and island artists, is located inside the liquor store.

Propane

Sid's Food Store Tel: 365-4055   Tanks may take a couple of days since they have to go to Marsh Harbour.

Seafood

Abaco Seafoods Tel: 365-4011

B & M Seafood York Street Tel: 365-4387   Excellent grouper, and lobster tails in season.

Sodas

Soda machine next to the *Red Door*, on Parliament Street, with Coke, ginger ale, orange, root beer, grape juice, and Goombay Punch for $1 in US quarters.

Videos

Porky's Next to the *Sea Garden Club*.

RESTAURANTS & BARS

Bluff House Beach Hotel at White Sound
Tel: 365-4247, ext. 228 • VHF 16
The Palms Beach Club is open for lunch from 11:30 am to 3 pm,

and for a barbecue on Thursday evenings when Kevin and the Gully Roosters provide live music. Please make your dinner reservations for the *Main House*, with choice of menu, by 5 pm daily. Fantastic sunset views and great food with Island Spice live music on Tuesday evenings.

Green Turtle Cay Club at White Sound Tel: 365-4271 • VHF 16 Breakfast from 7:45 am to 10:30 am, lunch from 11:30 am to 2 pm on a beautiful terrace overlooking White Sound. Dinner is served in their elegant dining room at 7:30 pm. Please make your dinner reservations by 5 pm. Live music on the patio with Kevin and the Gully Roosters on Wednesday evenings, and entertainment on Mondays and Fridays.

Ida's Take Away Tel: 365-4208

Islands Restaurant and Grill Tel: 365-4082   Above *Lowe's Grocery* on Parliament Street. Open daily, except Sundays, for breakfast, lunch, and dinner. Good pasta and salads, with fresh bread and soups. Take-out service.

Laura's Kitchen on King Street, opposite the *Shell Hut*
Tel: 365-4287 • VHF 16   Open from 11 am to 3 pm and 6:30 pm to 9 pm daily. A favorite meeting place for boaters, with good home cooking, and wine or beer by the glass. Daily menu changes; ice cream served all day. Complimentary transport is available for dinner.

McIntosh Restaurant and Bakery on Parliament Street
Tel: 365-4625 • VHF 16   Lunch and dinner; delivery, take away, or dine right there. Good Bahamian food, with seafood a specialty; delicious cakes and breads as well. Bar available.

Mike's Bar 'n' Restaurant Overlooking the anchorage
Tel: 365-4219 • VHF 16   Serving drinks all day, and home-cooked lunches and dinners to order from Josie Sawyer. A good place to watch the sunset, with their own dinghy dock.

Miss Emily's Blue Bee Bar Tel: 365-4181   Famous! Since Miss Emily died in 1997, the *Blue Bee Bar* has been run by Violet Smith who knows Miss Emily's secret recipe for a Goombay Smash.

New Plymouth Inn Tel: 365-4161 • VHF 16   Serving breakfast 8 to 9 am, lunch 11:30 am to 1:30 pm, and dinner at 7:30 pm, in the historic heart of town. An excellent Garden Brunch on Sundays, 11 am to 2 pm. Dinner reservations required by 5 pm; choice of three entrees nightly.

Paradise Restaurant (used to be *Ole B's*)   Open 10 am to 5 pm Monday to Saturday; 7 to 9 pm Fridays and Saturdays. Deli food and sixteen flavors of ice cream.

Plymouth Rock Liquors & Cafe Tel: 365-4234   Open 9 am to 6 pm Monday to Thursday; to 9 pm Fridays and Saturdays. Counter-style service for cold beer, sandwiches, and lunchtime snacks until 3 pm, in the liquor store.

Rooster's Rest Pub At the top of the hill on the road to Gillam Bay Tel: 365-4066   Open 11 am to 2 pm for lunch, to 9 pm for dinner. Drinks and Bahamian food, with live music by the Gully Roosters on Friday and Saturday nights until late.

Sea Garden Club Where Bert makes a brilliant Tipsy Turtle!

The Wrecking Tree On the southwest corner of New Plymouth harbor, overlooking the waterfront. Tel: 365-4263 • VHF 16 Serving baked goods, local seafood, and drinks from 8 am to 9 pm Monday to Saturday, to 11 am on Sundays. Their specialty house drink is a well-named Wrecker.

GETTING AROUND

Bicycle Rentals

Noel and Ivy Roberts, at the Albert Lowe Museum Tel: 365-4089

Brendal's Dive Center in White Sound   Tel: 365-4411 $12 per day.

Curtis Bike Rentals Tel: 365-4128   At the town dock, Monday to Saturday from 9 am to 5 pm.

Boat Rentals

Bay Street Rentals   Tel: 365-4070 • VHF 16   Call Janet Sawyer for canoes or a pontoon boat. Whalers and Makos available.

Dames Rentals VHF 16 "Louie Louie"

Donny's Boat Rentals in Black Sound Tel: 365-4271/4073 • VHF 16

Cart Rental

Bay Street Rentals   Tel: 365-4070 • VHF 16 "Bay Street Rentals"
Janet Sawyer has golf carts ($35 per day), and pontoon boats near the town dock. Visa or MasterCard accepted.

C & D Rentals in town   Tel: 365-4161/4311   Daily, three-day, or weekly rentals.

Ferries

Green Turtle Ferry Tel: 365-4128 (on Monday, Tuesday and Wednesday); 365-4166 (on Thursday, Friday and Saturday); 365-4151 (on Sunday) • VHF 16

Bolo ferries leave from their own dock in New Plymouth, or will collect you from any dock in Black Sound or White Sound to go to Treasure Cay for the airport, or a taxi to Marsh Harbour. Ferries connect with most flights in and out of Treasure Cay airport and leave daily at 8 am, 9 am, 11 am, 12:15 pm, 1:30 pm, 3 pm, and 4:30 pm. The 4:30 pm ferry leaves only from New Plymouth. Call for alternative timings, destinations, or where you need to be picked up. The fare is $7 one way or $11 round trip on a scheduled ferry from New Plymouth, $8 one way, $13 round trip from White Sound.

From Treasure Cay, the ferries leave for Green Turtle Cay at 8:30 am, 10:30 am, 11:30 am, 1:30 pm, 2:30 pm, 3:30 pm, 4:30 pm, and 5 pm.

Taxis

McIntosh Taxi Service Tel: 365-4309 • VHF 16 or 6
Cost between $5 and $10.

OMRI'S Taxi VHF 16

Travel Agent

A and W Travel Service Tel: 365-4140

SPORTS

Diving

Brendal's Dive Center in White Sound   Tel: 365-4411 or 800-780-9941 • VHF 16 • E-mail: brendals@grouper.batelnet.bs • Web site: www.bbrendal.com   Brendal and his wife Mary run an extensive dive operation. See our entry under *Green Turtle Club* for details. Two-tank dives from $70, snorkeling from $35. Guided reef trips including picnic lunches, sailboat cruises and rentals, kayaks, windsurfers, and full scuba instruction courses up to advanced SSI qualification. Diving is year round, with water temperatures from 76°F in the winter months, to 89°F during the summer, and an average visibility of 100 feet.

Dive Sites

The Tarpon Dive   Dive with Tarpon fish at 50 feet and feed a grouper called *Junkanoo* all along a coral wall. More schools of large grouper at 90 feet in Grouper Alley.

Coral Caverns   Winding caverns with schools of silversides.

The Catacombs   Sun-filtered catacombs with fish and turtles at 40 feet, brilliant for photography.

Hole in the Wall   Another photographer's dream, where you can swim through a huge coral head at 50 feet into more sun-filtered caverns.

Valley of the Sponges   You go down to 90 feet to see amazing tube and barrel sponges.

Violet Mitchell   A wreck that sank in the 1980s, at 45 feet with schools of fish surrounding it.

The Wreck of the San Jacinto   The first US steamship sank in 40 feet of water in 1865. You can even feed Goombay, a green moray eel.

Fishing

Playmate Charter Fishing with Rick Sawyer Tel: 365-4261 • VHF 16 "Playmate" or VHF 71 "Spindrift" • E-mail: pcfricle@batelnet.bs   Deep sea, reef, and bonefishing; snorkeling.

Joe Sawyer   Tel: 365-4173   Reef or bottom fishing in a 28-ft. Uniflite.

Ronnie Sawyer   Tel: 365-4070   Bonefishing and guided fishing trips.

Lincoln Jones Tel: 365-4223 • VHF 16 "I Lost It" 26-ft. Mako, day trips, fish fry on the beach, snorkeling, and fishing.

Eddie Bodie   Tel: 365-4387 • VHF 16 "The Rock"   Reef fishing, trolling for dolphin, marlin and tuna. Half day $200, full day $320.

FISHING TOURNAMENTS & REGATTAS

May/June

Green Turtle Club Fishing Tournament and the Bahamas Rendezvous at the *Green Turtle Club*. Call 242-365-4271 for more information.

July

Regatta Time in Abaco is held annually, the first week in July. Races form up in Green Turtle Cay, Man-O-War, Hope Town, and Marsh Harbour. Contact Dave or Kathy Ralph, Marsh Harbour, Abaco, Bahamas. Tel: 242-367-2677 • Fax 367-3677

Green Turtle Cay Regatta Week: The Bahama Cup, a race around Green Turtle Cay for visiting yachtsmen. Call the *Green Turtle Club* at 242-365-4271 for information.

November

All Abaco Sailing Regatta, a Bahamian workboat regatta, is held the first weekend. Contact Rev. Philip McPhee at 242-394-0445 for details.

ACCOMMODATIONS

Clubs and Inns

Bluff House Beach Hotel Tel: 242-365-4247 • Fax: 365-4248 • E-mail: BluffHouse@oii.net   Split-level suites from $135, two-bedroom villas from $385 per night, MAP $36. All new rooms and villas. Beach bar and clubhouse dining room above the marina.

Green Turtle Club Tel: 242-365-4271 • Fax: 365-4272   Single and double rooms from $145, villas from $160, MAP $36.

New Plymouth Inn Tel: 242-365-4161 • Fax: 365-4138   Single rooms from $95, double rooms from $130, year round. Prices include taxes, breakfast, and an excellent dinner. Surcharge of 4 percent on credit card payments. Closed in September.

Cottages and Apartments

Coco Bay Cottages   On Coco Bay between two beaches Tel: 242-365-5464 • Fax: 365-5465   From $150 per night, $800 per week for two-bedroom cottages.

Lintons Cottages On Long Bay Beach Tel: 242-365-4003 • Fax: 365-4002 $1,300/$1,500 per week.

Roberts Cottages Tel: 242-365-4105 • VHF 16   Jean Roberts has three cottages available on Black Sound, including dockage for boats under 25 feet. There is an extra charge for boats over 25 feet, plus an electricity charge. The cottages rent from $600 per week. She also has two apartments above Barclays Bank, from $60 per night, with a dock for small boats on the creek shore.

Sand Dollar Apartments   Above the Sand Dollar Shop in New Plymouth Tel: 242-365-4221 • Fax: 365-4046   From $175 per night, $1,000 per week for 1–2 people, three-night minimum stay.

South Beach Apartments Tel: 242-365-4283   Overlooking the Sea of Abaco, with dock facilities for small boats.

THINGS TO DO IN GREEN TURTLE CAY

- Visit the Albert Lowe Museum for a fascinating look back at the history of Green Turtle Cay.
- Walk over the hill to Gillam Bay and search for sand dollars at low tide.
- Enjoy an ice cream cone, and browse for souvenirs in New Plymouth.
- Shop for fresh food and provisions at the three excellent grocery stores.
- Have your boat hauled for a bottom job in Black Sound.
- Have your outboard motor fixed by the experts.
- Pamper yourself with a new hairdo at *Cuts 'n' Curls*.
- Enjoy a cool drink at *Miss Emily's Blue Bee Bar*, the *Sea Garden Club* or the *Wrecking Tree*.
- Jump up with Kevin and the Gully Roosters at the *Roosters Rest* on Friday or Saturday night.
- Take your dinghy around to Manjack Cay for some brilliant snorkeling and fishing.
- Make your dinner reservations at one of the restaurants by 5 pm, and enjoy some of the best food in the Islands.
- If you have books or magazines that you have finished, leave them at the library for others to enjoy.

COOPERS TOWN

Coopers Town has little to offer the cruising boat unless you need fuel: the approach to the fuel dock is easier and deeper than going in to Foxtown. It is a rolly anchorage, and there is nowhere to tie up other than alongside the fuel dock. Medious Edgecombe, who runs the Shell fuel dock, is most helpful and will assist you in any way possible. Coopers Town is not a Port of Entry for the Bahamas, so you cannot clear in through Customs or Immigration. It is an easy walk along the water-front to find everything in town.

SERVICES & SHOPPING

Accommodations
M & M's Guest House   Tel: 242-365-0142   With their own restaurant, on the main road leading south to Marsh Harbour.
Tangelo Hotel at *Wood Cay*   Tel: 242-365-2222   Twelve air-conditioned rooms from $65 per night, with their own restaurant and bar.

Bank
ScotiaBank Open 9 am to 2 pm, Tuesdays & Thursdays.

Bonefishing Guide
Orthnell Russell   Tel: 365-0125

Churches
Church of God's Cathedral
Friendship Mission
Pentecostal Church

Clinic
Tel: 365-0300/0301   In emergency out of hours, call Dr Biney at 365-0613. A short walk south of town, this fully equipped clinic has an X-ray, dispensary, two 2-bed wards, a morgue, and their own ambulance. Nurse Cornish and Nurse Adderley are there from 9 am to 5 pm Monday to Friday; Dr Biney is at the clinic on Monday, Wednesday, and Thursday.

Coopers Town Shell, with Medious Edgecombe.

Drugstore
Edgecombs, also sells gifts.

Fuel
Coopers Town Shell   VHF 16   Open from 7:30 am to 10 pm, and on standby on VHF 16 on Sundays, with 6 to 9 feet of water at low tide and an easy approach through deep water. Diesel and gasoline; Visa and MasterCard accepted, with a 3-percent surcharge. Medious Edgecombe has ice for $5 per bag or $10 per block, as well as oils and lubricants, snacks, liquor, sodas, a few spares for outboards, and a laundry that visiting boats may use.
Murray's Service Center   About a mile southeast of Coopers Town, with diesel and gasoline and a few groceries and ice, but very shallow water.

Groceries
Wright's Grocery Store, also has pies, bread, and cakes.

Liquor
Liquor and convenience store at the Shell gas station in town, open from 8 am to 8 pm.

Museum
Albert Bootle Museum   In a restored building near the dock in Coopers Town, ask the caretaker who lives nearby to open up this little three-room museum with local artifacts.

Police
Tel: 367-0002

Post Office
Open 9 am to 5 pm Monday to Friday, in the administration building.

Restaurants/Take-Out
M & M Restaurant and Bar at the *M & M Guest House*   Tel: 365-0142 Open for breakfast, lunch, and dinner.
Chilly's Take Out   Opposite the school.
Gelina's Pizza   Tel: 365-1022   Free delivery.
Valentine Take Away Snacks   Tel: 365-0438

Taxi
Jenson Edgecombe   Tel: 365-0161 • VHF 6   Ask Medious Edgecombe at the fuel dock to call one. Jenson also has six rental cars.

Telephones
There are two at the administration building. The *Batelco* office is closed.

GREAT GUANA CAY

Most of the action in this long, thin cay is centered around the quiet settlement, now with marinas at both sides, and the glorious Atlantic beach over the dunes with beautiful snorkeling only 75 yards from shore, which becomes a mobscene on Sundays during the weekly pig roast at *Nippers*. There are good beaches on both sides of Great Guana Cay, so you can nearly always find a sheltered spot. It is one of the larger Abaco cays, slowly developing, and well worth a visit. The holding is not good in the harbor, and there are no Customs or Immigration here for clearing in.

MARINAS

GUANA BEACH RESORT AND MARINA
Tel: 242-365-5133 • Fax: 365-5134 • VHF 16

This marina leads directly into the Guana Beach Resort, and their facilities are open to visiting boats. You are assured of a friendly welcome, though renovations in some areas would be welcome too. Not all the slips have shoreside power and water yet. If you come in from another island, the small boat tie-up fee is refunded when you have lunch or drinks at the resort.

Slips	21
Max LOA	65 ft., with 100 ft. on the T-dock.
MLW at Dock	5 ft.
Dockage	50¢ per foot per night.
Power	$12 per day for 30A, $22 for 50A.
Fuel	Diesel and gasoline at the fuel dock, open daily 8 am to 4:30 pm, credit card surcharge.
Restaurant	Pool-side and clubhouse dining, from 7:30 am to 9 pm. No in-between meal closings.
Bar	"Guana Grabbers" is the exotic rum-based specialty drink. Happy hour from 5 to 7 pm daily.
Ice	$4 a bag.
Swimming	Marina guests may use the pool; beaches are within easy walking distance.
Diving	*Froggies* is planning to open a dive shop with a new dive boat.
Boutique	A gift shop at reception with T-shirts, swimsuits, island maps, sunglasses, sunscreen, and jewellry. Open 8 am to 5 pm.
Credit Cards	Visa and MasterCard accepted.
Owner/Manager	Chris Sadler

ORCHID BAY YACHT CLUB AND MARINA
Tel: 242-365-5175 • Fax: 365-5166 • VHF 16 •
E-mail: orchidbay@yahoo.com

This new, state-of-the-art marina, at the southern point of the harbor with its protective sea wall, has brought a new cruising dimension to Great Guana Cay. Eventually this will be a private resort, but at the time of writing in 1999, cruising boats are privileged to enjoy all the benefits of new docks with power and water at every slip, and the excitement of seeing a new venture taking shape, with superb shoreside amenities. Call ahead for details of progress and to see if there is a slip available.

Slips	64
Max LOA	Space for two 124-ft. boats at the T-heads.
MLW at Dock	From 9 ft. on the outside dock to 4 ft. on the inner docks, with a 9- to 10-ft.-deep approach.
Dockage	On request

Power	30¢ per kWh, for 30A and 50A.
Fuel	Fuel dock open from 8 am to 5 pm daily, with diesel, gasoline, oil, and lubricants.
Water	25¢ per gallon, metered.
Telephones	Telephones and E-mail access available.
Showers	For marina guests only, immaculately clean.
Laundry	$3 for washer or dryer.
Ice	$4 a bag, cubes or block.
Swimming	Freshwater pool for marina guests; separate pool for hotel guests.
Ferry	*Albury's Ferry* to and from Marsh Harbour will call at the marina on request.
Coffee	Complimentary coffee in the marina reception area.
Accommodations	There will be 54 rooms at the hotel.
Credit cards	Visa, MasterCard, and Amex.
Resort Manager	David Yarbrough

SERVICES & SHOPPING

Church
Sea Side Gospel Church

Clinic
Nearest medical facilities are in Marsh Harbour.

Fishing
Henry Sands   Tel: 365-5140 • VHF 16 "PDQ"   Full- or half-day deep sea or bottom fishing in Henry's 22-ft. Baja.

Gift Shops
Bay View Gifts   Open from 9:30 am to noon, and from 1:30 to 5:30 pm Monday to Saturday.
The Bikini Shop
Milo's Gift Shop and Gallery   Open daily, with artwork, jewelry, wood objects, and T-shirts.
P & J Variety Store
Tom's T-Shirts   With a selection of gifts and souvenirs, as well as Nippers' T-shirts, tank tops, and shorts and caps. Open daily.

Groceries
Guana Harbour Grocery Tel: 365-5067 • VHF 16   Open 8 am to 5:30 pm, Monday to Thursday; to 6:30 pm Fridays and Saturdays. Well-stocked: fresh fruit and vegetables, canned and dry goods, meat and dairy; some pharmacy, stationery, hardware.

Hardware
Guana Cay Hardware   Monday to Saturday, 8:30 am to 5 pm.

Liquor
Fig Tree Wines and Spirits on the waterfront   Tel: 365-5058 Also has ice. Closed Sundays.

Post Office
Open from 9 am to 5 pm, Monday through Friday.

Telephones
One opposite *Tom's T-Shirts* (not working when we were there); one outside *Batelco*, by the school. Both are direct-dial telephones. The Batelco office is open from 9 am to 5 pm Monday to Friday.

GETTING AROUND

Bicycles and Cart Rental
Donna Sands   Tel: 365-5195 • VHF 16 "Young Lovers" Golf carts from $35 a day. Donna also has bicycles to rent, and cottages and property to sell or rent.
Guana Cay Cart Rentals   Tel: 365-5016

Ferries
Albury's Ferry Service   Leaves Great Guana Government Dock at 9 am, 11:30 am, 2:30 pm, and 4:45 pm, and takes 30 minutes to run to the *Union Jack Dock* and the *Conch Inn* at Marsh Harbour. $7 one-way fare; $10 same-day round trip. The ferry will drop you off at *Orchid Bay* on request.

Janet Wilson

Great Guana School mural.

RESTAURANTS & BARS

Guana Beach Resort and Marina Tel: 365-5133 • VHF 16
Open daily non-stop for breakfast, lunch, and dinner, poolside
or in the clubhouse. Wednesday night Conch Out, Friday night
BBQ, Saturday night Steak Out with Guana Daze grilled fish
and steak all day long, and rake and scrape music by tea time
on Saturdays. Good food, good ambience, good fun.

Guana Seaside Village Tel: 365-5106/5107 • VHF 16
Open daily for breakfast, lunch, and dinner. Call ahead for
dinner reservations by 5 pm, or for parties of ten or twelve.
Menu changes nightly. Tie your dinghy up at their dock.

The Mermaid Cafe at *Dolphin Beach Resort* Tel: 365-5137 • VHF
16 Anchor in Fisher's Bay and walk to the north side toward
the Junkanoo-colored cottages, with their own boutique and
dock. Open for breakfast, lunch, and dinner daily. Call ahead
for reservations.

Nippers Bar and Grill Tel: 365-5143 On the north side of the
cay, at the settlement. Bar opens at 10 am, lunch from 11 am
to 3:30 pm, dinner from 6 to 10 pm. Very casual, on the beach,
with a two-level swimming pool, one with a Tiki Bar with swing
chairs in the water. Michael and Johnnie Roberts have made
Nippers famous for their Sunday Pig Roasts, rain or shine, when
people come in from all over Abaco.

Purple Porpoise Open from 11 am to 3 pm Monday to
Saturday, and from 7 to 9 pm on Monday, Tuesday, Thursday,
Friday, and Saturday, for ice cream, hot dogs, nachos with
cheese, and more.

REGATTA

Regatta Time in Abaco is held during the first week in July.
Races form up in Green Turtle Cay, Guana Cay, Man-O-War,
Hope Town and Marsh Harbour. Contact Dave or Kathy Ralph,
Marsh Harbour, Abaco, Bahamas. Tel 242-367-2677 • Fax 367-
3677.

ACCOMMODATIONS

Dolphin Beach Resort Tel: 242-365-5137/800-ABACO-GO • VHF
16 On a spectacular Atlantic beach, a short distance from the
settlement, with beach-front cottages and a small hotel, nestled
among the trees. Rooms from $125 per night, individual two-
story cottages from $170 per night. All prices include breakfast;
the air-conditioned *Mermaid Cafe* is open for lunch and dinner
too. *Potcakes Boutique* is right there. Call Bruce and Nancy
McDaniel for details; they also have two rental cottages in the
settlement, where breakfast is not included.

Guana Beach Resort Tel: 242-365-5133 Eight beachfront rooms
from $125 per night, two-bedroom suites from $190 per night,
MAP $35 per person. All-day food service in the clubhouse
dining room, drinks and meals during the day at the pool.

Guana Seaside Village Tel: 242-365-5106/5107 • Fax: 365-5146
• VHF 16 Eight rooms from $90 per night, two-bedroom suites
from $145. Rooms face an attractive pool and bar, a restau-
rant, and a long dock leading out into the bay. It's a short walk
across to the beach on the northeast side of the island. Boat
rentals, golf carts, and fishing guides can be arranged.
Manager Glenn Laing welcomes visiting boaters for lunch,
showers ($3), or dinner by reservation before 5 pm.

Orchid Bay Hotel Tel: 242-365-5175 • Fax: 365-5166 At time
of writing in May 1999, was not yet built. Call ahead for
details.

THINGS TO DO IN GREAT GUANA CAY

- Walk on the seven-mile beach, and then snorkel the reef,
  which is close to shore and good for beginners.
- Take a picnic in the dinghy up to Baker's Bay, and have a
  fantastic time swimming without a crowd scene.
- Enjoy a Grabber by the pool at the *Guana Beach Resort* as
  the sun goes down over the anchorage.
- Take the dinghy over to the *Guana Seaside Village* for
  lunch or dinner, and have a change of scene.
- Stroll over to *Nippers* for an island feast set among the
  sand dunes. What about the pig roast one Sunday? Or try
  parasailing with *Abaco Watersports* in the ocean in front
  of *Nippers*. Call Beverly Sands at 365-5016 to find out
  more about it.

TREASURE CAY

Treasure Cay has the well-deserved reputation of being not
only a first-class cruising destination, with all the amenities you
would expect from a Florida resort, but also home to a great
many winter residents who come in for golf, tennis, and the
beaches, as well as for fishing and sailing. The marina is
pleasant and well organized, and everything is within walking
distance if you take a slip there for a few days. It is a good
place for a crew change, or to meet friends flying in, with
frequent flights to and from the US at nearby Treasure Cay
Airport. Treasure Cay is a Port of Entry, so if you are newly
arrived from Florida on your boat, the dock staff will call
Customs and **Immigration** for you.

MARINA

TREASURE CAY HOTEL RESORT AND MARINA
Tel: 242-365-8250/800-327-1584 • Fax: 365-8847 • VHF 16

Slips	150
Moorings	8 moorings on a first-come, first-serve basis for $10 per day.
Anchorage	$8 per day.
Max LOA	140 ft. on the T-dock.
MLW at Dock	5 ft.
Dockage	Under 70 ft., 85¢ per foot per day (Sept. 1–Feb. 28), $1 per ft. per day (Mar. 1–Aug. 31), $25 minimum per day. Over 70 ft., $1.25 per foot per day.
Long Term	From 40¢ to 55¢ per ft. per day, depending on LOA and time of year, payable in advance.

TREASURE CAY DIRECTORY

1. Treasure Cay Marina
2. Spinnaker Restaurant, Tipsy Seagull, Marine Shoppe, and Dockmaster's Office
3. Groceries, Post Office, shopping
4. Community Center and Clinic
⛽ Fuel
⛳ Golf Course

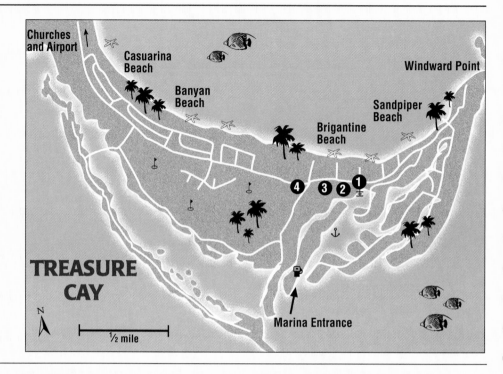

Churches and Airport

Casuarina Beach

Banyan Beach

Windward Point

Sandpiper Beach

Brigantine Beach

④ ③ ② ①

TREASURE CAY

N

½ mile

Marina Entrance

Power	30A and 50A from $9 to $30 per day, according to boat length. Boats using two 50A shore power cords will be charged double.
Fuel	Diesel and gasoline at the fuel dock on the approach into the marina, open 8 am to 5 pm daily.
Water	$5 to $12 per day according to boat length.
Telephones	At the *Treasure Cay Marine Shop* there are two for US direct calls, and two cardphones. There are four more phones by *G & M Variety Store* at the far end of the row of shops, and a *Batelco* office open from 9 am to 5 pm Monday to Friday.
TV	Cable hookup dockside. $30 deposit required. Charges are included in dockage fees.
Showers	Yes, clean but in need of renovation, for use by marina guests and registered mooring guests only.
Restaurants	*Spinnaker Restaurant and Bar* Tel: 365-8569 Breakfast 7:30 to 10:30 am, lunch 11:30 am to 2:30 pm, and dinner 6:30 to 9:30 pm. Dinner reservations requested. *Cafe La Florence*, in the long building, open daily from 8 am to 10 pm. *Coco Bar* on the beach, from 11 am to 4 pm daily. *Tipsy Seagull Bar and Grill* Open from 11 am to closing with live entertainment most evenings in high season. Open nightly from 6 to 9 pm for pizza, salad, and dessert, with a barbecue on Friday nights.
Barbecues	Barbecue pits are provided for marina guests. Pits are located at the entrances of docks L, T, N, and S. No barbecuing or open flame on boats or docks is permitted.
Swimming	Marina guests are welcome to use the freshwater pool by the *Tipsy Seagull*. Or walk over to the heavenly white sand beach.

Store	*Treasure Cay Marine Shoppe*, next to the marina office, open from 8 am to 5 pm daily, with some dive and snorkeling gear, logo shirts, and gifts with a nautical flavor.
Credit Cards	All major credit cards accepted.
Marina office	Open from 8 am to 5 pm daily.
Security	Contact VHF 19.
Dockmaster	Audrick McKenzie

MARINE SERVICES

Edgecombe's Marine Services Tel: 242-365-8454 • VHF 16 Engine repairs and boat delivery service back to Florida.

SERVICES & SHOPPING

Bank
Royal Bank of Canada Open from 10 am to 3 pm on Tuesdays and Thursdays.

Churches
Saints Mary and Andrew Catholic Church, on the road to the main highway. Mass at 5 pm on Sundays.
Church of St Simon by the Sea   Tel: 365-8422   Anglican/ Episcopal church, next to *Abaco Ceramics*, opened and consecrated in February 1999. Mass at 8 am on Sundays.
Treasure Cay Community Church   Sunday service at 9 am in the community building.

Clinic
The Corbett Medical Centre   Tel: 365-8288   Open 9 am to noon and 2 to 4 pm, Monday, Tuesday, and Friday; 9 am to noon on Thursday; 8:30 to 11 am Saturdays. In emergency call Dr. Ronald Wilson at 365-8286 or VHF 83A, pager 367-7243 or 367-2288.

Customs Tel: 365-8602   and **Immigration** Tel: 365-8604 Both at the airport.

Dentist
Treasure Cay Dental Clinic By the post office Tel: 365-8425/8625 or 800-224-6703 By appointment with Dr. Howard Spencer for the first and third weekends each month. Open Fridays 11 am to 5 pm, Saturdays 9 am to 5 pm, Mondays 9 am to 2 pm.

E-mail and Faxes

Frederick Sinclair, a homeowner on Ocean Boulevard, may be able to help you receive or send your E-mail. Call him at 365-8800. Faxes can be received at the front office at 365-8847. Outgoing faxes can be sent from the front office for $12 for the first page, and $1.50 per page thereafter to the US, $15 for all other countries.

Fruit and Vegetables

The stalls that used to set up along the road are now in a building on the edge of the shopping area, with a selection of locally grown fruit and vegetables.

Gifts & Souvenirs

Abaco Ceramics   Tel or fax: 365-8489   Next to the churches, on the road leading out of Treasure Cay past the golf course. Showroom workshop open from 9 am to 3 pm Monday to Friday, with attractive handmade ceramic gifts and souvenirs.

Bill's Canvas Bag   In the long building, next to the post office Tel: 365-8318   Marine upholstery renewed or replaced. Bill Carey and his wife, Margaret, have a selection of canvas bags and cards for sale, open between 8 am and 4 pm daily except Sundays.

Solomon's Mines   Open from 9 am to 5:30 pm Monday to Saturday, with duty-free watches, perfumes, jewelry, and more.

Treasure Cay Marine Shop   Open from 8 am to 4 pm next to the marina office.

Triple J Rentals and Gift Shop

Groceries

Treasure Cay Mini Market   Tel: 365-8350 • Fax: 365-8352 • VHF 16   Open from 8 am to 6 pm Monday to Saturday. Well stocked with meats, pharmacy, stationery, household goods, gifts, bread, water, and fresh and frozen vegetables and fruit.

G & M Variety Store   Open from 7 am to 10 pm daily. Soft drinks, water, dairy products, toiletries, ice.

Hardware

Treasure Cay Home Center   Open from 8 am to 4 pm Monday to Saturday, closed Sundays and from 1 to 2 pm daily. Hardware, housewares, and souvenirs.

Laundry

Annie's Laundry still sells "Fish and Conch," and can do your laundry too.

Library

Open 3 to 5 pm on Monday, Wednesday, and Friday in the Community Centre.

Liquor Store

Duty Free Liquor Store   Tel: 365-8082   Open from 10 am to 6 pm, Monday to Saturday.

Police

Tel: 365-8048

Post Office

Open from 9 am to 5:30 pm, Monday to Friday.

Telephones

Many close to the marina; the *Batelco* office is open for phone cards, faxes, etc. from 9 am to 5 pm, Monday to Friday.

GETTING AROUND

Airport

Treasure Cay International Airport is 7 miles away, with a 6,500-foot paved runway. Taxis are $14 for two people from the marina. There is a restaurant and bar at the airport called *Travellers Nest*, and a Texaco filling station.

Airlines

Air Sunshine   Tel: 365-8900 or 954-434-8900

Bahamasair   Tel: 365-8601 or 377-5505   Daily flights to Nassau at 9:05 am and 4:50 pm.

Continental Gulf Stream   Tel: 365-8615   Daily flight to Miami at 2:20 pm and to Fort Lauderdale at 2:30 pm.

Island Express   Tel: 354-8697   Flights to Fort Lauderdale.

Major's Air Services   Tel: 365-8616   Treasure Cay to Freeport at 7:50 am daily, and at 4:50 pm on Friday, Saturday, and Sunday.

Taino Air   Tel: 365-8245   To Fort Lauderdale.

US Air Express   Tel: 365-8686   To West Palm Beach daily at 2:25 pm, to Orlando daily at 3:15 pm.

Vintage Air   Tel: 365-8852

Bicycles

Wendell's Bicycles in the long building   Tel: 365-8687   Open from 8 am to 4 pm daily. $5 for half day, $7 full day, $40 per week.

Boat Rental

C & C Boat Rentals   Tel: 365-8582 • VHF 16   8 am to 5 pm. Call Mark Carroll. Dusky offshore 20–27-foot boats, sunfish, hobie cats, windsurfers, scuba & snorkel gear, spear fishing, island tours, picnics, and scooters.

JIC Rentals   Tel: 365-8465 • VHF 16 or 79   Call Josh Cash. 22-foot Angler, $130 per day; 24-foot Angler $159 per day; 26-foot Intrepid $160 per day; captains and guides available. Half-day guided trips to Shell Island and Guana Cay, or Green Turtle Cay. Day trips to Marsh Harbour, Man-O-War, and Hope Town.

Car Rental

Rental cars on Abaco cost around $70 per day.

Cornish Rentals   Tel: 365-8623

McKenzies Car Rental   Tel: 365-8849

Triple J Car Rental & Gift Shop   Tel: 365-0161 • VHF 6   Open from 8 am to 6 pm Monday to Saturday.

Cart Rental

Blue Marlin   Tel: 365-8687   In the long building, open from 8 am to 4 pm daily. Golf carts for half day $25, full day $40, weekly $245.

JIC Cash's Resort Carts   Tel: 365-8465 • Fax: 365-8508 • VHF 16 or 19 • E-mail: jic@oii.net   Open from 8:30 am to 5 pm daily, can be paged at the cart rental booth near the Convenience Store, until 8 pm daily. $25 for a half-day rental, $40 per day, $245 per week. Visa, MasterCard, traveler's checks, and cash accepted.

Ferries

The ferry to Green Turtle Cay leaves Treasure Cay Airport ferry dock at 8:30 am, 10:30 am, 11:30 am, 1:30 pm, 2:30 pm, 3:30 pm, 4:30 pm, and 5 pm. Fare is $7 one way, or $11 round trip to New Plymouth; $8 one way, $13 round trip to White Sound. Ferries from Green Turtle Cay return to Treasure Cay at 8 am, 9 am, 11 am, 12:15 pm, 1:30 pm, 3 pm, and 4:30 pm.

Motorscooters

C & C Scooter Rentals   Tel: 365-8582

R & A Scooter Rental   VHF 16   Open from 8 am to 5 pm daily.

Taxis

Call VHF 6. There are nearly always taxis waiting beyond the shops at the marina.

SPORTS

Diving

Divers Down   Tel: 365-8465 • Fax: 365-8508 • VHF 16 or 79 • E-mail: jic@oii.net   Two-tank dive from $80, blue hole dive $75, snorkelers $35. Reef and wreck dives, scuba instruction, air fills, and rental gear available. PADI or SSI referral and certification.

Fishing

Fish for marlin, dolphin, wahoo, tuna, snapper, grouper, and amberjack from Treasure Cay, or go out with Claud Burrows, Odonald McIntosh, Kingsley Murray, or Orthnell Russell, who all operate charters from Treasure Cay. Contact the marina office to find them.

Golf
An 18-hole Dick Wilson–designed golf course, with a golf pro and pro shop, open from 8 am to 5 pm. Greens fees at $60 for 18 holes, $50 if you are a hotel or marina guest. $25 for a shared golf cart, tee times not required.

Jogging
Beach, roads, and walkways set in 1,500 acres.

Tennis
$14 per person per hour, on four hard tennis courts, and $16 per hour on two clay courts. Racket rentals and lessons.

Water aerobics
In the pool on Tuesday, Thursday, and Saturday mornings at 9 am with Cathi Cash. $3 a class. Call her at 365-8467 for more information.

FISHING TOURNAMENTS

May
The Treasure Cay Billfish Championship with a golf tournament, cocktail parties, and local Arts and Craft Fair. The tournament encourages tagging and releasing the billfish.

ACCOMMODATIONS

Banyan Beach Club Tel: 242-365-8111/888-625-3060 • Fax: 365-8112 One-bedroom suites from $125 per night, two-bedroom suites with loft from $225 per night. Fully equipped kitchens, air-conditioning, and maid service.

Brigantine Bay Villas Tel: 242-365-8033
Treasure Cay Hotel Tel: 954-525-7711/800-327-1584 • Fax: 525-1699 or 800-327-1584 • E-mail: info@treasurecay.com Standard rooms from $130 per night, suites from $175, and villas from $385 per night. MAP $34 per day. At the time of writing, many of the rooms were being renovated. Golf and dive packages and private air charters available.

THINGS TO DO IN TREASURE CAY

- Take a short walk over to the beach, where you'll find over three miles of powdery white sand set in a magnificent, crescent bay. The swimming is glorious. Enjoy lunch at the *Coco Bar* while you're there.
- Play golf—or have a tennis game with friends.
- Explore the network of canals in your dinghy. These canals, incidentally, offer good hurricane protection.
- Shop for duty-free treasures at *Solomon's Mines*.
- Explore New Plymouth and discover the charm of Green Turtle Cay, by taking a taxi to the Green Turtle Ferry dock and going across for lunch. There is a frequent ferry service; see **Getting Around** for timings. Or take your own boat across and stay for longer!
- Treat your crew to dinner ashore at the *Spinnaker Restaurant*.
- Enjoy world-class fishing within easy reach.

Chapter 6
The Southern Abacos
Great Guana Cay to Cherokee Sound
South Great Abaco Island

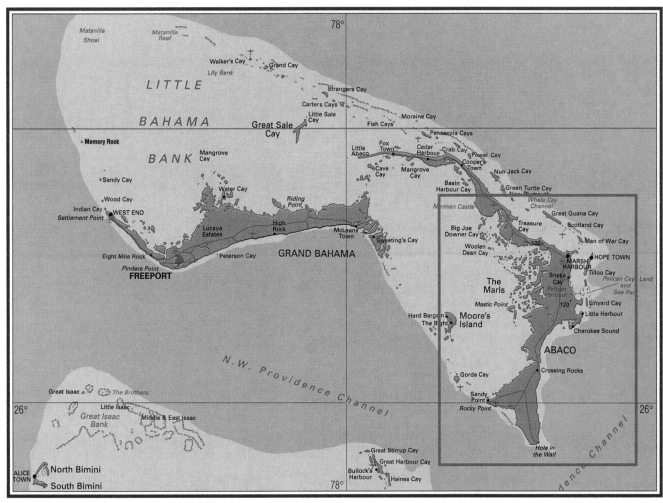

Ocean Passes

THE southern Abacos are well served by ocean passes. Man-of-War Pass serves the sports fishermen of Treasure Cay and Marsh Harbour; the two southern passes are the links to the Berry Islands and Eleuthera. If you've not already done so, read our warning about Rages on page 59.

with sand and reef to avoid, you can run into trouble. We choose the northern pass because it is a straightforward shot through a reasonably wide cut between Fish Hawk Cay and the northern tip of Man-O-War. A run of just over 1 nm on 030°M outgoing and 210°M incoming will get you through with no problems and 16 feet at MLW. Our waypoints refer to the Atlantic and Abaco ends of this northern pass.

Man-O-War Channel

Man-O-War Channel North		
MWCHN	26° 37' 50"/845 N	077° 01' 16"/273 W
Man-O-War Channel South		
MWCHS	26° 36' 49"/815 N	077° 01' 55"/928 W

Man-O-War has two passes through the barrier reef to the ocean. The southern pass is narrow, not a straight run, and

North Bar Channel

North Bar West		
NBARW	26° 23' 37"/615 N	076° 59' 10"/174 W
North Bar Channel		
NBRCH	26° 23' 23"/391 N	076° 58' 23"/379 W
North Bar Channel East		
NBARE	26° 22' 55"/929 N	076° 56' 51"/850 W

North Bar Channel is the preferred entry channel of the two South Abaco passes. It runs between the northern tip of Lynyard Cay, where there's reef extending offshore for a short distance, and the Pelican Cays to the north. There's reef all the way from the south end of Tilloo Cay linking the Pelican Cays like a daisy chain, so don't mistake the wide gap immediately east of Channel Cay as the pass. Immediately south of the southernmost Pelican there's more reef, and one isolated rock, Channel Rock.

Despite our forbidding description, the North Bar Channel is obvious. Two bearing marks, both posts, one on the south end of Channel Cay, and one on the north end of Cornish Cay, give you your line. 115°M outgoing, and 295°M incoming. You will have 16 feet at MLW.

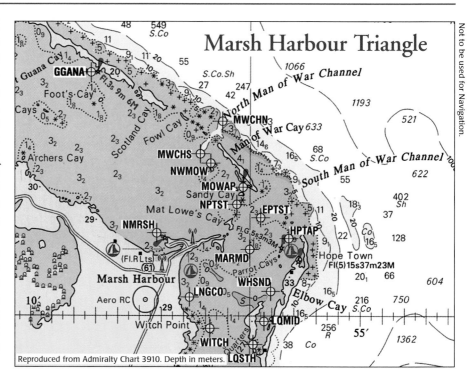

Reproduced from Admiralty Chart 3910. Depth in meters.

Not to be used for Navigation.

Little Harbour Bar Pass

Little Harbour North		
LHRBN	26° 20' 26"/432 N	076° 59' 40"/676 W
Little Harbour Bar Pass		
LHRBP	26° 19' 47"/793 N	076° 59' 19"/327 W
Little Harbour Bar East		
LHRBE	26° 18' 45"/747 N	076° 58' 45"/754 W

Little Harbour Bar presents no particular problems. Its depth at MLW is 16 feet. Running south from Goole Cay (the southern extension of Lynyard Cay) there's a reef that ex-

Man-O-War Channel, from the south.

tends for 0.75 nm. To the south a reef runs north from Little Harbour Point for 0.25 nm. Both reefs will show in any kind of weather. In between is the Little Harbour Bar itself and that 16-foot depth. A line running from the house on Bridges Cay through the pass, outgoing 165°M and incoming 345°M, is your median course.

Great Guana Cay to Marsh Harbour

IT'S an easy run down to Man-O-War Cay or Hope Town and Elbow Cay from Great Guana. A heading of 136°M for 5.83 nm will take you off the northwest end of Man-O-War Cay, leaving Foots Cay and the Fish Cays (that's another set of Fish Cays) to starboard and Scotland Cay and the Fowl Cays with Fish Hawk Cay to port.

FOOTS CAY
Foots Cay is private.

FISH CAYS
The Fish Cays have little to offer.

SCOTLAND CAY
Scotland Cay is a private resort with an airstrip.

FOWL CAYS AND FISH HAWK CAY
The Fowl Cays and Fish Hawk Cay are a Land and Sea Preserve. You may visit the park area, but you must use the

mooring buoys provided. You are not allowed to take anything from either land, beach, or water, and, hardly surprisingly, you're not allowed to fish there.

Man-O-War Cay and Dickie's Cay

From the Man-O-War waypoint that placed you off the northwest tip of the cay, 1.6 nm on a heading of 124°M will take you to the entrance to Man-O-War harbor. As we talk of two cays, Man-O-War Cay and Dickie's Cay, you may need reassurance at this point, for it's impossible to identify two separate cays to port. Dickie's Cay lies so close to Man-O-War that it might be a part of it, and even when you reach the point of entering Man-O-War harbor, it's still not apparent that a Dickie's Cay with a separate identity exists. At risk of offending local patriotism, treat them as one. To starboard you'll have no problems picking up Garden Cay and Sandy Cay.

Man-O-War Cay is famed for its boat building and a harbor that is reckoned to be one of the safest in the Abacos. The settlement itself, kept as clean as a new pin, reflects one of the most industrious communities in the Bahamas whose interests have always been primarily maritime: boat building, boat repairs, sail making, and ferry services. Inevitably Man-O-War has long featured on the tourist "must visit" lists, and has long been a port-of-call for every cruising boat passing that way, but somehow Man-O-War has maintained its integrity and kept its unique character. Part of the reason may lie in a strong religious sense of bonding that holds the little community somewhat apart from the ways of the outside world, not least of which is evidenced in a total ban on the sale of alcohol on the island.

Man-O-War Cay, from the southwest.

Man-O-War Cay Approaches and Anchorages

The northern entrance to Man-O-War harbor is for small boats or shoal draft boats only. The main entrance, which you will take, lies at the south tip of Dickie's Cay, and you go in between this point of land and the headland of the Man-O-War cove to the south. The entrance is narrow and hard to pick up from any distance away, but is marked by a prominent marker light on Dickie's Cay. You'll have 5 feet at MLW there. Expect tidal flow. As soon as you clear the entrance you must decide whether you're turning to starboard to go on into the southern harbor, aka American Harbour, to anchor or turning to port to go into the main harbor (where you may anchor, or go to the Man-O-War marina or boatyard of your choice). Be warned that Man-O-War harbor and its marina are always crowded, and if you want dock space, you should reserve it ahead of time.

Man-O-War Cay owes this double harbor to its hard-to-identify sibling. The west side of Man-O-War Cay is paralleled for a third of its length by Dickie's Cay, and this shielding produces the greater, northern part of Man-O-War harbor. The southern harbor lies wholly within Man-O-War territory.

Going on to Hope Town

To resume or stay on your course for Hope Town continue heading southeast on 160°M past and away from Sandy Cay for 1.38 nm, which will place you safely off Point Set Rock, on your starboard side, and well away from the shoal area that lies around Johnnie's Cay to port. From this last waypoint a heading of 138°M and 1.5 nm will place you ready to go visual and enter Hope Town harbor. The total distance run from Great Guana Cay will be around 13 nm.

SOUTHERN ABACOS I		
Man-O-War Cay		
NWMOW	26° 36' 00"/000 N	077° 02' 00"/000 W
Man-O-War Cay		
MOWAP	26° 35' 15"/250 N	077° 00' 25"/417 W
Point Set Rock North		
NPTST	26° 34' 20"/333 N	077° 00' 30"/500 W
Point Set Rock East		
EPTST	26° 34' 00"/000 N	076° 59' 45"/750 W
Marsh Harbour Entrance		
NMRSH	26° 33' 25"/417 N	077° 04' 00"/000 W
Hope Town Approach		
HPTAP	26° 33' 00"/000 N	076° 58' 30"/500 W

The final figures in each waypoint show seconds (00") and thousands (000) of a minute.

We've given waypoints and courses but in truth we go visual running between Great Guana Cay and Hope Town. The navigation data is just a useful backup. We were caught once on the final part of this run down to Hope Town by a heavy rainstorm that wiped out all trace of land and inked out the radar with clutter for over 45 minutes. We crawled along, stalling for time, and when the storm passed we'd hit the spot and were right there, on the mark, ready for Hope Town. Thank you GPS!

GARDEN CAY AND SANDY CAY

Both Garden Cay and Sandy Cay are private.

JOHNNIE'S CAY

Johnnie's Cay is also private.

Hope Town and the North of Elbow Cay

Hope Town is almost everyone's dream realized of how a place in the Abacos should look. A well-protected harbor, just big enough, watched over by the best-looking candy-striped lighthouse you ever did see, just how a lighthouse should look. The streets, other than the waterfront, are narrow concrete paths set between houses painted every color, in combinations your mother told you *never* to put together: pinks, greens, turquoise, salmon, yellows, blues, grey, and white are all there, together with gingerbread eaves and picket fences carved into hearts, whales, and pineapples. Flowers and flowering shrubs grow as if they're bent on staking their claim to exotic colors, co-equal with the houses. Beyond and behind this quiet riot of colors lies the Atlantic, deep dark blue on its far horizon, brilliant green closer to the shore, marked with inshore reefs the color of well-worn boat shoes, and then as clear as sparkling spring water at its edge. What of the beach, the sand? It's Hope Town. It has to be pink. It very nearly is. It's wide, and goes on forever.

Here in Hope Town you can wander at will, drink and watch the sun go down, and dine as the lighthouse starts its nightly cycle. You'll share your Hope Town with many others, visiting yachtspeople like yourselves, the renters of holiday cottages and apartments, and those staying at the Hope Town Harbour Lodge, the Club Soleil, the Abaco Inn, and other places, as well as day trippers from Marsh Harbour. Somehow, despite its small size, Hope Town seems to absorb this alien influx. Sometimes there seems to be too many of your own kind around, but it's rarely disturbing.

Hope Town has a pattern of life into which you'll fall, and soon, if you're anchored off, on a mooring, or at one of the three marinas, you'll realize that using your dinghy to get everywhere (for there's no other way to cross the harbor to get to the main town on the ocean side) is just a way of life. Go to the public dock at 7:30 in the morning to see the children gather to take the Albury ferry to get to school in Marsh Harbour. Many come in by small boat, just as you have. It's the way life goes in Hope Town. No stress. No tension. But the happy hours start at four in the afternoon, just in case it's all getting on top of you.

The Approach to Hope Town Harbour

The approach to Hope Town isn't difficult, but you have to get it right from the start because you have a comparatively narrow entry channel to negotiate with a 90-degree turn to starboard. This channel carries some 5 feet at MLW. When you're just off the northernmost Parrot Cay, head roughly toward the famous lighthouse marking Hope Town but setting slightly north of it, aiming to clear the headland on which the lighthouse is built. The entrance channel to Hope Town harbor won't become immediately apparent, but aim to clear that headland by at least 100 yards at this stage.

You'll see a prominent yellow house with a reddish-brown roof on the rocky islet called Eagle

Hope Town Harbour, from the east.

Hope Town Harbour.

There is a downside to most places, even Paradise probably has its problems, and Hope Town harbor is on our list of places where we never switch on our watermaker. The harbor, essentially landlocked as it is, has long passed its natural capacity to absorb pollution and cleanse itself with successive tides. There are too many boats there, one might question whether holding tanks are in use on every boat, and there is just too much boat traffic.

If you don't fancy a mooring in Hope Town Harbour you can anchor off outside between the Parrot Cays and Elbow Cay, roughly on the same latitude as Hope Town. Just stay clear of the Albury ferry routes on their runs between Hope Town and Marsh Harbour, and up to Man-O-War. You have about 6 feet there and reasonably good holding, but you are completely exposed to the north and the south.

ANNA'S CAY
Anna's Cay is the tiny islet off the west side of the northern peninsula of Elbow Cay.

PARROT CAYS
The Parrot Cays are the chain of five cays running down the west coast of Elbow Cay from the latitude of your approach to Hope Town Harbour. North Parrot Cay, your initial landmark on your approach to Hope Town, has what appears to be an incomplete dock on it, six pilings with no decking and a light. The fourth cay (counting from north to south, and the largest one) is the base of the Gale family's Island Marine Boat Rentals. They will collect you from wherever you are, take you to Parrot Cay, rent you an Albury 20, Boston Whaler, or an Aquasport, and at the end of your rental period, deliver you back to wherever you started. Call them on channel 16.

Rock as you get closer. At first you can't even see that the yellow house is offshore rather than on the main shoreline. The house is your first approach marker, which will be on your port side, and the lighthouse headland will be to starboard. The entry channel is marked and becomes more apparent as you get closer, as will two leading marks.

As you line up for the channel you'll see a concrete road that ends abruptly at the water's edge. It may well be that there's a Love Seat at the end of the road, set there for boat watchers. The alignment of the road itself is as good a leading mark as any, but to make it easier, there are two leading marks (to the port side of the Love Seat as you look at it). The first, by the Love Seat, is a white post with an upward facing white triangle on top of a red disk with a white, reflector tape cross. Further back down the road there's a second mark, a downward facing white triangle with its red disk on top of it. The disk, as before, has a white reflector tape cross on it. Get the two marks in line and you're right in the channel. Then you'll see your turn open up to starboard, and you're in Hope Town harbor. Keep your speed right down.

Hope Town Marinas and Anchorages
Lighthouse Marina comes up immediately to starboard, and further on, past a mini-headland of mangroves, is the Hope Town Marina and Club Soleil, and slightly further on is the Hope Town Hideaways Marina. The anchorage is to port as you enter, and most probably crowded. It's almost entirely taken up by moorings. See our **Yellow Pages** for your contacts.

White Sound, from the east.

South of Elbow Cay and White Sound

Hope Town so dominates Elbow Cay that it's easy to forget that Elbow Cay itself continues for over 2.5 nm south-southwest from Hope Town Harbour. If you leave Hope Town and run offshore between Elbow Cay and the Parrot Cays, at just under the 2-nm point, the entrance to Elbow Cay's own White Sound will open up. You'll have to stand off about 0.5 nm out from the Elbow Cay shoreline after passing the last of the Parrot Cays, because shoal water extends this far offshore at the entrance to White Sound.

The White Sound entrance channel is marked. Don't cut inside the northern outer channel buoy for you'll hit shoal. Stay in the clearly marked channel. At the Abaco Inn end, directly ahead, there are red disk leading marks. Before you reach the end a second channel to starboard leads directly south to the Sea Spray Marina. Their dock, if you want to plot it, is 26° 30' 34"/566 N 076° 58' 33"/550 W. Again very clear marking and a well-defined channel will lead you in. You can take it that all the White Sound channels will give you 5 feet at MLW.

The Abaco Inn is sited at the end of the initial entry channel at the point where, but for its rocky spine, Elbow Cay might well have been carved by the ocean into two

separate islands. The Abaco Inn dock has 6 feet and limited space. You must throw a stern anchor out as you come in and secure bow to (or come in astern, if you wish) but don't lie alongside. The Sea Spray Resort has the kind of space you'd expect at a marina, and is star quality. Attractive, and going places. But it is remote from Hope Town. There's no room for anchoring in Elbow Cay's White Sound, and the depths outside the channels are down to 2 feet in places. The best anchorage, if the wind is right for you, is just south of the White Sound entry point, well clear of the convergence zone if people are entering or leaving White Sound.

At the south end of Elbow Cay is Tahiti Beach (26° 30' 06"/100 N 076° 59' 16"/266 W), famed for its sandbar that virtually dries at low water, and a popular picnic spot for small craft. The apparent marina to the north of Tahiti Beach, partly shielded by Baker's Rock, is private. South of Elbow Cay lies the Tilloo Cut with Tilloo Cay, and to the west is Lubbers Quarters with the shallows of the Lubbers Quarters Bank.

Routes in the Marsh Harbour Triangle

Providing that you stay clear of the shoals extending to the west from Johnnie's Cay and Lubbers Bank to the south, as well as the obvious inshore shoal areas, there are no navigational problem areas in the Marsh Harbour Triangle. We define this area by placing the apex of our triangle at the northwest approach to Man-O-War Cay, then drawing one line down to hit Great Abaco Island southwest of Marsh Harbour, and another line to hit Elbow Cay south of Hope Town. If both these points are on Latitude 26° 32' N that's about right. Join them and there's your triangle. Within this triangle you have a web of routes, all short runs of a few nautical miles, linking Marsh Harbour to Man-O-War Cay and to Hope Town, and Hope Town to Man-O-War Cay, Marsh Harbour, and the Boat Harbour Marina, and so it goes on. Your network has Point Set Rock has it hub, and you could hardly wish for a better landmark. Though you may wish to take note of bearings and distances, as well as the principal coordinates, you'll probably go visual for every trip in this area.

POINT SET ROCK

Point Set Rock has what appears to be a concrete shed on it that is very prominent. The shed is, in fact, the terminal for an underwater power cable that runs across to Elbow Cay. You can't miss it.

MATT LOWE'S CAY

Matt Lowe's Cay is private and was up for sale the last time we were in the area. If you want something like 5 acres of island with five beaches, a tiny harbor, and a house, you might wish to bid for it if no one else has snapped it up in the meantime. We never checked the asking price.

SOUTHERN ABACOS II		
Marsh Triangle Mid Area		
MARMD	26° 32' 38"/646 N	076° 59' 59"/994 W
Marsh Boat Harbour Marina		
SMRSH	26° 32' 22"/373 N	077° 02' 32"/537 W
Long Cay		
LNGCO	26° 30' 43"/724 N	077° 02' 32"/536 W
White Sound		
WHSND	26° 31' 00"/000 N	076° 59' 00"/000 W

The final figures in each waypoint show seconds (00") and thousands (000) of a minute.

SUGAR LOAF CAY

Sugar Loaf Cay has private houses and rental properties with their own docks.

Marsh Harbour

We must admit to feeling schizophrenic about Marsh Harbour. Like it or not, sometimes you can't avoid it. You need that airport (unless you're set on using Treasure Cay) for crew changes. You may well be chartering a boat there from the Moorings fleet at the Conch Inn Marina, or from someone else. You may need its stores for re-provisioning. You may, if you're unlucky, need its backup services to fix faults, to put something right. But unless you fall into one of these categories, unless you've signed on for a fishing tournament or to take part in the annual Abaco Regatta, we feel you're unlikely to linger there for long.

The pluses are that Marsh Harbour has all these facilities, good restaurants, and even a traffic light in case you've forgotten what they look like. The minus side, simply put, is that it's not, we'd guess, what you had in mind when you set out for the Abacos. It's a hot, sprawling, disorganized town, noisy with road traffic, and the harbor is far from clean (we never use our watermaker there). Yet it seems to suit some cruisers who become semi-permanent residents, bonded by the 8:15 a.m. Marsh Harbour Cruisers Net on channel 68, which offers weather, advice, forthcoming attractions, and a kind of "Has Anyone Seen?" service if you've missed your friends somewhere up or down the line.

Approach to Marsh Harbour's Harbor

There are no problems in entering Marsh Harbour, other than identifying your headlands and recognizing exactly where you are. From your arrival waypoint you'll first see a thin island, Outer Point Cay, taking the form of a headland, which you'll leave to port. Outer Point Cay has shoals ex-

Marsh Harbour harbor entrance, from the southeast.

tending out in a hook to the northeast so stay sensibly clear of it, about 200 yards or so. It also has a light, which may or may not work, but if nothing else the light stake helps your identification.

Continue on in a gentle curve to take you south until a small string of islets forming a second headland, known as Inner Point, comes up repeating the line of the first small cay. There's a light here too. Once you've cleared Inner Point, keeping about two boat lengths off, the harbor opens up to the east. Favor the north side as you go in, and a fairway (where you must not anchor) becomes obvious. You have plenty of water, good anchorages on both sides of the fairway, and a multiplicity of choices in marinas.

Marsh Harbour Marinas and Anchorages

If we talk of marinas we'd put it simply. Boat Harbour Marina is the largest, arguably has the best facilities, but is also expensive. Conch Inn Marina is the most lively, has fuel, but its shoreside facilities still need a cash injection, despite recent upgrading. Mangoes is small, hangs its attraction on its restaurant and boutique, is perhaps the most attractive in its shoreside setting, but has no fuel dock. Harbour View Marina is as small as Mangoes, but other than a fuel dock, offers no particular pizzazz, although the floating Tiki Hut is on its doorstep. Triple J Marina is even smaller, but has a fuel dock. The Admiral's Yacht Haven is remote, but well run, and close by is a Pizza Hut that features conch pizza (the only conch pizza we've ever seen). If you want to distance yourself, the Marsh Harbour Marina on the north shore is the quietest, and wins a high score with its protection from Northers in winter and its exposure to the cooling southeast Trades in summer. It has a fuel dock, and a restaurant serving lunchtime snacks, but only gets its restaurant in gear for Wednesdays and Sundays if you want to dine there. See our **Yellow Pages** for the fine detail.

As for anchoring, the fairway is clearly defined and outside of its lanes you are free to pick your spot. You should find at least 8 feet at MLW, and you're within a well-protected harbor. However, under threat of a severe storm you may want to find somewhere more snug with less craft around.

THE CROWDING OF MARSH HARBOUR

In our overview of the Abacos scene from a cruiser's point of view, we mentioned the crowding of Marsh Harbour. This is no longer a casual concern, nor an occasional situation. The plain fact is that Marsh Harbour, right now, with its existing moorings and its tolerance of freedom of choice in anchoring, subject only to keeping the fairway clear, is no longer working. There are just too many boats inside the harbor basin. The expansion of the marinas and the increase in transients anchoring off have hit a critical point. Although most visitors are careful to anchor so that the fairway remains open, others, less skilled or less concerned, either use

Marsh Harbour, from the southeast, and Boat Harbour Marina in the foreground.

a short scope to squeeze in or, on the borderline of the fairway, ignore the possibility of a wind change.

Given a squall, or a change in wind direction, the fairway can be totally blocked, and the short scope anchorers endanger everyone else. It is no longer uncommon for an incoming craft of any size to be unable to identify and follow a clear path across the harbor, and the same applies for anyone setting out from a marina. Both have to hold and wait until someone can clear the log jam. Even a cross-harbor trip in a dinghy may involve weaving a track akin to a slalom course.

The solutions so far suggested have included marking the fairway and forbidding any infringement on it (as yet not unanimously agreed on at local level), and prohibiting anchoring within Marsh Harbour (feared to be too Draconian a measure). Moving the Government Dock to Snake Cay has also been proposed, though this is primarily because the draft of the new mailboats, the *Duke of Topsail* and the *Margarita*, limits them to high water entry only, and even then with carefully calculated loading. The Snake Cay, and an alternative Flag Swamp site, are unlikely to come about; but clearly dredging and some realignment of Marsh Harbour must take place, and this, inevitably, will have a knock-on effect on the cruising world.

An additional complication are the existing moorings inside the harbor, many of them dating back fifty years or more. They are for the most part heavy, secure moorings in deep water, and rightly prized. If a fairway were to be marked, and if free anchoring were to be controlled or even banned, it follows that the harbor space available for everyone, moored or anchored, is going to be squeezed. There is no easy solution. Banning anchoring and supplying moorings as an alternative would seem to be the best solution. Then it might

no longer be necessary to mark a fairway. But the money would have to be found for the new "visitor's" moorings, and the number that could be accommodated would be a significant reduction in the present Marsh Harbour fleet. We would guess that this last course will, eventually, be adopted. Maybe the critical state has to continue for another year or two, or the situation worsen, to trigger action.

APPROACH TO BOAT HARBOUR MARINA
Boat Harbour Marina is on the southwest side of the Marsh Harbour peninsula, and your access to it necessitates a totally different approach, which will take you to the east of Point Set Rock if you're coming from the north, then southeast of Matt Lowe's Cay and south of Sugar Loaf Cay. The marina is obvious and presents no difficulties. Its entrance is on the west side. Once you are there you're by no means marooned or separated from Marsh Harbour itself. A short walk to the main road and a turn to the left brings you right on the doorstep of the Conch Inn Marina.

Heading North to Treasure Cay
Approaching Treasure Cay from the south, our Fish Cay south waypoint is the focal point on all routes, unless you elect to go by way of Great Guana Cay and our Whale Passage waypoint (see **The Central Abacos, Treasure Cay and the Treasure Cay Triangle** on page 61). From Marsh Harbour to our Fish Cay waypoint it's 4.8 nm on 318°M. From North Point Set Rock it's 7.1 nm on 295°M. From Man-O-War it's 5.4 nm on 283°M. From Fish Cay it's 7.5 nm on a heading of 298°M to our Treasure Cay approach waypoint (1 nm southeast of the entrance to Treasure Cay marina).

Marsh Harbour Marina.

Peter Johnson sculpture, Little Harbour.

South Great Abaco Island

FOR many people the Marsh Harbour Triangle may be the turning point in cruising the Abacos, and if you started by crossing the Little Bahama Bank, you may well think of retracing your route when you get to Hope Town. For others, perhaps those who charter out of Marsh Harbour, the more immediate destinations, Hope Town, Man-O-War Cay, and perhaps Green Turtle Cay to the north, will satisfy a cruise itinerary.

If you decide to continue south from Hope Town, what's there? It's the last 10 miles of the Sea of Abaco (measured as a Brown Pelican might fly) but it comes out to more like 15 nm when you add up the legs of your courses down to Little Harbour. Great Abaco Island has another 30 miles to run before it ends, forbiddingly, in the unwelcoming South West Point with its lighthouse and Hole-in-the-Wall, which sounds like a cruiser's refuge, but is no safe haven. Unless you have the curiosity to visit Cherokee, effectively your Abaco cruising grounds end, as does the Sea of Abaco, at Little Harbour.

If you're bent on leaving the Abacos and carrying on south across the Northeast Providence Channel, the North Bar Channel or the Little Harbour Bar will be your point of departure for Spanish Wells and Eleuthera, Nassau and the Exumas, or the southern Berry Islands. If you're arriving from one of these cruising grounds, you're most likely to choose one of these ocean passes to gain the Sea of Abaco, rather than work your way offshore further north up the Abaco chain. These considerations apart, why head for Little Harbour? The answer is because of Little Harbour itself, the Pelican Cays Land and Sea Park to its north, and the anchorages of Lynyard Cay.

Just as the shoals off Spanish Cay and the Treasure Cay–Whale Cay shallows dictated your options on courses in those areas, similarly here, south of Elbow Cay, Lubbers Bank and the Tilloo Bank dictate that you either set off south running about 1 nm off the coast of Great Abaco Island or you thread your way between Elbow Cay and Lubbers Quarters Cay, and then around Tilloo Bank. Whichever route you choose, tide will be much in your mind for these are waters where you want a rising tide for your passage making, and at least a half tide to enter Little Harbour.

Elbow Cay–Tilloo Cay–Lynyard Cay–Little Harbour

Let's start at White Sound in Elbow Cay. From our waypoint there set an initial course of 192°M for 0.67 nm. This heading places Baker's Rock and Tahiti Beach on your bow. Look to port and a three-story house that has not been obvious as you set out from the White Sound waypoint appears around a little headland after you've run half a mile. You are close to your turn point, Lubbers Quarters north. It's here that we start jinking around Tilloo Bank.

SOUTHERN ABACOS III		
Lubbers Quarters North		
LQNTH	26° 30' 20"/333 N	076° 59' 05"/085 W
Lubbers Quarters Mid-Point		
LQMID	26° 29' 55"/916 N	076° 59' 30"/500 W
Lubbers Quarters South		
LQSTH	26° 29' 05"/084 N	076° 59' 45"/750 W
Tilloo Bank West		
WTILO	26° 25' 57"/961 N	077° 01' 07"/114 W
Tilloo Bank South		
STILO	26° 25' 23"/381 N	077° 00' 13"/221 W
North Pelican		
NPELI	26° 25' 22"/376 N	076° 59' 20"/339 W
Witch Point		
WITCH	26° 29' 40"/666 N	077° 01' 40"/666 W
North Bar West		
NBARW	26° 23' 37"/615 N	076° 59' 10"/174 W
North Bar Channel		
NBRCH	26° 23' 23"/391 N	076° 58' 23"/379 W
North Bar Channel East		
NBARE	26° 22' 55"/929 N	076° 56' 51"/850 W
Lynyard Mid-Point		
LYNMD	26° 22' 00"/000 N	076° 59' 40"/666 W
Lynyard Anchorages		
LYNAN	26° 21' 20"/333 N	076° 59' 10"/172 W
Little Harbour North		
LHRBN	26° 20' 26"/432 N	076° 59' 40"/676 W

The final figures in each waypoint show seconds (00") and thousands (000) of a minute.

Tilloo Bank Step-by-Step

Your route may sound complex, but it's simple and easy. See our chart.

Lubbers Quarters North

LQNTH	26° 30' 20"/333 N	076° 59' 05"/085 W

At LQNTH turn onto 222°M, which you'll hold for 0.5 nm. Aim for the slight dip in the skyline profile of Lubbers Quarters Cay (not the "first" low part you'll see on the port bow, which is the dip formed between the trees of the south tip of Lubbers Quarters Cay and the low scrub that takes over where the trees gave up). If you're in doubt, just go by the bearing and you have the reassurance of a house with a triple roof line, which is almost on your heading. After your run of 0.5 nm you're at LQMID.

Lubbers Quarters Mid-Point

LQMID	26° 29' 55"/916 N	076° 59' 30"/500 W

From LQMID head 195°M for 1.8 nm. This takes you on a direct course for the tip of Tavern Cay, easily recognizable because it appears to have a white castle tower on it, and later you'll see a large blue-roofed house complex. In fact the castle tower (and its blue house) is on Tilloo Cay and Tavern Cay, undeveloped, is on the market at an astronomical price. You can see it at closer range on your next leg.

Lubbers Quarters South

LQSTH	26° 29' 05"/084 N	076° 59' 45"/750 W

At LQSTH alter on to 200°M (no great change there) and at last you've got a chance to look at Tavern Cay. Hold 200°M for a relaxing 3.3 nm until you reach Tilloo Bank West.

Tilloo Bank West

WTILO	26° 25' 57"/961 N	077° 01' 07"/114 W

At WTILO turn onto 126°M for 0.9 nm, which places you at Tilloo Bank South.

Tilloo Bank South

STILO	26° 25' 23"/381 N	077° 00' 13"/221 W

At STILO turn to head 090°M for 0.8 nm, which places you off the north end of Pelican Cay (NPELI).

LUBBERS QUARTERS CAY

Lubbers Quarters Cay is useful to you navigationally, but is unlikely to feature as a destination unless you're thinking of buying a lot there. Like many of the cays the land has long since been staked out and all the title holder now needs is your money and whatever site you fancy (when you've done with the lawyers) is yours. There is what might appear to be a public dock at 26° 29' 29"/483 N 076° 59' 40"/666 W, but this is private and a communal facility for the Lubbers Quarters Cay property owners.

TAVERN CAY

Tavern Cay, as we've said, is up for grabs.

TILLOO CAY

Tilloo Cay, which seems to stretch on forever (its length is just over 4 nm) has good beaches on its southwest tip, and you can work your way in there just north of Tilloo Bank. There's an inshore route south you can take over the bank if you hug the shore, but we reckon you're in little more than 2 feet of water, so it's dinghy territory unless you have real shoal draft or zero draft. Tilloo Pond is private.

The Pelican Cays and Dropping South Toward Little Harbour

Once you've reached Pelican Cay it's plain sailing. You hardly need waypoints and courses to follow. At our North Pelican waypoint, 175°M held for 1.7 nm will place you right by

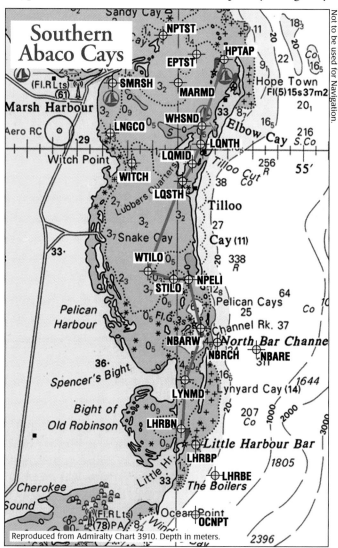

Reproduced from Admiralty Chart 3910. Depth in meters.

North Bar Channel. On this leg you'll see that Channel Cay, which at first sight looks uninhabited, has a house on it. Gaulding Cay becomes visible, and Cornish Cay with a house with a shiny roof. All of this is on your starboard side, as is Sandy Cay with its small boat moorings for snorkelers. To port you have the north–south run of the Pelican Cays and reefs, and the whole area you are transiting is the Pelican Cays Land and Sea Park. It would be a pity not to stop here and go snorkeling.

CHANNEL CAY
Channel Cay is private land.

THE PELICAN CAYS AND SANDY CAY
The Pelican Cays and Sandy Cay and the adjacent sea area form the Bahamian National Trust's Pelican Cays Land and Sea Park, which extends south to include the waters of North Bar Channel. You are allowed to anchor here, but *not* over coral and the holding on the east side of the Sandy Cay reef is not good. You must also be aware that swells coming in through North Bar Channel can make the Pelican Park sea area bumpy to say the least. If it's going to be rough there, forget it. The small boat moorings provided by the Bahamas National Trust may be used by you and if they're all taken, you must anchor independently over sand, not coral. It goes almost without saying that fishing, shell collecting, the taking of coral, or any predatory action is forbidden. Just snorkel and enjoy the reefs.

CORNISH CAY
Cornish Cay is private land.

NORTH BAR CHANNEL
North Bar Channel, just north of Lynyard Cay, has range marks set on Sandy Cay and Cornish Cay, and 16 feet of water. The range marks are not easy to see with the naked eye, but the lie of the cays themselves and the obviousness of North Bar Channel makes your navigation relatively easy. To your north is Channel Rock, and the only potential hazard are the rocks off the north tip of Lynyard Cay, but the range marks, the lie of the land, and your heading of 115°M will keep you clear. This pass is used by the mailboats.

From North Bar Channel to Little Harbour
Our North Bar Channel west waypoint could be your departure point if you were setting out into the Atlantic. Bound for Little Harbour from there hold 199°M to run for 1.71 nm to the midpoint of Lynyard Cay to port. To starboard you have a strange axe-like headland protruding out from Great Abaco Island. This was the site of Wilson City, a one time mega-forestry concern, which is now derelict.

From this mid-Lynyard point if you alter slightly on to 192°M, a run of just under a mile (0.67 nm) brings you level with the best Lynyard Cay anchorages, which are fairly well protected from the ocean swell that you'd expect to come in through the Little Harbour Channel. Bridges Cay (with a white house) is now on your starboard bow, and the Little Harbour Channel is opening up to port. You may be tempted to stop here, or you may wish to carry on with your approach to Little Harbour.

Going for Little Harbour head 193°M for just 0.59 nm, which brings you to the waypoint we'd choose if we were using Little Harbour Channel to gain the ocean, or to come in from it. For Little Harbour turn on to 180°M for 0.75 nm, bringing you to our last waypoint (LHRBN) in our Elbow Cay to Little Harbour list. From there you go visual.

LYNYARD AND GOOLE CAYS
Lynyard Cay, as we've hinted, has good anchorages on its southwest end, extending for the last third of its 2.5-nm length, which, at the south end, carry 15 feet of water surprisingly close to Lynyard Cay. There are houses on Lynyard that are private, but otherwise you can land there. Surprisingly the anchorages seem relatively well protected from the ocean swell. The reason for this may be that Goole Cay to its south, and the extensive reef extending 0.75 nm further south from Goole Cay, act as a breakwater. This reef, which does not always show (other than by an upheaval in swell pattern), together with the reef extending north from Little Harbour's Lighthouse Point, set your limits for passing safely through Little Harbour Bar.

LITTLE HARBOUR BAR
Little Harbour Bar has 16 feet of water as well, and is fairly straightforward. Goole Cay, to the north, has that 0.75-nm reef running south from its southern tip, and Little Harbour

Pete's Pub, Little Harbour.

Point has its reef running north for nearly 0.25 nm. If you set out from our Little Harbour north waypoint you should be fine, or position yourself so that a back bearing on the house on Bridges Cay reads 345°M, and you go out through the pass on 165°M.

When you reach our Little Harbour east waypoint you are set up either for going on to Cherokee, or setting out for Spanish Wells (Bridge Point north is 45.8 nm on 162°M, and Egg Island northwest is 47.3 nm on 176°M). Nassau, via Hanover Sound north is 74.5 nm on 192°M (a good route if you're bound for the Exumas). Nassau Harbour west is 75.5 nm on 196°M. The Berry Islands, a dogleg around Hole-in-the-Wall (30 nm on 197°M) lie a further 39.2 nm away on 270°M to Great Stirrup Cay or, for the southern Berrys, it's 44.1 nm on 233°M to just off Whale Cay light.

BRIDGES CAY

Bridges Cay is private property. The house on it is a useful landmark, particularly if you are entering Little Harbour Bar from the ocean.

Little Harbour

Approach and Anchorage

You can't miss the white beach to the east of the harbor entrance and Tom Curry Point is obvious on the port side. Just pause and check the state of the tide. The entry channel is shallow. If you need more than 3 feet of water, a half tide state is critical. If you're OK, swing easily to enter virtually in mid-channel and pick up the line of buoys marking the channel, four red and three green, to bring

you curving gently east into the harbor. Either pick up a mooring buoy or anchor. If you use a buoy, which are provided by Pete's Pub, you will be charged $10, which will be collected sometime during your visit. Someone will come out to you at your mooring. You're there. Twelve feet of water at high tide. A good 10 feet at low. The distance run from White Sound? 12.62 nm.

A Bahamian Dream

Little Harbour probably comes close to everyone's dream of a Bahamian hideaway, and it certainly met the critical demands of the extraordinary and dynamic Randolph Johnston, one of the great sculptors of this century. Johnston, who died in 1992 in his late eighties, spent the last forty years of his life in Little Harbour, pursuing his dream of living free to work in an unspoiled natural environment remote from the fetters, constraints, and pollution of twentieth-century life in the developed world.

Today much of Little Harbour remains in the hands of his three sons, of whom only Pete maintains a relatively high profile with a gallery devoted to his father's work and his own, as well as that of other local artists, and Pete's Pub, a shack bar on the beach. Little Harbour is almost completely enclosed, is protected from virtually all wind and surge, and has all the depth you need once you're in there. Don't forget that the entrance channel for most boats is a No-Go until at least half tide.

The harbor itself has a good beach, there's another good beach on the north side of the island, a small reef that is worth snorkeling, the remains of the old lighthouse on Lighthouse Point (together with a modern light on the old rusty light tower), and the caves on the east side of the harbor where the Johnston family, when they first migrated to a nearly deserted Little Harbour, first found shelter while building their home. The waters in the harbor and around Little Harbour, as well as the reefs, are dedicated to the Bahamas National Trust. You'll find turtles swimming in the harbor.

Pete's Gallery is well worth a visit. Randolph Johnston's work is powerful and moving, and Pete's own work, marine sculptures (many of dolphins) and his gold jewelry may have you reaching for your credit card. Remember that the island remains in private hands, there are a number of houses around Little Harbour now (many belonging to winter residents) and

Little Harbour, from the southeast.

there are no facilities for visiting boats other than the moorings. No stores, no fuel, no water, and no place to leave garbage. You are a guest there. Arrive quietly, enjoy your stay, and leave quietly.

THE BIGHT OF OLD ROBINSON

The Bight of Old Robinson to the west of Little Harbour, entered at any point between Bridges Cay and Tom Curry Point, has 7 feet of water in its central arc but otherwise is a maze of shallows with extraordinary blue holes with subterranean connections to the ocean, in which it's said that ocean fish like groupers may be found, far from their normal habitat. Sometime, we've promised ourselves, we'll devote a week to exploring this area but regret that to date the pres-

Sundowners at Pete's Pub.

sures of time have forced us to move on and stay with the main routes and main destinations.

The Alternative Great Abaco Side Route to Little Harbour

There's an alternative "inshore" route down to Little Harbour from Marsh Harbour. It's straightforward, and joins the Elbow Cay route at our West Tilloo Bank waypoint. If you're in the Marsh Harbour area, take our waypoint off Boat Harbour Marina (SMRSH) as your start point.

Marsh Harbour–Witch Point–Tilloo Bank

All you have to do is complete two doglegs to get you clear of Lubbers Bank and safely off Witch Point, and

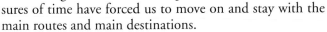

SOUTHERN ABACOS IV

Little Harbour Bar Pass		
LHRBP	26° 19' 47"/793 N	076° 59' 19"/327 W
Little Harbour Bar East		
LHRBE	26° 18' 45"/747 N	076° 58' 45"/754 W
Little Harbour		
LHRBO	26° 20' 10"/169 N	076° 59' 53"/886 W
Ocean Point		
OCNPT	26° 17' 02"/030 N	076° 59' 20"/342 W
Cherokee Point		
CHERP	26° 15' 40"/666 N	077° 03' 15"/250 W
Rock Point (Southwest Great Abaco Island)		
RCKPT	26° 00' 00"/000 N	077° 25' 51"/860 W
Hole-in-the-Wall		
HOLEW	25° 49' 43"/716 N	077° 08' 40"/666 W

The final figures in each waypoint show seconds (00") and thousands (000) of a minute.

then carry on as a straight run to West Tilloo Bank. Your initial course from the start waypoint is 194°M for 1.52 nm, and then off Witch Point change to 177°M and hold it for 3.88 nm, which will take you to West Tilloo. From then on, follow the route we've described running south from White Sound.

THE GREAT ABACO COAST BETWEEN MARSH HARBOUR AND SPENCER BIGHT

We've found nothing of interest on the Great Abaco coast between Marsh Harbour and Spencer Bight (just north of the Bight of Old Robinson) to tempt the cruising boat to stay awhile and explore, but the possibility remains that there may well be gunkholes worth visiting. Snake Cay in the middle of this stretch, whose rusting fuel tanks are conspicuous, is not worth considering and has poor holding.

Returning North Along the Great Abaco Coast

If you're heading north from Little Harbour inshore along the Great Abaco coast, simply reverse the route we gave south from Marsh Harbour Marina. If you're going on past Marsh Harbour to Man-O-War or further north, when you get to our original start point you have to dogleg part way to Hope Town before setting your course on for Point Set Rock. In this case, rather than going the whole way across the Marsh Harbour Triangle, we suggest you make use of our Marsh Triangle mid waypoint (MARMD) and then alter for East Point Set waypoint (EPTST). By then you'll probably know the area like the back of your hand and will be going visual. All this waypointing may seem unnecessary but, as we said some time back, rainstorms have wiped out all land while we've been in the Marsh Harbour Triangle.

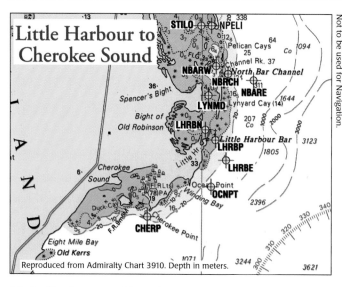

Reproduced from Admiralty Chart 3910. Depth in meters.

Little Harbour to Cherokee Sound

If you want to visit Cherokee, it's an easy 10-nm run from Little Harbour, but not one that you should undertake if the ocean is kicking up. In short, if you don't fancy going out over Little Harbour Bar, Cherokee would be no fun trip. The first stages are simple. From just off Little Harbour go on 000°M for just 0.75 nm to get to our Little Harbour north waypoint, opposite the Little Harbour Bar. From there head 158°M for 0.95 nm to reach our Little Harbour Pass waypoint, which takes you safely out over Little Harbour Bar.

Then you need to gain some offing to get well out from the reef known as the Boilers, which lies off the Great Abaco coast between Little Harbour and Ocean Point, halfway to Cherokee. Head 162°M for 1.1 nm to gain this offing, and then turn to clear Ocean Point on 207°M for 1.25 nm. After this you can relax for a while, safely offshore, and run on 247°M for 4.28 nm to clear Cherokee

Cherokee Sound, from the southeast.

Point, which is obvious.

Once you're around Cherokee Point, steer initially for its 250-foot Batelco tower. You can't miss it. You'll see water breaking on the reef and shallows to port. To starboard a beach will open up behind Cherokee Point with a small but precipitous cliff behind it. The water just off that beach is your anchorage, where you'll find a clean sand bottom that holds well and 8–10 feet of water. The anchorage is open to the south and southwest, and will take surge around the point if swells are running. This said, if the weather is right, it's one of the most pleasant places we've found. The beach is great. The water is fabulous.

Cherokee and Cherokee Sound

The Cherokee Point anchorage is, for all practical purposes, the *only* anchorage worth considering in Cherokee Sound. Though the Sound may appear inviting when looking at a map, it's far too shallow for anything other than shoal draft craft, and from Cherokee Point the only way you can reach the settlement is by dinghy.

If you do want to get your own boat as close in as it's humanly possible to get, at one time a call to Cherokee Radio on VHF 16 would produce a pilot, someone who'd come out and guide you in. We believe the privatization of Batelco may reduce the Cherokee station to an unmanned automated relay. If this does come about, try calling Cherokee Auto and Boat Haven on VHF 16. They have gasoline and diesel (in 55-gallon drums), as well as auto and boat spares. Above all, they'd be willing to help you in any way they can. See our **Yellow Pages**.

This apart, if you are anchored tucked in around Cherokee Point, think of taking your dinghy across to the old jetty you'll see stretching out from the beach in front of the Batelco station. Walk into the settlement. It's as neat as a new pin, and the people you'll meet could not be more friendly. And there you'll see a memorial to the twenty-nine famous Cherokee sailing smacks of the past. These people were once superb ship builders, and Cherokee Sound the place to have a ship built.

Cherokee Sound to South Abaco

From Ocean Point or Cherokee Sound, you have some 30 nm to run paralleling the eastern coast of Great Abaco to reach Hole-in-the-Wall, the southernmost Great Abaco peninsula. There is no shelter on this run, and no place, in our reckoning, where you would wish to stop. Our Hole-in-the-Wall waypoint (HOLEW) places you on the 100-fathom line 2.6 nm off Hole-in-the-Wall. From here, a 44-nm jump across the Northwest Providence Channel, running virtually east–west, will take you to the Berry Islands. Alternatively, you may wish to continue on south to North Eleuthera.

As ever, the direction and strength of the wind, and the sea state, particularly the set of the Atlantic, has a funda-

Hole-in-the-Wall, from the northeast.

cruising itinerary. If you're going past Hole-in-the-Wall, get the weather right, and you're fine. It is not a route for a quick sprint regardless of the weather.

SANDY POINT

Sandy Point is well-named. It's a low-lying sandy hook running about 2 miles north from Rocky Point, the extreme southwestern point of Great Abaco Island. It's a shoal area, bordered on the west by the dark blue Northwest Providence Channel but distanced from it by the sea green and brown of shoals. To the north and east there are mangrove flats. To the west, also on the edge of the Northwest Providence Channel, lies Gorda Cay (now renamed Castaway Island) the playground of the Disney Cruise Line.

Approaching from the south be aware that reefs run out to the southwest from Rocky Point (rightly named), and that you need to stand off the coast until you get your bearings. Sandy Point settlement is not hard to pick out. Far off, to port on the horizon, you may just see the tufts of the

mental impact on your planning. There's one potentially hazardous area in this route and that's around Hole-in-the-Wall. From a 1,000-fathom depth the ocean bed shelves to 100 fathoms within a hand span and, closer in, around Hole-in-the-Wall, to 3 fathoms. Any significant swell coming in from the open Atlantic, coupled with wind above 15 knots, can build up 10-feet-plus seas. It's one of the sea areas, which, like the Gulf Stream, require weather analysis before you set out, particularly because there's nowhere to run for shelter once you're out there.

HOLE-IN-THE-WALL

The Hole-in-the-Wall peninsula, which is south of the lighthouse, a wall of rock with the "hole in the wall" punched through it like an eye in a needle, offers no shelter other than in virtually calm conditions. You can tuck yourself behind it on the western side if the winds are light to zero from the east or southeast. Further to the west, Cross Harbour, on the south coast of Great Abaco Island, is a misnomer. It's a shallow, reef-filled bight. Don't even think of it as a potential refuge. Sandy Point, around the southwest tip (that's Rocky Point) of Great Abaco, might just serve. For this reason we cover Sandy Point in some detail. But make no mistake. Sandy Point would not feature on our

South Abaco

Reproduced from Admiralty Chart 3910. Depth in meters.

Not to be used for Navigation.

Sandy Point.

palms on Gorda Cay, and there may be a Disney Line ship anchored off. More immediately, to starboard on Sandy Cay's western beach there are two prominent docks running out, and a truncated ruin of a dock. Forget the stumpy dock. The first "for real" dock has a Texaco sign on the beach behind it, and is indeed a Texaco Starport (see our **Yellow Pages**). You can get fuel there, both gas and diesel, and get in to the outer head dock with 5 feet at MLW (coming in south of the white buoy that marks a wreck). But it is no safe haven.

Slightly further on the Government Dock, a wood structure, is a semi-permanent home for local fishing boats. Again, at the outer end, it will carry 5 feet at MLW. But again, it is no safe haven.

If you are running for shelter, you've got to work your way around Sandy Point into the "Creek" on the eastern side, between Sandy Point and Guana Cay. There you'll find the local fishing boats (certainly in severe weather) secured at three stub docks, but there'll be room to anchor, somewhere. It's tight, and it's shoal. But at least you'll be shielded.

The getting there is a matter of reading the water. The essential is that you take an apparent shoal course over "brown" water to gain a deeper entry channel to the Creek, and can expect to have breaking seas to port at one point, but also some 5 feet at MLW all the way around Sandy Point. We'd like to advise you, but were warned by Walter Lightbourne, the owner of the Texaco station, that the sand has been altering in each storm. Call him, if you like, on VHF 16 at Lightbourne Marina (despite the callsign, what he operates is not, certainly when we were there, a marina).

He will guide you. We have no depths for the Creek itself, but would guess that 5 feet will take you reasonably far in, certainly to a safe anchorage.

As for Sandy Point itself, again see our **Yellow Pages**. It has a Batelco office (the tower, as ever, is a landmark), a clinic, food, two bars, two restaurants, and an airstrip. But it's basic. This is one remote place, 60 miles from Marsh Harbour with nothing in between. But the connecting road is good.

CASTAWAY CAY

We must confess that we've not landed on Castaway Cay, aka Gorda Cay, but we've not failed to note the Disney ships in Nassau and anchored off on the Sandy Point horizon. It seems that their run down the Northwest Providence Channel to offer the castaway experience of a day on Gorda Cay is working out as planned. Sandy Point, which had at one time hoped that some benefit from this golden tide might come their way, have yet to see any kind of dividend materialize. Their local Texaco Starport with its one pump has been called on to refuel the Disney playcraft, but that, so far, is that.

Continuing South to North Eleuthera or the Berry Islands

A heading of 146°M taken from Hole-in-the-Wall (HOLEW) held for 22 nm will take you to Egg Island northwest (EGGNW), just off North Eleuthera. A heading of 270°M held for 40 nm will take you to Great Stirrup Cay (GSTRP) in the Berry Islands.

Sandy Point Creek.

YELLOW PAGES

This area received the full force of Hurricane *Floyd* in September 1999. Be aware that reconstruction and the restoration of normal services after a Category 4 Hurricane may take a considerable period of time to complete.

MAN-O-WAR CAY

This classic Abaco cay, steeped in the best boat-building and sail-making tradition, is well organized, self contained, and alcohol free. Man-O-War has much to offer cruising boats, with its good sheltered harbor and excellent marina and storage facilities where boats may be safely left for extended periods. Most buoys in Man-O-War harbor have a name and VHF callsign on them. You can pick up any that are not specifically marked PRIVATE or RESERVED. The charge is generally $7 per night. The frequent ferry service to and from Marsh Harbor makes it readily accessible to an airport. Everything closes down promptly at 5 pm and all day Sundays, so this is not a place with bright lights and night clubs. The island population numbers around 275, increased by winter home owners and visiting boats.

MARINA

MAN-O-WAR MARINA
Tel: 242-365-6008 • Fax: 365-6151 • VHF 16

Slips	26
Moorings	6, cost $7 per night or $150 per month, which does not include the use of marina facilities.
Max LOA	70 ft.
MLW at Dock	8 ft., but only 5 ft. at low water in the harbor entrance.
Dockage	70¢ per foot per day, 50¢ per foot per day on a monthly basis.
Long Term	45¢ per ft. per day over six months. Dry dinghy storage is $20 per month.
Power	40¢ per kWh, metered.
Fuel	Diesel and gasoline. Fuel dock is open 7 am to 5 pm, Monday to Saturday; 8 am to 3 pm on Sundays. The fuel dock also has oils, ice, and filtered water.
Propane	Refills take 48 hours.
Water	15¢ per gallon, metered.
Telephones	Two outside the *Dive Shop* at the marina, more at *Batelco*.
TV	Free hookup for cable TV.
Showers	In the office building, free to marina guests, otherwise $3. Open during office hours, key necessary in the evenings.
Laundry	Washer and dryer $3.50 each, open 24 hrs. Tokens from the marina office.
Restaurant	*Man-o-War Pavilion*, open for lunch and dinner daily except Wednesdays and Sundays.
Coffee	Complimentary morning coffee for guests.
Ice	$3.50 per bag, block or cubes.
Trash	Free to marina guests, otherwise $1 per bag.
Barbecue	Gas grill at the gazebo.
Social night	Social gathering at the gazebo on Thursdays at 6 pm. Take a beverage of your choice, and munchies to share.
Library & Videos	Book and video exchange in the office.
Mail	Mail can be held for you, and sent out.
Fedex and UPS	Can be arranged with the marina office.
Fax and Copy	In the marina office. Free to receive a fax, appropriate charge per page to send one. 25¢ per page for copies.
E-mail	Can be sent and received at: cruisers@oii.net.
Boat Cleaning	Bright work, varnishing, painting $22 per hour. Wash down and cleaning services for $15 per hour.
Boat Checks	$20 per check, every two weeks recommended.

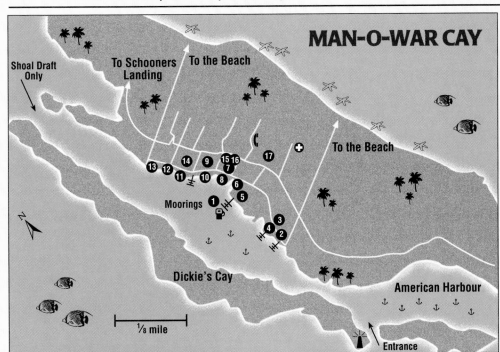

MAN-O-WAR CAY DIRECTORY

1. Man-O-War Marina
2. Public dock
3. Ena's Place
4. Albury's Ferry
5. Dive Shop and Pavilion Restaurant
6. CIBC Bank
7. Man-O-War Hardware
8. Edwin's Boat Yard II
9. Royal Bank of Canada
10. Albury Boat Builders
11. Albury's Harbour Store
12. Edwin's Boat Yard I
13. The Sail Shop
14. Hibiscus Cafe
15. Island Treasures
16. Man-O-War Grocery
17. Post Office
(Batelco
⌂ Fuel
✚ Clinic

Boat Provisions   The marina will see that provisions are put on your boat if you plan to return late evening or on a Sunday. Give them a list ahead of time.

Office   Open 7 am to 5 pm, Monday to Saturday; 8 am to 3 pm on Sundays.

Credit Cards   Visa, MasterCard, and American Express.

Owner/Manager   Tommy Albury

MARINE SERVICES

Boat Builders
Albury Brothers Boat Yard   Tel: 365-6086   Open 7:30 am to 5:30 pm, Monday to Friday.

Boat Rental
David and Shane Albury at *Conch Pearl Rentals* at the *Albury Boat Yard*   Tel: 365-6059 • VHF 16   Wide variety of boats to rent, as well as fishing guides and charters.

Boat Yard
Edwin's Boat Yard   Tel: 365-6006/6007   Full-service boat yard in two locations with hauling up to 65 ft. or 50 tons. Painting, welding, carpentry, and mechanical work.

Sail Maker
Jay Manni at *Edwin's Boat Yard*   Tel: 365-6171

SERVICES

Banks
Royal Bank of Canada   Open from 10 am to 2 pm on Fridays.
CIBC   Open from 10 am to 2 pm on Thursdays.

Beauty Salon
Bahama Waves   Tel: 365-6310

Churches
Gospel Chapel
Church of God
New Life Bible Church

Clinic
At time of writing, there was no nurse in Man-O-War. The nearest medical facilities are in Marsh Harbour.

Ferries
Albury's Ferry Service   Tel: 367-3147 or 365-6010 • Fax: 365-6487 • VHF 16   Leaves Man-O-War for Marsh Harbour at 8 am and 1:30 pm daily, as well as at 11:30 am and 2:30 pm Monday to Saturday. The ferry takes 20 minutes, runs absolutely on time, and will cost you $7 one way or $10 same-day round trip, taking you into the Albury Ferry Dock at Crossing Beach, Marsh Harbour. There are always taxis waiting there.

Golf Carts
Island Treasures   Tel: 365-6072   Next to *Man O War Grocery*. Golf carts and bicycles to rent.

Post Office
Open from 9 am to noon and 2 to 5 pm, Monday to Friday.

Telephones
Two outside the *Dive Shop* at the marina, and two at *Batelco*.

Trash
Can be left in the bins beyond *The Sail Shop* if you are not a marina guest.

Travel Agent
A and W Travel Service   Tel: 365-6002

SHOPPING

Bakery
Albury's Bakery   Tel: 365-6031   Opposite *Man O War Grocery*.

Clothing, Gifts, & Souvenirs
The Dive Shop at *Man-O-War Marina*   Tel: 365-6013   Open 9 am to 5 pm, Monday to Saturday. Some marine repair and maintenance supplies, beach accessories, footwear, rental and new

Man-O-War sign.

dive gear, and a wide selection of shorts, T-shirts, and light-weight clothes, as well as children's wear and Abaco books and charts.

Island Treasures next to *Man O War Grocery*   Tel: 365-6072   Open 9 am to 5 pm, Monday to Saturday. T-shirts, gifts, and jewelry, as well as bicycles and carts to rent.

Joe's Studio   Tel: 365-6082   Open from 9:30 am to 4:30 pm, Monday to Friday, and 9 am to 3 pm on Saturdays. Locally carved native woodcrafts, half models, books, hand-crafted gifts.

Mary's Corner Store   Tel: 365-6178   Open 9 am to 5 pm, Monday to Saturday. Books, gifts, hats, jackets, bags, and T-shirts.

The Sail Shop   Tel: 365-6014 • VHF 16   With their own dock, open 7 am to 5 pm, Monday to Friday, to 4 pm on Saturdays. World-famous canvas bags and accessories made by the Albury family. T-shirts and cards, too.

Seaside Boutique   Tel: 365-6384   Open from 9 am to 5 pm Monday to Saturday, with island fashions and accessories, greeting cards, and a wide selection of Androsia cloth and fashions.

The Shirt Shop   Tel: 365-6077   With souvenirs, T-shirts, household goods, and more; open 9 am to 5 pm Monday to Saturday.

Groceries
Albury's Harbour Store on the waterfront   Tel: 365-6004   Open 8 am to 5:30 pm, Monday to Friday; 8 am to 7:30 pm on Saturdays. Canned and frozen goods, sodas and ice cream, paper goods and some pharmacy; a good selection neatly displayed. Free delivery to the dock.

Man-O-War Grocery   Queen's Highway   Tel: 365-6016 • VHF 16   Open 8 am to 5:30 pm, Monday to Friday; to 9 pm on Saturdays. A very comprehensive grocery with homemade bread, soups and sauces, fresh fruit and vegetables, imported meats, fish, and dairy products. Free delivery to the dock.

Hardware
Man-O-War Hardware   Tel: 365-6011 • Fax: 365-6039 • VHF 69   Open 7 am to 4 pm, Monday to Friday, and to noon on Saturdays. Building, plumbing, and marine supplies, and fishing tackle. Inter-island delivery service.

RESTAURANTS

Restaurants post their daily menus on the telegraph poles along the street, or outside their doors. Alcohol is neither served, nor allowed to be brought in, to any restaurant on Man-O-War Cay.

Ena's Place   Tel: 365-6187   To the left as you walk up from the ferry. Open daily except Sundays, from 10:30 am to 9:30 pm. Sandwiches, conch fritters, nachos, homemade pies, ice cream, and yogurt, as well as Bahamian meals. Take-away or dine on the porch. Friday evening dinner by reservation.

Hibiscus Cafe, to your left as you walk up from the marina or ferry Open daily except Sundays, from 11 am to 9 pm, for lunch and dinner in the only air-conditioned restaurant in Man-O-War. No reservations necessary. House specialties include Hibiscus Petals (homemade potato chips) and a Works Burger, which is exactly that. Fish, chicken, steak, and shrimp also served, but no alcohol.

The Pavilion at the *Man O War Marina* Tel: 365-6185 Open 10:30 am to 2 pm, and 5:30 pm to 8:30 pm, Monday to Saturday. Serving sandwiches, hamburgers, and fried dishes, as well as local fish, chicken, and conch. Good homemade pies and cake too. Closed Wednesdays and Sundays. Barbecue nights on Fridays and Saturdays, when it might be a good idea to make a reservation.

REGATTA

July
Regatta Time in Abaco is during the first week in July. Races form up at Green Turtle Cay, Guana Cay, Hope Town, Man-O-War, and Marsh Harbour. Contact Dave or Kathy Ralph, Marsh Harbour, Abaco, Bahamas. Tel: 242-367-2677 • Fax: 367-3677.

ACCOMMODATIONS

Schooner's Landing Resort Tel: 242-365-6072 • Fax: 365-6285 Daily rates from $150, weekly from $850. Four two-bedroom, two-bathroom units with air conditioning on a white sand beach, with a tennis court nearby.

THINGS TO DO IN MAN-O-WAR CAY

- Have your boat repairs expertly and efficiently carried out.
- Stroll through town; go for a swim off the North Beach.
- Visit the *Sail Shop* and watch how beautifully the Albury family make their canvas bags. You could always make a start on your Christmas list?
- Dine in air-conditioned comfort at the new *Hibiscus Café*.
- Reprovision with groceries and baked goods
- Relax and enjoy this picturesque and hospitable island, where time stands still.
- Make new friends at the social hour on Thursdays at 6 pm at the Gazebo. Take munchies to share, and a beverage of your choice.

ELBOW CAY & HOPE TOWN

With the famous red-and-white-striped lighthouse beckoning you into its sheltered harbor on Elbow Cay, Hope Town can justifiably claim to be the Jewel of Abaco, and the dream come true for every cruising boat. It is picturesque and has some of the best facilities in the Abaco Cays, combined with a proximity to Marsh Harbour that provides good communications and ensures well-stocked stores and excellent restaurants. The village atmosphere with wooden houses painted the colors of Neapolitan ice cream, the glorious long beach with a safe reef to snorkel within easy reach of swimmers, and all the fishing and diving to enjoy in the surrounding waters will make you wish you could stay forever.

MARINAS IN HOPE TOWN HARBOUR

(As they appear on your starboard side, entering the harbor)

LIGHTHOUSE MARINA
Tel: 242-366-0154 • Fax: 366-0171 • VHF 16 •
E-mail: Lighthse@batelnet
Your welcome at the *Lighthouse Marina* by Craig and Linda Knowles will set the tone of your visit to Hope Town. Nothing is too much trouble for these two. You come in to this marina first on your starboard side, beneath the famous Hope Town Lighthouse. It has the only fuel dock in town, a well-stocked marina store, a laundry, charters and accommodations, and its own boat yard.

Slips	5
Max LOA	55 ft.
MLW at Dock	6 ft.
Dockage	75¢ per foot per day with 50A power, 65¢ per foot per day with 30A power.
Long Term	Over 2 months with no power, 60¢ per ft.; with 50A power 65¢ per ft., with 30A power 55¢ per ft.
Fuel	Fuel dock open from 7:30 am to noon, and from 1 to 5 pm daily. Ice, lubricants, and oils on the dock. Credit cards accepted, with a 3 percent surcharge.
Water	15¢ per gallon, for filtered water.
Showers	$3, and very clean.

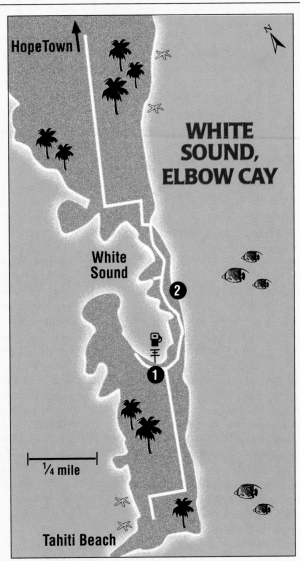

WHITE SOUND DIRECTORY

1. Sea Spray Resort and Marina
2. Abaco Inn
⛽ Fuel

Laundry	$3.50 per machine, tokens at the office.
Agency	Yamaha sales and service, with a Yamaha-trained mechanic on duty Monday to Friday.
Marina Store	Well stocked with fishing tackle and rod rentals, marine hardware, T-shirts, gifts, and souvenirs, many with a lighthouse motif.
Charters	*Sail Abaco* Tel: 366-0172 • VHF 16 • E-mail: charters@sailabaco.com Michael Houghton offers partial- or full-week charters, captained or bareboat, featuring PDQ catamarans.
Boat yard	Hauling and launching up to 25 ft. $1.25 per ft. one way; over 25 ft. $2 per ft. one way, maximum 9 tons. Dry storage up to 7 tons, $3 per ft. per month. Pressure cleaning up to 17 ft. $38, 18 to 30 ft. $50. Fiberglass repair $35 per hour. Carpentry and general repair, $35 per hour. Bottom painting, bright work: $20 per hour.
Accommodations	Apartment, cottage, and two very attractive houses available, well appointed and fully equipped, from $100 per night. Weekly rentals include use of a skiff. Ask Linda for details.
Credit Cards	Visa and MasterCard.
Dockmasters	Paul McDonald and Sam McPhee.

HOPE TOWN MARINA & CLUB SOLEIL RESORT
Tel: 242-366-0003 • Fax: 366-0254 • VHF 16

The second marina on your starboard side as you come into the harbor, *Hope Town Marina* is hard to miss with the pink and purple *Club Soleil Restaurant* behind it. Rudy Malone and his son Benji run both the marina and the resort. There is a pool at the hotel that is pleasant for marina and hotel guests; the restaurant no longer serves lunch but is open for breakfast and dinner and takes pride in its Sunday brunch.

Slips	12–14
Moorings	18 numbered red cylindrical buoys, marked **HT Marina** cost $10 per night. Call ahead.
Max LOA	Up to 125 ft.
MLW at Dock	6 ft.
Dockage	65¢ per foot per day.
Power	$8 per day for 30A, $15 per day for 50A.
Water	20¢ per gallon.
Telephone	Outside the restaurant.
Showers	$3 each. Key from the office.
Restaurant	*Club Soleil Restaurant,* open for breakfast, dinner, and Sunday brunch. Call ahead for reservations if possible.
Swimming	Pool available to marina guests.
Accommodations	*Club Soleil Resort* Six rooms and an apartment from $115 per night.
Credit cards	Visa and MasterCard.

HOPE TOWN HIDEAWAYS MARINA
Tel: 242-366-0224 • Fax: 366-0434 • VHF 16 and 63

The *Hideaway Villas* live up to their name, almost hidden among the lush plantings that run down to the pool and the marina. This is a pleasant, small marina on the edge of the harbor, and a good place to visit if you have friends who are more comfortable on land than on your boat.

Slips	12
Max LOA	Up to 60 ft.
MLW at Dock	4 to 5 ft.
Dockage	75¢ per foot per day.
Power	$12 per day for $30A, $17 per day for 50A.
Water	15¢ per gallon.
Swimming	Pool overlooking the marina.

HOPE TOWN DIRECTORY

1 Lighthouse Marina and Cottages
2 Hope Town Marina and Club Soleil
3 Hope Town Hideaways Marina and Villas
4 Sea Horse Marine
5 Abaco Bahamas Charters
6 School
7 Batelco
8 Hope Town Harbour Lodge
9 Wyannie Malone Museum
10 Public Dock
11 Post Office
12 Harbour's Edge
13 Harbour View Grocery; dinghy dock and propane
14 Captain Jack's Restaurant
15 Hope Town Sailing Club and dinghy dock
16 Public dock
17 Dave's Dive Shop and Boat Rentals
18 Bank
19 Vernon's Grocery
20 Hope Town Fire Station
⛽ Fuel
✚ Clinic

Accommodations	*Hope Town Hideaway Villas*, from $190 per night.
Dockmaster	Francis Joseph
Owners	Peggy and Chris Thompson.

MARINA IN WHITE SOUND

SEA SPRAY RESORT, VILLAS AND MARINA
Tel: 242-366-0065/0359 • Fax: 366-0383 • VHF 16

Only a few minutes from Tahiti Beach, within steps of the surf off Garbonzo Beach, and three-and-a-half miles from Hope Town (with complimentary transport to town), this marina enables you to enjoy everything that Elbow Cay has to offer, without being in the sometimes-crowded Hope Town harbor. With an excellent restaurant and good shoreside accommodations in pleasant villas, *Sea Spray* has become a resort in its own right.

Slips	60
Max LOA	84 ft.
MLW at Dock	6 ft.
Dockage	85¢ per foot per day.
Power	$12 per kWh for 30A, $20 per kWh for 50A.
Fuel	Diesel and gasoline. Open from 8 am to 5 pm daily.
Water	20¢ per gallon, metered.
Showers	$3 each, next to the office.
Laundry	$10 per load.
Restaurant	*The Boat House Restaurant* is open for breakfast, lunch, and dinner daily, under Patrick's direction, serving some of the best food on Elbow Cay. Alfresco dining by the pool, and open air *Garbonzo Bar* with a daily happy hour from 5 to 6 pm.
Ice	$4 per 10-lb. bag.
Swimming	A well-fenced pool, good for children; beaches within walking distance.
Catering	Available to your boat or villa.
Bakery	*Belle's Oven*
Bicycles	$10 per day.
Surfing	Garbonzo Beach has fabulous surfing and is only a short walk away.
Boat Rental	20-ft. Sea Spray for $90 per day, and a 22-ft. Sea Spray for $105 per day.
Fishing	Deep sea fishing for one to four people: $320 per half day, $500 per full day; reef and bonefishing $100 in your boat. Bait available.
Snorkeling	Rental equipment $7.50 per day.
Transfers	Complimentary shuttle to and from town.
Boat Storage	35¢ and 45¢ per foot per day.
Maintenance	$50 per hour.
Accommodations	*Sea Spray* villas from $910 weekly.
Credit cards	Visa and MasterCard.
Dockmaster	Junior Mernard
Owners	Monty and Ruth Albury

SERVICES IN HOPE TOWN

Bank
CIBC on Fig Tree Lane   Tel: 367-0296   Open 10 am to 2 pm Tuesdays, and 10 am to 1 pm on Fridays.

Churches
Assembly of God on Cemetery Road   Sunday service at 11 am.
Catholic Church Sunday Mass at 12 pm.
St. James Methodist Church on Back Street   Sunday service at 11 am.

Clinic
Tel: 366-0108   Nurse Forbes is at the clinic from 9 am to 5 pm daily, in the long, low building adjacent to the post office building, at the head of the town dock.

Dinghy Docks
You are welcome to tie up at the *Hope Town Sailing Club* dock during the day if you are under 24 feet, and tie away from the ladders. If you are shopping for groceries, you can tie up at the *Harbour View Grocery* dock. If you are going to the *Hopetown Harbour Lodge* for a meal, you can throw out a stern anchor from your dinghy and tie up to their dock. Many of the docks in the harbor are private. Don't tie up at the ferry docks!

Faxes
You can send faxes from *Malone Estates* on Back Street. They can also help you with rental accommodations.

Laundry
Suds Ahoy Laundromat   Tel: 366-0100/0060   Open 9 am to 4 pm, Monday through Saturday except Wednesday. Closed 1 to 2 pm. If closed, go into *Malone Estates* next door. Clothes can be washed, dried, and folded for $2 per lb.

Library
Open in the Jarrett Park Playground, next to the Government Dock from 10 am to noon on Thursdays, some weekdays after school, and frequently on Saturdays.

Moorings
Hope Town Marina VHF 16   Has 18 numbered red cylindrical buoys, marked HT Marina, $10 per night. Call ahead to find out if there is one available.
Truman Major VHF 16 "Lucky Strike"   Has the green moorings in the harbor. Call him when you have picked one up, if you haven't reserved one ahead of time. $10 per night.
Abaco Yacht Charters VHF 16   Sometimes have a spare white and blue mooring you can pick up if they are not fully booked with their own boats.

Museum
Wyannie Malone Historical Museum Tel: 366-0086 • VHF 16 "Museum"   Opening times are dependent on the volunteers who help at the museum, mostly winter residents. Usually open between 10:30 am and 12:30 pm on Monday, Wednesday, and Friday during the winter months. There is a $1 admission charge.

Police
In the same building as the post office.

Post Office
Open from 9 am to noon, and 1 to 5 pm Monday to Friday, upstairs in the green building at the head of the Government Dock.

Public Restrooms
To the right of the green post office and administration building at the Town Dock.

Telephones
One on the porch of the clinic at the Town Dock, one across from *Vernon's Grocery,* one on the deck of the *Club Soleil,* and a card phone outside the *Batelco* office up the hill beyond the *Hope Town Harbour Lodge.* The Batelco office cannot help you with E-mail at time of writing, but can receive and send faxes for you at 242-366-0000.

Travel Agent
A and W Travel Service   Tel: 366-0100

SHOPPING IN HOPE TOWN

Clothing, Gifts, & Souvenirs
Creative Native Studio Tel: 366-0309   Open from 10 am to 2 pm Monday to Friday, with hand-painted cards, paintings, and T-shirts. May be able to help you with surfing equipment.
Ebb Tide Gift Shop Tel: 366-0088   Open 9 am to 4:30 pm, Monday to Saturday
Edith's Straw Shop For hair braiding and straw work, open from 9 am to 6 pm Monday to Saturday.
El Mercado Gifts Tel: 366-0053   Open 9:30 am to 4:30 pm Monday to Saturday.

Fantasy Boutique Tel: 366-0537 Open for Cuban cigars and more from 9 am to 5 pm Monday to Saturday.

Iggy Biggy Boutique (formerly *Island Gallery*) Open 9:30 am to 5:30 pm Monday to Saturday.

Kemp's Gift Shop Tel: 366-0126 Open 10 am to 5 pm Monday to Saturday.

Water's Edge Studio Tel: 366-0143 Original native wildlife carving by Russ Ervin. Go in and talk with the artist as he works.

Fish Market

Lowe's Fish Market Tel: 366-0266 • VHF 16 "Seagull" In Nigh Creek, selling lobster tails, grouper, snapper, dolphin, tuna, wahoo, shark, and conch, as well as bait and block ice. This is also the home of *Seagull Deep Sea Charters* if you feel like going out with an expert guide to catch your own fish.

Groceries

Vernon's Grocery & Upper Crust Bakery Back Street Tel: 366-0037 • VHF 16 Open 8 am to 1 pm, and from 2 to 6 pm Monday to Friday, until 7 pm on Saturdays. Well stocked with fresh bread, pies and rolls, fresh fruit and vegetables, imported meats and cheeses, and all the news daily. If you want to be married on Elbow Cay, Vernon officiates at weddings too.

Harbour View Grocery Tel: 366-0033 With their own dinghy dock. Open 8 am to 1 pm and 2 pm to 6 pm, Monday to Friday; to 7 pm on Saturdays. A good selection of groceries, fresh vegetables and fruit, fresh bread, water, sodas, dairy, frozen foods, some pharmacy, propane, and batteries. Propane tanks fitted with a 10-percent valve can be filled here on the island; all others go to Marsh Harbour and may take 48 hours to return.

Hardware

Imports Unlimited Tel: 366-0136 Open from 8:30 am to 4:30 pm Monday to Friday, a short way out of town.

Liquor

Lighthouse Liquors Back Street Tel: 366-0100/0060/0567 • VHF 16 Open from 7 am to 9:30 pm Monday to Saturday, and from 11 am to 3 pm on Sundays.

Propane

Harbour View Grocery Tel: 366-0033 See under **Groceries**.

RESTAURANTS AND BARS ON ELBOW CAY

Abaco Inn at White Sound Tel: 366-0133 • VHF 16 Breakfast, lunch, and dinner is served in the dining room, or outside on their ocean-view terrace. Reservations required; complimentary transport available. They have their own dinghy dock.

Boat House Restaurant at *Sea Spray Resort* at White Sound Tel: 366-0065 • VHF 16 The restaurant is open daily for breakfast from 8 to 10 am, lunch from 11:30 am to 3 pm, and dinner from 6:30 to 9 pm. Complimentary transport available for dinner; reservations required. You can tie up at their dock. Chef Patrick, from Luxembourg originally, has revolutionized the restaurant, and now offers not only Bahamian barbecues on the deck every Monday night, but exciting salads and sandwiches for lunch daily, and superb, well-presented entrees for dinner. Live music on Wednesdays, and a happy hour from 5 to 10 pm on Thursday evenings at the *Garbonzo Bar*.

Captain Jack's overlooking the harbor Tel: 366-0247 • VHF 16 Breakfast 8:30 to 10 am, lunch from 11 am, happy hour 4:30 to 6:30 pm, and dinner until 9 pm. Casual atmosphere with live music on Wednesdays and Fridays, and satellite sports TV. Ice for sale. Visa and MasterCard accepted.

Club Soleil Resort at *Hope Town Marina* Tel: 366-0003 • VHF 16 Breakfast 8 to 10 am, dinner 6:30 to 9 pm. Reservations requested for brunch and dinner. Main entrees from $19, preceded by soup of the day and a salad. Sunday brunch served from 11:30 am to 1:30 pm with roast beef, smoked salmon, fresh fish, and ten different salads for $22.

Harbour's Edge on the waterfront Tel: 366-0292/0087 • VHF 16 Bar opens daily at 10 am. Lunch 11:30 to 3, dinner 6 to 9 pm. Happy hour 5 to 6 pm, appetizers served all day. Pizza and live music on Saturday nights; closed Tuesdays. Ice for sale, bicycle rental, pool table, and sports TV. Noisy and fun.

Hope Town Harbour Lodge Tel: 366-0095 • VHF 16 Breakfast daily 8 to 10 am. Lunch and happy hour by the pool at the *Reef Bar*. Dinner 6:30 to 9 pm, Tuesday to Saturday. Dinner reservations are appreciated. Their popular Sunday brunch by the pool offers Eggs Benedict.

Hollywood Temptations at *Malone Estates* on Back Street, next to *Lighthouse Liquors* Open from 7 am to 9:30 pm, Monday to Saturday, and from 11 am to 3 pm on Sundays, for deli sandwiches, cheeses, snacks, cookies, and Edy's ice cream.

Rudy's Place Tel: 366-0062 • VHF 16 Fine dining, open for dinner only, Monday to Saturday from 6:30 pm to 9 pm. A short way out of Hope Town, they offer complimentary transport. Reservations requested.

Munchies Tel: 366-0423 On Back Street, next to *Kemp's Gift Shop* and opposite *Vernon's Grocery*. Open daily from 11 am to 10 pm, with limited seating, but take-away service. Snacks, sandwiches, pizza, and ice cream.

RESTAURANTS ON LUBBERS QUARTERS

Cracker P's Patrick and Linda Stewart opened this new reastaurant with a floating dock and two moorings, for lunches only, at the end of 1999. They will specialize in smoked and grilled chicken and fish, with a volleyball court and playground for children; pets will be welcome.

Yahoes Sand Bar Tel: 366-3110 • VHF 16 "Yahoes" Open daily except Mondays, on the southeast shore of Lubbers Quarters, for lunch from 11 am, and for dinner by reservation. Daily fresh fish, which usually includes wahoo, mahi mahi, or blue crab, as well as lobster, grouper, conch, chicken, and a variety of burgers in paradise. Dinghy dock, and sandy beach only ten minutes from Hope Town. You can hear *Yahoes* on the Boaters' Net from Marsh Harbour in the morning.

GETTING AROUND

Bicycles

The Bike Shop at *Harbour's Edge* Tel: 366-0292/0087 Bicycles to rent for $8 a day.

Hope Town Harbour Lodge Tel: 366-0095

Boat Rental

Club Soleil Boat Rental Tel: 366-0003 • VHF 16 22-ft. Scandia $80 daily; 19-ft. Mako $70 daily

Dave's Dive Shop and Boat Rentals Tel: 366-0029 • Fax: 366-0420 • VHF 16 17-ft. Boston Whaler $80 daily; 22-ft. Paramount $100 daily; 20-ft. Privateer $90 daily. Complimentary delivery service to Hope Town, Marsh Harbour, or Man-O-War Cay. Pam and Dave Malone also offer dive and snorkeling trips and scuba rental equipment. Visa and MasterCard accepted.

Island Marine Boat Rentals Tel: 366-0282 • Fax: 366-0281 • VHF 16 Jeff, Dave, Phoebe, and Lory Gale have the largest fleet in the Bahamas, and offer complimentary delivery service to your house, hotel, or yacht in Hope Town, Elbow Cay, Marsh Harbour, or Man-O-War Cay. 17-ft. Boston Whaler $80 daily; 20-ft. Aquasport $95 per day; 20-ft. Albury $100 per day; and 22-ft. Aquasports $105 per day, all available for daily, three-day, or weekly rental. All boats are fully equipped with life jackets, anchor, lines, swim ladder, cushions, oars, cooler, compass, rod holders, and a large built-in gas tank. Visa and MasterCard accepted; deposit required on reservation.

Sea Horse Boat Rentals Tel: 366-0023 • Fax: 366-0189 • VHF 16 18-ft. Boston Whaler $95 per day; 18-ft. Privateer $85 per day; 19-ft. Hydra Sports $100 per day; 20-ft. Albury $105 per day; 22-ft.

Privateer $110 per day; 22-ft. Boston Whaler $125 per day; 24-ft. Privateer $140 per day. 25 boats available. Snorkeling gear and bicycles also available for $10 per day, and complimentary delivery of boats on request.

Hope Town.

Sea Spray Resort Boat Rental at White Sound   Tel: 366-0065 • Fax: 366-0383 • VHF 16   20-ft. Sea Spray $90 per day; 22-ft. Sea Spray $105 per day. Deep sea fishing $320 per half day, $500 per full day, for one to four people. Reef & bonefishing $100 in your boat for a half day, snorkeling equipment $7.50 per day.

Cart Rental
Golf carts are not allowed to drive through town.
*Hope Town Cart Rental*s   Tel: 366-0064
$35 per day, $210 per week, cash or traveler's checks.
Island Golf Carts   Tel: 366-0332 • VHF 16 $35 per day, $210 per week; Visa or MasterCard accepted, 50 percent reservation deposit required. Free delivery.

Ferries
Albury's Ferry   Tel: 367-3147 or 365-6010 • VHF 16   Daily ferries will pick you up from, or deliver you to, any dock in the harbor on request, or from White Sound. Fares collected on board.
Hope Town to Marsh Harbour at 8 am, 9:45 am, 11:30 am, 1:30 pm, 3 pm, 4 pm; also at 5 pm except Sundays and holidays. Ferries leave the Albury ferry dock at Crossing Beach. *Marsh Harbour to Hope Town at* 9 am, 10:30 am, 12:15 pm, 2 pm, 4 pm, 5:30 pm daily. Also at 7:15 am except on Sundays and holidays. One way $7, same day round trip $10. The journey takes 20 minutes, and is very punctual and reliable. The ferry from Marsh Harbour will drop you at any dock in the harbor on request, or in White Sound.

SPORTS

Diving
Dave's Dive Shop   Tel: 366-0029 • Fax: 366-0420 • VHF 16 Open from 8:30 am to 5 pm daily except Sundays. Pam and Dave Malone have daily dive and snorkel trips to Sandy and Fowl Cays. Two-tank dive $65, snorkelers $30. Scuba rental equipment available with their boats.
Froggies Out Island Adventure, next to the town dock Tel: 365-6494 • VHF 16   Half-day scuba trips with a PADI instructor, $50 for a two-tank dive, including tanks and weights. Half-day snorkel trips with gear provided, $35 per person. All-day trips go to Fowl Cay and Sandy Cay. *Froggies* also run trips to Guana Cay for drinks and lunch at *Nippers* for $45, and to Little Harbour for drinks and lunch at *Pete's Pub* for $45. Both trips include snorkeling stops and beach walks, but exclude the cost of lunch.

Fishing Boat Charters
Dave Malone of *Dave's Dive Shop*   Tel: 366-0029 • VHF 16 "Hope Town Dive Shop"   Takes out fishing trips on request in his 23-ft. boat.
Day's Catch Charters   Tel: 366-0059 • VHF 16 "Fox Chase"   Will Key, a licensed captain and guide, can take up to four people in his fully equipped 21-ft. Offshore, for reef, deep sea, or bonefishing, for $300 for a full day, or for $200 in your own or rented boat.
Lucky Strike   Tel: 366-0101 • VHF 16 "Lucky Strike"   Truman Major has a 30-ft. air-conditioned Sea Hawk, and will supply all bait, tackle, and ice for all types of fishing except bonefishing.

Rudy Malone at *Club Soleil and Hope Town Marina*   Tel: 366-0003 Can sometimes be persuaded to leave the *Club Soleil,* and share his love of fishing as a guide, using his own boat.
Seagull Deep Sea Charters at *Lowe's Fish Market*   Tel: 366-0266 • VHF 16 "Seagull"   Robert Lowe has over 30 years experience deep-sea trolling for billfish, dolphin, wahoo, and tuna, and can take up to six people in his 31-ft. Stapleton for a half day at $300 or a full day for $500.
Wild Pigeon Charters   Tel: 366-0234 • VHF 16   Maitland Lowe, aka Bonefish Dundee. Bonefishing, reef fishing, and bottom fishing $190 half-day, or $280 full-day charter in Mait's boat. $125 half day, or $200 full-day charter in your boat.

Fishing Tackle
Lighthouse Marina Store   Tel: 366-0154   Carries a good selection.

Sail Boat Charters
Abaco Bahamas Charters in Back Creek   Tel: 800-626-5690 in the US • VHF 16 in Abaco   Bareboat sailing yachts, with their own moorings in Hope Town harbor.
Sail Abaco at the *Lighthouse Marina*   Tel: 242-366-0172 • VHF 16 • E-mail: charters@sailabaco.com   PDQ Canadian catamarans, half-day sailing $200 for one to six people, full-day sailing with a captain, $300 for one to six people, includes snacks, light lunch, and beverages. Snorkeling gear for rent. Weekly charters available. Ask Mike Houghton, the manager, for details.

REGATTAS AND FISHING TOURNAMENTS

April
Abaco Anglers Fishing Tournament. The killing of billfish, sharks, and bonefish is prohibited. Trophies are awarded at *Sea Spray Resort and Marina.*

July
Regatta Time in Abaco is held during the first week in July. Races form at Green Turtle Cay, Guana Cay, Hope Town, Man-O-War and Marsh Harbour. Contact Dave or Kathy Ralph, Marsh Harbour, Abaco, Bahamas. Tel: 242-367-2677 • Fax: 367-3677
Independent Billfish Tournament is held at the *Sea Spray Resort and Marina* over the 4th of July weekend. Contact Monty Albury at 242-366-0065 for details of the tournaments.

ACCOMMODATIONS

Abaco Inn at White Sound   Tel: 242-366-0133 • Fax: 366-0113 • E-mail: abacoinn@batelnet.bs   22 rooms, including 8 new harborside rooms and 6 new oceanside rooms with patio and hammock, from $100 per night. With their own restaurant overlooking the beach, swimming pool, complimentary snorkeling gear, bicycles, transportation to town, rental boat dockage, and water sports.
Club Soleil Resort   Tel: 242-366-0003 • Fax: 366-0254 • VHF 16 Rooms from $115 per night and an apartment. Restaurant and bar, marina, swimming pool.
Hope Town Harbour Lodge   Tel: 242-366-0095 • Fax: 366-0286 • E-mail: harbourlodge@batelnet.bs • Web site: www.hopetownlodge.com   Single rooms from $110 per night with a harbor view, ocean-front from $130, $10 more for double occupancy or extra person. *Butterfly House* from $1,250 a week for four people, $50 each extra person per week, maximum six people. Two restaurants and bars, fabulous beach with snorkeling on the reef, swimming pool, bicycles to rent.
Hope Town Hideaways   Tel: 242-366-0224 • Fax: 366-0434 With their own 12-berth marina, and villas set in tropical gardens, $1,150 per week for two-bedroom villas for two people in high season. The villas are close to the marina, with its gazebo and swimming pool. Chris and Peggy Thompson

also handle rental accommodation all over Elbow Cay, and can help you with real estate.

Hope Town Villas Tel: 242-366-0030 Charmingly renovated 19th-century houses in town, from $150 per night for up to four people.

Lighthouse Marina Tel: 242-366-0154 • Fax: 366-0171 • VHF 16 Very attractive, secluded houses overlooking the harbor or the Sound, grouped around the Lighthouse Marina. Abaco Sound guest cottage from $1,100 weekly for two people, Abaco Sound house from $1,500 weekly for four people, Lighthouse Point house from $1,500 weekly for six people, Harbour apartment from $1,000 weekly for four people. All rentals include a 13-ft. or 16-ft. skiff with outboard motor. Reservations can be made through Craig and Linda Knowles at the marina.

Malone Estates Tel: 242-366-0100 • Fax: 366-0157 Vacation cottages and homes to rent.

Sea Spray Villas at White Sound Tel: 242-366-0065 • Fax: 366-0383 One-bedroom villas, harbor side from $910 per week, two-bedroom villas ocean side from $1,500 per week. Swimming pool, marina, boat rentals, clubhouse with cable TV, restaurant, yacht catering, free transport to and from Hope Town.

Turtle Hill Vacation Villas Tel and fax: 242-366-0557 Four new vacation villas to sleep four, with swimming pool, private beach access, and golf carts; from $260 per night, $1,500 per week.

THINGS TO DO IN ELBOW CAY

- Visit the much-photographed, candy-striped lighthouse. Built in 1864, there are 101 steps to the top. It is well worth the climb, not only to learn how the lighthouse works, with the unusual Fresnel lenses, but also to admire the stunning views over the harbor and neighboring islands.

- Swim and snorkel off the fabulous long beach running down the east side of Elbow Cay, or take your dinghy down to Tahiti Beach.

- Troll for sailfish, marlin, tuna, cobia, wahoo, and mackerel less than a mile offshore, or go bonefishing on the Tilloo Cay flats.

- Explore the town and admire the pastel-painted homes surrounded by colorful flower gardens.

- Take a trip over to Lubbers Quarters and enjoy island cuisine and native music as you sip tropical drinks and indulge in a festive lunch at *Yahoes,* overlooking Tahiti Beach and Tilloo Cut.

- Visit the *Wyannie Malone Museum* one morning to learn more about the history of this delightful town.

- Succumb to temptation at *Iggy Biggy's* and take home a memento of a happy visit.

- Indulge in Sunday Brunch at the *Hope Town Harbour Lodge* or the *Club Soleil.*

- Dive Johnnie's Cay reef, Fowl Cay reef, and Sandy Cay reef. Sandy Cay is part of the *Pelican Cay Land and Sea Park,* and Fowl Cay is part of the *Fowl Cay Bahamas National Trust Preserve.* Do not take any shells or coral from them, and fishing is absolutely prohibited. You can pick up one of the moorings at Sandy Cay, as the holding is not good there. There are also a few moorings at Fowl Cay. The reef buoys are intended only for boats less than 25 feet. Don't ever anchor on any reef, you could damage the coral.

MARSH HARBOUR

Not only the very heart of Great Abaco Island, but the center of commerce and trade for the Abaco Islands too, Marsh Harbour is the third-largest town in the Bahamas with a good road leading north and south to the rest of the island, and an international airport to town. It is perfectly suited to cruising boats needing stores or spare parts, with a wide choice of marinas, good shopping and medical facilities, as well as frequent ferry communications to the smaller cays and settlements in Abaco. Marsh Harbour is a Port of Entry, with **Customs** and **Immigration** on the south side of the main harbor. The customs dock is clearly marked with large pilings, and the customs office is in the building east of the dock. Customs can be called for you on arrival at your marina. Don't anchor in the channel or the approach to the channel of the Marsh Harbour public freight dock, as the freight boats cannot maneuver around anchored boats. Anchor east of the channel marker pilings.

MARINAS IN MARSH HARBOUR

As you enter, to starboard:
ADMIRAL'S YACHT HAVEN
Tel: 242-367-4242 • VHF 16
A quiet marina, west of the customs dock, with few facilities but a *Pizza Hut* overlooking the marina, and a 10-minute walk into town. Owner and dockmaster Silbert Mills reads the weather on Radio Abaco (93.5 FM) at 8 am daily. VHF 16 is only monitored occasionally, and there is no fuel dock here.

Slips	26
MLW at Dock	6 ft.
Power	36¢ per kWh for 30A and 50A.
Water	Yes
Showers	Yes, two
Restaurant	*Abaco Pizza Hut.*
Ice	Available from the restaurant.
Accommodations	Two villas, each with two bedrooms and two bathrooms at *Admiralty Court Villas.*

To port:
MARSH HARBOUR MARINA
Tel: 242-367-2700 • Fax: 367-2033 • VHF 16
This older marina, on the north side of the harbor, is under new management, but retains its original charm and peaceful atmosphere, with a feeling of being slightly away from the rest of the busy world of Marsh Harbour. The *Jib Room Restaurant* has been redecorated and still offers the outstanding Steak Barbecue on Sunday nights and Pork Rib Barbecue on Wednesday nights, with music and dancing. Many boats take advantage of the long-term dockage here, and there are plans to extend the docks. Make time to snorkel the famous Mermaid Reef, right across the road from the marina.

Slips	52
Max LOA	70 ft.
MLW at Dock	6 ft.
Dockage	60¢ per foot per day, 45¢ per foot per day with a Boat US discount.
Long Term	35¢ per ft. for the first 3 months, 28¢ per ft. after 3 months.
Power	34¢ per kWh.
Fuel	Diesel and gasoline. Fuel dock opens from 9 am to 6 pm daily, except closed on Tuesdays, and open from 11 am to 6 pm Sundays.
Propane	From *Corner Value* on Queen Elizabeth Drive
Water	$10 to docked boats.

(Photo credit, vertical text: Janet Wilson)

Telephone	Yes
Showers	$2 each for non-marina guests.
Laundry	$2.50 for washer or dryer.
Restaurant	*The Jib Room Bar & Restaurant* Open daily for lunch and dinner, with live music and barbecue on Wednesdays and Sundays.
Ice	$3.50 per bag.
Snorkeling	A five-minute walk to the beach to snorkel Mermaid's Reef.
Credit Cards	Visa and MasterCard with a 4-percent surcharge.
Dockmaster	Jason Davis

To starboard:

TRIPLE J MARINA
Tel: 242-367-2163 (store)/2287 (dock) • Fax: 367-3388
• VHF 16

This small marina, with simple facilities, has a well-stocked *Boaters' Boutique* and marine electronic repairs, with a laundry behind the store. *Flipper's Restaurant* (Tel: 367-4657) is open across the street from 8 am to 9:30 pm, serving local dishes and cosmopolitan cuisine.

Slips	26
Max LOA	55 ft.
MLW at Dock	5 ft.
Dockage	40¢ per foot per day, 35¢ per foot weekly.
Power	35¢ per kWh, 30A and 50A available.
Fuel	Diesel and gasoline. Fuel dock open from 8 am to 5 pm Monday to Friday, to noon on Saturday and Sunday.
Propane	From *Corner Value* on Queen Elizabeth Drive.
Water	$5 per stay, or per month.
Showers	Yes, for marina guests only.
Laundry	Behind the marine store, $3 tokens.
Ice	$3 per bag.
Electronics	*Pat* is an electronic wizard, fully trained by

	ICOM. Furuno, Garmin, and Simrad repairs, sales, and service available.
Marine Store	Open from 8 am to 5 pm Monday to Friday, to noon on Saturdays. Fishing tackle, dive gear, Androsia fabric, jewelry and gifts, electronic parts and repairs, and a book exchange.
Credit Cards	Visa and MasterCard, with a 5-percent surcharge.
Dockmaster	Martin Albury

To starboard:

HARBOUR VIEW MARINA
Tel and fax: 242-367-2182 • VHF 16

A very helpful and friendly marina, close to the amenities in town, with the *Tiki Hut, Sapodilly's,* and *Wally's* restaurants nearby and everything else within easy walking distance.

Slips	36
Max LOA	60 ft.
MLW at Dock	6 ft.
Dockage	40¢ per foot per day
Power	$7 per day for 30A, $14 for 50A
Fuel	Diesel and gasoline. Fuel dock open from 8 am to 5 pm daily.
Propane	From *Corner Value* on Queen Elizabeth Drive.
Water	10¢ per gallon.
Telephone	*Batelco* card phone on the street by the marina.
TV	Cable hookup, $2.
Showers	Free to marina guests, $2 each for visitors.
Laundry	Open from 8 am to 5 pm; $2 per load in tokens to wash or to dry.
Ice	$3 per bag.
Boat Rental	*Blue Wave Boat Rentals* Tel: 367-3910 • VHF 16 12-ft. Duskys and 26-ft. Paramounts to rent.

MARSH HARBOUR DIRECTORY

1. Marsh Harbour Marina and Jib Room
2. Conch Inn Marina and Dive Abaco
3. Mangoes Marina and Restaurant
4. Harbour View Marina and Blue Wave Boat Rentals
5. Triple J Marina and Boaters' Boutique
6. Admiral's Yacht Haven, Pizza Hut
7. Boat Harbour Marina and Abaco Beach Resort
8. Albury's Ferries
9. Doctors' Office
10. Abaco Markets (being rebuilt)
11. Post Office
12. Barclays Bank
13. Corner Value for propane
14. Tourist Office
15. Government Dock and Customs House
16. Master Marine
17. Rainbow Rentals
18. Wally's Restaurant
19. Sapodilly's Restaurant
20. Lofty Fig Villas
21. Rich's Rentals and The Outboard Shop
⛽ Fuel

Straw Market	Sets up next to the marina.
Teak Cleaning	*Frank* Tel: 367-2182 • VHF 16 Will re-varnish or clean teak for you.
Book exchange	In the marina office.
Credit Cards	Visa and MasterCard, with a 5-percent surcharge.
Dockmaster	Barbara Bethell

To starboard:

MANGOES MARINA
Tel: 242-367-4255 • Fax: 367-3336

A particularly pleasant marina, with well-landscaped shore facilities, boutique and liquor store, an excellent restaurant, and beautifully clean showers. This marina now caters primarily to long-term boats. It might be worth calling ahead to see if they have a slip available. *Lofty Fig Villas*, (Tel and fax: 242-367-2681) have six villas from $115 per night, just across the street, if you need accommodations.

Slips	30
Max LOA	60 ft.
MLW at Dock	6 ft.
Dockage	65¢ per ft. per day, 40¢ per ft. monthly.
Power	35¢ per kWh, $3 per day minimum unless on monthly dockage.
Water	$3 per day, $20 per month.
Telephone	Direct dial telephone.
TV	Cable hookup, $2 per day.
Showers	Yes, very clean. For marina guests only.
Laundry	Yes, $2 for each machine.
Restaurant	*Mangoes Restaurant*, open for lunch and dinner, with outside terrace or inside air-conditioned dining. Serving snacks all day and a Caribbean night on Tuesdays. Complimentary dinghy dockage.
Bar	*Patio Bar*, with Hurricane Libby as the specialty drink.
Ice	$3.50 per bag.
Liquor Store	*John Bull*, open 9 am to 5 pm Monday to Saturday.
Swimming	A very pleasant small pool set into the new deck patio.
Barbecue	Grill available for use by marina guests.
Boutique	*Mangoes Boutique*, well stocked with island fashions and interesting gift ideas.
Credit Cards	Visa, MasterCard, and Amex.

To starboard:

CONCH INN MARINA
Tel: 242-367-4000 • Fax: 367-4004 • VHF 16 • VHF 82 (for charter boats)

The largest of the marinas in the main harbor, the *Conch Inn Marina* plays host to the *Moorings* fleet and *Dive Abaco*, as well as the *Albury Ferry* running to Great Guana Cay. This combined with people on vacation staying at the *Conch Inn* makes it busier than all the others. The facilities are much improved recently with the newly renovated restaurant and small grocery store; its proximity to town and the airport makes it popular with bareboat charterers as well as visiting cruising boats.

Slips	80
Max LOA	Up to 110 ft.
MLW at Dock	5 ft. to 7 ft.
Dockage	60¢ per foot per day.
Power	35¢ per kWh, 100A, 50A, and 30A available.
Fuel	Diesel and gasoline. Fuel dock open from 7:30 am to 6 pm.
Propane	From *Corner Value* on Queen Elizabeth Drive.
Water	$1.50 per day or $25 a month.
Telephone	Upstairs in the marina and hotel office.
TV	Cable hookup $2.50 daily, $30 per month.

Showers	Key from reception. $2 per shower for non-marina guests.
Laundry	$2 tokens per machine.
Restaurant	*Bistro Mezzomare* Tel: 367-4444 Open from 8 am to 10 pm for breakfast, lunch, and dinner.
Bar	*Cabana Bar*, a friendly meeting place overlooking the marina.
Gifts	*Iggy Biggy Boutique,* open from 9:30 am to 5 pm Monday to Saturday, across the street from the *Conch Inn Hotel.*
Groceries	*Bahamas Family Market* Tel: 367-2257 Newly opened at the marina, from 8 am to 5 pm daily, with fresh breads, gourmet cheeses, coffee, jellies, gift baskets, and special Jamaica hot patties.
Mail	Can be held at the hotel and marina office.
Swimming	Pool by the hotel.
Bareboat Charters	*The Moorings Bareboat Charters* Tel: 800-535-7289 or 813-535-1446 Beneteau Oceanis and Jeanneau Lagoons from $2,310 per week.
Diving	*Dive Abaco* Tel: 367-2787 • VHF 16 Dive shop and daily dive trips; night dives. Two-tank dive $65, certification course $450, scuba introduction $125, snorkelers $35.
Rentals	Cars, scooters, and bicycles available.
Repairs	A *Moorings* technician may be able to help.
Sailboats	Charters from *The Moorings* in the marina.
Accommodations	*Conch Inn Hotel* Tel: 242-367-4000 Nine rooms from $90 per night.
Credit Cards	Visa and MasterCard.
Dockmaster	Nancy Russell

Marina facing Elbow Cay and the Sea of Abaco at Marsh Harbour:

BOAT HARBOUR MARINA
Tel: 242-367-2736 • Fax: 367-2819 • VHF 16

The largest of all the Marsh Harbour marinas, *Boat Harbour Marina,* a favorite with sports fishermen, offers full resort facilities as well as proximity to town, without being in the busy main harbor. It has the added advantage of being closer to Elbow Cay, if you are headed to Hope Town or White Sound. There is considerable development and building going on in the area surrounding the *Abaco Beach Resort,* including many new private residences at the *Great Abaco Club.*

Slips	180
Max LOA	Up to 200 ft.
MLW at Dock	10 ft.
Dockage	$1.50 per ft. per day.
Power	30A $10 per day, 50A $17.50.
Fuel	Diesel and gasoline.
Propane	Same-day refill.
Water	10¢ per gallon or daily rates.
Telephone	Complimentary hookup. 50¢ service charge for local calls, $2.50 for long distance. Four phone card and direct dial telephones by the showers.
TV	$5 per day for cable hookup.
Showers	Yes
Laundry	$3 for each machine.
Restaurant	*Anglers Restaurant* Open from 7:30 am for breakfast, lunch, and dinner, overlooking the waterfront.
Bar	*Sand Bar* with a swim-up Tiki bar
Groceries	*Boat Harbour Mini Mart* Tel: 367-4711 Open 8 am to 6 pm Monday to Saturday; to 10 am on Sundays. Well stocked, and very convenient.
Liquor	*Central Liquors* Tel: 367-2887 Open from 9 am to 6 pm Monday to Saturday.

Gifts	*T-zers Gift Shop* Open from 9 am to 5 pm next to the restaurant.
Diving	*Abaco Dive Centre* Tel: 367-4646 Dive trips, equipment rental, and charters. Two-tank dive from $70, full scuba course $450.
Tennis	Courts are available.
Swimming	Pools at the hotel and marina.
Golf	Can be arranged.
Bareboat Charters	*Florida Yacht Charters* Tel: 242-367-4853 Sailboats from $1,650 per week, catamarans from $2,310 per week, and motor yachts from $3,050 per week.
Rentals	*Sea Horse Rentals* Tel: 367-2513 Fleet of 25 boats, including Boston Whalers & Privateers from $95 pr day. Bicycles and snorkeling gear.
Shopping	*Solomon's Mines* and *Boat Harbour Marina Shop*, near the *Abaco Beach Resort* entrance, open from 9 am to 5:30 pm Monday to Saturday. *The Sand Dollar Shoppe* at *Royal Harbour Village*, across from the entrance, with gifts and Abaco Gold, locally hand-made jewelry, as well as *Tropical Treasures and Treats* selling ice cream, johnny cakes, and conch fritters along with local art, T-shirts, and Cuban cigars.
Accommodations	*Abaco Beach Resort* Tel: 242-367-2158 Rooms, villas, and the Grand Villa from $145 per night.
Credit Cards	Visa, MasterCard, Amex, and Discover.
Dockmaster	Cecil Ingraham

BOAT HARBOUR MARINA DIRECTORY

1. Entrance to Great Abaco Club homes only, not Boat Harbour Marina
2. Abaco Dive Centre
3. Florida Yacht Charters
4. Mini Mart and Liquor Store
5. Marina Office and Dockmaster
6. Showers
7. Tennis Courts
8. Shopping
9. Laundry
10. Sea Horse Rentals
11. Abaco Beach Resort
12. Anglers Restaurant and swimming pool
⛽ Fuel

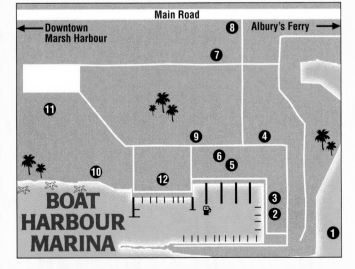

MARINE SERVICES

Cruiser's Net in Marsh Harbour VHF 68 at 8:15 am daily Radio Abaco FM 93.5 weather reports at 8 am, 1 pm, and 6 pm

Abaco Distributors Tel: 367-2265 • VHF 72 "Abaco Stereo" Marine and personal electronics, service, sales, installation.

Abaco Marine Props on Don MacKay Boulevard, beside *Western Auto* Tel: 367-4276 Recondition or re-hub propellers, aluminium, brass, or stainless, welding and sandblasting.

Abaco Outboard Engines half a mile west of the traffic light Tel: 367-2452 • Fax: 367-2354 Yamaha agents, repairs, mobile service, boat hauling up to 30 ft. or 8 tons, marine store, tackle shop. Dry storage, pressure cleaning, and repairs. Fuel, water, ice, and laundry.

Asterix for Diesels Tel: 367-3166 Gensets, marine, electrical troubleshooting.

B & D Marine Tel: 367-2622 • VHF 16 Open from 8 am to 5 pm Monday to Friday, to noon on Saturdays. A well-stocked marine store. Suzuki distributor, generators, marine hardware and supplies, fishing tackle, dive gear.

CJ's Welding on the waterfront at the end of the Key Club Road Tel: 367-4011 Marine items, boat T-tops, fuel, and water tanks.

Master Marine and Cycle on Front Street Tel: 367-4760 • VHF 16 Terrence Roberts and Richard Tigwell have a good selection of Suzuki outboards and Honda motorcycles, but they are also four-stroke outboard specialists, and can offer Yamaha outboard engine rebuilding and tuning, cylinder boring and honing, and can provide mobile service to north and south Abaco cays. Can help you with pumps, alternators, etc.

National Marine at Abaco Shopping Centre Tel: 367-2326 Mercury & Mariner outboard sales, service, marine accessories. Open from 7:30 am to 4:30 pm Monday to Friday.

The Outboard Shop next to *Rich's Rentals* Tel: 367-2703 • VHF 16 Evinrude motors and parts with factory-trained mechanics.

Sea Tow Abaco Tel: 242-365-4649/4226/4338 or 362-1236 • VHF 16 Stafford Morrison is Salvage Master for *Sea Tow Abaco* from Marsh Harbour, and can help with wreck removal, Caribbean deliveries, bottom cleaning, or propellers that need pulling, as well as towing from anywhere from Hole-in-the-Wall to Nassau and back to Florida if necessary.

SERVICES

Ambulance
Trauma One Tel: 367-4082 • VHF 16 or 80 • In emergency, page 367-7243-2911 There is no charge for this emergency service, though contributions are welcomed to ensure the future of this swift and professional rescue organization that operates seven ambulances throughout Abaco, the latest one based at Sandy Point.

Banks
Most banks are on or near Don Mackay Boulevard, and open from 9:30 am to 3 pm Monday to Thursday; to 5 pm Fridays.
Barclays Bank Tel: 367-2152/2153/2154
CIBC Tel: 367-2166
Commonwealth Bank Tel: 367-2370
Bank of Nova Scotia Tel: 367-2142
Royal Bank of Canada Tel: 367-2420/2421

Churches
Aldersgate Methodist Church Sunday service at 9 am.
Church of Christ Services at 11 am and 7 pm on Sundays.
Presbyterian Church of Abaco Services at 9 am on Sundays.
St. John the Baptist Anglican/Episcopalian Church Mass at 11 am on Sundays, other services during the week.
St. Francis de Sales Catholic Mission on Don Mackay Blvd Sunday Mass at 9 am.

Cinema

RND Cinemas Abaco 3 Tel: 367-4383

Clinic

Marsh Harbour Government Clinic on Don Mackay Boulevard, out toward the airport Tel: 367-2867 • Fax: 367-4470 In emergency call 367-2510. This is the largest and most comprehensive government clinic in the Abaco islands, with an X-ray, pharmacy, Trauma One ambulance, and two 2-bed wards. They are hoping the clinic will be rebuilt within the next two years. For Dr Ameeral, you can call 367-4880, or the nursing officer-in-charge, Nurse Cooper, at 367-3848. Clinic hours are from 9 am to 5 pm, Monday to Friday with Nurses Russell, Cooper, Joseph, Ferguson, and Mills to look after you.

Couriers

Fedex at *Travelspot* at the *Memorial Plaza*, Don Mackay Blvd.
UPS at the *Abaco Shopping Centre*, Don Mackay Blvd.
Tel: 367-2722

Customs

Tel: 367-2522/2525 At the customs house by the Government Dock; and

Immigration

Tel: 367-2536/2675

Dentists

Greater Abaco Dental Clinic Tel: 367-4070
Dr J. Denise Archer at the *Diamante Dental Centre*, Queen Elizabeth Drive Tel: 367-4968 Open from 9 am to 5 pm, Monday to Friday, and to 1 pm on Saturdays.
Dr Teresa Barnaby at the *Agape Family Dental Centre* Tel: 367-4355

Doctors

Dr Mark Binard and *Dr Frank Boyce MD,* at *Abaco Family Medicine* Tel: 367-2295/3028 An excellent medical center with a very helpful staff. Dr Boyce is much respected throughout the Abaco islands, and his partner, Dr Binard, has the added advantage of speaking Creole, Flemish, French, and German.
Dr Elaine Lundy, at the *Abaco Medical Centre* Tel: 367-4240/3933 In emergency call 367-3159.

Library

Marsh Harbour Community Library, off Don MacKay Blvd.
Tel: 367-2243 Open from 3:30 pm to 6:30 pm Monday to Friday, 9 am to noon on Saturday.

Police

Tel: 376-2560 or 367-2594

Post Office

Don Mackay Boulevard Tel: 367-2571 Open from 9 am to 5 pm, Monday to Friday.

Telephones

There are public telephones throughout Marsh Harbour.

Tourist Office

Tel: 367-3067 Wynsome Ferguson can help you with any questions about Marsh Harbour or the Abaco Islands. The office is open from 9 am to 5:30 pm Monday to Friday.

Travel Agent

A & W Travel at *Abaco Shopping Centre* Tel: 367-2806/2577 With agents at Hope Town, Man-O-War Cay, Treasure Cay, and Green Turtle Cay.
Travel Spot Memorial Plaza Tel: 367-2817

SHOPPING

Bakery

Flour House Bakery and Catering Service Tel: 367-4233 Open from 7 am to 5:30 pm, Monday to Saturday. A great variety of breads, cakes, pies, and pastries.

Drug Stores

Lowe's Pharmacy at *Lowe's Shopping Centre* Tel: 367-2667 With a wide selection of cosmetics, furniture, and household electrical goods.

Dry Cleaners

Vans Dry Cleaners Queen Elizabeth Drive Tel: 367-2275 Open from 8:30 am to noon and 1 pm to 4 pm, Monday to Friday; from 9 am to noon on Saturdays.

Groceries

Abaco Market Don Mackay Blvd. Tel: 242-367-2020/2081 Fax: 367-2242 *Abaco Market, Golden Harvest, Boat Harbour Mini Mart,* and *Abaco Wholesale* in Marsh Harbour, and *Treasure Cay Market* in Treasure Cay, are all part of *Abaco Markets* and offer galley stocking for boats with free dockside delivery. Talk to them, or fax them if you have special needs or delivery deadlines. The *Abaco Market* building burned down in June 1999, but a temporary convenience store was opening in the Sawyer Market building.

Bahamas Family Market Queen Elizabeth Drive Tel: 367-3714 Open from 7 am to 9 pm Monday to Saturday, to 5 pm on Sundays. Excellent, with a deli, bakery, and fresh produce; they will deliver to your boat dockside.

Frangipani, Marsh Harbour.

Bahamas Family Market at the *Conch Inn Marina* Tel: 367-2257 Open from 8 am to 9 pm Monday to Saturday, and to 5 pm on Sundays selling fresh bread, jamaican hot patties, gourmet cheeses, coffee, jellies, and fresh fruit and vegetables. Visa and MasterCard accepted.

Boat Harbour Mini-Mart at *Abaco Beach Resort* and *Boat Harbour Marina* Tel: 367-4711 Open from 8 am to 6 pm Monday to Saturday; well stocked, with free delivery to docks.

Food Store in *Memorial Plaza* Open from 8 am to 9 pm Monday to Saturday, and from 9 am to 4 pm on Sundays.

Golden Harvest Supermarket on Queen Elizabeth Drive Tel: 367-3079 Open 8 am to 6 pm, Monday to Thursday, to 7 pm Fridays and Saturdays, and from 9 am to 1 pm on Sundays, with meats, fresh fruits and vegetables, dairy products, and frozen foods.

Solomon's on Collins Avenue Tel: 367-2601/2602 • Fax: 367-2731 Fresh fruits and vegetables, choice meats, and dairy products.

Hardware

Abaco Hardware Don Mackay Blvd. Tel: 367-2170/2171 Open 7 am to 4 pm, Monday to Friday; to noon Saturdays. Marine & electrical, supplies, plumbing, hardware, paints, lumber.
Standard Hardware Queen Elizabeth Drive Tel: 367-2660/28ll Open 7 am to 5 pm Monday to Friday; to 1 pm Saturdays.

Liquor

Airport Liquor Store at the airport Tel: 367-3133 Open from 9 am to 9 pm, wholesale and retail.
A & K Liquor Queen Elizabeth Drive Tel: 367-2179 • VHF 16 Duty-free beer, liquor, wine, cordials; delivery.
Burns House Duty Free Liquor Store opposite *Memorial Plaza* Tel: 367-2172 Open 10 am to 6 pm, Monday to Saturday.
Central Liquors on Don Mackay Blvd. Tel: 367-2966 or 367-2881 at *Boat Harbour Marina* Open from 9 am to 6 pm Monday to Saturday.
John Bull at *Mangoes Restaurant* and *Marina* Open from 9 am to 5 pm Monday to Saturday.

Optician

Abaco Optical Services at *Lowe's Shopping Centre* Tel: 367-3546

Pharmacy

Lowe's Pharmacy on Don Mackay Blvd. Tel: 367-2667 Open 8:30 am to 5 pm, Monday to Saturday.
Chemist Shop Pharmacy Tel: 367-3106

Photographs

Snap Shop on Don Mackay Blvd. Tel: 367-3020   One-hour service.

Wally's Studio at *Abaco Shopping Centre*

Propane

Corner Value on Queen Elizabeth Drive, near the traffic light Tel: 367-2250   Open from 8 am to 5 pm Monday to Friday, to 1 pm on Saturdays. Allan Lowe's well-stocked store offers a propane tank refill service. If you take your tank in before 9 am, you can have it back, filled, at noon. Take it in before 1 pm and you can collect it at 4:30 pm. On Saturdays, there is only the morning refill service. *Please don't be impatient if the tanks are sometimes a little later arriving back at the store. This is a very generous free service to boaters.*

Seafood

The Fish House Tel: 367-2697   Conch, crawfish, grouper, snapper, shrimp, and bait.

Longs Landing Seafood Bay and William Street Tel: 367-3079 Open from 9:30 am to 6 pm daily, closed from 1 to 2 pm, with conch, grouper, and crawfish in season.

Sodas

C & A Variety Store and Soft Drinks, next to *Batelco,* around the corner from *Solomon Bros* Tel: 367-3131

Sawyer Soft Drinks Tel: 367-2797   Sodas & canned drinks; delivery to dock.

RESTAURANTS

Anglers Restaurant at *Abaco Beach Resort* Tel: 367-2158/2871 Open 7 am to 11 pm. Breakfast, lunch, and dinner overlooking the marina.

C & G Snacks and Bakery opposite *A & K Liquor Store* Tel: 367-3227

Golden Grouper Restaurant Dove Plaza Tel: 367-2301 Serves American and Bahamian food, with nightly specials.

The Jib Room at *Marsh Harbour Marina*   Tel: 367-2700 Lunch 11 am to 3 pm, happy hour 5 to 7 pm, and dinner from 7 pm. Closed Tuesdays, live music and barbecue Wednesdays & Sundays.

Kool Scoops, behind the CIBC bank, one block south of the traffic light Tel: 367-3880   Soup, salad, and hot dogs daily, with 30 flavors of ice cream and a variety of sundaes, splits, milkshakes, and snacks. Open from 11 am to 10 pm daily.

Mangoes Tel: 367-2366 • VHF 16 "Mangoes"   Serving lunch 11:30 am to 2:30 pm, dinner 6:30 to 9 pm. Appetizers and snacks served all day. Good food and casual elegance overlooking the harbor, with live music Tuesday and Thursday nights. Dinner reservations requested.

Mezzomare at *The Conch Inn*   Tel: 367-4444   Open for breakfast, lunch, and dinner daily. Serving both Italian and traditional Bahamian dishes, in the newly refurbished air-conditioned dining room, or outside on the shady terrace.

Sapodilly's Island Bar Tel: 367-3498   At the harbor's edge, between *Harbour View Marina* and *Lofty Fig Villas.* Serving lunch 11:30 am to 3:30 pm, dinner 6:30 to 9:30 pm. Exotic drink selection, as well as salads, sandwiches, hamburgers, fresh fish, pies. Live music and dancing.

Sharkees Island Pizza Tel: 367-3535   Delivery to your room or dock. daily until 10 pm, 11 pm Friday and Saturdays.

The Tiki Hut, a floating restaurant on the waterfront at *Harbour View Marina* Tel: 367-2575   Open for drinks from 3 pm and sunset dining from 6 to 10 pm daily, except Wednesdays, featuring island seafood. Happy hour from 3 to 7 pm on Fridays. Reservations suggested.

Pizza Hut at *Admiral's Yacht Haven* Tel: 367-4488/4242 Air-conditioned restaurant overlooking the harbor, carry out or delivery.

Wally's Tel: 367-2074 • VHF 16   On Bay Street. Lunch from 11:30 am to 3 pm, Monday to Saturday, dinner from 6 to 9 pm Tuesday to Saturday. Bar open from 11 am, with live music on Wednesdays and Saturdays. Boutique open 9 am to 9 pm. Closed on Sundays.

GETTING AROUND

Airport

Two miles south of the harbor, with a restaurant, bar, and liquor store. Taxis charge $12 to the ferry dock or into town, for two people.

Airlines

Abaco Air Tel: 367-2266   Daily flights between Abaco and Freeport. Air charter service from Abaco to all the Bahamas and Florida, air ambulance, search and rescue. Fifteen-seat turbo-prop aircraft.

American Eagle Tel: 367-2231 or 800-433-7300   Daily flights to Miami.

Bahamasair Tel: 367-2095   At Marsh Harbour Airport. Daily flights to Nassau, Freeport, and West Palm Beach.

Cherokee Air Tel: 367-2089/2613/2530   Charter flights to all points in the Bahamas and Florida.

Gulfstream Tel: 367-3415   *Continental Connection* with *Gulfstream:* 800-525-0280 (for Florida destinations), 800-231-0856 (for Bahamas destinations). Daily flights to Fort Lauderdale, Miami, and West Palm Beach.

Island Express Tel: 367-3597 or 954-359-0380   Daily passenger service from Fort Lauderdale to the entire Bahamas, with package express service.

Major's Air Services Tel: 367-4826 or 352-5778   Daily flights between Abaco and Freeport, charters, search and rescue, air ambulance, fifteen-seat turbo-prop aircraft.

Twin Air Tel: 333-2444 or 954-359-8271/8266   Passenger and freight service on eight-passenger Piper Navajo and sixteen-passenger Embraer Bandierante aircraft.

US Air Express Tel: 367-2231 or 800-622-1015   Daily flights to West Palm Beach at 3:05 pm, to Orlando at 2:30 pm, and to West Palm Beach at 4:15 pm on Saturdays.

Vintage Props & Jets Tel: 367-4852   Cheryl Clarke is the Abaco Agent.

Zig Zag Air Charters Tel: 367-2889

Bicycles

Rental Wheels Abaco near the entrance to the *Abaco Beach Resort* Tel: 367-4643 • VHF 16   Suzuki and Yamaha motorcycles from $10 hourly, and bicycle rentals from $2 hourly. Daily and weekly rates available. Visa, MasterCard, and Amex accepted.

R & L Rent-a-Ride at *Abaco Town by the Sea*   Tel: 367-4289/2744 Open from 9 am to 5 pm Monday to Friday, and from 10 am to 2 pm on Sundays. Yamaha motorcycles $40 per day, bicycles $8 per day.

Sea Horse Rentals at *Abaco Beach Resort* Tel: 367-2513 • VHF 16 Bicycles from $10 per day.

Boat Rentals

Blue Wave Boat Rentals at *Harbour View Marina*   Tel: 367-3910 • Fax: 367-3911 • VHF 16 "Blue Wave Rentals"   21-ft. Duskys from $95 per day, 26-ft. Paramounts from $140 per day.

Rainbow Rentals at *Bay Street* and *Union Jack Dock* Tel: 367-4062 • E-mail: rainbow@oii-net./go-abacos.com 22-ft. CDM White Caps, with freshwater shower system, 24-qt. coolers, glass-bottom buckets, compass, flares, VHF, life jackets, charts, fire extinguishers, dock lines, swim platform, anchors, and Yamaha motors. From $110 daily, $635 weekly. Ice, fishing rods, umbrellas, and snorkel gear available. Visa and MasterCard accepted.

Rich's Boat Rentals Tel: 367-2742 • VHF 16 "Rich's Rentals"
19-ft. Paramount $75 per day; 21-ft. Paramount $90 per day;
26-ft. Paramount $135 per day, with special monthly rates.
Open from 8 am to 5 pm daily. Also snorkeling gear, scuba
and fishing tackle, bait, ice. Credit cards accepted.

Sea Horse Rentals at *Boat Harbour Marina* Tel: 367-2513 • VHF
16 18- and 22-ft. Boston whalers from $95 per day; 18-, 22-
and 24-ft. Privateers from $85 per day; 20-ft. Albury from $105
per day; bicycles from $10 per day; and snorkel gear from $10
per day. Hope Town and Marsh Harbour locations. Complimentary delivery.

Car Rental
Remember to drive on the left! There is a 45-mph speed limit
throughout the island, 15 mph near schools, 20 mph in the
settlements.

A & P Rentals at *K & S Auto* on Don MacKay Blvd. (Airport Road)
Tel: 367-2655

H & L Rentals, one block south of the traffic light at the Shell
station Tel: 367-2854/2840   Open from 7 am to 6 pm,
Monday to Saturday. Cars from $70 per day, mini-vans from
$75 per day, motorbikes from $35 per day; credit cards
accepted.

Reliable Car Rentals at *Abaco Towns* centrally located between
Abaco Beach Resort and Marina and *Conch Inn Marina*
Tel: 367-4234   Open daily from 9 am to 5 pm, to 2 pm on
Saturday and Sunday. Mid-size cars from $70 per day, and
wagons with air-conditioning for $80 daily or $425 weekly
rental. Visa and MasterCard accepted.

Wilmac Rent A Car at the airport   Tel: 367-4313 or 367-3465 in
an emergency.

Ferries
Albury's Ferry   Tel: 367-3147 and 365-6010 • VHF 16   In addition
to their regular ferry service listed below, they also run to Green
Turtle Cay, Little Harbour, and Treasure Cay on request.
To **HopeTown** leave from the ferry dock at Crossing Beach at
9 am, 10:30 am, 12:15 pm, 2 pm, 4 pm, and 5:30 pm daily, as
well as at 7:15 am daily except Sundays and holidays.
To **Man-O-War** leave at 10:30 am, 4 pm, and 5:30 pm daily,
and 12:15 pm and 2:30 pm daily except Sundays.
To **Great Guana Cay** and **Scotland Cay** leave from the Conch
Inn and Union Jack Dock at 10:15 am, 1:15 pm, 3:30 pm, and
5:30 pm daily, and at 6:45 am except Saturdays, Sundays, and
holidays. Cost $7 one way, $10 round trip to all three places.

Taxis
Available at the airport and in town. You can call one on VHF 6
or 367-4395 for Beulah's Taxi stand. Prices are high in Marsh
Harbour because of union rules. Marsh Harbour to Treasure Cay
Marina costs $55 for two people, and $65 to the Treasure Cay
Ferry for Green Turtle Cay. Agree on the fare before you set off.

Tours
Abaco Delite Guide Service Tel: 367-4426   Fish, snorkel,
beachcomb, and island hop with *"Skipper" Captain James Sands.*
Sand Dollar Tours Tel: 367-2189   Daily tours all over Great
Abaco from $20 per person.

SPORTS

Bonefishing Guides
Capt. Justin Sands	Tel: 367-3526
J Sawyer	Tel: 367-2089
Patrick Roberts	Tel: 366-4286
Terrance Davis	Tel: 367-4464
Bonefish "Town"	Tel: 367-7123

Diving
Dive Abaco at the *Conch Inn Marina* Tel: 367-2787 •
Fax: 367-4799 • VHF 16 $65 for a two-tank dive, certification
course $450, $35 for snorkelers. Dive shop, rental equipment
including video camera with strobe, specializes in small groups.
Abaco Dive Centre at *Boat Harbour Marina*
Tel and fax: 367-4646/2736 • VHF 16 •
E-mail: info@greatabaco.com   Two-tank dive $70, snorkelers
$35. Air fills and rental equipment available; Nitrox, cave,
technical, deep, or night dives. Full certification courses.

Dive Sites
Favorite sites include *The Towers*, with 60-ft. tall coral pin-
nacles; *Grouper Alley*, with tunnels cutting through an
enormous coral head; *Wayne's World* outside the barrier reef;
and *The Cathedral*, a huge cavern where shafts of sunlight
dance on the floor.

Fishing Charters
Captain James Sands Tel: 367-4426 • VHF 16   Fishing,
snorkeling, beachcombing, or just island hopping.
Captain Bradley Russell at the *Harbour View Marina* Tel: 367-
2182 or 366-3010 (evenings)   Bottom fishing, bill fishing, or
island hopping, full and half days, rods and bait provided.
Lucky Strike Tel: 366-0101 • VHF 16 "Lucky Strike"   Truman
Major will take you fishing or sightseeing in his 35-ft. Maine
Coaster. $350 for a half day, $550 for a full day for one to four
people. There is a pick-up charge of $25 outside Hope Town.
Seagull Deep Sea Charters Tel: 366-0266 • VHF 16 "Seagull"
31-ft. Stapleton, $290 for half day, $490 for a full day with
Robert Lowe. Deep sea trolling for billfish, dolphin, wahoo,
tuna.

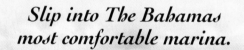

Fitness Center

Absolute Fitness Gym and Boutique, one block from the *Abaco Beach Resort* entrance Tel: 367-4613 Treadmills, bikes, single station units, and free weights. Open from 6 am to 9 pm Monday to Friday, from 7 am to 5 pm Saturday. $8 per day.

Sailboat and Motor Yacht Charters

Florida Yacht Charters at *Boat Harbour Marina*
Tel: 242-367-4853 or 800-537-0050 • Fax: 367-4854 •
E-mail: fla.yacht@grouper.batelnet.bs Family-run yacht and motor yacht charters operating out of Miami Beach and Key West, as well as Marsh Harbour. Captain Russell Williams, together with his daughters Susan and Nancy, offer a wide choice of bareboat Hunter sailboat charters from $1,650 per week, catamarans from $2,310 per week, and Mainship motor yachts from $3,050 per week. Sailing and power boat instruction courses available.

The Moorings at *Conch Inn Marina* Tel: 242-367-4000 or 800-535-7289 or 813-535-1446 Sailboats and catamarans from $400 daily. Provisioning plans, skippers and cooks available. Extensive bareboat charters. Customized Benetau Oceanis sailboats, Robertson & Caine and Jeanneau Lagoon catamarans.

Tennis

There are two courts at the *Abaco Beach Resort,* and at *Abaco Towns by the Sea.*

FISHING TOURNAMENTS & REGATTAS

January

Annual Bahamas Wahoo Championships at *Boat Harbour Marina.* Call 242-367-2158 for details.

April

Boat Harbour All Fish Tournament; South Abaco Championship

May

Bertram-Hatteras Shoot-Out Tournament and *Penny Turtle Billfish Ball* at *Boat Harbour Marina.* Contact *Abaco Beach Resort* at 242-367-2158 for details.

June

Annual Bahamas Billfish Championships and *Annual Boat Harbour All Fish Tournament* at *Boat Harbour Marina.* Contact *Abaco Beach Resort* at 242-367-2158 for details.

July

Regatta Time in Abaco is held during the first week in July. Races form up in Green Turtle Cay, Guana Cay, Man-O-War Cay, Hope Town and Marsh Harbour. Contact Dave or Kathy Ralph, Marsh Harbour, Abaco, Bahamas. Call 242-367-2677 or fax 367-3677.

October

Sunfish Discovery Day Regatta For information call Victor Patterson at 242-367-2344.

ACCOMMODATIONS

Abaco Beach Resort Tel: 242-367-2158 • Fax: 367-2819 • VHF 16 Rooms and villas from $145 per night.

Abaco Towns by the Sea Tel: 242-367-2227 Two-bedroom, two-bathroom villas sometimes available in this time-share development. Rooms from $130 per week.

Conch Inn Hotel Tel: 242-367-4000 • Fax: 367-4004 Rooms from $90 per night.

Island Breezes Motel Tel: 242-367-3776

Lofty Fig Villas Tel and fax: 242-367-2681 Six villas from $115 per person per night, single or double.

Pelican Beach Villas, close to *Marsh Harbour Marina*
Tel: 242-367-3600 Beachfront villas with dockage for small boats, from $165 per night.

THINGS TO DO IN MARSH HARBOUR

- Take advantage of large, well-stocked stores to reprovision your boat.
- Rent a car and explore the length of Great Abaco Island. As you head further south, and the road becomes rough, look out for parrots between Hole-in-the-Wall and Cross Harbour. The Abaco parrots have white heads and emerald green feathers, with a flash of red at their throats. They nest in rock crevices, while the Inagua parrots roost in trees. These are the only two islands with these rare birds, and their nesting ground in South Abaco is now a national park. You will need a tough car with good clearance if you go down to Hole-in-the-Wall, where Diane Claridge and her team of *Earthwatch* volunteers record the mammal sightings. The road north to Treasure Cay and on up to Coopers Town and Fox Town is good.
- Tune in to the cruiser's net on VHF 68 at 8:15 am to hear what's going on in Abaco.
- Sort out that pesky electronic problem on board.
- Take a ferry to explore another island that you may not have time to visit with your own boat. Go to Guana Cay or Little Harbour for their Sunday pig roasts, or over to Lubbers Quarters for lunch on the beach.
- Snorkel and dive one of the many fabulous sites nearby.
- Enjoy one of the "special" evenings put on by local restaurants. Or order a pizza to be delivered for dinner on board.

LITTLE HARBOUR

Little Harbour is a delight and a very special place. You feel like a guest from the moment you pick up one of the moorings in the crystal clear waters of the tiny bay, surrounded on three sides by hills dotted with private homes, and the fine studio devoted as a museum and art gallery by the Johnston family.

It was here that the charismatic and dynamic sculptor Randolph Johnston and his artist wife Margot found their escape from the world and a place to work in peace. The Johnstons lived in a cave when they first came to Little Harbour, while they were building their house and studios. You can still visit the cave.

Now that there is a full-time chef and bartender at *Pete's Pub*, 36 homes around the periphery, a scheduled *Froggies* expedition weekly, and a jitney service from Marsh Harbour twice a week, the character of Little Harbour is changing. But it is still a remote and attractive place to visit, without the amenities of public telephones, fuel, water, groceries, or showers/restrooms. There is only 3.5 feet of water in the channel if you come in at low tide, but there are radar reflectors at the entrance and on the final two buoys in the channel.

Charters

Albury's Ferry Tel: 365-6010 Will bring you to Little Harbour from Marsh Harbour if you don't have your own boat.

Froggies from Hope Town Tel: 365-6494

Gallery and Museum

Johnston Studios Art Gallery Open from 11:30 am to 4 pm Monday to Saturday; Pete Johnston is usually there on Sundays. A collection of Randolph Johnston's bronzes, together with Pete's current collection of dolphin sculptures and jewelry, which is for sale. Also wood carvings, prints, T-shirts, and postcards.

Jitney
On Sunday, the jitney leaves from *Sharkees* in Marsh Harbour at noon to bring you down to the pig roast at *Pete's Pub,* for $10. Transport from *Sapodilly's* on Wednesday and Sundays.

Moorings
There are 12 moorings, which you can pick up if one is available. Call VHF 16 "Pete's Pub" to check about a mooring. Someone will come around to collect your $10. You can also anchor in Little Harbour, if there is room. Put down two anchors to be safe.

Restaurant and Bar
Pete's Pub Open from 7 am till closing, under the able management of Aubrey Clark. A simple, open-sided, thatched beach bar overlooking the harbor, serving hamburgers, hot dogs, fresh fish, and more, with a pig roast on Sundays. Their specialty drink is a lethal Blaster, made with three types of rum and fruit juice. Dinner reservations are requested, or get there before sundown.

Trash
Please take your trash away with you. Little Harbour has no facilities to dispose of it.

THINGS TO DO IN LITTLE HARBOUR
- Visit the Gallery, and enjoy browsing through some very attractive artwork. Meet Pete when he's there on Sundays. Stroll through the Sculpture Garden.
- Walk over to the old lighthouse, now restored, overlooking the ocean.
- Explore the Johnston cave and imagine living in it.
- Take the dinghy around to explore the blue holes and shallow creeks in the Bight of Old Robinson.
- Snorkel the reef at the entrance to the harbor.
- Take a picnic across to Lynyard Cay for an exciting snorkeling day.
- Dive Sandy Cay Reef at *Pelican Cays Land and Sea Park.*
- Go to Cherokee Sound for the day.
- Enjoy good company and a Blaster at *Pete's Pub.*

CHEROKEE SOUND

Cherokee Sound has the most beautiful clear water in a sandy bay on the west side of Cherokee Point. The Sound once boasted a flourishing boat building yard, and the longest dock in Abaco. The dock is now rickety and unsafe to use, but the settlement is clean, neat, and tidy, with vegetables and fruit trees growing inside fenced gardens. You will find a good grocery store, but no restaurant or bar. There are ladies who would be happy to cook for you. A 10-mph speed limit is imposed in the narrow streets, and the road up to Marsh Harbour is now paved all the way. They hope that the clinic will soon be open again.

Catering
Wendy Sawyer (366-2115) *and Darlene Sawyer* (366-2025) will cook meals for boaters if you call them in advance. Or contact *Cherokee Food Fair* on VHF 16.

Church
Epworth Methodist Church

Fresh Bread
Diane Sawyer Tel: 366-2066 Bakes fresh bread daily.

Groceries
Cherokee Food Fair Tel: 366-2022 • VHF 16   Open from 7:30 am to noon, and from 1 pm to 6 pm Monday to Friday, to 7 pm on Saturdays. Well stocked with fresh fruit and vegetables, frozen and canned foods, sodas and juices, a card stand, some hardware, and a clothing corner.

Laundry
Cherokee Auto and Boat Haven Tel: 366-2092   Open from 7 am to 7 pm daily, from 10 am to 7 pm on Sundays, with coin-operated washers and dryers, $2 per machine in quarters. Double-load washers $3, double-load dryers $1 for 10 minutes.

Marine Supplies and Fuel
Cherokee Auto and Boat Haven Tel: 366-2092   Open on the creek, from 7 am to 10 am and 2 to 4 pm, Monday to Friday, and from 7 am to noon, and 2 to 5 pm on Saturdays. If there is no one at the store, call Trevor and Jennifer Sawyer at home at 366-2065 and they will always open up for you. Diesel is available in 5-gallon drums, with a hand-pump to your boat or fuel can. Gasoline is available at the fuel dock. The store has a good assortment of fishing tackle and marine supplies, with ballyhoo bait, sodas, and snacks. Ice $3 a bag.

Memorial
There is an obelisk overlooking the bay, commemorating the days of the old fishing sailing smacks.

Post Office
Open from 3 to 4 pm on Monday, Tuesday, Thursday, and Friday.

Telephone
The *Batelco* office, next to the tower, had been closed after their downsizing in May 1999.

THINGS TO DO IN CHEROKEE SOUND
- Swim in the glorious clear water.
- Take your dinghy and explore the narrow channel leading up to Mangrove Cay.
- Stroll through the settlement and admire the neat and tidy gardens with their mango trees.

SANDY POINT

Janet Wilson

This small village settlement, set out on a grid like a fish's backbone down the peninsula, was once home to a thriving lumber industry. Today there is little for the cruising boat, except a particularly good new Texaco Starport, operated by Walter Lightbourne, and *Pete and Gay's Guest House,* should you need food or accommodations if you are there for the bonefishing.

Clinic
Tel: 355-4110 Nurses Pinder, Bain, and Munnings give 24-hour coverage at the clinic. There is an ambulance in town, and even talk of an air ambulance service to take people more quickly to Marsh Harbour.

Fishing
For a bonefishing guide for South Abaco and Mores Island as well as Sandy Point, contact Paul Pinder at 366-4061 or Patrick Roberts at 366-4286.

Fuel
Lightbourne Marina VHF 16   Open from 7 am to 7 pm daily, with 5 feet of water at the T of the fuel dock; come in south of the white "market stalls." Diesel and gasoline, ice, oils, lubricants, sodas, and snacks.

Mailboat
M/V Mangrove Cay Express leaves Nassau weekly on Thursdays, returning on Sundays. Fare $30.

Chapter 7
Grand Bahama Island
Grand Bahama
Grand Lucayan Waterway

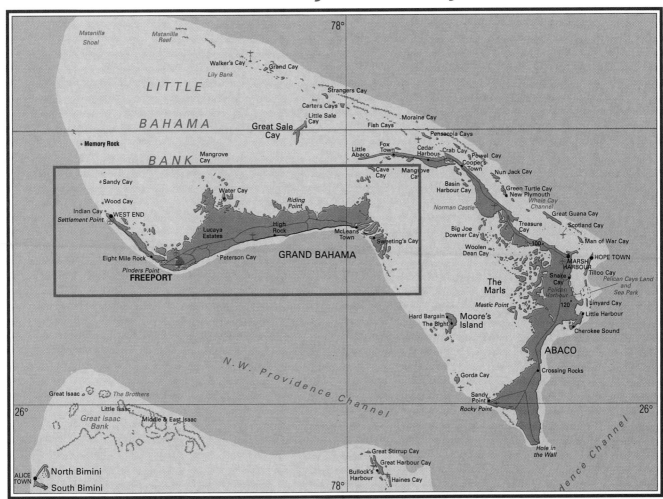

Grand Bahama

GRAND BAHAMA ISLAND, despite the fact that it seems to dominate any map of the Bahamas, is only fourth in size in the Bahamas chain (after Andros, Eleuthera, and Great Abaco). Grand Bahama runs east–west, sitting just above Latitude 26° 30' N, for well over one degree of longitude. Put another way, Grand Bahama Island is some 80 miles long and around 7 miles wide, with a girth stretching 16 miles at the widest point

For the cruising sailor Grand Bahama has been unlikely to feature in any projected itinerary. West End is a port-of-call on the main routes to the Abacos. Freeport is a commercial port, available to you in an emergency, but not a cruising destination. The marinas between Freeport and Port Lucaya (Xanadu, Running Mon, and the Ocean Reef

Yacht Club) are primarily geared to shoreside accommodation, or local boats. Essentially Port Lucaya is (apart from West End) the only port of call for the cruising visitor, whoever you are, power or sail. A tad to the east of Port Lucaya the Grand Lucayan Waterway offers a short cut through to the Little Bahama Bank, which those bound to or from the Abacos may find convenient.

Up to this time the entire energy and direction of Grand Bahama has rested in its Freeport commercial development and the lure of the Freeport–Lucaya area resort hotels with their casinos, and all the glitz that goes with a would-be Bahamian Las Vegas. Freeport Harbour, once virtually dedicated to BORCO (the Bahamas Oil Refining Company) has, with a decline in BORCO's fortunes, became a more general port with cruise ships calling in, container ships,

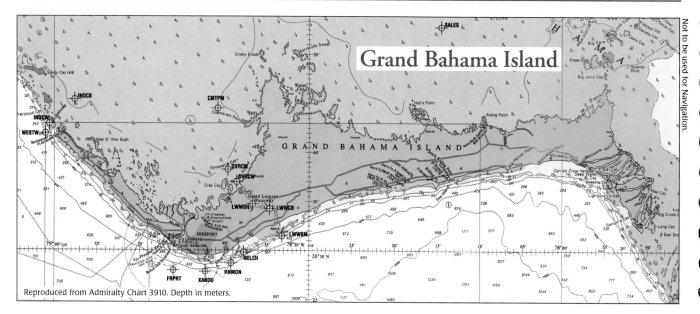

Grand Bahama Island

Reproduced from Admiralty Chart 3910. Depth in meters.

regular general freight runs from Florida, and hardly surprisingly, a regular port of call for a number of Bahamian mailboats. Customs and Immigration are there, as indeed they are at Freeport's International Airport, and between these offices offer an "on call" service to the Lucayan area marinas.

Now all this has changed. The one-time Hong Kong–based Hutchinson Whampoa Ltd. have as a new progeny the Freeport Harbour Company, a member of Hutchinson International Port Holdings Ltd. Add to this portfolio the Grand Bahama Port Authority and substantial real estate development interests in Grand Bahama, together with, through Hutchinson Lucaya Ltd. (their Bahamas Hotel & Resort Division), the greater part of the Port Lucaya strip. Much has changed and is changing in Grand Bahama Island.

It's difficult to define the Freeport–Lucaya area in terms

Queen Victoria, International Bazaar, Freeport.

that are easily comprehensible. It's a vast track of almost flat territory paralleling the coast for nearly 40 miles, some 7 miles deep. Development has been sporadic, centering on oases that have some reason to exist, such as Freeport Harbour, the International Airport, and the main tourist-seeking resort complexes. In between there's little but yellow pine and scrub. The road system on the main tourist-oriented routes is good, well landscaped and well kept. But there's nothing scenic there. Freeport International Airport, at this time still 1950s in vintage, offers reasonably good connections to the States but carries with it an $18 departure tax (as opposed to the all-Bahama standard rate of $15), and a taxi fare to Port Lucaya of $10–15 one way.

In Freeport the dominating development has been the complex built up by Princess Travel, which has culminated in a mini-city made up of the Princess Towers, the Princess Casino, the Princess Country Club, Castaways Resort, and the famous long-standing International Bazaar. Port Lucaya, beach rather than city oriented, has offered much the same vacation fare with its hotels, casino, and Marketplace, with parasailing, limbo dancers, and Pusser's Painkillers thrown into the cocktail. As a measure of the current zenith of this density in tourist-targeted activity, in the Marketplace complex (at our last count) there were 113 shops, restaurants, and bars. At the time we write the Port Lucaya beach hotels do not feature in our **Yellow Pages**, for all but one were demolished to make way for the construction of one multi-hotel resort. By 2001 much of it should be finished. Before we turn to Freeport and Port Lucaya in detail, we'll touch briefly on West End, for it's properly part of Grand Bahama Island.

WEST END AND THE ROUTE TO THE ABACOS

Location tells. Simply because of its position, we treated West End as the gateway to the Little Bahama Bank, the first landfall entry port on the route to the Abacos. For this reason West End is covered in Chapter 3, under the heading of **The Little Bahama Bank**.

An alternative route to the Abacos cuts out going around West End and has already been mentioned in passing. This is the Grand Lucayan Waterway, which runs across Grand Bahama Island from a point just east of Port Lucaya. This is covered in full later in this chapter, beginning on page 112.

The Southern Coast– Freeport and Port Lucaya

Freeport
Located at the bottom corner of the boomerang-shaped form of Grand Bahama Island, Freeport lies some 20 nm southeast from West End. The inshore coast between West End and Freeport is No-Go territory, shoal and reef strewn, so keep well out (ideally 4 nm or more), particularly if you are standing off at night, for you may be set toward the land.

Freeport is a major commercial port and is of no interest to the cruising skipper, other than as a possible refuge. If you do have to put in, Freeport's oil terminal, with its offshore tanker jetties and shoreside tanks and towers, is unmistakable. Aircraft approaching and leaving Freeport International Airport are also a sure indicator of where you are. There is a prominent radio mast to the west of the oil terminal, and the entry to the harbor (should you need it) lies just west of those oil tanker jetties. The sea approaches around the jetties is a Restricted Area. You should not transit it, nor anchor there. We would not enter Freeport Harbour without first contacting the Port Authority. Should you need them, there are (of course) Customs and Immigration facilities in Freeport.

Be aware that your charts may be out of date. If you have to enter Freeport Harbour at night your leading lights, under two original Fixed Greens, are two vertical white pipe lights, both visible out to 5 nm. Freeport Harbour is changing shape day by day, but the approaches (apart from the additional guidance of those two vertical pipe lights) have not changed.

GRAND BAHAMA ISLAND

West End		
WESTW	26° 42' 00"/000 N	079° 01' 00"/000 W
West End Harbour Hotel Marina		
HARBH	26° 41' 22"/366 N	078° 57' 58"/966 W
Freeport		
FRPRT	26° 29' 43"/721 N	078° 47' 25"/426 W
Xanadu		
XANDU	26° 28' 24"/399 N	078° 42' 22"/366 W
Running Mon		
RNMON	26° 28' 56"/933 N	078° 39' 22"/366 W
Ocean Reef		
OCNRF	26° 29' 22"/366 N	078° 39' 50"/833 W
Bell Channel		
BELCH	26° 29' 57"/949 N	078° 37' 48"/799 W

The final figures in each waypoint show seconds (00") and thousands (000) of a minute.

The Freeport–Port Lucaya Coast
Between Freeport and the Bell Channel to the east (which leads into Port Lucaya) there's a run of 7.5 nm, on which three marinas, given away only by their artificial entry-channel breakwaters, are hidden from view as you make your way along the coast. Taken from west to east, these are Xanadu, Running Mon, and Ocean Reef. The Bell Channel comes up a mile and a half after Ocean Reef. Stay in blue water 1–2 nm offshore until you turn to make an entry approach. This keeps you well clear of the inshore reef dive sites (some of which are marked by white mooring buoys), as well as parasailing and inshore water sports.

Freeport Harbour, from the south.

Signpost, International Bazaar, Freeport.

XANADU

After a run of about 5 nm from Freeport you'll come to Xanadu. Your landmark is a squarish hotel block, which, from a distance, appears to have a Chinese-looking roof with a peak in the middle. Getting closer you'll see that the roof is flat, topped by a white pyramid. Get even closer, and you'll see colors. The sides of the hotel appear vertically striped black and white from the ocean (in fact it's dark green balconies and the backing of dark solar-tinted glass set against pink walls), and the roof line has two clearly pink bands supporting it.

Once you've got all this, the entry to the Xanadu channel is straightforward. Xanadu carries 6 feet at MLW. It's classed as an on-call entry port. If you elect to go there, you are remote from the International Bazaar heartland and certainly remote from the Lucaya end. The Xanadu Marina has been in decline over the last two years, and it remains to be seen what the future holds for it. See our **Yellow Pages**.

RUNNING MON

Running Mon Marina comes up 2.7 nm after Xanadu. Its identification is hardly difficult for the architecture here is very different. Rather than having a single tower like Xanadu,

you pick up the Running Mon entry channel by a low-rise series of six white terraced apartment blocks, linked and all sloped back so that everyone's balcony gets some sun. A little further on, close to this terraced building, is what looks like a conventional (yellow) "clubhouse" type of building. The Running Mon beach looks good, and the whole scene is backed by casuarinas, which give it the appearance of seclusion and privacy.

By now, the entrance into the marina is apparent. Running Mon, which is not recognized as an entry port, has only 4.5 feet at MLW. It's too close to the safety margin for most cruisers, and those who risk it may find the marina disappointing at closer sight. The sloping apartments on the beach are timeshares. The resort, uninspiring and dull, faces its small dock area, built around pontoons. It's not, at this time, a place we feel you're likely to choose. Running Mon needs a massive cash injection, dredging, care, and considerable attention to put it in the league. We're not surprised to find it unfrequented save by local fishermen.

OCEAN REEF YACHT CLUB

After Running Mon there's a gap of about 0.5 nm or so, and you'll see what appears to be a huge white French chateau (complete with grey roof and turrets) come into view. As an aside, this is the home of Hayward Cooper, who built his fortune from a humble start running a small store on the road outside Freeport Harbour. A little later you'll pick up the breakwaters of the Ocean Reef Yacht Club marina. Again no problems here. This is not a port of entry.

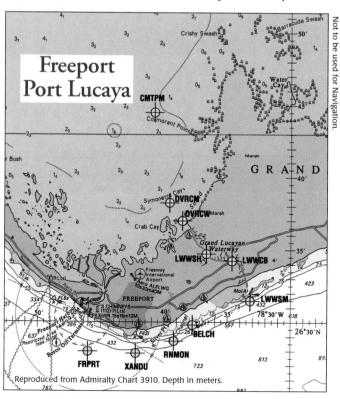

Reproduced from Admiralty Chart 3910. Depth in meters.

Not to be used for Navigation.

The Bell Channel and Port Lucaya, from the south.

The Ocean Reef Club is a gated timeshare community that has an integral marina available to visitors using their accommodations, but is not open for transients.

PORT LUCAYA (THE BELL CHANNEL)

At the time we write your primary Bell Channel landmark is the red and white "lighthouse" tower of the onetime Lucayan Beach Resort and Casino. Further on there's a cluster of pinkish townhouses, all huddled together, which are, in fact, on the east bank of the Bell Channel.

Bell Channel itself has a rust-colored marker buoy with a light (26° 29' 53"/883 N 078° 37' 44"/733 W). From a distance it's indistinguishable from six similarly rust-covered cruise ship mooring buoys, which come up close to your track before you reach the Bell Channel if you're coming in from the west. The familiar landmarks of the old hotels have gone, and over the next two years we shall see a new skyline take shape. However you'll have no problem getting your bearings. You'll have identified the two Bell Channel entry stakes, the line of the breakwater, and will probably be passing that rusty buoy with the light on it without any difficulty in fixing your position.

Once you're in the Bell Channel the Port Lucaya Marina lies to port around the built-on peninsula that juts out into the Bell Channel lagoon. The Lucayan Marina is to starboard as you come in. Both marinas are recognized as on-call ports of entry.

PORT LUCAYA MARINA

If you like to be in the center of the action, the long-established Port Lucaya Marina is the place to be. You can walk to the bars, restaurants, and shops that form the Market-place area. There's live music there, on your doorstep. There are snorkel trips, beach parties, dive trips, semi-submarine reef tours, and booze cruises chasing your custom, as well as the duty-free stores with everything you might need from liquor to Colombian emeralds.

The Port Lucaya Marina is a large complex. It has two conventional docks (both to port, as you make your way in) with a fuel dock, and ahead lies a radius of secondary docks on a separate peninsula ringing a low-rise circle of rooms built around a central swimming pool. This Garden Wing carries with it the use of the showers and pool, but no more than that. This means only one shower stall each for men and women, and one or three toilets (the females come out better there). If you take a Garden Wing room you're better off, but that kind of decision lies entirely in your court. The primary docks flanking the fuel dock are largely reserved for commercial use and mega-yachts. See our **Yellow Pages**.

THE LUCAYAN MARINA VILLAGE

If you want to remain detached from all this activity, go to the Lucayan Marina (part of the Lucayan Village development), which lies to starboard after you've passed through Bell Channel. The "Village" part of the title is continuing

Port Lucaya Marina.

to grow, albeit slowly. In its final form it'll be akin to something like Port Grimaud in Mediterranean France, a marina with a circling shorefront of multi-styled multi-colored houses, townhouses, and apartments. The architecture and landscaping are first class, as are the facilities offered: a pool and bar (with snacks served at lunchtime), telephones, laundry machines, immaculate showers and toilets, and a shuttle ferry that runs every half hour (8 a.m. to 11 p.m.) from the dockmaster's office across to the Marketplace side. At their ferry dock there's a full-service restaurant. Overall the Lucayan Marina, in its design, standard of construction, and state of maintenance is up to five-star international standards. See our **Yellow Pages**.

THE CRYSTAL BALL

So what's in the cards for the Freeport–Lucaya area? For Freeport, its establishment as one of the major container ports in the Western Hemisphere. With this development will come adjacent, vastly improved, cruise ship facilities, and hotels, shops, and restaurants. For the boating world, Bradford Marine have just opened a major repair facility with a 1,200-ton dry dock. See our **Yellow Pages**. Perhaps catering for smaller craft will follow. Link all this with Freeport International Airport, which Hutchinson Whampoa already owns (together with the land between the airport and the harbour), talk of a connecting monorail, and you can catch the flow of the tide without opening your Tide Tables.

The Grand Lucayan Waterway

IF you're setting out for the Abacos from Miami or Fort Lauderdale, your best route, unless size, draft, and masthead height prohibit it, is to use the Grand Lucayan Waterway as a shortcut to the Little Bahama Bank. The reverse applies if you're on your way home. The largest engineering feat ever attempted in the Bahamas, the 1967 dream of opening the heartland of Grand Bahama to development, as well as opening a direct route between Florida and the Abacos, cost $26 million. As a development it failed to get take off speed. As a canal, despite some shoaling and bank deterioration, it still serves. Now, at last, lots are beginning to move. Some four or five houses, approaching mini-palace size, are spearheading the long-delayed development in the area south of Casuarina Bridge.

The southern sector of Grand Lucayan Waterway is not so much a canal as the winding, 250-foot walled main artery of a canal system, which runs mostly north–south, with endless side basins, turning areas, and lesser canals opening off it. The northern sector is very different. It's more ditch-like with raw banks, and closes in to around 25 feet at its narrowest point. Some concrete walls feature again, briefly, in its final northern section.

You may find company there but often the Grand Lucayan Waterway, although it is used, appears to carry no traffic, and there are few signs of life on its banks. Each side there's nothing but scrub, a monolithic failed condominium (or was it a hotel?), and one or two houses apparently abandoned during construction. As we've said, the Waterway was envisaged as the Grand Canal of a whole new waterworld of development in the very heartland of Grand Bahama Island, a kind of Bahamian Venice. Perhaps, as we've said, all this is about to change. What has been built so far is some very expensive housing.

PLUSES AND MINUSES—THE GRAND LUCAYAN WATERWAY

The Grand Lucayan Waterway is not a difficult route but we wouldn't attempt it, simply for prudence, in anything over the mid-40s in LOA, and we'd be happier at or below the 40-foot mark. What are the bull points?

Vertical Clearance. Casuarina Bridge, the only bridge on the Waterway, has 27-feet clearance at high water. There

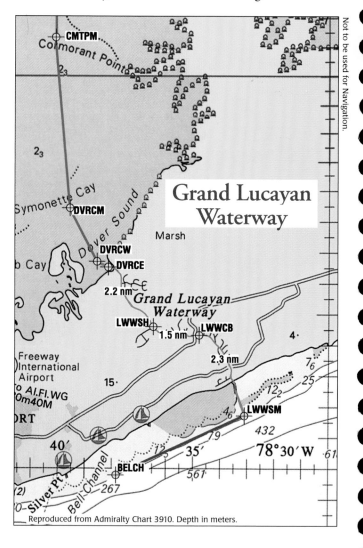

Reproduced from Admiralty Chart 3910. Depth in meters.

Not to be used for Navigation.

are no clearance gauges on its approach pilings.

Draft. You have 8–10 feet on average throughout the Waterway itself, but we've been unable to relate this accurately to a tidal state. See our next point. However the channel leading into Dover Sound is critical. At MLW you should not expect more than 4 feet.

Timing. There's a tidal difference of 2 hours between the south end and the north end of the Waterway. A further complicating factor is that strong tidal sets affect the choke points in the Waterway (essentially Casuarina Bridge and the first spoil narrows north of the bridge). This suggests that it's wise to avoid a transit of these points in hours 3 and 4 after high or low water. Fine in theory, but because the Waterway is a complex water basin linking two entirely different sea areas, it's not quite that predictable. In the end it's the tidal state in Dover Sound that's the critical factor. We reckon Port Lucaya as 30 minutes after Nassau, and Dover Sound as 2 hours 30 minutes after Nassau.

You might well say "That's it. Let's go by West End," but read on. We'd take the Waterway every time in preference to heading for West End provided that our boat fitted, and wind (see our note about Dover Channel) and tide were in our favor.

The time it will take you to transit the Waterway? You're asked to keep to a speed of 5 knots in the Grand Lucayan Waterway. Say a little over one hour. Whichever way you're travelling, to or from the Abacos, it's going to work out at about half the time it would take to get to West End from Port Lucaya, if you decided to go around that way. The West End–Mangrove Cay and the Mangrove Cay–Dover Sound Channel legs are just about equal length, at around 20 nm.

Is it worth taking the Waterway? We reckon it depends

Grand Lucayan Waterway, South Entry.

entirely on where you've come from or where you're heading. And, of course, whether Port Lucaya is on your visit list.

Approaches to the Grand Lucayan Waterway

From the South

From the Bell Channel entry buoy head 071°M to run parallel to the coast a safe 1.5 nm offshore for 4.5 nm. Keep in blue water, outside the line of white buoys you'll see running along the edge of the deeper water. (The white floats are UNESCO mooring buoys set there to be used by dive boats so that the reef along this stretch isn't ruined by random anchoring).

The Lucayan Waterway south mark buoy marking your turn-in point to access the Grand Lucayan Waterway carries red and white vertical stripes, has a red nose on top like a circus clown, and a white light. This is our waypoint LWWSM. At this point you can see the breakwaters, backed by casuarinas, very clearly. You'll be heading in on something like 000°M with just over 0.5 nm to run to the lights at the end of the breakwaters. As a fail-safe, just in case you miss that red-and-white-striped buoy entirely, if you see Peterson's Cay come up on your port bow (a tiny islet with four wind-blown trees on it) you've gone too far. Turn back.

From the North

From our Mangrove Cay waypoint (MANGR) head south on 195°M for 12.8 nm to Cormorant Point (CMTPM), where a lone piling gives you the reassurance that you're on a regular route, and not going on and on into a horizonless void.

THE GRAND LUCAYAN WATERWAY		
Lucayan Waterway South Mark		
LWWSM	26° 31' 48"/799 N	078° 33' 14"/233 W
Lucayan Waterway Casuarina Bridge		
LWWCB	26° 34' 21"/364 N	078° 34' 51"/862 W
Lucayan Waterway Spoil Hill Narrows		
LWWSH	26° 34' 49"/826 N	078° 36' 30"/501 W
Lucayan Waterway Dover Channel East		
DVRCE	26° 36' 37"/623 N	078° 37' 54"/906 W
Lucayan Waterway Dover Channel West		
DVRCW	26° 36' 48"/803 N	078° 38' 28"/462 W
Lucayan Waterway Dover Channel Mark		
DVRCM	26° 38' 16"/271 N	078° 39' 38"/643 W
Cormorant Point Marker		
CMTPM	26° 44' 38"/631 N	078° 40' 49"/812 W
Mangrove Cay		
MANGR 1.5 nm	26° 57' 00"/000 N	078° 37' 00"/000 W

The final figures in each waypoint show seconds (00") and thousands (000) of a minute.

The Grand Lucayan Waterway, from the south.

going. You'll notice there's a prominent sandy spoil ledge on the south side of the channel.

After the last pair of posts, incoming, turn to starboard by two concrete posts and you're in the Grand Lucayan Waterway.

The Southern Entry Breakwater to Spoil Hill Narrows (3.9 nm)

The major, southern part of the Grand Lucayan Waterway is straightforward. Once you're inside the breakwaters you're pretty well set. You've got maybe 14 feet there (if the tide is right) and you'll have 8–10 feet inside later. A warning sign, which you may not be able to read, tells you to stay at least 20 feet off the sides of the Waterway, and that if you're in trouble contact BASRA or the police on channel 16.

You don't need a map or a chart of the Grand Lucayan Waterway, despite its many side alleys. Just follow your nose. You'll not get lost. Just 2.39 nm after entering the south breakwater you'll come to Casuarina Bridge, which carries the main and only road (the East Sunrise Highway) linking the east and west halves of Grand Bahama Island. This fixed bridge gives you 27-foot clearance above the water at high tide, but has no clearance gauges on its piers to tell you what's there at the time of your arrival. It's the first "choke" point you come to where you can expect

The shallow bight you are crossing extends from West End to the Cormorant Point peninsula with Crishy Swash and Mangrove Cay to its immediate north. Closer in to Grand Bahama Island it's known as Dover Sound. The north running hook of land, of which Cormorant Point is a western outlier, is the widest part of Grand Bahama. The shore is low lying, broken up by swamp, mudflats, and small islands, and barely shows for much of the time. The entrance to the Grand Lucayan Waterway, masked by Crab Cay to the west and Sandy Cay to the east, is not evident until you are right there. The MLW depth over much of this area can be taken as 6 feet, but keep at least 3–4 nm offshore, for there is a definite shoal-depth contour running parallel to the coast.

From Cormorant Point you continue on 171°M for 6.4 nm to the Lucayan Waterway Dover Channel Mark (DVRCM), which is another lone piling. From there you head 144°M for 1.8 nm to the posts marking the west entrance to the Dover Channel.

The half-mile-long Dover Channel runs close to west–east (290°–110°). It's marked by seven pairs of marker poles (number 5, incoming from the west had lost its twin when we were there last), and the outer markers at each end have lights (red right returning from the west).

This channel is narrow and open to wind from the north. It's also shallow (as little as 6 feet at best and maybe 4 feet at worst). You can't hammer through it at speed to counter a side wind for you may dig your stern in too deep and take the water you need right out of the channel. It's best to take the best compromise speed if you have a side wind, but keep

Spoil Hill Narrows.

Spoil Hill Narrows.

to feel an appreciable tidal flow. Just keep motoring. Don't hang about.

The Waterway is much the same after Casuarina Bridge as it was before, but somewhat more straight in its course. After 1.51 nm you come to the second choke point. You'll find two conical mini-hills of spoil on each side of your bow flanking a narrow cut, and you won't be able to believe (at first sight) that you're supposed to go on and pass between them. At this point the Grand Lucayan Waterway changes character, and although there are no real problems lined up, you have to be a touch more alert in the northern part than the southern section requires.

Spoil Hill Narrows to Dover Sound (2.83 nm)

If there's a tidal set you'll really feel it at the Spoil Hill Narrows (the naming is ours). You have no room to maneuver and no room to pass oncoming traffic, for the width of the cut reduces the Waterway to something like 20 feet, if that, (albeit briefly) as you pass between the Spoil Hills.

At this point too you've lost your concrete embankments and the main course of the Grand Lucayan Waterway, now narrowed to 100 feet or less, becomes ditch-like in character. Stay in the center. You get a wall once again on the east side 1.28 nm after passing between the two spoil hills. When you reach this embankment favor the wall side, for the port bank deteriorates. Rocks and undredged ledges lie in the Waterway itself on your left-hand side.

On this stretch, on the port side, a wetland wilderness opens up to the west with signs of distant human activity (a sand mound from some excavation, a radio mast) but none of this must take your eye off the canal. To starboard the scrub area will show further mounds of spoil, the concrete walls will open into another dead-end basin, and then on the port side, as that west bank falls away completely, you'll come level with the first of two concrete posts.

You can see you're close to gaining access to the Little Bahama Bank. There are two more concrete posts that must be left to port, and then you're at the end of the Grand Lucayan Waterway and the beginning of a dredged channel leading you out onto the Little Bahama Bank. Your entry point, marked by two lighted posts (green to starboard and red to port as you're traveling, coming up from the south) are ahead of you. You'll have run 2.25 nm since passing between the two spoil hills, and will have another 0.58 nm to go before you gain the open water of the Bank.

Dover Sound—
Getting out on the Little Bahama Bank

The Little Bahama Bank channel turns you sharply to port on a heading of 295°M passing between 5 pairs of pilings (note that Piling 4 to starboard has lost its port twin) and a final pair of lighted markers (again green to starboard and red to port as you're traveling from the south) with a prominent sandy spoil ledge to port.

This channel is narrow and open to wind from the north. It's also shallow (as little as 6 feet at best and maybe 4 feet at worst). You can't hammer through it at speed to counter a side wind for you may dig your stern in too deep and take the water you need right out of the channel. It's best to take the best compromise speed if you have a side wind, but keep going.

What's the total distance you'll have run from entering that south breakwater to passing out of the channel on to the Little Bahama Bank? 6.73 nm, or 7.41 nm from the south entry buoy. The time it will take you? You're asked to keep to a speed of 5 knots in the Grand Lucayan Waterway. Say 1 hour and 15 minutes, or about half the time it would take to get to West End from Port Lucaya.

Dover Channel, looking west.

Going on to Mangrove Cay

You'll probably be disoriented at this point for it's hard to pick up your bearings on first coming out of the Grand Lucayan Waterway. The shallows you are crossing are known as Dover Sound. The low-lying land to port is Crab Cay (the land mass is sort-of crab shaped). The island off your starboard bow is Sandy Cay. Look at your chart. North of Sandy Cay is the headland called Cormorant Point, and north of that is the cay that marks the extreme north tip of Grand Bahama Island, called Crishy Swash. North of that is Mangrove Cay.

A whole area of shallows runs along the west side of the Cormorant Point–Crishy Swash peninsula, the western edge of which is just over 4 nm offshore at its widest point. To get to Mangrove Cay you have to dogleg to the northwest to give Cormorant Point and the shallows a wide berth before you can head safely for Mangrove Cay, so a Cormorant Point waypoint comes into play here as well as Mangrove Cay. Your first leg will be 327°M for 5.06 nm, and your second 020°M for 16.61 nm, a total distance (after exiting the Dover Sound channel) of 21.67 nm.

Once you reach Mangrove Cay you're set fair for going on to Walkers Cay by way of Great Sale, or to Great Sale and points east. See our **Routes Across the Little Bahama Bank** on page 32 and our **Options After Great Sale Cay** on page 36.

Flame trees, Grand Bahama.

YELLOW PAGES

This area was hit by Hurricane *Floyd* in September 1999. Be aware that post-hurricane repairs and reconstruction may still be in progress, and wind and storm surge damage may still be evident.

FREEPORT & PORT LUCAYA

There is an air of prosperity along the wide, tree-lined boulevards of Freeport and Port Lucaya that encourages the booming construction of elegant new homes, and the massive dredging of the hugely expanding commercial harbor, with its state-of-the-art container port and vastly improved cruise ship facilities. The older, high-rise hotels are giving way to newly landscaped luxury hotels with every possible resort amenity, including golf courses, superb restaurants, and casinos. This said, Grand Bahama is a sophisticated and well organized island for visiting boats, especially for those with children on board, with interesting places to visit and things to do on shore, together with excellent beaches, diving, and water sports. Freeport and Port Lucaya are Ports of Entry, and **Customs** can be called from any of the marinas to clear you in.

MARINAS

Marinas are listed west to east, from Freeport commercial harbor where you would not be welcome on anything much smaller than a cruise ship.

XANADU BEACH RESORT & MARINA
Tel: 242-352-6782 • Fax: 352-5799 • VHF 16
A resort popular with honeymooners, about fifteen minutes west of Freeport, the marina is attractively laid out with a friendly and helpful dockmaster. The actual docks are in need of updating. The hotel has much to offer with its water sports, dive center, mile-long beach, tennis courts, and games room. Most people don't leave the resort, except to go shopping or check out the night life. There are new port and starboard entry lights, 027°M from the entry buoy.

Slips	60
Max LOA	120 ft.
MLW at Dock	6.5 ft.; 13 ft. at low water in the entry channel.
Dockage	$40 per day up to 40 ft., $60 per day up to 60 ft., $100 per day over 91 ft.
Long Term	Dockage available, 45¢ per ft. per day for power boats, 35¢ per ft. per day for sailboats, 3-month minimum, payable in advance.
Power	Included in dockage fee.
Fuel	Diesel and gasoline. Fuel dock open from 8:30 am to 5 pm, with a 5-percent surcharge on credit cards.
Water	Included in dockage fee.
Showers	Hospitality room for showers and changing.
Laundry	Yes, at the hotel.
Restaurants	*Casuarina Cafe and Bar* and *Ocean Front Bar and Grill*
Facilities	Freshwater pool, 3 tennis courts, games room. Mile-long beach with watersports, car and scooter rental.
Diving	*Xanadu Undersea Adventures* Tel: 352-3811 or 352-6782, ext. 1421 Open 7:30 am to 5 pm daily. Two-tank dives from $55, snorkelers $25. Equipment rental available, full certification courses, night and shark dives.
Deep Sea Fishing	*Paradise Watersports* Tel: 352-4233/2887 • E-mail: pwsports@batelnet.bs See Colleen,

who, as well as fishing trips, can also arrange parasailing, reef and wreck snorkeling cruises, glass-bottom boat cruises, jet skis, banana boat rides, and canoes. They have a few marine stores and fishing tackle in their shop.

Taxis	Wait outside the hotel.
Accommodations	*Xanadu Beach Hotel*, the pink hotel with the pyramid-shaped roof. Rooms from $120 a night, MAP $35 a day.
Credits Cards	Major cards accepted.
Dockmaster	Keithlyn Russell

RUNNING MON MARINA AND RESORT
Tel: 242-352-6834 • Fax: 352-6835 • VHF 16
At time of writing, this somewhat run-down marina had just been sold. The new owner, Allan May, has many plans for rebuilding the docks, dredging the entry channel, and renovating the hotel. It is a quiet marina with repair facilities, but a shallow approach channel with only 4 feet of water at low tide. This is the marina to come into if you need mechanics to work on your boat.

Slips	66
Max LOA	75 ft.
MLW at Dock	4 ft.
Dockage	$1 per foot per day.
Long Term	35¢ per foot per day.
Power	Included in dockage fees.
Fuel	Diesel and gasoline; fuel dock open from 7 am to 5 pm.
Water	Included in dockage fees.
Telephones	Two pay phones on the dock.
Showers	Yes, and restrooms in the marina.
Laundry	Laundromat on site, tokens from the front desk. $2.50 for washer and dryer.
Restaurant	*Main Sail Restaurant* Open 7 am to 1 pm.
Store	A few snacks and sodas.
Repairs	Mechanics in the boatyard.
Fishing	*Deep Sea Fishing Charters* Tel: 352-6833 $70 per person half day, $840 per boat full day. Free transport from all Freeport Hotels.
Accommodations	32 guest rooms overlooking the marina.
Credit cards	All major cards except Diners/En route and Sun Card.

OCEAN REEF YACHT CLUB AND MARINA
Tel: 242-373-4661/2 • Fax: 373-8261 • VHF 16
This 52-slip marina has excellent facilities, but is for members only so we do not give details. Inquire about membership. Rental or interval ownership can be arranged. Contact Peter Mandt-Rauch for more information.

BELL CHANNEL CLUB AND MARINA
Tel: 242-373-2673/3801 • Fax: 373-3802 • VHF 16
This marina belongs to the owners of the pink condominiums you can see on the east bank of the channel as you approach the Bell Channel to come in to the *Port Lucaya Marina* and the *Lucayan Marina Village*.

PORT LUCAYA MARINA AND YACHT CLUB
Tel: 242-373-9090/9091/9092 • Fax: 373-8632 • VHF 16 • E-mail: port@batelnet.bs
The long-established and well-run Port Lucaya Marina is the busiest of all the marinas in Freeport and Port Lucaya, with a

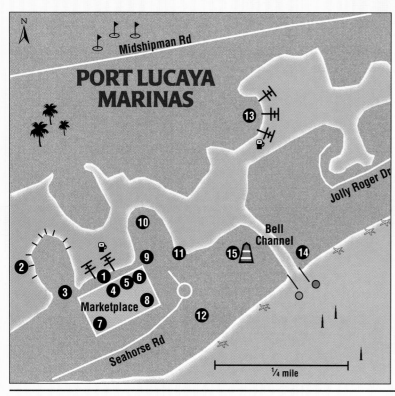

PORT LUCAYA MARINAS AND MARKETPLACE DIRECTORY

1. Port Lucaya Marina and Marketplace Wing
2. Port Lucaya Marina Sea Garden Wing
3. Port Lucaya Resort Hotel
4. Count Baisie Bandstand
5. Port Lucaya Yacht Club, on the second floor
6. Port Lucaya Marina Offices, on the second floor
7. Royal Bank of Canada
8. Drugstore
9. UNEXSO
10. Pelican Bay Hotel
11. Ferry House Restaurant
12. Lucayan Hotel
13. Lucayan Marina and Lucayan Marina Village
14. Bell Channel condomiums and private marina
15. Mock Lighthouse
⛽ Fuel
⚓ Golf Course

wide range of activities and facilities. It is on your port side as you come in through the Bell Channel, alongside the *Port Lucaya Marketplace* with its shopping crowds and limbo dancers. Restaurants are open all day, booze cruises come and go, and boat captains swap stories. If you prefer a quieter slip, ask to be put in the Sea Garden Wing. **Customs** and **Immigration** are on call in the marina. This is an official Port of Entry.

Slips	106
Max LOA	160 ft.
MLW at Dock	12 ft. in marina pool.
Entry Channel	6.5 ft. at low water.
Dockage	$1 per ft., $35 minimum, per day in slips. Choose between the peaceful Sea Garden Wing or the bustling Marketplace Wing. Long-term dockage by special arrangement. Alongside on end of T-docks, and parallel docking charges are $125 per day up to 100 ft., plus $1.25 for each additional ft., year round.
Power	25¢ per kWh for 30A, 50A, 100A, and 200A.
Fuel	Diesel and gasoline. Fuel dock open from 7 am to midnight, after midnight on request. Payment for fuel separate from dock charges. Bait, oils, and detergents at the fuel dock.
Propane	Same-day refills.
Water	$5 per day.
Telephone	$5 hookup charge.
Cable TV	$2 daily for 44-channel fiber-optic reception.
Showers	Next to the hotel restaurant by the pool, within the hotel's central garden.
Laundry	$1.25 washers, $1.25 dryers in quarters.
Restaurants	*Tradewinds Cafe* at the *Port Lucaya Resort* Tel: 373-6618 Breakfast and dinner buffets daily. *Pool Bar* at the *Port Lucaya Resort*, open daily 10 am to 6 pm. *The Brass Helmet* restaurant above UNEXSO is open from

7:30 am to 10 pm, with full-service dining, bar, and deli service. There are many restaurants in the Marketplace with a wide price range and choice. Some are open all day and late into the night.

Provisions	The marina office runs a bus that will take you to the *Winn Dixie* on Seahorse Avenue at 10 am and 3 pm daily except Sundays. Or you can take a cab, or a bus for 75¢ from the top of the main street outside the hotel and marina complex.
FedEx and UPS	Delivery available through the marina office.
Yacht Club	On registration, marina guests enjoy a two-month complimentary membership at the *Port Lucaya Yacht Club*, which is on the second floor, adjacent to the marina office, and opens from 5 pm to 1 am, serving meals daily. Private functions and parties can also be arranged and catered at the club.
Services	Domestic cleaning, laundry service, babysitting, catering, and long-term boat checks and maintenance.
Pump-out	At the fuel dock.
Accommodations	*Port Lucaya Resort and Yacht Club* Tel: 373-6618 Full-service resort hotel; 160 rooms overlooking either the pool or the marina. Rooms from $90 per night.
Deep Sea Fishing	*Reef Tours Ltd* Tel: 373-5880/5891/5892 Four hours fishing with only 4 to 6 people, from $70 per fisherman, $40 for spectators.
Diving	*Underwater Explorers Society* (UNEXSO) Tel: 373-1244 • Fax: 373-8956 At the end of *Port Lucaya Marketplace* boardwalk. Two-tank dive from $70, dolphin and reef two-tank dive from $169. Equipment rental and well-stocked dive shop with film processing and video service. See **Diving** in our SPORTS section for details.

Parasailing	*Reef Tours Ltd* Tel: 373-5880/5891/5892 $30 a flight.
Snorkeling	*Pat and Diane Cruises* Tel: 373-8681/1444 ext 4535 Also offer beach parties, booze cruises, and glass-bottom boat tours.
Submarine	*Deepstar* at *Reef Tours Ltd* Tel: 373-8940
Transportation	Courtesy transport to Freeport International Airport and local grocery stores.
Credit Cards	All major credit cards accepted.
Senior Dockmaster	Ryan Knowles

LUCAYAN MARINA AT THE LUCAYAN MARINA VILLAGE
Tel: 242-373-7616 • Fax: 373-7630 • VHF 16

To starboard after you enter through the Bell Channel, *Lucayan Marina* is a new, state-of-the-art marina with excellent facilities and a very helpful staff. It surrounds an imaginatively designed village community where the colorful homes are still under construction; no two are alike. *Lucayan Marina* acts as host to several major Boat Owner's Rendezvous. There is a no-tipping policy in the marina. **Customs** and **Immigration** are on call, and this is a Port of Entry.

Slips	125
Max LOA	150 ft.
MLW at Dock	7 ft.
Entry Channel	6.5 ft. at low tide.
Dockage	$1 per ft. per day.
Long Term	Rates are negotiable.
Power	25¢ per kWh, from 30A to 200A.
Fuel	Diesel and gasoline; fuel dock open from 7 am to 11 pm.
Propane	Same-day refill on weekdays.
Water	$5 per day. No charge for long-term storage boats.
TV	No charge for satellite hookup.

Telephone	No charge for hookup. Local and long distance calls billed at a nominal rate. Pay phones by the showers and laundry.
Laundry	$1.25 per load for washers and dryers.
Showers	Excellent and very clean showers, with handicapped-accessible toilets.
Restaurant	*The Pool Bar and Grill* serves lunch and snacks poolside and Bahamian Fish Fry Nights on Fridays. For breakfast, lunch, and dinner (and their Friday night specials!), the *Ferry House Restaurant* (Tel: 373-1595), open on the waterfront near the *Pelican Bay Hotel*, can be reached by the complimentary ferry from the marina dock or in your own dinghy from the marina.
Ice	$2 per bag.
Fax	$4 to send a fax, $3 per page to receive.
E-mail	Can be collected or sent from the sales office.
Maid services	Available
Office	Open from 7 am to 11 pm daily.
Swimming	Two-level pool with Olympic-length lap area and separate children's pool.
Barbecue Grills	There are grills set up for use in the grounds around the marina.
Bonefishing	Skiffs are available, with guides and special lunches each day, leaving from the *Pelican Bay.*
Fish Cleaning	Table available on the fuel dock.
Marine Mechanics	Can be contacted through the dockmaster.
Fishing Guides	Can be contacted through the dockmaster.
Pump Out	$20
Shuttle Service	Complimentary ferry runs between 8 am and 11 pm, to the *Ferry House, Port Lucaya Marketplace*, and the *Pelican Bay Hotel*.

Accommodations   *Pelican Bay Hotel*   Tel: 373-9550   Offers a special room rate of $90 per night for marina guests.
Credit Cards   Visa, MasterCard, and Amex.
Security   This marina is in a gated community, with 24-hour security staff on duty.
Dockmaster   Thomas Lockhart

MARINE SERVICES

BASRA Freeport   Tel: 352-6222 • VHF 16
Pager # 352-8339 for the Crew Chief
352-2628 for the Police Boat Yards

Boat Yards
Bradford Marine in Freeport Harbour   Tel: 352-7711 • Fax: 352-7695   Full-service boat yard with a 1,200-ton dry dock, and 30-foot depth with easy access. Call Freeport Harbour Control on VHF 16 before entering the commercial harbor.
OBS Marine Ltd at Queens Highway and Cedar Street Tel: 352-9246

Marine Weather Forecast
Freeport Weather Services   Tel: 352-9114 • Fax: 352-9432
For local and Gulf Stream weather forecasts.

SERVICES

Air Ambulance
Tel: 305-761-1512
Ambulance
Tel: 352-2689
ATMs
ScotiaBank Princess Casino, Freeport, gives US currency. All other *ScotiaBank* branches give US and Bahamian currency.
Royal Bank of Canada, main branch on East Mall and Explorers Way and at *Blvd Service Station* on Sunrise Highway, give Bahamian dollars.
All machines accept Visa, MasterCard, and cards connected to the Plus or Cirrus network.
ScotiaBank ATMs accept American Express as well as cards on the Novus network.

FREEPORT AND PORT LUCAYA DIRECTORY

1. Xanadu Beach Marina*
2. Running Mon Marina*
3. Ocean Reef Yacht Club (private)
4. Port Lucaya Marketplace; Port Lucaya Marina and Yacht Club*
5. Lucayan Marina*
6. The Lucayan Hotel
7. Lucaya Shopping Centre and Winn Dixie
8. International Bazaar

9. Airport
10. Rand Nature Centre
11. Garden of the Groves
12. Lucayan Medical Centre East
13. Sunrise Medical Centre
14. Lucayan Medical Centre West
15. Rand Memorial Hospital
⛳ Golf Courses
 * Marinas with fuel available

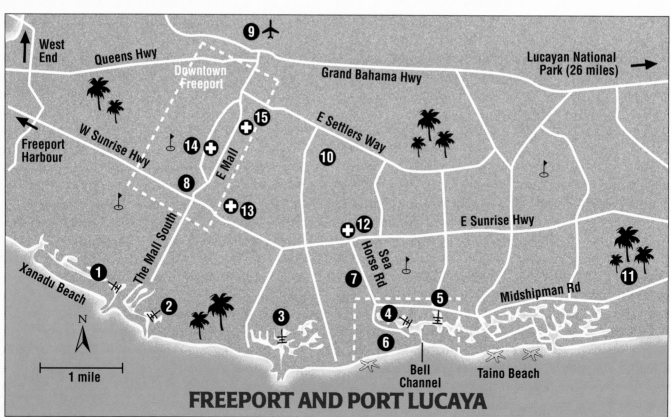

FREEPORT AND PORT LUCAYA

Banks
Most banks are open from 9:30 am to 3 pm, Monday to Thursday; to 5 pm on Fridays

Barclays Bank on Pioneers Way	Tel: 352-8391
Commonwealth Bank on The Mall Drive	Tel: 352-8307
At Lucaya	Tel: 373-9286

Royal Bank of Canada, Port Lucaya Marketplace Tel: 352-6631

ScotiaBank at Regent Centre Tel: 352-6774

Western Union at *British American Bank*, on the Mall, downtown
Tel: 352-6676/6677 Open 9 am to 4 pm daily.

Chamber of Commerce
Tel: 352-8329

Churches
There are 16 churches in the Freeport area, and only two of those are the same denomination, the Baptist churches of St. John's and the First Baptist. Every church has the times of services published in the Tourist Board's publication "What to do in Freeport," or posted outside the church itself.

Clinics
Lucayan Medical Centre West Tel: 352-7288

Lucayan Medical Centre East Tel: 373-7400

Sunrise Medical Centre Tel: 373-3333 Open daily from 8:30 am to midnight.

Consulates
Are all in Nassau.

American Embassy	Tel: 242-322-1181
British High Commission	Tel: 242-325-7471
Canadian Consulate	Tel: 242-393-2123

Customs
Tel: 352-8500, and

Immigration
Tel: 352-5454

Dentist
Tel: 352-8492 Dr Larry Bain is at the *Sun Alliance Building*, Pioneers Way.

Fire Brigade
Tel: 352-8888

Hospital
Rand Memorial Hospital On the Mall, downtown, with Emergency Room Tel: 352-6735/6736/6737/6738/6739

Library
Sir Charles Hayward Library, downtown on the Mall, next to *Rand Memorial Hospital* Open from 10 am to 5 pm, Monday, Wednesday, and Friday, and to 2 pm on Saturday.

Live Entertainment
Every evening from 8 pm to midnight, there is live entertainment at the central Count Baisie Square bandstand in *Port Lucaya Marketplace*. Dance the macarema along with everyone else, or compete with the fantastic limbo dancers. Gospel singing late Sunday afternoons.

Movies
Columbus 4 Theatres on East Mall Drive and Adventurer's Way Tel: 352-7478 Two-for-one admission on Wednesdays.

Performing Arts
Freeport Players Guild Tel: 373-8400 Presents three or four plays between September and June at the Regency Theatre.

Grand Bahama Players Tel: 352-7071 or 373-2299 Offers cultural productions featuring Bahamian, West Indian, and North American playwrights at the Regency Theatre.

Police
Tel: 352-8352 or dial 919 in an emergency.

Post Office
Explorer's Way, Freeport Tel: 352-9371 Open from 9 am to 5:30 pm, Monday to Friday. Stamps are also sold at *Crown Drugs* and *Oasis* in the *Port Lucaya Marketplace*, where there is a mailbox.

Recompression Chamber
At *UNEXSO* at Port Lucaya, but the chamber had been de-commissioned at time of writing. The nearest hyperbaric chamber would be in Florida, or the Lyford Cay Hospital in Nassau (Tel: 242-362-4025).

Telephones
All the hotels and marinas have telephones; there are 10 in the *Port Lucaya Marketplace*. $20, $10, and $5 phone cards are available from many stores, the *Batelco* offices in the *International Bazaar,* and downtown Freeport.

Theater
Regency Theatre Tel: 352-5533 For information about performances.

Tourist Information
Tel: 352-8044/8045 Pick up a street map, leaflets, and a free, comprehensive "What to do" booklet giving detailed descriptions of local places of interest, shopping, restaurants, sports, churches, etc. *The Tourist Office* at the *Port Lucaya Marketplace* was being relocated at time of writing, but there are others at the airport, the cruise ship terminal, and the *International Bazaar.*

SHOPPING

A wide selection of stores in the *International Bazaar* and *Port Lucaya Marketplace* offer something for everyone, and there are good shopping malls nearby.

Groceries
Winn Dixie at Lucaya Shopping Centre, Sea Horse Road
Tel: 373-5500 Closest to Port Lucaya.

Winn Dixie at Freeport Shopping Centre, downtown
Tel: 353-7901

Winn Dixie at Eight Mile Rock Tel: 348-2959
Stores open from 7:30 am to 9 pm Monday to Saturday, and from 7 am to 10 am on Sundays.
Free delivery to visiting boats for orders over $100.

Liquor Stores
Butler and Sands Duty Free Liquor Store on Port Lucaya waterfront. Open from 10 am to 7 pm, Monday to Saturday.

RESTAURANTS

Arawak Dining Room at the *Lucaya Golf and Country Club*
Tel: 373-1066 Serving very good French/Bahamian food overlooking the golf course. Open from 11:30 am to 3 pm daily, and from 6:30 pm to 10 pm Tuesday to Saturday. Closed on Sunday and Monday evenings.

The Princess Resort and Casino Sunrise Highway
Tel: 352-966l/6721/7811 A total of nine different restaurants.

Banana Bay Fortune Beach, Lucaya Tel: 373-2960
Chunky conch fritters and banana bread. Open 10 am to 6 pm; beachwear okay.

The Brass Helmet Tel: 373-2032 Upstairs at *UNEXSO*, at the end of the *Port Lucaya Marketplace* boardwalk. Self-service and full-service dining, open 7:30 am to 10 pm daily.

Captain's Charthouse East Sunrise Highway & Beachway Drive
Tel: 373-3900 or 373-3069 Tropical drinks, early bird specials, and a Bahamian Native Review feature at this unusual treetop-level restaurant. Reservations suggested. Open 5 to 11 pm, dinner and show at 7 pm. Free transportation for dinner guests.

The Ferry House, on the waterfront at the circle before *Pelican Bay Hotel* Tel: 373-1595 Ferry connecting to the *Lucayan Marina Village*, and dock space for boats up to 25 feet. Open daily from 7 am to 9 pm, excellent food, beautifully presented, with daily specials.

Port Lucaya Marketplace.

Giovanni's Cafe at the *Port Lucaya Marketplace* Tel: 373-9107 Italian chef Giovanni serves some of the best food outside Italy, as his wife Genny greets you and shows you to your table. Reasonable prices in a delightful atmosphere. Open from 7 am to 10 pm, closed Sundays.

Pier One Tel: 353-6674 Anchored on stilts in Freeport Harbour, with the best sunset on the island. Watch the cruise ships sail and the sharks being fed nightly at 7, 8, and 9 pm when the bell rings. Open from 10 am to 10 pm daily. Reservations recommended for the Shark Pit sittings.

The Pub at Port Lucaya Tel: 373-8450 Hearty pub fare, fresh seafood, and tropical drinks in a unique Victorian pub setting. Open from 11 am daily.

Pub on the Mall Tel: 352 2700/5110 There are three pubs at Ranfurly Circus, opposite the *International Bazaar. Islander's Roost, Prince of Wales Lounge* and *Red Dog Sports Bar*, serving Bahamian/Amercan food or pub fare.

Ruby Swiss European Restaurant Atlantic Way, opposite *Princess Resort* Tel: 352-8507 Gourmet menu and seafood with live entertainment nightly. Dinner special for two, $35 with gratuity. All-you-can-eat spaghetti bar for $9.75.

Silvano's Italian Restaurant Opposite the *International Bazaar* Tel: 353-5111 Serving homemade pasta. Reservations suggested.

The Stoned Crab on Taino Beach Tel: 373-1442 Dine overlooking the ocean. The nautical theme restaurant serves world-famous stone crab and seafood, as well as other dishes. Open 5 to 10:30 pm. Reservations suggested.

Zorba's Greek Cuisine at *Port Lucaya Marketplace* Tel: 373-6137 Freshly made authentic Greek dishes, as well as Ouzo and Retsina, accompanied by Greek music. Indoor and outdoor dining. Open from 8 am to 10 pm.

GETTING AROUND

Airlines
The departure tax from Freeport Airport is $18, not $15 as it is from every other airport in the Bahamas. Taxis charge around $14 for two people from Port Lucaya to the airport.

Air Canada (Nassau)	Tel: 377-8411 or 800-776-3000
American Eagle	Tel: 800-433-7300
Bahamasair	Tel: 352-8341/8346
Gulfstream Continental Connection	Tel: 800-231-0856 or 352-6447
Laker Airways	Tel: 352-3389

Air Charters
Major's Air	Tel: 352-5778	Aztec 402 or Beechjet 99.
Taino Air	Tel: 352-8885	Cessna 402

Buses
Cost 75¢ a journey around downtown Freeport or Port Lucaya, $1 between the two towns.

Car Rental
Don't forget! Drive on the left. Speed limit is 25 mph in town, 45 mph outside built-up areas.

Avis	Tel: 352-7666 at the airport
	Tel: 373-1102 in Port Lucaya
Bahama Buggies	Tel: 352-8750
Dollar	Tel: 352-9325
Hertz	Tel: 352-3297/9277
Thrifty	Tel: 352-9308

Cars cost from $49 to $119 per day with free unlimited mileage. Brightly painted dune buggies from *Bahama Buggies* can be rented from $50 per day.

Ferries
A daily scheduled auto and passenger ferry service was due to start, at time of writing, from North Riding Point to Crown Haven, Abaco, which is an hour's drive from Marsh Harbour. The journey would take about three hours. Cars can be driven on to the Water Bridge Ferry, which leaves North Riding Point, Grand Bahama, every morning, arriving on Great Abaco Island three hours later. Round trip rate per car is $300. Extra passengers are $50 for adults, and $25 for children. Call GSR Shipping at 373-1682 for details.

Mailboat
M/V Marcella III departs Freeport for Nassau at 5 pm on Fridays, a 12-hour trip, returning from Nassau on Wednesdays at 4 pm.

Scooters
Econo Motorbike Rental Tel: 351-6700

Taxis
Taxis charge $2 for first quarter mile and 30¢ for each additional mile. $2 per extra person. Most drivers will charge fixed fares for standard routes. From Port Lucaya to the airport will cost about $14 for two people.

Freeport Taxi Co Tel: 352-6666
Grand Bahama Taxi Union Tel: 352-7101

SPORTS

Bowling
Sea Surf Lanes on Queen's Highway Tel: 352-5784 Call for opening times.

Diving
Caribbean Divers Tel: 373-9111 Located at *Bell Channel Inn*, next to Port Lucaya. Rentals and specialty dives daily at 8 am, 10:30 am, and 1 pm. Two-tank dive $58; resort course daily at 9:15 am costs $79; snorkelers $20.

Underwater Explorers Society (UNEXSO) at the end of *Port Lucaya Marketplace* boardwalk Tel: 373-1244 or 800-992-DIVE in the US and Canada • Fax: 373-8956 One of the oldest dive operations in the Bahamas, UNEXSO was established in 1965, and administers diving access for the National Trust to the Lucayan National Park pre-Colombian underwater charted cave systems. UNEXSO have a very extensive and comprehensive dive shop, rental equipment, and a restaurant, *The Brass Helmet*, currently being remodeled at time of writing, at their Port Lucaya base. They also had the only recompression chamber outside Lyford Cay in the entire Bahamas. At time of writing this chamber was non-operational. Call *Lyford Cay Hospital* in Nassau at 242-362-4025 if you have a diving accident, or return to Florida.

UNEXSO offers over 35 dive sites including reefs, wrecks, caverns, walls, and blue holes, as well as night dives, courses in underwater photography, cavern diving, rescue diving, advanced open-water certification, marine awareness, and an exclusive four-day shark feeder program at *Shark Junction*, only ten minutes away from the Bell Channel entrance, for $2,495. If you prefer something less exhilarating, you can join the Dolphin Experience and swim with dolphins in several different programs. Two-tank dive $70, Dive Today $99, snorkelers $70 for two adventures, advanced open-water certification course $385, underwater photography course $189 with your own equipment.

Xanadu Undersea Adventures at *Xanadu Beach Resort and Marina*, Freeport Tel: 352-3811 or 352-6782, ext. 1421 Instruction, deep and wreck dive courses, night dives, shark dives, rental equipment, and repairs. Learn-to-dive classes every day at 8:30 am for $99. Two-tank dives $55, snorkelers $25 on the 10:30 am boat.

Bonefishing
Deep Water Cay Club, about 50 miles from Freeport
Tel: 353-3073 $1,310 for 3 nights and 2½ days fishing.
North Riding Point Club Tel: 353-4250 $1,315 for three nights and 2½ days fishing.
Pelican Bay Hotel Tel: 373-7616 $1,020 for three-night stay, with two fishing days, breakfast, and lunch included.
Sweeting's Cay Beach Resort
Tel: 353-3023 • E-mail: phllmel@batelnet. bs
Sam Taylor Tel: 352-8679

Deep Sea Fishing
Fisherman's Safari Tel: 352-7915 Captain John PM Roberts.
Ono Chase Tel: 373-2222 Day fishing with Captain Walter Kitchen on a 53-foot Hatteras for up to 6 people. Special trips to Walker's Cay, Chub Cay or Bimini for marlin or wahoo.
Paradise Watersports at *Xanadu Beach Resort*
Tel: 352-2887/4233 Half- or full-day charters on a 36-foot Chris Craft. Reef fishing $40 per person for two hours.
Reef Tours Ltd Tel: 373-5880/5891/5892 Four hours of fishing with only 4 to 6 people, from $70 per fisherman, $40 for spectators. Four custom sport fishing boats with tackle, bait, ice, and coolers provided.

Gaming
Princess Casino at the *Princess Resort* on West Sunrise Highway
Tel: 352-7811 Nearly 500 slot machines; blackjack, dice, poker, and baccarat tables.
A new casino will be opened at the end of 1999.

Golf
Fortune Hills Golf and Country Club Tel: 373-4500/2222
A picturesque 9-hole course; $43 for non-members for 18 holes. The restaurant is closed on Mondays.
Bahamas Princess Resort Tel: 352-9661/6721 Two challenging 18-hole PGA courses, the Emerald and Ruby. $65 for 18 holes.
Lucaya Golf and Country Club Tel: 373-1066 $80 for an 18-hole course. Designed by Dick Wilson with two lakes and the famous Balancing Boulders at the 18th hole. You can have lunch in the *Arawak Dining Room* daily from 11:30 am to 3 pm, and dinner from 6:30 pm to 10:30 pm Tuesday to Saturday.

Horseback Riding
Pinetree Stables Tel: 373-3600 $35 for an hour-and-a-half trail ride to the beach, accompanied by experienced guides. Dressage & jumping lessons; English saddles. Closed Mondays.

Parasailing
Reef Tours Ltd Tel: 373-5880 $30 a flight.
Paradise Watersports at *Xanadu Beach Resort* Tel: 352-2887
$30 a flight.

Sea Kayaking
Kayak Nature Tours Tel: 373-2485 Trips to *Peterson Cay*, the smallest National Park on Grand Bahama. Children must be over 10 years old. From $49 per person.

Tennis
There are more than 40 courts in the area, mostly at the hotels. Almost all are hard surface.

Water Skiing
Paradise Watersports at *Xanadu Beach Resort* Tel: 352-4233/2887
$20 an hour, lessons cost $40 for half an hour.

DIVE SITES

One of the best diving grounds in the Northern Bahamas, Grand Bahama proudly offers more than 36 dive sites within minutes of its southern shores. For ease of description, we list them in three categories; deep sites over 60 feet, medium sites between 40 and 60 feet, and shallow sites under 40 feet.

Deep Sites
There are caves to explore at *Littlehale's Lair*, *Pygmy Caves*, *Crystal Caves*, and the *Tunnels*, with a large blue hole at *Plate Reef*. *Blair House* has dramatic deep channels and wonderful deep-water staghorn, while *Theo's Wreck*, a 230-foot cement hauler, which was sunk in 100 feet of water in 1982, is now a main dive attraction. It is cloaked in sponges and teeming with marine life. *Ben's Caverns* make an exciting dive trip though part of the *Lucayan Cavern* complex; it is one of the most extensive underwater cave systems in the world, with incredibly clear water and some amazing stalactites and stalagmites.

Medium Sites
Shark Alley and the *Shark Encounter* are both for you if you are fascinated by sharks. If you prefer wreck diving, try *Etheridge Wreck*, a former car ferry sunk in early 1992 in 50 to 60 feet of water, or the *Papa Doc Wreck*, which sank in a storm in 1968 and now has the tugboat *Badger* lying alongside in 35 to 45 feet of water. Or another tug boat, *Doug's Wreck* lying upside down with the remnants of a cabin cruiser scattered around. *SPID City*, (standing for the Self-contained, Portable, Inflatable Dwelling which was used for short-term underwater living experiments in the '70s), is now home to schools of baracudas, horse eye jacks, snappers, and spadefish, with blue parrotfish on the bottom.

Shallow Dive Sites
Two of the best are the *Magic Kingdom* with a huge abundance of rays, eels, lobsters, octopus, squirrelfish, and butterflyfish, or *Silver Point*, a very attractive site with schools of grunts, parrotfish, angelfish, trumpetfish, and a beautiful variety of corals.

For exciting shark dives and dolphin dives, ask UNEXSO about their dive programs.

BEACHES

Xanadu Beach, with a mile-long stretch of white sand.
William's Town, where occasionally you may meet riders from *Pinetree Stables* riding along the sand.
Taino Beach, where you can treat yourself to a seafood feast at the *Stoned Crab Restaurant*.
Smiths's Point, with island specialties like *Mama Flo's* cracked conch, or fresh fish at *Outrigger's* Wednesday night native fish fry.
Fortune Beach, and those chunky conch fritters from *Banana Bay*.
Gold Rock Beach, at the end of the trail from the Lucayan National Park.

FISHING TOURNAMENTS & REGATTAS

February
Off Shore Deep Sea Fishing Tournament at *Xanadu Marina*
April
Port Lucaya Tuna and Dolphin Tournament. Contact the *Port Lucaya Marina* at 242-373-9090 for details.
June
Annual Grand Bahama Sailing Regatta. Contact Errol Ferguson at 352-9338 for details.
Bahamas Summer Boating Fling Flotilla. Call 800-327-7678 for details.

July

Port Lucaya Tuna and Dolphin Tournament. Contact the *Port Lucaya Marina* at 242-373-9090 for details.

Annual Bahamas National Bonefishing Championship, by invitation only, Call 800-32-SPORT for details.

Bahamas Summer Boating Fling/Flotilla. Call 800-327-7678. Contact the *Grand Bahama Tourist Board,* 242-352-8044, for more information.

ACCOMMODATIONS

Hotels in Freeport and Port Lucaya are changing and redeveloping so fast that we suggest you look in the current edition of "What to Do" or ask at one of the *Tourist Information Booths* if you need help finding accommodations. All the marinas have hotels on site, usually offering a discount for marina guests. See under **MARINAS** for details.

PLACES OF INTEREST

Bahamas National Trust Parks

Rand Nature Centre   Tel: 352-5438   Two miles from downtown, with guided tours through 100 acres of pine forest highlighting native plants and their medicinal uses, as well as migratory birds, reptiles, and a flock of flamingos. Open Monday to Friday, 9 am to 4 pm, Saturdays to 1 pm. Guided nature walks, Monday to Friday at 10 am and 2 pm; bird walks on the first Saturday of the month at 8 am; wildflower walk on the fourth Saturday at 8 am.

Lucayan National Park   Tel: 352-5438   Nature trails and one of the largest underwater cave systems in the world, 26 miles east of Freeport. *Ben's Cave* and *Burial Mound Cave* are habitats for rare underwater crustaceans and migratory bats in summer. Swimming is prohibited in the caves but you can dive them with UNEXSO. Open daily from 9 am to 4 pm, admission $3. Purchase tickets in advance at the *Rand Nature Centre*. Or you can take a *Kayak Nature Tour* (Tel: 373-2485) and enjoy a guided nature walk, visit caves, swim at Gold Rock Beach and kayak in a protected creek, for five hours, from $59.

Peterson Cay National Park Tel: 352-5438   About 15 miles east of Freeport and a mile offshore, this is an inviting cay for picnics, with surrounding reefs for snorkeling and diving.

Botanical Gardens

Garden of the Groves at the intersection of Midshipman Road and Magellan Drive Tel: 373-5668   Winding paths through 12 acres of mature tropical trees, waterfalls, fern gully, hanging gardens, and a chapel designed after the original church at Pine Ridge. Petting zoo with children's playground. Open from 9 am to 4 pm daily.

Hydraflora Gardens on East Beach Drive at Sunrise Highway Tel: 352-6052   Five acres of exotic tropical and subtropical plants, trees, and vines with a musical cave. Open from 9 am to 5:30 pm Monday to Friday, to 4 pm on Saturdays. Guided tours at 11 am Monday to Saturday. Admission $3 for an unguided tour, $6 for a guided tour.

THINGS TO DO IN GRAND BAHAMA

• Pick up your copy of the Bahamas Trailblazer map and "What to Do" in Freeport and Port Lucaya, to give you suggestions and ideas of what is going on here.

• Shop till you drop. Explore the *Port Lucaya Marketplace* and the *International Bazaar* for designer bargains and treasures from all over the world.

• Improve your golf game at one of three excellent courses.

• Take a kayak and paddle through Gold Rock Creek's mangroves, while bird spotting. Or discover the calm of Water Cay. Or bicycle along a coastal trail, watching birds and exploring caves. Call *Kayak Nature Tours* at 373-2485 for details.

• Have your hair braided.

• Dive some of the thirty-six regularly visited dive sites off the southern shore of Grand Bahama, within easy reach of Port Lucaya. Try your hand at shark feeding, or the Dolphin Experience, where you can interact with near-tame bottle-nosed dolphins.

• For a quick buzz, try skydiving or parasailing!

• Try your luck at the casinos.

• Rent a car for the day and explore the smaller settlements along the coast to West End. Or drive the other way out to the *Lucayan National Park* and *Barbary Beach*. Have a look at the *Grand Lucayan Waterway* as you pass and see whether you feel like taking your own boat through it.

• Join in the nightly dancing at the *Port Lucaya Marketplace*. All ages, lots of fun, especially the limbo dancers.

Casuarina Bridge on the Lucayan Waterway.

Part III

The Central Cruising Grounds

The Bimini Islands Group

The Great Bahama Bank

The Berry Islands

Nassau and New Providence Island

Eleuthera

North Andros

Bank water, about 20 feet deep, Sea of Abaco.

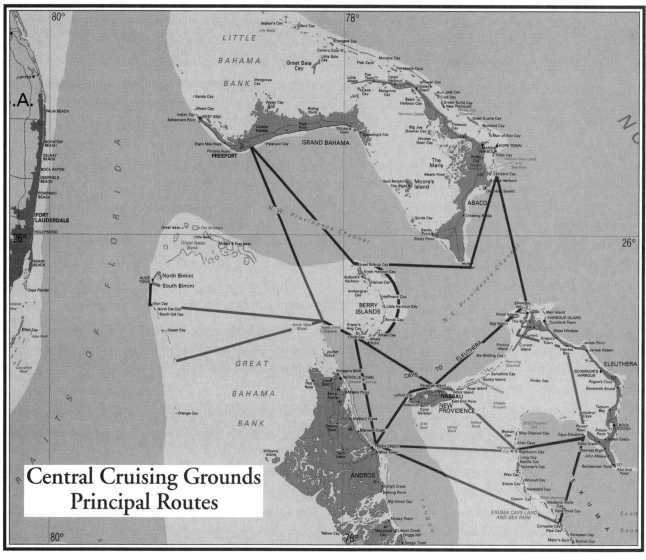

Central Cruising Grounds
Principal Routes

ROUTE TO/FROM		HEADINGS	DISTANCE NM	PASSAGE
Fort Lauderdale, Florida	Bimini	119°/299°M	48	Gulf Stream crossing
Fort Lauderdale, Florida	Gun Cay Cut	127°/307°M	52	Gulf Stream crossing
Miami, Florida	Bimini	095°/275°M	42	Gulf Stream crossing
Miami, Florida	Gun Cay Cut	106°/286°M	43	Gulf Stream crossing
Bimini	Gun Cay Cut	183°/003°M	09	Florida Strait coastal
Gun Cay Cut	NW Channel Light	095°/275°M	61	Great Bahama Bank
NW Channel Light	Chub Cay, Berry Islands	111°/291°M	15	NE Providence Channel
Chub Cay	Nassau	121°/301°M	35	NE Providence Channel
Chub Cay	Fresh Creek, Andros	167°/347°M	45	Tongue of the Ocean
Little Stirrup Cay	Chub Cay, Berry Islands	see text	40	Atlantic coastal
Fresh Creek, Andros	Highborne Cay, Exumas	092°/272°M	50	Tongue of the Ocean/Bank
Fresh Creek, Andros	Conch Cut, Exumas	114°/294°M	74	Tongue of the Ocean/Bank
Nassau	Allans Cay, Exumas	see text	38	Exuma Bank
Nassau	North Eleuthera	see text	43	NE Providence Channel
Spanish Wells	Harbour Island	see text	14	Devil's Backbone
Spanish Wells	Governors Harbour	see text	43	Current Cut/Bank
Governors Harbour	Cape Eleuthera	see text	28	Davis Channel/Bank
Cape Eleuthera	Highborne Cut, Exumas	255°/075°M	25	Exuma Sound
Cape Eleuthera	Conch Cut, Exumas	198°/018°M	33	Exuma Sound
South Eleuthera	Little San Salvador	096°/276°M	10	Exuma Sound
South Eleuthera	Hawk's Nest, Cat Island	131°/311°M	41	Exuma Sound

Distances exclude inshore close approaches at the start and end of a passage. The notation 'see text' indicates multi-leg passages that are fully covered in the text.

Chapter 8
The Bimini Islands Group

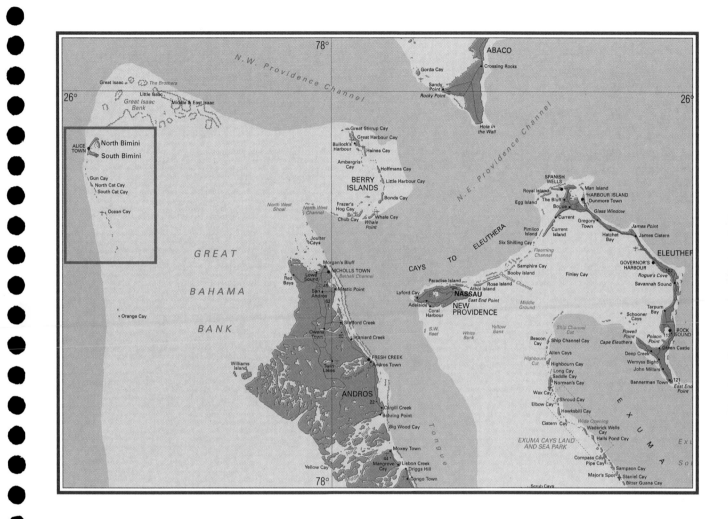

The Bimini Islands

BIMINI is a Bahamian name that rings a bell with most people. The immediate association is some kind of barefoot, laid-back island resort where anything goes, rum flows, deep sea fishing comes into it, together with the kind of weekend you wouldn't want your mother to know much about.

The name of the two small Bimini Islands (barely 9 square miles in land mass) serves as a convenient ID for the whole string of even smaller cays, rocks, and reefs that run south from North Bimini Island along the edge of the Gulf Stream for nearly 30 miles. However, when we talk of the Biminis, we really mean North and South Bimini Island, maybe with Gun Cay and Cat Cay thrown in. If we talk of Bimini, we mean North Bimini Island and Alice Town, but the town name is hardly ever mentioned. Bimini is the name that counts.

It wasn't always so. The Biminis didn't have a promising beginning. Juan Ponce de León passed that way in 1513 looking for the Fountain of Youth, but left disappointed. You might say he was ahead of his time. Now, almost five hundred years later, he might well have found the rejuvenating shot he needed in a place whose bars outnumber any other kind of store.

Bimini got its head start in the 1600s in the high days of piracy, went on to wrecking as a business until lighthouses were built, spoiling that game, and then learned all the tricks of blockade running during the US Civil War. Their new skills hit the jackpot during Prohibition (1920–33), and Bimini became the center of the rum-running trade targeted at the East Coast. When the 18th Amendment forbidding alcohol was repealed, Bimini might have slumped, but the luck of these islands still held.

BIMINI WAYPOINTS

North Rock		
NROCK	25° 51' 00"/000 N	079° 16' 30"/500 W
Bimini		
BMINI	25° 42' 30"/500 N	079° 19' 00"/000 W
Bimini Approach Range (not for navigation)		
BIMAP	25° 42' 05"/085 N	079° 18' 35"/583 W
Atlantis Dive Site (not for navigation)		
ATLDS	25° 45' 44"/733 N	079° 16' 44"/733 W
Gun Cay		
GUNCW	25° 34' 15"/250 N	079° 19' 30"/500 W
Cat Cay		
CATCE	25° 34' 00"/000 N	079° 17' 00"/000 W

The final figures in each waypoint show seconds (00") and thousands (000) of a minute.

By 1935 Ernest Hemingway and others found that the Bimini Islands were at the edge of one of the best ocean fishing grounds in the world. Since then tiny North Bimini, shaped like an upside-down fish hook and just over 7 miles long (and barely the equivalent of a mega-yacht LOA measured across the shank of the hook from coast to coast), has dominated the scattering of islands that share its name as a group. Today Bimini (and the Biminis) win on all counts as a cruising destination. What are the star points?

- The Biminis are the closest Bahamian islands to Florida. Just 50 nm away. Only two hours if you can do 25 knots, and ten hours if you can make 5 knots. Well within reach for weekend visits.

- Some of the best fishing you can find anywhere in the islands. It's world class.

- Great diving and good snorkeling, with dive sites that eclipse Florida's best.

- A place that *really* is different. There's no mistaking, as you walk up North Bimini's one-car-wide King's Highway (the main street), you are *not* in the USA!

- That Bimini "naughty weekend" atmosphere, which makes most people let down their hair the moment they land, if not one drink later.

- North Bimini and its southern neighbor, Cat Cay, are *the* obvious places to stop after your Gulf Stream crossing, clear in, and spend a night before setting off again across the Great Bahama Bank. They're equally obvious places to wait for the weather on your return crossing across the Stream.

Although there are many places where you can anchor in the Biminis (always with a sensible regard to the weather), there are only two places where you can secure alongside in a marina. The first, top of the list, is North Bimini with six marinas. The second is Cat Cay, or North Cat Cay to be

more accurate, with its Cat Cay Club.

If you're bound on bypassing the Biminis and carrying straight on across the Great Bahama Bank, North Rock (north of Bimini) and South Riding Rock (18 nm south of Cat Cay) may be your entry waypoints to Bank waters. Otherwise it'll be Gun Cay Cut, 9 nm south of Bimini and just north of Cat Cay, which will serve equally well as your access point to the Bank, whether you're staging in the Biminis, or riding past without touching land.

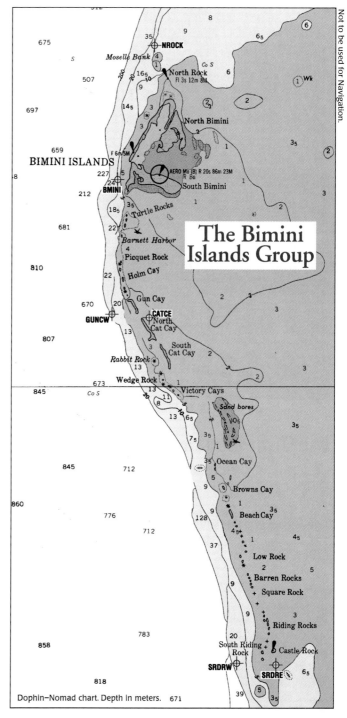

The Bimini Islands Group

Dophin–Nomad chart. Depth in meters.

Not to be used for Navigation.

Approaches to the Biminis

The geographical position of the Bimini Island group (Latitude 25° 40' 00 N as a median line), the run of the Gulf Stream, and the relative position of the Florida East Coast ports tell you with just a glance at the chart that it would be foolish, if you're heading for Bimini, to choose a Florida departure point anywhere north of Fort Lauderdale. Even from Lauderdale it's necessary to buck the Gulf Stream for 50 nm to reach the islands, and our own choice is to use the shortest course (just under 42 nm), which

Alice Town, North Bimini, from the northwest.

runs from the Miami harbor entrance to Bimini, and build an offset for the Gulf Stream into our course. We reckon Miami is the best jumping-off point for the Biminis, but we give you the options as we see them.

South Riding Rock (71.38 nm from Fort Lauderdale and 58.58 nm from Miami) offers no overriding advantages as a start point for your Bahamas cruise other than cutting some 6 nm in length from your Great Bahama Bank crossing. The Gun Cay Cut route is better and, even if you don't want to

call in anywhere, this route takes you past two potential havens, just in case you're in trouble.

North Bimini

If you're bound for Bimini Harbour, our landfall waypoint places you off South Bimini, a tad northwest of the approach range leading into the approach channel, so that you have a chance to pick up your bearings before going close inshore.

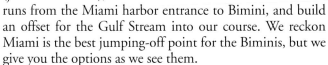

Bimini Cautions

Caution 1. Weather Conditions. Beware of trying to enter Bimini Harbour in southwest through northwest winds, particularly if the sea state is building up. In moderate conditions you should be fine, but you're exposed broadside on running along the beach from the entry markers. You're very close to the beach as you do this final leg. It is *not* sensible to attempt it in bad weather. Your best option is to divert to Gun Cay Cut, pass through, and seek shelter either behind Gun Cay or in Cat Cay Marina.

Caution 2. Approach Markers. The range markers leading you in are hard to see (particularly if you're being thrown around a bit). If you can't spot them, run slowly up and down to parallel the beach, keeping safely in deep water, until you have them fixed. Don't try to go in by guesswork. Neither of the two poles is significantly tall.

Caution 3. Shallow Water. The Bimini Sands development has now (1999) excavated a channel directly into an interior basin, which starts at the beach in the final third of your approach run in. Some local reports have it that the channel and its breakwaters have already altered the depth contours, and appear to be causing shoaling. If you have a significant draft, say over 4 feet, consider timing your entry and exit for High Water. In any event, go cautiously on you final run in, watch your depth, and be prepared to abort.

Caution 4. Chart Accuracy. Our GPS placed us on the sand by Pigeon Cay at the time we were in our slip in Bimini Bluewater Marina. As always, treat every GPS waypoint with caution, and the charts with reservation. It's your eyes that count every time you are close to shore or in shallow water.

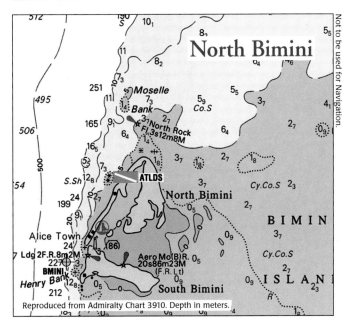

Reproduced from Admiralty Chart 3910. Depth in meters.

Bimini Approach Markers

At a distance out from South Bimini beach the most prominent landmarks are the pink townhouses of the Bimini Sands development, just south of the entrance to Bimini Harbour. There's a Texaco sign there that may stand out, and through binoculars you should be able to pick up the entry channel into the Bimini Sands basin with its green and red markers. The Bimini approach markers are at the southern end of that stretch of white beach, dwarfed by the background vegetation. Search carefully, looking for a straight stick, and you should be able to pick them up.

If you can't see the approach markers, pussy foot closer inshore to our BIMAP waypoint, which will place you in some 16 feet of water at low tide and about as close in as you want to be without knowing where you're going. The markers lie on a line of 075°M from that waypoint.

The range markers lead you straight in toward the white sand beach on the west shore of South Bimini. Turn to port having safely passed a sandbar on your port side and rocks and shallows on the starboard side. By then you'll be close to the beach, but in deeper water. Keep parallel to the beach and make your way up to the entrance to Bimini Harbour, which lies between North and South Bimini. You should have 5 feet at MLW, but go cautiously. Remember our caution about reports of shoaling in the Bimini Sands area. We found one shallow patch just to the north of the new Bimini Sands entrance where there would have been little more than 3 feet at MLW. Hence our advice to use the tide to your advantage.

If the wind is from the west and any kind of significant sea is running, this approach is not usable. Don't try it. Your immediate option is to divert to Gun Cay Cut and go to Cat Cay.

Bimini Harbour
MARINA AND ANCHORAGES

There are shoals extending out from both points of land at the entrance to the harbor. Choose your course carefully, staying mid-channel, and favor the mid-channel-to-port side of Bimini Harbour as you make you way up the fairway. The Chalks Airlines seaplane ramp and the marinas come up on your port side, and to starboard you have the Buccaneer Point Canal leading into the heart of South Bimini Island (about 4 feet MLW at the entry point) but there's nothing there for you. The Bimini marinas are first Harcourt Brown's (once derelict, but now apparently under renovation), Weech's Bimini Dock, then the Government Dock (with the Customs and Immigration), Sea Crest Hotel and Marina, the Bimini Blue Water Resort, and then the Bimini Big Game Fishing Club. To starboard you have nothing after that canal entrance but a shoal area that virtually dries at low water.

Bimini Harbour is used by the Grumman Mallard seaplanes of Chalks Airlines. You do *not* anchor in the main harbor freeway for this reason and also because local boats run fast through its length. The anchorage lies in the deeper water just past the Bimini Big Game Fishing Club. There's more than adequate depth there (8–10 feet) but take care that your anchor really sets, for the reversing tidal flow through Bimini Harbour is like a millrace. We mentioned speeding local boats. Don't swim too far away from your boat, or let a child stray too far, for the head of a swimmer would not be seen in time.

DOCK SPACE IN BIMINI

Bimini is crowded to capacity during its many fishing tournaments. It's crowded at Spring Break. It hits peak at any prime holiday weekend, particularly over the Fourth of July, and during the Summer Boating Flings. If you plan to visit Bimini at these times, book your marina space early.

The Gallant Lady *of Belize City, on the shore at Alice Town cemetery.*

ALICE TOWN

North Bimini's main settlement, Alice Town, is one place where you wouldn't even think of renting a bicycle. You can walk everywhere and cover the town in ten minutes. Alice Town is a strip of bars, shops, and market stalls that line the King's Highway, the main street running behind the marinas. It's pure island life there with an 80-proof rating, with the Compleat Angler Hotel (the Hemingway haunt) as its epicenter. A parallel road, the Queen's Highway, runs along the Gulf Stream coast, and there the Anchorage Hotel (don't be fooled: there's no anchorage that side) is the focal point. The beach is good.

In the last two years there are changes to note in Bimini, many of which are recorded in our **Yellow Pages**. A new visitor, likely to become a permanent resident, is the *Gallant Lady* of Belize City, now permanently lodged on the beach by the Alice Town cemetery (just north of the Bimini Harbour entrance). She must have been a handsome pocket trader in her time. Ashore the *End of the World* now bears a subtitle, the *Sand Bar*. Why? It's seems that many of its clients never realized that they'd hit the End of the World, but when gravity took over, soon realized what had been down there, under their feet. The PanAm Air Bridge has reverted to its ancient title, Chalks, and everyone is happy with that. Harcourt Brown's Marina is under renovation, but was not open for transient visitors (this at the time we write, April 1999). But see our **Yellow Pages**.

What is unpredictable is the future with regard to marinas lying outside the main strip in Alice Town Harbour. In North Bimini a new project, the Bimini Bay Hotel Marina and Resort promises everything in its title, and threatens a casino in addition. In South Bimini the Bimini Beach Club and Marina is closed, apparently awaiting a new life.

Atlantis or the Bimini Road Dive Site

You've heard that the Bahamas were the site of Atlantis? The evidence is right there. Want to dive it? There's a marker buoy there, waiting for you. Atlantis or the Bimini Road rock formation is on the sea bed in 15 feet of water off Paradise Point, North Bimini. We said "dive," but all you need is a mask and snorkel.

THE MARKER BUOYS

There are sixteen mooring buoys in the Bimini area, all placed to mark dive sites by Bill and Nowdla Keefe who run Bimini Undersea Adventures. They welcome you to make use of these buoys when you go diving, but ask that you call them first on VHF 6 (Bimini Undersea) and check that the buoy you would like to use is not required by them that day.

The End of the World, aka the Sand Bar in Bimini.

What's at the Atlantis dive site? A relatively small area of roughly rectangular flat rocks lying almost totally buried in the sand, which look like the paving stones of a ramp or road, or perhaps the cap stones of an ancient harbor wall. Certainly the stones have the appearance of having been fashioned and placed by man rather than a geological freak of nature. If you go for the Atlantis theory you're into wish fulfillment, for it's impossible to divine any plan in the site and, were it prehistoric, too much (one guesses) lies buried to permit analysis. This site has also been linked with the Moselle Bank, to the northwest of Bimini, which was also wrapped up in the Atlantis theory, as were the "lemon shark" sand mounds discovered in 1977 in the mangroves to the east of Bimini. These might be termed Bimini's version of the Nazca Lines, both of which can only be seen from the air.

South Bimini

You can dinghy across to South Bimini or take the water taxi from the Government Dock. There's little to see there, though someone will always be willing to show you where Juan Ponce de León's Fountain of Youth once flowed, and there's a major new development, Bimini Sands, townhouses with their own docks, but this has been a long time getting past the model house stage.

South of the Biminis—
Gun Cay and Gun Cay Cut

Turning south from South Bimini, a run of 9 nm takes you to Gun Cay. You're in interesting waters. For snorkelers there's Turtle Rocks and the far more striking wreck of the *Sapona*, the victim of a 1929 hurricane, which is a good shallow dive, too. For divers there are two more shipwrecks to explore, the *Bimini Barge* in 65–100 feet, and the *Bimini*

Trader. There's Picquet Rock and Holm Cay, and then, at the north end of Gun Cay, Honeymoon Harbour.

The rounded cove that forms Honeymoon Harbour is everyone's first dream of what a Bahamian anchorage should be like, with its sand beach and the Gulf Stream–side beach just across a spit of land. The downside is that the cove is exposed to wind wherever it comes from, and at peak Bimini visit periods, if you get there first and are anchored in virtual isolation or even get in with the first wave of a holiday invasion, you'll soon feel that you're in a boat jam worse than being caught in Friday afternoon Beltway traffic.

On the south end of Gun Cay there's the famous landmark Gun Cay Light, and the passage between Gun Cay and Cat Cay to its south is the access channel to the Great Bahama Bank known as Gun Cay Cut.

You can make your way south from South Bimini on the Great Bahama Bank side, but you have to feel your way. There are shoals to the east of Turtle Rocks, and shoals to the east of Gun Cay, and in places you'll find little more than 6 feet at MLW. We don't favor it, and take the deepwater route on the Gulf Stream side every time.

Gun Cay and Gun Cay Cut

Once you're at our Gun Cay west waypoint (GUNCW), turn to pass through Gun Cay Cut. The 2.5 nm or so you run through Gun Cay Cut must be taken visually, favoring Gun Cay Point and running in the deep water parallel to the shoreline (to avoid the shoal and reef extending north from Cat Cay) until you are through the Cut. Don't go too close in to Gun Cay as you go through the Cut, but there's

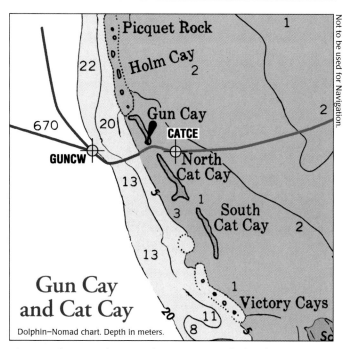

Gun Cay and Cat Cay

Dolphin–Nomad chart. Depth in meters.

plenty of water there and you can read the deeper water easily. Hold your course until, looking down the east coast of Cat Cay, you can see the entrance to Cat Cay Marina with its dwarf lighthouse.

Whether you're bound for a Bank crossing or for Cat Cay, turn to starboard at that point. Using the two lights, Gun Cay and Cat Cay as markers, one ahead and one astern, head south. This line will keep you clear of the shoal area close in to Cat Cay, and shoals that lie to the east of Gun Cay Cut. If you're going to Cat Cay, carry on into the marina.

If you're heading across the Great Bahama Bank, turn east to pick up your departure waypoint (CATCE) when you reach the line of Latitude 25° 34' 00 N. For routes across the Bank see **The Great Bahama Bank** on page 139.

Be aware that the holding behind Gun Cay (on the east) is fair weather only. There's some sand there, but it's not deep enough to hold an anchor if it blows. There's solid ledge underneath. Garry Miller of *Dad Bear*, whose advice has been invaluable more than once, told us that his 33-lb. Bruce with an all-chain rode failed to hold when the wind stepped out of the east. His 45-lb. CQR with 50 feet of three-eighths chain and three-quarter-inch nylon did hold. That's throwing metal down on the seabed, and not all of us carry that kind of ground tackle. Years back, in our *Terrapin* days, we dragged during the night anchored there. Conscious that more than one boat had gone on the rocks of Gun Cay, at that time we elected to go walkabout for the rest of the night, and eventually sought a haven in Honeymoon Harbour at dawn. It wasn't a good choice. The only sensible answer is this: anchor behind Gun Cay if conditions are favorable. If the wind changes, go to Cat Cay

Gun Cay Lighthouse.

Janet Wilson

Marina. It's the only safe option.

Cat Cay

Cat Cay is a private club situated on and wholly owning an island that is about 2.5 miles long and barely a mile wide. They welcome visitors (but not over the weekend of the Fourth of July) and you can clear in there, refuel, use all the marina facilities, and dine ashore in their restaurant. If you just call to clear Customs and Immigration into the Bahamas and then move on, you will be charged a $25 transient fee. Cat Cay have set out floating No Wake buoys running out from the entrance to Cat Cay Marina. While these are

Gun Cay Cut, from the northwest.

not channel markers as such, they serve as a useful entry line. Stay to the east of them (in other words, don't run between the markers and the beach). The first of these buoys comes up at 23° 33' 44"/733 N 079° 16' 57"/950 W.

For some cruisers, Cat Cay is preferable to Bimini. If you're not interested in diving in Bimini waters, the Bimini crowd scene, and the Bimini bars, you'll find Cat Cay not only meets your requirements, but gives you a more peaceful time. It could just turn claustrophobic if you get holed up there. The island, at least technically, is private turf and not a playground open to cruising visitors (unless they are members or guests). We spent nine days there once, holed up waiting for a chance to cross the Gulf Stream. Cat Cay was kind. We were allowed to walk around as we wished, but even then you can get to know one small island better than you ever intended. Have you heard of cabin fever?

South of Cat Cay

There's little of interest (other than some good diving) in the remaining 18-nm run of the line of the small cays and reefs that form the "trailing end" of the Bimini chain. After Cat Cay is its uninhabited sibling, South Cat Cay, then the Victory Cays (a popular dive site), Sandy Cay, Ocean Cay (an aragonite sea mining operation that is a high-visibility landmark), Brown's Cay, Beak Cay, and the Riding Rocks leading to South Riding Rock.

To the south of South Riding Rock there's the lonely Orange Cay, another 18 nm further on, but we've never been there.

SOUTH RIDING ROCK

We deal with the South Riding Rock approach on to the Great Bahama Bank in our section **The Great Bahama Bank** on page 142.

Returning to Florida

For courses and straight-line distances see **Crossing the Gulf Stream** on page 17.

Aragonite

DO you know what aragonite is? We didn't. Aragonite, named after Aragon in Spain, is an orthorhombic mineral made up of calcium carbonate, $CaCO_3$. It resembles calcite, but is heavier and harder, has less cleavage, and occurs less frequently. Our source is Webster's *New World Dictionary*.

Any wiser? Apparently it's a pure limestone, used for cement and fertilizers.

YELLOW PAGES

This area was hit by Hurricane *Floyd* in September 1999. Be aware that post-hurricane repairs and reconstruction may still be in progress, and wind and storm surge damage may still be evident.

NORTH BIMINI

If this is your first taste of the Bahamas, just 48 miles due east of Miami, then you're off to a great start. Despite a heavy influx of visitors throughout the year, Bimini retains an air of calm and relaxation. With all the shops and restaurants located on the King's Highway in Alice Town, only a minute's walk away from the brilliant white sand beach off the Queen's Highway on the west side, nothing is hard to find or to reach. Once the sport fishing capital of Ernest Hemingway's world, the tradition is carried on with pride, as keen fishermen pour in to attend the major sporting events of the season.

The **Customs** office, (347-3100), is in the large pink and white building at the Government Dock, and is open from 7 am to 7 pm daily. If you have just arrived from the US, the ship's captain should take the forms for everybody on board, already filled out, together with all the passports and the ship's documents, to the office. Your marina may well give you the forms on arrival if you have your yellow Q flag flying. Don't forget to keep it flying until you have completed the formalities at both Customs and Immigration. The **Immigration** office (347-3446) is now next door to the customs building, behind the Welcome Arch, within the new Straw Market. The office is open from 8 am to 6 pm Monday to Friday, and from 7 am to 6 pm on Saturday and Sunday. Only the captain is required to present the boat's papers and passports, crew are not needed and should stay on board until the boat is cleared in.

MARINAS

As they appear on your port side coming into Bimini Harbour:

BROWN'S HOTEL AND MARINA
The hotel has acquired a new roof and is slowly being refurbished, but the docks remain home only to Bill and Knowdla Keefe's *Bimini Undersea* dive boats, and a few local boats.

WEECH'S BIMINI DOCK
Tel: 242-347-3028 • Fax: 347-3508 • VHF 18
At this very small marina you will be welcomed by Dockmaster Morris Bowleg, and greeted by flowers as you enter the office area. The facilities are limited, but the welcome is warm.

Slips	15
Max LOA	100 ft.
MLW at Dock	5 ft.
Dockage	70¢ per ft. per day, $20 per day minimum charge, which includes use of washdown water, showers, and barbecue grills.
Power	$10 per day for 110V, $20 for 220V.
Showers	Yes
Ice	$2.50 per bag.
Fax Service	$5 per page outgoing, $1 per page incoming.
Boat Rental	Boston Whaler available for $60 for half day, $120 for a full day.
Credit cards	Cash only

SEA CREST HOTEL AND MARINA
Tel: 242-347-3477 (marina); 242-347-3071 (hotel) • Fax: 242-347-3495 • VHF 68
Home to Bimini's Gateway Wahoo Tournament, Dockmaster Michael, and Elaine in the hotel, will welcome you and your guests to Sea Crest. With *Captain Bob* serving breakfast from 6:30 am, there can be no better way to start the day's fishing.

Slips	14
Max LOA	105 ft.
MLW at Dock	5 ft.
Dockage	90¢ per ft. per day, $30 per day minimum.
Power	$12 per day up to 40 ft., $18 per day to 50 ft., $25 per day to 60 ft., and $30 per day over 61 ft.
Water	30¢ a gallon.
Showers	Yes
Barbecue	Grill on the dock for use by marina guests.
Accommodations	*Sea Crest Hotel* Tel: 242-347-3071 Rooms from $90 per day; 2-bedroom suites from $190 per day.
Fax	$5 per page outgoing, $1 per page incoming.
Credit cards	Visa and MasterCard.

BIMINI BLUE WATER RESORT
Tel: 242-347-3166 • Fax: 347-3293 • VHF 68
This small, very friendly marina has the added advantages of the *Anchorage Hotel* with a good restaurant, the *Compleat Angler* bar with its Hemingway charm, and easy access to the white sand beach on the ocean side of the island, where you can swim and relax after your Gulf Stream crossing.

Slips	25
Max LOA	100 ft.
MLW at Dock	5 ft.
Dockage	75¢ per ft. per day, $30 minimum per day.
Power	$10 per day up to 40 ft., $15 per day to 50 ft., $20 per day to 60 ft., $25 per day over 60 ft.
Fuel	Diesel and gasoline.
Propane	Yes
Water	40¢ a gallon.
Showers	Yes
Laundry	Ask at reception.
Restaurant	*The Anchorage Restaurant and Bar* at the hotel serves breakfast, lunch, and dinner.
Bar	*The Compleat Angler,* across the street from the marina, opens at 11 am.
Ice	$2.50 per bag.
Barbecue	Grill for marina guests on the dockside.
Swimming	Freshwater pool overlooking the harbor.
Accommodations	*The Anchorage, Bimini Blue Water Resort* Tel: 242-347-3166 Rooms, suites, cottages from $90 per night. Marlin Cottage, where Ernest Hemingway stayed, $285 per night.
Credit cards	Visa, MasterCard, Amex.

BIMINI BIG GAME FISHING CLUB
Tel: 242-347-3391 • Fax: 347-3392 • VHF 68

Slips	100
Max LOA	101 ft.
MLW at Dock	10 ft. to 12 ft.
Dockage	$1.25 per ft. per day.
Dockage (small craft)	On floating dock, $25 per day up to 30 ft., no water or electricity.
Power	$15 per day up to 39 ft., $20 per day to 49 ft., $30 per day to 59 ft., $37 per day to 80 ft., $50 per day over 80 ft.
Fuel	Diesel and gasoline.
Propane	Yes
Water	45¢ a gallon.
TV	Hookup to cable TV.
Showers	Yes, very clean.
Laundry	Yes, ask at the hotel.

Restaurant	*Gulf Stream Restaurant* open 7:30–10:30 am for breakfast and 7–10 pm for dinner.
Bars	*Big Game Sports Bar* serves lunch from noon; Bacardi drinks and 4 televisions for watching sports. *Barefoot Bar*, open poolside from mid-morning to late afternoon. *Gulf Stream Bar* with calypso music in the evenings.
Liquors	Liquor store near the front gate sells Bacardi rum products, beer, and soft drinks. Closed on Sundays. Deliveries to your boat.
Ice	Can be delivered to boats.
Barbecue	Grills for marina guests, near the cottages.
Box Lunches	Order from the restaurant for the next day.
Freezers	Limited freezer space for small boats to store bait.
Logo Shop	With many *Bimini Big Game Fishing Club* logo items; closed on Tuesdays.
Fishing	Sailfish, prize marlin, tuna, wahoo, kingfish, dolphin, and bonefishing available. Check with the dockmaster for recommendations.
Swimming	Pool in front of hotel building.
Tennis	Court available; lit at night.
Telephone	At the front office; a small service charge applies. There is a *Batelco* card phone outside the gate to the marina.
Credit cards	Visa, MasterCard, Amex. No personal checks.
Membership	Discount on charges for members.

SERVICES & SHOPPING IN ALICE TOWN

Bank
Royal Bank of Canada   On the King's Highway   Open 9 am to 3 pm on Monday & Friday, to 1 pm on Tuesday, Wednesday, and Thursday.

Churches
Community Church of God
Heavenly Vision Church of God
Holy Name Catholic Church
Mt. Zion Baptist Church
Our Lady and St. Stephen Anglican Church
Wesley Methodist Church

Clinic
Bimini Community Health Center in Bailey Town   Tel: 347-2210 Open 9 am to 5:30 pm Monday to Friday, with a doctor and nurse full time, and an 8-bed overnight facility. There is also a dentist in attendance. In an emergency, you can call Dr. Paul's residence at 347-2480, or the nurse at 347-2111.

Groceries
Brown's General Store in Bailey Town   Tel: 347-2305   Open 7:30 am to 2 pm and 4 pm to 8 pm Monday to Saturday, and 7:30 am to 10 am on Sundays.

The Alice Town cemetery.

Jontra's Grocery Store on King's Highway, close to *The Big Game Fishing Club*   Open from 7:30 am to 8:30 pm Monday to Saturday and from 7:30 am to 11 am on Sundays.
Roberts Supermarket   Tel: 347-3251   On King's Highway, beyond the pink administration building.
Watson's Supermarket on King's Highway   Open from 7 am to 7 pm, Monday to Saturday; to 10 am on Sundays.

Hardware and Marine Supplies
Bimini General Store   At *Weech's Bimini Dock*   Tel: 347-3359 Open from 10 am to 1 pm and 4 pm to 7 pm Monday to Saturday; closed Wednesday afternoons.

Laundry
Hinzey's, just past *Batelco* in Alice Town. Coin operated.
Porgy Bay Laundry has a pickup and delivery service.

Liquor Stores
Beverage Depot   Under the *Bahamas Art and Craft Boutique* and *Bimini Undersea* dive shop   Tel: 347-3112   Open 9 am to 5 pm Monday to Saturday, except Tuesdays to 2 pm.
Butler and Sands on King's Highway   Open from 9 am to 6 pm Monday to Saturday.
Sue and Joy Variety Store   Open 8 am to 9 pm Monday to Saturday and 8–11 am on Sunday. Liquor, pharmacy, souvenirs.

Police
Emergency: Dial 919 or Tel: 347-3144   Located in the pink administration building with the post office, just north of the *Bimini Big Game Fishing Club*.

Post Office
In the pink administration building, just north of the *Bimini Big Game Fishing Club*. Open 9 am to 4:30 pm, Monday to Friday.

Shopping
The new Straw Market next to the Customs House is a great source of T-shirts and souvenirs.

Telephones
All along the King's Highway. Some are coin operated, and some use phone cards, which are now on sale by the soft drinks machine in the pink administration building, just north of the *Bimini Big Game Fishing Club*. You will need a $20, $10, or $5 bill to purchase one here, or go to the *Batelco* office, a short walk further north.

Videos
Gesila Video Rentals in Bailey Town, opposite the baseball park.

RESTAURANTS

The Anchorage at the *Bimini Blue Water Resort*   Tel: 347-3166 Well-cooked food in an old home setting, with large windows overlooking the beach and ocean. Dinner reservations suggested.
Bimini Bay   At the Island's northernmost tip. A fantastic setting for a special evening. Call Basil or Antoinette Rolle at 347-2171 to make a reservation; they will send their own transport for you for $2 per person from any marina.
Captain Bob's   Across from Sea Crest Marina, serving the best breakfast in Bimini from 6:30 in the morning, sandwiches and more at lunchtime, and great Bahamian dinners. Popular with early-rising fishermen.
Fisherman's Paradise   At the south end of town, next to the *End of the World/ Sand Bar*. Serving Bahamian food for lunch and dinner, outdoors overlooking the harbor or inside with the *Star Disco* in the evenings.
Gulf Stream Restaurant at the *Bimini Big Game Fishing Club* Tel: 347-3391   Breakfast 7:30–10:30 am, dinner 7–10 pm. Live music; dinner reservations recommended. Good wine list; expensive.
Opal's Fish Restaurant   Very relaxed: the menu is announced to the entire room and then orders are taken. Lunch from 12 noon, dinner from 7 pm.
Red Lion Pub Restaurant and Bar   On the waterfront with home-cooked food in a cheery, friendly atmosphere. Bar opens at 5 pm.

BARS

There are many bars located in the marinas and attached to the restaurants. Everything is so accessible in Alice Town that it is fun to wander along and choose one that suits your mood.

Big Game Sports Bar at the *Bimini Big Game Fishing Club* Lunch from noon. Enjoy the best view in Bimini and a Big Game Conch Pizza. The *Gulfstream Bar* has calypso music in the evenings.

Compleat Angler Hemingway's favorite haunt, and a must visit. Sit under the tree or look at the photographs of early fishing tournaments in Bimini. Open 11 am to 1 am, with live calypso music on weekends.

End of the World Bar, at the southern end of the King's Highway has autographed walls and sand floors, and has now adopted the name *Sand Bar* after so many people asked the way to the bar with the sand floor!

Island House Bar opposite the *Red Lion Pub* Open 11 am to 3 am.

GETTING AROUND

Airlines
Chalks Tel: 800-424-2557, 242-347-3024, or 305-371-8628 Sea planes leave from the southern tip of North Bimini, using the harbor as a runway for the 25-minute flights two or three times a week to and from Watson Island, Miami, to Walker's Cay and Fort Lauderdale, and to Paradise Island for Nassau.

Bicycles
Bimini Undersea Tel: 347-3089 $7 per hour, $15 per half day, from 9 am to 1 pm or 1 to 5 pm, $25 per full day.

Boat rental
Weech's Bimini Dock Tel: 347-3028 • VHF 18 Boston Whaler available through the dockmaster, $60 for half-day rental, $120 for full day.

Buses
Frequent service up and down the length of North Bimini; hail a bumper sticker–covered jitney on the street. Fare is $3.

Ferries
Leave from the Government Dock every few minutes for South Bimini. Fare is $3, with transport on the other side it is $5. Taxis wait at both sides.

Golf Carts
Capt. Pat's at Sea Crest Marina Tel: 347-3477
Elvis Golf Cart Rental just north of the *Bimini Big Game Fishing Club* Tel: 347-3055/3056

Mailboat
M/V Bimini Mack sails to Bimini and Cat Cay weekly from Nassau. Fare $45.

Scooters
Bimini Scooters at *Watson's Supermarket.* Tel: 347-3089 $10 per hour, $50 per day.

Sea Kayaks
Bimini Undersea Tel: 347-3089 $15 per hour, $25 for half day either 9 am to 1 pm or 1–5 pm, $45 for full day.

Taxis
LCM Taxi Service VHF 68

SPORTS

Diving
Bimini Undersea Tel: 347-3089, 800-348-4644, or 305-653-5572 (for US reservations) • Fax: 347-3079 • VHF 6 • Web site: www.biminiundersea.com • E-mail: info@biminiundersea.com Bill and Knowdla Keefe offer a full range of dive experiences. One-tank dive costs $49, snorkelers $29, full range of rental equipment including underwater cameras, but no dive lights so bring your own for night dives. Their Wild Dolphin Excursion costs $99 for adults over 15, and $59 for children ages 8 to 14.

Dive Sites
Although there are more challenging sites around, the most famous site in the Bimini islands, or even in the Bahamas, is, of course, *Atlantis,* with its underwater pavement. *Hawksbill Reef* with schools of snapper and *Rainbow Reef* in around 25 feet of water, protected by the Bahamas Ministry of the Environment, lie northwest of Bailey Town, together with some caverns where you will meet lots of nurse sharks. There is also an exciting drift dive off the wall, right opposite Alice Town, which you can do with *Bimini Undersea.* The *Bimini Barge,* off South Bimini, lies in 100 feet of water, and the *Sapona,* part of which is still visible east of Turtle Rocks, both make good wreck dives; the *Sapona* is particularly good for snorkelers, but beware of the fire coral. *Bimini Undersea* have marked a number of sites with their own buoys, which not only make locating the dive site easier, but also protect the reef. You are welcome to pick up one of their buoys for your dive if they are not using it themselves, but please call them first on VHF 6. A list of GPS coordinates of dive site positions is available from them for $25, which goes to help maintain these buoys.

Fishing
Most marinas will arrange for charters or boat rentals. Expect to pay about $400 (half day) or $600 (full day) for deep sea fishing with a guide, tackle, and bait. Fishing guides for both deep sea and bonefishing are readily available.

FISHING TOURNAMENTS

There are fishing tournaments held almost every month in Bimini. For information and dates, call *Bimini Big Game Fishing Club, Bimini Blue Water Resort, Sea Crest Marina,* or contact the Bimini Progressive Sporting Club, PO Box 613, Bimini, Bahamas.

February
Mid-Winter Wahoo Tournament, Bimini Big Game Fishing Club
March
Bacardi Billfish Tournament, Bimini Big Game Fishing Club
April
Bimini Break Blue Marlin Tournament, Bimini Big Game Fishing Club
Annual Bimini Sailing Regatta
May
Bimini Festival of Champions, Bimini Big Game Fishing Club
June
Bahamas Summer Boating Fling at the Blue Water Resort
Big Five Fishing Tournament, Bimini Big Game Fishing Club
July
South Florida Fishing Club Rendezvous and *Latin Builders Fishing Tournament*, both at the Bimini Big Game Fishing Club
Bahamas Summer Boating Fling, Blue Water Resort
August
Bimini Native Fishing Tournament; Big Game Club Family Tournament; Bahamas Summer Boating Flings, all at the Bimini Big Game Fishing Club
September
Open Angling Tournaments, Bimini Big Game Fishing Club
November
Big Game All Wahoo Tournament, Bimini Big Game Fishing Club
Ossie Brown Memorial Wahoo Tournament, Blue Water Resort
Bimini's Gateway Wahoo Tournament, Seacrest Marina

ACCOMMODATIONS

The Anchorage at *Bimini Blue Water Resort* Tel: 242-347-3166 Rooms from $97.20 per day, Marlin Cottage $285 per day.
Bimini Big Game Fishing Club and Hotel Tel: 242-347-3391 Rooms from $149 per day, $298 for a penthouse.
Bimini Bay Tel: 242-347-2171 With a beautiful site at the northern tip of the island, this hotel is awaiting redevelopment and expansion. Meanwhile, there are one- and two-bedroom

condos and suites available from $75 per day midweek, $585 weekly.

Compleat Angler Tel: 242-347-3122 Rooms from $68 a night.

El Rancho Apartments $300 per month for a basic bedroom with bathroom, kitchen, and sitting room.

Sea Crest Hotel Tel: 242-347-3071
Rooms from $95 per day, suites from $200 per day.

Weech's Bay View Rooms Tel: 242-347-3028
Rooms from $63 per day, efficiency apartment to sleep four, $130 per day.

SOUTH BIMINI

Although separated by only 150 yards of water from its northern neighbor, South Bimini has hardly shared in its prosperity. You can visit Juan Ponce de León's supposed Fountain of Youth, though it is sadly overgrown. There are a few homes, a small grocery store called *Morgan's Drive Supermarket*, an automobile and small boat repair shop close to the airport, the currently closed *Bimini Beach Club and Marina*, and the little *South Bimini Yacht Club* that is on a narrow canal and plays host to *Scuba Bimini* dive guests. The pink townhouses you see as you approach Alice Town Harbour is the new development, *Bimini Sands*, with its own marina entrance clearly marked.

MARINA

BIMINI SANDS
Tel: 242-347-3500 • Fax: 347-3501 •
Web site: www.bimini.com
At the time of writing, some of the facilities in this new marina had yet to be completed, but the president of Bimini Sands, Frank Cooney, and his wife, Shirley, assured us that they would have everything in place by the end of 1999.

Slips	50, on floating docks.
Max LOA	100 ft.
MLW at Dock	8 ft.
Dockage	$30 daily up to 30 ft., $45 up to 40 ft., $50 up to 60 ft., $60 up to 75 ft., $75 up to 100 ft.
Power	Billed at prevailing rates and metered for usage, will include TV and phone hookup.
Fuel	Diesel and gas.
Propane	No
Water	Free up to 50 gallons, 20¢ per gallon after that. Reverse osmosis water supplied.
Telephones	Card and coin-pay phones within the marina, phone hookup at docks.
TV	Hookup at every dock, charges included with electricity.
Showers	6 showers and toilets.
Laundromat	Coin-operated washers and dryers on site.
Restaurant	*The Petite Conch*, with its attractive tables painted by a local artist, will be open for breakfast, lunch, and dinner overlooking the marina from the second floor, and will be happy to provide box lunches.
Bar	*The Healing Hole Bar*
Ice	$3 per bag.
Barbecue	There is a grill and a Tiki hut on the beach where you can cook your own catch of the day.
Swimming	Pool with its own bar.
Marine Store	Limited boat supplies.
Boutique	An imaginative selection of fun gifts and souvenirs.
Rentals	Golf carts, jet skis, bicycles, kayaks, and small boats available on site.
Bicycles	$12 for half-day rental, $15 for a full day.
Kayaks	$25 for a half-day rental, $40 for a full day.

Diving	*Bimini Undersea* (Tel: 347-3089) or *Scuba Bimini* (Tel: 347-4444)
Fishing	Charters can be arranged.
Snorkeling	Excellent snorkeling off the reef.
Storage	Storage racks for boats up to 25 ft.
Accommodations	*Bimini Beach Club Hotel*, harbor-view rooms from $90, ocean view from $95 per night. Condominiums can be rented from $150 per night, minimum 2-night stays. Dockage fees are reduced by 25 percent if you stay in one of the condos.
Customs	Customs and Immigration have an office within the marina, which makes *Bimini Sands* a Port of Entry on South Bimini.
Credit cards	Visa, MasterCard, Amex, personal checks.

SOUTH BIMINI YACHT CLUB
Tel: 242-347-4444 • Fax: 347-4511
This can hardly be called a marina, more a canal where you can tie up alongside. The entrance is to the east of the ferry dock, just follow the canal around. You will not have more than 6 feet under you at low tide. There is space for about 12 boats, providing none are more than 30 feet, and the dockage charge is 50¢ per foot per day. There are no restrooms, showers, or fuel, but the hotel alongside has a lively bar and a restaurant serving breakfast, lunch, and dinner. The hotel primarily serves groups who come to dive with *Scuba Bimini*, and has 16 rooms from $79 per night, which includes breakfast. Divers can go out on a one-tank dive for $49, snorkelers for $29, and rental equipment is available.

GETTING AROUND

Airport
BIA 954-938-8991 To Fort Lauderdale.

Island Air Charters 954-359-9942 or 242-347-4039 Four flights a week to and from Fort Lauderdale for $165 round trip. They also offer a weekly cargo run on Wednesdays from Fort Lauderdale to South Bimini, Cat Cay, and Ocean Cay.

Majors Air Service 242-347-3230 To Freeport. Private pilots and charter flights use the 5,000-foot South Bimini airstrip; a taxi and ferry will take you across to Alice Town for $5.

Sky Unlimited 242-347-2301/4029

THINGS TO DO IN NORTH AND SOUTH BIMINI

- Take off your watch and get accustomed to Bahamian time.
- Go fishing!
- Follow the Hemingway Trail to the *Compleat Angler* for a drink and discover the difference between a Bahama Mama and a Goombay Smash. Enjoy the historic photographs on the walls and dance the night away to calypso music.
- Go even further back in time: dive the *Bimini Road* and discover *Atlantis*!
- Dine as you watch the sunset from the *Anchorage Hotel*.
- Take a photograph of the Chalks seaplane landing or taking off in the harbor. You don't see many of them these days.
- Take your boat and your bride to Honeymoon Cove for the night.

Janet Wilson

CAT CAY

Cat Cay is an attractive island, privately owned by the members of the Cat Cay Club, with a good marina. Totally rebuilt after Hurricane Andrew, this marina welcomes visiting boats for a maximum of three nights, except over July 4th weekend when it is usually full of members and their friends. It makes a pleasant overnight stop after crossing the Gulf Stream from Florida, or having crossed the Banks from Chub Cay prior to returning to the States. You can clear in with **Customs** and **Immigration** at Cat Cay, but will be charged a $25 docking fee unless you stay overnight, when the fee is waived.

MARINA

CAT CAY YACHT CLUB
Tel: 242-347-3565 • Fax: 347-3564 • VHF 16

Slips	110
Max LOA	140 ft.
MLW at Dock	4 ft.
Dockage	$1.50 per ft. per day.
Power	30A, 50A, 100A available, 25¢ per kWh.
Fuel	Diesel and gasoline.
Water	35¢ per gallon.
Telephone	*Batelco* card phone on the dock.
TV	Satellite hookup on the docks.
Showers	Yes
Laundry	Yes
Restaurant	*The Nauticat Restaurant* is open for lunch and dinner, with a pleasant veranda bar for drinks; collared shirt and long trousers required at dinner.
Provisions	There is a small commissary.
Ice	Yes
Clinic	A Cat Cay Club member who is a doctor runs the clinic when he is on the island.
Fax	The office will send or receive faxes for you.
Office	Open from 8 am to 5 pm.

Shopping	The boutique has a good selection of clothing and some books.
Travel	STOL Islander aircraft fly daily to Fort Lauderdale using the 1,100-ft. landing strip.
Credit Cards	Major credit cards accepted.

SPORTS

Dive Sites

Tuna Alley is named for a cut in the reef where you can see barrel sponges and a host of different fish and coral; there are buoys marking the seven-mile site. *Victory Reef* has many different types of coral, and masses of caverns and holes and places you can swim through. The *Blue Hole* is for experienced divers only.

Cat Cay Club.

Chapter 9
The Great Bahama Bank

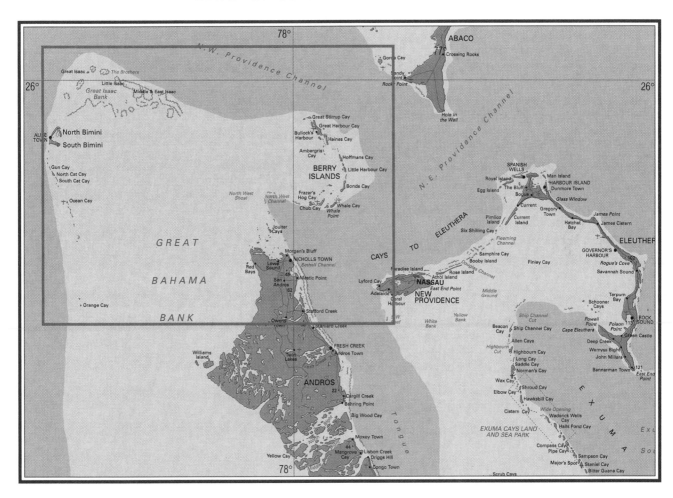

The Bimini Islands and Cat Cay

THE Biminis are prime cruising, fishing, and diving destinations in their own right. This apart, their proximity to Florida, together with the ongoing greater distances across the Great Bahama Bank, may well set them as the only possible Bahamian cruising ground within reach for those whose vacation time is short. In any event, these islands offer far more for the cruising visitor than simply serving as waypoints on the route to Chub Cay or Nassau. For this reason we decided to treat them separately, rather than including them under the heading of **The Great Bahama Bank**, to which they are the entry port. This chapter links with the Biminis and continues the story across the Great Bahama Bank.

The Great Bahama Bank

The Great Bahama Bank is, by any standard, a significant sea area. It's a great tableland of shallow water that has a pervasive influence on the tides and currents, wave patterns, navigable routes, and marine life of the central Bahamas, just as the Little Bahama Bank influences the north. Let's mention size first. The Great Bahama Bank starts (if you can put it that way) at its northwest corner, pinned in position by Northeast Rock and Great Isaac Island almost at the junction of Latitude 26° N and Longitude 079° W. In fact the real start of the Bank is between 6 and 9 nm to the northwest and north, parallel to the 100-fathom line, but you can see that on your charts. If you take the Bimini Islands as your markers to make it easy, the Great Bahama Bank begins 29 nm north of North Bimini.

The Bank runs roughly west–east along the line of Latitude 26° N with a pronounced set to the southeast as it curves down to sweep up and claim the crescent of the Berry Islands. Then, having grabbed the Berrys, the line of the Great Bahama Bank backtracks to drop south along the east coast of Andros. On the west side the Great Bahama Bank falls almost due south from Bimini down a barrier chain of small cays, rocks, and reefs that mark the east edge of the Florida Strait. Around Latitude 23° N the Great Bahama

GRAND BAHAMA BANK TRANSIT WAYPOINTS

Gun Cay		
GUNCW	25° 34' 15"/250 N	079° 19' 30"/500 W
Cat Cay		
CATCE	25° 34' 00"/000 N	079° 17' 00"/000 W
North Rock		
NROCK	25° 51' 00"/000 N	079° 16' 30"/500 W
Mackie Shoal		
MCKIE	25° 41' 30"/500 N	078° 38' 30"/500 W
NW Channel		
NWCHN	25° 40' 00"/000 N	078° 10' 30"/500 W
SW Edge of the Berry Bank		
SWEBB	25° 30' 15"/250 N	078° 10' 30"/500 W
Northwest Light Shoal (not for navigation)		
NWLSH	25° 29' 00"/000 N	078° 14' 00"/000 W
Northwest Channel Light		
NWCHL	25° 28' 45"/750 N	078° 09' 45"/750 W
South Riding Rock West		
SRDRW	25° 13' 30"/500 N	079° 11' 00"/000 W
South Riding Rock East		
SRDRE	25° 13' 30"/500 N	079° 08' 30"/500 W
Chub Cay South		
CHUBS	25° 23' 15"/250 N	077° 54' 50"/833 W
Nassau Harbour Northwest		
NASNW	25° 06' 30"/500 N	077° 23' 00"/000 W
Morgans Bluff		
MRGNE	25° 11' 00"/000 N	077° 59' 00"/000 W
Bethel Channel		
BTHEL	25° 08' 30"/000 N	077° 57' 30"/500 W
Fresh Creek		
FRESH	24° 44' 00"/000 N	077° 45' 00"/000 W

The final figures in each waypoint show seconds (00") and thousands (000) of a minute.

The Great Bahama Bank from Skylab, seen from the east.

Bank loses its geographic identity, and further south the Bahamian Out Islands are fragmented by a far more broken pattern of banks and shallows.

If you were to sum up the Great Bahama Bank, perhaps the easiest way is to say that it runs 50 nm across at its widest point and measures about 180 nm from north to south. Its waters are mostly 15–18 feet deep, but it spawns far shallower sandbars that are always changing, and for this reason the Bank is almost impossible to keep surveyed. There are navigation marks on the main routes across the Bank, but the constantly changing depth contours, as well as the loss of lights in storms or through human inattention, make these markers a bonus if they're in place, not signposts you should rely on.

For the cruising skipper the overriding factor comes with the size of the Great Bahama Bank and the consequent length of the three main navigational routes that cross it. Which-ever way you play it, there's some 75 nm of Bank to cross heading out or heading back home. This means, if you're sailing from, say, Cat Cay to Chub Cay, the distance to run may be greater than your achievable daytime range. If this is so, and it's impossible to squeeze that Great Bahama Bank passage into every available minute of daylight and com-plete the course, there's only one answer and that's to anchor out during the night.

Anchoring out on the Bank is not difficult, it's done of-ten, and it means that you don't risk sailing at night, for (as always) you needs your eyes to transit any area of shallow water. Just pick a spot well off the beaten track so that a Bahamian mailboat doesn't plough you down during the night, set two anchors, and have an anchor light that works.

In the way in which sea areas have their own characteris-tics, if you're going to get bounced by rough water crossing the Great Bahama Bank, it's highly likely that you'll meet this at the Northwest Channel Light and suffer it as you continue southeast. The Northeast Providence Channel particularly, which you cross to reach Nassau or Andros, is an area where confused seas are not unusual, a characteristic brought about by contrary tidal flows, the containment ef-fect of two dead-ends of deep ocean that are trapped by shallow seas (the northwest salient of the Providence Chan-nel and the Tongue of the Ocean), and wind, particularly Northers. Otherwise, like any shallow sea area, the Great Bahama Bank will kick up short, unpleasant seas when the wind hits 15 knots or so.

The tidal set across the Great Bahama Bank, like the set across its smaller twin to the north, is not the stuff of tidal atlases, but runs roughly northeast–southwest. Your auto-pilot may compensate for this or alternatively keep an eye on your cross track error and make continual adjustments, which will be needed both for tide and wind.

The Northwest Channel Light

Our NWCHL waypoint is set to the north of what was once the Northwest Channel Light, before it was destroyed one night by a vessel using the coordinates of the light as a waypoint. A marker buoy replaced the light, but in July 1999 the marker buoy parted from its mooring. Now there is no marker. The broken stumps of the old light tower show only at low water and even then are hard to see. Nonetheless, what remains is a potentially lethal underwater obstruction. BASRA strongly recommend that you do not cross the Bank at night, in poor visibility, or in poor weather conditions. Slow down in this area, and go carefully. Our NWCHL waypoint should serve as a safe line to take, but do not rely on it. Whatever you do, don't swing too far north or south of the original light tower's position, for there are reefs and shoals both to the north and to the south. The last time this marker disappeared two years passed before it was replaced. Be warned.

A Sunseeker, one guesses running at some speed, either attempted to run south of this mark, or failed to realize that he was running south of it. Suddenly realizing that all was not well, he went into reverse. Water was driven up his exhaust intakes flooding both engines. Two days later a tow boat set out from Florida to take him back to Fort Lauderdale. Stay to the north!

The Northwest Channel Light has claimed more than one casualty recently. This is not an isolated case. Most have ended in hull damage.

Clearing In— Your Options in the Central Bahamas

If you didn't clear in at Bimini or Cat Cay, you still have plenty of options, some of them a long haul if you're prepared to stay away from land and keep your Q flag flying. We'd guess that either Chub Cay or Nassau will be your choice.

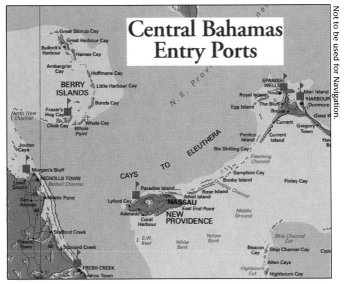

The Routes Across the Great Bahama Bank

THERE are three major west–east routes to the North west Channel Light. We'll take these first, and then cover the options once you pass the Northwest Channel Light.

North Rock to the Northwest Channel Light

If you want to bypass Bimini you can cross on to the Bank just north of North Rock (NROCK), which lies to the north of the Bimini Island chain (your entry route here must also take you north of the Moselle Bank, which lies to the northwest of North Rock). There's nothing difficult in gaining the Bank this way, and you're set fair once you're in green water but you can't set a direct course for the Northwest Channel Light. Two shoal areas lie across what would be the straight-line track. There's also the wreck of a ship with just 3 feet of water, shown on the chart at 25° 47' 00"/000 N 079° 06' 45"/750 W, which lies to the south of our route by 0.75 nm. But watch and correct your cross track error (XTE) on the first leg. The first of the shoal areas, the Mackie Shoal, lies across your path at the 35-mile point, so you have to head a little more north than you might wish at the outset. Then you alter on to your second leg just northwest of the Mackie Shoal to aim off to clear the second shoal area.

- From North Rock to the Mackie Shoal (MCKIE) area is 35.5 nm on a heading of 109°M.

- From Mackie Shoal to safely off the shoal by the Northwest Channel Light is 25.3 nm on 124°M. This second shoal area lies north of the Northwest Channel Light and is marked by a buoy at its northwest corner. Your run brings you not far off the Northwest Channel Light.

- The third leg is a straight run due east to the Northwest Channel Light on 098°M for 3.84 nm.

Your total distance from North Rock to the Northwest Channel Light is 64.74 nm. You might find the thought of turning a Banks run, which could be achieved as a straight shot, into a three-leg passage (four legs or more if you add in going on after the Northwest Channel Light), a touch of navigational overkill. But if nothing else the changes in course relieve the monotony of a run across the Great Bahama Bank (there's nothing there, nothing to see) and might give you a sense of progress, other than just looking at your distance run or distance-to-run log.

Cat Cay to the Northwest Channel Light (through Gun Cay Cut)

If you've come in through Bimini or Cat Cay, or just made these islands your Bahamian landfall, once you've passed through Gun Cay Cut (GUNCW) on to the Bank you can set a straight course for the Northwest Channel Light. You can set a departure waypoint off Gun Cay but we believe Cat Cay (CATCE) makes the better departure and arrival waypoint (particularly when you reverse the course and are running east–west), largely because of the shoals to the east of Gun Cay.

We give the Gulf Stream–side waypoint to the northwest of Gun Cay Cut as our landfall but this is for reference only. The 2.5 nm or so you run through Gun Cay Cut must be taken visually, favoring Gun Cay Point and running in the deep water parallel to the shoreline (to avoid the shoal and reef extending north from Cat Cay) until you are through the Cut and can see the entrance to Cat Cay Marina with its dwarf lighthouse. Using the two lights, Gun Cay and Cat Cay as markers, one ahead and one astern, head south until you are on the line of Latitude 25° 34' 00 N. Then turn east to pick up your departure waypoint. See **The Bimini Islands** under **Gun Cay Cut** on page 131 if you're in doubt about this passage on to the Bank. From Cat Cay to the Northwest Channel Light is 60.91 nm on a course of 099°M.

South Riding Rock to the Northwest Channel Light

Once again, if you have no interest in Cat Cay or Bimini you can pass on to the Bank just south of South Riding Rock. There are no problems gaining the Bank here, and you can set a direct course for the Northwest Channel Light, although we believe that you may find shallower-than-average water (perhaps as little as 6 feet in places) along this route. The 2.26 nm from the South Riding Rock west (SRDRW) waypoint to the east waypoint (SRDRE) must be taken visually, and the second waypoint is your departure point for the Great Bahama Bank crossing. The distance from this second waypoint to the Northwest Channel Light is 55.24 nm on a heading of 078°M.

Your Choice of Route

There's not a great deal of difference in the distance to run on all these routes, and your choice is bound to be set by your Florida departure port and whether or not you want to visit the Biminis, or overnight in Cat Cay. Don't forget too, if you've started calculating, that when you reach the Northwest Channel Light you still have at least 16 nm to run to get to Chub Cay, the closest of your destination options.

Options after the Northwest Channel Light

Chub Cay

Your first option and shortest leg (14.55 nm on a heading of 117°M) is to go to Chub Cay (CHUBS) and clear in there. If you have already cleared in, you may want to continue on a little way to Frazers Hog Cay, or to one of the southern Berry Island anchorages.

Nassau

The second option is to set a direct course for Nassau (NASNW), which gives you a greater distance to run, but if you're heading for Spanish Wells and Eleuthera or the Exumas, and have the daylight in hand, going straight for Nassau may make sense.

Your first leg will be 47.44 nm on a heading of 123°M. Then a short run of 1.69 nm on a heading of 132°M lines you up with the entrance to Nassau Harbour. The distance to run from the Northwest Channel Light is 49.46 nm to the Nassau Harbour entrance.

Andros

If you're going to Andros, we suggest you go first to the Chub Cay waypoint (CHUBS), and then set a course for your destination. It's a dogleg, but it's a safer route for it keeps you in deep water well away from the area of shoal, rocks, small cays, and reefs that lie to the north of Andros.

At the start you have 14.55 nm on a heading of 117°M to run to that Chub Cay waypoint. Then for Morgan's Bluff (MRGNE) it's 12.82 nm on 202°M. For Bethel Channel (BTHEL) and Nicholls Town it's 14.95 nm on 194°M. For Fresh Creek (FRESH), to our mind the most likely destination, it's 40.25 nm on a heading of 172°M. Don't enter Andros waters at night unless you're set on calling your insurance agent the next morning.

The Routes Across The Great Bahama Bank

Chapter 10
The Berry Islands
Great Stirrup Cay to Chub Cay

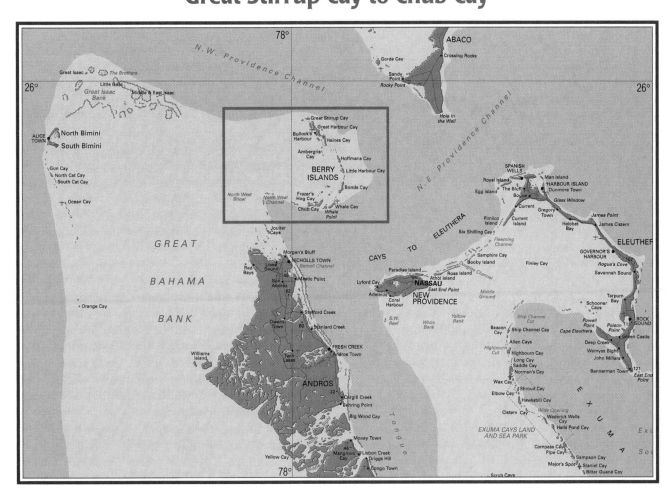

The Northern Berry Islands

WE'D suggest if you're bound for the Berry Islands from Palm Beach or anywhere north of Palm Beach that you head first for Grand Bahama, stage there, and cruise the Berrys starting in the north. If you're starting in Fort Lauderdale or Miami, go by way of Bimini or Cat Cay to Chub Cay, and do the southern Berrys first. We reckon it's always sensible to keep your open-water passages as short as you can, and we always try to keep our passage making in daylight hours, if the distances work out. As we're covering the Bahamas from north to south, we'll deal with the route from Grand Bahama Island first. We'll cover the southern route to the Berry Islands later in this chapter.

The Route from Grand Bahama Island

Crossing the Northwest Providence Channel is a simple run from the Bell Channel (BELCH) to Little Stirrup Cay

(LSTRP) of 54.56 nm on a heading of 142°M. Choose your weather, just as you do with every ocean crossing, and remember that you are passing through a major shipping lane. You'll have no problems in picking up both Great Stirrup Cay and Little Stirrup Cay from some 8 nm out. Once you are close to Little Stirrup Cay your navigation becomes, as it always is when making landfalls in the Bahamas, part GPS-dependent and part eyeball.

The Berry Island extension of the Great Bahama Bank, which lies to the west of the crescent of Berry Islands, is too shallow for anything other than shoal draft craft. If you're making for Great Harbour Cay Marina, you have to dogleg out to the west before turning in toward the harbor. If you are making for one of the Great Harbour anchorages you must work your way east around both Stirrup Cays, and enter the so-called "Great Harbour" between Great Stirrup Cay and the north tip of Great Harbour Cay.

At this point maybe we'd better make clear that Great Harbour (the sea area between Great Stirrup Cay and the north end of

Great Harbour Cay) is no harbor at all. You can anchor there. It has some protection. But that's it. If you're after a real harbor in the northern Berrys, there's only one, and that's Great Harbour Cay Marina on the west side of Great Harbour Cay (just about halfway down). Perhaps they should have cut down on the use of that name.

LITTLE STIRRUP CAY

Little Stirrup Cay, whose signs of habitation you may notice as you get closer to it (a white roof in the trees, and what appear to be litter bins on the west end beach as you round the point) is a Royal Caribbean Cruise Line playground. On Thursdays, Fridays, and Sundays the cruise ships deliver their passengers to Little Stirrup Cay for a day of swimming, volleyball, water sports, beach bar patronage, and buffet lunches. Everything is waiting for them, down to the glass-bottomed pedal boats and a First Aid station. For the rest of the week the Royal Caribbean "Coco Cay" beach staff look after the island, its deserted bars and cafeteria, its water toys, and several hundred sun loungers. And yes, there were litter bins on that beach.

GREAT STIRRUP CAY

Great Stirrup Cay has also been claimed as private property, by the Norwegian Cruise Line, but you can go ashore and take the path that leads to the white painted Great Stirrup lighthouse in its grove of palm trees at the east end of the island. There's a small, not-very-good beach at Panton Cove, and we're sure no one would keep you from using it if you were anchored there. The cruise line recreation ground is Bertram Cove on the north coast, which would make a great anchorage as long as nothing was coming from the north or west, but it's small, a little tricky to enter, and has barely 6 feet in depth. Not being able to go there is no great loss to the cruising community.

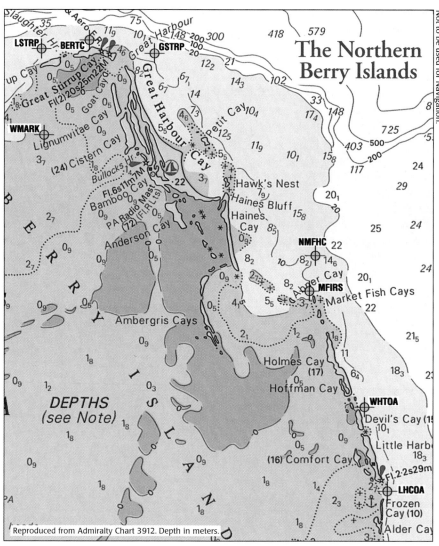

The Northern Berry Islands

Reproduced from Admiralty Chart 3912. Depth in meters.

NORTHERN BERRY ISLANDS

Little Stirrup Cay		
LSTRP	25° 49' 30"/500 N	077° 57' 00"/000 W
Off Bertram Cove		
BERTC	25° 49' 55"/927 N	077° 55' 01"/020 W
NW Great Stirrup Cay		
GSTRP	25° 49' 27"/450 N	077° 52' 16"/262 W

The final figures in each waypoint show seconds (00") and thousands (000) of a minute.

The Great Harbour Anchorages

PANTON COVE

Popularly there are reckoned to be three usable anchorages in the Great Harbour area. The first is Panton Cove, tucked up under the wing of the Great Stirrup lighthouse. It's shallow, 6 feet at best, and restricted by tiny little Snake Cay, which lies off the Great Stirrup Cay lighthouse dock. You can work your way in and lie there happily if you have shoal draft, otherwise you're forced to anchor further out, which can be rolly. You're protected from the north, but not much else. The holding around Panton Cove is not good, so check that anchor.

GOAT CAY

Goat Cay has good water, some 10 feet or more in places, off its east-facing side. This will shield you from the west, but otherwise you are in the open, exposed from all other directions.

SLAUGHTER HARBOUR

Slaughter Harbour is the deeper pocket of water (some 6 feet) that lies immediately to the west of Great Stirrup Cay. We see no value in it as an anchorage. It's OK for a day visit, to snorkel and maybe gunkhole around a bit in your dinghy. The only valid approach is from the north, between the east end of Great Stirrup Cay and the west end of the rock wall that lies between the two Stirrup Cays. To try to approach from the south (the Bank side) is shoal draft work at high tide and virtually impossible at low water.

The Approach to Great Harbour Cay Marina

If you're heading for Great

Great Harbour Cay Marina, from the southeast.

Harbour Cay Marina, once you're at our Little Stirrup Cay waypoint you have to run almost due south (on a heading of around 180°M) to pick up the first of the Great Harbour markers. Your course skirts the western edge of the extensive flats lying immediately to the south of the Stirrup Cays. From the LSTRP waypoint you should be able to pick up that first mark, which looks like a single pole some 3 nm ahead. (The wrecked fishing boat that used to lie off your port bow on this first leg of your route in no longer shows above the water.) Our West Mark waypoint (WMARK) places you a tad to the northwest of the mark itself.

We've called this first mark West Marker Piling and offer its waypoint as well (WMRKP). Originally a tripod of three pilings topped by a radar reflector, it is now just two pilings with no radar reflector, which, unless it is made good, may

well be taken out in a storm for it has lost its structural integrity. From here you alter course to run some 4 nm eastward in toward Great Harbour's harbor. At one time a well-spaced series of six markers took you to range marks just outside a cut leading in to the outer harbor. When we were last there the marks had suffered from weather, rather like the West Mark, and the total had reduced to four survivors. If this remains the case, you'll have no problems. Just use your eyes to pick up each marker in turn as you progress.

We give you the position of the surviving marks at the time we write. Plot them if you wish, but don't run in on autopilot, and don't go tearing in, for you never know what may have changed. Watch the color of the water and your

GREAT HARBOUR APPROACH MARKS		
West Mark		
WMARK	25° 46' 25"/417 N	077° 57' 00"/000 W
West Marker Piling (not for navigation)		
WMRKP	25° 46' 07"/125 N	077° 56' 41"/690 W
Marker Pole 2 (not for navigation)		
M2	25° 45' 37"/628 N	077° 55' 58"/972 W
Marker Pole 3 (BH) (not for navigation)		
M3	25° 45' 02"/305 N	077° 53' 41"/691 W
Marker Pole 4 (Red 8) (not for navigation)		
M4	25° 45' 00"/013 N	077° 52' 57"/957 W
Marker Pole 5 (not for navigation)		
M5	25° 44' 51"/851 N	077° 52' 32"/532 W

The final figures in each waypoint show seconds (00") and thousands (000) of a minute.

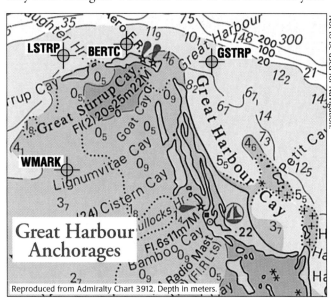

Great Harbour Anchorages

Reproduced from Admiralty Chart 3912. Depth in meters.

Not to be used for Navigation.

depth. Our waypoint sequence, used as a hand-steering guideline, will get you in. Now we'll take it stage by stage. All along the way you'll have 8 feet at MLW.

- At WMARK alter to about 115–120°M, roughly lined up with the Great Harbour Batelco mast, and hold that general line until you pick up the next mark, M2, a bare pole that lies 1.2 nm off. Go for the mark. From mark M2, you'll see, further on, a third marker, which lies 2 nm away on a heading of 099°M. This third marker, M3, is topped by a radar reflector and has a sign, half green, half red, with BH on it.

As you get closer to the land the houses you see off the port bow, and the dock there, which may or may not have a mailboat or fishing boats alongside, is Bullocks Harbour settlement, and is not your destination (at least not right now). The entrance to Great Harbour Cay's three connected basins lies concealed behind the headland with the Batelco mast, and will not be evident until you are almost ready to do a 90-degree turn to port to go in through a narrow cut.

- At the M3 (BH) pole, your heading alters to about 106°M toward a fourth marker, M4, about 1 nm on, which has a red triangle with an 8 marked on it. A fifth marker M5, a bare pole, comes up a short distance (0.1 nm) to the south of M4 (R8).

- From this last mark M5 look at the headland off your bow. You'll see the roof of a house on it. Look carefully below that roof, and hard to see at first, you'll pick up two red-and-white vertically striped range mark boards (the top one almost cloaked by vegetation), and in front of them, in the water, a single pole with a red triangle on it. If you can't see

The school in Bullocks Harbour settlement.

the range marks, don't worry. Just continue south until you see the entry cut to port and turn for it (see the next sequence).

At this last mark you'll realize that the Batelco mast that has been your primary landmark is in fact two masts, and that a Corinth Canal–like north-south cut through solid rock off to port is your entrance into Great Harbour. To help your local geography, the Batelco station is on the western side of the cut (your starboard), and a pink building (the clinic) is on the eastern side (to port). Entering Great Harbour is plain sailing, though you certainly won't be sailing at that point. It's a bit like going through the successive inner harbors the Spanish developed and fortified to protect their treasure ships in Cartagena, but at least you're not entering under the muzzles of hostile cannon.

- The entry cut has around 11 feet at MLW, and a tidal flow. Expect that. A swing bridge used to cross this cut, years back.

- The first inner basin (perhaps appropriately named the Bay of the Five Pirates) has the fuel dock to starboard. It's not the easiest of all fuel docks to approach. It's tucked right up into a corner under a small headland, with rock within feet of the eastern side, but they'll take your lines and walk you wherever they might want you to be if you come alongside the head of the dock.

- Your course across this first basin, and the next, a continuation of the bay, (a turn to starboard) is marked by a succession of poles, red right returning, which like the outside markers, have reduced in numbers. Nonetheless, they serve.

- The second basin has a white-roofed prominent house with its own dock to starboard and, ahead, a circular (restaurant) building, with a blue-painted balcony around it, and a grey shingle roof. The entry to the marina, still concealed, lies to port just before this building. You'll pass a No Wake sign, and then make a turn to port.

- You pass along a row of townhouses with their own docks to port, and turn again, a 90-degree turn to starboard. The Great Harbour Cay Marina is to starboard, and there's another line of townhouses with docks to port.

That's it. You've made it.

Great Harbour Cay Marina

Great Harbour Cay Marina has made a commendable effort to spruce up its facilities, and the shoreside restrooms, showers, and laundry were clean and well tended when we were last there. Shore power has been brought right up to date, and both drinking water (reverse osmosis) and washdown water (well water) is on tap. Hot and airless as this inner basin is bound to be at times, it remains a safe haven in severe weather, given that none of us can ever predict what might happen in a direct hit by a major hurricane.

Stores, nearby restaurants, and car rentals are covered in our **Yellow Pages**. If you're planning to be there for any length of time, you'll want wheels to get around. We hear reports that the marina is on the market, or open to offers, but this is a common story in the Bahamas, more so in places that have long received little attention in terms of significant

Market Fish Cay, inside channel approach.

continuing improvement. This very lack of attention in the past may add credibility to the rumors if "failure to develop" penalty clauses exist in the original contract. But we'll wait and see.

Great Harbour Cay and Cistern Cay

Nearly 6 nm long but hardly a mile wide, Great Harbour Cay is by geography and population (around the thousand mark) Top Dog in the northern Berry Islands. It has an airstrip, regular service to Nassau, and the townhouses around the marina, plus a slowly growing number of vacation homes, spell income for an island that has no resources other than conch taken from way out on the Great Bahama Bank.

The main settlement, Bullocks Harbour (sometimes called "The Village"), lies to the north, with the Government Dock you saw on the way in. The inn by the graveyard, once the epicenter of local entertainment that many visitors may remember, burned to the ground and exists no longer. Our **Yellow Pages** show what is there. Apart from the government services, such as the clinic and the post office, we doubt that you'll find much to detain you. Batelco, remote from the main village on the far side of the entry cut, can be reached by the road leading to the fuel dock from the marina.

Great Harbour Cay bears the marks of a failed development, with a hotel and golf course on the spine of the island just to the east of the marina. The golf course, despite its desert appearance, has refurbished tees and greens, and is used by the local expat community. Beautiful beaches lie on the east side (where all the new vacation-home building is taking place), and Petit Cay offers an attractive anchorage if the wind is from the east, but otherwise is exposed. You can

check it out from the Beach Club, a bar/restaurant built on the dunes due east from the marina (as the bird flies). The Beach Club itself, with a bar built around a massive cable drum, is rustic, showing signs of age, but attractive nonetheless and has good lunch snacks.

As we've suggested, getting around Great Harbour Cay is not easy. You can rent bicycles, dilapidated scooters, and maybe a jeep, but there are no taxis. There is a local bus, but you may never see it. We hitchhike. The walk from the marina to the beach bar, in the heat of the day, can make you wonder why you set out. If nothing else the necessary rehydration may double your bar bill.

Cistern Cay, which is almost a northwest extension of Great Harbour Cay, holds no particular attraction in cruising terms, nor does Lignum Vitae Cay to the north of Cistern Cay.

HAINES CAY, WATER CAY, AND MONEY CAY
Haines Cay (with a clutch of lesser islets, Anderson, Turner, and Kemp's Cays), as well as the slightly larger Water and Money Cays are fine for exploring in an inflatable or a Whaler, but are not a cruising ground.

THE AMBERGRIS CAYS, HIGH CAY, ABNER CAY, MARKET FISH CAYS
The Ambergris Cays, despite the attraction of their beaches, fall into the same category: good for exploration with swimming, snorkeling, and maybe even fishing, but no place for a live-aboard boat. The sands and shallows around the Ambergris Cays, and Ambergris Rock to the south, are No-Go territory if you need any kind of depth worth reckoning.

High Cay and Abner Cay offer nothing of interest, except maybe good fishing, and Market Fish Cays could be your

SOUTH FROM THE STIRRUP CAYS

North Market Fish Cay

NMFHC	25° 42' 10"/174 N	077° 45' 33"/549 W

Market Fish Cay Inside Route Startpoint

MFIRS	25° 40' 45"/750 N	077° 45' 45"/750 W

White Cay Ocean Approach

WHTOA	25° 36' 29"/484 N	077° 43' 29"/482 W

Little Harbour Cay Ocean Approach

LHCOA	25° 33' 30"/500 N	077° 42' 30"/500 W

Guano Cay Shoal Passage (not for navigation)

GCSHP	25° 34' 10"/166 N	077° 44' 05"/085 W

Southwest Comfort Cay Anchorage (not for navigation)

SWCCA	25° 34' 30"/500 N	077° 44' 05"/085 W

The final figures in each waypoint show seconds (00") and thousands (000) of a minute.

start point for taking the west, Bank-side route down to Little Harbour Cay (which we cover under the next heading).

Moving on South from the Stirrup Cays

Moving on south down the Berry Islands (or coming north) there's only one safe route and that's to stand well out to the east of the Berry Island chain. From a start point off Great Stirrup Cay (GSTRP), you want to gain and stay in deep water to clear Petit Cay, Hawksnest Cay, and Haine's Bluff as you head south. If you aim to keep about 1 nm offshore that's about right, or stay with the 30-foot depth contour.

Brenton Reef lies midway on a line from the south tip of Haines Cay to the north tip of Hoffmans Cay, so stand well clear of that. Watch out for a shoal that runs out from the north end of Hoffmans Cay, and there are offshore rocks halfway down it. There's a good anchorage behind White Cay, one of our favorites, which we'll cover in detail.

There is (as so often there is) a Bank-side route down (or up) the Berry Islands, but we're not attracted by it. These routes are rarely constant, for storms alter the lie of sandbanks and the nature of the cuts, and it would be misleading to pretend that we could offer useful guidance. If you want to try the inside route, either engage a local guide, or take it in stages, going ahead in your dinghy with a handheld GPS and a handheld depth sounder to prove each leg before you move.

This said, there is a "deep-" water channel that will take you from the Market Fish Cays down the west, Bank-side of Hoffmans, Devils, Little Harbour, *and Comfort* Cays. We italicize that "and Comfort." There's no way you can pass, other than in your dinghy, between Little Harbour Cay and Comfort Cay. Your northern start point for the inside route is close to the northern Market Fish Cay (MFIRS). Then it's eyeball all the way, and stay in the blue water.

There's a point on this route (just to the north of Comfort Cay) where you can see the Darville settlement (with its skyline grove of tall tousle-headed palm trees) and beyond it, the abandoned house on the south point of Little

Harbour Cay (also on the skyline, low and squat, like a fort) very clearly, and you're tempted to turn in between Comfort Cay and Little Harbour Cay. Don't do it. Keep to the west of Comfort Cay.

HOFFMANS CAY

Hoffmans Cay has a blue hole that you may wish to visit. It's easier to describe getting there from the south rather than the north, and if you use the White Cay anchorage, that's how you'll be going.

Round the south tip of Hoffmans Cay and follow the west coast up. Miss the first beach you see, and go to the second, around a headland. Near the right end of the beach you'll find the start of a trail that takes you heading south into the bush. The trail climbs up over the spine of the headland and just about the time you're beginning to think you've volunteered for a jungle warfare course, the trail splits. The right fork goes to the first beach, the one you ignored. The left fork leads you almost immediately to the rim of the blue hole.

If you've been to Chichen Itza in Yucatan and seen the Sacred Well, the Hoffmans Cay Blue Hole carries much the same sense of shock when you first come on it. Suddenly you're right on the brim of this great sheer-sided hole, the water far below you, unfathomable but looking deep. At

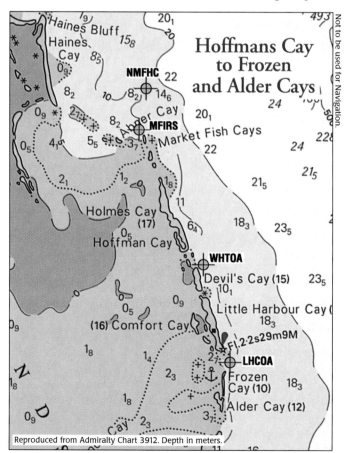

Reproduced from Admiralty Chart 3912. Depth in meters.

White Cay anchorage, from the east.

least in Hoffmans Cay there's no tradition of sacrificing living virgins, decked out in their best gold jewelry, by pushing them over the edge.

If you take the continuation of the trail that runs to your right along the rim of the hole, you'll find that within a few yards it takes you down under an overhang and you can reach the water there—and swim if you wish! Sacrificial virgins apart, it's said that someone once stocked the hole with just one grouper, but no one knows whether the fish found friends, died, or has survived in isolation. It could be, it just could be, that there's a world record giant grouper lurking there, if it found its new home agreeable!

THE WHITE CAY ANCHORAGE

Going down the outside, eastern route, after you pass the end of Hoffmans Cay you'll see a forbidding line of rock marking a low, pencil-like cay that fragments in rocks at its southern tip. This is White Cay, and if you get in behind it, you'll find one of the most attractive anchorages in the Berrys.

First of all, ignore the gap north of White Cay. You want to go in the south gap, midway between the rocks at the south of White Cay and the north tip of Devils Cay (your turning point will be around our waypoint WHTOA). As you turn you're on line for the south tip of Saddle Back Cay, which lies immediately behind White Cay. Beyond the south tip of Saddle Back, there's the south tip of another island lying behind Saddle Back. If you keep these two south tips in line as a rough transit, you won't go far wrong.

You'll have a good 18–24 feet of water, which will take you well inside. Once you come level with the sand of the beach on the north of Devils Cay, make a turn to starboard to head north between Saddle Back Cay and White Cay. The White Cay beach, roughly in the center of the cay, marks your anchorage. You'll find 12–18 feet of water there, and surprising depth close to the beach over sand. Otherwise it's grass all around. The beach itself, pure white sand backed with sea oats, is something to write home about. The anchorage is reasonably protected, but flanked as it is by two ocean passes, it can be rolly if the ocean is kicking up. Under those circumstances you wouldn't want to attempt running in there anyway. If wind and strong seas are running from the east, don't try it.

If you decide to travel on joining the inside route, you can do so here, or you can just pop around the corner to take in the Hoffmans Cay Blue Hole. In both cases go north around Saddle Back Cay. Don't even think of going around the south end—there's a reef running across there that acts like a doorstep. Not only is it too shallow for you to get over that sill, but the ocean water doesn't like it either. Any kind of sea running in results in spoils and tide rips on the ocean side, and a powerful up-swelling over the reef that will vacuum the depth from under you one moment, and threaten you with a wall of water the next.

The cay beyond Saddle Back Cay whose south tip we suggested you might use as a transit has a pretty palm-backed beach in the middle. Obviously there are others who think so too, for we found a stone-built barbecue grill built in the little palm grove, and two crude deck chairs.

Flo's Place, Chester Darville's settlement, Little Harbour Cay.

DEVILS CAY

We've found nothing of interest at Devils Cay.

COMFORT CAY AND LITTLE HARBOUR CAY

We take these two cays together as they are virtually joined at low water. The south end of Little Harbour Cay is shielded from the west by two further small cays, Guano in the north and Cabbage in the south. In the triangle formed by the Darville settlement on Little Harbour Cay, the north end of Cabbage Cay, and the southwest headland of Little Harbour Cay lies the Little Harbour Cay anchorage.

If you are coming in from the ocean side, the cut between Little Harbour Cay and Frozen Cay is wide and deep, but there is one reef (which normally shows with breaking seas) mid-channel. Once you've got it, you can pass either side of it. We favor turning in at our LHCOA waypoint for this gives you the chance to check out the anchorage behind the north end of Frozen Cay as well as the Little Harbour Cay anchorage, and depending on the set of the swell, go for the better-protected one.

Little Harbour ocean approach.

ANCHORAGES IN THE LITTLE HARBOUR CAY AREA

At first sight, particularly if you first see it at high water, the Little Harbour Cay anchorage looks the perfect place. Beware. Unless you are shoal draft there is only one place you can anchor and that is over the mid-channel sand patches level with the north end of Cabbage Cay. There's just room for two boats to anchor here, and you'll need to set two anchors because the tidal current is strong, runs north–south, and you'll achieve a 180-degree swing every six hours. Dive your anchors and make sure they set, and if you're in doubt, dig them in by hand.

If you have shoal draft two further options are open to you. You can tuck yourself just under the tip of Guano Cay, or you can go on (but not at low water) and anchor off the Darville settlement, where you will have just enough depth to stay floating when the tide is out.

If all this is too daunting, you can anchor off the southwest tip of Comfort Cay. As there is a shoal area in your path as you come in from the ocean, we offer two reassuring waypoints that may help. These are first the narrow passage through the south Guano shoal area, which is 25° 34' 10"/166 N 077° 44' 05"/083 W, and second, the location of the anchorage, which is 25° 34' 30"/500 N 077° 44' 05'/083 W. Of course if you're coming down the inside route you don't have to worry about that shoal area, at least until you head on south. Behind Comfort Cay you have plenty of sea room, and you can take your dinghy (which you would have had to do anyway) to get to Little Harbour Cay and the Darville settlement.

Although Frozen Cay falls under our heading of the southern Berry Islands, it's timely to note here that the nothernmost Frozen Cay anchorage, behind the northern tip of Frozen Cay, is your immediate alternative to Little Harbour and Comfort Cay. It's virtually on the doorstep and there are no problems getting there, but note our warning in the text on page 151.

LITTLE HARBOUR CAY AND THE DARVILLE SETTLEMENT

What's the attraction of Little Harbour? Well it's pretty much unfrequented, it's a good place to base yourself and go small-boat exploring, and Chester Darville's settlement, high on a spine of rock backed by the skyline of tousle-headed coconut palms we've already mentioned as a landmark, is worth visiting. You're welcome there for he runs a bar called Flo's Place (after his mother, Florence) and will serve meals too if you give him 3–4 hours advance notice.

There's nothing much unusual in this, but what is different is that the population of this settlement is just one family, with their hens and chickens, peacocks, sheep (some of whom must have had a goat or two in their ancestry), dogs, and cats. Talk to Chester about the hurricane that wiped everything off the island but the settlement his grandfather founded. Then sit outside, Kalik or one of his rum punches (regular or spicy) in hand, and watch the sunset.

The Southern Berry Islands

HAVING started the Berry Islands as if you arrived there from Grand Bahama and ended the northern Berrys with Little Harbour Cay, we start the southern Berrys with Frozen and Alder Cays, which lie immediately to the south of Little Harbour Cay.

To the vessel arriving in Chub Cay directly from Florida, this may seem vexing, but a reverse treatment would equally disadvantage the cruising visitor arriving from the north. Patently to work in toward the center from each end of the Berry Island crescent would be absurd, so we continue the broad direction we set from the beginning, to cover the Bahamas from north to south, and ensure that our approaches and fine detail, for want of a better word, are unisex.

The southern Berrys have the distinction of comprising some of the hottest property on the Bahamian market, and for this reason you could say that it's not the most hospitable cruising ground for the visiting yacht. Why? Out of the eight larger cays that form the major part of the southern Berrys, six of them are private property. So unless you have island-owning friends, your "visit ashore program" may be limited. But on the plus side, yes, there are anchorages, the water colors are fantastic, the snorkeling is good, and, if you're fishing, the fish bite.

Frozen and Alder Cays

We treat Frozen and Alder Cays together for they are all but joined and share a near landlocked bight that might look,

SOUTHERN BERRY ISLANDS		
Frozen Cay Anchorage (not for navigation)		
FRCAN	25° 32' 55"/916 N	077° 43' 03"/050 W
Bond Cay Reef		
BREEF	25° 29' 14"/240 N	077° 42' 29"/490 W
Bond Cay - Little Whale Cay Gap		
BLWGP	25° 27' 10"/176 N	077° 44' 19"/324 W
Bond - Little Whale Anchorage (not for navigation)		
BLWAN	25° 27' 45"/750 N	077° 46' 30"/500 W
Whale Cay Reefs		
OWCRS	25° 24' 48"/800 N	077° 44' 56"/943 W
Off Whale Cay Light		
OWCLT	25° 23' 14"/245 N	077° 47' 37"/625 W
Bird Cay Southwest		
BRDSW	25° 22' 58"/964 N	077° 50' 47"/785 W
Bird Cay Anchorage (not for navigation)		
BRDAN	25° 23' 40"/666 N	077° 50' 10"/166 W
Off Texaco Point (Frazers Hog Cay)		
OTXPT	25° 24' 05"/085 N	077° 50' 50"/833 W
Chub Cay Entry		
CHUBC	25° 24' 15"/250 N	077° 54' 50"/833 W
Chub Cay South		
CHUBS	25° 23' 15"/250 N	077° 54' 50"/833 W

The final figures in each waypoint show seconds (00") and thousands (000) of a minute.

on the chart, like a great anchorage. It isn't. It's shallow inside, you may find 4 feet there at MLW if you're lucky, and it's mostly grass. There is one patch of sand. What's not so good is that the approach shoals rapidly the closer in you get, and if there's a swell running outside in the ocean, or strong wave action, it will be rolly inside there for you're exposed to surge over the barrier rocks linking the two cays, and exposed to wind from the east. We suggest you strike this off your possible anchorage list and settle for the anchorage we suggested in the last section, which lies on the Bank side behind the north tip of Frozen Cay. You have sea room there, and you can choose your depth. We've found 20 feet and 12 feet around our waypoint FRCAN. But check that anchor. The bottom is hard. We've been told that there's one rock there, blazed with bottom paint, which in the words of our informant "we never knew existed, and we'd never have noticed but for the bottom paint." We were fortunate. We never encountered it in all our casting around for the ideal spot to drop

The Southern Berry Islands

Reproduced from Admiralty Chart 3912. Depth in meters.

Not to be used for Navigation.

our hook. Just be warned. There is a rogue rock somewhere in that area, which others, all too clearly, have found.

Both Frozen and Alder Cays are private. Frozen has undergone a major construction program, which if nothing else has given it two useful landmarks from the ocean side traveling from north to south: a green-roofed building and then a blue-roofed building, both set in clumps of coconut palms.

Bond Cay and Little Whale Cay

Like Frozen and Alder, as well as Whale and Bird to come, these cays are in private hands, and this places quite a stretch of the southern Berrys out of bounds on the land side. However there are two anchorages in

Whale Cay reefs, from the south.

the Bond Cay–Whale Cay gap area that you may want to use. We don't recommend taking the inside passage over the Bank, preferring (as we've said) to play safe on the ocean side. The ocean side does have hazards here, and you'll want to stay well out. Even if you are following the 30-foot depth contour, there are places where you may be caught short. Almost half way down Bond Cay a reef and shoal area suddenly reduce your depth to 16 feet around 25° 29' N 077° 43' W. Anticipate this and keep well offshore here. We reckon to stay out at least a mile, particularly if the set of wind and wave is pushing toward the shore. Use our BREEF waypoint.

The Bond Cay–Whale Cay Anchorages

If you're going to anchor in the Bond Cay–Little Whale Cay gap, you have the Sisters Rocks to take note of (they're easy to see) and a shoal area to the north of Little Whale Cay, which extends into the ocean. If you turn in at our BLWGP waypoint you should be well set for an anchorage that is more of a roadstead, in the old nautical sense, than a protected place. We wonder how such an open stretch of water gained the anchor symbol placed on the chart, for other than offering the right kind of depth and the sea room to accommodate a small armada, you're exposed to wind from every direction, as well as ocean swell.

But if the weather is kind, the Bond Cay–Whale Cay gap makes a good place to stop for a swim and lunch. Around BLWAN we've found 12–18 feet of water, but you don't need coordinates to help you decide where to drop your hook. You have all the space you could wish for, and the depth to settle anywhere you like.

A second anchorage lies tucked between Little Whale Cay and the north tip of Whale Cay. This offers some protection from north and south, but little from the other directions, nothing from the east and southeast, and is still open to ocean surge. It has a measure of shoal ground and reef to negotiate whichever way you choose to approach it. The ocean way takes you between two reefs, keeping more north than south, holding closer to Little Whale Cay. If there's any kind of wave action or swell coming in from the ocean, you'll find breaking seas here and the approach, particularly at low water, is not attractive. Don't consider it. From the Bank you have 4 feet at the most in some areas, maybe less. Just go slowly. Inside the anchorage you'll find 6–9 feet.

LITTLE WHALE CAY

Little Whale Cay, with virtually unlimited money lavished on it, looks good. A justifiable end, you might say, for the profits arising from the development of Freeport (for the developer of Freeport, Wallace Groves, took Little Whale Cay as his private kingdom). Just in case you need further identification, Little Whale Cay has a wind sock by its airstrip on the north end, and a truncated light house on the south end.

WHALE CAY

The ocean coast of Whale Cay is a potential nightmare with shoals and reefs extending off its two "elbows" where the lie of the island changes direction from north–south to southwest and then nearly west. The first elbow in particular has a singularly nasty shallow bight behind it. You're likely to run into it before you realize what's happening if you're not standing sufficiently far offshore (our waypoint OWCRS). Your warning of the second elbow is a sand cliff fronting on the beach. Just stand well out at this point, keeping in 60 feet of water. When you reach the end of Whale Cay and Whale Cay light with Bird Cay ahead, your position will be around our OWCLT waypoint.

BIRD CAY

Bird Cay is private. The ocean side (BRDSW) has no particular horrors, so take a fairly straightforward run to clear its southwest tip, and then head for the southernmost point of Frazers Hog Cay. There's a potential anchorage just behind the southwest tip of Bird Cay (BRDAN) with 10 feet of water, but from southeast to west it offers you no protection. If you have shoal draft you could creep further along the Bank-side coast of Bird Cay to escape the swells that can come around the corner, but Bird Cay doesn't rate on our list of anchorages. Like many other places, it's just somewhere you can drop your hook if the conditions that day are right.

Frazers Hog Cay and Chub Cay

The south headland of Frazers Hog Cay, known as Texaco Point, is a low-lying green whale of a mini-headland, which is hard to pick up from a distance. Waypoint OTXPT will place you just off it, ready to go up along the east coast of Frazers Hog Cay to anchor there, or to continue along the south coast of both Frazers Hog and Chub Cays if you're heading for Chub Cay Marina, or one of the two anchorages off Chub Cay.

Berry Islands Club Marina and Anchorage

There's now a definite alternative to Chub Cay. On the eastern shore of Frazers Hog Cay (which is essentially the eastward extension of Chub Cay, for the dividing channel between the two is now silted and mangrove-bound), the Berry Islands Club is in business. The name is a resurrection of the 1950s name of the first marina on this site, which has had more than one reincarnation since its demise. Many will know the site by its last name, the Frazers Hog Cay

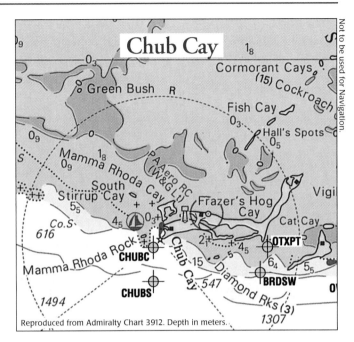

Reproduced from Admiralty Chart 3912. Depth in meters.

Marina. Now much has changed. There is a good dock with ten slips, and six well-laid moorings offshore. Onshore is a small, captivating little clubhouse with the kind of bar you dream about finding in the islands, a small restaurant with a reputation for fantastic food, good hosts, and three bedrooms.

They cater to visiting cruisers, and for visitors who fly in to stay and fish, or just relax. But see our **Yellow Pages**.

From our OTXPT waypoint just work your way around the point (there's an obvious shoal there running out a little way from the point) and you'll cross one "bump," a shallow spot that carries 8.5 feet at MLW. From there, parallel the shore, favoring (if anything) the sand to starboard, for that side has the deeper water. You'll have 9–10 feet at MLW, maybe more, all the way to their dock. The moorings are off your starboard bow. On your way in, if you want to be free, you can anchor. Or go past their dock and anchor. But don't, if you're dropping your hook, encroach into their mooring areas. That would be a big breach of etiquette.

Once there, you're open from northeast to southeast. It's not quite as bad as it sounds, for the flats to the north and east, as well as Bird Cay, shield you. You'll feel the wind. You may get a sharp chop. But you should survive. And the moorings, all one-time Chub Cay power station Caterpillar diesel generators, should hold you if you've picked one up.

Approaches to Chub Cay

Going along the south coast of Frazers Hog Cay and Chub Cay, it's hard to tell where Frazers Hog Cay ends and Chub Cay begins, but it hardly matters. Watch for the very obvious Diamond Rocks to port. Ahead you'll have the barren Mamma Rhoda Rock and the Chub Cay light (like a black stake) on Chub Cay Point. The Chub Cay Marina masts and a water

Sunset over Chub Cay.

tower will be all too obvious. Your Chub Cay entry waypoint is CHUBC, but you hardly need it because you should go visual. Go round Chub Point. An anchorage lies to starboard with 5–6 feet of water. Off your starboard bow you'll see the entry channel into the marina with its range marks. Be warned that we've found no more than 5 feet in patches in the approach channel and just 6 feet in the entry channel at Low Water. If you've failed to get hold of Chub Cay Marina on your way in, the reason is that they ignore channel 16 and stay locked on channel 68. Try it. The response time is rarely good, sometimes you draw a blank. If so, go ahead, enter, and see if you can attract attention.

If you want to anchor out away from the Chub Cay frontage, you have an alternative. Work your way past the Chub Cay entry into the channel between Crab Cay and Chub Cay. This is shallow, shoal draft stuff. We used to do this in our catamaran days when we were only drawing 2 feet 6 inches fully laden.

Chub Cay Marina

Chub Cay is at exactly the right geographic location to serve as a staging point for the Bahamas-bound boat coming from Florida to cruise in the Exumas, heading for Spanish Wells and Harbour Island, or content to remain in the Berry Islands. For the sports fisherman, intent on fishing the Northwest Providence Channel or the Tongue of the Ocean (between Andros and the Exumas Bank), Chub Cay couldn't be better placed. If you're sailing, Chub Cay comes at the limit of your daytime cruising range crossing the Great Bahama Bank. If you want to dive in the Bahamas, Chub Cay offers as wide a range of dive sites as the Bimini Islands. So Chub Cay, unusually, is one of the few places in the Bahamas where sailboats can sometimes outnumber visiting power boats, and the balance between trawlers and sports fishermen hangs on the season in the fishing calendar.

For all these reasons Chub Cay has modeled itself to serve some four different communities. From an initial desire to be a club resort catering to those who would wish to build there and keep a private dock, Chub Cay has a membership, a member's side to the marina, and favored rates and some

facilities to go along with their $1,500-a-year membership dues. The 130 or so members are primarily sports fishermen. Along with their members Chub Cay naturally attracts nonmember sports fishermen, and a stretch of dock space is reserved for them.

Chub Cay also caters to divers, who are accommodated in cabins on the non-member side of the marina, and it's this same side that has the berths for visiting boaters. The two transient docks extending out into the marina from the east side have no finger piers, so only the four slips alongside each T offer the facility of lying alongside. You have to come in having first figured out how you're going to get on and off your boat, over the bow or over the stern. Sailboats generally favor bow in and power boats, mostly, seem persuaded that stern first is best.

Chub Cay Marina has had its ups and downs, and like many places in the Bahamas, the attrition of climate alone, let alone severe storms, has made its effect felt. In 1992 Hurricane *Andrew* hit Chub Cay at the time when its material downslide was becoming critical, and providentially forced a reconstruction and modernization program that had become overdue. The recovery curve post-Andrew has been slow, but Chub Cay wins a Gold Star for what it has achieved to date. Dock power, once unstable and intermittent, is now working, as is cable TV. Shower and toilet facilities have been rebuilt (but we still consider the provision of just one toilet and one shower for the entire non-member side of the marina to be inadequate). The small store is looking better than we've ever seen it, and the Har-

Chub Cay Marina, from the southwest.

bor House restaurant, which you may use on your guest tab, has improved greatly in the last year.

Sadly, perhaps because of lax rules on holding tanks and a lack of shoreside facilities, the marina is polluted and urgently needs improved hydraulic engineering, perhaps a second channel, to help it self-cleanse and recover its natural state.

CRAB CAY AND SOUTH STIRRUP CAY
To the north and northwest of Chub Cay are Crab Cay and (to make the Berry Island crescent complete) a South Stirrup Cay. Neither of them hold particular interest.

You'll note, checking your chart, that there are cays we've missed writing about. These are the mid-Bank cays in the southern Berrys lying south of Latitude 25° 30' N, the Fish and Samphire Cays, Cockroach Cay, and the Cormorant Cays. They're all there, accessible by dinghy or shoal draft boat with the right tide, but surrounded by barrier girdles of shoals and sand bores. They are not a cruising ground.

Approaches to the Southern Berrys

The Chub Cay Entry Route from Florida
Chub Cay is right on the blue Interstate connecting Florida with the southern Berrys, Nassau, Spanish Wells and Harbour Island, and the Exumas as you swing past New Providence Island. Your route from Florida will first take you across the Gulf Stream to Bimini or Cat Cay, and then across the Great Bahama Bank to the Northwest Channel Light. As there may well be minor changes in your initial heading setting off across the Bank, we deal with these courses under **The Great Bahama Bank** on page 140. Here we'll just pick up the final legs.

From Northwest Channel Light (NWCHL), you head 116°M for 14.47 nm, which will bring you 1 nm south (CHUBS) of our Chub Cay entry waypoint. You can identify Chub Cay some 7–8 nm out by its trees, golf ball water tower (on the left), and radio mast (on the right).

Once you've got to that Chub Cay south waypoint, go north on 005°M for that 1 nm, which brings you ready (CHUBC) to enter Chub Cay Marina or to anchor off there. See **Frazers Hog Cay and Chub Cay** on page 153 for entry directions.

Chub Cay to Nassau (New Providence Island)
This is a simple route. At the outset run 1 nm south on a heading of 185°M to gain a reasonable offset from Chub Cay, and then turn to head 125°M for 34.99 nm, which will take you right to the entrance of Nassau Harbour (NASHW).

At that point call Nassau Harbour Control on channel 16 and request permission to enter the harbor area, giving them your destination.

Chub Cay to Andros
From Chub Cay down to Andros is a straightforward run from our CHUBS waypoint 1 nm due south of Chub Cay. For Morgans Bluff (MRGNE) it's 12.82 nm on 202°M. For Bethel Channel (BTHEL) and Nicholls Town it's 14.95 nm on 194°M. For Fresh Creek (FRESH), to our mind the most likely destination, it's 40.25 nm on a heading of 172°M (see page 140 for a list of waypoints).

Completing the Circuit—The West Side Route, Chub Cay to Great Harbour Cay
This alternative approach to Great Harbour Cay over the Bahama Bank is a route that takes you over shallow and largely uncharted waters, particularly around the Northwest Channel Light. The only certain factor is that each year the nature of the depths will change as sands move. You should plan to negotiate the shallowest section around the Northwest Channel Light and the start of the Northwest Channel at high tide. Our waypoints are there to help you set your courses, but are no guarantee of a safe route.

LEGS 1 AND 2
First, from your Chub Cay entry waypoint (CHUBC) head 1 nm south on 185°M to gain an offing. Then turn for the Northwest Channel Light (NWCHL) on a heading of 297°M, and you'll have 14.55 nm to run.

LEG 3
Alter to 341°M and you'll have 1.65 nm to run to our SWEBB waypoint.

LEG 4
Head due north on 005°M with 9.75 nm to run to our NWBAB waypoint.

LEGS 5 AND 6
You have a straight shot of 12.96 nm on a course of 065°M to get on the latitude of the first approach marker to Great Harbour Cay Marina. It should come up 1 nm to the east. Take that 1 nm to the marker (in fact it's 0.9 nm) on 095°M.

From then on go visual, following the directions we give in **The Northern Berry Islands** under **The Approach to Great Harbour Cay Marina** on page 145. This route gives you a total of 40.91 nm to that first marker, where you have about 5.5 nm to run. A total of 46.41 nm in all. You may have saved perhaps 10 nm by not going up the east-coast ocean route of the Berrys.

YELLOW PAGES

This area was hit by Hurricane *Floyd* in September 1999. Be aware that post-hurricane repairs and reconstruction may still be in progress, and wind and storm surge damage may still be evident.

GREAT HARBOUR CAY

The legendary Berry Island charm will captivate you as you are greeted with friendliness and kindness all around the Great Harbour Cay Marina, and Bullocks Harbour settlement a couple of miles away. What may be lacking in material goods here is more than compensated for by the willingness of local residents to share with you what they have. When looking for accommodations for a night, we were welcomed into someone's home; pulling over to let a car overtake in case we were dawdling, the driver got out and stopped to ask, with great courtesy, whether we were all right.

The Berry Islands are not well served in term of marinas, and anchorages are the name of the game. In the south, *Chub Cay Club* and the tiny *Berry Island Club* on Frazer's Hog Cay are the useful waypoints on the route between Bimini and Nassau. The only other marina is *Great Harbour Cay,* which is well located as a transit point between the northern and central cruising grounds. At the time of writing, the marina, which is independent from the surrounding townhouses and restaurants, was up for sale, and recent work had improved facilities greatly. There is a superb seven-mile long beach a short walk across to the eastern shore, with easy accessibility and glorious water colors, as well as some very good shelling. Great Harbour Cay is a Port of Entry, with **Customs** and **Immigration** able to clear you in when called from the airport.

MARINA

GREAT HARBOUR CAY MARINA
Tel: 242-367-8005 • Fax: 367-8115 • VHF 14/16/68
(in the USA) Tel: 561-585-0027 • Fax: 585-1998

This is a well-protected, sheltered marina once you have worked your way in, and makes a good refuge in a strong breeze. Rufus, the dockmaster, is wise and helpful, and the facilities surrounding the marina are very good for transient boats as well as for the owners of the townhouses with their own slips. The fuel dock (367-8113 and VHF 16 and 68) is on your starboard side after entering the first outer harbor, and can be called ahead if you want to refuel on your way in. It doubles as the only filling station in town, which makes access for boats needing gasoline cramped and difficult to get close enough to reach the same pump as cars on shore.

Slips	80
Max LOA	150 ft.
MLW at Dock	8 ft.
Dockage	From April 1st to August 31st, 80¢ per foot per day, or 70¢ per ft. per day monthly, or 50¢ per ft. per day quarterly. From September 1st to March 31st, 65¢ per ft. per day, 60¢ per ft. per day monthly, 40¢ per ft. per day quarterly.
Power	30¢ per kwh for 30A and 50A.
Fuel	Diesel and gasoline from the fuel dock in the outer harbor, open 8 am to noon and 1 to 4:30 pm daily, and 8 am to noon on Sundays. Visa and MasterCard accepted, with a 5-percent surcharge. Also oils and lubricants; pay independently of your dockage charge in the marina.
Water	30¢ per gallon for reverse osmosis water, $10 for washdown.
Telephones	By the marina office; a *Batelco* card phone next to *The Wharf.*
TV	Cable hookup available.
Showers	Seven very clean toilets and showers available to marina guests at no charge.
Laundry	Washers and dryers $2 each in US quarters.
Restaurants	*The Pool Bar* and *Restaurant* at *The Great Harbour Yacht Club,* open daily for lunch and dinner from noon, overlooking the swimming pool above the marina. Cash only. *The Wharf,* open for breakfast (7–11 am) and dinner (4 pm–midnight) every day except Tuesdays. *The Tamboo,* open on Wednesday and Saturdays for dinner; reservations required. No shorts or hats, and jackets preferred for Saturday nights.
Groceries	*The Marina Store* (367-8768), open daily from 9 am to 6 pm, and from 8 am to noon on Sundays, with a limited selection of canned and dry goods, baby food, nail polish, and oils. Fresh fruit and vegetables on Fridays when the mailboat comes in. $10 per bag.
Ice	
Liquor Store	*The Liquere Store,* next to the *Gift Shop,* is open from 9 am to 9 pm daily except Sundays.
Mail	There is a mail box outside the *Gift Shop,* and Ruth can sell you stamps and phone cards.
Gift Shop	Ruth Adderley, in *The Happy People's Gift Shop* (367-8117) has an enormous range of items for sale, including marine oils and some very good straw work of her own and her mother's. She can also help you with insurance, as subagent for *JS Johnson,* accommodations, fishing charters, and boat, car, and bicycle rentals.
Rentals/Charters	Bicycles, cars, jeeps, and small boats from *Happy People Rentals.*
Accommodations	*The Harbour Inn,* at the far end of the marina, behind *The Wharf Restaurant.* Five rooms with private baths, from $75 per night; 2-room efficiency from $125 per night. Call Ruth Adderley or Elorn Rolle at *The Happy People* (367-8117).
Library	Book swap in the marina office.
Credit cards	Visa, MasterCard, Amex.
Dockmaster	Rufus Pritchard, with Clarise in the office.

Happy People's Gift Shop, Great Harbour Cay Marina.

SERVICES AND SHOPPING IN BULLOCKS HARBOUR

Bus
Island Bus can be called on VHF 68 "De Boss."

Church
Church of God Prophecy

Clinic
Tel: 367-8400   Nurse Clark is at the clinic from 9 am to 2 pm Monday to Friday, in the government building with the post office. Turn left at the T-junction in Bullocks Harbour, and continue up the hill. A doctor comes in from Bimini via Nassau about once a month.

Customs
Tel: 367-8566, and

Immigration
Tel: 367-8112.   At the airport.

Golf
There is a maintained nine-hole golf course on the island, though the clubhouse by the bridge is derelict. Call VHF 16 "Even Par" for information.

Groceries
A & L General Store on the top of the hill toward the post office Tel: 367-8292   Open from 7:30 am to 8:30 pm Monday to Saturday, to noon on Sundays. A small selection of goods.
Pinder's Grocery in a pink building on the left-hand side toward the post office   Tel: 367-8262   Open from 7:30 am to 9 pm daily, with fresh fruit and vegetables when the mailboat comes in on Fridays. A limited choice, but very friendly.
Roberts Groceries   Tel: 367-8353   Scenically the best grocery store site in the Bahamas, on the ocean front, down by the Government Dock. No definite opening times, though pretty much 7:30 am to 6 pm Monday to Saturday, to 9 am on Sundays. Sparsely stocked shelves, but Mr. Roberts can help you with propane tank refills.

Liquor Store
Watergate Wholesale Liquor Store   Tel: 367-8244   Open 9 am to 10 pm daily. Wholesale and retail liquor and beers.

Police
Tel: 367-8344   In Bullocks Harbour, opposite the school.

Post Office
Open 9 am to 5:30 pm Monday to Friday in the pink administration building with the clinic.

Propane
Roberts Groceries   Tel: 367-8353   Leave your tanks with Mr. Roberts on Friday morning and he will send them to Nassau on the mailboat; they will be returned the following Friday.

Shopping
Lilly's Boutique at the airport   T-shirts and souvenirs.

Telephones
Batelco   Open 9 am to 5 pm at the foot of the towers, quite a hike from the marina. Ruth Adderley, at *Happy People's Gift Shop,* sells phone cards.

RESTAURANTS AND BARS

Great Harbour Yacht Club Pool Bar and Restaurant
Tel: 367-8051/8053   Known locally as the *Pool Bar,* open daily for alfresco lunches and dinners from noon on. The bar and restaurant overlook the swimming pool adjoining the marina, in a cloud of bougainvillea. Locally caught seafood, meats cooked expertly on the grill by Paul, Janet's fresh salads, and to-die-for homemade raisin and rum ice cream make this a choice restaurant in the Berry Islands. Dinner reservations preferred. No credit cards.
Mama and Papa T's Beach Club   Open daily for breakfast, lunch, snacks, and cocktails, under two circular thatched bars on the beach looking out to Petit Cay. Kitchen closes at 3 pm, bar stays open until about 5 pm. A short walk across from the airport on a heavenly site, this is the place to be during the day, with fabulous hamburgers or Angie's Special Sandwich washed down with a Goombay Smash, guaranteed to have you dozing the afternoon away.
The Tamboo is the large round building with a blue-painted circular deck that you see on your final approach into the marina. It is only open on Wednesdays and Saturdays for dinner, by reservation. Jackets required on Saturday evenings.
Watergate Bar and Restaurant in Bullocks Harbour   Tel: 367-8244 This is really a bar and liquor store, open 9 am to 10 pm, but the good Vernita Rolle will cook you conch fritters, chicken and chips, and more, if you ask her, or better still, call in advance.
Wharf Restaurant and Bar at the *Great Harbour Cay Marina* Tel: 367-8762   Open for breakfast from 7 to 11 am, and for dinner from 4 pm to midnight. Closed on Tuesdays. This attractively decorated and deservedly popular restaurant overlooking the marina, with its tropical frescoes on the walls, serves very good American/Bahamian food.
Whitewater Restaurant in Bullocks Harbour   Tel: 367-8050 This new restaurant and sports bar serves, according to local reputation, the best Bahamian seafood in Bullocks Harbour. The bar is open all day, with breakfast from 7 am, lunch from 11 am, and dinner from 6 pm. It is cavernous and plain inside, with a large satellite TV over the bar.

GETTING AROUND

Airport
With a 4,500-ft. runway, this makes a great place to stop for lunch if you happen to arrive in a small airplane. At the airport there is the *Killing Time Liquor Store* (367-8019); *Francis Electronics* (367-8088); *Grace's Ice Cream Parlor and Snack Bar,* which is open from 11 am to 5:30 pm daily except Sundays; and *Miss Lilly's Gift Shop,* selling T-shirts and souvenirs. *Mama and Papa T's Beach Club* is only a 5-minute walk.

Airlines
Bel Air   Tel: 954-524-0115/9814   Flights to Fort Lauderdale on Fridays and Sundays at 2 pm. $199 round trip, plus $37 US airport tax, or $15 departure tax leaving from the Bahamas. 50-lb. baggage weight limit.
Cat Island Air   Tel: 367-8021 (local) or 242-377-3318 (Nassau) • Fax: 377-3320   Daily flights from Nassau at 8 am and 4 pm.
Sapphire Aviation   Tel: 561-687-7967   Charter flights from Fort Lauderdale.
Tropical Diversions   Tel: 954-921-9084 • Fax: 921-1044   Can arrange charter flights for people using any of their rental properties in Great Harbour.

Bicycles, Cars, Motorcycles, and Small Boats
Happy People Rentals   Tel: 367-8117   Bicycles from $2 per hour or $15 per day, single-seat motorcycles $30 per day. Jeeps from $50 per day, cars from $65 to $85 per day. 15-foot Remington skiff from $100 per day, 19- and 20-foot Welcraft from $125 and $150 per day. Daily rates are from 8 am to 5 pm.

Mailboat
M/V Mangrove Cay Express leaves Nassau on Thursdays, returning on Sundays. Fare $30

Diving
There is very little diving off Great Harbour Cay because of the generally unfavorable weather conditions over the wall of the Northwest Providence Channel. No recognized dive facility on the island exists, but private dive trips can be arranged by *Happy People Rentals.* Ask Elorn Rolle or Ruth Adderley to help you.

Fishing
Percy Darville   Tel: 367-8818   He can take you either bone-fishing or deep sea fishing.

Bonefish.

FESTIVALS, FISHING TOURNAMENTS, AND REGATTAS

The fishing tournament has not been held for a couple of years, though there is talk of reviving it.

ACCOMMODATIONS

Harbour Inn behind *The Wharf Restaurant* at the marina Tel: 242-367-8117 • Fax: 367-8851   Ruth Adderley and Elorn Rolle have 4 rooms with bathrooms from $75 per night, and an efficiency with its own kitchen, living room, and separate bedroom for $125 per night.

Beach Villas   Tel: 242-367-8854   Paul and Janet Rich, who run *The Pool Restaurant,* have two delightful villas on the beach. One with two double beds and a sleeping loft, kitchen, bathroom, living room, and decks, costs from $125 per night. The other with double the accommodation and large family kitchen costs from $300 per night. Weekly and monthly rates available; cash or traveler's checks only.

Tropical Diversions   Tel: 954-921-9084 • Fax: 921-1044   This company offers air charter services to Great Harbour Cay, as well as rentals in some of the townhouses surrounding the marina and single and double studios and beach villas. Studios from $90 per night, villas from $175 per night, and townhouses at the marina with a dock underneath, from $180 per night.

THINGS TO DO IN GREAT HARBOUR CAY

- Take your inflatable north, up the Banks side of Great Harbour Cay, and visit Great Stirrup Cay Lighthouse. Wave to the parasailing cruise ship passengers as you go.
- Head south and go fishing off the Market Fish Cays.
- After an exhausting morning walking, swimming, and enjoying the pure white sand and shades of emerald water on the beach facing Petit Cay, treat yourself to a Goombay Smash and a hamburger with Mama and Papa T at the *Beach Bar.* Maybe you can persuade Papa T to play backgammon with you?

LITTLE HARBOUR

Flo's Conch Bar and Restaurant welcomes you as you drop the hook in Little Harbour. Chester Darville and his family are the sole survivors of the Little Harbour settlement, which was devastated by Hurricane *Andrew* in 1992. The food is cooked and prepared by Chester's mother, Florence, after whom the restaurant is named. Dinner requests should be sent in on VHF 68 by 3 pm. Fresh bread is available to order for $3 a loaf. Chester Darville is also the BASRA representative for Little Harbour, and can be reached on VHF 68.

Why have we chosen Little Harbour for one of our Yellow Pages when all that's there is just one house, one family, and yes, a bar and a small restaurant? It's true. There is nothing else. We could have scooped it up in the main text and forgotten about a Little Harbour Yellow Page entry.

We do it as a way of highlighting just one small family venture out of the many in the Bahamas who have made countless cruising visitors welcome over the years. Of course they earn their living that way, but the greeting and hospitality are the same, whether you have come to pass the time of day, have just one drink, or an evening meal. It is people like the Darvilles who are the Bahamas, and who are the reality behind our Yellow Pages. This single entry is done deliberately as a reminder of this, and as a tribute to them all.

THINGS TO DO IN LITTLE HARBOUR

- Join up with anyone else anchored off Little Harbour, and enjoy a delicious Bahamian meal cooked by Florence.
- Get acquainted with some of their animals.

CHUB CAY

The whole island centers around the *Chub Cay Club,* which although badly damaged by Hurricane *Andrew,* has been well restored and improved, with many new facilities added. Now that Bill and Donna Rossbach, who many people know from the *Green Turtle Club,* have taken over the management, we can expect an even higher standard at Chub Cay. It makes a convenient overnight stop if you have just crossed the Great Bahama Bank from Bimini or Cat Cay, and are on your way to Nassau or Andros. There are lovely beaches within walking distance of the marina, and some wonderful ones you can visit with your dinghy on nearby Crab Cay.

Charges differ greatly for members and transient boats in both the resort and the marina, though the staff are equally friendly and helpful. Prices quoted are for transient visitors. **Customs** and **Immigration** are available 9 am to 5 pm, Monday to Saturday, located at the airport. Dockmaster Gerreth Roberts will help you contact them. There is a $25 charge if you take a slip in order to clear customs, but this will be credited to your bill if you stay overnight. Since there are very few finger piers, decide before you go into your slip whether you want to get on and off over the bow or the stern. All registration and payment of bills must be done at reception, which is at the opposite side of the marina from the transient slips, beyond the restaurant. This marina answers on VHF 68.

MARINAS

CHUB CAY CLUB MARINA
Tel: 242-325-1490 • Fax: 322-5199 • VHF 68 and 71
Reservations only, 800-662-8555

Slips	60
Max LOA	110 ft.
MLW at Dock	7 ft.
Entry Channel	6 ft. at low water.
Dockage	$1 per ft. per day, plus 8 percent tax.
Long Term	Dockage from $620 to $1,000 per month.
Power	35¢ per kWh, 50A and 30A available.
Fuel	Diesel and gasoline.
Water	35¢ per gallon metered.
Telephones	*Batelco* card phones by the marina office, members' showers, the police station, and *The Island Shoppe*. There is also a pay phone outside the members' showers.
Showers	Separate facilities for members and non-members. There are still only two toilets and showers for transient boaters, which are not enough for a marina of this size.
Laundry	Washers and dryers, both sides of the marina; non-members $1.25 in quarters for each machine.
Restaurant & Bars	*Harbour House Restaurant* serves breakfast 7 to 9 am, lunch noon to 2 pm, and dinner 7 to 9 pm. The large, pleasant dining room is reserved for members, with a smaller section for non-members, though the food is excellent and the service is good in both. The bar is shared by everyone, with live entertainment at weekends. The chef's special fish coated with coconut and served with mango chutney is one of the best dishes in the Bahamas. *The Cay Bar* is a small, thatched palm bar by the marina swimming pool, open in the afternoons and early evenings.
Ice	Yes, from the dockmaster.
Mail	Reception will send mail for you.
Fax	Reception will send and accept faxes for you. $7 to send one page within the Bahamas.
Accommodations	*Chub Cay Club* has newly refurbished, attractive yacht club marina-side rooms from $135 per day, and three-bedroom beach villas from $500 per day at non-member prices.
Credit Cards	Visa, MasterCard, and Amex.
Dockmaster	Gerreth Roberts, who is always very busy.

SERVICES, SHOPPING, & SPORTS

Church
Chub Cay Chapel

Diving
Scuba Chub at the *Chub Cay Club* Tel: 323-2412 Most of the best diving is around Mamma Rhoda Rock, where you will find wall dives down to 230 feet, as well as canyons and caves abounding with sharks and rays. The actual Mamma Rhoda Reef is stunning, and brilliant for snorkelers. Further around off Whale Cay, another wall dive down into the Tongue of the Ocean is teeming with lobster.

Fishing
This is the closest marina to the Tongue of the Ocean, and a very popular fishing center.

Groceries and Gifts
The Island Shoppe Open 9 am to 1 pm and 2:30 to 5:30 pm, Monday to Saturday. Small supply of groceries, liquor, and

pharmacy goods, and a selection of gifts and logo items. For the first time there was bottled water for sale, but at $1.75 for a 12-oz bottle, it seemed expensive.

Police
The police station is behind *The Island Shoppe*.

Swimming
The pool by the marina is available to guests on visiting boats.

Tennis
There are tennis courts at the *Chub Cay Club*.

GETTING AROUND

Airport
A 5,000-ft. runway, used by private aircraft and some charters.

Airlines
Bel Air Tel: 954-524-0115 Flights to and from Fort Lauderdale on Fridays and Sundays.
BIA Tel: 954-938 8991 Flights into Fort Lauderdale Executive Airport.
Marco Aviation Tel: 941-394-0010 Flights into Naples, Florida.

Bicycles
10 bicycles available to rent from *Chub Cay Club* for $15 per day.

Bus
The *Chub Cay Club* minibus will take you over to the airport, or within the Club area.

FISHING TOURNAMENTS

March and April
Member/Guest Billfish Tournament
Bahamas Billfish Championship

July
All Billfish Classic
Blue Marlin Tournament

THINGS TO DO IN CHUB CAY

- Go gunkholing looking for shells between Chub Cay and Crab Cay.
- Fish along the 100-fathom line up to Rum Cay (the Berry Islands' Rum Cay!), which lies halfway to the Northwest Channel Light.
- Dive *Mamma Rhoda Rock* or over the *Wall* off Whale Cay Point.
- Take your dinghy and explore South Stirrup Cay.
- Relax and enjoy the beaches before moving on to Nassau, the Exumas, or Spanish Wells, or as you wait for weather before crossing the Great Bahama Bank.

FRAZER'S CAY

BERRY ISLANDS CLUB
Tel: 800-933-3533 (Collier Travel) in the USA • VHF 16

This utterly charming, tiny, remote marina, with only ten slips and eight mooring buoys, has re-emerged bearing its original 1940s name, after a brief incarnation as the Frazer's Cay Club. Two brothers from Louisiana, David and Donald Loupe, with Donald's wife, now offer well-appointed guest accommodations in three rooms with their own bathrooms above the club house. They can also serve up to fourteen people at a time with excellent, reasonably priced meals for lunch and dinner. This would be an ideal marina for people who like to avoid the crowd scene at *Chub Cay Club* around the corner, though the anchorage is exposed to anything other than a west wind, and there are few facilities. Just perfect peace!

Slips	10
Moorings	8, at $8 per day.
Max LOA	120 ft. on T-dock.
MLW at Dock	7 ft. at T-dock, 5 ft. on the inside docks.
Dockage	65¢ per ft. per day.
Long Term	40 percent discount on monthly rentals paid in advance.
Power	35¢ per kWh, 30A and 50A available.
Water	25¢ per gallon.
Showers	A good shower inside the clubhouse, $5 per person.
Laundry	$4 a load for the washing machine or dryer; clothes-line drying free.
Restaurant/Bar	Open for lunch and dinner daily, except the days when stocks are being replenished from Nassau. Their small vegetable garden produces salads, bell peppers, and tomatoes. Delicious food, with an emphasis on Cajun cooking, at reasonable prices. Daily fresh fish.
Ice	$4 a bag.
Trash	No charge to guests in the marina, or boats on the mooring buoys.
Library	Take a book, leave a book in the club house. Videos can be borrowed.
Fishing	Charters available. Bonefishing from $200 for a half day, $375 for a full day. Deep sea fishing from $400 for a half day, $800 for a full day.
Beaches	Lovely beaches within easy walking distance.
Accommodations	Two rooms, one with a four-poster bed and bathroom, from $75 per night. Double room with private bath and balcony overlooking the water, from $125 per night. All air conditioned.
Transport	From *Chub Cay Club*, you can be collected in the Swamp Buggy for dinner. Good photo op! If you need to fly out, there will be a charge of $10 to take you over to the *Chub Cay Airport.*

The Berry Islands Club.

Chapter 11
Nassau and New Providence Island

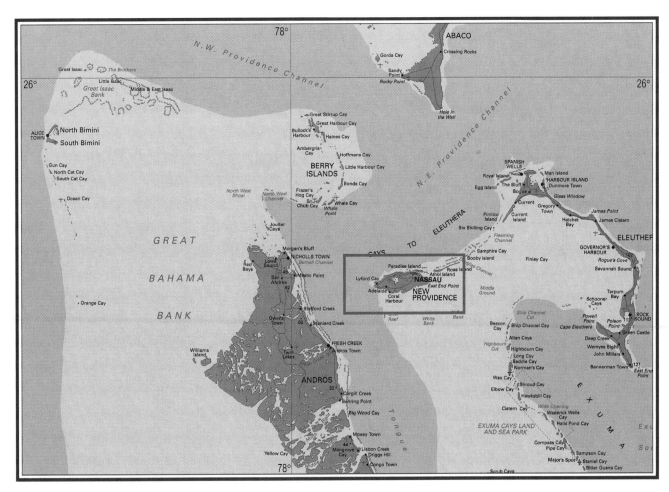

Nassau

NASSAU, capital and most highly populated city of the Bahamas as it is, dominates New Providence Island to the extent that New Providence Island has virtually lost its separate identity and its own name. Today when you speak of Nassau, you mean the whole island. If you mention New Providence, often you'll get blank stares. Nonetheless, we'll touch on New Providence Island, but only briefly, for Nassau (with Paradise Island included) is everything. For the cruising sailor, unless you're visiting friends living further afield in the island, it's going to be Nassau or nothing. At the time we write, Nassau and New Providence Island have been the focus of an unprecedented development boom over the last two years. The transformation shows even while you are still offshore in the greatly enlarged Atlantis Resort, which dominates the Paradise Island skyline. As you enter the harbor, you'll find not one but two Paradise Island bridges, and a new marina—yes, the Atlantis Marina—as you make your way up the harbor.

This is a cruising guide, not a travel guide. If we were to write about Nassau, like any city, let alone the capital of even a small nation, adequate coverage could run for pages, or form a book in its own right. We'll restrict ourselves to an overview. If you're going to spend time there, buy a set of guidebooks off the travel shelves.

New Providence Island is 27 miles long by 7 miles wide, taken as a rough measurement, and you can say that the eastern half, from Cable Beach to the quaintly named McPherson's Bend in the Eastern Road, is the urban area we call Nassau. Some 162,000 people live there. They own 85,000 motor vehicles, and use this almost incredible number of cars on a road system inherited from the British, 90 percent of which is still 1950s in form and barely adequate for 20 percent of this traffic load. Be aware right at the outset that if you need to get around Nassau in a hurry, or get to the International Airport with any degree of urgency, you won't make it in the rush hours. Nassau becomes gridlocked.

You'll find most things you need in Nassau, sometimes after a lot of legwork, but there are extraordinary, unexpected stock deficiencies and temporary shortages. If you're in urgent need of some replacement part, Miami, Fort Lauderdale, and Palm Beach are only an hour away by air and served by almost hourly flights.

ATLANTIS
From air or sea the enlarged 2,300-room Atlantis Resort dominates Paradise Island and indeed the Nassau frontage, making the low-rise run of downtown Nassau seem a straggling, sprawling, half-hearted attempt at settlement, with the one exception of the handsomely renovated ($100 million) British Colonial, now the British Colonial Hilton Nassau. There's no doubt that the sheer mass of the newly completed coral sand–pink Atlantis with its high-bridged towers, spired cupolas, domes, and leaping sailfish, makes a statement. It's amazing from afar (particularly at night with its spires tipped with aircraft warning lights, as red as Surinam cherries) and it's stunning seen close-to. Even if you have no interest in the hotel, the casino, the beaches, or its marina, you should go there. Why? Simply because if awards were given for the realization of a dynamic themed architectural concept on a major scale (round it off at $800 million with $480 million in the latest stage), Atlantis would head our list of contenders. It is achievement with a big A and, we would guess, success with a big S for Sol Kreuzner.

But there's another, marine-related reason why you should go there, and that's the aquarium. That lower case "a" word belies what has been done at Atlantis. The first "reef" with its walk-through tunnel was something to write home about. Now the new glass-sided fish preserve (there's no other word to adequately describe it), and the "tanks" centered around the Atlantis "Dig" (an archaeological fantasy) have far surpassed the original. Go there for that. Fathoms Restaurant (which serves, no surprise, seafood)

Nassau Straw Market.

is the one to choose if you want to watch, and eat!, fish.

And if you're thinking "oh . . . !" the answer is no, we're not on the Atlantis payroll, and our visit there was unannounced, and unescorted.

THE TWO PARADISE ISLAND BRIDGES
Entering Nassau Harbour by sea it's not immediately apparent that there are now two virtual look-alike Paradise Island toll bridges. As you progress further into the harbor, from either the west or the east entrances, you become aware that a double-image has formed arcing across your horizon. If you hadn't heard that a second bridge had been built and had not visited Nassau before, it could have you rubbing your eyes and wondering about your 20/20 vision.

The new western Paradise Island bridge runs from Bay Street at Church Street (by St Matthew's Church, a stone's throw to the east of BASRA's headquarters) to a Paradise Island landfall just to the west of the abutment of the original, but now eastern Paradise Island bridge. The Paradise Island jetties on the western side of the first bridge, which used to serve a miscellany of charter sportsfishers, tour, and booze cruise boats, now lie sandwiched between the two bridges. However the docks have been re-built, smartened up, and boast a terminal building cum shopping center.

The East Bridge serves traffic going to Paradise Island and the West Bridge carries traffic returning to Nassau. Both bridges have pedestrian walkways. Non-directional walkways!

DOWNTOWN NASSAU
Hardly surprisingly, there have been changes in Nassau since our First Edition. We're talking now primarily about the run of Bay Street. The good news is that a considerable reno-

Atlantis Resort, from the west bridge.

vation of Down Town Bay Street, essentially in the Prince George Wharf Area, has taken place. It's looking better. Plans apparently exist to continue this revitalization eastward, and there's every indication that this will happen. Additionally, making Bay Street, and its parallel Shirley Street a complementary one-way system has streamlined Nassau's harborside traffic flow, but has not solved the congestion.

The Coral World Tower is now the Crystal Cay Marine Observation Tower, part of the Marriott Crystal Cay water theme park. It follows, as you'll guess, that the cay we once knew as Silver Cay (to the northeast of Arawak Cay) has now, like so many other tourist targets, undergone a re-christening and Marriott would have it known as Crystal Cay.

If you appreciate at the outset that Nassau is not your town, not there to serve you, the cruising sailor, you'll have made a sensible start. It's a tourist mecca both on the land side with its resort hotel complexes that are as close to being self-sufficient kingdoms as you can get, and it's the "Grand Central Station" for many cruise lines. When you're talking of cruise line days, with maybe ten cruise ships in port, and you know that the big ones carry close to 3,000 passengers and a crew of a thousand, you begin to understand Nassau, and quickly learn to live with (or rarely visit) Bay Street and the downtown area.

Where might you go? Well for a start don't choose a cruise ship day, but see the historic parts of Nassau if you've never been there before. Go to Paradise Island and see the Cloister and the Versailles Garden. See the Atlantis Resort.

Don't wander around the back streets of Nassau at night. There is a high crime rate, and Nassau has endemic violent crime (which may be drug related), not just petty crime. More than one local resident spoke of the crime rate "soaring." Be sensible, street-smart as you would be in any city, and don't go around looking like a walking advertisement for Colombian emeralds. Be careful too, and think it through, if you're considering leaving your boat in Nassau for a time.

Ocean Approaches

One look at a chart will tell you that Nassau is well favored by its ocean approaches, and the reason it became the principal seaport and capital of the Bahamas is immediately obvious. Two great deep-ocean marine highways meet off the north coast of New Providence Island, the Northwest Providence Channel connecting to the Florida Strait and the Northeast Providence Channel connecting to the open Atlantic. To the south the whole run of the Exumas and the Out Islands slanting down to the southeast serve as waypoints on the maritime highway to the Caribbean.

In approaching Nassau from the north, there are essentially no problems. From any other direction you have a Bank approach and that means you must choose your course. But that done, you'll have plenty of water all the way. The one less-than-hospitable area in terms of depth is the south, which is for the most part too shallow for coastal cruising. Just avoid it.

Nassau Harbour, with St. George's Dock, from the west.

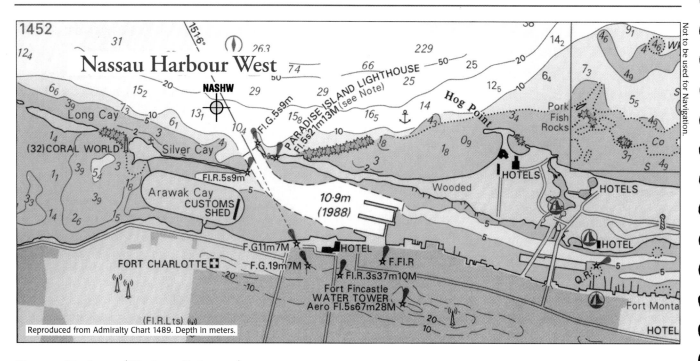

Nassau Harbour West

Reproduced from Admiralty Chart 1489. Depth in meters.

Nassau Harbour (Western Entrance)

Our NASHW waypoint places you right off the entrance to Nassau Harbour, within sight of the first entry buoys. It is mandatory that all vessels entering and leaving Nassau Harbour call Nassau Harbour Control on VHF 16, request permission to enter or leave, and give their destination.

The waypoint we give is the start of the standard western approach into Nassau Harbour, between the west tip of

Coral World tower and Arawak Cay on the right.

Paradise Island (with its lighthouse, now repainted all white rather than banded red and white as it was originally) and the line of Long Cay, Silver Cay, and the Silver Cay breakwater, which will be on your starboard side. The entrance is well marked with entry buoys, and as you carry on into the harbor you'll see the massive cruise ship berths of Prince George Wharf ahead to starboard, and beyond, the unmistakable elliptical spans of two Paradise Island bridges.

As you make your way into Nassau Harbour be conscious that you are moving into the Bahamian marine equivalent of O'Hare Airport. It's no longer the relaxed sightseeing ride up the harbor it once was. Do your homework first, and be quite certain that you've got the geography straight, you know where you're heading, and have anticipated your landmarks and turn points.

AN ALTERNATIVE APPROACH FROM THE WEST

There is an alternative oddball approach into Nassau Harbour from the west. If you've hugged the north coast

NASSAU AND NEW PROVIDENCE ISLAND I		
Nassau Goulding Cay		
GLDNG	25° 01' 30"/500 N	077° 35' 30"/500 W
Nassau Harbour Northwest		
NASNW	25° 06' 30"/500 N	077° 23' 00"/000 W
Nassau Harbour West Entrance		
NASHW	25° 05' 30"/500 N	077° 21' 30"/500 W
Coral Harbour		
COHBR	25° 58' 28"/465 N	077° 28' 30"/510 W

The final figures in each waypoint show seconds (00") and thousands (000) of a minute.

CHARTS AND NASSAU HARBOUR

Many of the charts showing Nassau Harbour currently on the market are out of date. Harbor development that has taken place over the last ten years is not shown. In particular, Potter's Cay may be shown as an island with only the central portion "squared off" as dock (the whole is now developed), the bridge connecting Silver Cay and the commercial Arawak Cay may not be not shown, nor may the Coral World observation tower on Silver Cay (this is one of the most prominent landfall marks, which is far more obvious than Paradise Island lighthouse).

Check your charts carefully and check any new chart or chart kit you buy. You can still use them if they are outdated, but you should overwrite them with your own corrections while you are in Nassau.

coming in from the west you'll arrive (on Longitude 077° 26' 00"/000 W) off Delaporte Point. Ahead of you to starboard will be the towering lilac-pink extravagance of the massive Cable Bay hotels, and to port will be one small island, North Cay. On your bow you'll see the white Crystal Cay underwater observation tower (a contradiction in terms there) with its flared base, and, yes, would you believe it, an elliptical bridge linking Coral Island (or Silver Cay) with Arawak Cay, the main commercial dock area.

The double-take is that the Arawak-Silver bridge is a mini look-alike of the Paradise Island bridges. Look hard. No, the white Coral World tower is **not** Paradise Island light. The bridge in front of you is **not** its big cousin, and Arawak Cay is **not** where the cruise ships tie up. But once you've got this all straightened out, you could go on into Nassau Harbour this way, although this route offers as little as 3 feet at MLW.

Nassau Marinas

Your choice of destination is likely to be one of five marinas:

ATLANTIS MARINA

If you're under 40 feet LOA, forget the Atlantis Marina. They set that 40 feet as a lower limit. Make no mistake, this is a mega-yacht marina, with $15 million invested in it. If you're up to 220 feet, whatever your beam (but with a 37-foot beam limit at the finger piers), you should consider it. Your only restrictions, if you could call them that, are a 100-foot-wide entry channel and 11.5 feet at MLW both in the entry channel and the marina. There are no limits on mast height, provided you come in from the west, and therefore don't have to pass under the two Paradise Island bridges.

The Atlantis Marina entry channel comes up, as you enter Nassau Harbour from the west, on your port side just before the western Paradise Island bridge. The entry is marked,

and they answer on VHF 16. See our **Yellow Pages** for all the detail on the Marina, and the Atlantis Resort.

EAST BAY MARINA

Virtually sandwiched on the New Providence shore between the two Paradise Island bridges is the long-standing East Bay Marina, at one time called the East Bay Yacht Basin. With just twenty-five slips, and long popular particularly with the sailing community, East Bay has often been pretty much fully booked in season. It has fuel and basic facilities, but is showing its age (a re-build is planned, pending a permit). If you have space here, be aware that the building of the western bridge has significantly affected your approach and exit.

Coming in from the west keep mid-channel until you are almost at the West Paradise Island Bridge, then turn to starboard. At this point you are crossing the mail and fishing boat approaches to the west end of Potter's Cay, and you may have to give way to commercial traffic. You should also look out for a sandbar that carries only 3–4 feet at MLW, which will come up on your starboard side. The bridge is still to port. The entry arch under the bridge is marked, like an Intracoastal Waterway bridge, as a channel, with a Tide Gauge Minimum Height Marker on its pilings (it also carries green lights above the arch at night). We suggest that your entry parameters to the East Bay Marina are simply these: your vertical clearance at High Water is 57 feet. Your depth at Low Water is 10–12 feet, which will carry you into the marina. Get the state of the tide, and work it out. Above all, don't head for that arch as you proceed further into the harbor having passed the cruise ships and the anchorage. If you take a curve in from that point, you'll be on that sandbar.

Atlantis Marina.

Statue of Queen Victoria in front of the Parliament Building.

HURRICANE HOLE

The Hurrican Hole is the next marina to come up, this time to port, on Paradise Island, immediately after that second Paradise Island bridge. Hurricane Hole has made its reputation meeting the needs of the mega-yacht fraternity, and hardly surprisingly its predilection (with somewhat limited space) lies with large white hulls and serious length. That's not to say you'll be turned from the door if they have room for you.

Once there you may find that Hurricane Hole is your heart's delight with the Atlantis Resort and its imitation reef, the white sand of the north shore beaches, and the Versailles Garden all within walking distance, and there's no doubt that Paradise Island is a great deal more pleasant as a background setting than East Bay Street on the other side of the harbor. Against this you are separated by that great span of bridge from mainland Nassau, its marine stores, the Bay Street heartland, and Nassau's historic sights.

NASSAU YACHT HAVEN

The Nassau Yacht Haven comes up almost as immediately to starboard. Recently expanded by thirty slips, it has everything that you'd expect, including an adjacent dive shop (we reckon the best), and the Poop Deck bar and restaurant on the second floor (by American counting). This has long been the epicenter of the boating world in Nassau. As for shoreside facilities, we'd class them as adequate. The Poop Deck, long popular, regularly exceeds its capacity at peak periods and in peak seasons. You can expect waits of 30 minutes or more for a table, and a waiting throng that may keep you an arm's length away from the bar. Be warned.

Any disadvantages? As ever with the East Bay Street marinas, as soon you as you step out into the street you wonder how long you need to spend in Nassau. It's busy, noisy, and not pedestrian friendly.

NASSAU HARBOUR CLUB

The fifth of our five primary choices is the Nassau Harbour Club, which is immediately recognizable, again to starboard, by its two open arms of main dock with a central heartland of club-like accommodations (but it's not a club) and a swimming pool. Like the Nassau Yacht Haven it too has a second-floor bar and restaurant, and indeed a ground-floor bar as well. Shoreside facilities (shared with the swimming pool) are barely adequate, and overall the Nassau Harbour Club is showing its age. On our last visit the shoreside facilities were patently in need of a major refit. The docks themselves, one would guess, must be the only reason it stays in business, for given alternative dock space in Nassau, and better facilities, the Harbour Club would surely stand empty. The restaurant, after a long closure, is now refurbished. We hope that this heralds a general renovation. If it does not, then we may all have to wait until someone, sometime, is ready to give the shore side of things a cash injection, or someone buys out the present ownership.

The Nassau Harbour Club offers good package berth-plus-accommodation deals if you have crew changes in mind, and there's a major shopping center immediately across the street if you're in Nassau to provision, which is well worth taking into account.

Versailles Garden.

OTHER DOCK SPACE

Between the Nassau Yacht Haven and the Nassau Harbour Club you'll find virtually all the marine facilities in Nassau devoted to cruising and sports boats, with Bayshore Marine/Maura's Marine, Lightborne Marine, Nautical Marine, and Brown's Boat Basin. Bayshore Marine has no transient berths, and the Texaco Harbour View Marina deals primarily with local long-term berths.

Your list can be expanded by including the Paradise Harbour Club and Marina (Paradise Island side, east end) who may have space, and the Nassau Yacht Club, right by Fort Montague (East Bay side, also east end), who offer

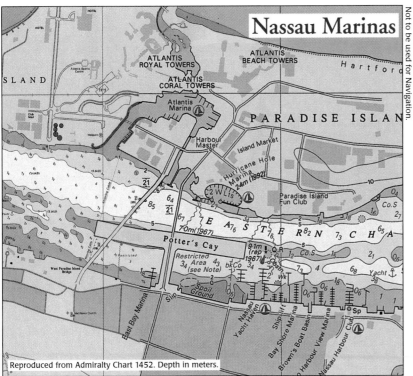

Nassau Marinas

Reproduced from Admiralty Chart 1452. Depth in meters.

Not to be used for Navigation.

for guidebook warnings and cautions. The next morning he couldn't raise it. He dived to find it "hooked under a length of old giant-sized anchor chain." "Did you fix the position?" we asked. "That's just what we all need. A guaranteed bad weather spot." "I should have done it, shouldn't I?" he said, "but I didn't. I was kind of busy after my swim."

Our cautions remain in force about anchoring in Nassau Harbour, and our reservations about Nassau as a port-of-call, certainly for any duration, also remain. You are in a tide and wind tunnel there, beset by almost continual man-induced surge, as constant traffic passes through the harbor at anything up to maximum speed. We would think that the need for speed limits was obvious, but we've heard no suggestion of it. Hurricane Hole, and now the Atlantis Marina, are the only two protected places. For the rest, or out at anchor, you take it as it comes.

We conclude with one final warning. We have a gut feeling that the Nassau Harbour anchorages will come under review in the foreseeable future. The harbor has become increasingly active, and increasingly crowded. The building of the second bridge, and the Atlantis Marina, the increased use of western Potter's Cay, and the freeway required for the approaches to the second (East Bay) pass under the western Paradise Island bridge, have all taken up hitherto relatively free space. In more than one instance, primarily due to random anchoring, craft on passage have fouled anchor lines. We would not be surprised if mooring buoys were put down and self-anchoring prohibited. Nor would we be entirely surprised if, within the limits of Nassau Harbour, every boat had to be secured at a regular dock, and both moorings and anchoring were forbidden.

space, if they have it, to members of foreign yacht clubs offering reciprocal hospitality. On your entry into Nassau Harbour you may have noticed the Sugar Reef Harbourside Bar and Grill to starboard, built out on the water, half way between Prince George Wharf (the cruise ships) and Potter's Cay. There's a small basin behind the restaurant with some slips. If you have nowhere else to go, you might find space there, but there are no facilities and no security.

NASSAU ANCHORAGES

The main Nassau Harbour anchorage remains essentially where it was before, on the starboard side as you pass Prince George Wharf (the place with the cruise ships) as you enter the harbor from the west. The anchorage, as before, is limited by the west end of Potter's Cay, and the prudence of allowing the mailboats and the fishing boats adequate turning space to enter or depart either side of the cay. So you could say the eastern limit of the anchorage comes up about two thirds of the way between Prince George Wharf and West Paradise Island Bridge.

A secondary anchorage still exists, again to starboard, between the Nassau Harbour Club and the Fort Montague area. It's a second choice, in our opinion. We are not convinced that the holding at either anchorage is sufficiently good to put your unreserved faith in a hook that appears reasonably set, and we would treat both anchorages as Fair Weather only.

Gary Miller of *Dad Bear*, a 33-foot Morgan Out Island, expecting this, was surprised to find his 33-lb. Bruce anchor had set rock solid in that second, east anchorage. Better, he said, than he had ever known it set. So much, he thought,

Nassau, eastern harbor.

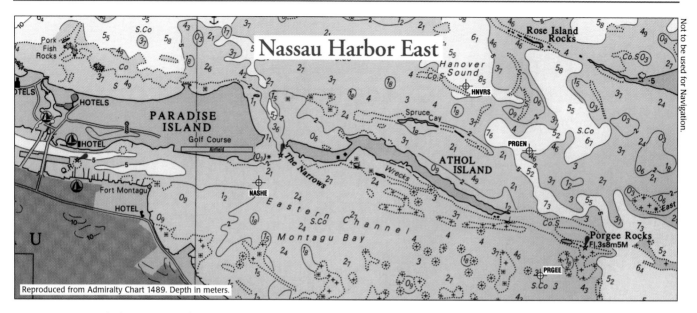

Reproduced from Admiralty Chart 1489. Depth in meters.

New Providence Island

AS the Lyford Cay Club, just north of Lyford Cay on the east peninsula, is the only facility open to visiting yachts in New Providence Island other than the marinas of Nassau Harbour, the south coastline of the island is likely to be of little interest to the cruising visitor. Coral Harbour, on the southwest end of the south coast, is the base of the Royal Bahamian Defence Force and is off limits, unless you have friends living further up the canals. Also marked out as off limits from time to time is the sea area boxed in by lines drawn 9 nm west and 8.5 nm south of Coral Harbour, which is used for gunnery practice. If you encounter any Defence Force vessel flying a red flag (or showing a red flashing light at night), live firing is taking place. It's best to stay clear of the area, period. This Danger Area is clearly shown on DMA Chart 26282 **Andros Island to San Salvador**, and noted on BA Chart 1489.

Lyford Cay is a private club, but you may be able to take a berth there if they have space, or if you are visiting friends who are members.

Nassau Harbour (Eastern Entrance)

Leaving or entering Nassau Harbour (NASHE) at the east end presents no problems as long as you favor the north shore. Fort Montague masonry runs out into the water as does a shoal in that area, and the deepest water parallels Paradise Island Airport's runway. This deep-water channel is also the landing and takeoff run for the Chalks seaplane.

Porgee Rocks (PRGEE) serve as a highly visual indicator of your departure waypoint whichever direction you are bound for, either northeast to Eleuthera or southeast to the Exumas. You may, if you are bound for the northeast, work your way out into ocean water between the east end of Paradise Island and the west end of Athol Island, but we see no particular advantage in taking a route that is shallow and requires careful eyeball navigation.

Once you've reached Porgee Rocks, if you're bound for Eleuthera, you still have four legs to go before you are in ocean water. If you're bound for the Exumas you can set a direct course to your Exuma waypoint from Porgee Rocks. For this reason we deal with each route separately.

Don't forget that it's mandatory that all vessels entering and leaving Nassau Harbour call Nassau Harbour Control on VHF 16, requesting permission to enter or proceed out, and give their destination or point of departure.

NASSAU AND NEW PROVIDENCE ISLAND II

Nassau Harbour East

NASHE	25° 04' 30"/500 N	077° 17' 30"/500 W

Porgee Rocks

PRGEE	25° 03' 45"/750 N	077° 15' 00"/000 W

Porgee Rocks North

PRGEN	25° 04' 45"/750 N	077° 15' 00"/000 W

Porgee Rocks Southeast

PRGSE	25° 03' 00"/000 N	077° 12' 00"/000 W

Hanover Sound South

HNVRS	25° 05' 15"/250 N	077° 15' 40"/666 W

Hanover Sound North

HNVRN	25° 05' 50"/833 N	077° 15' 45"/750 W

Chub Rock

CHBRK	25° 06' 45"/750 N	077° 15' 00"/000 W

Douglas Channel

DGLAS	25° 09' 31"/528 N	077° 06' 02"/043 W

Samphire Cays Channel

SMPHR	25° 12' 32"/532 N	077° 00' 51"/860 W

Junction White & Yellow Banks

WYBNK	24° 52' 00"/000 N	077° 12' 00"/000 W

The final figures in each waypoint show seconds (00") and thousands (000) of a minute.

Moving to Eleuthera after Nassau

This is the route you are most likely to take if you want to see Spanish Wells, move on to Harbour Island, or start cruising south down Eleuthera. If you are heading for the Abacos from Nassau, this is the only direct route and we'd guess that you'll elect to stage in Spanish Wells on your way.

Our initial legs taking you away from Nassau may seem unnecessarily complicated, but we have worked it and proved it as a low-water route, taking maximum advantage of the deeper water in Hanover Sound. Of course you can make changes. Anyway, the way we went is to take getting from Nassau Harbour to Chub Rock in five legs starting at our Nassau Harbour east waypoint, north of Fort Montague. So it came out as:

• LEG 1	to Porgee Rock (PRGEE)	114°M	2.31 nm
• LEG 2	Clearing the Porgee Reef area (PRGEN)	010°M	1.00 nm
• LEG 3	Getting to Hanover Sound (HNVRS)	315°M	0.78 nm
• LEG 4	Hanover Sound (HNVRN)	358°M	0.59 nm
• LEG 5	Getting to Chub Rock (CHBRK)	042°M	1.14 nm

After all this jinking around, the next leg is a straightforward 28.95 nm on a course of 048°M to take you (deep water all the way) to our entry waypoint to the Eleuthera Bank (LEGGI). You gain the Bank passing south of Little Egg Island, safely south of Barracouta Patch.

The next leg (3.09 nm on 059°M) takes you past Royal Island (ROYAL) and just north of the rocks that lie 1.25 nm south of Royal Island, and the final leg (3.75 nm on 076°M) places you north of Meeks Patch (MEEKP) ready to go visual to enter Spanish Wells. See **North Eleuthera** under **The Western Approach to Spanish Wells** on page 182.

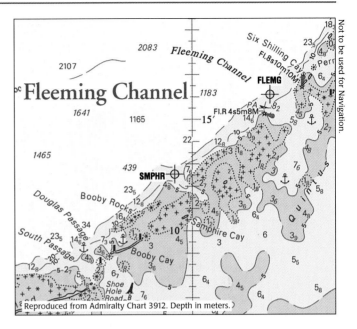

Reproduced from Admiralty Chart 3912. Depth in meters.

Moving to the Exumas after Nassau

Once you're at our Porgee Rocks waypoint you can set a direct course for Allan's Cay, Highborne Cay, Normans Cay, or anywhere further south in the Exumas. As the choices are many, we don't list the waypoints here. See **The Exumas** under **From Nassau** on page 228.

The Fleeming, Samphire, and Douglas Channels

In the past, running between Nassau and North Eleuthera, we've always taken it as a straight shot from Chub Rock (CHBRK), north of Nassau's Hanover Sound, to the pass through the reef to the south of Little Egg Island. We've neglected the 25–nm run of islands, rocks, and cays running along the northern edge of the Bank from Nassau's Salt Cay (now re-named Blue Lagoon Island) and Rose Island, through the Samphire Cays, to Eleuthera's Current Island. At the Nassau end, Salt Cay or "Blue Lagoon" is the playground of Dolphin Encounters, and Rose Island, the playground for Sea Island Adventures, also serves as the R&R destination for the majority of Nassau's weekend boaters. Extensive development plans have been drawn up for Rose Island, which, as with all Bahamian projects, may or may not mature. East-

Hanover Sound.

ward from Rose Island the Samphire Cays are, for the most part, barren rock. So for all these reasons we reckoned the cruising visitor would probably decide to bypass this part of the world.

Two major connectors between the Northeast Providence Channel and Exuma Sound run through this area. The Douglas Channel, with the Cochrane Anchorage, and the Fleeming Channel. The Samphire Cays offer a third deep-water inlet, through which it's also possible to get on the Bank. We went back there recently to reassess whether we'd made a mistake in leaving this part of the map blank. What we addressed was simply this: could we see any benefit in these channels for the cruising visitor?

The Douglas Channel (DGLAS) could be said to serve Nassau, and offers an alternative, if you're bound for Spanish Wells or the Abacos, to leaving from or coming in through Hanover Sound. A course set from the Douglas Channel to the southeast (some 22 nm on around 138°M) will take you to the head of Exuma Sound, south of the Sail Rocks, at Ship Channel. However this route entails crossing the Middle Ground, an area peppered with coral heads. It's not an attractive route. At the end of the day we could see no particular utility in the Douglas Channel. In the days of pure sail the Cochrane Anchorage probably served if you had to wait for the right wind to enter Nassau Harbour. But we're guessing.

The Samphire Cays (SMPHR) are a real muddle of an area, and may well be good for fishing, but we couldn't see many people enjoying poking around or anchoring there. We were happy enough to explore, amazed by the clarity and color of the water, at midday in near-calm conditions. Then the ebb tide brought Nassau's garbage. It spoiled the magic.

As for the Fleeming Channel (FLEMG), anciently it too must have been a sail route, a connector between the North-

The Fleeming Channel.

east Providence Channel and Exuma Sound (with some 24 nm on around 167°M to run to get to Ship Channel). We tried to figure out why anyone today might wish to go this way. We accept that it still offers its original purpose, but as we've indicated with the Douglas Channel route, we've never much cared for that part of the Bank. Coral heads strewn around like confetti after a wedding, as well as shoal areas, and we've yet to discover any chart covering it adequately. We reckon you're safer taking the well-tried, more commonly used routes that serve most of us today. Our survey ends on this kind of dismissive note. But we'd welcome your views. Final note. If you do take one of these routes, go slow. It's not Fast Boat Navigation territory.

YELLOW PAGES

NASSAU

Full of life and energy, culture and color, Nassau is the very heart of the Bahamas as its capital city and center of government. With cruise ships bringing visitors from all over the world, as well as hundreds of tourists staying at the hotels and playing the casinos, the relatively small islands of New Providence and Paradise Island host a large, cosmopolitan, transient population. There is the historical evidence of centuries of change and development in the islands to be found in Nassau's museums, rubbing shoulders with modern designer fashions and duty-free shops. As a tax haven, Nassau attracts the international banks and an expatriate community, while young Bahamians are enjoying a high standard of living and vastly improved education and health care. The island of New Providence is well worth exploring: there is much to do and see, and local bus transport is inexpensive. As you approach on your boat, don't forget to call **Nassau Harbour Control** on VHF 16 for permission to enter the harbor. Even if you plan to anchor in the harbor, you must come into a dock to clear **Customs** if Nassau is your Port of Entry; the dock staff will help, or you can call Customs at 322-8791.

MARINAS

On New Providence
approaching from the west:

EAST BAY MARINA
Tel: 242-394-1816 • VHF 16

East Bay Marina is next to Potter's Cay fish market, between the two Paradise Island bridges. There is only 57 feet under the span of the new bridge as you approach from the west, so your mast height could determine whether you stay at this marina. See our main text for details of how to come in. At the time of writing, the office and a few facilities are out on the end of the dock, but there are plans to completely rebuild the docks, with new shoreside facilities by the end of 1999. We wish them well, and write it as it was when we were there in April '99. Across East Bay Street from the marina there is a *Burger King, Domino's Pizza, Dunkin' Donuts,* and *Native's Restaurant,* with an *Outback Steakhouse* soon to be opened.

Slips	25
Max LOA	70 ft.
MLW at Dock	Deep water slips.
Power	$12 per day for 50A, $7 per day for 30A.
Fuel	Diesel and gasoline.
Water	50¢ per gallon for 5–25 gallons; 45¢ per gallon for 26–100 gallons, 40¢ per gallon for 101–200 gallons, and 35¢ per gallon for over 200 gallons.
Showers	Yes, but no toilets.
Ice	$2 per bag.
Credit Cards	Visa and MasterCard.
Dockmaster	Willie Meadows

NASSAU YACHT HAVEN
Tel: 242-393-8173 • Fax: 393-3429 • VHF 16

The *Yacht Haven* is a long-established, well-run marina in a good central position for visiting downtown Nassau and exploring New Providence. It is well situated if you need any parts or small repairs, with several marine stores within walking distance, and an excellent dive shop on site. The *Poop Deck* has long been a favorite watering hole for visiting boaters and local residents alike, with its upper-level bar and dining room overlooking the marina and the harbor. The dockmasters and all the staff are experienced, friendly, and very helpful. There is a pharmacy and liquor store across Bay Street opposite the entrance to the *Yacht Haven*; a 24-hour *CIBC* ATM within a few minutes walk; and the *Harbour Bay Plaza* with a good selection of stores, including a *City Markets* grocery store that will deliver to your boat, only a seven- or eight-minute walk to your left along Bay Street.

Slips	150
Max LOA	150 ft.
MLW at Dock	11 ft. inside marina, 18 ft. possible outside.
Dockage	$l per ft. per day, $35 minimum for transient boats, $1 "T-dock" rate.
Power	30A and 50A available, 35¢ per kWh, minimum $5 per day.
Fuel	Diesel and gasoline.
Propane	Same-day refill.
Water	Not metered. Boats up to 35 ft. pay $8 the first day and $6 each additional day; 36–60 ft. pay $10 the first day and $8 each additional day; over 61 ft. pay $16 per day. Water charges are automatic and include washdown water, filling holding tanks, and use of the showers.
Telephone	*Batelco* card phone and pay phone in the entrance way to the street.
TV	Satellite TV is included in the dockage fees.
Showers	Yes
Laundry	$2 tokens for washers and dryers from the office. A good laundry with plenty of machines.
Restaurant	*The Poop Deck Restaurant and Bar* serves lunch and dinner daily. Bar opens at 11 am. *The Pink Pearl Café,* in a recently restored historical house just across Bay Street, is also open for quieter lunches and dinners, with live music on the weekends.
Ice	Yes
Library	Paperback book exchange in the office.
Marine Supplies	The marine supply stores (listed under **MARINE SERVICES**) are a few minutes' walk to your left as you turn out on to Bay Street.
Repairs	Arrange with boat yards nearby. Brownie Third Lung repair and service on site.
Diving	*Bahamas Divers* run their dive operation from the *Yacht Haven*, with their own dive shop and rental equipment on site. Two-tank morning dive $65, snorkelers $25. Resort course $65, Certification $399. See **DIVING** for more information.
Taxis	Always plenty waiting outside the *Poop Deck*.
Credit Cards	Major credit cards accepted.
Security	The marina entrance from Bay Street is locked and guarded at night.
Dockmasters	Sidney Wilson and Dino Moss.

BAYSHORE MARINA
Tel: 242-393-8232 • VHF 16

Bayshore Marina is a working boat yard. It has only 12 slips for transient boats up to 60 feet, and there are few facilities for visitors.

Slips	175
Max LOA	60 ft.
MLW at Dock	6–7 ft.
Dockage	75¢ per ft. per day; long-term 50¢ per ft. per day monthly.

Power	$25 per kWh for 120v and 220v.
Fuel	Diesel and gasoline.
Water	$3 per day.
Telephone	Pay phone outside, or use the office phone.
Ice	Yes
Haul-out	For bottom painting. Repairs can be arranged.
Marine Supplies	*Marlin Marine* store on site.
Credit cards	Visa and MasterCard.

BROWN'S BOAT BASIN
Tel: 242-393-3331 • Fax: 393-3680 • VHF 16

This is a family-operated boat yard that rarely has space available for visiting boats, as it is primarily a working yard. *Brown's* marine supply store is opposite on East Bay Street.

Slips	60
Power	Yes
Water	Yes
Repairs	Specialize in general boat and yacht repairs.
Travel Hoist	Up to 40 tons, 18-ft. beam.

HARBOUR VIEW MARINA
Harbour View Marina is designed for smaller craft belonging to local owners needing long-term dockage. It runs from the Texaco Starport fuel dock, to the Texaco Starmart filling station on Bay Street, where you will find a telephone, ice, a few provisions, and toilets.

NASSAU HARBOUR CLUB AND MARINA
Tel: 242-393-0771 • Fax: 393-5393

This is a very attractive marina, well appointed and well run. It has the added bonus of full shopping facilities in the *Harbour Bay Plaza* directly across the street that offers restaurants, bank, supermarket, hardware, and liquor store, as well as being within easy walking distance of the marine supply stores. It is a good place to book into if you need shoreside accommodations as well as your own boat, with special rates if you have a slip in the marina. Though shabby and in need of renovation at the time of writing, the hotel is pleasant and friendly. The staff is helpful and marina guests are welcome to use the well-landscaped swimming pool. The re-opening of the restaurant will be a great improvement. Make sure you have reservations ahead of time, as this is a much sought-after marina.

Slips	65
Max LOA	Up to 200 ft. on the T-heads.
MLW at Dock	5 ft.
Dockage	$1 per ft. per day.
Power	35¢ per kWh for 30A and 50A.
Fuel	Diesel only at the fuel dock.
Water	$6 per day for boats under 40 ft., $8 per day for 40–60 ft., $10 per day over 60 ft.
TV	Satellite TV hookup available at no charge.
Showers	Shower rooms are by the swimming pool. Ask the office for the combination when you check in.
Laundry	Large machines; tokens $3 each, available from the office.
Restaurants	At time of writing, only the bar and grill at the marina level was open, from 11 am, serving snacks and light meals. *Tony Cheng's Restaurant* is planned for the upper level. The *Caffe Caribe* in *Logos Bookstore* opens at 7:30 am for delicious deli breakfasts and lunches until 6 pm, and *Le Carafe*, also at the *Harbour Bay Plaza*, is open 11 am to 8 pm for lunch and an early dinner; the *Texaco* filling station opens with hot coffee at 6:30 am.
Taxis	Mr. Moss has a desk by the hotel front desk, from where taxis can easily be called or tours arranged.

Marine Services	The marine stores and boat yards listed under our **Marine Services** for Nassau are within walking distance.
Swimming	This could be a very attractive pool with a good paved area for sitting out, overlooking the marina. But almost all the sunbed chairs were broken and there was a constant group around the bar the last time we were there.
Accommodations	*Nassau Harbour Club* has 50 air-conditioned rooms, with TV and telephones, from $90 per night. The hotel is sadly run down and in need of cleaning up and redecoration, but it still has the best site for a New Providence marina hotel, and offers a generous 35-percent discount for marina guests using a boat slip.
Credit cards	Visa, MasterCard, and Amex.
Security	The marina is only accessible from East Bay Street through the hotel, which is kept locked at night with a security guard on duty.
Dockmasters	Peter Attaloqlou and Ed Burrows with Lynette and Teresa in the office.

THE NASSAU YACHT CLUB and
THE ROYAL NASSAU SAILING CLUB

Both have small marinas near Fort Montague, but are not open for transient boats except by special arrangement.

Atlantis, Paradise Island.

On Paradise Island
approaching from the west:

THE MARINA AT ATLANTIS
Tel: 242-363-6068 • Fax: 363-6008 • VHF 16
(in the US) 800-ATLANTIS

An unparalleled yachting experience on Paradise Island with world-class services. Direct access from Nassau Harbour, with a 100-foot-wide entry channel to the west of the first Paradise Island bridge that you see, allows for unrestricted mast height on sailboats and easy approach for motor yachts. Full guest privileges at Atlantis are extended to marina guests, including the use of the waterscape, exhibit lagoons, pools, restaurants, entertainment complex and casino, spa and fitness center, golf course, and tennis courts.

Slips	63
Max LOA	160-ft. finger piers with 37-ft. beam; several lay-alongside berths with no beam restrictions.

MLW at Dock	Both the docks and the entry channel carry 12 ft. at low tide.
Dockage	$3 per ft. per day, 40 ft. minimum. $2.25 per ft. per day for slip rentals longer than 30 consecutive days.
Power	35¢ per kWh, single- and three-phase power.
Water	10¢ per gallon.
Telephones	Multiple phone/fax lines at each slip.
TV	Complimentary hookup
Showers	Excellent showers and toilets in the dockmaster's office building.
Laundry	Coin-operated washing machines and dryers in the dockmaster's office building. Dry cleaning service available.

Restaurants	The full range of *Atlantis* restaurants are only a short walk away.
Ice	Yes
Pump out	Sanitary sewer pump-out facility at each slip.
Newspapers	Complimentary daily newspaper delivery.
Services	Tie-up assistance for arrivals and departures. Dock assistance for transfer of luggage and provisions. Transportation between marina and resort. 24-hour room service to vessels. Private catering available. Faxes, UPS, and Fedex deliveries can be sent care of the dockmaster's office.
Crew facilities	A pleasant crew lounge in the dockmaster's office building has a pool table, drinks center, microwave, and television.
Security	24-hour security staff.

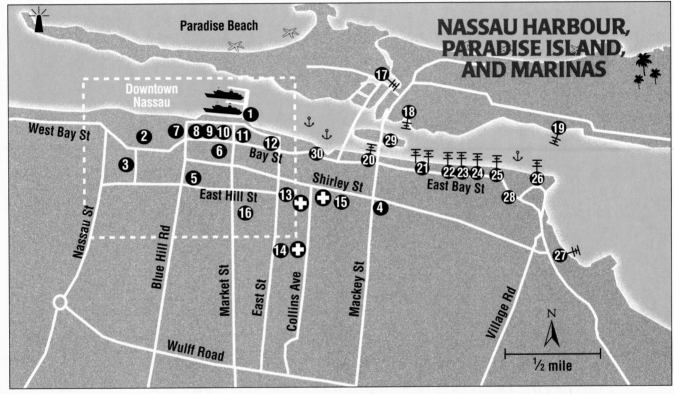

NASSAU HARBOUR, PARADISE ISLAND, AND MARINAS DIRECTORY

1. Cruise Ship dock
2. British Colonial Hotel and offices
3. US Embassy
4. Post Office
5. Government House
6. Batelco, Police, and British High Commission
7. Buses leaving from Bay Street for East Bay Street Marinas and New Providence destinations
8. Pompey Museum
9. Straw Market
10. Ministry of Tourism
11. Barclays Bank
12. Rawson Square
13. Princess Margaret Hospital
14. Walk-In Clinic
15. Doctor's Hospital
16. Queen's Staircase, Water Tower, and Fort Fincastle
17. The Marina at Atlantis and Atlantis Resort

18. Hurricane Hole Marina, Hurricane Hole Plaza, and Paradise Village Shopping Centre
19. Paradise Harbour Club Marina and Columbus Tavern
20. East Bay Marina and Burger King, Domino Pizza, Dunkin' Donuts and Natives Restaurant
21. Nassau Yacht Haven, Bahamas Divers, and the Poop Deck
22. Bayshore Marina and Marlin Marine
23. Brown's Boat Yard
24. Harbour View Marina and Texaco Starport
25. Nassau Harbour Club and Tony Cheng's restaurant
26. Nassau Yacht Club (not for transient boats)
27. Royal Nassau Sailing Club (not for transient boats)
28. Harbour Bay Plaza Shopping Centre
29. Potter's Cay mailboat dock, fish market and stalls
30. BASRA headquarters and office
⚓ **Fuel** available at *Atlantis, Hurricane Hole, East Bay Marina, Nassau Yacht Haven, Bayshore Marina, Harbour View Marina, Nassau Harbour Club* (diesel only), and at Lyford Cay.

HURRICANE HOLE MARINA
Tel: 242-363-3600 • Fax: 363-3604 • VHF 16 •
E-mail: hurrhole@mail.bahamas.net.bs

This protected marina, just east of the second bridge as you come in from the west, offers excellent service and facilities equal to those in the US, with well-landscaped grounds and a high standard of maintenance. It is also much less rolly than some of the marinas on New Providence, but do book space well in advance as Hurricane Hole is more popular than ever since the opening of *Atlantis*.

Slips	65
Max LOA	200 ft.
MLW at Dock	15 ft. on the T-head, 9 ft. on inside slips. 8 ft. in the entrance channel at low tide.
Dockage	$1.50 per ft. per day; $60 minimum daily transient dockage. Monthly $1 per ft. per day; $50 minimum daily dockage.
Power	35¢ per kWh for 110v and 110v; 440v available.
Fuel	Diesel, gasoline, oils and lubricants; open daily including Sundays and holidays.
Water	10¢ per gallon.
Telephone	Hookup $3 daily, $35 per month, plus calls.
TV	Cable hookup is $7 daily, $70 per month.
Showers	Yes
Laundry	Yes
Restaurants	*The Pool Bar and Grill* is open daily for drinks and snacks around the pool. *The News Cafe* serves breakfast, lunch, and a light dinner from 7:30 am daily in the *Paradise Village Shopping Centre* nearby. *The Blue Marlin* further along is only a minute's walk, serving lunch and dinner with a floor show in the evenings downstairs. An Italian restaurant is above, as well as *Anthony's Carib Grill* in the *Paradise Village Shopping Center*. The 19 new *Atlantis* restaurants and bars are within easy walking distance.
Groceries	*Paradise Supermarket and Deli* (363-1056) in the *Paradise Village Shopping Center*, open 8 am to 10 pm daily, and 9 am to 10 pm on Sundays and holidays.
Liquor	Liquor store open 9 am to 9 pm daily, 9 am to 6 pm on Sundays.
Ice	$3.50 per bag.
Shopping	*Hurricane Hole Plaza* has a *ScotiaBank* with an ATM opposite, *Tropic Traders, Calypso Fashions, Crown Jewellers, and Solomon's Mines*, and a whole range of stores from souvenirs and pharmacy to liquor and jewelry.
Casino	The casino at *Atlantis* is only a short walk from the marina.
Accommodations	The condominium apartments overlooking *Hurricane Hole* are usually booked at least a year ahead.
Credit cards	Visa, MasterCard, Amex, no personal checks.
Security	Security around the clock.
Dockmaster	Peter Maury

PARADISE HARBOUR CLUB AND MARINA
Tel: 242-363-2992 • Fax: 363-2840 • VHF 16

Winner of the prestigious RCI Gold Crown Award for the past seven years, this timeshare resort and marina has won an international reputation. With one staff member for every two guests, multi-lingual hosts, and excellent facilities, this is a much-sought-after, small marina.

Slips	20
Max LOA	120 ft. on the outer dock.
MLW at Dock	5 to 6 ft. on the inside slips.
Dockage	$1 per ft. per day, $45 minimum for transient boats. 85¢ per ft. per day monthly rate, 70¢ per ft. per day yearly rate.
Power	30¢ per kWh.
Fuel	Available nearby
Water	5¢ per gallon for reverse osmosis water.
TV	Hookup available for $5 per day, $50 per month.
Showers	Yes
Laundry	Yes
Restaurant	The friendly *Columbus Tavern* overlooking the marina serves breakfast, lunch, and dinner. You can charge your bill at the *Tavern* to your slip number.
Accommodations	Timeshare condominiums
Water Taxi	Complimentary water taxi service to the Straw Market, Cabbage Beach, and Rose Island. Transport on Mondays for the food store run.
Credit cards	All major cards accepted, with a 4-percent surcharge.
Security	Gate house at the entrance.
Dockmaster	Anthony Hall

MARINAS OUTSIDE THE NASSAU HARBOUR AREA

LYFORD CAY MARINA
Tel: 242-362-4131 • VHF 16

This is the most exclusive marina in the Caribbean, and is part of the privately owned *Lyford Cay Club* on the west side of New Providence island. The slips are reserved for members and their guests, though they can occasionally take in transient boats for three or four days maximum stay.

Slips	74
Max LOA	Over 100 ft.
MLW at Dock	9.5 ft.
Dockage	$2.10 per ft. per day.
Power	40¢ per kWh, 50A and 100A available.
Fuel	Diesel and gasoline.
Water	$5 per day up to 50 ft., $7 per day to 100 ft., $10 per day over 100 ft.
Telephone	Hookup on docks, $3 daily.
TV	Cable hookup, $5 per day.
Showers	Yes
Laundry	Yes, $1.50 tokens.
Restaurant	*The Captain's Table* in the marina is open to non-club guests.
Shopping	Just outside the marina there is a shopping center with a *City Markets* supermarket, as well as a bank, hardware store, liquor store, boutique, public telephone, travel agent.
Credit cards	Visa, MasterCard, Amex, checks.

MARINE SERVICES

BASRA monitors VHF 16 from 9 am to 5 pm, seven days a week. Nassau Harbour Authority monitors VHF 16 the remaining hours each day. In an emergency call 242-322-3877.

BASRA HQ (office on Bay Street), PO Box SS 6247, Nassau, NP, Bahamas   Tel: 242-325-8864 • Fax: 325-2737 • E-mail: co@basra.org • Web site: basra.org   The office is open from 9 am to 5 pm daily. Propane tanks can be filled for $3 if you take them to the office. Your e-mail can be held for you on maildrop@basra.org.

Are you a member? Why not call in at the office and join today. You never know when you might need BASRA's help.

Boat Yards, Marine Supplies, Agencies, and Repairs

Most of the agencies we list are found on Bay Street and East Bay Street, within walking distance of the Nassau Harbour area marinas. There are other marine stores in Nassau; ask the dockmasters or look in the Nassau telephone book for additional names if none of the Bay Street suppliers can help you.

Boater's Paradise Tel: 393-5713/3894 • Fax: 393-3592 • VHF 16 Formerly *Nautical Marine*, *Boater's Paradise* under the ownership of Barry and Dan Lowe offers a good supply of lines, hardware, spare parts, and lubricants. Agents for Wellcraft, Mariner outboards, Quicksilver inflatables, and Mercruisers. They provide full service on all major brands of gas engines, and will either come out to your boat, or have the boat hauled.

Brown's Boat Basin Tel: 393-3331/3680 • Fax: 393-1868 On East Bay Street, they have a small marine supply store across from their own boat yard, with hoists accommodating up to 40 tons and an 18-ft. beam. They can take 5-ft. draft boats at high tide. The fuel dock has diesel and gas and monitors VHF 16.

Cooper's Marine Tel: 393-7475 or 380-0706 On Abundant Life Road, Nassau. Michael Cooper builds 19-ft. Spirit Craft, and can help with fiberglass work, repairs, and boat painting. His brother, Ralph Hunter, specializes in marine upholstery and bimini tops.

Harbourside Marine Tel: 394-8360 • Fax: 394-7493 On East Bay Street. Specializing in Yamaha sales and full service, with marine supplies, lubricants, and cleaning materials in their marine store. By the end of 1999 they plan to have docking facilities for 40 boats, all privately owned by local owners. They will have a lift for 32-ft. and smaller boats, and be able to carry out repairs and service engines.

Lightbourne Marine Tel: 393-5285 • Fax: 393-6236 Open on East Bay Street from 8 am to 5 pm Monday to Friday, to 12 noon on Saturdays. Agents for Perkins diesel engines, Kohler generators, and Mercury outboards. Filters, electronics, pumps, paints, cleaning products, charts, lines, accessories, and fishing tackle in the well-stocked and friendly store across the street from their boatyard. Outboard motors, diesel engines, and generators serviced; haul and launch up to 25 ft.

Marine Diesel Tel and Fax: 322-7135 • VHF 16 On East Bay Street; agents for Westerbeke, Yanmar, and Lugger.

Marlin Marine (formerly *Maura's Marine*) and *Bayshore Marina* Tel: 393-7873/3874 • Fax: 393-0066 • VHF 16 On East Bay Street. A well-stocked store adjacent to their marina and working boat yard. Full service and parts for Johnson; agents for Evinrude, Boston Whaler, and Carolina Skiffs; a wide selection of fishing gear and equipment in the store. The boat yard is used primarily for bottom painting. The fuel dock has diesel and gasoline.

Marine Diesel Ltd. Tel: 322-7135 • Fax: 323-1825 On Bay and Armstrong Streets. Parts, sales, and service for Northern Lights, Yanmar, Volvo, Westerbeke, and Perkins engines. Waterfront service at their own dock, or they will come to your boat.

SOS Marine Tel: 394-5992 • Fax: 393-6264 Service and repairs on Johnson, Evinrude, Mercury, Suzuki, Yamaha, Sea Doo, and hydraulic steering systems.

SERVICES AND SHOPPING IN NASSAU

Accommodations
There are so many hotels, resorts, and guesthouses in Nassau, that it is better to ask for a complete list at the Tourist Information offices, where you can be helped and guided with prices and availability. At peak times, such as Spring Break and public holidays, accommodations in Nassau are at a premium.

Air Ambulance
Both these firms run land-based ambulances in addition to their air service; for a local ambulance call 322-2221.

Global Medical Rescue Tel: 394-2582/3388 • Cell: 359-2496 Helicopter and fixed wing, 24-hour medical rescue service. *Medevac Air Ambulance* Tel: 322-2881 24-hour service throughout the Bahamas, and worldwide. Local and foreign credit cards and insurance accepted.

ATMs
Citibank Dispenses Bahamian dollars at two branches on Frederick Street and Thompson Boulevard. These machines accept MasterCard and any bank card on the Cirrus network. Minimum $20 withdrawal.

Royal Bank These machines dispense US currency and accept Visa, MasterCard, and any bank card on the Plus or Cirrus network. Minimum $50 withdrawal. Locations:
   The Tourist Information Booth, Rawson Square
   Crystal Palace Casino on Cable Beach
   Lyford Cay Club
   Nassau International Airport at the US departures check-in

Royal Bank Dispenses Bahamian dollars, located at three Esso stations and scattered throughout the island.

ScotiaBank On Bay Street and in the casino at *Atlantis;* dispense US dollars for MasterCard, Visa, and any bank card on Plus or Cirrus networks. ATMs at other *ScotiaBank* branches dispense Bahamian dollars on the same networks. $20 minimum withdrawal.

Banks
Banking hours in Nassau are usually from 9:30 am to 3 pm Monday to Thursday, to 5 pm on Fridays. Most of the big banks are in downtown Nassau, many with offices on Bay Street, smaller branches in the other islands.

Bank of the Bahamas, Charlotte and Shirley Street Tel: 322-1210
Barclays Bank, Bay Street Tel: 356-8000
Barclays Bank, Harbour Bay Plaza Tel: 393-2334
Citibank, Thompson Boulevard Tel: 302-8500
Commonwealth Bank, East Bay Street Tel: 322-1154
Royal Bank of Canada, Bay Street Tel: 356-8500
Royal Bank of Canada, Lyford Cay Tel: 362-4540
ScotiaBank, Bay Street Tel: 356-1400
ScotiaBank, opposite *Hurricane Hole* Tel: 363-2591
Western Union, at *British American Bank*
   Cable Beach office Tel: 327-5170
   Frederick Street office Tel: 322-1084

Casinos
Atlantis Tel: 363-3000 On Paradise Island. A 50,000-sq.-ft. spectacular themed casino, open 10 am to 4 am, with 24-hr. slot machines.
Crystal Palace Casino Open 10 am to 4 am daily, also with 24-hr. slot machines.

Churches
Nassau has some 25 churches, representing 18 different religions. Most churches give their times of services outside the church, or you can look in the current edition of *"What To Do"* for information and times of services.

Clinic
The Walk-In Clinic Tel: 328-0783/2744 or 326-4026 • Fax: 356-9825 Up the hill on Collins Avenue, between Third and Fourth Terrace, opposite *JS Johnson and Co.,* if you just need to see a doctor or nurse for something minor. Open 7 am to 10 pm daily, including holidays, with no appointment necessary.

Couriers
DHL Worldwide Express Tel: 325-8266 • Fax: 325-7814 At 157 Nassau Steet South. Delivers documents and packages within the Bahamas and internationally.
FedEx Tel: 322-5656/5657 • Fax: 322-5659 At 3 Hillside Plaza, Thompson Boulevard. For pickup call 322-1791.
UPS Tel: 325-8227 • Fax: 328-0014 At Oakes Field Shopping Centre.

Customs and Immigration

Can be called from any of the marinas if you need to clear in, or on VHF 16. You are not required to clear out of any entry port **in person** when you leave, but you must return your Cruising Permit Number C39, Fishing Permit, and Immigration Card as soon as you reach the US or your home destination. Mail them to: The Comptroller of Customs, PO Box 155, Nassau, New Providence, Bahamas.

Dentist

The Walk-In Dental Clinic Tel: 393-6588 Open 11 am to 7 pm Monday to Friday, 9 am to noon on Saturdays with Dr. Ellen Strachan Moxey. Visa and MasterCard accepted. For a list of other dentists in Nassau, consult the yellow pages in the telephone book.

E-mail, Fax, Telephone, and Copy Service

ASAP Services Tel: 394-6447 • Fax: 394-8540 • E-mail: asap@bahamas.net.bs Open 9 am to 6 pm Monday to Friday, to noon on Saturdays. Located in the East Bay Shopping Center, at the foot of the east to westbound Paradise Island bridge, in a pink and white building on the left. Self-service computer rentals, e-mail access, international and local phone and fax service, Fedex, UPS, DHL, and EMS courier services, private mail box facility, stamps, and copy center. *BASRA* Visiting yachts can receive e-mail via BASRA at maildrop@basra.org.

Embassies & Consulates

American Embassy Tel: 322-1183

Canadian Consulate Tel: 393-2123

British High Commission Tel: 325-7471/7472/7473

For other consulates look in the yellow pages of the Bahamas telephone directory under *Diplomatic and Consular Representation.*

Emergency, Fire, or Police

Dial 919

Hospitals

Doctor's Hospital Tel: 322-8411 On Shirley Street. This is a private hospital with a 24-hr. emergency room and a complete range of medical facilities.

Lyford Cay Hospital Tel: 362-4025 • In emergency, call VHF 16 to any of the dive boat operators. The direct line to the Hyperbaric Chamber is 362-5765, but you should contact Dr. Dean or Dr. Ingraham first through the hospital.

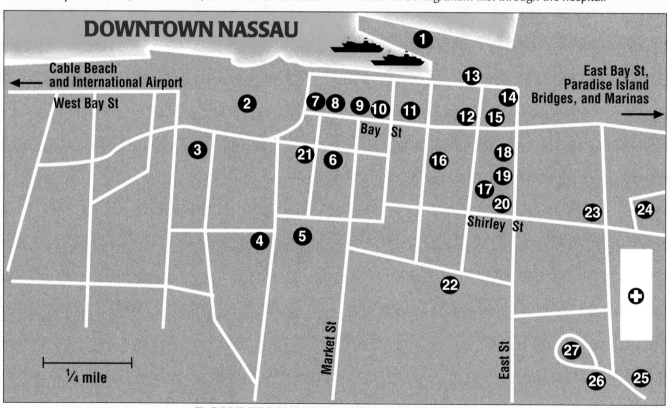

DOWNTOWN NASSAU DIRECTORY

1. Cruise Ship Dock
2. British Colonial Hotel and offices
3. US Embassy
4. Graycliff Hotel and Restaurant
5. Government House
6. Christ Church Cathedral
7. Cafe dell' Opera
8. Pompey Museum
9. Straw Market
10. Ministry of Tourism
11. Barclays Bank
12. ScotiaBank
13. Surreys at Woodes Rogers Walk
14. Tourist Information
15. Rawson Square
16. The Cellar Restaurant
17. Cafe Matisse
18. Police
19. Batelco
20. British High Commission
21. Pirates of Nassau
22. Main Post Office
23. Bahamas Historical Society Museum
24. Gaylords Restaurant
25. Queen's Staircase
26. Water Tower
27. Fort Fincastle
✚ Princess Margaret Hospital

Princess Margaret Hospital Tel: 322-2861 On Shirley Street. This is the Government Hospital and any visit may involve a wait.

Performing Arts
Dundas Centre on Mackey Street Tel: 393-3784 Plays by Bahamian artists are performed during the repertory season, January to May.

Police
Dial 919

Post Offices
Main post office at the top of Parliament Street, or the Shirley Street post office, open 8:30 am to 5:30 pm, Monday to Friday. Stamps are often available in the pharmacies on Bay Street.

Propane
Central Gas Tel: 361-2212
At the Gladstone Road Plant Tel: 364-0375
Tropigas Tel: 361-2695/2696
At the Gladstone Road Plant Tel: 361-0362
Shell Bahamas Ltd. Tel: 362-5417 Call the Clifton Terminal and talk to their LP Gas office.
BASRA If you are at anchor and can bring your tank to the *BASRA* office, one of the staff may well be able to fill it for you. The $3 charge goes toward feeding the dogs that roam around the BASRA compound.

Shopping
The length of Bay Street, from Rawson Square to the *British Colonial Hotel,* is a shopper's paradise. From fancy designer stores, duty-free shops, and glamorously expensive jewelry, to *Straw Market* souvenirs and T-shirts, there is something for everybody. When there are several cruise ships in port, it can be crowded. The *Straw Market* has everything imaginable in straw, some of it beautifully made and very individual. You can try bargaining, it's all part of the fun.

If it's history you're interested in, browse through the fascinating collection of antique maps and prints upstairs at *Balmain Antiques* (323-7421) on Bay Street. For more practical needs, there are several shopping malls on the island with good *City Markets* grocery stores. The closest one to the main marinas on New Providence is the *Harbour Bay Plaza,* where you will find:
City Markets supermarket, open 7:30 am to 9 pm Monday to Saturday, from 7 to 10 am on Sundays.
Barclays Bank, open 9:30 am to 3 pm Monday to Thursday, to 5 pm on Fridays.
John S George hardware store, open 9:30 am to 6:30 pm Monday to Saturday.
Harbour Bay Liquors, open 10 am to 8 pm Monday to Saturday.
Lowe's Pharmacy, open 8 am to 8:30 pm Monday to Saturday, and 9 am to 5 pm on Sundays.
Le Carafe restaurant, open 11:30 am to 8 pm daily, except closed for dinner on Mondays and all day Sunday. They have an imaginative choice of quiches that you can order ahead to take on your boat.
Caffe Caribe, open at 7:30 am for breakfast, with deli lunches and excellent coffees until 6 pm, within *Logos Bookstore.*
There is also a travel agent, beauty parlor, fashion store, and a children's store in the Plaza.

Telephones
Located at all the marinas, hotels, and many locations downtown. Most now take *Batelco* phone cards, which are available in $5, $10, and $20 denominations from the *Batelco* offices and some stores and marinas. For AT&T direct service from the Bahamas, call 1-800-872-2881.

RESTAURANTS

There are so many restaurants in Nassau and on Paradise Island that we suggest you look in the current issue of *"What To Do"* or the *"Dining and Entertainment Guide,"* issued by the Ministry of Tourism, for ideas and inspiration. There is a wide variety and the standard is generally very good, though prices can be a little higher than stateside. All the big hotels and resorts have restaurants of their own. *Atlantis* has 19 different restaurants, including dining within the world's largest aquarium, right next to the casino. We list a few that are easily accessible if you are on your own boat in the harbor area, but there are many more in other parts of town.

On New Providence Island:
Cafe dell Opera Tel: 356-6118
Upstairs in an old church, next to the *British Colonial Hotel* complex on Bay Street, serving their own homemade pasta and pizzas to the music of the Grand Operas, open for lunch and dinner daily.
Cafe Matisse Tel: 356-7012 On Bank Lane, behind Parliament Square, open daily from 10 am to 11 pm. Matisse prints and delicious Italian food are served indoors, or outside in a delightful courtyard. Reservations suggested. Proper dress for dinner.

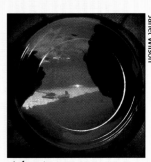
Atlantis.

The Cellar Tel: 322-8877 Located on Charlotte Street, just off Bay Street. Great quiches, salads, and more for lunch, either in their pretty courtyard or indoors, open 11 am to 4 pm daily, closed on Sundays. A good place for lunch if you are shopping downtown.
East Villa Restaurant Tel: 393-3377/3385 Open for lunch noon to 3 pm, dinner 6 pm to midnight, except Sundays 12:30 to 3 pm for lunch and 6 to 10 pm for dinner. Reservations suggested, proper dress required. Excellent Chinese food and New York strip steaks. Within walking distance of the *Nassau Harbour Club.*
Gaylords Tel: 356-3004 On Dowdeswell Street. Authentic Indian cuisine in a 125-year-old Bahamian mansion. Open daily for lunch and dinner. Reservations and proper attire requested for dinner.
Montagu Gardens Tel: 394-5347 Next to *Waterloo,* a short walk from the *Nassau Harbour Club.* Open for lunch 11:30 am to 3 pm and for dinner 6 to 11 pm, in an old Bahamian home and gardens on Lake Waterloo. Flame-grilled and blackened specialties, with mud pie for dessert.
The Pink Pearl Tel: 394-6143 Opposite the *Nassau Yacht Haven,* in an old Bahamian estate home. Elegant Caribbean and Bahamian dining for lunch and dinner, with live music on Fridays and Saturdays. Daily happy hour 5 to 7 pm, and weekend brunch. Reservations suggested.
The Poop Deck Tel: 393-8175 At the *Nassau Yacht Haven,* open from noon for lunch and dinner overlooking the marina. This is a cheerful, busy restaurant with long waits at peak times, serving good Bahamian and American food. Happy hour 5 to 7 pm daily.

Atlantis on Paradise Island:
DRESS CODE FOR ATLANTIS: *resort casual attire* is T-shirts, polo shirts, dress shorts, slacks or jeans, sundresses or skirts, or similar apparel; *resort evening attire* is polo or button-down shirts, slacks, sundresses or skirts, or similar apparel. No shorts, jeans, or T-shirts.

Atlas Bar and Grill Lunch and dinner are served either indoors or outside overlooking the marina, with oversized dinner favorites and broadcast sporting events. Resort casual attire for dinner.

Bahamian Club Steaks in a country club atmosphere, open for dinner only. Resort evening attire.

Cafe at the Great Hall of Waters Breakfast, lunch, and dinner looking into the underwater windows of the aquarium. Live entertainment. Afternoon tea served. Resort evening attire.

Cave Bar and Grill Hamburgers and sandwiches for lunch in an authentic re-creation of an actual Bahamian cave.

Fathoms Look into the underwater ruins of Atlantis through panoramic windows as you enjoy a raw bar and grilled fish and seafood for lunch or dinner. Resort evening attire.

Five Twins Exotic Asian cuisine, sushi and satay bar, cigars, rum bar, live music, and dancing. Adults only at dinner. Jackets required.

Lagoon Bar and Grill Pizza, salads, and sandwiches for lunch on the patio under the aquatic dome ceiling.

Mama Loo's Traditional Chinese dishes and exotic drink menu. Dinner only. Resort evening attire.

Marketplace Regional fare at made-to-order food stations. Bright, cheerful, and casual.

Seagrapes Tropical buffet with views of the waterscape, open for breakfast, lunch, and dinner. Sunday brunch. Resort casual attire for dinner.

Outside Atlantis on Paradise Island

Anthony's Caribbean Grill Tel: 363-3152 In the *Paradise Village Shopping Center*. Caribbean/American food, with specials such as Junkanoo Steak, Soca Tuna, Pasta Rasta, and Exuma chicken. Open daily for lunch and dinner from 11:30 am. Happy hour from 3 to 6 pm.

The Blue Marlin Tel: 363-2660 In the *Hurricane Hole Shopping Plaza*. Open 11 am to 10 pm daily, serving good Bahamian food, seafood, and exotic fruit daiquiris. Happy hour 4 to 6 pm daily. Reservations suggested for dinner. Evening entertainment with steel band and limbo dancing. Italian restaurant upstairs.

Columbus Tavern Tel: 363-2434/2992 At the *Paradise Harbour Club*. Open daily 7 am to 10:30 pm, serving breakfast, lunch, and dinner upstairs on an attractive, open veranda, overlooking the marina and Nassau Harbor. Good, international food. Happy hour 5 to 7 pm daily.

GETTING AROUND

Airports
There are two airports serving Nassau: the big international airport and the Nassau Jet Centre on the west side of New Providence Island. *Chalks International* flies seaplanes in from Miami, Fort Lauderdale, and Bimini. Private seaplanes land on Lake Nancy.

Airlines

Air Canada	Tel: 1-800-776-3000
Air Jamaica	Tel: 1-800-523-5585
American Airlines	Tel: 1-800-433-7300
American Eagle	Tel: 1-800-433-7300
Bahamasair	Tel: 242-377-7377/5505
British Airways	Tel: 1-800-AIRWAYS
Cat Island Air	Tel: 242-377-3318
Chalks	Tel: 1-800-424-2557
Cleare Air	Tel: 242-377-0341
Continental	Tel: 242-377-5486
Continental Connection	Tel: 242-356-7314
Delta/Comair	Tel: 1-800-221-1212
Le Air	Tel: 242-377-2356
Paradise Island Express	Tel: 242-377-2050
Sky Unlimited	Tel: 242-377-8993/8777
Sandpiper Air and Charter	Tel: 242-377-5751/5602
US Air	Tel: 1-800-622-1015

Buses
Buses run throughout the island, charging 75¢ wherever you go. Most of them leave from and run to Bay Street, a couple of blocks either side of the *Straw Market*, but there are bus stops marked out of town. The drivers will stop anywhere to pick up a fare. It is good manners to greet your fellow travelers as you board the bus, and then sit back and enjoy the music, usually played at full blast. Pay the driver exact money as you leave, or just hand in $1 and don't expect change.

Car Rentals
Don't forget to drive on the left!

Avis	Tel: 377-7121
Budget	Tel: 377-9000/7405
Dollar	Tel: 377-8300
Hertz	Tel: 377-8684

Carriage tours
Surreys are lined up by the cruise ship dock at Woodes Rogers Walk. They take you for a half-hour drive around town, usually with a cheerful commentary, for $10. Horses rest from 1 to 3 pm May to October, and from 1 to 2 pm November to April. Maximum three small adults, or two adults and a child in a carriage.

Conch Shell Roundabout, Nassau.

Ferries
The Cat Tel: 322-1340, 394-8747, or 323-2059 Departs Miami on Monday, Wednesday, Friday, and Sunday at 9 am, arriving Nassau at 2 pm. Departs Nassau at 4:30 pm, arriving Miami 9:45 pm. Round trip $119.
Departs Miami at 9 am on Tuesday, Thursday, and Saturday, arriving Freeport at 11:30 am. Leaves Freeport at 4:30 pm, arrives Miami at 6:45 pm. Round trip $99.

Bahamas Fast Ferries Tel: 323-2166 • Fax: 322-8185 Carries 200 passengers, fully air conditioned, travelling at 35 knots, 2.5 hours to Harbour Island. Daily scheduled service to Harbour Island and North Eleuthera costs $90 round trip. Leaves Nassau at 7:35 am, 2:30 pm, and 6:30 pm in the winter months, and 7:35 am, 1:30 pm and 7:30 pm in the summer months. A one-day excursion to Harbour Island, with a complimentary historical and cultural tour, lunch, and a visit to the Pink Sand beach, is $139 per person.

Taxis
Alan Major Tel: 361-2813
Howard VHF 16 "HT"
Meter Cab Tel: 323-5111
Bahamas Taxi Cab Union Tel: 323-5818
Taxis charge $2 for the first quarter mile, and 30¢ for each additional mile. Depending on the number of people in the cab, the fare can vary, so it is a good idea to discuss it before you set off. The taxis have to pay the bridge toll going over to Paradise Island, so that has to be included in the final bill.

SPORTS

Bowling
Village Lanes Bowling Club Tel: 323-2277 Located on Village Rd. $2.50 per game, 9 am to 5 pm, $2.75 after 5 pm. Shoe rental available.

Cricket
At Haynes Oval on West Bay St. Saturdays & Sundays at noon, from March to November.

Deep Sea Fishing
Chubasco Charters Tel: 322-8148
Captain Mike Russell. Deep sea and shark fishing.
Born Free Charters Tel: 363-2003
Captain Philip Pinder. Deep sea fishing and snorkeling.
Brown's Charters Tel: 324-1215
Captain Michael Brown has *Fantasea, White Cloud, and Nerina* to take you deep sea fishing or snorkeling as far as the Exumas and Harbour Island.
King Fisher Tel: 363-2335
Captain Jessie Pinder. Deep sea and shark fishing.
No Limit Tel: 361-3527
Captain Arthur Moxey. Deep sea fishing, sightseeing.

Diving
In emergency, call Lyford Cay Hospital at 242-362-4025 or contact VHF 16 for any of the dive operators. The direct line to the Hyperbaric Chamber is 362-5765, but you should contact Dr. Dean or Dr. Ingraham first through the hospital.
Bahama Divers at Nassau Yacht Haven Tel: 393-5644/1466 (reservations) 393-8724/6054 • Fax: 393-6078
• E-mail: bahdiver@bahamas.net.bs The most experienced dive operator in the Bahamas, with over 30 years in the business, and an excellent, well-stocked dive shop. Dive trips at 8 am and 1 pm daily, separate trips for beginners and experienced divers. Rentals, night dives, underwater videos. Two-tank dive $65, snorkelers $25.
Custom Aquatics Tel: 362-1492 25-ft. and 40-ft. dive boats, with 25 years of diving and cruising experience, professional Bahamian captain and PADI master. Private instruction for scuba, snorkeling, water skiing, aerobics, and swimming. Call Captain Frances Young for details.
Dive Dive Dive at Coral Harbour Tel: 362-1143/1401 Two-tank dive $70, shark dive $100, snorkeling $25.
Diver's Haven on East Bay Street Tel: 393-0869 Two-tank dive $65, snorkeling $30.
Nassau Scuba Centre at Coral Harbour Tel: 362-1964/1379 Two tank-dives $65, shark dive $110 or $295 for a Shark Suit Adventure, snorkeling $30.
Oceanus Sail and Dive
Tel: 426-6672 • E-mail: captbrucel@yahoo.com Week-long sailing and diving trips from Nassau to the Exumas with Captain Bruce Nelson. Cost from $1,000 per person. Scuba divers must bring proof of certification.
Stuart Cove's Dive South Ocean Tel: 362-4171/5227 With 16 instructors and guides and 11 dive boats; two-tank dive $70, shark dive $115, and snorkeling $30.
Sun Divers at the *British Colonial Hilton Nassau* Tel: 325-8927 Two-tank dive $65, snorkeling $20.
Sunskiff Divers at Coral Harbour Tel: 362-1979 One boat and one guide, for charter. Call for prices, they also offer kayak dives.

Dive Sites
From blue holes to wall dives to wreck dives, you have them all here!
Dive sites north, west and east of Paradise Island:
The *Blue Hole*, visible from the air east of Nassau, is exciting in the summer months with huge numbers of nurse sharks and stingrays. Often a second dive site after the *Blue Hole*, the *Cannonball Reef* is equally good for snorkelers in 20 feet of water with its elkhorn coral and zillions of fish and James Bond movie connections. The *Thunderball Barge* ran aground in the 1950s and snorkelers can see the outline of the ship lying upright in shallow water. Beware the fire coral! The *De La Salle* wreck, off Salt Cay, is lying in 70 feet of water along with two other boats, the *Grennen,* and the *Miranda,* which was sunk in 1980 to make an artificial reef. More wrecks north of Paradise Island are the *Mahoney,* the *Ana Lise,* the *Helena C,* and the latest, the *Bahama Shell.*

Dive sites off Lyford Cay and Clifton Point:
Lampton's Wall and *Tunnel Wall* are good for groups of divers with mixed experience levels, with a shallower wall dropping only 30 feet, plunging another 80 feet later and on down into seriously deep water. The *Oasis* is very exposed and for serious divers only, with many sharks. *Goulding Cay* has much to offer with its good snorkeling reef, as well as a dramatic wall dive, and further east is the *Willaurie* wreck, sunk intentionally in 1988. More wall dives include the *Black Forest Wall, Palace Wall* and the *Sand Chute,* with the wrecks used in the James Bond movies close in shore to Clifton Point.

Dive sites south of Coral Harbour:
A wrecked party boat, the *Bahama Mama,* lies in 50 feet of water, teeming with life. There is a mooring buoy. For some incredible snorkeling, try the *Southwest Reef* with its brilliant elkhorn coral stands. If it's sharks that turn you on, several of the dive operators run shark-feeding trips out to the *Shark Wall* and the *Arena.* More sharks abound at the *Valley* and *Jack's Jump,* where the wall height varies considerably before finally dropping down into the deep, deep water.

Golf
Cable Beach Golf Club at Cable Beach Tel: 327-6000
The 7,040-yard, par-72 course was designed by Emmet Devereux, and has been welcoming golfers since 1929. Pro shop, golf pro, and restaurant. Fees $100 for non-hotel guests.
Paradise Island Golf Club on Paradise Island Tel: 363-3925
Dick Wilson–designed, 6,780-yard, par-72 course overlooking Nassau Harbour, with a restaurant, golf pro, and golf shop. Fees $155, but price is subject to change.
South Ocean Golf Club at *Clarion Resort,* New Providence
Tel: 362-4391 Designed by Joe Lee, and steeped in history, this 6,707-yard course has lakes, and a blue hole by the 17th hole. Restaurant, snack bar, pro shop, and golf pro. Rates are $90 in the winter months.

Horseback Riding
Happy Trails at Coral Harbour Tel: 362-1820 $60 for an hour's ride, maximum weight 200 lbs. From 2 to 10 people per trail ride with experienced guides, English saddles. Cost includes transportation to the stables; children must be over 8 years old. No credit cards.

Jet-Skiing
Nassau Marriott Resort and Crystal Palace Casino Tel: 327-6200
Atlantis Resort, Paradise Island Tel: 363-2000
Superclub Breezes at Cable Beach Tel: 327-5356 20 minutes for 1 person $35, 2 people $45; 30 minutes for 1 person $55, 2 people $60. 1 hour for 1 person $110, for 2 people $120.

Parasailing
Costs around $35 for a 5–7 minute "flight."
Atlantis Paradise Island Tel: 363-2000
Nassau Beach Hotel, Cable Beach Tel: 377-7711
Radisson Grand Hotel, Paradise Island Tel: 363-3900

Power Boat Racing
Annual Bahamas Atlantis Superboat Challenge Held over three days in late September. Call the Ministry of Tourism at 242-302-2006 for more information.

Squash
The Village Club Tel: 393-1580 Open 8 am to 11:30 pm. Racket rental; courts $8 per hour. Also sauna and swimming pool.
Cable Beach courts, across from *Radisson Cable Beach*

Tennis
There are courts at most of the major hotels.

Water Skiing
Radisson Cable Beach Resort on Cable Beach Tel: 327-6000
$20 for 10 minutes.
Nassau Beach Hotel on Cable Beach Tel: 327-7711
$20 for three miles.
Windsurfing
Atlantis Paradise Island Tel: 363-3000 $25 per hour.
Superclub Breezes on Cable Beach Tel: 327-5356
Free for guests.
Nassau Beach Hotel on Cable Beach Tel: 327-7711
$14 per hour.

BEACHES

There are many to choose from, but a few suggestions on New Providence are Cable Beach and Goodmans Bay, Orange Hill Beach, Saunders Beach, and South Ocean Beach. On Paradise Island try Paradise Beach and Hartford Beach.

Potter's Cay, Nassau.

REGATTAS

December/January
New Year's Day is the grand finale of a week of championship racing in Bahamian built sloops, off Montagu Bay.
September/October
Annual Bahamas Atlantis Superboat Challenge

PLACES OF INTEREST

Ardastra Gardens and Zoo Tel: 323-5806 Five acres of gardens to wander through, and watch the marching flamingos perform at 11 am, 2 pm, and 4 pm. You can also see iguanas, monkeys, snakes, and rare Bahama parrots. Paths are signed, and many of the more interesting trees are labeled. Open daily from 9 am to 5 pm, admission $10.
Botanic Gardens With more than 600 species of tropical trees and plants. The curator can answer your questions. Open from 8 am to 4 pm, Monday to Friday, admission $1.
Canoeing at Lake Nancy Tel: 356-4283 An ecological adventure. Canoe rental available. You may see turtles, cranes, coots, ospreys, egrets, warblers, woodpeckers, and more!
The Cloister and *Versailles Garden* on Paradise Island Features a 14th-century arched walkway built by monks and brought in by Huntington Hartford as part of his initial island development. Overlooking the harbor, this makes a popular wedding site.
Crystal Cay Marine Observation Tower, part of the *Marriott Water Theme Park* Tel: 327-6200 See turtles, stingrays, and sharks at the world's largest man-made coral reef in an underwater

observatory. Restaurant and tower open 9 am to 6 pm daily. Admission $16 for adults, $11 for children.
Fort Montagu Built in 1741. It guards the eastern entrance to Nassau Harbour and was captured by the Americans during the American War of Independence in 1776.
Fort Charlotte Completed in 1789 to guard the western entrance to Nassau Harbour. Not a shot was ever fired against an invader by its 42 cannons, but there are still dungeons and a waxworks that you can visit free of charge.
Fort Fincastle Completed in 1793, built in the shape of a ship. Nearby is the 126-foot tall *Water Tower* with a dramatic view of the harbor.
Pirates of Nassau on King and George Streets Tel: 356-3759 Find out how pirates ruled the streets as well as the seas, in a historically accurate, interactive environment. Open 9 am to 5 pm, Monday to Saturday. Admission $15 for adults, $8 for children.
The Retreat, Village Road The headquarters of the Bahamas National Trust, set in 11 acres of lush tropical gardens, with the world's third-largest collection of rare and exotic palm trees. Half-hour guided tours available, or self-guided tours with a map. Open from 9 am to 5 pm Monday to Friday, and from 9:30 am to 12:30 pm on Saturdays. Admission $2.
Museums
Bahamas Historical Society Museum, Shirley Street and Elizabeth Avenue Tel: 322-4231 Displays depict Bahamian history from pre-Columbus to the present day, with Lucayan, Taino, and Arawak exhibits. Open 10 am to 4 pm Monday to Friday, and 10 am to noon on Saturdays. Admission $1.
Balcony House, Market Street Tel: 326-2566/2568 The oldest wooden house in Nassau dating from the 18th century. Fully restored. Open 10 am to 4:30 pm daily except Sunday, 1 to 4:30 pm. Admission by donation.
Pompey Museum of Slavery and Emancipation, Bay Street This was the old slave market until emancipation in 1834, and now has a post-emancipation exhibit. Open 10 am to 4:30 pm, Monday to Friday, and 10 am to 1 pm on Saturday. Admission $1.

THINGS TO DO IN NASSAU

- Pick up a copy of *"What To Do"* in Nassau, Cable Beach, and Paradise Island, and a Bahamas *Trailblazer* map, either from the Tourist Information office on Bay Street, many of the stores, or even from some of the marinas. It will give you current information as to what's going on, where and when.
- Buy yourself a hat in the *Straw Market*.
- Visit the newly reconstructed *Atlantis* on Paradise Island; take a $25 tour to the wonders of *The Dig* and to see the full beauty of the aquariums. Enjoy a meal at one of their many restaurants, or try your luck at the slot machines. Unless you are docked in the *Marina at Atlantis*, you will not be able to enjoy any of the water chutes or swimming facilities, which are reserved for guests at *Atlantis*.
- Climb the 66 steps of the Queen's Staircase leading up to Fort Fincastle, and photograph Nassau from above.
- Stock up on groceries and fresh provisions before heading out to less well-stocked islands.
- Have any repairs to your boat seen to, and replace spare parts you have used on board.
- Watch the marching flamingos at the *Ardastra Gardens Zoo*.
- Go for a 40-minute run with the Hash House Harriers on Monday evenings at 6:30 pm and Sundays at 10:30 am, from October to April. Call Brian Crick at 325-2832 or 327-5685 (evenings), or Ewan Tough at 323-4966 or 362-4654 (evenings).
- Become a BASRA member; you never know when you may need their help. Call their HQ at 324-8864 from 9 am to 5 pm, or write to them at PO Box SS 6247, Nassau.

Chapter 12
Eleuthera
Spanish Wells and Harbour Island
Hatchet Bay and Governor's Harbour to Cape Eleuthera

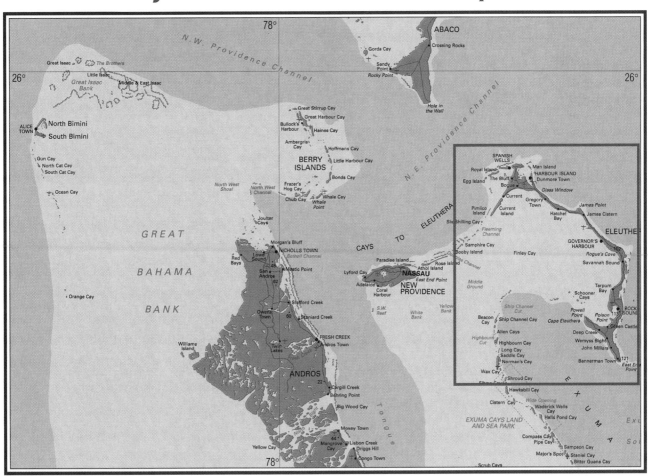

Approaches to Spanish Wells, Harbour Island, and North Eleuthera

THE north of Eleuthera is a distinct geographic area. You could say that it's an island in its own right, connected to "mainland" Eleuthera only by a bridge, and this is true. But more important to the cruising visitor are the problems set by the unique geography of North Eleuthera. To the north and west it's surrounded by coral reefs. In the south the waters of the North Eleuthera Bight are shallow, and the coast itself is low lying, without any natural harbor or viable anchorage. To the east the seabed plunges to ocean depths within a mile of land, and your approach problems, for there are reefs there too and fierce tides, are compounded by the pressures of three thousand miles of North Atlantic fetch.

All this sounds far from encouraging. It remains that there are only three approach routes into the North Eleuthera area. The first is from the west, taking advantage of a pass through the reefs lying to the south of Egg Island. The second is from the north through the reefs to the north of Bridge Point. The third is from the east, over a bar to the south of Harbour Island. There is only one approach that we recommend, and that's to go the Egg Island way. The north approach is not just difficult. It's dangerous. You need a pilot there. And we don't like the Harbour Island approach. If you ask "Is it worth going to North Eleuthera?," our answer is short and simple. You bet it is. We'll deal with the Egg Island approach first, as if we were coming in from Nassau, and we'll pick up the other two as we make our way around. Your initial destination, coming in this way, is bound to be Spanish Wells.

We list an Egg Island northwest waypoint (EGGNW) as a landfall (or departure point) for those arriving from or setting out for the Abacos. Your next waypoint, going in or out, is our Little Egg Island waypoint (LEGGI). Between the two, keep in deep water standing well off the Egg Islands, which are ringed by coral reef. In truth there is a 12–14-foot channel between the two Egg Islands, but we'd advise against your going that way. Use our approach, which is a wide, safely deep pass on or off the Bank. Your approach course coming from Nassau will be 048°M to reach our Little Egg Island waypoint, which places you 0.5 nm south of Little Egg Island. This wayoint was once marked by the wreck of the *Arimora*, high on the reef to the immediate north. This one-time 260-foot landmark has now been taken by successive storms, and only a small section of bow remains above the water, together with a horizontal section of deck. It's hard to see, and the triangular wedge of bow may have disappeared by the time you read this (Captain Edsel Roberts of Spanish Wells reckoned it would "go in the next breeze"). If it is there, it looks more like a rock than a piece of ship. Our message? Don't rely on it. To your south you also have reef, but as we've said, the pass is wide.

We'll take it in stages now. Rather than break the descriptive continuity of running from the pass directly to Spanish Wells, we'll deal with Spanish Wells first and then return, as it were, to cover Egg Island and Royal Island.

The Western (Little Egg Island) Approach to Spanish Wells (St. George's Cay)

From the Little Egg Island waypoint you have two straightforward legs to run setting you up ready to make your close approach to Spanish Wells. The first leg, 3.09 nm on 059°M, takes you just north of the rocks that lie 1.25 nm south of Royal Island. Here (ROYAL), if you're attracted by Royal Island's superb natural harbor and want an island to your-

Water towers, Spanish Wells Harbour.

NORTH ELEUTHERA		
Fleeming Channel		
FLEMG	25° 16' 20"/343 N	076° 55' 59"/983 W
Egg Island Northwest		
EGGNW	25° 31' 30"/500 N	076° 55' 30"/500 W
Little Egg Island		
LEGGI	25° 27' 32"/541 N	076° 53' 51"/848 W
Egg Island South		
EGGIS	25° 28' 47"/784 N	076° 52' 03"/055 W
Royal Island		
ROYAL	25° 30' 09"/161 N	076° 50' 28"/465 W
Meeks Patch		
MEEKP	25° 31' 30"/511 N	076° 48' 00"/000 W
Spanish Wells South Entry		
SPNWS	25° 32' 00"/000 N	076° 45' 39"/648 W
Spanish Wells East Entry		
SPNWE	25° 32' 38"/633 N	076° 44' 20"/333 W

The final figures in each waypoint show seconds (00") and thousands (000) of a minute.

self (or possibly shared with others) opt out of this routing and turn north. If you're bound for Spanish Wells, a second leg, 3.75 nm on 076°M, places you north of Meeks Patch (MEEKP) ready to turn directly for Spanish Wells harbor (SPNWS). Then take as your landfall mark the new Spanish Wells water tanks, which are silo-like in appearance just behind the entrance to the harbor. Your heading will be around 080°M, you have about 1.5 nm to run before you're going to enter the harbor, and you'll have 6 feet under you at MLW. Other than this water tank there are no quick-and-easy ID points on this approach leg.

Spanish Wells

The South Entry to Spanish Wells Harbour

By the time you've run 1 nm from that last waypoint you should have the skyline water tower plainly in sight, and in the last half mile you'll be altering more directly for the tanks (which you'll now see are dark blue with white tops) on a northeast heading. As you get closer you'll see the narrow channel between Russel Island (with a lot of dredging showing on what will be your port side as you enter) and Charles Island (shaggy green vegetation). Your best lead marks are the water tank on the skyline and a second larger but more squat water tank (also dark blue) slightly to the right and below it at harborfront level, but these two water tanks do *not* set up a transit. Your other confirmation of your landfall are the fishing boats (if they're in port, which is mostly April to July) you'll see to the right of the second, lower-level water tank.

What about channel markers? We're talking now about two approach markers (both steel I-beams), hard to pick up from any distance out. The port marker has heeled over and

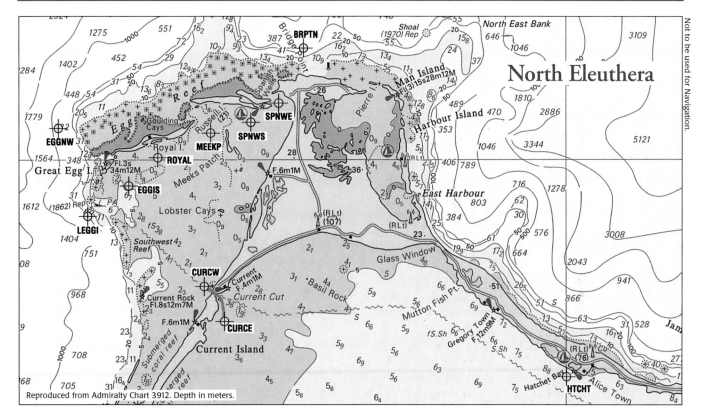

the starboard marker (still upright) bears a faded trace of red paint—these are both right at the entrance to the channel. More obvious is the line of dredged sand and marl you'll have on the port side, which gives the line of the channel more clearly than the indefinite shoreline of Charles Island.

Visitors still have trouble identifying this entry. Admittedly the I-beams are not easy to pick up at first (we've suggested coats of day-glow fluorescent red and green paint), but the confusion factor lies in the pilings that mark a water pipeline off toward the North Eleuthera coast. Don't get seduced by them and head that way. You'll run aground. Your fail-safe, by our reckoning, are those two blue water tanks. You can't miss them.

Once you're in the channel there's a further marker to starboard, and then you have two choices. Turn to starboard if you wish to anchor behind Charles Island, or turn to port (note the channel you must stay in, it's obvious, and there's a marker piling to be left to starboard) if you wish to go to Spanish Wells Yacht Haven, recognizable at once by its large shed. You'll have good depth on your approach all the way. Well over 6 feet, and mostly 10 feet or more.

The East Entry to Spanish Wells Harbour

There's an alternative route into Spanish Wells Harbour and that's to continue around Charles Island and pick up the channel (SPNWE) that leads east–west directly into the cut between St. George's Cay and Charles Island. If you do this, beware of the shallows on both sides. Pick up the three chan-

nel marks (to be left to port), which will take you in a curve around the shallows to port. Then you'll see two channel entry markers with, as a companion to the starboard one, a leaning telephone pole. When you get close you may see that the starboard entry piling has a single red reflector on it, one of the kind you use to mark your driveway.

By now you're heading almost due west and there's a line of four single posts to be left to starboard leading you straight

Spanish Wells Harbour, from the southwest.

Fishing boats, Spanish Wells.

into Spanish Wells Harbour. You have good depth in this channel, but we see no reason to take this route into the harbor if you've come from the west. Don't be confused by a continuation of these markers leading east from the entry pair. This is the route used by the Spanish Wells boats bound for Gene's Bay ferry landing on Eleuthera, directly opposite the channel entrance.

This is the entrance that you may prefer to use if you want to pick up a mooring, for the moorings (see our detail under the heading Spanish Wells Harbour) come up on your port bow as you proceed up the channel. They can, of course, be reached by running down the length of Spanish Wells Harbour from the south entry.

Spanish Wells Harbour

Spanish Wells Harbour is, in fact, just one long cut running between St. George's Cay (Spanish Wells) to the north and two islands, little peanut-shaped Charles Island to the southeast, and Russell Island to the southwest. It's not a natural harbor in the sense of being a cove or a landlocked bay, but it serves well with adequate protection from virtually all weather other than wind funneling in from the east. The open, free-to-all anchorage that once existed at the eastern end of Charles Island has now been converted into moorings, which in truth we feel is a better, and safer arrangement. Contact Edsel Roberts (*Dolphin)* or Bradley Newbold (*Cinnabar)* on VHF 16 if you want to pick up a mooring, or call them ahead of time (the latter, in season, is probably a wise course, as the total number available is nine in all). See our **Yellow Pages.** A second change has taken place, that there is now a speed limit of 4 knots in Spanish Wells Harbour. Keep to it!

Spanish Wells Yacht Haven is your only marina, but it's well found and well kept, a pleasant, agreeable place with every facility you are likely to need, including a circular swimming pool, and rooms if you wish to put up shoreside guests. Inexplicably the shore power outlets are 50A so if you're running 30A, you'll need a pigtail. They may be able to lend you one. If you carry on up the cut, between Russell Island and St. George's Cay, to port there are two openings into the Mud Hole, the local hurricane shelter where, when a hurricane threatens, the local boats are laced with a spider's web of lines into the mangroves (a practice that saw its toughest test when Hurricane *Andrew* hit in 1992). The technique works.

Spanish Wells Harbour, which is entirely weighted in its layout to favor the St. George's Cay side (the *'butment,* as it's called) is geared to supporting the fishing fleet. Counting from the east end, Ronald's Marine, the Anchor Snack Bar, Walton's Langousta Bar (it has been closed), Pinders Supermarket, Pool's Boatyard with its rail track into the harbor and its mini-drawbridge, the Texaco Service Center with Spanish Wells Marine and Hardware, and Jack's Outback (another snack-bar restaurant) are the main shoreside facilities on the waterfront between that east tip of St. George's Cay and the Yacht Haven. The fishing boat services and docks continue right up the harbor to the St George's Cay–Russell Island bridge, where the two islands have a road link, at the west end.

You can take a small boat out under this bridge at half tide or better to gain the open water of the bank between Pierre Rock and St. George's Cay, and from there head west to reach the gap between Russell Island and Royal Island. At less than half tide the area to the east of the bridge dries. If you go this way, beware of the old bridge (brought down by Hurricane *Andrew)* that lies on the north side of the channel, to the east side of the bridge.

SPANISH WELLS SETTLEMENT
(ST. GEORGE'S CAY AND CHARLES ISLAND)

St. George's Cay is so totally identified with and as being Spanish Wells that we deal with the island and the settlement (as well as little uninhabited Charles Island, which has no role to play other than in helping to form Spanish Wells Harbour) under the heading of Spanish Wells.

The name Spanish Wells sounds romantic. The legend that the Spanish filled their water casks from the sweet wells of the island now called St. George's Cay before setting off on the long haul to Spain sounds good, but is it credible? Look at the charts. Look at the reefs. Study the wreck history of the area. If you were a Spanish admiral with your pension coming up in six months time, would you lead your Treasure Fleet to Spanish Wells? But even if you doubt the legend, if you want to see the real Bahamas, Spanish Wells should be on your list. Go to its tiny museum. There's not much there but there's everything, from the house itself to the story the exhibits tell with unaccented simplicity. In

Spanish Wells, if you wander around and talk to people, you begin to get a feel for the history and the making of a place, rather as low tide reveals the inshore reef that made the beach.

Spanish Wells is no tourist resort. Hurricane *Andrew* in 1992 ended the modest attempt that had been made up to that date to encourage tourism as an income earner. Spanish Wells is fishing, serious fishing, with ocean-going craft and the whole infrastructure to support them. It is self-reliance taken as far as you can reasonably take it, that goes straight back to 1648 and the Eleutheran Adventurers, who were tough, ornery, independent of mind, and not prepared to live by the rules of the day just because that was the way it had always been. Spanish Wells *is* Bahamian lobster fishing with something like 75 percent of its annual production and exports that have long found markets worldwide. You can see the end result in new houses, new cars, and the reassurance that they got it right.

If you're looking for tourist attractions, bars to sit in watching the sunset, and gourmet restaurants, you'll find nothing there. What you will find is a settlement of sturdy, well-built, well-cared-for houses in Abaco colors (but then weren't they much the same people?), in which real grass, flower beds, and trees are tended with an un-Bahamian care. You'll find cultivation taken seriously, land taken into use for fruit trees and bananas, and young flowering trees started, ready for the future, in cans and buckets. You'll see the evidence now of the lobster fishing prosperity in new houses, and a gradual expansion into Russell Island.

Spanish Wells, northern beach.

You may conclude that isolation lasted perhaps a tad too long in this settlement. Certainly old customs endure and the division between the sexes, what the men do, and what the women do, reflects a simple, pragmatic way of going about the business of living, albeit a lifestyle that would be reckoned by today's torchbearers of individual emancipation to be hopelessly sexist. You'll find an island with far too many cars for its population, but the fishing brings money and what other status symbol would you choose if you already have a house? In the evening the cars are driven around the few streets in something like a Spanish paseo, endlessly and aimlessly it seems, round and round the circuit. Perhaps the Spanish really were there.

Above all, what you'll find is kindness, a readiness to talk, and one very attractive, small, close-knit community that has every appearance of having known where it was going since that magic date in its history, 1648, when they decided that Bermuda was too close to the British Crown politically and geographically to engender confidence in the future. They wanted freedom, and the right to determine how their own lives would shape. The story sounds familiar.

LITTLE EGG ISLAND AND EGG ISLAND

Little Egg Island is totally barren and Egg Island, despite a fishing shack that gives the appearance of habitation, has little to offer but a light that may, or may not, be working. You might find yourself drawn to the Egg Islands because the North Eleuthera reef, to which Egg Island has given its name, is easily accessible there, has good snorkeling, good diving, and there's good fishing, too.

ROYAL ISLAND

Royal Island (as you pass it) seems to go on forever, 4.5 nm long and 0.5 nm wide at its widest point. Its central, near-land-locked harbor, with the ruins of a house above it, is as perfect a natural haven as you could ever expect to find. On its north shore there are beaches and the protection (plus its attraction for snorkeling, diving, and fishing) of the Egg Reef, with little Goulding Cay as a playground to the north. The harbor is well protected from everything but the south and southwest, but you can tuck yourself up in the ends (beware the east end) even if you get it blowing straight in the entrance. You have 10–14 feet MLW in the harbor.

As for entering, you go in the central, obvious entrance favoring the west side between the little cay with its marker and the headland with its board. You have 8 feet there at Low Water. Don't take the other side, the east channel. There's a submerged rock there (which is marked). Further along the Royal Island coast there's another entrance to the east end of the harbor, but this is small boat stuff, and not for you. The east end is, in any event, shallow, far too shallow at low tide to serve anything drawing more than 12 inches.

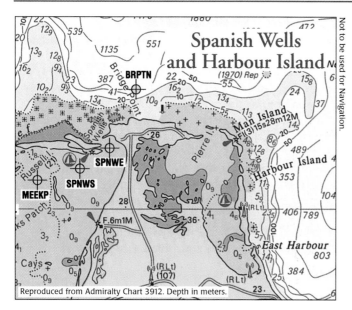

Spanish Wells
and Harbour Island

Reproduced from Admiralty Chart 3912. Depth in meters.

Not to be used for Navigation.

All reports tell us that Royal Island has now been sold. A marina is planned there, which is no surprise. No one, at the time we write, can provide any more information. A well-planned, well-managed marina and anchorage there should be a winner, as we've long said. In the meantime, (until it may be forbidden during construction?) Royal Island is still available (as of April 1999) as an anchorage.

RUSSELL ISLAND

Russell Island, at 3 nm in length, dwarfs St. George's Cay's 1.5 nm, but might best be considered the country estate of Spanish Wells. It has a considerable wealth of citrus and other planting under cultivation, some very handsome houses, two good beaches on the north side, and some fishing shacks.

Spanish Wells to Harbour Island– The Devil's Backbone Passage

THE FEARED DEVIL'S BACKBONE

Right at the start of the settlement of the Bahamas the Devil's Backbone claimed its first victim when the first shipload of Eleutheran settlers went on the reef, and ended up destitute, holed up in Preacher's Cave. It wasn't a good start. Since then the Devil's Backbone and the North Eleuthera reefs have claimed many victims, and gained a fearsome reputation.

We've done the passage in flat calm with perfect light. We've done it (with Edsel Roberts) in poor light, a bumpy sea state, and a 20-knot wind from the east–northeast. We've been caught there by a freak storm, halfway through the passage. We've checked it out from the shoreline. And we've overflown the whole run at low altitude, taking sequential photographs all the way from Spanish Wells to Harbour Island.

We know what it looks like, and we could even map it. But would we go it alone? If you've done it once, there are

some who say that given good conditions you can do it on your own. And yet . . . one boat owner, who'd taken a pilot the first time, reckoned he could go it alone on the return trip. He buckled two propellers and bent his shafts. Saving that Spanish Wells $60 pilot's fee cost him around $50,000 by the time his boat had been repaired in Florida.

Our conclusions are simply these. On that passage you're utterly dependent on good weather and perfect visibility, but however good your reading of the water, you've got to factor these parameters into your decision making:

- It's hard to distinguish between coral and grass.

- From a relatively short distance off it's almost impossible to guess the depth over sand, coral, or grass accurately.

- Generally your forward speed, even at 5 knots, will be sufficient (given average reaction time) to carry you exactly where you don't want to be.

- You have no room to maneuver on the critical sectors of this passage.

- The obstacle course is never quite the same. The sand, at the closest point of your run close to the shoreline, changes with each storm.

It's not supposed to be a test of character. Taking a pilot doesn't reflect on your competence and seamanship. You could say that it says a great deal for your pragmatic common sense. But of course you can try it alone, if you wish. For this reason, we offer a commentary on the Devil's Backbone Passage, with a set of ten **ballpark** waypoints.

THE DEVIL'S BACKBONE PASSAGE (WEST TO EAST)			
WPT01	Gun Point	25° 32' 57"/948 N	076° 44' 43"/712 W
WPT02	Ridley Head Stake	25° 33' 30"/500 N	076° 44' 24"/400 W
WPT03	Bridge Point	25° 33' 53"/887 N	076° 43' 26"/436 W
Bridge Point North			
BRPTN	outside reefs	25° 35' 00"/000 N	076° 43' 20"/333 W
WPT04	Devil's Backbone	25° 33' 38"/640 N	076° 42' 02"/043 W
WPT05	Preacher's Cave	25° 33' 39"/657 N	076° 41' 46"/765 W
WPT06	Hawk's Point	25° 33' 38"/633 N	076° 41' 09"/150 W
WPT07	Stake	25° 33' 33"/559 N	076° 40' 49"/816 W
WPT08	Current Point	25° 33' 05"/091 N	076° 39' 55"/915 W
WPT09	Stake	25° 32' 45"/744 N	076° 39' 33"/557 W
WPT10		25° 32' 31"/516 N	076° 39' 05"/086 W

The final figures in each waypoint show seconds (00") and thousands (000) of a minute.

Do not program our waypoints, and on no account even think of setting your autopilot. We accept absolutely no responsibility whatsoever if you go on the rocks, or your passage ends in disaster.

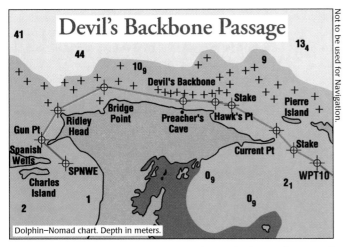

Devil's Backbone Passage

Dolphin–Nomad chart. Depth in meters.

Not to be used for Navigation.

The Devil's Backbone Passage through the reefs around the north coast of Eleuthera is an exercise in coastal navigation, which, rather like marriage, should not be lightly undertaken. It's potentially hazardous but not dangerous given the right conditions. Because the nature of the navigational problems presented change as you make your way around the coast, it makes sense to get a Spanish Wells pilot to take you around the first time you do it, if not every time, and talk you through the course. His services will cost you $60 but it's money well spent.

This advice given, what other cautions have we?

- *Never* attempt this passage in bad weather, particularly with wind, or wave, or ocean swells coming onshore out of the north.

- *Never* attempt it if the light is not good. Any time after 10 a.m., when the sun has got reasonably high in the sky, is OK, and around noon is best.

- *Never* attempt the passage from Harbour Island to Spanish Wells in the late afternoon with the sun in your eyes.

- *High water* is always an extra safety dividend. You could make it at low water, but it makes sense to have the reassurance of two feet or so extra under your keel.

- *If* you're in trouble, stay in 40 feet of water and call for help (the reason we say 40 feet is that the top of the reefs and isolated coral heads in this area rise about 25–30 feet from the seabed).

- *If* you're overtaken by weather use your best anchor and wait until it clears or alternatively call for a pilot.

Let's take the Devil's Backbone Passage in stages.

Spanish Wells Harbour to Ridley Head

Leave Spanish Wells by the eastern entry and, turning north, head for Gun Point (WPT01). Pass about 50 feet off Gun Point. Your next landmark is Ridley Head (WPT02), just over half a mile to run. You'll have 6 feet of water all the way (maybe 5 at the least if the moon isn't working for you). The dark patches ahead and to starboard as you cross the small bight between Gun Point and Ridley Head are grass. The dark patches to port are coral. Pass outside (offshore) Ridley Head stake leaving it a good boat length or so off to starboard (it stands on an isolated reef). You'll have some 30 feet of water there.

Be warned that if the weather is marginal and the wind has a north element in it, the worst area for high seas is from Ridley Head to just after the Devil's Backbone.

RIDLEY HEAD TO BRIDGE POINT

Immediately after Ridley Head you're going to alter to pass off the next headland, Bridge Point (WPT03), which is just under a mile away. At the start you'll find yourself paralleling a beach. The dark patches to port are reef. Keep favoring the beach side. When you run out of beach, you'll see four dark patches, which are reef, coming up on your starboard bow. Point out to sea slightly to leave these to starboard. You'll find yourself over or close to other dark patches, which are also reef, but you should have sufficient depth on your run to Bridge Point.

BRIDGE POINT

Stand reasonably well out from Bridge Point as the depth shoals close in. Bridge Point is not only a landmark on your Devil's Backbone Passage, but also your jumping off point for the Abacos (or alternatively your arrival point).

THE DEVIL'S BACKBONE

You now have just over a mile to run to take you past the actual Devil's Backbone Reef. After Bridge Point alter to starboard (maybe some 8–10°) and look out for Blowhole Rock, dark and cavelike, which you'll see off your starboard bow. When you're just about level with it a reef will come

BRIDGE POINT NORTH

Bridge Point North

Bridge Point North		
BRPTN outside reefs	25° 35' 00"/000 N	076° 43' 20"/333 W

Our Bridge Point North waypoint, lying outside the reefs is your actual point of departure, and the point at which, arriving in, you are advised to call Spanish Wells on VHF 16 for a pilot. We suggest you use a pilot to guide you out if you're leaving, rather than trusting your own eyeball navigation. If you've never been this way before, use a pilot. If the visibility or the weather is marginal, use a pilot. Also see our note **Moving on to the Abacos** on page 189.

The Devil's Backbone.

up on your port side. Keep inshore of that reef, and head for what appears to be the next headland, but it isn't a headland. It's the northern tip of Pierre Island.

You're now going to run in progressively closer to the shoreline to take you safely between the Devil's Backbone Reef and the beach. You'll see the Devil's Backbone, dark on your port side. The reef hooks inwards toward the shore, forcing you closer and closer to the beach. At what will be your closest point, you'll realize that the beach itself is hooking out toward the reef. Many people, scared of grounding on the sand (around WPT04), alter away from the beach and crunch on the Devil's Backbone. You've got to keep your cool, just hug that beach, about 150 feet out, and don't be scared of it.

After squeezing around the Devil's Backbone you can start easing out away from the beach, and flex your hands to get rid of your white knuckles. You've still got potential hazards ahead, but perhaps the worst leg is over.

PREACHER'S CAVE BEACH TO HAWK'S POINT

You have just over half a mile to run to clear the next low point. At WPT05 you are off Preacher's Cave beach, and in the limestone cliff face to starboard you can see the cave entrance. Your general line now is to continue moving out, further offshore, to pass around that low rocky point, Hawk's Point (WPT06). After that you're almost on the home stretch. Not quite. But getting there. There is grass underneath you, which you can pass over, and there are also two coral heads (which come up about the time you reach the end of Preacher's Cave beach), which you leave to starboard. Further offshore there are plenty of reefs. You're not out of reef country yet.

HAWK'S POINT TO CURRENT POINT

After reaching Hawk's Point head to pass off the next point of land, Current Point, which is obvious, just over a mile away. Stand out from the shoreline rather than paralleling close to it, for on the way there's an isolated stake that marks a ledge running out from the coastline. Our WPT07 is roughly where you should aim to be to pass safely around it. Don't shave it too close. You'll hit the ledge.

After passing the stake alter to take up a southeasterly heading to pass off Current Point (WPT08). You're pretty much fine now, with no particular problems to face. On this leg you'll have grass under you all the way. Leave Current Point passing 200 feet off it.

Current Point to just off Dunmore Town (Harbour Island)

After Current Point alter course to about 135–140°M to acquire a lone stake, half a mile away, marking a channel through sands that lie to the north of the Harbour Island "inland sea" area. The stake (WPT09) must be passed on the south side (left to port if you're inbound from Spanish Wells). Pass reasonably close to it, for you have shallows to starboard, which are easily seen. Your general direction, after passing the stake, should be toward the south beach on Man Island. Run on this heading for about half a mile, to around our WPT10, to get clear of the shallows and then you can take up a heading for Dunmore Town.

You have two final hazards to avoid, neither of them difficult. Look out for Eastmost Rock and Westmost Rock to starboard, and avoid them. Look out for Girl's Bank to port (which shows clearly) and skirt around that. Then you're all set to make your approach to either Valentine's or the Harbour Island Marina, or to anchor off wherever you wish.

Harbour Island Marina.

The pink sands of Harbour Island.

Harbour Island

Harbour Island is one of the fabled Bahamian hideaways, famous for its seclusion, relaxed life style, friendly atmosphere, pretty houses, and pink sands. Before the coming of air services Harbour Island won on the seclusion factor. It was three times removed from Florida, for you had to stage through Nassau and Spanish Wells to get there. Make that five times removed, for if you were sailing there the Biminis, the southern Berrys, Nassau, and Spanish Wells all came into the distancing process.

Now you can fly into North Eleuthera Airport and take a ferry from Three Islands ferry dock straight to Harbour Island and the streets of Dunmore Town. Has it lost anything because of this? Yes, of course it has. But if you still want to feel the magic of that distancing, of getting there and being remote, take the old route around North Eleuthera, make your way around the Devil's Backbone, and get to Harbour Island that way.

Dunmore Town Marinas and Anchorages

Previous visitors will note that the one-time pink customs building on the end of the Government Dock is now yellow. Lying immediately south of this dock, Valentine's Yacht Club and Inn is well established, well known, and has a bar and restaurant as well as a dive shop on the premises. Despite a disastrous fire that destroyed the shoreward end of Valentine's dock, a rebuild has taken place with consummate speed, and Valentine's, to their credit, stayed in business and hardly faltered a step. They are going strong, as ever. The Harbour Island Marina, rebuilt after Hurricane *Andrew*, is still developing. The marina, steadily being improved, is looking better each time we see it, and they have continuing plans in force to keep moving forward over the next two years. If you want to anchor off, the best place

is somewhere south of the Harbour Island Marina, away from all the traffic. Ferries from Three Islands (and North Eleuthera Airport) are running all day.

Harbour Island is a magnet in peak season, particularly at Easter. If you are intending to be there at a peak period, book your dock space early. It is limited! Both marinas, while well sheltered from the northeast, east, and southeast, are completely exposed to wind from any other direction. In the event of a Norther or strong winds from the west the Harbour Island marinas are virtually untenable and shelter may well have to be sought at anchor off the east coast of North Eleuthera.

PIERRE, MAN, AND JACOBS ISLANDS

The three islands to the north of Harbour Island have no particular interest, though anchorages may be found off them all. Beware that there are shallows on the west of all three islands and that there are no navigable gaps between them out into the Atlantic.

The Harbour Mouth Ocean Pass

The ocean pass known as Harbour Mouth lies at the south end of Harbour Island. A very extensive area of shoal (similar in extent to Girl's Bank) extends to the west from the south peninsula of Harbour Island as far as 25° 27' 50 N. To gain the ocean you have to run favoring the shore of North Eleuthera until you have passed the gap between Harbour Island and Whale Point, and then turn to go out into the Atlantic.

The route through Harbour Mouth carries little more than 6 feet even with a favorable tide, maybe less, and is beset by moving sandbanks, tidal currents, and ocean swell. An additional complication in your reading of the water color scheme is that a newly laid underwater pipeline has left a somewhat irregular sand scar running diagonally across the shoal area from Eleuthera to Harbour Island. The Harbour Mouth pass is best left to the locals, or learned from someone who is there and uses it. What does it offer you? Ocean fishing, and a good departure point for the Abacos or Cat Island. We would not use it as an arrival point.

During our last visit it became clear that the depth in this pass, though good for 20 feet in the mouth, shoals to no more than 4 feet at MLW. Though passable, we reckon it was never a good route to take in or out of Harbour Island/Dunmore Town, and in bad weather it is out of the question. Unless you have that local guide, or up-to-date local knowledge, we suggest you forget it.

Moving on to the Abacos

We believe Bridge Point is your best departure mark if you're setting out for the Abacos, and that your departure should be around our BRPTN waypoint to get you well into deep water before you set a course and settle down. We'd not come in this way from the Abacos. You would be chancing your luck with weather and on the time of day, and it makes no sense to put yourselves at risk. Take the route we recommend at the start of this section, going south of Little Egg Island, in which case our EGGNW waypoint is your best landfall or departure point.

A North Eleuthera Inland Tour

There are times when you should check your lines, or your ground tackle, and leave your boat to take a taxi tour of the hinterland, for otherwise you'll never get the feel of the place that has been your destination. North Eleuthera (and indeed the whole of Eleuthera, taken section by section) is one of them.

If you're in Spanish Wells, get to Gene's Bay ferry landing and take a taxi from there. If you're in Harbour Island, get to Three Islands ferry landing and do the same. Take Glass Window, the break point between North Eleuthera and Central Eleuthera, as your far out destination and turnround point. We're not writing a land tour guide, but we'll mention just three places you might feel worth your time. They don't come up precisely in the order we list them. Look at your road map. You'll see why.

UPPER AND LOWER BOGUE

The Bogues take their name from a corruption of the word "bog" or low-lying, nearly useless land. It was unclaimed, unwanted right from the start and it was there that the freed slaves staked out their tracts when they were turned loose after Emancipation. Drive through to see a part of the Bahamas that is far removed from either Spanish Wells or Harbour Island's Dunmore Town. Both Upper and Lower Bogue were hit hard by Hurricane *Andrew*, for they have no elevation, and no protection. You can still see the damage.

Glass Window, from the west.

THE CURRENT

The tiny settlement of The Current, "Population 131, Established 1648" as its welcoming sign advertises, was hit harder by Hurricane *Andrew* than anywhere else, and the traces are all too evident. Go there to reinforce what you learned from the Bogues and take a postgraduate course in real life in the Bahamas. While you're down that way go to look at Current Cut. Get the feel of it before you make use of it on your onward path down the west coast of Eleuthera.

THE GLASS WINDOW

The Glass Window is the point in the rock spine of Eleuthera, once no more than a natural arch undermined by the ocean, which became a real break. It was named for the facility to "look through" the window formed by the arch. There, today, the road crosses a rock gorge on a new bridge, the last in a series of storm-damaged bridges. Stop, and while your taxi turns around, look about you.

To the east, and right up to the concrete bridge itself (though well below it) you have the deep blue water of the Atlantic. To the west it's the turquoise green, far-shallower water of the Bahama banks. When the Atlantic rollers come surging in or the powerful swells of a distant mega-storm, three thousand miles of ocean fetch hit that rock spine beneath the bridge and can throw walls of water 100–120 feet high that will carry away anything on the bridge, and indeed (as has happened more than once) the bridge itself. It's a dramatic photo viewpoint at any time, and to see it in bad weather can lead to incredible shots. It can also lead to involuntary suicide if you venture too far out on the bridge. The Glass Window, in rough weather, has claimed victims almost every year.

Moving on to Central and South Eleuthera

SPANISH WELLS TO CURRENT CUT

This is a short, simple run of 7.29 nm from waypoint SPNWS on a heading of 099°M, which takes you safely to the west of Meeks Patch (MEEKP) and the Lobster Cays. You'll have no problems picking up the houses of The Current as a landmark, and Current Cut comes up (although it's well hidden at the start) about 0.5 nm south of The Current (CURCW).

CURRENT CUT

Current Cut West		
CURCW	25° 24' 27"/459 N	076° 48' 02"/040 W
Current Cut East		
CURCE	25° 23' 00"/000 N	076° 47' 15"/250 W

Current Cut is your Panama Canal to take you directly (or as directly as you can go) from Spanish Wells to Hatchet Bay. Current Cut looks rather like a canal when you first see

Current Cut, from the west.

it, broader than you thought it might be, and has dark blue water, which is always reassuring. It carries a tidal flow well-known in diving circles as giving you the greatest drift dive ever. As a diver you're rocketed totally out of control through the Cut at 6 knots or more, with an escort of fish who seem very much in control of their destinies.

Up on the surface you may have to contend with the full force of the tidal current and wind, and if you've not got the power to punch through it, you may regret taking Current Cut. The best time is slack water, and make it high tide, for you have shallows to cross on the east side. The tide in Current mouth is reckoned to be the same as Nassau (with Spanish Wells running 30 minutes after Nassau).

Other than taking these simple precautions, you'll have no problems in the Cut. We had 37 feet of water almost all the way. Just stay in the middle of the blue, and you'll realize that you're favoring the north side of the Cut. The mailboat dock is one certain indication that the deep channel runs that way. If you have wind against tide (not at all the best time to try to punch you way through) you'll see broken water and tide rips. Read what the surface patterns tell you, and get through the turbulence as directly, and as quickly, as you can.

- Pass the concrete dock where *Current Pride*, the mailboat ties up, and look out for two low rocks at the edge of the water, and then a sand track leading due north. Once you've passed these markers you're ready to turn south to pass to the east of the chain of barren cays lying just offshore to the south of Current Cut.

- You're in shallows here, and you must read the water and choose your path, heading to our Current Cut east waypoint (CURCE), which lies just north of the small bay that will open up to starboard. Then you're clear to set your course for Hatchet Bay.

It goes without saying that the Current Cut part of this passage from Spanish Wells to Hatchet Bay is visual. Our waypoints are useful for checking your position but *not* for navigation. One final note. As you pass through the Cut on a high tide you may see a fishing boat anchored on the east side, bow into the tidal flow, with its nets spread like welcoming arms. The fish, who to the diver seemed so certain that they had their environment checked out and under control, may yet meet their nemesis.

CURRENT CUT TO HATCHET BAY

A straightforward course of 105°M held for 16 nm will place you just off the entrance to Hatchet Bay (HTCHT), ready to make your way down the line of the coast for a mile or so, picking up landmarks. For a long time you'll have seen the Glass Window bridge off to port, and you'll pick up Gregory Town with no difficulty, and a scattering of houses to the south of it.

Hatchet Bay hides itself behind its cliffs and its narrow entrance, but its Batelco tower is a giveaway. A more interesting "lead-in" mark are the strange grey concrete silos on the spine of the island that are some 3 miles north of Hatchet Bay by road. A souvenir of a failed cattle-raising venture, these towers, set above the limestone cliff on a plateau of verdant green, can't fail to catch your eye. First three pairs become apparent, then later, about 2 nm off the final waypoint we give, another three silos come into view. They look like the remains of some vast prehistoric center of worship, a Bahamian stonehenge. By the time you've come to this conclusion you are off the entrance to Hatchet Bay, a light on a mast to port, some scruffy casuarinas to starboard, and that Batelco tower briefly in your gunsights before you lose sight of it as you straighten up to pass into the harbor.

We'll cover Hatchet Bay in the next section under **Central and South Eleuthera**.

Spanish Wells sunset.

Central and South Eleuthera

AS we said at the beginning of this Guide in **Where to Go? A Cruising Ground Analysis**, Eleuthera presents problems for the cruising visitor. Long and thin, Eleuthera has two coasts, the east (Atlantic) coast and the west (Eleuthera Bight) coast. The Atlantic coast has no shelter, near continuous offshore reefs, and, as we said in that analysis, isn't a cruising ground. As for the west coast, it has only three, true, all-weather havens: Hatchet Bay, Cape Eleuthera Marina, and Davis Harbour. In between there are places like Pelican Cay, Governor's Harbour, and Rock Sound where you can find some kind of shelter. If the prevailing southeast winds hold steady, you have no problems cruising along the west coast of Eleuthera, and you can safely anchor off most of the small villages. In unsettled weather you have just those three "safe" harbors as your safety net.

Eleuthera too presents real problems if you want to see the island. Unlike a small cay that can be covered in a day with some walking, Eleuthera's 110-mile length means that even if you carve it up into bite-sized chunks, you'll need wheels to get around. Renting a car for an entire day is one solution, and then doing the island from top to bottom. Having said this, we go for the bite-sized chunks, but this increases the cost. Whatever you decide, there are places to see and the Eleutheran landscape, and its small villages, have a character of their own.

We particularly like Unique Village at North Palmetto Point. The nearby hotel (which carries the same name) faces a pink beach that rivals Harbour Island's, and offers refreshment in a gazebo-like restaurant-bar set high over the Atlantic beach with a 180-degree view of ocean and reef. In all our travels we must admit we failed in one objective and that was to reach the lighthouse at Eleuthera Point, the south tip of the island. The road running south from Bannerman Town gets worse and worse and you soon find yourself driving over limestone ridges through a tunnel of scrub, barely as wide as the car. If we had no conscience we might have let the rental car take it, but after a realis-

tic assessment of the car's tires, suspension, steering, and probable mechanical reliability, and the fun factor if we had to walk back miles to Bannerman Town, we quit.

In this way the big island geographic factor does suggest that Eleuthera is not what we'd call a cruising ground in its own right, a destination (like the Abacos) that's enough in

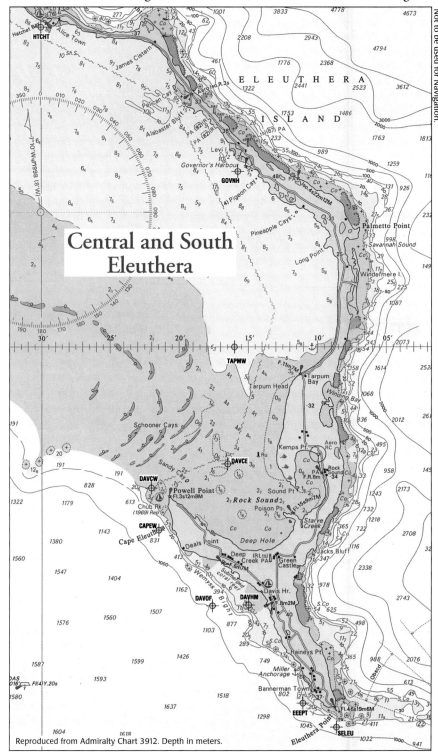

Central and South
Eleuthera

Reproduced from Admiralty Chart 3912. Depth in meters.

itself to occupy your cruising time. But if you're making your way from the Abacos to the Exumas, or southward to Cat Island, don't neglect Eleuthera.

Hatchet Bay

Hatchet Bay Harbour

Hatchet Bay Harbour was man-made, formed by cutting through the limestone cliff to form an entrance into a hitherto landlocked pond, thus giving the developing Hatchet Bay cattle-raising project a harbor it could use. The entrance to Hatchet Bay, kept well concealed from you by the cliffs, looks forbidding at first sight, far too narrow, but has good width (90 feet) and good depth (10 feet). Once inside swing easily around to starboard and head toward the two silver-colored propane tanks, favoring that far side of the east half of the harbor rather than the little island you'll leave to port. The Alice Town dock to starboard is not for you, nor the commercial dock (where *Current Pride* will secure), which lies on your starboard bow as you straighten to run up the harbor.

Your choices lie either with securing alongside the concrete wall of Marine Services of Eleuthera (if they have space), taking up one of their moorings, or anchoring. If you can get space alongside, they have shore power but little else. There's one shower.

You may find, if you're secured there, that opportunist teenagers and young adults try to touch you for money ("to help with school" or "to feed my children"). This is the only place in the Bahamas where this has happened to us. Other cruising visitors have found it so too. The "feeding chil-

Pineapple Festival stall in Gregory Town.

dren" request was made at 11 p.m. one night when the Harbour View Restaurant disco was in full swing, and the credibility of the request was questionable, to say the least. More disturbingly, while we were there two incidents of theft occurred. Oars were taken from a dinghy (the report had it that "it was only boys who were building rafts," but the oars were never recovered). The other theft was a backpack containing passports and money, left for a few minutes in a dinghy secured alongside the wall, while the owner was enquiring about a promised rental car.

Being inside Hatchet Bay Harbour is rather like finding yourself inside the flooded rim of a volcano. It's a strange feeling and the sense of security that should come with 360-degree protection is somewhat mitigated by the Hurricane *Andrew* wrecks still visible on the foreshore. Like all enclosed harbors it becomes hot during the day, it does not cleanse itself (we wouldn't use a watermaker there), and, come the evening, we hit the highest marks we've ever achieved on insect attraction.

Looking around it is clear that Hatchet Bay has seen better days, and shows every sign of being locked into a steady downslide. Yes, there is potential there, but it remains that the geographic advantages of Hatchet Bay, in terms of location and general protection, are almost totally negated by the way it looks and feels when you get in there. From Hatchet Bay to Governor's Harbour (GOVNH) is 15 nm on a heading of 125°M.

HATCHET BAY HINTERLAND

Hatchet Bay and Alice Town appear to have merged into a single Hatchet Bay identity. There's little in the village, in truth, to attract the particular interest of the cruising visi-

CENTRAL AND SOUTH ELEUTHERA		
Hatchet Bay		
HTCHT	25° 20' 32"/532 N	076° 29' 40"/665 W
Governor's Harbour		
GOVNH	25° 12' 00"/000 N	076° 16' 00"/000 W
Tarpum Bay		
TAPMW	25° 00' 00"/000 N	076° 16' 05"/085 W
Cape Eleuthera Marina		
CAPEM	24° 50' 15"/245 N	076° 21' 12"/204 W
Cape Eleuthera West		
CAPEW	24° 48' 13"/224 N	076° 21' 43"/720 W
Davis Harbour		
DAVOF	24° 43' 49"/816 N	076° 17' 50"/833 W
Davis Harbour Entry Marker (not for navigation)		
DAVHM	24° 43' 49"/816 N	076° 15' 05"/085 W
Eleuthera East End Point		
EEEPT	24° 37' 18"/310 N	076° 11' 02"/041 W
South Eleuthera		
SELEU	24° 35' 37"/615 N	076° 08' 44"/731 W

The final figures in each waypoint show seconds (00") and thousands (000) of a minute.

Governor's Harbour.

tor. If you want to see something of Eleuthera, your choice is to take a taxi or rent a car. Take care to find someone to keep an eye on your boat while you're away touring, or make certain that you have secured anything that might be tempting and removable.

Taking the main Eleuthera highway, if you go north through the silo country you can see Gregory Town and the Glass Window. You are also in a region of caves. You see one cave as you enter Hatchet Bay, on the cliff wall near the propane tanks. There are other, extensive caves in the limestone spine of the island in this part of Eleuthera, and a local guide can take you to them.

Going south of Hatchet Bay you find more abandoned gray concrete silos, grassland run wild, and scrub vegetation. It doesn't seem Bahama-like at all, but Eleuthera is in many ways atypical of the Bahama Islands. Some three miles south of Hatchet Bay you come to the Rainbow Inn, sitting on the low cliffs overlooking a shallow bight and a little island called Rainbow Cay. It is, by reputation, the "only" place to eat in the area. While not strictly true, the Rainbow Inn attracts tourists in its own right and is far from being solely dependent on cruising visitors. Further south the road takes you into Governor's Harbour, first going past its airport and Pelican Cay. Finally, if you want ocean beaches, the east coast, not a cruising ground as we know, has some beaches highly prized by surfers.

You might wonder at the lack of any development taking advantage of Hatchet Bay, which is arguably the only good "natural" harbor in Eleuthera. The reason seems to lie in that when the cattle-raising scheme failed in the 1970s, the land passed into the hands of the Bahamian Department of Agriculture. Wheels can turn slowly in governments

anywhere and, perhaps understandably, agriculture is rarely a torch bearer in promoting concrete development schemes. Despite proposals that cover the full range of options from resort hotels with golf courses to grand marinas, Hatchet Bay has remained locked in a time warp.

PELICAN CAY

Pelican Cay, which you'll pass on your way south, lies close to the coast just off Governor's Harbour Airport. It offers usable shelter from the west if the wind turns against you, but is no place you would wish to stay. Go around the south tip of Pelican Cay to find deep water, for behind the north end it's shallow, and in the center Pelican is almost joined to the mainland. If you do make use of Pelican Cay, even if you dinghy in to the shore there's nowhere (other than the airport) you can reach on foot.

Governor's Harbour

Governor's Harbour, despite its impressive name, is no harbor and has no facilities for visiting yachts. The holding off the main bay is poor to potentially disastrous, perhaps 2 feet of sand over hard rock, and no anchor will stay fixed there under stress. Levy Island offers two anchoring spots, one close to the island and one close to the mainland, but check the wind direction. What appears to be a third potential anchorage, tucking yourself under the southeast wing of Cupid Cay is not a valid option. It's shallow, the sea area is narrow, and Bird Cay offers little protection. In short, if the wind is from the southeast and is staying there, Governor's Harbour is fine. If not, don't risk it. Go to Hatchet Bay and take a taxi to get to Governor's Harbour.

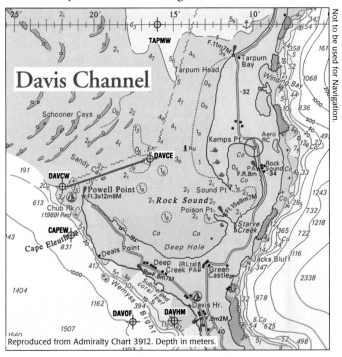

Reproduced from Admiralty Chart 3912. Depth in meters.

As we've indicated, Governor's Harbour does not feature on our list of safe anchorages, but it can be a calculated risk in settled weather. Much depends on the weight of metal you put down. Nonetheless it is an attractive and photogenic place, and one way or another, you should see it. Most things you might want are there, and there's even a dive shop, but they don't run a boat. They reckon there's nowhere safe to keep it. A run of 12 nm on 180°M will take you south from Governor's Harbour to our Tarpum Bay (TAPMW) waypoint.

TARPUM BAY

Tarpum Bay is very shallow and exposed to wind and weather over an arc of 180 degrees. Tarpum itself has very little to offer the cruising visitor that cannot be more safely and easily achieved in a rental car. We don't recommend it as an anchorage, and the Tarpum Bay dock is totally off limits on depth alone. A run of 7.5 nm on a heading of 185°M takes you from our TAPMW waypoint to the eastern entry to the Davis Channel. Alternatively you may wish to head southeast from this point and visit Rock Sound.

THE DAVIS CHANNEL

Davis Channel East		
DAVCE	24° 52' 27"/457 N	076° 16' 45"/755 W
Davis Channel South Sandbar Marker (Obelisk) (not for navigation)		
OBLSK	24° 51' 25"/414 N	076° 19' 36"/611 W
Davis Channel West		
DAVCW	24° 51' 06"/101 N	076° 21' 44"/735 W

Not entirely content with our First Edition treatment of the Davis Channel, we decided to re-run it and set some new waypoints. This was prompted in part by the restoration of the southern marker on the sand running parallel to the coast to the east of Powell Point, which is now a handsome stone marker. Coming down from the north, around our DAVCE waypoint, you are in some 15 feet of water, with scattered coral around that is easily seen. The Davis Channel at the start seems indeterminate, hardly a visible channel at all, but in time the sand marking the northern and southern limits becomes more visible, and the color of the water takes on a more positive indication of being deeper water.

From our DAVCE waypoint you have 4.7 nm to run on a heading of 253°M to bring you to our DAVCW waypoint. Your route takes you 0.26 nm due north of the new obelisk marker. By the time you are level with the obelisk it's obvious that you're in a channel, and gradually the water will take on a blue coloration, rather than a Banks green. To the north you'll see the Schooner Cays, which are clearly visible.

At DAVCW swing around gently to our CAPEM waypoint. You're then set to carry on toward the Exumas, or enter one of the South Eleuthera marinas.

If you're coming from the south, after you round that CAPEM waypoint you'll see what appears to be a bluewater channel off your starboard bow, which can be easily taken as the Davis Channel. If you turned at this point, which would be turning on to something like 065°M, you'd find yourself running south (rather than north) of the sand with the obelisk marker, and you'd eventually run into shallows and coral. The vital thing, coming into the Davis Channel from this direction, is to continue on for that DAVCW waypoint, and then turn to head for DAVCE. Your course, at that point, will be around 073°M. That southern "look-alike" channel can be deceptive coming up from the south.

ROCK SOUND

Rock Sound, which at first sight on a chart or a map looks as if it ought to be the ideal all-weather haven, other than in strong winds from the south, sadly fails to live up to its first promise. It's shallow, and your entry has to be made in a gentle curve in to the southeast favoring Poison Point (the south entry arm) rather than Sound Point (in the north) for there are coral heads that you must avoid. When you get closer in to Rock Sound itself, there's really nowhere to go. You can anchor off. The one-time choice spot used to be off Edwina Burrow's restaurant and bungalows to the north of the Government Dock but Edwina's place, which has some shops and a bank nearby, has closed, and the main reason for going there no longer exists. It's shallow off that jetty, and we wouldn't feel easy lying there for any length of time or even through a night.

South of the Government Dock there's a wooden jetty (the old Government Dock) right by the Harbour View restaurant. Tying up to the T of the jetty (the main run is too shallow on each side) brings no facilities and a depth that when we were there at one time had a sailboat bumping the bottom at low water (5 feet perhaps, less at extreme tides),

Ocean Hole, with Janet.

as well as bouncing to an unseasonable south wind. After looking at it in every way, and covering the shore side, we've concluded that unless you have some compelling reason to visit Rock Sound, we've seen little there that would persuade us to highlight it as a cruising destination.

This said, we counted six sailboats and one power boat anchored off while we were last there. Clearly some find Rock Sound attractive. Certainly you can find most of the necessities you might require. Just remember to dinghy in to the Government Dock (that's the north, concrete dock) if you want to clear in (which is unlikely), or need fuel, liquor, provisions, a laundromat, or to get your e-mail. Dinghy in to the wood dock (to the south, the one-time Government Dock), if you want the Harbour View Restaurant, or to see the Ocean Hole, which is within walking distance. But see our **Yellow Pages**.

Just be aware how shallow Rock Sound is over much of its area. Viewed from the air the scrape marks showing the entry tracks of many visitors is the most prominent feature of the sea bed. Larger craft, such as a mailboat, will generate a plume of sand like a contrail marking its course for as much as half an hour after its passing.

Cape Eleuthera and the South

Cape Eleuthera Marina
Cape Eleuthera Marina and its linked residential complex was allowed to go to ruin in the mid 1980s. It joins the list of the almost inexplicable Bahamian development failures. It could be one of the most attractive marinas in the Bahamas. Like West End, it has the twin benefits of a strategic geographic position (which in Cape Eleuthera's case would make it a natural port of call for virtually all traffic on the Exumas–Eleuthera–Abaco route), and a superb site. This

Rock Sound, South Eleuthera.

apart, its design is outstanding, a well-protected circular harbor, well laid out, and with a tidal through-flow (aided by a well-placed canal) that keeps it as clean as ocean water.

The sadness is that other than shore power (50A sockets only), water, and fuel, there's nothing there. Jungle-like scrub and bush have overtaken everything built around the marina, and now even the docks (concrete finger piers) are deteriorating. Across the marina area are a small lineup of townhouse condos, all that remains inhabited, huddled together looking beleaguered, rather like the last soldiers to remain on their feet at Custer's Last Stand. The condo owners have cars. You, without a car, are miles from anywhere, even the nearest restaurant.

The entry channel has 12 feet at Low Water, and the fuel dock has just 6 feet, but otherwise Cape Eleuthera Marina is satisfactorily deep all over. On entering and leaving be careful of a ledge that extends out from the north entry arm and don't cut this turn too close. Line up well out and run straight in, and on leaving keep going straight until that ledge falls away.

We hear expressions of high hopes for the future of the marina, but as yet nothing that we would consider as the clear evidence of coming change. In the meantime the concrete docks continue to deteriorate, year by year, and yet we remain convinced that its site and planning rate it as one of the best-positioned and best-designed marinas in the Bahamas.

Davis Harbour Marina
Davis Harbour is hard to locate offshore. After you've gone around Cape Eleuthera stay out in deep water, and for safety pass perhaps 1.5–2 nm off Bamboo Point as you head south to avoid the rocks lying 1 nm south of Bamboo Point. After passing the line of Latitude 24° 45' 00 N you're OK to start closing toward the shore, aiming at the waypoint we show for the Davis Harbour Marina approach (DAVOF).

You won't see the outlying Davis Harbour marker (DAVHM) until you're almost on top of it, and your first landmarks are the Deep Creek Batelco mast (some 2.5 nm north of Davis Harbour), a wrecked boat on a beach to the north of Davis Harbour, and a dense clump of casuarinas masking the harbor. The marker, when you pick it up, is a small red radar reflector on a white post planted on a large isolated coral head. By then you're going to be in 25 feet of water shoaling to 16 feet or less, and there are a number of isolated coral heads all around.

The Davis Harbour entrance, which bears 070°–075°M from the marker, should be obvious at this point. There's a double line of stakes marking the entrance and a Shell sign that shows against the trees, as well as a white painted signal mast. At regular MLW the entry channel has 3.5 feet, but during "Moon Tides" that can reduce to just 3 feet. The shallowest point is just before the first two markers. We sug-

Davis Harbour.

Moving on from South Eleuthera

South Eleuthera to Cat Island
Eleuthera (our waypoint SELEU) is a good jumping-off point for Cat Island. You're closer there than you'll be anywhere else, and Little San Salvador makes a good stop on your way, either for a break or for a more extended visit. But see our note under **Little San Salvador** in **The Out Islands North of the Tropic of Cancer** on page 274.

South Eleuthera to the Exumas
Either Cape Eleuthera Marina or Davis Harbour Marina makes an ideal departure waypoint for the Exumas, giving you single-leg runs straight across the deep water of Exuma Sound. Your choices in landfall extend virtually the entire length of the Exuma chain. For most people the destination normally lies between the Ship Channel to the north of Ship Channel Cay (a distance of some 25 nm from Cape Eleuthera) to Conch Cut, just north of Staniel Cay (some 35 nm). There are three or four other cuts lying between these two passes, and as there are so many options open to you we cover landfall waypoints under **The Exuma Cays** on page 229.

An Alternative Route Back to Nassau
If you choose to return to Nassau from Eleuthera and for some reason you don't wish to take the Current Cut–Little Egg Island route to gain the deep water of the Northeast Providence Channel, there is an alternative route. From Governor's Harbour or Hatchet Bay set a direct course for a point north of the south tip of Current Island. Get close to the shore of Current Island, in deep water, before you turn south to round the tip of the island, for there's a sand bar there, running out to the southeast from the end of Current Island.

Once you're around the island, if you want to anchor overnight, stay in deep water, turn north, and choose your spot between Current Island and the main Pimlico Island, just off the beach. Don't work too far to the north. There's a strong reversing tidal current there and you must set two anchors. If you don't want to stop, or when you're ready to move on, head toward the center of Little Pimlico Island, then parallel the coast of Little Pimlico running southwest until you've cleared its southern rock. Then head northeast into deep water and you're all set.

Unless the sun is right and conditions are good for eyeball navigation, we would not go this way. Apart from the sand we've mentioned, there is continuing reef, barely awash at low water, to the south of the deeper water lying immediately south of Little Pimlico, and it would be easy to find yourself temporarily trapped in a kind of sand-and-reef-locked swimming pool. With high water, and good visibility, you should have no problems. Just probe forward cautiously. Or take your dinghy and prove it first.

gest you check with the dockmaster on VHF 16 if you are in any doubt about the state of the tide. Inside the harbor you have 6–8 feet.

Davis Harbour Marina is not attractive to the eye, and does not clean itself well. This said, as a place to berth your boat you have power, water, fuel, restrooms, and showers. On this account it beats Cape Eleuthera. The downside is that like Cape Eleuthera you really are in the boonies there, miles from anywhere, and there's no restaurant at the marina. However there's a restaurant that will deliver pizzas within walking distance. See our **Yellow Pages**. All said, you may not want to spend days there, but Davis Harbour is a good passage stop (better than Cape Eleuthera Marina, as we've said, in its facilities at the time we write), and, if you're fishing, a good base for that area. And that wins it regular, in some cases constant, use by sports fishermen.

Bannerman Town and Princess Cay
We give this Eleuthera east end point (EEEPT) as a waypoint to satisfy your curiosity if you are on passage along the western coast of South Eleuthera. Just north of Bannerman Town you will see a blaze of glowing salmon red roofs, what appears to be two breakwaters, and behind them two blazes of brilliant white sand beach, lined with sun loungers. Behind, on the beachfront are three complexes of huts or houses. This is the "desert island" port-of-call of the Princess Cruise Line. Their ships anchor off for a day, and ferry their passengers ashore to soak up the sun, play with every conceivable water toy, eat, and drink.

YELLOW PAGES

SPANISH WELLS

Named for the Spanish galleons that were believed to have stopped here to take on fresh water, Spanish Wells has a long association with the sea. There are still many descendants of the early loyalist settlers among the nearly 1,500 people living in this premier Bahamian fishing port. Seventy percent of the annual Bahamian lobster harvest is caught by the Spanish Wells fishing fleet, who have to travel far afield to find them now.

Neat and tidy houses are surrounded by colorful gardens, carefully tended, many with prolific fruit trees and English and desert roses blooming side by side between the garden ornaments. Everything is very orderly here. All the shops close on Sundays and it shares the distinction, with Man-O-War Cay in Abaco, of having no liquor store on the island. There is a friendly rivalry between Spanish Wells and the other northern island off Eleuthera: Harbour Island views Spanish Wells as quiet and unsophisticated; Spanish Wells regards Harbour Island as a busy tourist town, while they are hardworking fisherfolk making their own way in the world without the need for the tourist dollar. Both islands have their pluses and minuses—we enjoy them both for their very different aspects.

There is an idyllic beach on the northeast side of the island that is easily accessible from any part of the main road running through Spanish Wells. It is reasonably sheltered and has good snorkeling off the reef further out, but otherwise it is just sand and crystal-clear shallow water. There are also good beaches on the northern tip of St. George's Cay, and all along the north side of Russell Island. Spanish Wells is a Port of Entry. **Customs** and **Immigration** are located in the same building as the post office.

MARINA

SPANISH WELLS YACHT HAVEN
Tel: 242-333-4255 • Fax: 333-4649 • VHF 16
This is one of the friendliest, safest, and most efficient marinas anywhere in the islands. From Anthony the dockmaster's welcome greeting, to help in docking and a quick smile, to all the back-up facilities of a busy fishing port if you need repairs or parts, everything is done to make you feel at home here. The covered storage shed makes it a good place to leave your boat if you need to return home for a few days in the middle of your cruising vacation.

Slips	40
Max LOA	100 ft.
MLW at Dock	5 ft.
Dockage	85¢ per ft. per day.
Storage	Covered storage available.
Power	35¢ per kWh for 50A and 30A.
Fuel	Diesel and gasoline, 5-percent surcharge on credit cards used for fuel.
Propane	From *Pinder's Tune Up* garage (333-4262), on Samuel Guy Street straight up over the hill behind the marina.
Water	15¢ per gallon for reverse osmosis and city water.
Telephone	Card phone behind the office.
TV	Hookup available for $5 per day.
Showers	Yes, $2.50 per boat for 2 people. Key from the office.
Laundry	Washers and dryers for marina guests only, $2 tokens for each machine from the office, open 8 to 5 daily.
Restaurant	Open for lunch from noon to 2 pm, and for dinner from 6:30 to 9 pm daily, except Saturdays, when dinner continues until 10 pm. Good, simple home cooking using fresh ingredients.
Bar	Open from noon until closing.
Store	*Uncle Mike's Lil General Store* at the marina has a selection of snacks, sodas, water, and some pharmacy items, and is open 10 am to 10 pm Monday to Thursday, to 11 pm on Saturdays. Closed Sundays.
Ice	$3 for a small bag, $6 for a large bag.
Swimming	Salt-water pool for marina guests, due to be remodeled in 1999 using fresh water.
Bicycles	$6 for a half day, $10 for full day, available from Leroy Kelly at the office.
Library	A small selection of books to exchange in the office.
Accommodations	Three air-conditioned rooms and two apartments available with satellite TV. The rooms are quite simple, but clean. There are plans for refurbishment during 1999.
Credit cards	Visa, MasterCard, Amex, and Esso.
Dockmaster	Anthony Bethel is a most pleasant and helpful dockmaster.
Manager	Leroy Kelly, with Angela and Cassandra in the office.

MOORINGS

There are nine moorings off the east end of the island, owned jointly by Edsel Roberts and Bradley Newbold. They are good and strong and cost $8 per night. Call Edsel on VHF 16 "Dolphin" or Bradley on VHF 16 "Cinnabar" if you need to pick one up. Since both these gentlemen are experienced pilots, they may well be out guiding people around the Devil's Backbone, or to or from Harbour Island, but their wives will always answer your questions.

MARINE SERVICES

Chris Electronics on the Main Road   Tel: 333-4638   Call Jane Forsythe to arrange for all types of electronic problem solving. They will come out to your boat if necessary.

On Site Marine and Auto Service   Tel: 333-4382 • Fax: 333-4772 • VHF 16   Charlie Pinder and Charlie Sands can help you with diesel engines, generators, auto pilots, watermakers, winches, pumps, exhaust systems, and marine plumbing.

Ronald's Service Centre on the waterfront   Tel: 333-4021 • Fax: 333-4594 • VHF 16   Diving and marine supplies, fuel, Johnson outboards, apartments to rent on the beach, and fresh fish for sale.

Spanish Wells Marine and Hardware Store on the waterfront   Tel: 333-4122   The best-stocked marine store in the Out Islands. Open 8 am to noon, and 1 to 5 pm, Monday to Saturday, but they monitor VHF 16 and will stay open late in an emergency. They can repair Mercury and Mariner engines and have hauling facilities for boats up to 30 ft. There are also four air-conditioned apartments above the store, which can be rented for $55 per day, and $330 per week.

Boat Yard
R&B Boatyard   Tel: 333-4462   Diesel and gasoline, electricity, showers, and boat storage, as well as a marine railway extending into the harbor that can haul very large boats.

PILOTS

for *The Devil's Backbone*
Due to the very complicated route through the reefs as you go around to Harbour Island, it really is a good idea to take a

pilot with you, at least the first time. We suggest you contact one. Edsel Roberts and Bradley Newbold have more than 20 years experience each.

Edsel Roberts	VHF 16 "Dolphin"
Bradley Newbold	VHF 16 "Cinnabar"
A1 Broadshad	VHF 16 "A1"
David Roberts	VHF 16 "Blue Marlin"
Woody Perry	VHF 16 "Little Woody"

SERVICES AND SHOPPING IN SPANISH WELLS

Bakery
Kathy's Bakery on the main road, across from *Spanish Wells Food Fair* Tel: 333-4405 Wonderful fresh bread and baked goods.

Cecile Dunnam Tel-333-4596 Cakes and bread.

Beryl Pinder Tel: 333-4259 Breads.

Gloris Roberts, Edsel's wife Tel: 333-4209 • VHF 16 "Dolphin"
Makes delicious bread, which keeps well and makes good toast.

Bank
Royal Bank of Canada Open 9 am to 3 pm on Monday, to 1 pm on Tuesday, Wednesday, and Thursday. Fridays 9 am to 5 pm. Visa accepted for cash.

Churches
Gospel Chapel
Methodist Church
People's Church

Clinic
On the main road, across from the *Food Fair*
Tel: 333-4064/5145 A general practice clinic with 24-hour emergency service. Open 9 am to noon and 1 to 5:30 pm Monday to Friday. There is a nurse full time, and the doctor comes in once a week on Thursdays.

Customs
Located above the post office, next to the school, but they can be called to the *Yacht Haven* to clear you in.

Dentist
Dr. Mark Davies Tel: 333-4609

Dive Shop
Manuel's Dive Station, half a block west of *Generation Gap* on Main Street Tel: 333-4495 Taken over by Edmund Pinder, who sells masks, fins, compressors, tanks, spears, hooks, wetsuits, etc. There is no recreational dive facility on Spanish Wells.

Doctor
Dr. Stephen Bailey Tel and Fax: 333-4868/4869
He practices from home, with his own laboratory, EKG, etc..

Fishing
Ask any of the pilots listed for advice or if they can take you out fishing. Both *A1 Broadshad* (333-4427 and VHF 16) and *Woody Perry* (333-4433 and VHF 16 "Little Woody") specialize in deep sea, reef, and bonefishing.

Fresh Fish
Ronald's Service Centre Tel: 333-4021/4022 Has fresh fish most days. Closed on Sundays.

Groceries
CW's Groceries Tel: 333-4856 In the same building as the old *Captain's Diner* on Central Street. Open 9 am to noon and 1 to 6 pm daily except Sundays. A convenient little corner store.

Pinder's Supermarket on the harborfront Tel: 333-4048 Open 9 am to noon and 1:30 to 5 pm on Monday, Tuesday, Thursday, and Friday. Open 9 am to noon on Wednesday, and 9 am to 6 pm on Saturday. Well stocked, with some fresh fruit and vegetables, and they will deliver for you.

Spanish Wells Food Fair and Pharmacy Tel: 333-4675 • VHF 16
On the west end of Central Street. Open 8 am to 5 pm Monday, Thursday, and Friday, to 6 pm on Saturdays. The pharmacy is closed all day Wednesday, and the whole store closes at noon on Wednesdays and all day Sunday. Excellent choice of well-stocked groceries, meats, fresh fruit, and vegetables; one of the best selections in the Out Islands, comparable with many small US supermarkets. Free delivery service.

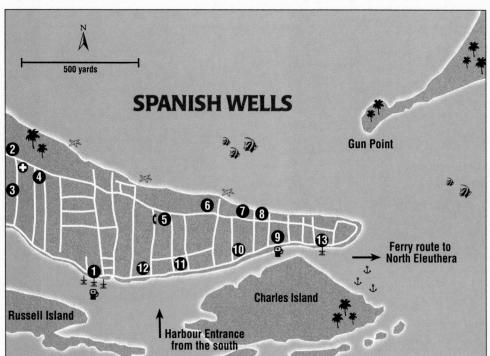

SPANISH WELLS DIRECTORY

1. Spanish Wells Yacht Haven
2. Spanish Wells Food Fair and Pharmacy
3. Adventurer's Resort
4. Pinder's Tune-Up for propane
5. Batelco
6. Museum
7. Post Office; Customs
8. Spanish Wells Furniture Company
9. Ronald's Service Centre
10. Pinder's Supermarket
11. Spanish Wells Marine and Hardware
12. Jack's Outback
13. Public Dock
⛽ Fuel
✚ Clinic

Laundromat
There are still apartments to rent, and a laundromat, in the old *Captain's Diner* building on Central Road. For marina guests, the *Spanish Wells Yacht Haven* has a good laundromat.

Liquor Store
There is no liquor store in Spanish Wells. The nearest one is at Gene's Bay, at the dock where the ferry leaves for North Eleuthera.

Museum
Spanish Wells Museum Next to the *Islander Shop* in a Spanish Wellsian house; ask at the shop to open up. Fascinating insight into the life and history of this island. Admission $5.

Pharmacy
Spanish Wells Food Fair and Pharmacy George is the only pharmacist in the whole of Eleuthera, and the pharmacy in the store is open the same hours as the *Food Fair*, except for Wednesdays when he takes a day off. The store is also closed on Sundays.

Police
Tel: 333-4030 On Central Road, next to the All-Age school.

Post Office
In the government building next to the All-Age School, open 9 am to 5:30 pm, Monday to Friday.

Propane
Pinder's Tune Up garage on Samuel Guy Street. Tel: 333-4262

Shopping
The Islander Shop Tel: 333-4104 Open 9 am to noon and 1 to 5:30 pm daily except Sundays, with a great selection of clothing, swimsuits, souvenirs, T-shirts, notions, and greeting cards.
Lynette's Tel: 333-2405 Open 9 am to 5 pm, Monday to Friday, to 6 pm on Saturday. Jewelry, watches, clothing, and accessories.
Three Sisters Variety Store Tel: 333-4618 Open 9 am to 5 pm Monday to Saturday. Clothes, gifts, swimwear, and T-shirts.

Taxi
Pinder's Taxi Service Tel: 333-4068/4041 For transport to and from North Eleuthera airport.

Telephone
Batelco has a telephone outside the office on Central Street, which is open from 9 am to 4:30 pm.

RESTAURANTS & BARS

Anchor Snack Bar On the harborfront. Open daily from 9 am to 10 pm, closed 3 to 5 pm, serving snacks and entrees. Busy on Saturday and Sunday with local people.
Jack's Outback Tel: 333-4219 On the waterfront, east of the *Yacht Haven* and west of the anchorage and moorings. Open 9 am to 4 pm for breakfast and lunch, and at 6 pm for dinner. Reasonably priced, delicious, home-cooked food. Good atmosphere in simple, friendly surroundings. Fantastic fresh lobster in season.

Janet Wilson

Generation Gap On the main road. Open 10 am to 2 pm with an arcade that looks like an American diner in the '50s, and 7 to 11 pm in the dining room. Catering mainly to the young with lots of loud music.
L & B Cookouts on Saturday nights Tel: 333-4681 Call ahead to order barbeque dinners.
The Restaurant at *Spanish Wells Yacht Haven* Open for lunch from noon to 2 pm and for dinner from 6:30 to 9 pm daily, except Saturdays when dinner continues with specials until 10 pm. Enjoyed by residents as well as boaters, the simply decorated restaurant is clean and neat, with good home-cooked food served overlooking the marina. There are tables outside and a bar next door that opens up in the afternoons. You can order wine with dinner, but no spirits.

GETTING AROUND

Airport
There is no airport on Spanish Wells; you have to go to North Eleuthera by ferry to Gene's Bay, then by taxi to the airport. The ferry costs $4 from the steps, $5 from the *Yacht Haven,* per person. The taxis waiting at the other side charge $20 to the airport, unless you are leaving on a scheduled flight when a Pinder's Taxi will take you for less if you are sharing. For airline details, see under **North Eleuthera.**

Bicycles
Spanish Wells Yacht Haven Ask Leroy Kelly at the office, which is open from 8 am to 5 pm. $6 per half day, $10 for a full day.

Car Rental and Golf Carts
M & M Car Rentals at *Spanish Wells Furniture Company* Tel: 333-4585 • VHF 16 Open 8 am to 5 pm Monday to Friday, to noon on Saturdays. Golf carts available for $20 per hour, $35 for 3 hours, $50 per day, and $270 per week. If you really need one, cars are available for the same rate.

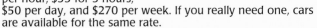
Janet Wilson
Advertisements at the Spanish Wells Ferry.

Ferries
Government ferries run from Spanish Wells to Gene's Bay all day from 7 am to 5:10 pm, costing $4 one way from the steps, and $5 on to the *Yacht Haven*. Call Thad Underwood at 333-4213 or VHF 16.

Mailboat
M/V Eleuthera Express leaves Potter's Cay in Nassau on Thursday at 7 am for Spanish Wells and Harbour Island, and returns to Nassau on Sunday at 1 pm. Fare $20.

Taxis
Anthony and Joanie Tel: 333-4222 • VHF 16 "Buddha"
Pinders Transportation and Taxi Service Tel: 333-4068/4041 Transport between the ferry dock and North Eleuthera Airport, or on to Three Islands Harbour for the Harbour Island ferry.

Water Taxi
Knight Rider Water Taxi Tel: 333-4291 • VHF 16 "Knight Rider" Daniel Higgins will take you across to Gene's Bay, charges the same as the government ferry, and will pick you up from any point.

DIVE SITES

For a complete list of sites in the area, see **Dive Sites** under **Harbour Island**. Fantastic elkhorn coral grow on the reef off Egg Island.

SPORTS

Boat Charters
Ronald's Service Centre Tel: 333-4021 Boat charters and fishing trips.

Diving
Manuel's Dive Store Carries basic diving equipment, but there is no dive center on Spanish Wells since Hurricane *Andrew*. Harbour Island is the nearest source.

Fishing
A-1 Broadshad Tel: 333-4427 • VHF 16 Boat rentals, fishing guide, pilot, and snorkeling.
Captain John Roberts Tel: 333-4171 Offers charters, pilotage, and deliveries.
Spanish Wells Marine and Hardware Store Inquire about fishing trips.

ACCOMMODATIONS

Adventurers Resort Tel: 333-4883 • Fax: 333-5073 Newly rebuilt after Hurricane *Andrew* on the site of the old Harbour Club at the west end of town and within walking distance of the beach, this attractive small hotel has nine rooms, four single apartments, and three double apartments. The rooms are well-equipped and nicely decorated from $75 per night; double apartments, which have two double rooms with their own bathrooms, a third bedroom, and a fully equipped kitchen with living and dining area, are from $150 per night.
Spanish Wells Yacht Haven Tel: 333-4255 • Fax: 333-4649 Three air-conditioned rooms and two apartments with satellite TV, to be refurbished in 1999, from $75 per day.

THINGS TO DO IN SPANISH WELLS

- Go to the Museum; it's one of the best, maybe *the* best, settlement museum in the Bahamas.
- Take time to walk around the whole of Spanish Wells. The houses offer a photo opportunity at every corner.
- Find out about the Spanish Wells lobster industry. If they have time, maybe they will tell you how it works. Spanish Wells is a world leader in the lobster market.

Unloading lobsters, Spanish Wells fishing fleet.

- Ask a Spanish Wells pilot to teach you how to get around the Devil's Backbone Passage.
- Go snorkeling along the northern reef, anywhere from Spanish Wells to Egg Island in the west. There is some of the best elkhorn coral there you will ever see.
- Join in and help quilt, or just chat with the ladies at the Quilting Bee held every afternoon opposite the Museum.

HARBOUR ISLAND

This fabled Bahamian island is known affectionately as "Briland" to several generations of visitors who return each year to their pastel-painted cottages sprinkled like colored Easter eggs throughout the now well-populated island. It has maintained its relaxed and welcoming air, despite the bumper-to-bumper golf carts during holiday periods. Narrow flower-lined streets, artists, and restaurants, boutiques, and straw work in Dunmore Town give way to the quiet luxury of the big resorts lining the edge of the legendary powdery pink sand beach, glowing in the dawn light. Harbour Island is a Port of Entry; the Customs office is in the yellow building on the government pier, but **Customs** and **Immigration** can be called from the marinas if you need to clear in.

MARINAS

VALENTINE'S YACHT CLUB
Tel: 242-333-2142 • Fax: 333-2135 • VHF 16
At the time of writing, work was starting on the rebuilding of the docks, dockmaster's office, bar, dive shop, and showers, which were damaged by fire in February 1999. Great credit goes to the courage of Dockmaster Marcus Pinder and his team who swam out at 2 am to wake up owners and move 28 boats away from the burning docks, with no loss of life or damage to boats. The marina was fully operational again a month later, and the new facilities will be a whole lot better. This marina is particularly enjoyed by sports fishermen and those who prefer to be close to the action of Dunmore Town, with the added benefit of the dive shop and the hotel with its pool, bar, and restaurant across the street.

Slips	39
Max LOA	165 ft.
MLW at Dock	13 ft.
Dockage	$1 per ft. per day.
Power	40¢ per kWh; minimum charge $15 up to 30 ft., $40 per day for boats over 80 ft.
Fuel	Diesel only at the fuel dock.
Propane	Yes, from *Chacara Lumber*.
Water	$10 per day.
Telephone	At the hotel.
TV	Cable hookup available, $12 a day.
Restaurant	Open 7:30 to 10 am for breakfast, noon to 3 pm for lunch and 7:30 to 10 pm for dinner.
Bar	*The Reach Bar* is being rebuilt, and will be open daily for breakfast, lunch, and light dinners until 10 pm.
Ice	$4 per day.
Swimming	Freshwater pool & Jacuzzi at the hotel.
Tennis	One court at the hotel.
Diving	*Valentine's Dive Center* Tel: 333-2309 • VHF 16 • E-Mail: vdc@batelnet.bs Resort dive $75, two-tank dive to sinkhole and bat cave $120, drift dive through Current Cut $75. Rental equipment, Hobie Cats, and Waverunners available from the dive shop.
Fishing	With *Bonefish Joe*; inquire at marina office.
Accommodations	*Valentine's Yacht Club and Inn* Tel: 333-2080/2142 • Fax: 333-2135 Air-conditioned double rooms from $190 per night.
Credit Cards	Visa, MasterCard, and Amex.
Dockmaster	Marcus Pinder

Ruined mansion at Harbour Island Marina.

HARBOUR ISLAND CLUB AND MARINA
Tel and Fax: 242-333-2427 • VHF 16
• E-mail: RAment8072@AOL.com

A delightful, small and quiet, well-run marina, a short walk from the hustle and bustle of Dunmore Town, situated on the southeast part of the island. With its own charmingly decorated bar and restaurant and attractive landscaping that even includes a haunted house, this is definitely a place to relax and enjoy Harbour Island.

Slips	32
Max LOA	18-ft. to 22-ft. beam can be accommodated.
MLW at Dock	10 ft., 15 ft. on outside slips.
Dockage	$1 per ft. per day.
Power	30A and 50A at every slip, 40¢ per kWh.
Fuel	Gas and diesel, fuel dock open daily 8 am to 6 pm. A new 40,000-gallon fuel facility is being installed that will allow "in slip" refueling.
Propane	Available from *Chacara Lumber*.
Water	$10 per day.
Telephone	Yes
Showers	Two good restrooms and showers free to marina guests, located in the main building.
Laundry	Wash, dry, and fold service.
Restaurant	*Devil's Backbone,* open 11:30 am to 7:30 pm, with a Sunset Getaway 5:30 to 7:30 pm on Sundays. The enlarged kitchen will mean extended dining facilities and longer dining hours by the end of 1999.
Groceries	*T & K Grocery* and *Water Depot* is a very short walk from the marina.
Swimming	Pool overlooking the marina.
Diving	*Ocean Fox Diving* Tel: 333-2323 Diving with Jeff Fox.
Accommodations	Guest villas are to be constructed on the property, but meanwhile marina guests are offered a 20-percent discount at the neighboring *Romora Bay Club* (333-2325), only a three-minute walk away.
Credit cards	Visa, MasterCard, and Amex.
Dockmasters	Dick and Gail Ament

SERVICES AND SHOPPING IN DUNMORE TOWN

Bakeries
Arthur's Bakery Tel: 333-2285 Open Monday to Saturday, from 8 am to 5:30 pm. Wonderful fresh bread and cakes with a cafe at the back of the store.

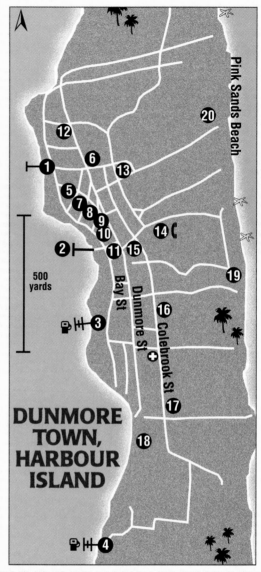

DUNMORE TOWN, HARBOUR ISLAND

DUNMORE TOWN DIRECTORY
1. Fisherman's Dock
2. Government and Ferry Dock
3. Valentine's Yacht Club, Hotel, and Dive Center
4. Harbour Island Marina and Ocean Fox Diving
5. Liquor Store
6. Sawyer's Food Store
7. Dunmore Deli
8. Bank
9. Chacara Lumber for propane
10. Tourist Office
11. The Landing
12. Angela's Starfish
13. Vic Hum's
14. Batelco
15. Post Office
16. Library
17. Ma Ruby's and Tingum Village
18. Romora Bay Club and Dive Shop
19. Runaway Hill Club
20. Pink Sands Hotel
⛽ Fuel
✚ Clinic

Sybill's Bakery Tel: 333-2523 On the corner of Dunmore and Duke Street for the "best baked goods in Briland." Fresh-baked pastries, cake, or donuts under the Royal Poinciana tree during the morning, or fried shrimp with peas and rice, among other good dishes, from 3 pm.

The Landing Hotel and Restaurant Tel: 333-2707 Sourdough bread for $8 a loaf; order the night before you need it.

Bank
Royal Bank of Canada on Murray Street Tel: 333-2250 Open Monday to Thursday 9:30 am to 3 pm, Fridays to 5 pm.

Boutiques
Brilands Androsian Boutique, on King Street, next to *Piggly Wiggly.* Tel: 333-2342 Batiks, souvenirs, T-shirts, and Bahamian-made goods.

Churches
on Dunmore Street:
Blessed Sacrament Catholic Church Sunday services at 9:30 am and 7 pm.

Methodist Church Built in 1843, the largest Out Island church. Sunday services at 11 am and 7 pm.

St Johns's Anglican Episcopal Church Built in 1768, this is not only the oldest building on Harbour Island, it is also the oldest church in the Bahamas. Sunday services at 8 am and 7 pm.

Clinic Tel: 333-2227/3073 The new government clinic is on Colebrook and South Streets, open 9 am to 5 pm Monday to Friday, with a doctor and registered nurse.

Deli
Dunmore Deli on King Street Tel: 333-2644 Open daily 7:30 am to 4 pm. This "must-visit" deli serves light meals at small tables either inside or outdoors, as well as meals to go. Tasty breakfasts, box lunches, and a good place to stock your boat with special treats, which can be delivered to you at the marinas.

E-mail, Internet, Faxes, Copies
Island Services on Dunmore Street Tel: 333-3032 • Fax: 333-3045 Dake Gonzales can help you send or retrieve your e-mail, send faxes, or make phone calls and copies.

Gift Shops
Briland Browser on King Street, whose proceeds go to help the Harbour Island Day Nursery; staffed by volunteers.

Sugar Mill on Bay Street below the tourist office, with a tempting selection.

Miss Mae's on Dunmore Street Open 9 am to 6 pm Monday to Saturday, with beautiful *Whistles* clothes from London, some interesting antiques, and fine, elegant accessories from the Orient.

There are also small stalls along Bay Street selling delicious fresh fish, straw hats, and conch shells.

Groceries
on Dunmore Street:
Johnson's Grocery Tel: 333-2279 Open Monday to Saturday, 7:30 am to 1 pm and 3 to 7 pm, Sundays 8 am to 10 am.

Sawyer's Food Store Tel and Fax: 333-2358 Open Monday to Thursday 8 am to 6 pm, Friday and Saturday to 8 pm, Sunday to 10 pm. A good selection of groceries, boat provisions, fresh meat, frozen foods, and vegetables; they will deliver to your boat.

on King Street:
Piggly Wiggly Food Store and *Tip Top Grocery* offer limited selections of a wide range of goods.

Laundry
Seaside Laundromat on Bay Street
Chris and Carmen's on Dunmore Street. Dry cleaning and pressing.

Library
Sir George Robert Memorial Library on Dunmore Street Open 3:30 to 5 pm daily. A small, well-stocked library with changing photographic exhibitions.

Liquor
Bayside Liquor Store on Bay Street
Briland Booze next to the *Dunmore Deli* on King Street. Open daily except Sundays and holidays, from 9 am to 6:30 pm. Liquors, wines, beers, cigars. Free delivery to boats.

Pharmacy
Harbour Pharmacy Tel: 333-2174 Open Monday to Friday from 9 am to 5:30 pm, except 9 am to 1 pm on Wednesdays, 9 am to 6 pm on Saturdays.

Police
Tel: 333-3111 In the same building as the post office, on Gaol Street!

Post Office
Tel: 333-2315 Open 9 am to 5:30 pm, Monday to Friday, on Gaol Street.

Propane
Tel: 333-2176 *Chacara Lumber* on King Street can refill tanks for you, but only if you have the right connection and are there between 8 am and 1 pm, or 2 and 5 pm, Monday, Tuesday, Thursday, and Friday, or between 8 am and 1 pm or 2 and 4 pm on Saturdays. They close at 1 pm on Wednesdays.

Straw Market
On Bay Street, *Curline, Eva, Patricia, Dorthea, Jacqueline, and Sarah* sell straw work.

Telephones
At the *Batelco* office on the corner of Gaol Lane and Colebrook Street. Open Monday to Friday, 9 am to 4:30 pm.

Tourist Office
Above the *Sugar Mill* gift shop on Bay Street. Good for local maps and information.

Vegetables and Fruit
Patricia's on Pitt Street Tel: 333-2289 Fresh fruits and vegetables, as well as homemade jams, bread, island spices, and hot sauce. Open Monday to Saturday, 7 am to 10 pm; Sunday 7 am to noon, and 1 to 4 pm. No credit cards.

Percenties on Dunmore Street across the street from *Johnsons Grocery* Tel: 333-2195 Open Monday to Saturday, 9 am to 6 pm. Fresh vegetables and a barber's shop.

Pineapple Fruit 'n Veg Tel: 333-2454 Open Monday to Saturday, 7 am to 9 pm; Sunday to noon.

RESTAURANTS
With so many to choose from, Harbour Island is a delightful gastronomic experience. All the hotels have good restaurants, which will welcome you for lunch, and for dinner with reservations. Offerings range from conch fritters and grouper fingers to international gourmet dining. A few suggestions:

Angela's Starfish Restaurant Tel: 333-2253 Located on Grant Street, at the north end of Dunmore Street. Open from 8:30 am to 10 pm. The bell signals last orders at 8:30 pm. The menu is written up on a blackboard and you order by writing down what you would like to eat. A good choice of dishes in a great atmosphere, with a garden area. No credit cards.

Bayside Cafe on Bay Street   Tel: 333-2174   Open daily from 7:30 am to 9 pm. No credit cards.

Dunmore Deli on King Street   Tel: 333-2646   Open daily from 7:30 am to 4 pm. Tasty breakfasts and box lunches to go as well as delicious deli foods, with free delivery to your boat.

Harbour Lounge Restaurant and Bar on Bay Street   Tel: 333-2031 Open Tuesday to Sunday from 11 am to 11 pm for lunch and dinner. Fresh meats and seafood, distinctive homemade soups, and drinks, served on their cool, breezy veranda.

The Landing   Tel: 333-2707/2740   On Bay Street, greeting you as you step off the Government Dock. A traditional 1800s house and garden, slowly being restored. Open for lunch and dinner. Dine in an elegantly understated dining room, or in their charming courtyard garden, with an enthusiastic Australian crew running the hotel and the restaurant. Superb food, well worth the wait, and fantastic sunsets from the verandas. Call ahead for reservations.

Ma Ruby's at the *Tingum Village Hotel*   Tel: 333-2161   Serving Bahamian food in a cheerful setting, famous for Jimmy Buffet's "Cheeseburgers in Paradise." Open from 8 am.

Runaway Hill Club on Colebrook Street   Tel: 333-2324   Open to the public for dinner only, by reservation, at 8 pm. Jackets required. Set menu, but alternatives to the main entree.

Pink Sands Island Outpost Bahamas, on Chapel Street and Ocean Tel: 333-2030   Lunch served daily at the *Blue Bar on the Ocean* from 11:30 am to 4 pm. Dinner by reservation at *The Garden Restaurant,* $70 per person for a four-course meal.

Romora Bay Club   Tel: 333-2325   World-class *Fabrice Gomet's* cuisine at *Ludo's.* Reservations, please.

Bars

Sea Grapes Club on Colebrook Street   Open from 7 pm for music, dancing, snacks, cocktails, beer, and wine. Home of "The Funk Gang" band with live music Wednesdays through Saturdays.

George's Bar on Colebrook Street   Satellite TV and a pool table, open daily from noon to 2 am.

Gusty's on Grant Street   Add your name to the vast collection of signatures on the walls, and try Gus's latest alcoholic concoction even if he doesn't know what goes into it . . .

Vic-Hum's or The Great Briland Forum on Barracks Street. Bahamian license plates cover the yellow walls where Humphrey Percentie (street name Hitler) will show you the world's largest coconut. He runs his bar with the conviction that every visitor will want to write about it.

Willy's Tavern on Dunmore Street.

GETTING AROUND

Airport
For airline details see under **North Eleuthera.** To get there, take a ferry from the town dock across to Three Islands, which costs $4, and then a taxi to the airport for about $5 per person.

Bicycles
Michael's Cycles   On Bay Street   Tel: 333-2384 • VHF 16 Open from 8 am to 6 pm daily with bicycles for $10 per day, motorbikes for $25 per day, and a 13-ft. boat for $70 per day. Free delivery of motor bikes and bicycles to the marinas or hotels. Visa and MasterCard accepted.

Martin Hudson   Motorbikes to rent.

Carriage Tours
Sunset Carriage Tours with Rupert Davis on Colebrook Street. Tel: 322-2337

Golf Carts
Cars, scooters and bicycles are often available from these people, as well as golf carts.

Big Red	Tel: 333-2045
Dunmore Rentals	Tel: 333-2372
Johnson's Rentals	Tel: 333-2376
Ross's Rentals	Tel: 333-2122
Sunshine Rentals	Tel: 333-2509

Red Apple Rosie	Tel: 333-2750
R & G Rentals	Tel: 333-2116

Mailboats
Briland Provider   Leaves Nassau at 6 pm on Monday, returns at 8 pm on Tuesday. Fare $30.

Bahamas Daybreak   Arrives from Nassau on Thursdays, leaving again on Sundays at 8 am.

Eleuthera Express   Arrives from Nassau on Thursdays at 7 am. Fare to Nassau is $25.

Yeocomico 11   Arrives bi-weekly from Florida with freight. Call G & G Shipping (954-920-0306) for more information.

Taxis
Wayne Major's The Big M Taxi Service

	No 20	Tel: 333-2043	VHF 16
Danny Major	No 9		VHF 16 "The Minister"
Jen's	No 8	Tel: 333-2116	
Percival Johnson	No 173	Tel: 333-2174	
Reggie's	No 24	Tel: 333-2116	VHF 16 "No Problem"
Spooner Grant	No 10		VHF 16

Water Taxis
All the water taxis stand by on VHF 16. Call in advance if you need night service.

Jarrod Johnson	Tel: 333-2160	"White Lightening"
Jack Higgs	Tel: 333-2472	"Sea Jack 1"
Michael Higgs	Tel: 333-2466	"Sea Jack 2"
Andrew Higgs		"Lucky Too"
Duke's	Tel: 333-2337	"Briland Queen"
Dwight Stewart	Tel: 333-2159	"Commander One"
Sean Major	Tel: 333-2043	"Lady M"
Kenneth Stewart	Tel: 333-2287	"Keva"
Uncle Sam	Tel: 333-2394	"Uncle Sam"
Paul Percentie	Tel: 333-2097	"Briland Sea Breeze"

SPORTS

Deep Sea Fishing
Tel: 335-5357   Captain Gregory Thompson has a 32-foot Stamas sport fish boat called *Gone Fishing,* and charges $400 for a half day and $600 for a full day for 1 to 6 people. Visa and MasterCard accepted.

Diving
Ocean Fox Diving   Tel: 333-2323   Diving and Fishing with Jeff Fox.

Romora Bay Dive Shop at the *Romora Bay Club*   Tel: 333-2325 Individualized dive trips to suit special interests. Dive packages include 7 nights at the hotel, transfers from the airport, breakfast and lunch, initiation and/or certification, and 5 double-tank dives: from $1,720 per week single, $1,350 per person double. Rental gear available.

Valentine's Dive Center   Tel: 333-2309 • E-mail: vdc@batelnet.bs • Web site: www.valentinesdive.com   Daily dive trips, newly rebuilt dive shop, dive instruction, and full rental gear available. Two-tank dive from $65, snorkelers $20, boat ride only $15. Trips depart at 9:30 am and 2 pm daily. Open-water certification $425, introduction to scuba class $75. Excursions to Sink Hole and Bat Cave $120, Current Cut high-speed drift dive (three passes) and one anchored dive with lunch and drinks $90, or $75 for the drift dive only. Or dive the Eleuthera Wall for $220. Sunset cruises leave 45 minutes before sunset every Friday, for a cruise around the harbor with wine, cheese, and fruit served. All divers are required to purchase a token at a cost of $3 that is good for one year. The money is used to support Harbour Island Reef Relief, a not-for-profit organization that puts in and maintains the mooring system. Part of the fund is applied to recompression chamber membership. Talk to Rosa Liva or Bob Beregowitz to plan your dives.

Fishing
Patrick Roberts   Tel: 333-2213   Bonefishing and bottom fishing.

BEACHES

The famous pink powdery sand beach stretches for three glorious miles along the eastern side of the island. This is a perfect beach for children, well protected by the reef, with some good snorkeling you can easily swim out to, and a magical rosy glow in the dawn light. Although the main hotels border the beach, there is public access to it.

Children on the Dunmore Town Beach.

DIVE SITES

The Arch, a coral bridge at around 60 to 110 ft., for experienced divers.

The Canarvon Wreck, whose stern you can swim through, This 186-ft. freighter sank in 1895, and lies between 15 and 35 ft. below the water.

The Cave, a cavern dive from 75 to 125 ft.

The Cienfuegas Wreck, a wrecked passenger liner that sank in 1895 in from 5 to 35 ft. of water, complete with all her china, glass, and silverware. Sadly, even if you find any, it is illegal to take them from Bahamian waters.

Current Cut, a fast drift dive that sends you through at up to 10 knots.

Glass Window Bridge, under the bridge on Eleuthera, from 25 to 55 ft. Maybe drive down to see it from above before you try the dive . . .

Man Island, good for beginners. There seem to be octopus and sea cucumbers in every crevice, in 0 to 15 ft. of water.

Pink House , an especially busy reef with a breathtaking elkhorn forest, used in TV commercials, in 1 to 25 ft.

Pinnacle, a deep, bluewater dive in 99 to 130 ft. of water, with trees of black coral at 100 ft.

Potato and Onions, a natural wreck. Swim through boilers on a 200-ft.-long reef.

Sea Gardens, with fantastic elkhorn coral in 10 to 35 ft. of water, perfect for snorkelers too.

Sink Hole and Bat Cave, close to Preacher's Cave. You leave by land for these cavern dives, which are for experienced divers only.

Eleuthera Train Wreck, a train that slid off a barge during the American Civil War in 25 to 35 ft. of water. You can still see the sets of railroad wheels and other parts of the train, though they are covered with fire coral.

FESTIVALS, FISHING TOURNAMENTS, AND REGATTAS

June
Bahamas Billfish Harbour Island Championship Tel: 954-920-5577 • Fax: 920-5530 • E-mail: bbc@albehrendt.com

October
North Eleuthera Sailing Regatta, with five days of racing locally

built sailing sloops from all over the Bahamas between Harbour Island and Three Island Bay on North Eleuthera. Call Rev. Philip McPhee (394-0455) or Mr. Glenroy Aranha (333-2281) for details.

ACCOMMODATIONS

All hotels levy a 10-percent service charge in lieu of tipping, 4-percent government tax, and 4-percent resort tax.

Coral Sands Hotel Tel: 242-333-2350/2320 • Fax: 333-2368 33 ocean-front rooms from $195, 2-bedroom suites from $275 per night. MAP $50.

Dunmore Beach Club Tel: 242-333-2200 • Fax: 333-2429 12 cottages from $370 per night in the summer months, from $420 per night December to April. Collared shirt required for dinner. Early dining for children under 12. Full MAP.

The Landing on Bay Street Tel: 242-333-2707/2740 • Fax: 333-2650 9 gracious rooms overlooking the harbor in Dunmore Town, from $85 per night, continental breakfast included.

Pink Sands Hotel Tel: 242-333-2030 One- and two-bedroom cottages from $305 per person, including MAP.

Romora Bay Club on the Bay side of Harbour Island Tel: 242-333-2325 • Fax: 333-2500 • Toll Free: 800-688-0425 • In France: 331-45-67-10-30 Garden-view rooms from $190 with breakfast and lunch, or $210 with breakfast and dinner. Honeymoon weeks, Dive weeks, and other packages available. Full dive operation at the hotel, as well as the *Parrot Bar, Sloppy Joe's Bar,* and *Ludo's Restaurant.* Room discount of 20 percent for guests at the *Harbour Island Club Marina.*

Runaway Hill Club Tel: 242-333-2150 • Fax: 333-2420 10 rooms in the main houses from $180 single in low season to $240 for a double room in the winter months. Villas from $215 for two people. MAP breakfast and dinner $60. Optional lunch by request $15 per person. Jackets for gentlemen are required at dinner.

Tingum Village Hotel in Dunmore Town   Tel: 242-333-2161   In a tropical garden setting, single rooms from $50 per night, double from $75, and a three-bedroom cottage from $175 per night. MAP $35. *Ma Ruby's Restaurant,* serving her famous "Cheeseburgers in Paradise," featured in Jimmy Buffet's Parrot Head Hand Book, is on site. Monthly Goombay Festivals with a street party, calypso dancing in the streets and seafood.
Valentine's Yacht Club and Inn opposite the marina, on Bay Street Tel: 242-333-2142 • Fax: 333-2135   21 air-conditioned garden and poolside rooms from $90 per night, MAP $35, with their own restaurant and bar overlooking the pool and Jacuzzi. This is a good hotel for friends who may prefer to stay ashore in Harbour Island while your boat is in the marina.

THINGS TO DO IN HARBOUR ISLAND

- Walk through the town and take photographs of some of the prettiest streets and houses in the Bahamas.
- Go to the fabled pink beach, walk that too, and swim. Enjoy a leisurely lunch at one of the hotels.
- Cross over on a ferry to North Eleuthera. Visit Preacher's Cave on the north coast. While you're there, you could make a day of it and head south to visit Upper and Lower Bogue, The Current, and the Glass Window, or even drive down to Governor's Harbour and explore this very attractive old town.
- Take advantage of a fantastic choice of dive sites with experienced dive operators on the island, or dive the Bat Cave and Sink Hole with the *Valentine's Dive Center* team. Or try an exhilarating drift dive through Current Cut.
- Ask one of the Spanish Wells pilots to come with you in your boat to teach you the secrets of the Devil's Backbone Passage as you work you way around to Spanish Wells.
- Enjoy a spectacular sunset with drinks on the veranda of one of the many waterfront restaurants and bars.

THE ISLAND OF ELEUTHERA

Talk of Eleuthera and most people will think of Harbour Island and pink sands, but there is more to it than that. Sailors will think of the dreaded Devil's Backbone reef, which claimed its first victims in 1648. These were the Eleutheran Adventurers who crawled up the beach and took refuge in Preacher's Cave. You can see it today. The island is rich in history as a result of this early settlement, and has long been enjoyed by families who return each year to their winter homes. Think of Eleuthera and you think of beaches, as well as pineapples, which remain Eleuthera's most famous crop, though their fresh vegetables are highly prized too.

The main centers of population in the North Eleuthera area are its two offshore settlements, Spanish Wells and Harbour Island, both served by North Eleuthera Airport. Spanish Wells is important as a fishing port, and Harbour Island is a prime tourist destination, so we have covered these two places in their own right. Eleuthera is long and thin, but you can explore the length of it by car in one day. Your problem is to find a rental car. We found them only in Governors Harbour, Hatchet Bay, and Cape Eleuthera Marina, but you may be able to find someone to help you at the airports.

Central and South Eleuthera, though less frequented by visitors, still retain their early charm, with traces of a once-flourishing agriculture. Governor's Harbor and Rock Sound have **Customs** and **Immigration** at their airports, which can be called to clear you in. Hatchet Bay is served by Governor's Harbour and Cape Eleuthera by Rock Sound. Call 322-2250 for **Governor's Harbour Customs**, or 334-2183 for **Rock Sound Customs**.

The extreme length of Central and South Eleuthera and the relatively few safe harbors and good anchorages en route would make it confusing to cover the land survey of Eleuthera taking it in isolated bites. So we have taken it in one sweep, as if you were driving from north to south.

NORTH ELEUTHERA

As you step off the Spanish Wells ferry on to North Eleuthera at **Gene's Bay**, only the liquor store, a telephone, and the Pinders' taxis are waiting for you. From the Harbour Island ferry, you come into **Three Islands** ferry dock, with the Pineapple Cafe and a telephone. Or, you may have flown in to **North Eleuthera Airport,** where a small community of cafes and gift shops has sprung up.

SERVICES AND SHOPPING IN NORTH ELEUTHERA

Airport
North Eleuthera Airport   Tel: 335-1241   With its 4,500-ft. runway, this airport serves not only the northern part of Eleuthera but also Harbour Island and Spanish Wells. Connecting ferries and taxis from both islands are reliable and efficient. For details of how to get to the airport from Harbour Island or Spanish Wells, or how to get back to them from North Eleuthera, see under **Getting Around** in both islands. From North Eleuthera Airport to the Hatchet Bay area, a taxi will cost around $30 for two people.

You should confirm all airline reservations two days in advance, and be at the airport an hour before departure. If you are leaving the Bahamas don't forget the $15 departure tax.

The Junkanoo Lounge (Tel: 335-1605) is open daily for breakfast, lunch, dinner, and snacks from 7 am to midnight, with parties continuing until 2 am on weekends. Gregory Stuart has recently arrived to take over this happy scene for arrivals and departures. *The Calypso Lounge* serves good meals in a calm atmosphere and *Dis 'n Dat* is happy to sell you souvenirs and gifts. There is a liquor store between the two restaurants.

Airlines
Bahamasair to Nassau   Tel: 335-1152
USAir Express to Fort Lauderdale   Tel: 335-1152
Sand Piper to Nassau   Tel: 335-1475
Continental Connection to Fort Lauderdale and Miami Tel: 335-1278
Twin Air to Fort Lauderdale   Tel: 335-1278
For local *Twin Air* reservations, contact Calvin Pinder (333-4041) or Miss Cartwright (333-1475)

The closest settlements are the Bogues, **Upper** and **Lower Bogue**, both of which suffered severe hurricane damage several years ago, still visible in the topless houses. The main North Eleuthera crossroad is close to the airport, and there you will find the *North Eleuthera Service Station*, which is a good place to pick up gas if you need it (closed on Sundays), and a *ScotiaBank* that is open from 9:30 am to 3 pm Monday to Thursday, to 5 pm on Fridays, but with no ATM. **Lower Bogue** is a thriving community, which hosts a very popular annual homecoming, as well as a clinic, post office, liquor store, laundromat, *Aggie's Bakery, Brendee's Mini Food Store,* the *First and Last Bar,* and *Gullie's Restaurant* (Tel: 335-1437).

To the southwest you have the settlement of **The Current**, close to Current Cut, which you will undoubtedly pass through on the water, but is well worth stopping at if you have the time. It is an enchanting small, neat settlement with colorful bougainvillea dripping from well-maintained wooden houses, with the *Griffin Snack Bar* and *Lim's Take Away* if you need sustenance before or after you do a drift dive through Current Cut. There is a glorious beach on the west side of the settlement.

On your way south to Gregory Town and on to Hatchet Bay, stop for a moment to look at the **Glass Window**. This narrow road-bridge is the only land link between the north end of this very long, thin island, and the southern two thirds of the island, and in stormy seas the Atlantic waves come crashing through the rocky cliffs and beneath the road.

ALICE TOWN, HATCHET BAY, AND GREGORY TOWN

Alice Town and Hatchet Bay are officially two separate settlements, though the dividing line between them is blurred, and the whole is now generally referred to as Hatchet Bay. We have listed Gregory Town in with Hatchet Bay too, since it is the closest village with a greater selection of shops and services that you might find useful. With its brightly painted houses, churches, and the school surrounding the tiny harbor (which is really only suitable for dinghies), it also plays host to the Annual Eleuthera Pineapple Festival, a cheerful June event not to be missed if you are around at the time. Hatchet Bay itself is now somewhat rundown, and we heard reports of minor theft. Don't leave anything in your dinghy when you come ashore for provisions or to collect fuel, especially not oars or fishing tackle, which are highly prized.

Janet Wilson

MARINA

MARINE SERVICES OF ELEUTHERA
Tel and Fax: 242-335-0186 • E-mail: pbell@batelnet

Dockage	Alongside the concrete wall is 50¢ per ft. per day, 35¢ per ft. per month, and 25¢ per ft. long term, minimum 3-month stay.
Power	$7 per day from 20 to 30 ft., $10 per day from 30 to 40 ft., $18 per day from 40 to 50 ft., $25 per day from 50 to 60 ft. Add $5 per day for air conditioning.
Fuel	Diesel on the dock, and motor oils.
Propane	Available on a 24-hr. turn-around for refills, or same day on Friday morning when tanks can be collected later in the day.
Water	10¢ per gallon.
Shower	Yes, for $1.
Laundry	A washing machine at the back of a workshop for $2, but no dryer.
Trash	$1 per bag.
Faxes	$4 per page to the US, $6 per page to Canada, and $8 per page to Europe.
E-mail	$2.50 per minute to the US, $4.50 per minute to Canada, $6.50 per minute to Europe.
Credit cards	Cash or traveler's checks accepted.
Owner	Pat Bell is very helpful.

SERVICES AND SHOPPING IN HATCHET BAY

Accommodations
The Cove Eleuthera Tel: 242-335-5142 • Fax: 335-5338
• E-mail: george@thecoveeleuthera.com
• Web site: www.thecoveeleuthera.com 26-room beachfront resort set in 28 acres, between Hatchet Bay and Gregory Town. Rooms from $99 per night. MAP $33. Tennis, kayaking, bicycles, swimming pool, hammocks, and their own restaurant serving 3 meals daily. Boaters are welcome to anchor off their beach and come up to the hotel for lunch.
The Rainbow Inn Tel and Fax: 242-335-0294
• Web site: www.rainbowinn.com Only 3 miles from Hatchet Bay, delightful cottages within a garden setting, overlooking Rainbow Point, with tennis court, bicycles, salt-water pool, and an excellent restaurant that is open daily except Sundays and Mondays in the summer, and Sundays in the winter. Rooms from $115 per night.
Cambridge Villas Tel: 242-335-5080 • Fax: 335-5308
In Gregory Town, with its own restaurant. 25 single, double, triple, or quad rooms, from $80 per night and MAP $30 per day.

Bakery
Thompson Bakery on the hill overlooking Gregory Town Tel: 335-5053 Monica and Daisy Thompson offer pizza, pastries, sandwiches, fresh bread, jams, and dinners.

Boat Charters
Charter Cats of the Bahamas Tel: 335-0186 or 937-835-5829
• Fax: 937-835-3171 • E-mail: chartercat@aol.com

Clinics
In Hatchet Bay:
Tel: 335-0091 • VHF Rescue 3 Open 9 am to 3:30 pm daily. Or call 335-0341 for Nurse Scavella or 335-0521 for Nurse Pinder. Closed Saturdays and Sundays except for emergencies.
In Gregory Town:
Tel: 335-5108 The doctor from Governor's Harbour visits Alice Bay and Gregory Town on Tuesdays.

Car Rental
Dewitt Johnson Rental Service Tel: 332-2568 at the airport or 335-0211 at home.
Larry Dean's Taxi Service & Car Rentals Tel: 332-2568 or 335-0059
Marine Services of Eleuthera Tel and Fax: 355-0186 • VHF 16 Pat Bell can arrange a rental car for $60 per day.

Fishing Charter
Capt Gregory Thompson on *Gone Fishing* Tel: 335-5369/5357 or stop by *Island Made Gift Shop* in Gregory Town. 32-ft. Stamas Sportfish. Full day $600, half day $400 for 1 to 6 people.

Fishing Tournament
The *Gregory Town Annual Fishing Tournament* is held in April. Contact Mr Denis Johnson (Tel: 332-2714) for details.

Gift Shop
Island Made Gift Shop in Gregory Town Tel: 355-5369 Open 9 am to 7 pm Monday to Saturday and 10 am to noon on Sundays. Manager Pat Thompson has a wide selection of driftwood paintings, Androsia clothing, hand-crafted dolls, native straw work, and lots of island stuff.

Groceries
Sawyer's Grocery Store in Hatchet Bay Tel: 335-0417 Groceries, frozen foods, meats, and fresh vegetables.
Thompson Brothers Supermarket in Gregory Town Tel: 335-5009 Fresh produce, beef, poultry, canned foods, dairy products. Open 8 am to 6 pm Monday to Saturday, and 10 to 11 am on Sundays.

Laundromats
Jay's Laundromat in Gregory Town Tel: 335-5236
The Half Way Laundromat next to *Rosey's Bakery*, south of

Hatchet Bay, in James Cistern. Very good, brand new, open 9 am to 6 pm daily except Sundays. $2 tokens for washing machines and dryers.

Mailboats

M/V Current Pride leaves Potter's Cay in Nassau on Thursdays at 7 am for North Eleuthera, Hatchet Bay, and James Cistern.

M/V Captain Fox leaves Potter's Cay on Fridays at 1 pm for Governor's Harbour and Hatchet Bay, and leaves for Nassau on Tuesdays. Fare $25.

Moorings

Marine Services of Eleuthera Tel: 335-0186 • VHF 16   10 mooring buoys for $10 per day, $200 monthly unoccupied, $150 per month occupied.

Post Office

In Alice Town, open from 9 am to 5:30 pm, Monday to Friday.

Propane

Marine Services of Eleuthera, ask Pat Bell.

Restaurants and Bars

Chatters Place in Gregory Town Originally intended to be Charters Place in honor of the boat charters, the newly painted sign returned as Chatters and has remained so ever since. Adequate Bahamian food, served in a dark, rather gloomy atmosphere, with a television in the corner showing female wrestling at top volume, much to the amusement of the locals the night we were there. But it is open for dinner on Sundays when everything else is closed.

Sugar Apple Restaurant and Bar and *Cushings Place Restaurant* Tel: 335-5301   Both between Hatchet Bay and Gregory Town.

Elvina's Restaurant and *Washateria* in Gregory Town

The Cove Eleuthera Tel: 335-5142   Restaurant open 8 to 10:30 am for breakfast, noon to 2:30 pm for lunch, and 6 to 8:30 pm for dinner. Boaters are welcome to drop a hook in favorable weather and use the restaurant, beach, and hotel facilities. If you are in Hatchet Bay and need a ride up for dinner, or back afterward, call ahead to let them know.

The Rainbow Inn Tel: 335-0294   The restaurant and bar has a nautical theme and is 2.5 miles from Hatchet Bay. With stunning sea views it serves some of the best food in Eleuthera. Evening specials include pizza on Mondays, BBQ ribs and music on Wednesdays, steak and music on Fridays and the best Seafood Newburg in the world. Ken Keene and Charlie Moore make great hosts at this lively and fun meeting place. Open for breakfast, as long as you are there between 8 and 8:55 am, and for dinner from 6 to 9 pm. No reservations, just first-come-first-served in their booths with tables made from bows of old boats.

The Harbour View Restaurant and *Tasty Treats Ice Cream* overlooking Hatchet Bay Tel: 335-0212   They advertise that they are open for breakfast, lunch, and dinner, but they seemed to be more closed than open on our last visit.

Forget Me Not Club Tel: 335-0054 Much favored by locals in the center of the settlement.

Surfing

Surfers Beach, east on Ocean Boulevard about 2 miles south of Gregory Town. A rocky track leads you over to a long, sandy beach with fantastic surfing when the wind comes from the southwest, we are told. Better to take a 4WD vehicle if you can. If the road at the bottom of the hill is too rough, park your vehicle and walk to the bottom. Turn right and walk 25 yards, turn left and walk up the hill to the beach. Surfer Pete Fox from New Hampshire has a bar there, and can rent you surfboards.

Taxi

Hilton Johnson at James Cistern Tel: 335-6241   He may be able to help with a rental car too, and accepts Visa and MasterCard. A taxi to North Eleuthera Airport will cost around $30 for two people; to Governor's Harbour Airport about $40.

Telephone

Batelco in town is open from 9 am to 4:30 pm. Pat Bell at *Marine Services* is very kind about letting you use her telephone. There is a card phone next to the clinic.

JAMES CISTERN

Six miles from Hatchet Bay is the wonderful *Big Rock General Store,* owned and operated by Mr Bernard Bethel. Call them at 335-6355. They have a filling station outside their general store, which is well stocked, and a deli and restaurant open for breakfast, lunch, and dinner, 7:30 am to 7:30 pm daily except Sundays, when they close at 11 am. In James Cistern you will find the *Halfway Laundromat,* alongside *Rosey's Bakery,* which is open for breakfast and lunch until 5 pm, serving hot dogs and hamburgers, sandwiches, grouper, conch fritters, and chicken dishes, as well as fresh-baked coconut, raisin, whole wheat, and white breads, and coconut and pineapple tarts. Call ahead (335-6248) to order.

GOVERNOR'S HARBOUR

One of the most attractive, well-established communities in the Bahamas, Governor's Harbour has great charm. The holding is not particularly good in the harbor, though it is possible to find better holding toward the Club Med watersports area if you can put up with the buzzing water-ski boats and jet skis. The best beach is on the Atlantic side, up and over the hill through town. Well-stocked grocery stores make this a good place to re-provision, as well as to find a bank, post office, UPS, and other useful amenities within easy walking distance.

SERVICES AND SHOPPING IN GOVERNOR'S HARBOUR

Accommodations

The Buccaneer Club Tel: 242-332-2000 • Fax: 332-2888 Perched on a hill above Governor's Harbour. A converted Bahamian farmhouse with six double rooms from $80 a night, and its own restaurant and swimming pool.

The Duck Inn Tel: 242-332-2608 • Fax: 332-2160 • E-mail: duckin@batelnet.com   Emily Duckworth runs this inn with its 3,500 rare orchids. Flora's Cottage sleeps 8, from $220 per night; Hunnie Pot Cottage is a one-bedroom efficiency from $110 per night; and Cupid's Cottage, which sleeps 2 and overlooks Governor's Harbour beach, is from $110 per night.

Laughing Bird Apartments Tel: 242-332-2012   Efficiency apartments overlooking the beach, from $65 per person.

Airport

At Governor's Harbour:

American Eagle	Tel: 332-2703	Flights to Miami
Bahamasair	Tel: 332-2648	Flights to Nassau
US Air Express	Tel: 332-2648	Flights to Fort Lauderdale
Twin Air	Tel: 332-2425	Flights to Fort Lauderdale

Bakery

Governor's Harbour Bakery Tel: 332-2071   Opposite the *Blue Room Restaurant,* with a wide assortment of cakes, breads, and pastries. Open 9 am to 6 pm Monday to Friday, and 9 am to 5 pm Saturdays.

Bank

Barclays Bank Tel: 332-2300   Open 9:30 am to 3 pm Monday to Thursday, to 5 pm on Fridays.

Royal Bank of Canada on the Queen's Highway east of town Tel: 332-2856   Open 9:30 am to 3 pm Monday to Thursday, to 5 pm on Fridays.

Boutiques

Brenda's Boutique Tel: 332-2089

Nicole's Dress Shop

Car Rental
Edgar Gardiner Tel: 332-2665
Highway Service Station and Rental Cars Tel: 332-2077 • VHF 9
Johnson's Car Rental Tel: 332-2226/2778

Churches
Methodist Church
St. Patrick's Anglican Church
St. Paul's Catholic Church

Clinic
Governor's Harbour Medical Clinic Tel: 332-2774   Open 9 am to 5 pm Monday to Friday, with their own ambulance. To contact Dr Bacchus, call 332-2020.

Dive Shop
Clear Water Dive Shop Tel: 332-2146 • Fax: 332-2546   Charles Sands has complete sets of dive equipment to rent from $36 per day, snorkel equipment from $8 per day, tanks from $12 a day, or he can refill yours for $6. There is no dive operation in Governor's Harbour, but Charles can put you in touch with people who can guide you. Their store is open from 8:45 am to 4:45 pm Monday to Friday, and from 8:30 am to 2 pm on Saturdays.

Fishing Guides
Gladstone and Paul Petty Tel: 332-2280

Gift Shop
Norma's Gift Shop

Groceries
Eleuthera Supply Shopping Centre Tel: 332-2026   Very well stocked with a good selection of canned and fresh goods, as well as a pharmacy section and separate hardware store.
Sawyer's Food Store Tel: 332-2836   Groceries, frozen foods, meats, and fresh vegetables.

Laundromat
Sands Laundromat

Library
The Haynes Library in a historic 1897 building overlooking the harbor.

Janet Wilson

Liquor Stores
Butler and Sands Liquor Store
Pyfrom's Liquor Store
Ronnie's Smoke Shop Tel: 332-2307   Cigars from all over the world, as well as a sports bar and liquor shop.

Mailboats
M/V Eleuthera Express leaves Potter's Cay in Nassau at 5 pm on Mondays for Governor's Harbour and Rock Sound, and leaves for Nassau on Tuesdays at 8 pm. Fare $30.
M/V Day Break III leaves Potter's Cay on Mondays at 5 pm for Rock Sound, Davis Harbour, and South Eleuthera, and departs for Nassau on Tuesdays at 10 pm. Fare $25.
M/V Captain Fox leaves Potter's Cay on Fridays at 1 pm for Governor's Harbour and Hatchet Bay, and departs for Nassau at 5 pm on Tuesdays. Fare $25.

Police
Tel: 333-2111

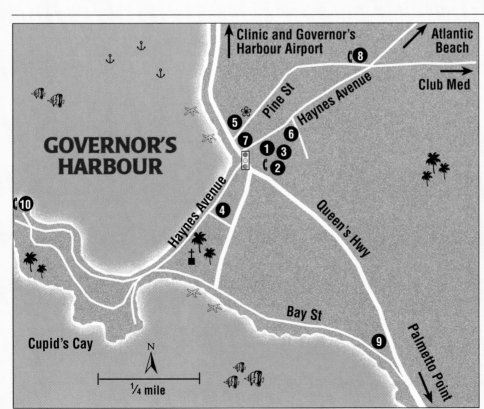

GOVERNOR'S HARBOUR DIRECTORY

1. Eleuthera Supply Shopping Centre
2. Barclay's Bank
3. UPS; Clear Water Dive Shop
4. Post Office
5. Duck Inn and Orchid Garden
6. Buccaneer Inn
7. Tourist Office
8. Batelco
9. Highway Service Station
10. Government Dock
‡ St. Patrick's Anglican Church

Post Office

In the pink administration building next to the Haynes Library, open 9 am to 5:30 pm Monday to Friday.

Restaurants

The Blue Room   Tel: 332-2736

The Harbour Inn   Tel: 332-2686

The Buccaneer Club   Tel: 332-2000   Specializing in native and American dishes, which can be ordered for take-away. Dwight Johnson, the owner and operator, can also help you find a bonefishing guide.

Pammy's Snack Bar and Take Away   Tel: 332-2843

Taxis

Taxis will charge about $25 to the airport.

Arthur H. Nixon   Tel: 332-2568 or 332-1006

Tommy Pinder   Tel: 332-2568 or 332-2216

Telephones

There are telephones in town and on the Government Dock, and up the hill at *Batelco*, where the office is open from 9 am to 4:30 pm Monday to Friday.

Tourist Office

Tel: 332-2142/2868   Just along from the only traffic light in Eleuthera. Jacqueline Gibson is very helpful and can give you useful information about Governor's Harbour.

Travel Agent

Mundy Tours   Open 9 am to 5 pm Monday to Friday, to 1 pm on Saturdays.

UPS

Tel: 332-2454 • Fax: 332-2453   UPS and GWS can hold deliveries for you at their office, near *Barclays Bank*, if the package is addressed "Hold for Arrival" with your name and your boat name. Deliveries take two working days from the US. If it is a spare part for your boat, have it labeled as such to avoid customs duty.

PALMETTO POINT AND TARPUM BAY

Palmetto Point is three miles further southeast of Governor's Harbour. There the *Unique Village* has a restaurant on a superb site, perched on a cliff overlooking a fantastic beach and a stretch of ocean with coral reefs close to shore that are good for snorkeling. It's well worth visiting. The *Unique Village Restaurant and Lounge* (332-1830) has 10 rooms from $100 a night, MAP $35, and a restaurant that is open from 7:30 am to 10 pm, specializing in native dishes, steaks, and seafood. Palmetto Point is also home to *Unique Hardware*, a liquor store, and *Sands Enterprises Supermarket* (332-1662), which carries everything from food, gifts, and furniture to electrical fixtures and auto accessories.

Palmetto Shores Vacation Villas (332-1305) with self-catering villas opening directly on to the beach, start from $90 a night. Sadly, they no longer have slips to offer for visiting boats. Check out *Mate and Jenny's Restaurant* in Palmetto Point (332-1504) and try their special Conch Pizza.

About 15 miles from Palmetto Point, at **Tarpum Bay**, you come somewhat unexpectedly to two art galleries, the *MacMillan Hughes Art Gallery* and, two miles south of Tarpum Bay village, to the *Mal Flanders Art Gallery*. Tarpum Bay's

From Tarpum Bay to ?

most visible landmark is the remarkable castle-like tower built by artist-sculptor Peter MacMillan Hughes, whose work has long attracted attention. His studio is near his "castle." Here, too, is Mary Hilton's hotel, the *Hilton's Haven Motel* (334-4231), which has 10 suites from $65 year round and MAP $17, with its own restaurant. At Kinky's Corner in Tarpum Bay there is a hardware store, *Carey's Groceries* at the Shell Station, and *Bayside Liquor*, as well as *Shine's Seafod Restaurant and Bakery*. Call *Ingrahams Beach Inn* (334-4285) if you need accommodations.

From Tarpum Bay, the road drops due south to **Rock Sound**, past the airport. Rock Sound is a diverse settlement, closest to the two southern marinas, with the famous *Ocean Hole*, an inland blue hole that is believed to be connected to the ocean. Rock Sound holds the *Eleuthera Junkanoo* in December, and their *Homecoming* in April. Call the Eleuthera Tourist Office (242-332-2142) for details on all the Eleuthera Festivals and Regattas.

ROCK SOUND

The southern dock, close to the little white Anglican church, is a wooden dock useful if you are going to the *Harbour View Restaurant* or to visit the Ocean Hole. For shopping, Customs, and "downtown" Rock Sound, tie up at the northern, concrete Government Dock.

SERVICES AND SHOPPING IN ROCK SOUND

Airport

Bahamasair   Tel: 334-2125 Flights to Nassau.

Twin Air   Tel: 334-2142 Flights to Fort Lauderdale.

Bakery

The Haven Bakery   Tel: 334-2155

Bank

Barclays Bank on the Queen's Highway, adjacent to the *Market Place*   Tel: 334-2022

ScotiaBank next to the *Market Place*, open from 9:30 am to 3 pm Monday to Thursday, to 5 pm on Fridays.

Church

St. Luke's Anglican Church

Clinic

Rock Sound Medical Clinic on the main Queen's Highway in town   Tel: 334-2226 or 336-2182   With their own ambulance, open 9 am to 5 pm Monday to Friday. Dr Gainor can be contacted in an emergency at 334-2226.

Diving

Tim Riley at *South Eleuthera Divers*   Tel: 334-4083   We couldn't track him down when we were there.

Fax and E-mail

Eleuthera Stationery and Office Supplies   Tel and Fax: 334-2494   Open 9 am to 5 pm Monday to Saturday. Michelle is very helpful and efficient, and will help you to retrieve and send your E-mail or faxes. They stock basic office, school, and business supplies.

Fishing Supplies

Eleuthera Fish and Farm Supplies, a short way north of town   Tel: 334-2489   Open 8 am to 6 pm Monday to Thursday; Fridays and Saturdays to 7 pm.

Fuel

Esso fuel at *Dingle Motor Service*, who also rents cars.

Shell filling station at the *Market Place*.

There is also a NAPA store, which could be useful for engine spares, etc.

Gift Shops

The Almond Tree Arts and Crafts

Goombay Gifts

St. Luke's Anglican Church, Rock Sound.

Groceries

Rock Sound Super Market in the *Market Place*.

Nat's Produce Store Fresh vegetables and fruit.

Sawyer's Food Stores Tel: 334-2123   Groceries, frozen foods, meats, and fresh vegetables.

Hardware

Rock Sound Hardware in the *Market Place* Tel: 334-2253

Laundromat

C and C next to *Elite Customs Brokers* Open 9 am to 5:30 pm Monday to Friday, 8 am to 5:30 pm on Saturdays, and 1:30 to 5 pm on Sundays. $2 tokens each for washer and dryer.

Liquor store

Burns House Liquor Store

Sturrup's Liquor Store in the *Market Place*.

Mailboat

M/V Bahamas Daybreak III leaves Nassau at 5 pm on Mondays for Rock Sound, Davis Harbour, and South Eleuthera, returning on Tuesdays at 10 pm. $25 fare.

Marine Spares

Elite Customs Brokers Tel: 334-2275/2600/2039   James Gibson will be able to help you with many different services, including Customs clearance, 5-gallon jugs of water for $5, ice for $3, $5, or $9 per bag, and spare parts for engines and outboards. If he doesn't have spares in stock, he can get them for you within 48 hours.

Police

Tel: 334-2244

Post Office

At Rock Sound Airport.

Restaurants

Harbour View Restaurant Tel: 334-2278   At the head of the dock on Fish Street, overlooking the waterfront, serving American and Bahamian food, with a disco on Thursday, Friday, and Saturday evenings. Three beers for $6 on Saturdays. Closed on Sundays.

North Side Restaurant and Bar Tel: 334-2573 • VHF 16   Open for breakfast, lunch, and dinner. They can collect you from a dock.

Sammy's Place Tel: 334-2121   A casual restaurant with an extensive lunch and dinner menu, and a wide selection of beer.

Vita's Blue Diamond Restaurant Tel: 334-2425

Telephone

Batelco office near the tower, open 9 am to 4:30 pm Monday to Friday.

MARINAS IN SOUTH ELEUTHERA

To reach Cape Eleuthera by road, just follow the outline of the Bight, which will lead you northwest from Waterford.

CAPE ELEUTHERA MARINA
Tel: 242-334-6327 • Fax: 334-6326 • VHF 16 "Cape E"

This has to be the most perfect, crescent-shaped marina in the entire Bahamas, with good, deep-water, easily visible entrance, and wonderful, clear, clean water inside. Unfortunately the amenities are few at this time, but the all-girl dockmaster team of Monique and Janice more than make up for the current lack of showers, toilets, marine stores, or restaurants. Now that the new Island School has opened up next door, using the marina for its dive boat operation, they are hopeful that they will soon have a telephone on the dock, and maybe even a laundromat by the end of 1999. Cape Eleuthera is a Port of Entry.

Slips	25
MLW at Dock	9 ft., with a 12-ft. entrance depth at low water.
Dockage	45¢ per ft. per day, $15 minimum, 25¢ per ft. per day monthly.
Power	30A, 50A, and 100A available at 42¢ per kWh, $10 per day minimum.
Fuel	Diesel and gasoline.
Water	20¢ per gallon.
Laundry	6 miles up the road.
Restaurant	*Sheril's Inn* in Deep Creek Tel: 334-8111 • VHF 16 Serves Bahamian/American food or will deliver meals to your boat on request.
Provisions	The dockmasters have sodas, candy, and ice for sale, but there is *Pinder's Dry Goods Store* in Deep Creek that monitors VHF 16, and *Thompson's Food Store*, both carrying dry goods. Or try *Brown's Grocery Store* in Green Castle. For more than food, you will have to go 25 miles to Rock Sound to find a bank, post office, hardware store, bakery, or well-stocked food store.
Liquor Store	*Friendly Bob's Liquor Store*
Ice	$3.50 per bag.
Trash	Collected weekly, no charge.
Medical	There is a nurse in Wemyss Bight, and a doctor and nurse on duty in Rock Sound. Tel: 334-2226 or 334-2182, or ask the dockmasters.
Charters	20-ft. boat available from $300 per day for fishing.
Car rental	From $60 a day. The dockmasters can help you organize a car.
Diving	Contact David Carey through Monique or Janice.
Boat cleaning	Cleveland Delancy Tel: 334-0142
Credit cards	Visa and MasterCard, 3-percent service charge added.

DAVIS HARBOUR MARINA or HOBO YACHT CLUB
Tel: 242-334-2280 • Fax: 334-6303 • VHF 16

This marina is over 30 years old, surrounded by brightly painted boat-owners' storehouses, with some of the friendliest staff we met anywhere. It has arguably the worst water, floating with disgusting looking flotsam, and no facilities apart from fuel and power, but very clean drinking water and good showers. Dockmaster Delroy Richards will help you all he can, and Davis Harbor is still a good jumping off (or in) point for Cat Island and Little San Salvador, and for some spectacular fishing. If you are prepared to walk, the settlement of Waterford is only about a mile to your north once you join the main highway. There is a small pink grocery store, *Down Home Pizza*, and Mr. Watson, in a little house on the left-hand side, who has the most delicious freshly roasted peanuts, and grapefruit from his own tree for sale.

Children in Waterford settlement, South Eleuthera.

Slips	30
MLW at Dock	7 ft., but a 4-ft. entrance at low water.
Dockage	$1 per ft. per day
Power	$15 per day for 30A, $20 per day for 50A.
Fuel	Diesel and gasoline.
Water	$6 per day under 40 ft.; $12 per day over 40 ft.
Telephone	In the dockmaster's office.
Showers	Yes, good ones with plenty of hot water but no shower curtains.
Laundry	The washing machine was filled with stagnant, rusty water when we were there, with assurance that a new machine was on its way.
Restaurant	The once-attractive second-floor restaurant and bar is now derelict. You can either order a taxi that will cost you about $25 or $30 and go off to *Sheril's Restaurant* in Deep Creek (Tel: 334-8111), or order in pizza from *D and N Down Home Pizza* (Tel: 334-6401) allowing at least 1½ hours for delivery.
Provisions	In Green Castle and Deep Creek or walk into the Waterford settlement and see what you can find.
Ice	$7 a bag, which seemed expensive, but they were out of it anyway, so don't rely on it.
Trash	Collected free
Dive site	Nearby *Bamboo Point* is probably one of the most dramatic and pristine wall dives in the Bahamas. The wall stretches down to Little San Salvador and Cat Island, dropping from 40 to 230 ft. and deeper off the edge.
Credit Cards	Visa and MasterCard.

Security	There is a security guard on duty all night. This is a gated marina.
Dockmaster	Delroy Richards

BEACHES IN ELEUTHERA

Preacher's Cave There is a pretty beach opposite the entrance to the cave, which overlooks the Devil's Backbone.

Gauldin Bay Continue north of Gregory Town until you pass the salt ponds, and look for a pasture on the second dirt road. Follow the road around to the right looking for the overhead power lines, until you come to the beach.

Rainbow Bay Drive east on Hidden Beach Drive from Queen's Highway, which deadends at the beach. Good snorkeling close in, or below the tennis court at the *Rainbow Inn*. Go in at the boat ramp and swim to the left, about fifty yards around the point staying close to the cliff, but don't swim if the waves are too big.

James Point If you turn east on Johnson Street in James Cistern, go to the top of the hill and then follow the dirt road to the right, you will find a wonderful beach. Coming in from the Governor's Harbour direction, this would be after the first speed bump.

Ten Bay Beach between Savannah Sound and Palmetto Point.

Ocean Side South from the airport at Governor's Harbour. Take the first dirt road on the left at the end of the runway where you will find miles of beach in both directions.

THINGS TO DO IN ELEUTHERA

- Rent a car and drive the length of this attractive island.
- If you're in Gregory Town in June, check the date of the Pineapple Festival. If you're lucky and it's on at the time, go and join in the fun. Even if it's not on, Gregory Town is still worth a visit.
- Take your photographs of the *Glass Window*, but not in bad weather. It can be dangerous there if heavy swells and high seas are coming in from the Atlantic.
- Stock up on art work in Tarpum Bay!
- Drive out on the sand road to Preacher's Cave and see where it all started in 1648. Swim off the beach. Snorkel the Devil's Backbone!
- Visit the Bogues and see real Bahamian villages.
- Go to The Current at low water and search the long east beach for sand dollars. Go a short way further south and check Current Cut before you run it in your own boat.
- Stop and admire the orchids at *The Duck Inn* as you wander the flower-lined, narrow hillside streets in Governor's Harbour.
- Visit the Ocean Hole in Rock Sound. You can sit on the steps and feed the fish too.

Chapter 13
North Andros

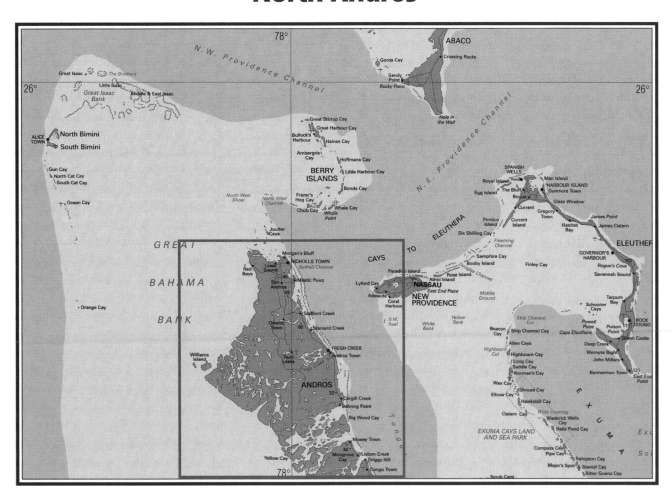

Andros Island

ANDROS ISLAND, over 100 miles in length and 40 miles wide (reckon it the size of Puerto Rico, but without the mountains) is the largest island in the Bahamas. It has about 5,000 inhabitants living in a scattering of isolated village clusters on the east coast, no road system to speak of, four small airfields, one marina, and about three (maybe five, depending on your classification) small resorts. The rest of the island is a wilderness of mahogany and pine forest, scrub, marsh, tidal inlets, and flats. Andros, the least favored (by its government) of all the big Bahamian islands, has long been known as "The Sleeping Giant" or "The Big Yard." Why the sparse population and why just the east coast? The answer is that the west coast, a maze of wetland and mud flats, is uninhabitable. The interior, tangled, hot, and rife with insects, has no prevailing cooling winds and is almost uninhabitable. The east coast has the cooling wind, and it has the ocean, both as a means of communication (long before aircraft) and a means of sustenance, primarily by fishing.

If you look at the geography of Andros, you can see that three lateral physical divisions, where three bights of water cut right across the island from east to west, make Andros even less cohesive and less attractive as a ground for settlement. Effectively the land below the North Bight (from Behring Point to the south) is more remote than the fabled boondocks, and both Central Andros (Mangrove Cay) and South Andros can only be reached by boat and air.

All this said, it is water that has saved Andros. First the ocean. Running little more than a mile off the east coast, at well over 100 miles in length, Andros has the third-largest continuous barrier reef in the world (after Australia's Great Barrier Reef, and the Belize Reef). The extraordinary coral of this reef, and its marine life, has brought marine biologists and divers to Andros from all over the world. Long ago this reef should have been given the status of a World Heritage Site. Each year that the reef continues to lack the environmental protection of the world community highlights our failure to take elemental steps to preserve this frail water planet for our descendants.

Outside the reef, a singular and almost unique inlet of deep ocean water, known as the Tongue of the Ocean, divides Andros from the shallow bank to the east of the Exuma Cays (see chart below). The Tongue of the Ocean is abysmal (some 6,000 feet deep) and suddenly you're there, off the reef in water space, hanging off sheer walls that plummet into blackness. This ocean inlet has brought almost every kind of pelagic fish to the waters off Andros, and with them, the sports and commercial fishermen. This phenomenal deep inlet has also brought the US Navy and the Royal Navy, jointly interested in undersea testing and evaluation programs, the purpose of which may be guessed, but is secret. This has also helped Andros survive.

Perhaps the third blessing that water has brought the island is abundant fresh water. Andros now supplies Nassau and New Providence Island with over 50 percent of the fresh water they require, shipped by tanker from North Andros. Now in Andros they'll tell you that both the naval testing and the export of fresh water have barely benefited their island directly, because the rent for the naval bases is paid into the accounts of the Bahamian government, and the water is taken as a Bahamian birthright. Perhaps a greater annual dividend for Andros might have helped the Sleeping Giant attend to its yard.

Andros is, above all, a strange place. The reasons why Andros is as it is today are clear, and yet it puzzles. In a way it defeats logical explanation and falls, rather like Ireland, into the field of intuitive acceptance: that is how things are. An island where the ghosts of the Arawaks remain almost within touch (evidence of a mass suicide in an inland blue hole), a land the Spanish named but gave up as hopeless, a base for pirates like Henry Morgan whose treasure, so legend has it, remains buried in Andros, a refuge for the hard-pressed Florida Seminoles who were not enchanted by finding themselves and their territory included in the US (whose descendants allegedly survive in Red Bay to this day), a place in which tourist de-

NORTH ANDROS		
Morgans Bluff		
MRGNE	25° 11' 00"/000 N	077° 59' 00"/000 W
Morgans Bluff Entry Buoys (not for navigation)		
MRGNB	25° 11' 09"/150 N	078° 01' 02"/033 W
Bethel Channel (not for navigation)		
BTHEL	25° 08' 30"/500 N	077° 57' 30"/500 W
Fresh Creek		
FRESH	24° 44' 00"/000 N	077° 45' 00"/000 W

The final figures in each waypoint show seconds (00") and thousands (000) of a minute.

velopment has never taken root other than in remote fishing camps and latterly one or two dive resorts. Andros is a mystic, still largely unexplored place, fearsome in the remoteness of the interior, the home of the dreaded *chickcharnies*, a short-tempered feathered Androsian lepre-

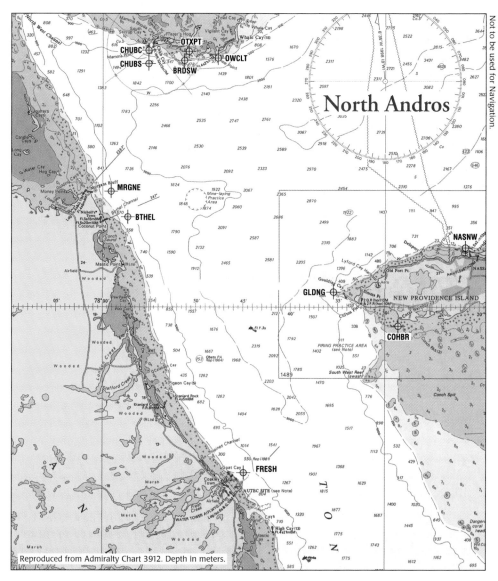

Reproduced from Admiralty Chart 3912. Depth in meters.

chaun with powerful psychic influence, whose habit it is to live hanging upside down from trees.

We had hoped to write with enthusiasm of changes in North Andros, but if anything the last two years have brought little improvement, save for some of the snazziest settlement signs we've ever seen decorating the Queen's Highway, each one a veritable work of art. In Fresh Creek the Lighthouse Marina remains the flag carrier, and indeed remains the only conceivable destination for any cruising or sports-fishing visitor. It now has the added attraction of a well-run new dive enterprise, Andros Undersea Adventures. The Chickcharney Hotel, that great yellow stranded whale of a building on the North Bank, remains in business pursuing its commercial destiny in unfathomable ways, sometimes barred and grilled, sometimes open for casual business. See our **Yellow Pages**. Hank's Place has gone fancy with a deck and loud music. There's not much else to report from Fresh Creek.

Morgans Bluff, which has gained one of the snazzy new signs (this one marking Morgans Cave) has remained locked in a time warp. Walking into Willy's Bar, that's exactly how it seems. Perhaps our greatest disappointment was to find the Andros Beach Hotel in Nicholls Town in a state where total demolition must precede the rebirth of this once well-sited facility, and the dock is now unusable. Don't even think of it. But nothing is permanent save change, and the owner of the Green Windows Inn (as well as the Texaco station, a car rental agency by the Inn, and the dive shop in Nicholls Town), is talking of a new dive shop in Morgans Bluff, and a car rental agency in Fresh Creek, all of which could benefit the boat-borne visitor. See our **Yellow Pages**.

What is going on in Andros is the development of a rash of bonefish lodges, which clearly are the Flavor of the Day. There may already be too many to meet demand spread over any twelve-month period, and they may be pricing themselves out. We have that feeling, but then we're no more than dispassionate observers.

For us, in this Edition, two messages come out of our return to Andros.

THE INSIDE REEF PASSAGE
The first is a note of admiration and congratulation, and a caution. We have always maintained that cruising territory can be classed as an area where no unusual hazards exist. The vagaries of weather, for most of us, are quite enough to deal with whether you've got 1,000 feet under your keel or 15 feet. For this reason we wrote off as quite outside our set parameters the consideration of passage making inside the Andros Barrier Reef. Stephen Pavlides, in his 1997 *On and Off the Beaten Path. The Central and Southern Bahamas Guide*, has pioneered just such a route, which takes you from Morgans Bluff to Fresh Creek. It's a remarkable voyage of exploration. Take his hand in guidance if you have a mind to go this way. But maybe square it with your insurers first?

The Predators

THE new dive operators in Fresh Creek, Andros Undersea Adventures, were pressured to provide the GPS references of dive sites they recommended. The visitors, scuba divers, did not require rental dive gear, and were prepared to dive unescorted. Not entirely happy about it, out of goodwill and an unfortunately misplaced belief in the conservation awareness of all divers, the visitors were given the locations of a selection of reefs.

One of these was a shallow dive site, well stocked with all the normal, healthy population of an inshore reef. The fish population, never harmed by Man, were curious, unafraid. The visitors dived with spear guns. Three days later the dive shop operator found a desolation. There were no adult fish left. The juveniles were scared by the divers. The reef had lost its population, and its life. Today it is no longer visited. There is no point in going there.

MARINE CONSERVATION
In our First Edition we made the point that for every day that passed the failure of the Bahamas government and the World at large to ensure that the Andros Barrier Reef was declared a World Heritage Site, was near-criminal, in terms of global conservation. The situation has not changed. There are no marked, buoyed, and protected dive sites. There are no protection rules. There are no conservation areas. Each year more damage is done. It is impossible, in our human time span, to reverse such damage. We will say no more at this point, for what we say is too great an issue to come simply under the heading of **Andros**. See our Editorial, and our **Green Pages**.

THE TONGUE OF THE OCEAN AND THE ANDROS BARRIER REEF

The Tongue of the Ocean, whether you approach it from the shallow green waters of the Bank off the Exumas or directly from the Andros Coast is extraordinary, a color change that goes from green to ultramarine to ink blue almost instantly as your depth sounder goes ape and then gives up. If you're bent on fishing, there's nothing that can't be found in that deep blue water and you'll stop fishing for dolphin (not dolphin as in Flipper, but the fish the Spanish named *dorado*: we got it wrong in translation) for you'll catch too many. In the southern circlet of the Tongue of the Ocean they say that marlin, who somehow took a wrong turn off the Marlin Ocean Interstate Highway, are hanging out there and hungry.

As for the naval side, if you're around Andros Town you'll soon learn that AUTEC (the Atlantic Underwater Test and Evaluation Center) is everywhere you look, and manifests itself in an array of buoys (which attract the dolphin), strange towers, forbidden harbors, and communication masts. Other than using AUTEC facilities as landmarks, there's not much to be gained from their presence if you're a cruising visitor and you're likely to fall short of a welcome if you take an AUTEC harbor as a storm refuge. AUTEC is not for you.

The barrier reef is (the word comes up again and again) "awesome." We're talking about visibility (100 feet is minimal), coral formations, dropoffs and walls, blue holes, marine life, and the whole quintessence of the scuba world. You can dive the reef without guides, but you're wise to go guided. Your anchor depths off the reef are deep (45 or 50 feet), and your dive depths can be deep too (120 feet to even 185 feet if you wish). The blue holes can be hazardous, sucking in water and expelling water with the tide. You could be stuck in one for a tide change, which could spoil your day if you're on a single 80-cubic-foot tank.

Andros as a Cruising Ground

We're not surprised that Andros has remained a land apart in the Bahamas, and not surprised that the name Andros doesn't come forward often in cruising circle conversation. We've had a hard enough time trying to figure out the nature of the place and a newcomer to Andros might well be forgiven for believing that chickcharnies built the square offshore towers (as fishing shacks?) and strange creatures called autecs haunt the forests of the interior. Taking a cool

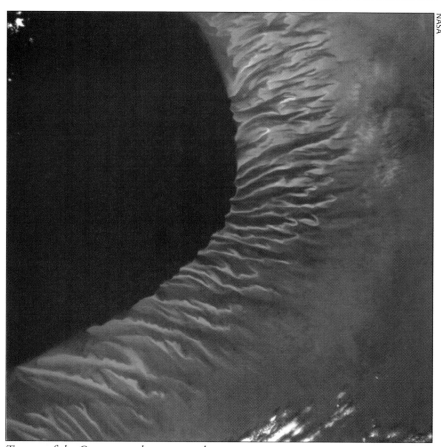

Tongue of the Ocean, southeastern end.

dispassionate look at navigation in Andros is as difficult an exercise in comprehension.

Andros certainly falls into the big island category. It's Big Island magnified. What's the cruising analysis? There's just the one (east) coast that's approachable, (plus a shoal draft trans-Andros passage through the South Bight). That one coastline, with its barrier reef, presents problems. There are very few places you can enter through the reef, and very few places where you can navigate with safety running inside the reef. There are too many coral heads, shallows, and the overall depth is mostly shoal draft at best. Support facilities for the cruising vessel are minimal in Andros. You could say virtually non-existent. Fresh Creek is the only place anywhere close to development and it's small (we were told "small is beautiful, and we want to keep it that way") and has little to offer in the support line.

We debated at length how best to handle Andros. We concluded that if we worked our way along the east coast, whichever way we took it, we'd end up writing a land guide to Andros, for there's almost no navigation advice we could give other than to say "once you're in Andros water, you're on your own—get someone local to guide you if this scares you." A negative approach, you might say, but there are plenty of straight travel guides out there if you want to read about the island. Think it through. The essence of cruising is safe, enjoyable navigation, not setting yourself the ultimate testing experience. Other factors come into the cruising "wish list," none of which are soft or decadent: airports for crew changes, marinas with telephones and shore power, fuel, and backup facilities (however minimal) coming up somewhere on your route every now and again. You might reasonably expect landfalls worth discovery trips ashore, and to be able to find transport to make your way around if you wish. Safe anchorages will be high on your list if you want to be alone, or away from telephones and shore power. Continue the analysis for yourself if you wish, but the greater part of Andros (while reachable by boat and often only by boat) is not, in our opinion, an area we would class as a cruising ground.

North Andros is the only part of the island that comes even remotely close to satisfying any of these parameters. We've concentrated on two areas that might feature on your visit list for one reason or another. The first is Fresh Creek, and the second (far less well-favored) is the north tip of Andros, Morgans Bluff and the Bethel Channel area (Conch Sound and Nicholls Town). In future editions, as Andros develops, we'll keep pace and we'll add more. Nothing we've said denies the fact that the whole east coast of Andros offers superb fishing (deep sea, reef, and flats) and superb diving. Central and South Andros offers tiny remote settlements where you can tuck yourself in (but carry insect repellent that works—you'll need it) and fish the flats. If this is your life, go for it; and if you're one of the small band who commute from Florida to the Exumas by way of the South Bight (where you may have 4 feet at high water) go

for it. In our catamaran days, with a 2-foot-6-inch draft and no compelling requirement for shore power, we would never have hesitated to explore these unfrequented waterways. But for the reasons we've given, and as Fresh Creek is the only place in Andros with the facilities to take cruising boats, we start there and work our way north to cover the other options.

Approach Routes to Andros

The Mid-Exumas to Fresh Creek

The route from the mid-Exumas, just north of Staniel Cay, is an easy one (73.32 nm on a heading of 301°M) that avoids the worst of the coral head–cluttered areas lying on the western edge of the Exuma bank, just before you gain the deep water of the Tongue of the Ocean. We tried to find a course that could be taken as one straight run with the minimum of eyeball navigation on the way, and think we achieved it.

There are two areas where you should keep a particularly sharp lookout for coral heads. The first is around 24° 25' 00"/000 N 077° 00' 00"/000 W. There are a few there. The second area is just before you reach the Tongue of the Ocean. Around 24° 30' 22"/366 N 077° 13' 00"/000 W you'll find yourself in 12–13 feet of water with a minefield of coral heads all around you. Most of them are safely beneath the surface but don't trust any of them. Go slowly, and hand steer for a while. Within 2 nm you'll hit the 100-fathom line, and two miles later you'll have 500 fathoms under your keel.

Nassau to Morgans Bluff, Bethel Channel, or Fresh Creek

From Nassau, having cleared the west entrance of Nassau Harbour, you want to get offshore, something like 2 nm, before setting your course for Andros. If you're heading for Morgans Bluff (MRGNB), you'll have 32.9 nm to run on a heading of 283°M. If you're heading for Bethel Channel (BTHEL), Nicholls Town, and Conch Sound, it's 31.3 nm on a heading of 279°M. If you're going to Fresh Creek (FRESH), after leaving Nassau Harbour the best way is to go coastal, visual all the way, to just 1 nm west of Goulding Cay on the west tip of New Providence Island. Then set a direct course for Fresh Creek. You'll have 19.51 nm to run from Goulding Cay (GLDNG) on a heading of 211°M.

Chub Cay to Morgans Bluff, Bethel Channel, or Fresh Creek

From Chub Cay (CHUBC) down to Andros is a straightforward run from our waypoint 1 nm due south of Chub Cay. For Morgans Bluff it's 12.82 nm on 202°M. For the Bethel Channel (Nicholls Town and Conch Sound) it's 14.95 nm on 194°M. For Fresh Creek, to our mind the most likely destination, it's 40.25 nm on a heading of 172°M.

Andros Reef, 30 feet down.

Fresh Creek
(Andros and Coakley Towns)

Andros Town and Coakley Town are Siamese-twin settlements linked by a bridge over Fresh Creek, and the whole settled area can be called Fresh Creek. Andros Town, to the south, has the Lighthouse Yacht Club and Marina, and the outlet for Androsian batik fabrics, tucked away behind in the trees. Other than the old lighthouse on the south entrance to the Creek, which is in a sad state of neglect, that's Andros Town.

Across the bridge Coakley Town boasts two hotels, the Chickcharney and the Landmark, both with bars and restaurants and a kind of mid-Western rail town feel to them. There's a "supermarket" and there are a number of small shops, but Coakley Town is sprawling, awaiting better days, and has little to offer but the watering holes adopted by off-duty AUTEC personnel. Hank Roberts, the one-time dockmaster at the Lighthouse Marina, has just opened a new watering hole with a small restaurant (which has clearly won AUTEC favor).

Fresh Creek is not fresh, not river water as we know it. This despite the impressive river-like characteristics of Fresh Creek seen from the bridge, particularly at ebb tide. It's saline. Not drinking water, not even clothes-washing water.

Approach to Fresh Creek

The approach to Fresh Creek is simple. There are two radio masts, one (AUTEC) some way south of Fresh Creek (and there's the AUTEC harbor there too, and an orange-and-white-checkered water tower) and one radio mast (Batelco) north of Fresh Creek. There are two AUTEC towers (like square huts on stilts), one south of the entrance channel, and one north (right on the edge of it). To the north a string of some seven barren rocks (with a little green on some of them) run north–south, ending in a channel light marker. You pass out of deep water as you get closer to the channel light, and the rocks on your starboard side mark the line of

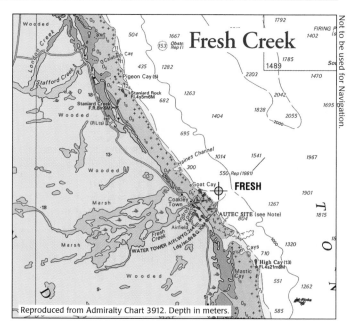
Reproduced from Admiralty Chart 3912. Depth in meters.

the inshore reef. Of course that reef continues on your port side too, but it's not so obvious. Favor the light side (the north), and favor that AUTEC tower to the north too (but don't get closer to it than 200 feet).

As you get closer to the entry to the Creek, you'll see a rock promontory running out a little way from the north point, and there's shallow water to the south (there's a ledge there, about 100 feet out in the narrows). Just swing around that rock promontory, which can be clearly seen, stay safely off the ledge, and make your way up Fresh Creek holding center channel.

ANCHORAGE AND MARINA

The Lighthouse Marina comes up almost immediately on your port side. If you want to anchor, go on past it, and find a place in the basin before the road bridge, and far enough off the Government Dock (which is to starboard, past the yellow Chickcharney Hotel) so that the mailboats have a turning circle. It's said that the holding there is not good, which comes as no surprise for dredging in the past and the swift-running tides must have scoured the bottom clean.

The tidal flow is formidable (over 6 knots at extreme tides) and making your way into the Lighthouse Yacht Club and Marina at any time other than slack tide demands well applied power and a degree of seamanship not normally called for at most marinas. It's worth holding off momentarily to check the direction and force of the stream before committing yourself to an approach. Once you're there, and tied up, you're fine. You have hotel accommodations with its bar and restaurant, showers, laundry, fuel, and willing attention. There is no other place like it, no other marina, in Andros. If you are using your boat day by day, be aware that AUTEC broadcast warnings of areas they have declared off limits over channel 16 each day.

Approach to Fresh Creek.

THE FRESH CREEK HINTERLAND

Explorers venturing out into the Fresh Creek hinterland will not find a multiplicity of excitements. In the south there's the AUTEC base. To the north, some 3 miles out of Coakley Town, you come to the mini-settlement of Small Hope Bay where, on a beach promontory, the Canadian Dick Birch opened his Small Hope Bay Club in the 1960s. Devoted primarily to SCUBA diving and the pursuit of a simple life that could be summed up as sarongs and bare feet, for over thirty years the charismatic Birch, with the assistance of three successive wives (who all stayed on with the team), built up a business that has a 60 percent repeat rate and gave birth to Androsian batik. Peter Birch has now taken over the reins on the death of his father, and the little resort continues unchanged. It's small, family, totally informal, communal in its life-style, and your welcome will be friendly.

The Small Hope dive staff don't follow the PADI/NAUI/ DAN rules for recreation diving and 185-foot dives are regularly on the program, but you're not compelled to go deeper than you wish. Nor are C-cards asked for, or dive logs. All that's required before you dive with them is a simple check-out to ensure that you can remove and replace your mask and regulator under water.

Fresh Creek to the Bethel Channel and Morgans Bluff

As a straight course from Fresh Creek, our Morgans Bluff waypoint is a run of 29.83 nm on a heading of 340°M. This course keeps you in deep water all the way. If you elect to try the Bethel Channel (for Conch Sound or Nicholls Town), your run on this heading stops short at 26.99 nm. We're not entirely happy with the Bethel Channel or with Conch Sound and Nicholls Town.

Fresh Creek Lighthouse Marina.

The Bethel Channel

The Bethel Channel is the only viable boat channel through the Andros barrier reef between Fresh Creek and Morgans Bluff. It had importance in the past when the mailboat used the channel to serve Conch Sound settlement to the south of the Bethel Channel and Nicholls Town to the north. Now the Bethel Channel is a route for local, small-draft boats and is not an entryway to anchorages, docks, shoreside facilities, or any of the infrastructure of value to a visiting boat. Why do we mention it? Because the Bethel Channel is identified on the charts, and if we ignore it, you'll wonder why we missed it.

The Channel has an entry range (lighted, with white lights), which will bring you in through the passage (reckon 4 feet at MLW but the locals claim a greater depth) into inshore water. Keep going until you are about 100 feet from the shore, but use your eyes judging the water depth rather than measuring that distance off so precisely. Then turn north if you want Nicholls Town or turn south for Conch Sound, staying inshore (100–150 feet) all the while.

CONCH SOUND

Only the old Government concrete Dock with a survey mark embedded in it remains to remind the straggling Conch Sound of its mailboat days, but even then the mailboat couldn't get in right up to the dock and passengers and goods had to be tendered ashore and embarked. They'll tell you that Conch Sound is a good anchorage, all along that coastline south of Bethel Channel, and has 7 feet of water if you don't get too far south and too close to Scotts Cays. Just off the cays, on the reef, you can see the 1926 wreck of the *Potomac*. Wrecks are always an encouraging sign when you're trying to work out routes through a reef, but the *Potomac* is a great dive site.

The same reef that stranded the *Potomac* is the prime reason for local faith in the Conch Sound anchorage, in that the barrier reef gives protection even in onshore weather and (we quote) "it don't never get rough in here." The craft we found using Conch Sound were all Whaler-size local boats. As for Conch Sound as a place to visit, even though it has the somewhat surprising, newish, and upmarket Conch Sound Resort Inn (tucked away well inshore, in the village), we'd advise leaving it off your list of ports of call.

NICHOLLS TOWN

Nicholls Town is so spread out that it has no comprehensible cohesive identity. On the shore side, the very heart was taken out of Nicholls Town when the Andros Beach Hotel and its Dive Shop closed and the vandals started to take over. It has a great site on a pretty sand beach, and the hotel's docks (now deteriorating fast) were at least a place where you could secure alongside, although there was no power or water, you were open to the northeast and south, and exposed to surge.

There's another small dock in Nicholls Town, immediately after you round the point after heading north from Bethel Channel and enter the shallow Nicholls Town Bay, but this is for local boats and you should not consider it. Until such time as the Andros Beach Hotel regains life and its docks are rebuilt, cross Nicholls Town off your list.

MORGANS BLUFF

You can't miss Morgans Bluff, a great 40-foot high spine of limestone that's the final marker of Andros Island. To its north there's the water maze of the Golding and Joulter Cays, but if nothing else Andros ends in style with its one long gray, jagged headland. The entry channel to Morgans Bluff is well marked with conventional buoys and you'll have no problems. The outer buoys lie at 25° 11' 09"/150 N 078° 01' 02"/033 W and are easy to pick up.

Around the corner behind the bluff, to port you have the long Government Dock, which is off limits to all but mailboats, traders, and the water tankers. The anchorage lies off the curve of sand beach, giving around 8 feet or more at MLW, and is completely exposed to the north. If you are there in a Norther, unless you have shoal draft and can work your way behind one of the cays to the north, or further around to the west into Lowe Sound, you're going to be uncomfortable if you stay. The anchorage is large, so you're unlikely to be crowded, but even if there's room to swing, you should set two anchors.

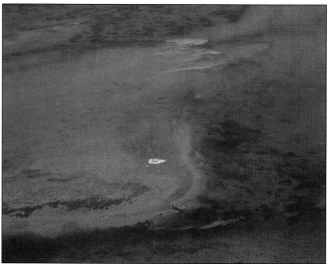
Joulter Cays. Fishing boat grounded on reef.

There's one small commercial harbor in Morgans Bluff, approached through an entry channel that carries a good 8 feet of water (as far as we could tell), and an interior depth greater than that. This has one concrete wharf, given to the mailboats and traders who are rejects from the major Government Dock outside, and the rest is a crude excavated basin, still unwalled but lined with old car tires with a surprising run of rustproof-painted iron bollards hammered into the bare soil. It is there that you'll find fuel. We hesitate to say a fuel dock, for you have to come alongside the car tires closest to the fuel pumps, and jump the gap to shore, but this is the only marine fuel in Andros until you reach Fresh Creek.

What of Morgans Bluff itself? There's Willie's bar by the fuel place, which, if nothing else, has atmosphere. Further inland there are the derelict buildings of a failed wood pulp enterprise, whose smarter housing, high on the bluff, has now become the enclave of local government servants, police officers, schoolteachers, and the like. Apart from Henry Morgan's Cave (not very striking or believable), which lies off the main road in the limestone strata under the housing estate of the police officers and the schoolteachers, there's nothing more in Morgans Bluff.

Why go there? Go there if you need fuel. Go there for shelter (but not in a Norther). Go there to get a night's sleep at anchor, if your passage planning works out that way. Finally, if you're interested in Bahamian sailing regattas, go there for the Morgans Bluff Regatta in June. You'll be there with some 3,000 others, but if that's your scene, you'll find a place transformed. Like a sub-tropical Brigadoon, Morgans Bluff, which otherwise appears to have perhaps twenty visible inhabitants, takes off over one wild weekend and is jumping.

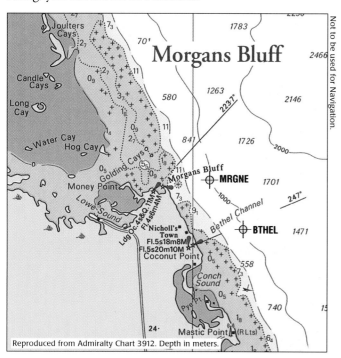
Reproduced from Admiralty Chart 3912. Depth in meters.

YELLOW PAGES

FRESH CREEK
(ANDROS AND COAKLEY TOWNS)

Despite being the largest island in the Bahamas, stretching some 100 miles from top to bottom, with some of the best scuba diving in the world, together with superb fishing and more than 50 varieties of orchids growing here, little is known about Andros in the cruising world, due mainly to the lack of good anchorages or marinas. Andros is still a mysterious and largely unexplored island, and our Yellow Pages cover only the areas that are accessible to cruising boats. There are other bonefishing lodges and resorts on different parts of the island, but they are difficult to reach unless you have a shoal draft boat and good local knowledge. As the main harbor for the island, it is still a surprise to find Fresh Creek so quiet. It attracts those who have known of its hidden charms for many years, while cruising boats looking for excitement and glamour tend to ignore Andros altogether. **Customs** and **Immigration** can be called from the airport by the *Lighthouse Marina* if you need to clear in on arrival.

MARINA

LIGHTHOUSE YACHT CLUB AND MARINA
Tel: 242-368-2305
• Fax: 368-2300 • VHF 16
Owned and run by the Bahamian government, the *Lighthouse Yacht Club and Marina* is still the only marina on Andros. The pink hotel, overlooking the few slips, is well maintained, with a pleasant dining room and helpful staff. Don't rely on the dockmaster answering your call on VHF 16 as you come in, but there will always be someone around to help you if you have booked a slip. Anchoring is not always possible further up the creek toward the road bridge; it is largely scoured out and the current runs at about 6 knots

Old lighthouse near the Yacht Club.

in and out every day, which makes holding difficult. And, of course, you have to leave room for the mailboats. But there is still an interesting and largely unexplored island awaiting you when you choose to come in here. For many visitors, it is the excitement of the fantastic diving; for others it is a place that is trying hard to put its past behind it, and show its new face.

Slips	17
MLW at Dock	8 ft. to 10 ft.
Dockage	65¢ per ft. per day.
Power	$12 per day for 50A and 30A.
Fuel	Diesel and gasoline.
Water	$5 per day.
Telephone	Public telephone
Showers	Yes, just adequate.
Laundry	$2 per washer or dryer. Ask the dockmaster how to start the machines.

Restaurant	Open at 7:30 am for breakfast, lunch, and dinner with a bar, and indoor or terrace dining overlooking the marina.
Swimming	Pool for marina guests.
Bank	*Royal Bank of Canada* in the hotel grounds.
Diving	*Andros Undersea Adventures* at the marina Tel: 368-2795
Accommodations	*Lighthouse Yacht Club* Tel: 368-2305 Has 20 well-appointed rooms, from $130 per night, overlooking the gardens or the marina.
Credit cards	Visa, MasterCard, and Amex.
Dockmaster	Don Goodman

SERVICES

Bank
Royal Bank of Canada Tel: 368-2071 Behind the hotel, open 9 am to 3 pm on Monday, Thursday, and Friday, to 1 pm on Tuesday and Wednesday.

Clinic
Health Centre in Fresh Creek Tel: 368-2038 On the first road left after you cross the bridge from the *Lighthouse Marina*, with a doctor and a nurse.
Ragnasbah Medical Clinic in Fresh Creek Tel: 368-2051 Open Fridays between 9 am and 2 pm to make appointments for Saturdays from 9 am to closing.

Laundromat
Adderley's Bargain Mart and Washerette Tel: 368-2201 Open 8:30 am to 10 pm Monday to Saturday, to 12:30 pm on Sundays. $1 tokens to wash or dry, from the *Bargain Mart* next door.

Police
Tel: 368-2626

Post Office
In the new pink administration building for Calabash Bay and Fresh Creek, a short walk out of town on the right side of the road. Open from 9:30 am to 1 pm, and 2 pm to 4 pm, Monday to Friday.

Telephones
Batelco, opposite *Skinny's Landmark Hotel and Bar*, open 9 am to 4:30 pm Monday to Friday. Sells phone cards and has two card phones outside, and two telephones inside. They will not accept US $100 or $50 bills.

SHOPPING

Clothing, Gifts & Souvenirs
Androsia Factory Outlet Store, at the Androsia Factory outside the entrance to the *Lighthouse Marina.* Tel: 368-2080 Open from 8 am to 4 pm, Monday to Friday, to 1 pm on Saturdays. Superb hand-screened batik that is exported worldwide; tours available.
Straw Shop On the front street, almost opposite the road down to *Chickcharnie's*, a little shop selling locally made straw baskets, hats, toys. There is talk that one day soon a Straw Market will open in Fresh Creek to encourage straw making on Andros.

Groceries
Adderley's Bargain Mart Tel: 368-2201 Open 8 am to 10 pm Monday to Saturday, to 12:30 pm on Sundays. An amazing variety of merchandise, including bottled water, canned and dried goods, and some fresh vegetables and fruit.
Charlie Gay at the *Chickcharnie Hotel* Tel: 368-2025 A general store carrying a surprising assortment of things. Opening hours seem to be during the morning, and then again late afternoon.

Gaiter's   A limited selection of food stuffs.

Penn's Meat Market and Convenience Store   Open from 8 am to 11 pm Monday to Saturday, to 1 pm on Sunday, with a selection of frozen meats and a few groceries.

Liquor

Skinny's Wholesale Liquor next door to *Skinny's Landmark Hotel* and opposite *Batelco*. Open 9 am to 5 pm, Monday to Friday.

Vegetables

Some mornings, Magnolia, or Maggie as she likes her friends to call her, brings fresh fruit and vegetables to sell from the back of a

Janet Wilson

WELCOME TO BEAUTIFUL FRESH CREEK THE HEART OF TOWN

pickup near the bank at the *Lighthouse Yacht Club*. Otherwise, it is difficult to find any fresh produce locally.

RESTAURANTS & BARS

Chickcharnie Hotel   Tel: 368-2025   Open for meals on demand.

Golden Conch Restaurant, up the hill

Hank's Place   Tel: 368-2447   On the waterfront next to the bridge serving good Bahamian food from 11 am to 10 pm Monday to Saturday; and Sunday special dinners of wild hog and fish, from 5 pm. Hank Roberts used to be dockmaster at the *Lighthouse Marina*, and he and Eva have recently rebuilt the restaurant. There is a pleasant deck outside overlooking the water for dining or just enjoying their aptly named special drink, a Hanky Panky—or two. A dinghy dock was planned at time of writing.

Lighthouse Yacht Club Restaurant   Open 7:30 am to 10 pm serving good American and Bahamian food in a very pleasant dining room, or outdoors on the terrace overlooking the creek.

Skinny's Landmark Hotel and Bar and *Treat's Bar* are both noisy and well frequented.

Small Hope Bay Lodge   Tel: 368-2014   3 miles north of Fresh Creek, where you dine family style. Call ahead for dinner reservations.

Square Deal Restaurant

GETTING AROUND

Airport

Andros Town Airport is three miles south of the town.

Bahamasair   Fifteen-minute flights twice daily to and from Nassau; only one flight on Wednesdays. The fare is $42.

Small Hope Bay Lodge

Charter flights to Fort Lauderdale.

Major's Air   Tel: 329-4309   Fly to and from Freeport to Fresh Creek, San Andros, and Mangrove Cay.

Car Rental

Bill Adderley   Tel: 368-2514/2560   Cars from $70 per day.

Donalds Rent A Car and *Five Rent A Car* may also be able to help you. Ask at the Lighthouse Yacht Club.

Mailboats

M/V Lady D leaves Fresh Creek at 7:30 am on Saturdays, and returns at 6 pm on Tuesdays.

M/V Lady Gloria arrives on Tuesdays at 4 pm, and leaves at 7 pm for South Andros, returning Thursdays at 1 pm until Saturdays at 7:30 am. The fare to Nassau is $30 one way.

Taxis

There are many taxis operating in Fresh Creek, but a few names to ask for are:

Lynden Farrington   Tel: 368-5183/2339.

Or *Linwood Johnson, John Saunders, Rupert Leadon, Paul Roberts, Floyd Newmour, Irwin Mackey,* or *Adolphos Leadon*.

SPORTS

Diving

Andros Undersea Adventures   Tel: 242-368-2795 • Fax: 368-2796 • E-mail: androsmm@aol.com • Web site: www.divebahamas.com Martina and Matthias Mueller, with Mark's help, are running a highly organized, bi-lingual dive operation here, with previous experience in the Red Sea and the Maldives. As open water dive instructor and master scuba diver trainer/divemaster, these two can show you some of the wonders of the world's third-largest barrier reef, in either German or English. One-tank dives from $40, snorkelers from $25 on their 38-ft. dive boat, the *Santa Fe*, which is fully equipped for diving with a Bauer Compressor, 80-cu-ft. tanks, and full rental equipment. A resort course will cost you $125, an Advanced Open Water course $240.

Dive Sites

This is one place where it really is advisable to dive with experienced operators, such as Martina and Matthias, rather than try to find the sites on your own. The wall dives such as *Diana's Dungeons, Hole in the Wall,* the immense *Ocean Blue Hole,* and *Skeebo's Surprise* are all stunning dives, while *Klein's and Peter's Reefs* are shallower reef dives. And a comparatively recent wreck, the *Marion*, a mobile crane that fell off a barge, lies in 70 ft. of water after sinking in 1987. Or try *Brad's Mountain,* a honeycombed coral mountain in 50 ft. of water with schools of Atlantic spadefish and Bermuda chub. In perfect weather conditions, and if you are an experienced diver, you might be lucky enough to be taken out to the AUTEC buoy for an open water dive, where there is a chance of meeting up with silky sharks as you dive in the 6,000-foot-deep waters.

ACCOMMODATIONS

Chickcharnies Hotel   Tel: 242-368-2025   Waterview rooms from $75 per day; simply furnished, rooms without a view from $60 per day. Restaurant opens on demand. Five new cottages for weekly rental are under construction along the waterfront. There is a concrete dock outside that has space where you can tie up alongside, but there are no facilities and you will need extra fat fenders to hold you off against the tidal creek flow.

Coakley House   Tel: 242-368-2013 or 800-223-6961 • Fax: 368-2015   Three air-conditioned bedrooms in the former Commander of the Royal Navy's house, at the entrance to Fresh Creek, from $1,750 per week, with its own dinghy dock and once-a-day transport to *Small Hope Bay Lodge*. Cook and maid service available.

Lighthouse Yacht Club Hotel   Tel: 242-368-2305   In a garden setting, overlooking the creek and the boats, with 20 pleasant rooms available from $130 per day.

Small Hope Bay Lodge   Tel: 242-368-2013 • Fax: 368-2015 Twenty beachfront cottages from $175 per day, including three meals daily. Diving, bonefishing, windsurfers, kayaks, lasers, bicycles, and their own flights into Andros from Florida.

NICHOLLS TOWN

There is a Customs office, a police station, and *The Andromed Medical Centre* (Tel: 329-2171) on the Nicholls Town Highway, which opens from 6 am to 8 pm, Monday and Wednesday, and on Saturdays from 3 to 8 pm. The doctor is there from 8 am to 4 pm on Fridays, and every other Saturday. The dentist is there every other Saturday. There is a *Batelco* office with telephones inside and outside, and a post office in Nicholl's Town, as well as a *CIBC* bank (329-2382). *The Green Windows Inn* (Tel: 242-329-2194 • Fax: 329-2016), with its peacocks and orchids, has 10 simple rooms above the bar and restaurant, some with shared bathrooms, from $70 to $86 per night. The owners of *The Green Windows Inn,* Patrick and Kenny Robinson, are now starting a dive operation in Morgans Bluff, and a bonefish lodge, as well as refurbishing their hotel rooms. The diving will start from their *Andros Scuba Centre and Dive Resort* at Morgans Bluff and the bonefishing from their *Bonefishing Resort.* They plan to open another car rental in Fresh Creek soon, and will sell LP Gas in Nicholls Town and Fresh Creek. They have a filling station adjacent to the hotel, as well as their grocery and liquor store and *Tropical Car Rental* (Tel: 329-2515/2194). The two main resorts here, the *Andros Beach Hotel* and the *San Andros Hotel,* have been closed down for the last few years, and show little sign of reopening. Diesel and gasoline are available at the commercial harbor.

Bahamasair and *Majors* use San Andros Airport, and there are charter flights as well. Daily flights to and from Nassau. The mailboat, *M/V Lisa J,* leaves Nassau at 3:30 pm on Tuesdays, calling at Nicholls Town, Mastic Point, and Morgans Bluff. The fare is $30.

MORGANS BLUFF

Willy's Water Lounge is a good starting point for information. For transport, Evan Rolle (329-7293) offers trips out to the reef in his whaler, as well as a taxi service. *Willy's Water Lounge* will direct you to the grocery store, send you off in a taxi, and put you in touch with Philip, who takes dive trips to the reef. *Henry Morgan's Cave* is near Morgans Bluff, but sadly overgrown, so take a flashlight with you. The settlement of Red Bay, home to the descendants of Seminole Indians, is 40 minutes away by car.

Janet Wilson

RESTAURANTS

Big Josh Seafood and Restaurant at Lowe Sound
Conch Sound Resort Inn Tel: 329-2060
Green Windows Inn and Restaurant, Nicholls Town Tel: 329-2194 Restaurant, bar, hotel; call Kenny for reservations.
Joe's Seafood Grill at Lowe Sound. A new venture by a young local Androsian, the liveliest place to go with music every night, except Sundays.
Morgan's Treasures Tel: 329-2072 Call Evie for reservations. Open for dinner daily, serving Bahamian food overlooking the bluffs.
Rumours Restaurant and Disco on the road to Nicholls Town. A popular local restaurant.
Willy's Water Lounge at Morgans Bluff commercial harbor. Offers helpful advice, a pool table, and Bahamian food.

FISHING TOURNAMENTS AND REGATTAS

June
Inter Island Fly Fishing Tournament at Cargill Creek Bonefish Lodge, Cargill Creek. Contact the Andros Tourist Office at 242-368-2286.
North Andros Regatta, at Morgans Bluff. Contact the commissioner's office at 242-368-2340.
July
Mangrove Cay Independence Regatta Contact Mr. Earthel Greene at 242-369-0164 or Fax: 369-0365.
All Andros and Berry Islands Independence Regatta, Andros Regatta Village, Morgans Bluff. Contact Mr. Frank Hanna at 242-323-4531 or Barbara J. Deveaux at 242-328-6133.
Mangrove Cay Emancipation Day Regatta Contact the Commissioner's office at 242-369-0494.
September
Annual Bahamas Free Diving Championship at Nicholls Town.
October
Nicholls Town Regatta and Homecoming Contact Chief Councilor, Alphonso Smith, or Ms. Clara Evans at 242-329-2308.
November
North Andros Thanksgiving Bonefish Tournament

THINGS TO DO IN ANDROS

- Dive and snorkel the third-largest barrier reef in the world.
- Explore the creeks and lakes on this unspoiled island.
- Take advantage of the brilliant bonefishing or deep sea fishing, both within a short distance. Fish to your heart's content.
- Watch out for the chickcharnies; special elves with three fingers, three toes, red eyes, and feathers. Oh yes, and beards too. If you laugh at them, you may find your head is turned backwards.

Part IV

The Southern Cruising Grounds

The Northern Exuma Cays

The Southern Exuma Cays
and Great Exuma Island

The Out Islands North
of the Tropic of Cancer

Long Island

Exuma Bank water, about 8–10 feet deep, Barracouta sandbores.

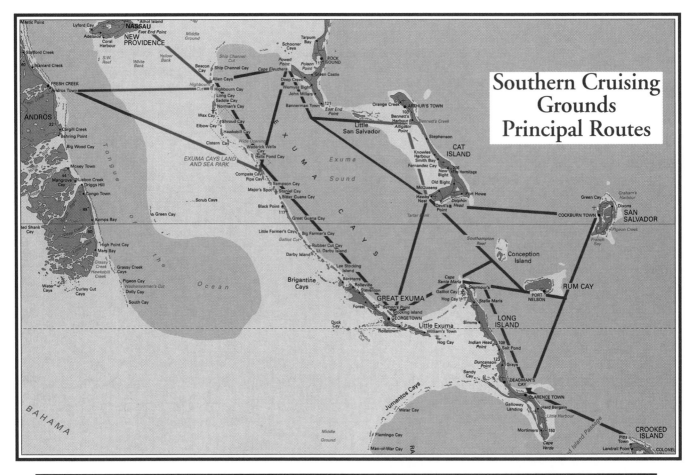

Southern Cruising
Grounds
Principal Routes

ROUTE TO/FROM		HEADINGS	DISTANCE NM	PASSAGE
Fresh Creek, Andros	Highborne Cay, Exumas	092°/272°M	50	Tongue of the Ocean/Bank
Fresh Creek, Andros	Conch Cut, Exumas	114°/294°M	74	Tongue of the Ocean/Bank
Nassau	Allans Cay, Exumas	see text	38	Exuma Bank
Cape Eleuthera	Highborne Cut, Exumas	255°/075°M	25	Exuma Sound
Cape Eleuthera	Conch Cut, Exumas	198°/018°M	33	Exuma Sound
South Eleuthera	Little San Salvador	096°/276°M	10	Exuma Sound
South Eleuthera	Hawk's Nest, Cat Island	131°/311°M	41	Exuma Sound
Allans Cay, Exumas	Warderick Wells, Exumas	see text	36	Exuma Bank
Highborne Cay, Exumas	Conch Cut, Exumas	147°/327°M	30	Exuma Sound
Warderick Wells, Exumas	Staniel Cay, Exumas	see text	18	Exuma Bank
Conch Cut, Exumas	George Town	138°/318°M	58	Exuma Sound
Staniel Cay, Exumas	Farmers Cut, Exumas	see text	19	Exuma Bank
Farmers Cut, Exumas	George Town	130°/310°M	37	Exuma Sound
George Town	Cape Santa Maria, Long Island	054°/234°M	23	Exuma Sound
George Town	Hawk's Nest, Cat Island	024°/204°M	37	Exuma Sound
George Town	Conception Island	055°/235°M	37	Exuma Sound
Little San Salvador	Hawk's Nest, Cat Island	141°/321°M	34	Exuma Sound
Hawk's Nest, Cat Island	Conception Island	125°/305°M	32	Atlantic open
Hawk's Nest, Cat Island	San Salvador	see text	58	Atlantic open
Cape Santa Maria, Long Island	Conception Island	056°/236°M	14	Atlantic open
Conception Island	Rum Cay	see text	14	Atlantic open
Rum Cay	San Salvador	see text	30	Atlantic open
Rum Cay	Clarence Town, Long Island	191°/011°M	31	Atlantic open
Cape Santa Maria, Long Island	Clarence Town, Long Island	152°/332°M	40	Atlantic coastal
Clarence Town, Long Island	Bird Rock, Crooked Island	115°/295°M	35	Crooked Island Passage

Distances exclude inshore close approaches at the start and end of a passage. The notation "see text" indicates multi-leg passages that are fully covered in the text.

Chapter 14
The Northern Exuma Cays
Sail Rocks to Little Farmer's Cay

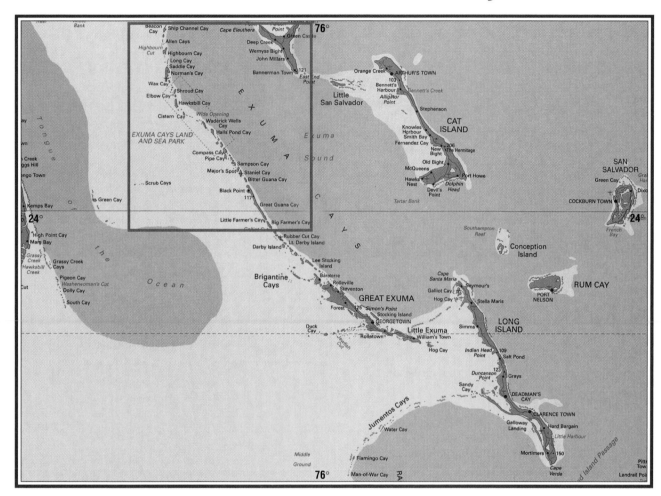

An Introduction to the Exumas

THE Exuma Cays and Great Exuma Island rate, with the Abacos, as one of the two most popular cruising destinations in the Bahamas. Both, as it happens, are roughly the same length measured as a chain of islands (the Exumas at some 95 nm are slightly longer) and both offer much the same attractions to the cruising boater: Bahamian water at its best, an apparently endless succession of small cays where if you feel escapist you can be on your own, and way stations where you can find fuel, food, and the rest of the cruising world if you've missed them.

It's a hard choice to say which cruising ground is the most attractive. The Abacos are easier to reach from Florida, for the Gulf Stream and the Little Bahama Bank are your only positioning passages. To reach the Exumas you have the Gulf Stream, the far greater extent of the Great Bahama Bank, the Northwest Providence Channel, and the Yellow Bank transit southeast from Nassau before you reach the top of the chain. There are differences when you reach your destination. The Abacos are more settled and have many more "pit" stops where you can find all the trappings of stateside life. In the Exumas, apart from Great Exuma Island with George Town, a three-figure population is exceptional and you could say that the facilities you'll find pretty much match the needs of the population.

The Exumas run northwest to southeast from 25° 00' N to 23° 25' N, the chain starting some 35 nm southeast from Nassau and New Providence Island, and ending at the point where the Out Islands (the truly remote southern Out Islands) start. In some ways the Exumas are not dissimilar to the Florida Keys as a cruising ground, for you have two sides, an east coast and a west coast, both navigable, and a number of cuts between the islands that allow you to play the flexibility of switching sides to advantage in the light of the prevailing winds.

In the Exumas the east side is the deep-water side, Exuma Sound. Here you have no problems about coral heads, sand banks, and shoals, but you may have to face higher seas (for you are more open to the ocean) and the southeast prevailing wind may give you waves on top of those swells. To the west the Exuma Bank is protected from the prevailing wind, but it's the shallow side with every problem that Bahamian waters can give you, just to test your skills. You have to feel your way there. The difficult part of your decision making, if you can put it that way, is that the navigation is better on the Exuma Sound side, easier, simpler, no problem areas, and generally the cuts are easier to identify and enter from the east, *but* the prevailing weather is southeast and so much of the time the Exuma Bank offers you less wind, a gentler sea state, better conditions.

Our advice is simple. If you're in a hurry to reach George Town, go down Exuma Sound unless the weather is adverse. If you want to cruise the Exumas in the time-honored fashion, island by island, cay by cay, go the Banks route. Make your initial choice to fit the weather, and bear in mind you can switch from side to side, through the cuts, as you wish.

Just one glance at a map or a chart will tell you that the primary approach routes to the Exumas lie from Nassau and New Providence Island to the northwest, from Andros to the west, from South Eleuthera to the east, and in the south from the open ocean to the east of Long Island. We'll deal with each one in turn.

From Nassau

As you leave Nassau for the Exumas, there are many choices open in choosing your landfall, but a waypoint off the Allan's Cays is probably a sound choice. This gives you the options of visiting Allan's Cay (where you can anchor, and see the iguanas), going on to Highborne Cay (for their anchorage, or the marina), going through Highborne Cut (to gain Exuma Sound), or continuing south along the Bank. Although just one landfall waypoint off the Allan's Cays would serve all these options, we list two waypoints, the first for Allan's Cay, and the second for Highborne Cay and Highborne Cut.

THE DIRECT ROUTE OVER THE YELLOW BANK

Porgee Rocks to Porgee Southeast	2.82 nm	110°M
Porgee Southeast to Allan's Cay	26.38 nm	139°M

On this approach your problem area is the Yellow Bank. There are many coral heads in this area, the shallowest of which lie some 3 feet below the surface at MLW. The average depth on the Yellow Bank at MLW will be around 6 feet. The bad news is that you cannot afford to run the Yellow Bank on autopilot. You must keep careful watch, you need the sun in the right position, you need favorable weather, and you must be prepared to thread your way around the coral heads as you cross the Yellow Bank.

Reckon that the tide on the Yellow Bank will be one hour behind Nassau. Your optimum time to gain the Yellow Bank is around 11 a.m., so that the sun is to your advantage. Finally, if the wind is going to be on your head and 20 knots or more, you'll get steep, nasty seas. You would be better off waiting for more favorable weather.

AVOIDING THE YELLOW BANK

If you are prepared to set a dogleg course directly south from our Porgee Rocks southeast waypoint (PRGSE 25° 03' N 077° 12' W), after a run of 11 nm you'll reach a point midway between the Yellow and White Banks. From this waypoint you can alter course and head for your chosen landfall. Although this route is generally believed to be clear of keel-threatening coral heads and rock ledges, *don't* take it on trust. There are isolated coral heads there. From the time you pass on to the Bank (around 25° 55' 35"/583 N 077° 12' 00"/000 W) go slowly and keep a lookout until you are well past the junction between the Yellow and White Banks on your new heading (116°M for Allan's, 120°M for Highborne) and safely southeast of the Yellow Bank. Read the chart, and use your eyes. The depth of water is a good indicator, perhaps 9–12 feet at MLW where you should take it slowly, and 5 feet more than the depths we've quoted elsewhere. Take it slowly once again on your close approach to your final waypoint.

Porgee Rocks to Porgee Southeast	2.82 nm	110°M
Porgee Southeast to Yellow-White Junction	11.00 nm	185°M
Yellow-White Junction to Allan's Cay	20.39 nm	116°M
Yellow-White Junction to Highborne West	23.97 nm	120°M
Through Highborne Cut		Go Visual

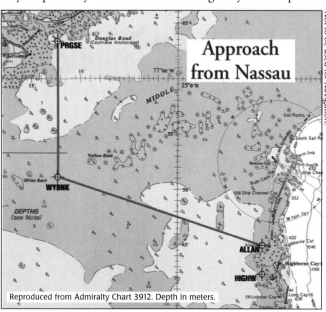

Approach from Nassau

Reproduced from Admiralty Chart 3912. Depth in meters.

Not to be used for Navigation.

Allan's Cay native iguana.

From Andros

From Andros we'd assume that Fresh Creek is your most likely departure point, and the most useful arrival waypoint you could choose is off Conch Cut, giving you the options of turning north for Warderick Wells or south for Sampson or Staniel Cays, turning north or south for other points, or going through Conch Cut to get into Exuma Sound.

On this approach route there's one area where you will find reefs and coral heads and *must* go slowly, keeping a sharp lookout, and that's the point where you leave the deep water of the Tongue of the Ocean and come on to the Bank. We mark this as a waypoint to remind you. A second area where you must go carefully is after reaching our Conch Cut west waypoint, where you have sandbores to north and south as you go visual to Conch Cut itself. See our sections on Conch Cut on pages 230 and 238.

Fresh Creek to Edge of Bank	40.77 nm	119°M
Edge of Bank to Conch Cut West	25.08 nm	120°M
Through Conch Cut	Go Visual	

From Eleuthera

From Eleuthera we reckon the best departure points are either just off Cape Eleuthera (which also suits Cape Eleuthera Marina if you use it) or just off Davis Harbour,

NORTH ELEUTHERA (CURRENT ISLAND) AND THE FLEEMING CHANNEL

The area of Bank to the immediate north of Exuma Sound in the Middle Ground–Finley Cay–Schooner Cays triangle is more shoal, and more hazardous, than the charts suggest.

We recommend you do not attempt this route.

taking either Highborne Cut or Conch Cut as your arrival waypoints. You then have the choice of staying in Exuma Sound, or making your way on to the Bank.

Cape Eleuthera to Highborne East	25.82 nm	257°M
Davis Harbour to Highborne East	29.96 nm	273°M
Cape Eleuthera to Conch Cut East	32.15 nm	203°M
Davis Harbour to Conch Cut East	28.37 nm	217°M
All passages through the Cuts	Go Visual	

From the South

Making your way into the central Bahamas from the south, all routes can be said to converge at Cape Santa Maria, the northernmost point of Long Island. Here you have to stand well out from land to avoid the reefs, and from here you can set a straight course for the entry point to George Town Harbour, which is almost bound to be your chosen entry point to the Exumas, if not to the Bahamas.

Cape Santa Maria to George Town	22.24 nm	239°M

The Principal Navigable Cuts Between the Exuma Cays

There are almost as many cuts or passes between the Exuma Bank and Exuma Sound as there are cays and islands in the Exumas. Some are navigable, in the fullest sense, given the right conditions. Others are more difficult passes, which you may explore in your dinghy, but are not transits between the Exuma Bank and Exuma Sound that we'd recommend. Even the navigable ones, as we've said, are subject to weather, and by that we mean the state of the tide, wind direction, wind strength, and the angle of the sun. Wind against tide will inevitably set up adverse seas, which at best will be uncomfortable, and at the worst, something approaching an Abaco Rage—meaning dangerous seas that could, particularly in some passes, be life threatening.

What we now list are the principal cuts we use. Other passes, which you may bring into use once you have gained the knowledge and confidence to negotiate them, are mentioned in our sections dealing with each geographic area. To help you in your route planning we give the approximate latitude of each cut.

The Northern Exumas

HIGHBORNE CUT 24° 42' N

At the south end of Highborne Cay. At least 6 feet at MLW and straightforward, but you need good light in your favor. As with almost all the Exuma cuts, it can develop a short chop with wind against tide.

WARDERICK WELLS CUT 24° 24' N

At the north end of Warderick Wells Cay. Apart from strong currents, it's a fine, wide pass.

CONCH CUT 24° 17' N

Between Cambridge Cay and Compass Cay. Again a strong current, and in this case a rock awash in the middle, but there's plenty of room, no other hazards, and good depth. But stay north of that rock in the middle of the pass.

DOTHAM CUT 24° 07' N

At the north end of Great Guana Cay (named after Dotham Point). Sandbores on the Bank side dictate swinging north or south almost as soon as you are clear of the pass and the reef that extends west from the south tip of Gaulin Cay/Bitter Guana Cay.

FARMER'S CUT 23° 57' N

Narrow but good depth. Used by the mailboats.

GALLIOTT CUT 23° 55' N

Again narrow, but good depth. Also a mailboat route.

The Southern Exumas

CAVE CAY CUT 23° 54' N

Deep (over 20 feet) but strong currents.

RUDDER CUT 23° 52' N

Straightforward. While a muddle of small cays and reef clutter the southeast on the Bank side, these present no problem.

RAT CAY CUT 23° 44' N

An unusual north–south pass between Rat Cay and Boysie Cay. If the wind gets up from the east, this is the best cut.

CONCH CAY CUT 23° 34' N

This pass is the west (and best) entrance into George Town Harbour.

The waters of the Exumas cuts. Prime Cay–Bock Cay Gap, from the east.

The Most Popular Destinations

In the northern Exumas there's enough to keep you happily gunkholing for months, if not years, and if you're bent on snorkeling and diving, as well as shoal-water exploration, you could go on almost forever without running out of new places to explore. Mindful that we are writing a cruising guide to the whole of the Bahamas, which necessarily implies a measure of selection, we put our money on four areas in this sector. All of them should feature high on your visit list. The first is the Allan's Cay–Highborne Cay area. The second is Normans Cay. The third is Warderick Wells and the Exuma Land and Sea Park, and the fourth is the Compass Cay–Staniel Cay area.

Sail Rocks to Conch Cut

LOOK at your chart. If you decided to cordon off an area of rocks, reefs, and coral heads where no one lived and few people visited, and said, "OK, let's call this a marine sanctuary and let the fish and lobsters get on with the business of regeneration," the sea area from the Sail Rocks down to and including Ship Channel Cay would be a good choice. Despite the Ship Channel that passes through connecting the Exuma Bank with Exuma Sound south of Beacon Cay and north of Ship Channel Cay, we rate it as an area the prudent cruising navigator is better off avoiding. It's a maze of bare rock, reefs, coral heads, and tide rips that has never been charted accurately and, if you get into trouble there, it's uninhabited. We know of no anchorages there that we'd recommend.

So, on the face of it, you might well declare it as a sea reserve. It is unlikely to happen, for the only people who do frequent the area are Bahamian fishermen, and they might well object. More seriously, in settled weather if you want an area for exploring, snorkeling, and fishing that has little been touched by visiting boaters, you might decide to anchor off and dinghy in to look around.

SHIP CHANNEL

Ship Channel passage is a genuine pass, and the light on Beacon Cay (if it works) is there for guidance. But don't, even if the light is working, risk that passage at night. For the cruising yachtsman we see no utility in this cut through the northern Exumas. It is, of course, the direct route from Nassau to Cape Eleuthera (or the reverse), but your track will take you through the worst part of the Yellow Bank. Even if we were going this way with no interest in visiting the Exumas, we'd elect to go through Highborne Cut and make use of the route we've already listed that avoids the Yellow Bank.

PIMLICO CAY AND ROBERTS CAY

Pimlico Cay is almost an extension of Ship Channel Cay. It has a house, sometimes used, at the southern end and there is a resident caretaker there. Roberts Cay, its tiny neighbor, also has a holiday house. Consider both cays as private property. There is a small potential anchorage between the two cays, only suitable for shoal draft (less than 3 feet) craft. Enter it from the south *only* at high tide and go in first by dinghy, checking the depth and noting rocks and reef as you go. This could serve as a refuge in bad weather, particularly in a Norther.

The Allan's Cay Group

Allan's Cay is often the first destination of cruisers visiting the Exumas for two good reasons. It offers the first anchorage that can accommodate a number of boats in most weather, and it's the home of the iguanas, the prehistoric-looking large-size lizards that live here and in some of the more remote Out Islands, but nowhere else in the Bahamas.

In talking about Allan's Cay, in truth most people are referring to a group of three cays, Allan's Cay, Southwest Allan's Cay, and Leaf Cay, in which the sheltered water lies between them. Immediately south of the group there is a navigable cut between the Bank and Exuma Sound, but there are many reefs and coral heads in that pass.

Your approach to the Allan's Cay group, and your landfall recognition from either side, Bank or Sound, is not difficult, because when you're still some distance off the humpy higher ground of Highborne Cay to the south becomes visible, together with Highborne's 260-foot Batelco tower. If you are coming in from Exuma Sound our advice is to take Highborne Cut, swing out into the deeper water of the Bank to avoid the shoals and reefs to the northwest of Highborne Cay, and then make your way in to the Allan's cays from our Allan's waypoint. From the Bank side simply make for that Allan's waypoint. If there are other boats in the Allan's Cay anchorage you will see their masts showing above Allan's Cay.

Take the obvious way in between Allan's Cay and South-

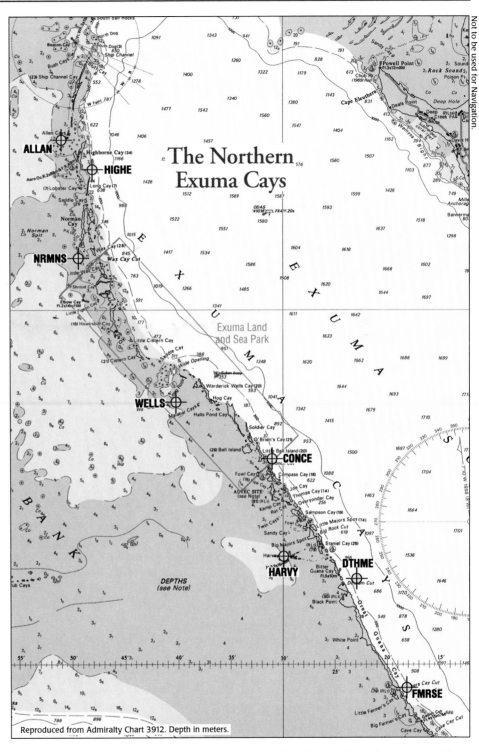

Reproduced from Admiralty Chart 3912. Depth in meters.

west Allan's Cay, south of the little rock to the south of Allan's Cay. Then turn to anchor either in the bight of Southwest Allan's Cay to starboard or between Allan's Cay and Leaf Cay to port. Don't go further up the channel than the final part of Leaf Cay for it shoals rapidly. Check your anchor, as we have seen anchors drag there, and make sure it's well bedded. Then launch your dinghy and go to meet the iguanas. Do *not* take a pet on shore, and *no* garbage. The islands are a protected reserve.

Allan's Cay to Normans Cay

FROM ALLAN'S CAY TO HIGHBORNE CAY

To make for Highborne Cay from the Allan's group the safest way is to head out southwest on to the Bank and swing around to avoid the reefs and shoals that lie to the west of the Allan's Cay Cut. There is a direct route that shoal draft craft *could* take at high tide, but we see no point in trying to prove it. Save that for your exploration later on in your dinghy.

HIGHBORNE CAY

Lining up to enter Highborne Cay is not difficult. Highborne has a long white beach on the west side, the humpy high ground we've already mentioned, a white house and trees on one of the humps, and that 260-foot Batelco tower. The anchorage and the Highborne Marina are to the south of the tower, and as you get closer you'll see boats at the dock. Ahead you'll see two rocks, one with a white stake on its north tip. You are going to leave that stake to starboard as you enter, and beyond these rocks, on the shore of Highborne itself, you'll see two orange range marks. Once you've got your bearings, there are no problems. Go in reading the water, particularly at low tide, and swing easily north toward the marina once you're safely past that stake. Keep in the deep water (there's a sand bar to port) and go on past the end of the concrete dock to where you plan to secure. The fuel dock is hard to starboard past the concrete dock.

If you want to anchor off you have two choices. Just behind the southeastern tip of Highborne Cay on the west side, and along the line of the western coast of Highborne Cay (off that fine beach), remembering that at the north end there are reefs and shoals. Both anchorages are obviously weather dependent, but otherwise have good depth (about 12 feet MLW) and good holding.

Highborne Cay is private, but limited privileges and the use of the store are extended to visiting boaters. For details see our **Yellow Pages** on page 247. If you are at anchor you may land on the beaches, but respect the privacy of the island as a whole. With the Allan's Cay group, Highborne Cay rates as one of our favorite places in the Bahamas.

HIGHBORNE CUT

Highborne Cut, just to the south of Highborne Cay, is a relatively straightforward "read-the-water-as-you-go" pass between the Exuma Bank and Exuma Sound. Look at the chart, and then use your eyes. You should have no problems. Just remember that wind against tide produces turbulence, and that like all passes anywhere in the world, the current can run fast.

Highborne Cay to Normans Cay

If you are shoal draft, with the tide and the right light you can work your way south from Highborne Cay on the Bank side, past Oyster Cay, Long (sometimes called Spirit) Cay,

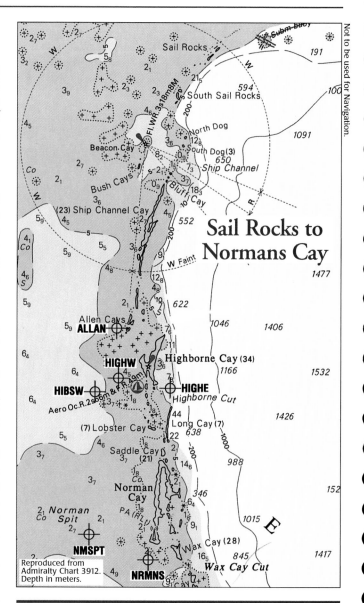

Reproduced from Admiralty Chart 3912. Depth in meters.

NORTHERN EXUMAS I

Allan's Cay		
ALLAN	24° 44' 50"/833 N	076° 51' 00"/000 W
Highborne Cut West		
HIGHW	24° 42' 30"/500 N	076° 51' 00"/000 W
Highborne Cut East		
HIGHE	24° 42' 00"/000 N	076° 48' 15"/250 W
Highborne Stake		
HSTKW	24° 42' 30"/500 N	076° 50' 00"/000 W
Highborne Southwest		
HIBSW	24° 42' 00"/000 N	076° 52' 00"/000 W
Normans Spit		
NMSPT	24° 35' 45"/750 N	076° 52' 00"/000 W
Normans Cay		
NRMNS	24° 34' 40"/666 N	076° 49' 30"/500 W

The final figures in each waypoint show seconds (00") and thousands (000) of a minute.

Allan's Cays from the west.

Lobster Cay, and Saddle Cay to the north tip of Normans Cay. There the shoals to the west of Normans Cay will oblige you to detour to the west out into deeper water again before you can work your way in to the Normans Cay anchorage around its south end.

As both Long Cay and Saddle Cay are private, unless you are particularly concerned with exploring this area, we suggest you take an easy loop out to the west to run from Highborne to Normans. All we would point out, just in case you need it, is that Long (Spirit) Cay offers an anchorage accessible from the Bank on its southwest tip (but open

to the west) and Saddle Cay has an anchorage accessible from both the Sound and the Bank (the Bank approach is more difficult). Those who know this anchorage, to the southwest of Saddle Cay and just north of Norman's Cay, should be aware that the southern Saddle Cay beach, a once pristine and unfrequented spot, has now become a popular playground. Island World Adventures bring day trippers in a fast "cigarette-type" ferry from Nassau daily, to discover the Exumas. If you don't know the area, you can't mistake Saddle Cay. The name was well chosen.

The safe route from Highborne to Normans involves getting well out on to the Bank from a start point just off the Highborne Cay Marina entrance, and staying out until you have cleared the shoal area known as Normans Spit, which runs out westward from the southeast tip of Normans Cay. Our courses work out as something like this:

From Highborne to gain that offing	1.88 nm	260°M
From this waypoint to off Normans Spit	6.52 nm	190°M
To a close approach waypoint	2.39 nm	114°M

This last point places you ready to go visual into Normans Cay's southern anchorage. It sounds like a lot of jinking around, but the plain truth is all you have to do is take one easy loop out on to the Bank to get to Normans from Highborne, keeping about 3 nm offshore. And read the water!

NORMANS CAY

Normans Cay won fame, or rather infamy, as the base of the Colombian drug runner Carlos Leder during the bad days of Bahamian drug trading. The end result before the Leder barony was brought to an end was a tally of unproven murders (when cruising boaters came too close to the Leder operation); a ruined development (once the heart of Lederland) on the south tip of Normans Cay with a dock falling into deterioration; the remains of a "Berlin" wall, which once guarded the northern boundary of Leder's territory (just north of the airstrip); a runway closed to traffic; a ditched aircraft in the southern anchorage; and an evil feel to the

Highborne Cut, from the south.

whole place. The Batelco-type mast you'll see on the south-west tip of Normans Cay is a disused radio mast, yet another souvenir of the Leder regime.

Today the visible signs of those days remain, but Normans Cay has a great deal to offer as a cruising destination. The approach to the southern anchorage is easy from either Exuma Sound or the Bank. On the Sound side the channel is nar-row, carries about 7 feet, but is straightforward. Coming in from the west keep a touch to the south as you go in, follow-ing the obvious deep-water channel. Then you can follow a branch of this channel that runs roughly between the ruined dock and the ditched aircraft, or stay in the main stream (a pass through to Exuma Sound), which runs just north of a pretty little cay with white sand, a hillock, one teenage palm tree, and two baby palm trees. The depth overall in the an-chorage is 6–8 feet at MLW. You are well protected there, other than from the southwest. If you are in the main tidal flow, expect a reversing current and 180-degree swings as the tide changes, but the holding is good. Don't go further up the apparent anchorage than the line running between the dock and the ditched aircraft, for it shoals.

The gunkholing around Normans Cay is good, the wa-ter is beautiful, and just north of the ruined dock (which is unsafe) there's a little beach. You are welcome to land, but the north end of six-mile-long Normans Cay is private. On the west of the airstrip, now open to charter traffic, there is MacDuffs, a pocket-sized beach resort that offers cruising visitors highly praised hamburgers, and you can buy ice there. See our **Yellow Pages** on page 247.

Normans Cay has a second northern anchorage, Normans Pond, which is accessible only from Exuma Sound. Its ap-proach is not easy. You would be foolish not to take your

dinghy to reconnoiter the route in before you attempt it (we've seen two boats ground there at high water), and go in *only* with a high tide. Even then we've found only 4 feet 6 inches over the shallowest part of the entry passage, although there's a safe 15 feet inside. It's certainly well protected and even has a reputation as a hurricane hole. We'd go there to escape bad weather, but a hurricane? No. Not by deliberate choice.

NORTH HARBOUR OR NORMANS POND

If you want to try it, the entrance lies at the break in Normans Cay's east shore just to the north of Latitude 24° 37' 00"/000 N. The entry channel lies between the two larger islets or rocks you'll see, each of which has a fallen marker on it, both looking rather like cannon facing in-ward at the pass, and on the far shore there's a conspicuous white house. After an unfortunate visitor spent longer than he intended in Normans Pond, he determined to set up, once and for all, markers to guide other cruisers safely in *and out* of the Pond. Hopefully these markers will stay. The marked course, going in, runs like this. When you are be-tween the two "cannons" (in fact angled pipe), immediately look to your right and you'll see two markers. If you don't look to your right immediately, you'll fail to see both mark-ers for they will merge as one, and you'll run in too far and ground waiting to pick up the second marker.

The bottom one is float shaped, and white. The second is a white pole with a circle on the top. Just use them as leading marks and turn to starboard.

So you bear to starboard almost immediately after pass-ing through the entry and feel your way over a shoal (that 4-feet-6-inch depth we wrote about), working your way closer to the shoreline to starboard. As you do this you'll enter deeper water and notice a pronounced shal-low water contour running parallel to the shore. Stay in that deep water, keep going parallel to the shore, and you'll soon be in the basin of the North Harbour. The first of two caves that will come up to starboard is, if you like, the signal that you've made it. Thereafter you're free to roam.

On going out, at the "cannon" point, there are two markers on the rock to the right of the "cannon." The lower marker has a black aircraft tire on the top, and the upper one is white.

A third option in anchoring at Normans Cay is to make your way in north of Normans Spit to anchor off the airstrip beach, where you'll

Normans Cay anchorage, from the south.

see the three houses of the MacDuff development, or anchor further up the coast north of Skipjack Point.

Normans Cay to Warderick Wells

The Wax Cays, Wax Cay Cut, Shroud Cay, Elbow Cay, Hawksbill Cay, the Cistern Cays, and the gap known as the Wide Opening lie on your route south from Normans Cay to Warderick Wells and the Exuma Land and Sea Park. Wax Cay, we reckon, falls into the Normans Cay gunkholing area. It has good rocks and reefs for exploring. Wax Cay Cut is not one we'd take to gain the Sound or come in from it. Little Wax Cay (part

Normans Pond entry, from the east.

of Exuma Park) marks the northern boundary of the Exuma Land and Sea Park, and at that point you pack your fishing gear away. The first significant island in the Park area is Shroud Cay (part of Exuma Park), a curious three-mile long atoll surrounded by coral reefs with a heartland of mangrove swamp. No part of it is cruising boat ground, but you might want to poke your nose in somewhere in your dinghy to see what's there.

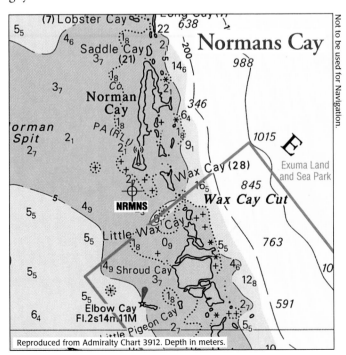
Reproduced from Admiralty Chart 3912. Depth in meters.

THE INSHORE BANK ROUTE FROM NORMANS CAY TO WARDERICK WELLS

If you elect to hug the coastline, what have you got there? We mentioned Shroud Cay. If you're there in March and April, that's the time Tropic birds nest there, recognizable by their white tails. Little Pigeon Cay, between Shroud and Elbow Cay, is private. Hawksbill Cay has great beaches and popular anchorages off the beaches on the east side from the center down to the south, but these are open to the southwest through to the north. Little Hawksbill Cay has been taken over by ospreys as their nesting territory. Cistern Cay is private. All of these cays are within Exuma Park. South from Cistern Cay the gaps out into Exuma Sound known as the Wide Opening (all of it part of Exuma Park) is a dream world for the experienced diver with drift dives and dives off Brad's Reef to the east of Long Rock, but tidal current dictates that this is no territory for the inexperienced. Hawk Fish Rocks, like Little Hawksbill Cay, have been claimed by the ospreys.

We have done this route in a shoal draft boat and even then sand bores, areas of shoal, and reefs oblige you to detour, heading out to the west and coming back in again. Much of the shoreline, such as the Hawksbill Cay anchorages, are accessible to vessels with "normal" draft, but you are wise to take the state of the tide, as well as the angle of the sun, into your calculations before setting your general course.

THE WIDE OPENING

The Wide Opening is a viable route between the Bank and the Sound, and in many ways, the easiest approach route to

Warderick Wells. The best cut lies at the north end of Warderick Wells Cay, and is wide, deep, and easily identifiable.

THE BANK ROUTE FROM NORMANS CAY TO WARDERICK WELLS

If you're bound southward on the Bank from Normans Cay to Warderick Wells, rather like the swing out on to the Bank from Highborne, you're much in the same game, particularly because Elbow Cay, a mile southwest of Shroud Cay, forces you out at that point. You'll note the prominent light stake on Elbow Cay. Your safe route on the Bank side will take you well off Shroud Cay, Hawksbill Cay, and the Cistern Cays to the south. The Cistern Cays have spawned sandbores that run far out to the west, and there's no point in attempting to work any closer to land than 3–4 nm along this route. The track we take is probably further out than you need to go, but we like the sea room and passage legs where you can relax to some extent. Our courses run something like this:

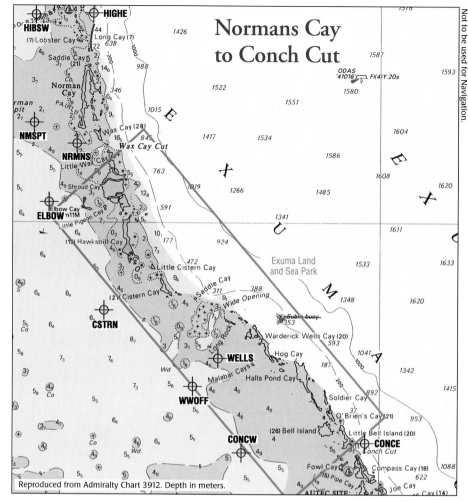

Reproduced from Admiralty Chart 3912. Depth in meters.

Not to be used for Navigation.

From Normans Cay to just off Elbow Cay	3.86 nm	199°M
From Elbow to off Cistern Cay	6.79 nm	158°M
Cistern to 5 nm off Warderick Wells	6.41 nm	134°M
And then to our final waypoint	2.19 nm	052°M

The approach into Warderick Wells anchorage from this waypoint is simple. You'll find you have a very obvious sandbore to starboard. Keep it that way. To port, in time, you'll realize you have another sandbore. Favor the first one. Your heading will be around 065°M, but more importantly, in the Wide Opening ahead of you will be two rocks, the left one looking flat like a table top and the right one rounded, a bit like an upturned salad bowl. Once you've got them identified, head toward the north tip of Warderick Wells just south of the salad bowl rock. As you get closer a small, highly visible sand beach just south of Warderick Wells' northern point makes a good lead-in mark. Just head toward it. You have deep water all the way, and don't go in the first entrances you see to starboard. Take the last one in, where you'll see a line of marker buoys start, white, red, blue, and then the line of white mooring

buoys with maybe other boats already on them.

On turning in there are first two white floats, then two floating post channel marks, a red and a green (red right returning).

Call Exuma Park on VHF 16 and declare yourself as you

NORTHERN EXUMAS II		
Elbow Cay		
ELBOW	24° 31' 00"/000 N	076° 51' 00"/000 W
Cistern Cay		
CSTRN	24° 25' 00"/000 N	076° 47' 30"/500 W
Warderick Wells West		
WWOFF	24° 21' 00"/000 N	076° 42' 00"/000 W
Warderick Wells Southwest		
WELLS	24° 22' 30"/500 N	076° 40' 15"/250 W
Conch Cut East		
CONCE	24° 17' 30"/500 N	076° 31' 00"/000 W
Conch Cut West		
CONCW	24° 17' 00"/000 N	076° 39' 00"/000 W

The final figures in each waypoint show seconds (00") and thousands (000) of a minute.

enter. You should, by then, have already asked for and been allocated a mooring buoy by number. As you enter the northern harbor the darker, deep-water blue channel that curves ahead of you is as obvious as the Yellow Brick road leading to Oz. Just stay in the channel and pick up your allotted buoy (which are numbered from your entry point, the colored ones included). Then take your dinghy and check in at the Park HQ.

A new Park pamphlet is due out in late 1999, which will summarize all the existing leaflets. On the enforcement side, after a bad period in which Ray Darville, the Park Warden, was more than once threatened and put at grave personal risk in carrying out his duties, two members of the Royal Bahamas Defence Force are now stationed at Park Headquarters on active duty.

Warderick Wells northern anchorage, from the southwest.

WARDERICK WELLS AND
THE EXUMA LAND AND SEA PARK

The Exuma Park, a world-first in marine conservation, was set up in 1958 and covers 176 square miles of cays, rocks, and reefs running from Little Wax Cay in the north to Conch Cut in the south, and is bounded by Exuma Sound on one side and the Exuma Bank on the other.

Warderick Wells Cay is the site of the Park HQ and the principal visitor center with twenty-two moorings (anchoring is not allowed there). There are also four moorings in the southern anchorage. All these are reserved through Park HQ. See our **Yellow Pages** for the latest mooring fees, which are based on LOA. You may anchor wherever you wish in the Park area, but not, as we've said, in the north anchorage, and *not* on coral. For anchoring your dinghy when you go snorkeling or diving the same rule applies. You may anchor where you wish, but *not* on coral.

It's a hard choice to decide whether to opt for the northern anchorage or the southern Warderick Wells anchorage, which lies between the southeast tip of the island and Hog Cay. Here the best approach is from the north, from Exuma Sound. The tip of Hog Cay is marked by a stone cairn, and you'll have deep water all the way in. Entering from the south, from the Bank, is better done at high tide with some judicious reading of the water, but it's possible. If you like relative isolation, this is the place for you and in slow periods of Park business you could well be alone here, with just the ospreys nearby on Little White Bay Cay for company. The Bank-side route between the two anchorages, inside Emerald Rock, London Gin Rock, and the Malabar Cays is shoal draft work, better explored in your dinghy.

We cover the Exuma Park in greater detail in our **Yellow Pages** on **The Exuma Land and Sea Park** on page 248. It is sufficient to say that a visit to Exuma Park is a must. We know of no anchorage more beautiful than Warderick Wells, and the stately crescent of boats in line on their moorings at sunset makes a mental photograph that will stay with you for life as the archetypal cruiser's dream. The swimming and snorkeling are superb.

WARDERICK WELLS AREA: THE MALABAR CAYS

There is a hazard to navigation just to the west of the Malabar Cays. It is either a boat-shaped reef or a sunken boat, and we would give it a wide berth. Its position is 24° 21' 30"/500 N 076° 38' 30"/500 W. We've not been aware of this potential

Nurse sharks.

obstacle before, but as it's comparatively small (30–40 feet in length and roughly boat beam in width) it could be that our track has never run close enough before. Note the position. Mark it. And draw a safe circle around it.

Warderick Wells, north anchorage.

Warderick Wells to Sampson and Staniel Cays

Having left Warderick Wells we'd guess that your next stop is likely to be either Sampson Cay or Staniel Cay, both lying south of Conch Cut. It is at Conch Cut that you leave the Exuma Land and Sea Park area.

Our courses will take you well out to the west, further offshore than you might think necessary. The reason for this is the sandbores that lie to the west of Bell Island and the Rocky Dundas–Fowl Cay area, which extend out as far as Longitude 076° 37' W.

THE HALLS POND CAYS, THE BELL ISLANDS, SOLDIERS AND O'BRIEN'S CAYS, CAMBRIDGE CAY

Halls Pond Cay (part of the Exuma Park) is marked by the derelict Exuma Cays Club that stands on a headland above its northwestern point. A beach there (with some mobile-type housing evident) offers an anchorage protected from northeast to southeast, but is open to surge from the Halls Pond Cay Cut. Better anchorages, but still shielded only from the east, can be found opposite the two sand beaches further down the west shore of Halls Pond Cay. However bear in mind that the cay is private.

We've been told that a government writ has halted further construction on Halls Pond Cay. Additionally restoration to make good environmental damage has been ordered before any further legally permitted work is allowed to proceed.

Also private territory are Little Halls Pond Cay, Soldier Cay, Bell Island, and Cambridge Cay (although they are all part of Exuma Park). O'Brien's Cay is the only one in this group to remain public land. Sadly but predictably it's the least attractive of the group lying south of Warderick Wells and north of Conch Cut, and few people go there. Anchorages can be found off Bell Island (on both the east and west side) and on the west of Cambridge Cay, if you work your way in behind a line of rocks running north–south down the west coast of the cay.

Conch Cut

Conch Cut East		
CONCE	24° 17' 30"/500 N	076° 31' 00"/000 W
Conch Cut West		
CONCW	24° 17' 00"/000 N	076° 39' 00"/000 W

Our Conch Cut west waypoint (CONCW) is unusually far offshore. The reason for this is the sandbores extending out to Longitude 076° 37' W from Bell Island to the north and Rocky Dundas–Fowl Cay to the south. A waypoint closer in would not usefully serve Conch Cut itself, Warderick Wells

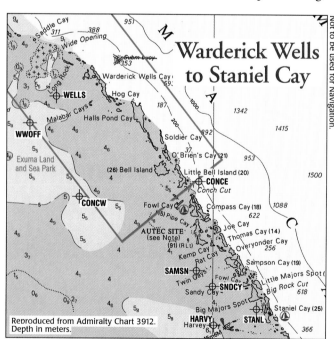

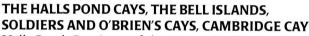

Reproduced from Admiralty Chart 3912.
Depth in meters.

Poachers

VISITING yachtsmen have been caught taking fish, lobster, and souvenirs from the Exuma Land and Sea Park. Do *not* do it. Apart from the mandatory $500 fine per person on board per incident (a single fish, lobster, or shell counts as one incident), your boat is liable to confiscation. *The Park Wardens have taken action against cruising visitors and will continue to patrol, make arrests, and impound vessels for violations regardless of the flag they fly.* The rules are absolute. Enjoy everything that is there. But leave it as you found it.

to the north, and Sampson or Staniel Cay to the south without doglegs. Once you are at Conch Cut west your route to and through the pass is direct and obvious.

Conch Cut is one of the best Exuma cuts, lying between Cambridge Cay and Compass Cay. It has, like all the Exuma cuts, strong tidal flows, and its one hazard is a rock, barely awash, in the middle. But there are no other hazards, good depth, and plenty of room. Your course through the Cut must run to the north of that rock in mid-pass.

Conch Cut from the west, just south of the main Pass. Rocky Dundas and Fowl Cay are in the foreground.

Conch Cut to Little Farmer's Cay

WHEN you move south of Conch Cut, you must start to think seriously, if you are traveling on the Bank side, about the cut you will select to gain access to Exuma Sound if you're going on south to George Town. The most important of these from a routing point of view are Dotham, Farmer's, and Rat Cay Cut. None of these cuts pose any particular navigation problems, but all the Exuma Cuts are subject to strong reversing tidal flows which, when running against wind, wave, and swell can kick up extremely turbulent, short, and potentially hazardous seas. The effect of this kick back can be felt as far as a mile or more off the cut, and if you're sensible, you won't force the issue and try to punch your way through. Hold off, wait for the slack, and then move.

These conditions affect the smaller cuts equally, and if anything make them even more hazardous under unfavorable conditions, for you have shallower, narrower passes, more rocks and shoals around your approaches, and at times sharp turns to hit the right deep-water channel at the right moment. Don't be put off by all this. Simply take it into account and pre-plan your cruising. Get the time of the tides, think of the wind, and study the geography of your chosen cut. If it's A-OK, go for it.

To save endless repetition we're not going to warn about tidal flows and the effects of tide against wind each time we list a cut. Take it as read that what we've said applies to them all. We have listed only one east waypoint (incoming from Exuma Sound) and one west (Bank-side) waypoint for each cut. A single waypoint works well in the Sound, but on the Bank side the channels threading between reef and sand often demand a succession of waypoints. But channels can change as the sand changes. Rather than list an endless stream of directions, as in any event you'll be eyeballing your way, we give you just one fix for reassurance. It should be enough.

Utility of the Exumas Cuts

The more we look at the geography of the Bank side and the real utility of the Exumas cuts, the more we are led to three conclusions.

- The primary passage-making cuts we identified in our introduction on pages 229–230 are vital to you whether you are on the Exuma Bank or in Exuma Sound. Other than the dubious importance of Rat Cay Cut, these passes are your best way of switching from one side to the other.

- The real utility of the secondary cuts is to open up anchorages on the Bank side if you're out in the Sound, or, if you've worked your way far enough south on the Bank, to give you your last opportu-

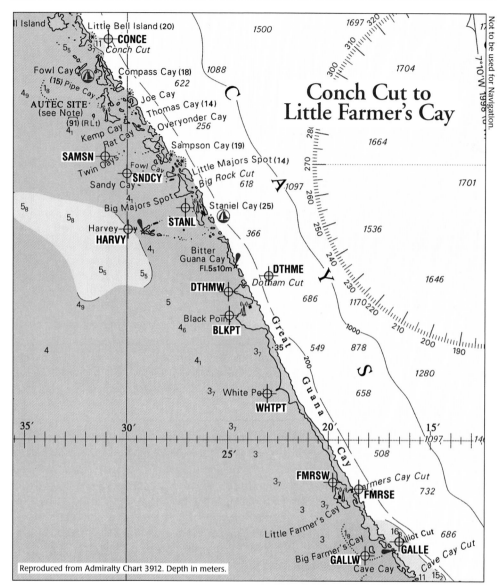

Conch Cut to
Little Farmer's Cay

Reproduced from Admiralty Chart 3912. Depth in meters.

cays. From our Conch Cut west waypoint (you're on the Bank side) you'll run 8.66 nm on a heading of 128°M to get to the Twin Cays waypoint, and then if you're bound for Sampson Cay turn to a heading of 095°M to pass south of Twin Cays and the line of rocks and reef to their east. You'll see the Sampson Cay Club buildings ahead of you.

If you're going on to Staniel Cay, Sandy Cay serves as a waypoint in the same manner as Twin Cays. You have another 1.24 nm to run on a course of 138°M to get to the Sandy Cay waypoint from Twin Cays. Then go around Sandy Cay to the west, and go visual for 3 nm toward Staniel Cay, with its 260-foot Batelco tower, on a heading of 118°M.

PIPE CAY ALLEY

The cays between Compass Cay and Sampson Cay enclose a protected inner passage that we've always termed Pipe Cay Alley. Although much of the enclosed water is shoal draft or dries at low tide, there are deeper channels on both inner sides. It's an area of almost unbelievable water color, everything from white to turquoise to sapphire blue, with a clarity of water that can only be described as gin clear. However be aware that Compass Cay, Little Pipe Cay, Wild Tamarind Cay, and Overyonder Cay are private and your freedom to roam is not only limited by water depths.

From the Bank side the best approach into the area is north of Sampson Cay, taking the channel between Wild Tamarind and Overyonder Cays. There are three navigable cuts between Exuma Sound and Pipe Cay Alley, the first two north and south of Joe Cay, and the third between Thomas Cay and Overyonder Cay. The last is very narrow. The best area for anchoring, well shielded from the prevailing southeast winds, lies in the channel running along the west coast of Thomas Cay.

COMPASS CAY

We've long felt that Compass Cay Marina had all the potential to hit "Dream Class" as a pocket marina. The site is good, virtually all-weather, the beach arguably one of the best in

nities to get out into the Sound. But the more difficult eyeball navigation needed on the west side in many cases reduces their attractiveness for spur-of-the-moment changes in route.

- The Exuma Bank is no cruising ground south of Rudder Cut. In truth the practical limit to relatively straightforward Exuma Bank cruising comes at Cave Cay Cut. From then on making your way south is a slow business. It's fine if you want to take your time and poke around wherever you fancy, but it's time consuming and best avoided if you have dates to keep.

Conch Cut to Staniel Cay

Both Conch Cut west and our Sampson Cay waypoint give you access to the whole area lying between Compass Cay and Staniel Cay. In fact the waypoint might be better described as Twin Cays, for it's just west of these landmark

NORTHERN EXUMAS III		
Sampson Cay		
SAMSN	24° 12' 20"/333 N	076° 31' 00"/000 W
Sandy Cay		
SNDCY	24° 11' 15"/250 N	076° 30' 00"/000 W
Staniel Cay		
STANL	24° 10' 15"/250 N	076° 27' 15"/250 W
Harvey Cay		
HARVY	24° 09' 15"/250 N	076° 30' 00"/000 W
Dotham Cut East		
DTHME	24° 07' 00"/000 N	076° 23' 00"/000 W
Dotham Cut West		
DTHMW	24° 06' 30"/500 N	076° 25' 00"/000 W
Black Point		
BLKPT	24° 05' 25"/417 N	076° 25' 00"/000 W
White Point		
WHTPT	24° 02' 00"/000 N	076° 23' 00"/000 W
Farmer's Cut East		
FMRSE	23° 57' 50"/833 N	076° 18' 30"/500 W
Farmer's Cut West		
FMRSW	23° 58' 05"/085 N	076° 19' 40"/666 W

The final figures in each waypoint show seconds (00") and thousands (000) of a minute.

the Exumas. Compass Cay has become a role model mini-haven, setting standards that few other places can match. Dock space has been expanded, power and water are on tap, and there are moorings as an alternative to lying at one of the docks. See our **Yellow Pages**. What impresses is the owner Tucker Rolle's concern for the environment. There is no trash, no spoil. Fishing is banned. As far as it's humanly possible to ensure (given that property rights end at the high water mark), Compass Cay is a nature reserve. You too are protected there, and at peace. And if you do not need or want the crowd scene, you should go there.

The entry routes from both Exuma Sound and the Bank are now well marked. The Bankside way in is the shallower, and we suggest taking the Exuma Sound route and going in and out at high water. The MLW depth is 6 feet. Neither route is a straight run: you have a series of legs to follow, stage by stage, and both coral and sand to avoid, but the route marking is exact. All you have to do is follow the markers and don't get distracted. Just keep your eyes on the ball, and call Compass Cay Marina on VHF 16 if you have any problems.

The Exuma Sound Route into Compass Cay Marina

Compass Cay Exuma Sound Approach		
CMPSA	24° 15' 31"/520 N	076° 29' 56"/940 W

From the area of our approach waypoint you are going to enter Joe Cay Cut, on the north side of Joe Cay, favoring the Compass Cay side. Your initial guidance is two red leading marks on a small unnamed rocky cay lying roughly level with the north end of Joe Cay, and further in, to the west of Joe Cay. Don't go in to the cut itself until you have picked up these marks. When you've got them, read the water, make sure you're OK, and you'll find that you are taken in along the 210°M line or close to it.

SAMPSON CAY

Sampson Cay is also private but has long been in business as a pocket-sized marina, and the Sampson Cay Club offers not only slips on an outer dock and moorings, but also a totally protected inner dock area where many people keep their boats on a long-term basis. In many ways Sampson Cay is a dream destination for the cruiser. Small enough to be a home, it has all the facilities you need: bar, restaurant, small store, and accommodations ashore.

Compass Cay and Sampson Cay are the only places we know along this stretch of the Exumas with almost total protection. You might want to tuck this away in the back of your mind, just in case. That's not to say that you'd weather a direct hit from a hurricane in either place but in a severe storm you'd be better off there than anywhere else in the area.

Sampson Cay, so we have been told, has just changed hands, with Little Sampson Cay and the marina passing into new ownership. Perhaps it will prove timely. The attrition of a subtropical climate was becoming more and more apparent in Sampson Cay, which, nonetheless, still holds its basic attraction as a mini-haven. Paul, long one of our favorite dockmasters, has moved back to his native Eleuthera, and at the time of writing we're not entirely certain what names will feature as the Sampson Cay cast over the next two years. A new landmark, a new house high on the ridge to the south of the marina, south of the existing Tower and the Hill House, has added to the shoreline profile as you run toward Sampson from the west. These changes apart, Sampson Cay remains very much in business, and, we'd guess, will stay essentially as it was. See our **Yellow Pages** for the fine detail.

Breadfruit tree at Staniel Cay.

FOWL AND NORTH GAULIN CAYS
AND THE MAJORS SPOTS

Between Sampson Cay and Staniel Cay you have a virtual repeat of Pipe Cay Alley. The protected channel between Big and Little Majors Spots offers yet another deep channel and shoal-water playground, culminating in the famous Thunderball Cave in the south, on the doorstep of Staniel Cay. In this alley between the two Majors Cays you have anchorages on either side, and can play these to advantage with the weather. However be aware that a strong reversing tidal flow courses down this conduit, and that heavy swell can bring in surge. The holding is not always good, and you'd be foolish to fail setting your anchor by hand if it hasn't taken satisfactorily, or quitting to find another place. To the west of Big Majors Spot there is good holding, and it's no bad place to anchor.

Staniel Cay

Staniel Cay, with its landmark 260-foot Batelco tower, has long been the cruising mecca of the central Bahamas because it's there, it's central, because it has a 3,000-foot paved airstrip, and because good facilities, two marinas, some moorings, sheltered anchorages, and adequate-though-simple stores are all at hand. It is also a very attractive settlement, neat, compact, and well planted with trees, not the least of which is a handsome breadfruit (remember the *Mutiny on the Bounty*?). Any more pluses? Well there's the legendary Thunderball Cave that would be a pity to miss. See our **Yellow Pages.**

Problems have been reported to us concerning approach tracks into Staniel Cay. Apparently a waypoint has come into use in one of the guides that places anyone coming from the north on the Bank side too far south before they turn in. Equally, anyone coming up from the south is going to turn east toward Staniel Cay too soon. The problem lies in sand, which is more than likely to ground you, between this quoted turning point and Staniel itself.

If you're coming from the north, the approach, reduced to its simplest form, is this: round Sandy Cay safely off, and then turn directly for the Staniel Cay marker stake on the southern rock. If you're coming up from the south, stand safely off Harvey Cay and continue northward, gradually turning northeastward in a gentle curve until you intersect the course line running in from Sandy Cay. Then go in on that line. Our waypoints show you the way it is.

There were some sixty boats in the Staniel Cay area at the time we were there last. For some time now we've become aware that Staniel, or more accurately, the Majors Spot anchorages, have become a mirror, albeit on a reduced scale, of George Town as a cruising destination. We've seen the development of a VHF social net, with its 8 a.m. weather forecast, and broadcast of the program of the day, the naming of beaches (no Volleyball yet, but a Picnic), and a cohesive, mutually supporting, community afloat. Those we met there, time and again, expressed the opinion that George Town was "too crowded." It seems, as ever, that people vote with their feet, move on, and a new town develops.

Approaches to Staniel Cay

Either Sandy Cay (SNDCY to the northwest) or Harvey Cay (HARVY to the southwest) are your lead marks to gaining Staniel Cay (STANL). From either of these you should be able to pick up that Batelco tower and steer for it. Go easy once you pass Longitude 076° 27' 30 W, and pay attention to the color of the water, particularly on your port side, for a sandbar bulges down from the north as you get closer in. Your heading now should be fixed on the larger of the low-lying rocks ahead, which has a hard-to-define stake on it. Short of this rock you'll become aware that deeper-water channels fork off to the north and south. The north channel leads you toward the Staniel Cay Yacht Club and, if you go on "around the corner," to the moorings of Club Thunderball. If you turn south you are heading directly toward the Happy People Marina.

Staniel Cay, from the southwest.

Staniel Cay Yacht Club cottages (and Batelco tower).

To gain Staniel Cay Yacht Club you must parallel the line of rocks heading up your deep-water channel, and then round a reef that extends north from the last visible rock. In effect you go past the docks, and then do a 180-degree turn to come back to them. If you're after the Club Thunderball moorings, you carry on around the shoulder of Staniel Cay. The approach to the Happy People Marina is straightforward.

If you wish to anchor off, the southwest edge of the bulging sandbank (on your port side on the way in to the Staniel Cay Yacht Club) is good, as is just off the Yacht Club (but there's little room here for more than two boats). The Club Thunderball has eleven Sleep Tight moorings, all blue buoys. If you're interested, contact them on VHF 16. The moorings off the northern of the three cays you'll pass going this way are temporary moorings for visitors to Thunderball Cave. The cave is, in effect, the center of that island. The anchorages between and around the Majors Spots have already been covered.

The Marinas

The Happy People Marina has been a staple of Staniel Cay, and with its hotel, restaurant, and bar has always been popular. Staniel Cay Yacht Club had a shot in the arm with a near-total transformation of the docks, the Club itself, its satellite cottages, and even its landscaping. It's an ambitious undertaking, aiming for the upper strata of the market, and you'll see more mini-mega yachts there than humble cruisers.

Around and About

We've already touched on Staniel Cay in capsule. It remains to say that Thunderball Cave is fun to dive, and dramatic. But you need sunlight. Ideally strong, overhead sun to work its magic. The cave has two entrances, on the west side (the primary one) and on the east, and at high

water the lintels of both entries form sumps, and you have to duck underwater to clear them. Inside you have surface air space, a high dome above your head with shafts of sunlight slanting down into the water. But it's what you see under your feet that counts. These shafts of sun reaching down into the depths, creating a blaze of neon blue in contrast to the outer blackness, and the Thunderball fish population, curious, maybe waiting for handouts, are not at all afraid of you.

The best time to dive it? At low water, and wait for the slack. The tidal current is strong there. We say dive, but we mean snorkel. All you need is a mask and fins. Take some bread in a plastic bag to feed the fish, and an underwater camera if you have one. At peak times you'll find Thunderball Cave a forest of fins and snorkels, which can spoil the magic. If all the world is there when you arrive in your dinghy, come back another time and try to see it without the crowd scene.

Staniel Cay to the Farmer's Cays

HARVEY CAY TO DOTHAM CUT AND BLACK POINT SETTLEMENT

Harvey Cay, a short run of 3.46 nm on 170°M, is rather like Elbow Cay in the northern Exumas, an outlying cay that makes staying out to the west necessary if you are passage making on the Bank side. From Harvey Cay to Dotham Cut west is a short run of 5.13 nm on a heading of 123°M.

BITTER GUANA AND GAULIN CAYS

Bitter Guana and Gaulin Cays are virtually one. Uninhabited, there's not much there other than a memory of disaster and sadness, for a boat carrying Haitian refugees was wrecked just off Bitter Guana Cay. Its crew and passengers, who all lost their lives, were buried there in a mass grave.

The entrance to Thunderball Cave, Staniel Cay.

Dotham Cut

Dotham Cut East		
DTHME	24° 07' 00"/000 N	076° 23' 00"/000 W
Dotham Cut West		
DTHMW	24° 06' 30"/500 N	076° 25' 00"/000 W

Dotham Cut is recognizable as a wide clear opening as you run south on to this heading, which takes you to just off Dotham Point, a touch further south than you might think necessary at first. There's a sandbore running out to the west from the south point of Gaulin Cay, which you must avoid. With wind and tide fighting over this shoal, Dotham Cut can produce millrace conditions on the Bank side, but the Cut itself is fine, deep, and holds no other hazards. Your recognition of Dotham Cut is further aided by a light stake on Gaulin as well as white cliffs, rather like a mini-Table Mountain, further north up the cay. As with all passes, go through it visual.

DOTHAM CUT TO GEORGE TOWN

From Dotham Cut east to the northwest entrance to George Town Harbour is a straight offshore Exuma Sound run of 45.42 nm on 142°M. We reckon this is the most simple route to take to George Town from the Staniel Cay area. It presents no navigation problems and Dotham Cut is, as we've said, not a difficult pass.

DOTHAM CUT TO BLACK POINT SETTLEMENT

To go on to Black Point settlement from the north, just go visual heading southeast on the Bank side to ease around Dotham Point and run parallel to the shore to anchor off the bay. Black Point's 100-foot Batelco tower is a good marker if you can't pick up buildings immediately. If you veer off toward Black Point you'll find yourself in another shoal area, and the best line to take is favor Dotham Point and then go straight for the Government Dock, which should then be visible.

A regatta racer built in Black Point.

BLACK POINT SETTLEMENT

Black Point settlement, perhaps surprisingly, is the largest center of population in the Exumas after George Town. There seems to be no particular reason why this has come about, and the brief analysis put to us is probably right on the button: "It's good here. None of our children want to go to Nassau. We get bad stories of what it's like there. So they stay. There's not much here, but it's better than Nassau. And we fish a bit. We know the places, where to go."

The Black Point settlement area, on its wide east-facing bight formed by Dotham Point in the north and Black Point in the west, is attractive at first sight, and holds its attraction close in. You can anchor virtually where you wish, best leaving a fairway open to the Government Dock, for that is used by the mailboat and by fishing craft. However, it is possible to come alongside there if you want. The depth is 6 feet at MLW around the outer half of the dock, shoaling to 3–4 feet closer to the shore. There is no fuel, but Black Point has good water, offered free. All you have to do is bring your cans or jugs. If you elect to anchor off, as almost every visitor does, you'll find yourself over sand with 7 feet of water at MLW even quite close in, and it's good holding.

An alternative anchorage lies off the community dock, the smaller dock to the west tucked off a knob of land called Adam's Point. Here too, if you draw 4 feet or less, you could come alongside the dock but anchoring off in 12–15 feet of water is probably better. The little bay itself shoals past the dock. Again, other than an open shelter built for local partying, there are no facilities there, but it's a pleasant, well-shaded and quiet place, no further from the center of the settlement than the Government Dock.

Wherever you choose to go, you're exposed to the southwest through west to north in that bight, but in prevailing southeast winds, we reckon Black Point is a good place to call. If you were caught there by the onset of unfavorable weather, your choices are either to make a break for Little Farmer's Cay or for Staniel Cay, if either look right to you, or do what the locals do. Go east around Dotham Point and enter Little Creek and hole up there. We were assured you have 4 feet at MLW but we've not tried it. What you do have there is total protection. The settlement, apart from its lack of fuel of any kind, has what you'd expect to find in any similar community. See our **Yellow Pages** for the detail.

Black Point to Little Farmer's Cay

GREAT GUANA CAY

At something over 10 nm in length, Great Guana Cay dominates the central Exumas. You expect more from it, but there's really nothing there for the cruising visitor. Black Point is the only settlement. You can anchor off the west coast at many places, and will be protected from northeast to southeast; there are beaches and places to explore, but go cautiously as you parallel the coast for there are reefs and coral heads that must be avoided. It's strange. There must be something in the name. Guana Cay in the Abacos at just over 5 nm can't quite rival its Exuma cousin in length but equally has a coastline that seems to go on forever.

Local reports have it that a new marina has been planned, is under construction, and may be operating with a year or so on the southwestern tip of Great Guana Cay. The project was not sufficiently advanced for us to write helpfully about it at the time we were in Little Farmers Cay (March 1999).

Little Farmer's Cay, from the northwest.

Farmer's Cay Cut

Farmer's Cut East		
FMRSE	23° 57' 50"/833 N	076° 18' 30"/500 W
Farmer's Cut West		
FMRSW	23° 58' 05"/085 N	076° 19' 40"/666 W

The Little Farmer's Cay 260-foot Batelco tower is a clear indicator of the proximity of Farmers Cay Cut. The entrance to the Cut from the east is well defined, and your entry route lies to the south of the small cay in the center of the Cut, aiming for the beach on Little Farmer's Cay. Once you're in, you must avoid the patch of shoal and reef that lies immediately to the southwest of the little cay, and make your turn to starboard or port in the deeper water that is divided, a bit like a rotary, by that patch. From then on you have no problems. The water is clear and easy to read. Taking the Cut from west to east is relatively straightforward, for the deeper water shows clearly.

Little Farmer's Cay

Little Farmer's Cay could be the ideal, archetypal Bahamian settlement, or maybe it's just everyone's dream vision of just what a small Bahamian settlement should look like. It has a superb site, the enhancement of two harbors (though both tend to shoal), enough land elevation to add interest, and attractive houses in a blaze of colors set among palms and flowering shrubs. It's something close to Polynesian. Unexpected. A surprise.

ANCHORAGES, MOORINGS, AND MARINA

Your choices there are to anchor off the southwest tip of Great Guana Cay, where a narrow tongue of deeper water places you just off the beach. The holding is not so good, but there are two moorings you can take up, and more are planned. See our **Yellow Pages** on page 253 for more information. Slightly better holding may be found to the west side of the sand bar enclosing that tongue of deeper water. You could drop south to the northwest cove of Big Farmer's Cay, but this places you the full width of the cut away from the settlement, and in line for surge. Neither of the two harbors, Small Harbour and Big Harbour, are open to you as an option. Both shoal rapidly, and the good ground is already taken by local boats. The Government Dock in Small Harbour is in use by fishing boats, and of course the mailboat.

Alternatively you can go alongside the Farmer's Cay Yacht Club and Marina dock on the northeast tip of Little Farmer's Cay. It's a big title for one comparatively small dock with just one building there and two fuel tanks, but read on. Here over the past few years the owner, Roosevelt Nixon, has patiently built the nucleus of what is intended to be a larger facility. His work to date has provided a good dock, albeit subject to the reversing current of the cut, with water, fuel, a telephone, and a restaurant and bar, all well built and well run.

To get from there into the settlement you have two options. The first is to cross a bridge over the creek that runs behind the yacht club and take a beach walk along Big Harbour. The other is to walk along the sand road that runs to the north end of a 2,200-foot paved airstrip, and walk down the strip to the road running from its south end into the settlement. We go into this kind of detail because the plans for the future hinge on the geography of this site, the existing dock, with almost half a mile of creek behind it, and the good fortune of the existing airstrip. In time the creek may well offer an all-weather harbor, a small colony of low-rise efficiencies may offer shoreside accommodations, a further bar may be built, and the airstrip is there. The plans are sympathetic to the environment, and the best in this regard we have seen in the Bahamas, but at the time we write remain "on paper."

THE SETTLEMENT

We've already given an initial view of the settlement and our **Yellow Pages** give the detail. Perhaps the focal point of Little Farmer's Cay from the visitor's point of view may well be the Ocean Cabin restaurant and bar, whose owner, Terry Bain, was the initiator of the First Friday in February Festivals in 1986, and has been the driving force behind them since them. As often happens in the Bahamas, some two or three cruising boats have made Little Farmer's Cay and the

Ocean Cabin their winter home, and you'll find a small world there that may well attract you to join them.

Small Harbour, Little Farmer's Cay.

YELLOW PAGES

This area received the full force of Hurricane *Floyd* in September 1999. Be aware that reconstruction and the restoration of normal services after a Category 4 Hurricane may take a considerable period of time to complete.

HIGHBORNE CAY

Shaped like the H in Highborne, this 2½-mile-long private island, with its small marina and welcoming hosts, Ian Macbeth and Barbara Thrall, is a tiny Exuman paradise for your first stop after leaving the Nassau metropolis. There are only nine residences, four of which can be rented, and a grocery store. If you are a marina guest you are allowed to walk on the island; there are roads and trails to pristine beaches marked on the map you are given in your welcome pack when you sign in. Aloes can still be found on the cay, a legacy from an earlier aloe plantation, when watermelons flourished here as well. For visiting yachts at anchor, you can come into the dinghy dock, or fuel dock to refuel, but will be discouraged from exploring the island and charged $2 per bag to dispose of garbage. Reservations are important; call ahead of time to make certain there is space for you.

MARINA

HIGHBORNE CAY
Tel: 242-355-1008 • Fax & Residence: 355-1003 • VHF 16

Slips	16
Max LOA	100 ft. or more alongside the piers.
MLW at Dock	10 to 12 ft., less in the channel.
Dockage	$1.25 per ft. per day in the slips, $1.50 per ft. at the slips alongside the long pier. Tenders are charged dock space.
Power	$15 per day for 30A, $25 per day for 50A, and $60 per day for 100A.
Water	40¢ per gallon for reverse osmosis water.
Fuel	Fuel dock open from 8 am to noon and 2 to 5 pm, except Wednesday afternoons.
Propane	Refills available on a 24-hour turnaround.
Telephone	Public telephone with US-direct access, next to *Cheap Charlie's*.
Laundry	Done by one of the island's housekeepers after 5 pm for $10.
Bar	There are plans to build a bar and snack bar; *Cheap Charlie's* on the dock sells cold sodas, cigarettes, beer, and snacks.
Provisions	Open 9 am to noon, and 2 to 4 pm, Monday to Saturday. Canned foods, produce, frozen meat, liquor, fish & lobster in season, T-shirts.
Ice	$5 for a 10-lb. bag.
Sewerage	Please use holding tanks in the harbor.
Accommodations	Four houses available to rent from $200 per night, for four to six people.
Catering	*Janet's Catering Service* Tel: 355-1010 or call "Cool Runner" on VHF 16 for homemade bread and a delicious selection of appetizers, entrees, cakes, and other desserts delivered to your boat.
Facilities	Every morning at 7:30 am Ian gives the weather report from NOAA, and from Nassau for the Bahamas. Listen on VHF 16 and switch to channel 6. Barbecue and outdoor dining area on shore; dogs are welcome on a leash provided you scoop the poop into the bushes. Pooper scoopers provided. Marked trails and walking paths lead to fabulous beaches. Brilliant snorkel-

	ing and deep sea fishing five minutes away.
Credit Cards	Visa, MasterCard, Discover, checks, or cash.
Dockmaster	Eric with his wife, Darnelle, run the Marina and *Cheap Charlie's*.

THINGS TO DO IN HIGHBORNE CAY

- Choose a new beach to visit every day.
- Snorkel staghorn and elkhorn reefs and the *Octopus's Garden*.
- Dive down more than 230 feet off the *Highborne Cay Wall*, the vast wall stretching down the eastern side of the Exuma chain, largely unexplored by divers. But keep a lookout for sharks. Or try *Basketstar Reef* and *Filefish Reef*, and the sixteenth-century *Highborne Cay Wreck*.
- Take the dinghy up to Allan's Cay and introduce yourself to an iguana. Please don't feed them. They are prehistoric to look at, a protected species, and may nibble your ankles (which hurts) if you try to give them Cheerios for breakfast. And don't take your dog with you, either; they are banned on Allan's Cay, which is a Bahamas National Trust reserve. Why not snorkel *Barracuda Shoal* while you're up there?

NORMANS CAY

This is a favorite anchorage for yachts, where a partially submerged aircraft, a legacy from drug-running days, lies in four feet of water within the lagoon. There is a tumble-down dock and some deserted buildings at the south end of the six-mile long cay. Although it is a private island, you are allowed to walk on the southern end. There is ice available from *MacDuff's of Norman's Cay*, a quarter of a mile north, who has oceanfront villas to rent (Tel: 242-357-8846) at what is fast becoming a favorite lunch spot in the northern Exumas, easily accessible from either side of Normans Cay. Go ashore and try their hamburgers!

There is a designated area on the south end of Norman's Cay for trash. Please leave a $1 donation in the honesty box (or with the barman at *MacDuff's*) to help the residents with the cost of removing it to a landfill.

Janet Wilson

MacDuff's.

WARDERICK WELLS
EXUMA CAYS LAND AND SEA PARK

The Exuma Park covers 176 square miles of spectacular subtropical waters, coral reefs, and cays, from Wax Cay at the northern end to Conch Cut at the southern end, with a broad spectrum of natural vegetation and wildlife. It was established in 1958, and is supervised by the Bahamas National Trust. Some of the islands within the Park are privately owned so please respect their privacy. The Park Warden and his staff operate from the Headquarters building at the north end of Warderick Wells. You should check in at the headquarters building, where the staff can answer questions and provide information about the Park.

If you would like to take a mooring in the Park overnight, call "Exuma Park" on VHF 16 at least a day in advance so that when moorings are allocated at 9 am each morning, you can talk to them and ensure your mooring. If you join the Support Fleet you can stay for two nights free each year, and enjoy the facilities provided through membership and donations, together with a newsletter and a chance to volunteer your time for them. Volunteers may choose to receive credits to offset their expenses while staying in the Park; see Ray and Evelyn about this. The Park has recently introduced User Fees of $5 per day for boats anchoring anywhere within the Park area, with honesty boxes on Hawksbill, Shroud, and Cambridge Cays.

At Warderick Wells, the island is covered with walking trails and a huge diversity of wildlife, while the snorkeling within easy distance of the anchorage is breathtaking. The Park itself is the largest protected fish-breeding ground in the Caribbean, hence the problem with the two P's: Pollution and Poaching. Pollution is the responsibility of every visitor to the Park to keep to a minimum. Absolutely no trash, maximum use of holding tanks, minimum noise from jet-skis, radios, and rowdy parties (except at the Saturday evening happy hour at the headquarters with other visitors). Everything you bring with you, take away with you. Be responsible and maintain and nurture this environmentally and ecologically superb site. And don't for one minute think that because you have made a $100 donation that you can go off and catch just *one* big fish. Or a lobster. Or a conch. You can't. Not only is it morally wrong, it's illegal too, and you can be fined. Big time. Your passport can be taken away. And your boat impounded. End of a happy vacation? You bet.

Warderick Wells, North Anchorage.

FACILITIES

Wardens
Ray and Evelyn Darville will do everything they can to help you. Evelyn allocates moorings for the day on the radio every morning, and Ray is a hard-working and knowledgeable warden with dedicated conservationist ideals.

Moorings
There are 22 in Warderick Wells near the headquarters, and 4 in the idyllic south anchorage on a first-come-first-served basis.

Cost of Mooring
Includes the $5 daily User Fee: less than 45 ft., $15 per day; 45 to 54 ft., $20 per day; 55 to 70 ft., $30 per day; 71 to 90 ft., $50 per day; over 90 ft., $100 per day. Anchoring fees and mooring fees for private charters, corporate vessels, dive charters, kayaks, and sea plane charters are all the same at $1 per foot per day in order to encourage the use of moorings. The daily user fee remains the same. Bahamian pleasure vessels, tours and charter boats are not charged for park use.

Booking
Call "Exuma Park" on VHF 16 at least 24 hrs. in advance. They announce mooring allocation at 9 am on VHF 16, switching to channel 9, each morning.

Park Headquarters
Open 9 am to noon and 1 to 5 pm, Monday to Saturday; 9 am to 1 pm on Sundays. The headquarters has a communication center with VHF radio and cellular telephone (no public telephone), as well as maps and nature displays, but it is the Darville's home as well so please respect their privacy.

Library
In the headquarters, T-shirts and post cards also for sale. Ray's own book, written with Stephen Pavlidis about the Land and Sea Park, is for sale, giving an in-depth appreciation of what is in the Park and why it's so important to conserve it.

Lectures and Nature Walks
Given at the headquarters. Volunteers are encouraged to help with Park Management projects.

Credit Cards
Only cash, checks, traveler's checks.

Support Fleet Membership
If your boat is:

less than 45 ft.	$50 per year
45 to 54 ft.	$60 per year
55 to 70 ft.	$80 per year
71 to 90 ft.	$120 per year
over 90 ft.	$220 per year

Support Fleet Members receive two free days on moorings. Any contribution of $500 or more allows for free moorings for one calendar year, and does not incur daily user fees. Contributions may be sent to *The Bahamas National Trust,* for The Exuma Cays Land and Sea Park, PO Box N 3189, Nassau, Bahamas.

SNORKELING & DIVE SITES

Reefs equal land mass in the Bahamas, so treat them with respect. Don't touch, harm, or take anything you see. As visitors, we are privileged to enjoy the splendor of this underwater spectacle; leave it exactly as you find it for others to enjoy. Take only photographs; leave only footprints.

Off Hawksbill Cay, which also has good anchorages off the central west coast, and an excellent freshwater well near the anchorage. There are rare, white-tailed Tropic birds nesting here in March and April, providing spectacular flying displays. Between *Little Cistern* and *Cistern Cay*.

Brad's Cay on the east side of *Long Cay*, with a cave on the northeast side.

Between *S. Hall's Pond, O'Brien's,* and *Pasture Cay* where there is a sunken drug-smuggling plane.

Cambridge and *Little Bell Cay*, which are private but have good reefs to the east and south.

Rocky Dundas, with dinghy moorings near the caves and reef.

And the Park's own *Sea Aquarium,* which you can locate by a sign on a small rock, with a dinghy mooring.

THINGS TO DO IN WARDERICK WELLS

- Swim off your own boat in some of the clearest water in the world.
- Snorkel or dive the unbelievably beautiful and diverse reefs.
- See how many birds you can hear in the total peace and quiet of Warderick Wells, and spot them from the Bird Check List given out at the headquarters.
- Walk to the top of Boo Boo Hill and leave your boat's name as a memento. Keep to the marked "Shaggy Dog" trail to protect new indigenous plant growth, and wear sturdy shoes to protect your feet across the moonscape. Maybe you'll meet a Hutia on the way? Don't forget to take a camera; the views from the top are glorious, and you have to be photographed nailing your boat name to the great collection up there.
- Ask how you can help with volunteering in the Park.
- Listen for the ghosts of Warderick Wells on moonlit nights!

COMPASS CAY

This small island is a tiny corner of paradise, beautifully tended by its owner, your host Tucker Rolle. Tucker's thoughtful stewardship of the land and surrounding waters are an example of the highest ideals in ecological conservancy. The sheltered harbor with its docks and moorings would make for good hurricane protection and is popular for long-term boat storage. The approach channels have been well marked by Tucker, and you should be able to bring in a 8-foot-draft boat without problems on a high tide from Joe Cay Cut, or 5 feet at low tide. Well-marked trails, with attractively painted driftwood signs, guide you over the walking paths that criss-cross the cay, and "the prettiest beach in the Bahamas" is no false claim to their idyllic crescent beach.

MARINA

COMPASS CAY MARINA
Tel and fax: 242-355-2064 • VHF 16
• E-mail: compasscay@aol.com

Slips	13
Moorings	4, cost $15 per night.
Max LOA	Up to 120 ft.
MLW at Dock	Shoal draft approaches, 8 ft. at the dock.
Dockage	$1 per ft. per day for transient boats; 30¢ per ft. per month.
Power	$15 per day for 30A, $25 per day for 50A.
Fuel	No
Water	50¢ per gallon; new water tanks installed in 1999.
Telephone	There is no public telephone; ask Tucker if you need to make a call in an emergency.

Trash	Recycling is practiced here! All trash is separated into glass/metal and burnable.
Marina Shop	The dockside store has a few provisions, beer, and liquor, as well as T-shirts and charming maps of the island.
Accommodations	*The Lodge* is a three-bedroom house that can be rented for $1,450 per week for two people; $100 per week per extra person up to a total of six. This includes use of a boat. Plans are to have two apartments available as well by the end of 1999 to accommodate guests on board who prefer to stay ashore.
Facilities	Beach parties and potluck suppers on the beach with other guests. This beach is superb, with good snorkeling on reefs that you can almost walk out to. Marked walking trails on the island. Both Sampson and Staniel Cays are easy to reach in your dinghy if you need supplies or service.
Credit Cards	Cash or traveler's checks only.

THINGS TO DO IN COMPASS CAY

- Enjoy lazy days on that gorgeous beach. Snorkel out to introduce yourself to the colonies of fish living on the reefs.
- Make new friends at a dockside potluck supper.
- Take the dinghy to explore some of the little bays and inlets among the neighboring islands.

SAMPSON CAY

Sampson Cay is still a tiny, privately owned gem of an island. The main dock and the fuel dock are easy to spot, as are the moorings on your port side as you come in. Through the narrow gap is a second, sheltered harbor where you can safely leave your boat for a while if you have to return home. This is a perfect center for exploring the central Exumas, with fantastic fishing and diving within easy reach, and snorkeling within dinghy reach.

MARINA

SAMPSON CAY CLUB AND MARINA
Tel: 242-355-2034 • VHF 16 "Sampson Cay"

Slips	11
Moorings	4, cost $10 per night.
Max LOA	160 ft.
MLW at Dock	8 ft., but less in the channel.
Dockage	$1 per ft. per day under 100 ft., $1.25 per ft. per day over 100 ft.
Power	$25 per day for 50A, $15 for 30A, and $10 for 20A.
Fuel	Diesel and gasoline.
Propane	Can be brought in from Staniel Cay.
Water	50¢ per gallon.
Telephone	No public telephone
Laundry	$16 per load. See Eulease.
Restaurant	An attractive bar with pennants flying, and a lounge and restaurant that opens daily at 8 am for breakfast, lunch, and dinner, where you dine at a long table with other guests. See Eulease, or Mark at the bar, and choose from a delicious menu before 3:30 pm for dinner, which is served at 7 pm. Eulease serves the best lamb chops in the islands!

Groceries	The marina store has a small selection of groceries, liquor, gifts, and T-shirts, as well as a tiny amount of fresh produce. Cabbage was $2 per lb. when we were there.
Ice	$4 a bag.
Trash	Only marina guests may leave trash. Put it by the front-end loader.
Boat Rental	13-ft. Boston Whaler: $20 per hour, $50 for a half day, $80 full day, plus gas and oil. 21-ft. Boston Whaler with local guide or captain: $75 per hour, $185 per half day, $300 for a full day, plus gas and oil. This boat is not available for bareboat charter.
Kayaks	$25 for a full day, $15 for half day.
Diving	Rental tanks and refills are available.
Storage	$13 per ft. per month, pro-rated 2-week minimum. Includes daily fender and waterline check, storm watch, etc. for non-live-aboard boats in the inner harbor. Electricity not included.
Salvage	*Overseas Salvage* Tel: 242-355-2034, 359-1464, or 331-2845 Marcus Mitchell runs the *M/V Victoria* salvage vessel operation from Sampson Cay.
Accommodations	Two cottages to rent overlooking the marina, and a hilltop villa with two bedrooms (one with bunk beds) and living room with stunning views on three sides, from $125 per night.
Credit Cards	Cash or traveler's checks only.

Janet Wilson

Sampson Cay Club.

THINGS TO DO IN SAMPSON CAY

• Enjoy an excellent dinner with new friends.
• Snorkel and dive the many reefs within easy reach of Sampson Cay as you explore Pipe Creek.
• Leave your boat in this safe place if you have to go off to attend to the outside world.
• Watch Eulease feed the sharks swimming at the dock by floodlight after dinner.

STANIEL CAY

With its good anchorages, moorings, and marinas, and its central position in some of the most spectacular waters in the Exuma chain, Staniel Cay is fast becoming a mini-George Town. Brightly painted houses and friendly people await the boating visitor, with the relaxed informality that makes for a very popular cruising destination. Listen out for the Boaters' Net on VHF 16, switching to 14, at 8 am for weather and local information.

MARINAS

STANIEL CAY YACHT CLUB
Tel: 242-355-2024 • Fax: 355-2044 • VHF 16

Slips	15
Max LOA	150 ft.
MLW at Dock	7.5 ft.
Dockage	80¢ per ft. per day. The dock is open from 8 am to 5 pm Monday to Friday, to noon on Saturdays, and to 10 am on Sundays.
Power	$35 per day for 50A, $25 per day for 30A.
Fuel	Diesel and gasoline
Propane	From *Isles General Store.*
Water	50¢ per gallon.
Telephone	Card phones beside the restaurant. Only one of the two working when we were last there, but it's just a short walk up the hill to *Batelco.*
Restaurant	Open from 8:30 to 10 am for breakfast, 11:30 am to 3 pm for lunch, and from 7:30 pm for dinner, when reservations are requested. Box lunches for picnics can be provided. Closed for lunch on Sundays.
Ice	$3.50 per bag.
Trash	Can be left behind the Club. $1.50 per 15-gallon bag, $3 for a 33-gallon bag, and $5 for a 50-to-60-gallon bag.
Store	Within the restaurant, selling mostly liquor and logo T-shirts.
Boat Rental	SCYC has a 13-foot Boston Whaler for cottage guests to rent for $50 a day, excluding fuel.
Diving	There are dive guides available, though there is no dive shop on the island.
Accommodations	Four air-conditioned cottages, a houseboat cottage, and a guest house from $135 per day, MAP $30.
Credit Cards	Visa and MasterCard.
Manager	Nicole Ferguson
Dockmaster	Kuenson Rolle

HAPPY PEOPLE MARINA
Tel: 242-355-2008 • VHF 16

This really is the happiest marina in the Exumas. Kenneth and Theazel make the most wonderful hosts with all the best in Bahamian hospitality. Kenneth is dredging outside the marina to make a little sandy beach in front of the rooms in order to create a bigger turning basin and increase the entrance channel to 8 feet, while Theazel continues to cook up a storm in the restaurant. Their two-bedroom efficiency, with a stunning panoramic view out over the Staniel Cay entrance, comes complete with a crib for new members of the boating world who might prefer to spend a night or two ashore with their parents.

Slips	17
Max LOA	177 ft.
MLW at Dock	7 ft.

Dockage	80¢ per ft. per day.
Power	$25 per day for 50A, $18 per day for 30A.
Propane	From *Isles General Store*.
Water	50¢ a gallon.
Telephone	On the dock.
Showers	Yes
Restaurant	Theazel is in charge of the *Royal Entertainer Restaurant*, which is open for breakfast and lunch on request, when she serves her famous Theazel Burgers, and for dinner by reservation. Great Bahamian food!
Ice	$3 a bag.
Accommodations	8 simple, clean, air-conditioned rooms from $90 per day, and a well-equipped two-bedroom efficiency from $200 per day.
Credit Cards	Cash and traveler's checks only.

MOORINGS

CLUB THUNDERBALL
VHF 16 "Thunderball"

Moorings	11, from $10 a day according to boat length. Call ahead to see if they have one available.
Dock	There are two dinghy docks.
Restaurant	*Club Thunderball Restaurant and Bar* open from 11:30 am Tuesday to Saturday, and from 1 pm on Sundays, with a happy hour on Tuesdays from 5 to 7 pm and Friday night barbecues.
Laundry	Three coin-operated machines.

Inside Thunderball Cave.

SERVICES & SHOPPING IN STANIEL CAY

Accommodations
Happy People Marina Tel: 242-355-2008 Eight double rooms, simply furnished, with bathrooms and views over the harbor, from $80 per night. Two-bedroom efficiency with air-conditioned bedrooms, overlooking Staniel Cay harbor. Two weeks notice to reserve rooms.

Staniel Cay Yacht Club Tel: 242-355-2024 • Fax: 355-2044 • E-mail: watermak@safari.com Four waterfront cottages for two people from $800 per week, one cottage for four people from $1,200 per week, one houseboat cottage for two people, plus two guests, from $800 per week. MAP $30 a day. Flights from Nassau or Fort Lauderdale can be arranged, with complimentary transport from the Staniel Cay Airport to the Yacht Club. Small boat rentals are available.

Airport
No scheduled air service to this paved 3,000-foot runway, but local pilots include:
John Chamberlain, with a six-seater Piper Lance
Tel: 242-355-2043 • VHF 16 "Himalaya"
Bill Hirsch, flies from Miami to Staniel Cay
Tel: 305-944-3033 • Fax: 944-8033
Solomon Robinson, with a six-seater Piper Cherokee
Tel: 242-355-2012 • VHF 16 "Club Thunderball or DJ"
Roland Smith, with a six-seater Piper Cherokee
Tel: 242-355-2013 • VHF 16 "295"
Dorothy Westby, of Professional Flight Transport Inc. will fly you from Ft. Lauderdale to Staniel Cay, for $320 per person round trip. Tel: 954-938-9508 • Fax: 938-9509

Beauty Parlor
Natajia's Unisex Salon Tel: 355-2005 • VHF 16 "Nikki"
Call Nikki to make an appointment or see her at the Staniel Cay Yacht Club where she is the manager.

Boutique
Lindsay's Boutique Tel: 355-2050
Next to *Happy People Marina.* T-shirts, bags, some clothes.

Church
Mt. Olivett Baptist Church

Clinic
St. Luke's Clinic Tel: 355-2010 • VHF 16 "St Luke's Clinic" or "Nana 2" Mary Lou Fadden is still the wonderfully competent nurse on Staniel Cay, with the doctor who visits once a month from Steventon. St Luke's is funded by private donations, so do support their fundraising activities if you hear on the Boater's Net that one is being held. Open 9 am to 12 pm and 2:30 to 5 pm on Monday, Tuesday, Thursday, and Friday; from 9 am to 12 pm on Wednesday and Saturday.

Groceries
Both stores are up the hill within easy walking distance of the two marinas.
The Blue Grocery Store Tel: 355-2014 Open 7:30 am to 7:30 pm Monday to Saturday. Burke Smith has a good selection of groceries, liquor, vegetables, and household supplies and fresh bread. Let him know if you need laundry done, or special mailboat orders.
Pink Pearl Supermarket Tel: 355-2040 • VHF 16 "Pink Pearl" Hugh Smith's store is open 7:30 am to 7:30 pm Monday to Saturday, with bread, groceries, household items, and some frozen goods.
Isles General Store Tel: 355-2007 • VHF 16 Open 7:30 am to 12 pm, and 1:30 to 7 pm, Monday to Saturday. Burkie Rolle has a well-stocked store located over the bridge across the creek selling everything from hardware, marine supplies, groceries, ice, propane and homemade bread. There is a concrete dock inside the creek where you can tie up, and bagged garbage can be left for a small fee.

Ice Cream
Frosty's Ice Cream and *Chamberlain's Arts* on the waterfront opposite the brightly painted picnic area.

Library
Built in 1776, this is the oldest building on the island. Open on Tuesday and Friday from 11 am to 12 pm and 3 to 5 pm.

Mailboat
M/V Etienne & Cephas calls weekly from Nassau on Tuesday evenings. Fare $50.

Propane
Refills available from the *Isles General Store*.

Post Office
Near the *Blue Grocery Store*.

Regatta and Fishing Tournament
Staniel Cay Cruising Regatta in January, headquarters at the *Happy People Marina*. Contact Kenneth Rolle, 242-355-2008 for information.

Annual Staniel Cay Bonefish Tournament and Homecoming held over four days in late July or early August. Call Tony Gray at 242-355-2018 or the Exuma Tourist Office at 242-336-2430.

Restaurants and Bars

Royal Entertainer Lounge and Restaurant at the *Happy People Marina*   Tel: 355-2008 • VHF 16 "Happy People"   Open from 8 am on request for breakfast and lunch daily, and for dinner at 7 pm. Call ahead for dinner reservations to let Theazel know what you would like to eat, and how many people are coming. Famous for her "Theazel Burger," Theazel Rolle was awarded the 1983 Bahamas National Tourism Achievement Award. There is a pool table in the bar, music, and a great atmosphere.

Staniel Cay Yacht Club Restaurant and Bar   Tel: 355-2024 • VHF 16   Open for breakfast from 8:30 am and lunch daily, except closed for lunch on Sundays. Open for dinner every night from 5 pm, for excellent American and Bahamian meals. Call ahead to make dinner reservations. The bar has a pool table and satellite TV, and is well frequented by visiting boaters.

Club Thunderball   VHF 16 "Thunderball" or "DJ"   Open 11:30 am to closing Monday to Saturday, from 1 pm to closing on Sundays, dinner reservations requested before 4 pm. Call a day ahead, or by 1 pm on Fridays, for reservations for the not-to-be-missed Friday night barbecue. Serves Bahamian dishes with an emphasis on seafood, burgers, and sandwiches. Occasional pig roasts, and a Super Bowl party. The bar has a pool table, satellite TV, and dancing on weekends with local DJ and occasional live music. They have two dinghy docks.

Telephones

Batelco   Tel: 355-2060 • Fax: 355-2063   Open Monday to Friday 9 am to 4:30 pm. They sell phone cards, will handle faxes. Phones also at the *Happy People Marina* and the *Staniel Cay Yacht Club*.

Trash

Trash has become such a problem on this small island that it may only be left, tied in bags, behind the two marinas or at the *Isles General Store*, for a small fee of $1.50 for a 15-gallon bag, $3 for a 33-gallon bag and $5 for a 50/60-gallon bag.

THINGS TO DO IN STANIEL CAY

- Dive *Thunderball Cave*, a spectacular underwater cave with shafts of sunlight illuminating it, attracting schools of fish. It was made famous in the James Bond movie, *Thunderball*. Time your dive for slack tide, since the currents are strong here. Take a bag of bread crumbs left over from breakfast or a bag of frozen peas 'n' corn in with you and watch the fish flock toward you, almost nibbling your fingers in their excitement. You can tie your dinghy up to one of the two mooring buoys at the west end of the site.
- Live it up with the in-crowd at *Club Thunderball's* Friday night barbecue, but make your reservations early; this is a popular evening.

BLACK POINT

This friendly settlement has the second-largest population in the Exumas, after George Town. Anchor off, come in with your dinghy, and tie up to the government pier to explore Black Point. Highlights of the year are the *Black Point Homecoming* in April and the *Black Point Regatta* in August. Turn right at the head of the dock as you walk in for the main street in town. At time of writing, there was talk of putting mooring buoys down in the bay off Black Point. Check with Zhivargo Rolle, 355-3003 or VHF 16 "Scorpio," for information.

Small boats at Black Point settlement.

SERVICES & SHOPPING IN BLACK POINT

Accommodations

De Shamons   Tel: 355-3009 • VHF 16   Three rooms to rent with own bathrooms and TV from $80 per night above *De Shamons Restaurant*.

Scorpio's Cottages   Tel: 355-3003 • VHF 16 "Scorpio"   Five brightly painted cottages with full bath and air-conditioning, across the street from the *Scorpio Inn*, from $75 per night. Visa accepted.

Churches

St. Luke's Baptist Church
Gethsemany Baptist Church

Clinic

Tel: 355-0007   The clinic is just across from the school, open Monday to Friday from 9 am to 1:30 pm. A nurse is on duty. The doctor comes in from Steventon once a month.

Fishing

Clayton Rolle will take you bonefishing, snorkeling, and sightseeing in the Exuma Cays. Contact him through *Lorraine's Café*, Tel: 355-33012 or VHF 16.

Fresh Bread

Ask at *Lorraine's Cafe* or call her on VHF 16. Her mum bakes bread daily.

Groceries

Anita's Convenience Store   Tel: 355-3045   Fruit and vegetables, dairy products, hot dogs, and baby items. Take a left as you leave the dock, *Anita's* is a short way along on your right.

Adderley's Friendly Store   Tel: 355-3016   Where "a smile awaits you." Open from 9 am to 6 pm Monday to Saturday, and after church on Sunday. Well stocked with groceries, fruit and vegetables, fresh milk, ice cream, and outboard engine oil.

Darlene's Grocery Store   Tel: 355-3026   Open most days; go to the house and ask her to open up.

Ice

Lorraine's Café $3 for a 10-lb. bag.

Laundry

Ask at *Lorraine's Cafe*; Lorraine's mum, who also bakes bread, will do it for you.

Mailboats

M/V *Etienne & Cephas* leaves Nassau weekly for the Exuma Cays at 2 pm on Tuesdays. Fare $50.

Post Office

Tel: 355-3043   Facing the head of the dock, open from 9 am to 5 pm, Monday to Friday.

Regatta

Annual Black Point Regatta is usually held the first weekend in August. Contact the Exuma Tourist Office, 242-336-2430 for more details.

Restaurants

De Shamon's Restaurant Open from 11 am, serving lunch and dinner. Diane and Simon Smith have recently opened this restaurant, with three rooms above to stay in, and serve Bahamian meals with the emphasis on freshly caught fish. Simon is a diver and catches most of the fish himself. He is happy to take people out on his boat to watch how a diver can work without the benefit of scuba equipment.

Lorraine's Cafe Tel: 355-3012 • VHF 16
Opens at 8 am, serves breakfast, lunch, and dinner with fresh baked breads, pastries on request and free water for boaters. Take your own containers. Arrange for breakfast the night before. Lorraine will also cater for you on board, and can supply ice at $3 a bag.

Scorpio's Restaurant and Bar Tel: 355-3003 • VHF 16   Bar and restaurant serving Bahamian food. Open daily from 9 am, Sundays after church. Visa accepted. This is where it all happens in Black Point!

Sculpture Garden

Willie Rolle's Garden, past *Lorraine's Cafe* and the school, on the left-hand side of the street. Willie is happy to let you wander through his garden and admire the sculptures, though a small token of appreciation for a guided tour is always acceptable.

Straw Market

J and D's have straw goods and souvenirs. *Eunice Wright* lives in the little green painted house, fourth along on the left-hand side as you leave the dock and turn right into town, and sells straw hats of her own creation. There are many ladies weaving and plaiting throughout the settlement.

Telephone

Batelco Tel: 355-3060 • Fax: 355-3063   Open Monday to Friday 9 am to 5 pm with a card telephone outside the office. Phone cards are for sale.

Trash

Can be left in the bins by the dock. No charge.

Water

Free water for boaters from the well outside *Lorraine's Cafe*. This is good, clean water; bring your own containers to fill.

LITTLE FARMER'S CAY

Famous for its *Five F's Festival*, Little Farmer's Cay boasts its own flag, too. Settled originally by freed slaves from Exuma, there are approximately fifty-five residents on the island today, some of whom are descendants from those early days. This one-and-a-quarter-mile long island is the quintessential Bahamian cay, largely undeveloped so far, with moorings in a sheltered anchorage and an independent, self-sufficient lifestyle.

MARINA

FARMER'S CAY YACHT CLUB
Tel: 242-355-4017 • VHF 16

Slips	5
Moorings	There are six moorings between Little Farmer's Cay and Great Guana Cay. Cost is $10 per day. The southern buoys are owned by *Terry Bain* who can be called on VHF 16 "Ocean Cabin" or 355-4006. The northern ones near Great Guana Cay, where a new development with 16 rooms and a marina has just started, are owned by *Hallan Rolle*. Call him at 355-4003 or VHF 16 "Little Jeff."

Max LOA	110 ft.
MLW at Dock	8 ft.
Dockage	$1 per ft. per day.
Power	$25 per day for 50A, $20 per day for 30A.
Fuel	Diesel and gasoline.
Propane	From Hallan Rolle.
Water	50¢ per gallon.
Telephone	Card phone at the restaurant.
Restaurant	Serves breakfast, lunch, and dinner.
Ice	$5 per bag.
Mail	Will be held for your arrival.
Repairs	Small repairs
Accommodations	Three double rooms, from $80 per night in the Club building.
Credit Cards	Visa, MasterCard, and Amex with a surcharge, traveler's checks, or cash.
Owner/Dockmaster	Roosevelt Nixon, with his wife Shirley, who is also the nurse for Farmer's Cay.

SERVICES & SHOPPING IN LITTLE FARMER'S CAY

Accommodations

Farmers Cay Yacht Club Tel: 242-355-4017   Three double rooms, to be refurbished at time of writing, with twin beds and bath, from $80 per night. Book at least two weeks in advance.

Ocean Cabin Tel and Fax: 242-355-4006
• E mail: oceancbn@batelnet.bs   Two cabins on the hill in the village from $100 per night, book at least three weeks in advance.

There are also five Addison cottages to rent; ask locally for more information.

Church

St. Mary's Baptist Church

Clinic

Tel: 355-4015   Call FCYC in an emergency. Located up the hill near the Batelco office. Open Monday to Friday, 9 am to 1 pm. Shirley Nixon, wife of Roosevelt Nixon at the *FCYC*, is the nurse at the Government Clinic. The doctor from Steventon calls in once a month, and a dentist twice a year.

Fishing

Cely Smith Tel: 345-2341   Will come up from Stuart Manor to take you bone or reef fishing.

Fresh Bread

Call ahead through *Ocean Cabin* to Earnestine Bain. Shirley Nixon will also make cakes and desserts. Contact her through *FCYC.*

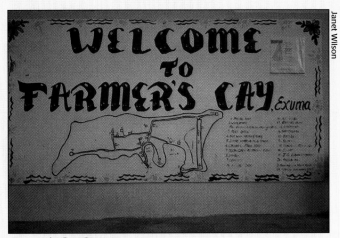

Farmer's Cay Sign.

Janet Wilson

Groceries
Little Harbour Supermarket Tel: 355-4019 Open 8 am to 7:30 pm.

Corene's Grocery Store Up the hill toward Ocean Cabin. Terry or Ernestine Bain will open up for you.

Most islanders have their supplies delivered by the weekly mailboat, *M/V Etienne & Cephas,* so the stores do not carry large stocks. If you need something specific, contact *FCYC* or *Ocean Cabin* to order it for you.

Laundry
Ask at *JR Woodcarvings.*

Liquor Store
Little Harbour Liquor Store Tel: 355-4019 Open 9 am to 5 pm, Monday to Saturday. Ask Eugenia Nixon Percentie at *Little Harbour Supermarket* to open it up for you.

Post Office
Near the Government Dock by *Corene's Grocery Store.* Open on Wednesday, handling incoming mail off the mailboat, and on Thursday, handling outgoing mail for the Friday mailboat.

Propane
Hallan Rolle Tel: 355-4003 or VHF 16 "Little Jeff" Take tanks in early for a same-day fill; available 9 am to 5 pm, Monday to Friday.

Restaurants
Farmer's Cay Yacht Club Tel: 355-4017 • VHF 16 Call at least an hour ahead to ask Joycelyn to prepare a delicious dinner. She will also serve breakfast and lunches on request.

Ocean Cabin Tel: 355-4006 • VHF "Ocean Cabin" Call Ernestine at least an hour ahead for lunches and dinners, and make breakfast arrangements the night before. *Ocean Cabin* also hosts the rowdy and fun 5 F's party annually, on the first Friday in February. Call 324-2093 or 355-4006 for information.

Telephones
Tel: 355-4060 • Fax: 355-4063 Two telephones in the *Batelco* office. Open from 9 am to 5 pm, Monday to Friday; also sells *Batelco* phone cards. There is a card phone on the waterfront in Little Harbour, and one at the *FCYC.*

Trash
Trash can be left by the pink government building at the Government Dock.

GETTING AROUND

Airport
There is no scheduled air service to this 2,300-foot paved airstrip, but Harvey Nixon flies twice a week to Nassau for $60 at time of writing.

Mailboats
MV Etienne & Cephas calls weekly on Tuesday or Wednesday from Nassau. Fare $50.

Water Taxi
Hallan Rolle Tel: 355-4003 • VHF 16 "Little Jeff" He will take you to Barraterre or to explore the surrounding islands.

Cecil Smith VHF 16 "Lamonde" Will also take you to Barraterre to pick up a taxi at *Fisherman's Inn* (Tel: 255-5016) to take you down to George Town Airport. Cecil is a local government representative who is also a superb free diver and spear fisherman. There is no scuba dive operation or scuba gear rental in Little Farmer's Cay.

THINGS TO DO IN LITTLE FARMER'S CAY

- Join the fun for *The First Friday in February Farmer's Cay Festival,* also known as the Five Fs party, held the first weekend in February. Call 242-324-2093 or 242-355-4006 for more information.
- Take the Great Guana Cay cave tour with Stanley Rolle, and explore the 90-foot land cave.
- Visit JR's woodcarving shop up near the Batelco office, and take home a memento of Little Farmer's Cay with one of his carvings from the *Ocean Cabin.*

Chapter 15
The Southern Exuma Cays and Great Exuma Island
The Farmer's Cays to Little Exuma Island

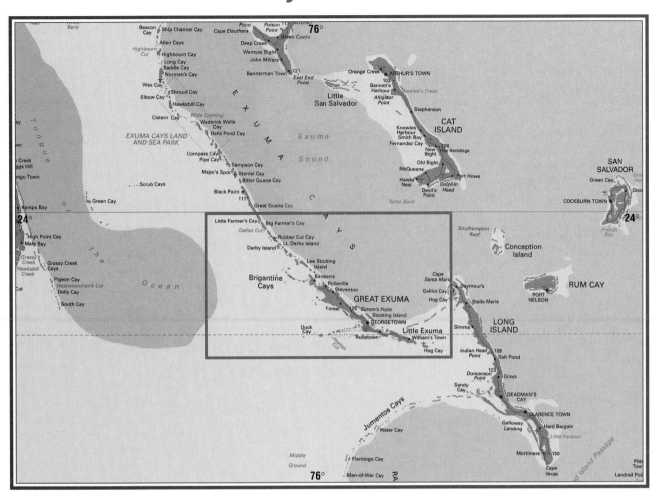

An Overview of the Southern Exumas

THE southern Exumas continue the northwest to southeast line of the Exuma chain from Galliot Cut, just south of Farmer's Cay, to Hog Cay and White Cay, just off the southeast tip of Little Exuma Island at 23° 23' N 076° 25' W. On the Bank side, south of Rat Cay Cut, sandbores and shoal water set limits on cruising territory, and in effect, on that side, you've gone as far as you can go. Rat Cay Cut is your last chance to switch to Exuma Sound to enter George Town. The cays and islands extending south from Rat Cay to Great Exuma Island on the Bank side offer a good area for shoal draft exploration, but if you carry any kind of draft it could turn into a nightmare ground of deceptive channels, shoals, sand, and reef. Leave it to the locals. The west coast of the two Exuma Islands, masked by

flats, mud, and mangroves, as we've said is no cruising territory, but it's good for bonefishing. This may seem a bleak report, but in the southern Exumas everything pales into insignificance compared to George Town and Stocking Island, the Shangri-La of the Bahamas. Little Exuma Island itself is so diminished by its larger twin that it hardly features on the itinerary of most cruising boats.

George Town is, in itself, either the end stop and turn-around point on your cruise south from Florida, the launch pad for your voyage to the Caribbean, or a winter or summer haven. Whatever your plans, cruising in or passage making through the Bahamas takes on a fundamental change at George Town. Continuing south you're committed to serious bluewater passages with Atlantic swells and waves, a diminishing number of safe havens on your route, and few, if any, resources available until you reach the Turks and Caicos. Cruising in the Bahamas north of George Town, as we all know it, has plenty of places to stop, shoal draft and deep water–passage options, and very often a lee side and a windward side to your chosen route. Perhaps unfairly, George Town has long been known as "Chicken Harbor," for many bound for the Caribbean find their first passage after George Town less than pleasant, and return to venture no further south. But as in all sailing, it's weather and timing that make the difference. There's nothing inherently dangerous about going on past George Town, and the span of Out Islands running south from Long Island to the Turks and Caicos form one of the least-spoiled tropic transits in the Western Hemisphere.

For all these reasons, George Town dominates the southern Exumas and is all things to all people. Taking an opinion poll of the cruising community, some like it, some can't stand it for long, but almost every craft on passage between the Virgin Islands and the East Coast of the US will call in at George Town, Great Exuma Island, and no one cruising in the Exumas will miss it. The tide in the southern Exumas runs about the same as Nassau times.

Big Farmer's Cay to Great Exuma Island

BIG FARMER'S CAY AND THE GALLIOT CAYS

Big Farmer's Cay, despite its size, holds nothing to excite the cruising visitor other than shoals and sand extending west into the Bank for over 1 nm. There are no anchorages in its 2.5-nm length other than the northwest-facing cove that opens into the Farmer's Cut basin. If you choose to go in here, you are close enough to the Cut to suffer surge if any kind of sea is running outside. The Galliot Cays, which gave their name to the Cut, are largely unapproachable due to sand, reefs, and tidal flow, but an anchorage can be found by the edge of the sand off the northwest tip of Little Galliot Cay.

Galliot Cut

Galliott Cut East		
GALLE	23° 55' 40"/666 N	076° 16' 35"/583 W
Galliott Cut West		
GALLW	23° 55' 00"/000 N	076° 18' 00"/000 W

Galliot Cut is not hard to pick out from the east with High Cay standing proud to its immediate north like an aircraft carrier, and a highly visible light on the north tip of Cave Cay. However, beware that this light is not at the extremity of the lowlying rock that runs north from this point, and a much smaller stake has been placed nearer the north tip of this reef. A continuing shoal area contours around the north tip of Cave Cay. Stay well clear of it. Once you're through the Cut, there's sand on both sides of the little unnamed cay that lies ahead, and more sand behind Little Galliot Cay off your starboard bow. You must turn fairly immediately either to starboard or port and pick your way from then on.

We don't like Galliot Cut. Ebb tide flows can build a wall of water there, rather like a standstill tsunami, and it's just too fast running for

Not to be used for Navigation.

The Southern Exuma Cays

Reproduced from Admiralty Chart 3912. Depth in meters.

comfort. It seems to offer no particular advantage over its neighboring cuts. Why not use Farmer's Cut?

CAVE CAY AND MUSHA CAY

Cave Cay is private, as is Musha Cay to the south. Both are being developed. There's an anchorage to the west of Cave Cay, which also has a shallow hurricane hole opening off the west coast. At one time this was an option open to you, but no longer. The hole is being set up as some kind of marina for private use. The area around Musha Cay, although visually attractive simply because of the contrasting colors of the water, is almost totally shoal save for the one north–south channel, which itself at any time other than high water, is a shallow-draft route. There are no anchorages there.

Cave Cay Cut

Cave Cut East		
CAVEE	23° 54' 10"/166 N	076° 15' 10"/166 W
Cave Cut West		
CAVEW	23° 53' 55"/916 N	076° 16' 05"/085 W

Cave Cay Cut looks narrow and appears unattractive for that reason, but it's deep and straightforward. The shore of Cave Cay is well-weathered and looks like a cave-breeding shore, if nothing else. To the south the demarcation of the Cut rests on the flank of the unnamed small cay lying to the north of the reef, rock, and shoal area to the north of Musha Cay. There was, and still might be, a Christian-type cross on the rock to the south, which was put there as a marker. It might well act as a deterrent rather than encouragement!

RUDDER CUT CAY

Rudder Cut Cay, another long one at over 2 nm in length, is private. Distinguished by the architecture of its guardian house set on a spine of rock, Rudder Cut Cay has a spawn of reefs off its southeast headland. See our notes on Rudder Cut. There are anchorages along the west coast of Rudder Cut Cay, and, rather like Cave Cay, Rudder Cut Cay also has its hurricane hole midway along its length, but this one is also no longer open to casual visitors.

Rudder Cut

Rudder Cut East		
RUDRE	23° 52' 15"/250 N	076° 13' 25"/417 W
Rudder Cut West		
RUDRW	23° 51' 50"/833 N	076° 13' 40"/666 W

A large prominent house on the north tip of Little Darby Island marks Rudder Cut, and for additional ID the beaches fronting east on this property show white sand backed by palm trees. The actual cut lies between Rudder Cut Cay in the north and the plug of a cay (no name) that sits in the

Galliot Cut, from the west.

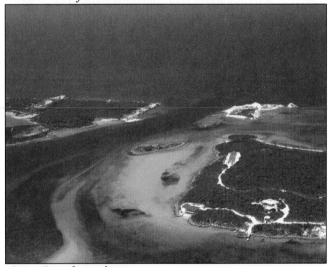

Cave Cut, from the west.

Rudder Cut, from the west.

apparent middle of the Cut. Go north of this cay. Deeper inside the Cut, on the Bank side, are a cluster of rocks anchored, as it were, by a massive rock whale look-a-like (the whale is swimming north). You can pass to either side of the whale and its babies, but the south channel is narrow.

Entering Rudder Cut from the Sound, or exiting to the Sound, look out for the reefs around the southeast hammerhead of Rudder Cut Cay. Rudder Cut really is a pass to nowhere if you're in Exuma Sound, for every route accessing Rudder Cut on the Bank side is shoal draft, and tide becomes critical. It's at this point, south of Rudder Cut Cay, that the Exuma Bank side, unless you have the right draft and a passion for shoal-water exploration and bonefishing, really becomes a no-no as a cruising ground.

THE DARBY ISLANDS, GOAT, LIGNUM VITAE, PRIME CAY, MELVIN, AND BOCK CAYS

The Darby Islands are private and other than the anchorage between them, there is little for the cruising visitor there. Goat Cay and Lignum Vitae Cays are private. There's a neat little anchorage tucked up in the north mouth between the two Darby Islands, but it's shoal draft.

As you go further south, Prime Cay is private, as is Neighbor Cay and Melvin Cay. Bock Cay (the 100-foot radio mast is not a Batelco tower) is also private and under development. So the land is out of bounds, there are few anchorages worth marking as such, and the whole area is such a maze of shoal-draft channels that we can see little point in attempting to thread your way around the shallows. The next reasonable point at which you can access the Bank side from Exuma Sound with purpose is Adderley Cut.

Adderley Cut

Adderley Cut East		
ADDYE	23° 47' 15"/250 N	076° 06' 25"/417 W
Adderley Cut West		
ADDYW	23° 46' 45"/750 N	076° 07' 25"/417 W

Adderley Cut is primarily your access to Lee Stocking Island and the Caribbean Marine Research Center. Well marked with a stone beacon on Adderley Cay and a prominent house off the north headland of Lee Stocking Island, you can't miss the entrance. There's also a house almost at beach level on the north shore of Lee Stocking Island, which will become apparent as you get closer in. Your main hazards are the reefs extending north from Lee Stocking Island, which mercifully show awash in part, so you can take a line well to the north to avoid them. Beware too of the shoal area in the central part of the Cut as you gain the Bank.

NORMANS POND CAY, LEAF CAY, AND LEE STOCKING ISLAND

Normans Pond Cay, once worked for salt, has native iguanas. If you land there, pets are prohibited. Leaf Cay is shoal to the

Adderley Cut, from the northwest.

east, but has a useful anchorage to the west. Lee Stocking Island, running south from Normans Pond Cay, is important as the base of Caribbean Marine Research Center, one of NOAA's National Undersea Research agencies. Located on the northwest tip of the island, just under the anvil head of its northern promontory, the Research Center is open to visitors on request (call *Bahama Hunter* on VHF 16). You are asked not to go on shore without permission. Childrens Bay Cay, to the south of Lee Stocking Island, is private. Immediately south lies Rat Cay, and Rat Cay Cut, the only north–south cut in the Exumas.

THE BRIGANTINE CAYS

The Brigantine Cays, some forty in total, typify the Bank side at this point in the Exuma chain. A confusion of islets, banks, mangroves, and channels, which may well tempt the

Rat Cay Cut, from the north.

bonefisher and the explorer, are tidal to a degree and boat mobility ends with the start of an ebb tide.

Rat Cay Cut

Rat Cay Cut North		
RATCN	23° 44' 05"/085 N	076° 02' 05"/085 W
Rat Cay Cut South		
RATCS	23° 43' 45"/750 N	076° 01' 55"/916 W

Rat Cay Cut earns distinction as being your last option to switch between the Bank side and Exuma Sound. For this reason alone we listed it with our primary passage-making cuts, but in truth Rat Cay Cut is hardly on the main road to anywhere, for on the Bank side you are already deep into sand-maze territory. Nonetheless it offers access to good anchorages behind Childrens Bay Cay, Rat Cay, and Square Rock Cay to the south.

The Cut itself, unusual in that it runs almost north–south, has no approach problems. From Exuma Sound the bulk of Square Rock Cay looks like a detached bung held ready to close the passage if need be. Rat Cay and Boysie Cay both appear low lying and the entrance to the Cut seems diminished in importance through a lack of height on either side. Perhaps the distant Square Rock Cay is compensation.

CHILDRENS BAY CAY, RAT CAY, AND THE CAYS LEADING TO GREAT EXUMA ISLAND

As we've said, Childrens Bay Cay is private and Rat Cay offers anchorages but little more. Better anchorages in this area might be found behind Square Rock Cay. We would go no further toward Great Exuma Island on the Bank side than Square Rock Cay.

Heading South to George Town, Great Exuma

RAT CAY CUT TO GREAT EXUMA ISLAND

Heading for George Town your arrival waypoint will be our George Town Harbour west (GTAW1) entry waypoint. A scattered line of minor cays lead south from Rat Cay Cut to Rokers Point on Great Exuma Island. Inside these cays there is a shoal-draft channel, but it's primarily of interest only to local fishermen. On your way south stand well offshore (at least 1 nm off the line of barrier cays and reef along the east coast of Barraterre and Great Exuma Island), and watch out for the Three Sisters Rocks (23° 43' N 076° W). At Channel Cay you can close your offing to a third of a mile, and then pick up that waypoint, between Channel Cay and Conch Cay.

At one time an island in its own right, Barraterre is now joined by a bridge to Great Exuma Island. The 150-foot Batelco tower, just north of Barraterre settlement, is a useful landmark at this point, as is the Farmers Hill 40-foot Batelco tower on Great Exuma Island, just south of Rokers Point.

George Town, Great Exuma Island

GEORGE TOWN, despite being host to one of the highest annual cruising visitor totals in the Bahamas, strangely carries the reputation of a difficult, if not dangerous place to enter. It seems totally at odds with its popularity. Almost every sailing guide urges caution, and entry instructions can seem complex and daunting. Let's take a satellite view of George Town first. If you understand the way it is, the worries diminish. George Town does not have a harbor. The "harbor" is a 9-by-1-nm-wide strip of water between the mainland of Great Exuma Island and, for the most part, Stocking and Elizabeth Islands.

Three Sisters Rocks, northeast of Great Exuma Island.

An Introduction to George Town

George Town Harbour Entrance West		
GTAW1	23° 34' 30"/500 N	075° 48' 30"/500 W
George Town Harbour Entrance East		
GTAE1	23° 30' 00"/000 N	075° 40' 00"/000 W

Inside this strip you can find shelter, one side or the other, whatever the wind, but not all places are sheltered all the time, and in some you are even exposed to the prevailing southeast wind. In old-fashioned terms, it would be called a *roadstead*, a place where a large number of vessels can lie up and find better shelter than they would outside. Right from the start we have two harbor names, Stocking Harbour and Elizabeth Harbour, but they are essentially a continuance of each other.

It's easier to think of George Town, or George Town Harbour. You'd think it would be one of the best-developed harbors in the Bahamas, but with the failure of the early plantations in the Exumas, there never was the need to improve on what nature offered as a partly sheltered area.

The Government Building, George Town.

Back in 1942, in the early days of the Second World War, the UK-US Lend-Lease agreement gave vital military hardware to Britain in exchange for bases for the US Navy in the British Atlantic and Caribbean colonies. George Town became a US naval patrol base, and the harbor was dredged to make it safe for seaplanes. Today that dredging has slowly infilled, and the bottom profile of George Town Harbour is much as it was at the start, shoal areas, rocks, and reefs scattered around, as well as dredged hollows.

What is inexplicable is that no project has been commissioned to set up navigation marks to take vessels safely in and out of George Town. Hurricanes are blamed, which can take out marks. Almost every year some attempt, often private initiative, is made to set up some marks, none of which endure for long. You are better off expecting none, and perhaps even ignoring those you do see, unless you're absolutely certain of their meaning. For guidance you have two easy-to-distinguish distant landmarks. The stone beacon on Stocking Island, looking like a shorn-off mini lighthouse, and the Batelco tower, 180 feet tall with its two large satellite dishes, on the ridge to the south of George Town. However, the harbor depth profile prevents you steering directly for either of these, except on certain legs.

CLOSE APPROACHES

The George Town Harbour area has two principal entrances. The west entrance serves if you are coming down the Exuma chain. The east entrance serves if you are coming from the south or heading toward Long Island. Both have reefs and rocks, and in bad weather are not to be attempted. By bad weather we mean high winds, high seas, and bad visibility. To be safe you must be able to read your way in, and have absolute control over your boat. You would also be prudent, dependent on your draft, to take advantage of a favorable tide.

Because of the absence of marks, the only way to enter is by a series of legs from GPS waypoint to GPS waypoint, which will position you at or near each point where you should alter course. *Don't even think* of programming and setting on autopilot. This is eyeball navigation with GPS used as a helping hand rather than a set of old-fashioned position lines and fixes. Be mindful that your GPS and mine will never agree. With this caveat, we'll take each entrance in turn and then deal with marinas and anchorages.

With such a list of waypoints it looks like a potential nightmare, but it's not difficult. Just take it easily, in bite-sized chunks, and get your first mate to call it out as you go. You'll have at least 6 feet on this route.

The West Entrance

STAGE 1: GETTING THROUGH CONCH CAY CUT

George Town Harbour Entrance West		
GTAW1	23° 34' 30"/500 N	075° 48' 30"/500 W
West Approach Waypoint 2		
GTAW2	23° 33' 40"/666 N	075° 48' 40"/666 W

Two simple half-mile legs will take you through Conch Cay Cut (don't confuse this with the Conch Cut already discussed further to the north). GTAW1 places you about 0.5 nm north of Conch Cay Cut. From there steer 199°M for 0.68 nm to clear the reef (on your port side), which runs northwest from Conch Cay. Conch Cay (or rather its outlier) has a light on it. The Smith Cays, right on your nose on Leg 1, are to starboard and are easily identifiable. There are houses on the hill behind the Smith Cays.

At GTAW2 you'll be safely past that first reef. Turn to port on a heading of 138°M, which has you running parallel to Conch Cay and its reefs on the port side, and off the reefs that you'll see to starboard. There may or may not be a marker on the reef you pass on your starboard side. Follow this course for 0.62 nm to GTAW3.

STAGE 2: THE SIMON'S POINT LEGS

West Approach Waypoint 3		
GTAW3	23° 33' 15"/250 N	075° 48' 10"/166 W
West Approach Waypoint 4		
GTAW4	23° 32' 45"/750 N	075° 48' 00"/000 W

Two easy legs around Simon's Point sets you up to enter the George Town Harbour area. From GTAW3 turn to starboard and head on 169°M for Simon's Point, which has two highly visible pink houses. Run for 0.52 nm on this leg to reach GTAW4 (standing safely off the point). At GTAW4 turn to port on a heading of 148°M, and run parallel to the Great Exuma coast for 0.74 nm to reach GTAW5.

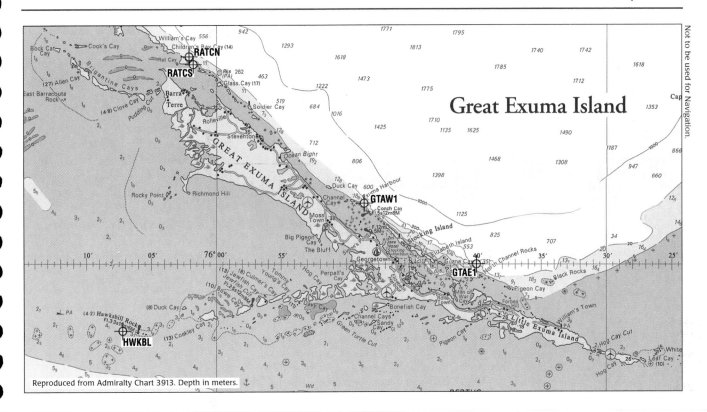

Reproduced from Admiralty Chart 3913. Depth in meters. ⚓

STAGE 3: CROSSING TO STOCKING ISLAND

West Approach Waypoint 5		
GTAW5	23° 32' 10"/166 N	075° 47' 30"/500 W
West Approach Waypoint 6		
GTAW6	23° 31' 55"/916 N	075° 46' 30"/500 W

One further leg sets you up to continue on your own. At GTAW5 turn to port, and identify that Stocking Island beacon. Head for it. A run of just about 1 nm on this heading will take you across to the deep-water channel to GTAW6, which is on the main fairway running parallel to Stocking Island. Once you're there, turn to starboard and run something like 140°M to where you wish to go. Follow or head for the other boats. You can hardly go wrong. It's safe where everyone else has gone.

If you're bound for the George Town side, when you're just about level with the entrance to the Stocking Island basins, turn to starboard and head for the pink buildings of the Peace and Plenty Hotel if you want to anchor there. Head for the Batelco tower to take you south of Regatta Point for Kidd Cove or the Exuma Docking Services.

There are other simpler ways of making this entry from Conch Cay Cut. It can be reduced to as little as three legs. In any event once you've done it once or twice you'll get your bearings, so that you can go visual much of the next time, rather than taking note of GPS readouts and your distance log. We give what we've found to be a safe approach as a starter pack.

The East Entrance

The east entrance also produces a list of waypoints, but once again these are not daunting if you take them in stages. Also, once again, do *not* attempt to go in or out on auto. What is important is that you are right on top with your eyeball navigation, for you are passing through reef country at the start. However, you should find at least 12 feet the whole way.

STAGE 1: THE INITIAL ENTRY

George Town Harbour Entrance East		
GTAE1	23° 30' 00"/000 N	075° 40' 00"/000 W
East Approach Waypoint 2		
GTAE2	23° 29' 10"/166 N	075° 40' 15"/250 W

As you approach the east entrance, you'll pick up the prominent isolated skyline house on Man-O-War Cay from some distance out, which will be off your starboard bow, and North Channel Rocks, off your port bow, show plainly and black. From GTAE1 a course of 200°M held for 0.75 nm takes you safely in through a wide, deep, 20-foot cut to GTAE2.

STAGE 2: RUNNING UP TO RED SHANK CORNER

East Approach Waypoint 3		
GTAE3	23° 29' 25"/417 N	075° 42' 00"/000 W
East Approach Waypoint 4		
GTAE4	23° 29' 25"/417 N	075° 42' 35"/583 W

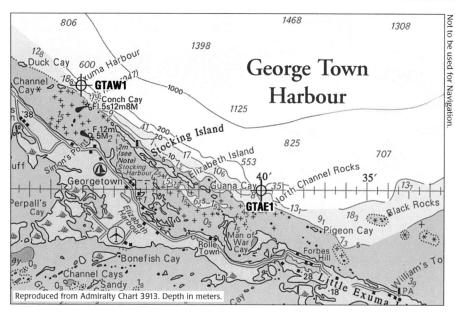

Reproduced from Admiralty Chart 3913. Depth in meters.

If anything the situation could be said to have got worse rather than better, as Exuma Docking Services have continued to decline and the number of cruising boats anchored off, in season, has increased. Regatta Week in April 1999 hit close to an all-time high in boats in the George Town area, with shoulder-to-shoulder conditions in every bar and restaurant. If you're not keen on the crowd scene, stand away until the forest of masts has thinned out. The one new star, George Town Marina & Repair in Master's Harbour (south of the Red Shank Cays) has brought a haul-out service to George Town, and the first general repair facility in town. In time more may be added. See our write-up. In the meantime, this is how it is in George Town at the time we go to press.

At GTAE2 turn to starboard on 285°M for 1.5 nm to reach GTAE3, which lies just short of a coral reef to port and patches of isolated heads to starboard. At GTAE3 alter course just a tad to 280°M and eyeball your way for 0.5 nm to reach GTAE4, which we call Red Shank Corner.

From this waypoint, if you want Red Shank Cays, you would work your way southwest around the coral to tuck yourself in behind the Red Shank Cays or Crab Cay. This waypoint also serves as the approach marker for Masters Harbour and the George Town Marina and Repair Yard.

STAGE 3: THE FINAL RUN IN

East Approach Waypoint 5

GTAE5	23° 30' 27"/460 N	075° 44' 34"/572 W

From GTAE4 you have a comparatively long run of just over 2 nm on a heading of 305°M to reach GTAE5, which is between Stocking Island (to starboard) and Rolle Cay (to port). This run is *not* coral free, and you pass close between two reefs (about 23° 30' 05"/083 N 075° 44' 00"/000 W) that lie midway between Elizabeth Island and Crab Cay. The passage between these reefs has been marked by two buoys (red/white to starboard, green/white to port **as you enter**) but these could be missing.

A barrel marker has also been placed on the reef to the north of your route just short of our GTAE5. From here you can carry on, taking it visually to the Stocking Island anchorages, or swing around Rolle Cay and the little Moss Cays for Kidd Cove, the Exuma Docking Services, or the Peace and Plenty anchorage.

Dock Space and Anchoring

Essentially George Town's facilities in terms of dock space and anchor room for visiting boats has remained unchanged.

ANCHORING

Your choices for anchoring are almost unlimited but boil down to five broad options:

1. Anywhere off Stocking Island clear of the harbor fairway.

2. One of the linked Stocking Island basins.

3. Off the Peace and Plenty Hotel.

4. In or just off Kidd Cove (south of Regatta Point).

5. Tucked in behind the Red Shank Cays or Crab Cay.

If you choose the remoter reaches of Stocking Island or the Red Shank area you are in for a longish dinghy ride to George Town to get your provisions or enjoy time ashore. In good weather this may be fine. In protracted bad weather, it may be too bumpy, too wet, and too uncomfortable to be worth attempting. Off Stocking Island take care not to anchor in the fairway. Off the Peace and Plenty you must keep clear of the Government Dock (on the north side of Regatta Point) and the turning basin. In the Kidd Cove area you must not obstruct the harbor fairway.

The three Stocking Island basins are well protected, but if you're lying off Stocking Island you'll feel anything from south through the western quadrants to north. It's almost exactly the reverse on the George Town side. To reach the distant but well-protected Red Shanks area remember that if you've come in through the west entrance, you must carry on and pick up the reverse course of our east entrance instructions to take you to Waypoint GTAE4, the place we call Red Shank Corner. From then on you are dependent on your eyeball navigation. You will find that there are other anchorages that may be found with careful reconnaissance, behind Rolle Cay, in the north bight of Crab Cay, and so on. Much depends on your curiosity, and skill.

EXUMA DOCKING SERVICES

The one long-established marina, Exuma Docking Services, is showing its age and, perhaps for too long now, it's been the only act in town. "Service is our thing" is advertised, but a working power hookup and constant voltage is not always certain, water is turned on only during the day and water pressure is often low, and the facilities on shore can best be described as just adequate. The marina as a whole is exposed from the northeast through to east, and you can expect discomfort, which can be acute, if you're unlucky and get these winds while you're there. Some recent seawall refurbishment engendered a downside, for reflected waves in strong easterlies create an evil crosshatch for those secured closest to the shore. Under bad conditions the marina can become almost untenable, and your only hope, if you are on a small boat, is to find a slip in the lee of a megayacht and hope that your shielding big friend never moves.

These comments apart, Exuma Docking Services has the best site in George Town and the potential, more so with its Sam's Place Restaurant, to rival Nassau's Yacht Haven with its Poop Deck Restaurant and bar, if there were the will to do so.

GEORGE TOWN MARINA AND REPAIR

The new facility we mentioned, George Town Marina and Repair, is sited on Master's Harbour, just to the south of the Red Shank Cays. Your approach to it is to take the course that would take you out of the George Town harbor east

George Town Marina and Repair.

entrance, that is if you're in George Town Harbour or if you've entered from the west. If you're coming in from the east, you're set fair. At our waypoint GTAE4, which is just south of Fowl Cay, turn to head roughly 235°M to pass off the east end of Red Shank Cay. You have just over 1 nm to run. At this point you should pick up a red buoy. From there look ahead on a rough heading of 229°M and you'll see the west end of Isaac Cay, about half a mile off. There are further marker buoys leading you in, and the boatyard, with its main shed building and its travel lift, should be apparent on the Exuma Island shore. From that GTAE4 waypoint in you'll have 8–9 feet at MLW off Red Shanks, and 5 feet at MLW off Isaac Cay. There is coral around on your course in. You pick your own line initially, and then follow the markers.

When you get there you'll find the travel lift we've already mentioned, and inside that main shed, the offices, a workshop, rest rooms, showers, washing machines, and storage areas for those who wish to leave their boats on shore. If you leave a boat on shore, it will be cradled in a frame built to fit. It's not guaranteed to be storm proof, but it is one step above simply chocking it up for a bottom paint job. At present some fifteen–eighteen boats are stored on the hard during the hurricane season.

Not in hand when we visited, but in the cards for late 1999, was the construction of between five and ten floating dock slips, primarily intended for those who want work done, or want to work on their boats, but do not require hauling. There are no moorings (although early printouts of their leaf-

Lake Victoria, Regatta Point, and Kidd Cove.

George Town, from the west.

George Town has taken a leap forward. Our one final note about George Town is on security. We are now less happy about leaving a boat unattended, be it at a dock, on shore, or at anchor, than we have been in the past. Just take care, and take precautions. And if you are leaving a boat for some time, make sure your insurance policy covers what you would regret not having had included . . . just in case.

THE GEORGE TOWN MIGRATIONS

George Town is also an extraordinary place. Year after year Great Exuma and Stocking Island play host to a seasonal floating population equivalent to a small town. Each winter, in November, the first armada of George Town–bound winter residents sets out from Florida. They make their return passage in May. By midwinter some three hundred visiting yachts are anchored off Stocking Island, in the Stocking Island basins, off the Peace and Plenty Hotel, and in Kidd's Cove off George Town itself. In Regatta weeks you can add another hundred boats to this total. The majority of the boats, once they've dropped their anchors, never move until it's time to leave.

A permanent "transient" population of this size is bound to generate its own dynamic. If you're new to George Town, listen to the Cruisers Net that opens on VHF 16 (later switching to VHF 68) at 8:10 each morning. You'll discover a whole new world of boat people with a lifestyle that has evolved over the years into a community with its own social events, recreational programs, a safety net of mutual assistance, and what almost amounts to a territorial stake on the beaches of Stocking Island. Almost unnoticed, the cruising boats inbound from the Caribbean, or on their way there, come and go. To a lesser extent much the same migration takes place in the summer months, and there are those who reckon the summer there is the best season.

Is there a knock-on effect? Of course there is. In one word, pollution. The contamination problem that is ruining the marine ecology of the George Town area must be addressed *now*. Up to four hundred boats discharge raw sewage into a four-square-mile area (if that), part of which (the Stocking Island basins and Kidd Cove) is not well cleaned by the changing tides. Does it make sense? No. It's madness to let it continue. Would it be permitted by any community in the

let mention moorings), and the holding in the Master's Harbour area is poor. It's slightly better off Isaac Cay. Once you are there, you're five miles by road from George Town, and a taxi there will cost you $15 one way.

At some time in the future plans for a one-hundred-slip marina and rental cottages on Isaac Cay may be realized. At this time George Town Marina and Repair is, basically, a working boatyard offering storage on land. All of this, but no more than that. See our **Yellow Pages**.

George Town

There's no doubt that George Town is the best waystop in the southern Bahamas, and if you're heading further south, little short of a compulsory stop, for after that you're in the Bahamian boondocks, on your own. As we've mentioned, George Town has both its *aficionados* and those who limit their time there to the minimum. It's a good harbor in prevailing winds, particularly on the Stocking Island side. It's a good place to restock, fill your tanks, get in touch with the world, and take a run ashore to stretch your legs, and you can dine well there. The airport is well served and you can get crew out, friends in, and yourself home in a hurry if you need. See our **Yellow Pages** for details.

The establishment of the George Town Marina and Repair facility, remembering that the realization of that word "marina" in the title is still on the Wish List, is a significant plus, both for passage makers on transit and seasonal visitors. A good general repair facility is now at hand where you can get work done, or work on your boat yourself. And you can leave it there, cradled, for as long as you wish. In this respect,

United States? No. Then why do we do it here? Even if the Bahamian government fail to enact and enforce discharge legislation, we, the cruising visitors, ought to follow our own national code. Use your holding tank in harbor. When it is full, take a day trip out into the ocean. Three miles or more out, flush your tanks. If we, you and I, fail to take preventive action, George Town will become a marine Chernobyl within our lifetime. The bottom line is that it is not our land and not our sea to trash.

GREAT EXUMA ISLAND

For all its size, there is not a great deal in Great Exuma or Little Exuma Islands to draw the interest of the cruising visitor. There are the ruins of abandoned plantations (notably on Crab Cay), early graves (Rolle Town), and good beaches (particularly on the doorstep, on Stocking Island). It's worth taking an island tour, but renting a car may seem wasteful at the end of the day.

Little Exuma Island

Little Exuma, like Barraterre, is no longer an entity but is now joined by a road bridge to its larger sibling. The settlements, sparse and far apart, show a lifestyle close to subsistence living. George Town has it all. It is the magnet, the center of all that counts in the southern Exumas, and the hinterland is abandoned.

THE REMAINING SOUTHERN EXUMA CAYS

Hog Cay and White Cay, lying south of Little Exuma Island, are the two last cays in the Exuma chain. Difficult to access either on the Exuma Sound or the Bank sides because of shoal water and coral, they are best left unvisited unless you elect to anchor off and take your dinghy in to explore. If you do decide

to feel your way along the coast, the Williams Town 200-foot Batelco tower is a useful mark, but we would be very wary of going this way. Once we are clear of the east entrance to George Town Harbour, we are bound for the Out Islands.

Not yet mentioned in the guide are the Jew Fish Cays that run west from Great Exuma Island roughly on the same latitude as George Town, and form a spur out into the Great Bahama Bank rather in the same manner as the Brigantine Cays. These cays are in no way a cruising destination.

George Town is the only place between Nassau and Providenciales in the Turks and Caicos Islands where you can touch base with the world by telephone, fax, e-mail, UPS, and air, buy provisions, and seek backup facilities you may well need. We see no value whatsoever in bypassing George Town. The Jew Fish route is difficult for navigation, which is an understatement, and this, if nothing else should persuade you that George Town would not have developed into the focal point it has become, were there not good reasons for it.

Stocking Island, the end of the day.

YELLOW PAGES

This area received the full force of Hurricane *Floyd* in September 1999. Be aware that reconstruction and the restoration of normal services after a Category 4 Hurricane may take a considerable period of time to complete.

GEORGE TOWN

Over the years George Town has gained the reputation of being not only a maritime hub for the southern Bahamas, but in many cases the ultimate destination for cruising visitors keen to avoid the cold, northern winter. Hundreds of boats gather annually, some for several months, to enjoy the facilities and the ambience of this boater-friendly harbor and small town, to the point that overcrowding, garbage, and water pollution are becoming a problem. On our last visit, we were distressed to hear of theft creeping in too, but that said, George Town is still a beautiful place, with plenty to do and much to enjoy.

When you reach George Town, coming in to Elizabeth Harbour from any direction will feel like coming home. The reassurance of a forest of masts, seen from the Sound, will encourage even the most timid navigators to sharpen their navigating skills and come in to drop anchor for a few days, or even several months, of lotus eating within the protected harbor. After all, you can always pull up the hook and move to a more sheltered spot if the wind switches around. And there is the whole of Great Exuma to be explored when you take your dinghy ashore. There are useful things like water, the best grocery store in the southern Bahamas, and telephones too, quite apart from restaurants, medical help, and those much-needed spare parts. Tune in to the net at 8:10 am on VHF 68 to keep abreast of daily activities as well as weather and services. Many boaters volunteer in town projects during the winter; you can listen for ways to help out locally.

George Town is a Port of Entry. Incoming captains may clear **Customs** at the pink two-story administration building, between 9 am and 5 pm, Monday to Friday. If you arrive on a weekend, a public holiday, or outside office hours, you will be charged overtime. If the customs officer is at the airport, call for an appointment at 345-0071. The **Immigration** office is also in the administration building, open 9 to 5:30, Monday to Friday. Call the immigration officer at the airport (345-0073) to set up an appointment at any other time. There will be a $20 fee if the officer has to come into town outside business hours.

GUIDES AND PILOTS

If you are concerned about coming into George Town, don't worry. There are people out there who can help you.

Wendell Cooper	VHF 16 "Interlude"
Clifford Dean	VHF 16 "Gemini II"
Wendell McGregor	VHF 16 "Little Toot"

MARINA

EXUMA DOCKING SERVICES
Tel: 242-336-2578/2101 • Fax: 336-2023 • VHF 16 "Sugar One"

This marina is the only act in town, and can be unbelievably uncomfortable if the wind is from the northeast through east to southeast. The new dock wall has been completed, but the rest of the facilities lag far behind other marinas in the Bahamas. At time of writing, the toilets and showers were a disgrace, although new washing machines and dryers have been installed in the laundromat and most of them are working. The filling station on the street has been rebuilt, from where you carry jerry cans of gasoline back to your dinghy. You are only allowed to tie up at their dinghy dock while you are doing this. If your boat has inboard tanks, you fill up at the fuel dock. On their own admission, many of the slips are without power, there is a security problem, with several reports of theft from boats tied up here, and the water is turned off when the dockmaster goes home and at weekends and holidays. The best part of the marina is the cheerful service in *Sam's Place Restaurant*, looking out to the harbor and the marina, and its proximity to *Exuma Markets* and the facilities in town.

Slips	50
Max LOA	100 ft.
MLW at Dock	8 ft.
Dockage	60¢ per ft. per day
Power	Up to 40 ft.: $8 per day for 30A, $12 for 50A
	41 to 50 ft.: $12 per day for 30A, $17 for 50A
	51 to 60 ft.: $16 per day for 30A, $22 for 50A
	61 ft. and up: $20 per day for 30A, $27 for 50A.
Fuel	Fuel dock is open 8 am to 5 pm, with diesel and gas for inboard engines. For outboard fuel, or fuel for sailboats, jerry cans have to be filled at the roadside gas station. You may tie up at their dock only when you are doing this.
Propane	Available from the filling station between *Marshall's Liquor Store* and the *Towne Cafe*.
Water	10¢ per gallon. Turned off at night, holidays, and weekends.
Telephones	*Batelco* card phone, and US-direct phone.
Showers	Not good at time of writing; open during dock hours.
Laundry	Much improved. $1.50 tokens from the office.
Restaurant	*Sam's Place*, upstairs overlooking the docks, is open from 7:30 am for breakfast, lunch, and dinner to 10 pm.
Trash	Only boats tied up in the marina may leave their garbage in the skips provided.
Ice	$2.75 per bag.
Liquor	*Sam Gray's Liquor Store* is open from 9 am to 5 pm, Monday to Saturday.
Marine Supplies	There is a limited selection of stores next to the marina office with paints, boat cleaners, etc.
Taxis	Wait outside the marina.
Car Rental	*Sam Gray's Car Rental* Tel: 336-2102 Cars from $60 per day.
Perfumes	*Scentuous Perfumes* has a small selection of perfumes and cosmetics on the first floor of *Sam's Place Restaurant*.
Credit Cards	Visa, MasterCard, and Exxon.
Dockmaster	Falandez Aristide, with Sheila in the office.

DINGHY DOCKS

Elizabeth Harbour at the Government Dock. Be sure to avoid the mailboat dock.

On *Lake Victoria*, reached by an 8-foot cut with an 8-foot clearance under the road bridge, which is to the north of *Exuma Docking* marina as you approach from the harbor.

You can tie up at the long *Exuma Markets* dinghy dock immediately to your left as you come in under the bridge. They are generous to boaters, and you can leave bagged trash (no used oil, even in containers, please) in their large red roadside dumpsters.

You can tie up at the *Two Turtles* dock if you are coming in for drinks or meals.

There is still a dock at *Harbour View Apartments*, although the laundromat has closed and the apartments are being rebuilt inside.

MARINE SERVICES

Repairs

George Town Marina and Repair Ltd.   Tel: 345-5116 • Fax: 336-2528
A new facility in Masters Harbour, 5 miles southeast of George
Town, with a 50-ton Acme marine hoist for a maximum draft of
8 ft., a maximum beam of 22 ft. Kelly Wilson and Mark
Turnquest offer general repairs, fiberglass repairs, refrigeration
repairs, rental tools and equipment, spare parts, and dry storage
for short or long-term stays. A pump-out facility is planned.

Haul and launch, including 3 days on land: $7 per ft.
Additional days on land, if working or living aboard: 50¢ per ft.
from day 4 to day 21, 40¢ from day 22 onward.

Storage from day 4 to day 90, left unattended: 25¢ per ft.
per day. Storage from day 90 onward, left unattended: 20¢
per ft. per day.

Cradle rental for boats stored in hurricane season: $200.
Brown's Auto and Brown's Marine   Tel: 336-2883/2928   Call
Perry Brown for marine and fiberglass repairs, painting, and
engine work.

Top II Bottom   Tel: 336-2200/2114   Open 8 am to 5 pm with a
wide range of marine supplies and household goods.

Naamon Forbes   Tel: 336-2857/2484   If you have a problem
with roaches on your boat, or it needs a really thorough interior
cleaning to include upholstery and floor covering, Naamon will
come out to your boat. He has an extractor so that no solvents
reach the water. He can also help with customs brokerage and
delivery of spare parts imported from the US.

Minn's Water Sports, on Lake Victoria   Tel: 336-2604 •
Fax: 336-3483   OMC products, sales and service, boat and
engine sales, dock service fueling, dock space rental, and dry
storage, boat and outboard engine service. Annual dockage
and storage $50 per ft. per year. Weekly dockage and storage
$4.50 per ft.

Super Sea Marine   Tel: 345-2319   State-of-the-art 16-ft. bonefish
boats, built by Eugene Smith.

Towing

If you need assistance entering the harbor, and some limited
towing, contact *Wendell Cooper* on VHF 16 "Interlude."

Yacht Sewerage Pumping

Exuma Waste Management   Tel: 336-2324

SERVICES & SHOPPING IN GEORGE TOWN

Bank

ScotiaBank   Located opposite *Exuma Markets*, open 9 am to
3 pm, Monday to Thursday, and 9 am to 5 pm on Friday.

Beauty Salons

My T Fine Beauty Salon   Tel: 336-2295

Tranee's Beauty Salon   Tel: 336-2620

Churches

St. Andrew's Anglican Church   Painted white and blue, a landmark on the hill above the *Club Peace and Plenty*.

St. John's Baptist Church   On the edge of Lake Victoria.

St. Theresa's Catholic Church   Overlooking Lake Victoria.

The Church of God Prophecy

The Seventh Day Adventist Church

Times of services are posted outside the churches.

Clinic

Government Clinic   Tel: 336-2088   Staffed by a doctor, a
dentist, and nurses. General clinics from 9 am to 1 pm Monday
to Friday, and a children's clinic on Thursday. Two, two-bed
wards. As a nonresident, the standard consultation charge is
$30. Out of clinic hours, you can call Dr. Appiah at 336-2606.

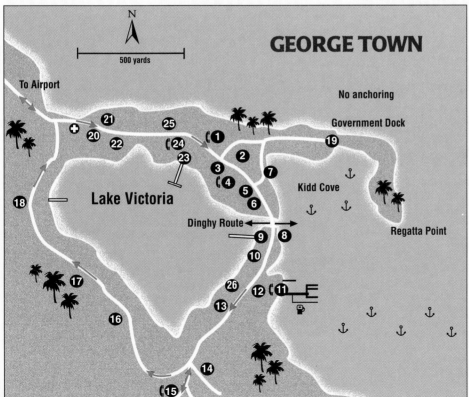

DIRECTORY

1. Customs, Immigration, Police, Post Office
2. Regatta Park
3. School and Library
4. Two Turtles Inn
5. Town Cafe, Filling Station, Propane
6. Liquor Store
7. Exuma Cleaners
8. Bank, Travel Agent
9. Exuma Markets and dinghy dock
10. N & D Fruits and Vegetables
11. Exuma Docking Services and Sam's Place
12. Mom's Bakery
13. Baptist Church
14. Corner Laundromat
15. Batelco
16. Eddie's Edgewater
17. Catholic Church
18. Harbour View Apartments
19. Fruit and Vegetable Market
20. Community Centre
21. Tourist Office
22. St Andrew's Anglican Church
23. Minn's Water Sports
24. The Sandpiper
25. Club Peace and Plenty
26. Exuma Dive Centre
⛽ Fuel
✚ Clinic

Island Med Medical Clinic Tel: 336-2220/2221 This is a private clinic just past the *Peace and Plenty Beach Inn* on the left-hand side as you go out towards the airport from George Town. Dr. Fox comes in once a week from Nassau on Thursdays from 9 am to 2 pm and from 3:30 to 9 pm, but his secretary, Mrs. Elder, is there on Mondays and Wednesdays from noon to 4 pm, so you can contact her to make an appointment. The doctor has his own pharmacy at the clinic.

Couriers
UPS Tel: 336-2148 Daily deliveries and pickups from its office in *Wally's Photography* building, opposite Regatta Park. A package can only be held for three days before being returned to sender.

Fedex There is no Fedex dispatch office in George Town, but a package sent via Fedex can be delivered c/o *Exuma Markets*, who will hold it for your arrival. There will be a collection charge of $5 for having it brought in from the airport.

Fashions
Exuma Fashion Shop Tel: 336-2616 Clothing for men, women, boys, and girls, opposite the Baptist Church.
Muck a Mucks Tel: 336-2858

Faxes and E-mail
Exuma Markets Fax: 242-336-2645 Will accept incoming faxes for boats. The list is read out on VHF 68 at around 8:10 am each morning, during the boaters' net. Faxes can also be sent from here.

Ferg's Business Center Tel and Fax: 336-2915 Open from 9 am to 5 pm Monday to Friday, to 2 pm on Saturdays. Office and business center in Lovely House, just beyond *Batelco* next to the *Sports Bar* on the edge of Lake Victoria. Faxes for boaters are accepted free, and can also be sent out. Inah Gray can help you with this, as well as with photocopying and a typing service. You can collect or send your E-mail here for $1.50 per minute, plus $1.50 service charge to the US.

Batelco Office Open from 9 am to 4:30 pm, Monday to Friday, with two card phones outside, and telephones inside where you can collect or send E-mail. Not all *Batelco* stations in the Bahamas allow you to use their phones for E-mail, so this service is much appreciated.

Fresh Bread
Mom's Bakery
Tel: 345-4062 Arrives daily from Williamstown with her van full of wonderful homemade breads, cakes, doughnuts, and pastries; parks right outside *Exuma Docking Services* at around 8:30 am. Listen out for her special of the day on the boaters' net. She will greet you with a big hug when you choose your "Bread of the Day."
Town Cafe Tel: 336-2194 Located behind the filling station. Not only has very good homemade bread in the mornings, but also serves an excellent breakfast and lunch.

Fresh Fish
Fishin' Good Seafood Tel: 336-2966 Open from 10 am to 1 pm daily except Sundays, beside the Baptist Church. Fresh seafood, condiments, jams and jellies, and Christmas tree ornaments.

Fruit and Vegetables
A small selection of fresh local produce is available from the *Straw Market* ladies. Delicious tomatoes, as well as red and green peppers, potatoes, grapefruit, and vegetables in season. *N and D Fruits and Vegetables* Next to *Exuma Markets*, has a little produce.
Fruit and Vegetable Market at the Government Dock Open daily from 8 am to 5 pm with a good selection of whatever is in season, mostly from local sources.

Exuma Markets dinghy dock, Lake Victoria.

Gift Shops
Art and Nature at the *Two Turtles Inn*
Peace and Plenty Boutique at the *Peace and Plenty Inn* Open from 8:30 am to 5 pm, closed on Sundays, with a selection of Androsia clothes, T-shirts, post cards, and some guide books.
The Sandpiper opposite *Peace and Plenty Inn* With a wide selection of books, gifts, pottery, fashions, post cards, and much more. Louise will help you in this well-stocked and attractive store. Open from 8:30 am to 5 pm daily, except Sundays.

Groceries
Exuma Markets Tel: 242-336-2033
• Fax: 336-2645 With their own dinghy dock under the bridge and behind the store on the pond, and dumpsters where you can leave bagged garbage. Open 8 am to 6 pm Monday to Friday, to 7 pm
on Saturdays, and to 10 am on Sundays. This is the best-stocked store in the Exumas. Fresh fruit and vegetables, dairy and cheeses, imported meats, a great selection of canned and dried goods, bottled and canned juices and sodas, water, batteries, film, household cleaners, some pharmacy, daily newspapers, and more. Michael and Sandy Minns are extremely generous to boaters in holding mail and faxes, and reading out lists of faxes over the boaters' net on VHF 68 at about 8:10 am each morning. You can also use their VHF should you need to contact a boat while in town.
Shop Rite Mart opposite Regatta Park Tel: 336-2670 Open from 7:30 am to 7 pm Monday to Saturday, and to 10 am on Sundays.
Smitty's Convenience Store Tel: 336-2144 and *L N K Liquor* Tel: 336-2145 At Hoopers Bay, open 8 am to 6 pm daily and to 10 am on Sundays.

Hardware
Clarke's Hardware opposite the Baptist Church
Darville Lumber Tel: 336-2114
At Hoopers Bay, about three miles out of town. Open from 9 am to 5 pm, Monday to Friday. Builders' supplies, with a good range of plumbing, electrical, hardware, fishing equipment, cleaning fluids, oils, garden and some marine supplies. Customer pickup at *Exuma Markets* at noon on Tuesdays and Thursdays.

Ice Cream
Rowshe's Ice Cream Parlour With hot dogs, baked goods, and guava duff, as well as ice cream and barbecues some days.

Laundry

Corner Laundromat Tel: 335-2094 In Lover's Lane, opposite *My T Fine Beauty Salon.* Open from 7 am to 11 pm daily with ten new washing machines and ten dryers, two extra large dryers. Counter for detergents with snacks and cold drinks planned. Tokens $1.50 per machine.

Exuma Cleaners Tel: 336-2038 • VHF 16 Behind Regatta Park. Open 8 am to 5 pm Monday to Saturday. If you take your laundry to them before 8:30 am, they will wash, dry and fold it for you by 4:30 pm the same day, for 95¢ per lb. Dry cleaning also available.

Exuma Docking Services $1.50 tokens from the office, for washers or dryers. Open during dock hours.

Liquor

BGS Liquor Store, just south of the *Batelco* tower.

Sam Gray's Liquor Store at *Exuma Docking Services.*

John Marshall's Liquor Store, next to the gas station.

Liquor stores are open 9 am to 5 pm, Monday to Saturday.

Mail

Exuma Markets They will hold mail for you. Have it addressed to: your name, c/o your boat name, Exuma Markets, George Town, Exuma, Bahamas and mark it HOLD FOR ARRIVAL. There are boxes with incoming mail addressed to boaters inside the store.

Police

Tel: 336-2666, emergencies dial 919. Located in the pink administration building.

Post Office

Located in the pink administration building. Open from 8 am to 4 pm, Monday to Friday.

Straw Market

T-shirts, locally woven baskets, shell jewelry, fresh vegetables & fruit, sold Monday to Saturday under the trees by Regatta Park.

Telephones

There are many telephones in town. Where there are two, one is usually a *Batelco* card phone, and the other a coin box where you can dial US direct on your credit card, using an American or Bahamian quarter to connect you to an operator. There are two card phones outside the *Batelco* office, two outside the *Club Peace and Plenty*, two at *Exuma Docking Services*, two outside *Exuma Markets*, two in the administration building, and two outside the *Two Turtles Inn.*

Tourist Office

Tel: 336-2430 Ona Bullard is very helpful in the Government Tourist Office, opposite the community center, open 10 am to 4 pm Monday to Friday. It is well worth a visit to find out what is going on throughout the Exumas, and for any local information you may need.

Trash

If you are in a slip at *Exuma Docking Services*, you may leave trash in their bins. If you are at anchor, *Exuma Markets* allows boaters to bring trash ashore to their big red dumpsters beside the store.

Travel Agent

HL Young Tel: 336-2705 Located above the *ScotiaBank.*

Water

Coral Springs Tel and Fax: 336-2830 • VHF 16 Delivery of water, ice and juices, catering to the yachting community. Will refill your drinking water containers. Listen for their advertisement on the boaters' net at around 8:10 am on VHF 68 or contact Peter or Andrew Burrows.

RESTAURANTS & BARS

There is something for everybody here, from a casual hot dog out of the back of the yellow bus to elegant dining at the hotels. Many of the restaurants further out of town will send transport on request. Dinner reservations are preferred at the major restaurants.

Big D's Conch Spot Tel: 358-0059 Out at Steventon, where Daron Tucker serves island delicacies and runs a catering service.

Castaways in Moss Town Tel: 345-0088 Restaurant and bar specializing in cracked conch and other native dishes, open from 8 am to midnight Monday to Friday, and to 1 am on Saturdays.

Chat 'n Chill Beach Club on Stocking Island Tel: 358-5010 • VHF 16 Open daily for lunch and dinner on the beach, with sandwiches, breads, drinks, and picnic items. Water available for 60¢ per gallon.

Club Peace and Plenty Tel: 336-2551 Serves breakfast, lunch, and dinner poolside and in the dining room downtown, and at their *Beach Inn* and *Bonefish Lodge*. As a guest, you can ask for the free shuttle to take you for dinner at any of their restaurants. Snacks are also available at the Stocking Island *Beach Club*. Dinner reservations requested.

Coconut Cove Hotel Tel: 336-2659 • VHF 16 Serving elegant food in delightful surroundings, 1.5 miles west of George Town. Open for breakfast, lunch, and dinner, with *The Sandbar* open 3 to 9 pm, and their own dinghy dock. Call ahead for dinner reservations and complimentary transport to and from George Town.

Eddie's Edgewater Bahamian cuisine and local color on the edge of the pond, with a bar and restaurant specializing in Eddie's famous fried chicken, Angie's turtle souse, and turtle steaks. Open for breakfast, lunch, and dinner. Join in on Monday and Thursday evenings for rake and scrape live music.

Jean's Dog House Tel: 345-5055 A social place to meet and enjoy hot dogs and daily specials from the back of the yellow bus, parked opposite the pink administration building from early morning.

Higgins Landing Tel: 336-2480 On Stocking Island. Enjoy romantic, candlelit, fixed-menu, multi-course gourmet dinners for nonresident guests, served at 7 pm. Closed on Tuesdays. Price $55 per person, plus gratuity. Call before noon for a reservation. Transport from George Town is available for $5 per person.

Hilltop Sports Bar and Lounge Tel: 336-2288 Local bar, with scouse a specialty.

Iva Bowe Restaurant and bar in Jimmy Hill. Open from 10 am to 10 pm, Monday to Saturday for the best native dishes in town.

Kermits Airport Lounge Tel: 345-0002 Open for breakfast, lunch, and dinner from 7:30 am to 8 pm. Bahamian cuisine, fast food, and takeout.

La Shante Tel: 345-4136 Open for breakfast and lunch, and dinner by reservation.

Sam's Place Tel: 336-2579 Open from 7:30 am for breakfast, lunch, and dinner overlooking the marina.

Silver Dollar Restaurant and Bar Tel: 336-2939 East of *Batelco* in town, serving native dishes with rake and scrape on Wednesdays.

Town Cafe Tel: 336-2194 Behind *Shop Rite* grocery store, next to the gas station. Open for breakfast & lunch from 7:30 am, serving their own bread, delicious sandwiches, salads, and Bahamian entrees.

Two Turtles Inn Tel: 336-2545 A central, popular, meeting place for a drink and casual dining. Fish nights and barbecues on Tuesdays and Fridays.

GETTING AROUND

Airport
Exuma International Airport, with a paved 8,000-ft. runway, is 9 miles out of town at Moss Town, a $23 taxi ride into George Town. *Kermits Airport Lounge* serves drinks and snacks at the International Bar across from the terminal building.

Strachan's Aviation Service Tel: 345-0641/0519 Has an office at the airport, where they can be contacted for charter flights. This is the only fuel stop between Nassau and South Caicos Islands.

Airlines
American Eagle Tel: 800-433-7300. Daily flights from George Town to Miami at 1:30 pm, and from Miami to George Town at 11:30 am daily.

Bahamasair Tel: 345-0035
Flights from Nassau to George Town at 8:15 am on Monday, Tuesday, Wednesday, Friday, and Saturday. Return flights to Nassau at 9:10 am on the same days. Daily flights from Nassau to George Town at 6:45 pm, and from George Town to Nassau at 7:40 pm. Flights to Stella Maris on Long Island leave on Thursdays and Sundays. Leave Nassau at 7:15 am, arrive Stella Maris 8 am; leave Stella Maris at 8:15, arrive George Town at 8:30 am. Flights leave George Town at 1:15 pm, arrive Stella Maris at 1:30. Leave Stella Marris at 1:45 pm, arrive George Town at 2:30.

Lynx Tel: 345-0108 Fly from Fort Lauderdale at 9:30 am on Mondays, arriving in George Town at 10:45 am. Leaving George Town at 3:15 pm, arriving in Fort Lauderdale at 4:35 pm. On Fridays and Sundays, they leave Fort Lauderdale at 12:40 pm, arriving George Town at 2 pm, leaving George Town at 3:50 pm, arriving Fort Lauderdale at 5:10 pm. Cost $185 round trip.

Bicycles
N & D Fruits and Vegetables Tel: 336-2236 Next to Exuma Markets. They have some bicycles for $18 per day, $10 for a half day.

You could also try *Regatta Point* for bicycles. Call Nancy at 336-2206.

Boat Rentals
Exuma Dive Centre and Watersports Tel: 336-2390
• Fax: 336-2391 17-ft. Polar craft with bimini top for $80 per day, $375 per week. Security deposit and prepayment required, fuel to be purchased from *Exuma Dive Centre*, boat for use in the harbor, from 8:30 am to 5 pm daily, other hours on request. Office open 8 am to 5 pm daily.

Minn's Water Sports Tel: 335-2604 • Fax: 336-3483 17-ft. Boston Whaler from $80 per day, or $400 per week, and an 18-ft. Boston Whaler from $110 per day, or $550 per week, as well as dockage and storage, ice and gasoline at their dock in Victoria Harbour, opposite and down the hill from *Club Peace and Plenty*. Security deposit required. Visa and MasterCard accepted. Open 8 am to 5 pm Monday to Friday, to noon on Saturday, and to 11 am on Sunday.

Buses
There is no actual bus service in Great Exuma, but Naamon Forbes runs a jitney service from George Town to Moss Town and *The Palms* at *Three Sisters*, leaving at 8:15 am and 2:30 pm, arriving at 9 am and 3:15 pm. Call Naamon at 336-2857 or 336-2484 for details. Charters are available on request for his 26-seater bus. A fare to Barraterre, for example, would cost around $20 per person.

Car Rental
Don't forget to drive on the left! There is a one-way system around the pond. An average speed of 35 mph out of town is recommended. Valid driver's license and security deposit required to rent a car. Average car rental costs $60 per day.

Airport Rentals at the airport Tel: 345-0090

Sam Gray's Car Rentals at *Exuma Docking Services* Tel: 336-2101
Don Smith Rentals

Thompsons Rentals Tel: 336-2442 Located above the *Scotia Bank* and has cars, scooters, and bicycles.

Mailboats
M/V Grand Master and *M/V Etienne & Cephas* run to George Town weekly from Nassau. Fare $50. The *M/V Lady Roslyn* and the *M/V Sea Hauler* call in on a charter basis. The *M/V Captain Moxey* goes throughout the Exuma Cays. All mailboats come in to the Government Dock.

Motor Scooters
Exuma Dive Centre Tel: 336-2390 • Fax: 336-2391 From $35 per day, or $240 per week with a $25 deposit. Deposit will be refunded if there is no damage to the scooter on return.

Thompsons Rentals Tel: 335-2442 Located above *ScotiaBank*.

Taxis
The minibus taxis all have numbers; call one on VHF 14. Several usually wait outside *Exuma Docking Services, Exuma Markets,* and *Club Peace and Plenty.*

Towing
If you need assistance entering the harbor and some limited towing, contact *Wendell Cooper* on VHF 16 "Interlude."

SPORTS

Beaches
Hamburger Beach and *Volleyball Beach* are popular with boats at anchor off Stocking Island. There are literally dozens of glorious beaches the whole length of the Exuma chain.

Bonefishing
La Shante Beach Club at Forbes Hill Tel: 345-4136 Call Marvin or Trevor Bethel for snorkeling, trolling, spinfishing, and sightseeing.

Peace and Plenty Bonefish Lodge at the Ferry Tel: 345-5555/5556 Complete bonefish packages and vacations, with Bob Hyde as your guide. Weekly packages from $2,326 per person at the *Bonefish Lodge,* and from $2,088 per person at the *Peace and Plenty Beach Inn.*

Private bonefish guides:

Garth Thompson	Tel: 345-5062
Wilfred Rolle	Tel: 345-5106
JJ Dames	Tel: 345-5049
Cairy "Poop" Mc Kenzie	Tel: 345-0053
Ernest "Abby" McKenzie	Tel: 345-2312
Cely Smith	Tel: 345-2342

Janet Wilson

A school band at the Family Island Regatta, George Town.

Michael Rolle	Tel: 345-5008
Samuel Rolle	Tel: 345-5011
Wilmore Rolle	Tel: 345-5008
Reno Rolle	Tel: 345-5003
Christopher Rolle	Tel: 345-5057
Quinton Clarke	Tel: 345-0053
Henry Rolle	Tel: 345-5053

Deep Sea Fishing

Coopers Charter Services Tel: 336-2711• VHF 16 "Interlude"
Contact *Wendell Cooper* aboard the *Interlude*, or the *Peace and Plenty* at 336-2551. *Interlude* is a 34-ft. Flybridge Sport Fisherman. Deep sea fishing for kingfish, tuna, dolphin, wahoo, and bonita, from $400 for half day or $600 for full day, for two to four people. Still fishing for grouper and snapper, $250 for half day, $500 for full day for two to five people. This includes bait, the use of fishing equipment, and your catch cleaned and filleted for you. Snorkeling for three hours, from $20 per person for two to ten people. If conch or lobster (in season) is caught, your catch will be cleaned for you. Shark fishing by special request.

Fish Rowe Charters Tel: 345-0074   Call Captain Doug Rowe for professional sport fishing, bone/flats, and deep drop fishing, scuba diving, snorkeling, and sunset cruises. 37-ft. Hatteras, with dead bait, tackle, and an experienced captain from $400 for half day, and $650 for a full day.

Rev AA McKenzie at Barraterre Tel: 355-5024   Fishing, shelling, snorkeling, exploring, iguanas. A 17-ft. Boston Whaler with a 70-hp engine for hire, and Taxi No. 27 available for transport.

Shadow Pleasure Tours Tel: 336-2968/2144   Call Captain Craig Parotti for deep sea and line fishing, snorkeling, sightseeing, or a custom trip.

Diving

Exuma Dive Centre and Water Sports Tel: 336-2390 • Fax: 336-2391 Open from 8:30 am to 5 pm Monday to Friday, and from 9 am to 1 pm Saturday and Sunday. Johnny and Connie Dey offer a wide range of blue holes, walls, and shallow reefs for all levels of divers, in small groups of six people in their two dive boats. Full range of rental equipment available with a 50-percent discount if you dive with them. Dive trips start at $60, with snorkelers at $30.

Dive Sites

Closest to Stocking Island:

Stingray Reef, northeast of Conch Cay.

Angelfish Blue Hole, which can be accessed from Stocking Island but should only be dived when the current is flowing **out.** There are two buoys that mark the location of the Blue Hole, attached to a chain that you can follow down to a line showing the inner passageway.

Mystery Cave, opposite *Angelfish Blue Hole.*

Crab Cay Blue Hole should also only be dived when the tide is flowing out, and with great caution. Do not to go into the caverns without local and specialist knowledge.

Further south:

Guana Reef and *Fowl Cay Reef* both make fascinating snorkeling sites, together with *Pigeon Cay* off Forbes Hill on Little Exuma.

North of George Town:

Flat Cay Wall, down to 230 feet over a wall covered with sponges, sea fans, and plumes, off Flat Cay and Channel Cay.
Duck Cay, southeast of the settlement of Ramsey on Great Exuma, is good for snorkelers too.

Tennis

Courts at *The Palms* at *Three Sisters Resort* at Mount Thompson
Tel: 358-4040 • VFH 16

REGATTAS

George Town is famous for its two annual Regattas. In March each year the *George Town Cruising Regatta* attracts over 500 yachts for a week of racing and festivities. For information contact the Exuma Tourist Office (336-2430), Mr. Kermit Rolle (345-0002), Mrs. Mary Dames (336-2176), or Ms. Eulamae Knowles (336-2435).

The Shacks, George Town at Regatta Time.

In April the *Annual Family Island Regatta* hosts scores of locally built sloops, representing each of the major islands, for four days of fierce racing for the coveted *Best in the Bahamas* title. The carnival-like atmosphere in town includes a beauty pageant, fashion shows, volleyball, and weight lifting. Contact Mr. Stephen Hall (336-2685) or Christopher Kettel (336-2690).

Bonefish tournaments are held in July and October. Contact the *Peace and Plenty Bonefish Lodge* or any of the guides for more information.

ACCOMMODATIONS

Hotels

Club Peace and Plenty Tel: 242-336-2551 and 1-800-525-2210 • Fax: 336-2093   As well as a charming, historical downtown location, the *Peace and Plenty* also has its *Beach Inn* and the *Bonefish Lodge*. There is a shuttle service to and from both locations for dinner, and a regular ferry service to their private *Beach Club* on Stocking Island for swimming and snorkeling during the day. Restaurants, swimming pools, and bars at the hotels. Rooms from $140 per night, packages from $1,690 per week.

Coconut Cove Hotel Tel: 242-336-2659 • Fax: 336-2658 An idyllic setting, with gourmet dining, and all the facilities of a resort hotel. Rooms from $128 per night.

Two Turtles Inn Tel: 242-336-2659 • Fax: 336-2658   A small Inn with atmosphere in the heart of George Town. Simple accommodations with a noisy restaurant crowd on busy nights. The bar is a local meeting place. Rooms from $88 a night.

Hotel Higgins Landing Tel: 242-336-2460   The only hotel on Stocking Island. Accommodates ten guests in cottages with spacious verandas. From $175 per person, double rooms, includes breakfast and dinner.

The Palms at *Three Sisters* Tel: 242-358-4040 • Fax: 358-4043 Fourteen beach-front rooms from $105 per night at Mount Thompson. Three miles from the airport, with its own restaurant and tennis court. Transport to George Town provided.

Regatta Point Tel: 242-336-2206 • Fax: 336-2046   Beautifully furnished rooms and two apartments overlooking the harbor, with a private beach and bicycles and boats to enjoy. From $122 per night.

La Shante Beach Club and Resort Tel: 242-345-4136   Rooms from $85 per night, at Forbes Hill, 12 miles east of George Town. This small hotel has its own private beach, open-air bar, and restaurant. Boat charters, deep sea fishing, and bonefishing can be arranged with Trevor and Marvin Bethel, and Garth Thompson. There is a courtesy bus into town once a day.

Apartments

Ask Ona Bullard at the Tourist Information Office (Tel: 366-2430) for an up-to-date list of the many apartments in the area available to rent.

THINGS TO DO IN GEORGE TOWN

- Reprovision your boat with a wide selection of fresh island produce and imported stores.
- Dive the famous Stocking Island caves. Take care not to walk on the 4,000-year-old stromatolites on the island, or crush their fragile surface. They are the oldest evidence of life on Earth, the dominant reef-building structure for about 3 billion years.
- Enter your boat for the Cruising Regatta in March next year. Or share the excitement of Family Island Regatta Week in April.
- Make new friends and share your boating experiences through the boater's net on VHF 68 in the mornings.
- Try a different restaurant for lunch or dinner each day.
- Rent a car for a day and explore Great Exuma, Little Exuma, and Barraterre. See the *Cotton House* at Williamstown and the ancient tombs at Rolletown. Have lunch at the *Fisherman's Inn* at Barraterre. Or go on tour with Christine Rolle and learn all about the herbal medicine of the islands.
- Read the "Shark Lady's" book, and then go and meet Gloria Patience in her own home at The Ferry, and see St. Christopher's Anglican Church nearby, the smallest church in the Bahamas.
- Go bonefishing in the flats on the south side.
- Meet up with friends on Volleyball Beach.
- Relax and enjoy being on this fabled island.

BARRATERRE & ROLLEVILLE

Although Barraterre is a separate island at the northwestern tip of Great Exuma, it is joined by two causeways. Despite this road link it has an identity of its own. The small community of Rolleville, with the *Hilltop Bar* and a couple of grocery stores, is surrounded by pothole farms producing bananas, tomatoes, onions, and peppers. If you've driven up from George Town the term "pothole farming" may cause you to wonder if it doesn't apply to the road itself, rather than local agricultural methods. There is no marina here, and it is very shoal, but you can tie up a dinghy at the *Fisherman's Inn* and enjoy the friendly atmosphere and good food. **Rolleville** hosts an annual regatta, usually the first weekend in August. For information call Kermit Rolle at 242-345-0002.

Clinic

There is a nurse at the government clinic. Dr. Swamy, who looks after other island clinics in the Exumas is based at the Steventon Clinic, south of Rolleville.

Fishing

Rev A. A. McKenzie Tel: 355-5024 • "Taxi 27" He has a 17-ft. Boston Whaler and will take you fishing, shelling, snorkeling, to see iguanas, or just exploring, as well as provide a taxi service.

Groceries

Mc Kenzie's Store Groceries, liquors, and good fresh produce from local pothole farming, as well as gasoline.
Ray Ann's Variety Store Canned goods, sodas, fresh vegetables.

Restaurant

Fisherman's Inn Tel: 255-5017 Two rooms to rent, as well as a bar and very pleasant restaurant overlooking the water. Taxi service to the airport and water and ice from Norman Lloyd (Tel: 255-5016).

Telephone

There are public phones by the *Batelco* station, and at the *Fisherman's Inn*.

LITTLE EXUMA

Southeast of George Town, Little Exuma is a charming, smaller edition of its larger namesake, and well worth a visit. It is joined to Great Exuma by a narrow bridge at **The Ferry**, so named because for years that was the way you crossed between the two islands. Even now you can see the remains of the old haulover ferry alongside the new bridge.

The most famous inhabitant of The Ferry today is Gloria Patience, the Shark Lady. Do buy a copy of her book from *Exuma Markets*, and go visit this fascinating lady who has created a living museum at her house. Nearby is the smallest Anglican church in the Bahamas, St. Christopher's.

If you don't want to take your boat down to Little Exuma, one of the taxis will drive you or, if you are feeling energetic, you could make it a real adventure on a bicycle. Or include it on your day out with a rental car. But don't miss going on to **Williamstown**, where you can see the remains of an old Loyalist plantation, and the impressive, Greek-looking column that was built to guide the ships in as they picked up their cargoes of salt. There is a restaurant, *Kelson Point* (345-4043) at Williamstown, as well as another *Hilltop Bar*, a grocery store, and the very pretty St. Mary Magdelene Anglican church.

There is also excellent bonefishing along the flats on the south side of Little Exuma; the *Peace and Plenty* has its *Bonefish Lodge* there. Goats and slightly strange-looking sheep wander among what remains of stonewalled pastures as a reminder that this island has been farmed since the 1700s. Visit the *Cotton House* if you have time, and the ancient tombs at **Rolletown** on your way back to George Town.

Chapter 16
The Out Islands North of the Tropic of Cancer
Little San Salvador, Cat Island, Conception Island, Rum Cay, and San Salvador Island

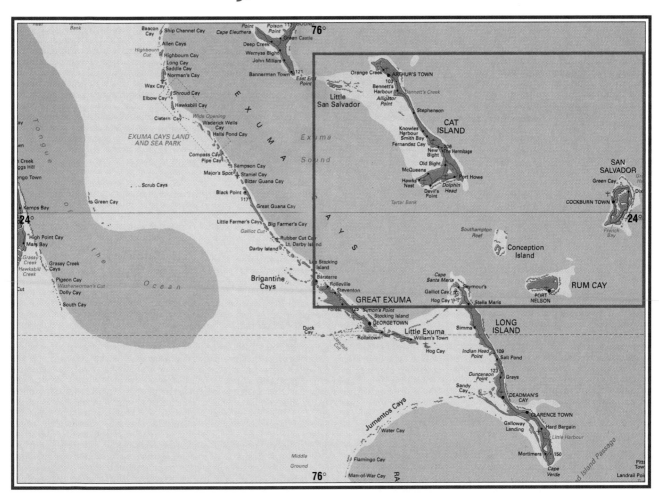

Approaches to the Out Islands from Eleuthera

South Eleuthera to Eleuthera Point	139°M	6.01 nm
Eleuthera Point to Little San Salvador	113°M	11.0 nm
Little San Salvador to The Bight	134°M	30.0 nm
The Bight to Hawk's Nest	204°M	6.5 nm

FROM the north, Eleuthera and Cat Island form a route that takes you into the center of the Out Islands lying north of the tropic of Cancer (that magic line of latitude running 23° 30' N). Going on from the south of Cat Island you have decisions to make over the route you wish to take. We cover the broad options open to you at the end of our entry on Cat Island.

For planning purposes, so that you can start reckoning time and distance to wherever you want to go, if you were to take all our waypoints as the legs of a passage, it would work out something like this:

In reality in leaving Eleuthera for Cat Island you'll probably use the leg to Little San Salvador and will want to stop there (but read what we say about West Bay). Thereafter everything depends on what you're intent on doing. Making your way slowly down the coast of Cat Island, or taking a straight shot for Hawk's Nest? If the straight run south is your plan, then you've no need to go by way of The Bight and the two legs we show (simply to give an idea of the distance you have to cover) are invalid.

Little San Salvador Island

LITTLE SAN SALVADOR

Little San Salvador

| LSSAL | 24° 34' 39"/646 N | 075° 58' 00"/000 W |

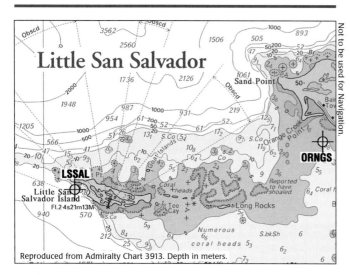

Reproduced from Admiralty Chart 3913. Depth in meters.

Little San Salvador, a one-time inhabited 5-nm-long ridge of limestone, lagoon, and reefs, lies almost midway between Eleuthera and Cat Island, and for this reason alone was always reckoned to be a picnic stop if you passed that way. At 10 nm southwest of Eleuthera Point and 14 nm west of Bennett's Harbour, Little San Salvador is a fair-weather destination, primarily because the whole sea area to the north and east of Little San Salvador is a maze of coral heads and reefs, and in weather in the less-than-gentle category you'd wish to keep well out in Exuma Sound. Long Rocks, a line of rocks and reef lying 4.5 nm east of Little San Salvador, is a good marker warning you to keep to the south on your passage to or from Cat Island. The only attractive Little San Salvador anchorage is the bay on the west side, open from south through to northwest, which has a great beach, some good sand, and patches of coral that are easily avoided.

For these reasons, because Little San Salvador was on your way, because it had that attractive (but not all-weather) anchorage, and simply because it was a "desert" island, Little San Salvador was perennially popu-lar as a stop for both power and sail yachts. Now you have to share it. The Carnival "Family" (Carnival, Costa Cruises, Cunard, Holland America, Seabourn, and Windstar) have the title to the island, have lodged their staff there, developed West Bay into a one-day-stop water playground for their passengers, and renamed it (in their cruise literature) "Half Moon Cay."

We feared Little San Salvador might be declared off limits to visiting boats, but to their credit, so far everyone we've met has been allowed to put in and anchor off West Bay. It is polite to make contact and call the cruise ship also anchored off (if one is there) or the shore staff (if there is no ship) and ask permission. Don't crowd into their water sports area. That goes without saying. But these points made, you are welcome. As one cruise ship captain put it "We like to have you there. You add local color."

The island's inside lagoon is in the process of being opened up, and its eventual purpose is unclear at this time. We've always reckoned it would make a perfect marina. Otherwise the interior of Little San Salvador is for the most part matted secondary scrub, and is barely walkable. The reefs lying to the north and east of the island, extending out toward Long Rocks, are superb snorkeling and shallow dive territory.

Cat Island

Cat Island, some 45 miles long with a width never exceeding 4 miles, fits the archetypal mold of the Bahamian Atlantic barrier island, like its kindred neighbors Eleuthera to the north and Long Island to the south. In essence its primary characteristics are identical: long and thin, a hostile east coast that is not cruising territory, and a west coast that is pass-

West Bay, Little San Salvador.

able but almost completely devoid of good anchorages and with few natural harbors. On the face of it you could say that Cat Island doesn't rate high as a cruising destination, and the fact that only one marina has been established on the entire length of the island would perhaps support this judgement. But hold on. Let's look at it again.

First of all Cat Island is a stepping stone on the eastern route to the south, from the Abacos to Eleuthera, on to Cat Island, and then Conception, Rum Cay, and Long Island. It's your alternative to the Exumas, and Cat Island is also your bridge to San Salvador, the real outlier when it comes to Out Islands. But all this is geography. Is Cat Island itself worth a visit? The answer is "yes." Why? Because it has a mood and a feel of its own. There is almost no tourist development. It's an island of small settlements strung along its east coast, in which the ruins of abandoned houses often seem to outnumber those that are inhabited. Its length and the run of its limestone spines, which produce the highest land in the Bahamas, combine to divide the island into three parts, the north with Arthur's Town as its administrative center, the center, with New Bight furnishing the seat of government for the whole of the south, and the south itself, that low-lying hammer head running out to the west, which until comparatively recently was the back of beyond. As if to reinforce this division into three, Cat Island has three regularly used airfields, Arthur's Town, the Bight, and, although not used by commercial airlines but still carrying plenty of traffic, Hawk's Nest in the south.

The cruising geography of Cat Island is simple. Its western coastal waters are shallow, averaging 12 feet and barely half that close in. Further out, toward the dropoff, there's deeper water. Apart from the northern third it's largely free of reefs and coral heads. The holding generally is not good, the ground being hard sand over coral, and you should check and if necessary set your anchor by hand. Sandbores extend westward in the Orange Creek area, from Bennett's Harbour (Alligator Point), from just south of Fernandez Bay, and from the point just north of Hawk's Nest Creek. It's at that point that the dropoff comes within half a mile of the shore. The south coast is not navigable.

Like Eleuthera and Long Island, the

only way to see Cat Island is by car. You need a rental car, or a new friend with wheels, and for this reason alone your landing place is critical. Gain your mobility and you'll find more than enough to keep you happy exploring for a day or more, and a friendliness that delights and surprises. However, weather is bound to dictate the length of your stay. Southwest through west to northwest and north rules Cat Island right out, except for one all-weather haven and that's Hawk's Nest. Choose your weather and you'll be fine, but maybe it's fortunate that you can, if need be, cover Cat Island in a day. If you're dreaming of weeks at anchor somewhere idyllic, perhaps with some regret you'll need to find a place other than Cat Island.

The North of Cat Island

As we've said the north of Cat Island has Arthur's Town as its center, and there you can find most of the basic support services you may require including an airport served by

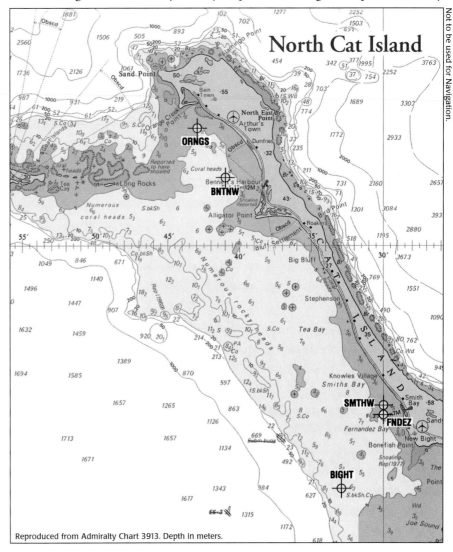

Reproduced from Admiralty Chart 3913. Depth in meters.

CAT ISLAND		
Orange Creek		
ORNGS	24° 37' 00"/000 N	075° 43' 00"/000 W
Orange Creek Dock		
ORNGE	24° 38' 48"/800 N	075° 42' 45"/750 W
Bennett's Harbour		
BNTNW	24° 34' 00"/000 N	075° 41' 00"/000 W
Bennett's Harbour Dock		
BNNTS	24° 33' 33"/600 N	075° 38' 24"/400 W
Smith Bay		
SMTHW	24° 20' 00"/000 N	075° 30' 00"/000 W
Smith Bay Government Dock		
SMITH	24° 19' 58"/966 N	075° 28' 32"/533 W
Fernandez Bay		
FNDEZ	24° 19' 30"/500 N	075° 30' 00"/000 W
The Bight		
BIGHT	24° 15' 00"/000 N	075° 33' 00"/000 W
New Bight Dock		
NBGHT	24° 17' 15"/250 N	075° 24' 54"/900 W
Hawk's Nest		
HWKN1	24° 08' 45"/750 N	075° 35' 00"/000 W
Hawk's Nest		
HWKN2	24° 08' 45"/750 N	075° 32' 00"/000 W
Hawk's Nest Marina Entry		
HWKNM	24° 08' 46"/766 N	075° 31' 36"/600 W
Hawk's Nest Beach		
HWKNB	24° 09' 19"/316 N	075° 31' 25"/417 W

The final figures in each waypoint show seconds (00") and thousands (000) of a minute.

Bahamasair and a Batelco office, under its 200-foot tower. Your access to this area by boat is not easy, however.

ORANGE CREEK

Orange Creek, to the north of Arthur's Town, is the site proposed for a marina by Nicholas Cripps, who at one time ran the Marsh Harbour Marina. At the time of our last visit (March 1999) the plans had been passed by the central government but were stalled at the local level. The creek carries a reasonable depth of water in its final run, but an extensive sandbar that can be taken only by shoal draft craft, together with narrow width and shoaling inland, limit the utility of Orange Creek in its natural state.

Orange Creek already has an excellent general store that would be a windfall adjunct to a marina. We would welcome a northern haven, for one is sorely needed to complement Hawk's Nest in the south, and with both operative, Cat Island cruising would take on a new aspect. There seems to be no positive indication that the scheme will move forward.

In the meantime, reports have it that Club Med is interested in buying land on the West Point of the Orange Creek promontory, and a long-proposed Anguilla development on the Atlantic coast is being pushed by its promoters. If it moves forward, whether the envisaged condominiums, docks, and even a proposed casino, will materialize remains one big question. Local opinion seems set against it.

BENNETT'S HARBOUR

The only anchorage at this time giving direct access to northern Cat Island is Bennett's Harbour, on the north side of Alligator Point. The name is illusionary. We would not describe this opening into Bennett's Creek as a harbor. What you have there is a narrow cut, marked by a light, leading directly to a small dock used by the mailboat, the *North Cat Island Special*. Beyond this dock there's room for perhaps two boats and thereafter the creek shoals. The downside is the narrowness of this channel, barely 100 feet in width, and the tidal flow that sluices through it. If you try it, be aware of the sand and reef running out for some distance both from Alligator Point and the entry cut to Bennett's Harbour. It is not a straightforward approach. Go in at slack tide, preferably high, and secure yourself aligned with the channel with both a bow and stern anchor as well as lines taken across to each side, for there's no room to swing. Don't block the mailboat.

Bennett's Harbour may be hardly worth the effort. The restaurant by the dock is closed. There is no telephone. The settlement is half a mile up the sand road, and apart from one small "convenience" store, there's nothing there. The ultimate factor on the downside is that you are surrounded by mangroves, and that means bugs.

There is a reasonable anchorage further inshore just to the north of Bennett's Harbour, where in southeast weather you can lie off the beach. But this hardly solves your access to shoreside facilities, for you are in a tract of Cat Island where there is very little in conventional support terms. Arthur's Town, further north, whose Batelco tower is clearly visible, is your only source of food, water, and fuel.

The Center and South of Cat Island

SMITH BAY

Should you have to declare Cat Island as your port of entry, you are bound to land at only one place and that is Smith Bay. A cut opening into a creek, again marked by a light, serves a Government Dock built to accommodate mailboat services (in this case the *Sea Hauler*) and the exportation, though the adjacent Department of Agriculture warehouse, of Cat Island produce. At first sight Smith Bay seems a good harbor but its usable depth extends only from the entry channel to parallel the dock; the rest shoals rapidly, and you are not protected from surge or from the west.

Nonetheless it's here that Customs will clear you in, and it's only here (other than at Hawk's Nest) that you can obtain diesel and gasoline, which will be delivered by truck from the Shell service station in New Bight. To request clearance in, and to request fuel, call New Bight Service Station on VHF 16. They in turn will contact Customs at New Bight airport. However, other than securing these services, Smith Bay is no place we'd recommend and it's just too far from New Bight. If you do elect to anchor there, the Shell station is also a car rental agency.

FERNANDEZ BAY

To the south of Smith Bay, set in a cove-like hook of land, is the Fernandez Bay Resort. An upscale and attractive small resort, Fernandez Bay has been disappointed by its experiences with the boating community. For the boater, Fernandez Bay, given anything but the dreaded west weather, looks idyllic. Good depth, fair holding, a great beach, and of course the Fernandez Bay Resort itself, right on your doorstep. Seen from the beach, the view is somewhat different. It is a very small resort, and underline that word small. Sharing their hard-won retreat with boaters is not always appreciated by the paying guests, and

Smith Bay, from the east.

when, as has happened, the honor bar system has been abused by nonresidents and the one telephone is used as a boater's hotline, a sense-of-humor failure is almost inevitable.

Of course there's freedom of the seas and no one can stake out even one small bay as their private turf. What it really boils down to is the consideration to avoid intrusion in personal space, and the sensitivity to avoid swamping by numbers. Normal boating etiquette should serve, just plain good manners, but sadly it hasn't. Fernandez Bay may be a place where you can anchor but it's not a charted anchorage, nor is the resort in the business of hosting visiting boats. Perhaps they would welcome a cruising visitor if permission to anchor off were requested, and if the visitor made arrangements to use their facilities, bar, restaurant, dive shop, etc., and ran a credit card. But just swinging in, dropping a hook, and running a dinghy on the beach with a sackful of garbage? That's a real social no-no. And there's another problem too. Do you use your holding tank? They swim off that beach.

NEW BIGHT AND MOUNT ALVERNIA (THE HERMITAGE)

Your final option, and the only real option in central Cat Island is to anchor off the settlement of New Bight. Of course you're open there, wide open from south right through the west to north. But if you anchor off that 230-foot Batelco tower you're right in the heart of the settlement, with pretty much everything within walking range. Ignore the small concrete dock, which has rock

Reproduced from Admiralty Chart 3913. Depth in meters.

Father Jerome
(aka John Hawes) 1876–1956

THE builder of the Hermitage on Comer Hill at New Bight in Cat Island, the place he called Mount Alvernia, was by any measure an extraordinary man. English by birth, born of a comfortably affluent family, he studied architecture and suddenly switched to theology. He was ordained in the Church of England early in the twentieth century. In 1908 he arrived in the Bahamas, where he combined his architectural expertise with bare-hands skills and his Anglican faith, and devoted himself to traveling the islands and repairing storm-devastated churches.

A John Hawes church (as he was then) had unmistakable characteristics. It was always stone built, thick walled, often Romanesque in style. His approach to religion was modeled on St Francis of Assisi, a barefoot simplicity, which, among other tenets of his faith, had no time for distinctions between black and white, poor and affluent, and he undoubtedly challenged the status quo of the Bahamian social order at that time. Perhaps it was social rejection or dissatisfaction that took him out into a wider world, both as a sailor, and into virtually any employment that came his way. There was time spent in Canada. In 1911 he made a second abrupt move in his vocation. He went to Rome, studied Catholicism, became a priest, and adopted a new name.

As Father Jerome he went to Australia as a bush priest and remained there for almost a quarter of a century. Then, perhaps sensing his own mortality after a heart attack, he returned to the Bahamas in 1939. He settled in New Bight, chose Comer Hill, the highest point in the Bahamas, as the site of a hermitage, and started to build the place you see today. He died, and was buried there, barefoot in a bare grave, seventeen years later.

His memorials are not only the Hermitage. There are four other Father Jerome churches in Cat Island, and five churches in Long Island, which include the two highly visible Clarence Town churches, the Anglican St Paul's, and, in an extraordinary marriage of Greek Island, Celtic, and Romanesque architecture, the Roman Catholic church of Saints Peter and Paul.

Plantation House, New Bight.

around it, and run your dinghy right up on the beach. You can walk from there to Mount Alvernia, the extraordinary hilltop (206 feet) hermitage of Father Jerome, the famed architect and builder of the two Clarence Town churches on Long Island. That hilltop is the highest point in the Bahamas, and that, whatever your religion and your interest in Jerome churches, should make Mount Alvernia (aka Comer Hill) a place of pilgrimage.

We cover Mount Alvernia more completely in our **Yellow Pages**. We're glad to report that some repair work and care have reversed what was a steady deterioration of the site. Although not yet restored to pristine condition, Father Jerome's memorial is in good hands at this time and should yet endure.

HAWK'S NEST

When we first wrote about Hawk's Nest it was in the early days of the near-total rebuild of the original, essentially airstrip-based, resort. That the place had potential, particularly in the development of the marina in Hawk's Nest Creek, was obvious. The only question was whether the development plans could be carried through, and the management would match the ideas. The answer is a definite "yes" on both counts. Let's now look at the way it is.

The first plus is location. OK, there are no other all-weather marinas in Cat Island, but beyond this, Hawk's Nest is one of the key points in the Greater Exuma Sound cruising area. Take a map. Draw a line and connect Powell Point in South Eleuthera with Highborne Cay in the Exumas. Draw that Exuma line down to George Town, then across to Cape Santa Maria in Long Island, and on to Rum Cay. Now complete the box back to Eleuthera. Hawk's Nest is right there, on the line. Location counts. And it's on the doorstep of the Tartar Bank, one of the best fishing grounds in the southern Bahamas.

We said "all-weather," and although no one can forecast the effects of a direct hit by a hurricane, we reckon Hawk's Nest Marina is safe for severe weather, and Hawk's Nest Creek might well be one of the best hurricane holes you could find. More of this later.

These factors apart, what have you got there? A small but supremely well-run resort, restaurant, and marina complex. You have access by air (charter or private aircraft only), or sea, a rental car available for Cat Island exploration, and golf carts if you find it tiresome walking between marina and resort. There are good beaches, snorkel and scuba equipment, the fishing we mentioned, with boats to rent or charter if you wish, and bonefishing too. There's fuel and water, rooms for crew changes, and a rental house. But see our **Yellow Pages** for all this detail.

In the past our one reservation about Hawk's Nest was the entry to Hawk's Nest Creek, and therefore into the marina, which was widely held to be a no-no in westerly weather. Popular wisdom had it that you had to turn briefly broadside to weather during your entry run. It's just not so. The entry channel has now been surveyed and re-marked, and we've been that way. It's a straightforward, no-problems, run in.

THE APPROACH TO HAWK'S NEST MARINA

Our HWKN1 waypoint is probably redundant, but we give safe offshore landing waypoints for approaches made in poor visibility. The first critical point, HWKN2, is at the dropoff, which is close inshore at this point. From here you can see exactly what lies ahead, and you've got just over 0.5 nm to run in to the marina. Your principal landmarks are a yellow house (Point House) on the point of land to port and a red ball, together with a radar reflector on a stake, on the rock spine to starboard. In between you have Hawk's Nest Creek (off your starboard bow) and a shallow bay (which drys partially at low water) off your port bow.

From HWKN2 you run in visually for the Creek. Your heading will work out to be around 062°M. Your first marker is a red float, which you leave to starboard. The dark bottom in this area is grass, not reef. A clear sand bottom shows to port at this point, but there's no need to swing off taking this to be the safer course. You can stay on your heading. Pass between the rock with the red ball and the radar reflector and a green marker that will come up to port. You're in the Creek. Carry straight on, the fuel dock (diesel and gas) is on your port side, and just after the fuel dock, swing to port to enter the marina, which up to that point has remained concealed. In the marina you have power, water, and an added bonus, a mini (West Marine–stocked) marine store.

Ahead of you, further up the Creek, are the Hawk's Nest mooring buoys. Three of them while we were there, probably five in total by the time you read this. You will have 6 feet at MLW in the entry channel to the marina. The fuel dock, and the moorings, have 7.5 feet at MLW. If you elect to find yourself a pocket in which to anchor further up the Creek, there are deep places there. We suggest you explore by dinghy first and take soundings. It's quite possible to work yourself surprisingly far in, and in severe weather the surrounding mangroves are your protection, your mooring, and your "air bags" if you get carried by wind or surge. Anchored up there in normal conditions, set two anchors. The tidal flow is strong, about 4 knots, and it reverses, like all Bahamian cuts and creeks.

Is there any downside to all this? Yes, you're in the mangroves there, be it in the marina, moored, or anchored. Maybe the mosquitoes and no-see-ums might leave you in peace. Maybe not. Be prepared.

MOVING ON FROM CAT ISLAND

Hawk's Nest is well placed for moving on to the other Out Islands, or indeed making your way to George Town. It lies at the apex of a triangle whose base runs from George Town through Cape Santa Maria (the northern point of Long Island) to Conception Island, all of which are just about equidistant from Hawk's Nest. If you want to head directly for San Salvador from Hawk's Nest, we suggest you create a waypoint north of Conception Island to accommodate your turn to run east somewhere above the line of 24° N. Our "standard" route

Hawk's Nest Creek, from the west.

Conception Island, from the north.

THE NORTHERN ANCHORAGE

The most-often-used anchorage lies on the northwest tip of the island proper, shielded in part by West Cay. You are exposed there from the northwest through west to the south, and you may find surge from easterly ocean swell, particularly if the set is from the northeast. The depth is 30 feet running to shoal draft off the beach, and there are isolated reefs and coral heads in the area, which can be easily seen. Enter with the light in your favor. Just to the north of this anchorage there is the 4-mile run of Southampton Reef, which, for divers, is a prime destination. Snorkeling or diving on any reef or coral head will be equally rewarding. The creek halfway down the west coast of Conception Island is shoal draft and not a viable anchorage.

to San Salvador goes from Rum Cay, which we reach by way of Conception, but there's no reason why you should follow our tracks. Your distances and bearings in the triangle are:

Hawk's Nest (3 nm W) to George Town (West)	207°M	36.5 nm
Hawk's Nest (3 nm W) to Conception (Northwest)	133°M	30.9 nm
Hawk's Nest (3 nm W) to Cape Santa Maria	160°M	28.9 nm

Conception Island

Conception Island itself is barely 3 nm by 2 nm in land area, but sits in a surrounding shield of reefs that extend 4.5 nm to the north, 4 nm to the east, and just over 1 nm to the south. The island itself rises to 60 feet in part, which as you make your landfall can deceive you into thinking that this high land is your aiming point. It may be, but rather like the bull's eye being just the center of a target, you must be acutely conscious of those rings of surrounding reefs and go cautiously as you draw close to the island. The whole island, with its reefs, is a marine park, protected exactly under the same terms as the Exumas Land and Sea Park, and is uninhabited. You are welcome to visit Conception Island, may anchor and land there, and may dive its reefs. Take nothing from this pristine and beautiful site, and leave footprints, but no trash.

Approaches to Conception Island

George Town Harbour East to Cape Santa Maria	059°M	22.24 nm
Cape Santa Maria to Conception (Northwest)	063°M	13.87 nm
Cape Santa Maria to Conception (Wedge Point)	074°M	13.33 nm

CONCEPTION ISLAND

Conception Northwest Anchorage		
CONNW	23° 50' 56"/929 N	075° 07' 44"/732 W
Conception Wedge Point		
CONWG	23° 48' 00"/000 N	075° 07' 00"/000 W

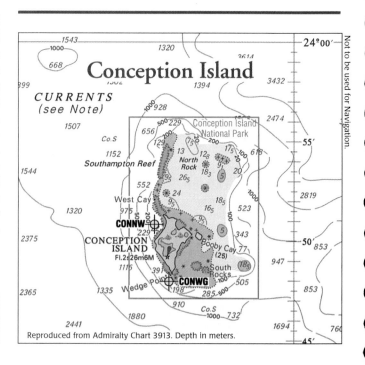

Reproduced from Admiralty Chart 3913. Depth in meters.

Not to be used for Navigation.

Sandy Point, Rum Cay, looking southeast.

THE EASTERN ANCHORAGE

It is possible to work up along the east coast of the island, eyeballing around Wedge Point (you'll note the wedge-shaped rock formation that led to the name) and pick your way up toward Booby Cay. In calm weather, with nothing threatening, this presents no problems other than the need for careful navigation. We'd hesitate to select this east anchorage as our base for an extended stay unless we had confidence in stable conditions, with nothing changing in the middle of the night, simply because you can't cut and run from there.

Rum Cay

Rum Cay, a 9-by-5-nm chunk of an island, has a reassuringly solid appearance from the ocean. It too has surrounding reefs, but these are tucked close to its shoreline, and only one reef, extending 2 nm north from the northwest tip, is a significant offshore hazard (and its last victim, a Haitian boat that foundered there two years back, is still visible as a warning). However, the inshore reefs have claimed many vessels over the years, and continue to do so. Our waypoints are chosen to set up two approaches to St. George Bay and the Port Nelson–Sumner Point area, which is your destination if you're visiting Rum Cay. We cover these approaches in detail but two factors are vital for a safe arrival or departure. The first is good weather, and the second is the sun, which must be in your favor. If it turns out that you can add the advantage of a high tide to these two factors, you have a winning combination.

With a head count of fifty-two Bahamians and eight to ten Americans (some of them part-time residents), Rum Cay is uninhabited for its greater part, has an airstrip (which may be extended one day) on the west side of Port Nelson, and no road system. The extended settlement of Port Nelson, with its dock, is the whole of Rum Cay in human terms. The one exception, ten minutes walk from Port Nelson, is a new marina, the only one on Rum Cay, at Sumner Point. We devote some time to Rum Cay, which up to this date has been largely avoided by cruising yachts because its only anchorage was open to prevailing winds, the reefs had a bad reputation, and all in all, Rum Cay just seemed to be a detour that was not worth taking. In fact, geographically Rum Cay is well placed as a waypoint on the route to and from the Caribbean, and our own feeling is that with the continuing development of the Sumner Point Marina, Rum Cay is on the map.

RUM CAY		
Rum Cay Sandy Point		
RUMSP	23° 38' 45"/750 N	074° 57' 30"/500 W
Rum Cay Southeast		
RUMSE	23° 37' 15"/250 N	074° 47' 30"/500 W
Rum Cay Port Nelson		
RUMPN	23° 37' 15"/250 N	074° 51' 00"/000 W
Sumner Point Marina Approach		
RUMAP	23° 37' 51"/846 N	074° 51' 02"/035 W

The final figures in each waypoint show seconds (00") and thousands (000) of a minute.

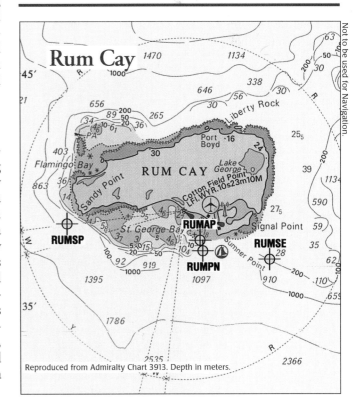

Reproduced from Admiralty Chart 3913. Depth in meters.

Approaches to and from Rum Cay

Conception (Wedge Point) to Rum Cay (Sandy Point)	143°M	12.70 nm
Rum Cay (Sandy Point) to Conception (Wedge Point)	323°M	12.70 nm
San Salvador (Cockburn) to Rum Cay (Southeast)	214°M	28.60 nm
Rum Cay (Southeast) to San Salvador (Cockburn)	034°M	28.60 nm
Clarence Town to Rum Cay (Sandy Point)	006°M	30.75 nm
Rum Cay (Sandy Point) to Clarence Town	186°M	30.75 nm

FROM THE SOUTHWEST

The southwest point of Rum Cay, Sandy Point, can be rounded reasonably close in, between a quarter and half a mile offshore, and a course set from there to Sumner Point, which will be the southernmost tip of land you see. You have deep water all the way until you cross Longitude 074° 51' 30"/500 W, which brings you level with Cotton Field Point, with a prominent house on it. Ahead of you, at the most half a mile away, you'll see an orange-red buoy. This is the outer marker of the route into Sumner Point Marina, and it's also the point at which you can turn to port toward the anchorage. Adjust your heading to approach this outer buoy, as if to leave it to starboard. Your position at this time should be around 23° 38' 10"/166 N 074° 51' 00"/000 W, standing safely clear of the buoy in around 20 feet of water. Now you have a decision to make. Anchorage? Or marina?

Wherever you're bound, it's not a bad idea to check out your orientation at this stage. Cotton Field Point, with the prominent house, is 345°M. Summer Point bears 100°M. The marina is just north of it. You'll see the white sand from the dredging, the Texaco sign, and the oil tanks. Port Nelson hardly shows. A few houses, some palm trees, and its new (1997) 200-foot Batelco tower. The settlement dock is lost against its background.

If you want to anchor off, turn for Cotton Field Point, favoring the house to the east with the shiny tin roof bearing at around 005°M. To the right of this house you'll see the ruined buildings of the Rum Cay Club. The anchorage lies between the house with the shiny roof and the dock at Port Nelson, which will become apparent as you get closer. Make your way in eyeballing as you go, and then turn to parallel the beach if you want to be closer to Port Nelson.

There's an inshore route from Sandy Point to the an-

chorage, but we see no point in it. There is coral on the way, Cotton Field Point is hard to identify right at the start, and you're making life unnecessarily difficult. Take the deep-water route we've outlined.

If you're bound for Sumner Point Marina a series of entry markers will lead you in from the outer reef. It is vital that you identify the outer marker accurately, for if you mistake an inner marker for the first one, you will end up on the reef. In effect you have three legs from that outer marker, and then you are virtually at the entry channel. You have plenty of sea room as you go in, although you have coral on both sides. Your depth will go from 20 feet to 10 feet, and then 8 feet. We are talking MLW depths.

The entry channel itself (as of April 1999) had 6.5 feet at MLW. At that time plans had been made to dredge the channel to 12 feet MLW in the fall of 1999. (Because this date is after we go to print, you would be wise, if you are entering at low water and depth is critical to you, to call Sumner Point Marina on VHF 16 and check the depth). Short of the entry there's a good place to anchor and wait for the tide.

If you cannot identify the marker buoys, or if it appears that one is missing, call Sumner Point. They will always guide you in. Storms have taken markers away, and people have run over them and cut the lines. These things happen.

FROM THE SOUTHEAST

Coming into St. George Bay from the southeast you must avoid the reefs that run west for just over 1 nm from Sumner Point. The only safe approach is to run on an east–west line almost 1.5 nm south of Sumner Point straight to

Sumner Point Marina.

our Port Nelson waypoint. *Don't* be tempted to turn in sooner than Longitude 074° 51' W, even if you see what you take to be the entry buoys leading you into the marina. Our air photograph shows very clearly the line of reef running east–west to the south of Sumner Point. This *must* be rounded to the west.

At our Port Nelson waypoint turn to run due north on Longitude 074° 51' W. We strongly recommend that you contact Sumner Point Marina on VHF 16 at our Port Nelson approach waypoint, or before proceeding more than half a mile north of it, tell them where you are, and ask whether there are any special instructions on entering. About 1 mile ahead from our approach waypoint you should be able to pick up, off your starboard bow, the first of the orange-red buoys marking the route in to the Sumner Point Marina. Don't run too close to this buoy, which you leave to starboard. Keep well to port. It marks the outer limit of the reef. Once you're at that mark, follow the instructions we've already given in the last section.

PORT NELSON ANCHORAGE

The Port Nelson anchorage is the bight of St. George Bay running along the frontage of the settlement from the dock westward toward Cotton Field Point. You may anchor virtually wherever you fancy in suitable depth anywhere along the beach. There are two pockets of slightly deeper water that will become apparent. Don't go west of Cotton Field Point. You're open from southeast through south to west in St. George Bay, and you can get thrown around if the wind comes from these quadrants in any strength. Don't be fooled by the name Port Nelson. There's no port there. In the past it was the risk of changing weather, let alone the openness of St. George Bay to prevailing winds, that put many cruising visitors off Rum·Cay.

SUMNER POINT ANCHORAGE AND MARINA

Sumner Point Marina, small, still under construction, is a surprise and a delight. With fuel, water, and power it has all the basics, but the real delight is a clubhouse-like restaurant and bar, its friendly owners and their gourmet evening meals that win unreserved and well-deserved praise. Over the last two years the fuel dock (at the entry) has been extended and opened on both sides. A second inner basin has been dredged, but is not yet finished. Ultimately it will be primarily devoted to residents, for building lots have been sold and house construction, at least on one prize lot, has already started. For facilities as they are at the time of writing, see our **Yellow Pages**.

The one problem that has plagued Sumner Point to date has been sand building up on the southern side of the entry channel itself, right by the fuel dock. It's controllable, and presents you, the visitor, with no problems. You'll see the sand clearly as you go in. Favor the fuel dock side of the channel. For Bobby Little, it presents an interesting problem in hydraulic engineering. It's worth noting that so far two hurricanes have hit this new marina. At the time of *Erin* in 1995 eleven boats sought shelter and survived. With *Lily* in 1996 the marina sheltered eight boats. One of them, a delivery boat fitted out with just four 15-foot lines and one anchor, was driven ashore but refloated later, undamaged. The others went through it unharmed.

HMS Conqueror

In 1860 HMS *Conqueror* was one of the Royal Navy's latest ships, and took pride of place in the British line of battle in that day. She was a 101-gun battleship, capable of throwing a prodigious weight of metal from a broadside, still very much a three-decker with the masts and full rig of a ship of the eighteenth century, but with the incongruous addition of a smokestack amidships and a vast, primitive, coal-burning engine driving one great screw. Still virtually on her maiden voyage, she was lost on Sumner Point Reef, Rum Cay, on December 13, 1861. Her crew of 1,400 all survived.

She was 20 nm out in estimating her position and, after making her landfall, cut rounding the southeast point of Rum Cay too fine and went hard on the reef. Her captain, fearing that his crew (most of whom could not swim in those days) would drink themselves insensible when it became obvious the ship was lost, ordered all ale, wine, and spirit casks to be broken and their contents ditched. He then sent the two largest ship's boats, rigged with sail as well as oars, to Nassau and Jamaica requesting help. For the next two days the ship's company unloaded everything they could salvage, and set about making a camp on the island. The captain remained on board with one midshipman and ten seamen until the ship broke up. Then all of them, less the boat parties, were marooned on Rum Cay. They were rescued soon after the news of the disaster was known.

HMS *Conqueror* is still there. You can dive her, in some 30 feet of water.

Illustrated London News, *Feb. 8, 1862.*
HMS Conqueror.

Courtesy Balmain Antiques, Nassau

Longer-term plans for the Sumner Point Marina include a secluded mega-yacht dock with a private apartment ashore and a private beach, a number of residential homes with docks, some of them rentable, and stores offering fresh vegetables and provisions as well as lubricants and marine spares.

PORT NELSON

Port Nelson has spread itself along its loosely aligned grid of sand roads, and its two small stores, three bars, and two restaurants are distanced as if proximity were forbidden by local zoning. You can find most staples in Port Nelson, there's a Batelco office, and those bars and restaurants. Don't expect to find much, though. There's not much there. Rum Cay suffered when its salt pond operation became economically nonviable, leading to a population drop from 5,000 to 60. It has suffered from its isolation and from hurricanes. What Rum Cay does have to offer is superb snorkeling, diving, and fishing. It has, in addition to its reefs, the wreck of the ill-fated HMS *Conqueror*, the Royal Navy's first propeller-driven warship, which came to an untimely end on the reef off Sumner Point. The one-time Rum Cay Club, an ambitious and well-set-up diving resort to the west of Port Nelson, ran into a reversal of fortune, closed some years back, and its buildings were totally devastated by *Lily*. With this final blow the certainty of employment for every adult on the island came to an end. Now the developing Sumner Point Marina, and vacation-home construction associated with it, has engendered a new spirit, employment, and the chance to learn and master new skills. Rum Cay is going forward.

San Salvador

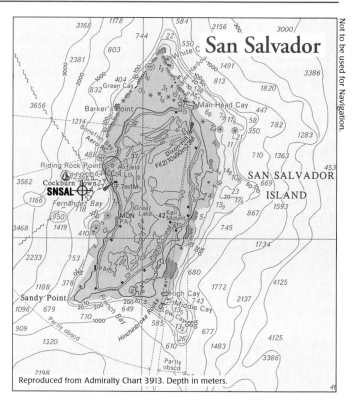

Reproduced from Admiralty Chart 3913. Depth in meters.

SAN SALVADOR ISLAND

San Salvador		
SNSAL	24° 02' 45"/750 N	074° 33' 45"/750 W

New Government Dock, San Salvador.

Approaches to and from San Salvador

Rum Cay (Southeast) to San Salvador (Cockburn)	034°M	28.60 nm
San Salvador (Cockburn) to Rum Cay (Southeast)	214°M	28.60 nm

San Salvador, roughly 12-by-6 nm, is a strange mix of elevation, hills and bumps (140 feet at the highest) and creeks and lakes that take up most of the interior land area. It might well be just another Out Island clinging to subsistence but for two strokes of fortune. The first was the alleged First Landing of Christopher Columbus after his 1492 Atlantic voyage. Many now dispute this attribution (see the **Green Pages** under **The Columbus Controversy** on page 394) but long- established official endorsement that San Salvador was indeed his first stop brought the island a star role in a set of Bahamian Quincentennial postage stamps. The second benefit dealt by fortune is simply the spin-off of fame. With the aura of being the "Columbus Island" has come four commemorative memorials (one of these to the landing of a *Santa Maria* replica in 1991); selection as the offshore transit site of the Olympic flame on its way

VHF

San Salvador, exceptionally, has always had an island VHF net on channel 6. You may get no response on 16 if you use it. We suggest, while you're in San Salvador waters, using VHF 6 as your calling channel.

from Greece to Mexico; two resorts, the Riding Rock Inn, and a Club Méditerranée; an airfield now extended to 8,000 feet, capable of taking just about anything in the charter business with the exception of the *Concorde*; regular Bahamasair service; and cruise ship visits.

Comparatively tightly bound by its fringing reefs except in the north, where the coastal reefs extend out for 3 nm, San Salvador is famed in the diving world for its almost incredible dropoffs, where the bottom contour hits 600 feet within a hand span and 6,000 feet within a second hand span. Only 5 nm out from that fringing reef you'll have 24,000 feet under your keel. Its relative isolation and geographic location well off the beaten track between Florida and the Caribbean, however, has meant that San Salvador has never been a popular cruising destination. This is reinforced by the absence of natural harbors and the sole alternative of one small marina that, given weather from the westerly quadrants, may present entry and exit problems, and is open to surge.

ANCHORAGES
The only anchorages are Grahams Harbour in the northeast, which is completely exposed to the north, an uneasy anchorage off Cockburn Town or Fernandez Bay on the west coast, and French Bay, not easy to enter and coral strewn, in the south, open from the southeast through south to the west.

RIDING ROCK INN MARINA
San Salvador's only marina, part of the Riding Rock Inn complex north of Cockburn and to the immediate north of the marina, has ten slips plus space for an unquantified number of boats lying alongside their newly constructed south basin wall. The marina is divided into two basins, which open up each side of the entry channel. The north basin, long completed, has the more conventional layout with both finger piers and a wall, primarily used by their own dive boats. The south basin has a recently constructed wall on the eastern side, but otherwise is unfinished. The governing depth in the entry channel is 6 feet at MLW with perhaps slightly more, 6.5 feet or maybe 7 feet overall, in the two basins at MLW. Don't forget they work on VHF 6.

All the facilities you would expect to find in a marina are there, and the backup facilities on the diving side are second to none. See our later remarks, and see our **Yellow Pages** for further details on the marina, particularly regarding booking dock space (which has to be done through their Florida office), and the Riding Rock Inn. The marina's surge problems stem from a lack of a well-sited breakwater, and the extension of the north arm of the entry channel has done nothing to solve it. Not only does this raise the issue of the comfort factor in the marina as a serious consideration if you're thinking of going there, but also, if there's any significant swell, particularly from the west and southwest, your entry or exit through the 50-foot cut is perilous. The channel has range markers and is not difficult in calm conditions.

Riding Rock Inn built its trade on diving, and in the past its marina served adequately for its three dive boats and the occasional visiting yacht. Now the attention of the sports fishing community has turned to San Salvador with the realization that San Salvador waters offer blue marlin, yellowfin tuna, and wahoo (the last record breakers) right on the doorstep, and the island is now a fishing destination.

The sports fishermen now outnumber all other boating visitors to San Salvador, and we reckon that limited space alone has prevented greater expansion.

GOVERNMENT DOCK
There is a new Government Dock midway between the Riding Rock Marina and Cockburn Town, but although you could enter and secure here, and we doubt that anyone would turn you away, you'll find yourself with high walls, no pilings, some surge, and no shoreside facilities. This newly cut basin is where the mailboat comes in, and this alone suggests it's better not to use it. In an emergency, it's another alternative.

San Salvador's west coast, with the Government Dock and Riding Rock Marina.

Shell has built a large complex close to the Government Dock. At present gasoline and diesel tanks are there, and a roadside gas station. It is believed that avgas and propane may follow. With Shell's continuing Bahamas-wide interest in marinas, it would not surprise us to see the new Government Dock basin developed into both a commercial dock facility and a marina. There is room for both. As they say, "Watch this space."

COCKBURN TOWN

Cockburn (pronounced "Coburn") Town is recognizable offshore by its Batelco tower (200 feet) and large satellite

The colors of San Salvador, Sandy Point.

dish, and the ruins of its old Government Dock. Cockburn is an entry port, has the range of facilities you expect to find in the main Out Islands, a Batelco office, a relocated and much-improved clinic north of the airport (see our **Yellow Pages**), a bank, and food stores, but there's nothing of substance there. Even the little museum is run down and appears to have been abandoned. For visitors arriving by air, the two self-contained resorts provide everything for their clients.

It remains to say that the color of the water all around

San Salvador is outstanding. The ocean dropoff runs so close to the land all around the island that it brings deep ultramarine blue water virtually within swimming distance of the beaches. You have three bands of vivid color almost wherever you look, the white sand, the aquamarine of the shallows, and then this deep, deep blue. But despite this gemlike brilliance, the cruising visitor, unless taken up with big game fishing or diving the walls, is unlikely to rate San Salvador high on their visit list.

YELLOW PAGES

This area received the full force of Hurricane *Floyd* in September 1999. Be aware that reconstruction and the restoration of normal services after a Category 4 Hurricane may take a considerable period of time to complete.

CAT ISLAND

Like most of the Bahamian islands settled for many centuries, over the years the name has changed. Cat Island was originally called Guanahini by the Lucayan Indians, then San Salvador by the Spanish, and finally Cat Island by the British after noting the huge number of cats imported by the Spanish to rid the islands of its rat population. Or could it be named after Arthur Catt, one of Blackbeard's contemporary brigands? Whatever the origin of the name, plantation houses still stand as reminders of earlier prosperity on the island, when cotton, pineapple, and sisal grew here in such abundance that ships called in at the Cat Island ports from New England and Europe, and the railroad (the only one ever constructed in the Bahamas) at Old Bight was kept busy. It is undoubtedly one of the most beautiful islands in the Bahamas, and still largely unspoiled. The west coast is lined with narrow beaches, and if you drive along the main (and only) north–south road you will be mesmerized by the extraordinarily attractive coastline, and the small village settlements, several still with derelict slave cabins standing among pothole farms. And, of course, there is the Father Jerome Hermitage to visit and admire. The snorkeling and diving off Cat Island, as well as the deep sea and bonefishing, all contribute to make this historically interesting island a fascinating place to visit. Anchor off New Bight in good weather, or tie up in secure *Hawk's Nest Marina*, and take time to explore.

THE NORTH OF CAT ISLAND
From Orange Creek to Smith Bay

Orange Creek, the northernmost settlement on Cat Island, is home to the *Orange Creek Inn* (354-4110) with its food store, and laundromat (closed on Saturdays); the *Sea Spray Hotel* (354-4116) where rooms cost from $65 a night; and a clinic (354-4050).

Arthur's Town, the center of government for Cat Island, and briefly the boyhood home of Sidney Poitier, has an airstrip served by *Bahamasair* (354-2049 on days of flight) three times a week; a *Batelco* office (with a card phone outside); a clinic (354-4050); a police station (354-2046); and restaurants and liquor stores. Motor scooters can be rented from Pat Rolle, at *Cookie House Rentals* (354-2027), who also runs the *Cookie House Restaurant,* and bakes homemade bread daily.

Traveling south through **Zion Hill** and **Dumfries**, you come to **Bennett's Harbour**, which is really an apology for a harbor since it is so shoal that nothing much more than a 3-ft. draft can get into it, and even then you'll be high and dry at low tide in the protected part to starboard after you come in. Once you're in, you are then a hot hike away from the main road with no facilities within walking distance. The *North Cat Island Express* calls in weekly, but only on a high tide.

The settlements of **Rokers** and **The Bluff**, with its small *Island General Shopping Center*, lead south to **Industrious Hill, The Cove,** and **Knowles Village** with the *Bachelor's Restaurant*. Some of these settlements have original slave cabins and traces of early Loyalist settlers, until you come to **Smith Bay.**

CENTRAL CAT ISLAND
From Smith Bay to New Bight

Accommodations and Restaurant
Haulover's Inn and Restaurant Tel: 242-342-2028   Opposite the Government Dock, open for local food with a bar.

Hazel's Seaside Bar
Litle Bay Inn Tel: 242-342-2004
Clinic
Madeline Smith Community Clinic Tel: 342-3026   This is the main clinic for the whole of Cat Island, with a resident doctor and full-time nurse. Open 9 am to 4 pm Monday to Friday.
Customs
Customs and Immigration can be called to the Government Dock from New Bight Airport on VHF 16 to clear you in here, before you proceed to anchor off New Bight. If you need help to contact Customs, call "New Bight Service Station" on VHF 16. The service station will also truck in fuel to you at the Government Dock if you need it.
Mailboat
M/V Sea Hauler calls in weekly from Nassau and ships out island produce.

Further south, between **Smith Bay** and **New Bight**, lies the attractive *Fernandez Bay Village (*Tel: 242-342-3043 • Fax: 342-3051), a remote and low-key luxury resort owned and run by the Armbrister family, with a heavenly crescent-shaped white sand beach, and nine villas with garden baths as well as private baths inside, starting at $210 per night. They are not too keen on having boats at anchor in "their" bay, but the restaurant opens for breakfast, lunch, and dinner daily; dinner reservations are requested**.**

NEW BIGHT AND MOUNT ALVERNIA

If you plan to anchor in the Bight, your best bet is to position off **New Bight** where everything is within walking distance. If you have not cleared in, remember that Smith Bay is your Port of Entry, and you must go there first to have these formalities completed.

Mount Alvernia is particularly interesting because of its church. A young priest, Father Jerome, trained as an architect at the end of the last century, and then decided to become an Anglican missionary. Not too many years later, he switched to the Roman Catholic faith, and in 1908 arrived in the Bahamas to rebuild local, but frail, wooden churches that could not withstand hurricane-force winds, reconstructing them in stone. When he was 62 years old he decided to build the Hermitage, modeled on scaled-down European monastic buildings, on the top of the highest hill in the Bahamas, Mt. Comer, aka Mount Alvernia, standing 206 feet above sea level. Here he lived out the rest of his life, until he died in the late 1950s. There are fantastic views from the top of the hill, and it is well worth the short climb up to his chapel, the Bell Tower, and his own monastic quarters. You can see other examples of his work in the Catholic Church of St. Francis of Assisi at Old Bight, and in the two churches of different faiths at Clarence Town on Long Island.

Accommodations
Bridge Inn Hotel and Restaurant Tel: 242-342-3013 • Fax: 342-3041   Rooms from $70 per day without air conditioning, and from $100 with air conditioning.
Airlines
Bahamasair Tel: 342-2017   Call on day of flights, which are from Nassau on Sunday, Monday, and Wednesday.
Air Sunshine Tel: 342-3117   Flights from Ft. Lauderdale and Sarasota on Monday, Tuesday, Wednesday, and Thursday. Connecting flights to Turks and Caicos, Dominican Republic, San Juan, and USVI.
Cat Island Air Tel: 377-3318   Captain Albert Rolle.

Bakery
McKinney Town Bakery in the pink house   Open from 8 am to 6 pm with fresh bread, coconut pies, Danish pastries, and on weekends, souse, chicken, and fries.

Car Rental
New Bight Service Station   Tel: 342-3014 • VHF 16   Eight cars to rent for $80 per day. If you need one for longer than three days, the rate drops to $70 per day.

Customs Officer
Bradley Dorsett   Tel: 342-2016

Fuel
New Bight Service Station   Tel: 342-3014 • VHF 16   Open 8 am to 6 pm Monday to Saturday. Call ahead if you need to clear in with Customs, buy fuel for your boat, or rent a car. They will truck diesel for boats to Smith Bay, and have diesel and gasoline for cars. Propane tanks can be sent to Nassau.

Gift Shop
Gina's Gift Shop   Tel: 342-3017   Virginia Romer has an interesting selection of gifts, some locally made. Open 7 to 9 am and from 3:30 to 9 pm.

Groceries
New Bight Food Market and Liquor Store   Open 8 am to 7 pm. Groceries, bread, fruit, vegetables, pasta, sodas, small pharmacy.
Romer's Mini Mart   Some groceries, meats, and sodas.

Liquor Store
Harry Bethel's Wholesale Liquor Store

Police
Tel: 342-3039   Office open from 8 am to 5:30 pm.

Post Office
In the administration building with the police and Tourist Information Office.

Propane
Tanks have to be sent to Nassau on the mailboat to be filled, so will take a week to return.

Restaurants and Bars
Blue Bird Restaurant and Bar   Tel: 342-3095/3023   A delightful, small restaurant by the water, run by three sisters, Neacker, Grace, and Jennie (the latter sadly had a stroke just before we visited last time but is making good progress). Open from 8:30 am for breakfast, lunch, and dinner. Dinner reservations requested three hours ahead. Excellent Bahamian food with special fish dinners and souse at weekends. Closed Sundays.
Bridge Inn Motel and Restaurant   Tel: 342-3013   Breakfast, lunch, and dinner daily, featuring fresh seafood, garden-picked vegetables, and tropical fruits. Barbecue night on Fridays.

Derek's wood carvings.

Sailing Club Bar and Restaurant   Open from 9 am to 9 pm, serving Bahamian dishes. Dancing Friday and Saturday nights, closed Sundays.

Telephone
Batelco   Tel: 342-3060   Card phone at the *Batelco* office, behind the police station.

Tourist Information Office
Next to the post office in the administration building.

SOUTHERN CAT ISLAND
New Bight to Hawk's Nest

In years gone by, **The Village** was the end of the railroad used to bring farm produce to the port for export. There is little to be seen of it now, since many miles of rail track were torn up and shipped to England to produce armaments during WWII.

At **Old Bight** you will find St. Mary's Church, donated by Governor Balfour, who read the Emancipation Proclamation, standing as a monument to Emancipation. There are still ruins of former plantations to be seen east of the settlement, and St. Francis of Assisi Catholic Church, another of Father Jerome's churches. Opposite the *Pass Me Not Bar*, stop by to see Winiefred Rolle, who has some of the best straw work in the Islands. And a little further south, woodcarver Derek Wells carves wonderful fish and birds from tamarind wood, opposite the *Peter Hill Bar and Restaurant*. You will find *Dawkins Food Store, Hart's Convenience,* and *BJ's Payless* along the way, and a new restaurant at the beach called *Beaches Delight*.

On the remote east coast, *The Greenwood Inn Beach Resort* (Tel and fax: 242-342-3053) has 20 beachfront rooms on an eight-mile-long beach with good elkhorn coral for snorkeling, and the only full dive facilities on the island. Rooms start from $79 for a single in high season, with MAP an additional $40 a day. Alfresco dining overlooking the beach. German is spoken, as well as English and other European languages.

HAWK'S NEST

Reached by a bumpy road overland from **McQueen's**, Hawk's Nest is unique in that it joins the exclusive list of the small Bahamian resorts that offer both their own private airfield, and a full marina for visiting boats. It has the advantage of a large, dramatic site, with tiny secluded beaches and some brilliant snorkeling and diving off the point, as well as the amenities of the resort. Whether you arrive by sea or by air, nothing is too much trouble for your hosts, Curtis and Patti Clark.

MARINA

HAWK'S NEST RESORT AND MARINA
Tel: 242-342-7050 • Fax: 342-7051 • VHF 16

This sheltered marina, far up the creek and cut out of mangroves, has hurricane-protection potential, although on still days it can be hot and airless. This minus factor is entirely offset by the benefit of the *Hawk's Nest Resort*, built near the site of a seventeenth-century settlement, only a short walk away, with its bar, good restaurant, friendly staff, and air-conditioned rooms if you want them. Please use holding tanks; they have no pump-out facility, and the creek is slow to clean itself. Pets are welcome, so long as they are on a leash off your boat and, on their early morning walks, use the wooded area away from the marina. Plans are going ahead to create extra slips, as well as a Tiki Hut and Bar, which makes this a well-appointed, small marina.

Slips	8
Moorings	5 just up the creek past the marina, $10 per night.

Max LOA	100 ft.
MLW at Dock	7 ft.
Dockage	$1 per ft. per day, minimum $50 from April 1st to July 30th.
Power	39¢ per kWh for 50A and 100A. No 30A power, but a splitter is available.
Fuel	Diesel and gasoline
Propane	Tanks can be filled for $25 at Port Howe.
Water	25¢ per gallon, filtered well water.
Telephone	Card phone outside the hotel; phone cards available from the bar.
Showers	Cold shower free at the marina, $3 for a hot shower at the hotel.
Laundry	$2.50 each for washers and dryers.
Restaurant	At the hotel. Make your dinner reservations by 2 pm if possible. There are golf carts available if the walk over to the restaurant seems too far!
Provisions	The best grocery store is *New Bight Food Market* at New Bight. If you run short of something, Patti may be able to help you from their own stores at the hotel.
Fresh Foods	Local fruit and vegetables, as well as freshly baked breads, are brought into the marina on Thursday evenings.
Ice	$3.50 per bag.
Marina Store	The new ship's store at the marina is a mini *West Marine*. Well stocked in a modest way with all sorts of boat essentials.
Straw Market	One of the basket ladies can be called in to the marina.
Fishing Guide	Nathaniel Gilbert "Top Cat" from Devil's Point.
Tennis	Tennis and badminton courts at the hotel.
Credit Cards	Visa and MasterCard accepted, with a 2-percent discount for cash.

SERVICES

Accommodations
Hawk's Nest Resort Tel: 242-342-7050 • Fax: 342-7051 Ten ocean-view rooms from $140 per night, double occupancy, year round. If your boat is in the marina the room charge is $100 per night for up to 4 people. There is also a house that can sleep 6 people, on the point of land overlooking the creek and the ocean, that can be rented for $2,200 per week, or $370 per night.

Airfield
At *Hawk's Nest Resort*
4,600-foot hard-surfaced air strip for private and charter aircraft. Hawk's Nest is not a Port of Entry. The nearest public airport with Customs and Immigration is at New Bight.

Boat Rental
There is a 35-ft. Viking, a 25-ft. Dusky, a 26-ft. Nautica inflatable with dual outboards, and a Caribe with a 15-hp outboard available to rent, as well as four kayaks.

Doctor
Smith's Bay Clinic 342-3026

Restaurant and Bar
Hawk's Nest Resort Curtis and Bryan are now the master chefs in the kitchen. A wide selection of American, Bahamian, and Italian meals are served in the attractive dining room, which opens for breakfast, lunch, and dinner. Tables of like-minded guests are matched up after cocktails before dinner, or you can dine alone. Catch of the day may be served at dinner, imaginatively presented. Reservations are requested for dinner by 2 pm. If you are at anchor off Hawk's Nest, call ahead on

VHF 16 to make your reservations; you can bring your dinghy right up on their beach.

SPORTS

Diving
Greenwood Dive Center at the *Greenwood Inn*   Tel: 342-3053
Three guided dives daily, with shore diving from the beach. Two dive boats, with only ten people aboard each one. Rental equipment and instruction in both German and English.
Hawk's Nest Resort Tel: 357-7257 Equipment and boats for rent, but no full-time instruction classes.

Dive Sites
Other than *Tartar Bank* and *Devil's Point*, most of the favorite dive sites are off Port Howe. Many of these are dropoffs, going down to 230 feet with huge black coral bushes, some with sharks, such as *The Cave* and *Big Blue*. *Tartar Bank* is absolutely spectacular, but it is about 16 miles offshore from *Devil's Point*, and you need calm seas. The *Devil's Point* is another brilliant site, closer in shore, where the wall drops off very quickly, and there are masses of fish and sea fans.

Fishing
Excellent bonefishing on the west side of Cat Island.

Fishing Guides
All the resorts offer fishing, but there are also some guides:

Orange Creek	Lincoln & Willard Cleare	Tel: 354-4143
The Cove	Jeffrey Smith	Tel: 342-2029
Smith's Bay	Jeffrey Smith	Tel: 342-2029
Devil's Point	Nathaniel Gilbert	Tel: 342-7003
Port Howe	Charles Zonicle	Tel: 342-5005/5011

THINGS TO DO IN CAT ISLAND

- Make time to climb the rough track leading out of **New Bight** up Comer Hill (Mount Alvernia) to see the Hermitage built by Father Jerome. There are steep steps as you approach, with hand-carved stations of the cross, but the 360-degree view from the top is well worth the short climb, especially at sunset.

- Attend the annual *Cat Island Regatta* in August, with sailboat races at The Bight, and lots of rake and scrape, festivities, and fun. Call Philip McPhee at 394-0445 for details.

- Go around to **Port Howe** and **Bailey Town**, the most historic area on the island. In pirate days it was ringed by fortresses against such infamous brigands as Augustino Black and Blackbeard, Black Caesar and Josephus, and American privateers. The Deveaux plantation, the house of which still stands, is sadly in ruins. (See our **History of the Bahamas** in the **Green Pages**).

Janet Wilson

- Enjoy some of the best fishing and diving in the islands, and some of the most interesting people.

RUM CAY

At one time way off the beaten track, Rum Cay is now becoming an increasingly popular cruising destination. When you could only anchor off, exposed to weather, few boaters stopped here, but the new *Sumner Point Marina* has now made all the difference. Although there are only fifty-two residents, traces of an earlier prosperity can still be found dating from the days of salt production. It is believed that the name Rum Cay derives, of course, from a ship wrecked off the shore while carrying that precious cargo. The diving off the Rum Cay reefs, largely unexplored, places Rum Cay as one of the premier dive destinations in the Bahamas. But beware, you must be self-sufficient. For snorkelers, the inshore coral, with some superb coral heads and elkhorn, is some of the best we've seen. For sport fisherman, there are blue marlin, tuna, and record-size wahoo. *Sumner Point Marina*, where Jon Jones and Bobby and Jeni Little will give you a warm welcome, is very much in service, and still expanding. This small, family-run marina has possibly the greatest potential and enthusiasm of any marina in the Bahamas. Slowly but surely they are developing the site into a first-class marina. What is there now is a delightful welcome, from them and their fifteen cats and four dogs, and a well-decorated restaurant serving delicious, imaginative dinners. Call ahead on VHF 16 for instructions and any help you may need entering, and also to check that they do have space available.

MARINA

SUMNER POINT MARINA
Tel: 242-331-2923 • Fax: 331-2824 • VHF 16

Slips	16
Moorings	No mooring buoys, but space for 20 boats inside the marina, Mediterranean moored. The charge is 50¢ per foot per day.
Max LOA	140 ft.
MLW at Dock	7 ft.
Dockage	95¢ per foot per day.
Power	$25 per day for 50A, $15 per day for 30A
Fuel	Diesel and gasoline. The fuel dock is open from 10 am to 4 pm daily.
Water	30¢ per gallon.
Telephones	There is a US-direct-dial phone at the marina, and a *Batelco* card phone at the town dock.
Laundry	Arrangements can be made.
Restaurant	Open daily for excellent dinners and fun. Make your reservations before 4:30 pm, either by calling up on VHF 16, or by writing your names on the chalkboard outside. The restaurant is beautifully decorated, with hand-painted tables and stenciled bar decoration. The menu consists of daily fresh-baked bread, two different appetizers and an entree for about $30.
Ice	$5 per bag.
Trash	On the east side of the building, in the painted cans. For marina guests only, please.
Repairs	Limited service available.
Compressor	Air tank refills available.
Aircraft	Private charters available, call ahead for details.
Accommodations	One-bedroom, air-conditioned studio available, and a two-bedroom cottage. Call ahead for details.
Credit Cards	Visa, MasterCard, checks; 6-percent discount for cash.
Dockmasters	Bobby, Jeni, or Jon will guide you in over the radio if you need help, and will welcome you when you arrive.

SERVICES & SHOPPING IN PORT NELSON

You can walk to **Port Nelson** from the marina in 10–15 minutes.

Churches
St. Christopher's Anglican Church
St. John's Baptist Church
Both have 11 am services on Sundays.

Groceries
Last Chance Market Open 9 am to 4 pm daily.
Terry Strachan's One Stop Shop Open 9 am to 5 pm Monday to Saturday.

Mailboat
M/V Lady Francis calls weekly from Nassau.

Post Office
In the government building.

Restaurants
Kayes Restaurant Open daily, but call ahead on VHF 16. Last meal served at 8 pm, but bar will stay open.
Ocean View Restaurant Ruby and Ted Bain open daily, but call ahead on VHF 16 for dinner reservations.
Sumner Point Marina Restaurant Open daily for dinner, serving Jon's New World Caribbean Cuisine. Make your reservations by 4:30 pm, please; the menu changes daily.

Telephone
Batelco office at the foot of the *Batelco* tower and a card phone at the town dock.

Variety Store
Hermie Bain's Variety Store With a little of everything.

DIVE SITES

Grandpa Grouper is a deep wall site, over 230 feet, *The Chimney* has a 100-foot vertical shaft; and *Barracuda Junction* are all at the edge of the dropoff on the southeast corner of Rum Cay. *Snowfields*, on the western tip of the island, is good for snorkeling, and the two wrecks, *HMS Conqueror* opposite Sumner Point and the *Tatoo Express* off Gin Hill on the north side of the island, are both interesting and sufficiently shallow for snorkeling given perfect weather conditions.

THINGS TO DO IN RUM CAY

- Dive or snorkel some of the best and least-known reefs in the islands.
- Go for a walk around the settlement of Port Nelson. Its sand roads are attractive, and you are seeing the real Bahamas as every island once was.
- Explore the wreck of the Royal Navy's first steam-powered ship, *HMS Conqueror*, which sank in 1862 in 30 feet of water off Sumner Point. See our picture on page 283.
- Ask Bobby Little to take you surfing on the eastern shore of Rum Cay!

SAN SALVADOR

San Salvador needs no introduction as the island that is widely believed to have been the first landfall of Columbus in the New World. With its deserted beaches and spectacular wall dives, it boasts some of the finest diving year round, with normal visibility between 100 and 200 feet, as well as museums and historic monuments to mark the 1492 arrival of the European Discoverer of the Americas. Cockburn Town (pronounced *Coburn* Town), is a Port of Entry. **Customs** (331-2131) and **Immigration** (331-2100) are here if you need to clear in, and can be called from *Riding Rock Inn* on VHF 16 when you arrive.

MARINA

RIDING ROCK INN RESORT AND MARINA
Tel: 954-359-8353 or 242-331-2631 or 800-373-1492
• VHF 16 and 6 • E-mail: ridingrock@aol.com

Slips	10, with space for 4 sailboats at the south end of the marina.
Max LOA	110 ft.
MLW at Dock	6.5 ft, at low water.
Dockage	90¢ per ft. per day, or $5.40 per ft. per week.
Power	$10 per day up to 40 ft., $15 per day to 50 ft., $20 per day over 50 ft.
Fuel	Diesel and gasoline available. Fuel dock open 9 am to 4 pm daily.
Propane	Will be available from Shell in Cockburn Town.
Water	$10 per day up to 40 ft., $15 per day to 50 ft., $18 per day over 50 ft.
Showers	Yes
Laundry	$2 tokens for washer or dryer.
Restaurant	At the *Riding Rock Inn,* a short walk from the marina.
Ice	$3 a bag.
Bicycles	$6.50 for a half day, $10 for a full day from the *Riding Rock Inn.*
Rental Cars	$85 per day also from the *Riding Rock Inn.*
Diving	*Riding Rock Divers* on site, with three boats and three dives daily, dive shop and rental gear.
Swimming	Freshwater pool
Tennis	Court available
Accommodations	*Riding Rock Inn* has poolside and oceanfront rooms, as well as beach villas.
Credit cards	US checks drawn on US funds payable 30 days in advance to hold booking; then Visa, MasterCard, Amex, Discover, or Diners cards accepted.
Dockmaster	Chris McLaughlin, who is also a dive instructor and runs the dive operation with his team, from the marina.

SERVICES & SHOPPING IN COCKBURN TOWN

Accommodations
Club Med Columbus Isle, two miles north of town Tel: 242-331-2000 From $1,050 to $1,700 per person per week; requires advance booking.
Riding Rock Inn Tel: 1-800-272-1492 or 954-359-8353 • Fax: 954-359-8254 Single, double, triple, and quad rooms, as well as poolside or oceanfront rooms and newly refurbished villas, from $110 per night. Breakfast $11, lunch $14, and dinner $27 daily.

Bank
Bank of the Bahamas Tel: 331-2237 Open from 9 am to 3 pm on Fridays.

Churches
Holy Saviour Catholic Church, painted pink, by the Museum.
Church of God Prophecy
St. Augustine Anglican Church

Clinic
The new clinic is a little way out of Cockburn Town beyond the airport, open 9 am to 5:30 pm Monday to Friday, with a delivery room, three-bed male and female wards, an x-ray machine, morgue, and their own ambulance. Nurse Burrows (Tel: 331-2109) and Nurse Lewis assist Dr Sidney Smith, who can be called in an emergency at 331-2033. A dentist comes to the island every two months.

Drug Store
J's Discount Drugs Tel: 331-2570

General Store
Laramore's Tel: 331-2282 Open Monday to Saturday from 9 am to 5:30 pm.
Jake Jones Food Store

Library
On the corner of First Avenue, open 4 to 6 pm Monday, Thursday, and Saturday.

Museums
New World Museum, about 3 miles north of *Riding Rock Marina* at North Victoria Hill, is now, sadly, hardly worth a visit. It used to contain a small collection of Lucayan pottery.

San Salvador Museum, next to the Catholic Church in Cockburn Town. This former jail was turned into a small, two-room museum devoted to a Columbus display and some Lucayan artifacts. Ask at *Batelco* to have it opened.

Police
Tel: 331-2010, or 331-2919 in an emergency. Office open from 9 am to 5:30 pm Monday to Friday.

Restaurants and Bars

Club Med Columbus Isle Tel: 331-2000 Just north of town, will take reservations for dinner if they have space available.

Harlem Square Club Bar and wholesale liquor. An island "Rip" is held on Friday nights.

Riding Rock Inn Restaurant and *Driftwood Bar* Tel: 331-2631 The appropriately decorated *Driftwood Bar* is open from 11 am daily, alongside the waterfront restaurant of the hotel. Breakfast costs $11, lunch $14 (served at 12:30 pm), and dinner is $27. Lunch includes soup, homemade bread, entree, dessert, and coffee or tea. Dinner includes a glass of wine, soup, salad, entree, homemade Bahamian bread, dessert, and coffee or tea.

The Three Ships Restaurant and Bar Tel: 331-278 • VHF 6 Breakfast, lunch, and dinner.

Telephones

There is a telephone at the dock, one at the *Riding Rock Inn,* and at *Batelco* in town. The *Batelco* office is open 9 am to 5 pm Monday to Friday.

GETTING AROUND

Airport

Newly completed 8,500-foot paved runway, with Avgas and Jet A fuel usually available. This is a Port of Entry.

Airlines

Both the *Club Med* and *Riding Rock Inn* charter in their dive groups, usually on Saturday mornings from Fort Lauderdale or Miami, for around $300 round trip. Divers on a pre-paid package are only allowed 70 lbs of baggage; all others are limited to 44 lbs. Excess baggage may be carried on a space-available basis for $1 per lb.

Bahamasair Tel: 331-2631 Daily flights to Nassau; Thursday and Sunday flights to Miami.

American Eagle Tel: 331-2076 Operate the charter service for *Club Med* flights on weekends.

Bicycles

Riding Rock Inn Tel: 331-2631 $6.50 for a half day, $10 for a full day.

Mailboat

M/V Lady Francis leaves Nassau on Tuesdays and arrives in Cockburn Town on either Wednesday or Thursday.

Rental Cars

Riding Rock Inn Tel: 331-2631 From $85 per day.

Scooters

K's Scooters Tel: 331-2125 At the airport.

Taxis

Available at *Riding Rock Inn* and the airport.

DIVING

Club Med Columbus Isle Tel: 331-2458 Have their own dive boats and schedule.

Riding Rock Divers Tel: 331-2631 An experienced team leading three dive trips daily on their three boats. Two-tank dive $60. Snorkelers $20. Open water certification, underwater photography courses, camera and video rentals. Dive shop with full rental equipment, T-shirts and more, with a photo shop and meeting room within the marina. No airfills. Dive packages available through the *Riding Rock Inn,* from $1,070 per diver for 8 days, 7 nights, and 18 dives. Call 800-272-1492 in the US for more details.

Dive sites

All these dive sites are within easy reach of *Riding Rock Marina:*

Riding Rock Wall, with a 66-foot drop off the wall.

Telephone Pole, where you might be lucky enough to meet Oscar, a friendly grouper who likes to pose for underwater portraits.

Vicky's Reef and *Snapshot Reef*, both good for photography.

Devil's Claw with its wire corals, groups of chubs, and shark sightings.

Shangri La with depths from 40 to 230 feet, and *Frascate Wreck*, which lies strewn over a large area, from the British freighter *Frascate,* that sank in 1902.

Off the southwestern shores of San Salvador you will find *Double Caves,* an exciting cave dive; *La Crevasse*, with huge vertical crevasses; *Dr John's*, where the wall drops 130 feet from 40 feet; and *Great Cut.*

Reef Survey

At the old navy base field station at North Point, the *Earthwatch Institute* has a study center for monitoring and testing water temperatures, and photographing and mapping selected reefs in order to determine the reason for coral bleaching. Dr Garriet Smith, from the University of South Carolina in Aiken, directs the center with Tom McGrath, who has written an article for this guide (see page 404). If you want to help with the project, which takes place in February, July, and November, contact the *Earthwatch Institute*, 680 Mount Auburn Street, Box 9104, Watertown, MA 02272. Tel: 800-776-0188.

REGATTA

October

San Salvador Sailing Regatta For more information, call Rev. Philip McPhee at 242-394-0445.

THINGS TO DO IN SAN SALVADOR

- Walk the Long Bay beach where Columbus and his sailors are believed to have landed in their longboat more than five centuries ago. You can swim and snorkel, and there is a monument placed on the floor of the ocean in Long Bay marking the exact spot where Columbus dropped anchor on October 12th, 1492. You can photograph the simple white Columbus Cross erected in 1956, and the Mexican Olympic Monument close by; it's only three miles out of Cockburn Town.

- Visit Watling's Castle, actually the ruins of an eighteenth-century Loyalist plantation, and the lookout tower at Sandy Point Estate, which was built to spot any unfortunate ship that ran aground on the reefs below.

- On the east coast of the island, the mouth of Pigeon Creek is good for shelling and snorkeling, and further north, past Snow Bay Beach with its views of High Cay and the white sand beach, you come to the Pigeon Creek archaeological site. This was one of the largest Arawak Indian villages in the Bahamas, people who thought Columbus and his men were gods from the sky, and were later carried off by the Spanish to work in the mines of Cuba and Haiti.

- Further north, the Chicago Herald Monument poses the question as to how Columbus could possibly have anchored off in the maze of reefs there, and planted his cross in honor of Spain? And at Dixon Hill, visible for 19 miles, the lighthouse is still lit by a kerosene light that has to be refilled by hand twice nightly. You can visit the lighthouse.

- Dive, dive, and dive again!

Chapter 17
Long Island

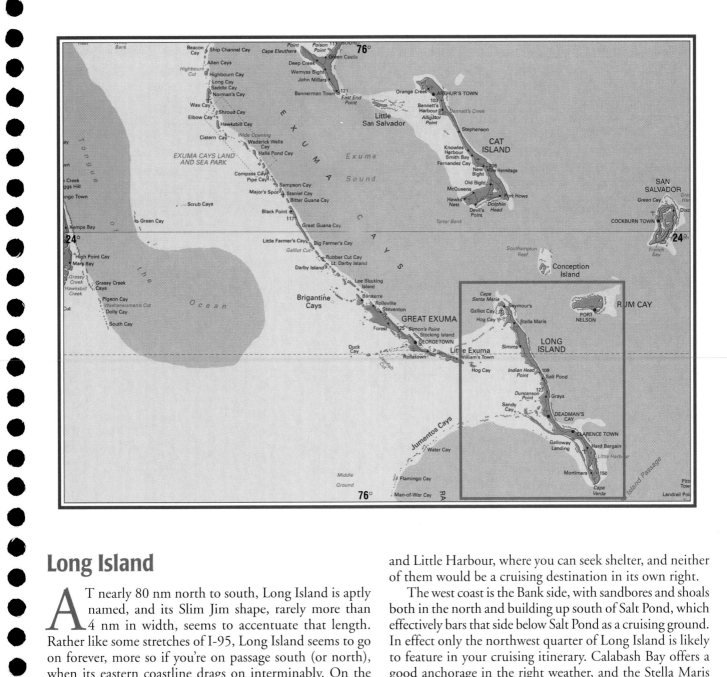

Long Island

AT nearly 80 nm north to south, Long Island is aptly named, and its Slim Jim shape, rarely more than 4 nm in width, seems to accentuate that length. Rather like some stretches of I-95, Long Island seems to go on forever, more so if you're on passage south (or north), when its eastern coastline drags on interminably. On the island itself, perhaps it's the constriction of that narrow width, but there's little there in terms of major settlement.

Geography has dictated that Long Island was not dealt a favorable hand in cruising terms. Your negotiation of Cape Santa Maria, the northern tip of Long Island, requires caution and understanding. The east coast is rocky, steep, and weather beaten, best held at arm's length well offshore. All along that coastline there are only two places, Clarence Town

and Little Harbour, where you can seek shelter, and neither of them would be a cruising destination in its own right.

The west coast is the Bank side, with sandbores and shoals both in the north and building up south of Salt Pond, which effectively bars that side below Salt Pond as a cruising ground. In effect only the northwest quarter of Long Island is likely to feature in your cruising itinerary. Calabash Bay offers a good anchorage in the right weather, and the Stella Maris Resort and Marina, some 6 nm south of Calabash, is well worth visiting. Another 15 nm further on Salt Pond, host to the annual Long Island Regatta, will probably be as far south as you will wish to venture down the western shore.

At first sight you might be inclined to write off Long Island as a potential destination as you plan your Bahamas cruise itinerary. The passage maker, heading south to the Caribbean or returning north from there, is almost certainly going to mark Clarence Town as a possible port-of-call, more so if the proposed marina developments, or even one of them, now on the books for Clarence Town achieve reality. What about the cruising visitor?

The attractions are simply these. Long Island has a unique character and attraction. It's a place that has developed in its own way and keeps its ways. Its quiet, self-reliant people depend on agriculture not only for themselves, but as a major export to the rest of the Bahamas. Their environment is better tended. Their friendliness (you raise your hand in greeting to everyone you meet as you travel the Queen's Highway) is, even in the friendly Bahamas, something you'll not have encountered elsewhere. Long Island has always made its way in the world, primarily through agriculture, but lately there is a new feeling of optimism abroad. Power lines, telephone services, and tax breaks for new construction, as in many islands, has produced a renaissance.

In Long Island the advent of tourists other than those tied to the two resorts, essentially small groups bent on bonefishing, has encouraged a new growth in "small inn" and apartment accommodations, small restaurants, renters of cars (no agencies yet!), and the like. Those who come express surprise and delight at the quietude, lack of stress, ease, and trust apparent in Long Island life. In short, doors are left unlocked. We can think of many places where the reverse is true.

What is there for you? The settlements are spread out and hardly likely to grab your heart but the churches all along the way are stunning, white with red shutters, and white with blue shutters, ranging from wayside chapel size to full parish church, fit for a major wedding. Each one is quite unique, the focal building, and the pride, of each community. And there are the Father Jerome churches (of Cat Island fame), some six in all, of which the Clarence Town churches are a "Must See."

Cape Santa Maria, seen from the land, is a stunning white cliff, with a "to-die-for" beach tucked around the corner to the east. Calabash Bay is dream world. The diving offered by Stella Maris is legendary. Geographically, at first sight, Long Island can disappoint. There are very few good beaches on the Atlantic side. It's all rock and inshore reef. The western side is flats. Mangrove and sand for the most part. But the bonefishing of the western flats is unequalled. And there's the Salt Pond Regatta, caves to explore, and blue holes to be seen. We reckon it's worth going there. Where will you go? Just read on and decide. Rather like visiting Cat Island, the ideal plan is to find the place where you are content to leave your boat while you are sightseeing, and rent a car.

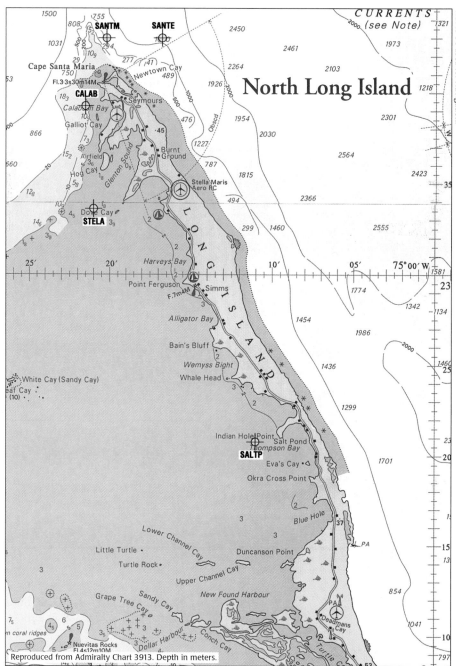

Reproduced from Admiralty Chart 3913. Depth in meters.

The North of Long Island

Cape Santa Maria

The northern point of Long Island, Cape Santa Maria, is dangerous. Reefs surround the cape and run out for a mile north of it, and a bank with barely 50 feet of water extends a further two miles offshore. As the surrounding ocean has depths averaging 6,000 feet, you can understand that savage breaking seas can develop around this cape even under conditions of moderate swell. For this reason we set our Cape Santa Maria waypoint 1.5 nm north of the reefs, close to the northern limit of this bank. In bad weather we'd add another mile north to this, and for a night passage, for prudence, add one more mile of northing.

If you are turning south down the east coast of Long Island, it's prudent to take our Cape Santa Maria East waypoint as your turning point, for this will give you some 2 nm offing at the outset as you run down the Long Island coastline. Your actual course obviously depends on your destination. If you're coming up from the south and heading for George Town or the shelter of Calabash Bay, the natural temptation to round the cape within a mile or so is hard to resist, but **don't** do it. Stand well out. Our Cape Santa Maria East waypoint is a good one to choose to keep you well off the reefs and the Santa Maria shoal.

Cape Santa Maria itself is easily recognizable (it is, after all, the only land in sight) and the light stands on the top of a prominent white cliff. It is around this cape, if you're outward bound, that you'll meet ocean swells and waves for the first time. You will also experience a strong set to the northwest, particularly if you are heading for Conception Island or Rum Cay, and your cross track error can build up rapidly unless you take this into account early in the passage.

Cape Santa Maria.

CAPE SANTA MARIA AND THE COLUMBUS MONUMENT

The closest anchorage from which you can visit Cape Santa Maria and explore the north of Long Island, or indeed the whole of Long Island, is the Cape Santa Maria Beach Resort on Calabash Bay (more detail later). From there, in your rental car, make your way past their airstrip to the Queen's Highway (the Long Island north–south road) and turn left. You enter the hilltop settlement of Seymours, and turn off the road at a sign "Columbus Monument." From there rough track (in parts very rough, trucks or 4WD, unless you're prepared to wreck someone's car) takes you 1.7 miles to the base of the Santa Maria headland.

LONG ISLAND NORTH		
Cape Santa Maria		
SANTM	23° 43' 00"/000 N	075° 20' 30"/500 W
Cape Santa Maria East		
SANTE	23° 43' 00"/000 N	075° 17' 00"/000 W
Calabash Bay		
CALAB	23° 39' 15"/250 N	075° 21' 39"/656 W
Stella Maris (not for navigation)		
STELA	23° 33' 30"/500 N	075° 21' 00"/000 W
Salt Pond (not for navigation)		
SALTP	23° 21' 00"/000 N	075° 11' 00"/000 W

The final figures in each waypoint show seconds (00") and thousands (000) of a minute.

Cape Santa Maria, from the north.

Stella Maris Marina entry channel.

The Columbus Monument, a 1989 construction, is high and in front of you, together with the Cape Santa Maria light. Walk the lagoon beach around to your right to get a better view of the cliff and the memorial before you climb up there, and as a warning not to get too close to the cliff edge while you are up there! Sadly the memorial has lost its inscription, a dedication not only to Columbus but also a late apology to the indigenous people of Long Island. The beach we first mentioned is a great swimming and picnic spot.

If you want to continue to the north end of the Queen's Highway you'll find the road ends at the eastern mouth of the lagoon, a narrow neck of mangrove swamp crossed by a small footbridge. You've gone as far as you can go.

Calabash Bay

Calabash Bay, some 2 nm to the southwest of Cape Santa Maria, an attractive temporary haven from prevailing winds, has to be entered through its fringing reefs. The entry passage is not difficult, but requires care and attention. We suggest a Calabash Bay waypoint as a indicator, but don't make a compass course serve as a rigid leg. From roughly the position we suggest, initially point toward the north end of Galliott Cay and settle to latitude sailing along 23° 39' 15"/250 N, or thereabouts, on a heading of 090°M until you're through the reefs. But remember this is eyeballing, not a straight-line guaranteed safe course. Once through the reef you can anchor where you will. There's good depth, 15 feet going down to 9 feet, as you move in toward the beach.

Slightly further south, following much the same "feel-your-way-in" technique, you can find some good places to tuck yourself up close to Hog Cay.

CAPE SANTA MARIA BEACH RESORT

The Canadian-built and operated Cape Santa Maria Beach

Resort, right on Galliot Cay at Calabash Bay, is holding itself deliberately small (twenty rooms) with its accent on the last two words of its title. It's well planned, well built, and well run, certainly up in the top rank of its kind. While it is in no way seeking to tempt cruising visitors, if you are anchored off you may take meals there and use the bar and the lobby telephones. If you dive, they have a compressor to fill your tanks. If you want to go fishing, or diving, they can arrange it. If you want a rental car, they will fix it for you. And of course if you want shoreside accommodations, subject to their bookings, they can provide it.

If your crew changes are air-charter dependent, they have a 2,600-foot airstrip, and Stella Maris airport, with Bahamasair service, is about half an hour down the road. See our **Yellow Pages** for details. Play their open-door policy with sense, discretion, and gratitude. Don't impinge on their living space, or their quietude. Tread gently and softly, and we, the cruising community, may always be welcome there.

STELLA MARIS

The Stella Maris Marina, an adjunct of the Stella Maris Resort, lies under a protective hook of shoal water just south of Dove Cay. After passing about 500 yards to the west of Dove Cay make sure you clear the shoal (known as White Sand Bank) to port, and turn on to a heading of 090°M keeping the shoal on your port side. Our Stella Maris waypoint may be helpful as an indicator. About 1 nm after your turn you'll pick up the Stella Maris marks, and follow the deeper water channel into the marina. Stella Maris can take only twelve boats and much of this space may be taken up by Stella Maris regulars. Call ahead.

Once you are in the Stella Maris Marina you're in the hands of a very competent German-managed upscale resort organization, primarily centered on the Stella Maris Resort, which nestles on the limestone spine of Long Island about

Stella Maris Marina.

Millerton church.

2.5 miles to the northeast. Their specialty has long been diving, and in a sense, the marina is both the child of this specialization and a vital support facility for it. They have a compressor there, but more importantly a marine railway haul-out that can take boats 75–80 feet LOA and a beam of 25 feet (which counts in most catamarans). Above this, their boat shops are there to carry out virtually any task, and replacement parts can be ordered and flown in to Stella Maris from Florida within 48 hours.

Our **Yellow Pages** tell you the rest of it. All you have to remember is that the entry channel, which is marked, carries 4.8 feet at MLW. The marina has 5 feet at MLW.

As for the Resort itself, again our **Yellow Pages** tell the story. By and large just about everything you might require is there if you wish to make use of their facilities. Rooms, restaurant, bar, rental cars, rental scooters, and the airport with its scheduled and charter services. With the airport comes all the facilities of an entry port, plus a bank, post office, and a snack bar. A general store lies not far distant, and, near the marina, a restaurant named Potcakes.

The Tropic of Cancer

If you're touring Long Island by road, stop in Simms, a tiny settlement south of Stella Maris. For two reasons. The first is that the tropic of Cancer, that magic 23° 30' line, passes right through it. So that places you in the real tropics, not the subtropics, and the next line down (admittedly out of reach in your rental car, but in reach if you take your boat?) is the equator. The second is that the administrative center of Simms has to be seen to be believed. A neat quadrangle of pink one-story buildings, the administrator's office, a post office, the police station, the magistrates court, and, right by it, Her Majesty's Prison. The Batelco office, close by, has clearly declared independence and painted itself yellow. The Simms churches, active and ruined, are also interesting.

Further south, Salt Pond, the home port of a sizeable fishing fleet, is more difficult to compass with its broad

sweep, and normally much preoccupied with its principal business. At regatta time it's a different story. Deadman's Cay, still mainland Long Island despite that name, is so spread out that it's hard to define its start and finish. If you want banks, Bahamasair, Batelco, or general provisioning, most things are there. But one feature of Long Island is the well-stocked (we're talking of staples now) general stores that come up regularly, every five or six miles or so. You'll not die of thirst or hunger, but watch that fuel gauge. You can get gas at only Burnt Ground (north of Stella Maris), at the Stella Maris Marina, in Sims, at Salt Pond, and Deadman's Cay.

SALT POND

Salt Pond is the best-protected anchorage on the west coast of Long Island, although it's wide open to the west. The clutch of small cays off the settlement offer limited local shelter if the wind works into the west, and all the Salt Pond boats not riding to all-weather moorings migrate from one side to another, playing the cays to advantage. It could be crowded bunching up there with the local boats.

Salt Pond was hit hard by Hurricane *Lily* but has rebuilt and is back on line in all respects with fuel, water, and all the normal shoreside facilities, including an excellent marine store, that you expect to find in a settlement devoted to being the support base for a fishing fleet and the hosts of the annual Long Island Regatta. However, other than coming alongside to take on fuel or to take on supplies, there are no marina facilities in Salt Pond. You are unlikely to want to stay long there, although the proximity of Deadman's Cay airport with its Bahamasair service may be worth noting. See our **Yellow Pages**.

Calabash Bay.

The South of Long Island

Clarence Town

Clarence Town has long had a reputation of being one of the best-kept settlements in the Bahamas, as well as the site of two Father Jerome churches, each as interesting, and as different, as his Cat Island Mount Alvernia Hermitage. There's no doubt that Clarence Town itself has a spectacular site with its twin hills and surrounding limestone ridges fronting a harbor partly shielded from the Atlantic by outlying cays and rocks. It's a surprise and a delight, coming in by sea or by land, and most people are taken by Clarence Town at first sight. In marine terms though, despite its Government Dock (the linchpin of South Long Island trade), Clarence Town has been no more than a "possible" diversion stop. Firstly because there have been no facilities for passage making or cruising visitors, and secondly its anchorage, which with anything bad coming in from the Atlantic, can be adrenaline producing. Now changes are in the wind. Read on.

As you approach Clarence Town from a mile out it's almost impossible to pick up your bearings, and your orientation comes as you pass the outlying Booby Rock. The anchorage, an ill-defined area off the Government Dock, has an entrance to the north nearly a mile wide, which narrows between reefs to a quarter of this on the line between Strachan Cay and Harbour Point. Initially head to leave Booby Rock well to port, and pick up your bearings when you draw level with Booby Rock (bearing 085°M). You should be about 23° 06' 50"/833 N 074° 57' 30"/500 W

Saints Peter and Paul Church, Clarence Town.

at this point. You'll pick up two landmarks: the white twin-spired (round towers) Catholic church bearing 220°M; and a red-roofed prominent house bearing 195°M.

Steer for the apparent middle of the open channel ahead of you on a course of about 180°M. Your approach line is simply to head for the center of this wide opening, spotting the breaking surf on your starboard bow, and tending to favor that side if you cannot see the reef to port that runs out to the west from the north of Strachan Cay. Treat Harbour Point (aka Lighthouse Point) and Lark Point (the northwest tip of Strachan Cay) as the entry arms to a harbor and stay between them, mindful of their reefs. Just read the water and don't head for the Clarence Town front until you've cleared Harbour Point and have the Government Dock in plain view. That's all there is to it. To make

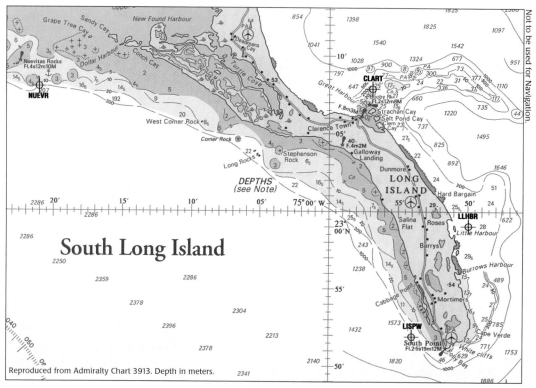

South Long Island

Reproduced from Admiralty Chart 3913. Depth in meters.

LONG ISLAND SOUTH		
Clarence Town		
CLART	23° 08' 00"/000 N	074° 57' 00"/000 W
Little Harbour		
LLHBR	22° 59' 00"/000 N	074° 50' 00"/000 W
Long Island South Point East		
LISPE	22° 51' 00"/000 N	074° 45' 00"/000 W
Long Island South Point West		
LISPW	22° 52' 00"/000 N	074° 54' 00"/000 W

The final figures in each waypoint show seconds (00") and thousands (000) of a minute.

your way out of Clarence Town steer for the house with the palms (the only house) on Strachan Cay at the start, and then turn to port when you're in mid-channel. Steer due north watching out for those reefs. You should have no problems. It's an easy exit.

ANCHORAGES
Clarence Town anchorage owes its protection to this less-than-effective shielding in the north and the line of reef and cays to the east (Booby Rock in the north, with Strachan Cay and others unnamed on the charts), but there's scant shelter from wind other than from the west, and no real protection from wind and surge from northwest through to east. Even southeast weather will bring surge into the anchorage. It is perhaps a timely reminder, if you call in here, that you are now on an Atlantic coast and even distant Atlantic storms may bring heavy ground swell a day or two later into Clarence Town Harbour, with rollers carrying right through the anchorage on to the beach.

Nonetheless Clarence Town is not unvisited, and has an alternative anchorage across the way under the south tip of Strachan Cay, known as Sandy Point, which some prefer. Your depth in the anchorage will be around 8–15 feet, depending on how far you work your way in, and the ground is mostly grass with a few sand hollows, which are the best places to go for. An anchor digs in well there with encouragement, and by that we mean diving. In anything approaching stronger winds (15 knots or more) keep a close check on your position. Many boats have found that they are dragging. When you select your spot, keep clear of the direct approach to the Government Dock, which is used by the mailboat.

GOING ASHORE
Ashore you'll find fuel is on request at the Government Dock, the Harbour Restaurant, Batelco, basic foodstuffs, and the two Father Jerome churches with their twin spires. Visit the churches. Their architecture is remarkable, and both carry their size (unusual in the Out Islands) dominating the settlement as if they were medieval cathedrals sited in a rural village. The Roman Catholic church with its round towers, white paint and blue windows, looks as if it had been lifted from the Greek Cycladic Islands. Inside it's plain, quite unadorned, and simple. In contrast the Anglican church is more ornate, and certainly shows the kind of decoration more normally associated with Catholicism. It's a strange reversal, and both churches, for those who have an interest in such matters, are fascinating.

THE CLARENCE TOWN AREA PROJECTED MARINAS
We've long commented on the total lack of marina facilities south of George Town, and in particular singled out Clarence Town as one place where this void might be most logically first filled. It now seems that the tide in the Clarence Town area may yet turn in the millennium.

Turtle Cove
For some time Turtle Cove, the next bight in the coast north of Clarence Town (on the east coast), has been earmarked as the site of a new housing development in which the ultimate aim is declared to include a hotel, a golf course, and a marina. Two houses have been built. A third is under construction. There have been problems with securing title to the lots offered for sale, and perhaps a slow start is under-

Clarence Town approach, from the east.

Clarence Town Harbour, from the east.

passage to and from the far south of the Bahamas and beyond, and will place the Crooked–Acklins area within the reach of those who are happier breaking their open-water passages into relatively short, weather-window-assured legs.

Our only reservation is the openness of Clarence Town Harbour to weather from the east, and the southeast. That north shore has often taken breaking waves as well as surge. The breakwater will be critical, and 200 feet may not achieve its purpose. We await reports.

CLARENCE TOWN MARINA

A second Clarence Town marina is apparently in the cards and the land is already staked out, the point to the south of the Clarence Town Government Dock. Here plans call for twenty slips, a 100-feet LOA as a maximum, and 15 feet at MLW. Fuel, water, power, and all the standard facilities are to be available, and some eighteen cottages are planned as shoreside accommodations. The name is likely to be the *Clarence Town Marina*, and its completion date sometime in 2000.

We know some of its backers, and don't doubt their determination to go ahead. We believe that the partnership of an oil corporation may be vital, and know that it has been solicited. But more than this we can't tell you.

LITTLE HARBOUR

Little Harbour, some 11 nm south of Clarence Town has been reported as an all-weather anchorage. Once isolated, Little Harbour has now been connected to the main Long Island highway by a rough dirt road, but it remains that the

standable. Our own guess is that the whole project will be a slow mover, each step forward financed, we'd guess again, by property sales and house construction. We'd reckon too that water considerations on an island where rain is vital, are going to rule out that golf course unless they're prepared to go into reverse-osmosis in a big way.

What about the marina? Turtle Cove is shoal draft, shielded only at its southern end by a spine of rock. You'd need to dredge, and you'd need a breakwater, and you'd need an entry channel, and maybe even a kind Atlantic, ready to play pussy cat, to let you get into it. Once again, money counts. Maybe we'll see something when a sizeable number of lots have been sold. Look again in ten years?

LIGHTHOUSE POINT

Work has already started on a projected marina on the north shore of Clarence Town Harbour. Mario Cartwright's plans for his *Flying Fish Marina* call for fourteen slips, a maximum LOA of 100 feet, 8 feet at MLW, and full support services: diesel, gas, water, power, together with ice, provisions, a marine store, and laundry, as well as five apartments. The target date was set as the end of 1999.

At the time we write (April 1999) work on the first shoreside building had reached shoulder height. Vital to the plan is a 200-foot breakwater, seen as following the line of and extending from the Harbour Point/Lighthouse reef, to shield the marina from surge and the worst of bad easterly weather, together with dredging to achieve that 8 feet MLW depth overall.

We're delighted to see it start, and keep our fingers crossed. We all need a facility of this kind on the Atlantic coast, and particularly at Clarence Town, the Long Island halfway mark. It will offer a diversion port to anyone on

Little Harbour, from the south.

Little Harbour, the south entrance, from the east.

closest settlement, on the intersection of the dirt track with the main road, is twenty minutes away by car or truck, although there are two or three isolated houses on the way. Not only is Little Harbour disappointing in its remoteness but, attractive in terms of shelter as it might seem looking at the chart, it fails on most counts as a refuge.

There are three entrances to Little Harbour, of which the southernmost is usable if you favor the north side, but all these entrances break heavily in weather from northeast through to southeast and we wouldn't attempt an entrance (or an exit) in anything other than calm, high-visibility, good-light conditions. Inside Little Harbour shoals totally to the south, and about as far as you get tucked into the southern end is the raw blaze where the newly dozed track ends, but we're talking of 2–3 feet at MLW. Another alternative is to turn north and seek a deeper spot behind the island, but you are in the surge channel here. Bear in mind that even if you entered Little Harbour under ideal conditions, a change of weather could keep you there for anything up to two weeks.

Little Harbour appears to be home to two local fishing boats, both flat bottomed, whose traps are piled on the shore and, when we were there one time, a Performance 40 open cockpit cigarette look-alike with four 250-hp Yamaha outboards on the back, the whole outfit painted something approximate to a non-reflecting Navy grey camouflage. The owners of this remarkable boat take a close interest in visitors. We give Little Harbour as a listing because it is there. Only a dire emergency would lead us to use it.

The South by Road
Continuing south by road from Deadman's Cay your first stop might well be Hamilton's Cave (see our **Yellow Pages**) or the blue hole just south of Turtle Cove. Go into the Turtle Cove development, drive straight to the beach, turn right,

and right again at their beach gazebo. The track you take ends at the Blue Hole Beach. There you can walk ankle deep on fine white sand and leap, almost in one bound, into blue water 660 feet deep. It's something. We reckon that the Turtle Cove–Blue Hole beaches are the best on the Atlantic coast of Long Island. Bar none.

Further on, Clarence Town with its two Father Jerome churches is one place (that's if you haven't arrived in Clarence Town!) you must not miss. Beyond Clarence Town, Lochabar Bay (another blue hole) is a fantastic beach, known for its color, but then, other than a run of small settlements and three more Father Jerome churches, there's little to tempt you further south. But you may want to take in Little Harbour, just to see it. Turn off the Queen's

The Bahamian Sailmaker

MARK KNOWLES of Mangrove Bush in Long Island makes sails for boats. Principally sails for Regatta boats, but he will turn his hand to any sailmaking requirement. Do you want a yardstick to measure the kind of test his sails must stand?

The typical Bahamian "A" Class racing sloop is 28 feet LOA, with a mast height between 55 and 60 feet, a 28–30-foot boom, and a draft between 5 and 6.5 feet. There can be 925 square feet of overstressed canvas up there, with the high-stress points not just doubled over, but sewn through up to five thicknesses of sail cloth. And we're talking old-fashioned canvas. Nothing high tech. The racing rules, bent on the wholly traditional Bahamian boat, won't allow that. The crew of a Class A? Up to fifteen, many of whom, "sitting outboard on a plank" are there for one critical contribution. Body weight.

Mark Knowles is not alone. There are other sailmakers in the Bahamas. But rest assured, if you need to go to one of them, they know their trade.

Ministry of Tourism

Highway at Roses. But remember that your only source of fuel is Clarence Town.

THE KEEL PRINT OF COLUMBUS

Long Island south of Clarence Town may hold little attraction for the land tourist, but the cruising voyager is in waters of great interest. Anciently the indigenous Lucayans were competent inter-island voyagers, and according to Columbus, knew of Crooked Island to the southeast, and the giant, Cuba, to the southwest. Arcing away from mid-Long Island on the western side are the Jumentos Cays, and the Ragged Island Range, which head that way. Nuevitas Rocks at the start of the chain offer a

Turtle Cove, Blue Hole Beach.

safe pass between Great Bahamas Bank water and the ocean on that side, and a straight run to Cuba. On the east side a chain of larger islands, Crooked, Acklins, Mayaguana, and the Turks and Caicos serve as stepping stones to and from the Dominican Republic, Puerto Rico, the Virgin Islands, and the Caribbean.

Columbus sailed these waters on his First "Discovery" Voyage in 1942. Did he sail to the east or the west of Long Island? The experts are certain about his route, but none agree with each other. See our **Green Pages, The Columbus Controversy**.

What about you? We cover this ground in **Part V, Far Horizons**, starting with two link waypoints off the east and west coast of the south of Long Island. Our passages south are routes that the Lucayans, and Columbus (albeit in part) traveled. Come and voyage on with us.

YELLOW PAGES

This area received the full force of Hurricane *Floyd* in September 1999. Be aware that reconstruction and the restoration of normal services after a Category 4 Hurricane may take a considerable period of time to complete.

THE NORTH OF LONG ISLAND

Long Island was called Yuma by the Indians, and Fernandina by Columbus, who described this still largely undeveloped island as "the World's most Beautiful Island." It stretches for more than 80 miles, with farming communities, steep cliffs, and shallow bays, and represents the best of the old, Out Island traditions with its historic churches and long-established, essentially family villages. The beaches of Cape Santa Maria at the northern tip are winners, perfect for beachcombing and exploration. It is such a very long island that it is fun to explore by renting a car; so much of it is not readily accessible from the water. *Stella Maris Airport* is the Port of Entry for Long Island. **Customs and Immigrations** can be called on request via *Stella Maris Marina* from the airport on VHF 16, switching to VHF 6, if you need to clear in here when you arrive.

The south of Long Island is rarely visited by cruising boats. The west coast waters are too shallow, and Salt Pond is as far as you can go on this side. But perhaps the Long Island Regatta held there each year will attract you? The east coast may feature in your plans if you are bound for the Turks and Caicos or the Caribbean, but Clarence Town is the only place you can put into on this coast.

We give the Yellow Page information for Long Island working from north to south.

MARINA

STELLA MARIS MARINA AND RESORT CLUB
Tel: 242-338-2050/2051/2053/2054 • Fax: 338-2052
• VHF 16

Slips	12
Max LOA	90 ft.
MLW at Dock	5 ft., but only 4.8 ft. in the approach channel at low water.
Dockage	70¢ per foot per day, with long-term retroactive discounts.
Power	36¢ per kWh, minimum $7 per day for 110v, $11 per day for 220v. Some power limitations apply; contact the dock staff.
Fuel	Diesel and gasoline.
Propane	Is available. Ask at the marina office.
Water	At time of writing water is being trucked to the marina. Please use sparingly. Drinking water is available from the hotel at no charge to fill "normal" containers.
Telephone	At the marina.
Showers	Complimentary to marina guests.
Laundry	Coin laundromat opposite the marina, full-service laundry at the hotel.
Restaurant	*Pot Cakes,* next door to the marina complex, open Wednesday to Sunday from 3 pm.
Services	Hotel facilities are open to marina guests, who are encouraged to take part in the activites and entertainment.
Transportation	Call Stella Maris Taxi on VHF 16, going to VHF 6.
Marine Services	Boat Hauling and Launching: marine railway haul out 75 to 85 ft., with 25-ft. max beam; $8 per ft. boat length, plus labor charges.
Small Boat Hoist	$100 up to 18 ft.
Ramp Storage	$5 per foot per day if owner performs work. $2.50 per foot per day if Stella Maris Marina technicians are working on the boat.
Out Storage	$5 per foot per month, open air storage.
Labour Charges	Carpenters $20–24 per hour, electrical/ injection $48 per hour, fiberglass $30 per hour, painters $20, power plants/gear-boxes $36–48 per hour
Credit Cards	Visa, MasterCard, and Amex.

SERVICES & SHOPPING AT STELLA MARIS

Accommodations
Stella Maris Resort Club   Tel: 242-338-2051 or (In the US) 800-426-0446 • Fax: 338-2052   Thirty rooms and apartments, 24 bungalows and villas, available from $135 per night, plus $10 per person government tax and service charge and resort levy. MAP $44 per day. Three swimming pools, private beaches, complimentary shuttle to beaches, bicycles, tennis courts, table tennis and volleyball, scuba diving, fishing, island tours, videos, evening entertainment.

Airport
The airport offers a 4,050-foot paved runway, av-gas, light ground services, cafeteria, post office, bank, and air charter office.

Bahamasair at Stella Maris Airport   Tel: 338-2015   Leaves Nassau at 1:45 pm on Monday, Tuesday, Friday, and Saturday, arriving in Stella Maris via Deadman's Cay at 2:45 pm. Leaves Nassau at 9:45 am on Wednesdays, arriving in Stella Maris at 11:10 am. On Thursdays and Sundays, *Bahamasair* flies from Nassau at 7:15 am, leaves Stella Maris at 8:15 am for George Town, and from George Town back to Fort Lauderdale at 8:45 am. A second flight leaves Fort Lauderdale on Thursdays and Sundays at 11:15 am, into George Town at 12:45 pm, arriving Stella Maris at 1:30 pm, returning to Nassau at 1:45 pm.

Island Express runs a service five times a week from Fort Lauderdale, and *American Eagle* or *Gulfstream* run from Miami to George Town, where you can connect with a *Bahamasair* flight on Thursdays and Sundays.

Bank
ScotiaBank at the airport   Tel: 338-2000   Open from 9:30 am to 2 pm on Tuesdays and Thursdays.

Bicycles
Available from the hotel.

Car Rental
From the *Stella Maris Resort.* $65 per day, plus mileage.

Charter Aircraft
Hawkline Aviation   Tel: 338-2006   Al and Jane Wehrenberg
Island Wings   Tel: 338-2022/0028   Captain Marty Fox has a five-passenger Aztec.

Clinic
Tel: 338-8488   The nearest clinic is at Simms and is open from 8:30 am to 4 pm Monday to Friday. To contact the Long Island (North End) government doctor, or in emergency, call the front desk at *Stella Maris Resort.*

Groceries and Hardware
Stella Maris General Store on the road between the marina and the hotel   Tel: 338-2020   Open from 8 am to 6 pm Monday to Saturday with groceries, hardware, plumbing and electrical goods, and pet food.

Liquor Store
Next to the *Stella Maris General Store*.

Mailboat
M/V May Dean and *M/V Windward Express* bring mail and passengers from Nassau.

Police
Tel: 337-0999 or 338-8555

Restaurants
Pot Cakes at the Marina   Open from 3 pm Wednesday through Sunday.

Stella Maris Resort Club Dining Room and Garden
Breakfast 7:30 to 10 am, lunch from noon to 2 pm and dinner from 7 to 9 pm. Bahamian and European cuisine, with cave parties, lunch boxes to order, Rum Punch parties on Wednesday evenings, and a Saturday dance.

Scooters
Three mopeds from *Stella Maris Resort*. $30 for a half day, $46 for a full-day rental.

Taxis
Call Stella Maris Taxi on VHF 16, switching to VHF 6.

SPORTS

Diving
Stella Maris Resort Club Tel: 338-2051• Fax: 338-2052   Full day (2 to 3 dives) $75. There is no dive instructor at time of writing, but two divemasters with boats can take you out. They also have a compressor for tank refills.

Dive Sites
Shark Reef between Long Island and Sandy Cay, west of Stella Maris marina, if you feel like meeting sharks in only 30 feet of water.

Three Sisters, west of Hog Cay, where more sharks may greet you expecting to be fed.

Flamingo Tongue, good for snorkelers.

Comberbach Wreck in 100 feet of water, half a mile off Cape Santa Maria Beach, deliberately sunk by Stella Maris as a dive site.

Long Island north and east walls, rivalling Andros with depths from 90 feet down.

Fishing
Stella Maris Resort Club Bonefishing from $200 per day on 13- to 16-ft. skiffs for two people with guide. Bottom and reef fishing from $200 per day on 16 to 21-ft. boats. Deep sea fishing on 28- to 32-ft. boats from $550 per day. Group fishing trips from $40 per person.

Regattas
The *Stella Maris Resort* hosts the *Bahamian Outer Islands International Gamefish Tournament* in late May/early June.

Tennis
Hard tennis courts available, with night lighting.

Water Skiing
From $40 per person, minimum three people.

CAPE SANTA MARIA

Cape Santa Maria Beach Resort Tel: 242-338-5273 or from US and Canada 800-663-7090 • Fax: 338-6013
• E-mail: capesm@batelnet.bs   Highly praised by those who have come to know it, this is the kind of place for a holiday that most people hope to find in the Bahamas. Unlike some resorts, they are happy to welcome those who anchor off. With its 4,000-foot runway, it is readily accessible to pilots wanting to share the fun with their boating friends. Rooms from $715 per person, double occupancy, for 4 nights. Deep sea fishing for 1 to 6 persons $550 for half day and $800 for a full day. Reef fishing from $450 for a half day, and $600 for a full day. Bonefishing from $200 for 2 people for a half day, and $250

for a full day. Snorkeling trips from $10 per hour per person. Their restaurant is open for breakfast, lunch, and dinner. Call ahead for reservations.

SIMMS

Simms is a small settlement south of Stella Maris, with a *ScotiaBank* (338-2000); post office; *Batelco* office; *the Blue Chip Restaurant* (338-8106) under the rubber tree; *Mario's Liquor Store;* the *MGS Food Store* (338-8255); and the clinic (338-8488) that serves Stella Maris as well. On the way down, you may want to stop at *Cartwright's Grocery and Straw Work* as well as *C & M's Total Mart and Straw Work,* at Scrub Hill, and *Lula Pratt's Straw Work* at O'Neals.

Her Majesty's prison at Simms.

WEST COAST

THOMPSON BAY

Thompson Bay is very quiet, with activity centered around the *Thompson Bay Inn.* It is about two miles north of Salt Pond, with a peaceful anchorage outside Regatta time and bad weather.

Accommodations and Restaurant
Thompson Bay Inn Tel: 242-338-0052 • VHF 16 "Aquarius" Tryphena Knowles has great plans for the renovation and expansion of the hotel, which currently has 12 rooms with shared bathrooms, from $50 per night. You can have home-cooked Bahamian meals there, and enjoy a rolicking game of pool, as well as enjoy the live band or disco most weekends. You can also rent a car for $65 per day, and let them know if you want scuba diving trips, bone or bottom fishing trips, cave tours, or directions for exploring historic ruins nearby.

SALT POND

Fuel
Long Island Petroleum Tel: 338-0032 • VHF 16 "Docking Services"   Distributor for Esso products, batteries, and tires. Ask for manager Basil Fox if you need fuel.

General store
Harding Supply Center Tel: 338-0333/0042   Open 8 am to 8 pm Monday to Saturday, and 10 am to 8 pm Sundays. Some groceries, cold drinks, lumber, and marine supplies. They are also a Johnson and Evinrude/OMC outboard distributor.

Mailboat
M/V Sherice M leaves Nassau on Mondays at 5 pm for Salt Pond, Deadman's Cay, and Seymour's, returning to Nassau on Thursdays. Fare $45.

Regatta
Long Island Regatta is held over five days each May at Salt Pond, accompanied by a series of sports events, rake and scrape bands, junkanoo parades, and dancing the Maypole. For more information contact Mr. Henderson Burrows (242-394-1535) or Mr. Geoffrey Treco (242-328-2495).

DEADMAN'S CAY

Airport
Bahamasair Tel: 337-0877   Flies in to Deadman's Cay via Stella Maris from Nassau on Monday, Tuesday, Friday, and Saturday.

Banks

Royal Bank of Canada at Gray's north of Deadman's Cay
Tel: 337-1044

Royal Bank of Canada at Cartwright's south of Deadman's Cay
Tel: 337-0001 Open from 9 am to 1 pm Monday to Thursday, and 9 am to 5 pm on Fridays.

ScotiaBank at Buckleys Tel: 337-1029 South of Deadman's Cay, open 9 am to 1 pm Monday to Thursday and 9 am to 5 pm on Fridays.

Clinic

Deadman's Cay Health Centre Tel: 337-1222 The main clinic for southern Long Island, with a doctor and nurses. Out of hours, you can call the doctor at 337-0555 or the nurses at 337-0666.

Groceries

Caroll's has snack food, soft drinks, groceries, and some household items.

Deadman's Cay Supermarket has some clothing, as well as groceries and cleaning supplies.

Rental Cars

Mr T at the airport Tel: 337-1054

MANGROVE BUSH

Marine Supplies

Under the Sea Marine Supplies Tel: 337-0199 • Fax: 337-0341
Run by Francis and Cathy Darville, open 7 am to 6 pm Monday to Saturday, for Yamaha sales and service, general marine supplies, and some diving equipment.

Restaurant

Kooters Restaurant, with a good location on the waterfront, overlooking the bonefish flats. Open from 8 am Monday to Saturday, and from 6 to 10 pm on Sundays, with inside and outdoor dining. *Kooters* serves the best BLTs and good Bahamian food, too.

Sailmaker

Mark Knowles

HAMILTON'S

Accommodations

Hamilton's Inn and Restaurant Tel: 242-337-1264 Madge and Herbert Turnquesst have good, clean rooms for $75 per night, and can help with rental cars for $60 per day. They have their own bar and restaurant, and if you tell them ahead of time what you would like to eat, they will cook it for you.

Cave Tours

Legend has it that the Arawak Indians once inhabited the Hamilton Caves north of Clarence Town, which were more recently used to mine bat guano for fertilizer. An authenticated Arawak chair from here resides in a Minnesota museum, thanks to a traveling clergyman who took it back to his home town. All of this you will learn if you take the hour-long cave tour with Leonard Cartwright. You can call him on VHF 16 "Cave Man," or stop by his house in Hamilton's, which has a sign CAVE TOURS outside it.

Hamilton's Cave.

Grocery

Long Island Wholesale Groceries Tel: 337-0249

Marine Store

Fisherman's Marine Center Tel and fax: 337-6226 • VHF 16
Violet Cartwright Major has set up this excellent marine store in Hamilton's, which is open 8 am to 6 pm Monday to Saturday, for Evinrude, Johnson sales and service, general marine supplies, fishing equipment (particularly for bone and fly fishing), Boston Whalers, and Carolina Skiffs.

EAST COAST

CLARENCE TOWN

Clarence Town is famous for its two skyline churches designed by Father Jerome. If you have visited Cat Island this name will be familiar to you. Father Jerome was a young priest, trained as an architect at the end of the last century, who became an Anglican missionary. In 1908 he arrived in the Bahamas to rebuild local, but frail, wooden churches that could not withstand hurricane winds and reconstructed them in stone. Here in Clarence Town you find two examples of his work, one Anglican, the other Roman Catholic, the faith he later adopted.

CLARENCE TOWN DIRECTORY

1. Police, Batelco, Government Offices
2. Harbour Grocery, Milander Auto, Skeeter's Bar
3. Harbour Restaurant, Agriculture Warehouse
✝ St Paul's Anglican Church
✝ St Peter and Paul Catholic Church
⛽ Fuel pump on street
✛ Clinic

Bakery
Oasis Bakery and Restaurant   Tel: 337-3003   One mile north of town on the Queen's Highway. Call to ask what's baking; it could be fresh breads, pies, and buns.

Car Rental
Red Major, who is also a diesel mechanic, has cars to rent. Tel: 337-3004

Milander's Auto   Tel: 337-3227   Carlos Milander, centrally located by the *Harbour Grocery*, is very helpful, and has apartments to rent as well as cars.

Churches
St. Paul's Anglican Church, west of town.
Sts. Peter and Paul Catholic Church, where it is possible to climb the narrow tower with caution.
Both have services at 7:30 am on Sundays.

Church window detail, Clarence Town.

Clinic
Tel: 337-3333   By the dock in Clarence Town, open 9 am to 3:30 pm, Monday to Friday. The nurse is highly regarded.

Fuel
Tel: 337-3936   Henry Major at the Shell station by the Clarence Town Government Dock has diesel and gasoline.

Groceries
Harbour Grocery   Tel: 337-3934 • Fax: 337-3935 • VHF 16 Open from 8:30 am to 7:30 pm Monday to Saturday, 8 to 10 am Sundays. Well stocked with meats and vegetables, canned & dry goods, cold drinks, and insect repellent, which is a must in Clarence Town.

Mailboat
M/V Mia Dean leaves Nassau at 8 pm on Tuesdays for Clarence Town, returning to Nassau at 7 pm on Thursdays. Fare $45. Talk to Dockmaster Henry Major for more information.

Marina
Flying Fish Marina at Lighthouse Point Road   At the time of writing, this new marina was being started in Clarence Town. For more information, call Mario Cartwright, the owner, at 352-3126 or 351-2240.

Marine Supplies and Repairs
Milander's Auto   Tel: 337-3227 • VHF 16   Open 8 am to 5 pm Monday to Saturday. Carlos Milander has limited spare parts in store, but can help with most repairs. He can also put you in touch with two diesel mechanics to come to your boat. One is Red Major, who can be contacted at *Oasis Bakery* (338-3003); his wife runs the bakery. The other, Rudolph Pratt (338-2378), lives in Cabbage Point, but will come to Clarence Town. He

also runs a mobile diesel fuel operation if Clarence Town dock is out of diesel. Extra charge for delivery.

Police
Tel: 338-3919   Open 9 am to 5:30 pm Monday to Friday.

Post Office
Tel: 337-3030   Open from 9 am to 5:30 pm Monday to Friday.

Restaurant and Bars
Harbour Restaurant and Bar   Tel: 337-3247   Open from 9 am Monday to Saturday, and from 2 to 8 pm on Sundays; specializing in Bahamian dishes, as well as cakes, pies, pastries, and guava duff. Sells beer and liquor to drink on his small patio, or to take away.

Skeeters   Sells beer and liquor to drink on his small patio, or to take away.

Taxi
Lawrence Major   Tel: 337-4005   Transportation to Deadman's Cay Airport, or anywhere else.

Telephones
At the *Batelco* office   Tel: 337-3000 • Fax: 337-3100   Open from 8:30 am to noon, and 1:30 to 5 pm Monday to Friday, with phone cards for sale.

Vegetables and Fresh Fruit
The Department of Agriculture runs a warehouse consolidation facility at the docks. You can find bananas, limes, peppers, pumpkins, and watermelons almost all year. In the spring there will be tomatoes, onions, and sweet peppers; in the summer, mangoes and pineapples too. This is open most days from 9:30 am to 5 pm, but you can call ahead at 337-3276 to check. The stocks are best when the mailboat arrives.

DIVE AND SNORKELING SITES

There are two idyllic blue hole sites for snorkeling or diving within easy reach of Clarence Town. One is just north at Turtle Cove, aka Dean's, between Clarence Town and Hamilton's, where you turn east off the main road at the sign advertising the development. Drive to the beach, turn right at the gazebo and take the track half right across the headland and you are on the beach by the blue hole.

To the south, the Lochabar Bay Blue Hole has more greenish water, due to the shallowness of the surrounding lagoon, but it is fun to snorkel there, and also a little further north from the hotel where there is a sunken boat that attracts some fabulous fish. Ask at the *Lochabar Beach Lodge* for help to find the site. Both blue holes are more easily approached from the land.

SOUTH OF CLARENCE TOWN

Accommodations
Lochabar Beach Lodge on Lochabar Bay   Tel: 242-337-3123

THINGS TO DO IN LONG ISLAND
- See the Columbus Monument at Cape Santa Maria.
- Swim in Calabash Bay.
- Go diving or snorkeling with one of the Long Island resorts.
- Have your boat repairs done in Stella Maris.
- Photograph the Long Island churches and visit the Clarence Town Father Jerome churches.
- See Hamilton's Cave.
- Swim in the blue hole at Turtle Cove, the next bight in the east coast north of Clarence Town.
- Buy the wonderful Long Island fruit and vegetables, and some fabulous straw work.

Part V

Far Horizons

The Bahamas South of the Tropic of Cancer

The Unexplored Bahamas

Ocean water dropoff, San Salvador.

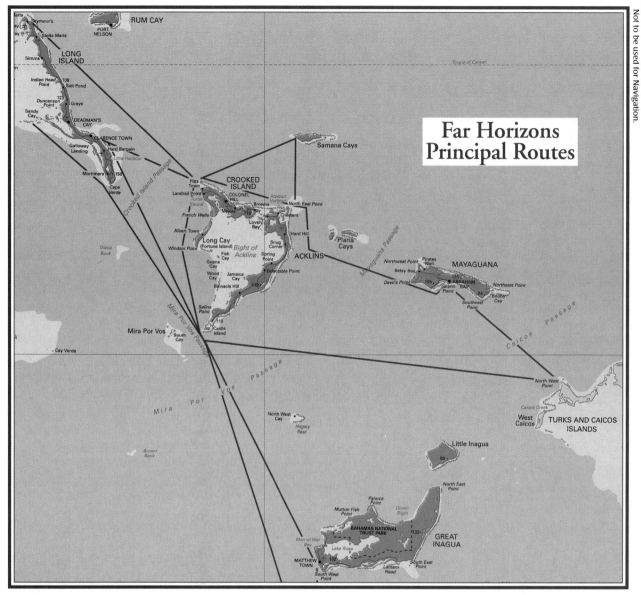

Far Horizons
Principal Routes

Not to be used for Navigation.

ROUTE TO/FROM		HEADINGS	DISTANCE NM	PASSAGE
Cape Santa Maria, Long Island	Bird Rock, Crooked Island	135°/315°M	71	Atlantic open
Clarence Town, Long Island	Bird Rock, Crooked Island	115°/295°M	35	Crooked Island Passage
Bird Rock, Crooked Island	Acklins Northeast	101°/281°M	38	Atlantic open
Bird Rock, Crooked Island	Semana Cay	075°/255°M	36	Atlantic open
Semana Cay	Acklins Northeast	170°/350°M	17	Atlantic open
Acklins Northeast	Plana Cays South	180°/000°M	16	Atlantic open
Plana Cays South	Mayaguana West	106°/286°M	39	Mayaguana Passage
Mayaguana West	Providenciales North	121°/301°M	47	Caicos Passage
Mayaguana West	Sandbore Approach	136°/316°M	47	Caicos Passage
Long Island South Point East	Mira Por Vos Passage	157°/337°M	49	Crooked Island Passage
Bird Rock, Crooked Island	Long Cay	185°/005°M	21	Crooked Island Passage
Long Cay	Mira Por Vos Passage	180°/000°M	26	Crooked Island Passage
Nuevitas Rocks	Mira Por Vos Passage	140°/320°M	81	Crooked Island Passage
Nuevitas Rocks	Long Island, South Point West	123°/303°M	30	Atlantic pocket
Long Island, South Point West	Mira Por Vos Passage	149°/329°M	53	Crooked Island Passage
Long Island, South Point West	Long Cay	126°/306°M	34	Crooked Island Passage
Mira Por Vos Passage	Matthew Town, Great Inagua	151°/331°M	80	Atlantic open
Matthew Town, Great Inagua	Windward Passage North	190°/013°M	28	Atlantic open

Distances exclude inshore close approaches at the start and end of a passage.

Chapter 18
The Bahamas South of the Tropic of Cancer

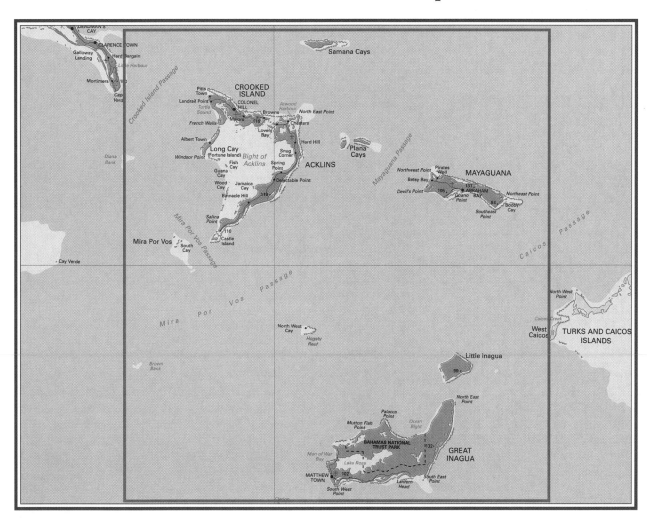

South of Latitude 23° 30' N

THE generally perceived wisdom that it's different south of George Town is true. For good reason we draw the bottom line of the Southern Cruising Grounds along the tropic of Cancer, Latitude 23° 30' N. The Exumas and the north of Long Island (so we included the whole) fell within the Southern Cruising Grounds, as did the Out Islands (Cat Island, both San Salvadors, Conception Island, and Rum Cay), which we covered. Our Far Horizons title covers the extreme south of the Bahamas, south of Latitude 23° 30' N.

So what about this line? Why is it so special? Well, perhaps it's academic that it happens to be the tropic of Cancer (that's as far north as the sun travels above the Equator during our summer). From this at once you realize that below the line you're in the Tropics. The real Tropics. Not the sub-

tropics. The difference on the ground, as it were? Not much. Not immediately. What about the marine side? Once you head south of the 23° 30' N line you're in a different game. You're exposed to the Atlantic, you have legendary passages to negotiate, all of which carry a weather factor (rather like crossing the Gulf Stream), there are almost no all-weather anchorages, few settlements, and over much of the area, no sources of fuel. It goes without saying that you shouldn't venture into these waters in a craft that isn't well found and well equipped. The sailboat really comes into its own here, for it's not fuel dependent. The power boat must calculate fuel and endurance, and keep a 20 percent reserve in hand.

What it boils down to is this. This area lies across the direct path to and from the Caribbean. If you're going that way (or returning), then fine. Choose the best route suited to you, and do it. If you have no purpose other than poking around to see what it's like down there, maybe think twice about it. That is if passage making or cruising in an area like this lies outside your experience. But let's look at two basic considerations before you set out.

Fuel

Between George Town or Rum Cay and Providenciales (Provo) in the Turks and Caicos Islands, your *only* sources of fuel are **Long Island** (Clarence Town), **Crooked Island** (Landrail Point), **Mayaguana** (the Government Dock), and **Great Inagua** (Matthew Town). The first three run out of fuel time and time again. You must check ahead if you hope to tap what they hold, for they may be waiting for resupply.

Air Links

There's another consideration above fuel that may be worth taking into account, and that's air links with the outside world. You're unlikely to schedule crew changes during your transit from George Town to Provo, but you might have to fly someone out in an emergency. Where can you do it? Bahamasair serves **Crooked Island**, **Acklins Island**, **Mayaguana**, and **Great Inagua**. Just keep it in the back of your mind.

The Interstate Highways to the Caribbean

A quick glance at the chart will tell you that the obvious direct route, you could say the I-95 to the south, is to parallel Long Island's east coast, leave Crooked and Acklins to starboard and Semana to port, leave the Plana Cays to port, maybe stop in Mayaguana, and go on to Providenciales. Of course if you're heading for the Windward Passage, you'd drop south down the Crooked Island Passage and wouldn't want to fool around in the Turks and Caicos, and maybe you'd stop in Great Inagua. But every route has options at every waypoint.

On the face of it, the Crooked–Acklins–Long Cay Archipelago might be considered as a definitive route-setter. If you're going to or coming from Provo or the Turks and Caicos, you'll pass to the east. If you're bound to or coming from the Inaguas and the Windward Passage, you'll pass to the west. But in truth it's not so. The archipelago is best seen as a rotary (that's a "roundabout," for British readers), and this is why. It's the weather factor. Generally your weather is incoming from the Atlantic, from the east to west. The east coast of Long Island offers no shelter, although there are two places where, in a last resort, you might find refuge if you entered before the onset of bad weather. The north coasts of Acklins and Crooked islands offer nothing. No shelter. Anywhere. And it's not only wind, wave, and swell. You've got other excitements on that route that make it appear like the endless hazards in Homer's *Odyssey*, the tide-rips and seas off Cape Santa Maria, and a mean current running through the Mayaguana Passage.

It sounds alarming? Read on. We're not trying to engender panic. In settled weather we'd always take the eastern

The east coast of Long Island.

route bound to or from Provo, and the western route bound to or from the Inaguas and the Windward Passage. But destined for Provo or heading north from there, if the weather kicked up we'd switch to the west of the archipelago, taking the Crooked Island Passage. The reason? To use the land mass and the Bight of Acklins as a shield from weather and current, and because tucked up behind the southwest tip of Long Cay, in French Wells (Crooked Island), and around Salina Point (the south of Acklins Island) you can find shelter (but read our detailed notes!). You still have the east coast of Long Island to face, but that leads us to the next section. Is there an alternative?

AN ALTERNATIVE ROUTE?

In our First Edition we raised the subject of a viable north–south route for cruising yachts across the Bank to the west of Long Island, based on the belief that in years past it was possible to gain the deep pocket of ocean water to the northwest of the Crooked Island Passage by a transit from the southern Exumas or Salt Pond in Long Island. We now believe that the proven Bank transit path we envisaged does not exist. This is not to say that local captains cannot safely cross the southeast corner of the Great Bahama Bank. Underline that word "<u>local</u>." It requires local knowledge. Storms can alter the whole lie of the sand, and it's not possible for a cruising guide to offer waypoints and say "you can go this way."

We have, however, identified one longer route, which, in theory, will take you on the Bankside from west of Harvey Cay in the mid-Exumas to the deep water south of Nuevitas Rocks. This could be attractive as an alternative to the east coast of Long Island. We'll now start with the traditional Eastern Route, and we'll turn to this option later when we cover the Crooked Island Passage and the route to the Inaguas and the Windward Passage lying to the west of the Crooked–Acklins–Long Cay archipelago.

The Eastern Route South: George Town to the Turks and Caicos Islands

YOU'LL see by our route and our waypoints that your start point is probably George Town, and the route takes you by way of Cape Santa Maria down the east coast of Long Island. As we've covered all the Long Island detail under the Southern Cruising Grounds, we won't repeat it here. Your pick-up point, at it were, lies somewhere around our Long Island southeast waypoint (LISPE), which in all probability you won't use. It's just a marker, there if you want it. So we'll pick up the story after you've made your 30-nm transit across the Crooked Island Passage, in the Crooked–Acklins–Long Cay Triangle.

EASTERN ROUTE I

George Town Harbour Entrance East		
GTAE1	23° 30' 00"/000 N	075° 40' 00"/000 W
LONG ISLAND		
Cape Santa Maria		
SANTM	23° 43' 00"/000 N	075° 20' 30"/500 W
Cape Santa Maria East		
SANTE	23° 43' 00"/000 N	075° 17' 00"/000 W
Clarence Town		
CLART	23° 08' 00"/000 N	074° 57' 00"/000 W
Little Harbour		
LLHBR	22° 59' 00"/000 N	074° 50' 00"/000 W
Long Island South Point East		
LISPE	22° 51' 00"/000 N	074° 45' 00"/000 W
Mid-Crooked Island Passage		
MIDCP	22° 51' 00"/000 N	074° 35' 30"/500 W
CROOKED ISLAND		
Bird Rock Northwest (not for navigation)		
BRDRK	22° 53' 00"/000 N	074° 23' 00"/000 W
Bird Rock		
BRDRE (exact)	22° 50' 42"/700 N	074° 21' 34"/566 W

The final figures in each waypoint show seconds (00") and thousands (000) of a minute.

Headings °M and Straightline Distances

The figures we show below are no more than an approximation of distance to run, a set of ballpark figures, and an indication of direction. We know, if you're a sailor, you can't sail a pencil line on a chart, just like that. Even a power boat has to take account of the sea state and, yes, the wind too. It's up to you to vector in the weather, choose your route, and decide where you might stop. For this reason we take the Eastern Route and all your options in bite-sized steps.

But first, the rough figures, the way it looks overall as you head south on this route.

George Town Harbour E	Cape Santa Maria	055°M	22 nm
Cape Santa Maria	Santa Maria East	090°M	3 nm
Santa Maria East	Clarence Town	150°M	40 nm
Clarence Town	Bird Rock	115°M	35 nm
Bird Rock	Atwood	105°M	30 nm
Atwood	Acklins Northeast	090°M	10 nm
Acklins Northeast	Plana Cay West	180°M	10 nm
Plana Cay West	Plana Cays South	180°M	7 nm
Plana Cays South	Mayaguana West	105°M	39 nm
Mayaguana West	Providenciales North	120°M	47 nm
Mayaguana West	Sandbore Approach	135°M	47 nm
Mayaguana West	Mayaguana East	visual	6 nm
Mayaguana East	Providenciales North	125°M	44 nm
Mayaguana East	Sandbore Approach	140°M	45 nm
George Town East	Turks & Caicos Approaches		240 nm

The Crooked–Acklins–Long Cay Triangle

Seen from Space, the triangular atoll formed by Crooked Island, Acklins Island, and Long Cay is spectacular. All around is the deep blue of deep ocean. A thin line of breaking white seas define the fringing barrier reefs, which are almost continuous around the archipelago. Then there's a

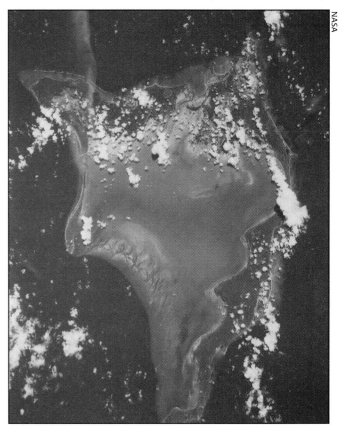

NASA

The Crooked–Acklins–Long Cay archipelago from Skylab.

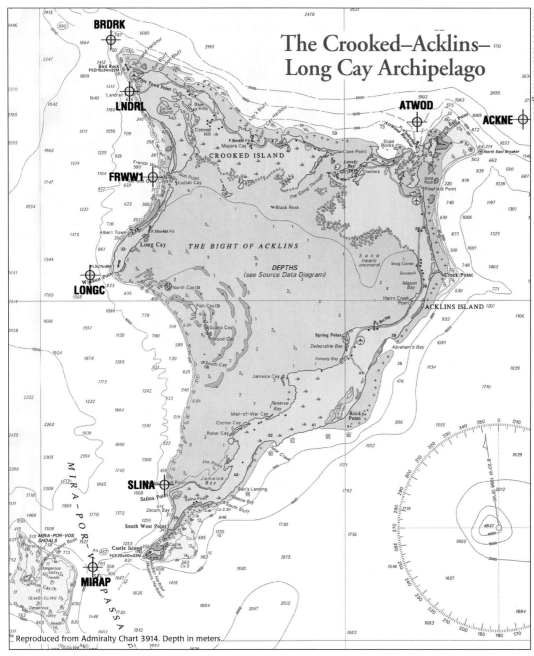

The Crooked–Acklins–
Long Cay Archipelago

Not to be used for Navigation.

Reproduced from Admiralty Chart 3914. Depth in meters.

narrow band of brilliant light blue shallow water, and the green of the land. Inside this frame, almost like a jewel in a setting, are the turquoise waters of the Bight of Acklins forming a virtual lagoon. One snippet to add to your intelligence file, if you're a Campari drinker, is that these islands are the world source of cascarilla bark, the ingredient that gives Campari its bitter, astringent taste.

As you make your way south of Long Island, you meet the first of the West Indian Passages, all of which slant in from the Atlantic, ancient deep-water channels. Ocean swells, together with high seas in unsettled weather, can produce surprising and less-than-welcome bumpy rides as

you cross each passage. Or it can be pussy cat.

Counting the passages as you go south, the Crooked Island Passage is the first. Then it's the Mayaguana Passage. And then the Caicos Passage. Further to the southwest is the closest entry point to the Caribbean, the Windward Passage.

Heading for Providenciales, one way or another, you are going to cut across the first three passages. As for the land, watch out for the barrier reefs and stand well offshore everywhere unless you are definitely closing for a specific destination. Our advice is to stand 5 nm off any coastline, and add more miles to that if you are passing the southeast point of Great Inagua Island.

Nature, in a sense, has ill-served the passage maker. In a perfect world, the Crooked–Acklins–Long Cay archipelago should offer havens if you want to rest or wait out the onset of unfavorable weather. In reality your choices there are very limited and, as is true with most of the Bahamas, all-weather anchorages do not exist. The one exception lies with true shoal draft craft, who can play the Bight of Acklins to advantage.

Crooked Island

BIRD ROCK

Bird Rock, the northern of the two Crooked Island Passage lighthouses, is dated 1876. It's not only a fine landmark but a triumph of construction built from Crooked Island stone quarried from nearby Gun Bluff. At one time its mecha-

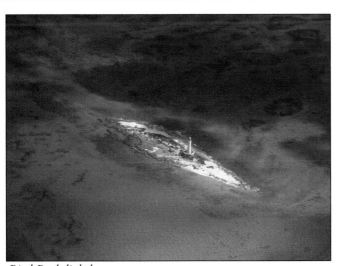
Bird Rock lighthouse.

nism and lenses were a match to Hope Town lighthouse in the Abacos (which is still operating in its original state), but when the Bird Rock lighthouse was electrified, its nineteenth-century machinery and museum-quality Fresnel lenses were trashed. Recently the lighthouse, having survived over 100 years up to its modernization, was deteriorating rapidly and, despite its strategic position, was no longer working. The Bahamas Defence Force, in a brief visit, made an attempt to get Bird Rock Light working, but despite initial success, it failed. The owners of Pittstown Point Landings have cleared up a mess of abandoned secondary batteries littered around the foot of the lighthouse, but their plans to go further and turn the accomodation into an "out-of-the-way" refuge have yet to take a step forward.

PORTLAND HARBOUR AND PITTSTOWN POINT

Portland Harbour at the northwest tip of Crooked Island is, in truth, the perpetuation of mistaken identification. There's no harbor, just a ring of circling reef where if the wind's from the south, you can find a pleasant anchorage off the beach just to the east of Pittstown Point. You'd be uneasy there at any other time, and crazy to think of it when the wind was either west or north. Your entry point lies to the south of Bird Rock. Working your way in, you have 20 feet of water, and keeping the obvious coral to starboard, when you're "inside" Bird Rock, turn to starboard toward the center of the first white sand beach. It's eyeball stuff, the coral easily seen and easily avoided, with the main reef lying on your starboard side. Anchor over sand as close in as you desire, comfortably off the beach and over sand, about midway between Pittstown Point and the next mini-point to the east (22° 49' 59"/983 N 074° 20' 32"/533 W). There'll always be some motion inside Portland Harbour, but with south winds and no significant ocean swell, it's fine.

Pittstown Point is the location of a small, relaxed low-rise resort known as Pittstown Point Landings, just 2 miles north of Landrail Point, up a sand road that has the feel of Florida's A1A years back in time. The twelve-room hotel is centered on its 2,000-foot paved airstrip (to be extended to 4,000 feet), and guests arrive piloting their own aircraft or fly Bahamasair to Colonel Hill, the Crooked Island airport. Pittstown Point Landings (extraordinarily the site of the first post office in the Bahamas) has had a checkered past. Now, after more changes in ownership and management than you might believe, it has hit its stride. It's a delight, certainly on our short list of the remoter places that, for setting and ambiance, win instant stars as an island retreat. Not surprisingly, over the years a small colony of some sixteen or seventeen houses, hardly noticeable at first sight, have tucked themselves under the wings of the small resort.

We had hoped that Crooked Island, with its strategic position, might one day offer better facilities for cruising boats, and the Pittstown Point area would be our choice. Despite talk at one time that Salt Pond between Pittstown and Landrail might be opened to the ocean and dredged to accommodate a marina, it seems that nothing is in the cards yet. It would be an expensive undertaking. We're not certain how many cruising boats (as opposed to just those on passage to or from the Caribbean) would venture that way, but as a voice in the boating community, we'd welcome it. An all-weather marina, with fuel and all the normal resources of a full-service marina, would be a signal gain for the Bahamas south of the tropic of Cancer. Until this comes about, if indeed it does materialize, you can still put in to Pittstown's Portland Harbour and to Landrail Point, but if you choose to visit you must find the weather to fit, and trust your own hook in one of these two exposed anchorages.

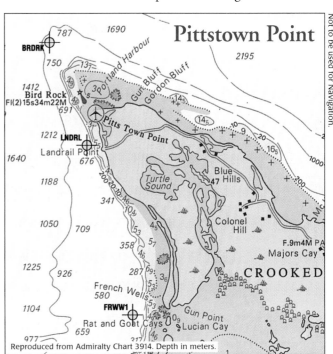

Not to be used for Navigation.

Reproduced from Admiralty Chart 3914. Depth in meters.

Portland Harbour, from the northeast.

LANDRAIL POINT

Landrail Point, about 4 nm south of Bird Rock, appears the most unlikely place to construct a Government Dock to serve the mailboat *United Star*, but it's there with a small settlement behind it. The geography of this part of the coast is that the dropoff of the Crooked Island Passage runs close and parallel to the shore at Landrail, while further south the margin of offshore shallows gradually increases until you're held well off the coast by a shallow shelf. There's no protecting reef off Landrail, and both the mailboat (and you) can make your way in from deep water to virtually within a stone's throw of the shoreline.

The Government Dock is no real option for you (because of surge) except for a short visit to take on fuel. Your landmark for the dock, which doesn't stand out clearly from the shore and is not looking as good as it was before Hurricane *Lily*, are the fuel tanks (three large and one small) just to the north of the dock, and a yellow building with blue shutters just by the dock. If you want fuel, call *Early Bird* on VHF 16. If the quantity is small, you can fill your cans at the nearby gas station. If you need more than can be handled can by can, they'll send the fuel truck (carrying both diesel and gasoline) to the dock to meet you.

The best place to anchor lies to the north of Landrail Point, halfway to Pittsdown Point, off the white sand beach just opposite the only mid-beach stand of casuarinas. However, the absence of a reef doesn't mean there's no coral there, and you must read your way in. You'll anchor in 20–30 feet of water over good sand, and only one anchor should be necessary. Here you'll be OK in east to northeast winds, and wind from the south at no significant strength. There were seven yachts anchored off in this area, an unusually large number at one time, during our last (April 1999) visit. Anything from the north is a real put-off. Don't be tempted to move closer to Landrail Point. The bottom there looks OK, sand in part, but it's thin sand over rock. A grapnel might eventually hold, but you're likely to drag.

EASTERN ROUTE II		
Portland Harbour Entry (not for navigation)		
PTLNH	22° 50' 24"/400 N	074° 21' 15"/250 W
Portland Anchorage (not for navigation)		
PTLNA	22° 50' 12"/200 N	074° 20' 47"/783 W
Landrail Anchorage (not for navigation)		
LNDAN	22° 49' 10"/166 N	074° 20' 48"/800 W
Landrail Point		
LNDRL	22° 48' 30"/500 N	074° 21' 15"/250 W
Landrail Small Boat Dock (not for navigation)		
LNDSB	22° 48' 18"/300 N	074° 20' 29"/483 W
Landrail Government Dock (not for navigation)		
LNDGD	22° 48' 07"/116 N	074° 20' 22"/366 W
French Wells West		
FRWW1	22° 41' 00"/000 N	074° 19' 00"/000 W
French Wells (not for navigation)		
FRWW2	22° 41' 05"/085 N	074° 18' 00"/000 W
French Wells Anchorage (not for navigation)		
FRWAN	22° 41' 04"/066 N	074° 16' 29"/483 W

The final figures in each waypoint show seconds (00") and thousands (000) of a minute.

Old cannon at Marine Farm, Crooked Island.

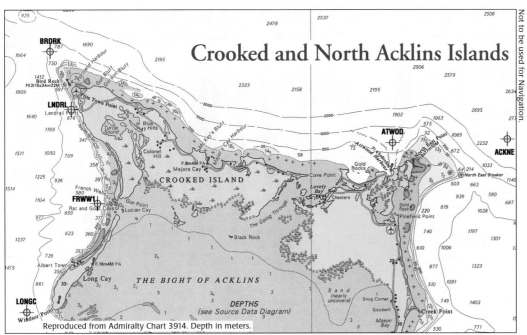

There's a small-craft basin cut into the rock at the north end of the settlement that you can enter in your dinghy, but you may prefer to run your dinghy right up on the beach. Landrail Point is a small, compact settlement spread around a short triangle of roads, one marked *Pittstown* and the others *Inland* and *Airport*. There's a clinic, a one-room school, the Seventh Day Adventist church, the gas station (smart and up to date), which we've already mentioned, and Gibson's Lunch Room (longstanding and well reputed), run by Marina Gibson, the BASRA representative. Thunderbird's can take you fishing and scuba diving, and there's a Batelco card phone by the Government Dock. The people of Landrail, mostly Seventh Day Adventist, are friendly and approachable. Just remember that their Saturday figures as your Sunday, and that alcohol is not part of their life style.

FRENCH WELLS

Although not directly on the Eastern Route, weather or the desire simply to take a break from passage making may prompt you to divert to French Wells at the south tip of Crooked Island. French Wells, despite its alluring name, has long lost its population. Nonetheless, it offers what is arguably the best all-weather anchorage in the Crooked–Acklins–Long Cay archipelago. Follow the deep water of the Crooked Island Passage dropoff and then, when you're off French Wells, turn in between Crooked Island and Rat and Goat Cays (to the immediate north of Long Cay) and head almost due east on 090°–095°M. To port and starboard you have sandbars reaching out toward the dropoff, and you have a shoal area to cross with perhaps just 12 feet at MLW. Then, passing the south point of Crooked Island you'll find yourself in a deeper channel bordered by shoal on both sides.

We add one caution. Feel your way in to French Wells. Sand is the governing factor, and, as we all know, sand moves. French Wells, in the words of one Bahamian captain, "comes and goes." Much of the time you can get in there. Sometimes it's a No-Go. But it worked for Columbus in 1492.

Work your way in and anchor in 15–20 feet over sand. The further in you go, within reason, the more protected you'll be and the better the sand underneath you. You're shielded by sand virtually on all sides, and only really vicious west weather could rock you. We're told it "never gets really bad in there." If you're lucky, flamingos will join you at dusk and at the turn of the tide, the bottom fishing is good. On the west side of Crooked Island, running north from its tip for just over 3 nm, is one of the most fabulous continuous runs of pure white sand beach facing pure white sand–bottomed turquoise water we've seen in the islands. Talk about perfect swimming beaches? That's it.

The Rest of Crooked Island

Colonel Hill, a strung-out settlement resting securely notched into its north coast spine of limestone, is (we were told by a proud schoolteacher) the capital of Crooked Is-

French Wells, from the west.

land, and the center of the island's population of 300 lies spread along on the Colonel Hill–Cabbage Hill ridgeline. To the east, in the low ground, is the airport, and in the west, high on that spine, a Batelco tower with three great dish antennae. Crooked Island may well be set for significant change. Together with road improvement, the age of centrally generated electricity has arrived (every generator in the island is now relegated to stand-by status) and they're ready to take off.

LONG CAY

Logic would dictate that we cover Long Cay, running south from French Wells and the south tip of Crooked Island, at this point in our text. However as it's not part of the Eastern Route from George Town to Providenciales, we leave it until later. It remains that if you elect to take the Crooked Island Passage and are making directly for the Windward Passage, you'll continue on south, paralleling Long Cay. To see our comments on going this way, please turn to the **Western Route** on page 323. We now continue with the Eastern Route.

Acklins Island

The North of Acklins Island

Acklins Island, with a population of around 500 spread over 150 square miles, has a look of depopulation if not almost total dereliction at first sight. The center of Acklins in terms of government, airport, clinic, communications, and police is Spring Point, sited on the Bight of Acklins, almost exactly halfway down the west coast. This at once places it out of reach of any cruising boat. Roads on the island are poor but were improved with the advent of centrally generated electricity; nonetheless getting around is not easy, and is difficult to say the least if you have no wheels. The east (ocean) coast has a virtually continuous inshore reef and there is no place into which you could, with safety, bring a boat.

It remains that if you're taking the Eastern Route between George Town and Providenciales, the only place in Acklins that has any utility to you is Atwood Harbour in the northeast. As the south of Acklins Island is only relevant to those taking the Western Route, we leave this to be covered under that heading.

ATWOOD HARBOUR AND NORTHEAST POINT

Atwood Harbour, a cup-shaped bay behind the reef some 2 nm southwest of Acklin's Northeast Point, is just about the only anchorage worth that name in the Crooked–Acklins area. It has good protection once you get in there, except from the north when it should not be attempted, but the getting in requires care and attention. It's unfortunate that Atwood lies at the limit of a natural passage length in either direction, in other words, it's a good midpoint resting place. This means that many people reach Atwood just too late to

Atwood Harbour, from the north (above) and the south (below).

North Acklins from the east (above) and the northwest (below).

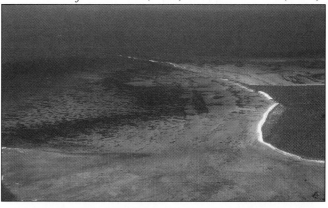

SEMANA CAY		
Semana Cay		
SMANA	23° 02' 00"/000 N	073° 46' 00"/000 W
ACKLINS ISLAND		
Atwood Harbour North		
ATWOD	22° 46' 00"/000 N	073° 53' 00"/000 W
Atwood Harbour (not for navigation)		
ATWIR	22° 43' 40"/666 N	073° 53' 05"/085 W
Northeast Point		
ACKNE	22° 46' 00"/000 N	073° 43' 00"/000 W

The final figures in each waypoint show seconds (00") and thousands (000) of a minute.

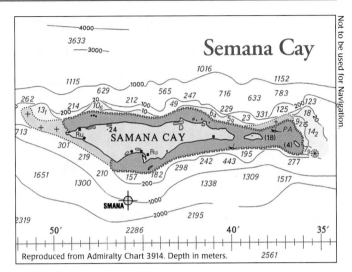

Reproduced from Admiralty Chart 3914. Depth in meters.

have good light and are, most probably, tired. In the last few years about a dozen boats have run into trouble entering Atwood. Be warned; but don't be put off.

The break in the reef is well-defined but you have no particular leading mark as you enter the harbor, other than to steer almost due south leaving Umbrella Rock and the white light on the headland to port. Look out for the coral inside the harbor area, and once inside the curve of the anchorage, turn to port and find your chosen place to drop your hook. There are two houses there, on the foreshore. There's a small settlement, Chesters, about two miles to the west, with little or nothing but one small store, a telephone, and sandflies. A second small settlement, Pinefield Point on the east coast some 4 miles south of Northeast Point, is primarily a fishing village. If you wish to find a local guide try Newton Williamson answering on VHF 16 as Holiday Inn or use Batelco and call 344-3210.

The reef known as Northeast Breaker lies 4 nm east of Northeast Point. It's marked on the chart, and it shows as breaking seas. A spine of underwater reef runs between Northeast Point and the Northeast Breaker. Stay well clear, and round the Northeast Breaker to the east.

Semana Cay

Semana Cay, some 35 nm from Bird Rock and 20 nm from Acklins' Northeast Point, is not on your route, but we include it as you may wish to divert there purely out of interest. Semana Cay, no longer populated, lies 30 nm northeast of Crooked Island, and is 9-by-2 nm in land area with a sibling mini-cay to the east. Its surrounding reefs extend the sea area of the whole Semana Cay landmass to something like 16-by-4 nm. Semana Cay, despite apparently protected bays on both the north and the south coasts, has no easy-to-enter anchorage. The problem is simply those surrounding reefs that have no breaks, no apparent cuts through the coral.

Why go there? Perhaps because you're a maritime history buff, interested in the Columbus Voyages, and a member of the "It Wasn't San Salvador" school? See **The Columbus**

Controversy on page 394. on page 394. There's a compelling case for believing that Semana Cay was where Columbus made his first transatlantic landfall. Alternatively you might elect to go there simply because it's there, or because it's remote and largely unvisited, except occasionally by fishermen from Acklins Island.

Forget the bay in the north. The only place to attempt a landing is the one in the south. The first point to register is that you have to find your way through the coral. Hopefully you can anchor off and scout the area by dinghy first, and hopefully too you'll have the dividend of the extra 2 feet that a high tide will give you. Mark your way in with temporary buoys. Even the Acklins fishermen do this, and if you find other people's markers there, be wary of using them. Check the whole thing out yourself. Once in, you'll be safe if the wind is from the north. Forget Semana Cay if the wind is northwest or southwest, and forget it whenever high seas are running.

Two open boats from Acklins went to Semana fishing. On the passage back the engine of one boat failed. By the time the other realized something had gone wrong, the miss-

Semana Cay, south bay.

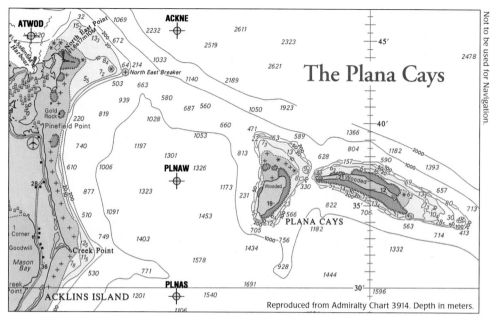

The Plana Cays

Not to be used for Navigation.

Reproduced from Admiralty Chart 3914. Depth in meters.

ing boat was over the horizon. They backtracked, but failed to sight the lost boat. They had no VHF. They searched, but failed. Five men were on board the missing boat. Over the next five days the weather worsened, with winds reaching 35–40 knots on two of those days. The missing boat was given up for lost. On Day 5 a tanker sighted the boat off the Long Island coast. The five men were still alive.

The Plana Cays

West Plana Cay offers a good anchorage on the west side in northeast to east winds, but you'll feel swell there, so expect to roll. Avoid it in northwest and southwest winds. In favorable weather West Plana's a good place for beachcombing, but you're unlikely to want to stay there long. It's twin, East Plana Cay, has poor anchoring, by repute,

but we've not tried it. We reckon there could be a fantastic drift dive site between the two cays, but again we've not tried it. Watch it if you do. The current there could be strong, and potentially dangerous.

East Plana is the only undisturbed habitat of the hutia, a small native Bahamian cat-size rodent. How did they get there? One can only guess that one day, way back in time, the hutias were great swimmers. By all accounts the Arawaks rated hutia hot dogs, hutia hamburgers, and just plain roast hutia as gourmet fare. No wonder the unfortunate hutias learned to swim, and their selection of East Plana Cay as a desirable residence was, perhaps, no accident.

Mayaguana

Mayaguana marks the midway point between Acklins Island and Providenciales. Sizeable though it is at some 24 nm in length and a good 6 miles in width at the fatter western end, the island is for the most part a low-lying tangle of scrub and trees and has very little to offer the cruising visitor, other than shelter. Its population of 500 is spread between three settlements: Pirate's Well on the northwest coast; Betsy Bay on the west coast, just 2 miles south of a new Government Dock where the weekly mailboat *United Star* calls; and Abraham's Bay, the largest settlement, in the center of the island on the south coast. Mayaguana was once part of the US missile-tracking network, which left the dividend of an 11,000-foot runway (of which only 7,700 feet are now usable) located 5 miles west of Abraham's Bay, and

EASTERN ROUTE IV

PLANA CAYS		
Plana Cays West		
PLNAW	22° 37' 00"/000 N	073° 43' 00"/000 W
Plana Cays South		
PLNAS	22° 30' 00"/000 N	073° 43' 00"/000 W
MAYAGUANA		
Government Dock (not for navigation)		
GOVD	22° 26' 57"/949 N	073° 07' 45"/750 W
Betsy Bay		
BETSY	22° 25' 00"/000 N	073° 09' 00"/000 W
Mayaguana West		
MAYAW	22° 19' 12"/200 N	073° 03' 20"/333 W
Mayaguana East		
MAYAE	22° 20' 45"/750 N	072° 58' 04"/067 W

The final figures in each waypoint show seconds (00") and thousands (000) of a minute.

Plana Cays, from the east.

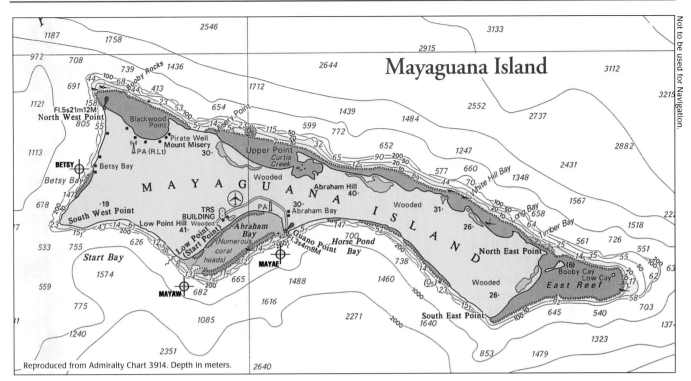

Reproduced from Admiralty Chart 3914. Depth in meters.

Not to be used for Navigation.

a dock that serviced the USAF fuel tank farm on Start Bay, which was known locally as POL (port of landing? or petrol, oil, and lubricants?). Once used by the mailboat, the USAF dock is now in a state of advanced decay. Little else of this period remains. Four stripped-out aircraft, which you'll see on the apron if you visit the airfield, are seized drug runners of the post–USAF base period.

Were Mayaguana anywhere else other than right on the main cruising path to and from the Caribbean, it would probably remain almost totally unvisited, but it's there, right on your route, and you may wish to call in. Its isolation is also broken by the weekly mailboat calls, and twice-weekly Bahamasair visits (Mondays and Fridays), for Mayaguana has the good fortune to be a brief stop on the scheduled Nassau–Inagua service. Add these pluses, together with centrally generated power, regraded and surfaced roads, a Batelco station, a police post, and a government clinic, and Mayaguana wins status as a diversion refuge, if for no other reason. Therefore we cover it in some detail.

Turning to navigation, the chart of Mayaguana can frighten at first sight. The island is surrounded by an almost continuous reef that forms great bights at the northwest tip, the east, and at Abraham's Bay in the south. Look at the chart and you'll see no less than eight shipwrecks marked on the reef, but the Mayaguana total is far higher than this. Your options boil down to two alternatives. The first is to anchor off the west coast, where from Northwest Point down to the first sand beach south of Betsy Bay there's no barrier reef. The depth is good, and you're protected from the prevailing winds, east and southeast, but it's a real no-no in

northwest and southwest weather. The second option is to go into Abraham's Bay.

Northwest Point to Betsy Bay

Northwest Point is low lying, but is marked by a light pole close to its tip, and shows even more prominently by the breaking seas on its barrier reef. If you have shoal draft you can work your way inside the reef close to Northwest Point, and anchor somewhere off the foreshore running east to Pirate's Well. The downside is that it's shallow there and you're open to the north. Pirate's Well, with just one small store, is not geared to receiving guests, although there is a small low-rise beach hotel now under construction (with no apparent deadline), which may, one day, be completed. It's a surprising location for it. Despite the promise of the advent of tourism, we suggest Pirate's Well is left off your potential haven list.

A new Government Dock 1 nm south of Northwest Point has been cut through the beach rock and coral to provide a square basin with one concrete wall for the mailboat. The beach reef on the north side was not completely cut away and remains a hazard, but there are range marks, two triangles on stakes on the land behind the dock. The depth at the dock is good, 6–8 feet at MLW by guess, and there is some surge. This is the best place where you can easily take on fuel, either diesel or gasoline, if you need it, *if* the island has fuel in stock. The fuel will be brought to the dock in drums. There's no filtration. You either come alongside, or bring your fuel cans ashore having anchored off (remember there's no offshore reef there). The Government Dock is untenable, even for the mailboat, in southwest and northwest winds of any strength, and under these conditions the mailboat will divert to Abraham's Bay where whatever can be easily offloaded is cross-decked into small boats.

The best way to call for fuel, or indeed for anything in Mayaguana, is to call Batelco on VHF 16, and they'll look after you. If for some reason you get no response, try the police, who also monitor channel 16.

Betsy Bay is recognizable offshore by its shortish 104-foot Batelco tower with a dish antenna coupled to it. The settlement parallels the beach, which has an

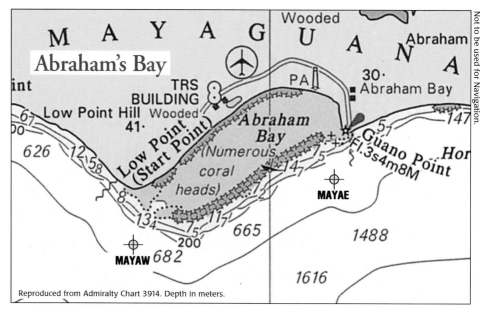

Reproduced from Admiralty Chart 3914. Depth in meters.

inshore reef about 100 feet out. Anchoring off is fine in prevailing southeast winds, but out of the question if the weather is southwest to northwest. There's plenty of depth, but check your holding. The settlement has little to offer the cruising visitor, and lost its dock to a hurricane.

Abraham's Bay

Abraham's Bay, at just over 5 nm in length with a width of nearly 2 nm is an all-weather anchorage, accessed by two passes through its barrier reef. Apart from its very obvious reef, two landmarks are useful in defining each end of Abraham's Bay. In the west are what appear to be two towers, the still-standing buttress walls of a larger ruined ridgeline building once part of the USAF missile-tracking complex, and the remains of two water tanks. In the east, there's the 175-foot Batelco tower in Abraham's Bay settlement. The bay itself virtually dries along its shoreline, has an inner near-continuous run of beach reef just offshore,

Abraham's Bay, Mayaguana.

and a generous scattering of random coral. But its navigable part has water depths running 6–8 feet and more than this in deeper pockets, plus the benefit of that broad band of shielding coral on the ocean side. But you are open to wind from southeast through to southwest.

ABRAHAM'S BAY WEST (THE START POINT–LOW POINT ENTRY)

The entry at the west end of Abraham's Bay is just under a mile slightly southeast from Low Point. If you choose to put in here it places you furthest away from the Abraham's Bay settlement but it's certainly the easier of the two cuts to negotiate and carries some 12 feet at MLW. The break in the reef is easily defined, and it is this entry that is used by the mailboat if it has to divert to Abraham's Bay. Your primary coastline landmark, just to the west of Low Point, is the remains of the US missile station dock (22° 20' 06"/100 N 073° 03'51"/850 W) with a tank farm behind it. The range marks still stand, but the dock is unusable. Nonetheless, this docking facility, partly kept in use, is the island's source of fuel. The fuel tanker anchors off, runs its discharge hoses over the sea to the dock, where they are connected to working pipelines running back to two in-use fuel tanks in the farm. Low Point itself, by no means a well-defined feature, is your second landmark.

Our Mayaguana west (MAYAW) waypoint lies just over 1 nm from the Start Point dock, which bears 330°M from the waypoint, and 0.7 nm from Low Point, which lies on a bearing of 342°M. The pass through the reef is wide and clearly defined by its blue color. You have plenty of sea room and good depth for the first half mile, which you'll take on a heading of around 052°M and then you're in around 12 feet of water. At this point alter slightly to around 076°M and carry on to give yourself shelter behind the barrier reef. Just another half a mile or so should do it. But if you want

Start Point Pass from the northwest (above), and the south (below).

Guano Point Pass from the south (above), and from the east (below).

to take your dinghy to the Abraham's Bay settlement dock you have a long haul, just over two miles, to get there. Don't attempt it at low tide. You could be walking long before you get anywhere near the dock.

You might consider working your way eastward to anchor closer to the Abraham's Bay dock, but we see little advantage in it. If you really need the settlement, choose the Guano Point Pass to enter the bay.

ABRAHAM'S BAY EAST (THE GUANO POINT ENTRY)

At the east end of Abraham's Bay, under Guano Point, which has a light, you have another well-defined break in the reef but less water, only 6 feet at MLW, and the opening turns out to be deceptive. At first sight it seems wide and fairly well defined, but after the initial pass through the outer barrier reef there is a secondary reef, known as Middle Reef, lying right in the middle. There appears to be the option at this point of passing Middle Reef on either side, for apparent deeper water seems to run each way, but under no circumstances should you choose to pass between Middle Reef and Guano Point. You'll wreck yourself. That way runs right into a coral trap.

From our Mayaguana east (MAYAE) waypoint, which lies 1 nm due south of Guano Light, take a heading of around 315°M and follow the deeper water that runs in a northwesterly direction, leaving Middle Reef to starboard. You'll have 6–8 feet of water. Just short of a mile in there are two shallow shelves or steps where the water depth will reduce by half, but both are avoidable. Just use your eyes as you go in. At this point you are just about level with Middle Reef, and Guano Light will bear about 90°M. Start heading more to the west, following the deeper water, and run in behind the barrier reef to drop anchor wherever you fancy.

Don't head toward the Abraham Bay concrete dock that lies to the northeast, nearly a mile off. In no time at all you would be in 3 feet of water. Despite a scar with the semblance of a channel carved by a local fishing boat, the dock is only approachable by dinghy, and, as we've said earlier, don't even try it at low tide. You'll barely find a foot of water there. Don't be fooled by the fishing boat if it's at the dock.

ABRAHAM'S BAY SETTLEMENT

A ten-minute walk from the Abraham's Bay dock will bring you into the settlement by the Batelco tower and the government offices. Abraham's Bay is now an official Port of Entry, but Customs and Immigration, although offices exist for them, may not be present (they commute from Great Inagua); the Commissioner has vested powers to act in their absence. The Batelco office is open seven days a week, and further into the settlement you'll find the police station, the government clinic (staffed by a nurse—a doctor from Inagua visits once a month), two small stores, and two places where you can get food or a drink. The Batelco office will guide you.

Elsewhere in Mayaguana

There are places where in settled conditions you can work your way in through cuts in the reef, around Northwest Point as we've already mentioned, or almost due south or due north of Booby Cay in the Eastern Bight, but we think you'd be crazy to attempt it.

A stillborn US development on North Beach (22° 24' 22"/366 N 072° 58' 50"/833 W), launched under the curious cover title of the Mayaguana Ecological Group, has yet to produce more than the frame of one half-completed Italianate house and some foundations. There was talk of a cut in the reef, some dredging, and a marina. The bight is shallow there, and ideas of constructing anything approaching a marina, quite apart from the exposure of the northern coast to weather, seem unlikely to achieve reality.

Is this why we go cruising? The stuff of dreams. Location secret!

Approaches to Providenciales in the Turks and Caicos Islands

Whether the Turks and Caicos Islands are your turnaround point or just a waypoint on an extended passage makes little difference to the geography of your approaches in the early stages, unless you are going to bypass the Turks and Caicos completely as some do, who don't want to transit the Caicos Bank. If you elect to stop in the Turks and Caicos, you're bound to make Providenciales (known as Provo) your first stop and your port of entry. Why? Because it's there, right on your path. And Provo has everything. Nowhere else in the Turks and Caicos has as much to offer the transient boater.

You have two landfall options, as Provo is a barrier island, one of the circlet of islands bordering the Caicos Bank starting at West Caicos in the west and continuing around to South Caicos in the southeast. If you elect to stay outside the Caicos Bank initially, PROVN off Northwest Point will be your approach waypoint after crossing the Caicos Passage. If you want to get on the Caicos Bank at the outset, you must pass between Provo and West Caicos, through the Sandbore Channel (aka Caicos Creek). Here our Sandbore Channel Approach mark (SBORA) is your waypoint.

For details, turn to our section on the **Turks and Caicos Islands**, in which we also give the location of an anchorage that may be found in darkness if, arriving early, you wish to drop your hook rather than stand off waiting for daylight. However this option is weather dependent. Your cruise planning should call for a daylight landfall.

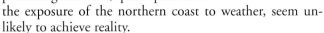

TURKS AND CAICOS ISLANDS APPROACHES

PROVIDENCIALES
North West Point

PROVN	21° 55' 00"/000 N	072° 20' 00"/000 W
Tiki Huts Anchorage		
TIKIA	21° 49' 50"/833 N	072° 20' 30"/500 W
Sandbore Channel Approach		
SBORA	21° 46' 00"/000 N	072° 28' 30"/500 W

The final figures in each waypoint show seconds (00") and thousands (000) of a minute.

A Cautionary Tale

A SMALL sailboat was wrecked on the reef leaving Abraham's Bay through the Guano Point Pass. Her captain sailed late in the day, despite heavy surf breaking along the reef, and realized too late that the seas were too much for him. He turned back, but had lost his light by then and with it his ability to read the water. It hardly mattered, for in turning he was swept sideways. He hit Middle Reef.

The state of the surf at the Guano Pass entry tells you everything. If there's a lather of white water there, forget it.

The Western Route South to the Windward Passage

IF you're heading for the Windward Passage you have a choice at the start. The "standard" route is to go by way of George Town and the east coast of Long Island and turn to take the Crooked Island Passage south. Your route plan is straightforward. Pass Cape Santa Maria safely off, and keep your distance off that Long Island east coast. Clarence Town is there as a port-of-call (but not an all-weather haven!) halfway down Long Island if you want it. When you reach the Crooked Island Passage, head for the Mira Por Vos Passage. If you want stops along the way (none of them problem free), there's Crooked Island with the so-called Portland Harbour, Landrail Point, and French Wells. We covered this route as far as French Wells in Crooked Island, under the **Eastern Route South, George Town to the Turks and Caicos**, beginning on page 311.

There is an alternative if you're heading for the Windward Passage, or coming north from it, and that's to transit the southeast corner of the Great Bahama Bank. The Bankside route was and is used by Bahamian captains when unfavorable weather makes exposure to the Atlantic a real no-no. For this reason even if the Turks and Caicos, rather than the Windward Passage, are your destination, a Bank transit may prove attractive.

But let's be clear at the start about the downside of going the Bank way. First, it dictates that you bypass George Town, your ultimate stop for fuel, provisions, spares, etc. (or, coming north, your entry port). Going west of the Exumas and Long Island you have nothing. Nothing at all. Secondly it's not a straight run clear of obstacles. Your route crosses snake-like sandbores in the area of the Barracouta Rocks, which may or may not bar your passage, coral scattered like coarse-ground black pepper in the area of Hawksbill Rock, and reefs and isolated coral heads around the Nuevitas Rocks. In short, it's no playground. But it has been navigable in the past, and, depending largely on whether the Barracouta sand has moved as the result of storms, may still be navigable at the time you read this.

We repeat that the Long Island east coast transit is the standard, safe route to follow. However, whichever way you go, either going south or coming north, both routes are the same from the Mira Por Vos Passage to the Windward Passage.

One additional note. There are charts in circulation showing Bankside routes passing through Jew Fish Cut (in the Jew Fish Cays to the west of George Town) and Hog Cay Cut (between Little Exuma Island and Hog Cay). These cuts are shoal draft and could be said to lead from nowhere to nowhere. They have no utility for the passage maker.

George Town or the Mid-Exumas to the Windward Passage

Headings °M and Straightline Distances

Once again we repeat our warning given under the **Eastern Route**. The figures we show below are no more than an approximation of distance to run, a set of ballpark figures, and an indication of direction. We know, if you're a sailor, you can't sail a pencil line on a chart, just like that. Even a power boat has to take account of the sea state and, yes, the wind too. It's up to you to vector in the weather, choose your route, and decide where you might stop. For this reason we take the Western Route and all your options in bite-sized steps. But first, the rough figures, the way it looks overall as you head south on this route.

FROM GEORGE TOWN			
Clarence Town	Little Harbour	145°M	11 nm
Little Harbour	Long Island South Point East	150°M	9 nm
Long Island	Mira Por Vos Passage	160°M	50 nm
FROM HARVEY CAY			
Harvey Cay	Barracouta Sand	160°M	27 nm
Barracouta Sand	Hawksbill Rock	150°M	22 nm
Hawksbill Rock	Nuevitas Rocks	110°M	45 nm
Nuevitas Rocks	Long Island South Point West	125°M	30 nm
Long Island	Mira Por Vos Passage	150°M	53 nm
THE ROUTE IN COMMON			
Mira Por Vos Passage	Great Inagua (Matthew Town)	150°M	80 nm
Great Inagua	Windward Passage North	190°M	28 nm
TOTAL DISTANCES			
George Town East	Windward Passage North Approach		240 nm
Harvey Cay	Windward Passage North Approach		284 nm

From George Town Heading for the Windward Passage

We won't duplicate our Long Island port information and the first stage notes on the Eastern Route south to the Turks and Caicos. If you're setting out from George Town, or heading that way, the information you need is there. We've fixed a Long Island South Point east waypoint (LISPE), at which you can turn to take the Crooked Island Passage and make for the Mira Por Vos Passage. Crooked Island lies to port for much of your way after you've taken up your new heading, and our Crooked Island landfalls, particularly French Wells, offer places where you may wish to call in to take a break. If you choose to fish as you're going south, try running along the line of the Crooked Island–Long Cay dropoff. It could be good. Just remember that your potential stops are, as ever, weather dependent, and the entry to French Wells is sand-governed and can change from year to year.

We'll deal now with the Western Route in full, taking it from the Great Bahama Bank off the Exuma Cays down to the Windward Passage. The George Town startpoint option (which, as you've appreciated, amounts to going east rather than west of Long Island), links up with the full run of the Western Route at the Mira Por Vos Passage.

WESTERN ROUTE I
GEORGE TOWN TO THE WINDWARD PASSAGE

George Town Harbour Entrance East

GTAE1	23° 30' 00"/000 N	075° 40' 00"/000 W

LONG ISLAND
Long Island South Point East

LISPE	22° 51' 00"/000 N	074° 45' 00"/000 W

LONG CAY
Long Cay (Windsor Point)

LONGC	22° 32' 30"/500 N	074° 25' 00"/000 W

HARVEY CAY TO THE WINDWARD PASSAGE

Harvey Cay

HARVY	24° 09' 15"/250 N	076° 30' 00"/000 W

GREAT BAHAMA BANK
Barracouta Sandbores (general area)

BRCTA	23° 44' 00"/000 N	076° 20' 00"/000 W

Hawksbill Rocks

HWKBL	23° 25' 00"/000 N	076° 07' 00"/000 W

Nuevitas Rocks

NUEVR	23° 08' 00"/000 N	075° 21' 00"/000 W

LONG ISLAND
Long Island South Point West

LISPW	22° 52' 00"/000 N	074° 54' 00"/000 W

LONG CAY
Long Cay (Windsor Point)

LONGC	22° 32' 30"/500 N	074° 25' 00"/000 W

The final figures in each waypoint show seconds (00") and thousands (000) of a minute.

The Western Route South—
Harvey Cay to Nuevitas Rocks

Your first leg is a straight shot from a position safely to the west of Harvey Cay to the area of the Great Bahama Bank lying off the Brigantine Cays, and by extension East and West Barracouta Rocks. In this first part of your transit the critical parameter is that you should be running along a general line to pass no closer than 8 nm to the west of Darby Island, and by projection, the rest of the coastline as you proceed south. Keep your eyes open for sand, but you should have 6–7 feet of water all the way.

In the Barracouta Rocks area you'll come across a wide band of sand that has worked its way in from the west. At

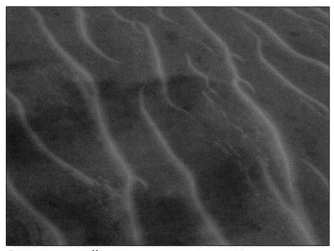
Barracouta sandbores.

first it appears Sahara-like, albeit an underwater Sahara, a broken pattern of dunes and ridges, which gives way to a snake pattern of sand ridges, yellow-white against an electric blue background. It's some of the most extraordinary water we have found in the Bahamas. The sand has advanced in recent years, and this unceasing eastward movement was much accelerated by Hurricane *Lily*. You should, with luck, have 6 feet at MLW there. It might be more. But be warned, for it keeps changing.

Your next target is to pass to the west of Hawksbill Rock. Coral reefs and isolated coral heads lie both east and west of Hawksbill Rock. You should aim to pass to the west of Hawksbill Rock, fairly close to it without hugging the rock, and you'll find a channel there relatively clear of coral in which you will have 6 or 7 feet at MLW.

Set a straight course to pass to the east of Nuevitas Light. You'll have no problems there, for the Nuevitas Rocks are obvious, and you have a well-defined blue-water pass to take

Nuevitas Rocks.

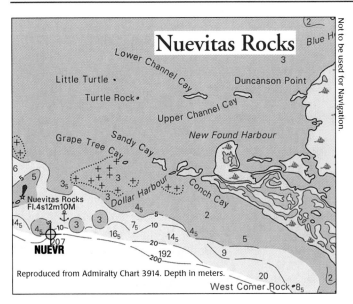

Reproduced from Admiralty Chart 3914. Depth in meters.

you out into deep ocean water. It goes without saying, but we'll say it: you must have good light to do this transit south from Harvey Cay or northbound from Nuevitas Rocks. You must use your eyes, for the underwater pattern is constantly changing, and if you can't read the water, you must stop, anchor, and go no further until you have useful light.

Nuevitas Rocks to the Mira Por Vos Passage

Once you're in deep water you're free to set your courses to take you past the southern tip of Long Island, across the Crooked Island Passage, past the southwest point of Long Cay, and through the Mira Por Vos Passage, leaving Castle Island and Acklins Island to port. The first leg takes you safely to the east of the Diana Bank, the only shallow area in this deep pocket of ocean water. If conditions are right, you might wish to visit the Diana Bank area, for it is a fishing ground, good enough to be the target of both Long Island and Crooked Island fishermen. If you need to seek shelter there are two options open to you. The first is anchoring off the west coast of Long Island about 1 nm north of South Point, and the second is French Wells (see the **Eastern Route**), although it lies off your direct course.

Further south you are not well served with shelter. Although the east coast of Long Cay, about 1 nm north of Windsor Point

(the southern point), has long been regarded as a potential anchorage. In theory you're protected from the west there and the shoal water of the Bight of Acklins offers some protection from most other directions, but in practice it doesn't work out so well. As one local fisherman put it "the ocean is too close there." The shallow bights on the west side of the southern end of Acklins Island each side of Salina Point offer another option, but like so many potential anchorages, are weather dependent.

LONG CAY

Long Cay (see the chart on page 312), with a population of around twenty-five, is yet another once-prosperous Bahamian island that has fallen on hard times, and its overly large church is sad evidence of this decline. In the past Long Cay was a pit-stop for sailing vessels taking the Crooked Island Passage, a spongeing center, and like so many islands, had a hand in salt production too. Albert Town on the west coast is protected from the east but is open to surge and has no clear anchorage, and there's very little that Albert Town itself has to offer. We don't recommend it.

WESTERN ROUTE II		
ACKLINS ISLAND		
Salina Point		
SLINA	22° 14' 00"/000 N	074° 18' 00"/000 W
Mira Por Vos Passage		
MIRAP	22° 06' 30"/500 N	074° 25' 00"/000 W

The final figures in each waypoint show seconds (00") and thousands (000) of a minute.

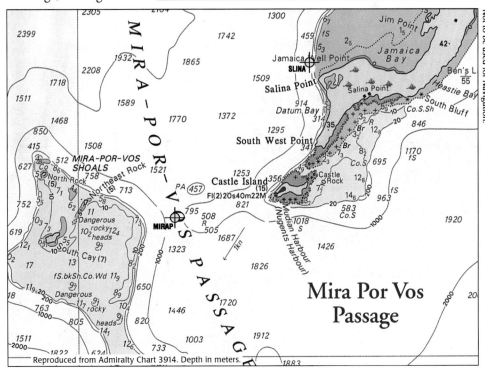

Reproduced from Admiralty Chart 3914. Depth in meters.

Acklins Island, Southeast Point.

NORTH CAY, FISH CAY, AND GUANA CAY

To the southeast of Long Cay on the edge of the Bight of Acklins lie North Cay, Fish Cay, and Guana Cay. These three cays are the last refuge of the local species of iguana, which for reasons yet unknown have suffered a devastating population drop in the last few years. The iguanas are currently the subject of a scientic study hoping to determine the cause for this reversal. If you call there, tread carefully. Land no animals. And leave no garbage.

THE BIGHT OF ACKLINS

Spectacular as it may be from Space, unless you're hot on shoal draft exploration, the Bight of Acklins is not a cruising ground.

Castle Island lighthouse.

ACKLINS ISLAND

We covered the north of Acklins Island under the **Eastern Route**. The south of Acklins is not tourist territory and even in Spring Point the local inhabitants admit they rarely venture down that way. This leaves, in near total isolation, the one southern settlement of Salina Point. Confusingly Salina Point itself is the headland projecting to the northwest while Salina settlement lies on the opposite (Mayaguana Passage) shore. The shallow bights on each side of the point have both been, at one time or another, labelled Jamaica Bay on charts, but it hardly matters which one is the original.

It's entirely possible to work yourself in to the first one, and you can probe further, moving around Salina Point, but if you carry any kind of draft local advice is against it. A clear route is not easy to find, and if the weather turns you may have a tough time getting out and away. If you anchor off this coast you can make contact with the Salina settlement, but there's not much they can offer other than fresh bread and, yes, there is a telephone. How do you get there? Not by dinghy. Walk up the beach heading northeast. You'll come to a straight road crossing the width of that Acklins promontory, which runs right into the settlement. It's a long walk. And it could be hot. Maybe someone might give you a lift back.

The Mira Por Vos Passage

Mira Por Vos! Look Out for Yourself! The Spanish must have been terrified by the Mira Por Vos area, a nightmare of coral and sand almost bang in the middle of the southern entrance to the Crooked Island Passage. If you couldn't slip between the Mira Por Vos Cays and Castle Island, a tough shot for the captain of a lumbering galleon to call, you had to go to the west of the Mira Por Vos Cays. But if the set, which runs that way, and the wind forced you too far west, you'd be on the Columbus Bank. If you clawed your way off that, but got taken too far to the northwest, you'd end up in the deepwater trap ringed from the west to the northeast by the Jumentos Cays and Long Island. You could regret the day you got the captaincy of that galleon, or even worse, command of that fleet of treasure ships.

An alternative translation has been offered to me as *Look Out For Us!* In other words, be wary of us. I think the end effect of both messages is one of total accord, and could be summed up as "Keep Away!"

Small wonder that the Spanish decided to take the Gulf Stream route from Havana, settled on St. Augustine as a take-off point into the Atlantic, and quit trying to play it as a straight shot through the Bahamas.

CASTLE ISLAND

The Castle Island lighthouse, the southern complement to Bird Rock in the north, marks the southern exit of the Crooked Island Passage. Sadly this lighthouse, in its conversion to power, suffered the same vandalism as the result of bureaucratic ignorance or disinterest as Bird Rock. Beware of the currents around Castle Island. As always at a place that is the focal point of a deep-water passage, here compounded by the shallows of the Mira Por Vos reefs, shoals, and cays, the currents are strong and unpredictable. Expect anything from southwest to northeast.

We've come across charts, and indeed a guidebook, showing an anchorage to the south of Castle Island. Don't believe it. The shallow bay there is chock full of coral. You might get in. You'd lie uneasily there. If it blew, or you suffered surge, you'd be in serious trouble. And you might never get out.

The east or ocean coast of Acklins is forbidden territory. It's a long run of nothing but near continuous reef and coral heads. Keep well clear of it.

South of the Mira Por Vos Passage

At this point on the Western Route your only sensible course, if you're heading south, is to make a straight run for the Windward Passage, standing well to the west of Hogsty Reef and well off Great Inagua. You'll be setting off on something like 169°M with something plus of 100 nm to go, a run that can be broken with no great cost in diversionary miles at Great Inagua.

If you're bound for the Turks and Caicos you've already gone out of your way, but a straight run to Sandbore Channel passing well north of Hogsty Reef and, of course, well north of the two Inagua Islands, is possible. Your course should be something in the order of 108°M and a run of

Hogsty Reef.

110 nm or so will place you at our Sandbore Approach waypoint. It's not an efficient way to reach Providenciales when you compare it to the Eastern Route, and, more times than not, you'll be heading into weather. However, on a reverse course it could be a different story, and the Crooked Island Passage, and indeed the Bank Route, could be an attractive option using the shielding of the Crooked–Ackings–Long Cay group and Long Island to advantage.

We'll conclude this section on the Western Route with brief coverage of the remaining two Bahamian territories that lie in this area of ocean but are not on your direct track, whichever heading you follow.

HOGSTY REEF

About as remote as you can get in Bahamian waters, over 30 nm from land in any direction, Hogsty Reef is a one-off in the Western Hemisphere, a near perfect atoll, barely 5 nm east to west and 3 nm north to south. It has also, in its time, been a mean ship-cruncher and no one knows how many vessels have fixed the exact position of Hogsty Reef more

WESTERN ROUTE III		
HOGSTY REEF		
Hogsty Reef		
HGSTY	21° 41' 00"/000 N	073° 54' 00"/000 W
GREAT INAGUA ISLAND		
Matthew Town		
INAGA	20° 57' 00"/000 N	073° 44' 00"/000 W
WINDWARD PASSAGE		
Windward Passage Approach North		
WINDN	20° 30' 00"/000 N	073° 42' 30"/500 W

The final figures in each waypoint show seconds (00") and thousands (000) of a minute.

Cautionary Tales

A TRIMARAN with four on board ran on the reef attempting to enter the lagoon some time back. There was no one else there. Hogsty Reef was deserted. Five days later a small Bahamian fishing boat passed, and stopped. They could take no more than one person on board. Three of the trimaran crew were left to trust that their companion would reach some place where he could make contact with the outside world. It must have been an unnerving period. They were lucky. Eventually they were rescued by the US Coast Guard.

❖ ❖ ❖

You could say that Hogsty Reef is (1) so remote and (2) such a well-known hazard that the probability today that anyone should run on to the reef was close to zero. On the night of Wednesday December 9, 1998 the mail-boat *Lady Mathilda* was bound from Mayaguana to Great Inagua on her regular run in the southern Bahamas. She was carrying her normal load, vehicles as deck cargo, drums of fuel, and frozen food, as well as whatever had been requested for delivery from Nassau. It was a routine trip she had done time and time again. She ran straight on to the southeastern circle of the reef.

The weather was OK. Good visibility, five days after a full moon, scattered cloud, moderate southeasterly winds, and a sea state that was within her limits. But none of this would have helped if she came within sight and hearing of the surf breaking on Hogsty's barrier reef at passage speed. Our immediate reaction is to wonder about the course steered, and more particularly, the compensation made for a relatively strong set to the northwest. But we make no comment. There, but for the grace of God, go any one of us.

Lady Mathilda on Hogsty Reef.

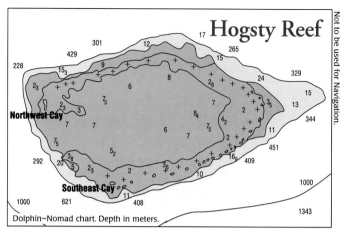

Dolphin–Nomad chart. Depth in meters.

Not to be used for Navigation.

accurately than they might have wished. Two highly visible, long-abandoned, rust-red wrecks remain there, high and dry on the reef, at the time we write. It's one of the fabled remote Bahamian dive sites, visited occasionally by live-aboard dive boats, but otherwise you might wish to give it a miss. If you do elect to go there, it's entirely possible to make your way into the lagoon through a pass on the west side to the south of Northwest Cay and anchor wherever the depth suits you. You'll find anything from around 18 feet down to 6 feet in there. What it might be like being caught there in bad weather is not the stuff of pleasant dreams. Hogsty is deadly in southwest and northwest weather. For a long time Hogsty Reef has been on our Dive Destination List. We'll get those dives in one day.

The Inagua Islands

Great Inagua, which dwarfs its smaller sibling to the northeast, Little Inagua Island, also dominates the southern Bahamas by land mass alone, some 40 nm wide running east to west by 26 nm north to south. Its baby sibling, just 5 nm away across a strait, is a stout 10 nm wide by 8 nm running north to south. Despite the total land mass perhaps it's a blessing that the two islands lie on no direct track, for there's nothing there, and both islands are surrounded by reefs.

LITTLE INAGUA

Other than one possible anchorage off its southwest point, there's absolutely nothing in Little Inagua to attract the cruising or passage-making visitor.

Great Inagua

Great Inagua has far more to offer than its sibling. Its only settlement, Matthew Town on the southwest tip, has an airstrip and small harbor. The island is the source of raw product for Morton Salt, and over a million tons of it are exported each year, 99.4–99.6 percent pure. This good fortune (which the ghosts of Rum Cay must envy) brings a salt-loading dock to Man of War Bay (on the west coast to the north of Matthew

Town), where the backdrop of stock-piles of salt give the disorienting appearance of snow-covered peaks. Matthew Town has the stamp of a company town, and potential advantage comes in better-stocked stores than most Out Islands, a regular air service, and arguably better back-up facilities, as well as a US Coast Guard station.

But for the visiting yachtsman there are few attractions. The reefs around the island are formidable, particularly at Southeast Point where they run out for 5 nm, and there are are no anchorages anywhere, save off Matthew Town where there are no reefs, but wind and ocean swell could make any extended visit hellish.

MATTHEW TOWN HARBOUR

The good news of 1999 was that Matthew Town Harbour, which has an entry channel open to weather and suffers from surge, was at last to receive remedial attention. In Matthew Town we were told work would start in the summer of 1999, but it seems that nothing will change in the short term. At press time we heard work has not started, and that the funds allocated to this project had been diverted to Matthew Town school. If one day the proposed changes come about, we believe it will amount to a change in alignment of the entry channel, possibly the addition of a breakwater, and perhaps the im-

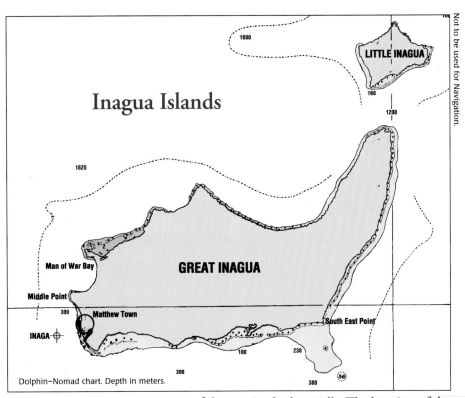

Dolphin–Nomad chart. Depth in meters.

provement of the existing harbor walls. The location of the harbor remains unchanged.

If you're going to enter the harbor, go carefully. The slanted entry into this small concrete and rock basin has a single leading mark at its southeast corner. Watch out for the reef to starboard that runs out from the shore as you approach. Once inside you have an advertised 10 feet at MLW. To starboard you have the concrete dock used by the mailboat, which has a short arm on the seaward side and a longer run on the land side. But apart from the fuel facility near the range marker in the southeast corner, there's nothing there other than the Bahamas Defence Force office and a Batelco telephone box. This is essentially a Government Dock used by the mailboat. It is not, and was never intended to be, a facility for cruising boats.

You will also find the US Coast Guard in Matthew Town, but they are there as "guests." If you run into trouble, the responsibility for monitoring channel 16 lies in the hands of the Bahamas Defence Force.

What is there to draw you in? Crew changes and air delivered spares featured high on the list of the two boats in harbor when we were there. Maybe fuel, and possibly back-up engineering from the workshops of the Morton Salt Company, if you can persuade them to help you. Maybe medical help (there is a small hospital there) and air evacuation is always possible. That alone may be worth an entry in your What If? file. If you do need to put in, remember that your coastal landmarks are the lighthouse on the coast to the south of Matthew Town and the two Batelco dishes to the north of Matthew Town and Matthew Town Harbour.

Matthew Town. Anchoring off.

INAGUA NATIONAL PARK

If none of this sounds particularly encouraging, perhaps, in settled weather, there is a good reason for visiting Great Inagua. The Inagua National Park, given a boost by the Audubon Society, is now home to the largest colony of West Indian flamingos in the world, narrowly saved from extinction. The pink birds share their habitat with a number of other native birds now virtually extinct, not the least of which is the cute little Bahamian Parrot.

An early cruising visitor, a Genoese sailor working for Spain, reported that the parrots circled them in flocks as they approached each island. His name? It doesn't often feature in works on wildlife, but you might have heard of him for other reasons. It was Christopher Columbus.

For all these reasons we have covered Great Inagua in our **Yellow Pages.**

Morton Salt.

YELLOW PAGES

This area was hit by Hurricane *Floyd* in September 1999. Be aware that post-hurricane repairs and reconstruction may still be in progress, and wind and storm surge damage may still be evident.

CROOKED ISLAND

For the sailor, the Landrail Point area has the only settlement where you can access Crooked Island that can offer even basic facilities. There is a small boat harbor through a narrow cut, suitable only for dinghies, which will bring you into Landrail settlement where you will find a rundown Government Dock, a filling station, *Batelco*, and the Gibson and Scavella families, who are delighted to meet visitors, and will help in any way they can.

Some 2.5 miles north of Landrail Point, on a superb site, is *Pittstown Point Landings,* one of the best-kept secrets in the Bahamas. Private and charter aircraft can come in here on the *Landings'* own 2,300-foot paved landing strip.

Today, if you call in, you'll find a warm welcome. In the settlements there's usually water, some fuel in drums or cans, and very basic food stores. But the lack of safe anchorages probably dictates that you'll soon move on, and your ability to move around the islands, to move from one settlement to the other, is limited to the endurance of your dinghy or hitching a ride. The only bonus is that both Crooked and Acklins Islands are served by *Bahamasair* if you need to fly in or out, and of course there's always *Batelco* if you need to contact the outside world, and clinics in the larger settlements. There is no bank on either island, so make sure you have enough cash to cover your needs before you arrive.

For these reasons we don't cover the islands exhaustively, but give a brief review of "what's there" in the places where you are most likely to make a landfall.

LANDRAIL POINT

Church
Seventh Day Adventist Church   Saturday service at 11 am.
Clinic
Nurse Beulah Carrol runs the clinic, and can be contacted through *Batelco*. The doctor from Acklins comes over every two weeks.
Ferry
A government ferry runs between the southeast tip of Crooked Island and Lovely Bay on Acklins Island. The ferry times are posted as 8 am and 4 pm Monday to Saturday, but the ferry is notoriously unreliable and you have to get there in the first place. If it does run, the fare will be $5.
Fuel
Scavella's Filling Station   Usually has diesel and gasoline, but you will have to carry it out to your boat in jerry cans.
Groceries
Scavella's Grocery Store next to their filling station   A limited supply of canned and dried goods, and occasionally fresh fruit and vegetables.
Pittstown Point Landing   Tel: 344-2507 • VHF 16   If you are in great need of something in particular, they may be able to help you.
Restaurants
Gibson's Lunch Room   Tel: 344-2676   From her tiny kitchen, Marina Gibson serves delicious, freshly cooked Bahamian food. She specializes in fish and steaks for breakfast, lunch, and dinner. And make sure to try her bread pudding! She is also the local BASRA representative, answering emergency calls on VHF 16 "Basra Landrail Point." Call ahead for dinner if you can. By the end of 1999 there will be another Gibson's

Restaurant in town. Marina's daughter, Wilhemena, plans to open her own restaurant, closer to the shore, called *Little Willie*, so be sure to check it out.

ACCOMMODATIONS

Crooked Island Beach Inn at Cabbage Hill   Tel: 242-344-2321   Very simple rooms from $50, no credit cards. Serves Bahamian meals on request.
Gibson's House at Landrail Point   Tel: 242-344-2676   A two-bedroom cottage with a shared bathroom across the street from *Gibson's Lunch Room*. From $80 a night, which includes three meals a day.
Pittsdown Point Landings at Pittsdown Point   Tel: 242-344-2507   Ask for Tammy Coy, the dynamic manager of this well-run resort. Twelve rooms from $125 per day. Full American plan $55 per day. This small resort, much dependent on its own airfield and pilot loyalty, but welcoming to visiting boaters, is centered around a bar and restaurant that has, as its origin, the oldest post office in the Bahamas. The detached, cottage-type, simple rooms, with their own verandas, face either one of the two beaches with fantastic snorkeling or the palm grove garden. Excellent homebaked bread and freshly caught seafood are their specialty. They are happy to cook your catch if you've had a successful day trolling the dropoff contour. Special dietary needs can be accommodated. Bonefishing available for $160 for a half day, $320 for a full day. Contact Carter Andrews, the fishing director, or Andy Gibson, one of Marina Gibson's sons, at *Pittstown Point* for fishing details. Andy can also take you diving, act as a tour guide, and find you fresh conch salad.

If you anchor off their beaches in a favorable wind, come ashore at the end of the runway in your dinghy for dinner. If you are at anchor off Landrail Point, call VHF 16 "Pittstown Point" ahead of time and you can be collected from the town small boat harbor. Tammy may be able to help you with provisions from their own supplies if you have a problem finding what you need locally.
Scavella's Guest House   Four rooms to rent; ask at the gas station or the grocery store.

THINGS TO DO ON CROOKED ISLAND

- Go to see French Wells. Maybe anchor there for two days or so and go gunkholing and fishing.
- Take your dinghy out to Bird Rock. If you have an interest in lighthouses, you'll be fascinated by *Bird Rock Lighthouse,* which may or may not be working.
- Find someone to guide you across the lagoon to see ruins and the few old cannon at the *Marine Farm*, a one-time British fortification.
- Ask Tammy or Andy to take you to visit the bat caves about 4 miles east of Pittsdown Point.

ACKLINS ISLAND

Acklins Island is, if anything, poorer than Crooked Island. Until the cotton crops were wiped out by blight in the last century, large, working plantations covered this island. No longer heavily populated, Acklins has little to show for its former prosperity. The local tarpon and bonefishing is some of the best in the Bahamas, but there are few onshore facilities and the ones we list are throughout the island, rather than in the individual settlements.

The only places you can access Acklins is at Atwood Harbour in the north and anchoring off Jamaica Bay in the south. This gives you Chesters settlement for the first point of contact, and Salina for the second. Neither are in the front rank. The center of the island is Spring Point, which you can reach only by road, for the ocean side offers no viable anchorage and the bight side is accessible only by shoal-draft craft. Spring Point is a *Bahamasair* stop and offers most back-up facilities, such as they are.

SPRING POINT

Airport
Bahamasair flies to and from Nassau twice weekly.
Accommodations
Central Guest House at Mason's Bay
Tel: 242-344-3628 • VHF 16 "Central" Contact Ethlyn Bain.
Nais Guest House at Spring Point   Tel: 242-344-3089 • VHF 16 "Nais Place" Four double rooms, call a month ahead for reservations. Contact Naomi Mackey, or call the *Batelco* office at Spring Point if you have problems getting in touch.
Bonefishing
Greys Point Bonefishing Inn at Pinefield Point   Tel: 1-800-99-FLATS
Joe Deleveaux   VHF 16 "Lovely Bay" or call Elijah Beneby at 344-3087 to pass a message.
Newton Williamson   Tel: 344-3210 • VHF "Holiday Inn"
Churches
Most settlements have Sunday morning gathering places. Services are mainly Baptist.
Clinics
Main Island Clinic at Spring Point   Tel: 344-3550 This is the *Batelco* number, but they will contact a doctor during working hours. In an emergency or on weekends the number is transferred to his home phone. The clinic is open from 9 am to 5:30 pm, Monday to Friday.
Clinic at Mason's Bay   Tel: 344-3169, or 344-3628 after hours and on weekends. Nurse Ethlyn Bain is the nurse in charge.
Clinic at Chester's   This clinic is not staffed at the moment, but a doctor visits twice a month.
Clinic at Salina Point   VHF 16 "Hummingbird" Contact is clinic aid Pandora Williams.
Med-Evac is handled through Spring Point Airport.
Contacts
These people can act as contacts in the various settlements:

Chester's	Edmund Johnson	Tel: 344-3108
Hard Hill	Leonard Collie	Tel: 344-3613
Lovely Bay	Elijah Beneby	Tel: 344-3087
Mason Bay	Ethlyn Bain	Tel: 344-3628 VHF 16 "Central"
Pinefield Point	Newton Williamson	Tel: 344-3210 VHF 16 "Holiday Inn"
Delectable Bay	Leon Cooper	Tel: 344-3543 VHF 16 "Highway Inn"
Salina Point	George Emmanuel	Tel: 344-3671

Ferry
A government-owned ferry runs between Lovely Bay and Crooked Island at about 8 am and 4 pm. Trips cost $5.

Fuel
Diesel and gasoline are available at the Government Dock. Call VHF 16 "Central," or contact Felix at *Batelco* at Spring Point. Fuel at the settlements has usually been trucked in.
Groceries
McKinney's Grocery and Meats in Spring Point   Tel: 344-3614 Open from 7 am to 9 pm, Monday to Saturday, and from 7 am to 10 am, and 2 pm to 9 pm on Sundays. Well stocked.
Edmund Johnson's General Store in Chester's   Tel: 344-3108 The only store in Chester's; no set opening hours.
Police
In Spring Point   Tel: 344-3666   Open 9–5:30, Monday to Friday. There is also a police office at the airport, same hours.
Post Office
Tel: 344-3169 In Mason's Bay, since a fire destroyed the main office in Spring Point.
Restaurants
Nais in Spring Point   Tel: 344-3089 • VHF 16 "Nais Place" Call ahead for serving time and menu selection of Bahamian dishes. A bar, with satellite TV & pool table, has music most nights.
Bluebird Bar and Restaurant at Salina Point   Serves drinks, can provide lunch and dinner. Reservations must be made.
Telephone
Batelco at Spring Point   Tel: 344-3550/3536 • VHF 16 Open from 9 am to 5 pm, Monday to Friday.
Water
In Spring Point. Contact Mr. Heastie in town, by the tamarind tree, on the corner of the main road and the road leading to *Batelco*. Or you can use the government well, near the beach.

THINGS TO DO ON ACKLINS ISLAND

- Go bonefishing.
- Visit the caves in Havel Hill. Contact Leonard Collie at 344-3613 to put you in touch with guides.

MAYAGUANA

As far as Yellow Page information is concerned, Mayaguana falls into the same category as the islands in the Crooked–Acklins–Long Cay archipelago. Mayaguana is large, 24 miles long by 6 miles wide, and as you pass along its coast it seems to go on forever. There are only two sensible access points, the first on the west coast where the small settlement of Betsy Bay offers a fair-weather anchorage and a new Government Dock, just two miles north of the settlement. The new dock is of no value to you unless you want to call in to take on fuel, which in most cases has to be achieved can by can because the surge tends to make coming alongside perilous. The other access point on Mayaguana is Abraham's Bay, which offers good anchorages behind its barrier reef, but no direct access to Abraham's Bay settlement, which lies a hot ten-minute walk inland from its public dock. Don't be misled by the apparent convenience of that dock. You can't get close to it other than in a dinghy, and at low water even that can be difficult. Getting around Mayaguana is difficult, too. There are no taxis or buses, so you'll have to hitch rides; it's too hot and too far to walk.

So what can Mayaguana do for you? Well, there are the Abraham's Bay anchorages, which are as close as you can get to all-weather anchorages (but not severe-weather havens). There is a clinic, *Batelco*, basic food stores, and a twice-weekly *Bahamasair* service to Nassau. There is fuel in drums if they have it in stock. No bank, so everything is paid for with cash. The pluses are wonderfully friendly and kind people who will do everything they can to help you and make you feel welcome on their own special island.

ABRAHAM'S BAY

Church
Zion Baptist Church

Clinic
Tel: 339-3109   Open daily Monday to Friday from 9 am to 5 pm, with three nurses on call.

Customs and Immigration
Open daily from 9 am to 4:30 pm Monday to Friday at the administrative office, next to *Batelco*, a ten-minute walk up from the jetty.

Groceries
Brook's, Brown's, and *Farrington's* are open almost all day, every day, with a few groceries and supplies, mostly canned and dried goods.

Telephone
At *Batelco,* who also monitor VHF 16 and sell phone cards. The office is open from 8 am to 5 pm Monday to Friday, and 9 am to 5 pm on Sunday. If you need to talk to anyone in the settlement, *Batelco* will pass a message to them and they can be called to the phone in the office.

RESTAURANTS AND BARS

Paradise Villas Restaurant   Open for breakfast and lunch by arrangement, and for dinner most nights. Good Bahamian home cooking.

Reggie's Bar   Open daily for drinks and Bahamian meals.

Janet Wilson

ACCOMMODATIONS

Paradise Villas in Abraham's Bay   Fred Moss, with his wife Emmeline and daughter Jessie, have twenty simple rooms, as well as a bar and restaurant with a pool table and cable TV. The rooms cost $85 per night, and Emmeline will prepare you delicious home-cooked meals. You can contact them through *Batelco*.

Mayaguana Sheraton Guest House in Abraham's Bay   Cap'n Brown has two guest rooms in his own home, for which he charges $85 per night. Call *Batelco* to contact him.

Buccaneer's Inn at Pirates Wells   Tel: 242-339-3605   Sixteen rooms on the beach, with their own drinking water and restaurant and bar. Call Mrs. Brown.

THINGS TO DO IN MAYAGUANA

- Go fishing, or better still go crabbing with new friends from Abraham's Bay, any time between the months of March and August.
- Finish that good book you've been meaning to read.

GREAT INAGUA

Ministry of Tourism

Famous for its salt and flamingos, Great Inagua is one of the largest islands in the Bahamas. For the cruising visitor, it lies almost directly on the Windward Passage route between the Bahamas and the Caribbean. This said, few marina support facilities have ever been developed on the island. Great Inagua owes its continuing prosperity to the Morton Salt Company, which exports around a million and a half tons of Great Inagua salt each year. Morton Salt has its own company houses, backup facilities, and dock here. **Matthew Town** is very much a satellite to this activity. In Matthew Town, which is a Port of Entry, you will find facilities that are available at any Bahamian settlement. The commercial harbor was designed to accommodate the Royal Bahamas Defence Force and the United States Coast Guard, both based at Matthew Town Harbour. However, the USCG is there as a guest. The waters around the Inaguas are Bahamian territory, and distress calls must be directed to the RBDF.

MATTHEW TOWN

Matthew Town Harbour
Tel: 242-339-1427/1550 • Fax: 339-1670
• VHF 16 "Harbour Pilot"
Although this can hardly be called a marina, the little harbor offers some protection from all but the northwest winds, and a friendly welcome. It is a short walk into town.

Dockmaster and owner of the filling station next door and the *Crystal Beach View Hotel*, Leon Turnquest, told us that the government will extend the dock 80 to 90 feet on the north side, and 30 to 40 feet on the east side. The entrance will change from northwest to southwest with a breakwater to protect from northwest seas, and after dredging they will be able to take a 200-foot boat inside the harbor. Plans are to have showers and restrooms on shore. As of August 1999, work had not started, so call ahead to make sure of how to approach if there is building in progress.

Slips	8 ft. alongside the L-shaped wall.
Depth at Entrance	16 ft. at high water, 13 ft. at low water, 50 ft. width in the entry channel.
Dockage	$8 per day, including power.
Fuel	Diesel and gas available from Leon Turnquest. Cash only, but the bank will cash money on a Visa or MasterCard. The bank is closed on Wednesdays and weekends.
Water and Ice	Yes
Propane	From the *Inagua General Store*.
Mechanics	Newell Ingraham or Clive Claire may be able to help you; ask Leon to contact them

SERVICES & SHOPPING

Accommodations
Crystal Beach View Hotel   Tel: 339-1550
North of town, with its own restaurant, but closed at time of writing.

Morton Bahamas Ltd. "Main House" Tel: 339-1267 Six rooms from $55, four with a bathroom; reservations necessary.
Walkines Guest House Tel: 339-1612 Five double rooms from $50, in town, but call ahead for reservations.

Airport
Bahamasair Tel: 339-1415 Flights to Nassau.

Bank
Bank of the Bahamas Tel: 339-1264 Open 9 am to 2 pm on Monday, Tuesday, & Thursday; 10 am to 5:30 pm on Fridays. Closed Wednesdays.

Bicycles
Rentals through Mr. Bertram Ingrahams at one of his stores.

Churches
St. Philip's Anglican Church Built in 1885, it is the oldest church on the island.
Wesley Methodist Church
Zion Baptist Church
Greater Bethel Temple Mission Church

Commissioner's Office
Tel: 339-1271 Open from 9 am to 5:30 pm, Monday to Friday.

Customs
Tel: 339-1254 in Matthew Town or 339-1605 at the airport. Open from 9 am to 5:30 pm, Monday to Friday.

and Immigration
Tel: 339-1234 in Matthew Town or 339-1602 at the airport. Open from 9 am to 5:30 pm, Monday to Friday. Immigration officials advise boats to call the Royal Bahamian Defence Force on VHF 16 to announce their arrival, and request entry. The RBDF monitors channel 16 around the clock, and they will notify Customs and Immigration for you.

Inagua General Store

Fuel
Far East Enterprise Petroleum Tel: 339-1427 A new filling station at the harbor.

Groceries
Inagua General Store Tel: 339-1460 Open from 9:30 am to 5:30 pm. This is a well-stocked and good-sized store.

Hospital
In Matthew Town
Tel: 339-1249 For emergencies out of hours, call 339-1226; clinics held 9 am to 5:30 pm with Dr. Mukerjee & Nurse Patty Fawkes, who can be called at 339-1808 in emergency.

ILibrary and Museum
Erickson's Public Library and Museum Tel: 339-1683 Ask about opening hours.

Mailboat
From Nassau.

Liquor Store
Ingrahams Liquor Store Open from 8 am to 8 pm Monday to Saturday, after church on Sundays. This store is owned jointly with *Ingrahams Variety Store,* so check both if one is not open. The *Variety Store* carries food and household goods.

Photo Shop
Abby's Photo Shop Tel: 339-1750 Film and developing.

Police
Emergency call 919 or Tel: 339-1263
In Matthew Town, 339-1444; at the airport, 339-1604.

Post Office
Tel: 339-1248 Open 9 am to 5:30 pm, Monday to Friday.

Repairs
In an emergency, the *Morton Salt Company* might be able to help from its machine shop. Call 339-1300 or 339-1849.

Restaurants
Cozy Corner Restaurant and Bar Tel: 339-1440 Opens at 10 am Monday to Saturday, and 1:30 pm on Sundays. Bahamian food, snacks, pool table, satellite TV, weekend DJ.
Snake Pit Bar Open from 10 am Monday to Saturday, and from 2 pm on Sundays. Weekend music, large, local crowd. Snacks.
Topp's Restaurant and Bar Tel: 339-1465 • VHF 16 Open from 9 am to 10 pm Monday to Saturday, and from 6 pm to 10 pm on Sundays. Bahamian dishes and fantastic cracked conch. Call ahead for reservations and to check menu availability.

Telephone
Batelco Tel: 339-1000/1007 • Fax: 339-1323 Office open 9 am to 5:30 pm, Monday to Friday, with phone cards for sale.

Tours
Great Inagua Tours Tel and Fax: 339-1862 Larry Ingraham organizes tours to the *Inagua National Park,* where huge numbers of flamingos and many types of birds can be seen, as well as donkeys and ducks, and maybe even wild boar. He can also, for around $80, take you on an all-day tour from the manually operated lighthouse on the southwest coast to Arawak Indian sites and noisy bat caves.

DIVE SITES

Both wall dives down to 230 feet, *Devil's Point* and *South Bay* offer exciting diving. If you are coming down from Crooked Island, *Hogsty Reef* would make an interesting diversion to dive one of the many wrecks there. Some of them are visible above the water.

INAGUA NATIONAL PARK

The Bahamas National Trust, with help from the Audubon Society, maintains the *Inagua National Park.* It is home to more than 60,000 flamingos, the largest nesting colony of West Indian Flamingos in the western hemisphere, as well as many other birds such as roseate spoonbills, rare reddish egrets, hummingbirds, blue herons, tree ducks and Bahamian parrots. More than 250 species of plants and animals live on Great Inagua. You can also visit the *Caves,* the *Bonsai Forest,* and the inland *Blue Hole.* The road leading to the park is open to the public but you will need a guide. Henry Nixon (339-1616) is a contact for tours.

THINGS TO DO IN GREAT INAGUA

- Go and see the massive salt piles awaiting further action. These huge crystalline mountains look like snow.
- Take a bicycle ride down to the lighthouse, which became necessary after 65 boats met their final destination on the reef in one year, 1859.
- Dive the wall sites, at the edge of the Great Bahama Wall. *Devil's Point* particularly, has a pure sand dropoff with giant coral heads that tumble toward a vast abyss.
- Take a tour through the *Inagua National Park.*
- Walk down to *Kiwanis Park* in Matthew Town on a Saturday morning to share freshly cooked meals, with money going to local charities.

Chapter 19
The Unexplored Bahamas
South Andros
The Jumentos Cays

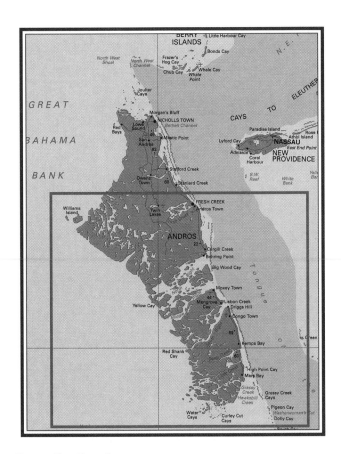

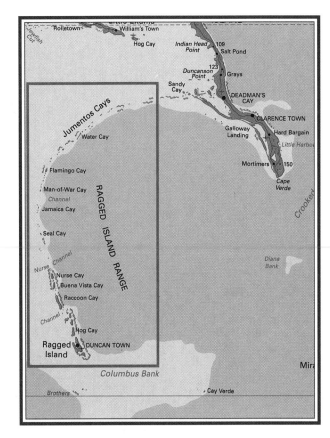

South Andros

TAKE an airline flight from Miami to George Town in the Exumas and look down all the way once you've crossed the Gulf Stream. The almost unbelievable maze of shallows, deeper-water channels, tidal inlets, coral heads, shoals, mangrove swamp, and land is the area we're talking about. South Andros. The land itself is almost totally devoid of settlement, for the most part tangled low-growth forest, scrub, sink holes, and shallow ponds. But winding through all this confusion there are channels that can offer you transits across Andros, and ways in which you can probe your way up and down, and part way inland, along both the west and the east coast.

Somehow we don't think we're likely to add this area to this Guide. But it's there, if you want to try it.

The Jumentos Cays

THE Jumentos Cays are the great 50-nm arc of cays that start just north of the Ragged Island range in Latitude 22° 30' N, and swing northeast toward Long Island, to end some 18 nm south of Little Exuma. They are bordered on the east by a pocket of deep water north of the Columbus Bank, and on the west by the southeast edge of the Great Bahama Bank. The Jumentos form an area for real exploration, shelling, fishing, and diving that remains largely untouched, although we've heard that the fishing there has been hard hit in recent years, given the mobility of a Bahamian skiff with an outboard.

Largely unvisited, except by fishermen, you are on your own there. There are no backups. Take note of your weather before you set out, and watch the sky while you're there.

Part VI

The Turks and Caicos Islands

Introduction

Providenciales

The Caicos Bank and South Caicos

Grand Turk Island and the Turks Bank

Ocean water, about 100 feet deep, Turks Island Passage.

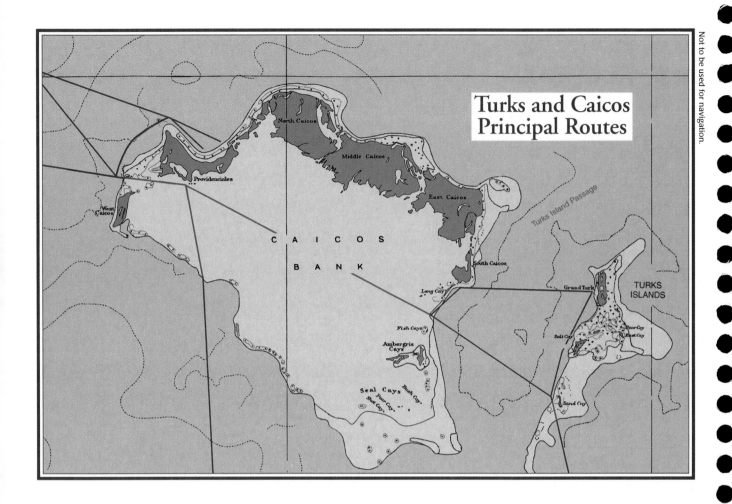

Turks and Caicos
Principal Routes

Not to be used for navigation.

ROUTE TO/FROM		HEADINGS	DISTANCE NM	PASSAGE
Mayaguana West	Providenciales North	121°/301°M	47	Caicos Passage
Mayaguana West	Sandbore Channel Approach	136°/316°M	47	Caicos Passage
Mira Por Vos Passage	Providenciales North	095°/275°M	117	Caicos Passage
Mira Por Vos Passage	Sandbore Channel Approach	100°/280°M	110	Caicos Passage
Providenciales North	Sellars Cut Approach	133°/313°M	10	Atlantic coastal
Providenciales North	Leeward Cut Approach	117°/297°M	10	Atlantic coastal
Providenciales North	Sandbore Channel Approach	221°/041°M	12	Atlantic coastal
Sandbore Channel	South Dock	see text	10	Caicos Bank
South Dock	French Cay	see text	15	Caicos Bank
South Dock	Fish Cay Channel	see text	44	Caicos Bank
French Cay	Luperón, DR	Not covered in this Guide	90	Atlantic open
Fish Cay Channel	South Caicos	046°/226°M	6	Turks Passage
Fish Cay Channel	Sand Cay	125°/305°M	23	Turks Passage
South Caicos	Grand Turk	090°/270°M	21	Turks Passage
Grand Turk	Sand Cay	see text	19	Turks Passage
Sand Cay	Luperón, DR	Not covered in this Guide	90	Atlantic open
Sand Cay	Mona Passage	Not covered in this Guide	270	Atlantic open
Sand Cay	San Juan, PR	Not covered in this Guide	360	Atlantic open
Sand Cay	St Thomas, USVI	Not covered in this Guide	390	Atlantic open

Distances exclude inshore close approaches at the start and end of a passage. The notation "see text" indicates multi-leg passages that are fully covered in the text.

Chapter 20
Introduction

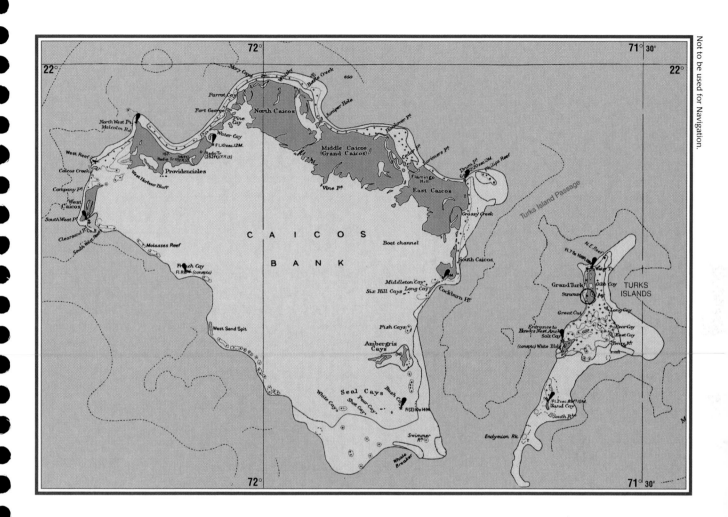

Where Are These Islands?

OPEN an atlas. Take a straight edge and lay it on the map, to connect Fort Lauderdale or Miami with the Virgin Islands. Take, if you like, St Thomas, as your target. It hardly matters which one you choose as all the Virgins lie pretty much within arm's length of each other. Your straight-edge line will pass Long Island's Cape Santa Maria, pass between Semana Cay and Crooked Island, go past Mayaguana, cross over North Caicos in the Turks and Caicos, and continue on across open water to St Thomas.

Now North Caicos is unlikely to feature on your potential port-of-call list, but the Turks and Caicos Islands as a whole lie right there, on your path, whichever way you are voyaging, northwest to southeast, or southeast to northwest. Almost at the halfway mark.

This, a matter of simple geography, is the main reason why the Turks and Caicos are important to anyone voyaging in either direction on the route between the east coast of the United States and the Caribbean at large. It doesn't matter whether you are sailing single-handed, or driving a mega-yacht. What is vital to you is that these islands can provide just about everything that will be on your contingency list.

The Turks and Caicos offer much to the passage maker bound to the Caribbean or heading north from it. But most Bahamas-bound cruising sailors, quite rightly, reckon that the Turks and Caicos are just too far, too remote, to be attractive as a destination. Yes, there's logic in that conclusion, but think again. So much depends on who you are, what you level of experience is, and how you choose to tackle this cruising business. In short, if you want to push the envelope that little bit, to voyage out, to find new places, you might well decide to visit the Turks and Caicos.

Yes, it means bluewater passages, but none of them are overly long. George Town to Crooked and Acklins Islands. Acklins to Mayaguana. Mayaguana to Providenciales. None of them are significantly greater in distance than crossing the Gulf Stream. If you only have two or three weeks, forget it. But for those who have the luxury of time?

Are They Part of the Bahamas?

Let's nail down one misconception right now. It's sometimes believed that the Turks and Caicos, at least physically, are part of the Bahamas. It's not true. Just as the Bahamas are made up of shallow sub-sea platforms and some isolated sub-sea mountain peaks, separated by deep ocean troughs, so are the Turks and Caicos. Geologically the two areas may be cousins, but a connection, a continuance of the same mould? Not so. They're quite distinct.

The same holds true politically. A common ancestry as British colonies suggests that, but for the vagaries of decisions made as the British shed former possessions worldwide, the two areas, in logic, could well have been linked. But this doesn't hold true. Historically they are very different. A different settlement pattern, a different development, and the result is a different personality today. As for political status, the Turks and Caicos are still a part of the United Kingdom. On a day-to-day basis they are, in effect, semi-autonomous.

That link with Britain remains, and with it comes some very tangible benefits, not the least of which is linkage with the European Community and the handouts that come with this membership. In general the accent is on development funds. In 1998 the leading project was setting up a freshwater pipeline grid for Providenciales, together with a significant expansion in desalinization capability. Under another heading a marine park warden service was set up and funded. More of this later, for it holds considerable import for the cruising visitor. Just keep reading!

Turks and Caicos Coat of Arms, Cockburn Town.

by the deep water of the Turks Passage, is outlying Grand Turk with Salt Cay, and a number of smaller cays. In the Turks and Caicos at large the island count numbers some eight large cays, of which only six are inhabited, and a scattering of small cays, spread over some 166 square miles. The land is low lying, coral and limestone, and barely shows beyond sea-level sight range. The highest elevation, in Providenciales, is 163 feet. Native vegetation is scrub, savanna, and marsh swamp, and native wildlife is essentially Caribbean with iguanas and flamingoes as exotic extras, and the islands are a main stop on the route of migrating birds.

For the cruising visitor only three cays, Providenciales, commonly called "Provo," South Caicos, and Grand Turk, offer shoreside facilities and shelter. The rest, unless you are bound on shoal draft exploration, are better ignored.

The Banks and the Ocean

You'll not go wrong if you think of the Caicos Bank as a great near-circular atoll, some 60 nm wide, fringed all around by reef. Inside water depths run from around 20 feet in parts to zero in some areas at low water. You can find transit routes across the bank that carry about 8 feet, and these have been surveyed. However most of the Caicos Bank is unsurveyed, and there is both reef and sand there. For navigation you need your eyes, and you need good sunlight with the sun high in the sky. This at once means that the sailboat crossing the Caicos Bank must, most probably, anchor for one night in transit.

The Turks Bank is lozenge shaped, running from northeast to southwest for some 36 nm. It has much the same characteristics as the Caicos Bank. It is navigable in parts. Both areas, like the Bahamas, have claimed many ships as victims since Juan Ponce de León discovered the islands for the European World in 1512. As always, your safety lies in choosing your weather, never attempting a night passage, and using the sun to advantage. Yes, you can run on an autopilot on a bank transit, but you need your eyes as well, full time, otherwise you too may join the list of Turks and Caicos wrecks.

The Turks and Caicos Islands at a Glance

The Turks and Caicos Islands lie between 21° and 22° N and 071° and 072° 30' W. There are two groups of islands, the greater part forming a crescent around the northern edge of the Caicos Bank. To the east, separated from the Caicos Bank

The ocean waters around the Turks and Caicos are seriously deep, plunging to 12,000 feet between the Dominican Republic and these islands, to 9,000 feet in the Caicos Passage to the northwest, and 15,000 feet in the open Atlantic. To the southeast three banks, the Mouchoir, Silver, and Navidad Banks, shoal to 60 feet or less and have coral that is awash at low water. These banks are the winter breeding ground for the Atlantic humpback whale population, which takes off bodily, adults and calves, to migrate to the New England coast for the summer. The Turks Passage, 22 nm wide and 6,000 feet deep, is part of their long-established ocean highway.

What really makes the Turks and Caicos is the water world. The colors, clarity, and warmth of the ocean and bank waters are unbelievable. The reefs are pristine. Innumerable. And the diving is world class, from shallow reef dives to awesome wall dives. The fishing is good. Turn shoreward, and the Turks and Caicos beaches are "to die for," gently shoaling water and soft white sand.

The Weather

The climate is tropical, with temperatures averaging 75°–80°F (24°–27°C) in winter (November to April), and 85°–90°F (29°–32°C) in summer (May to October). The prevailing winds are the Trades, easterly to southeasterly, but these winds, which do much to moderate both temperature and humidity, are rarely rain-bearing (the annual average rainfall is some 29 inches). The islands have no underlying aquifers, cannot survive on rainfall, and desalinization is vital to both the local population and the tourist industry.

During the winter season the islands, albeit to a far lesser degree than the Bahamas, are effected by Northers. Cold fronts from the northwest are heralded by a period of calm, invariably followed by the standard wind switch to the southwest, then to the northwest as the front moves through. It will bring disturbed skies and disturbed seas, making reef passes temporarily impassable and anchorages, depending on their location, unpleasant if not untenable. A day or longer may elapse before the weather returns to normal.

As with the Bahamas, the hurricane season runs from May through to November. Statistically the Turks and Caicos seem well favored by nature, for they have been hit by a hurricane, on average, only every ten years.

The People

Ninety percent of the population of some 15,000 are the descendants of former slaves, and the only two centers of population of any significance are Providenciales and Grand Turk. Strange as it now may seem, Grand Turk, the outlier, is the capital. It's one of those rare places that appears to have been by-passed by the political genesis and pressures of the Southwest Atlantic–Caribbean region, and is, per-

haps, a quarter of a century behind in time. Providenciales is where the action is, all the tourist development, and where, right now, much of the development money is targeted.

Population Figures

Providenciales	7,000
Grand Turk	3,500
North Caicos	1,275
South Caicos	1,400
Middle Caicos	270

The Turks and Caicos Islanders call themselves "Belongers," a self-protective definition perhaps necessary in Providenciales as flight after flight of tourists arrive at Providenciales International. Along the northern sweep of Grace Bay beach the resort hotels dominate the entire coastline. Elsewhere virtually the entire island appears to be

Turks and Caicos

WHY Turks? The answer lies in a cactus plant that grows on Grand Turk Island. It looks pretty normal, green, fattish, and prickly most of the time. But in flower it produces a red top that looks just like a Turkish fez, those round red hats with a tassel that Attaturk banned when he took Turkey into the twentieth century. The plants clearly impressed the early Western European navigators. So Grand Turk got its name.

What about Caicos? Maybe it's Arawak or an Arawak-Spanish derivation, rather like *cay*, or maybe it came from the coco plum tree, *cay icoco*. No one knows for sure.

Janet Wilson

sub-divided into building lots, and new houses, built for winter visitors, tax exiles, and housing for offshore bankers, crowd the most desirable sites.

Anciently the Turks and Caicos population depended on fishing (largely conch and lobster), boatbuilding, and salt. Today their income depends almost entirely on tourism and a "tax free status," which has attracted some 7,000 foreign financial institutions to nail up corporate signs in Providenciales. But as we've said, it's different in Grand Turk. If you go to South Caicos, there you'll find yourself even more remote from the glitter, glitz, drive, and dust of Providenciales with its would-be Gold Coasts.

National Marine Parks

The Turks and Caicos, to the best of our knowledge, are world leaders in the field of marine conservation. To date six Marine Parks have been established, as well as a further fifty sites designated as Land Parks, Reserves, Sanctuaries, and Historical Sites. For the cruising visitor this legislation has a significant impact on where you go, and what you do there. In brief, in the conservation areas, except in designated anchorages, vessels over 60 feet LOA are prohibited. No vessel is permitted to anchor other than over sand, and not within 300 feet of a dive site and within 400 feet of the Low Water mark. The penalties, particularly for damaging coral by grounding or anchoring, are severe. The highest fine on record, levied against a US yacht for damaging coral with an anchor, was $40,000. Yes, that figure 40 and the three zeros are not typos.

The Marine Parks cover most of the western and the northern waters of Providenciales, West Caicos, Chalk Sound, the Pine Cay area (between Providenciales and North Caicos), South Caicos, and Grand Turks. Four protected areas of small cays, of particular interest to boaters because they are important transit waypoints, are French Cay, the Ambergris Cays, the Fish Cays, and Sand Cay.

We'll cover this subject more fully, and list the regulations, under our **Green Pages** section titled **Parks and Wildlife Preserves** on page 401.

How We'll Cover the Turks and Caicos

We covered the Bahamas choosing to run from north to south, simply because most cruising visitors take their voyaging in the Bahamas that way, at least in the outward passages. Rather than break that pattern, we'll deal with the Turks and Caicos the same way. This may not make sense to the voyager coming up from the Caribbean, but once you've decided how to cut the cloth for your suit, you've just got to get on with it and fit the pieces together. In truth, if this is any reassurance for those who may feel aggrieved and want a south–north orientation, yes, when we first visited the Turks and Caicos we too were on passage, from Bridgetown, Barbados, to Jupiter, Florida.

Planning Your Voyaging

Straightline Distances

The distances we show are straight-line ballpark figures to kick off your Time and Space considerations. The reality, recorded in your log, will be different. It could be very different, for as always the variables lie in whether you're voyaging under sail or power, your average SOA, the wind speed and direction, the sea state, the incidence of bad weather, your endurance, and the continuing seaworthiness of your vessel.

APPROACHES TO THE TURKS AND CAICOS		
George Town	Providenciales	250 nm
Mayaguana	Providenciales	55 nm
Mira Por Vos Passage	Providenciales	115 nm
CAICOS BANK TRANSITS		
Providenciales	French Cay	15 nm
Providenciales	Fish Cays	50 nm
Providenciales	South Caicos	60 nm
TURKS PASSAGE TRANSITS		
South Caicos	Grand Turk	22 nm
Fish Cays	Sand Cay	25 nm
TURKS BANK TRANSITS		
Grand Turk	Sand Cay	18 nm
MOVING ON		
French Cay	Luperón, DR	120 nm
Sand Cay	Luperón, DR	80 nm
Sand Cay	Puerto Plata, DR	90 nm
Sand Cay	Mona Passage	270 nm
Sand Cay	San Juan, PR	360 nm
Sand Cay	St. Thomas, USVI	390 nm

Landfall and Departure Points

As we've said, only three of the inhabited cays offer any facilities to the cruising visitor. Providenciales (with five possible ports of call) is the most important, and where you are most likely to go. South Caicos might serve as short-term shelter, and Grand Turk, pleasant though it is, lacks any significant marine facilities. Grand Turk's North Creek could be listed as a hurricane hole, but don't think of it if you can't get there before the onset of severe weather.

There are a handful of other cays, one sparsely populated, the others uninhabited, that can offer you shelter in reasonably good weather and a chance to get some sleep before you continue on passage, or the chance to swim, snorkel, dive, and go beachcombing. French Cay or the Fish and Ambergris Cays on the rim of the Caicos Bank are the most obvious choices, and Salt Cay or Sand Cay are your best bets on the Turks Bank. French Cay, the Fish Cay Channel, and Sand Cay are good approach or departure waypoints.

Coming in from or Heading North

Whether you're on passage or cruising, Providenciales is almost bound to be your number-one destination in the Turks and Caicos. As Providenciales is a barrier island, one of the half-circle of islands and cays bordering the Caicos Bank, you have a choice to make: to approach Providenciales from the north, ocean side, or approach from the south, over the Caicos Bank. If you're on passage, you may well wish to maximize your time in blue- water, and avoid the shallows. As it happens, the best facilities for visiting boats are on the north coast of Providenciales, the bluewater approach. For years the south coast, although the most frequented by visitors, be it cruis-

Sitting Pretty Beach, Grand Turk Island.

ing or on passage, has had virtually no significant marine facilities. This now may be changing.

This then is your first decision. You can, of course, have both worlds. Put in to the north, and then backtrack back into bluewater, and make your way on to the Caicos Bank from the west or the east, as you would in a direct ocean approach. There is no connector between the north and south of Providenciales. See our coverage in the next chapter.

Entry Ports — Providenciales	
North Coast:	Turtle Cove and the Leeward Marina
South Coast:	South Dock (for Sapodilla Bay and the Caicos Marina)

Coming in from or Heading South

French Cay is a good starting block for Luperón in the Dominican Republic, some 120 nm away. However you can't play it as a straight shot from there, because the Caicos Bank extends to the southeast for another 30 nm. You have to run south-southeast for about 10 nm, say to 21° 20' N 072° 10' W, before taking up your bluewater heading.

Entry Ports — South Caicos and Grand Turk Island	
South Caicos	Cockburn Harbour (Government Dock or Shell Fuel Dock)
Grand Turk	South Dock

South Caicos is a well-placed start point for the Dominican Republic, Puerto Rico, and the Virgin Islands, but it's short on facilities. Unless you particularly want to put in to South Caicos, or for some reason decide to clear in here (which you can do), you're unlikely to come this way. The Fish Cay Channel and Sand Cay (aka Big Sand Cay) on the Turks Bank offer better jumping-off places,

unless you choose to go north around Grand Turk and take it to Puerto Rico or the Virgins as a straight shot passing north of the Mouchoir, Silver, and Navidad Banks.

So, if you're going south down the Turks Island Passage, in reality your departure (or arrival) waypoint is likely to be either the Fish Cay Channel, or Sand Cay. From the Fish Cay Channel, southward bound, for comfort's sake I think we'd run the 25 nm or so to Sand Cay, and rest there before going on. From Sand Cay, Luperón is 80 nm, Puerto Plata 90 nm, and the Mona Passage, between the Dominican Republic and Puerto Rico, if you want to take it as a straight

APPROACH AND DEPARTURE WAYPOINTS
PROVIDENCIALES

North West Point		
PROVN	21° 55' 00"/000 N	072° 20' 00"/000 W
Sandbore Channel Approach		
SBORA	21° 46' 00"/000 N	072° 28' 30"/500 W

CAICOS BANK

French Cay		
FRNCH	21° 30' 00"/000 N	072° 12' 30"/500 W
Fish Cay Channel		
FCCHN	21° 25' 00"/000 N	071° 35' 40"/668 W
South Caicos		
SCAIC	21° 28' 37"/631 N	071° 31' 40"/664 W

GRAND TURK

Grand Turk		
GTURK	21° 28' 22"/375 N	071° 09' 24"/396 W
Sand Cay		
SANDC	21° 11' 45"/757 N	071° 15' 24"/408 W

The final figures in each waypoint show seconds (00") and thousands (000) of a minute.

shot, is 270 nm. You can exit over the Turks Bank from this waypoint, but be sure you don't match HMS *Endymion*'s 1790 misfortune (a fate shared by at least two other vessels at a later date) and hit the reef 5 nm to the southwest of our waypoint.

It's not a remote possibility! Captain Bob Gascoigne, the publisher of the Taicos and Caicos charts we list, has found that earlier BA and DMA charts misplace the Endymion reef by about one mile. Your safest course is to draw a 2 nm radius circle around 21° 07' N 071° 18' W and stay out of this area. If you wish to dive the wreck, Salt Cay Divers, who operate out of the Mount Pleasant Guest House on Salt Cay, can take you there.

Grand Turk is well placed for the Dominican Republic, Puerto Rico, and the Virgin Islands. Much the same considerations apply to Grand Turk as they do to South Caicos. If you clear in here, you must report at South Dock, 2 nm to the south. Read our detail on Grand Turk before you decide whether this is your place.

Final Thoughts

As always, season, weather, as well as your endurance, will dictate the way you choose to go. It's that, and, if you're sailing, whether you're trying to ride Northers to get south, or running with the Trades to reach the Bahamas. Be aware that the Turks Island Passage can be a millrace, with the current taking you northward on a faster track than you might desire. We logged it a 7 knots. And, at the edges of the Banks, like all deep-water/shallow-water interfaces, it can kick up like mad when the wind piles the water the wrong way and stacks it up against the tide.

CHARTS AND LIGHTS

British Admiralty and DMA charts of the Turks and Caicos Islands are based, as are most charts, on surveys carried out in the past, which, because of the state of the art at the time, were inaccurate. While a chart may show an "updated to" and a recent publication date, it does not mean that the chart has been 100 percent checked and revised. It means that known errors, brought to notice, have been corrected.

There are areas, principally on the banks, where no detailed surveys were carried out, simply because it was taken that they were off the shipping routes and could be ignored. A blank area showing no reef and no sand is no guarantee that it is so.

At the time of our writing, other than Grand Turk Light and Sand Cay Light, no other Turks and Caicos lights marked on the charts were working. Additionally, the entry lights marking the approach pass into South Caicos showed the opposite of "red right returning."

The answer to these problems? Don't cross the Banks at night. Stay in deep water if you make your landfall during darkness. And by day, use your eyes.

At risk of overkill on this topic, let's just mention GPS and waypoints again. Don't believe your GPS shows you exactly where you are on the chart. It shows where you are on the surface of this planet, and the chart may be out of kilter with the real world.

Chapter 21
Providenciales

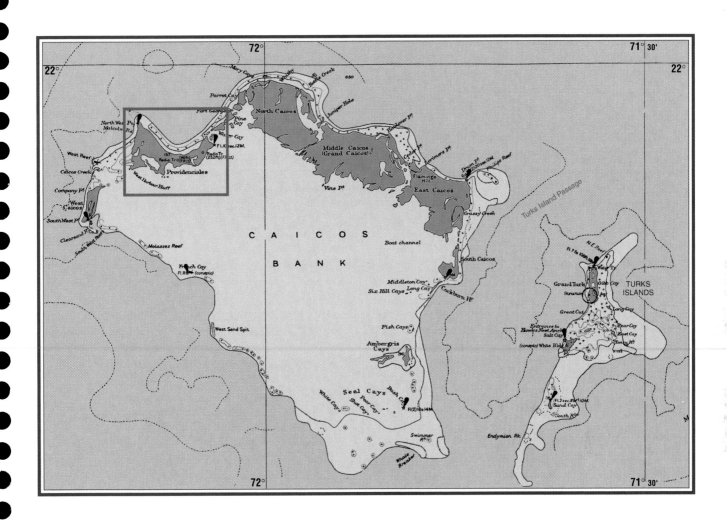

Providenciales

PROVIDENCIALES is one of the Dream Destinations. Any way you look at the sand, water colors, and coral of Grace Bay, it's poster material. This kind of impact can hit hard when you're in Month Two of digging yourself out of each successive snow storm, and this kind of imagery spurs the bookings for the tourist-hungry resort complexes, the *Club Med Turkoise*, *Beaches* (a new Sandals resort), the *Grace Bay Club*, the *Turkoise Beach Resort*, and, by our last count, four new condominium resorts. This is Providenciales (call it Provo), the north coast scene.

Elsewhere development (mostly new housing estates and small shopping centers) seems haphazard, but continuous. Provo, as a town rather than an island (for the name serves both), appears to have no plan, no form, and no controlling hand. Small isolated mini-malls, investment banks, gas sta-

tions, and liquor stores are scattered randomly, chaotically, for over three miles between the airport and the Leeward Highway, the island's backbone road, and two to three miles eastward on each side of highway. At first sight, and on better acquaintance, the island appears to be one great construction site from which the only escape is to take flight (literally), or put out to sea.

What then about the incoming sailor? Unless you're bound on gunkholing around the Caicos Bank or the Turks Bank, Providenciales is going to be your pit stop, because almost everything you might require is there. Your problems, if we can call them that, lie in deciding where you want to put in, and once you've arrived, how you'll get around. Provo is not pedestrian oriented. The distances, and the distances between each stop you'll need to make, are too great to use boat shoes as transport.

Choosing Your Destination

Your initial choice is simple. Either the north coast or the south coast. On the north coast you have Turtle Cove Marina, and further on the Leeward Marina. Turtle Cove is the only place in the Turks and Caicos to have the appearance, facilities, and "feel" of a US-type marina, with restaurants, a dive shop, and accommodations all there, and it's the closest to "downtown" Provo. But you still need wheels to get there. The Leeward Marina is as far as the road runs from the business center, but if you want to explore in a dinghy, swim, dive, and fish, you are probably better off there. No north coast anchorages exist, but you can anchor in the Leeward Going Through.

Both north coast marinas have one apparent disadvantage. If you are passage making to or from the Caribbean, to get there you have to divert from your direct course. Then you have to put out again, through the reef, and backtrack to take up your desired course, be it across the Caicos Bank or to bypass the islands. There may be a day or so in it.

On the south coast, previously almost totally undeveloped, there are now more options. The first is the long-standing anchorage of Sapodilla Bay, with no facilities nearby and over two miles to go to the supermarkets, shops, banks, and restaurants of downtown Provo. South Dock, slightly further on, is your entry port but it's a commercial dock, and only occasionally will it accept the temporary presence of a private craft. Slightly further on the Five Cays offer an alternative anchorage. Then, on the next hook of land, the new South Side Marina is getting into business on Cooper Jack Bight, and further on, the still near-derelict Caicos Shipyard and Marina remains in business. A change in ownership, now in progress, may lead to rejuvenation there. The latter two options, like the Leeward Marina, are

PROVIDENCIALES NORTH COAST

North West Point		
PROVN	21° 55' 00"/000 N	072° 20' 00"/000 W
Sellars Cut Approach		
SLLRA	21° 48' 30"/500 N	072° 12' 30"/500 W
Leeward Cut Approach		
LWRDA	21° 50' 30"/500 N	072° 10' 30"/500 W

The final figures in each waypoint show seconds (00") and thousands (000) of a minute.

light years away from commercial Provo.

On this last thought, local taxis cost the earth. It's cheaper to rent a car for a day than it is to take two taxi rides. The rental car agencies will bring the car to you, and will deliver you back to your boat when you turn the car in.

Navigation

The North Coast

From our Providenciales north waypoint (PROVN) you have some 8.5 nm to run to the Sellars Cut entry waypoint (for Turtle Cove) on something like 137°M, and about 10 nm to run to the approach waypoint for the Leeward Going Through (for the Leeward Marina) on around 125°M. Both runs are in deep blue water.

TURTLE COVE MARINA

At our Sellars Cut waypoint, SLLRA, you can, if you know the way, follow the markers in to Turtle Cove. You have 2.07 nm to run, there are channel markers, red to starboard and green to port, and the depth at the shallowest point reduces from between 6–8 feet and 5.5 feet at MLW, so if you fit these parameters, you can make it.

Against this, the pass itself is clear but has mid-pass coral. Some of the markers (6-foot-tall vertical floating posts) may be missing (while we were updating this Guide two were claimed by a storm), and the marked entry route consists of nine legs before you alter into a final 180-degree curve, which will take you to the marina entrance. If you get swept sideways by wind or wave, you can end up on the rocks. It's a series of doglegs around coral, and, at one point, a narrow pass through an artificial cut (blown in the years before such engineering was forbidden) known as the English

Dolphin–Nomad chart. Depth in meters.

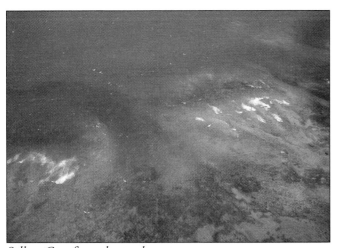

Sellars Cut, from the south.

Channel. Above all, you can't sail in, and to attempt it would lead to disaster. Northerly weather, any kind of set from the north, dictates "Forget It."

But let's be encouraging. The largest user of the marina has been a 110-foot dive boat in the Aggressor fleet with a 6-foot draft and a single screw. Why not call Turtle Cove on VHF 16 and get a guide to lead you in?

Turtle Cove itself, built in the natural lagoon called Sellars Pond, offers total protection from wave and surge, and protection from all wind save that coming out of the northern sectors. Like every place in Providenciales, it's a construction site. Much is finished, and has been long established. Much, including repair facilities and a lift, remains to be done. This apart, virtually all you could wish for is there, and there are bars and restaurants within walking distance, and rental bicycles, motorcycles, and cars on your doorstep. See our **Yellow Pages** for the fine detail.

LEEWARD MARINA

Much the same considerations on entry apply to the Leeward Marina. At our approach waypoint LWRDA you can iden-

Turtle Cove Marina, from the southwest.

tify the Leeward Cut and there are no particular problems there. Inside the reef there's some scattered coral, but you'll see the markers set out by the Leeward Marina and could make your own way in. Here it's not coral but sand that's your main concern. Currently there are four markers defining two possible, alternative, routes. Apart from the possibility of missing marks, in the words of the dockmaster "the sandbars are always shifting." You'd be wise to call on VHF 16 for advice, and check the state of the tide. If the channel has held, you should have 9 feet at MLW all the way.

In the Leeward Going Through the marina comes up to

Leeward Going Through, from the north (above), and from the south (below).

starboard roughly halfway down. Don't confuse the marina with the entry channel into the housing development that comes up first. If you reach the Conch Farm, you've gone too far.

Despite the attraction of "going through" to gain the Caicos Bank we reckon it's a no-no. To the east and southeast the Caicos Bank is plagued by sand, and to the south you have the Leeward Reef. Our recommendation is that if you're going south, go north first, retrace your entry track, and then set out around Providenciales.

The Leeward Marina has ambitious plans to rebuild itself

into a major marine resort complex. At the moment it's simple, and very remote. See our **Yellow Pages**. What it does offer is immediate dinghy access to the Fort George National Park and Historical Site, and the Princess Alexandra Nature Reserve, all of this protected area centered around the Water Cays, Fort George Cay, Mangrove Cay, and Donna Cay.

The South Coast

Now let's look at the south coast of Providenciales, and we'll take it as if you were coming in from Mayaguana, because we want to include one possible anchorage before you make your Sandbore Channel (Caicos Creek) approach mark landfall. For as long as we can remember Sapodilla Bay has been *the* Turks and Caicos anchorage on the route to and from the Caribbean. There never has been much there, other than the entry facilities of nearby South Dock, the chance to buy some stores, and one small beach. With the prevailing wind it has proved a good anchorage, but it's not an all-weather haven. Most of the time, for most people, it served. It certainly helped when the Mariner Hotel was there, but this is now closed. In contrast to this apparent dereliction, the immediate shoreline has blossomed into endless property developments spread westward from Sapodilla Bay along the Silly Creek peninsula, which runs between the Caicos Bank and Chalk Sound.

When the Caicos Shipyard and Marina, further along the coast to the east, came into business, for the first time the islands had a travel lift, a repair facility, and an alternative to Sapodilla. Like Sapodilla, the Yard was remote. Even further away from the supermarkets and banks, and either lack of drive or lack of adequate funding left the Caicos Yard looking like a development in Year 1. Now a new marina has been opened in Cooper Jack Bight, just about

Tiki Huts Anchorage, from the south.

halfway between Sapodilla and the Caicos Yard, and the south coast is beginning to show promise for the cruising visitor. The downside as we see it? You are still so far from your provisioning, and all the rest. In time, if the marinas attract or develop a support infrastructure around them, that could change. But it remains that the south coast of Providenciales is right on your route, south or north.

Now we'll switch back to the start and look at your route in from Mayaguana. There is one anchorage off the west coast that you may wish to note.

TIKI HUTS ANCHORAGE

Tiki Huts Anchorage		
TIKIA	21° 49' 50"/833 N	072° 20' 30"/500 W

Running south from North West Point the western shore of Providenciales is shielded by reef until Latitude 21° 50' N. There the reef disappears for about 2 nm, and then builds up again to continue south to the edge of the Sandbore Channel. The coastline that runs south to this break in the reef has long been known as Malcolm Roads. It was inaccessible overland until a French TV company built a mock-Polynesian village, improbably called Atlantis, on a small headland just east of our waypoint TIKIA. The enterprise failed, the site is now in ruins, and the access road from central Provo is a rough sand track. It remains that this is an anchorage that might serve you well in northwest through southeast weather, and could be approached (with caution) at night, if you are waiting for sunlight to negotiate the Sandbore Channel.

The 50-fathom-line in this area has a string of dive site buoys (rated for vessels up to 50 feet LOA), and it is legal to secure to one of these, if you wish to, on a temporary basis. You must move off if a dive operator requires it.

SANDBORE CHANNEL (AKA CAICOS CREEK)

Sandbore Channel has suffered from bad PR on occasion and quite wrongly been considered a difficult pass. It's a good, relatively straight, 10–15-foot-deep half-mile-wide cut through the reef some 2 nm north of the northwest point of West Caicos. It's a pity that the wreck of a freighter, which provided the best nav mark ever, a mile and a half to the north, vanished in a storm, but this sudden disappearance of a wreck is not uncommon. Our waypoint SBORW, at the western entrance of the channel, is just a tad over 2 nm southeast of our initial approach waypoint SBORA.

If you elect to enter by daylight, with the sun high, you'll find yourself tripping along a broad blue highway running almost due east, better by far than the Yellow Brick Road that led to Oz. You'll want to favor the north side of the channel, for it's better defined, with the blue of your deepwater road and the white of the sandbore. Don't wander off toward the south, for it's harder to pick up your line there.

Sandbore Channel, from the west.

It should go without saying, but we'll say it, don't attempt the Sandbore Channel with the sun in your eyes. We tried it once. Never again!

Our east entry waypoint SBORE, lies 2.5 nm southwest of West Harbour, but marks no recognizable feature. The Sandbore Channel loses its color and peters out, and suddenly you realize that you're there, you've made it, and you're on the Caicos Bank. That waypoint serves to establish a line. From this point you want to head on roughly 102°M to run to Sapodilla Bay (our waypoint SPDLA) or on to South Dock (SDCKA), although South Dock itself is unlikely to be your destination. You have about 9 nm to run, depending on where you're going. This is not a course that we would run on autopilot, nor would we run on autopilot anywhere on the Caicos Bank. Our bearing is an indication of your heading if you're bound for Sapodilla Bay.

PROVIDENCIALES SOUTH COAST		
Sandbore Channel Approach		
SBORA	21° 46' 00"/000 N	072° 28' 30"/500 W
Sandbore Channel West Entrance		
SBORW	21° 44' 33"/550 N	072° 27' 00"/000 W
Sandbore Channel East Entrance		
SBORE	21° 44' 30"/500 N	072° 24' 00"/000 W
Sapodilla Bay Approach		
SPDLA	21° 44' 15"/250 N	072° 17' 30"/500 W
South Dock Approach		
SDCKA	21° 44' 10"/166 N	072° 17' 00"/000 W
Five Cays Anchorage		
FIVE	21° 44' 05"/084 N	072° 16' 00"/000 W
South Side Marina Approach		
PSSMA	21° 43' 51"/855 N	072° 13' 51"/851 W
South Side Marina Turning point		
PSSMT	21° 45' 24"/400 N	072° 13' 52"/860 W
Caicos Shipyard		
CAIYA	21° 44' 40"/660 N	072° 10' 05"/085 W
Caicos Shipyard Channel Entry		
CAIYE	21° 45' 39"/650 N	072° 10' 03"/050 W

The final figures in each waypoint show seconds (00") and thousands (000) of a minute.

Your aim on this run is to hold off at least 1 nm south of West Harbour Bluff, being conscious of Bluff Shoal, which extends for nearly a mile to the southwest from this point. Stay at least one-quarter mile south of Turtle Rock, which is clearly visible. In general you should not edge toward the coastline more than one-quarter mile north of the 21° 44' N line, and if you hold this track you'll have 9–10 feet along your route. Sapodilla Hill (sometimes called Mariner Hill) and some of the Five Cays show clearly off your port bow, and Turtle Rock, mentioned earlier, is a good marker.

SAPODILLA BAY

Sapodilla Bay has had its ups and downs as its supporting shore establishments have changed hands, or, in the case of the Mariner Hotel, simply closed its doors. South Dock, further on around the headland, is the entry port you must use, and you've either got to walk there, or take your dinghy. On days when South Dock has freighters stacked up, the customs office can go stratospheric. You, and your ship's papers, may not rate highly on their priority list.

If you want to get to the center of Provo from Sapodilla you have to hitch a ride, pay the market rate for a taxi, or rent a car. The airport, if you need it, is five miles away, and, if you elect to walk to the business center of Provo you'll cover some three miles or so getting there, and may not be too enchanted by the prospect of a return march, loaded up. See our **Yellow Pages** to find out what lies ahead of you if you set out. Sapodilla Beach is pleasant, though shared now with many local snowbird residents, but just as they might affect the quality

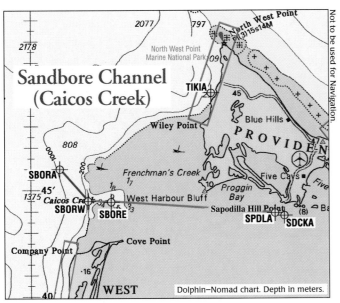

Sandbore Channel (Caicos Creek)

Dolphin–Nomad chart. Depth in meters.

Not to be used for Navigation.

Sapodilla Bay, from the southeast.

of your beachcombing, too great a concentration of boats has, at times, markedly affected the quality of Sapodilla Bay water. As an alternative to beach life, you might want to explore and climb the hill behind the old Mariner Hotel. Find the trail that leads up there from the hotel, and on the top you'll find flat rocks carved with the names, ship names, and dates of mariners who, the story has it, were shipwrecked on that coast. The earliest we have found is eighteenth century. You get a good view of the Bay and of Chalk Sound from the top, and South Dock too, which is not so photogenic.

Finally, as an anchorage Sapodilla has reasonable holding in 5–6 feet of water, but it's open from south-southeast to west and you'll suffer the fetch of whatever short seas build up over the Caicos Bank. However the Five Cays can offer alternative anchorages where you might ride this out. There's talk that moorings may well be put down in Sapodilla Bay to restrict numbers in the anchorage and, we'd guess, provide a source of revenue. It could happen during the validity of this edition of this Guide.

SOUTH DOCK

South Dock is Providenciale's one commercial dock, devoted to fuel (you'll see the highly visible Texaco and Shell fuel tanks) and general cargo (you'll see the two cranes and the containers). It's not a pretty place. The customs office is in the administrative building, which is not difficult to find.

South Dock currently handles ships of up to 225-feet LOA with a draft of 12 feet, and the sea area off South Dock is used as an anchorage by vessels waiting their turn to lie alongside one of the two wharves. Plans have been drawn up to improve port facilities in the Turks and Caicos, and it's highly likely that Providenciales South Dock will be the first to be revamped.

FIVE CAYS

The Five Cays—William Dean, Pussey, Sim, Bay, and Middle

Cay—lie about one mile east of South Dock, and just over one mile north of the waypoint we call FIVE. Sometimes marked on charts as Bermudian or Mudjon Harbour, the cays offer alternative protection if Sapodilla Bay became uncomfortable, but you might not want to base yourself there in total isolation. Or at least we think not. You'd be wise to take a reconnaissance trip there first in your dinghy, and you'll find that you can work yourself in between Pussey and Sim Cays, or behind the northeast tip of Middle Cay. There is plenty of coral around there. Move only in good light.

SOUTH SIDE MARINA

Two miles further east on the northeast inward curve of Cooper Jack Bright, the channel connecting the interior canals of a proposed new housing development has been dredged, and a new marina, called South Side, is now in business. At the time we write the approach through Cooper Jack Bight is unmarked, and you must find your own path through the coral. The entry channel itself is narrow, and has a 2 knot + tidal runoff, but at slack high water you should have plenty of depth, and no problems. The MLW depth over the entire approach and entry route is 4.5 feet.

Our approach waypoint PSSMA is the start of your close approach. To reach this point stand out well from Five Cays, something like a mile, and then turn in rather than cutting across. There is coral. Watch for it.

- At waypoint PSSMA take up a heading of 030°M. Ahead, on the land, you will see a tower with an antenna two miles inland, and on the same bearing, close to the shore the right-hand house of three houses, with, in line behind it, a tree. All this lines up on 030°M. You are going to our waypoint PSSMT, which is a turning point, not the entry channel. The entry channel is off your starboard bow. Don't head directly to it.

Mariner Hill rock carving.

Southside Marina, from the south.

- Your approach track will take you over two distinct lines of dark grass and coral. The first comes up at 21° 43' 59"/990 N 072° 14' 24"/410 W and extends to 21° 44' 15"/260 N 072° 14' 20"/340 W.

- The second band of grass and coral comes up at 21° 44' 43"/730 N 072° 14' 09"/150 W and extends to 21° 44' 53"/890 N 072° 14' 04"/070 W. Watch out for the coral and don't assume your heading is safe all the way.

After passing through these two bands you'll reach our waypoint PSSMT. There are coral heads in that area, and a wreck lies ahead. A distinctive white scar of excavation is to port. You turn east, almost 90 degrees, and line up the two range markers outside the entry channel (they have red tops and yellow bases). Proceed in line with the markers, and then turn 90 degrees into the channel. The South Side Marina basin is directly ahead and to starboard, and the house on the port side is a Marine School.

Does it sound daunting? The guidelines often make it seem worse than the reality. You have VHF 16 if your nerve fails, and remember, you're not out there proving your courage or to provide work for the Caicos Yard.

Inside there is fuel, some basic repair facilities, and room for thirteen boats, principally alongside a wall, with space for Mediterranean mooring when the wall is occupied. Although full-keel sailboats can be accommodated, as well as power

boats, the primary emphasis at this time is in offering dry storage (lift outs with a crane/cradle) to craft under 30 feet, and, in the main, outboards. However further developments, including more berths and an enlarged turning area, are planned. See our **Yellow Pages** for the state of the marina at the time we were there.

There are plans, which we have seen, for a second marina to be constructed further up the canal system, just south of Turtle Lake, but we would guess that this is tied to success or failure in the sale of the surrounding building lots.

CAICOS MARINA AND SHIPYARD

Waypoint CAIYA places you one mile south of the Caicos Yard entrance. At one time there were marks to lead you in, but they no longer existed when we were there last. Rather like the approach into South Side Marina, you either call for guidance, or feel your way in. The coral is more random, and we have no approach path to suggest. All we can say is that we, and many others, have made it without undue stress.

The entry channel, CAIYE, lies at 21° 45' 39"/650 N 072° 10' 03"/050 W. The governing depth is 6 feet at MLW, and the prize at the end, if you want it, is a 75-ton travel lift. Space for visitors is limited to maybe twelve boats, simply because development was halted. It's one deep-frozen construction site (to be honest, one sun-baked wilderness littered with a lot of expensive scrap metal) but they will look after you, and if you do need help, they are your best bet at this time. However don't forget how remote you are there from downtown Provo. The taxi fare, if you're foolish enough to try it for size, could spoil your day.

And we'd like you to enjoy your time in Providenciales!

Caicos Yard.

YELLOW PAGES

PROVIDENCIALES

If this is your first visit to the Turks and Caicos Islands, Provo, as it is often called, will delight you with its brilliant waters and wide variety of amenities. If this is a return visit, after several years' absence, you will be amazed by the upmarket building development and noticeable increase in traffic. Lacking an island center, Downtown remains as close to being a hub as you will find; everything else is very spread out in a long, urban sprawl along the Leeward Highway, and you need wheels to get around. The hotel strip plays host to tourists from all over the world, many of whom come specifically for the spectacular diving. The desalination plant, installed originally by the Sheik of Qatar to water the golf course, is now providing piped water throughout the island. The Turks and Caicos have legislated more protected areas per square mile than any other country in the world, with 33 areas separated into National Parks, Nature Reserves, Areas of Historical Interest, and Sanctuaries, so there are miles of pristine beaches, healthy reefs, migrant and wading birds, and crystal clear seas to enjoy. Don't forget, take only photographs and leave only bubbles or footprints behind! See our **Parks and Wildlife Preserves** section in the **Green Pages**, on page 401.

Customs are based at South Dock, and you must clear in if this is your arrival point in the islands. You will need a passport or photo ID with a birth certificate, as well as your boat papers. There is a boarding fee of $5 during working hours, which are from 8 am to 12:30 pm and 2 to 4:30 pm Monday to Thursday, and to 4 pm on Fridays. Outside these hours, you will be charged $15, plus $6 overtime on weekends or public holidays. Cruising permits are issued for three months free of charge; you are allowed three permits per year. When you arrive at either the *Leeward Marina* or *Turtle Cove Marina*, Customs can be called to clear you in.

MARINAS

On the north coast:

TURTLE COVE MARINA
Tel: 649-946-4303 • Fax: 946-4326 • VHF 16

For many years the only marina in Provo, Turtle Cove is an attractive and friendly marina that has ambitious plans for the future. The details we give below are based on time of writing; there could be many improvements when you get there. It makes a good place for a crew change, with the *Turtle Cove Inn* set in its attractively landscaped gardens, and the excellent *Tiki Hut* and *Terrace Restaurants*, as well as good dive facilities and the *Internet Cafe* for collecting E-mail. If this is your first visit to Turtle Cove, it's recommended that you call VHF 16 "Turtle Cove Marina" to be guided in through the reef. Turtle Cove Marina is a Port of Entry; Customs will come over from South Dock to clear you in.

Slips	24 on hotel side, 22 on island side
Max LOA	Up to 130 ft.
MLW	6 ft. at docks and in the channel.
Dockage	90¢ per ft. per day.
Long Term	Monthly 75¢ per ft. per day, yearly $500 under 45 ft., $650 over 45 ft.
Power	30A, 50A, and 100A; 45 cents per kWh.
Fuel	Diesel and gasoline. Fuel dock open from 8 am to 12 pm and 1 to 5 pm.
Propane	Yes; ask dockmaster.
Water	12¢ per gallon.

Turtle Cove Marina.

Telephone	3 telephones dockside; phone cards available from *Tiki Hut* and *Banana Boat*.
Showers	New and clean, only two. Key from dockmaster.
Laundry	Can be sent out. A new laundromat is proposed by the year 2000.
Restaurants	*The Banana Boat Bar and Grill* serves lunch and dinner, and the bar is open all day. *The Tiki Hut* opens at 7 am for breakfast and remains open all day for drinks, lunch, and dinner until 10 pm. It is a meeting place for divers and boaters, and serves good food and an excellent Sunday brunch that many residents come in for. *The Terrace Restaurant* above the *Tipsy Turtle Liquor Store* in the *Turtle Cove Inn*, opens daily except Sundays, for lunch and fine dining. Caribbean cocktails and home-made ice cream served all day. *The Sharkbite Bar and Grill*, built out over the water at the east end of the marina, is open daily for lunch and dinner, serving a traditional English lunch on Sundays.
Groceries	*Quality Supermarket* on Leeward Highway is about a ten-minute walk away, or rent a car for a day and reprovision at one of the downtown supermarkets.
Liquor Store	*Tipsy Turtle Liquor Store* at the *Turtle Cove Inn*, open 9 am to 6 pm, closed Sundays.
Ice	From the *Tipsy Turtle Liquor Store*.
Marine Supplies	*Walkin Marine Store* Tel: 946-4411 • VHF 16 "Walkin Marine" On Blue Hills Road, just off Leeward Highway.
Repairs	A mechanic can be called to help you.
Transport	Jitneys will stop for you outside the hotel entrance, and take you where you need to go for $3, but they don't run to a schedule. Just wait for one to come along!
Tennis	Clay tennis courts and fitness center a five-minute walk away.
Diving	Art Pickering's long-established *Provo Turtle Divers* Tel: 946-4232 • Fax: 941-5296 Dive shop at *The Turtle Cove Inn*; daily dive trips and classes.

Caicos Adventures   Tel and Fax: 941-3346
Offer personal service with complimentary food and beverages, and snorkeling and beach barbecues in West Caicos.
Flamingo Divers   Tel and Fax: 946-4193
See Diving in our SPORTS section for details

Boat Rentals   *Provo Turtle Divers*   Tel: 946-4232   See Art Pickering for rentals or fishing charters.
Fishing   *Capt. Bob Collins*   Tel: 946-4065 • VHF 16 "Sakitumi"   43-ft. Hatteras docked behind the *Tiki Hut* for full or half-day charters.
Capt. Phil Williams on Gwendolyn
Tel: 941-0412 or 946-5321   Offers full or half-day trips, leaving from behind the *Tiki Hut.*
Pump Out   It will be mandatory to use holding tanks when the marina extension and renovations are completed. A pump-out facility is being installed.
Shopping   *The Tourist Shop* next to the *Internet Cafe* has gifts, T-shirts, and a few toiletries.
Communications   *The Internet Cafe,* adjacent to the *Banana Boat,* where you can connect, receive, and send your E-mail. You can reach them at iai@tciway.tc or cybercare@tciway.tc or at www.turkdsandcaicos.tc.
Credit cards   Visa, MasterCard, and Amex or traveler's checks.
Dockmaster   Kyle
Director   Bengt Soderquist

LEEWARD MARINA
Tel: 649-946-5000 • Fax: 946-5674
Dock Office Tel: 946-5553 • VHF 16 "Leeward Marina"

This is going to be a spectacular marina by the year 2000 if all the projected plans go through. They are planning to build 100 slips, 54 feet long, with dry stack facilities, haulage, a ships' chandlers, and a new restaurant with a cafe on the first floor. The sandbar will be dredged to carry 11 feet of water throughout the whole marina and within the basin, with permanent lighted buoys. It is a spectacular site, though at time of writing, facilities are limited, and it is hardly a marina; more somewhere to tie up, either alongside or stern to. It is best to call up VHF 16 "Leeward Marina" as you come in through the 30-foot cut in the reef, marked by a green ball, for current recommendations on the route in to avoid the sandbars. They suggest making a reservation in advance for space dockside. Otherwise, you can anchor off in Leeward Going Through, and for $10 a day you can use their dinghy dock to load up with groceries, friends, passengers, and take your garbage ashore. You need to rent a car for a day to reprovision, since it is too far to walk and jitneys are scarce; why not keep the car overnight and enjoy a fabulous dinner at one of the many good restaurants in Grace Bay? Leeward Marina is a Port of Entry; Customs can be called on arrival. We give details as we find it at time of writing.

Slips	28
Max LOA	60 ft.
MLW at Dock	9 ft. in the channel; the sandspit off the north shore moves the low water level on the sandbar to around 4.5 ft.
Dockage	Stern to: 50¢ per ft. per day short term, $3 per ft. per month long term. Dockside: $1 per ft. per day short term, $7.50 per ft. per month long term. All dock fees must be paid in advance.
Power	220V and 110V available, 45¢ per kWh.
Fuel	Diesel and gasoline.
Propane	Tanks can be refilled at Shell or TCGas.
Water	15¢ per gallon.
Telephone	Card phones dockside.
Showers	Clean restrooms, but no showers at time of writing.
Laundry	Can be arranged.
Restaurant	*Gilley's* at Leeward opens from 8 am to 5:30 pm Monday to Thursday, and to 7 pm on Fridays and Saturdays, for drinks and light meals, and will cook your catch of the day for you. Closed on Sundays.
Ice	$2.75 a bag.

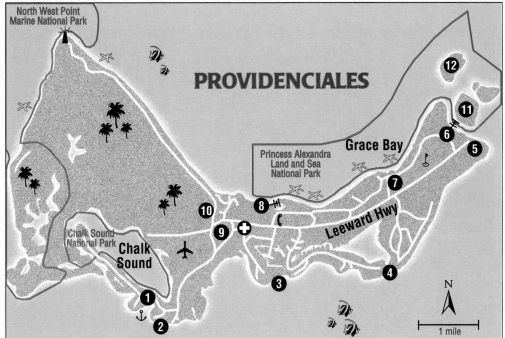

PROVIDENCIALES DIRECTORY
1. Sapodilla Bay and anchorage
2. South Dock and Customs
3. Cooper Jack Bight and South Side Basin Marina
4. Caicos Marina and Shipyard at Juba Point
5. Conch Farm
6. Leeward Marina, restaurant and fuel
7. Ports of Call Shopping Plaza, and restaurants
8. Turtle Cove Marina and Inn, fuel, restaurants, dive shops, tourist information
9. Downtown shops, banks, post office and supermarkets
10. Walkin Marine Store
11. Mangrove Cay
12. Little Water Cay
✛ MBS Medical Centre
✈ Airport
✆ Cable and Wireless
☼ Northwest Point Light
Red line: National Park areas

Leeward Marina.

Boutique	Small store with film, snacks, and T-shirts.
Repairs	Mechanics can be called.
Fishing	*Silver Deep* Tel: 946-5612 or 941-5595 Offers full or half-day excursions for fishing or scuba diving, with beach barbecues and picnics.
	J & B Tours Tel: 946-5047 Offers island exploration excursions and private fishing or dive charters, and will take you over to Little Water Cay.
	Hammerhead Charters VHF 16 "Hammerhead" Capt. Joe Stubbs will take you for bonefishing, snapper or grouper, or to troll for wahoo and barracuda.
	Black Diamond Fishing and Boat Tours Tel: 946-5225 • VHF 6 Bottom or bonefishing.
Sailing	*Sail Provo* Tel: 946-4783 • 941-6178 Private charters available on either *Arielle* or *Two Fingers*, starting at $450 for half day, up to 12 people.
Wave Runners	*Sun and Fun Seasports* Tel: 946-5724 Prices start at $65 per hour.
Credit Cards	Visa, MasterCard, and Amex.
Manager	Judd Clarence
Dockmaster	Dwayne Pratt

On the south coast:

SOUTH SIDE BASIN MARINA   Discovery Bay
Tel: 649-946-4200/4747 • Fax: 941-5955

With a Marine School on site, and soon to be home to the Marine Police, this small marina is being developed by Robert Pratt inside Cooper Jack Bight. At the time of writing there are 13 spaces alongside a 260-foot concrete wall. He has taken a 90-foot boat in there, but the entrance channel only carries 4.5 feet of water at low tide. There is power for 35¢ per day, and water at 10¢ per gallon available dockside, and plans for TV and phone service to be installed. Gas and diesel fuel are already there; restaurant and bar, laundromat and showers are planned. There will also be a 15-ton crane to haul small boats and trailer-driven craft, as well as storage racks for boats up to 30 feet. Reservations in advance are absolutely necessary. Clear Customs at South Dock before coming in. You will have to rent a car or jeep to give you mobility on shore, as it's too far to walk for provisions. Visa and MasterCard accepted.

CAICOS MARINA AND SHIPYARD   Juba Point
Tel: 649-946-5600 • Fax: 946-5390 • VHF 16

Although this is primarily a working shipyard, we give details in case you come in needing repairs and have to spend time here, but there are very limited facilities. Call ahead if you need help coming in. Taxis charge $25 one way to take you downtown, but all the rental car companies will deliver a car to the dock. See under Car Rentals in GETTING AROUND for details. We visited shortly after the owner had passed away, and the yard was up for sale. The office administrator is Carrington Williams.

Slips	Up to 12 boats.
Max LOA	110 ft.
MLW at Dock	6 ft., with 6 ft. in the channel at low water and 8 ft. at high water.
Dockage	70¢ per ft. per day under 50 ft.; $1 per ft. per day over 50 ft.
Power	110v and 240v; 50¢ per kWh.
Fuel	Diesel available
Water	20¢ per gallon for reverse osmosis water; 15¢ per gallon for washdown water.
Telephone	Card phone dockside; cards available from the office.
Showers	Showers and restrooms very basic.
Laundry	Washer and drier, $3 each. Tokens from the office.
Ice	$2 per bag.
Repairs	Outboard and diesel mechanics in yard. Fiberglass repairs and bottom painting. Sailmaker on call.
Travelift	Up to 75 tons; can take 24-ft. beam. $9 per ft. haul-out charge under 30 ft.; $12 per ft. haul-out charge for 30 to 50 ft.
Mail	Caicos Marina and Shipyard is a mail, Fedex, DHL, and UPS drop off. Write "Boat in Transit" on packages containing spare parts to avoid paying customs duty.
Credit Cards	Visa, MasterCard, and Amex.

SAPODILLA BAY ANCHORAGE

This most fabled and beautiful crescent bay, long chosen by visiting yachts and larger boats as their corner of paradise on the island, has seen a spectacular housing boom during the 1990s. It is still magnificent, though the land is dotted with small, and not so small, houses overlooking the water, and the beach is no longer your own at sunset. Taxis or rental cars are the only way to get around once you're on shore. Provo Taxi Association monitors VHF 6, though it will probably cost you $25 to go downtown. Call **Customs** on VHF 16 "Harbour Master" at South Dock to clear in.

SERVICES IN PROVIDENCIALES

Emergency Numbers	999 and 911
Police	946-4259
Fire Department	946-4444

Air Ambulance
RedJet International Tel: 649-941-3274/3275 or 1-888-473-3538 ICU/CCU-equipped jet fleet, rapid emergency response with physicians and ACLS flight paramedics. 24-hour dispatch center.

ATMs
There are ATMs at *Barclays Bank* in Butterfield Square, and at *ScotiaBank* next to *Island Pride Supermarket* at *Town Centre Mall*, both downtown.

Banks
Off-shore banking plays a large part in the economy of the islands, so there are many banks here. For simple transactions like cashing traveler's checks, the main ones are:

Barclays Bank in Butterfield Square   Tel: 946-4245   Open 8:30 am to 2:30 pm, Monday to Thursday, and to 4:30 pm on Fridays.

ScotiaBank in Town Center Mall   Tel: 946-4750   Open 8:30 am to 2:30 pm Monday to Thursday and to 4:30 pm on Fridays.

Western Union at Cheshire Square   Tel: 941-3702   Open 8:30 am to 4:30 pm Monday to Friday, and to noon on Saturdays.

Bookstore

Unicorn Bookstore at *The Market Place* on Leeward Highway   Tel: 941-5458   Books, magazines, newspapers and some nautical charts. Any book can be ordered. Open 10 am to 5:30 pm Monday to Saturday.

Churches

St. Monica's Anglican Episcopal Church on Leeward Highway has a 9 am service on Sundays.

Our Lady of Divine Providence, Roman Catholic Church, almost opposite on Leeward Highway, has a 9 am Mass on Sundays. There are many other churches on the island, including the large *Faith Tabernacle Church of God*, also on Leeward Highway.

Courier Services

DHL Worldwide Express   Tel: 435-4255   Butterfield Square

Federal Express   Tel: 946-4682   Atlas House, Leeward Highway

UPS is only available for incoming package delivery.

Decompression Chamber   Tel: 946-4242   At the *MBS Medical Centre* with the Red Cross on the building, on Leeward Highway. Hyperbaric decompression chamber with fully trained staff.

Dentists

Dr. Johann Pretorius and Dr. Roxanne Jeffries   Tel: 946-4321   At the MBS Group Medical Building on Leeward Highway.

Doctors

Mrytle Rigby Health Clinic   Tel: 941-3000 • VHF 82 • Pager 1094   On Leeward Highway. Government doctor and nursing staff available, X-ray, laboratory services, and a casualty department.

MBS Group Medical Practices   Tel: 946-4242/4222 or 941-5252   On Leeward Highway, with a Red Cross on the building. Full-service general practice, emergency room, air ambulance, dentists, chiropractor, optometrist, pharmacy, and X-ray including trauma stabilization.

Dr. Steven Bourne Tel: 941-0000 and Pager 2222

Dr. Euan Menzies Tel: 941-0642

Dr. Sam Slattery   Tel: 941-0525

Gaming

Port Royale Casino   At the *Turkoise Reef Resort* on Grace Bay Road   Tel: 946-5555   Blackjack, Caribbean stud poker, roulette and slot machines.

Groceries and Provisions

Island Pride Supermarket   Tel: 941-3329   Town Centre Mall, downtown   Open from 7:30 am to 7:30 pm Monday to Thursday, and to 9 pm on Fridays and Saturdays. Closed on Sundays. A large store, very well stocked with a good range of fresh fruit and vegetables, housewares, and pharmacy section.

Payless Wholesale Provisions   Tel: 941-3912   Central Square

People's Choice, IGA Supermarket   Tel: 941-5000   Leeward Highway   Open daily. Well stocked with fresh produce, fresh bread daily, meats, dairy products, dry goods, and a liquor store.

Provo Eats Ltd.   Tel: 941-5184/5880 • Fax: 941-5028   South Dock Road, opposite Five Cays Turn   Offers a delivery service for their wholesale and retail fresh and frozen meats, seafood, ice cream, and breads.

Quality Supermarket   Tel: 946-4600   Leeward Highway   Open 7 am to 9 pm Monday to Thursday, and to 10 pm on Fridays and Saturdays. Open on holidays until 5 pm.

Liquor Stores

Carib West   Tel: 946-4215   At the corner of Airport Road

Discount Liquor   Tel: 946-4536   On Leeward Highway

Tipsy Turtle   Tel: 941-5016   At the Turtle Cove Inn

The Vineyard   Tel: 941-5100   On Leeward Highway, next to NAPA   Open for fine wines 10 am to 6 pm Monday to Friday, and to 5 pm on Saturdays.

Marine Repairs

Caicos Shipyard   Tel: 946-5600 • VHF 16   For details see under MARINAS.

Caribbean Marine and Diesel Ltd.   Tel: 941-5903 • Fax: 941-5902   Southside Basin, Venetian Road, Discovery Bay   Detroit Diesel, Westerbeke, Perkins, John Deere Marine, Isuzu Marine, mobile welding, aluminum and stainless steel tower and top repairs, and full propeller repair.

Marine Store

S Walkin and Sons   Tel: 946-4411 • Fax: 946-4945   Marine Building, off Blue Hills Road   Distributors for Evinrude out-boards and Pursuit, Mako, and Boston Whalers. They also carry boat cleaners and coolers, spare parts and oil, fishing line and tackle, paints, varnish and marine batteries, and have a well-stocked boat-shoe department.

Pharmacies

Island Pharmacy   Tel: 946-4150   At Medical Building on Leeward Highway

Sunset Pharmacy Plus   Tel: 941-3751   In Times Square

Photo Shops

Island Photo   Tel: 946-5417   Grace Bay

Pennylaine Photo Studio   Tel: 941-3549   Central Square   Developing, portraits, and aerial and commercial photography.

Post Office

At the corner of Airport Road, downtown. Open 8 am to 4 pm Monday to Thursday; to 3:30 pm on Fridays. US post cards cost 50¢, to Canada and the UK 60¢, to Europe 80¢ to mail; letters cost 60¢ to the US, 80¢ to Canada and the UK and $1 to Europe for the first half ounce.

Propane

General Trading Company   Tel: 946-2355 • Fax: 946-2799   On Airport Road   Shell distributors for gas, diesel, kerosene, and avgas as well as propane.

TC Gas   Tel: 941-3216   Or the marinas will help with refills.

Shopping

There is no shortage of shops on the island, but they are very spread out in small shopping plazas, and you really do need a car to get around, or be very lucky with the jitneys. Grocery stores are well stocked and people are very helpful. Most stores close at 5 pm, though the supermarkets and small local stores may be open later. Almost everything is closed on Sundays.

Telephones

The area code for the entire Turks and Caicos is now 649, and calling within the islands you only dial 7 digits, *e.g.* 946-2200.

Cable and Wireless provide communication services throughout the Turks and Caicos Islands. Almost all the public telephones need a phone card. These are widely available in $5, $10, and $20 denominations, usually from a store or restaurant near the telephone, or from the Cable and Wireless office on Leeward Highway, which is open 8:30 am to 4 pm Monday to Thursday, and to 3 pm on Fridays. There is no tax on pre-paid phone cards. For more information on Telephones, see our **Turks and Caicos ABC** on page 418.

Tourist Board

Turtle Cove Landings   Tel: 946-4970   Mr. Ralph Higgs and Mrs. Michelle Simons are both very helpful with maps of the islands and copies of *Where, When, How*, which gives you invaluable local information.

RESTAURANTS

The imaginative use of fresh, locally caught fish and the high standard of food throughout the island is an unexpected delight. Dining out is a pleasure! Restaurants generally close slightly earlier and the cost of your meal may be very slightly higher than stateside, but it is fun to try different ones, and there is plenty of choice. Pick up a copy of *Where, When, How* to give you ideas. You will need wheels to get to most restaurants, unless you happen to be in the *Turtle Cove Marina*, where there are several within walking distance. We have grouped a few geographically to make it easier, and have not covered the restaurants at the hotels, all of which are very elegant; some require passes for non-guests. A 10 percent government tax is added to all meals bills, of which 1 percent goes to help finance and staff the National Parks; a I5 percent tip is customary.

AIRPORT ROAD

Rolling Pin   Tel: 941-5023   Open for lunch and dinner seven days a week, serving Indian and Caribbean food. Eat in or take out.

BLUE HILLS

Pub on the Bay   Tel: 941-3090   On the beach in Blue Hills settlement under a thatched cabana   Some of the best local food on the island is served by Charlie and Zennith Parker. The seafood buffet served on Tuesday evenings, 6:30 to 10 pm, is accompanied by live music, and transportation is available. Open daily 11 am to 5 pm for lunch, and 6 to 10 pm for dinner; closed on Sundays.

GRACE BAY AREA

Bella Luna Ristorante   Tel: 946-5214
The Glass House   In Grace Bay across from the Allegro Resort on Governor's Road   Open from 6:30 pm to 10 pm nightly with Italian and Continental specials; closed on Mondays.
Caicos Cafe   Tel: 946-5279   Across from the Allegro Resort on Governor's Road   Terrace dining daily for lunch and dinner with superb grilled fresh local seafood and meats; choose from their daily chalkboard specials. A favorite with both residents and visitors.
Coco Bistro   Tel: 946-5369   In Provo's only coconut grove on Grace Bay Road   Serving lunch and dinner under the palm trees, with an exotic Mediterranean and Moroccan influence, and their house punch served, naturally, in a coconut. Reservations suggested.

PORTS OF CALL SHOPPING MALL at Grace Bay

Angela's Deli   Tel: 946-5023   Open for breakfast and lunch; fresh baked bread, Cappuccino, bagels, over-stuffed subs, soups, and salads. Angela also has a Deli called *Top o' the Cove* next to NAPA on Leeward Highway (Tel: 946-4694).
Barefoot Cafe   Tel: 946-JAVA   Opens at 6:30 am for breakfast and lunch, serves Sunday brunch from 8 am to 2 pm, Sunday supper 6:30 to 9:30 pm. They will make up picnic lunches for you.
Calico Jack's   Tel: 946-5278   On the upper level at *Ports of Call*. Offers all-you-can-eat pasta on Monday nights and live music on Fridays until 1 am, as well as pizzas and local cuisine. Open 5:30 to 10 pm, closed Sundays.
Latitudes   Tel: 946-5832   Open daily 11:30 am to 10 pm for lunch, happy hour, and dinner. Jeff and Diane have returned to the island after three years in the US, and are pleased to be back serving their salads, wraps, pizza, and ribs.

LEEWARD

Gilley's   Tel: 946-5094   Pleasant setting over the water for lunch and dinner, serving American and local food, with happy hour 4:30 to 6:30 pm. Wilbert will prepare and cook your catch of the day for you.

ON THE LEEWARD HIGHWAY

Dora's Restaurant and Bar   Tel: 946-4558   Next to Power House   Open daily until late, with live music on Thursdays and Saturdays. Specializing in seafood buffets on Monday and Thursday nights, from 6:30 pm, costing $22 per person, which includes a taxi for four people.
Hey Jose's   Tel: 946-4812   Central Square   Mexican-American restaurant, open daily, noon until closing, except Sundays, for pizzas and margaritas.
Pizza Pizza   Tel: 941-3577   Provo Plaza   Fresh pizzas baked to your instructions, eat in or carry out, closed on Mondays.
Tasty Temptations   Tel: 946-4049   Butterfield Square   The downtown cafe for coffee and French breakfasts, with home-made sandwiches and fresh salads at lunch time.

TURTLE COVE AREA

Banana Boat Restaurant and Bar   Tel: 941-5706   Dockside at Turtle Cove Marina   Very casual, serves snacks, lunch, and dinner; music on Sundays. Happy hour 5 to 7 pm.
The Erebus Inn   Tel: 941-5445   Above Turtle Cove   Open for breakfast, lunch, and dinner with Pacific Northwest–style menu, wood-burning pizza oven, burgers, and Sunday brunch. Happy hour from 5 to 7 pm.
Sharkbite Bar and Grill   Tel: 941-5090   On the water at Turtle Cove   Daily happy hour 5 to 7 pm, separate sports bar and game room, varied menu, Sunday lunch a specialty.
The Terrace Restaurant   Tel: 946-4763   At the *Turtle Cove Inn*   Overlook the gardens as you dine upstairs, on the plant-shaded terrace. Creative conch dishes and superb seafood; Saturday specials of sushi and sashimi. Wickedly good home-made ice creams and Caribbean cocktails during the day. Open for lunch and dinner 11:30 am to 10 pm, closed Sundays.
Tiki Hut Cabana and Grill   Tel: 941-5341 • VHF 16 "Tiki Hut"   Dockside at the *Turtle Cove Inn*; a popular meeting place for breakfast, lunch, and dinner, daily 7 am to 10 pm. Black Angus beef, pizzas, fresh fish and pasta combos, and excellent salads. Box lunches on request. Chicken-and-Rib special for $10 on Wednesday nights.

GETTING AROUND

Airlines

There is a departure tax of $15 per person, except for children under 12.
American Airlines   Tel: 649-946-4948 • 1-800-433-7300 (reservations and information)   Local office, Butterfield Square   Flights leave Miami at 1:20 pm and 5:10 pm, arriving in Providenciales at 3:03 pm and 6:45 pm; flights leave Providenciales at 7:40 am and 4:04 pm, arriving in Miami at 9:25 am and 5:25 pm.
SkyKing   Tel: 649-941-5464   Inter-island service and inter-Caribbean flights between Cuba, Providenciales, Grand Turk, Haiti, Jamaica, South Caicos, Bahamas, and Dominican Republic. Scheduled and charter flights.
Lynx Air International   Tel: 1-888-LYNX-AIR or 649-946-1971
Turks and Caicos Airways   Tel: 649-946-4255   At Provo International Airport with daily flights to Grand Turk and each of the Caicos Islands, connecting to American Airlines, Bahamasair and Air Jamaica, as well as flights to Cuba, Haiti, and Dominican Republic.

Bicycles and Scooters

Provo Fun Cycles and Autos   Tel: 946-5868   At *Ports of Call Plaza*
Scooter Bob's   Tel: 946-4684 and 941-0262 • VHF 22   Beside the *Tiki Hut* at the *Turtle Cove Marina*; open 9 am to 5 pm Monday to Saturday, and to noon on Sundays; Yamaha scooters from $35 per day, bicycles $12.50 per day.

Buses

Jitneys run throughout the island, charging a $3 fare. They don't always come around just when you need one, and you may have to wait.

Car Rentals

DON'T FORGET TO DRIVE ON THE LEFT! Government Stamp Duty of $10 is payable on each agreement; liability insurance $2.50 per day, collision damage waiver from $10 per day. You will need to show a valid driver's license.

Avis   Tel: 946-4705 and 941-0226   Leeward Highway   Free unlimited mileage, free pickup and delivery.

Budget   Tel: 946-4079   Town Centre Mall   Free pickup and dropoff. One day free on weekly rentals. Economy cars from $44 per day, 4WD Samurai from $54 per day. Office open 8 am to 5 pm Monday to Saturday, and 10 am to 4 pm on Sundays.

Provo Fun Cycles and Autos   Tel: 946-5868 and 941-3312   At *Ports of Call Plaza*   Jeeps, Honda, scooters, and motorcycles.

Provo Rent-a-Car   Tel: 946-4404   At the airport   Free pickup and return. Sub-compact auto from $39 per day, 4WD Jeeps from $52.

Rent-a-Buggy   Tel: 946-4158   Leeward Highway   Jeeps from $52 per day, free pickup and delivery.

Scooter Bob's   Tel: 946-4684 and 941-0262 • VHF 22
Beside the *Tiki Hut* at *Turtle Cove Marina*   Open 9 am to 5 pm Monday to Saturday, and to noon on Sundays. Cars from $55 per day, scooters from $35 per day, bicycles $12.50 per day. Free pickup and return, instruction to novices, map, helmets, and airport dropoff.

Tropical Auto Rentals   Tel: 946-5300   Grace Bay Road

Turks and Caicos National Car Rental   Tel: 946-4701 and 941-3514   Airport Plaza

Taxis

Taxis are expensive. $25 from Sapodilla Bay to downtown, one way, was quoted to us, so check the fare before you set off. It is so easy to drive on the island that it makes sense to rent a jeep or motor scooter for 24 hours and explore.

Island's Choice Taxi/Tour   Tel: 941-0409

Nell's Taxi   Tel: 941-3228 or 946-4971

Paradise Taxi Company   Tel: 941-3555

Provo Taxi Association   Tel: 946-5481 • VHF 6

Leave only footprints. Sapodilla Bay.

SPORTS

Beaches

With more than twelve miles of some of the most beautiful beaches in the world to choose from, there is plenty of room for everyone to enjoy themselves. As in any other part of the world, don't leave valuables in your beach bag while you go off for an hour's snorkeling.

Sapodilla Bay Beach   A gentle crescent of almond sand when you come in from the anchorage.

Taylor Bay Beach   Northwest of Sapodilla Bay, secluded and shallow.

Long Bay Beach   Nearest to the *Caicos Shipyard*.

Malcolm Roads   A two-mile-long stretch of white sand, south of Northwest Point, with tiki huts for shade. Please no litter, which applies to all beaches. Excellent, pristine snorkeling.

Erebus Beach   At the entrance to Turtle Cove Pond, with Smith's Reef just off the point for snorkeling. This beach leads up to the seven-mile stretch of beach, including Grace Bay and the hotels, which ends at Leeward.

Diving

Art Pickering's Provo Turtle Divers   Tel: 946-4232/4994 and 1-800-833-1341   *Turtle Cove Marina and Ocean Club*; two-tank dives from $70, night dive $45, open-water PADI certification $350. Dive shop, equipment rental, tank fills, and still and video cameras available. Private dive courses and charters, and hotel dive packages. Art can also provide boat rentals and fishing charters.

Caicos Adventures   Tel and Fax: 941-3346   *Turtle Cove Marina*
Pride themselves on their small groups, flexibility, and attention to detail with "dive you crazy" as their catch phrase.

Dive Provo   Tel: 946-5040   *Leeward Marina*   Dive boats can pick you up from Sapodilla Bay for daily two-tank dives to West Caicos, Northwest Point, Grace Bay, and Pine Cay.

Flamingo Divers   Tel and Fax: 946-4193   Turtle Cove   Small groups and personalized service, with fast boats and complimentary snacks.

Fishing

Black Diamond Fishing   Tel: 946-5225/4451 • VHF 6 "Black Diamond"   At *Leeward Marina*   Bonefishing and bottom fishing include: grouper, snapper, barracuda, and shark.

Bonefish Unlimited   Tel: 946-4874 and 941-0133   Fish with Captain Barr Gardiner.

Gwendolyn   Tel: 941-0412 or 946-5321   At *Turtle Cove Marina*
Go fishing with Captain Phil Williams for marlin, sailfish, tuna, dorado, wahoo, and more, and have your catch prepared by an island chef on your return.

Hammerhead Charters   VHF 16 "Hammerhead"   At *Leeward Marina*   Fish for bonefish, snapper, and grouper or troll for wahoo and barracuda with Captain Joe Stubbs.

J & B Tours   Tel: 946-5047   At *Leeward Marina*   Bonefish, shark, barracuda, or night fish for jack and tarpon, and bottom fish for snapper and grouper. The chef at *Gilley's Restaurant* at the *Leeward Marina* will prepare your catch for you.

Sakitumi Charters   Tel: 946-4065 • VHF 16 "Sakitumi"   At *Turtle Cove Marina*   From 8 am to 4 pm fish for marlin, sailfish, dorado, tuna, wahoo, shark, mackerel, barracuda, or kingfish with Captain Bob Collins.

Silver Deep   Tel: 946-5612 and 941-5595   Full- or half-day charters from *Leeward Marina* or *Turtle Cove Marina*.

Golf

Provo Golf Club   Tel: 946-5991 • Fax: 946-5992   Grace Bay
A Karl Litten–designed, 6,560-yard, par-72 course, watered by an irrigation system using 300,000 gallons of desalinated water daily. Greens fees $95 per person for 18 holes with shared cart. Rental clubs $18 for 18 holes. Pro shop, driving range, professional instruction. Breakfast and lunch served daily at the *Fairways Bar and Grill*.

Gym

Fun and Fit Health Club   Tel: 941-3527   Next to the *Erebus Inn* at Turtle Cove   Weights, treadmills, Lifecycle, stair climber, aerobic/step or water aerobics. Two clay tennis courts and squash court.

Parasailing

Captain Marvin's Turtle Parasail   Tel: 946-4956   Single rides from $60, tandem from $110. Daily 9 am to 5 pm, weather permitting.

Sailing

Beluga   Tel and Fax: 946-4396   Full- or half-day charters with French-speaking Captain Tim Ainley, on board his 37-ft. catamaran "Beluga."

Sail Provo   Tel: 946-4783 and 941-6178   At Leeward Marina "Arielle," a 52-ft. catamaran, and "Two Fingers," a 36-ft. catamaran. Half-day cruises from $42, sunset cruises from $35, and full-day cruises from $75. Private charters for 12 people from $450 for a half day.

Tao Charters   Tel: 941-6767   Fun on the "Tao," offers dinner cruises, Brunch a la Mer, overnight dive and sail from $235 per person, seven-day excursions for six people, live-aboard from $6,275.

Skydiving

Skydive Provo   Tel: 946-4201 and 941-0901   Off the Club Med beach in Grace Bay   Tandem skydiving with Andy Fell. The thrill of a lifetime with photographs or a video to prove it. $350 includes a video and still photographs; $250 for a tandem jump without pictures. All accompanying instructors have made at least 1,000 jumps!

Wave Runners

Sun and Fun Seasports   Tel: 946-5724   At Leeward Marina 1998 model Sea Doo's from $65 per hour.

NATIONAL PARKS, NATURE RESERVES AND HISTORICAL SITES ON PROVIDENCIALES

For Park Rules and Regulations, see Turks and Caicos Parks and Wildlife Preserves in our Green Pages.

Princess Alexandra National Park   Reef and wreck diving, all water sports, spectacular thirteen-mile beach.

Chalk Sound National Park   Bonefishing, small boat sailing, and photography.

NW Point Marine Park   Spectacular wall diving and deserted beaches.

NW Point Pond   Breeding and migrant waterfowl.

Pigeon Pond and Frenchman's Creek   Tidal flats, mangrove creeks, shorebirds, and waders.

Cheshire Hall   1790 Plantation House.

Sapodilla and West Harbour Bluff Rock Carvings   Carvings by shipwrecked sailors.

Fort George   Late 1790s British fort, north of Pine Cay.

ACCOMMODATIONS

A wide variety of hotels and inns cater to all tastes and pocket books, and the Tourist Board will be happy to give you a complete list. For a crew changeover, the most convenient and pleasant would be to bring your boat into *Turtle Cove Marina*

and stay with Tom and Jo Buck at the *Turtle Cove Inn* (Tel: 649-946-4203 or 800-887-0477 • Fax: 946-4141). Set in its own gardens facing the marina, with twenty-eight rooms from $90 per night, you have most amenities within walking distance. Make reservations ahead of time.

THINGS TO DO IN PROVIDENCIALES

- Dive, Dive, and Dive again; some of the best diving in the world is here!

- Climb Sapodilla Hill where flat slabs of rock lie carved with an assortment of names and initials, engraved, it is thought, by sailors who had the misfortune to be shipwrecked on Providenciales, atop a rugged hill leading up the track to your right between the gates to South Dock and the old Mariner Hotel. 360-degree views from the site make it well worth the climb for the view out over Sapodilla Bay, South Dock, and Chalk Sound, quite apart from the interest of the carvings themselves.

- Explore the Cheshire Hall Ruins. A short walk from the Leeward Highway you will come to the ruins of an early Loyalist Plantation on Providenciales. Their crops of Sea Island cotton and, later, sisal were wiped out by a combination of depleted soils, devastating insects, and the 1813 hurricane. The planters were forced to move on, leaving behind many of their slaves who became the settlers and developers of the Caicos Islands. What remains of the 1790s construction is an interesting reminder of an earlier, pioneering lifestyle, and some of the hardships they had to endure.

- You have heard of conch, but have you ever heard of Island Princess, Ocean Escargot, and Pacific Rim? To learn more about these new members of the mollusk family that are being developed by Chuck Hesse, and to visit the only successful conch hatchery, under its geodesic dome, take a trip to the Conch Farm at the western end of the Leeward Highway on Leeward Going Through. Open 9 am to 4 pm, Monday to Friday. Admission $6 for a 30-minute tour; gift shop.

- Within the *Princess Alexandra National Park* lies Little Water Cay with its Rock Iguana nature trails. This little gem of a cay is given over entirely for the benefit of some 1,500 to 2,000 of these threatened Cyclura carinata, or Rock Iguanas. Walkways thread through the 150-acre cay from beach to mangrove estuary, through native palms and shrubs, with viewing towers on both the North and South Shore Trails to highlight osprey nests and the surrounding reef. Do keep to the boardwalks, so as not to disturb the iguanas' many burrows and underground nesting chambers. You need a $3 access pass before visiting this nature reserve. *J & B Tours* (Tel: 946-5047) at *Leeward Marina* will help you plan your trip.

- Jo Jo the Dolphin is Provo's mascot and everybody's friend. If you like dolphins, and want to know more about swimming with Jo Jo, call Dean Bernal at the *JoJo Dolphin Whale and Wildlife Project* (Tel: 941-5617).

- Give yourself a thrill and show everyone at home the video of you freefalling a couple of thousand feet in seconds as you tandem skydive with Andy Fell at *Skydive Provo* (Tel: 941-0901). Good luck!

Chapter 22
The Caicos Bank and South Caicos

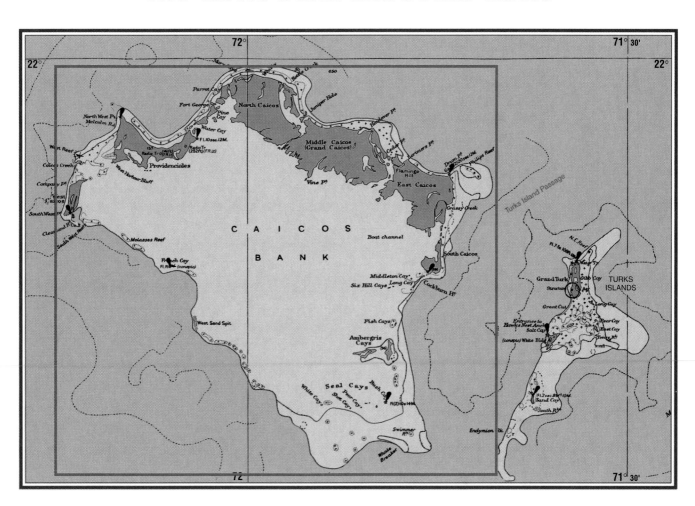

The Caicos Bank

REPORTAGE has it that two natural features and one man-made feature, given clear skies, head the list of the most stunning sights from space. Taking it in reverse order, the hand of Man wins with the Great Wall of China. It's incredible, because of its length. The other two might be difficult to guess. One is the stark terracotta beauty of the barren wind-blown sand formations of Saharan Africa. The other is the stunning sight of the Turks and Caicos, brilliant in their shallow water colors, set in the indigo blue of the deepest water in the North Atlantic. The star in this extraordinary piece of natural jewellery is the major gemstone, the aquamarine waters of the Caicos Bank.

Let's describe the Caicos Bank. It's virtually an atoll, almost circular, some 60 nm across at its widest point, something like 6–12 feet in depth, and peppered with reefs and coral heads. For this reason you must cross in good daylight, and don't tempt Fate by heading straight into the

sun, particularly when it's low in the sky. So, if you're slow, you may not be able to cross the Caicos Bank in a single daylight shot. There's no particular problem in that. Just anchor out. It's a strange feeling to anchor for the night out of sight of land, and far removed from the loom of shore lights, in water that's around 10 feet deep. If you have no moon, the stars are Fantastic. That's a capital *F*.

For some strange reason many people refuse to consider making this crossing, but we count it as one of the most memorable legs of our passage making. If you want to preview what the Caicos Bank looks like from above, and you're not enrolled in the NASA astronaut training program, try it another way. Fly from Miami to San Juan in Puerto Rico, or the reverse. Most probably your track will pass directly over the Caicos Bank. Just make sure you have a window seat and good weather.

In this section on the Caicos Bank our plan is to cover the no-go areas first, then the transit routes, covering the waypoints we would use.

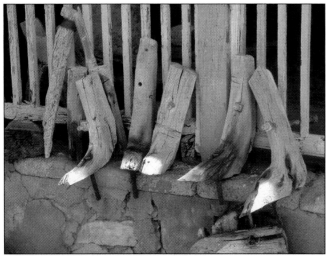

The bones of those who didn't make it.

The No-Go Areas

There are three areas we wouldn't venture, save in exploration in a shoal draft craft, prepared to ground. The first is the full run of the northeastern segment, that is the Caicos Bank bordering North Caicos, Middle Caicos, and East Caicos, all the way to South Caicos. There is a transit route from the Leeward Going Through to South Caicos, used by local craft, but to our mind it has no utility to the cruising yacht, and you could regret attempting it. You're just too far from home to start altering the pitch of your wheels, or changing the profile of your keel.

The second area is the whole sector south of the Ambergris Cays, centered on the Seal Cays. Yes, explore it if you wish and if you're prepared for it, but don't go straight through the middle of it heading from the Caicos Yard to Luperón.

The third area is the edge of the Caicos Bank running southeast from French Cay. It's largely unsurveyed. It could be that it offers superb routes on and off the Bank, brilliant fishing and diving, and even fair-weather anchorages, but we've never had the time to work along it. For this reason we hold back. In flying over it to get some idea what it was like (this in a light aircraft at low altitude, not at 28,000 feet bound for

San Juan), it seems that "all the above" could be true. We'd welcome feedback.

There's one final area we should mention, and that's the shoals and coral in the center of the Caicos Bank around 21° 35' N 72° 05' W. It's not a no-go area, but it's an area where, if you don't take the Pearl Channel, and try to work your way around the shallower water, you might be in trouble. You can bypass it, but we think the simplest and best transit route is to take one central waypoint right in the channel, and go that way.

Navigation

FRENCH CAY

As we said in the **Introduction**, our chosen waypoint to go from Providenciales to Luperón in the Dominican Republic could well be French Cay, particularly if we wanted to anchor for the night there, rather than carry on directly. The Bank transit is short, some 15 nm, and straightforward. Remember French Cay is a Wildlife Sanctuary, which governs your activities while you are there, and remember too that you can't play your onward course as a straight shot from there, because the Caicos Bank extends to the southeast for another 30 nm. You have to run south-southeast for about 10 nm, say to 21° 20' N 072° 10' W, before taking up your bluewater heading.

CENTER BANK

Crossing the Caicos Bank from Providenciales to the Turks Island Passage, or the reverse, the Pearl Channel (our CMBCH waypoint) through the shallows and reef lying just about smack in the middle of the Caicos Bank, around 21° 35' N 72° 05' W is your best way to go. It's a kind of grand name for a run of water that is average Caicos Bank depth running between two unattractive shallower and more hazardous areas. One way or another this effectively dictates that your Bank transit will be taken as two or more legs, for the alignment of this channel doesn't match up neatly with every Bank transit course.

We suggest no courses here, for our chart would look like a spider's web if we were to start plotting every option. Other than your projected route, the only other decision to take into account, if you are going to have to spend the night on the Caicos Bank, is where will you be at the time you want to anchor? We've spent a comfortable night in 12.5 feet of water close to 21° 30' N 72° 00' W (we'll leave out the seconds and thousandths for simplification). We anchored at 7:30 p.m., and, immensely idle (waiting for sunlight!), didn't move until 8 a.m. the next morning. The only downside was that the only fish we caught on Transit Day 1 were two barracuda, which we released. We dined on canned tuna that night from our increasingly unpopular, but seemingly inexhaustible stock.

CAICOS BANK		
French Cay		
FRNCH	21° 30' 00"/000 N	072° 12' 30"/500 W
Caicos Mid-Bank Channel		
CMBCH	21° 36' 00"/000 N	072° 05' 00"/000 W
Fish Cay Channel		
FCCHN	21° 25' 00"/000 N	071° 35' 40"/668 W
South Caicos		
SCAIC	21° 28' 37"/631 N	071° 31' 40"/664 W

The final figures in each waypoint show seconds (00") and thousands (000) of a minute.

THE FISH CAYS AND THE AMBERGRIS CAYS

Our Fish Cay waypoint is that of Fish Cay Channel, which is your exit to the Turks Island Passage. The point at which you move off the Bank into the deep water needn't be quite as exact as that, and there are other equally good crossing places between Long Cay and the Fish Cays. You are about 30 nm from our CMBCH waypoint in this area, and about 23 nm from the place where we overnighted. Working backward, CMBCH to Providenciales is roughly 15 nm (to Sapodilla). Our chosen stop was almost exactly at the halfway point.

The Fish and Ambergris Cays may well be a place you want to go, either for fun, or for rest before setting out again. The area, like French Cay, is a Protected Place.

South Caicos

South Caicos becomes the oddball in destinations as you figure Caicos Bank transits. You can come in from the west and make a landfall on the northwest of Long Cay, but there's an awful lot of mess around that area, and the more we look at it, the less attractive we find it. Quite possibly we're losing our spirit of adventure but, bound from Providenciales for South Caicos, we'd probably take that Fish Cay

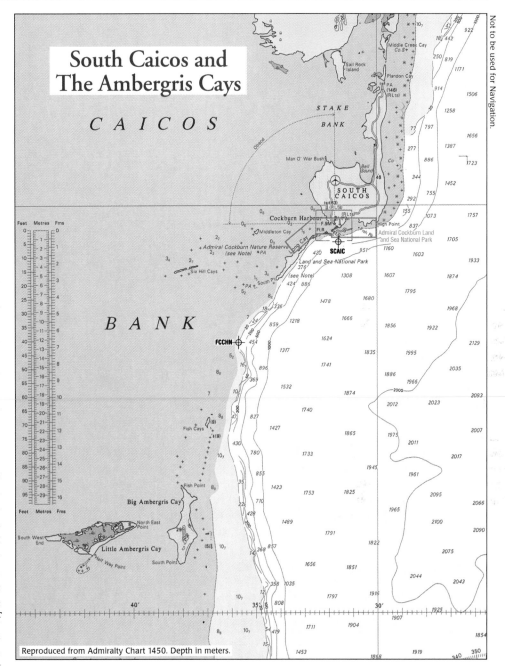

Reproduced from Admiralty Chart 1450. Depth in meters.

waypoint, and then head northward up the Turks Island Passage for 5 nm and turn in through the regular harbor entrance, between Long Cay and Dove Cay.

South Caicos, in the salt trade days, was the Gold Rush port of the Turks and Caicos. Not only did the island have salt pans, but it also had the finest natural harbor of them all, strategically sited right on the edge of the Turks Island Passage. What more could you ask for? Just that the harbor, a prime requirement for a ship with sails, was only two steps away from unobstructed deep water where you really could spread your canvas. It was. It still is. The harbor's there, but South Caicos itself has the look of Cinderella's kitchen after

the ball. It's been a downhill ride.

Today the thousand or so islanders who still live there make a seasonal and uncertain living from conch and lobster. The stocks are depleted and may, in time, be exhausted unless a total ban is imposed for a number of breeding cycles, followed by strict limits, but this would effectively draw the curtains on South Caicos as it is now. Attempts to develop tourist trade, particularly dive associated, have failed to take off, eclipsed by what Provo has to offer. It may be that tourism could yet provide a shot of adrenalin into South Caicos, but indirectly. See our final feature on the Turks and Caicos, **The Future,** on page 371.

So what about South Caicos as it stands right now? It's an entry port, the harbor is there, an open roadstead, of which more later, and there are two docks of interest to you, the visitor—the Government Dock (for clearing in), and the Shell dock. The old small boat harbor, just past the Government Dock, is still in use, but has the air of a derelict maritime museum with beached and abandoned vessels taking up much of the space, and is used only by small outboard craft. Round the corner, as it were, the recently built Shell dock complex, called the Seaview Marina, offers concrete walls, fuel, and has the look of greater promise. In reality much of this second mini-harbor is devoted to the fishing fleet and its wharfside factory. Despite that name *marina* South Caicos is not in the business of hosting cruising migrants.

Nor is the town, which shows every indication of exhaustion and the wear of tear of a tropical climate. There's a surprisingly good supermarket, two small restaurants, and that's about it. A marine training center, the School for Field Studies, occupies a one-time hotel, and runs courses focused on resource management. The airport, grandly named South Caicos International, lies a mile and a half to the north.

To do a 360 and look around the island of South Caicos, to the north lies East Caicos, almost linked by a string of small cays. To the east, the Turks Island Passage, with a con-

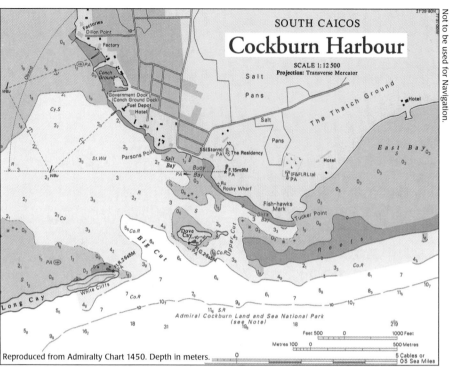

Reproduced from Admiralty Chart 1450. Depth in meters.

tinuous wall dive reef, which you would write home about. To the south, little Dove Cay, and the long thin Long Cay which give Cockburn Harbour its shielding. And to the west, the sands, coral, and shoals of the Caicos Bank. Part of this bank is the Admiral Cockburn Land and Sea National Park, a protected zone that is backed up by three other Nature Reserves in the South Caicos sea/land area, and one Historical Site.

Navigation

COCKBURN HARBOUR

The underwater contours passing beneath your keel as you turn to enter Cockburn Harbour could be described as sensational. Within half a mile you pass from 3,000 feet to 50 feet, which barely has time to register, and then you're into the 20s. From our waypoint your close approach into Cockburn Harbour is on about 330°M, a line that takes you between Long Cay to port and Dove Cay to starboard. We doubt that you'll be entering at night, but if you are, we'll repeat the warning we gave on page 344 that the colors of the entry lights on Dove Cay and Long Cay were at one time reversed, and Dove Cay may show green and Long Cay may show red. There are no other navigation lights in this area at the time we write.

You have at least 20 feet going in, which gradually reduces to 12 feet and then 8–9 feet off the town. The Government Dock has 8 feet. The anchorage is where you are on arrival and the sea area behind the northern end of Long Cay, where you'll find 6 feet. To the west the Caicos

South Caicos Harbour.

Bank shoals to give around 3 feet with a lot of sand running northwest from South Caicos itself, and the southern half of Long Cay, where the main sandbar embraces Middleton Cay.

The holding in the Cockburn anchorages is not so good. Find a pocket of sand to drop your hook in, but be aware it's hard limestone down there and it probably won't dig in far. Why then this reputation as the finest harbor around? Because it has protection from high seas all around. What you don't have is protection from wind from the southwest through to northwest, but of course these quadrants are normally the downwind sectors of your compass.

It is because Cockburn Harbour is a usable anchorage, and because South Caicos is an entry port, that we suggest you consider it. South Caicos offers you that real estate premium quality "location, location, location," not only as a staging point if you want to visit Grand Turk, but also as a departure point. Finally, if you're coming up from the Caribbean passing to the north of the Navidad, Silver, and

One that did make it—a Puerto Rican boat.

Mouchoir Banks, you'll round Grand Turk Island to the north. South Caicos would be no bad place to put in. If we'd used our heads and really thought it through when we were on that track, we would have done it that way.

YELLOW PAGES

SOUTH CAICOS

South Caicos boasts the best harbor in the islands, but very few facilities for boats when you get there. Friendly people, a School for Field Studies, and a wandering cow population greet you. And, as a Port of Entry, you would be unlucky to find a long line waiting to clear in at **Customs**.

SEA VIEW MARINA IN COCKBURN HARBOUR
Tel: 649-946-3219

The word marina conjures up an image of well-maintained lines of sleek, expensive yachts, tied up at wooden docks with power, fresh water, and TV at every slip. This is not the case here. The Sea View Marina is at the Shell fuel dock in South Caicos harbor, with 12-foot depth at low water, and a primarily commercial harbor shipping out fresh conch and lobster, and bringing in fuel and supplies to the island. But it is a Port of Entry and you can clear in here with some of the most helpful Customs and Immigration officers that we found in the Turks and Caicos Islands.

The Sea View Market, with a telephone outside, opens from 6:30 am to 11 pm, is well stocked, and can sell you ice. Dwain, from *Bayside Autoparts* can help you if you need repairs to your boat. *Lloyd Stubbs Liquor Store* is just across the street. There is diesel at the *Shell fuel dock*, and gasoline and water can be delivered.

Just a short walk into town, *Barclays Bank* is open on Thursdays, and you will find a post office, another grocery store, and the *Club Caribe* (Tel: 946-3444) with its 16 rooms and a restaurant serving generous portions of local conch, fish, and lobster. On the Airport Road, *Pond View Restaurant* will also feed you, and so will *Dora's* at the airport, and *Muriel's* in town. If you need medical help, there are two nurses you can call at 946-3216, and a visiting doctor. The town itself is charming, very quiet and unassuming with a couple of pretty churches and cows wandering the streets. There is a School for Field Studies here, bringing in college and high school students doing field research. Most of them vowed never to leave—or at least to return soon.

The Admiral Cockburn Land and Sea Park offers some excellent diving, while the *Belle Sound and Admiral Cockburn Cays Nature Reserve* provides you with bonefish, mangroves, and tidal flats, as well as shorebirds and waders to admire. Or you can go over to see the *Boiling Hole*, a tidal-powered solar salt works. All these are within the National Parks of the Turks and Caicos. See our **Parks** section in the **Green Pages** for **Park Rules and Regulations**.

Chapter 23
Grand Turk Island and the Turks Bank

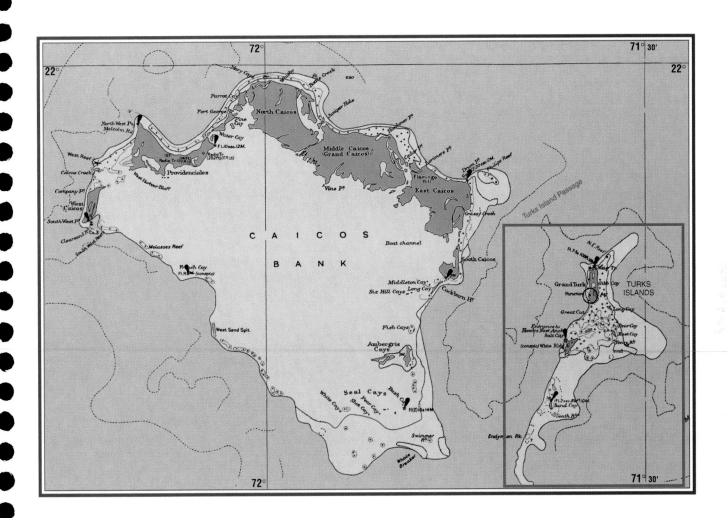

Grand Turk Island

I T'S the height of international fashion to raise your flag of state in the place where all the action is, the center of population, the center of attention, the place served by your best airport, and the best international airline connections. You know the way it goes. On this kind of evaluation the visitor to the Turks and Caicos would reckon Providenciales must be the Top Dog island every time. How wrong they'd be. It's Grand Turk Island, and Cockburn Town, home for some 3,500 people.

Why is this? The answer goes back 400 years. What was important in those days? Much the same criteria as today. The "A" points. Access, and All the Action. Try to get to Provo in the seventeenth or eighteenth centuries in a three master and you'd probably leave your bones on the reef. Grand Turk won the vote, and it took the air age before beach length (measure Grace Bay) and runway length (mea-

sure Providenciales International) became critical parameters. And none of them fitted into Grand Turk Island. This was the time of the final, definitive passing of the Salt Trade and the development of international air traffic, the growth of tourism with a big T, and the guaranteed seasonal flights south of exhausted snow shovelers, seeking nothing but sun beds and sand. Grand Turk Island failed to fit the template. Perhaps thankful that it had escaped attention and remodeling, Grand Turk has largely survived "as it was." And Cockburn Town remained the capital.

The government, and the governor, are still there. The Turks and Caicos government runs its front offices in Cockburn Town, but much of the grunt work takes place in South Base, the old USAF base that was used to support the initial orbital flights in the Space program (that's the young John Glenn, and others) with splashdowns in the adjacent ocean waters. In contrast to this recycling of property, North Base, up on the northeast corner of the island is now aban-

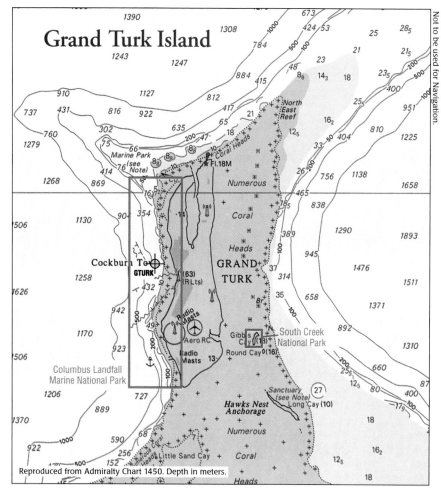

Reproduced from Admiralty Chart 1450. Depth in meters.

doned. We can't help feeling that some role could have been found for so much well-constructed real estate when the US government handed it over. But there's also a fine lighthouse there that you should go to see. It's a rare one indeed, constructed of ship plate sent to Grand Turk in kit form, but that's not its only unusual feature. Four massive steel springs support the tower to flex and right it under storm stress, and serve as lightning conductors, each spring grounded by a chain dropped into a cistern dug deep in its supporting platform.

Much of Cockburn Town is like this. Some things new, but buildings and houses with a charm you won't find anywhere else in these islands spread easily along the simple pattern of just two narrow roads leading through the town, connected by lateral lanes or streets. Behind the town still-

flooded salt pans or salinas give a curious Venetian look to the whole site, lagoon on one side, ocean on the other. There, on the ocean side the old dock in the center has long fallen into disuse, and South Dock (at South Base) is now the Port of Entry and the only commercial dock.

The maritime world is not well served by Cockburn Town. Perhaps South Caicos's Cockburn Harbour, although "across the water" was the only option, for Grand Turk has no natural harbors. This said, we'll disprove it later. But as it stands right now, other than one out-of-sight marina in its start-up stages, with little to offer except a dock to lie alongside, that's it for the cruising world in Grand Turk Island. We like the place. We like it for what it is, as is, and we'd like to see change come about as gently as such trauma can be brought about, for change there will be.

An Overview

Now let's look wider, briefly, before we focus down again. A 360-degree orientation. To the west the deep, deep, waters of the Turks Island Passage are on the doorstep, at the closest point, a quarter of a mile offshore. There's a wall there (great for divers) and coral between that 50-fathom line and the shore. Between the coral and the beach, there's anchoring potential, over sand. And you're shielded from the prevailing winds on that side. To the north, every wind recorded in history can come your way. A great hook of Turks Bank extends to the northeast for 3 nm, with 60-foot banks after that for another five miles. What you have there, veterans of Long Island's Cape Santa Maria, is a similar situation. Magnified. Watch out. There's three thousand miles of Atlantic coming your way if you're putting out, but it can be quite a roller coaster coming in. Depending on the wind!

To the east of Grand Turk Island there's weather, reef, and Atlantic. Close to, that's not your scene. And to south? The Turks Bank, of which more later. Now let's return to Grand Turk.

Navigation

COCKBURN TOWN

As we've indicated, to clear in at Grand Turk Island your reporting station is South Dock, 2 nm to the south of our GTURK waypoint. It's prominent, and stands out from the coast. If you have any landfall problems the airport, Grand

GRAND TURK		
Grand Turk		
GTURK	21° 28' 22"/375 N	071° 09' 24"/396 W
Sand Cay		
SANDC	21° 11' 45"/757 N	071° 15' 24"/408 W

The final figures in each waypoint show seconds (00") and thousands (000) of a minute.

Grand Turk's South Dock.

Turk International, lies just about halfway between the town (our waypoint) and South Dock, with its runway aligned east–west. The approach paths of incoming aircraft can lead you in.

The largely coral-free area to the immediate north of South Dock is the anchorage used by freighters serving that dock, and we suggest, if you have cleared in, you move further north and anchor off Cockburn Town if you want to stay. There's a near continuous belt of coral along the west coast between the wall and the beach, but the old Town Dock, a quarter of a mile north of the 21° 28' line, can only have been built where access was not only possible, but relatively safe. Another relatively coral-free area comes up just south of the 29' line. Be aware that anchoring is prohibited under the approach path to the airport.

For whatever you need, Cockburn Town is it. Go to see the Turks and Caicos National Museum. It's great, and it's marine oriented. Otherwise, just wander around. Relax. And eat well. See our **Yellow Pages**. However, we class this as a temporary daytime stop, and we would not hang around unless we were convinced that the weather was settled. Stable. Nothing in the wind (and indeed no wind there!) for at least forty-eight hours.

North Creek

We said Grand Turk has no natural harbors. Now we'll counter our assertion. Look at the north end of the island. The inland lagoon that connects to the ocean through a narrow channel is known as North Creek. Anciently, before a hurricane at the end of the nineteenth century,

All Those Cockburns

WHAT about all these Cockburns. Cockburn Harbour in South Caicos, just across the road, and now Cockburn Town, with those 22 miles of fast-running deep ocean passage between them? Admiral Cockburn is the man. Just one Go Everywhere Admiral. The naming seems a touch of overkill, but then think of all the (Admiral of the Ocean Seas) Columbuses. These namings just happen.

that connecting channel was wider, and was navigable. There are two problems that probably prevented North Creek's development as a harbor. The first is the close approach offshore. The full force of the Atlantic could hit you broadside on as you run in. The second is the coral reef a quarter of a mile off the entrance, much of which lies deep enough to pass under your keel, but some heads are high enough to have you grounded.

North Creek extends for 2 nm running almost due north–south, measured from the coral at the entry point to its southern limit. The entry channel, at the time we write, is three-quarters of a mile in length, narrow but able to take most craft below the seriously big category (say under 50 feet LOA), and has 3 feet at MLW, reduced to around 2.5 feet at the southern end by a sand hump.

We hesitate to be specific about the beam that can be taken into North Creek because one sandbar, by a little beach about one-quarter of the way in on the port side as you enter, is encroaching into the channel. That MLW depth dictates use of the channel at High Water, which will give you another

North Creek approach.

The North Creek Story

LOOKING at Grand Turk Island you don't need anyone to tell you that North Creek would make a superb all-weather harbor and no bad choice as a hurricane hole. Some ten years ago a Rothschild from New Jersey held this view. At that time the run-off between the lagoon and the ocean was no more than a trickle of water and clearly what amounted to the excavation of a canal had to be set in hand. He had money at his disposal and extraordinary mechanical aptitude. He was hooked on heavy plant, and enjoyed nothing better than putting it to work, hands on, himself. He proposed opening up North Creek to make it a harbor, and wanted no more in return than the title to the land each side of the entry channel he would excavate. The proposal was accepted.

At his own expense, the equipment needed was shipped to Grand Turk. He started work, and took the channel down to 8–10 feet, using the spoil to build a breakwater extending out into the ocean on the western side of the entrance to the Creek. At the lagoon end a continuation of the entry channel for 3/8ths of a mile took the channel through the northern shallows to reach deeper interior water. At last North Creek was open to boats, but Rothschild quit at that point.

Perhaps the effort had been too great. Perhaps it had become evident that the new channel was already threatened. At the ocean end wind and waves eroded the spoil bank and silted the entrance. The coral remained an unsolved problem. All the length of the channel the banks were collapsing, and the water depth achieved was short lived. Later, in a desperate move to halt this continual erosion, every derelict vehicle in the island was taken and dumped along the spoil bank to reinforce it. The rusted frames are there to this day, together with the rusting hulks of the abandoned Rothschild plant. At the ocean end the flamingos now take advantage of sand flats that at one time were never there.

2 feet. It should be slack High Water, for the tidal flow runs fast, some 5–7 knots at peak. This flow certainly scours the channel and keeps it clean, but the sand is still building up year by year, and the prognosis is that unless action is taken soon, North Creek will become unnavigable.

Inside, North Creek has 15 feet of water in the middle. Its western half shoals rapidly to 2–3 feet. Don't be fooled by the fact that the Marine Police have their base on that side, about half way down, and that a clutch of boats (their own patrol craft, and seized or abandoned craft) may be clustered around their dock, which extends to the deeper water. The median line is as far as you want to go toward the western side. As it happens, the eastern side is the best side to go in all respects. You have 6 feet almost up to the shoreline (10 feet under the "White Cliffs"), and are protected from the prevailing wind by the limestone ridge that runs northward to Northeast Point, the iron lighthouse, and the ruins of North Base. The bottom is soft, swamp muck and sand, and your anchor will dig in easily. Maybe too easily, for if you don't get into anything with some cohesion you could drag. You would have to have strong winds in there for that to happen and in truth, if you did drag, unless you hit another boat (or the police dock!), you'd come to little harm in North Creek.

Just over half a mile from the southern exit of the entry channel, on the eastern side, is the dock of the only marina in Grand Turk Island. The Flamingo Cove Marina was hit hard by a storm in its start-up period, and took a step back. At this time you can lie alongside their dock, or anchor off, but otherwise there are few facilities on offer. See our **Yellow Pages**.

We've dealt at some length with North Creek. Why? Because you can get in there now, and it's the best storm refuge we know existing on the route from Florida all the way to the Dominican Republic. You may want to take note of that. If you are going to make use of it, you're a mile or more out of town. You've got nothing up there. Not right now. And there are some cautions to remember:

- You must enter before the onset of severe weather. Anticipate. Even the swell from a storm in the southern Bahamas can make the entry impassable. Don't wait for the sky to tell you that bad weather is coming your way, and if the wind and set is already northerly, forget it.

- Go in only at slack high water (while we think of tides, inside North Creek the highs and lows run about twenty minutes after ocean times).

- Watch out for the coral. You should have enough water at high tide, but use your eyes. There are two rogue heads out there.

- Be prepared for a longer stay than you might expect. You cannot exit until the ocean has settled down. This may be as long as two to three days after the storm has passed through.

Salt "The Salinas" pans in South Caicos.

What of the Future for North Creek?

The Turks and Caicos government want to develop North Creek as a viable harbor and, we believe, would like to see both a marina or marinas and moorings there, as well as supporting facilities on shore. At this time there are no funds available to take this on. A preliminary study on the ocean approach to North Creek, and a survey of the entry channel, has already been carried out. The desired depth overall has been stated as 8 feet, and it is fairly clear, on the construction side, what has to be done to ensure that North Creek does not self-destruct a second time.

We believe Turks and Caicos Investments hold a file on this, and may already have found someone prepared to pick up the action. If not, if nothing comes about, here's your chance.

South Creek

At the south of the east coast of Grand Turk Island there is another creek called South Creek, which has linkage with one of the interior salinas of the island. We have seen highly colorful and ambitious plans drawn up by a Nevada-based US consortium seeking investment in the development of South Creek.

A massive series of housing projects is envisaged with a hotel, restaurants, a golf course, and one or more marinas on the land lying between the airport and Cockburn Town. South Creek, and the central salinas, are envisaged as becoming an interior waterway, linked to the Red Salina to the east of Cockburn Town itself. There the island, and the eastern shores of the Red Salina, will become part of the same development.

The approach in from the ocean is not directly addressed, nor proximity to the Grand Turk Cays Land and Sea National Park, nor the fact that South Creek is a National Park and the wetland is vital to both island wildlife and migrat-

ing birds. It's not for us to comment, but were this proposal to come about, its ecological effect on Grand Turk Island would be cataclysmic.

The Columbus Landfall

Did Columbus make his landfall on Grand Turk Island? A plaque in the Plaza of Cockburn Town (the Government Square) will tell you so. The sea area off the western coast of Grand Turk Island has been designated the Columbus Landfall National Park. Yet many maritime historians, interested in fixing the exact location of the Columbus Landfall for all time, don't subscribe to the Grand Turk Island claim.

And yet? The Grand Turk Island theory has one extraordinary premise. The island he named *San Salvador* was said, in its overall shape, to resemble a bean pod. In Spanish, a *haba*.

Now in a 1636 book titled *Herbal*, written by a biologist called Gerard, there is an illustration of the 'wild Greeke beane' which if you're into wish fulfillment, could be said to look like the outline of Grand Turk Island. Fluke? The rest of the supposition starts to become more tenuous as we move on from beans to the later sequence of the Columbus log.

We'll not take up the Turks Island case here, but what we have done is allow others to take up the argument, which still focuses on the Bahamas. Not the least amongst the theorists is Arne Molander, who has some compelling and cogent theories to support his hypothesis.

He has written for us. Turn to those **Green Pages** and see how it goes. And join in the debate, if you wish!

The Turks Bank

THE Turks Bank, though significantly smaller in area than the Caicos Bank, is nonetheless a significant feature. Some 36 miles in length and 15 miles across at the widest point, it has depths running from 50+ feet to the near-zero of ship-wrecking reefs, of which there are many. Grand Turk and Salt Cay are the two principal land features, and the Grand Turk Cays and Sand Cay (aka Big Sand Cay), down in the south, make up the rest.

In our opinion this area is not a cruising ground. It's exposed to the Atlantic, there are (at this time) virtually no back-up cruising facilities in the area, and, other than North Creek in Grand Turk Island, no place we would recommend in severe weather. What the area does offer is the entry port facility of South Dock in Grand Turk Island, re-supply and communications facilities there, including its air services, hospital, etc, and Sand Cay as a convenient jumping off waypoint for heading on toward the Caribbean. Those coming up from the Caribbean are likely to come around the north of Grand Turk Island if they have elected to pass on the northern side of the Navidad, Silver, and Mouchoir Banks. If you're one of them, be aware that the Turks Bank hooks wickedly to the northeast from its North East Point for a distance of 9 nm. Make that an even ten or go to twelve. Keep clear of it, for you can get reflected waves if you pass too close.

You can count on superb fishing and diving on the Turks Banks and around its dropoffs, but when we stop to think about it, we have some hesitancy about going it alone, just mooching around to see what it's like around the bank. Our inclination would be to put into Grand Turk and Salt Cay, and go with the local operators, who know their home territory, and are good.

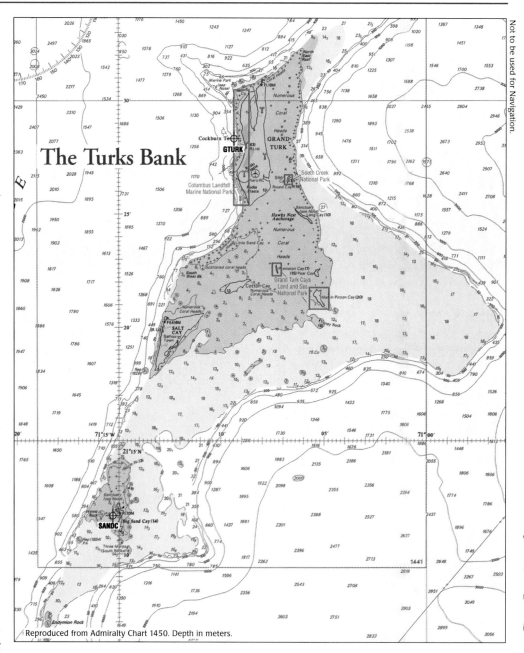

Reproduced from Admiralty Chart 1450. Depth in meters.

For these reasons our navigational offering on the Turks Bank is mean and minimal. We have no wish to tempt you into trouble with a deceptive blindfold of waypoints tied up with courses.

Navigation

SALT CAY

Salt Cay, barely three miles in length, was at one time nothing but salt ponds and drying salt, and holds a one-time crown as the world leader in the salt business. Much of their product went straight up north to pack the cod of the Grand Banks fishing fleets. Today Salt Cay is still salt ponds, the salinas, and with it the ruins of sluices, sluice gates, and windmills, as well as the old storage sheds. About 125 people live on the island, which has now become fashionable with Non-Belongers, refugees from harsher, more northern climates, who find the isolation of Salt Pond, and its lack of any of the trappings of the industrial world, refreshing and agreeable, and prefer a low profile life.

For the visiting boat there's not much there that is likely to detain you long, although the wall diving (off the west coast) is said to be sensational. The anchorage, roughly at the latitude of the Town Salinas, is fair and safe in settled weather, but no more than that. Both north and south of this point coral starts to work out from the coast, markedly at North West Point, and at South Point, where the reef extends southward for a good half mile.

Salt Cay has an airstrip, which is used for regular flights from Providenciales, and a clinic.

SAND CAY (BIG SAND CAY)
We covered Sand Cay at some length in our **Introduction**. We see no reason why you would choose to go there other than on passage, using the shelter of Sand Cay (if the weather's right) for some rest before you set off, or, exceptionally, to explore and dive Endymion Reef. The cay itself, just over a mile and a quarter in length, is uninhabited. Its

navigation light shared with Grand Turk Island the distinction of being the only working light in the Turks and Caicos at the time of our writing. The popular anchorage is over sand just to the southwest of the light, where you'll find 12–15 feet of water, just about 0.3 nm southeast of our approach waypoint.

The east coast of Sand Cay is bad news, with too much coral to encourage blind exploration. Otherwise the Three Marys rocks to the southwest are visible, as indeed is the line-up of rocks and cays running to the north of Sand Cay. What is not so obvious is Endymion Reef, 5 nm to the southwest. Unless you are going to the reef deliberately to dive there, as we said earlier your safest course is to draw a 2 nm radius circle around 21° 07' N 071° 18' W and stay out of this area. If you wish to dive the wreck, Salt Cay Divers, who operate out of the Mount Pleasant Guest House on Salt Cay, can take you there.

Protected Areas
The Turks Bank is protected by the Columbus Landfall Marine Park off Grand Turk Island, the South Creek National Park, and the Grand Turk Cays National Land and Sea Park. Long Cay, to the southeast of Grand Turk Island, is a Sanctuary, as is Sand Cay. Salt Cay itself, and the *Endymion* wreck, are listed as Historical Sites. For the full list of these areas, and the regulations governing the visitor, see our section on **Turks and Caicos Parks and Wildlife Preserves** in the **Green Pages** on page 402.

The Future
TWO or three years ago it would have been hard to believe how much would change in the Turks and Caicos Islands. Oh yes, we'd guess that there was bound to be more tourist development along Grace Bay. Providenciales was almost bound to get a renovated or rebuilt airport terminal, and the offshore financial community was bent on drumming up more important business. But anything else? Not much, in truth, at least very little that was going to affect the cruising sailor. Perhaps we were short sighted.

It's not in our charter to give a grand economic overview but as we know, our boating world is largely dependent on the fortunes of the larger world. If it all goes well, so we profit. If the Turks and Caicos continue to ride the present wave of development that has hit the shores of Provo, the spin-off for us will materialize in south coast marinas, in an expanded Turtle Cove, in navigation lights, and in active environmental controls that will ensure the coastal waters stay unpolluted, the reefs are undamaged, and fish populations survive.

If we were to petition for a specific dividend, we would put forward two requests. The first would be for navigation

Reproduced from Admiralty Chart 1450. Depth in meters.

Sitting Pretty window view.

marks on both the Caicos and the Turks Banks. Day marks. Night marks could lead to danger. Marks to help people find the Sandbore Channel, the major cuts, and cross the Caicos Bank with confidence.

The second would be for moorings in places like French Cay, the Fish Cays and the Ambergris Cays, and Sand Cay. The places that are both landfall/departure points and protected areas. This could be a win-win situation for both the conservationists and the visitors.

We have a third wish. A hope that one day there may be a full-service marina either in South Caicos or in Grand Turk. There's a vacuum there, and in small-boat terms, it's a hard day's run to Provo. We believe this could, together with the development of the Providenciales marinas, set the seal on the establishment of the Turks and Caicos as a cruising ground.

But the vacuum might not exist for long. At this time a Vancouver, BC–based corporation has a multi-million-dollar development proposal in hand, which is close to getting a green light. The key element lies in the construction of a major cruise ship facility on the east coast of East Caicos, together with attractions to cater for large numbers of cruise ship passengers. Apart from whatever is built for this purpose, the island will be subdivided into 2,000+ building lots centered on a golf course, and land will be set aside for shopping centers and the like.

To kick off the East Caicos Cruise Port project, South Caicos will be turned into a base camp. Ships bring-ing in plant and materials will unload there. A road will connect South Caicos with its bigger twin to the north, running bridge by bridge over those little cays. South Caicos International will come into its own and South Caicos will enjoy a boom the like of which was unknown even in the Salt Trade days. The $450 million required to kick the scheme off is reckoned to be worth it, for the projected returns quoted are substantial. All that is required is that the Caribbean cruise ships call in, the building lots sell, and the houses are built.

East Caicos is virgin untenanted land, but for a handful of squatters. You could say it's uninhabited, which is a great plus. No potential hang-ups there. It's even more encouraging to have a green field site at the very edge of deep ocean water on a shipping route. A stretch of reef may have to go, but this is nothing. The East Caicos flamingos who live there will lose, but if all this comes about, maybe we'll not want that marina in West Caicos. We too, like the flamingos, may have to find other places to spread our wings and walk the beaches.

Let's alter our focus to the world seen from deck level. The Turks and Caicos has 166 square miles of the waters that rate as an Earth Spectacular seen from Space. That's some rating for a Blue Planet, a water world that's seven-eighths ocean. Have we any problems? Simply where to go next when we're in the islands. Have we any certainties? Just that the water visibility is the best we've ever known, anywhere. That the reefs are world class. And that when the sun sets over the unbroken open waters of the Caicos Bank, we know we'll see the stars that night as we've never seen them before, anywhere, anytime. And if there are no stars, the moon.

Have you ever gone swimming under a full moon in tropic waters thirty miles from the nearest land?

Go there. Try it!

Caicos Bank sunset.

YELLOW PAGES

GRAND TURK

Full of history and charm and wandering donkeys, Grand Turk is the long-established center of government for the Turks and Caicos Islands. Running alongside a magnificent beach where the wall drops off the edge of the reef protecting the island and producing a daily delight of water colors, historic Cockburn Town stretches with brightly painted Bermudan-style houses one street deep, making everything easy to find the length of Duke and Front Streets. Parallel lie the Red Salina and the Back Salina, testaments to the importance of salt in earlier days, now surrounded by town. Although facilities for boats are limited at the present time, it would be sad to pass by an island with so much to offer.

Customs is at South Dock, the commercial shipping dock, and it is here you must clear in if you are arriving in the islands for the first time. If you have come from one of the other Turks and Caicos Islands, you will only need to show the harbormaster your cruising permit. Cruising permits are issued free of charge for three months. You will need a passport or photo ID with a birth certificate, as well as your boat papers, to obtain one.

Working hours are 8 am to 12:30 pm and 2 to 4:30 pm, Monday to Thursday, and to 4 pm on Fridays. You will pay a $5 boarding charge within these hours; $15 outside working hours, plus $6 overtime fee on weekends and public holidays.

MARINA

FLAMINGO COVE MARINA IN NORTH CREEK
Tel and Fax: 649-946-2227 • Cell: 946-641-0376
If tide, wind, and weather are in your favor and you can get into the creek, there is room for a couple of boats to Mediter-ranean moor at the dock, which lies beyond the Police Dock, on the port side as you come in. You will have 3–4 feet in the channel at low water, other than over the "bump" that leaves you with only 2.5 feet, and virtually 6 feet at high tide, with about 5.5 feet dockside at low water. Or you can anchor in 10-foot water under the wryly named White Cliffs. There is water and diesel available, and a taxi into town costs about $6. Plans are to build a guest house on the site, but at the moment the closest accommodation would be *Island House Hotel* on Lighthouse Road (Tel: 946-1519). Overlooking North Creek, this Mediterranean-style villa hotel has eight rooms from $100 a night, which includes the use of a golf cart, free laundry service, and a swimming pool.

The owner of *Flamingo Cove*, Kirk Graff, also runs *MPL Enterprises* (same telephone and fax numbers) on Duke Street, selling and servicing Yamaha outboard motors and generators, and selling Carolina Skiffs, so he should be able to help you if you need something fixed on your boat.

SERVICES & SHOPPING

Emergency Numbers
Police   Tel: 946-2299
Fire   Tel: 946-2233
Hospital   Tel: 946-3333

ATM
Barclays Bank on Front Street.

St. Thomas's Anglican Church.

Banks
Barclays Bank   Tel: 946-2831   Front Street
ScotiaBank   Tel: 946-2506   Harbour House on Front Street
Banks are open 8:30 am to 2:30 pm Monday to Thursday and to 4:30 pm on Fridays.
Western Union   Tel: 946-2324   Upstairs at Dot's Enterprises
Open 9 am to 8 pm Monday to Friday, to noon on Saturday and Sunday.

Churches
St. Mary's Cathedral Church on Front Street is used for Sunday services. The oldest church, *St. Thomas's Anglican Church*, now used infrequently, is well worth the walk around Back Salina, if only to see the old headstones in the cemetery surrounding it. The newer *Methodist Church* overlooks the Salina.

Clinic
Government Clinic   Tel: 946-2328   Cockburn Town   Open 8:30 am to 12:30 pm and 2 to 4:30 pm.

Courier Services
Cee's Messenger Services   Tel: 946-2030   Provides the on-island courier service.
DHL offer daily service from Providenciales   Tel: 946-4352
UPS has incoming package delivery only.
Fedex   Tel: 946-2542/4682   Harbour House, Front Street

Groceries and Provisions
Cee's Wholesale Grocery and Sundries   Tel: 946-2030   Pond Street
Dot's Enterprises   Tel: 946-2324   Pond Street
Sarah's Shopping Centre   Tel: 946-2370   Frith Street across the Salina   A good selection of canned and dried goods, as well as fresh fruit and vegetables, a coffee shop with a deli, and pharmacy section.
Turks Islands Importers (TIMCO)   Tel: 946-2480   Front Street

Hospital
Grand Turk Hospital   Tel: 946-2040   One mile north of Cockburn Town   Four doctors and full-time nurses, surgery, X-ray, laboratory, and general medicine.

Library
Victoria Public Library, in the pink building on Front Street
Open 8 am to 5 pm Monday to Thursday, to 4 pm on Fridays, and 9 am to 1 pm on Saturdays.

Liquor Store
Carib West   Tel: 946-2044   Harbour House

Marine Supplier and Repairs
MPL Enterprises   Tel and Fax: 946-2227 • Cell: 941-0376   Duke Street   Distributors for Yamaha outboard motors, motorcycles, generators, water vehicles, and Carolina Skiffs.

Philatelic Bureau
Tel: 946-1534   At Church Folly

Post Office
In the handsome blue building on Front Street, open 8 am to 4:30 pm.

Propane
Available from South Dock.

Telephones
Cable and Wireless on Front Street   Open 8:30 am to 4 pm Monday to Thursday, to 3 pm on Fridays. $5, $10 and $20 phone cards for sale. For details of services, see under telephones in our **Turks and Caicos ABC** in the **Buff Pages**.

Tourist Office
Tel: 946-2321   At the old Town Dock   Lindsey Musgrove and Valerie Jennings will give you ideas and advice to make your time in the islands special.

RESTAURANTS

A 10-percent government tax is added to all meals, and a 15-percent tip is customary.

Arawak Inn Restaurant and Bar   Tel: 946-2277   Governor's Beach   Local and American cuisine. Open for breakfast, lunch and dinner, with daily specials, seafood, and Saturday night barbeque. Spectacular sunsets.

Peanuts Pepper Pot   On the beach next to the old Town Dock, now the new Tourist Office   Sodas, beer, snacks, and Peanuts' own Rhythm Pills, aka conch fritters!

Secret Garden Restaurant   Tel: 946-2260   At the *Saltraker Inn* on Duke Street   Delightful courtyard setting for breakfast, lunch, and dinner. Barbecue on Wednesdays and Saturdays; sing-along with live music on Wednesday and Sunday evenings.

Shipwreck Restaurant and Lounge Tel: 946-2135   At the *Guanahani Beach Resort*   Breakfast, lunch, and dinner served in a tropical setting. Credit cards accepted.

Turks Head Inn   Tel: 946-2466   On Duke Street   Drinks in *Calico Jacks*, dinner in the walled garden on the terrace, or in the attractive dining room of this one-time governor's house, newly refurnished with antiques. Interesting, international food in elegant surroundings.

The Water's Edge   Tel: 946-1680   Jan Stegner and David Church open their very successful, laid-back and relaxed *Conch Cafe*, right on the beach on Duke Street, for lunch from 11 am until about 2:30 pm, opening again for dinner overlooking the ocean with music from 5:30 pm. Bar and snacks all day. Happy hour on Wednesdays and Fridays.

GETTING AROUND

Airlines
There is a departure tax of $15 per person, except children under 12.

American Airlines   Tel: 1-800-433-7300   Twice-daily flights to Providenciales from Miami.

Bahamasair   Flights direct to Florida.

InterIsland Airways   Tel: 649-946-1667 (Grand Turk), 941-5481 (reservations)

Lynx Air International   Tel: 649-946-1971 • 1-888-LYNX-AIR   Several flights a week between Grand Turk and Fort Lauderdale.

Sky King   Tel: 649-946-1520 (Grand Turk), 941-KING (reservations)   Daily scheduled service and charter flights take 30 minutes between Grand Turk and Providenciales. Salt Cay is a five-minute flight.

Bicycle Rentals
Island Fun Cycles   Tel: 946-1680   Duke Street   Ask at the *Water's Edge*.

Sea Eye Diving   Tel: 946-1407
Salt Raker Inn   Tel: 946-2260
Turks Head Inn   Tel: 946-2466

COCKBURN TOWN DIRECTORY

1. Sea Eye Diving
2. Blue Water Divers
3. Oasis Divers
4. Turks Head Inn
5. Barclays Bank
6. Post Office
7. Government Offices
8. Library
9. Prison
10. ScotiaBank
11. Town Dock and Tourist Office
12. Museum
✝ St. Thomas Anglican Church
Red line: National Park area

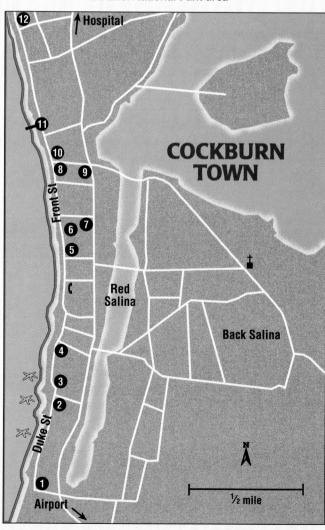

Car Rentals

Don't forget to drive on the left and watch for one-way streets in Cockburn Town.

Dutchie's Car Rental   Tel: 946-2244
Sunshine Auto Leasing   Tel: 946-1588

Scooter Rentals

Island Fun Cycles   Tel: 946-1680   Open noon to 10 pm daily, scooters from $25 per day.

Taxi and Tour Services

Henley's Cab Service   Tel: 946-2331
Sand Dollar Tours   Tel: 946-2018
Jackie Williams   Tel: 946-1860

SPORTS

Diving

Blue Water Divers   Tel and Fax: 946-2432   Daily dives on the Grand Turk Wall, special dive trips to South Caicos, cay trips, and picnics. Dive shop on Duke Street. Full PADI instruction and certification.

Oasis Divers   Tel: 946-1128   Captains Everette Freites and Dale Barker will show you some of the best dive sites, while teaching you about migrating patterns of humpback whales! Small groups, two-tank morning dive $50, PADI open water course $325, advanced open water course, rescue, first aid, and divemaster courses offered. Equipment rental from their Dive Shop on Duke Street.

Sea Eye Diving   Tel and Fax: 946-1407   Cecil Ingham and his team have been diving the Grand Turk Wall for a combined 35 years. They are the only land-based facility in the islands offering Nitrox diving and training, and specialize in teaching underwater photography and video, and extended range diving. Two-tank morning dive $50, Nitrox package $150. Snorkel trip to Gibbs Cay which includes barbecue lunch and a stingray encounter, $40.

Dive Sites

Some of the best are: *The Anchor, Coral Garden, Black Forest, Amphitheatre, Tiki Hut, Sand Canyons, The Library, McDonalds,* and *Tunnels*. Or try the wreck of *HMS Endymion*, which sank in 1790, and lies at 21° 6.95 N/071° 18.51 W in a groove at the approximate center of the reef, with two more modern wrecks close by. And a few snorkeling suggestions: off Governor's Beach, South Dock, the Old Dock, Harold Wreck, Water's Edge, South Point, and Gibbs Cay.

Fishing

Sand Dollar Tours with Captain Ossie Virgil   Tel: 946-2018
21-foot and 34-foot sports fishing boats for full- or half-day charters. Ossie also runs a taxi service.

Golf

Waterloo Golf Club   Tel: 946-2308   At the Governor's Residence at Waterloo   Clubs can be rented, greens fees are $25 for nine holes.

Horseback Riding

Tel: 946-2214/2277   Call Gail for trail and beach rides from $25, or a paddock ride for $15.

FISHING TOURNAMENTS

August

Grand Turk Game Fishing Tournament   Call Ossie Virgil for details at *Sand Dollar Tours* (Tel: 946-2018) or at 649-941-0199.

NATIONAL PARKS, SANCTUARIES, NATURE RESERVES AND HISTORICAL SITES

Grand Turk Cays Land and Sea National Park

Gibbs, Penniston, and Martin Alonza Pinzon (East) Cays   Nesting gulls, terns, Turk's Head Cactus, picnicing, swimming, snorkeling.

Columbus Landfall Marine National Park   Wall diving, swimming, snorkeling, picnicing, shorebirds, and raptors.

South Creek National Park   Wetlands and mangroves; breeding, migrating shorebirds, and waders; walks and viewpoints.

Big Sand Cay Sanctuary   Nesting of seabirds, shorebirds, and turtles.

Molasses Reef Wreck   Site of the earliest known shipwreck in the Western Hemisphere.

Wreck of HMS Endymion, south of Big Sand Cay   1790s British Man-o-War in 40 feet of water.

For park rules and regulations, see Turks and Caicos Parks in our Green Pages.

ACCOMMODATONS

Arawak Inn   Tel: 649-946-2277   Fifteen rooms from $120 per night.

Beachcomber House, B & B   Tel: 649-946-2470   One room from $75 per night.

Island House   Tel: 649-946-1519   Eight rooms from $100 per night.

Guanahani Beach Resort   Tel: 649-946-2135   Sixteen rooms from $95 per night.

Sadler's Seaview Apartments   Tel: 649-946-2569   Three rooms from $70 per night.

Salt Raker Inn   Tel: 649-946-2260   Thirteen rooms from $45 per night.

Sitting Pretty Hotel   Tel: 649-946-2232   Twenty-four rooms from $115 per night.

Turks Head Inn   Tel: 649-946-2055   Seven rooms from $80 per night.

Water's Edge Club   Tel: 649-946-2466   Three, two-bedroom units.

A house on Grand Turk.

Janet Wilson

THINGS TO DO IN GRAND TURK

- *Turks and Caicos National Museum*   Visit the 160-year-old Guinep House, home to the museum (Tel: 946-2160), on the north end of Front Street. Did you know that the oldest shipwreck in the Americas was found on the rim of the Caicos Bank? You can see the remains of the ship's hull and rigging, as well as cannons, tools, and personal possessions of the crew in the museum's central exhibit. Did you know that the highest mountain in the Turks and Caicos is more than 8,000-feet tall? But only 140 feet of it is above sea level, the reason for the breathtaking wall dives. The natural history room in the museum explains and re-creates reef formation. And did you know that the first human inhabitants, the Lucayan Tainos, arrived here by boat more than 1,000 years ago? Find out about pirates and salt rakers, cotton planters and Yankee traders, sisal farmers, and ship wreckers, even about Astronauts, by visiting this gem of a museum. Open 10 am to 4 pm Monday to Friday, until 6 pm on Wednesdays, to 1 pm on Saturdays. Entrance $5 donation. Small gift shop with a good selection of books, maps, postcards, and island handicrafts.

- Dive the wall! and dive as many of the fantastic sites as you have time for; try Nitrox diving, or take a course and improve your dive qualifications. This is world-class diving.

- Return home with a set of the unusual and attractive island stamps, from the Philatelic Bureau at Church Folly.

Janet Wilson

Northeast Point lighthouse.

- Perched on the clifftop at Northeast Point, the light from the Grand Turk Lighthouse shines out for 20 miles. Built in 1852 of cast iron shipped from England, the original eight small burners produced such a dim light that ships continued to be wrecked until 1894 when kerosene lamps and a Fresnel lens were installed. Today the newly restored lighthouse, keeper's quarters, interpretive signs, and magnificent sea views make this National Trust site well worth a visit.

- Take a stroll along Duke Street early in the morning for some soft light photographs of the many colored Bermudan-style houses. Or stroll out in the evening, and enjoy drinks, dinner, and oceanside music under the stars.

Part VII

———

Reference Sections

Blue Pages:
Putting Out to Sea

Green Pages:
History, Wildlife, and Fishing and Diving

Buff Pages:
Infrastructure and Government

Sand and channels, the Exuma Cays.

Reference Sections
Table of Contents

Chapter 24
Blue Pages
Putting Out to Sea

Man-O-War schooner William H. Albury, *built 1963.*

Seamanship and Preparation

WHAT are the qualities that go to make up the ideal boat for the these islands? For a start, the ability to cross the Gulf Stream safely, even if the weather turns against you. You'll want a draft that will take you safely over the Banks and into the anchorages and harbors. You need the endurance to take you from fueling point to refueling point, and the water-tank capacity to match your endurance. It goes without saying that you need a boat that's seaworthy, in prime condition, and well equipped. Nothing, you hope, will go wrong; but you need a measure of self-reliance. You'll want a reasonable stock of spares, and the tools to carry out your basic servicing.

Turn to the comfort side. Ventilation and shade from the sun come high on your list, particularly if you've not got air conditioning. Hopefully you'll have the capacity to accommodate everyone comfortably, for overcrowding and hot climates don't go well together. A swim platform is a plus, as is a dinghy you can use to get ashore, get provisions, and go gunkholing.

The boats that meet these parameters form a long list, covering both sail and power. We've cruised in the islands happily in a sail catamaran that was just 22 feet on the waterline, to take the bottom of the scale, and in a 49-foot motor yacht with three double cabins with bathrooms (there's no other way to describe them) and every appliance you could find in a house, which is heading toward the top end. Did they have anything in common? Let's check the list:

- seaworthiness
- sound engines
- tankage to carry sufficient reserves of fuel and water
- draft under 6 feet (though you can get by with an 8-foot draft)
- good navigational equipment
- VHF radio, and, of course
- full safety equipment above the basic US Coast Guard requirements

One time when we were in West End someone was towed in by a Bahamian fishing boat shortly after dawn. The weather had been unsettled and the Gulf Stream had not quieted down, but it was by no means rough out there.

The boat being towed in was a 17-foot center-console open boat with just one man on board. He had set out from Palm Beach the evening before for a week in the Abacos. He'd run out of fuel during the night, was being thrown around a bit by the seas out there, and fired off the only two flares he had. He was lucky. A Coast Guard helicopter passing to the south saw the flares, and radioed West End to get help to him.

Despite his timely rescue, he wasn't altogether happy when his rescuer charged him $3,000 for the ride. Asked why he hadn't got enough fuel to cross the Stream, the reply was simple: "I didn't think it was that far."

Is there an ideal boat for the Bahamas? It's the boat that will take you safely there and back, and let you have all the fun you want while you're there. The rest (even the hull color!) is up to you.

Pre-Departure Checks

- Check diesel, outboard fuel, reserve oil and lubricants, water.
- Check engine oil levels, coolant, hoses, belts, bilges.
- Check navigation lights, spotlight, deck lights, all interior lights.
- Check man overboard (MOB) equipment, flares and smoke signals, EPIRB, life raft, and survival equipment.
- Check that dinghy and outboard are OK, scuba tanks filled, fishing rods and fishing gear on board.

Complete Navigation Work

- Waypoints.
- Courses, times, and distances—alternatives if bad weather.
- Lights listed and tides known.
- Weather forecast checked.
- Set watch and ship's clock to USN Observatory time (call 900-410-8463).
- Set barometer.
- Complete provisioning; list stores and spare parts.
- Entertainment: videos, CDs, cassettes, and books.
- Q flag and Bahamas courtesy flag.
- Check that ship's papers are complete: documentation or state registration, insurance, passports, money.
- Check that crew passports or proofs of citizenship are set for entry into the Bahamas; open log and list crew.
- Complete Float Plan and leave with a relative or friend.
- Prepare first day/night-on-passage food.
- Stow for rough weather and clear decks. Secure open ports and hatches.
- Garbage ashore.
- Obtain marina or (if necessary) port authority departure clearances.

- Turn on radios and navigation instruments.
- Take a head count before sailing.
- Hold a new crew safety briefing, including MOB drill, use of VHF, and abandoning ship.

Float Plan

The person in whose hands this Float Plan is left is to keep it handy until *you* telephone and report your safe arrival. You should set a "fail safe" time, and if he or she has not heard from you by then, they are to call the US Coast Guard and report that you are missing at sea. A sample Float Plan is included in **Appendix A** on page 428.

Coming into Port

- Have approach chart, coastal pilot, harbor chart on hand. Know location of reporting dock.
- Check on any special timings: bridges or the like.
- Know the state of tide and tidal stream, and the local wind pattern.
- List navigation aids in order of likely utility: lights, marks, bottom contours and depths.
- Have VHF, binoculars, hand-bearing compass, loud hailer, and air horn on hand.
- Have Q flag if it's your Port of Entry, courtesy flag ready to fly after clearance.
- Prepare anchor, fenders, and lines.
- Keep navigation instruments on until log data is recorded.
- Arrival clearance if it's your Port of Entry—did you leave a Float Plan? If so, call and report your safe arrival.

After clearance

- Write up log
- Check bilges and engines
- Garbage ashore
- Fill water and fuel tanks
- Wash down decks
- Washing and laundry?

Clearing In on Return to the US

Immediately on arrival the captain must call US Customs at:

Miami	Tel: 305-536-5786
Fort Lauderdale	Tel: 954-356-7241
Palm Beach	Tel: 561-844-4393
Fort Pierce	Tel: 561-461-1733

If you have non-US residents on board, call Immigration at:

Miami	Tel: 305-536-5290
Fort Lauderdale	Tel: 954-356-7790
Palm Beach	Tel: 561-845-6898
Fort Pierce	Tel: 561-461-1733

Additionally, US Customs has an 800 number that gives you access to the office responsible for the whole area from

Sebastian to Key West. This is 1-800-432-1216. No one should leave the boat until after US Customs clearance has been given. Fly your Q flag, and keep it flying until your have clearance. Be prepared to give all your vessel and crew details:

- Boat type, model, year.
- US documentation number or state registration number with state decal number.
- Registered name of vessel and the declared home port.
- Your FCC call sign.
- Your hull identification number.
- LOA, LWL, beam, draft (for comparison with your registration).
- Your US Customs decal number (if you have one).

Details of the owner/captain:
- Nationality, passport number, date and place of issue.
- Social security number (if a US citizen).

Details of the crew:
- Total number and nationality.
- Full names, dates of birth, social security numbers (US citizens), and passport details (US visas if applicable).

Passage details:
- Date sailed from your US departure port.
- Ports of call.
- Last port of call before returning to the US.

Firearms:
- Any firearms on board?
- Detailed list of ammunition on board.

US Customs decals are required for any boat over 30 feet long, other than non-US boats and one-time entries from the Bahamas or elsewhere. If you've not already paid your annual Customs User Fee and got your decal, add it to your list. It will simplify your return entry into the US.

CLEARANCE NUMBER
When you have been given your clearance number, record it in your ship log. Everyone is now free to go ashore.

Bahamas Boating Regulations

POWER BOATS
- It is illegal to drive a power boat within 200 feet of the shore of any Bahamian island unless you are approaching or leaving a dock or marina.
- Within this 200-foot coastal zone speed is limited to 3 knots.
- It is illegal to drive a boat in a reckless manner, or while under the influence of alcohol or drugs.
- No one under 16 years of age may drive a boat with an engine greater than 10 hp, although 14- and

15-year olds may if they are under the supervision of someone over 16 years of age.

WATER SKIING
- Water skiing is forbidden within the 200-foot coastal zone, unless it is taking place in a lane clearly marked with buoys and lines.
- Water skiers are required to use flotation jackets.
- A lookout, in addition to the driver, is required in the tow boat. The lookout must be 16 years of age or older.
- Water skiing is forbidden at night.

Turks and Caicos Boating Regulations
On the face of it, the regulations governing boating in the Turks and Caicos are essentially what you would expect, pretty much in line with what is the North American standard, what you find in the Bahamas, and, where international regulations apply, in the world at large. However very strict rules are in force in respect to anchoring in the Turks and Caicos, and particularly in the many protected areas designated as National Parks, Nature Reserves, Sanctuaries, and Historic Sites. A significant part of the coastal sea area of the Turks and Caicos is protected and for this reason alone, it's sensible to review the regulatory side of the more important aspects of cruising there, or just passing through on passage.

- No vessel over 60 feet LOA is allowed to anchor in a National Park area except at a permitted Large Vessel Mooring. For this you must first contact the local harbormaster or the Department of the Environment.
- You may anchor only over sand.
- You are nor permitted to anchor close to reefs, within 300 feet of any marked dive site, and within 400 feet of any area designated as a Nature Reserve or Sanctuary.
- Damaging coral, either by anchoring over or near coral, or by grounding, is an offence. The fines levied in such cases can be substantial.

Turks and Caicos Mooring Buoys and Markers

Large Vessel (80 ft LOA) Dive Site	White cylinder, 2 Blue Bands
Standard Dive Site	White Ball, 1 Blue Band
Private Mooring	Red Ball
Danger Mark	Red Ball with a Black Band
Park Boundary Mark	White Post
Anchorage Zone	White Post, 3 Blue Bands
Channel Marker	Red or Green Post

- Dive sites controlled by the Turks and Caicos Department of the Environment are buoyed. You may pick up on of these buoys if it is unused, but if it is required by a dive boat, you must leave at once. (The peak period for dive site use is 8 a.m.–3 p.m. hours daily). If you use a dive site buoy the custom is to secure your own line or bridle (about a 20–25-foot length should serve) to the buoy pickup line.

LANDING IN SANCTUARIES

Take note that you are NOT allowed to land in a Sanctuary without a permit from the Department of Natural Resources.

DIVE SITES

Dive sites are numbered. Generally private mooring buoys will bear the name of the owner's vessel. Danger buoys may identify the threat (RF for reef, WRK for wreck, and BAR for bar) but you may not want to get that close! Park boundary markers may say just that, and anchorage zone markers should bear the letter "A."

The Turks and Caicos government are in the ongoing process of setting up their marine marks and indeed establishing a full Park Warden service, so what we have outlined may change in some respects, and may become formalized to an even greater extent.

If all this sounds forbidding, remember the aim is to protect the marine environment for all time. You are welcome. It is for their own people and their children, *and for you and people like you and your children*, that the legislation has been enacted.

Anchoring and Mooring

- *Never* anchor in coral. You'll kill the reef.
- If other boats are already in your chosen anchorage, try to stand off as far from everyone else as possible. This isn't just for safety. They might not share your taste in music, or enjoy the noise you make during your midnight swims.
- If the shore is covered in vegetation, scrub, or mangroves, you'll be wise to anchor well out of insect range. Getting too close can spoil your night.
- Be prepared for 180- and 360-degree swings, and strong tidal flows, which are not uncommon in Bahamian anchorages. Do you need two anchors out? Don't wait until there's a crisis to decide you *did* need that second anchor.
- Always dive to check that your anchors have set, or check them using a dive mask or a glass-bottom bucket from your dinghy. Sometimes, if the bottom is hard-packed sand or rocky, you may have to dive and set an anchor by hand.

- Continue this checking daily, look at your anchors and the free run of your anchor rodes to ensure that all is OK, and that your two rodes (assuming you are lying to two anchors) are not twisted together, which could give you a nightmare situation if you wanted to get up and go in a hurry.
- Don't run your generator after sunset unless you're alone, or have a super-quiet generator. Sound carries at night. And it's antisocial to run your generator during the "cocktail hour" (unless it really is sound-proofed) for you'll spoil the magic of that special time of day for everyone else.
- Always set an anchor light. Your light warns latecomers to stay away from you. However remote you may be, however unlikely it is that another cruising boat will join you. In high-traffic areas you'll soon discover that local Bahamian boats go about their business at all hours of the night, often at high speed. We reckon the conventional mast head light is just too high to warn off someone racing along at sea level, who may have had one Goombay Smash too many. Consider mounting an anchor light not much more than 10 feet above the water, and see how that looks to you. It could be just the most sensible precaution you ever took.
- Take anchor bearings or your GPS fix and keep them displayed at your helm station so that you can check that you've not dragged. If the risk is high, make out a roster and keep checking throughout the night. Set an anchor alarm if you have one.

SEVERE STORM CONDITIONS

If you're unlucky and have to weather a severe storm at anchor, avoid exposed harbors and crowded anchorages. Try to find a hurricane hole, something like a channel in mangroves where you can secure lines to the mangroves. Use every line you have, making a spider web of lines allowing 10 feet of slack for tidal surge, and use all your anchors fanned out at 90–120 degrees to complement your spider's web.

Use chafe protectors on your lines where they come on board. Reduce your windage. Take down your canvas, your sails if you are a sailboat, your flybridge canvas and curtains if you are a power boat, lower your antennas, remove your davits if they are removable, and deflate and store your inflatable below deck. Lash down everything that must remain on deck. Make the hull watertight. You might even consider plugging your engine and generator exhaust ports: but don't forget that you have done this!

If you can't find a hurricane hole (and there are very few places that are ideal) you can anchor out to face the wind, setting three anchors in a 120-degree fan. Ideally lead the three rodes to a swivel, and then run line from the swivel to the boat. Try for a 10:1 scope. If you use all chain, put a nylon snubber (equal to 10 percent of the chain length) in the chain to absorb shock.

All of this is a "last ditch" defensive measure in very severe conditions. You should never have to experience anything like this, and if you are caught out when hurricane or near-hurricane conditions are imminent, your boat is of secondary importance to your life and the lives of those with you. Your action should be to secure the boat if you can do so, but find a better place to take shelter ashore and leave the boat to take what comes.

How to prevent this kind of crisis situation? *Just listen to daily weather forecasts!*

GROUND TACKLE

We all dream of idyllic, calm, isolated, and uncrowded anchorages. You'll find some in the Bahamas. But you don't win perfection all the time. Your Bahamian anchorage may well turn out to be swept by reversing tidal currents, open to squalls, or already crowded with other boats by the time you get there. We reckon you need to carry three anchors cruising in the Bahamas:

1. A plow type for rock and sea grass
2. A Danforth type for sand and mud
3. Maybe a second plow as a storm and reserve anchor

Fit your anchor to your boat length, and go oversize if in doubt. Go one anchor size heavier if you anticipate heavy weather, or your planned passage is going to take you to more open anchorages.

With a nylon rode we always have 50 feet of chain to prevent anchor rode abrasion and to get the optimum catenary curve so that the direct pull on the anchor is flattened

Anchoring: Depth and Scope						
Depth	3:1	4:1	5:1	6:1	7:1	8:1
10 ft	30	40	50	60	70	80
15 ft	45	60	75	90	105	120
20 ft	60	80	100	120	140	160
25 ft	75	100	125	150	175	200
30 ft	90	120	150	180	210	240

to near-horizontal at the shank. In the Bahamas you can get by with 15–20 feet of chain, but don't go below that. Experienced skippers, especially those on larger and heavier boats, use an all-chain rode, and of course have the windlass for retrieving it. You should know the *safe working load* and the *breaking point* of your ground tackle.

BAHAMIAN MOOR

The Bahamian Moor is designed to keep you secure against the reversal of a tidal stream and prevent you swinging into your neighbors in a crowded anchorage.

Set your first anchor upstream, motoring into the current, and then let the stream take you back (or motor back if the wind is blowing you off) to set your second anchor downstream from the first, ideally 180 degrees apart. You can settle for a 90-degree separation if sea room is limited.

Once you have set the second anchor, pull yourself back on the first rode to get your desired scope on each rode and then make fast. Some skippers find it easier to set the first anchor normally, and then use their dinghy to take out and place the second anchor. You can add a third anchor, which will further reduce your radius of swing.

TIDAL RISE AND FALL

Work on a tidal rise and fall of 3 feet and you'll be about right. Remember you will get your highest tides with a full moon. If you have tide tables, check them.

SCOPE

Scope (the length of anchor rode you put out measured from the entry point of the rode into the water to the anchor) helps determine how well your anchor will hold under most conditions. Generally the greater the scope, the better. With an all-chain rode 3:1 (that's 3 feet of anchor chain for every foot of depth at high tide) may well be sufficient in sheltered water. With nylon and chain 5:1 scope is good. 7:1 is even better.

Both tidal current and crowding in an anchorage may dictate that you should use a Bahamian Moor and lie to two anchors, in which case you'll be unlikely to achieve anything like a 7:1 scope.

Pull in Pounds: Boat Length x Wind Velocity				
LOA (feet)	Wind Speed (knots)			
	15	30	40	60
25	125	490	980	1960
30	175	700	1400	2800
35	225	900	1800	3600
40	300	1200	2400	4800
50	400	1600	3200	6400
60	500	2000	4000	8000

Tides and Currents

TIDE is the vertical movement of water, while current is the horizontal movement of water. Both tides and currents will affect you in the Bahamas. As skipper and navigator, it's up to you to be aware of the state of the tide, particularly when entering and leaving harbors and negotiating passages. Even an inch can make the difference between being afloat and aground, but we try not to play it so close. If your boat draws more than 4.5–5 feet, you'll need to pay a lot of attention to tides in the Bahamas.

Bahamian Tides

Bahamas tides are what's known as semi-diurnal, which means two high tides and two low tides in 24 hours, in other words two tides a day, with about six hours from high to low and low to high. You can easily chart the tide without a tide table. Just remember that at full moon and at new moon, high tide comes at 8 a.m. and 8 p.m. local time, and high tides then occur roughly an hour later each day, and use the Rule of Twelfths (see **Conversion Tables and Useful Measurements** on page 446) to plot the rise and fall.

The mean tidal range in the Bahamas is 2.6 feet. When the moon is full or new the range increases to around 3.1 feet. At the lowest range, the *neap* tides, which occur at the first and third quarters of the moon, you get your lowest levels, about six inches below the mean tidal range.

The time of high and low tides throughout the Bahamas varies only 40 minutes or less, except for the west coast of Eleuthera and the Bank side of the Grand Lucayan Waterway on Grand Bahama, both of which are about 2.5 hours behind Nassau. All Bahamian tides are based on Nassau. High winds can have a significant impact on tides, particularly in the Bahamas, sweeping water up much higher than normal in enclosed areas or, conversely, blowing away the water to produce what will appear to be much lower tides than normal.

If you tried to produce a "Tidal Atlas of the Bahamas," you might go insane. Perhaps that's why no one has done so. The Banks shed their water in every direction, and draw in ocean water from every direction when the flow reverses. How does this work? While this is a far from scientific explanation, here's a simplified view. Imagine the Bank as a great shallow plate with an uneven rim, surrounded by ocean. The high bits of the rim are the islands. On a rising tide, ocean water rises up on to the Bank over all the low bits of the rim and flows in trying to fill the plate from all directions. On a falling tide the plate sheds its water in all directions.

Figuring it out on the Banks

You can understand why that tidal atlas could be difficult to draw. When you're on the banks, what you need to know is where the nearest low part of that plate rim is, and of course where the "center" of the plate lies. A line between the two gives you an idea of the current you can expect, in one direction or the other depending on the state of the tide. In some places you'll find that the current is surprisingly strong and can take you well off course. If you make use of the cross track error capability of your GPS you will see it, can correct it, and you'll have no problems.

Turks and Caicos Tides

Tidal information is based on Hawk's Nest anchorage (21° 26' N 071° 07' W), which is the sea area immediately to the southeast of Grand Turk Island.

The mean range is 2 feet 10 inches. The tide set on the Caicos Bank is reckoned to be about 1 knot +, running northeast on flood and southwest on ebb. The Turks Island Passage has a strong northerly set. As far as we know, no tidal atlas has ever been compiled for the Turks and Caicos Islands.

What Else Should You Know?

Be aware that reef passages and cuts between the islands and cays can produce rip tides that will run from 2.5 to 4 knots, and can occasionally reach 6 knots in places. If the wind is against this current, this can produce a narrow mill race of water you're better off avoiding. Heavy offshore swells can compound the problem and produce the very dangerous seas known as a "Rage" (see page 59), which makes reef passages out into the ocean, like Whale Cay Passage in the Abacos, impassible. Make your transits through restricted waters and choke points only when wind and current are right.

Be cautious approaching an unfamiliar anchorage or harbor, and check the depth it carries and the state of tide before you commit yourself to an approach channel. If you are in doubt when you arrive, use your VHF and ask for local guidance. But if you're off the beaten track on your own, that's where eyeball navigation becomes vital. The best procedure, when you get in close, is to anchor where you're safe and then do your surveying in your dinghy.

VHF Radio

WE'VE all been well trained and pay strict attention to the international rules governing the use of VHF radio. We use channel 16 for distress and calling (and channel 9 now, in the USA, for recreational boat calling). We keep a listening watch on channel 16 the whole time we're at sea. When we make contact with someone on 16, we switch to a designated working channel immediately. On any channel we're conscious that other people are also out there, somewhere within range, and they too may want to use the radio. We keep our conversations brief, to the point, we don't use marine VHF radio as a telephone, and we never use VHF radios on land.

Distress Calls

Channel 16 is the distress call frequency. We show the form a distress call should take for those not familiar with it. The codeword MAYDAY is the international alert signal of a life-threatening situation at sea. **After a MAYDAY message is broadcast Channel 16 must be kept free of all traffic, other than those directly involved in the rescue situation, until the rescue has been completed.** If you hear a Mayday message, if no one else is responding, it is **your** duty to step in to answer the call, relay it to the nearest rescue organization, and get to the scene to help.

Remember a Mayday distress call can only be used when life is threatened. If you have run on the rocks but no one is going to lose their life, however grave the damage to your boat, that is not a Mayday situation.

Distress Call

Hello All Ships. MAYDAY! MAYDAY! MAYDAY!

This is [give your Vessel Name and Callsign].

Our position is [read it off the GPS, or give it as something like "2 miles southwest of Royal Island." Your rescuers **must** be able to find you!].

We are [then say what's happening: on fire? have hit a reef and are sinking?].

We have [say how many people there are on board].

At this time we are [say what you're doing about the crisis: abandoning ship?]

For identification we are [say what your boat is: type, length, color, so that your rescuers can identify you at a distance more easily].

We have [say what safety equipment you have on board: flares? smoke? ocean dye markers? an EPIRB?]

We will keep watch on Channel 16 as long as we can.

This is [repeat your vessel Name and Callsign]. *MAYDAY! MAYDAY! MAYDAY!*

Wait for an answer. If no one responds, keep repeating your distress call until you receive an answer.

VHF in the Bahamas

All this goes out of the window in the Bahamas. Bahamians, especially in the Out Islands, use VHF radios like party-line telephones, and take their pick of the channels in the recreational boating frequencies. Almost every house, certainly everyone in business in the Out Islands, makes use of VHF as a primary means of communication. You don't just stop at arranging a berth in a marina over the radio. You check menus at a restaurant, book a table, find a taxi to pick you up, ask for someone to do your laundry, or repair your outboard. Even channel 16 is no longer sacred and carries far more traffic than it should. Is this legitimate? Don't let the answer to this question disturb you, because that's the way it is in the Bahamas. Yes, there is cellular telephone service there, just as there is Batelco's (the Bahamas Telecommunications Company) conventional telephone service. But VHF radio is cheaper than paying Batelco bills.

Newcomers soon learn that in the main centers where visiting yachts concentrate (like Marsh Harbour and George Town) VHF radio has become a bonding lifeline. Cruising nets open at a set time each morning, provide weather, local information such as future events and social get-togethers, and offers of services or pleas for help with problems. Don't be outraged by it. The bottom line is simple. You are in an island nation that makes use of VHF radio as a telephone service and you are part of a cruising community where VHF radio is one piece of equipment every boat has in common. Forget the normal contraints on using VHF radio. Ignoring the rules makes sense. Ride along with it. Don't get mad if you can't stand it. Just turn your radio off.

This said, essentially the International Maritime Organisation conventions on VHF channel allocation remain in force, and your "standard" list of channel allocation applies Bahama-wide. The primary reserved frequencies are shown below.

RESERVED CHANNELS

Nassau Harbour Control	09
Distress and Calling	16
US Coast Guard	21–23A
Marine Operator Nassau (radio telephone)	27

UNAUTHORIZED USE

In some areas of the Bahamas, notably the Abacos, common usage has resulted in a rash of so-called reserved channels, such as 6 for taxis, 65 for Dolphin Research, 68 as the calling channel, 72 for the Hope Town Fire Brigade, and 80 for Trauma One. These adoptions of air space are unauthorized. Nonetheless this is the way it is, and you should take note of them if you are in waters where local channel designation has become customary.

VHF in the Turks and Caicos

Generally the international rules apply, and most importantly, VHF 16 is the distress and primary calling frequency. Otherwise channel usage is:

Commercial vessels	68
Working frequencies	09, 12, 14, 65, 69, 74
Taxis	06
Public bus	70

Weather Broadcasts

In the Bahamas (apart from Grand Bahama and the Biminis) you are out of range of the US NOAA weather broadcasts. You may be able to access the Weather Channel on a dockside TV hookup or through a satellite antenna. Your principal sources of weather information will be Radio Bahamas (the ZNS stations), the broadcasts of Mobile Marine Radio (WLO) and the US Coast Guard (NMN), weather facsimile broadcasts, and a number of other miscellaneous sources. If you're unable to receive SSB broadcasts or do not have access to most of the sources we list, generally you'll always find someone on shore or another cruising boat willing to share weather information with you.

All sources of weather information are consolidated in one comprehensive section. This is in **Appendix C** on page 443. Together with this we include a Weather Plotting chart for use during the broadcasts.

A Pilot House Booklist

IN addition to your charts, your shipboard library should contain these "standard" works most of us carry on a cruise, as well as manuals for all equipment on board.

Federal Requirements and Safety Tips for Recreational Boaters

NOAA Chart No 1. Nautical Chart Symbols and Abbreviations.

Reed's Nautical Almanac, North American East Coast Edition and *Caribbean Edition.*

Reed's Nautical Companion.

Navigation Rules.

Chapman Piloting, Seamanship & Small Boat Handling. Elbert S. Maloney.

Chapman Emergencies at Sea.

Heavy Weather Sailing. Adlard Coles, revised by Peter Bruce (International Marine, 1996).

Mariners Weather. William P Crawford (W.W. Norton, 1995).

Admiralty List of Radio Signals. Volume 3. (United Kingdom Hydrographic Office, NP283, annual).

Marine Diesel Engines. Nigel Calder (International Marine, 1997).

Boatowner's Electrical and Mechanical Handbook. Nigel Calder (International Marine).

12V Bible. Miner Brotherton (Seven Seas).

Handbook of First Aid and Emergency Care. American Medical Association.

Advanced First Aid Afloat. Peter F. Eastman (Cornell Maritime Press, 1995).

A Medical Guide to Hazardous Marine Life. Paul S. Auerbach (Best Publishing Co., 1997).

Where There Is No Doctor: A Village Health Care Handbook. The Hesperian Foundation.

DAN Emergency Handbook.

A cruising guide of this scope cannot, unless it is to run into more than one volume, cover the inshore waters in exhaustive detail, and we recommend that you carry in addition one of the special-to-area guides now on the market. Under this heading we would list:

The Cruising Guide to Abaco. Steve Dodge (White Sound Press). The long-standing, detailed guide to the Abacos.

The Explorer Chartbooks. Monty and Sara Lewis. (Lewis Offshore Ltd.) These well-known chartbooks cover the Central Bahamas and the Exumas.

The Pavlides Guides. (Seaworthy Publications.) Stephen Pavlides first covered the Exumas in 1995, and has now extended his area of interest to cover from South Florida to the Dominican Republic. His titles cover the Abacos, the Central and Southern Bahamas, the Exumas, and the Turks and Caicos. You may wish to check these out.

Day-to-Day Living in the Islands

IN the Bahamas you can buy almost anything you can buy in the US. If it's not there, in stock, someone will order it for you. Depending on where you are, you can sometimes get it within twenty-four hours. But there is a BUT in all this. It will cost you. It will cost you more than you would pay in the states, both for what you buy off the shelf in the islands, and whatever you might order specially.

Other than fish, conch, and lobster tails, chicken, eggs, bread, beer, rum, soft drinks, Bahamian "spring" water, and a seasonal but slender stock of locally grown fruits and vegetables, the Bahamas produces almost nothing you require for your day-to-day living. Almost everything the Bahamanians themselves need to sustain their daily lives has to be imported. Hardly surprisingly it carries prices way above those of stateside supermarkets. Marine spares are high priced, as is marine fuel.

The knock-on effect generally means that the cost of living in the Bahamas is high. Meals in a restaurant cost more than you would pay at home (with rare exceptions), the price of accommodations (if you need shoreside accommodation) is high in the winter season, taxis charge the earth for a short ride from an airport to a ferry dock, and refueling a power boat will make you wish you owned a sailboat.

Above all this, fresh water is desperately scarce. In many places the water table has been so reduced by demand that salt water has permeated into the aquifers and turned all well water forever brackish. Islands rely on rainfall, water brought in on a barge, or desalination. Water is expensive.

Before you set out for the Bahamas, the first and obvious conclusion is to take everything you can, leave with full fuel and water tanks, and take extra fuel if that is possible. In practice we're all limited by what we can take on board. There's another consideration that may not weigh much with you initially, but you become conscious of it in the islands. The Bahamians, in comparison to their visitors, have nothing. Tourists (and this includes cruising yachtsmen) underpin the Bahamian economy. If you never buy anything in the islands, you leave resentment in your wake. Buy some things there, put some money into their economy, for you are using their waters, their beaches, and their islands for your enjoyment. The price of a cruising permit is an entry ticket, not a pass for a free ride.

Locker and freezer space, and the length of your cruise, will dictate what you stow on board, but in drawing up your provisioning list, leave some things for that local store. Bahamas bread is delicious, fresh baked each day and free of artificial preservatives. The rum and the beer are good. Fresh produce is hard to find outside the larger towns. You pay the prices Bahamians pay themselves, and you'll get to know them as you do your marketing. Isn't that what cruising is all about?

MAJOR PROVISIONING STOPS

Freeport and Port Lucaya, Grand Bahama
Marsh Harbour, Abacos
Nassau, New Providence
Harbour Island and Spanish Wells, Eleuthera
George Town, Exumas

RE-STOCKING THE LARDER

Alice Town, Biminis
Great Harbour Cay, Berry Islands
Fresh Creek, Andros
Green Turtle Cay, Abacos
Man-O-War Cay, Abacos
Hope Town, Abacos
Staniel Cay, Exumas
New Bight, Cat Island
Cockburn Town, San Salvador
Clarence Town, Long Island
Matthew Town, Great Inagua
Providenciales, Turks and Caicos

The Bahamas: Population and Tourism

AT the start of the twentieth century, in 1901, there were just over 50,000 Bahamians living in the islands. Since then that figure has increased by 200,000. Where are they all living? The 1990 census showed:

ALL-BAHAMAS

Total Population	254,685

THE MOST HEAVILY POPULATED

New Providence	171,542
Grand Bahama	41,035

THE NEXT LEVEL

Eleuthera, including Harbour Island and Spanish Wells	10,524
Abaco	10,061
Andros	8,155

THINNING OUT

Exumas	3,539
Long Island	3,107
Cat Island	1,678
Biminis	1,638
Great Inagua	985

NOT MANY PEOPLE AROUND

Berry Islands	634
San Salvador	486
Acklins Island	428
Crooked Island	423
Mayaguana	308
Ragged Islands	89
Rum Cay	53

THE VISITORS

Cruise Ship Visits (Peak)	April, June, July
Cruise Ship Visits (Low)	September
Annual Cruise Ship Visitors	over 500,000
Average Spending per Visitor	about $60 per day
Fly-In Visits (Peak)	April, June, July
Fly-In Visits (Low)	September
Annual Fly-In Visitors	over 100,000
Average Spending per Visitor	about $134 per day

Priorities in Southern Waters

The priority is to leave with your fuel tanks and water tanks full, but there's nothing new in this. It's our standard drill, wherever we are, wherever we go. Let's turn to the broader field of general provisioning. A check list that you may find useful is on page 447, but it's still worthwhile running over the basic considerations you should have in mind before setting out.

A reasonable quantity of oil and lubricants should go with you. Boat spares are vital, for quite apart from expense, a local dealer may not have them in stock, or you may be miles away from civilization when something breaks down. Bulbs, fuses, belts, impellers, filters, spare pumps, spark plugs, injectors, gaskets, and distilled water for your batteries. Go through your lists and ensure that you have a reasonable self-sufficiency, particularly in the line that everyone hopes will never malfunction, your marine sanitation system.

What then of foodstuffs? If you have a deep freeze, take ground beef, steaks, chicken breasts, chicken thighs, and the like. Don't take frozen seafood. You can buy it there, frozen if you wish, or fresh. But why not catch it yourself? Take frozen vegetables. Stock your refrigerator with a start-out quantity of eggs, cheeses, butter, margarine, fresh vegetables, and salad. Take as much fresh fruit as will last, for that can be hard to come by in the islands.

Some canned food is worth taking, like tuna, mushrooms, corned beef, beans, and maybe soups. Dry goods like rice, flour, pastas, and sugar make sense, and so do sauces and mustards, mayonnaise, salad dressings, spices, dried herbs, and cooking oils. Take tea and coffee, mixers for your drinks, and all your alcoholic beverages except beer and rum. If you're going to run short in the alcoholic drink line, the local prices are not exhorbitant. Bottled water is essential until you can re-stock in the larger towns.

The only other goods we would place on the priority list is drugstore stuff. Your own medication, if nothing else. Sunscreens, aftersun lotion, insect repellent, and the like. Even your own brand of toothpaste. It's easier to take your own stock. And while you're in the pharmacy don't forget to check your medical pack and build it up so that you have everything you might need for the length of your cruise, and a good book on first aid.

What Else Could You Take?

Otherwise what remains? The list of what you could take would be almost endless. Dry goods like paper towels, toilet paper, Kleenex, cleaners, and garbage bags all come into it. Lemon Joy is popular for dishwashing because it lathers in salt water.

Perhaps if you are going cruising for the first time, the best answer is to walk round your house with a legal pad noting everything you need. For some time before your departure start recording the date you take a new bar of soap or tube of toothpaste into use. How long does a pack of five razor blades last? What about shampoo? Like Lemon Joy, Head and Shoulders lathers in salt water. But watch the quantities as you push your cart around the supermarket. It's so easy to overstock.

Just remember you can get everything you are likely to need in all the major centers of population, but if you're going off into the Out Islands, your provisioning at once takes on a different aspect. Then you should handle it rather as you would handle stocking up for a bluewater passage.

WHAT COULD YOU TAKE THEM?

Don't arrive empty handed. In the islands both the libraries and the schools welcome gifts of books. Maybe a child somewhere might welcome a toy. Have something, if you can, just to say "Thank You," particularly if you plan to stay in one place for long.

Finally, Back to Water and Fuel

The price of fresh water in some islands runs as high as $1.25 a gallon. If you're considering extensive cruising in the Bahamas or further south, down to the Turks and Caicos, it might be worth thinking about reducing the size of your water tank(s), fitting a watermaker, and, if you've gained tank space, increasing the size of your fuel tankage. Work it out.

Chapter 25
Green Pages
History, Wildlife, and Fishing & Diving

Commemorating the Loyalist settlement of Green Turtle Cay in 1783.

The Story of the Bahamas

"THIS *island is very large and very flat. It is green, with many trees and several bodies of water. There is a very large lagoon in the middle of the island and there are no mountains.*"

"*I was alarmed at seeing that the entire island is surrounded by a large reef. Between the reef and the island it remained deep . . . there are a few shoal spots, to be sure, and the sea moves in it no more than the water in a well.*"

"*I have no desire to sail strange waters at night . . .*"

"*You must keep your eyes peeled where you wish to anchor and not anchor too near shore. The water is very clear and you can see the bottom during the daylight hours, but a couple of lombard shots offshore there is so much depth that you cannot find bottom.*"

You could say there you have it, in four bites. An introduction to cruising in the Bahamas, with all the vital lessons set out.

Don't expect any significant elevation in the land to guide you in. You can expect reefs around the islands, but you can find deep water inside the reefs and the reef itself will offer shelter. It's dangerous to sail Bahamian waters at night. Generally anchoring too close to a beach is a mistake, but you can choose exactly where you wish to drop your hook. The water is so clear. The dropoffs run closer to land than you'd expect, and are profound.

⁂

The author was Christopher Columbus and the date was 1492.

With 50 men you could subject everyone and make them do what you wished . . . (Columbus, in the Bahamas. Sunday, October 14, 1492)

His "handsome" islanders "as naked as their mothers bore them" are described as "very simple and honest, and exceedingly liberal with all they have; none of them refusing any thing he may possess when he is asked for it . . . they exhibit great love towards all others in preference to themselves; they also give objects of great value for trifles, and content themselves with little or nothing in return . . ." His simple people lived to regret the spotlight. The Arawak dividend from this first contact with European Man was extinction within a quarter of a century.

The Arawaks left no ruins in the Bahamas in which you can imagine their presence, but the unspoiled landscape and the seascape, the deep blue, green, and turquoise waters, are just as they were when the Bahamas was their land. If you go quietly and gently you can assume an affinity with their life style, for the daily concerns of their world were much the same as yours in the Bahamas. Theirs was a low-stress littoral life, in which boats and fishing were everything, with the freedom to move from island to island at will, even as far afield as Haiti and Cuba. Perhaps it's fitting that part of

A seventeenth-century Spanish galleon.

their language remains with us to this day, words that Columbus and his successors had to adopt, for there was no other way to name or describe the New World they had found. We have inherited avocado, barbecue, cannibal, canoe, Carib, cay, guava, hammock, hurricane, iguana, maize, manatee, potato, and tobacco, among others.

Once the terrible genocide of the Bahamian native population had been achieved through mass abductions into slavery, disease, and starvation, the Bahamas became a wasteland in Spanish eyes. A disappointment to Ponce de Leon in his search for the Fountain of Youth, and a trap for their treasure galleons lumbering north from Havana on the long haul back to Spain. One hundred and fifty years passed. Then in 1648 the quaintly named Eleutheran Adventurers, seeking a Mayflower Pilgrim–type fresh start and religious freedom, literally hit Eleuthera. You could say their vessel was the first known victim of the Devil's Backbone. From then on, the Bahamas were on the map. By the end of the seventeenth century the slow re-population of the Bahamas had begun with over a thousand settlers divided between Eleuthera and its twin haven, New Providence Island. It was tough going. The new immigrants soon found that the Bahamas were no self-sustaining Garden of Eden, and their primary needs were imports, and vital imports needed hard cash. Happily the regular Spanish-galleon run provided windfall jackpots, as did the wrecks of other ships unfortunate enough to be ill-set by wind and current in Bahamian waters. But there was a downside to this marauding. The sharks joined in.

My name was William Kidd, and so wickedly I did, when I sailed . . . (The Ballad of William Kidd)

The sharks were not the ones with triangular dorsal fins, though undoubtedly the shipwrecks attracted them too, but two-legged ones with names like Henry Morgan (of Morgans Bluff, in Andros), Edward Teach (the dreaded Blackbeard), Jack Calico Rackham, and a pair of terrifying Amazons, Anne Bonney and Mary Read, who, scuttlebutt had it, fought naked to the waist. Nassau paid host to enough real pirates and would-be pirates to fill the Bay Street waterfront bars every night and in consequence was hammered in retaliation by the Spanish four times in just a quarter of a century. The dreams of a simple, peaceful, agricultural God-fearing community had been totally eclipsed. It got so bad that eventually the British government showed some interest in a territory it had arbitrarily claimed way back in 1629. An ex-privateer, Woodes Rogers, was given a clean Bill of Health and sent out to govern the islands and end piracy. By 1720 he was a long way down the road, yet another Spanish attack had been repulsed, life on shore became quieter, but was no easier. The wrecking went on.

Fort Montague, Nassau, captured by US Marines, 1776.

Edward Wilson

If this be treason, make the most of it . . .

(Patrick Henry, Williamsburg, Virginia.
May 29, 1765)

The foment of the watershed events of the end of the eighteenth century as the European Powers started to lose their hold on the New World rocked the Bahamas like a succession of tidal waves. In 1776 the new American Continental Navy attacked the Bahamas, captured Fort Montague, and occupied Nassau. Why? Because it was British. But there was little profit in it, and they left after two weeks. Two years later the Americans returned to raise their new flag over Nassau, but yet again had second thoughts, and left. There was a four-year gap. Then in 1782 the Spanish came back in strength, and that was it. The Bahamas became Spanish.

Meanwhile back in Europe at the Treaty of Versailles the British had conceded independence to the North American colonies, had hung on to Canada, traded a tenuous claim to Florida with the Spanish, and reclaimed the Bahamas. But an American Loyalist, Andrew Deveaux, unaware of the horse trading in France, set out from South Carolina to win the Bahamas back, and achieved it through a brilliant, simple, deceptive display of quite false overwhelming strength. His lead opened the doors to a rush of migration as Loyalists, unhappy at the prospect of living in a new United States, fled with all their worldly goods, their slaves, and sometimes even the bricks of their houses to start a new life, secure under the British flag. Deveaux himself took the southeast of Cat Island as his reward (you can still see the empty shell of his great house) and one by one all the larger islands were settled as plantation land. It

was a disaster. Within ten years crops had failed, the thin soil was exhausted, and many frustrated, ruined planters quit. Some, in leaving, set their slaves at liberty. They had no further use for them.

The fortunes of the Bahamas had been set in a cyclic pattern from the first ill-fated resettlement of the islands in the mid-seventeenth century. Ignoring moral justification about good guys and bad guys, rights and wrongs, the first high spot was the success of piracy in the first part of the eighteenth century. That was a boom time. If you were a pirate. The second boom, short-lived, came with the migration of the American Loyalists. The plantation era, when it had seemed at first that Bahamian land was almost worth its weight in gold, barely lasted that decade. And then the Bahamas became a backwater. The only living that could be won came from the reefs and shoals of the shallow seas, and wrecking was the mainstay of survival.

Shall be thenceforward and forever free . . .

(Abraham Lincoln, Washington, DC.
September 22, 1862)

The character of the Bahamas had been formed. By the early 1830s permanent settlements existed on seventeen of the islands, and there was precious little land of agricultural value even in them. The black population outnumbered the white, but figures were hard to establish. A census of slaves in the 1820s, as the Abolitionist movement developed a ground swell, showed more than 10,000 in the Bahamas. By 1838

Courtesy Balmain Antiques, Nassau

Illustrated London News, *April 30, 1864. Confederate blockade runner unloading cotton in Nassau.*

slavery was ended, and the Royal Navy added to the Bahamas population the human cargo they had captured in slave ships. The newly-landed joined the newly-freed in scratching out a living somewhere near the survival line. As the hands of time moved closer to the twentieth century the Bahamas, at grassroots level, was foundering.

The outbreak of the American Civil War was a wake-up call and a shot of adrenaline for the Bahamas. For five years it was like a Gold Rush boom or a return to the days of Bonney and Read as Nassau played host and haven to Confederate blockade runners. Strange it was that the emancipated slaves of the Bahamas should combine in commercial enterprise with the oppressors of the Deep South, but pragmatism wins over the contemplation of an empty bowl. When the guns fell silent it was curtains again over the Bahamas. Even the wrecking business was no longer a fail-safe. The rule of law was enforced, lighthouses were built, the islands at last were charted. A market for sponges kept the Bahamas alive, as did relatively productive, easy-to-grow crops such as pineapples. But the sponges became diseased and US import preferences along with the Hawaiian pineapple soon negated any regeneration through aquaculture or agriculture.

Prohibition comes into force.

US Headline. January 16, 1919

Another recession followed, not even alleviated by the First World War, when many Bahamians volunteered for service. Once again US internal politics were to catapult the Bahamian economy to another all-time high. In 1919 the Volstead Act was passed, prohibition was imposed, and the manufacture, sale, and consumption of alcohol in the United States became illegal. The Bahamian rum runners saved the day for those whose day was ruined without a martini, and Nassau and Bimini were back in a Civil War mode, this time with power boats. Nassau boomed, offering new hotel rooms, bars, and gambling, and PanAmerican, only too happy to print and sell the tickets, flew in regularly from Miami. In 1933 it all ended with the repeal of Prohibition. Nassau closed down, and Bimini went to sleep.

Roosevelt signs Lend-Lease Bill.

Headline. March 11, 1941

The Lend-Lease bases of the Second World War, the fame of the Duke of Windsor, the unusually high-ranking governor of the Bahamas (to say nothing of the Duchess, for whom a throne was surrendered), and the infamous Harry Oakes affair put the Bahamas on the map once again. There were hopes that with postwar affluence the benefits of tourism might come to the Bahamas, more so after the earlier spear-

The Duke and Duchess of Windsor on his arrival to assume the appointment of Governor of the Bahamas in 1940.

heading by PanAm, but the Bahamas relapsed again. The time was not ripe. The Bahamas had yet to work out a political *modus vivendi*, racial relations were as strained as the imbalance of domestic wealth, independence was clearly in the cards but worrisome, Florida was far from reaching capacity in attracting sun-seekers, Havana was more exciting than Nassau, and air tourism had yet to find its wings.

This is my island in the sun . . .

Calypso

By the mid-1950s it was time for another boom. Most of the ducks, other than independence, had come in line. With the development of Freeport, West End, Nassau Harbour, new air services, and the enactment of legislation deliberately designed to attract offshore investment, the Bahamas hit a boom period spurred by tourism, investors, and speculators. Private cays, once a dime a dozen, became premium property. It seemed there was no holding back. But the pace slackened. The builders stopped building. It had worked, but then the momentum failed. In place of the materialization of this new boom, drug running became an all-too-viable, and too visible, alternative route to riches.

A sudden demand for cigarette boats and used C-47s . . .

Market trends in the 1960s

The shades of piracy, blockade running, and rum running resurfaced. For the first time the remoter parts of the Bahamas became hot property, new airstrips spread like a rash over the Exumas and the Out Islands, and suddenly some people were becoming very rich. There was money to burn, and in an uneven distribution, the Bahamas enjoyed some kind of minor boom. It ended when the downside, not least of it the murder of anyone who happened to be in the wrong place at the wrong time, became intolerable.

A used C-47.

I simply do not know where to go next . . .

Columbus, in the Bahamas.
Friday, October 19, 1492

Why did the Freeport initiative stall? Perhaps three prerequisites had to come before the dreams of the 1950s initiatives were achieved. One was the resolution of the political future of the Bahamas. It was. The Bahamas became independent on July 10, 1973. The second was the halting of the drug trade, as far as traffic built on addiction can be halted, for it was debilitating the nation and distorting the economy. The third was the realization that wrecking, cotton, sisal, pineapples, and agriculture in general, as well

as sponging, were no ways to fortune. What the Bahamas had to offer were two immutable blessings that had come as a package deal with their environment. The first, the natural dividend of a multi-island people, was a maritime tradition dating back three hundred years. The second was also a natural dividend. It was the most brilliant waters in the Western Hemisphere.

Today the Bahamas is at the threshold of another boom period, which, unless there is a global catastrophe or enormous mismanagement, will eclipse and outlast any previous gold rush. It's a time of change, and you can see it in Nassau, on the docks and on Bay Street, and on Paradise Island. Grand Bahama is about to hit high stakes far beyond the expectations of the Freeport founders, with a totally reconstructed harbor and airport, vast new housing developments, the reconstruction of the Port Lucaya hotels, and the long overdue resurrection of West End.

Two private sky harbours for executive jets are being developed . . .

1997 Bahamas Business Report

Why has all this come about? We've suggested three reasons. What are the contributory factors? The 1997 change of government in the Bahamas. The upsurge and stability of the US economy. In tourism terms a growing disillusionment with the Caribbean. The continuance of the Castro regime, and the certainty that Cuba, even freed of communist dictatorship, will take years to find its feet. There are the motive pluses, the Bahamas is on the US doorstep, right there, just 50 miles across the Florida Strait. The language is English, and the law is English too. The banking laws are favorable and absolute. And Florida has now hit its zenith in constructing beach-obliterating shoulder-to-shoulder condominiums. There is no more coastline.

Is there any other factor? Yes, there is one. Not to be underrated. It lies in the lessons of another British colony founded on piracy, smuggling, and drug running, which turned to trading and tourism. Now after the handover of Hong Kong to the Chinese, the former colony may well continue as a potent commercial center, but it remains that the most successful self-regulating entrepot in the world has gone.

We may well see the Bahamas take the torch from Hong Kong, and make a bid to become the banking, shipping, and trading epicenter of the Western Maritime World with links to Europe, North America, South America, and, through the Caribbean and Panama, into the Pacific. The first indication lies in the Hong Kong money that even now has been, and is being, invested in Grand Bahama. The writing is on the wall. Let's hope that the wall itself is well built, and maintained.

Meanwhile back on board . . .

Let's change the focus. What's in this for the cruising visitor? Better shoreside facilities. More marinas. Isn't this going to bring about the Floridization of the Bahamas, and spoil its attraction as a cruising ground? No. We think not. The total sea area is too great, there are so many islands, there will always be remote places. Those who want to hook up to shore power will be better served, and those who wish to drop a hook will still be able to find that magic anchorage.

As the words of the song go, "Who Could Ask For Anything More?"

The Columbus Controversy

IN November 1986 the National Geographic Society detonated a bomb under conventional theories about the track and landfalls of the First Voyage of Columbus. In a well-researched, cogent analysis *Where Did Columbus Discover America?* a compelling argument was advanced that his first landfall was Semana Cay, not San Salvador. The first serious attempt to identify the site of the Columbus landfall in the Americas was published in 1625, and concluded that it was Cat Island. Since then there have been no less than nine different contenders for the honor of selection, of which the perennial frontrunner was Watling Island or San Salvador, as we call it today.

The Landfall. An Island Called Guanahani.

As for Columbus, his description of his landfall is hardly sufficiently explicit to identify one single island, but then try to write descriptions of each Bahamian island and cay as you come to them. The natives called his landfall *Guanahani*. Columbus renamed it San Salvador, for the standard operating procedure of the Spanish discoverers and *conquistadors* was an automatic assumption that the population of the places they found had no significance, other than as slave labor, and rechristening the land they found was tantamount to takeover. Guanahani, Columbus said, was surrounded by a large reef that had a narrow entrance, it was fairly large, very flat, green, covered in vegetation, and had several bodies of water (ponds? swamps?) as well as a large central lagoon. An inlet? Mangroves? The description could fit any number of the 723 islands and cays of the Bahamas. Out of the nine

Columbus landing in the Bahamas. Artist unknown.

"possibles" the spotlight eventually rested on just two places, Watling Island and Semana Cay.

The Columbus Landfall Contenders

The list runs from Cat Island, Conception Island, East Caicos Island (Turks and Caicos Islands), Egg Island and/or Royal Island, Grand Turk Island (Turks and Caicos Islands), Mayaguana, the Plana Cays, Semana Cay, to Watling Island.

THE WATLING SCHOOL

You could say that the renaming of Watling Island as San Salvador in 1926 was the grant of *de facto* title as the proven landfall. Largely through the advocacy of early heavyweight naval historians, later joined by Samuel Eliot Morison, one of the premier authorities in this century on American maritime history, Watling Island was "it." Not everyone agreed. A small band of disbelievers said Columbus's re-

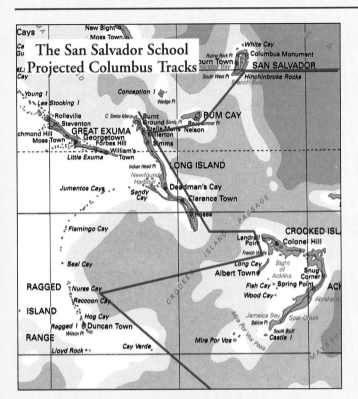

corded onward track didn't fit the geography of the Out Islands to the north of the tropic of Cancer. Everyone acknowledged that Columbus kept his log secret from his crew for fear of alarming them about their distance run from Spain, and everyone agreed that there were translation confusions, particularly about *leagues* run and *miles*. But it remained that however you projected his track after San Salvador, the Columbus log didn't fit. There were fundamental errors in distances and direction.

THE SEMANA SCHOOL

In 1880 Captain Gustavus Vasa Fox, President Lincoln's Assistant Secretary of the Navy from 1861 to 1866, published an article in which for the first time Semana Cay was proposed as the landing site. Despite the fact that suddenly the Columbus log fitted neatly into the Bahamian map like the long missing piece of a jigsaw puzzle, the Fox theory won little backing, even though in 1894 the National Geographic Society published a reinforcement of his argument. The debate continued with Conception Island, East Caicos, and the Plana Cays thrown in as confusion factors. In November 1975 the National Geographic Society threw in the towel and joined the San Salvador support group.

The Quincentennial Analysis

The advent of the Quincentennial of the Columbus Landing reawakened interest in the controversy, and the National Geographic Society took another long, hard look

at Fox and Semana Cay. A highly skilled team was put together to make the ultimate comparison between the San Salvador and Semana Cay theories using technology to advantage. The detailed study rested initially on a computer-drawn analysis of the always-suspect Columbus Atlantic log with winds, currents, and leeway taken into account. Every projection run ended at Semana Cay.

A detailed analysis of his America log started. Columbus reported sending small boats to scout around his landfall. The boats returned in seven hours. Even a champion Eights crew couldn't make a round trip up the only part of San Salvador that half-fits his description (the 15-nm northwest coastline up to Grahams Harbour) in seven hours. But Semana (some 16 nm in total circumference) matches. And it fits in many other ways.

From Semana the recreation of Columbus's track led to northeast Acklins, to Crooked Island (Pittstown Point, Landrail, and French Wells), on to the southeast coast of Long Island (Little Harbour and Clarence Town), and then back to Crooked Island (French Wells again) and Long Cay (Windsor Point). He tried the Bight of Acklins (it was too shallow), headed west, bumped into the Jumentos Cays, turned south, and so "discovered" Cuba. In his three subsequent voyages he never returned to the Bahamas. Later Spanish expeditions were mounted to take Arawak males away to slavery in Española (Haiti and the Dominican Republic), which resulted in the total extinction of the Bahamian population within a generation. The islands that had marked, shared, but not enjoyed the First (Euro-

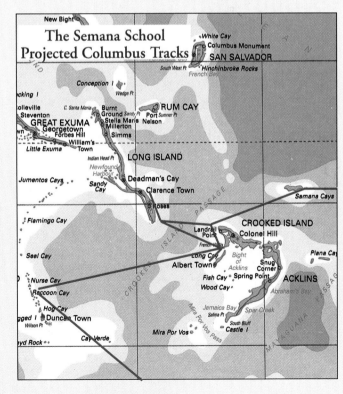

The Columbus Log

FOR those who venture into the Bahamas south of the tropic of Cancer, we highlight and comment on some brief extracts from the log of Columbus's First Voyage.

Northeast Acklins Island (never named by Columbus)
The coast that faces San Salvador [the east coast facing his Guanahani landfall] *lies in a north-south line and extends for 15 miles. The other coast* [the north coast] *which I followed, runs east and west and is more than 30 miles long.*

Crooked Island (Santa María de la Concepción)
. . . the western cape. I anchored at sunset near the cape [Portland Harbour, probably just southeast of Bird Rock in the deep water inside the reef just off Pittstown Point] *in order to find out if there was gold there.*

Passage to Long Island (Fernandina)
Judged by the clouds and the signs made by the men from San Salvador [Guanahani men captured to serve as guides] *this large island to the west was about 27 miles distant.*

Long Island
It is very big and about 24 miles due west of Santa María de la Concepción [Crooked Island]. *This entire part where I am anchored runs NNW-SSE. It appears that this coast runs for 21 miles or more, and I saw 15 miles of it but it did not end there. It is very level without any mountains . . .*

Little Harbour
After I had sailed six miles from the island's cape [South Point] *where I had been anchored, I discovered a very wonderful harbor* [Little Harbour] *with one entrance, one may say two entrances, for there is an island in the middle. Both passages are very narrow, but once within, the harbor is wide enough for 100 ships. I did not think that either the entrance or the harbor was deep enough, however nor did I feel that the bottom was clear of rocks. It seemed reasonable*

to me to look it over well and take soundings, so I anchored outside and went in with the small boats. It was fortunate that I did, for there was no depth at all.

Clarence Town. *After taking on water* [at Little Harbour] *I returned to the ship and sailed to the NW until I had explored all that part of the island as far as the coast that runs east-west* [from Booby Cay, just north of Strachan Cay, westward to Longitude 075° N].

The weather turned against Columbus and he was forced to put about and run before the wind. He retraced his track and eventually anchored off French Wells in Crooked Island.

Crooked Island—French Wells (Cabo del Iseo)
Before we had sailed three hours we saw an island to the east for which we steered, and before midday all three ships reach a small island [Rat Cay] *at the north point* [of Long Cay]. *There is a rocky reef at this island that runs to the north, and between the reef and the large island to the north* [Crooked Island] *there is another island* [Goat Cay]. *To the NE of this small island there is a great bay* [the northwest corner of the Bight of Acklins] *. . . I wanted to anchor in that bay . . . but the water is shallow and I could not anchor.*

Long Cay (Isabela)
The coast trends west for 12 miles from this small island to a cape [Windsor Point, named Cabo Hermoso]. *It is round, and the water is deep with no shoals offshore.*

The Bight of Acklins
I thought I might sail around the island [Long Cay] *to the NE and to the east, from the SE and the south . . . but the bottom is so shallow* [the Bight of Acklins] *that I cannot enter or sail . . .*

pean) Discovery of the New World were then ignored.

Columbus wanted to head for northern Acklins where *"the men from San Salvador tell me there is a king with a lot of gold . . ."* but was foiled by the shoal waters of the Bight of Acklins. He returned to French Wells, and this time tucked himself further in, probably just south of the French Wells Creek or the Turtle Sound Creek, off Gun Point, which he named the Cabo de la Laguna. They spent three days there, discovered the Bahamas boa constrictor, and killed two of them *"the people here eat them and the meat is white and tastes like chicken."* Then they sailed west-southwest for a large island they had been told was called Cuba, *"which I am told is magnificent with gold and pearls."* After bouncing off the southern Ragged Is-

lands and adjusting their course to run almost due south, Columbus's small fleet made their Cuban landfall four days later. Perhaps by then Columbus was running out of names for his islands. Somehow Cuba escaped the ritual discovery rechristening.

To Join the Debate

Where does this leave us boating visitors some five hundred years after these events? If nothing else, with a fine project if you're intent on cruising in the Bahamas south of the tropic of Cancer. Get a good, readable translation of Columbus's Log of his First Voyage. We'd recommend the Robert Fuson version published by International Marine–McGraw-Hill in 1987. Get a copy of that November 1986

National Geographic with its map. Then make like Columbus. Or not quite like him as far as today's inhabitants of the islands are concerned.

We asked Arne Molander to write for us. He's a retired engineer who has spent the past 30 years researching this subject, and has cruised in the Bahamas many times searching for islands that match the descriptions in the Columbus Log. In short, his conclusion is that Columbus made a North Eleuthera landfall, and eventually headed southward, reaching Cuba by way of the Tongue of the Ocean and the west coast of Long Island. It's a compelling theory. We've long been interested in finding connectors between the Tongue of the Ocean and the Crooked Island Passage. Anciently they were said to exist. A 1780 French map in the Library of Congress, discovered by Arne Molander in his research, shows such a route. Our charts today, in their namings of channels to the immediate route southeast of the Tongue of the Ocean, suggest navigability, as well as exits from the Great Bahama Bank, such as Pear Cay Pass.

Read what he says. Look at our NASA photograph of the southeast Tongue of the Ocean on page 216, look at your charts, and turn back to our Northeast Eleuthera and North Andros charts to analyse what he says. And maybe go the way he suggests? We think we shall, one day.

Columbus statue, Nassau.

Cruising in the Wake of Columbus

by Arne Molander

AFTER Columbus reached the New World on October 12, 1492, he explored four islands in the Bahamas—San Salvador, Santa Maria de la Concepcion, Fernandina, and Isabela—before sailing on to Cuba. Although the identity of these four islands has long been in dispute, the Bahamian government now accepts Samuel Elliot Morison's theory that Watling Island was the first landfall. They have officially renamed that island San Salvador, although that honor had always belonged to Eleuthera prior to 1800. In 1986 the National Geographic Society (NGS) reopened the controversy by espousing a landfall at Semana Cay. Advocates of the Northern Route— based on the premise that Columbus used latitude sailing to maintain a due west Atlantic crossing—have long held that Columbus left his first footprints on the beaches of Egg Island at the northwest corner of Eleuthera.

You can easily trace the northern route through the Bahamas and decide for yourself if the Columbus descriptions of courses and islands ring true.

To fully relive the excitement of that momentous night of discovery, you should sail east–northeast from Harbour Island about six nights after a full moon. When you reach a location six miles east of Man Island at 2 a.m., the moon should be high enough to reflect off Eleuthera's surf, just as it did for Columbus' lookout 500 years off.

After shouting "tierra!" to mark your landfall, coast cautiously along northern Eleuthera's reef into the Northeast Providence Channel. On your way you'll note three important landfall features—unique to Eleuthera—are Harbour Island's entrance, the shallows behind it, and the equally spaced triple cusps on the north coast of Royal Island.

At first light you should keep an eye out for the same benthic (bottom-growing) seaweed Columbus *"found in the gulf when he arrived at his discovery."* There is no gulf at either Watlings or Samana Cay. When you reach the end of

Columbus Naming	Morison's Conventional	National Geographic	Northern Route
San Salvador	Watlings	Samana Cay	Eleuthera
Santa Maria	Rum Cay	Crooked-Acklins	New Providence
Fernandina	Long Island	Long Island	Andros
Isabela	Crooked-Acklins	Fortune Island	Long Island

Eleuthera's reef shortly after dawn you will see Columbus's first lee anchorage opportunity southwest of Egg Island.

Now you can begin following 30 features uniquely matching descriptions Columbus himself recorded in his Journal of Discovery.

The Landfall at San Salvador

1 Anchor near the south end of Egg, "… an islet of the Bahamas." Egg's 250 acres puts it comfortably within Columbus' definition of islet as opposed to a full-sized island, such as Watlings, which sprawls over more than 40,000 acres.

2 Columbus wrote, "in the island's center there is a very large lagoon." From Columbus' Egg Island anchorage you too can look eastward across the 20,000-acre roadstead centered between you and the main island of Eleuthera.

3 Columbus "rowed along the island in a north-northeast direction to see the other part, that other part which it has to the east." Eleuthera's roadstead is now accurately charted, so a small yacht can safely follow the Admiral's rowboats north-northeast the full length of Egg's coastline to Royal Island, the "other part … to the east."

4 Some Royal Island natives hailed his boat but Columbus wrote: "I was afraid (to come ashore) seeing the great ledge of rocks that encircled the whole of that island." You won't meet any Indians beckoning you ashore, but Royal Island's south coast is still lined with the jagged aeolian limestone ledge that kept Columbus away.

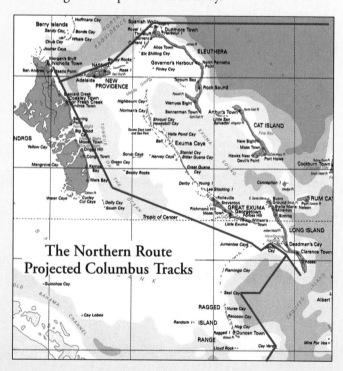

The Northern Route Projected Columbus Tracks

5 According to his log, the Admiral saw "a harbour large enough for all the ships in Christendom …" Eleuthera's lagoon (roadstead) is big enough—much larger than the Cuban lagoon Columbus later described as a harbor "large enough for all the ships in Spain."

6 "… and halfway there was a narrow entrance … the sea no more disturbed than the water in a well." Precisely centered on Royal's south coast is a narrow opening from the roadstead into one of the Bahamas' best-protected harbors. You'll find its surface like a mirror under almost all wind conditions, so unlike the exposed "harbors" at Watlings and Samana.

7 In returning to your Egg anchorage, Rat Cay at Royal's West End will also seem at first glance the ideal location he sought for a fort. To him it was "formed like an island although it is not one, on which there are six houses; it could be converted into an island in two days." Your closer inspection will also show that it's bridged to Royal by marl-covered shallows not deep enough to keep Indians at bay. Columbus quickly realized that this marl could easily be scooped out deep enough to make it into a useful island. By contrast, thousands of tons of limestone would need to be dynamited to convert the Watlings peninsula into an island. (Resist the temptation to search for brass hawks bells and other trading truck Columbus might have left at these six houses. It is against the law to conduct unauthorized archeology.)

8 "Near the said islet, moreover, there are the loveliest group of trees." Although that nearby grove of coconut palms wasn't there in 1492, its wind-sheltered and well-watered location remains one of the most favored arboreal sites in the eastern Bahamas. At corresponding Watlings and Samana locations you'll search in vain for "lovely" trees.

9 Columbus says "I stood off that night." If you trust your engine and the trade winds, there's no need for you to stand off from Egg island's morning tide that Columbus observed flowing against him nine days after the full moon.

Southwest to the Second Island, Santa Maria de la Concepcion

10 On the advice of Indian guides, "I resolved to go to the southwest … about 21 miles … to the (second island)." From your Egg anchorage take a 235-degree course about 22 miles to the 100-fathom line off the end of Rose Island.

11 Columbus noted that "the tide was against me, so it was midday when I arrived at the island." Time your Rose Island arrival for noon—a few hours before high tide—

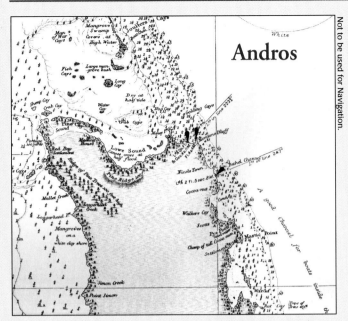

Andros

Reproduced from Admiralty Chart 1496 (now outdated). Soundings in fathoms and feet. See our note on this chart in the Chart List in Appendix A.

to observe the same battle he saw there between the tides and the secular ocean current. There's no tidal current along any other proposed route to the second island.

12 From there, "I saw another and larger one to the west. I set sail to go all day until night since otherwise I would not have been able to reach the western cape." As you sail westward toward New Providence's protected West Bay, you'll see the same Blue Hills behind Nassau revealing this as a larger island. Note the north coast's lack of anchorage and consider the impracticality of an anchorage in the swiftly flowing tides at Nassau. Compare Morison's proposed route along the south coast of Rum Cay and ask why Columbus would have passed up a relatively comfortable mid-afternoon anchorage at Port Nelson to barely reach an exposed one at dusk.

13 Of the island he saw to the southwest, Columbus wrote "the side which lies toward the islet of San Salvador runs north/south for a distance of 15 miles, and the other side, which I followed, runs east/west for more than 30 miles." As you sail 30 miles past the string of islets to New Providence's West Bay, consider how early Spanish maps often grouped all islets with the shoal's main island.

14 The next morning "a small canoe came from the other cape." From your secure anchorage near Lyford Cay you can easily imagine that Indian canoe being launched from Clifton Point, the "other cape" only a mile away. No other second-island candidate has the requisite double cape.

Across the Tongue of the Ocean to Fernandina, the Third Island

15 "This (third) island is distant about 24 miles, almost from east to west." Set your course almost due west 23 miles across the Tongue of the Ocean toward Andros Island.

16 Columbus estimated that "the coast may extend for some 84 miles or more." Verify on your charts that Andros island is roughly 90 miles in length, compared with only 60 for Long Island, advocated as the third island by both Morison and the NGS.

17 "This cape where I came, and all this coast runs north-northwest and south-southeast." If conditions are quiet, anchor along the reef in front of Mastic Point and verify Columbus' description of this truly unique geographic configuration.

18 Columbus marveled that "3,000 yards from land, the water off all these islands is so deep it cannot be sounded." From your anchorage, identify the continuous reef defined by the breakers parallel to Andros' coastline at 3,000 yards.

19 Columbus noted "fish of the finest colors in the world." As you row over to Mastic point, note the myriad of brilliant reef fish clearly visible from the boat. How could Columbus have possibly seen such fish in the pounding surf at Long Island?

20 "The coast is all beach…and the island flat and fertile." Enjoy the verdant scenery of low-lying Andros Island. The comparable location at Long Island is dominated by "dramatic" high cliffs.

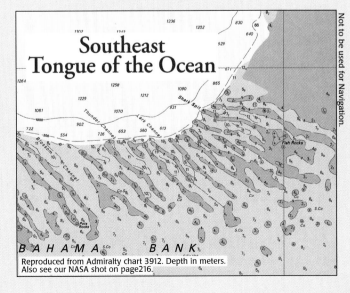

Southeast Tongue of the Ocean

BAHAMA BANK

Reproduced from Admiralty chart 3912. Depth in meters. Also see our NASA shot on page 216.

Discovery of America by Christopher Columbus. Salvador Dali.

©Salvador Dali Museum, Inc. St. Petersburg, Florida.

21 Columbus marveled at "mastic trees with many branches of different kinds." The mastic trees which gave Mastic Point its name are still garlanded by epiphytic plants and laced with tall grasses.

22 The admiral surmised that "the island could be rounded more quickly to the north-northwest." Check your charts for the shallows south of the Tongue of the Ocean that frightened Columbus' Indian guides out of a direct route to Cuba. Apply these instructions to Long Island's East Coast and realize how silly they would have been.

23 Sailing northwest "six miles from the head of the island I found a wonderful harbor for 100 ships … but it proved shallow. I thought it was the mouth of a river." If you sail northwest along the reef to within six miles of Morgan's Bluff, you'll see that the entrance to Conch Sound is large, shallow, and actually looks like the mouth of a river. None of Long Island's East Coast harbors meet any of these criteria.

24 "The (north) coast runs east and west." Continue past Morgan's Bluff to where the north coast of Andros truly runs east and west, a feature lacking at Long Island's narrow North Cape.

Reversing Course to Isabela, the Fourth Island

25 With uncharacteristic brevity Columbus wrote that he "… sailed all that night." A strong Norther arrived that afternoon and drove him at eight knots the length of the Tongue of the Ocean soon after sunrise. His arrival shortly after dawn positioned him for a daylight run across the shallows, so you may need a head start from north Andros.

26 In his briefest entry he wrote that he "anchored when it was not well to navigate, but I did not land." After a difficult crossing of the bank through Thunder Channel, neither will you have the time or inclination to explore barren No Bush Cay.

27 To the east he "saw an island … and another between it and the main island." Sailing ESE from No Bush Cay the next morning, you should spot Dollars and Conch Cays off the northwest corner of Long Island within a few hours. No such dual islets exist at Morison's Crooked-Acklins candidate.

28 Coasting offshore he notes "in the middle of the island a large cove curves to the northeast." Squarely in the middle of Long Island you'll see a large cove curving to the northeast.

29 Columbus spotted "one elevation … which serves to beautify the rest of the island." Behind the large cove you too may enjoy the beauty of a gracefully sloping miniature version of Mount Fuji.

30 Continuing to the southeast he sailed "36 miles to a beautiful cape." Time your 36-mile sail along Long Island's west coast to arrive at its southern cape by late afternoon. You'll see for yourself why Columbus gave its glistening limestone cliffs the name Cabo Hermoso as they reflected the bright sunlight.

You've done it! Using the words of Christopher Columbus as your only guide, you've now retraced the very first exploration of the New World.

Arne Molander is a retired engineer who has spent the past 30 years researching the voyages of Christopher Columbus. He has cruised the Bahamas in search of those island features that best match the detailed descriptions recorded by Columbus 500 years ago. This article, one of dozens published by him, presents his conclusion that there's strong evidence that the Columbus landfall was off Northern Eleuthera, and that the Columbus tracks accepted in the past are incorrect.

The Climate of the Bahamas

CLIMATICALLY the Bahamas can be divided into three zones: the north, the central Bahamas, and the south. The climate line between north and central dips southward to include both North Andros and New Providence Island (Nassau), with the Biminis, the Berrys, Grand Bahama Island, and the Abacos in the northern zone. The dividing line between Central and South runs almost due east–west just below the South Point of Long Island, placing the Crooked–Acklins archilpelago, and everything on the same latitude and to the south in the southern zone.

THE NORTHERN ZONE

In the north you can expect colder winters, wind, and marginally more rain. You are too close to the North American continent not to be effected by American weather. If an Alberta Clipper comes south, you'll feel it, and the temperature can fall to as low as 50° F (10° C). The good news is that these blasts of cold continental air never last for long. In the summer the north enjoys much the same climate as the rest of the Bahamas. Overall, year long, the north has the highest rainfall in the Bahamas, an average of 115 days per year. The summer months are the primary rainfall producers.

THE CENTRAL ZONE

In the center you win a better average temperature in winter, and if a Norther comes, you'll feel it less than you will in the north. Generally your temperature in winter will not fall below 70° F (21° C). The summers are Bahamian standard: hot, tempered by the Trade Winds, and wet at times, for those are the rainfall months. In this zone your average works out at 95 days of rain each year.

The Bahamian Climate Average Figures

WINTER (NOVEMBER TO MID-APRIL)

Month	Nov	Dec	Jan	Feb	Mar	Apr
Temperature (°F)	74.90	71.40	69.90	70.00	72.00	74.20
Humidity (%)	0.78	0.78	0.78	0.78	0.76	0.74
Sun (Hours)	7.40	6.90	7.10	7.60	8.30	9.20
Rainfall (Inches)	2.23	2.04	1.86	1.59	1.57	2.12
Wind Speed (Knots)	8.10	7.80	8.00	8.60	8.90	8.30

SUMMER (MID-APRIL TO OCTOBER)

Month	May	Jun	Jul	Aug	Sept	Oct
Temperature (°F)	77.50	80.40	82.30	82.20	81.10	78.70
Humidity (%)	0.77	0.79	0.77	0.79	0.81	0.80
Sun (Hours)	8.70	7.70	8.80	8.60	7.10	7.20
Rainfall (Inches)	4.58	9.17	6.21	8.50	6.75	6.91
Wind Speed (Knots)	7.90	7.20	7.10	6.90	6.20	7.40

Source: Bahamas Government Statistics 1961-1990

THE SOUTHERN ZONE

In the south you will rarely be affected by continental weather, save possibly by the whip end of higher winds if the weather is bad up north. Your winter temperatures are higher, 75° F (24° C) to around 80° F (28° C), and in summer you can add 10° F to that. The south has less rainfall annually than the two more northern zones, and the average works out at around 90 rain days a year. Most of this rain falls in the spring and the autumn.

To boil it all down in simple terms, reckon that the north is sub-tropical with a Florida Palm Beach County climate. The central zone, still sub-tropical, is like the Florida Keys. And the south is low island (as opposed to high or volcanic island) Caribbean tropical. For greater detail on Bahamian weather see **Chapter 2, The Lessons of 500 Years of Voyaging in Bahamian Waters** on page 11.

Parks and Wildlife Preserves
The Bahamas
The Northern Cruising Grounds

ABACO NATIONAL PARK
On Great Abaco Island between Cherokee Sound and Hole in the Wall. The preserve of the Bahama Parrot.

BLACK SOUND CAY NATIONAL RESERVE
A thick stand of mangroves in Black Sound, Green Turtle Cay, in the Abacos.

FOWL CAYS LAND AND SEA PRESERVE
An area of cays (the Fowl Cays and Fish Hawk Cay) just north of Man-O-War Cay in the Abacos.

PELICAN CAYS LAND AND SEA PARK
The area south of Tilloo Cay and north of Little Harbour, in the southern end of the Sea of Abaco.

TILLOO CAY NATIONAL PROTECTED AREA
A nesting site for tropical birds, north of Pelican Cay and south of Marsh Harbour in the Abacos.

LUCAYAN NATIONAL PARK
A 42-acre reserve with nature trails and boardwalks in Grand Bahama. The park area contains one of the world's largest charted cave systems.

PETERSON CAY NATIONAL PARK
A small cay with a coral reef off the south coast of Grand Bahama, just east of Port Lucaya.

RAND NATURE CENTER
One hundred acres of pine forest and wildlife gardens, two miles from Freeport, with flamingos and guided nature walks. The headquarters of the Bahamas National Trust.

The Central Cruising Grounds

THE RETREAT

An 11-acre site in Nassau devoted essentially to palm trees.

The Southern Cruising Grounds and Out Islands

EXUMA CAYS LAND AND SEA PARK

A well-known and much-visited 160-square-mile nature reserve, primarily devoted to the sea, in the mid-Exumas.

CONCEPTION ISLAND LAND AND SEA PARK

The largest "whole island" reserve in the Bahamas. Conception is almost 3 miles long by 2 miles in width, rises to 60 feet in the center, and is surrounded by shoals and reefs that extend as far as 5 miles offshore. It is uninhabited, notable for its birds and nesting turtles, and a visit allegedly paid by Christopher Columbus in 1492.

INAGUA NATIONAL PARK

The largest colony of West Indian flamingos in the world.

UNION CREEK NATIONAL RESERVE

A seven-square-mile area of tidal creek in Great Inagua.

WILDLIFE PARK REGULATIONS

As you would expect, conservation rules in the park areas are strict. Essentially you are not allowed to fish, hunt, remove any living or dead animal, fish, vegetation, plant life, and coral, or in any way damage, alter, or leave a footprint on the environment. Most of the marine parks have moorings that you are required to take up. If you do anchor, you are required to anchor in sand well clear of any reef. You are not allowed to discharge any waste, nor to dump your garbage.

If you break the rules, not only are you in line for a $500 fine, but your boat may well be confiscated.

The Turks and Caicos

National Parks

COLUMBUS LANDFALL MARINE NATIONAL PARK, GRAND TURK

Wall diving, swimming, snorkeling, picnicing, shorebirds, and raptors.

GRAND TURK CAYS LAND AND SEA NATIONAL PARK

Gibbs, Penniston, and Martin Alonza Pinzon (East) Cays. Nesting gulls, terns, Turk's Head Cactus, picnicing, swimming, and snorkeling.

SOUTH CREEK NATIONAL PARK, GRAND TURK

Wetlands and mangroves; breeding, migrating shorebirds and waders; walks and viewpoints.

ADMIRAL COCKBURN LAND AND SEA NATIONAL PARK, SOUTH CAICOS

Excellent diving and large marine life.

CONCH BAR CAVES NATIONAL PARK, MIDDLE CAICOS

An extensive cave system with lagoons, bat colonies, and Arawak sites.

EAST BAY ISLANDS NATIONAL PARK, NORTH CAICOS

Scenic views, picnic area, coastal flora, shorebirds, and waders.

FORT GEORGE LAND AND SEA NATIONAL PARK, PINE CAY

Cannons from the 1790s in 3 feet of water, wall diving, iguanas, and ospreys.

CHALK SOUND NATIONAL PARK, PROVIDENCIALES

Bonefishing, small boat sailing, and photography opportunities.

NORTH WEST POINT MARINE NATIONAL PARK, PROVIDENCIALES

Spectacular wall diving, deserted beaches.

PRINCESS ALEXANDRA LAND AND SEA NATIONAL PARK, PROVIDENCIALES

Reef and wreck diving, all water sports, and a spectacular 13-mile beach.

WEST CAICOS MARINE NATIONAL PARK

Wall diving from shore, good snorkeling.

Sanctuaries

BIG SAND CAY SANCTUARY, GRAND TURK

Nesting seabirds, shorebirds, and turtles.

LONG CAY SANCTUARY, GRAND TURK

Gulls, terns, iguanas, and tropical flora.

THREE MARYS CAYS SANCTUARY, NORTH CAICOS

Flamingos, osprey nesting sites.

FRENCH, BUSH AND SEAL CAYS SANCTUARY, CAICOS BANK

Conch, lobster, and nurse shark nursery; frigate birds, osprey, and nesting seabirds.

Nature Reserves

BELLE SOUND AND ADMIRAL COCKBURN CAYS, SOUTH CAICOS

Bonefish, mangroves, and tidal flats; shore birds and waders; rare rock iguanas.

VINE POINT (MAN-O-WAR BUSH) AND OCEAN HOLE, MIDDLE CAICOS

Frigate bird breeding colony. Seventy-meters-deep by 400-meters-wide marine sinkhole with turtles, bonefish, and sharks.

COTTAGE POND, NORTH CAICOS

Fresh and salt water, 50-meters-deep sinkhole. Botanical walk, grebes, and West Indian whistling duck.

PUMPKIN BLUFF POND, NORTH CAICOS
Flamingos, Bahamian pintail, waders.

DICK HILL CREEK AND BELLEFIELD LANDING POND, NORTH CAICOS
West Indian whistling duck, flamingos.

NORTHWEST POINT POND, PROVIDENCIALES
Breeding and migrant wildfowl.

PIGEON POND AND FRENCHMAN'S CREEK, PROVIDENCIALES
Tidal flats, mangrove creeks, shorebirds, and waders.

PRINCESS ALEXANDRA, LITTLE WATER CAY, MANGROVE CAY, DONNA CAY, NORTH OF PROVIDENCIALES
Iguanas, ospreys, tropical flora.

LAKE CATHERINE, WEST CAICOS
Scenic views, flamingos, ospreys, ducks, and waders.

Historic Sites

SALT CAY
Solar salt industry of 1700s to 1900s, salinas, windmills, waterfront buildings (including the White House), and an old whaling station.

MOLASSES REEF WRECK
The earliest known shipwreck in the Western Hemisphere (pre-1509). Excellent museum of artifacts in Grand Turk.

HMS ENDYMION, SOUTH OF BIG SAND CAY
1700s British man-o-war ship in 40 feet of water.

BOILING HOLE, SOUTH CAICOS
Tidal powered solar salt works.

RAMSAR SITE
Wetlands on south side of Middle, North, and East Caicos. This reserve of international importance is protected under the international Ramsar Convention. Water birds, intertidal and shallow water flora, lobster, conch, and fish nursery.

FORT GEORGE
Late 1790s British fort, north of Pine Cay.

CHESHIRE HALL, PROVIDENCIALES
Ruins of 1790s Loyalist plantation.

SAPODILLA AND WEST HARBOUR BLUFF ROCK CARVINGS, PROVIDENCIALES
Rock carvings by shipwrecked sailors.

Anchoring and Mooring in Marine Parks
Anchoring is allowed only on a clear sandy bottom. Check anchors to avoid dragging over the coral, as damage from anchors will result in a fine. Boats more than 60-feet LOA are not allowed to anchor in any of the marine national parks, other than in the designated anchorage zones. No boats can anchor within 400 feet of the low-water line surrounding any national park cay or sanctuary. No boat may anchor within 300 feet of scuba dive-site moorings, which are marked by white balls or cylinders with blue bands. Boats carrying divers or snorkelers must use a 20-foot mooring extension line to attach to dive site moorings. Commercial dive boat operators have the right to use the moorings before private boat owners. Peak time for dive boats is between 8 a.m. and 2 p.m.

DIVING AND SWIMMING
Do not allow your fins, knees, or tank to touch the coral. Touching live coral damages its fragile polyps and delicate mucous tissue. Remain 1 meter (3 feet) above the reef at all times. You can be fined by a park warden if you damage anything within the marine park.

Be extra cautious not to impact corals when using a camera or video. Unfortuanately, divers and photographers are most likely to impact the coral. Wear proper weights and maintain neutral buoyancy at all times. Ask a dive master if you need assistance.

The national parks are for people. Scuba diving, snorkeling, sightseeing, and photography are encouraged. Take only pictures and leave only bubbles! It is good practice to touch nothing and treat all underwater life with respect. It is punishable by law to harass any living creature in the park, including whales, turtles, mantas, or Jo Jo, the dolphin.

PARK REGULATIONS
It is prohibited to:
- Remove any land or sea animal or plant from the parks, including seabird eggs.
- Damage or destroy (hunt or fish) any animal or plant in the parks.
- Remove animal or plant products including timber, corals, sponges, rocks, and sand from the parks.
- Remove any man-made artifact from the parks.
- Litter or dump on land or sea in any park.
- Enter a sanctuary without a permit from the Director of Parks, Heritage and Environment.
- Use spear guns, fish traps, pole spears, seine nets in marine parks.
- Use jet skis, wave runners, or hovercraft in marine parks.
- Moor vessels over 60 feet unless attached to a fixed buoy in the marine parks.
- Water ski except in designated areas in marine parks.
- Drive boats within 100 yards of the shoreline.

Our thanks to Judith Garland, Project Manager of the Coastal Resource Management Project in Providenciales, and to Mr. Tomlinson Skippings from the Ministry of Natural Resources in Grand Turk, for their valuable help and encouragement in allowing us to use their maps and information in this Guide.

Coral Reefs of the Bahamas
by Thomas A. McGrath

CORAL reefs are the heart of the Bahamas. Most Bahamian islands are fringed by them, and you have to find safe, deep-water passages through them to get in to port. Even in what seems to be open water on the Great Bahama Bank, you can find yourself surrounded by patch reefs reaching up from the shallow bottom to grab your hull. Coral reefs can be a nuisance. They can also be pure pleasure once you don your snorkeling gear and jump overboard to see what's out there. Whether you see them as nuisance or pleasure, coral reefs are the reason the Bahamas exist and the reason so many pleasure craft are drawn to these islands.

In the 1980s worldwide concern grew over what appeared to be the decline in the health of coral reefs, with increasing incidences of a phenomenon known as coral "bleaching." Corals bleach when they experience various stresses—they expel their algae, or the algae themselves lose pigment, and the result is that the white limestone skeletons show through. Exposure to too much heat, too much cold, too much salt, too little salt, too much sunlight (UV), and too much sediment in the water can cause corals to bleach. If conditions don't return to normal quickly enough the corals can die, destroying the structure of the reef—in some cases, thousand of years in the building. When this happens, bigger waves hit the shoreline, eroding it; the fish disappear, resulting in serious declines in the fishing industry; and of course, tourists cross those spots off their lists. Thus bleaching can have profound economic impacts. Before the 1980s, coral bleaching was localized and the causes were easy to find, but recent events have been widespread and have no clear causes. A few scientists have suggested that the increase in bleaching events is a result of higher than usual ocean temperatures. Maybe coral bleaching, then, is like the canary in the coal mine for global climate change. This idea has not been substantiated but it certainly has sparked many people's interest.

Since 1997 new concerns over the health of coral reefs have been raised. A raft of newly described coral diseases and some increasing incidences of others, known for a long time, have been reported. Only a few of these diseases have been

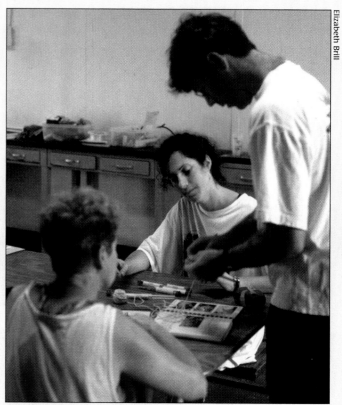
Earthwatch volunteers in the lab in San Salvador.

traced to a causative agent and, even then, little is known of the ways that they infect or progress. It is not certain that all phenomena being described are diseases in the strict sense, being caused by an infective organism, nor is it even clear whether these phenomena are truly new or just new to us. It is certain that some of these diseases are of real concern, though, as one such disease, for instance, has completely killed off sea fans in parts of the southern Caribbean.

In 1991 we started a long-term study of the patch reefs around San Salvador Island with the help of Earthwatch, an organization that supports biological, geological, archeological, paleontological, anthropological, and sociological research projects throughout the world. They link volunteers from all walks of life to these projects. Under the supervision of professional researchers, these volunteers collect data, while at the same time learning more about the field and, specifically, of course, about the particular project on which they are volunteering their energies. A portion of the fees they pay is used to provide grants that fund Earthwatch research projects.

The reefs we are studying are the inshore patch reefs, which are most often used by islanders and tourists alike. San Salvadorans fish and swim on these reefs. Tourists have been snorkeling and diving these reefs for decades. Thus, as with many other tropical islands, the reefs that surround San Salvador have long provided a source of food and tourist revenue, as well as helped to protect the small land mass

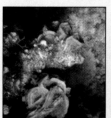  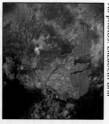

Left to right: normal and a bleached leaf coral, Lindsay's Reef, San Salvador; sea fan disease, Rocky Point Reef, San Salvador.

Elizabeth Brill

All photos: Elizabeth Brill

of the island itself from the potential ravages of the ocean. We need to understand what is going on in these reef systems both under normal circumstances and during periods of bleaching or disease.

Over the years of our study we have discovered that small corals (less than ½ inch) come and go on the reef at a steady rate. While as many as 10 percent of the small corals on a reef die off in a year, there is usually a 10 percent increase in new colonies as well. This means that coral numbers and types have remained relatively constant over time. It is also impor-

tant to note that these comings and goings affect less than five percent of the total coral cover on any of the reefs. We have also found that there is a normal "background" level of bleaching on our reefs. Again this background bleaching rarely affects more than five percent of the hard coral on a reef and has not been shown to affect the overall health of the reef in any way. This information is beginning to give us an idea of what is normal for these patch reefs.

During the early part of our study we found little coral disease and no significant coral bleaching. Most scientists

Corals and Coral Reefs

ALL Bahamian islands are nothing more than calcium carbonate (limestone) sand turned to stone. The Bahama Banks are huge, limestone sand flats that lay under a shallow sea. Where did all this limestone come from? Almost all of it has come from coral reefs. The animals and plants that live in these underwater cities have pulled calcium out of the ocean water and carbon dioxide out of the air to make skeletons for protection. These skeletons become the sand and the sand becomes the rock that forms the islands.

At the center of these reefs are the corals. Corals are animals that contain algae—dinoflagellates called zooxanthellae—inside the cells that line their gut. The algae give the coral its color and some of the food that they make from water and carbon dioxide through photosynthesis. The corals, in turn, give the algae a place to live and some nitrogen and phosphorus from some of the things that they pull out of the ocean to eat. Working together, the corals and their symbiotic algae lay down a limestone shell and grow.

There are some other requirements for this to happen, however. Some of them are the environmental conditions that surround them. Corals like the waters of the tropics for some of the same reasons you do. They like it warm, between 70 and 88 degrees Fahrenheit. They also like the water to be extremely clear so that sunlight can reach the algae. Tropical waters are so poor in nutrients—often likened to deserts—that they remain unclouded by sediment and floating life, plankton.

Corals grow slowly. Big boulder corals grow only slightly each year, and even the "weedy" types like staghorn and elkhorn corals grow less than 5 inches a year. Needless to say, the sand and rock that have created the Bahamas have been produced over a very long period of time. So when you are looking at coral reefs, you are looking at a very old system: coral reefs grew and produced sand, which became rock, which created islands—a very lengthy "manufacturing" process!

Many Bahamian islands are surrounded by fringing reefs that protect the shore line from the open ocean.

You usually can see the crest of these reefs as a line of waves breaking around the edges of the islands.

Between these crests of fringing reef and shore are patch reefs, smaller stands of coral reef that rise from the sand flat. Beyond the fringing reef can be a precipitous drop off called "The Wall." The Bahamas have some of the best wall formations in the western Atlantic and attract divers who love the experience of thousands of feet of nothing under them as they slide down the edge of these coral dropoffs.

Associated with coral reefs are seagrass beds on the ocean floor and mangrove swamps on the shore. Both are important parts of the whole system. Seagrass beds trap and release food for corals and many of the reef creatures. Seagrasses are real flowering plants just like the grasses that make up your lawn. Many reef fish feed on the grass beds but hide in the reefs. The mangrove swamps trap sediment, protecting the reef and serving as a nursery for the developing young of a whole range of reef creatures.

Elizabeth Brill

Elkhorn coral forest, Gaulin Cay, San Salvador.

Earthwatch volunteer collecting data on San Salvador's reefs.

around the world believe that the reefs were protected from bleaching by cooler-than-normal temperatures. They theorize that the clouds of dust from the volcano Mt. Pinatubo, which erupted in June 1991, shielded the earth from the sun for several years, and caused a drop in the temperature of the planet's surface. In October/November 1995 a mass bleaching event began throughout the Western Atlantic. NOAA reported higher-than-normal sea temperatures for some areas at that time; however the temperatures taken locally near San Salvador were not elevated. Nonetheless, on our November 1995 Earthwatch expedition, volunteers found bleaching on our reef study sites to be well above the "normal" levels we had been tracking.

After a year and a half of study we found that not all of our reefs behaved in the same way during this event. Lindsay's Reef (south of the monument in Fernandez Bay), was more affected than our other two study reefs, Rice Bay (inshore of Manhead Cay at the northeast end of the island), and French Bay Reef (west of the Government Dock at the south end of the island). None of our measurements of temperature, salinity, pH, water clarity, or other environmental conditions accounted for any of the differences we recorded in the severity of bleaching. We also found that not all coral species responded the same way, either, with lettuce leaf coral much more susceptible to this event than any other species.

Despite widespread, high levels of bleaching recorded in 1995, in 1996 our volunteer teams found that the reefs had returned to normal. No significant damage or death occurred on the coral patch reefs of San Salvador as a result of this event.

Another bleaching event began in the fall of 1998 and this one was worse than anything seen there before. Extremely high sea temperatures lasting for several months was the driving force behind this event. We have already documented the loss of major stands of staghorn and elkhorn corals and we are anxious to see how the rest fare as the event plays out.

Our volunteers have documented an increase in the amount of large algae on our study reefs over the years. Other areas of the world are reporting this too. It may be that algae are starting to take over the reefs. If this is true, it could mean that the reefs will stop growing, thus compromising the integrity the whole system.

We have also been looking for evidence of the coral diseases that are being described around the region, only two of which have been found in any abundance by our volunteers. Sea fan disease is found quite often around San Salvador, but the good news is that we know what is causing it: a soil fungus, related to the green mold in your refrigerator, appears to be the culprit. Around San Salvador, at least, sea fans seem to be able to mount a defense against this infection and to halt the spread of the disease. White band disease on staghorn and elkhorn corals is also periodically a problem. Even so, during the time of our study this disease has not wiped out significant stands of these corals.

All of these conditions—bleaching, algae growth, and diseases—may be compromising the health of reefs, or they may be acting as a creative force. Some scientists have suggested that such challenges may be forcing the corals to adapt to new environmental conditions. Others fear that the may lead ultimately to the reefs' death—and to the resulting impact on cultures and economies as well as the surrounding ecology. These concerns were highlighted when 1997 was declared the International Year of the Reef and 1998 was declared the International Year of the Ocean.

There are good arguments on both sides of that question. But there is very little long-term information. And so we continue to collect and analyze data, and ask still more questions. The long-term survival of these essential and beautiful tropical resources requires that we find some answers.

Corals at Lindsay's Reef, San Salvador.

Thomas A. McGrath is a professor of biology at Corning Community College in Corning, New York, and a certified diver. He holds an M.S. in biology from Duquesne University, and has done further graduate work in marine biology at Cornell University, and in ethology at the University of Maryland. Information about Earthwatch Institute can be found at www.earthwatch.org.

Fishing

Fishing in the Bahamas

Heading the list of the great gamefish are marlin. **Blue marlin** top the list with an average body weight of 250–300 lbs. The chance of catching a fish weighing 800 lbs. or more is always within the realm of possibility. **White marlin** follow with an average weight around 100 lbs, and make up for their lesser weight as a prize catch by a fighting stamina that outclasses the blue. **Sailfish** rank with the marlin, matching the blue marlin in dramatic performance when hooked.

Tuna, and particularly migrating **bluefin tuna**, are the next on the list. The bluefin, who pass through the Bahamas on their way north each year, can weigh anything up to nearly 1,000 lbs. and once hooked, you're in for a serious battle that can last hours. The other varieties of the tuna family, **blackfin, yellowfin,** and **bonito,** are Bahamian residents rather than visitors in transit, and not as spectacular nor indeed in the heavyweight class of the bluefin.

Dolphin (not the Flipper variety but the fish the Spanish called *dorado*, whose name we adopted but got wrong) are next on the gamefish list. Around 10–15 lbs. in weight, tough fighters, with iridescent skin colors like a rainbow, the dolphin is prized both for its fighting qualities and its quality as an eating fish, reckoned by many to be better than swordfish or tuna.

The mackerel family is next with **wahoo**, the fastest fish in the ocean, and **King mackerel**, which can come close to 5 feet in length and are never taken without a fight. The fighting list also includes the marauders, **barracuda** and **sharks**. We see little point in shark fishing and we've found barracuda, only too ready to strike at any lure, more of a curse on a line than a

blessing. **Tarpon**, who will often take a trolled line and fight fiercely, complete our gamefish list but, like the marauders, have no place on a food list.

Turning away from trolling to fishing the depths, **groupers** top the list of the prize fish for weight and for food value. After them come **snappers** and **amberjack**; the last respond to live bait and will take your line, when hooked, deep into a wreck or the holes of a reef if they have the chance.

The fish of the Bahamian shallows or flats, **bonefish** and the less widely known **permit**, are considered by many anglers to be the best prizes of all. You won't stock your larder with them, but once you get hooked by the lure of bonefishing, you'll spend hour after hour fishing the flats.

Fishing Regulations

- Boats with a valid cruising/fishing permit are allowed 20 pounds of scale fish, ten conch and six crawfish (in season) per person, at any time.

- A combined total of six fish per person per vessel of kingfish, dolphin, and wahoo may be taken. All other migratory fish shall be returned to the sea alive unless it is to be used immediately. No grouper or rockfish weighing less than three pounds may be taken.

- No spear fishing within one mile of the coast of New Providence, one mile of the southern coast of Grand Bahama, or 200 yards of any island in the Bahamas. It is illegal to use any type of underwater air supply for spear fishing or collecting of any marine life. This includes scuba gear and air compressors.

- Spear fishing is restricted to free dives only and only with the use of a Hawaiian sling. It is illegal to take coral, tropical fish, or sea fans.

- The capture or molesting of dolphins, whales, and manatees is probited.

- It is illegal for non-Bahamians to use any type of fishing net, *except* a cast net.

- It is illegal for non-Bahamians to use fish traps or to sell marine products of any type.

- The use of bleach or similar stunning or poisoning chemicals is forbidden.

- Nothing may be taken from any Bahamas National Park at any time.

The Northern Cruising Grounds

The Abacos

OFFSHORE FISHING

The 100-fathom line from Walkers Cay down to Elbow Cay (Hope Town) and on to Southwest Point offers excellent

---

Seasons and Sizes

- **Spiney Lobster** (Crayfish). Closed season is April 1–July 31. Carapace length is limited to 3⅜ inches with a tail length of at least 6 inches. No berried females (egg carrying) are allowed. The limit is six per person.

- **Conch.** Harvested conch must have a well-formed, flaring lip (*i.e.*, be adult). The limit is ten per person.

- **Stone Crab.** Closed season is June 1–October 15. The minimum harvestable claw length is 4 inches.

- **Turtles.** Are expressly forbidden.

- **Fish Sizes**

Blue Marlin	86 inches
White Marlin	62 inches
Sailfish	57 inches
Grouper	Over 3 lbs. in weight
Rockfish	Over 3 lbs. in weight

fishing for blue marlin, white marlin, sailfish, bluefin tuna, blackfin tuna, dolphin, and wahoo. The sea area off Hope Town is particularly promising, for the "elbow" in the Abaco Cays produces an underwater shelf that extends some 10 miles out into the ocean with dropoffs on all sides.

BOTTOM FISHING

The entire area, rich with reefs, offers ideal fishing grounds for grouper, snapper, lobster, and all kinds of reef dwellers.

SHALLOW WATER FISHING

The Abacos has extensive flats. Grand Cays and Great Breasted Cays offer good fishing. South of Marsh Harbour the inlets into the Great Abaco coast are good, and the entire area of the Marls, the swamp-like water maze to the west of Great Abaco Island, is a bonefish paradise.

Little Bahama Bank and Grand Bahama Island

OFFSHORE FISHING

As with the Abacos, the primary offshore fishing ground parallels the 100-fathom line, in this case the line running from West End northward to Matanilla Shoal. The edge of the Gulf Stream between West End and Memory Rock is the best fishing, with migrating bluefin tuna.

A secondary offshore fishing ground lies south of Freeport, along the run of the dropoff extending east–west from a point offshore of Bell Channel to the intersection of this line with the edge of the Gulf Stream. This fishing ground covers the intersection of the Northwest Providence Channel with the Gulf Stream, the confluence of these ocean highways producing the right conditions for a concentration of gamefish.

The Best Fishing Months

Blue Marlin	June–July
White Marlin	Winter–Spring
Sailfish	Summer–Fall
Allison Tuna	June–August
Bluefin Tuna	May–June
Blackfin Tuna	May–September
Yellowfin Tuna	June–August
Bonito	May–September
Dolphin	Winter–Spring
Wahoo	November–April
King Mackerel	Mostly winter months
Barracuda	Year round
Tarpon	Year round
Grouper	Year round
Amberjack	November–May
Bonefish	Year round

BOTTOM FISHING

The west edge of the Little Bahama Bank, for the most part north of Memory Rock, is a largely uncharted maze of innumerable runs and twists of reef with mini dropoffs, short cuts, holes, and shoals. For the most part it forms an ideal environment for grouper, snapper, and lobster, and is well worth attention.

SHALLOW WATER FISHING

The entire run of the north coast of Grand Bahama forms an ideal shallow-water fishing ground, and the east coast of Grand Bahama Island is reckoned to be particularly good for bonefish and permit.

The Central Cruising Grounds

The Bimini Islands

OFFSHORE FISHING

The main offshore fishing ground parallels the 100-fathom line from Great Isaac in the north to South Riding Rock in the south. The big game territory also continues, hooking around to the east and southeast from Great Isaac, running along the 10-fathom line bordering the southern edge of the Northwest Providence Channel.

BOTTOM FISHING

The best area for grouper and the medium-depth fish are the whole run of rock, reefs, and islands running from Great Isaac to the Gingerbread Ground along the southern edge of the Northwest Providence Channel. Immediately north of North Bimini the 3-fathom line running east from North Rock marks the edge of a good fishing area with a number of wrecks, such as the *Seminole*, which lies some 10 nm east of North Rock.

The wreck of the *Sapona* marks the best fishing grounds immediately south of the two Bimini Islands, but over the years both diving and fishing have overworked the area. Better alternatives lie further away down the line of reefs and rocks to the south of the Cat Cays.

SHALLOW WATER FISHING

The Great Bahama Bank side of the Bimini Islands is good for shallow-water fishing. A line drawn connecting the easternmost points of North Bimini and South Bimini defines the general run of the best grounds for bonefishing.

The Berry Islands

OFFSHORE FISHING

Predictably the offshore fishing grounds off the Berry Islands lie to the east of the island chain. The Berrys don't rate highly as a fishing destination with one exception, and that's southwest of Chub Cay in the southern Berrys. There the Tongue of the Ocean hooks toward the Northwest Providence Channel, forming a deep-water dead-end that has the fish milling around with nowhere else to go. It's made even better when a southeast wind pushes water and fish that way.

BOTTOM FISHING

Bottom fishing in the Berrys is better in the north and central islands, with the best area from the Market Fish Cays down to Little Harbour Cay.

SHALLOW WATER FISHING

For shallow-water fishermen the whole "inside" arc of the Berry Islands offers almost unlimited fishing grounds, with the best areas in the south around the Cormorant and Fish Cays. These really are shallow waters. You're almost bound to get grounded sooner or later, and your problems may be compounded by isolated coral heads and rocks. If you're careful (or take a guide), you should be OK.

New Providence Island

OFFSHORE FISHING

The Tongue of the Ocean offers more miles of big-game water than you can cover adequately in a week. If you want a focal point, the ocean buoy 15 nm southwest off Clifton Point in New Providence Island is the Times Square for baitfish in the area. The gamefish, wise to this, use the buoy as a fast-food stop. You can find them hanging out there much of the time.

BOTTOM FISHING

The best area for bottom fishing is the line of islands, reefs, and rocks running east from Paradise Island to Pimlico Island. You could also try around the isolated coral heads and small reefs on the White Bank and the Yellow Bank.

SHALLOW WATER FISHING

New Providence is not as good for shallow-water fishing, although the southeast tip of the island may be worth trying.

Eleuthera

OFFSHORE FISHING

On the Atlantic side, the Eleuthera 100-fathom line should be a natural fishing ground, but it hasn't been greatly exploited, probably because it's a potentially hazardous shoreline. There the reef shielding the east coast of Eleuthera is near-continuous, and the prevailing weather, both wave and current, sets onshore. It's no place to be in bad weather.

To the north of Eleuthera, outside the reefs of the Devil's Backbone Passage area, there's a reasonable fishing ground, but once again the area is not easily accessible and it's weather dependent, a real no-no in wind or seas coming in from the northern quadrants. As for the south of Eleuthera, reports have it that the gap between Eleuthera Point and Little San Salvador is good. There's a shelf there with deep water on both the Atlantic and Exuma Sound.

BOTTOM FISHING

We've not found any particular area we'd recommend above all others for bottom fishing. Just as the geography of Eleuthera doesn't really fit the offshore fishing criteria, so there are few places that are a real setup for grouper and snapper. The fish are there, but you have to find your spot.

SHALLOW WATER FISHING

For bonefish and the like the best areas lie along the west coast of Eleuthera, particularly from Tarpum Bay down to Rock Point, and across the bight toward Powell Point.

Andros

OFFSHORE FISHING

Naturally the Tongue of the Ocean is the number-one offshore fishing ground for Andros, easily accessible from either Chub Cay or Fresh Creek. You can run down to South Andros along the 100-fathom line, or try the 1,000-fathom contour off North Andros. One way or another you shouldn't miss.

BOTTOM FISHING

Bottom fishing is good either side of the Andros Barrier Reef, although the navigation inside the reef can be difficult. Bottom fishing is also good in the maze of shallows, reefs, and rocks running through the Joulter Cays to the north of Morgans Bluff.

SHALLOW WATER FISHING

Despite the premium usually placed on big game fishing, Andros should win its accolades for the best shallow-water fishing in the Bahamas. The bonefish grounds start with the Joulter Cays in the north, include just about every inlet and bight on the east coast of Andros, and the entire west coast. For the greater part these fishing grounds are rarely visited, largely uncharted, and you are on your own. If you don't want to go it alone, find a local guide in the nearest settlement and take him with you.

The Southern Cruising Grounds

The Exuma Cays

OFFSHORE FISHING

The Exumas, spectacular cruising ground as they are, are not the top of the list when it comes to big game fishing. The place to try is along the lines of the 100- and 500-fathom contours running along the depths of Exuma Sound.

BOTTOM FISHING

For bottom fishing the reefs off great Exuma and south of Little Exuma are reputed to be good for grouper, and the reefs between Great Exuma and Long Island may be worth trying. If you want to venture further afield, try the reefs lying to the south and southeast of the Exuma chain. At the time we write, there is a ban on grouper fishing in the Highbourne Cays.

SHALLOW WATER FISHING
The best bonefish areas in the Exumas are Normans Cay Pond, in the shallow areas around Sampson and Staniel Cays, Compass Cay, Pipe Creek, and Harvey Cay in the central Exumas, and in the shallows off Great Exuma.

THE EXUMAS LAND AND SEA PARK
Don't forget that the entire sea area lying between the south of Normans Cay to the north of Conch Cut is designated as the Exumas Land and Sea Park and is closed to all fishing.

The Out Islands North of 23° 30' N
The Out Islands are remote cruising grounds and remote territory for the sports fisherman. The areas we mention are fishing spots that have come to our attention. There must be a thousand other places, rarely visited dropoffs, reefs, and shallows, in such a vast area, all of them worth attention. If you find somewhere that the fishing is great, and you don't care to keep it secret, will you let us know?

OFFSHORE FISHING
Cat Island. Off Garnsey Bank to the northeast of the island, and the deep-water contour off the south coast, the dropoff south of Northeast Point, and the southeast point, Columbus Point, around the 1,000-fathom line. Tartar Bank, to the west of this area may also prove productive.
Long Island. Try the deep water along the 500-fathom contour off the north tip of the island.
Rum Cay. The ocean dropoff to the east of the island.
San Salvador. The deep-water contour to the north and west of the island.

BOTTOM FISHING
Cat Island. Try the south of the island, off Columbus Point and Tartar Bank.
Long Island. The inshore reefs, and the reefs between Long Island and Little Exuma.
Rum Cay. The reefs to the north of the island.
San Salvador. The close-in reefs, particularly to the north of the island.

SHALLOW WATER FISHING
Cat Island. The Moss Town bight.
San Salvador. The southeast coast of the island.

Far Horizons

The Out Islands South of 23° 30' N
For most people this is really over the horizon and out of reach. You could say why go that way when there are many other productive fishing grounds all the way along your route south? The answer must be "because it's there" and maybe

"because no one else goes there." Well, that's not entirely true, for generations of Bahamians have come to know and fish these waters, and the Cubans and the Haitians have come that way too. There's no virgin territory, and in each island the senior generation will tell you that the stock of fish, lobster, and conch has been significantly depleted in their lifetime. Even there, far from any center of population.

OFFSHORE FISHING
The Crooked Island Passage dropoff running south off Crooked Island from Bird Rock down to Long Cay.

BOTTOM FISHING
The Semana Cay reefs and the Mayaguana reefs.

SHALLOW WATER FISHING
The Bight of Acklins.

You'll note that we've left unmentioned the Jumentos Cays and the Ragged Island Range, Hogsty Reef, and the Inaguas. The last two are too remote to be considered accessible fishing grounds. As for the arc of the Raggeds and the Jumentos Cays, years back it was the place for reef fish and lobster. It's been hit hard now, we're told, but in truth we've yet to try it.

CIGUATERA

The possibility always exists of ciguatera poisoning from eating fish you have caught in the Bahamas. See our warning and advice that is given in detail in the **Buff Pages** under **Medical Facilities and Health Hazards** on page 419.

Fishing in the Turks and Caicos
The Turks and Caicos Islands attract the majority of their visitors by the superb underwater environment that surrounds every cay, every reef, the vast expanse of the two great banks, the whole span of it from the plummeting abysses of ocean walls to coral so shallow you can barely glide over it with fins, mask, and a snorkel. The diving undoubtedly rates as the top attraction, but the fishing, from bonefish flats to the ocean track of the large gamefish, is no less. It's just not that well frequented, well promoted if you like, at this time. Our own private feeling is that we wouldn't be upset if it remained this way, but the first few through the doors of the Sea Gardens of Paradise always want to close them to others, and hang out the No Vacancy signs.

We also list the charter boats offering deep sea or other fishing, most of which are Providenciales based. For you, on your own boat, be aware that both spear gun and spear sling fishing is illegal, and it's illegal to fish using scuba or surface-supplied air.

Everyone over age 16 intending to fish is required to buy a fishing license ($10 for 30 days), which limits you to line fishing only; you are prohibited from selling your catch, and you may not take more than 50 lbs. weight of fish.

It almost goes without saying that fishing is not allowed in the protected areas. A wider ban, which you must be aware of, is that you, the visitor, are forbidden to take conch or lobster, which are reserved entirely for the local population.

Diving
Diving in the Bahamas
The Bahamas are one of the best destinations for diving in the world. The islands offer everything from shallow reef dives to wall dives, with ocean dropoffs, blue holes, drift dives, and encounters with dolphins, rays, and sharks. The potential dive sites in the Bahamas are endless. Andros alone has the third-largest barrier reef in the world. Above all, not only is the marine life everything you've always dreamed about, but the sea temperature is in the 80s, and the visibility is beyond belief. One hundred feet is not uncommon.

Many cruising visitors may prefer to explore and find their own favorite areas for diving, rather than signing on with a dive operator for scheduled dive trips. However most of us need to touch base at a dive shop sometime to fill tanks, fix equipment if something goes wrong, or seek local advice. So we've listed the dive operators in the islands to help your planning. For local information, telephone numbers, and suggested dive sites, see the **Yellow Pages** for that island. Live-aboard dive boats are not included in our listing.

We would have to write an encyclopedia to list every dive site in the Bahamas. With regret this is beyond our scope. We list two sources of information in our recommended reading later in this chapter, under Marine Reference. We suggest, particularly in cases of deep dives (over 80 feet) and specialist dives (such as wrecks) that you seek advice from the local dive operator, and join one of their dive trips to gain familiarization before setting off on your own.

Dress and Protection
In the winter months the ocean temperature will drop from the summer 80s to the 70s. A 2mm wetsuit is your best bet for the winter months. During the summer you hardly need a wetsuit for shallow dives (80 feet or less), but a wetskin is sensible to give you some protection in case you accidentally brush against fire coral or encounter sea lice.

Diving Emergencies
All dive operators in the islands have rescue-trained personnel and oxygen. Any island with an airfield or airstrip can provide air evacuation. If you need a recompression chamber, call Lyford Cay Hospital at 242-362-4025 or contact any of the dive operators on VHF 16. The direct line to the Hyperbaric Chamber is 242-362-5765, but you should contact Dr. Dean or Dr. Ingraham first through the hospital. If you are diving in the Bahamas, first read our cautions and notes in the **Buff Pages** under **Medical Facilities and Health Hazards** and the **BASRA** section.

Live-Encounter Diving
This statement may not be politically correct in today's world, but we have strong reservations about live-encounter diving. We do not believe that live feeding should be carried out to produce a circus display and increase dive trip revenue.

Why do we take this stand? Let's deal with the shark dives first. The longer-term effects of this are unquantifiable, distort the pattern of nature, and bring predators into waters they did not frequent before. Inevitably the shark population will come to associate divers with food. The prognosis for such an automatic association is not good. Somewhere, sometime, quite possibly in a place not associated with feeding dives, a shark will turn on innocent divers who fail to provide a free meal. Beyond this, there are always mavericks, unstable and unpredictable creatures, just as the human race produces its psychotics. Is shark feeding wise? The only sensible, logical answer must be "No."

We also believe that playing with dolphins should not be encouraged, and that dolphin captivity, in any form, should be banned. Dolphins are highly intelligent, intuitive, tolerant, gentle, and playful creatures with a very strong sense of family and pod (clan) bonding. They are used to ranging far, born free and swimming free, over a vast range of water, where other than sharks, they have no enemies. They are dependent for their navigation and communication on a long-range sonar system that eclipses our best submarine sound ranging and communications. To pen a dolphin is cruelty, and to confine a dolphin within a tank, where its sonar re-echoes on all sides like a scream in a prison cell, is torture. As divers we should enjoy random encounters with dolphins in the open ocean and bless our good fortune when these happen.

Let's ban the circus acts.

Diving in the Turks and Caicos
There are some of the best dive sites in the world here, and many excellent dive operators, who will provide a list of sites. Or you can tie up to one of the dive site buoys (a white ball with one blue band) if no on else is using it. The buoys are most likely to be in use by the dive boats between 8 a.m. and 3 p.m. Larger vessels (over 80 feet LOA) may tie up to the buoys marked with a white cylinder with two blue bands.

There's not a wall, not a stretch of reef, nor a single coral head that's not worth diving. Dive where you will, but take care. Keep that buoyancy under control, keep your fins and your hands away from the coral, and enter the magic environment of this fantastic underwater world gently. Most of the local population you will meet down there will be totally unafraid of you, if you are quiet and unaggressive. Don't take liberties and treat them as your new life-long friends. They are born free and living remote from your world, sharing no part of your social culture and encounter codes.

Diving Emergencies

On Providenciales there is a recompression chamber (Tel: 946-4242) at the MBS Medical Centre on Leeward Highway, with fully trained staff.

Recommended Reading

The Bahamas

So many books have been written about the Bahamas, but one of the most delightful stories that at the same time gives you all the flavor of Bahamian history is Robert Wilder's *Wind From the Carolinas*, which has been republished by Bluewater Books & Charts. It's a classic. You could say it's the "Gone With the Wind" of the Bahama Islands. Other books you may wish to add to your Bahamas bookshelf (some of them obtainable only in the Bahamas) are:

General Reading

Abaco, History of an Out Island and Its Cays. Steve Dodge (White Sound Press).
The Bahamas, A Family of Islands. Gail Saunders (Caribbean Guides).
Bahamas: Out Island Odyssey. Nan Jeffrey (Avalon House).
Bahamas Rediscovered. Nicholas Popov (MacMillan Caribbean).
Eleuthera: the Island called Freedom. Everild Young (London: Regency Press).

My Castle in the Air. Evans W. Cottman (Rehor Publishing).
Mystical Cat Island. Eris Moncur (Available from Balmain Antiques, Nassau).
Out-Island Doctor. Evans W. Cottman (Landfall Press).

Marine Reference

The Dive Sites of the Bahamas. Lawson Wood (Passport Books).
Diving and Snorkeling Guide to the Bahamas, Family Islands, and Grand Bahama. Bob & Charlotte Keller (Pisces).
Fishes of the Atlantic Coast. Gar Goodson (Stanford University Press).
Guide to Corals and Fishes: the Bahamas, and the Caribbean. Idaz & Jerry Greenberg (Pen and Ink Press).
Reef Coral Identification Guide. Paul Hunan (New World Publishing).
Reef Creatures Identification Guide. Paul Hunan (New World Publishing).
Reef Fish Identification Guide. Paul Hunan (New World Publishing).

General Reference

Bahamas Handbook and Businessman's Annual. Etienne Dupuch (E. Dupuch).
Insight Guide to the Bahamas. Insight Guides (Houghton-Mifflin).

(Bahamas bibliography courtesy of Bluewater Books & Charts, Fort Lauderdale, Florida, 1-800-942-2583).

The Turks and Caicos

Turks Islands Landfall, A History of the Turks and Caicos Islands. HE Sadler (Available from Marjorie Sadler, PO Box 31, Grand Turk, for $30, plus $6 for overseas shipping.)
Turks and Caicos Pocket Guide. Edited by Julia Blacke and updated annually. A very informative pocket guide to these islands, available from local stores for $5, including the Unicorn Bookstore in Providenciales.

Chapter 26
Buff Pages
Infrastructure and Government

The Bahamas National Flag.

Infrastructure

A Bahamian ABC

AIRLINE TELEPHONE NUMBERS

Abaco Air	242-367-2266
Air Canada	800-776-3000
American Eagle	800-433-7300
Bahamasair (Nassau)	242-377-5505
Bahamasair (Freeport)	242-352-8343
British Airways	800-AIRWAYS
Cat Island Air	242-377-3318
Cleare Air	242-377-0341
Continental Connection (Gulfstream)	242-356-7314
Delta Air Lines	800-221-1212
Island Express	954-359 0380
LB Ltd (formerly Laker)	242-352-3389
Major's Air Services	242-352-5778
Chalk's International (sea planes)	800-424-2557
Sandpiper Air Charters	242-377-5751
Sky Unlimited	242-377-8993
Stella Maris Resort Aviation	242-338-2051
Paradise Island Helicopters	242-363-4016
USAir Express	242-327-8886

AIRPORTS

Airports shown in **bold type** have regular, scheduled flights, with Customs at the airport. Airports shown in normal type are used by charter and private aircraft. Private airstrips are not listed.

A $15 departure tax must be paid by every passenger leaving the Bahamas by air, which is collected at the airline desk on check-in. There is an additional $3 security fee at Freeport International Airport.

ABACO: **Marsh Harbour**, Sandy Point, Spanish Cay, **Treasure Cay**, Walker's Cay

ACKLINS ISLAND: **Spring Point**

ANDROS: **San Andros, Fresh Creek, Andros Town, Congo Town**

BERRY ISLANDS: Chub Cay, **Great Harbour Cay**

BIMINI: **Alice Town** (sea plane only), **South Bimini**, Cat Cay

CAT ISLAND: **Arthur's Town**, **New Bight**, Hawk's Nest

CROOKED ISLAND: Pittstown Point, **Colonel Hill**

ELEUTHERA: **Governor's Harbour**, **North Eleuthera** for Harbour Island and Spanish Wells, **Rock Sound**

EXUMAS: Normans Cay, Sampson Cay, Staniel Cay, Black Point, Farmer's Cay, **Moss Town** for **George Town**

GRAND BAHAMA: Deep Water Cay, **Freeport**

GREAT INAGUA: **Matthew Town**

LONG ISLAND: **Deadman's Cay**, Cape Santa Maria, **Stella Maris**

MAYAGUANA: Mayaguana

NEW PROVIDENCE: **Paradise Island, Nassau International**

RUM CAY: Rum Cay

SAN SALVADOR: **San Salvador**

BANKING

The Bank of the Bahamas, ScotiaBank, Barclays Bank, Canadian Imperial Bank of Commerce, Chase Manhattan Bank, Citibank N.A, and the Royal Bank of Canada are all active in the Bahamas. All of them accept and change traveler's checks (you will need your passport for verification) and some have ATMs.

There is no restriction on the amount of money that you may bring into the Bahamas and the amount you may take out; it's prudent to overestimate your expenditures and carry traveler's checks in reserve.

Banking hours are usually Monday to Thursday from 9:30 a.m. to 3 p.m., and Fridays 9:30 a.m. to 5 p.m. We list ATMs and banks' specific hours in the **Yellow Pages** for each port of call.

BUSINESS HOURS

Government offices are open Monday to Friday, from 9 a.m. to 5 p.m. There may be minor changes, and don't necessarily expect that these hours will be kept by a small customs office that may be a one-man or one-woman band, and the office holder, to complicate matters, may well be double-hatted, running a second office at the same time.

Generally the business hours set by the government offices set the pace for most businesses in most places, save where financial interests dictate more flexible, often extended, opening hours. We have tried to give precise times in our **Yellow Pages** but it's not always possible to tie people down to a declared schedule.

CREDIT CARDS

MasterCard and Visa are widely accepted, although a credit card surcharge (sometimes as much as 5 percent) can be added. You can always refuse and use your traveler's checks or cash. American Express and Diners Club are not so widely accepted. The smaller islands and cays may well not take credit cards, and you should be prepared for this. In general you could say that as you go down the scale in size and up the scale into remoteness, first of all the utility of credit cards fades out, then the utility of traveler's checks. Make sure you have adequate cash on hand, and if your destination is really remote, favor them with the currency of their own land, for US dollars may be rare currency there.

CURRENCY

The Bahamian currency is the Bahamas dollar, which rates on par with the US dollar. Both Bahamian and US currency are accepted universally in the Bahamas, although as we've said, in remote settlements the Bahamian may well be preferred. A curious anomaly is that many Batelco coin phones will only operate on a US quarter (25¢) and fail to work with a Bahamian quarter. Save your US quarters. You may need them.

DRESS CODES

The Bahamas are informal and the jacket and tie of normal business attire is rarely required, although the upper strata of restaurants often prefer men to wear a blazer or a sports jacket in the evening. Check if you have doubt. In such places a shirt with a collar is invariably preferable to a T-shirt, and long trousers rather than shorts. Otherwise you may dress casually virtually wherever you are.

Remember that just because **you** are on vacation and wearing beach clothes much of the time, it's not the way you should dress to tour Nassau or even an outlying settlement. The Bahamians have a deeply ingrained sense of propriety and are offended by nudity and near-nudity; bikini bras and short cut-offs do not go down well as street attire. Respect the life style. You are a guest in their islands.

DRIVING

Visitors may drive in the Bahamas for up to three months on their own driver's licence. The Bahamas adheres to the British system of driving on the left side of the road. As most vehicles are imported from the US with the steering wheel on the left of the vehicle, a "co-pilot" is often useful to help the driver see the road ahead. It takes some concentration to get used to the "keep left" rule, and it's easy to forget which side of the road you should be on in remote stretches in a place like Eleuthera, when you meet no other traffic for quite a while.

Speed limits are 25 mph in built-up areas and 30 mph everywhere else, except for some specified sections of new road in Nassau and Freeport where a 45-mph limit has been set. There are no seat belt rules. Motorcyclists are required to wear helmets.

DRUGS

Drugs that are illegal in the US (marijuana, LSD, cocaine, morphine, opium, and the like) are also illegal in the Bahamas. If you are caught in possession, at the least you will face a fine of $100,000 and anything up to five years in prison. Under US rules, it may well be that the boat is confiscated with no appeal possible. There's only one way to go: *don't do drugs*.

DUTY FREE

Generally in the Bahamas china, crystal, fine jewelry, luxury leather goods, linens, tablecloths, liquor, perfume, cologne and toilet water, photographic equipment, sweaters, watches, and wine are classed as duty-free goods.

ELECTRICITY

Electricity supply is 1 phase 3 wire 120V 60 cycle AC, which is the same as in the US. Power in the small islands is provided by locally owned generators and you can expect inexplicable surges and occasional low voltage. If you're operating sensitive equipment like a computer, you would be wise to have a good surge protector in use when you're hooked up to shore power. Otherwise, generate your own power.

GARBAGE

We put garbage in our ABC with no apology. Garbage is always a problem for the cruising sailor, and the disposal of garbage is an ongoing and vexing problem for the Bahamas, who have no land mass to play with and cannot excavate landfills. For your part, *never* dump plastic at sea or anywhere else. Don't even think of burying your garbage on a deserted island. Anything that is truly biodegradable may be jettisoned at sea, well offshore, in deep water. If you must, glass bottles (broken first) may be disposed of in this way, and cans (cut open at both ends) other than aluminum cans. For the rest you must carry your garbage with you until you can dispose of it, bagged, wherever there is a recognized disposal site.

Walk the beaches of the Bahamas and you will see what the heedless disposal of garbage, particularly plastics, has already done to the environment. What you will not see are the seabirds and turtles who have died caught in six-pack rings, and the fish who have died ingesting the detritus of passing boaters.

LANGUAGE

Yes, of course English is spoken. But you may take some time to get used to the lilt, catch phrases, and inflection.

LIQUOR LAWS

The drinking age is 18 at present, though there are suggestions that it may soon be raised to 21.

MAIL

You must use Bahamian stamps (which are pretty)! A one-half-ounce letter to the US costs 65¢; to Europe and Central and South America 70¢; to the rest of the world 80¢. Postcards to all destinations are 50¢.

PORTS OF ENTRY

Customs and Immigration working hours are usually from 9 a.m. to 5 p.m., Monday to Friday. Outside these hours, you will be charged overtime. In some places, like Chub Cay or Port Lucaya or Treasure Cay, the marina will call the officer to your boat. In other places, like North Bimini, Green Turtle Cay, or George Town, the captain alone must take all the boat papers and passports to the customs office in town. See our Yellow Pages for individual ports. This list gives Ports of Entry accessible to boats. All major airports have customs officers as well. Keep your yellow flag flying until you have been cleared by Customs on entering the Bahamas.

ABACOS: Green Turtle Cay, Marsh Harbour, Spanish Cay (on request), Treasure Cay Marina, and Walker's Cay Marina

ANDROS: Fresh Creek, Andros Town; San Andros Airport for Nicholls Town or Morgans Bluff

BERRY ISLANDS: Chub Cay Club Marina, Great Harbour Cay Marina

NORTH BIMINI: Alice Town

SOUTH BIMINI: Bimini Sands Marina

CAT CAY: Cat Cay Club

CAT ISLAND: Smith Bay

ELEUTHERA, HARBOUR ISLAND AND SPANISH WELLS: Governor's Harbour, Harbour Island, Rock Sound, Spanish Wells

EXUMAS: George Town

GRAND BAHAMA: Freeport Harbour*, Lucayan Marina, Old Bahama Bay, West End, Port Lucaya Marina, Running Mon Marina, and Xanadu Beach Marina

GREAT INAGUA: Matthew Town

LONG ISLAND: Stella Maris Marina

MAYAGUANA: Abraham's Bay

NEW PROVIDENCE/NASSAU: Clifton Pier*, East Bay Yacht Basin, John Alfred Dock*, Kelly's Dock*, Lyford Cay Marina, Nassau Harbour Dock West*, Nassau Harbour Club, Nassau Yacht Haven, Union Dock*

NEW PROVIDENCE/PARADISE ISLAND: The Marina at Atlantis, Hurricane Hole Marina

SAN SALVADOR: Cockburn Town

Denotes Ports of Entry primarily for commercial shipping.

REFUELING

Call ahead on VHF 16 in remote islands to check that there is fuel available.

Northern Cruising Gounds

ABACO: Cherokee Sound *Cherokee Auto and Boat Haven;* Coopers Town *Cooper's Town Shell;* Elbow Cay; Hope Town *Lighthouse Marina;* Elbow Cay; White Sound *Sea Spray Marina;* Fox Town *Fox Town Shell and Fox Town Starport;* Grand Cays *Rosie's Place;* Great Guana Cay *Guana Beach Resort Marina, Orchid Bay Yacht Club Marina;* Green Turtle Cay, Black Sound *The Other Shore Club;* Green Turtle Cay, White Sound *Bluff House Marina, Green Turtle Club;* Man-O-War *Man-O-War Marina;* Marsh Harbour *Boat Harbour Marina, Conch Inn Marina, Harbour View Marina, Marsh Harbour Marina, Triple J Marina;* Sandy Point *Lightborne Marina;* Spanish Cay *Spanish Cay Marina;* Treasure Cay *Treasure Cay Marina;* Walker's Cay *Walker's Cay Marina.*

GRAND BAHAMA: Freeport *Running Mon Marina, Xanadu Beach Marina;* Port Lucaya *Lucayan Marina, Port Lucaya Marina;* West End *Harbour Hotel Marina, Old Bahama Bay Marina.*

Central Cruising Cruising Grounds

ANDROS: Fresh Creek *Lighthouse Yacht Club;* Morgans Bluff contact *Willy's Water Lounge.*

BERRY ISLANDS: Chub Cay *Chub Cay Club;* Great Harbour Cay *Great Harbour Cay Marina.*

NORTH BIMINI: *Bimini Big Game Club, Bimini Blue Water.*

SOUTH BIMINI: *Bimini Sands Marina.*

CAT CAY: *Cat Cay Club Marina.*

ELEUTHERA: Central Eleuthera (Hatchet Bay) *Marine Services of Eleuthera* (no dockside refueling); Harbour Island *Harbour Island Club, Valentine's Yacht Club;* South Eleuthera *Cape Eleuthera Marina, Davis Harbour Marina;* Spanish Wells *Robert's Marine, Spanish Wells Marine and Hardware, Spanish Wells Yacht Haven.*

NASSAU/NEW PROVIDENCE ISLAND: *Bayshore Marina, Brown's Boat Basin, East Bay Marina, Harbour View Marina, Lyford Cay Marina, Nassau Harbour Club* (diesel only), *Nassau Yacht Haven.*

NASSAU/PARADISE ISLAND: *Atlantis, Hurricane Hole Marina*

Southern Cruising Grounds

CAT ISLAND: Hawk's Nest *Hawk's Nest Resort and Marina;* Smith Bay Government Dock, *New Bight Service Station.*

EXUMAS: George Town in Great Exuma *Exuma Docking Services;* Highborne Cay; Little Farmer's Cay *Farmers Cay Yacht Club;* Sampson Cay *Sampson Cay Club;* Staniel Cay *Staniel Cay Yacht Club.*

LONG ISLAND NORTH: *Stella Maris Marina.*

LONG ISLAND SOUTH: Clarence Town Government Dock *Clarence Town Shell;* Salt Pond.

RUM CAY: *Sumner Point Marina.*

SAN SALVADOR: *Riding Rock Inn Marina.*

Far Horizons

CROOKED ISLAND: Landrail Point *Landrail Service Station.*

GREAT INAGUA: Matthew Town *Far East Enterprise*s

MAYAGUANA: contact *Batelco*

TAXES AND TIPPING

A tax of 8 percent is added to all hotel bills and villa rentals. An energy surcharge of $3 per person per day and other local charges may be added to a hotel bill. Tipping? The standard rate is 15 percent. Be aware that a 15-percent gratuity is often added to your restaurant bill. Always check to see if this has been done. If you are paying by credit card, the space for recording a tip on the card slip will be left blank, but the food and drink total may already reflect the service charge. If you then add 15 percent, you will have paid a 30-percent gratuity.

TELEPHONES

The area code for the Bahamas is 242. Gradually card phones are replacing coin phones in all public telephone booths. Batelco telephone cards ($5, $10, or $20) are a useful buy, particularly as a reserve resource, and are available at any Batelco office. You may dial foreign direct calls from any of these telephones, and from any of the public telephones used for purely local calls, which, like a domestic telephone, are straight touch-tone phone with no coin or card payment linkage. If you are using a coin phone, your 25¢ will be returned on getting through to a foreign direct operator. Beware that in the Bahamas, US 800 calls carry a charge. They are not toll free.

Useful numbers are:

Long Distance Operator	0
Directory Assistance	916
Weather	915
Time	917
Phone card locations (in Nassau)	328-0990

The principal foreign direct call numbers are:

AT&T USA Direct Service	1-800-872-2881
MCI Call USA	1-800-888-8000
Sprint Express	1-800-839-2111
Canada Direct	1-800-389-0004
United Kingdom Direct	1-800-839-4444

TIME ZONE

The Bahamas are in the same time zone as the east coast of the United States, which is Eastern Standard Time (EST), five hours behind UT or Greenwich Mean Time. When it's noon in the Bahamas, it's noon in Washington, DC, 9 a.m. on the west coast of the United States (Pacific Time), and 5 p.m. in London, England.

The Bahamas change to Daylight Savings Time (EDT) on the first Sunday in April and revert to EST on the last Sunday in October (as does the US).

TOURIST OFFICES

Abaco Tourist Office, Marsh Harbour	367-3067
Bimini Tourist Office, Alice Town	347-3529
Eleuthera Tourist Office, Governor's Harbour	333-2142
Exuma Tourist Office, George Town	336-2430
Freeport, Grand Bahama, Ministry of Tourism	352-8044
Harbour Island Tourist Office, Harbour Island	333-2621
Ministry of Tourism Hotline (9 a.m. to 11:30 p.m.)	377-6833
after 5:30 pm in Nassau	377-6806
Nassau, Ministry of Tourism	322-7501

WEIGHTS AND MEASURES

Weights and measures for linear, dry, and liquid measurement used in the Bahamas are the same as in the United States. Fuel is sold in US gallons. The Bahamas is likely to follow any moves made by the US government toward adopting the metric system, but as yet this has amounted to no more than the requirement that consumer goods are labeled in both metric and US measurements.

A Turks and Caicos ABC

AIRLINES

American Airlines	800-433-7300
	or local 649-946 4948
Caicos Air Services	649-946-3283
SkyKing	649-941-5464
Lynx Air International	1-888-LYNX AIR
	or 649-946-1971
Turks and Caicos Airways	649-946-4255

AIRPORTS OR AIRSTRIPS

Airports shown in **bold type** have regular, scheduled flights, with Customs at the airport. Airports shown in normal type are used by charter and private aircraft. Private airstrips are not listed. There is a departure tax of $15 per person, except for children under twelve years of age.

Grand Turk International Airport
Providenciales International Airport
South Caicos Airport
North Caicos Airport
Pine Cay

AIR AMBULANCE

Air Ambulance Red Jet   1-888-473-3538

BANKING

Banking hours are usually from 8:30 a.m. to 2:30 p.m., Monday to Thursday, and from 8:30 a.m. to 4:30 p.m. on Fridays.

Barclays Bank and ScotiaBank have offices on Grand Turk and Providenciales. Barclays Bank also has a branch on South Caicos that opens on Thursdays.

There are ATMs at both banks on Providenciales, and at Barclays Bank on Grand Turk.

CREDIT CARDS

Visa and MasterCard are widely accepted; American Express much less so. You still need cash in some of the smaller stores.

CRUISING PERMITS

Granted free of charge. You may have three a year, for three months at a time.

CURRENCY

US dollars accepted at par.

DRESS CODE

Very informal, unless you are dining out somewhere elegant. Nude and topless bathing and sunning is not encouraged.

DRIVING

Drive on the left! These islands are still a British Crown Colony. Visitors can drive for 30 days with a valid driver's license from their own country. After that, a three-month permit can be issued for $30. Government stamp duty of $10 is payable on each rental car agreement. Liability insurance is charged at $2.50 per day, and collision damage waiver from $10 per day.

ELECTRICITY

110V/60 cycle, the same as the US. Outlets fit all US appliances.

ENTRY PROCEEDURE

Boats that clear in or out during working hours only pay a $5 boarding fee. Working hours are from 8 a.m. to 12:30 p.m. and 2 to 4:30 p.m. Monday to Thursday, to 4 p.m. on Fridays. Outside these hours you will have to pay $15 for clearing in or out and an overtime fee of $6 on weekends or public holidays. The Harbormaster can give permission to stay for seven days. If you want to stay longer, you can ask for a three-month cruising permit, which is issued free during working hours. You are allowed three of these in a year. Show your cruising permit to each harbormaster as you move between the islands. You can call them on VHF 16 "Harbormaster." (See also **Ports of Entry** in this listing.)

FISHING PERMITS
For line fishing only, $10 for 30 days. No fishing is allowed in any of the national parks.

HOLIDAYS
New Year's Day	January 1st
Commonwealth Day	2nd Monday in March
Good Friday, Easter, Easter Monday	March/April
National Heroes Day	4th Monday in May
HM The Queen's Official Birthday	Monday after the 2nd Saturday in June
Emancipation Day	1st Monday in August
National Youth Day	4th Friday in September
Columbus Day	2nd Monday in October
International Human Rights Day	4th Monday in October
Christmas Day, Boxing Day	December 25th and 26th

LANGUAGE
Although English is the first language, you may hear French, German, Italian, Spanish, Norwegian, Swedish, or French Creole spoken by residents from all over the world.

LIQUOR LAWS
The drinking age is 18.

MAIL
Post offices are generally open between 8 a.m. and 4 p.m., but watch for lunchtime closing and early closing on Fridays for the weekend.

A one-half-ounce letter to the US costs 60¢, to Canada and the UK 80¢, to Europe $1. Postcards cost 50¢ to the US, 60¢ to Canada and the UK, and 80¢ to Europe.

PETS
Current health certificate, within the last 30 days, required. Your pet will be examined by a health inspector on arrival.

PORTS OF ENTRY
(See also **Entry Procedure** in this listing.)

GRAND TURK: Government Dock and Airport.

PROVIDENCIALES: South Dock, Leeward Marina, Turtle Cove Marina, Sapodilla Bay, Caicos Marina and Shipyard.

SOUTH CAICOS: Government Dock, Shell Dock at the Seaview Marina.

REFUELING IN THE TURKS AND CAICOS
GRAND TURK: *Government Dock, Flamingo Cove Marina* (diesel only).

PROVIDENCIALES: *Turtle Cove Marina, South Side Basin Marina, Leeward Marina, Caicos Shipyard* (diesel only).

SOUTH CAICOS: *Seaview Marina.*
Propane gas is available from *South Dock* (Government Dock) in Grand Turk, and *General Trading Company* at Airport Road in Providenciales.

TAXES AND TIPPING
A 10-percent government tax will be added to all restaurant and hotel bills, and it is customary to tip 15 percent for good service.

TELEPHONES
The area code for the Turks and Caicos is 649. Cable and Wireless provide communication services throughout the Turks and Caicos Islands, and almost all the public telephones take a phone card. These are widely available in $5, $10, and $20 denominations, usually from a store or restaurant near the telephone, or from the Cable and Wireless offices on Leeward Highway, Providenciales, or Duke Street in Cockburn Town, Grand Turk, which are open from 8:30 a.m. to 4 p.m. Monday to Thursday, and from 8:30 a.m. to 3 p.m. on Fridays. There is no tax on pre-paid phone cards.

Calling within the islands you must dial seven digits, *e.g.,* 946-2200. Peak rate charges are $2.50 per minute to the US, off-peak charges $1.95 per minute. You can call using American Express, Discover, MasterCard, or Visa by dialing 111. Telephones also accept AT&T, Bell Canada, Teleglobe, BT, C&W Communications, and MCI World cards.

For information about using your cellular phone, dial Cable and Wireless at O-SEND. You can be connected by quoting a major credit card number, and call details will be mailed to your home address monthly. For more information, call 1-800-955-8512.

Internet and fax services are widely available throughout the islands. The Internet gateway is www.turksandcaicos.tc.

TIME ZONE
Eastern Standard Time, or five hours behind Greenwich Mean Time. The islands change to and from Daylight Saving Time the same days as the US.

TOURIST OFFICES
Old Dock, Grand Turk	Tel: 946-2321
Turtle Cove Landings, Providenciales	Tel: 946-4970

Medical Facilities and Health Hazards

Medical Facilities

Hardly surprisingly, the best medical facilities are found in the centers of population, Nassau, Freeport, and Marsh Harbour. In Nassau, there are two main hospitals; the government-owned Princess Margaret Hospital, and the ever-expanding privately owned Doctor's Hospital, with seventy-two beds and one hundred physicians. The latter plans to open a second hospital in Marsh Harbour, and a new out-patient clinic in western New Providence, near the airport. There is also Lyford Cay hospital, with the only hyperbaric chamber in the Bahamas at time of writing, and the Bahamas Heart Institute. In Freeport, there is the Rand Memorial Hospital, and in Marsh Harbour a large government clinic and the excellent Abaco Family Medicine practice.

Throughout the rest of the Bahamas, medical facilities are available in most of the populated islands. In the larger settlements, there are very good government clinics, which have been greatly improved in the last few years. As a non-resident, you will be charged $30 for a routine visit to see a nurse or doctor at any of the clinics. The new ones generally have full-time nurses with a doctor on call, two-bed wards, a dispensary, X-ray equipment, a morgue, and a few have their own ambulance. It remains that if you are not in either New Providence or Grand Bahama, and someone needs urgent attention in the event of a serious medical condition or injury, they will probably have to be flown to Nassau or back to the US. This might not be the first step in their medical evacuation, for the casualty may have to be taken first by boat (it could be in your boat) to the nearest island or cay with a clinic, and from there, after stabilizing treatment, by boat once again to the nearest airfield or airport, and then moved by air to a hospital.

Two broad conclusions can be drawn from this:

- You should carry the fullest possible medical pack on board, together with first-aid manuals, so that you (or your crew) are able to respond with effective immediate first aid after any accident or medical crisis. As a preventive measure you should ensure that everyone on board has an adequate stock of prescription medication to last the voyage. Your aim, even before you set out on your cruise, must be to achieve the medical capability of being able to deliver someone, in an emergency, in a no-worse state to the nearest clinic or health center from wherever you might be, or to an airfield with a waiting air ambulance.

- If the casualty is in serious danger, rather than risk the trauma of repeated inter-island moves, it may be better to seek direct air evacuation from the nearest airport (such as Marsh Harbour or Treasure Cay in the Abacos, George Town in the Exumas) straight to a hospital in Florida. To this end the Divers Alert

Network (DAN) and other organizations offer insurance with emergency air evacuation included. It's well worth considering. Failing this cover, it would be sensible to travel with an air evacuation service contact number listed in your Log Book. Take care of this before you set out for the Bahamas.

If you need an air ambulance, you can call:
Global Medical Rescue Tel: 242-394-2582/3388; Cell: 359-2496 in Nassau, or 351-3333 in Freeport.
MedEvac Air Ambulance Tel: 242-322-2881 in Nassau,
Air Ambulance Professionals Tel: 954-491-0555 (call collect) in Fort Lauderdale, Florida or 800-752-4195 in the Bahamas.
AAA Advanced Air Ambulance Tel: 305-232-7700 (call collect) in Miami, Florida, or 800-633-3590.

A number of other operators offer similar services.

For local medical help, see our **Yellow Pages.** We list dental facilities where they exist, although there are few outside the three main towns. For this reason, we always carry a dental first-aid kit, and hope never to have to use it.

Health

You should have no particular health problems in the Bahamas. There are three health hazards, all marine related, which we'll deal with separately, but taken across the board the Bahama Islands are a healthy environment. Although Bahamas piped water is not always good, and may well be brackish in many places, there are plentiful supplies of bottled drinking water in the larger towns and settlements. It is not always easy to find in the remote islands. Stock up wherever you can. Food in the Bahamas is generally good and wholesome, and there are no problems there. Both daytime and nightime temperatures, and humidity, are normally well within your comfort zone.

Are there any areas for concern? Yes, watch the sun. You wouldn't believe how many people get sunburned. Whatever sun lotion, cream, or gel you use, it should have a sun protection factor of at least 15. It should be waterproof. If your skin is sensitive or your complexion is fair, the chances are that you should use a PABA-free product to prevent blistering. In the evenings and at night, particularly if you fall into that "fair skin and attractive to insects" category, protect yourself against mosquitos and No-See-Ums.

Is there anything else to watch? Yes, watch your drinking. We're not talking about counting your Goombay Smashes here (though it's not a bad idea to try) but your water intake. We reckon on, and get through, one gallon of drinking water per person per day, just to keep normally hydrated.

Health Hazards

CIGUATERA

Top of our list, though mercifully we've escaped it so far, is ciguatera, poisoning by eating seafood. The name comes from the Spanish "cigua," a marine snail that the early Spanish settlers in Cuba tried to add to their diet and found poisonous. That particular snail is no longer a part of our diet, but fish carrying ciguatoxin may well be part of your catch. It's a naturally occurring toxin that passes along the food chain and, if it reaches you, will cause nausea, vomiting, and vertigo at best (after an initial tingling and numbness), and paralysis at worst.

The most suspect species are reef fish: barracuda, eels, red snapper, amberjack, sea bass, and grouper. Since grouper is a staple Bahamian food (every menu features fried grouper, grilled grouper, and grouper fingers) this sounds like bad news. The key is to go for the smaller fish (5 lbs. or less), and don't eat the internal organs. Fine, you might say, but who ever heard of anyone saying "small is beautiful" in the commercial fishing stakes and going for the 3-lb. groupers? Point taken, we'd say. The carry-on is this: listen to local advice. The Bahamians are not immune to ciguatera. If they catch a grouper and reckon it's OK for them, it's OK for you too.

Can you test for ciguatera? The answer is no. Not yet. People are working on it. Can cooking neutralize it? The answer, once again, is a no. Neither cooking, freezing, marinating, or pickling kills the ciguatera toxin.

Finally, if you do get ciguatera? What can you expect? Symptoms within 2–12 hours after eating the affected fish. Seek help at a clinic, or call the DAN Ciguatera Hotline in the states. You have two points of contact. Call 305-661-0774 or fax 305-667-2270 (Dr. Donna Blythe), or 305-361-4619 (Dr. Donald da Sylva). Rest assured, however bad it is, ciguatera is rarely fatal.

SEA LICE
Sea lice or jellyfish larvae can "bloom" in sea areas at times on a very local basis. Often the larvae come from seagrass that has been kicked up or disturbed, bringing the larvae to the surface. In contact with the human skin both sea lice and jellyfish larvae parasites burrow into the upper layers of the skin causing a rash, sometimes tenderness, sometimes small pimples, but always irritation and itching. This condition will last a week or so and then disappear. The only counter is to wash yourself thoroughly in fresh water, but by then it may be too late.

DECOMPRESSION SICKNESS
The deep dives of places like the Abaco Barrier Reef (where regular dives to 185 feet are offered by local dive operators) can produce at best narcosis with all its dangers and at worst, decompression sickness. If you are not in training, and not experienced in deep diving, do *not* attempt it. If you do go along for the ride, pay particular attention to your safety stops on your ascent, and keep it *slow, slow, slow*. Don't ne-

glect to have that extra tank with a regulator hooked up hanging on a line at your last stop, so that anyone low on air can stay there until your degassing is complete.

Just in case you need it, the only working hyperbaric chamber in the Bahamas at time of writing this edition of the Guide (mid 1999) is at Lyford Cay Hospital on New Providence at 242-362-4025.

Cellular Telephone in the Bahamas
The Bahamas Telecommunications Corporation (Batelco) does not as a matter of routine provide roaming facilities for the cellular telephones that most cruising visitors may have on board. Batelco has a list of US, Canadian, and Mexican cellular companies with whom they have roaming agreements, which is available from their Roaming Department at 242-394-3685 or 242-394-4000. Most of these companies tend to be relatively small, local US cellular services rather than the giants, and as the list is changing constantly, we think it better that you check with your own cellular company and ask if they have a roaming agreement with Batelco, or check with Batelco directly.

Batelco offers the cruising visitor full roaming facilities in the islands through their own facilities. To arrange this you need to produce:

- A passport or valid ID such as a voter's card or driver's license.

- A credit reference letter from your bank.

And you are required to pay the following charges up front:

Security deposit	$500.00
Activation fee	50.00
Inter-island roaming fee	20.00
Programming fee	50.00

Thereafter Batelco's charges are:

Monthly access charge	48.00
Rate per minute 7 a.m.–7 p.m.	0.45
Rate per minute 7 p.m.–7 a.m.	0.30

Your monthly charges are deducted from your initial deposit. When you choose to close your Batelco account, the balance remaining will be refunded to you.

These arrangements can be set up ahead of your visit by faxing the relevant identification and credit information to Batelco, but on your arrival it is necessary to call at Batelco to complete the process. We give the details of their Nassau office with whom you should first deal. If your landfall is planned for an island other than New Providence, Batelco will advise you where you should complete the formalities they require.

Their address is: Bahamas Telecommunication Corporation, Wireless Department, PO Box N-3084, The Mall at Marathon, Nassau, Bahamas. Tel: 242-394/5000; roaming department: 394-3685; fax: 393-3516/4798.

Coastal Radio Stations

There are only two specified Public Correspondence (Marine Operator) radio stations in the Bahamas. These are:

CALL SIGN	FREQUENCY	NAME
C6N2	2182 kHz	Nassau Public Correspondence
C6N3	VHF 27	Nassau Public Correspondence

Government

Entering the Bahamas

You are required by law to clear in with Customs and Immigration on entering the Bahamas. The geographic spread of Bahamian entry ports gives you options that allow you to approach the Bahamas from any direction. You may sail on past one entry port and clear in later at another as you wish, provided that no one in your crew lands until you have cleared in.

When you reach your chosen port of entry you'll be flying your yellow Q (quarantine) flag, which will have been flying from your starboard spreader (or the equivalent position on a power boat) ever since you entered Bahamian waters. You have 24-hours grace to clear in from your time of arrival at your entry port, and that Q flag stays flying until you've cleared in.

Only the captain of the vessel is allowed on shore to report for clearance. He or she should take the ship's papers, and the passports (or acceptable proof of ID) of all on board.

Passports or Proof of ID

US citizens: Valid passport, voter registration card, birth certificate
Canadians: valid passport
UK citizens: valid passport
Additionally, if any member of your ship's company is planning to leave while you are still cruising in the Bahamas, they require a valid air ticket for the return journey. This should be taken by the ship's captain with the passport of the person concerned.

The Paperwork

One way or another, it takes some time to clear in, but the Bahamas government have tried to simplify it by legislation passed in July 1999. Instead of the old cruising permit, fishing permit, Customs clearance charge, and departure tax that each incoming boat was required to pay separately, there is now a flat fee of $100 per boat with four people or less on board. If there are more than four people on board, there will be an extra charge of $15 per person to cover their departure tax. This flat levy is intended to simplify

and speed up the entry process for pleasure vessels entering the Bahamas.

Bahamas Customs Department—Inward Report, Pleasure Vessels This is a straightforward declaration but requires a full crew and passenger list, with addresses and nationality, and the details of any arms and ammunition on board.

Bahamas Immigration—Inward Passenger and Crew Manifest, Pleasure Ship This again requires a full crew and passenger list with addresses and nationality.

Bahamas Immigration Arrival/Departure Cards (for each person on board). You complete your Immigration card. Each person has to complete and sign their own card, which must be presented with their passport. The passport is stamped, the card is stamped twice, and the arrival part of the card is retained by the immigration or customs officer. The passport is returned with the departure part of the card, which has to be surrendered on leaving the Bahamas.

Bahamas Customs—Maritime Declaration of Health This is a question-and-answer form that requires you to account for the state of health of everyone on board. We feel that the form itself has been overtaken by time, but consider it an interesting insight into earlier days. Among the matters you're required to address or furnish are:

- A report on cholera, yellow fever, and small pox cases.
- A report on the unusual death of rats and mice during your voyage.
- How many people died on board (on the reverse of the form you are asked what you did with the bodies).

Application For a Permit to Engage in Foreign Fishing for Sporting Purposes.
At the end of all this you should emerge with:
(1) A cruising and fishing permit valid for 12 months.
(2) Your own stamped passport with your immigration departure card.
If you're lucky, you may be able to have your passengers and crew at hand during this procedure so that you can have them fill out their immigration cards while you are tackling your mountain of paperwork. So much depends on where you are. If the customs officer is clearing you on board, then that's fine. They're right there with you.

If you have to hike to an office further afield, much depends on the drill in that place. Some entry ports don't mind if your crew tag along and sit on a bench outside. Others play it straight. Check with other people who've already cleared in to see how it works where you are. If you're unlucky, you have a second trip to make to the customs office with those passports and immigration cards.

Once you have your cruising permit, take down your Q flag and fly the Bahamas Ensign (*not* the National Flag) in its place. See **The Bahamas Flag and Flag Etiquette**, page 423.

What You May Bring In

ALCOHOL AND TOBACCO
You may import alcoholic drinks for your own use (nominally 1 quart of spirits and 1 quart of wine) and 1 lb. of tobacco, or 200 cigarettes, or 50 cigars.

BOATS
For your own boat, your cruising permit is obviously your authority to cruise in the Bahamas for up to one year without paying import duty on your vessel. Thereafter you would be liable for 7.5 percent (30–100 feet LOA) or 22.5 percent (less than 30 feet LOA) of its value if you import the boat. Alternatively you can extend your cruising permit for up to three years for a fee of $500 per year.

An important new change has been made in respect to the duty-free importation of boats for cruising in the Bahamas. In the past, to get your cruising permit, you had to bring the boat in under its own power and import it in person to qualify for a cruising permit. Now you, a non-Bahamian national, may have your boat shipped in by freighter and imported as cargo for temporary use, provided that it is going to be reshipped out of the Bahamas. This change applies to boats of not less than 23 feet LOA.

The Bahamian customs have put in effect a procedure in which the boat is unloaded from the freighter bringing it in at the port of entry and, for a flat fee of $50, is granted a cruising permit (under Duty Exemption Clause 23 listed in Part B of Schedule 4 of the Bahamas Tariff Act). Those who do not want to face a Gulf Stream crossing may now fly in to pick up their boat, use it in the islands, and then ship it out.

BOAT SPARES
You may import marine parts for your own use fully exempt from customs duty. Just make sure that the shipper labels the package for you as the captain of your vessel, and that your boat name, as well as your temporary address, is clearly displayed. If you sell one of your boat spares to someone else, Bahamas law considers that to be a dutiable transaction. There is no import duty on the spares you carry for use on board your own boat.

DRUGS
You may bring in your own prescription drugs. Otherwise it's a big *no* to anything that is illegal in the US.

FIREARMS
You may import firearms (rifles, shotguns, and hand guns) and ammunition provided that they are declared, and kept on board under lock and key. Automatic weapons, such as assault rifles, are banned. If your cruise is to extend over three months, you must report to the police to obtain a firearms certificate. Firearms may not be used in Bahamian waters nor taken ashore.

FOOD
You are permitted to bring in food in bulk for your own cruising requirements. If you are inspected and have abnormal quantities of food, it might be suspected that you intend to barter or sell your surplus, and you may be asked to explain why you are so well stocked. Try to buy as much food as you can locally, thereby putting something back into the local economy of the country you are visiting.

MOTORCYCLES AND BICYCLES
These are subject to import duty and must be licensed in the Bahamas and insured before you may use them on shore. If you do not wish to pay import duty, a bond in lieu (such as a cash deposit or a bank guarantee) may serve. We reckon it's not worth the trouble. Forget it and rent a local bicycle, golf cart, or car when you need wheels.

PETS
Dogs and cats over the age of six months may be admitted with you to the Bahamas. You will need to start work on the import papers required for a pet about two months ahead of your cruise. First you must apply to the Director, Department of Agriculture, PO Box N-3704, Nassau, Bahamas (Tel: 242-325-7502/9 or fax: 325-3960) for an application to import your pet. Return the form with a $10 fee (use an international money order). You should get your import permit.

You also need a certificate of health (issued within 48 hours of your embarkation for the Bahamas), and a rabies certificate. The rabies certificate, if issued with a one-year validity, should be valid from not less than one month and not more than ten months before your entry to the Bahamas. If the validity of your rabies certificate covers three years, the acceptability bracket is not less than one month prior to entry and not more than 34 months.

There have been changes in these rules, and you would be wise to check before starting any inoculation process. Nonetheless, it remains that if you get your paperwork in order *before* you declare yourself in to the Bahamas, your pet should be able to remain signed on as part of the crew while you're in the islands.

Technically it can be argued that if your pet remains on board, you are not importing into the Bahamas. In practice, the Bahamian authorities do not seem much concerned about the rules regarding animals.

BARTERING—A WARNING
The Bahamian customs have become increasingly intolerant of bartering carried out by cruising boats in which otherwise dutiable goods, allowed in duty free with the issue of a cruising permit, are traded for local goods or services. If you are caught in this kind of activity, you'll be in trouble.

Leaving the Bahamas

You don't have to report to Customs and Immigration to clear out of the Bahamas. If your last port is an entry port, you may hand in your cruising permit and the immigration departure cards of everyone on board, just before you leave. However if you do this, and if you have to put back for any reason, you may have set yourself a problem with your premature surrender of these vital forms. Alternatively, you may mail your cruising permit and the immigration cards back to the Bahamas government from the US (or your next landfall). The address to use is on the reverse of the cruising permit.

See the **Blue Pages** under **Clearing In on Return to the US** on page 380–381.

The Bahamas Flag and Flag Etiquette

The Bahamas flag was taken into use on Independence Day in 1973. Its design rests primarily on three equal bands of color. Two aquamarine stripes, one at the top and one at the bottom, represent the colors of Bahamian skies and waters, with a central yellow stripe representing sand and shore. The three bands have a black triangle superimposed on the left (the staff side), which represents unity. This is the national flag, which is not flown as a courtesy flag.

Courtesy Flag

The courtesy flag flown by visiting yachts is a variation of the ensigns flown by Bahamian craft. The civil ensign, which you will fly, is based on a white St. George's cross on a red background (a variation of the English national flag), with the Bahamas national flag superimposed in the upper left quarter.

Normal flag etiquette dictates that you fly a courtesy flag immediately after you are granted clearance to cruise in the Bahamas. You take down your Bahamian courtesy flag when you leave the Bahamas, normally when you are three miles out in international waters.

War Ensign

You may see a variation of this ensign on Bahamian warships. In the War Ensign the background is white (again taken from the British, this time the Royal Navy) with a red cross on it. The War Ensign also has a national flag superimposed in the upper left quarter.

Q Flag

Remember it is international law that you fly a yellow Q flag on entering territorial waters from another country. This applies to you entering the Bahamas, and returning to the United States, regardless of your nationality and registration. You take down your Q flag as soon as you are granted clearance.

The Bahamas Air-Sea Rescue Association (BASRA)

The Bahamas Air-Sea Rescue Association (BASRA) is the leading marine rescue organization in the Bahamas. It is a volunteer service, very similar in its conception to a volunteer fire service. Its members contract to respond to

BASRA Emergency Stations in the Bahamas (24-Hour Monitoring)

LOCATION	VHF CHANNEL OR SSB FREQUENCY
Abacos	
BASRA Green Turtle Cay	VHF 16 "Bluff House"
BASRA Hope Town	VHF 16 "Seahorse Marine"
	VHF 16 "Island Marine"
	VHF 16 "Lucky Strike"
BASRA Man-O-War Cay	VHF 16 (Denise McDonald)
BASRA Guana Cay	VHF 16
BASRA Little Harbour	VHF 16
BASRA Marsh Harbour	VHF 16
Grand Bahama	
BASRA Freeport	VHF 16 or Tel: 352-6222
	Pager # 352-8339 for the
	Crew Chief, or 352-2628
	for the Police
Berry Islands	
BASRA Great Harbour Cay	VHF 16 or 68 "Great Harbour Cay"
Chub Cay & Frazer Hog Cay	VHF 16 or 68
BASRA Little Harbour	VHF 68 "Chester Darville"
Nassau	
BASRA HQ Nassau	VHF 16 "BASRA Nassau"
	Harbour Authority will respond on VHF 16 outside office hours.
Eleuthera	
BASRA Spanish Wells	VHF 16
& Harbour Island	or any of the Spanish Wells pilots
BASRA Governor's Harbour	VHF 16
Exumas	
BASRA Black Point & Compass Cay	VHF 16 "Tucker Rolle"
BASRA Staniel Cay	VHF 16
BASRA George Town	VHF 16
BASRA Highbourne Cay	VHF 16 "Highbourne Cay"
Cat Island	
BASRA Hawk's Nest	VHF 16 "Hawks Nest"
Rum Cay	
BASRA Rum Cay	VHF 16 "Sumner Point Marina"
San Salvador	
BASRA San Salvador	VHF 16 "Riding Rock Marina"
Crooked Island	
BASRA Landrail Point	VHF 16
Long Island	
BASRA Deadman's Cay	VHF 16 "Gemini"
BASRA Clarence Town	VHF 16 "Dockmaster"
BASRA Salt Pond	VHF 16 "Sunseeker"

emergency calls at any time of the day or night, and, very often, will use their own boats, and on occasion seaplanes, to effect a rescue. BASRA does not, however, operate in isolation and has close and constant links with the Royal Bahamas Defence Force and the US Coast Guard.

BASRA would wish, we believe, to make plain that they are not a fallback service for those who run out of fuel, nor are they a towing service if you have mechanical failure. Your primary responsibility is to look after your own vessel and your crew, and solve your own problems. BASRA are there to step in when lives are in danger.

May we make a plea that all cruising visitors make a point of becoming members of BASRA? Life membership is $500. Sponsorship is $250 and above, each year. Individual membership is $30 per year. Other than its fundraising activities, BASRA has no source of income. Do you know the cost of running BASRA? An air search costs over $100 an hour. A rescue boat costs $60 an hour to operate. Do you think those rescued by BASRA ante up this kind of money to say "thank you" for their lives or their vessel? Sadly and regrettably not.

It just may happen that one day your contribution to BASRA may save a life. It could be your own.

If you join, you're not committed to playing an active part in BASRA if you don't wish to do so. If you are semipermanent in the Bahamas in one area and willing to help, you may be welcome as a Boat Captain, Boat Crew, for the Air Wing, for help in fundraising, or for some other activity. Contact:

The Bahamas Air-Sea Rescue Association
PO Box SS-6247, Nassau, NP, Bahamas

BASRA Headquarters (open 9 a.m. to 5 p.m. daily)
Tel: 242-325-8864 • Fax: 242-325-2737
24-hour number: 242-322-3877
E-mail: co@basra.org • www.basra.org • mail drop for visiting boats: maildrop@basra.org

The Turks and Caicos Search and Rescue Association (TACRA)

The Turks and Caicos Rescue Association is not a full-time 24-hour, on-watch rescue service with its own rescue craft. It is essentially a voluntary association of HF and VHF marine radio operators, dive and fishing boat captains, local mariners, and onshore volunteers who will respond in any emergency. On call is the TACRA 50-foot patrol vessel *Sea Quest*, the Fisheries Department 19-foot patrol craft *Osprey*, and a police aircraft (callsign *Skyhawk*), as well as the backing of the US Coast Guard helicopters in Great Inagua (flying time 90 minutes).

If you are in trouble, or reckon that events are snowballing that way, you would be prudent to warn ahead of time so that TACRA is briefed and can be standing by, rather than waiting until the critical moment comes. Use VHF 16 or 68, 2182 kHz on SSB, or any active Ham or correspondence frequency.

The Royal Bahamas Defence Force

An armed force combining naval and air elements, the Royal Bahamas Defence Force is charged with the protection of the Bahamas, fishery protection, countering illegal immigration and drug smuggling, and search and rescue. It's a tall order for a small force faced with the operational responsibility for 100,000 square miles of Bahamian territorial water, with the complication of some 700 islands and well over 2,000 nm of coastline. Under a bilateral agreement with the US government, joint patrols are conducted in the Biminis with US Customs, and Royal Bahamian Defence Force personnel also serve on board US Coast Guard cutters, when required, to give the US Coast Guard jurisdiction in Bahamian waters.

The Royal Bahamas Defence Force has a fleet of twenty-six coastal and inshore patrol craft ranging from PO 1, HMBS *Marlin*, a 103-foot patrol boat, to 29-foot patrol boats and a handful of cigarette boats. All the patrol boats are painted naval gray, carry their pennant numbers (PO 1, etc.) on the sides, and bear that HMBS designation, standing for Her Britannic Majesty's Bahamian Ship. The honor goes to the Queen of the United Kingdom as the head of the British Commonwealth, to which the Bahamas belongs. The Force also has two fixed-wing aircraft, a Cessna Golden Eagle 421C, and a Cessna Titan Ambassador 404, which are used for reconnaissance, patrols, search and rescue, and in a transport role.

All told the Royal Bahamas Defence Force numbers some 850 officers and other ranks, 71 of whom are women. Their working dress may be naval blue fatigues or tropical white full dress uniforms, or may be camouflaged combat dress. All personnel may be armed. The Force is based in Coral Harbour on the southwest coast of New Providence Island, where they have a sea firing range (see our section on **Nassau and New Providence Island** on page 168).

The Royal Bahamas Defence Force has the right to board and inspect any vessel in Bahamian waters. They will be armed during such inspections. If you are boarded, you'll be asked to sign a certificate at the end of the inspection to state that it was carried out politely, correctly, and that the captain of the vessel boarded (or his or her representative) was allowed to be present throughout the inspection.

The members of the Royal Bahamas Defence Force are well trained (often graduates of the Britannia Royal Naval College in Dartmouth, England, or the US Coast Guard Officer Candidate School in Yorktown, Virginia), friendly, and approachable. All patrol boats monitor channel 16. Channel 22A is their primary frequency. Coral Harbour has a 24-hour watch on 22A, and to broaden their range there are repeater stations in the Berry Islands (at Chub Cay), the Abacos (at Hole-in-the-Wall), and in the Exumas (at Highborne Cay).

The Royal Bahamas Police Force

The maintenance of law and order in the Bahamas rests with the Royal Bahamas Police Force, whose current strength is 2,023 police officers, who are supported by a clerical staff of 220 civilians. While the main strength of the Force is based in the centers of population, with Nassau and New Providence Island hardly surprisingly rating the greatest police presence, isolated detachments are stationed in virtually all the settlements.

Royal Bahamas Police Force Band drummer.

Bahamas police normally are unarmed, but the carriage of weapons is not unknown. Violent crime, much of it drug related, has increased in recent years. The Bahamas Police Force Drug Enforcement Unit works closely with the Royal Bahamas Defence Force, the US DEA, and the US Customs Service. The Force was computerized for record keeping in 1990, maintains a forensic science laboratory, and on a more human note, also runs a canine section and believes strongly in community policing, which suits their island environment well. Outside the Bahamas the police force is generally better known for its ceremonial activities, especially in the form of the Royal Bahamas Police Force Band, which has won acclaim both on state duties in the Bahamas and abroad. If they are on parade while you are in the Bahamas, be sure to see them. Check with the Ministry of Tourism in Market Place, Bay Street, in Nassau. They have a program of forthcoming events.

Bahamian Holidays and Special Events

Public Holidays

New Years Day. January 1.
Easter. In March or April. **Good Friday, Easter Day** and **Easter Monday**
Labour Day. The first Friday in June.
Whit Monday. The first Monday seven weeks after Easter.
Independence Day. July 10.
Emancipation Day. The first Monday in August.
Discovery Day. October 12.
Christmas Day. December 25.
Boxing Day. December 26.

If a public holiday falls on a Saturday or a Sunday, it will be switched to the Friday before or the following Monday.

Special Events

JANUARY
New Years Day (January 1).
Junkanoo. Just before dawn on New Year's Day the Bahamian *Junkanoo Festival* kicks off. It's the party of the year over most of the islands. Nassau and Freeport–Port Lucaya, as the centers of population, stage the largest events, but you can be swept up into Junkanoo just about anywhere. It's a carnival time with extravagant costumes, parades, wild dancing, and all that goes with it, and has its roots in a mix of African drumming, Mardi Gras, Carnival in Rio, and Haitian frenzy, just about anything you care to name in that line, rolled into one wild celebration.
Exumas (Staniel Cay). New Year's Day Cruising Regatta.
Nassau (Paradise Island). New Year's Day Regatta.

FEBRUARY
Exumas (Farmer's Cay). Annual Farmer's Cay Festival.

SPRING BREAK
The spring break vacation, wherever it falls, sometime between February and April, has the Bahamas as a premier destination, at least for east coast colleges. The Bahamas in turn does much to attract this influx of visitors bent on celebration. Charter boats are a favored means of reaching the islands, but time and distance dictate that the Biminis, the northern Abacos, Chub Cay in the southern Berrys, and Nassau are about as far as this traffic will reach. Dock space along these routes, and popular anchorages such as Honeymoon Cove in the Biminis, may well be crowded.

MARCH
Easter. Could be in April. Date changes annually.
Exumas (George Town). Annual Cruising Regatta on Exuma.
Long Island (Stella Maris). Out Islands International Game Fish Tournament.

APRIL
Easter. Could be in March. Date changes annually.
Exumas (George Town). Annual Bahamas Family Island Regatta.

MAY
Whit Monday. Date (linked to Easter) changes annually.
Long Island (Salt Pond). Long Island Regatta.

JUNE
Labour Day. First Friday in June.
Goombay Summer Festival. A kind of summertime Junkanoo, the Goombay Summer Festival starts in June but continues through the summer months generating parades, street festivals, and whatever may be decided to whet the appetite of the locals or tempt the tourists.

Eleuthera (Gregory Town). Eleuthera Pineapple Festival.
Grand Bahama. Annual Grand Bahama Sailing Regatta (could be held June–July or in July).

JULY
Independence Day (July 10). Celebrated by a week of events. Parades, fireworks, regattas, and partying above all, Kaliks and Goombay Smashes, mark the remembrance of the ending of 300 years of British rule.
Abacos (Green Turtle Cay). Bahamas Sailing Cup.
Abacos (Marsh Harbour). Regatta Time, with a nine-day series of races starting from Marsh Harbour, Green Turtle Cay, Man-O-War Cay, Great Guana Cay, and Elbow Cay.
Andros (Morgans Bluff). Independence Day Regatta.
Cat Island Regatta, held the last weekend in July.
Exumas Regattas at Black Point and Rolleville.

AUGUST
Emancipation Day (the first Monday in August). Emancipation Day marks the setting free of all slaves in 1834, and is celebrated with a Junkanoo Rushout that starts a 4 a.m. from Fox Hill Village in Nassau, and continues all day.

OCTOBER
Discovery Day (October 12). The date in 1492 when Christopher Columbus made his landfall in the Bahamas. It's still disputed which island was his initial landing, but San Salvador holds the official title at this time. We believe it was Semana Cay. Be that as it may, October 12 is a Public Holiday.
Abaco All Abaco Sailing Regatta from Green Turtle Cay.
Eleuthera North Eleuthera Sailing Regatta (held between Harbour Island and Three-Island Bay).
San Salvador Sailing Regatta.

NOVEMBER
Guy Fawkes Day (November 5). As a curious link with their one-time British overlordship, the Bahamas celebrates Guy Fawkes Day each year. Guy Fawkes, the leader of a "Gun-

Bahamas Tourist Office Summer Boating Flings
In June, July, and August regular Summer Boating Flings take off from Florida for the Bahamas. These are flotillas of small boats (not less than 24 feet LOA or, for the Biminis, a 22-foot minimum is permitted) guided by a lead boat, which set out from the Radisson Bahia Mar Marina in Fort Lauderdale for either the Biminis or Freeport–Port Lucaya in Grand Bahama, and may extend their range to include either the Abacos or the southern Berry Islands. The purpose is to encourage those who might not otherwise dare to cross the Gulf Stream but have always wanted to cruise in the Bahamas.

Departures are scheduled almost weekly through the summer. For information contact the Bahamas Sports and Aviation Center at 800-327-7678 or 305-932-0051.

powder Plot" to blow up the British Houses of Parliament in 1605, failed and was cruelly executed. The anniversary is commemorated in a macabre but traditional form with firework displays and the burning of a Guy Fawkes effigy.

DECEMBER
Christmas Day (December 25) and Boxing Day (December 26) are celebrated throughout the island during December, with tree lightings, concerts with Christmas music under the stars, carol singing, and a Masked Ball, together with a Junkanoo Rehearsal for New Year's Day, on Boxing Day morning.

FURTHER INFORMATION AND FIRM DATES
As this Guide is republished every second year and at the time of going to print for each edition the dates of many Bahamian annual fixtures have not been set, we show the events that normally fall in each calendar month, which gives guidance on the places where you may want to be, or perhaps, if you don't want the crowd scene, places you'll want to avoid! Detailed calendars covering the regattas, fishing tournaments, Summer Boating Flings, and holidays are obtainable from: Bahamas Tourist Board, One Turnberry Place, Suite 809, 19495 Biscayne Boulevard, Aventura, Florida 33180-2321 (Tel: 305-932-0051); Bahamas Out Islands Promotion Board, 1100 Lee Wagener Boulevard, Suite 206, Fort Lauderdale, Florida 33315 (Tel: 954-359-8099); The Bahamas Sports and Aviation Center, 255 Alhambra Circle, Suite 415, Coral Gables, Florida 33314 (Tel: 800-327-7678 or 305-932-0051); Bimini Big Game Fishing Club, 866 Ponce de Leon Boulevard, 2nd Floor, Coral Gables, Florida 33134 (Tel: 800-737-1007 or 809-347-3391).

LOCAL INFORMATION ABOUT SPECIAL EVENTS
Rev. Philip McPhee, Ministry of Youth, Sports and Culture (Tel: 242-394-0445; Fax: 394-5920); Ministry of Tourism, Nassau (Tel: 242-322-7501; Fax: 328-0945); Exuma Tourist Office (Tel: 242-336-2439; Fax: 336-2431; Eleuthera Tourist Office (Tel: 242-332-2124; Fax: 332-2480). For Fishing Tournaments, see our Yellow Pages for each area in the Bahamas.

Those Strange Bahamian Names

JUNKANOO AND GOOMBAY
Have you ever wondered where those oddball names, Junkanoo and Goombay, came from? There are many theories, many explanations. Our preferences are these. The word *Junkanoo* came from Haiti. In French (which is the Haitian language) it was the festival of the *Gens Inconnus,* the "Unknown or Disguised People" from the masks the dancers wore and wear today. *Goombay* seems firmly African. It's a kind of drum, and we've been told, the Bantu word for rhythm.

Part VIII

Appendices

Appendix A
Planning

Appendix B
Waypoint Catalog

Appendix C
Blue Pages Supplement

Shoal water, the Abaco Cays.

Float Plan

Boat Name and Port _____

Year, Type, and Model _____

Radios _____ **Callsign** _____

LOA _____ **Color** _____

Registration # _____ **Flag (if not US)** _____

Engines _____ **Other Means of Propulsion** _____

Port and Date of Departure _____

Destination and Estimated Date and Time of Arrival _____

_____

Route Planned _____

_____

Persons on Board with addresses (note if young children) _____

_____

_____

_____ (continue list as necessary)

Safety Equipment (list flares, smoke, strobes, EPIRB (and type), life raft, dinghy)

_____

_____

_____ (continue list as necessary)

If a 406 MHz EPIRB   **Model** _____

                         Category _____

                         Unique Identifier # _____

Your name, Home Address, and Telephone Number

_____

_____

_____

Signature _____ **Date** _____

Appendix A
Planning

Planning Your Gulf Stream Crossing

What Kind of Boat Do You Have?

If you have a powered craft that can average 12 knots or more, the drift effect of the Gulf Stream is no great concern. A relatively small initial offset, around 10 nm or so, or continual minor on-course adjustments, can take care of it.

If you are slower, you must do your figuring more carefully and ensure that your Departure Port is the right one for you. You don't want to fight the Gulf Stream all the way across; you want to use it to advantage. Let's keep it simple, stage by stage.

STEP 1. WHERE ARE YOU HEADING?

Northern Cruising Grounds
- Abacos
- Port Lucaya–Grand Bahama

Central Cruising Grounds
- Biminis
- Berry Islands
- Nassau
- Eleuthera
- Andros

Southern Cruising Grounds
- Exumas

STEP 2. PICK A LANDFALL

Northern Cruising Grounds
- **Abacos:** Memory Rock (for Walkers Cay, Great Sale Cay, and beyond)
  West End (for Great Sale Cay and beyond)
  Port Lucaya (for the Lucayan Waterway)
- **Grand Bahama:** Port Lucaya

Central Cruising Grounds
- **Biminis:** North Bimini, or Cat Cay
- **Berry Islands, Andros:** North Bimini, or Cat Cay
- **Nassau, Eleuthera:** North Bimini, or Cat Cay

Southern Cruising Grounds
- Treat as Central

STEP 3. CHOOSE YOUR DEPARTURE PORT

For	Depart From
• Memory Rock	Palm Beach
• West End	Palm Beach
• Bimini	Fort Lauderdale or Miami
• Cat Cay (Gun Cay Cut)	Fort Lauderdale or Miami

STEP 4. KNOW YOUR DISTANCE TO RUN

Straight Line Distances
(offsets and close approaches excluded)

• Stuart–Memory Rock	56 nm
• Palm Beach–Memory Rock	49 nm
• Palm Beach–West End	53 nm
• Fort Lauderdale–Bimini	48 nm
• Fort Lauderdale–Gun Cay Cut	52 nm
• Miami–Bimini	42 nm
• Miami–Gun Cay Cut	43 nm

STEP 5. FIGURE OUT THE GULF STREAM EFFECT FOR YOUR CROSSING

- Take the total Distance to Run, and divide it by your Average Speed to find your Passage Time:

$$\text{Palm Beach–West End} = \frac{53 \text{ nm}}{\text{Average Speed 8 knots}} = 6.62 \text{ hours}$$

  For simplicity we reckon the Stream will affect you throughout that passage, flowing from south to north at 2.5 knots.

- Take the Passage Time and multiply it by 2.5. So 6.62 x 2.5 = 16.55. If you set a direct course, the Gulf Stream would carry you 16.55 nm (round it off and say 17 nm) north of your desired landfall.

- So lay off a course for a point 17 nm south of your target landfall, head for that, and let the Gulf Stream take you "off course" and carry you to your destination. All that remains is to figure out when to leave, when you'll make your landfall, and what you plan to do after that.

We reckon to make our landfalls around 1100 when the sun is high in the sky and the underwater colors are easiest to read. With a sailboat your Crossing Time will probably dictate a night passage, and your arrival could well be sometime around first light. Time it so that the rising fireball is not right in your eyes when you're making your close approach, and you should be fine.

The one period you don't want to select is an arrival time after 1600. If anything goes wrong while you're on passage, you may find that you're making your landfall after last light. Unless you really know the waters around your destination, that could be disastrous.

Don't forget that **Float Plan**!

Bahamas and Turks and Caicos Chart List

British Admiralty

BA 398	Freeport Roads/Freeport Harbour
BA 390	Approaches to Freeport
BA 2866	Cape Canaveral to Key West including the Western Part of the Bahama Banks
BA 3907	Passages between Mayaguana Island and Turks and Caicos Islands, including northern approaches to Haiti and Dominican Republic (new chart expected to be published in 2000)
BA 3908	Passages between Turks and Caicos Islands and Dominican Republic (new chart expected to be published in 2000)
BA 3910	Little Bahama Bank including North West Providence Channel
BA 3912	Bahamas, North East Providence Channel and Tongue of the Ocean
BA 3913	Bahamas, Crooked Island Passage and Exuma Sound
BA 3914	Turks and Caicos Islands and Bahamas, Caicos Passage and Mayaguana Passage
BA 1441	Turks and Caicos Islands, Turks Islands
BA 1450	Turks and Caicos Islands, Turks Island Passage and Mouchoir Passage
BA 1452	Nassau/Eastern Approaches to Nassau (new edition due to be published in September 1999)
BA 1489	Bahamas, New Providence Island
BA 1496	The Great Bahama Bank. Sheet I: from Great Isaac to 23° 40' N (outdated).
BA 4400	West Indies
BA 1496*	

Defense Mapping Agency

DMA 400	West Indies
DMA 25720	Monte Cristi to Cabo Francés Viejo
DMA 26190	Windward Passage
DMA 26240	Crooked Island Passage to Punta de Maisi
DMA 26257	Plans in the Bahamas
DMA 26260	Passages between Acklins Island, Haiti, and Caicos Island
DMA 26261	Turks Island Passage and Mouchoir Passage
DMA 26262	Grand Turk Island and Adjacent Cays

DMA 26263	Plans in Southeastern Bahamas. Mayaguana Island, Abraham's Bay, Plana Cays, Hogsty Reef
DMA 26267	Great Inagua and Little Inagua Islands
DMA 26280	Eleuthera Island to Crooked Island Passage
DMA 26284	Cat Island, Rum Cay, and Conception Island
DMA 26286	Elizabeth Harbour and Approaches
DMA 26288	Bird Rock to Mira Por Vos Passage
DMA 26290	Tongue of the Ocean and Exuma Sound
DMA 26300	Little Bahama Bank to Eleuthera Island
DMA 26303	Tongue of the Ocean-Southern Part
DMA 36305	Eleuthera Island & Northern Part of Exuma Sound
DMA 26306	Eleuthera-West Part
DMA 26307	Eleuthera-East Part
DMA 26308	Tongue of the Ocean-Northern Part-Bahama Islands
DMA 26309	Nassau and Approaches
DMA 26320	Northern Part of Straits of Florida and Northwest Providence Channel
DMA 26321	Hope Town Approaches
DMA 26323	Freeport Riding Point and Approaches
DMA 26324	Bimini Islands
DMA 26328	Berry Islands
DMA 27040	Cayo Verde to Cabo Lucretia
DMA 27060	Cayo Lavela to Cayo Verde

Waterproof Charts, Inc (Punta Gorda, Florida)

38	North Bahama Islands
38A	Grand Bahama and the Abacos
38B	Bahama Crossing – Bimini
38C	Central Bahamas
38G	Western Grand Bahama and the Berry Islands
38H	Nassau, Bahamas
120F	Fish/Dive Chart. Bahamas

Wavey Line Publishing Ltd (Turks and Caicos Islands)

TC-001	Turks and Caicos Islands
TC-002	Turks and Caicos Islands. Providenciales

Electronic Charts

British Admiralty	The Bahamas (ARCS portfolio 10 charts)
C-Map NT	The Bahamas & Bimini Islands (NA-B601.03)
C-Map Standard	Bahamas (J129.05)
	Bahamas Islands/North (J135.04)
	Bahamas Islands/South (J136.04)
	Great Bahama Bank to Windward Passage (J146.00)
Laser Plot 84	Western Bahamas and Miami
Laser Plot 85	Eastern Bahamas and Bermuda
Maptech MCP-07	The Bahamas (includes the Turks & Caicos)
Maptech ECK 09	The Bahamas and Bermuda

---

*BA Chart 1496 was surveyed in 1836–1842 and published in 1844. The last new edition was published in July 1907. It has been updated many times during its currency, but has remained, essentially, a chart of the last century. It's fascinating for a "hand-drawn" feel and a wealth of detailed observation. It is the Bahamas as they were seen almost 200 years ago, a third of the way back in time to that first Columbus voyage. Andros would not have appeared very different to him. That is, if he went that way. You may, or may not, agree with Arne Molander.

Routes and Distances

In general the distances shown are rounded up to a whole nautical mile, and exclude the initial approach to a route start point and the final approach to a destination. The actual distance to run may be 1 nm or more greater than the figures given. On longer passages the distance logged may well be increased by cross track error.

Part I. Gulf Stream Crossing

Stuart	Memory Rock North	55 nm
	Memory Rock South	57 nm
	Sandy Cay	60 nm
	West End	66 nm
	Port Lucaya	93 nm
	Walkers Cay	96 nm
	Great Sale Cay	106 nm
Palm Beach	Memory Rock North	49 nm
	Memory Rock South	49 nm
	Sandy Cay	49 nm
	West End	53 nm
	Port Lucaya	77 nm
	Walkers Cay	90 nm
	Great Sale Cay	98 nm
Fort Lauderdale	Bimini	48 nm
	Gun Cay Cut	52 nm
	West End	69 nm
	Port Lucaya	83 nm
	Chub Cay	130 nm
Miami	Bimini	42 nm
	Gun Cay Cut	43 nm
	Chub Cay	120 nm

Part II. Northern Cruising Grounds

Little Bahama Bank

West End	Indian Cay Passage	2 nm
	Sandy Cay area	9 nm
	Memory Rock South	15 nm
	Freeport	18 nm
	Memory Rock North	20 mn
	Mangrove Cay	28 nm
	Port Lucaya	28 nm
	Walkers Cay	45 nm
	Great Sale Cay	46 nm
	Palm Beach, Florida	53 nm
	Stuart, Florida	66 nm
	Fort Lauderdale, Florida	69 nm
	Allans-Pensacola Cay	82 nm
	Green Turtle Cay	106 nm
Indian Cay Passage	Length overall	3.6 nm
Indian Cay Passage	West End	2 nm
	Mangrove Cay	22 nm
Sandy Cay	Mangrove Cay	27 nm
Memory Rock South	Mangrove Cay	27 nm
	Walkers Cay	42 nm
	Great Sale Cay	48 nm
	Palm Beach, Florida	49 nm
	Stuart, Florida	57 nm

Memory Rock North	Mangrove Cay	28 nm
	Walkers Cay	41 nm
	Great Sale Cay	49 nm
	Palm Beach, Florida	49 nm
	Stuart, Florida	55 nm
Mangrove Cay	Cormorant Point	13 nm
	Dover Sound Channel	20 nm
	Great Sale Cay	21 nm
Great Sale Cay	Carters Cay	19 nm
	Walkers Cay	20 nm
	Hawksbill Cays (Fox Town)	29 nm
	Allans-Pensacola	36 nm
	Moraine Cay	37 nm
	Crab Cay	41 nm
	Green Turtle Cay	57 nm
Little Sale Cay	Double Breasted Cay	8 nm
	Carters Cay	14 nm
	Walkers Cay	15 nm
	Hawksbill Cays (Fox Town)	30 nm
	Allans-Pensacola Cay	35 nm
	West End	46 nm
Carters Cay	Little Sale Cay	14 nm
	Hawksbill Cays (Fox Town)	15 nm
	Moraine Cay	18 nm
Moraine Cay	Allans-Pensacola Cay	4 nm
	Carters Cay	18 nm
Allans-Pensacola Cay	Moraine Cay	4 nm
	Crab Cay	5 nm
	Hawksbill Cays (Fox Town)	7 nm
	Great Sale Cay	36 nm
Hawksbill Cays (Fox Town)	Allans-Pensacola	7 nm
	Crab Cay	12 nm
	Carters Cay	15 nm
	Great Sale Cay	29 nm
Crab Cay (Angel Fish)	Green Turtle Cay	17 nm

Abacos

Walkers Cay	Grand Cays	10 nm (shoal 4 nm)
	Little Sale Cay	15 nm
	Great Sale Cay	20 nm
	Memory Rock North	41 nm
	West End	45 nm
	Palm Beach, Florida	90 nm
	Stuart, Florida	96 nm
Grand Cays	Double Breasted Cay	8 nm
	Walkers Cay	10 nm (shoal 4 nm)
Double Breasted Cay	Grand Cays	8 nm
	Little Sale Cay	8 nm
Great Sale Cay	Carters Cay	19 nm
	Walkers Cay	20 nm
	Hawksbill Cays (Fox Town)	29 nm
	Allans-Pensacola	36 nm
	Moraine Cay	37 nm
	Crab Cay	41 nm
	Green Turtle Cay	57 nm
Little Sale Cay	Double Breasted Cay	8 nm
	Carters Cay	14 nm
	Walkers Cay	15 nm
	Hawksbill (Fox Town)	30 nm
	Allans-Pensacola Cay	35 nm
	West End	46 nm

Carters Cay	Little Sale Cay	14 nm
	Hawksbill Cays (Fox Town)	15 nm
	Moraine Cay	18 nm
Moraine Cay	Allans-Pensacola Cay	4 nm
	Carters Cay	18 nm
Allans-Pensacola Cay	Moraine Cay	4 nm
	Crab Cay	5 nm
Hawksbill Cays (Fox Town)	Allans-Pensacola Cay	7 nm
	Spanish Cay	9 nm
	Crab Cay	12 nm
	Coopers Town	14 nm
	Carters Cay	15 nm
	Green Turtle Cay	23 nm
	Great Sale Cay	29 nm
Crab Cay (Angel Fish)	Spanish Cay	4 nm
	Coopers Town	7 nm
	Green Turtle Cay	17 nm
Spanish Cay	Powell Cay	4 nm
	Allans-Pensacola Cay	9 nm
	Coopers Town	6 nm
Coopers Town	Powell Cay	3 nm
	Spanish Cay	6 nm
	Green Turtle Cay	12 nm
Powell Cay	Coopers Town	3 nm
	Spanish Cay	4 nm
	Manjack Cay	10 nm
Manjack Cay	Green Turtle Cay	3 nm
	Powell Cay	10 nm
Green Turtle Cay	Manjack Cay	3 nm
	Whale Cay Passage	5 nm
	Great Guana Cay*	12 nm
	Treasure Cay*	14 nm
Treasure Cay	Marsh Harbour	12 nm
	Green Turtle Cay*	14 nm
	Man-O-War Cay	14 nm
	Hope Town	18 nm

Whale Cay Passage	Length overall	6.8 nm
Whale Cay Passage	Great Guana Cay	4 nm
	Green Turtle Cay	5 nm
Great Guana Cay	Whale Cay Passage	4 nm
	Man-O-War Cay	8 nm
	Green Turtle Cay*	12 nm
Man-O-War Cay	Hope Town	3 nm
	Marsh Harbour	5 nm
	Great Guana Cay	8 nm
Hope Town	White Sound (Elbow Cay)	3 nm
	Man-O-War Cay	3 nm
	Marsh Harbour	6 nm
	Little Harbour	15 nm
Marsh Harbour	Man-O-War Cay	5 nm
	Hope Town	6 nm
	Treasure Cay	12 nm
	Little Harbour	14 nm
White Sound (Elbow Cay)	Hope Town	3 nm
	Little Harbour	12 nm

Little Harbour	Cherokee Sound	10 nm
	White Sound (Elbow Cay)	12 nm
	Marsh Harbour	14 nm
	Hope Town	15 nm
	Hole-in-the-Wall	33 nm
	Bridge Point North, Eleuthera	48 nm
	Egg Island NW, Eleuthera	50 nm
	Nassau	78 nm
Cherokee Sound	Little Harbour	10 nm
Hole-in-the-Wall	Rocky Point	5 nm
	Little Harbour	33 nm
	Great Stirrup Cay, Berrys	40 nm

Grand Bahama Island

West End	Indian Cay Passage	2 nm
	Sandy Cay area	9 nm
	Memory Rock South	15 nm
	Freeport	18 nm
	Memory Rock North	20 nm
	Mangrove Cay	28 nm
	Port Lucaya	28 nm
	Walkers Cay	45 nm
	Great Sale Cay	46 nm
	Palm Beach, Florida	53 nm
	Stuart, Florida	66 nm
	Fort Lauderdale, Florida	69 nm
	Allans-Pensacola Cay	82 nm
	Green Turtle Cay	106 nm
Port Lucaya	Lucayan Waterway	5 nm
	West End	28 nm
	Little Stirrup Cay, Berrys	55 nm
	Allans-Pensacola Cay**	65 nm
	Palm Beach, Florida	77 nm
	Great Sale Cay**	81 nm
	Fort Lauderdale, Florida	83 nm
	Green Turtle Cay**	90 nm
	Stuart, Florida	93 nm
	Walkers Cay**	95 nm
	Nassau	116 nm

Grand Lucayan Waterway	Length overall	7.4 nm
Port Lucaya	South Entrance	4.5 nm
South Entrance	Casuarina Bridge	2.3 nm
Casuarina Bridge	Spoil Hill Narrows	1.5 nm
Spoil Hill Narrows	Dover Sound East	2.5 nm
Dover Channel East	Dover Channel West	0.5 nm
Dover Channel West	Cormorant Point	7 nm
Cormorant Point	Mangrove Cay	13 nm

Part III. Central Cruising Grounds

Biminis & Great Bahama Bank

Bimini	Gun Cay Cut	9 nm
	South Riding Rock	23 nm
	Miami, Florida	42 nm
	Fort Lauderdale, Florida	48 nm
	Chub Cay, Berrys	88 nm
	Nassau	121 nm
Gun Cay Cut	North Cat Cay	3 nm
	Bimini	9 nm
	Miami, Florida	43 nm

*via Whale Cay Passage

**via Lucayan Waterway

	Fort Lauderdale, Florida	52 nm
	NW Channel Light	64 nm
	Chub Cay, Berrys	80 nm
	Nassau	113 nm
North Cat Cay	NW Channel Light	62 nm
South Riding Rock	NW Channel Light	56 nm
NW Channel Light	Chub Cay, Berrys	15 nm
	Nassau	50 nm

Berry Islands

Little Stirrup Cay	Great Stirrup Cay	5 nm
	Great Harbour Marina	8 nm
	Port Lucaya	55 nm
Great Stirrup Cay	White Cay Anchorage	16 nm
	Little Harbour	20 nm
	Chub Cay	40 nm
	Hole-in-the-Wall, Abacos	40 nm
	Little Harbour, Abacos	73 nm
White Cay Anchorage	Little Harbour	4 nm
	Great Stirrup Cay	16 nm
Little Harbour	White Cay Anchorage	4 nm
	Bond-Whale Anchorage	8 nm
	Great Stirrup Cay	20 nm
	Chub Cay	23 nm
Bond-Whale Anchorage	Little Harbour	8 nm
	Bird Cay Anchorage	11 nm
	Chub Cay	15 nm
	Great Stirrup Cay	28 nm
Bird Cay Anchorage	Chub Cay	4 nm
	Bond-Whale Anchorage	11 nm
	Great Stirrup Cay	39 nm
Chub Cay	Bird Cay Anchorage	4 nm
	Morgans Bluff, Andros	15 nm
	NW Channel Light	15 nm
	Nassau	35 nm
	Great Stirrup Cay	40 nm
	Fresh Creek, Andros	45 nm
	Gun Cay Cut, Biminis	80 nm
	Spanish Wells, Eleuthera	80 nm

Nassau

Nassau	Coral Harbour	21 nm
	Morgans Bluff, Andros	33 nm
	Fresh Creek, Andros	33 nm
	Chub Cay, Berrys	35 nm
	Current Cut West, Eleuthera	36 nm
	Allans Cay, Exumas	38 nm
	Highborne Cay, Exumas	39 nm
	Spanish Wells, Eleuthera	43 nm
	NW Channel Light	50 nm
	Gun Cay Cut, Biminis	113 nm
	Port Lucaya	116 nm
	Bimini	121 nm

Inshore Route Nassau– North Eleuthera	Length overall	40 nm
Nassau Harbour East	Chub Rock	6 nm

Chub Rock	Douglas Channel	10 nm
Douglas Channel	Samphire Cays	6 nm
Samphire Cays	Fleeming Channel	6 nm
Fleeming Channel	Little Egg Island, Eleuthera	12 nm

Eleuthera

Little Egg Island	Egg Island NW	5 nm
	Royal Island	5 nm
	Spanish Wells	11 nm
	Fleeming Channel	12 nm
	Little Harbour, Abacos	54 nm
Royal Island	Little Egg Island	5 nm
	Spanish Wells	6 nm
Spanish Wells	Royal Island	5 nm
	Current Cut	11 nm
	Little Egg Island	11 nm
	Harbour Island (Dunmore Town)††	14 nm
	Hatchet Bay†	28 nm
	Governor's Harbour†	43 nm
	Nassau	43 nm

Devil's Backbone Passage	Length overall	10 nm
Harbour Is (Dunmore Town)	Spanish Wells††	14 nm
Current Cut	Length overall	2 nm
Current Cut	Spanish Wells	11 nm
	Hatchet Bay	16 nm
	Nassau	36 nm
Hatchet Bay	Governor's Harbour	15 nm
	Spanish Wells†	28 nm
Governor's Harbour	Tarpum Bay	12 nm
	Hatchet Bay	15 nm
	Cape Eleuthera	28 nm
Tarpum Bay	Davis Channel East	8 nm
	Governor's Harbour	12 nm
Davis Channel	Length overall	5 nm
Davis Channel East	Davis Channel West	5 nm
	Cape Eleuthera	8 nm
Davis Channel West	Cape Eleuthera	3 nm
	Davis Channel East	5 nm
Cape Eleuthera	Davis Harbour	9 nm
	South Eleuthera	18 nm
	Highborne Cut, Exumas	25 nm
	Little San Salvador	27 nm
	Governor's Harbour	28 nm
Davis Harbour	Cape Eleuthera	9 nm
	South Eleuthera	12 nm
	Little San Salvador	22 nm
	Conch Cut, Exumas	29 nm
South Eleuthera	Little San Salvador	10 nm
	Cape Eleuthera	18 nm
	Orange Creek, Cat Island	27 nm
	Hawk's Nest, Cat Island	41 nm

North Andros

Morgans Bluff	Chub Cay, Berrys	15 nm
	Fresh Creek	31 nm
	Nassau	33 nm

†via Current Cut   ††via Devil's Backbone Passage

Fresh Creek	Morgans Bluff	31 nm
	Nassau	33 nm
	Chub Cay, Berrys	45 nm
	Allans Cay, Exumas	50 nm
	Conch Cut, Exumas	76 nm
	Staniel Cay, Exumas	81 nm

Part IV. Southern Cruising Grounds

Exuma Cays

All routes are Exuma Banks passages unless noted as Exuma Sound or transits to destinations outside the Exuma chain

Allan's Cay	Highborne Cay	5 nm
	Nassau	38 nm
	Fresh Creek, Andros	50 nm
Highborne Cay	Allan's Cay	5 nm
	Normans Cay	11 nm
	Cape Eleuthera	25 nm
	Nassau	39 nm
Normans Cay	Highborne Cay	11 nm
	Warderick Wells	20 nm
Warderick Wells	Conch Cut	6 nm
	Sampson Cay	14 nm
	Normans Cay	20 nm
Conch Cut	Warderick Wells	6 nm
	Sampson Cay	7 nm
	Staniel Cay	12 nm
	Davis Harbour, Eleuthera	29 nm
	Cape Eleuthera	35 nm
	George Town (Exuma Sound)	58 nm
	Fresh Creek, Andros	76 nm
Sampson Cay	Staniel Cay	5 nm
	Conch Cut	7 nm
Staniel Cay	Sampson Cay	5 nm
	Dotham Cut	9 nm
	Fresh Creek, Andros	81 nm
Dotham Cut	Black Point (Great Guana)	2 nm
	Staniel Cay	9 nm
	Farmer's Cut	10 nm
	George Town (Exuma Sound)	53 nm
Black Point (Great Guana)	Dotham Cut	2 nm
	Farmer's Cut	10 nm
Farmer's Cut	Galliott Cut	4 nm
	Black Point (Great Guana)	10 nm
	George Town (Exuma Sound)	37 nm
	Hawk's Nest, Cat Island	42 nm
Galliott Cut	Cave Cut	2 nm
	Farmer's Cut	4 nm
	George Town (Exuma Sound)	40 nm
Cave Cut	Galliott Cut	2 nm
	Rudder Cut	3 nm
	George Town (Exuma Sound)	38 nm
Rudder Cut	Cave Cut	3 nm
	Adderley Cut	8 nm
	George Town (Exuma Sound)	35 nm

Adderley Cut	Rat Cay Cut	6 nm
	Rudder Cut	8 nm
	George Town (Exuma Sound)	26 nm
Rat Cay Cut	Adderley Cut	6 nm
	George Town (Exuma Sound)	20 nm

Great Exuma Island

George Town	Rat Cay Cut (Exuma Sound)	20 nm
	Calabash Bay, Long Island	20 nm
	Cape Santa Maria, Long Island	23 nm
	Stella Maris, Long Island	26 nm
	Adderley Cut (Exuma Sound)	26 nm
	Rudder Cut (Exuma Sound)	35 nm
	Hawk's Nest, Cat Island	37 nm
	Conception Island	37 nm
	Farmer's Cut (Exuma Sound)	37 nm
	Cave Cut (Exuma Sound)	38 nm
	Galliott Cut (Exuma Sound)	40 nm
	Salt Pond, Long Island	42 nm
	Rum Cay	48 nm
	Dotham Cut (Exuma Sound)	53 nm
	Conch Cut (Exuma Sound)	58 nm
	Clarence Town, Long Island	63 nm
	San Salvador	80 nm

The distance to run to Kidd Cove (that is George Town itself) from either entrance of George Town Harbour can be taken as ± 4 nm.

Little San Salvador

Little San Salvador	South Eleuthera	10 nm
	Orange Creek, Cat Island	17 nm
	Davis Harbour, Eleuthera	22 nm
	Cape Eleuthera	27 nm
	The Bight, Cat Island	30 nm
	Smith Bay, Cat Island	30 nm
	Hawk's Nest, Cat Island	34 nm
	Conch Cut, Exumas	35 nm

Cat Island

Orange Creek	Bennett's Harbour	4 nm
	Little San Salvador	17 nm
	South Eleuthera	27 nm
Bennett's Harbour	Orange Creek	4 nm
	Smith Bay	18 nm
Smith Bay	Fernandez Bay	1 nm
	The Bight	7 nm
	Hawk's Nest	14 nm
	Little San Salvador	30 nm
Fernandez Bay	Smith Bay	1 nm
	The Bight	6 nm
The Bight	Fernandez Bay	6 nm
	Hawk's Nest	10 nm
Hawk's Nest	The Bight	10 nm
	Smith Bay	14 nm
	Conception Island	32 nm
	George Town, Exuma	37 nm
	San Salvador	58 nm

Conception Island

Conception Island	Rum Cay	14 nm
	Cape Santa Maria, Long Island	14 nm
	Hawk's Nest, Cat Island	32 nm
	San Salvador	35 nm
	George Town, Exuma	37 nm

Rum Cay

Rum Cay	Conception Island	14 nm
	Cape Santa Maria, Long Island	28 nm
	San Salvador	30 nm
	Clarence Town, Long Island	31 nm
	George Town, Exuma	48 nm

San Salvador

San Salvador	Rum Cay	30 nm
	Conception Island	35 nm
	Hawk's Nest, Cat island	58 nm
	Clarence Town, Long Island	60 nm
	George Town, Exuma	80 nm

Long Island

Cape Santa Maria	Calabash Bay	4 nm
	Stella Maris	10 nm
	Conception Island	14 nm
	George Town, Exuma	23 nm
	Salt Pond	26 nm
	Rum Cay	28 nm
	Clarence Town	40 nm

West Coast Long Island

Calabash Bay	Cape Santa Maria	4 nm
	Stella Maris	6 nm
	Salt Pond	22 nm
Stella Maris	Calabash Bay	6 nm
	Salt Pond	16 nm
	George Town, Exuma	26 nm
Salt Pond	Stella Maris	16 nm
	George Town, Exuma	42 nm

East Coast Long Island

Clarence Town	Little Harbour	11 nm
	Rum Cay	31 nm
	Bird Rock, Crooked Island	35 nm
	Cape Santa Maria	40 nm
	San Salvador	60 nm
	George Town, Exuma	63 nm

Part V. Far Horizons

The Eastern Route South
George Town to Providenciales, Turks & Caicos Islands
DIRECT ROUTE

George Town Harb. East	Cape Santa Maria, Long Island	22 nm
Cape Santa Maria	Santa Maria East, Long Island	3 nm
Santa Maria East	Clarence Town, Long Island	40 nm
Clarence Town	Bird Rock, Crooked Island	35 nm

DIVERSION TO CROOKED ISLAND WEST COAST

Bird Rock	Landrail Point	5 nm
Landrail Point	French Wells	8 nm
French Wells	Bird Rock	13 nm

Diversion Distance Run:	Bird Rock–Bird Rock	26 nm

ROUTE SWITCH OPTION TO THE WESTERN ROUTE

French Wells	Long Cay	11 nm

[Join Western Route South to the Windward Passage]

DIRECT ROUTE

Bird Rock	Acklins Northeast	38 nm
Acklins NE	Plana Cays West	10 nm
Plana Cays West	Plana Cays South	7 nm
Plana Cays South	Mayaguana West	39 nm
George Town East	Mayaguana West	194 nm
Mayaguana West	Providenciales North	47 nm
	Sandbore Approach	47 nm
Mayaguana West	Mayaguana East	6 nm
Mayaguana East	Providenciales North	44 nm
	Sandbore Approach	45 nm
George Town East	Turks & Caicos Approaches	245 nm

The Western Route South
George Town or Harvey Cay to the Windward Passage

START FROM GEORGE TOWN

George Town Harb. East	Cape Santa Maria	22 nm
Cape Santa Maria	Santa Maria East	3 nm
Santa Maria East	Clarence Town	40 nm
Clarence Town	Little Harbour	11 nm
Little Harbour	Long Island, South Pt East	10 nm
Long Island, South Pt East	Mira Por Vos Passage	44 nm
George Town	Mira Por Vos Passage	130 nm

START FROM HARVEY CAY

Harvey Cay	Barracouta Sand	27 nm
Barracouta Sand	Hawksbill Rock	23 nm
Hawksbill Rock	Nuevitas Rocks	46 nm
Nuevitas Rocks	Mira Por Vos Passage	81 nm
Harvey Cay	Mira Por Vos Passage	177 nm

(For overall time and space calculations:
Harvey Cay–George Town 61 nm)

DIVERSION TO LONG CAY AND SOUTH EAST
ACKLINS ISLAND (SALINA POINT)

Nuevitas Rocks	Long Island South Pt West	30 nm
Long Island South Pt West	Long Cay	34 nm
Long Cay	Salina Point (Jamaica Bay)	20 nm
Salina Point (Jamaica Bay)	Mira Por Vos Passage	10 nm
Additional Distance Run to Mira Por Vos Passage		13 nm

DIRECT ROUTE

Mira Por Vos	Windward Passage North	102 nm
George Town East	Windward Passage North Approach	232 nm
Harvey Cay	Windward Passage North Approach	279 nm

OPTION SOUTH OF THE MIRA POR VOS PASSAGE

Divert to Hogsty Reef and Great Inagua add	10 nm

WARNING

The Bank Route Passage south from Harvey Cay to Nuevitas Rocks is subject to changing sand and the effects of hurricanes, as well as severe storms. It is in no way a guaranteed passage. If you elect to go this way, you are exploring. Even if you prove a viable route, it may not remain valid after your departure from the area.

Part VI. Turks and Caicos

Northwestern Approaches

Providenciales North	Tiki Huts Anchorage	6 nm
	Sellars Cut Approach	10 nm
	Leeward Cut Approach	10 nm
	Sandbore Approach	12 nm
	Mayaguana East	44 nm
	Mayaguana West	47 nm
	Mira Por Vos Passage	117 nm
Tiki Huts Anchorage	Providenciales North	6 nm
	Sandbore Approach	9 nm
Sandbore Approach	Sandbore Channel West	2 nm
	Tiki Huts Anchorage	9 nm
	Providenciales North	12 nm
	Mayaguana East	45 nm
	Mayaguana West	47 nm
	Mira Por Vos Passage	110 nm

Sandbore Channel	Length overall	2.78 nm
Sandbore Channel West	Sandbore Channel East	3 nm

Providenciales North Coast

Providenciales North	Sellars Cut Approach	10 nm
	Leeward Cut Approach	10 nm
Sellars Cut Approach	Leeward Cut Approach	3 nm
	Providenciales North	10 nm

Leeward Cut Approach	Sellars Cut Approach	3 nm
	Providenciales North	10 nm

Caicos Bank

Sandbore Channel East	Sandbore Channel West	3 nm
	Sapodilla Bay Approach	7 nm
Sapodilla Bay Approach	South Dock Approach	1 nm
	Sandbore Channel East	7 nm
South Dock Approach	Sapodilla Bay Approach	1 nm
	Five Cays	1 nm
	Caicos Mid-Bank Channel	14 nm
	French Cay	15 nm
Five Cays	South Dock Approach	1 nm
	South Side Marina Approach	2 nm
French Cay	South Dock Approach	15 nm
	Luperón, DR	120 nm
South Side Marina	Five Cays	2 nm
	Caicos Shipyard	4 nm
Caicos Shipyard	Five Cays	4 nm
Caicos Mid-Bank Channel	South Dock Approach	14 nm
	Fish Cay Channel	30 nm
Fish Cay Channel	South Caicos	6 nm
	Sand Cay	24 nm
	Caicos Mid-Bank Channel	30 nm

Turks Island Passage And Turks Bank

South Caicos	Fish Cay Channel	6 nm
	Grand Turk	21 nm
Grand Turk	Sand Cay	18 nm
	South Caicos	21 nm
Sand Cay	Grand Turk	18 nm
	Fish Cay Channel	24 nm
	Luperón, DR	90 nm
	Mona Passage	270 nm
	San Juan, PR	360 nm
	St Thomas, USVI	390 nm

Appendix B
Waypoint Catalog

The waypoints we give in this Guide are shown in Degrees and Minutes north of the Equator (26° 43'), and west of Greenwich (079° 20'), followed by both Seconds (30"), and Thousandths of a Minute (500), separated by an oblique stroke (30"/500). That Minute, remember, is 1 nautical mile (1.15 Statute Miles or 6,078 feet). The two different systems of showing final values are just different ways of carving up that final fractional Minute.

We all work in Degrees and Minutes. When we get to that last figure, you may work in Seconds. Many charts are still calibrated that way. Or you may have followed the trend and gone to Thousands (500), or, most probably, Hundreds (50), the first two figures of the Thousands value. You must take care in entering waypoints that the list you import matches the default setting of your GPS, or matches your chosen setting if your GPS offers you both systems. If you're working in Hundreds don't confuse Seconds and Hundreds. The fail-safe indicator that the final two figures in a list of waypoints are in Hundreds is when values above 59 occur.

If you do chartwork in the old fashioned way, use Seconds. If you are primarily electronic dependent, go for Thousands or Hundreds. What about accuracy? Here's how it pans out:

1 Second	101 feet
1 Hundredth	60 feet
1 Thousandth	6 feet

We reckon Thousands are fine for land surveying, but no-one one can shave it that close at sea. Sixty feet (one boat length? two boat lengths?) is as close as we want to call it. The Seconds value rates "as close as you could call it" in days gone by. Even then, we've lived with that one too. What's 100 feet? About 30 yards? Again, that's as close as we want to take whatever, in navigational terms, comes our way. The choice is yours.

Our navigational waypoints are intended to help you set your routes. Sometimes a waypoint may appear to be set unnecessarily far off the apparent course. If this strikes you as strange, look forward or back along our suggested track. What we've tried to do is simplify navigation by reducing waypoints to a minimum, in other words going for slightly longer single legs rather than using a whole clutch of waypoints and short legs, with endless changes of heading, to work round No-Go areas.

You're free, we need hardly say, to write your own route plans. We hope you do, and if something seems blindingly obvious that we don't seem to have thought about, will you let us know? And if typos have crept in to our waypoints, despite our checking and rechecking, for sometimes the computer has a mindset of its own, will you let us know?

Part I: Florida Departure/Arrival Ports
East Coast

Stuart	LUCIE	27° 10' 00"/000 N	080° 08' 00"/000 W
Jupiter Inlet	JUPTR	26° 56' 30"/500 N	080° 03' 15"/250 W
Palm Beach	PPALM	26° 46' 00"/000 N	080° 00' 00"/000 W
Fort Lauderdale	LDALE	26° 05' 30"/500 N	080° 05' 15"/250 W
Miami	MIAMI	25° 46' 00"/000 N	080° 05' 00"/000 W

Part II: Northern Cruising Grounds
The Little Bahama Bank
ENTRY POINTS FROM FLORIDA

Memory Rock North	MEMRN	26° 59' 15"/250 N	079° 08' 00"/000 W
Memory Rock Light	MEMRK	26° 57' 00"/000 N	079° 07' 00"/000 W
Memory Rock South	MEMRS	26° 55' 00"/000 N	079° 07' 00"/000 W
Sandy Cay	SANDY	26° 49' 30"/500 N	079° 05' 30"/500 W
West End	WESTW	26° 42' 00"/000 N	079° 01' 00"/000 W

INDIAN CAY PASSAGE

ICP West (Ocean side)	INDCW	26° 43' 00"/000 N	079° 00' 26"/433 W
ICP Pass	INDCP	26° 43' 10"/166 N	079° 00' 15"/250 W
ICP 2nd Mark	INDC2	26° 43' 42"/698 N	078° 59' 46"/773 W
ICP 3rd Mark	INDC3	26° 44' 45"/750 N	078° 59' 10"/166 W
ICP Barracuda Shoal	INDCB	26° 45' 51"/847 N	078° 58' 00"/000 W

LITTLE BAHAMA BANK TRANSIT WAYPOINTS

Mangrove Cay	MANGR	26° 57' 00"/000 N	078° 37' 00"/000 W
Cormorant Point Marker	CMTPM	26° 44' 38"/631 N	078° 40' 49"/812 W
Triangle Rocks	TRIRK	27° 11' 00"/000 N	078° 25' 00"/000 W
Sale Cay West	SALEW	27° 04' 00"/000 N	078° 14' 30"/500 W
Sale Cay North	SALEN	27° 03' 22"/375 N	078° 11' 10"/167 W
Great Sale Cay	GSALE	26° 58' 45"/750 N	078° 14' 30"/500 W
Great Sale Anchorage	GSANC	26° 59' 52"/867 N	078° 12' 54"/900 W
Sale Cay South	SALES	26° 52' 49"/828 N	078° 14' 30"/500 W
Mid-Carters	MCRTR	27° 03' 00"/000 N	078° 01' 00"/000 W
South Carters Cay	SCRTR	27° 00' 00"/000 N	078° 01' 00"/000 W
Fish Cays	FISHC	27° 01' 19"/324 N	077° 49' 00"/000 W
Veteran Rock	VETRK	26° 55' 45"/750 N	077° 52' 16"/275 W
Hawksbill Cays	HAWKB	26° 56' 48"/805 N	077° 48' 30"/500 W
Center of the World Rock	CNWLD	26° 56' 05"/091 N	077° 41' 40"/671 W

The Abacos
PRINCIPAL OCEAN PASSES

Walkers Cay Channel	WLKCN	27° 19' 05"/086 N	078° 29' 42"/699 W
	WLKCS	27° 13' 48"/795 N	078° 29' 10"/175 W
Walkers-Gully Rocks–Seal Cay Channel			
	SELCN	27° 16' 14"/239 N	078° 21' 35"/582 W
	GLRKS	27° 15' 18"/309 N	078° 23' 25"/423 W
Seal Cay Channel	SELCN	27° 16' 14"/239 N	078° 21' 35"/582 W
	SELCS	27° 15' 20"/341 N	078° 21' 45"/758 W
Moraine Cay Channel	MORCN	27° 03' 53"/886 N	077° 44' 49"/824 W
	MORCS	27° 02' 06"/109 N	077° 44' 49"/824 W
Powell Cay Channel	PWLCE	26° 56' 22"/365 N	077° 28' 42"/699 W
	PWLCW	26° 55' 53"/889 N	077° 30' 45"/759 W
Nunjack Channel	NUNCN	26° 52' 52"/864 N	077° 23' 06"/096 W
	NUNCS	26° 50' 52"/877 N	077° 24' 22"/376 W
Whale Cay Passage 1	WHLP1	26° 42' 30"/500 N	077° 17' 00"/000 W
Whale Cay Passage 2	WHLP2	26° 43' 30"/500 N	077° 14' 15"/250 W
Whale Cay Passage 3	WHLP3	26° 42' 30"/500 N	077° 12' 25"/417 W
Whale Cay Passage 4	WHLP4	26° 42' 15"/250 N	077° 12' 10"/166 W
First Deep Channel Marker	DMKR1	26° 42' 00"/000 N	077° 12' 00"/000 W
Second Pair of Markers	DMKR2	26° 41' 52"/866 N	077° 11' 53"/883 W
Man-O-War Channel North	MWCHN	26° 37' 50"/845 N	077° 01' 16"/273 W
Man-O-War Channel South	MWCHS	26° 36' 49"/815 N	077° 01' 55"/928 W
North Bar West	NBARW	26° 23' 37"/615 N	076° 59' 10"/174 W
North Bar Channel	NBRCH	26° 23' 23"/391 N	076° 58' 23"/379 W

The final figures in each waypoint show seconds (00") and thousands (000) of a minute.

North Bar Channel East	NBARE	26° 22' 55"/929 N	076° 56' 51"/850 W
Little Harbour North	LHRBN	26° 20' 26"/432 N	076° 59' 40"/676 W
Little Harbour Bar Pass	LHRBP	26° 19' 47"/793 N	076° 59' 19"/327 W
Little Harbour Bar East	LHRBE	26° 18' 45"/747 N	076° 58' 45"/754 W

The Northern Abacos

Walkers Cay Channel	WLKCN	27° 19' 05"/086 N	078° 29' 42"/699 W
	WLKCS	27° 13' 48"/795 N	078° 29' 10"/175 W
Walkers-Gully Rocks – Seal Cay Channel			
	SELCN	27° 16' 14"/239 N	078° 21' 35"/582 W
	GLRKS	27° 15' 18"/309 N	078° 23' 25"/423 W
Seal Cay Channel	SELCN	27° 16' 14"/239 N	078° 21' 35"/582 W
	SELCS	27° 15' 20"/341 N	078° 21' 45"/758 W
Walkers Cay Approach	WLKRA	27° 12' 55"/913 N	078° 25' 27"/451 W
Walkers Cay	WLKRS	27° 14' 00"/000 N	078° 24' 09"/148 W
Grand Cays	GRAND	27° 12' 00"/000 N	078° 19' 30"/500 W
Grand Cays Anchorage	GCANC	27° 13' 10"/166 N	078° 19' 18"/299 W
Double Breasted Cays	DBRST	27° 11' 00"/000 N	078° 16' 30"/500 W
Mid- Carters	MCRTR	27° 03' 00"/000 N	078° 01' 00"/000 W
Carters Cay	CRTRS	27° 04' 00"/000 N	078° 01' 00"/000 W
Carters Anchorage	CTANC	27° 05' 03"/050 N	078° 00' 07"/116 W
South Carters Cay	SCRTR	27° 00' 00"/000 N	078° 01' 00"/000 W
Fish Cays	FISHC	27° 01' 19"/324 N	077° 49' 00"/000 W
Moraine Cay Channel	MORCN	27° 03' 53"/886 N	077° 44' 49"/824 W
	MORCS	27° 02' 06"/109 N	077° 44' 49"/824 W
Moraine Cay Approach	MORAP	27° 01' 02"/043 N	077° 46' 07"/123 W
Moraine Cay	MORAI	27° 02' 06"/108 N	077° 46' 07"/123 W
Allans-Pensacola Cay	ALPEN	26° 59' 15"/250 N	077° 42' 15"/250 W

The Central Abacos North of Whale Cay Passage

Crab Cay	CRABC	26° 56' 00"/000 N	077° 36' 00"/000 W
Spanish Cay	SPNSH	26° 56' 30"/500 N	077° 32' 15"/250 W
Powell Cay Channel	PWLCE	26° 56' 22"/365 N	077° 28' 42"/699 W
	PWLCW	26° 55' 53"/889 N	077° 30' 45"/759 W
Powell Cay	PWELL	26° 54' 19"/317 N	077° 29' 05"/083 W
Coopers Town	CPSTN	26° 53' 00"/000 N	077° 30' 00"/000 W
Ambergris Cay Warn. Stake	AMSTK	26° 51' 35"/583 N	077° 25' 50"/833 W
Nunjack Channel	NUNCN	26° 52' 52"/864 N	077° 23' 06"/096 W
	NUNCS	26° 50' 52"/877 N	077° 24' 22"/376 W
Manjack-Crab Cay Anchorage	MANCR	26° 49' 03"/050 N	077° 21' 47"/783 W
Green Turtle North	GTNTH	26° 47' 00"/000 N	077° 23' 00"/000 W
Green Turtle Cay	GTRTL	26° 46' 00"/000 N	077° 21' 00"/000 W
Green Turtle Cay Southwest	GTCSW	26° 45' 30"/500 N	077° 20' 30"/500 W

WHALE CAY PASSAGE

Whale Cay Passage 1	WHLP1	26° 42' 30"/500 N	077° 17' 00"/000 W
Whale Cay Passage 2	WHLP2	26° 43' 30"/500 N	077° 14' 15"/250 W
Whale Cay Passage 3	WHLP3	26° 42' 30"/500 N	077° 12' 25"/417 W
Whale Cay Passage 4	WHLP4	26° 42' 15"/250 N	077° 12' 10"/166 W
First Deep Channel Marker	DMKR1	26° 42' 00"/000 N	077° 12' 00"/000 W
Second Pair of Markers	DMKR2	26° 41' 52"/866 N	077° 11' 53"/883 W
Baker's Bay 1	BKRS1	26° 41' 25"/417 N	077° 10' 15"/166 W
Baker's Bay 2	BKRS2	26° 41' 05"/085 N	077° 10' 05"/085 W

The Central Abacos South of Whale Cay Passage

Great Guana Cay	GGANA	26° 39' 31"/519 N	077° 07' 22"/374 W
Treasure Cay Entrance	TREAS	26° 39' 30"/500 N	077° 15' 45"/750 W
Fish Cay South	FISHS	26° 37' 14"/232 N	077° 09' 16"/270 W

The Southern Abacos

Man-O-War Channel North	MWCHN	26° 37' 50"/845 N	077° 01' 16"/273 W
Man-O-War Channel South	MWCHS	26° 36' 49"/815 N	077° 01' 55"/928 W
Man-O-War Cay	NWMOW	26° 36' 00"/000 N	077° 02' 00"/000 W
Man-O-War Cay	MOWAP	26° 35' 15"/250 N	077° 00' 25"/417 W
Point Set Rock North	NPTST	26° 34' 20"/333 N	077° 00' 30"/500 W
Point Set Rock East	EPTST	26° 34' 00"/000 N	076° 59' 45"/750 W
Marsh Harbour Entrance	NMRSH	26° 33' 25"/417 N	077° 04' 00"/000 W
Hope Town Approach	HPTAP	26° 33' 00"/000 N	076° 58' 30"/500 W
Marsh Triangle Mid Area	MARMD	26° 32' 38"/646 N	076° 59' 59"/994 W
Marsh Boat Harb. Marina	SMRSH	26° 32' 22"/373 N	077° 02' 32"/537 W
Long Cay	LNGCO	26° 30' 43"/724 N	077° 02' 32"/536 W
White Sound	WHSND	26° 31' 00"/000 N	076° 59' 00"/000 W
Lubbers Quarters North	LQNTH	26° 30' 20"/333 N	076° 59' 05"/085 W
Lubbers Quarters Mid Point	LQMID	26° 29' 55"/916 N	076° 59' 30"/500 W

Witch Point	WITCH	26° 29' 40"/666 N	077° 01' 40"/666 W
Lubbers Quarters South	LQSTH	26° 29' 05"/084 N	076° 59' 45"/750 W
Tilloo Bank West	WTILO	26° 25' 57"/961 N	077° 01' 07"/114 W
Tilloo Bank South	STILO	26° 25' 23"/381 N	077° 00' 13"/221 W
North Pelican	NPELI	26° 25' 22"/376 N	076° 59' 20"/339 W
North Bar West	NBARW	26° 23' 37"/615 N	076° 59' 10"/174 W
North Bar Channel	NBRCH	26° 23' 23"/391 N	076° 58' 23"/379 W
North Bar Channel East	NBARE	26° 22' 55"/929 N	076° 56' 51"/850 W
Lynyard Mid Point	LYNMD	26° 22' 00"/000 N	076° 59' 40"/666 W
Lynyard Anchorages	LYNAN	26° 21' 20"/333 N	076° 59' 10"/172 W
Little Harbour North	LHRBN	26° 20' 26"/432 N	076° 59' 40"/676 W
Little Harbour Bar Pass	LHRBP	26° 19' 47"/793 N	076° 59' 19"/327 W
Little Harbour Bar East	LHRBE	26° 18' 45"/747 N	076° 58' 45"/754 W
Little Harbour	LHRBO	26° 20' 10"/169 N	076° 59' 53"/886 W
Ocean Point	OCNPT	26° 17' 02"/030 N	076° 59' 20"/342 W
Cherokee Point	CHERP	26° 15' 40"/666 N	077° 03' 15"/250 W
Rock Point (SW Great Abaco)	RCKPT	26° 00' 00"/000 N	077° 25' 51"/860 W
Hole-in-the-Wall	HOLEW	25° 49' 43"/716 N	077° 08' 40"/666 W

Grand Bahama Island

West End	WESTW	26° 42' 00"/000 N	079° 01' 00"/000 W
Harbour Hotel Marina Dock	HARBH	26° 41' 22"/366 N	078° 57' 58"/966 W
Freeport	FRPRT	26° 29' 43"/721 N	078° 47' 25"/426 W
Xanadu	XANDU	26° 28' 24"/399 N	078° 42' 22"/366 W
Running Mon	RNMON	26° 28' 56"/933 N	078° 39' 22"/366 W
Ocean Reef	OCNRF	26° 29' 22"/366 N	078° 39' 50"/833 W
Bell Channel	BELCH	26° 29' 57"/949 N	078° 37' 48"/799 W

GRAND LUCAYAN WATERWAY

South Mark	LWWSM	26° 31' 48"/799 N	078° 33' 14"/233 W
Casuarina Bridge	LWWCB	26° 34' 21"/364 N	078° 34' 51"/862 W
Spoil Hill Narrows	LWWSH	26° 34' 49"/826 N	078° 36' 30"/501 W
Dover Channel East	DVRCE	26° 36' 37"/623 N	078° 37' 54"/906 W
Dover Channel West	DVRCW	26° 36' 48"/803 N	078° 38' 28"/462 W
Dover Channel Mark	DVRCM	26° 38' 16"/271 N	078° 39' 38"/643 W
Cormorant Point Marker	CMTPM	26° 44' 38"/631 N	078° 40' 49"/812 W
Mangrove Cay	MANGR	26° 57' 00"/000 N	078° 37' 00"/000 W

Part III: Central Cruising Grounds

The Bimini Island Group

Bimini	BMINI	25° 42' 30"/500 N	079° 19' 00"/000 W
Bimini Approach Range	BIMAP	25° 42' 05"/085 N	079° 18' 35"/583 W
Atlantis Dive Site	ATLDS	25° 45' 44"/733 N	079° 16' 44"/733 W
Gun Cay	GUNCW	25° 34' 15"/250 N	079° 19' 30"/500 W
Cat Cay	CATCE	25° 34' 00"/000 N	079° 17' 00"/000 W

The Grand Bahama Bank
GRAND BAHAMA BANK TRANSIT WAYPOINTS

North Rock	NROCK	25° 51' 00"/000 N	079° 16' 30"/500 W
Mackie Shoal	MCKIE	25° 41' 30"/500 N	078° 38' 30"/500 W
NW Channel	NWCHN	25° 40' 00"/000 N	078° 10' 30"/500 W
SW Edge of the Berry Bank	SWEBB	25° 30' 15"/250 N	078° 10' 30"/500 W
North West Light Shoal	NWLSH	25° 29' 00"/000 N	078° 14' 00"/000 W
NorthWest Channel Light	NWCHL	25° 28' 45"/750 N	078° 09' 45"/750 W
South Riding Rock West	SRDRW	25° 13' 30"/500 N	079° 11' 00"/000 W
South Riding Rock East	SRDRE	25° 13' 30"/500 N	079° 08' 30"/500 W

The Berry Islands
NORTHERN BERRY ISLANDS

Little Stirrup Cay	LSTRP	25° 49' 30"/500 N	077° 57' 00"/000 W
Off Bertram Cove	BERTC	25° 49' 55"/927 N	077° 55' 01"/020 W
NW Great Stirrup Cay	GSTRP	25° 49' 27"/450 N	077° 52' 16"/262 W

GREAT HARBOUR APPROACH MARKS

West Mark	WMARK	25° 46' 25"/417 N	077° 57' 00"/000 W
West Marker Piling	WMRKP	25° 46' 07"/125 N	077° 56' 41"/690 W
Marker Pole 2	M2	25° 45' 37"/628 N	077° 55' 58"/972 W
Marker Pole 3 (BH)	M3	25° 45' 02"/305 N	077° 53' 41"/691 W
Marker Pole 4 (Red 8)	M4	25° 45' 00"/013 N	077° 52' 57"/957 W
Marker Pole 5	M5	25° 44' 51"/851 N	077° 52' 32"/532 W
North Market Fish Cay	NMFHC	25° 42' 10"/174 N	077° 45' 33"/549 W
Inside Route Startpoint	MFIRS	25° 40' 45"/750 N	077° 45' 45"/750 W

The final figures in each waypoint show seconds (00") and thousands (000) of a minute.

White Cay Ocean Approach	WHTOA	25° 36' 29"/484 N	077° 43' 29"/482 W
Little Harbour Cay Approach	LHCOA	25° 33' 30"/500 N	077° 42' 30"/500 W
Guana Cay Shoal Passage	GCSHP	25° 34' 10"/166 N	077° 44' 05"/085 W
SW Comfort Cay Anchorage	SWCCA	25° 34' 30"/500 N	077° 44' 05"/085 W

SOUTHERN BERRY ISLANDS

Frozen Cay Anchorage	FRCAN	25° 32' 55"/916 N	077° 43' 03"/050 W
Bond Cay Reef	BREEF	25° 29' 14"/240 N	077° 42' 29"/490 W
Bond Cay–Whale Cay Gap	BLWGP	25° 27' 10"/176 N	077° 44' 19"/324 W
Bond–Whale Anchorage	BLWAN	25° 27' 45"/750 N	077° 46' 30"/500 W
Whale Cay Reefs	OWCRS	25° 24' 48"/800 N	077° 44' 56"/943 W
Off Whale Cay Light	OWCLT	25° 23' 14"/245 N	077° 47' 37"/625 W
Bird Cay SW	BRDSW	25° 22' 58"/964 N	077° 50' 47"/785 W
Bird Cay Anchorage	BRDAN	25° 23' 40"/666 N	077° 50' 10"/166 W
Texaco Pt. (Frazers Hog Cay)	OTXPT	25° 24' 05"/085 N	077° 50' 50"/833 W
Chub Cay Entry Waypoint	CHUBC	25° 24' 15"/250 N	077° 54' 50"/833 W
Chub Cay South	CHUBS	25° 23' 15"/250 N	077° 54' 50"/833 W

Nassau and New Providence Island

Nassau Goulding Cay	GLDNG	25° 01' 30"/500 N	077° 35' 30"/500 W
Nassau Harbour NW	NASNW	25° 06' 00"/500 N	077° 23' 00"/000 W
Nassau Harbour West	NASHW	25° 05' 30"/500 N	077° 21' 30"/500 W
Coral Harbour	COHBR	25° 58' 28"/465 N	077° 28' 30"/510 W
Nassau Harbour East	NASHE	25° 04' 30"/500 N	077° 17' 30"/500 W
Porgee Rocks	PRGEE	25° 03' 45"/750 N	077° 15' 00"/000 W
Porgee Rocks North	PRGEN	25° 04' 45"/750 N	077° 15' 00"/000 W
Porgee Rocks SE	PRGSE	25° 03' 00"/000 N	077° 12' 00"/000 W
Hanover Sound South	HNVRS	25° 05' 15"/250 N	077° 15' 40"/666 W
Hanover Sound North	HNVRN	25° 05' 50"/833 N	077° 15' 45"/750 W
Chub Rock	CHBRK	25° 06' 45"/750 N	077° 15' 00"/000 W
Douglas Channel	DGLAS	25° 09' 31"/528 N	077° 06' 02"/043 W
Samphire Cays Channel	SMPHR	25° 12' 32"/532 N	077° 00' 51"/860 W
White/Yellow Bank Junction	WYBNK	24° 52' 00"/000 N	077° 12' 00"/000 W

Eleuthera
NORTH ELEUTHERA

Fleeming Channel	FLEMG	25° 16' 20"/343 N	076° 55' 59"/983 W
Egg Island North West	EGGNW	25° 31' 30"/500 N	076° 55' 30"/500 W
Little Egg Island	LEGGI	25° 27' 32"/541 N	076° 53' 51"/848 W
Egg Island South	EGGIS	25° 28' 47"/784 N	076° 52' 03"/055 W
Royal Island	ROYAL	25° 30' 09"/161 N	076° 50' 28"/465 W
Meeks Patch	MEEKP	25° 31' 30"/511 N	076° 48' 00"/000 W
Spanish Wells South Entry	SPNWS	25° 32' 00"/000 N	076° 45' 39"/648 W
Spanish Wells East Entry	SPNWE	25° 32' 38"/633 N	076° 44' 20"/333 W
Bridge Point North	BRPTN	25° 35' 00"/000 N	076° 43' 20"/333 W
Current Cut West	CURCW	25° 24' 27"/459 N	076° 48' 02"/040 W
Current Cut East	CURCE	25° 23' 00"/000 N	076° 47' 15"/250 W

CENTRAL AND SOUTH ELEUTHERA

Hatchet Bay	HTCHT	25° 20' 32"/532 N	076° 29' 40"/665 W
Governor's Harbour	GOVNH	25° 12' 00"/000 N	076° 16' 00"/000 W
Tarpum Bay	TAPMW	25° 00' 00"/000 N	076° 16' 05"/085 W
Davis Channel East	DAVCE	24° 52' 27"/457 N	076° 16' 45"/755 W
South Sandbar Obelisk	OBLSK	24° 51' 25"/414 N	076° 19' 36"/611 W
Davis Channel West	DAVCW	24° 51' 06"/101 N	076° 21' 44"/735 W
Cape Eleuthera Marina	CAPEM	24° 50' 15"/245 N	076° 21' 12"/204 W
Cape Eleuthera West	CAPEW	24° 48' 13"/224 N	076° 21' 43"/720 W
Davis Harbour	DAVOF	24° 43' 49"/816 N	076° 17' 50"/833 W
Entry Marker	DAVHM	24° 43' 49"/816 N	076° 15' 05"/085 W
Eleuthera East End Point	EEEPT	24° 37' 18"/310 N	076° 11' 02"/041 W
South Eleuthera	SELEU	24° 35' 37"/615 N	076° 08' 44"/731 W

North Andros

Morgans Bluff	MRGNE	25° 11' 00"/000 N	077° 59' 00"/000 W
Morgans Bluff Entry Buoys	MRGNB	25° 11' 09"/150 N	078° 01' 02"/033 W
Bethel Channel	BTHEL	25° 08' 30"/500 N	077° 57' 30"/500 W
Fresh Creek	FRESH	24° 44' 00"/000 N	077° 45' 00"/000 W

Part IV: Southern Cruising Grounds
The Exuma Cays
THE NORTHERN EXUMAS

Allan's Cay	ALLAN	24° 44' 50"/833 N	076° 51' 00"/000 W
Highborne Cut West	HIGHW	24° 42' 30"/500 N	076° 51' 00"/000 W
Highborne Cut East	HIGHE	24° 42' 00"/000 N	076° 48' 15"/250 W
Highborne Stake	HSTKW	24° 42' 30"/500 N	076° 50' 00"/000 W
Highborne SW	HIBSW	24° 42' 00"/000 N	076° 52' 00"/000 W
Normans Spit	NMSPT	24° 35' 45"/750 N	076° 52' 00"/000 W
Normans Cay	NRMNS	24° 34' 40"/666 N	076° 49' 30"/500 W
Elbow Cay	ELBOW	24° 31' 00"/000 N	076° 51' 00"/000 W
Cistern Cay	CSTRN	24° 25' 00"/000 N	076° 47' 30"/500 W
Warderick Wells West	WWOFF	24° 21' 00"/000 N	076° 42' 00"/000 W
Warderick Wells SW	WELLS	24° 22' 30"/500 N	076° 40' 15"/250 W
Conch Cut East	CONCE	24° 17' 30"/500 N	076° 31' 00"/000 W
Conch Cut West	CONCW	24° 17' 00"/000 N	076° 39' 00"/000 W
Sampson Cay	SAMSN	24° 12' 20"/333 N	076° 31' 00"/000 W
Sandy Cay	SNDCY	24° 11' 15"/250 N	076° 30' 00"/000 W
Staniel Cay	STANL	24° 10' 15"/250 N	076° 27' 15"/250 W
Harvey Cay	HARVY	24° 09' 15"/250 N	076° 30' 00"/000 W
Dotham Cut East	DTHME	24° 07' 00"/000 N	076° 23' 00"/000 W
Dotham Cut West	DTHMW	24° 06' 30"/500 N	076° 25' 00"/000 W
Black Point	BLKPT	24° 05' 25"/417 N	076° 25' 00"/000 W
White Point	WHTPT	24° 02' 00"/000 N	076° 23' 00"/000 W
Farmer's Cut East	FMRSE	23° 57' 50"/833 N	076° 18' 30"/500 W
Farmer's Cut West	FMRSW	23° 58' 05"/085 N	076° 19' 40"/666 W

THE SOUTHERN EXUMAS

Galliott Cut East	GALLE	23° 55' 40"/666 N	076° 16' 35"/583 W
Galliott Cut West	GALLW	23° 55' 00"/000 N	076° 18' 00"/000 W
Cave Cut East	CAVEE	23° 54' 10"/166 N	076° 15' 10"/166 W
Cave Cut West	CAVEW	23° 53' 55"/916 N	076° 16' 05"/085 W
Rudder Cut East	RUDRE	23° 52' 15"/250 N	076° 13' 25"/417 W
Rudder Cut West	RUDRW	23° 51' 50"/833 N	076° 13' 40"/666 W
Adderley Cut East	ADDYE	23° 47' 15"/250 N	076° 06' 25"/417 W
Adderley Cut West	ADDYW	23° 46' 45"/750 N	076° 07' 25"/417 W
Rat Cay Cut North	RATCN	23° 44' 05"/085 N	076° 02' 05"/085 W
Rat Cay Cut South	RATCS	23° 43' 45"/750 N	076° 01' 55"/916 W

Great Exuma Island
WEST ENTRANCE TO GEORGE TOWN HARBOUR

George Town Harbour West	GTAW1	23° 34' 30"/500 N	075° 48' 30"/500 W
West Waypoint 2	GTAW2	23° 33' 40"/666 N	075° 48' 40"/666 W
West Waypoint 3	GTAW3	23° 33' 15"/250 N	075° 48' 10"/166 W
West Waypoint 4	GTAW4	23° 32' 45"/750 N	075° 48' 00"/000 W
West Waypoint 5	GTAW5	23° 32' 10"/166 N	075° 47' 30"/500 W
West Waypoint 6	GTAW6	23° 31' 55"/916 N	075° 46' 30"/500 W

EAST ENTRANCE TO GEORGE TOWN HARBOUR

George Town Harbour East	GTAE1	23° 30' 00"/000 N	075° 40' 00"/000 W
East Waypoint 2	GTAE2	23° 29' 10"/166 N	075° 40' 15"/250 W
East Waypoint 3	GTAE3	23° 29' 25"/417 N	075° 42' 00"/000 W
East Waypoint 4	GTAE4	23° 29' 25"/417 N	075° 42' 35"/583 W
East Waypoint 5	GTAE5	23° 30' 27"/460 N	075° 44' 34"/572 W

Out Islands North of the Tropic of Cancer (23°30' N)
LITTLE SAN SALVADOR

Little San Salvador	LSSAL	24° 34' 39"/646 N	075° 58' 00"/000 W

CAT ISLAND

Orange Creek	ORNGS	24° 37' 00"/000 N	075° 43' 00"/000 W
Orange Creek Dock	ORNGE	24° 38' 48"/800 N	075° 42' 45"/750 W
Bennett's Harbour	BNTNW	24° 34' 00"/000 N	075° 41' 00"/000 W
Bennett's Harbour Dock	BNNTS	24° 33' 33"/600 N	075° 38' 24"/400 W
Smith Bay	SMTHW	24° 20' 00"/000 N	075° 30' 00"/000 W
Smith Bay Gov't Dock	SMITH	24° 19' 58"/966 N	075° 28' 32"/533 W
Fernandez Bay	FNDEZ	24° 19' 30"/500 N	075° 30' 00"/000 W
The Bight	BIGHT	24° 15' 00"/000 N	075° 33' 00"/000 W
New Bight Dock	NBGHT	24° 17' 15"/250 N	075° 24' 54"/900 W
Hawk's Nest	HWKN1	24° 08' 45"/750 N	075° 35' 00"/000 W
Hawk's Nest	HWKN2	24° 08' 45"/750 N	075° 32' 00"/000 W
Hawk's Nest Marina Entry	HWKNM	24° 08' 46"/766 N	075° 31' 36"/600 W
Hawk's Nest Beach	HWKNB	24° 09' 19"/316 N	075° 31' 25"/417 W

CONCEPTION ISLAND

Conception NW Anchorage	CONNW	23° 50' 56"/929 N	075° 07' 44"/732 W
Conception Wedge Point	CONWG	23° 48' 00"/000 N	075° 07' 00"/000 W

The final figures in each waypoint show seconds (00") and thousands (000) of a minute.

RUM CAY

Rum Cay Sandy Point	RUMSP	23° 38' 45"/750 N	074° 57' 30"/500 W
Rum Cay SE	RUMSE	23° 37' 15"/250 N	074° 47' 30"/500 W
Rum Cay Port Nelson	RUMPN	23° 37' 15"/250 N	074° 51' 00"/000 W
Sumner Point Marina	RUMAP	23° 37' 51"/846 N	074° 51' 02"/035 W

SAN SALVADOR ISLAND

San Salvador	SNSAL	24° 02' 45"/750 N	074° 33' 45"/750 W

Long Island

Cape Santa Maria	SANTM	23° 43' 00"/000 N	075° 20' 30"/500 W
Cape Santa Maria East	SANTE	23° 43' 00"/000 N	075° 17' 00"/000 W
Calabash Bay	CALAB	23° 39' 15"/250 N	075° 21' 39"/656 W
Stella Maris	STELA	23° 33' 30"/500 N	075° 21' 00"/000 W
Salt Pond	SALTP	23° 21' 00"/000 N	075° 11' 00"/000 W
Clarence Town	CLART	23° 08' 00"/000 N	074° 57' 00"/000 W
Little Harbour	LLHBR	22° 59' 00"/000 N	074° 50' 00"/000 W

EXUMA BANK ROUTES

White/Yellow Bank Junction	WYBNK	24° 52' 00"/000 N	077° 12' 00"/000 W
Edge of Bank North	EBNKN	24° 27' 30"/500 N	077° 04' 00"/000 W
Edge of Bank Central	EBNKC	24° 16' 10"/163 N	077° 09' 55"/914 W
Edge of Bank South	EBNKS	24° 13' 44"/743 N	077° 03' 49"/828 W
Harvey Cay	HARVY	24° 09' 15"/250 N	076° 30' 00"/000 W
Barracouta Sandbores	BRCTA	23° 44' 00"/000 N	076° 20' 00"/000 W
Hawksbill Rocks	HWKBL	23° 25' 00"/000 N	076° 07' 00"/000 W
Nuevitas Rocks	NUEVR	23° 08' 00"/000 N	075° 21' 00"/000 W

Part V: Far Horizons
The Route South to the Turks and Caicos Islands
GEORGE TOWN TO THE TURKS AND CAICOS

George Town Harbour East	GTAE1	23° 30' 00"/000 N	075° 40' 00"/000 W
LONG ISLAND			
Cape Santa Maria	SANTM	23° 43' 00"/000 N	075° 20' 30"/500 W
Cape Santa Maria East	SANTE	23° 43' 00"/000 N	075° 17' 00"/000 W
Clarence Town	CLART	23° 08' 00"/000 N	074° 57' 00"/000 W
Little Harbour	LLHBR	22° 59' 00"/000 N	074° 50' 00"/000 W
South Point East	LISPE	22° 51' 00"/000 N	074° 45' 00"/000 W
Mid-Crooked Island Passage	MIDCP	22° 51' 00"/000 N	074° 35' 30"/500 W
CROOKED ISLAND			
Bird Rock NW	BRDRK	22° 53' 00"/000 N	074° 23' 00"/000 W
Bird Rock	BRDRE	22° 50' 42"/700 N	074° 21' 34"/566 W
Portland Harbour Entry	PTLNH	22° 50' 24"/400 N	074° 21' 15"/250 W
Portland Anchorage	PTLNA	22° 50' 12"/200 N	074° 20' 47"/783 W
Landrail Anchorage	LNDAN	22° 49' 10"/166 N	074° 20' 48"/800 W
Landrail Point	LNDRL	22° 48' 30"/500 N	074° 21' 15"/250 W
Landrail Small Boat Dock	LNDSB	22° 48' 18"/300 N	074° 20' 29"/483 W
Landrail Government Dock	LNDGD	22° 48' 07"/116 N	074° 20' 22"/366 W
French Wells West	FRWW1	22° 41' 00"/000 N	074° 19' 00"/000 W
French Wells	FRWW2	22° 41' 05"/085 N	074° 18' 00"/000 W
French Wells Anchorage	FRWAN	22° 41' 04"/066 N	074° 16' 29"/483 W
SEMANA CAY			
Semana Cay	SMANA	23° 02' 00"/000 N	073° 46' 00"/000 W
ACKLINS ISLAND			
Atwood Harbour North	ATWOD	22° 46' 00"/000 N	073° 53' 00"/000 W
Atwood Harbour	ATWIR	22° 43' 40"/666 N	073° 53' 05"/085 W
NE Point	ACKNE	22° 46' 00"/000 N	073° 43' 00"/000 W
PLANA CAYS			
Plana Cays West	PLNAW	22° 37' 00"/000 N	073° 43' 00"/000 W
Plana Cays South	PLNAS	22° 30' 00"/000 N	073° 43' 00"/000 W
MAYAGUANA			
Government Dock	GOVD	22° 26' 57"/949 N	073° 07' 45"/750 W
Betsy Bay	BETSY	22° 25' 00"/000 N	073° 09' 00"/000 W
Mayaguana W	MAYAW	22° 19' 12"/200 N	073° 03' 20"/333 W
Mayaguana E	MAYAE	22° 20' 45"/750 N	072° 58' 04"/067 W
PROVIDENCIALES			
North West Point	PROVN	21° 55' 00"/000 N	072° 20' 00"/000 W
Tiki Huts Anchorage	TIKIA	21° 49' 50"/833 N	072° 20' 30"/500 W
Sandbore Approach	SBORA	21° 46' 00"/000 N	072° 28' 30"/500 W

The final figures in each waypoint show seconds (00") and thousands (000) of a minute.

The Routes South to the Windward Passage
GEORGE TOWN TO THE WINDWARD PASSAGE

George Town Harbour East	GTAE1	23° 30' 00"/000 N	075° 40' 00"/000 W
LONG ISLAND			
Cape Santa Maria	SANTM	23° 43' 00"/000 N	075° 20' 30"/500 W
Cape Santa Maria East	SANTE	23° 43' 00"/000 N	075° 17' 00"/000 W
Clarence Town	CLART	23° 08' 00"/000 N	074° 57' 00"/000 W
Little Harbour	LLHBR	22° 59' 00"/000 N	074° 50' 00"/000 W
South Point East	LISPE	22° 51' 00"/000 N	074° 45' 00"/000 W
LONG CAY			
Long Cay (Windsor Point)	LONGC	22° 32' 30"/500 N	074° 25' 00"/000 W
ACKLINS ISLAND			
Salina Point	SLINA	22° 14' 00"/000 N	074° 18' 00"/000 W
Mira Por Vos Passage	MIRAP	22° 06' 30"/500 N	074° 25' 00"/000 W
HOGSTY REEF			
Hogsty Reef	HGSTY	21° 41' 00"/000 N	073° 54' 00"/000 W
GREAT INAGUA ISLAND			
Matthew Town	INAGA	20° 57' 00"/000 N	073° 44' 00"/000 W
WINDWARD PASSAGE			
Approach North	WINDN	20° 30' 00"/000 N	073° 50' 00"/000 W

HARVEY CAY TO THE WINDWARD PASSAGE

EXUMA CAYS			
Harvey Cay	HARVY	24° 09' 15"/250 N	076° 30' 00"/000 W
GREAT BAHAMA BANK			
Barracouta Sandbores	BRCTA	23° 44' 00"/000 N	076° 20' 00"/000 W
Hawksbill Rocks	HWKBL	23° 25' 00"/000 N	076° 07' 00"/000 W
Nuevitas Rocks	NUEVR	23° 08' 00"/000 N	075° 21' 00"/000 W
LONG ISLAND			
South Point West	LISPW	22° 52' 00"/000 N	074° 54' 00"/000 W
LONG CAY			
Long Cay (Windsor Point)	LONGC	22° 32' 30"/500 N	074° 25' 00"/000 W
ACKLINS ISLAND			
Salina Point	SLINA	22° 14' 00"/000 N	074° 18' 00"/000 W
Mira Por Vos Passage	MIRAP	22° 06' 30"/500 N	074° 25' 00"/000 W
HOGSTY REEF			
Hogsty Reef	HGSTY	21° 41' 00"/000 N	073° 54' 00"/000 W
GREAT INAGUA ISLAND			
Matthew Town	INAGA	20° 57' 00"/000 N	073° 44' 00"/000 W
WINDWARD PASSAGE			
Approach North	WINDN	20° 30' 00"/000 N	073° 42' 30"/500 W

Part VI: The Turks and Caicos Islands
Providenciales

North West Point	PROVN	21° 55' 00"/000 N	072° 20' 00"/000 W
Sellars Cut Approach	SLLRA	21° 48' 30"/500 N	072° 12' 30"/500 W
Leeward Cut Approach	LWRDA	21° 50' 30"/500 N	072° 10' 30"/500 W
Tiki Huts Anchorage	TIKIA	21° 49' 50"/833 N	072° 20' 30"/500 W
Sandbore Approach	SBORA	21° 46' 00"/000 N	072° 28' 30"/500 W
Sandbore West Entrance	SBORW	21° 44' 33"/550 N	072° 27' 00"/000 W
Sandbore East Entrance	SBORE	21° 44' 30"/500 N	072° 24' 00"/000 W
Sapodilla Bay Approach	SPDLA	21° 44' 15"/250 N	072° 17' 30"/500 W
South Dock Approach	SDCKA	21° 44' 10"/166 N	072° 17' 00"/000 W
Five Cays Anchorage	FIVE	21° 44' 05"/084 N	072° 16' 00"/000 W
South Side Marina Approach	PSSMA	21° 43' 51"/855 N	072° 13' 51"/851 W
South Side Turning Point	PSSMT	21° 45' 24"/400 N	072° 13' 52"/860 W
Caicos Shipyard	CAIYA	21° 44' 40"/660 N	072° 10' 05"/085 W
Caicos Shipyard Entry	CAIYE	21° 45' 39"/650 N	072° 10' 03"/050 W

Caicos Bank

French Cay	FRNCH	21° 30' 00"/000 N	072° 12' 30"/500 W
Caicos Mid-Bank Channel	CMBCH	21° 36' 00"/000 N	072° 05' 00"/000 W
Fish Cay Channel	FCCHN	21° 25' 00"/000 N	071° 35' 40"/668 W
South Caicos	SCAIC	21° 28' 37"/631 N	071° 31' 40"/664 W

Grand Turk Island

Grand Turk	GTURK	21° 28' 22"/375 N	071° 09' 24"/396 W
Sand Cay	SANDC	21° 11' 45"/757 N	071° 15' 24"/408 W

Batelco Towers

Visual navigation in the Bahamas and identifying your land-fall after a passage is not always easy, simply because the islands are relatively featureless and low lying. Cat Island is the only place in the Bahamas where the elevation of the land rises above 200 feet. Taking the twenty-three largest islands or island groups, Cat alone hits that 200-foot mark. Just three islands top 150 feet. Thirteen islands rise above 100 feet, but are less than 150 feet in height. The five remaining islands in our list have elevations between 50 and 100 feet. Your problems are eased considerably by the Bahamas Telecommunications Company. Batelco's radio towers are, more often than not, the greatest boon to your visual navigation, for where there is a tower, there is surely a settlement near it.

Batelco, in providing us with this information, have made the point that they are not responsible for the accuracy of the positions given. We have not thought it necessary to take a hand-held GPS receiver to double check each one.

LOCATION	HEIGHT IN FEET	POSITION	
ABACOS			
Cherokee	235	26° 16' 48" N	077° 03' 12" W
Coopers Town	200	26° 52' 26" N	077° 30' 52" W
Crossing Rocks	200	26° 07' 25" N	077° 11' 07" W
Fox Town	200	26° 55' 03" N	077° 47' 44" W
Grand Cay	275	27° 14' 20" N	078° 19' 30" W
Green Turtle Cay	100	26° 45' 25" N	077° 19' 32" W
Guana Cay	50	26° 41' 10" N	077° 08' 16" W
Hope Town	40	26° 32' 07" N	076° 57' 30" W
Man O War Cay	40	26° 25' 44" N	077° 00' 15" W
Marsh Harbour	200 & 250	26° 33' 35" N	077° 03' 25" W
Moores Island	200	26° 18' 51" N	077° 23' 53" W
Sandy Point	260	26° 01' 30" N	077° 23' 53" W
Treasure Cay	200	26° 40' 08" N	077° 17' 29" W
GRAND BAHAMA			
Basset Cove	400	26° 37' 15" N	078° 19' 21" W
Eight Mile Rock	200	26° 32' 51" N	078° 49' 17" W
Freeport	200	26° 31' 45" N	078° 41' 47" W
Mcleans Town	200	26° 39' 02" N	077° 57' 24" W
South Riding Point	225	26° 37' 44" N	078° 14' 21" W
West End	150	26° 41' 44" N	078° 58' 27" W
BIMINI			
Bailey Town	265	25° 21' 00" N	076° 27' 20" W
BERRY ISLANDS			
Bullocks	235	25° 49' 20" N	077° 53' 20" W
Chub Cay	200	25° 24' 39" N	077° 54' 03" W
NEW PROVIDENCE			
Coral Harbour	100	25° 00' 08" N	077° 28' 12" W
Delaporte	200	25° 04' 41" N	077° 31' 15" W
Lyford Cay	200	25° 01' 43" N	077° 31' 15" W
Paradise Island	150	25° 04' 50" N	077° 19' 10" W
Perpall Tract	2x80 2 x 150	25° 04' 16" N	077° 21' 43" W
Poinciana Drive	200	25° 03' 41" N	077° 21' 41" W
Soldier Road	260 & 220	25° 02' 47" N	077° 19' 10" W
Pinewood	100	25° 01' 25" N	077° 19' 45" W

LOCATION	HEIGHT IN FEET	POSITION	
ELEUTHERA			
Current Island	40	25° 22' 53" N	076° 47' 00" W
Current	50	25° 24' 28" N	076° 47' 00" W
Governors Harbour	180	25° 11' 56" N	076° 14' 30" W
Green Castle	240	24° 46' 37" N	076° 12' 54" W
Harbour Island	40	25° 30' 01" N	076° 38' 11" W
Hatchet Bay	265	25° 21' 18" N	076° 28' 50" W
Lower Bogue	200	25° 26' 56" N	076° 42' 56" W
Rock Sound	100	24° 52' 00" N	076° 09' 30" W
Savanah Sound	200	25° 05' 17" N	076° 07' 58" W
Spanish Wells	120	25° 32' 34" N	076° 44' 56" W
Tarpum Bay	200	24° 58' 51" N	076° 11' 02" W
ANDROS			
Cargil Creek	100	24° 29' 42" N	077° 43' 30" W
Fresh Creek	225	24° 43' 44" N	077° 47' 13" W
Kemps Bay	180	24° 05' 28" N	077° 32' 58" W
Mars Bay	100	25° 52' 06" N	077° 31' 00" W
Mastic Point	100	25° 03' 52" N	077° 58' 08" W
Nichols Town	255	25° 08' 42" N	078° 02' 40" W
Staniard Creek	200	24° 49' 35" N	077° 54' 07" W
EXUMA			
Barraterre	150	23° 41' 50" N	076° 02' 55" W
Black Point	100	24° 05' 45" N	075° 24' 05" W
Farmers Hill	40	23° 36' 56" N	075° 54' 33" W
George Town	260	23° 30' 06" N	075° 46' 16" W
Highbourne Cay	260	24° 42' 53" N	076° 49' 21" W
Little Farmers Cay	260	23° 57' 21" N	076° 19' 13" W
Rolle Town	40	23° 27' 54" N	075° 42' 25" W
Rolleville	260	23° 40' 28" N	075° 59' 11" W
Staniel Cay	260	24° 10' 20" N	076° 26' 30" W
Williams Town	200	23° 25' 22" N	075° 33' 36" W
CAT ISLAND			
Arthur Town	200	24° 37' 23" N	075° 40' 31" W
The Bight	230	24° 17' 26" N	075° 24' 53" W
LONG ISLAND			
Clarence Town	60	23° 05' 50" N	074° 48' 05" W
Deadman's	225	23° 09' 36" N	075° 05' 31" W
Roses	50	22° 57' 10" N	074° 52' 00" W
Simms	230	23° 29' 45" N	075° 14' 02" W
Stella Maris	50	23° 33' 40" N	075° 14' 30" W
RUM CAY			
Port Nelson	260	23° 40'00" N	078° 48' 00" W
SAN SALVADOR			
Cockburn Town	150	24° 03' 07" N	074° 31' 57" W
CROOKED ISLAND			
Cabbage Hill	220	22° 45' 58" N	074°12' 38" W
ACKLINS			
Spring Point	220	22° 27' 43" N	073° 57' 30" W
MAYAGUANA			
Abraham's Bay	175	22° 22' 03" N	072° 58' 05" W
Betsy Bay	110	22° 24' 52" N	073° 57' 30" W
GREAT INAGUA			
Matthew Town	100	20° 56' 04" N	073° 40' 55" W

The final figures in each waypoint show seconds (00").

Appendix C
Blue Pages Supplement

Tidal Differences

Our plan was to publish full tide tables for the years 2000 and 2001 in this edition, both for the Bahamas and the Turks and Caicos. With regret we have set this intention to one side as we needed the space to accommodate our post-1999 hurricane season report, and we are bound to a finite limit in pages. Tide tables are available from sources such as *Reed's* and, in electronic form, *Nautical Software's Tides and Currents*. In the Bahamas tide tables are published in the *Abaco Journal*, and often available in pamphlet form in marine stores and dive shops.

The Bahamas

Tides in the Bahamas are based on Nassau, New Providence Island 25° 05' N 077° 21' W.

In practice we find that you do not necessarily require full tide tables in the Bahamas. What you do need are the Day One times of High and Low Water in Nassau. Thereafter you can predict the daily tides simply by advancing those times by six hours day by day. It will be sufficiently accurate for general cruising. Then all you have to calculate is whatever tidal difference may apply in the area in which you are cruising. The tides in most of the Bahamas run within thirty minutes of Nassau time. In effect, measured against an average 2-foot 6-inch rise and fall, that thirty minutes amounts to approximately 1.5 inches. In short, it's too small a variation to take into account. What you must be aware of are the places where the tidal difference is significant, such as the north end of the Grand Lucayan Waterway. For this reason take note of our Tidal Difference Table.

Tidal Differences After (+) or Ahead (-) of Nassau

The time differences we quote below are rounded off. For the exact times of high and low water, together with the predicted height and range of each tide, you must refer to full tidal data based on NOAA harmonics and correction tables. In practice, particularly as wind and barometric pressure affect all tides, our figures should serve for all normal cruising and passage-making calculations.

Tide Changes in Passes and Cuts

Do not expect that a slack tide followed by a current reversal will occur at predicted high and low water times in passes and cuts. More often than not the moment of change will come about after the forecast time. Much depends on bottom contours, depth, width, and other factors.

NORTHERN CRUISING GROUNDS

Marsh Harbour, Abaco	+	30 mins
Abaco Cays, North Bar Channel	+	30 mins
Memory Rock	+	30 mins
Grand Bahama, West End	+	25 mins
Grand Bahama, North End Lucayan Waterway	+	2 hrs 30 mins

CENTRAL CRUISING GROUNDS

North Bimini	+	20 mins
North Cat Cay	+	30 mins
Berry Islands, Whale Cay	+	40 mins
Spanish Wells	+	30 mins
Eleuthera, Current Mouth		Nassau Time
Eleuthera, East Coast	+	20 mins
Eleuthera, Central, West Coast	+	2 hrs 25 mins
Andros, Fresh Creek	+	8 mins

SOUTHERN CRUISING GROUNDS

Exuma Cays, Highborne	+	20 mins
Exuma Cays, Warderick Wells	+	30 mins
Exuma Bank, Great Exuma Island	–	2 hrs
George Town		Nassau time
Long Island, Salt Pond	+	2 hrs 30 mins
Cat Island, The Bight	–	25 mins
San Salvador, Cockburn Town		Nassau time
Long Island, Clarence Town	+	50 mins
Long Island, Salt Pond	+	2 hrs 30 mins

FAR HORIZONS

Acklins Island, SW Point	–	10 mins
Mayaguana, Abraham's Bay	+	10 mins
Great Inagua, Matthew Town	+	20 mins

Tidal Ranges
North of George Town reckon on height of tide 0.3 ft below Nassau.
South of George Town reckon on height of tide 0.5 ft below Nassau.

Neap Tides		
(first and third quarters of the Moon)	–	0.5 ft
New and Full Moons	+	0.5 ft
Spring Tides	+	0.5 ft
Spring Full Moon Tides	+	1.0 ft

To be safe, reckon on a rise and fall of 3 feet. The Exumas' average is approximately 2 feet 6 inches. This means that the state of the tide becomes a factor worth taking into account at mid-tide when we are talking about just over 1 foot. But we assume that no one out there will call their passage shots so close than the difference of just 12 inches is critical. However that 2-foot 6-inch difference can, of course, make all the difference if you are entering, say, Black Sound in Green Turtle Cay.

The Turks and Caicos Islands

Tides in the Turks and Caicos are based on Hawk's Nest Anchorage in Grand Turk Island 21° 26' N 071° 07' W.

Weather Information

Florida, Bahamas, and Southwest North Atlantic Ocean South of 32°N and West of 65°W

All times shown are EST or EDT depending on the season. Where the time is UTC this is shown. For conversion to EST subtract five hours. For conversion to EDT subtract four hours.

In the Bahamas, apart from Grand Bahama and the Biminis, you are out of range of the US NOAA weather broadcasts. You may be able to access the Weather Channel on a dockside TV hookup or through a satellite antenna. Your principal sources of weather information will be Radio Bahamas, VHF radio, and SSB radio as well as a number of other miscellaneous sources. Generally you'll always find someone on shore or another cruising boat willing to share weather information with you.

Radio Bahamas

ZNS-1	1540 kHz	Principal Radio station
	107.1 & 107.9 MHz	Nassau and Southeast Bahamas
ZNS-3	810 kHz	Northern Bahamas
		Grand Bahama, Abacos, Berry Islands,
		Biminis

RADIO BAHAMAS WEATHER BROADCASTS

The first weather reports of the day are broadcast around 0615 and 0645 (sometimes 0735 and 0755) on ZNS-1 and ZNS-3. Brief weather reports are normally scheduled either before or after the news at 1200 and 1800. The 0645 ZNS-1 broadcast was at one time the best and often gave a three-day forecast. However the timings of the morning reports may slip from day to day, may occasionally be missed, and Sundays are a blank. If a tropical storm or a hurricane is threatening the islands, full weather reports and warnings are virtually continuous.

Radio Abaco

| Radio Abaco | 93.5 MHz | Weather at 0800, 1300, & 1800 Mon–Sat |

NOAA Radio Stations

KEC-50	NOAA Weather Radio, West Palm Beach	WX-3	162.475 MHz
KHB-34	NOAA Weather Radio, Coral Gables	WX-1	162.55 MHz
WXJ-95	NOAA Weather Radio, Key West	WX-2	162.40 MHz

Gulf Stream data broadcasts:

| Monday, Wednesday, and Friday | between 1600 and 2000 |
| Tuesday, Thursday, and Saturday | between 0400 and 0800 |

VHF Radio Broadcasts

NORTHERN CRUISING GROUNDS

| Marsh Harbour | 0815 | VHF 16/68 | Cruisers Net |

CENTRAL CRUISING GROUNDS

| Nassau | 0715 | VHF 72 | BASRA (Ranger) |
| Nassau | 0800 | VHF 27 | Nassau Marine Operator |

Nassau Marine Operator broadcasts weather on even hours and on request on VHF 27.

SOUTHERN CRUISING GROUNDS

Highborne Cay	0730	VHF 16/06	Dockmaster
Staniel Cay	0800	VHF 16/14	Cruisers Net
George Town	0810	VHF 16/68	Cruisers Net

Time Signal Radio

WWV FORT COLLINS, CO

2500 & 5000 kHz	best at night
10000 kHz	night or day
15000 & 20000 kHz	best by day

Storm warnings at 0500, 1100, 1700, and 2300 hours.

SSB Radio Reports

0700	4003 kHz	USB	BASRA	Full Ocean and Coastal Areas
0720	3696 kHz	LSB	Offshore Weather Net	Full Ocean and Coastal Areas (C6AGG)
0745	7268 kHz	LSB	Waterway Net	Full Ocean and Coastal Areas
2000	1239 kHz		Herb Hilgenburg	Full Ocean and Coastal Areas
UTC	Advisory service		(Southbound 2)	

USCG SSB Radio Offshore Broadcasts

US COAST GUARD STATION NMN

0330 UTC	4316 kHz, 4426 kHz, 6501 kHz, 8502 kHz, 8764 kHz, 12788 kHz
0500 UTC	4316 kHz, 4426 kHz, 6501 kHz, 8502 kHz, 8764 kHz, 12788 kHz
0930 UTC	4316 kHz, 4426 kHz, 6501 kHz, 8502 kHz, 8764 kHz, 12788 kHz
1130 UTC	4316 kHz, 6501 kHz, 8502 kHz, 8764 kHz, 12788 kHz, 13089 kHz
1600 UTC	4316 kHz, 6501 kHz, 8502 kHz, 8764 kHz, 12788 kHz, 13089 kHz
1730 UTC	4316 kHz, 8502 kHz, 8764 kHz, 12788 kHz, 13089 kHz, 17314 kHz
2200 UTC	4316 kHz, 6501 kHz, 8502 kHz, 8764 kHz, 12788 kHz, 13089 kHz
2300 UTC	4316 kHz, 6501 kHz, 8502 kHz, 8764 kHz, 12788 kHz, 13089 kHz

Marine Radio SSB Offshore Broadcasts

WLO MOBILE MARINE RADIO

At present WLO broadcasts NOAA-generated weather three times every 24 hours. These reports, treated as one "global" broadcast are lengthy, and can be even more extended during the hurricane season. WLO are presently actively considering breaking their broadcasts into specific area reports tied to set times. This is likely to come about during the currency of this Edition. Their frequencies will remain the same. For up-to-date information on the services they offer call WLO 334-666-3487; fax: 334-666-8339; or visit their website: http://www.wloradio.com; or tune in to one of their broadcasts. We now list their frequencies and current broadcast schedule (as of August 1999). WLO Weather Broadcasts at 1200 UTC, 1800 UTC, and 2400 UTC on ALL frequencies: Select the best frequency range for the time you are tuning in, and then find the best frequency for reception at that time. If it doesn't work in that range, keep searching.

2572 kHz	8806 kHz	17362 kHz
4369 kHz	8713 kHz	17368 kHz
4396 kHz	13110 kHz	17380 kHz
4411 kHz	13149 kHz	19773 kHz
4351 kHz	13152 kHz	22804 kHz
6519 kHz	13173 kHz	22819 kHz
8788 kHz	13179 kHz	22831 kHz
8803 kHz	17260 kHz	26151 kHz

AT&T Reorganization

At the time we go to print we have been informed that Marine Radio Stations WOM (Florida), WOO (New Jersey), and KMI (California) are to be closed by the end of 1999. This closure, long forecast, has been postponed in the past and may yet be prevented by the Federal Communications Commission. However we believe, particularly in view of the reduction of these stations to skeletal staffing, that in all probability these stations will cease broadcasting in 2000. For this reason we do not list their last advertised weather broadcast schedules and transmission frequencies.

Anyone interested in checking whether a reprieve has been won for the stations may wish to try telephoning WOM in Fort Lauderdale (954-587-0910). If they are still in business, the stations will gladly fax you their broadcast schedules.

Weather by Telephone

Nassau Meteorological Service	242-377-7040	(in Nassau dial 915)
Freeport Weather Service	242-352-9114	
US NOAA Weather Network	see your local Blue Pages	
National Hurricane Center, Coral Gables	305-229-4483	
Marine Forecasts	305-229-4502	
Gulf Stream Analysis	305-229-4444	(contact Stephen Baig)
National Climatic Data Center	704-271-4800	

WeatherFax

For weatherfax services for the current year covering the ocean and land areas of interest to anyone cruising or passage making in the Bahamas and Turks and Caicos, see *Reed's Nautical Almanac* for the North American East Coast and the Caribbean, as these schedules may change. Normally there are four broadcasts each 24 hours.

Weather by Internet

FEMA Stormwatch	http://www.fema.gov/fema/weathr.htm
Michigan State University	http://rs560.cl.msu.edu/weather
National Hurricane Center	http://www.nhc.noaa.gov
National Weather Service	http://www.nws.noaa.gov/om/marine/forcast.htm
NOAA Climatic Data Center	http://www.ncdc.noaa.gov
USA Weather	http://www.intellicast.com
The Weather Channel	http://www.weather.com
WXP: The WeatherProcessor	http://www.atms.purdue.edu
Yahoo! Weather	http://www.yahoo.com

Weather Plotting Chart

A Weather Plotting Chart covering the southwestern North Atlantic Ocean, the Caribbean, and the Gulf of Mexico is provided on the following page. Use this to follow broadcasts, and plot the track and predicted track of severe storms. For best results, use the "photo" setting when photocopying the chart.

Weather Plotting Chart

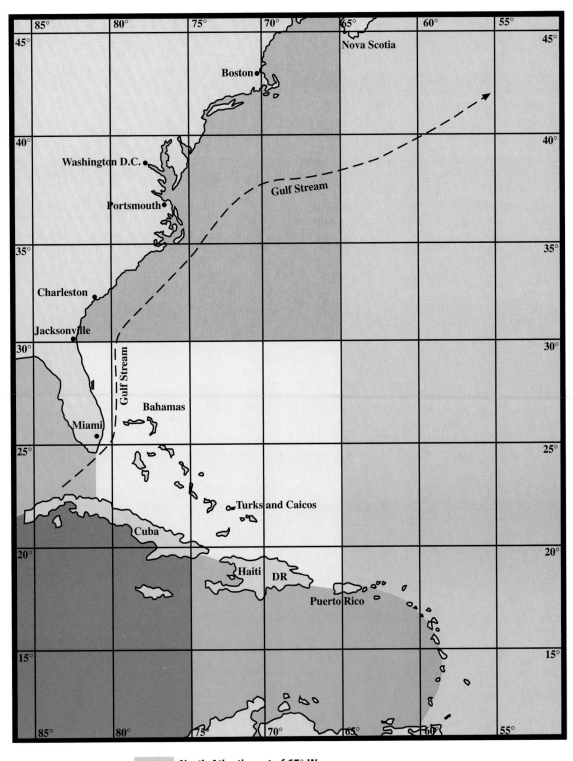

North Atlantic east of 65° W

Southwest North Atlantic south of 30° N, and west of 65° W

East Caribbean east of 75° W

Northwest Caribbean north of 15° N and west of 75° W

Southwest Caribbean south of 15° N and west of 75° W

Conversion Tables and Useful Measurements

DISTANCE EQUIVALENTS

1 Degree of Latitude	60 nm	111.120 km
1 Minute of Latitude	1 nm	1.852 km

SECONDS TO THOUSANDS (LATITUDE)

SECONDS	THOUSANDS	IN TWO FIGURES	LOG COUNT
5	083.33	8	0.083
10	166.66	17	0.166
15	249.99	25	0.249
20	333.32	33	0.333
25	416.65	42	0.416
30	499.98	50	0.500
35	583.31	58	0.583
40	666.64	67	0.666
45	749.97	75	0.750
50	833.30	83	0.833
55	916.63	92	0.916
60	999.99	00	0.999

1 second = 101.33 feet = 33.77 yards = 30.88 meters

Thousands to Seconds   divide by 16.6666

Seconds to Thousands   multiply by 16.6666

DEPTH

1 fathom = 6 feet = 1.83 meters
1 foot = 0.305 meters
1 meter = 3.281 feet

MAGNETIC VARIATION

VARIATION WEST	VARIATION EAST
True to Mag: ADD VARIATION	True to Mag: SUBTRACT VARIATION
Mag to True: SUBTRACT VARIATION	Mag to True: ADD VARIATION
[Variation West Compass Best]	[Variation East Compass Least]

WEIGHTS

Diesel oil	1 US gallon	7.13 lbs
Fresh water	1 US gallon	8.33 lbs
Gasoline	1 US gallon	6.1 lbs
Salt water	1 US gallon	8.56 lbs

NAUTICAL MILES TO STATUTE MILES

1 nm = 1.15 mile. 1 mile = 0.86 nm

NMS	MILES	MILES	NMS
1.0	1.15	1.0	0.86
5.0	5.75	5.0	4.30
10.0	11.50	10.0	8.60

METERS–FEET

METERS	FEET
1	3
2	7
3	10
4	13
5	16
6	20
7	23
8	26
9	30
10	33
11	36
12	39
13	43
14	46
15	49
16	52
17	56
18	59
19	62
20	66
25	82
30	98
40	131
50	164
100	328

TIDES: RULE OF TWELFTHS

HOUR	RISE/FALL	SUM
1	1/12th	1/12
2	2/12th	3/12
3	3/12th	6/12
4	3/12th	9/12
5	2/12th	11/12
6	1/12th	12/12

Provisioning Checklist

FRESH FOODS
milk
orange juice
butter or margarine
yogurt
sour cream
eggs
meats for sandwiches
hot dogs

CHEESE
cheese slices
hard cheese
Parmesan

FRUIT & VEGETABLES
cabbages
carrots
cucumbers
garlic
grapefruit
green bananas
green beans
green peppers
Iceberg lettuce
lemons
limes
melons
onions
oranges
potatoes
squash
sweet potatoes (yams)
unripe tomatoes
zucchini
fresh herbs in pots
flowers or pot plant(s)

FREEZER
bacon
best ground beef
chicken pieces
frozen vegetables
ice cream
frozen yogurt
sausages
shrimp

CANS
baked beans
chick peas
peas
chili beans
coconut milk
corn
corned beef
corned beef hash

ham
mushrooms
red kidney beans
tomatoes
tomato paste
pasta sauces
olives
salmon
spaghetti sauce
tuna
water chestnuts
variety of canned
  soups

DRY GOODS & PASTA
rice (plain, brown, and
  wild)
granola bars
cereal
flour
packet soups
instant mashed potato
dried lentils and beans
bouillon cubes
sugar
variety of pastas

SAUCES
chutney, jams, and
  marmalade
mustards, Marmite,
  and mayonnaise
soy sauce and Worces-
  tershire sauce
Tabasco and tomato
  ketchup
variety of oils and
  vinegars

HERBS & SPICES
salt
black pepper
black peppercorns
chilli powder
curry powder
dried basil
dried chives
dried mint
dried parsley
Italian seasoning

COFFEE, TEAS
tea and coffee (bags or
  ground)
sugar substitute
UHT milk

SNACKS
mixed nuts
nachos
potato chips
cheese balls

DRINKS
bottled water
fruit juices
mixers
sodas
beer, wine, or liquor

PAPER GOODS
foil
garbage bags
paper towels
plastic wrap
plastic bags
  (different sizes)
tissues
toilet paper

CLEANERS etc.
ant and roach traps
air fresheners
cold water soap
  powder
cleaning cloths and
  handy wipes
Joy dishwashing liquid
matches and cigarette
  lighter
mosquito coils
Murphy's Oil Soap
nightlights
rubber gloves
scouring pads
white vinegar for the
  heads
window cleaner
wood polish
bilge cleaner
boat soap, Spray 9,
  fender cleaner
bucket with lanyard
clothes hangers
clothes pegs and
  clothes line
deck swab, squeegee,
  sponges
dust pan and brush,
  small wet/dry
  vacuum
holding tank biode-
  gradable active
  agent
scrubbing brush
sponges
sewing kit
toilet brush, toilet
  plunger

DRUGSTORE
after sun lotion
antiseptic cream
Band Aids
body lotion/hand
  cream
dental floss
deodorant
insect repellant
mouthwash
shampoo
soap
sunscreen
toothpaste and
  toothbrushes
vitamins
*check ship's medical
  pack*

BASIC GALLEY EQUIPMENT
nonstick cooking pans
  including fry pan,
  medium and small
  saucepan, kettle,
  baking tray, and
  pressure cooker
plastic bowls and
  plates, coffee mugs,
  glasses
knives, forks, spoons
kitchen knives,
  wooden spoons,
  ladle, grater, bottle
  opener, can opener,
  corkscrew, ice pick
sieve
mixing/serving bowls
plastic food and drink
  containers
measuring cup
chopping boards
kitchen timer
garbage pail
washing up brush

LINEN AND BEDDING
pillows, blankets
sheets or sleeping
  bags
towels, beach towels
drying up cloths

PAPERWORK
Passports
Health certificates
  (only if going on)
Ship's Papers
FCC license
Log Book

credit cards
cash and traveler's
  checks
camera(s) and film
Polarized sunglasses
Bahamas courtesy flag
Q flag
US ensign

SWIMMING GEAR
masks, snorkels, fins,
  gloves
scuba gear
pole spears
spare rubber slings

FISHING GEAR
rods, reels, lures
handlines
spare leaders and
  hooks
gaff

MISCELLANEOUS
tool kit
flashlights
spare dry batteries
tender anchor and
  rode
inflatable repair kit
binoculars
hand-held compass

BOAT SPARES
oils and lubricants
bulbs, fuses
impellers
filters (fuel and oil)
spare pumps
spark plugs
spare belts
rebuild Heads kit
spare injector
gaskets, hose clamps
duct tape

ABANDON SHIP PACK
pre-prepared Panic
  Bag or
pre-list items to take

BOAT SAFETY
flares and smoke
dye markers
distress flag
EPIRB
MOB equipment

COMMUNICATIONS
hand-held VHF
cellular telephone

Afterword
The Cruising Guide Team

The Idea behind the Guide

This guide is the product of almost a decade of passage making and cruising in the Bahamas and the Turks and Caicos Islands, seafaring carried out in a variety of boats, sail and power, ranging from 26 feet to just under 50 feet in LOA. Much of this early sailing was pure pleasure. The accent changed with the determination that an entirely new approach in cruising guides was needed in the marine world, and that this area, the Bahamas, and the Turks and Caicos, needed a new pilot book, and a new way of putting a cruising guide together. The last four years have been spent devoted to this book.

MATHEW WILSON

After a career in the British Army with a service record covering every quarter of the globe, Mathew Wilson became the Executive Director of the Wilderness Foundation (UK) and pioneered the concept of eco-travel in Kenya and India. Moving to the USA, he sailed the Atlantic in a 26-foot boat, and turned to writing and lecturing on *Man and the Ocean*. His small boat voyaging was the subject of a 1994 book *Taking Terrapin Home*, and his lectures have been given for five of the premier cruise lines on voyages in the Atlantic, Pacific, and Indian Oceans and the Aegean, Mediterranean, and Caribbean Seas.

Mathew is a certified Divemaster, and a member of the Explorers Club. He and his wife Janet have a home in Jupiter, Florida, and spend the summer months in Vermont, where they have restored a long-neglected small farm.

JANET WILSON

Janet Wilson has shared these ocean travels as well as traveled widely independently, taking in both Russia and China. A talented gardener she would tell you that her Vermont paradise carries a far higher rating in her heart than boats and cruising, but the long Vermont winters with five feet of snow on the ground can reinforce the attraction of coral seas.

Janet provided the inspiration, the framework, and the targets for the Yellow Pages, the "shore" side of the Guidebook and, hardly surprisingly, the advice on commissioning and provisioning. Her dedication and her painstaking research has made this Guide the best single source of information on the Bahamas and the Turks and Caicos on the market, and her name, rightly, should feature on the cover. She refuses to have it placed there.

THE SUPPORT TEAM

Krov Menuhin earns our thanks for some superb piloting during three extensive periods of air photographic reconnaissance, which took us from Walkers Cay to Grand Turk Island, much of it slow flight at low altitude. The pilots amongst our readers will understand what that entails. With his help we have now acquired a unique archive of over five hundred air photographs of the islands, many of them targeted specifically on the approaches, cuts, and areas where we have found safe navigation difficult and charts inadequate guidance.

Sophie Bell, who joined us twice in our research for the First Edition, returned to the Bahamas and once again contributed to our Yellow Pages, and recorded and catalogued our first air photographic mission. Her enthusiasm for the islands and island life can turn a working week into a seven-day carnival. We enjoy her company, and thank her for it.

The names of those who have contributed to our information bank, and provided us with much-appreciated comment on the First Edition, are recorded under **Acknowledgements**.

FEED BACK

We welcome your comments and we welcome information to add to our data bank for the next edition of this Guide. You can contact us at:

The Bahamas Cruising Guide
Dolphin–Nomad Publications
Norwich Commerce Park, Route 5 South
PO Box 875
Norwich, Vermont 05055

Tel: 802-649-1995
Fax: 802-649-2667

e-mail: info@bahamasguide.com

We also have a website at www.bahamasguide.com

Quick Reference Index